Tyndale Concise Bible Commentary

Tyndale
CONCISE
BIBLE
COMMENTARY

◆◆◆◆◆

Robert B. Hughes
AND
J. Carl Laney

Tyndale House Publishers, Inc.

WHEATON, ILLINOIS

The authors wish to acknowledge all those who have had an influential or direct part in the production of this book. Numerous colleagues, especially Dr. Donald Launstein and Dr. Stanley Ellisen, and students through the years have greatly influenced the approach taken in this book. We also wish to acknowledge Mrs. Nancy Nasution, a Tyndale editor who worked many hours on this project. Although she did not live to see the completion of this book, her edits will be appreciated with each new page read. Our editor, Mr. Mark Norton, has skillfully led us through the entire editorial process. We are also happy to acknowledge his expertise, scholarship, and clarity of thought.

Library of Congress Cataloging-in-Publication Data

Hughes, Robert B., date.
  Tyndale concise Bible commentary / Robert B. Hughes and J. Carl Laney.
    p. cm.—(The Tyndale reference library)
Rev. ed. of: New Bible companion. 1990.
Includes index.
  ISBN 0-8423-5444-1 (alk. paper)
  1. Bible—Commentaries. I. Laney, J. Carl, date. II. Hughes, Robert B., date. Tyndale concise Bible commentary.
III. Title. IV. Series.
BS491.3 .H84 2001
220.7—dc21   2001002653

Printed in the United States of America.

ISBN 0-8423-5444-1

09 08 07 06 05 04 03 02 01
10 9 8 7 6 5 4 3 2 1

To DANIELLE ELLEN HUGHES
A daughter full of grace and beautiful moments
and
To JOHN, ELISABETH, LAURA, *and* DAVID LANEY
(2 Peter 3:18)

CONTENTS

INDEX OF BIBLE-WIDE THEMES

All of the following themes are Bible-wide in scope and could easily be traced through many, if not all, of the books of the Bible. This index connects these "Bible-wide" themes to the biblical books where they are discussed in the *Concise Bible Commentary*. See the Bible-Wide Concepts sections in the books mentioned for more information on the listed themes.

PREFACE

INTRODUCTORY SECTIONS

The *Concise Bible Commentary* presents each Biblical book by means of an introductory section followed by an outline and interpretive notes. The introduction to each Biblical book contains four subsections. First, the *BASIC FACTS* section discusses the book's historical setting, authorship, date, and essential purpose. Second, the *GUIDING CONCEPTS* section provides keys to understanding how the book's message unfolds and to identifying its major emphasis. Third, the *BIBLE-WIDE CONCEPTS* section explains how the book fits into the unified message of the Bible as a whole. Finally, a fourth section pinpoints the major *NEEDS MET BY* a particular book for its original hearers and for readers today. A fifth section discussing geographical concerns has been added to books in which geography plays a significant role. The idea of these introductory sections is to take the reader to the original time and setting of the book, to how the author developed his message, to the book's place in the entire scope of God's revelation, and, finally, to the major applications of its message—then and now.

OUTLINES AND NOTES

The introductory sections are followed by an overall outline of the book and then specific notes on each section of the book. The notes at the beginning of each major section of the book summarize the development of the author's thought over a major section. The interpretive notes that follow these *overviews* contain historical, geographical, and archaeological insights and help with major interpretive problems. We have tried to distill the essential message of each book without adding extensive and overly technical data. While the notes are quite readable on their own, our hope is that you will read them in close conjunction with the Biblical text. We also hope that you will keep this volume close at hand to provide an initial orientation to particular books of the Bible before you begin reading them and to answer your questions as they arise along the way.

INTRODUCTION
THE BIG PICTURE

Every book from Genesis through Revelation has a special way of fitting into the Bible as a whole. Wonderful when studied one by one, the Biblical books form an even more enriching whole when viewed together. Like a diamond's facets, each book makes its own special contribution to God's unfolding revelation. It is beautiful to see how the smaller facets—verses, chapters, and books—contribute to and receive meaning from the whole of God's revelation. The benefit of studying passages in the full light of their immediate, bookwide, and Bible-wide contexts is great. And an investigation of Scripture with the narrow and wide contexts in mind is the best foundation for accurate interpretation and effective application. The following overview of the Bible's big picture will help the reader make applications that will be based on the truth revealed in the whole of God's word.

THE NEED FOR A BIG PICTURE

A BIBLE MAP
As tourists need maps to avoid getting lost in foreign cities, Bible readers need a map to keep from getting lost between the books of Genesis and Revelation. They need to see how the whole Bible is laid out—how Scripture's main freeways interconnect with its smaller streets and avenues. Although a child may recognize the houses where he and his grandparents live, he may not know how to get from one to the other. Likewise, Bible readers may know one Bible book here and another there, but have no real sense of how the one is connected to the other. How does Genesis lead to 1 and 2 Samuel? Or how are 1 and 2 Chronicles crucial for understanding Matthew? The books of Scripture are extremely diverse, yet in their diversity, they form a unified whole that reveals God's amazing work to save and redeem mankind. The *Concise Bible Commentary* will provide a bird's eye view of the Bible, recognizing the diversity of its individual books and revealing how its diverse parts form a wonderful unity.

DIVERSITY WITHIN THE BIBLE
Different authors. The Bible was finished nearly two thousand years ago. Many different human authors wrote it over a period covering at least fifteen hundred years and including three different languages (Hebrew, Aramaic, and Greek). During that long period, history and culture changed radically—from the time of Moses, writing some fourteen hundred years before Christ, to the time of the apostle John, writing in the Roman Empire around A.D. 80. In addition to different cultures and languages, the

Biblical writers had their own different personalities and abilities. Moses was a prince of ancient Egypt—Matthew was a Roman tax collector. Solomon lived securely in a palace—Ezekiel was a prisoner of war. Paul was highly educated—Peter was an unschooled fisherman.

Different purposes. Each Bible book was written with its own specific purpose in mind. Each author wrote to meet specific needs. He selected, under God's guidance, appropriate truths that matched the particular needs of God's people at that time. Therefore, many different needs and situations are represented from book to book: announcements of God's discipline, loving God for his redemption, the problem of family hatred and jealousy, wandering in the desert, wars with the Philistines, captivity in Babylon, church squabbles, and dealing with personal sin. Some books were written to individuals, others to large groups. Some were for singing, while others were poetry or narrative to be read aloud. Some were written to bring correction, while others were for information or historical record.

Different topics. Because the purposes differ from book to book, so does the subject matter. God did not present his Word in long and organized lists of simple principles for living, detached from real people and their ancient historical situations. He wrapped his truths in greatly varied everyday history, language, and life. God gave us his truth in ancient books like Exodus, Joshua, Malachi, Romans, and 1 and 2 Peter. He did not give us books like 1 and 2 Thought Life or The Epistle To Parents. God's principles and truth are embedded in the events of God's salvation history and the diverse experiences of God's people.

Neither life nor God's truth comes in a neat, self-contained package. Just as our daily experiences contain diverse situations and needs, the books from Genesis to Revelation contain a diverse presentation of truth; the Bible is not a systematized card file of questions and answers. Its diversity is important to consider when interpreting and applying the Bible. God presented his eternal truth in the context of communities and people with concerns and needs defined by distant places and cultures. Thus, Bible readers cannot ignore the various cultures and situations of the Biblical text. Part of the task of interpreting the Bible is to see how its ancient context actually sharpens and clarifies its message. Seeing how God's truth helped ancient people in the struggles of their varied lives shows how we can apply the same truths today. Understanding the diversity of the Bible's message and context is vital to properly interpreting and applying Scripture.

Different relevance. Becoming aware of the Bible's diversity may cause us to make a mistake. We may tend to ignore those parts of the Bible that seem strange or difficult to apply. When we read the New Testament, especially Paul's letters, God seems to be speaking directly to us. But in the Old Testament we may find it difficult to apply things like bloody battles, ancient rituals, and long genealogies. In the face of the Bible's strangeness, it is possible that we may read only the New Testament—and just parts of it, at that. But such a neglect of the difficult and culturally distant parts of Scripture is wrong. To correct this neglect that grows out of the Bible's cultural distance and diversity, we need to look to another truth—the Bible's essential unity.

THE UNITY OF THE BIBLE

But how do the various books of the Bible fit together? Although the Bible was written book by book over a period of around fifteen hundred years, the end result is a single work, each part of which contributes perfectly to the whole. Therefore, it is not enough to study only a book here or there. The Bible should be understood as a logically ordered whole, moving from Genesis through Revelation. Although there are many different historical contexts and human authors in the Bible, God is the unifying author behind it all. Behind each diverse passage of Scripture stands our unchanging God. Behind the Bible's many human authors stands the single divine Author. And he is the real solution to the needs of the people in the Bible and those living today. Since God intended for the diverse books of Scripture to fit together as a unified whole, the interrelationships of the various books are significant for understanding God's revelation as a whole.

It would be somewhat odd to begin reading a current best-seller in the middle of the fifth chapter, skip to the last chapter, and then go back and read the end of the third chapter. Although a reader could make some sense of what he had read, he would not have an accurate picture of what the book was all about. The reader would have to see why the chapters were arranged in their present order and how each chapter fit into the entire book. Likewise, Bible readers need to determine how each Bible book fits into Scripture as a whole. Then they will be able to understand how the Bible's development has resulted in a beautiful and cohesive whole, from Genesis through Revelation, that meets the practical needs of believers.

GETTING FROM THE BIBLE MAP TO LIFE

Questions concerning how the different books of the Bible are interrelated are not just academic questions. The question of how the Bible fits together is crucial for a believer's practical application of Scripture. In order to understand the relationships between the various books of Scripture it is important to emphasize God's single authorship and the literary unity of Scripture. An understanding of the unifying message of Scripture should serve as a Bible map, revealing the unity of God's revelation amidst its diversity. Without a sense of how each book relates to the others, historically and literarily, interpretations and applications are open to a number of potential problems.

First, verses or books might be taken out of their larger Biblical context. They might be read as if they can be properly interpreted without understanding their original God-given literary context. This approach sees the Bible as if it were just a long list of detached Christian principles. Scripture becomes like a stack of cards, each with a principle for living. This approach denies the true nature of the biblical text and can be a cause for great misinterpretation.

One slightly humorous example of such misinterpretation would be to read Psalm 91:4, "He will shield you with his wings. He will shelter you with his feathers," and conclude that God has wings and feathers. To convert these bare words into a meaningful interpretation demands placing the words in their original context. When that is done, it is clear that the key element of the context is poetry that involves figurative language. Thus, the feathers and wings are not spoken of in a scientific sense but in a poetic sense describing God's love and care using the imagery of a mothering bird.

A less humorous example is found in Matthew 5:29: "If your eye—even if it is your good eye—causes you to lust, gouge it out and throw it away." The gouging out of the eye might appear to solve the problem of sin, especially lust (see Matt. 5:27-28). But a look at the broader context of Jesus' entire Sermon on the Mount (Matt. 5:1–

7:29) shows that God is against the notion that sin problems can be solved by external remedies. The context calls believers away from external actions (called hypocritical in Matthew 6:2, 5, 16) to making changes of the heart (Matt. 5:28; 6:21). Hands and eyes do not cause people to sin. They are just instruments, controlled not by themselves, but by man's inner desires and will. Removing them would not remove the inner bent of people toward sin. The context shows that the problem of lust is solved by correcting the warped vision of the spiritual eye ("eye" as symbolic of one's worldview, Matthew 6:22) not the gouging out of the physical eye.

If readers ignore the literary and historical context for the verses they study, they will inevitably pile up misunderstandings about God's original message. Each verse must be read in its immediate literary context (chapter and book) and then interpreted within the context of the entire Bible—a formidable but necessary and lifelong task.

Second, failing to study Scripture with its unity in mind creates a greater possibility of coming up with many conflicting interpretations. Without the control of the broader Biblical context, interpretations will be built on the interpreter's own experiences and ideas. The interpreter will tend to project his own needs and solutions into the text and, in doing so, miss what God originally intended. Interpretations may end up being as numerous and as creative as the interpreters themselves.

Third, fragmentary Scripture knowledge leaves the interpreter deficient when coping with the transition between Old and New Testaments. A great change came about at the coming of Christ, and that change is reflected in differences between the Testaments. But only a firm grip on the Bible-wide context can help interpreters move accurately from the Old to the New. How should Christians view the Old Testament laws and rituals? Why do some Christians still keep them while others do not? How are Christians supposed to use Genesis through Malachi?

Fourth, a Bible-wide picture is necessary for understanding how and why Christ, Paul, John, and the rest of the New Testament authors continually referred to the Old Testament in order to explain the fullness of God's redemption in Christ. What did the New Testament authors, who had known and experienced the person and work of Jesus Christ, find the same as they looked back to the Old Testament times of Moses? What had changed? How did they connect Christ with the Old Testament? How did they use the Old Testament to define Christian behavior? The identity of Christians rests on their appreciation of how the New Testament grows out of the Old. Without that appreciation they may make the mistake in day-to-day practice of treating the content of Genesis through Malachi as somewhat inferior, if not excludable, information.

Discovering how the whole Bible fits together will help Bible readers avoid these four problems and others. It will become clear that in the New Testament the Bible developed progressively, both by adding new truth and by reinterpreting the old. After readers have become oriented to God's map from Genesis to Revelation, they will have accurate directions for avoiding interpretations rooted solely in their own situations or personalities, and they will find themselves nearer to God's intended truth.

FINDING PRESENT POWER IN ANCIENT SCRIPTURE

God made no mistakes when he chose the means for communicating his truth. He purposely used history, different kinds of literary form (poetry, prose, proverb, hymns), culture, the authors' personalities, and three languages (Hebrew, Aramaic, and Greek).

These things are both antiquated and foreign to the world we live in today. Since God's word is conveyed in an ancient medium, what part should it play in contemporary interpretation and application of the Bible? Must we pay attention to the ancient forms used in Scripture to apply God's word today? How can God speak today through such a diverse and ancient document? Why did God not give his word in lists of timeless truth, rather than in truth wrapped up in time-bound language and culture?

Actually, we should be glad that God chose to communicate the way he did. He did not bring his message around the specifics of history. Rather, he brought his word right into the middle of the miracles and the messes of human life. So, rather than seeing the foreign people and cultures of Scripture as confusing, we need to see them and their occasional strangeness as part of the very message God intended for us to receive. The earthy quality of the Bible is a vital part of its divine message. It is not something to be ignored or peeled off in order to get at a supposed "real" and "timeless" Biblical message. Just as our Lord in his full humanity became the perfect medium for the message of God, so the written word of God, with all its ancient, diverse, and sometimes strange qualities, is the perfect expression of God's mind. God did not want to simply present truth. He wanted to present truth in the context of life's events. In that way God revealed truth in application, not in the abstract. And the applications of the Bible to its original readers should provide direction for our own applications. God wrapped his truth in the real world because he wants us to learn it and live it in the real world. And appreciating both the familiar and the foreign in the Bible is the best way to appreciating the fullness of God and his will for the world. If we fail to recognize Scripture's historical distance and diversity, we might interpret Scripture from the limited standpoint of modern culture—much like the artists of the Renaissance who painted all Biblical characters, whether Abraham or Paul, in the clothing and setting of contemporary Europe—thus distorting the true message of Scripture.

THE FOCUS OF GOD'S RULE

The entire Bible consistently develops God's three-part promise of his *presence*, his chosen *place*, and his redeemed *people*. God's presence, place, and people form the focus through which readers can discover and profit from the Bible's "big picture." Bible readers can use this threefold framework at each point in Scripture to discover how that section develops God's promises and speaks to believers today. Although many different and sometimes strange things happen in Scripture, they can all be unified around the three aspects of presence, place, and people.

PLACE
The first aspect, God's promised place, relates to the physical universe, and earth in particular. God's will and power stand behind the existence of the earth, sea, trees, birds, and animals. The physical creation perfectly manifests God's will and reveals much about his character and abilities, for example, his sheer power and incredible creativity. The earth also became the exciting arena in which God reveals his will and where humans respond to that will with either a yes or a no. God began with a perfect earth, cursed it with thorns and groanings (Rom. 8:22), gave a piece of it to Israel as a Promised Land, and promised to ultimately re-create an entirely new heaven and earth.

The progressive revelation of what God wants to do with the physical earth is a unifying theme from Genesis through Revelation.

PEOPLE

The second aspect of the Bible's focus is God's desire for his people. He creates, rules over, and seeks intimacy with them. Under God's rule, his people experience a vast variety of situations, problems, and needs. His special beginnings with Adam, Noah, and Abraham are summed up and brought to completion in Christ. The progressive revealing of how God works through his people's needs is a unifying theme from Genesis through Revelation.

PRESENCE OF GOD

The third and most important aspect of the Bible's focus is God himself. The crown of the Bible is the proclamation of who God is. Believers know who God is both by what he does and by what he says. Although the physical universe reveals much about its Creator, reading the Creator's words shows in even more detail who he is. When God reveals what he wants, he reveals something about himself—God's will reveals his character.

And when believers look closely at what God wants, they are brought close to his character and heart. The presentation of God's character by means of his deeds and words is the comprehensive unifying theme from Genesis through Revelation. He is consistently characterized as a king ruling from his throne. And the Bible clearly explains what the rule of God looks like from Genesis through Revelation. It is a story of how the King became more intimately present with his estranged kingdom by following a consistent pattern through differing times and cultures. A series of interrelated agreements, or covenants, between God and his creation brought his promises concerning his *presence, place,* and *people* to ultimate fulfillment.

THE MAP OF GOD'S RULE

THE SIGNPOSTS OF GOD'S COVENANTS

From the time of the apostles, the sacred writings were collected under two names that greatly illuminate the big picture of Scripture: the Old Testament and the New Testament. The Bible is about two testaments, or covenants. The old covenant was given under Moses. The new covenant came through Christ. A covenant is an agreement to do something, like a contract or a promise. Some biblical covenants are like contracts where both parties, God and people, have responsibilities and conditions for the contract to be fulfilled. Other covenants place all the responsibility to carry out the conditions on God alone. Instead of being like contracts, these covenants are more like unconditional promises.

Although the two covenants of Moses and Christ receive the most attention in the Bible, several other covenants complete God's revelation. In fact, God's covenant promises form the basis for all of his redemptive actions throughout Scripture. The covenants inform and explain virtually all of the events and speeches in the Bible and frame the development of God's plans for his *presence,* chosen *place,* and *people.* A covenant is at the backbone of every book of the Bible and, taken together, the covenants form the blueprint of the entire Bible.

Covenants also pave the way to understanding how each book interrelates with the rest of the Bible. Each new covenant is a sign-post that shows the next major route opening up in Scripture and how to understand all the little side roads of biblical history. Because each book was written from the perspective of the covenant or covenants operating at that time, knowing the main promises of those covenants will help the reader understand a book's particular emphasis and point. It will also help him to avoid making major points out of minor details and keep him from missing the heart of God's message. From Genesis through Revelation the unfolding interrelationship between the covenants is the key to understanding and applying the Bible. This overview of how God expressed his rule of love and justice through his promises begins with the sad fact of a divinely blessed creation being broken under a divine curse.

Goodness. In Genesis 1 God evaluated his creative work as being very good. In Genesis 2 God sanctified the completion of his creative work with a great Sabbath rest. In Genesis 3 God cursed everything he had made and damned it to an eternity in hell. What caused the goodness of creation? And what caused the badness of the curse?

Creation was good because it was exactly the way God wanted it. The pattern in Genesis 1 is "God said, 'Let there be . . .' and so it was." God got what he asked for. When he commanded that there be light, there was light, pure and simple. When he called for fish and birds, he got fish and birds. And when his word was perfectly obeyed, he recorded his response: "God saw that it was good." This reveals the relationship between what God wants and who he is. What he wants springs from his essential good-ness. When his will is accomplished it reflects the goodness of his divine character.

From its first lines, the Bible defines what makes something good. Things and people are not good because they are beautiful, smart, rich, productive, or fun. Goodness is that which matches up with what God wants and the standards he sets. To the extent that people and the earth are the way God wants them—to that extent, they are good. And what God wants reveals who he is—powerful, sovereign, and good.

Badness. In Genesis 3, God cursed the world because of Adam's sin. The pattern of "God said . . . and so it was" was broken. God wanted obedience, but he did not get it. He said, "You may freely eat any fruit in the garden except fruit from the tree of the knowledge of good and evil." But Adam and Eve said, "No." They did not shout it, and they probably had, in their own views, very good reasons for saying no. But, while all creation had resounded up to that point with a very good yes to God, Adam quietly brought in the first no. God could not say "It was good" to that response. He could only say, "Cursed." Adam's sin infinitely offended God's infinitely holy character. God responded with an infinitely devastating curse.

From its first lines, the Bible defines what makes something bad. Things and people are not bad because they may be unattractive, ignorant, poor, unproductive, or no fun. Badness is that which does not match up with what God wants and the standards he alone sets. God's curse provides Scripture's constant background of brokenness and need for restoration. Behind each act of hate, lust, murder, or lying stand human sin and divine curse. Not only are the Bible's characters shot through with a sinful nature, they also have to labor in a world damned at every turn by God's own curse.

GOD'S PROMISE OF ULTIMATE VICTORY

Along with the curse, the Bible reader needs to keep God's promise continually in view. The curse was not the end of the human story; it became the reason for God's plan to offer worldwide salvation to a fallen creation. What could ever remedy the infinite offense of sin and remove the infinite curse? Only a correspondingly infinite sacrifice would be sufficient to do so. The entire scope of the Bible is about how God moves from the *good* creation into the *bad and cursed* creation and out again into a new and blessed second creation. It is a story of how God, at great cost, removed his offense at mankind's sin and restored a relationship of blessing with his creation. The Bible is first and foremost a story of God dealing with his problems with human sin. To put it another way, it is a simple story of two acts, one of offense, the other of forgiveness. It is about an intensely personal transaction between God and humanity.

Right in the middle of his curse regarding Adam, God gave a promise of ultimate victory (Gen. 3:15). He said that someday a son of Adam would crush the head of the serpent. Ultimately, the son of Adam was Christ, and the serpent was Satan. Amazingly, God's curse and Satan's hatred would culminate in the crucifixion of Christ, an act that satisfied God's offense at sin and defeated Satan's power. But God did not move immediately to the fulfillment of his promised redemption in Christ. Thousands of years came between the promise to Adam and Christ's resurrection. And nearly two thousand years have passed since then.

THE COVENANTS AND GOD'S CHARACTER

How could Adam, Eve, and all people who have followed them know that there would be ultimate victory as the process of conflict with personal and world evil lengthened from days to thousands of years? As generations came and went through the cursed world, their faith had to be based on a God who would keep his word. To his original word of promise in Genesis 3:15, the Creator, who was by nature a sufficient object of trust, added many more words of promise.

Those words of redemptive promise blossom within the framework of the covenants recorded in Scripture. Behind each covenant stands the trustworthy character of God. God takes nearly all the responsibility in some covenants and shares it with his people in others. Biblical contracts form a blueprint that unifies the diverse Scriptural elements of *people, place,* and God's *presence* around God's faithful character. Also, those covenants clarify how believers may apply the truth of any passage.

THE COVENANTS AT A GLANCE

The grand scriptural movement from infinite curse to eternal blessing is directed by a series of covenants between God and sinful mankind. Through these contracts, God brings promises of hope and blessing to a world that has been separated from its Creator by sin. See the accompanying chart.

As Bible readers discover what the Bible says about why God made contracts, three questions should continually be asked. (1) What can be learned about God in each covenant? (2) What does he want from the people he brings into those contract relationships? (3) In what way do God's conditions continue or change from covenant to covenant? These questions will provide a solid basis for applying the Bible to a reader's own situation. Each covenant contains the basic elements that provide signposts for tracking change and development from one covenant to another. These guidelines also show how the passages properly apply to a reader's own personal situation.

GOD'S COVENANT WITH NOAH

THE FOUNDATIONS OF LONGSUFFERING

God made a contract with Noah (Gen. 9:1-17) that, in part, echoed what he had originally said to Adam in Genesis 1:28. God restated his original commission to the human race. Though Noah, God was giving humankind a second start with a second "first family." The contract with Noah was necessary for all the others that would follow because in it God said he would never again destroy the entire earth by flood. Without that promise of restraint, humans could expect God to vent his global wrath at any moment. Every so often, God would have to destroy the world again. Why? Because the human problem of saying no to God still persisted. God would have had to punish sin.

By making a contract with Noah, God showed he could withhold his righteous retribution. And though God at times in Scripture judged some sins in order to warn and instruct, he let the vast majority of human sin go unpunished throughout the course of history. God refrained from immediate judgment by exhibiting the characteristic of longsuffering. From the time of Noah, Bible readers should appreciate the concept of longsuffering in a new way. The holy God, whose attitude of loathing and grief toward sin had not changed, would now live with sin for a long time. Why?

THE COST OF LONGSUFFERING

The covenant with Noah reveals a God who is more concerned with the restoration of the human race than with its destruction; God is more concerned with humankind's salvation than he is with venting his own rightous anger. God's decision to be longsuffering toward sinful people was costly. It left his reputation open to human scoffing that he was powerless or indifferent regarding evil. It would cost him his own dear Son. Longsuffering would also become the only acceptable model for the life-styles of his followers.

Even after the flood, the earth was still under God's curse. And, as Noah's children show, people had not miraculously become any less sinful as a result of the flood. Above all, God had certainly not changed his mind about sin. He still hated it. But, in the contract with Noah, God determined to hold back the flood waters of his wrath in order to make room for his grace in the cross of Christ.

In Genesis 3:15 God had promised ultimate victory over the serpent. Through Noah, God promised to withold his global wrath on the road to ultimate victory. The next step toward that great victory was God's covenant with Abraham.

GOD'S COVENANTS WITH MANKIND

Promise of ultimate victory	Genesis 3:15
Noah	Genesis 9:8-17
Abraham	Genesis 12:1-3; 13:14-17; 15:1-21; 17:1-14
Moses	Exodus 20—Numbers 6; explained and elaborated throughout the Old Testament
David	2 Samuel 7:8-17
Christ	Jeremiah 31:31-34; Ezekiel 36:22-32; Hebrews 8:1–10:18; explained and elaborated throughout the New Testament

GOD'S COVENANT WITH ABRAHAM

THREE ELEMENTS

The basic elements of the covenant with Abraham are found in Genesis 12:1-3 (cf. also Gen. 13:14-17; 15:1-21; 17:1-14). Abraham was promised a *place*, the land of Israel; a *people*, the nation of Israel; and the blessings that come from the special *presence* of God. These three elements—place, people, and God's presence—were God's focus in the original creation, and they direct the way to his future final restoration of world-wide blessing. Although this promise begins with Abraham, eventually "all the families of the earth" will find blessing (Gen. 12:3). The Abrahamic promise included every place and people of the entire earth. From this point on, each book of Scripture will be understood by finding out how it shows God's progress in fulfilling his promises to Abraham of place, people, and presence.

The Place. The initial place of Abrahamic promise, the Promised Land—Israel—was just a starting point. It began with Palestine, but it will eventually extend to the entire earth. In the beginning of history, God gave, as a starting point, a little patch of the earth to Adam and Eve. Although their ultimate goal was dominion over the entire earth, they had to start somewhere. The Garden of Eden was a small starting point. The finish line would be of global proportions. Likewise, the place of Abrahamic promise, beginning with the Promised Land of Israel, will also ultimately be global and will one day extend to the new heavens and earth. Each book of Scripture needs to be searched as to what it says about God's progress in giving the Promised Land to Israel and then about giving the new earth to all the saints.

The People. The starting point of the people aspect of the Abrahamic covenant was Abraham's children: from Isaac and Jacob to the twelve tribes of Israel. But it did not end there. It would eventually grow to include all the people of the earth. At creation, God gave his original commission for world dominion to just two people, Adam and Eve. But through them he addressed all the human race who would follow after them. In a similar way, God's promises were given to one man, Abraham. But through Abraham God addressed all peoples. The people of the Abrahamic promise are international. Each book needs to be searched as to what it says about how God extends his people from Abraham, to Israel, and finally into all nations.

The Presence of God. God promised Abraham great blessing. Blessing is not defined throughout Scripture as simply the material things God gives. The essence of blessing is having God present in a special way. Blessing is God's presence, not just his gifts. The blessings offered to Abraham were based on a new intimacy with God. God often told Abraham, "I am with you" or "I will be with you." Later, God would be with his people in greater intimacy as he moved from thundering Mount Sinai into the tabernacle at the center of Israel's camp. That initmate presence would later be extended to all lands and peoples in the new covenant in Christ. God would move from the tabernacle and temple into the center of believers' hearts. Finally, the joy of eternity will be the unhindered presence of God in the new earth. The divine presence of the Abrahamic promise is universal. Each book can yield rich truths about the conditions required for God's presence and how he became increasingly more intimate with his people on the basis of each new covenant.

ABRAHAM AND THE BIBLE

All the rest of the Bible is about how God fulfilled the three aspects of his great promise to Abraham. The next covenants, centered around Moses, David, and Christ, all flesh out and fulfill the great promises to Abraham. From Abraham on, the geographic starting places of Eden for Adam and the newly dried earth for Noah were replaced with the focus on the Promised Land of Israel. The human starting points, Adam and Noah, were replaced with Abraham. And the work of God to reverse his curse and restore his unhindered presence took a great leap forward in his deepened intimacy with Abraham. Long after Abraham, the apostle Paul would call him the spiritual father of all believers (Rom. 4:12).

THE PRESERVATION OF THE PROMISED NATION AND LAND

Nation. Once God had marked out his chosen man, Abraham, and his chosen line through Sarah's children, the history of Abraham's covenant revolves around how Abraham's descendants respond to God's grace and demands for obedience. Although God always remained faithful, more often than not his people were uncooperative and placed themselves at great risk. God had promised Adam ultimate victory. The covenant with Noah had shown that God was more interested in redemption than in destruction. But how would God preserve his continually rebellious people in order to bring in his promised blessings? That drama brings excitement to many portions of the stories of the Patriarchs and of Israel. Here are just a few examples of the drama of God's preserving his people despite their sins: Would Sarah be married off to the wrong man before she could bear the promised son (Gen. 12:10-20; 20:1-18)? Would Rebekah be married off to the wrong man in a similar way, putting a stop to God's chosen family (Gen. 26)?

In addition to individuals like Sarah and Rebekah, the drama of preserving Abraham's line also relates to the nation of Israel as a whole. God used Joseph's captivity in Egypt as the very thing needed to bring his family down out of Canaan and into Egypt to preserve the kernel nation of Israel from starvation during a great famine. God caused the tribe of Israel to increase miraculously while in Egypt. He preserved Israel from Pharaoh's army and from starvation in the wilderness after the Exodus.

During the conquest of Canaan under Joshua, God preserved the nation and gave it great victory. God preserved Israel through the devastating Assyrian and Babylonian captivities. He once again saved the entire nation from being wiped out through the heroic efforts of Esther during the time of Persian rule.

Much can be learned about God and people from these events of preservation. God is faithful and is able to keep his words of promise no matter how many years and harrowing events pass. God preserved his chosen people, not because of their faithfulness, but because he remained faithful to his promise to Abraham.

Land. The drama of Israel's preservation also involves the second aspect of the Abrahamic covenant, the preservation of the land. Would God be strong enough and faithful enough to give Israel the land? Or would the constant failures of his people void the land promise?

The Old Testament gives great attention to the ups and downs involved in God's people and their land. Abraham received the promise, though he never owned any significant part of the land. The land was taken by Joshua, though it was never very secure until David's conquests and Israel's consolidation under Solomon.

But all of that security evaporated in the face of Assyrian and Babylonian devastation and captivity. Even when the people were allowed to return from the Babylonian captivity, the Promised Land was not their own. Until the time of Christ, Israel would be under a sequence of foreign domination by Persia, Greece, and Rome. God's promises of victory, peace, and international blessing seemed very far off.

GOD'S COVENANT WITH MOSES

THE DIVINE PRESENCE PROMISED TO MOSES

Long after Abraham, God made another covenant, this time with Moses. Moses' covenant developed the promises and demands God had originally given to Abraham. The Mosaic covenant clarified two critical aspects of God's redemptive plans given through Abraham: human obedience and divine presence. God would be present only with a people obedient to his will.

Under Moses, the rituals surrounding the tabernacle defined the obedience required for remaining in God's blessed presence (Lev. 11:45; 15:31). The great festivals of the covenant clarified the major elements of God's promised blessing through Abraham. The Day of Atonement pictured a perfect forgiveness of sin (Lev. 16). The Jubilee, or Sabbath year, pictured the restored and perfect creation Sabbath (Lev. 25). The blessings and curses spoke of the pleasure and pain arising from either keeping or breaking the covenant (Lev. 26:27-45). God would be with the nation for its blessing only if the people loved and obeyed him. God's law found its source in his love and was designed to lead to an improved relationship between God and his people.

HOLINESS

The tablets of the Ten Commandments, placed in the Most Holy Place of the tabernacle, summed up the grace and demands of the new relationship with God under Moses. Human obedience and God's presence rested on the demands arising from God's absolute holiness. Because God was holy, he would be redemptively present only with an obedient people. From Adam on, it was always clear that the believer's obedience was indispensible for enjoying the blessing of divine fellowship. The laws of the Mosaic covenant spelled out in black and white the holiness of God's character and how to have a redemptive relationship with him. The detailed laws of Exodus showed how far the people had fallen into lawlessness. The detailed sacrifices of Leviticus showed the gracious way back to obedience and holiness. All of these laws and sacrifices sprang from, and blazingly illustrated, God's holiness. His holiness demanded the believers' conformity to it. But that conformity of obedience was to spring from the heart (Deut. 6:4-9).

In the face of the Mosaic covenant's many laws and regulations, one point must not be lost. The Mosaic covenant grounded blessing squarely on a deep inner love for God which issued in doing what he wanted. While carrying out all the requirements of the Mosaic covenant, the believers' hearts were to match their external conformity to God's law. Only through heartfelt obedience would the curse on God's *people* and *land* be lifted. Sincere obedience alone could bring holiness and salvation from war, famine, and disease.

Adam was the source of humanity's fall. Noah's covenant opened up time for grace to overtake judgment. Abraham's promises outlined the route to international blessing. And Moses' covenant visualized the solutions to the two road-blocks to experiencing that blessing: forgiving human sin and perfecting human obedience. The covenant that God would make with David continued to clarify how God would remove those two roadblocks.

GOD'S COVENANT WITH DAVID

THE KING AS MEDIATOR FOR GOD'S PEOPLE

God's covenant with David was made during the most secure period of Israel's history. It was a special word of God's promise, not to the whole nation of Israel, but to the special kingly line of David. To Abraham, God had promised blessing on his offspring. To Moses, God had continued the blessing to Abraham's offspring, then known as the nation of Israel. But under David the personal blessing promised to Abraham and Moses focused on one man within the nation of Israel, the king. And that king functioned as the representative for the entire nation of Israel. As the king went, so went the people of Abrahamic promise. In the Davidic covenant a new drama arose in Scripture: the preservation of the kingly line. That drama is clearly seen throughout the books of Samuel, Kings, and Chronicles and reaches its height in the attempts on the life of the King of Israel, Jesus, during his life as a baby and as a man.

Under the Davidic covenant the king of Israel held a critical place of mediation between God and the nation. The king was responsible to ensure civil justice and the sanctity of the temple services. The preservation of the nation depended upon the king's obedience to God's commands. The whole story of how God enthroned his chosen king, David, is climaxed by the king's mediation for the entire nation of Israel. When the king did right in God's sight by keeping his commands, he answered prayers for the preservation of the people and the land (cf. 2 Sam. 21:14; 24:25). The king became the person through whom the nation experienced the rule of God. That rule finds its fulfillment in the sacrificial mediation and exalted rule of the ultimate seed of David, Jesus the Messiah.

THE KING AS GOD'S SON

In 2 Samuel 7:8-19, God promised that a royal line would extend from David onward forever. The critical emphasis was that each Davidic king of Israel would have a special father-son relationship with God. Each king was a special son of God, blessed with a potentially close and powerful relationship with the Father. The kings of David's line realized that potential in degrees varying from better to worse. But the power of divine sonship found its fulfillment in the Son of God, Jesus, who had a perfect and unique form of sonship with God.

Through Christ, that sonship has been shared with his followers. The victory promised to Adam, the international blessing promised to Abraham, and the forgiveness and obedience required under Moses all zeroed in on one man. And that man was the second Adam, the single seed of Abraham, the prophet greater than Moses, and the perfect son of David. Where Adam, Abraham, Moses, and David failed, Christ succeeded. God's redemptive focus narrowed to one man, Christ, so that from his singular perfection it could expand outward into the international blessing promised to Adam and Abraham. Because of Christ's redemptive work, now all believers have the privilege of being called sons and daughters of God. See 2 Corinthians 6:18–7:1 where Paul applies the Davidic covenant to Christian believers (Paul quoted 2 Sam. 7:8, 14).

One man, Adam, brought sin and God's curse into the world. He received a promise that someday his son would crush the head of the serpent. To get to that ultimate victory, Noah was promised a period of patient and longsuffering grace. Abraham was given the promise of a special place, nation, and blessing that someday would extend around the world. Moses received the details of maintaining that blessing through forgiveness and obedience. And to David came the hope of one Israelite who would be the perfect king and mediator for the nation and the world. That one would bring in the fullness of the kingdom of God. But until he came, the nation went through traumatic times of failure, always warned, encouraged, or condemned by a long series of prophets.

GOD'S PROMISES AND THE PROPHETS

The Old Testament prophets primarily focused on the conditions for blessing found in the covenant with Moses. They inevitably spoke out because God's kings, priests, and people had broken their promise to love and obey God. Obedience to the commands in Moses' covenant was the key condition for God's people to be preserved in his land. The prophets are best arranged around the times during which they prophesied: *before, during,* and *after* the exile to Babylon.

BEFORE THE BABYLONIAN EXILE

Before the Exile, the nation of Israel still had a chance to avoid destruction. The prophets who spoke before the Babylonian exile warned of impending judgment for unfaithfulness to the covenant with God (for example, see Isaiah, Jeremiah, and the minor prophets from Hosea through Zephaniah). Their message to Israel was to stop being like the nations that surrounded them. Their message to the nations was to repent and do justice to all men, especially Israel. The exhortations to the nations rested not on the Mosaic covenant, which was made only with Israel, but on God as the Creator who had rights to command and correct all of his creation. Also, God continually had more on his mind than just the well-being of the little nation of Israel. The Abrahamic covenant had shown God's ultimate intentions to bless all nations.

Another important prophetic message to Israel was that of the promise of exaltation after a period of chastisement and humiliation. Israel would have to undergo both deserved and undeserved suffering, after which God's people would be raised up and eternally blessed. That great truth is continually emphasized throughout Scripture, especially by the prophets, the Lord Jesus, and Paul: suffering before relief, humility before praise, perseverance before reward.

DURING THE EXILE

The prophets who spoke during the Babylonian exile told captive Israel to submit to and learn from God's chastisement (see Daniel, Ezekiel, and parts of Jeremiah; the books of 1 and 2 Kings were also written from the perspective of the exile). The prophets told Israel not to hope in the nations for deliverance. Israel was warned to make sure that idols were scrubbed out of their hearts (see Ezek. 14 with reference to the curses of Deut. 28). The captive Israelites in Babylon were not to hope in the temple still standing in Jerusalem. The temple was not a good luck charm against the consequences of Israel's rebellion. It was only a symbol of God's presence and would soon fall. The real issue of God's presence would hinge on their present obedience, no matter where in the world they might be. Wherever they were obedient to God's laws, God was with them.

Daniel brought a special message of the need to wait for the restoration to the Promised Land. After the seventy years of captivity another type of seventy would come, only this time it would be seven times seventy. Four hundred and ninety years of oppression under the nations would have to pass before the great king of Israel, the Messiah, would come.

AFTER THE EXILE

The prophets who spoke to Israel after she had returned from exile to the Promised Land called upon the nation to persevere (see Haggai, Zechariah, and Malachi; the books of 1 and 2 Chronicles were also written from the perspective of positive restoration after the exile). Daniel had told the nation about the years of oppression to come, but Israel had also been told to continue on in obedience to the requirements of the Mosaic covenant. So, lest Israel's courage fail, the prophets gave comfort and warning. The day of God would eventually come, bringing destruction to the rebellious but salvation and rest to the faithful remnant. That time of final restoration would be according to the Abrahamic covenant as it had been gradually elaborated in later revelation to Moses, David, and the prophets. In that final day: (1) God's *land* will be restored; (2) God's *people* will be saved; (3) God's *presence* will dwell with his people once again.

All of God's promises to Abraham would be fulfilled. But a final covenant, mentioned in Jeremiah and Ezekiel but not inaugurated until Jesus' life, addressed the major problem blocking the dawning of the kingdom of God: sin. All the sacrifices of the Mosaic covenant did not secure perfect and final forgiveness. Guilt persisted. All the laws of the Mosaic covenant could not ensure perfect obedience. Sin persisted. How could the infinite offense of past sin be removed? And how could people stop sinning in the future?

JESUS: THE NEW COVENANT

The new covenant was designed by God to remedy the long-standing problem of sin in Israel and the world. First, the new covenant brought a sacrifice that removed God's offense at human sin from Adam onward (Jer. 31:34). The basis of the new covenant is the better sacrifice of Christ (Heb. 8–9).

Second, through Christ, God created people who would no longer echo Adam's original no to God. God's people always had a bad habit of doing what he did not like. Adam ate the fruit. Abraham lied. Moses got angry. The nation of Israel grumbled and complained. David committed murder and adultery. Solomon supported idolatry.

Peter denied his Lord. Church after church continued to fall prey to pride, bickering, and lapses in faith. Even in the face of God's great redemptive events from the Exodus to the Cross, his people persisted in falling down on their responsibility to respond in gratitude and obedience.

The new covenant in Christ aimed at correcting the weak link of disobedience. And that was begun by putting the law of God into the human heart by means of the interior regeneration of the human soul. The law was placed inside (Jer. 31:33-34). God had told Israel to put his will into their hearts (Deut. 6:4-6). But in the new covenant, God does the interior decorating himself. Humans receive a new heart, and the Spirit of God moves believers to obedience to his laws (Ezek. 36:26-27). Obedience becomes an instinctive response.

The Old Testament promised the fulfillment of the promises to Abraham: a restored earth and people enjoying God's unhindered presence and blessing. And the new covenant is the means for fulfilling those promises. The entire New Testament is an explanation and application of the new covenant for the people of God. Every New Testament book emphasizes the significance of Christ's sacrifice and its implications for past history, present salvation, and future hope.

In Revelation 21:1-7; 22:3 all the strands of covenant promise come together. The ruined creation, both people and earth, are re-created. Then God's place and people will experience the greatest blessing: unhindered divine presence. The curse will be lifted, disobedience will end, and all aspects of God's promises will be realized. God's kingdom will have come and his will will be done on earth just the way it is done in heaven—perfectly and from the heart.

THE PRESENT

But until that great day of heaven on earth, believers live in the challenge of a world still under God's curse and human sinfulness. Forgiven believers can experience the power of new hearts and the Holy Spirit. All sin is forgiven. The power for obedience is present. And a day will come when all who believe will cease to disobey. But for the present, as the apostle Paul explained in Romans 8:22-23, believers groan, awaiting the glorification of their all-too-mortal bodies. While much of God's promise has been completed, some critical areas await completion. Earth remains a maverick, prone to earthquakes, floods, droughts, and famines. And people continue to be their own worst enemies, prone to the jeopardy of their flesh and Satan's attacks.

But Scripture was written for people just like these, people caught in the weakness and pain of living on a cursed earth. They need Scripture's redemptive truth. The task in Bible study is to find out what redemptive help each section was designed to give. The map of the Bible outlined above will help Bible readers see how a text fits into the flow of God's redemptive plan. As they work to understand what has changed since the text was written and what remains the same, they will be able to link how it was designed to help its original readers to how it can relate to believers today.

GENESIS

BASIC FACTS

HISTORICAL SETTING

Genesis was written for the people of Israel, who had just been redeemed out of Egypt under the leadership of Moses. They had been living on God's provisions in the wilderness and had seen his awesome appearance on Mount Sinai. They were being introduced to a new relationship with their God through his covenant and through worship of him at the tabernacle.

AUTHOR

The Authorship of Genesis through Deuteronomy

The authorship of Genesis is an integral part of the larger question of who wrote the first five books of Scripture (called the Pentateuch by scholars). Scholars agree that these five books have an overall thematic and literary unity and that Scripture and tradition place these books under Moses' name. But scholars disagree as to the editorial process his material underwent to arrive at its present form. The question hinges on the relationship between the material's present and original forms.

A more conservative view tends to see only minor differences between the forms of the original and final compositions. According to the conservative view, the books of Genesis through Deuteronomy contain, with the exception of later minor additions, essentially what God transmitted through Moses. A more liberal view sees a long and complex history of editorial development and a vast difference between the bits and pieces of the original materials and their final edited form. Scholars have presented positions on the authorship of the Pentateuch ranging all the way from direct dictation by God to Moses to seeing the books as a fragmented collection of bits of tradition only brought into its present form after the Babylonian captivity.

Several key biblical passages, however, support Moses' significant part in the original shaping of the Pentateuch. First of all, Moses was highly educated (Acts 7:22). Then, after the Exodus from Egypt, God told Moses to write a specific message concerning the destruction of the Amalekites (Exod. 17:14). Moses first spoke and then recorded God's law given at Mount Sinai (Exod. 24:3-4; 34:27-28). He recorded the stages of the wilderness journey (Num. 33:2). He wrote the "Book of the Law" that probably refers to virtually all the Pentateuch except the last chapter of Deuteronomy, which recounts the event of Moses' death (Deut. 31:24-26; see also Neh. 13:1).

After Moses died, God referred Joshua to "all the laws Moses gave you" and the "Book of the Law" (Josh. 1:7-8; see also 1 Kings 2:3; 1 Cor. 9:9). Although it cannot be proven that the written material mentioned in these passages is identical to the present Pentateuch, it is clear that Moses left for Joshua a comprehensive written record of the laws of God that would encompass the general material now known as the Pentateuch.

Much later, when Jesus referred to the incident of Moses and the burning bush, he revealed that Moses' name was also attached to the book of Genesis ("the writings of Moses, in the story of the burning bush," Mark 12:26). Luke reflects the common tradition of putting the "law of the Lord" (in this case specifically referring to Exod. 13:2, 12 and Lev. 12:8) under the broad heading of "law of Moses" (Luke 2:22-24; see also Acts 13:39). When Jesus said that Moses wrote of him, he again reflected the conventional view of Moses as the author of Genesis through Deuteronomy (John 5:46).

The first five books of the Bible were also commonly referred to simply as "Moses" (Luke 16:29; 24:27, 44; Acts 26:22). Although biblical connections between the Pentateuch and Moses' name do not prove that Moses wrote every word of these books, they do affirm him as both the chief figure in the books of the Pentateuch and as their primary human author. Any others who had a later part in editing Moses' work remain unnamed. Moses was viewed as the human transmitter of the laws of God and the chief literary figure behind the Pentateuch.

The Authorship of Genesis

The book of Genesis itself does not name its author, who is therefore anonymous. And although Moses was viewed as the figure behind Genesis, in the book, and throughout the Pentateuch, he is always referred to in the third person "he," not in the first person "I." The Pentateuch unfolds its message from a biographical, not an autobiographical, perspective. But the central issue in authorship is the nature and authority of the message.

The question of authorship is usually closely linked to the question of authority. Although it cannot be proven, nor does it need to be proven exactly what Moses or other possible editors wrote, believers can have absolute confidence that Genesis comes with the full authority of God as transmitted through its original human author, Moses. If, after Moses, others had a hand in editing his material, the crucial issue of the book's divine authority through Moses is not altered. But that process of editing, however it may be conceived, is never mentioned in the Bible. Moses and Moses alone is viewed as the author and the mediator of God's authority inherent in the Pentateuch.

DATE

Because the book of Genesis builds up to and ends with Israel's bondage in Egypt and her hope of return to the Promised Land, it is clear that its purpose was to lay out the background of Israel's election by God and her exodus from Egypt. Therefore, the date of the book is from a time shortly after the Exodus. Because Moses had a significant hand in writing the material, it initially must have been composed in the wilderness period prior to his death. The two most commonly accepted dates for the wilderness wanderings of Israel, and therefore for the composition of Genesis by Moses, are an early date of around 1446–1406 B.C. and a later date of around 1220–1180 B.C., depending on when one dates the Exodus. See the introduction to the book of Exodus for the issues involved in dating Israel's exodus from Egypt.

PURPOSE

The general purpose of Genesis is to preserve an accurate record of the beginnings of the human race and the Hebrew nation. More specifically, it is designed to record man's initial rebellion against God's rule and the beginnings of his redemptive program through Israel. Genesis records the origins of the world, plants, animals, humans, sin, death, and redemption. These origins were recorded to provide the necessary background for Israel's appreciation of her election in Abraham, her redemption from Egypt, and her obedience to the Mosaic Law. In essence, the book of Genesis was designed to help God's redeemed people to respond to their Redeemer in gratitude, love, and obedience.

GEOGRAPHY AND ITS IMPORTANCE

The Bible is a book about the entire world. Genesis begins with the creation of the universe—the background against which all the little places in the Bible will be set. Several places in Genesis cannot be identified today, like the Garden of Eden or where Noah lived. But the major places where Abraham, Isaac, Jacob, and Joseph lived have been found. Geographically the Genesis narrative moves from Adam and Eve in the Garden, to Abraham in Ur and then in Israel, and to Joseph in Egypt. Genesis makes the first important step in God's redemptive movement that spans from Eden, to Israel's exodus from Egypt, to the Cross of Christ in Judea, and finally to the new heavens and earth found in the book of Revelation. See the introductory map.

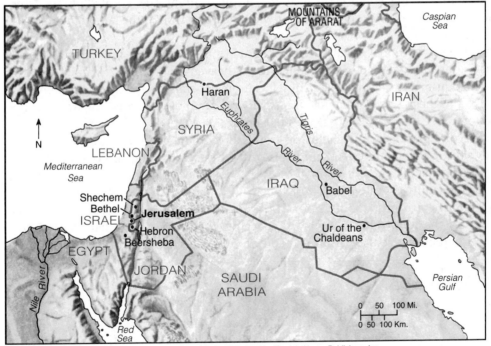

Modern names and boundaries are shown in gray. Copyright © 1986, 1988 by Tyndale House Publishers, Inc.

GUIDING CONCEPTS

FROM EDEN TO EGYPT

Genesis is full of contrasts. It begins with the creation of the universe and ends with Joseph's corpse in a coffin in Egypt. At the beginning of Genesis, Adam and Eve were living in the purity and security of the Garden of Eden; at the end of the book, the little family of Jacob was dwelling in the foreign land of Egypt. Adam and Eve were offered the world and God's unhindered presence; the family of Abraham was offered the promise of eventual deliverance out of Egypt. The earth was created and cursed, destroyed and repopulated. Genesis tells the story of human failure and divine help given to a special family on a journey from Eden to Egypt.

FAMILY ACCOUNTS IN GENESIS

2:4	The account of the heavens and the earth
5:1	The account of Adam
6:9	The account of Noah
10:1	The account of Shem, Ham, and Japheth
11:10	The account of Shem
11:27	The account of Terah
25:12	The account of Ishmael
25:19	The account of Isaac
36:1	The account of Esau
37:2	The account of Jacob

PEOPLE: ADAM TO JOSEPH

The main interest in Genesis is the history of a single family. The repeated phrase, "this is the account of," or "history of," helps divide the book around the family members (see chart above).

The Hebrew word that is translated "account" (this word is also commonly rendered "generations") is first used with reference to the heavens and earth (2:4) and represents more than just a list of descendants. It refers more generally to family origins and history. In Genesis such "accounts" are usually made up of two parts. The first part is a genealogy. (See the chart "Genealogies in Genesis.")

The second part of each "account" section is a record of important events in the family's history. Sometimes the family history comes before the genealogy, as in the following format: (1) family history (2:4–4:26); (2) the catchphrase "history of" (5:1); and (3) the family genealogy (5:2-32).

The phrases "account of" and "history of" can refer both to what precedes and to what follows—to the family history and to the genealogy that follows from that history. The histories and lineages of God's chosen people form the backbone of the book of Genesis.

GENEALOGIES IN GENESIS

5:1–9:29	From Adam through Noah
10:1-32	Noah's three sons: Shem, Ham, and Japheth
11:10-26	From Shem through Abram and his brothers, Nahor and Haran.
11:27-32	From Terah through Abram in Haran
25:12-18	From Ishmael through his twelve tribes
36:1-19	From Esau through his sons, the chiefs of Edom

THE CENTRAL PERSON: ABRAHAM

The emphasis and main point of Genesis can be seen by the book's interest in certain people. The section 1:1–37:2 emphasizes Adam, Noah, Abraham, Isaac, and Jacob. The human sin against God. All of God's great acts of love toward Abraham, Moses, David, and others were steps that led to the only satisfactory means for removing sin's offense: the sacrifice of Jesus Christ.

Not until the events described in Revelation 22:3 take place, however, will the full weight of the curse be lifted in the recreated heavens and earth. All that takes place between the beginning in Eden and the end in the new heavens and earth illustrates the pain of the curse and the joy of redemption. The Bible is the story of how God reverses his curse upon sin. Although individuals and groups can experience aspects of God's blessing and presence now, the curse continually crouches behind the scenes as the awful spoiler that keeps believers from experiencing the fullness of a true relationship with him. Some humans perform beautiful acts of sacrifice and obedience, but God's full glory will remain hidden until he removes the curse at his own sovereignly appointed time. Even at the best of times the curse and its resultant human and cosmic brokenness are continual threats to the well-being of people and society.

CONFLICT BETWEEN GOD AND SATAN

The continual turbulence created by human sin and the divine curse clearly manifests itself in the conflicts found throughout Scripture. Those conflicts may be between individuals (Cain and Abel, Jesus and Satan), groups (Joseph and his brothers), nations (Israel and the Philistines), or within ourselves (flesh and spirit). Genesis 3:15 sketches the process of conflict that runs throughout the Bible. God caused Satan and Eve's descendants to be enemies. The chart below, "Victory through Conflict," sketches out the basic direction that the conflict between the children of evil and the children of God takes throughout Scripture.

VICTORY THROUGH CONFLICT: ENMITY BETWEEN SATAN'S AND EVE'S SEED

Genesis 4:1-12	Cain with Abel (cf. 1 John 3:10-12)
Genesis 21:10	Ishmael with Isaac (cf. Gal. 4:28-29)
Genesis 3:15	Satan with Jesus (cf. Gal. 3:16)
Genesis 6:3-6	flesh with spirit (cf. Rom. 16:20; Gal. 5:16-17)

Genesis explains the conflict between good and evil from two perspectives: (1) humans chose to say no to God; and (2) disobedience was an immense and infinite offense to God's love and holiness. Genesis provides the answer to why life is tragic and futile in so many ways. The curse and its ensuing conflict are behind all of the conflicts recounted in the Bible.

NEEDS MET BY GENESIS

Who were the original hearers of Genesis and what did they need? Genesis was written to people who needed to know about three things: creation, Abraham, and Egypt. The original hearers had a rich religious history preserved from Abraham onward. They were also face to face with God, who had redeemed them out of Egypt and now thundered in glory from Mount Sinai. God had redeemed Israel from Egyptian slavery and took them directly into another difficult situation in the wilderness. There, Israel had to rely solely upon God to guide and provide. The material in Genesis helped flesh out who God was and what the roots and purpose were for his people. The structure and content of Genesis show that it was written to give clear answers to questions like these.

- How did the Israelites get into Egypt in the first place?
- Who is the God who saved Israel out of Egypt?
- Who is the nation of Israel and why did God choose to come to them?
- What is the purpose for the earth?
- Why are there problems in the created world?
- What is the solution to the curse of sin?
- What is the basis of God's salvation for believers?

Believers ask many of these questions today, especially the last four. Although we were not redeemed out of Egypt in the first exodus, in a similar way we do stand before God, having been redeemed out of the bondage of sin and guilt in the second exodus in Christ. Like Israel, believers today need to understand how their future hope for the Promised Land of the new heavens and earth is directly rooted in the original purposes of the first creation. The rest of Scripture provides the answers to the questions of Genesis—questions that relate to the brokenness of God's creation and its eventual healing.

OUTLINE OF GENESIS

I. GOD'S PLAN FOR HIS CREATION (1:1–2:25)
   A. The Place: Eden As Earth's Place of Beginnings (1:1-25)
   B. The People: Adam and Eve As Parents of the World's Population (1:26–2:25)

II. GOD'S CURSE ON THE VIOLATION OF HIS CREATION (3:1–7:24)
   A. Primary Recipients: The Earth Cursed and Adam and Eve Cast Out of Eden (3:1-24)
   B. Secondary Recipients: The Creation Destroyed by Flood (4:1–7:24)

III. GOD'S COVENANT FOR A NEW CREATION (8:1–50:26)
   A. God's Covenant through a New People: Noah (8:1–11:32)
   B. God's Covenant through Abraham (12:1–21:34)
   C. God's Promises through Abraham's Son Isaac (22:1–26:35)
   D. God's Promises through Abraham's Grandson Jacob (27:1–36:43)
   E. God's Promises through Abraham's Great-grandson Joseph (37:1–50:26)

GENESIS NOTES

1:1–2:25 GOD'S PLAN FOR HIS CREATION

Overview: The first half of this section opens with a title, "In the beginning God created the heavens and the earth" (1:1), and closes by again identifying itself as a report of that creation: "This is the account of the creation of the heavens and the earth" (2:4). The words of 2:4 restate the title of 1:1 and end the opening section on creation.

Genesis 1:1–2:4 shows the original nature of creation in three ways. First, the creation revealed the character of its Creator. The nation of Israel and redeemed people of all ages need to know that God is the supreme Creator of the universe, the One who creates merely by speaking a word. Second, the original creation was very good. Believers need to know that everything God created was very good. God is not one who only approximates what is best in his creation, nor does he need help to finish a good job. All that he touches by his creative power is supremely good. Third, the original creation displayed its purpose. Believers need to know that creation was intended to continue being very good and that humanity's role in that process was one of working together with God to rule the earth and, in ruling, to obey God's guidelines.

1:1-25 The Place: Eden As Earth's Place of Beginnings

Overview: The heart of the creation account is revealed by the repetition of these three phrases: (1) "And God said. . . ." God's word was the potent force behind creation and it laid the foundation for the authority of his future words (see, for example, Heb. 11:1-3). (2) "And it was so." God speaks and it happens. The sure and potent force of the Creator is behind any other words he will speak, whether for judgment or for salvation. (3) "And God saw that it was good" (Gen. 1:4, 10, 12, 18, 21, 25, 31). Why is there a repetition of these words? What made creation good? It was the fact that it was exactly the way the Creator wanted it to be. It was a perfect manifestation of his will and purpose. The repeated declaration of creation's goodness forms one pole; the second pole is the recreation of the new heavens and earth at the end of the age. The goodness of the first and last creations forms the framework for understanding both the horror of the evil and the hope for restoration that comes to believers today who stand between these two poles.

1:1 THE BEGINNING

Two major and differing translations of Genesis 1:1-2 are believed to be true today. The first reads: "When God began to create the heavens and the earth, the earth was formless and empty." This translation focuses on the state of the earth before God began the creative activity that is recorded in the Genesis account. Those who accept this translation believe that God's historical involvement with creation began after the earth already existed in a formless and empty state. That is, the earth was formless and empty, and then God began to create. According to this view, Genesis does not address how the earth originally came into existence in its formless and empty state, but what God did with a world already in existence.

The second translation reads: "In the beginning God created the heavens and the earth. The earth was empty, a formless mass. . . ." This traditional translation teaches that God created everything out of nothing. Therefore, his first step was to create the earth, which prior to that time did not exist, and he created it without form and population (empty). God then proceeded to shape and populate the world he had made as witnessed by the Genesis account.

Although the validity of either translation cannot be proven by grammar and syntax alone, the second translation is preferred for several reasons. First of all, a literary comparison of "In the beginning God created the heavens and the earth" (1:1) and "This is the account of the creation of the heavens and the earth" (2:4*a*) supports the idea that Genesis 1:1 is the first part of a literary framework within which the creation account is presented. Genesis 2:4*a* stands as the closing phrase for this literary unit and it refers backward, not forward, ending the account of creation begun at 1:1.

This framework with its beginning and ending statements substantiates the argument for 1:1 ("In the beginning God created the heavens and the earth") being independent of 1:2 ("The earth was empty, a formless mass") and standing alone as a comprehensive statement of God's creative work. Genesis 1:1 is a title that refers to the whole creative process described in Genesis 1:2–2:3. It is not a simple introduction that notes when God began to create. Literary form supports the conclusion that Genesis 1:1 is an independent and general statement of God's total creative activity from its start to its Sabbath wholeness.

Another argument supporting the second translation points out that the phrase "heavens and the earth," in 1:1, functions much like the English idioms "A to Z" or "top to bottom." It is a phrase that covers not only the "heaven" and the "earth," but everything in between as well. This reveals that God created, that he created in the beginning, and that his creative work involved the heavens, the earth and everything in between.

1:2-25 SEVEN DAYS OF CREATION

Some see a time gap between 1:1 and 1:2 in which they place long geological ages and the chaos stemming from the fall of Satan to earth. If, however, God originally created the earth as formless and empty, there is no need for such a gap.

Verse 1:2 introduces three environments for God's first step in creation: (1) an empty and formless earth, (2) a formless mass cloaked in darkness, and (3) the Spirit of God hovering over the surface.

account one step further by clarifying the following three roles which mankind was to fill: Mankind's first role was to populate the earth (1:28). This reveals some aspects of the nature and abilities of men and women: people were created to be members of families. Everyone was created to be a social creature. The image and likeness of God

---

THE DAYS OF CREATION

Formation	Population
Day 1 light	Day 4 Lights
Day 2 Waters/Expanse	Day 5 Fish/Birds
Day 3 Land	Day 6 Animals/People

The words "formless" and "empty" can be literally translated "unformed and unfilled." This phrase is the literary key to the creation account. In the first three days the earth was "formed," and in the second three it was "filled." The arrangement of those first six days shows a clear order in God's creation (see chart).

Days one, two, and three move creation from a formless to a formed state. Days four, five, and six move creation from an empty to a filled state. Order and population form the thrust of God's creative work.

(1:26-27) is most immediately linked to humanity's power to rule over creation (1:26) and to reflect the nature and graces of male and female gender (1:27). Human rule over the earth reflects God's perfect and sovereign rule over the universe. Human gender reflects God's infinitely deep character as the potent Creator and the perfectly wise, loving, and nurturing Person. God's likeness passed on to Adam's son Seth (5:1, 3). Ultimately, every human shares in God's likeness (James 3:9), but the redeemed person undergoes a process of more perfect conformity to God's image (Col. 3:10). That

---

THE DAY-AGE THEORY
Many argue that the six creative days of Genesis 1 involved millions of years, not literal twenty-four-hour days. This view is essential to the evolutionary hypothesis that requires long time periods for mutation and natural selection. However, the terms "evening" and "morning" suggest days of a normal length. Throughout the Old Testament the word "day" is never used figuratively when accompanied by a number. But whether they are interpreted as literal or figurative days, God fashioned the literary portrayal of his creation of the universe around six literal days. If something other than literal days is in view, then the text uses the term "day" as a figure of speech. Although normal word usage upholds the argument for literal days, the creation narrative's literary form of elevated and poetic prose and the desire to correlate the days of creation with the long geological ages posited by science leave room for a figurative use of the word "day."

1:26–2:25 The People: Adam and Eve As Parents of the World's Population
Overview: Some believe that 2:4-25 records a different account of creation than the account given in 1:1–2:3. This belief arises, in part, from viewing 2:4 as an introduction to what follows it rather than as a conclusion to what preceded. Whichever view is taken, these verses actually presuppose and elaborate on events that happened on the sixth day of creation as mentioned in 1:24-31. Thus, Genesis 1 outlines God's creation of the world and everything in it, while Genesis 2 details the creation of man and woman.

1:26–2:17 HUMANITY'S PHYSICAL AND MORAL LIMITATIONS
It is important to notice that the end of Genesis 1 and the beginning of Genesis 2 take the creation

image is more fully described as conformity to being "righteous, holy, and true" (Eph. 4:24).

The second role for humanity was that of subduing the physical earth (1:26, 28). Subduing means taming the earth and caring for it so that it will continue to be of profitable use. Subduing is not destroying. The Hebrew word translated "subdue" is used in 2 Samuel 8:11 to describe the activity of overcoming nations, and in Jeremiah 34:16 the same word describes the activity of making people slaves. The idea carried here by "subdue" is to tame and train, not to destroy or consume.

The third role given to man was his rule over the animals, but not over other humans (1:26, 28). Eden was to be the starting place for a society of sinless development that would eventually encompass the entire world; what was just a small garden was to expand to worldwide proportions. The method of starting small but having a plan with worldwide intentions appears again in God's plans for the world, starting with the small family of Abraham, and once more in the smallness of the hidden kingdom of God that will someday grow into God's complete and righteous rule over the entire earth.

This section also explains the moral context for humanity. God displayed his right to dictate: (1) where humans lived; (2) what they were to do; and even (3) what they were to eat. God alone is the sovereign King. The great expressions of his will in the laws of Moses and the teachings of Christ would continue his right to determine how believers live, what they do, and even what they eat. God originally made all his creatures to be vegetarians (1:29-30). His command regarding this would change only after the flood (9:3).

God rested on the seventh day because all his work was completed (2:1-2). This completion of his incredible work of creation is the reason he set the seventh day apart as blessed. God's rest became the basis for human rest under the Mosaic covenant (Exod. 16:23; 20:11; 31:15-16); for redemptive rest in Christ's salvation (Matt. 11:28); and for eternal rest in the new heavens and earth (Heb. 4:8-9). God's rest on the seventh day meant that he stopped creating, not that he stopped doing everything. He continues to maintain his creation and works of redemption every day, including the Sabbath, as John 5:17 shows.

Adam was to till and take care of the garden (Gen. 2:15). The original earth presented sinless man not with thorns and frustrations, but with a real and healthy challenge to tame it and to bring it to its inherent potential. The meaning of the tree of knowledge of good and evil is understood by the consequences that Adam and Eve experienced by eating from it (2:16-17). God had said that eating from it would bring death. Thus, the knowledge regarding the tree was knowledge gained by committing a negative act; Adam and Eve gained firsthand knowledge of evil by doing evil. That kind of knowledge brought deadly enlightenment.

2:18-25 MALE AND FEMALE UNITY AS CORULERS OF THE EARTH
Adam had no human person-to-person relationships, so God made a "companion who will help him" (2:18), one who was nearly a mirror image of him. The female was not inferior, she was, literally, "one corresponding to him"—like an image in a mirror. By saying, "she will be called 'woman'" (2:23), Adam discerned her character. Of everything created, only woman was qualified to be called by a term related to the Hebrew word for

man, *ish*. The word "woman" is formed simply by adding the feminine ending *ah*, thus making *ishah*, or "woman."

God instituted marriage for the human family (2:24). Marriage may be defined as a God-ordained, blessed, permanent, one-flesh, covenant relationship between a man and a woman. The permanence of the relationship is implied in the word "united" (2:24; cf. Mal. 2:14,16; Matt. 19:6-9; Mark 10:6-9; 1 Cor. 7:39). The close unity between man and woman is demonstrated in the one-flesh relationship of 2:24. That was a unified physical, emotional, and spiritual relationship between male and female. Before sinning, they were not ashamed of their bodies. Their awareness of self was without guilt and shame. There were only two limitations on their relationship: physical (the universe in which they lived) and moral (the forbidden tree).

3:1–7:24 GOD'S CURSE ON THE VIOLATION OF HIS CREATION
3:1-24 Primary Recipients: The Earth Cursed and Adam and Eve Cast Out of Eden
3:1-7 SATAN'S STRATEGY
Satan denied God's word (3:4) and led Eve to doubt God's will (3:1) and his good intentions (3:5). Satan had argued that restrictions were not good and had told Eve that because God's plan contained restrictions, it was flawed. The serpent had brought into force a will other than God's by directly contradicting God's commandments and telling Eve that she would not die if she ate of the forbidden tree. The test of the serpent was an ethical one. It was a test that caused Adam and Eve to question the authority of God's perfect will, and thereby moved them to act against God's will and everything that they knew was right.

The created quality of Adam's and Eve's wills was indeed "very good." They had free wills that were in need of expression and maturity, and which were originally in line with God's command to subdue and rule the earth. Satan's subtle encouragement was for Eve to ask herself, "What do I think?" No doubt all that she observed was that the tree was beautiful and good for food. No created thing could be bad in itself, for God had created it. But she became the standard-maker. Sin, in this case, was the wrong use of good things—her own will and the beautiful, though forbidden, tree.

The desire for wisdom (3:6) is a theme that pervades all of Scripture and is the foundation for books like Proverbs and Ecclesiastes. This recurring theme of the "wise man," very prominent in the Old Testament, reaches its high point in the person and work of Jesus—the perfect wisdom of God (1 Cor. 1:24).

3:8-2 THE TWOFOLD CURSE

Each curse was twofold. The serpent was directly cursed; it received a physical curse and the promise that it would ultimately be crushed by the seed of the woman (3:15). God promised that he would execute his rule through the seed of the woman and Christ came as a fulfillment of that promise. The victory of Christ was a direct crushing of Satan in fulfillment of this curse, for Satan was behind the serpent in Eden (Rom. 16:20; Rev. 12:9; 20:2).

The woman received the consequences of her actions, though they were not called a curse. The conflict between the man and the woman, foretold in the words "desire" and "master" in Genesis 3:16, is seen in the same Hebrew words used in 4:7. The strain that would occur between man and woman was in regard to the man's ruling and supremacy over the woman. The world of man-woman relationships specifically and all relationships generally had fallen prey to the upside-down chaos that resulted from Adam's sin. The consequences for women also included suffering great pain in childbirth. Thus, the only means of fulfilling God's promise to crush the serpent's head with the heel of someone born of a woman was through the childbearing sufferings of a woman.

Adam also was not directly cursed, but the earth was cursed on his account, as Paul later noted in Romans 8:20-22. The curse on the earth has caused toil and frustration for humanity. Work is not a result of the curse; toil and frustration are. Another result of Adam's sin was physical death (Gen. 3:19). Paul also noted that the root of death was in Adam's sin (Rom. 5:14-15).

Adam exercised faith and hope when he named the woman Eve (Gen. 3:20), for he looked to the life that the woman would bring forth. Adam and Eve could now only hope in the promise that someone born to Eve would undo the curses that they had caused through disobedience. The issue of Adam and Eve's shame at their nakedness confirmed the split between man and woman. They were no longer the original and pure "one flesh" that God had created them to be. God confirmed their instincts of shame by making clothing and covering them (3:21; cf. 3:7).

3:22-24 THE ISSUE OF ETERNAL LIFE

Another tree, the "tree of life," was then mentioned. But Adam and Eve were banished from the garden to keep them from it. That mysterious tree will not appear again until the dawn of the new heavens and earth spoken of in Revelation 2:7; 22:2, 14, 19.

4:1–7:24 Secondary Recipients: The Creation Destroyed by Flood

4:1-26 THE GENERATIONS OF CAIN

The genealogies of Genesis were designed to show both the multiplication of evil in the world and

God's plan of redemption. In 4:16-24 the line from Cain through Lamech shows the spread of murderers. In 5:3-32 the narrative moves from Adam, through Seth, to Noah and his sons. Noah's father said about him, "Lamech named his son Noah, for he said, 'He will bring us relief from the painful labor of farming this ground that the Lord has cursed.'" (5:29). These family trees separate the world into two categories: the descendants of Adam through Cain and those through Seth.

The fighting between the godly and ungodly lines that were born of the woman was manifested when Cain murdered Abel. The apostle John later used Cain to typify those who murder and show hatred toward the righteous (1 John 3:12). The ground already had been cursed by God; then Cain was cursed from the ground that had soaked up Abel's blood (Gen. 4:9-15), revealing that God still held sovereign right and protection over life. Lamech's killing of a man (4:23) shows that moral advancement did not keep pace with cultural progress, for there was a growing presumption among mankind on God's protective grace.

5:1-32 FROM ADAM THROUGH NOAH

The purpose of the genealogy in 5:1-32 was to show the development of the human family from Adam through Noah and to illustrate the falsity of Satan's claim, "you won't die." Some have used the Bible's genealogies in an attempt to reconstruct a chronological record back to creation. On this basis, James Ussher (1581–1656) dated creation at 4004 B.C. However, the problem with such efforts is that biblical genealogies were not intended to present a full chronology, but to trace a family line back to a chief ancestor. Furthermore, there is evidence of some gaps in the genealogies of Scripture (e.g., compare Gen. 11:13 with Luke 3:36).

6:1-4 SONS OF GOD AND DAUGHTERS OF MEN

The "sons of God" mentioned in Genesis 6:2 have been identified in three different ways: (1) as Seth's apostate descendants who intermarried with the depraved descendants of Cain, (2) as fallen angels who took on physical bodies to cohabit with women of the human race, and (3) as despotic chieftains of Cainite descent who married a plurality of wives in order to expand their dominion.

Although each of the three views has its problems, those of the "angel" view can be most satisfactorily resolved. The expression "sons of God" is used exclusively in the Old Testament of angels (Job 1:6; 2:1; 38:7). According to this view, the Nephilim (from a Hebrew word meaning "to fall") were the monstrous offspring of these unnatural unions. (For more on the Nephilim, cf. Num. 13:33.) Although they were big, they were not stronger than God, who blotted them out (Gen.

6:7; 7:23) in the flood, along with the rest of the world.

In Genesis 6:3 a question arises. Evil mortals were striving with God, yet at the same time their lives were sustained by God alone. Why did God allow such enemies to continue existing? In answer, note that the meaning of the name *Israel* is "the one who strives with God." Even Israel (Jacob) and the Israelites, God's chosen people, often questioned God's will. If God destroyed all those who resisted his will, all people would soon be destroyed as they were in the flood. In contrast, Noah was one man who followed God's will totally.

6:5-12 NOAH IN THE CONTEXT OF AN EVIL SOCIETY
The Hebrew root for Noah is the same root behind the English words "comfort" and "grieved." Both God and humanity shared in the pain caused by sin. Both also shared in the pain of what their hands had labored over. And each in their own ways would share in the comfort brought by God's redemption. It is interesting to compare 6:6 with 5:29. Both verses use the same two Hebrew root words in a similar order. "Relief" (5:29) and "sorry" (6:6) come from the same Hebrew root. "Labor" (5:29) and "made" (6:6) are related similarly.

Although God is perfect, he can still experience genuine sorrow over what he has created. He can grieve over his creation just as he can rejoice over it (cf. Gen. 1). In the same manner his perfect Son could also experience genuine sorrow over the lost condition of his world (Matt. 23:37). God's love and his hatred of sin form the indispensable foundation of his plans for redemption through the incarnation of Christ.

6:13-22 THE ARK
While God was grieved with mankind in general, there was one man, Noah, who pleased him. Therefore, God told him to make an ark to save him from the coming flood and destruction. Actually, the ark was more of a barge than a ship. It was 450 feet long, 75 feet broad, and 45 feet high, giving it a capacity of 1,400,000 cubic feet. As many as 522 modern railroad boxcars could have fit inside. But only 150 boxcars would have been sufficient to house two of every air-breathing creature, including animals now living and those that are now extinct. The covenant that God told Noah he would make with him (6:18) related to Noah's salvation (9:9-16) and contrasted with everything else on earth that would perish in the flood. God told Noah, "But I solemnly swear to keep you safe in the boat."

7:1-24 THE FLOOD
Was the flood universal or local? Indications for a universal flood include the depth of the water (7:19), the death of all flesh (7:21-22), the duration of the flood (371 days), and the need for the ark. Had the flood been only a local one, God could have directed Noah, his family and the animals to migrate to a safe place. The ark's contents are emphasized in 7:13-16. The phrase "every kind of breathing animal" refers back to the event of creation recorded in Genesis 1. There is repeated emphasis on the flood or waters and on the earth in 7:17-18; note also the mention of heavens. The water moved progessively higher; the ark was lifted up above the ground; the water greatly increased (7:18); all mountains under the heavens were covered (7:19); and finally the water was twenty-two feet higher than the mountaintops (7:20).

Every living thing was "wiped out" (7:23), just as God had said (6:7). All that had the breath of life—man, cattle, beasts, and swarming things—died. This portrays the unraveling of the act of creation recounted in Genesis 1. The rain (7:12) continued for 40 days; the ark rested on Ararat after 150 days (7:24; 8:4); and all the waters did not recede for a year and 10 days (7:11; 8:14).

8:1–50:26 GOD'S COVENANT FOR A NEW CREATION
Overview: The historical narrative moves quickly from Noah through Babel to Abraham. After Abraham received the great Abrahamic covenant, he went down to Egypt because a famine had occurred in Canaan. The relationship between the Promised Land and Egypt pervades Genesis 12–50 and makes preparation for understanding the book of Exodus. In Egypt Abraham saw God's power and miracles and was sent out of Egypt with great wealth from Pharaoh. At the end of Genesis a famine in Canaan would bring Abraham's children once again down into Egypt. Hundreds of years later their ancestors also would see the power of God and be sent out of Egypt by another pharaoh. Many years afterward a baby, Jesus, would make a trip with Mary and Joseph to Egypt in order to escape murder by Herod the Great.

Egypt functions not only as the place where Israel was placed into bondage but also as the place where God preserved his chosen line from famine and threat of death. For Abraham, Egypt served as a place of preservation. For Israel (Jacob), Egypt provided food in a time of famine and made possible the multiplication of his family into a great nation. For Jesus, Egypt provided a place of safety from Herod (cf. Hos. 11:1; Matt. 2:15). Egypt, therefore, often functions in the Bible as a place of preservation and salvation—preservation from the evils in the Promised Land (famine, death threats) until God's appointed time of salvation. A simple lesson for all eternity can be learned here: God does control and preserve the lives and destinies of all men according to his eternal plan.

But why did God choose not to sustain his people in the very land he had promised them? Why did they have to travel to the land of Egypt? The reason is that Egypt not only served as a place of preservation, but also functioned as a place of experiencing God's physical salvation. There are both physical and spiritual elements to salvation. In the history of God's people, they were often physically saved from human wrath and oppression. And through that history believers now can discern, along with the Israelites themselves, that the essential reality of God's spiritual salvation is release from divine wrath and satanic oppression. In addition, since Egypt was a land of "old" things and ways, it served for the Israelites as a place for learning things that they would later use while in the wilderness and the Promised Land.

8:1–11:32 God's Covenant through a New People

8:1–9:17 THE COVENANT WITH NOAH

After the earth had been flooded for 150 days, God remembered Noah. The word "remembered" (8:1) is one of the great words for expressing redemption and salvation in the Old Testament (cf. Exod. 2:24-25). Although the flood story ends with 8:22, there is a spiritual as well as physical watershed at 8:1 where the reader is reminded, "But God remembered Noah. . . ." In Scripture when something is said about God remembering, this signals a major act of redemption for the ones remembered (cf. 9:15-16; 19:29; 30:22; Exod. 2:24; 6:5). God's remembering of Noah explicitly begins his major design for bringing about worldwide redemption; the record of that design stretches from Genesis 8 through Genesis 50.

In some ways the flood returned the earth to a condition that was similar to its state at the beginning of God's creation. Although the earth still retained its basic form and probably had not changed drastically under the floodwaters, water covered the earth as it did in the beginning. Also, it was again empty of people and animal life, except for the handful of people and animals that were aboard the ark. After Genesis 8:13, time began to be reckoned by Noah's age. He was the head of a new race and father of a new beginning of history. He, like Adam, was commanded to be fruitful and multiply (8:17; cf. 1:28).

God's covenant with Noah was foundational for his grace seen later in the cross. (See the discussion of God's covenant with Noah in the introductory section, "The Bible's Big Picture.") In the flood, God displayed his hatred and vengeance toward sin. In the rainbow he showed that man's deserved punishment for his acts of sin would not be immediately fulfilled. He also revealed that his hatred of sin would not be expressed until his plan of grace

was completed. How then, could God stand to face mankind's continued sin? The answer lies in his character: though God is holy and just, he is also longsuffering. God is always more interested in salvation than in damnation.

9:18–10:1 NOAH'S DESCENDANTS

The story of Noah's offspring recounts a curse placed on Ham (Canaan). This curse would be very important for the Israelites, who were in the wilderness, about to enter the Promised Land where they would run up against the Canaanites. The sin of Ham was disrespect toward his father, Noah. The curse of Ham's son, Canaan, was actually a curse on all of Ham's descendants. Thus, the curse on Canaan was not specifically directed against the man Canaan himself, but against the Canaanite people in general. Ham's sin was his frivolous look upon his naked father, an act in which he abandoned God's moral code. Canaan's descendants acted as their ancestor had—with moral abandon (Lev. 18:24-30). The curse on Canaan was fulfilled in the destruction and the conquest of the land by the Israelites led by Joshua.

10:2-32 THE GENEALOGY THROUGH SHEM

Genesis 10 is a table of the ancient nations that reveals where the different peoples were scattered, and 11:1-9 tells why they were scattered. The sons of Japheth (10:2-5) are the Indo-Europeans; the sons of Ham (10:6-20) are the Africans and various peoples of Babylon, Assyria and Palestine; and the sons of Shem (10:21-32) are the Semitic peoples. "Eber," the son of Shem, is singled out in 10:24-25 and 11:16-17 and is probably the chief ancestor of the Hebrew people.

The genealogy in 10:2-32 serves two purposes: (1) It begins to focus on Abraham's line: the order is Japheth, Ham, and then Shem, the ancestor of Abraham. (2) It prepares for the story of the Tower of Babel, which explains how the "earth was populated with the people of these nations after the Flood" (10:32). This genealogy does not mention all the names or identify all the peoples (cf. 10:5, 20, 31-32). Shem is mentioned last in order to clear the way for Abraham. This shows that the story about Babel was included as part of the preparation for the story of Abraham. The unity of the human race was shattered and many nations were formed. This prepares the reader for the promise that all nations will be blessed in Abraham (Gen. 12:3). Babel is also traced to Ham (10:10; NASB, TLB), and thus stands as one of the results of the curse on Canaan. The people of Babel, along with Ham, failed to show respect toward their father, who was ultimately God.

11:1-9 THE TOWER OF BABEL

The "plain in the land of Babylon" (11:2) is the fertile plain of Babylonia (modern Iraq) that lies between the Tigris and Euphrates rivers. The Tower of Babel may have been an early type of Babylonian ziggurat; these pyramid-like towers served as shrines for mountain-dwelling deities. The story of Babel shows how people banded together in an evil effort to block God's plan for mankind to fill the earth. (See "scattering all over the world,"11:4.)

11:10-32 FROM SHEM TO ABRAHAM
At this point, the Genesis narrative begins its focus on the family of Abraham (around 2166–1991 B.C.). The genealogies in Genesis 5 and 11 both move respectively toward the next key figures in God's redemptive history: Noah (5:29) and Abraham (11:26). Both of these men had a special part in God's plan to recreate his kingdom on earth. Ur, Abraham's hometown (11:31), was the ancient capital of the Sumerian kingdom, the earth's first great civilization (see introductory map). Situated on the bank of the Euphrates River, it was an important commercial center with two harbors. Nanna, the moon god, was the city's patron deity.

was offered the spoils of war. Would Abraham take the spoils from the king of Sodom (14:21-24)? No, because it would show that he lacked faith in God. Afterward God confirmed his great reward to Abraham (15:1).

The major focus of 16:1–21:34 is the birth of the promised son of Abraham and Sarah. That son would become the first of many in the Abrahamic line that would stretch out until God would fulfill his promise to bless all the earth in Abraham through the greatest of all Abraham's descendants, Jesus Christ. The twists and turns leading to the birth and establishment of Isaac as Abraham's sole heir show God's sovereignty over human frailty. Then, during the bondage of Jacob, Isaac's son in Paddan Aram, God would increase the tribe of Abraham into the majority of the twelve tribes of Israel.

12:1-9 THE FOUNDATION OF THE ABRAHAMIC PROMISE
Abraham's initial call was at Ur in Chaldea (11:31; Acts 7:2-3), but the call was renewed at Haran

---

GOD'S BLESSINGS TO ABRAHAM

12:1-3	Blessings promised
12:7	Land identified
13:15-16	Land and seed emphasized
13:17-18	Land surveyed
15:5	Seed reemphasized
17:9-14	The sign of the covenant
17:15-21	Seed reemphasized
18:l0	Seed reemphasized
21:1-7	Seed given
22:1-18	Certainty of the covenant reemphasized

12:1–21:34 God's Covenant through Abraham
Overview: The section 12:1–21:34 emphasizes the personal and property aspects of the Abrahamic covenant. Abraham would gain the land promised to him and an heir to inherit it. His blessing would extend to those closely associated with him, which at first included his nephew, Lot (13:10). Two potential conflicts are noted. First, even though Lot was not Abraham's own son, Abraham did not strive with him over how they would divide the land between them for the grazing of their flocks and herds. Instead, he relied on God, not quarreling with his relatives for the land he would receive. Readers may have wondered whether Abraham would fight with Lot over the land (13:5-8). Abraham allowed Lot to take the best land because he did not need to fight for the land that he believed God had given him. Later God would confirm his promise of giving the land to Abraham (13:14-17). The second potential conflict arose when Abraham

(12:1) (see introductory map). God revealed his will for worldwide redemption, and all the nations would find their blessing in what he would do through his promises to Abraham. (For an overview of the covenant with Abraham, see the introductory section, "The Bible's Big Picture.") God reinforced his promises to Abraham several times and in a number of different ways (see chart).

The promises would not come instantly or all at once, but they would gradually be realized over a period of thousands of years. Because that slow unfolding of God's promises could cause believers to weaken in their faith and desire an affirmation of God's faithfulness, God consistently and repeatedly affirmed his promises to Abraham and his offspring.

12:10-20 ABRAHAM'S EXODUS
Abraham and Sarah's departure from Egypt (12:10-20) is an event parallel to Israel's later national exodus from that land. Both events reveal something of God's might and plan. Since the bondage

of God's people was not accidental, deliverance and preservation were sure. Abraham had gone to Egypt because of a famine (12:10). Famines were frequent in Palestine, a land with a marginal climate, where agriculture was dependent upon rainfall. Since the Nile River furnished a more certain supply of water for cattle and crops, it made Egypt a haven from hunger in times of famine. God inflicted Pharaoh and his household with diseases (12:17) and miraculously preserved Abraham and his family, especially Sarah, God's chosen bearer of the promised son. The great plagues on Egypt that occurred just before the exodus of Israel were not the first that God had sent upon an Egyptian pharaoh. This fact would have confirmed to the readers of Genesis, who had just witnessed another pharaoh's defeat at the exodus from Egypt, that nothing is accidental with God. Even great and powerful pharoahs could not keep him from doing his promised work.

13:1–15:21 ABRAHAM RESCUES LOT

Because their flocks and herds had become so large, Abraham and Lot divided the land (13:1-18). Lot chose to reside in the Jordan Valley. This valley, while barren and desolate today, was well watered before God destroyed Sodom and Gomorrah (13:10). A major environmental change appears to have taken place as a result of God's judgment.

Hebron, founded around 1700 B.C., did not exist as a city in Abraham's day (see introductory map). The site Abraham visited was called Mamre; the mention of Hebron (13:18) is a later scribal note indicating where Mamre was located.

Genesis 14 tells of an early invasion of Palestine by a coalition of four Mesopotamian kings who invaded the plain of the Jordan, subjugating the five cities there, including Sodom (14:1-3). Lot, Abraham's nephew, was among those taken captive. But God is sovereign over the nations, and Lot was saved because of his relationship to Abraham (cf. 12:3). In future generations when the nation of Israel was attacked and her people taken captive by Assyria and Babylon, nations also from Mesopotamia, she would find that her preservation as a nation was assured in much the same way— because of her relationship to Abraham.

When Abraham returned from defeating the four kings, he was met by Melchizedek, the king of "Salem" (14:18). "Salem" is believed to be an early name for Jerusalem (see introductory map). Melchizedek was not just a king; he was also a priest of the Most High God (cf. Ps. 110:4; Heb. 5:5-10; 7:1-10).

In Genesis 15 God confirmed his covenant with Abraham and foretold Israel's future enslavement in Egypt. This chapter's importance in placing the Egyptian enslavement squarely in God's sovereign and predetermined plan for redemption can scarcely be overestimated. Abraham was told that a 400-year period of enslavement and oppression would come upon his family. The 400 years is a round figure that is given more exactly as 430 years in Exodus 12:40. After four generations (of 100 years each) Abraham's descendants would return to the land. At that time the oppressing nation (Egypt) would be judged (Gen. 15:14) and Israel would come out with many possessions.

After that prediction, the covenant between God and Abraham was finalized. This fact would be highly significant for the Israelites who, under Moses, had just been released from Egyptian bondage. Note that Israel's return to Canaan was linked to God's plan for the Amorites (Gen. 15:16), "Amorite" being a general term for the inhabitants of Canaan. Therefore, Israel's return and the end of the Amorite's iniquity were closely linked.

16:1-16 ABRAHAM'S MISGUIDED EFFORTS AT GAINING A SON

Ishmael was a son of Abraham but not of the promise (16:1-16). The Nuzi tablets, cuneiform documents dating from about 1500 B.C., shed light on why Sarah did what she did (16:1-4). Giving Hagar to Abraham was in keeping with an ancient custom that allowed a wife who was unable to bear children to give a concubine to her husband in order to gain an heir. What was missing, as noted in 16:2, was a request for the Lord's advice. Abraham's action was not rebellious, just hasty and unwise. Note the parallel between the statement, "And Abram agreed" (Gen. 16:2) and God's words to Adam, "you listened to your wife" (Gen. 3:17). Would a son by Hagar be the answer? No. But her son, Ishmael, was greatly blessed anyway.

Why was Ishmael blessed (16:10)? Because the Abrahamic covenant stated that any offspring of Abraham would be blessed, even if that offspring was not received according to the promise. The descendants of Ishmael are modern-day Arabs, blessed with incredible wealth that silently existed beneath their tents even at the time of Hagar: the wealth of oil.

17:1-27 THE COVENANT SIGN OF CIRCUMCISION

Abraham aligned himself with God's covenant sign of circumcision in an account that is sandwiched between two responses of his faithlessness: his attempt to gain a son through Hagar (16:1-4) and his reaction of falling down and laughing when God said he and Sarah would have a child (17:17-18). Circumcision, a sign pointing away from itself to something else, was the external mark or evidence of Abraham's covenant relationship to God. In view was God's intention to create a pure race of obedient people who would fill, rule, and subdue the earth—a race bearing a mark that showed they were followers of God's way.

18:1–19:38 SODOM AND GOMORRAH

Abraham still had to learn about God's wrath against sin and of his grace toward the righteous. God desired to share with Abraham how he would vent his wrath against Sodom and Gomorrah (18:16-33). God initiated the conversation (18:17), for he wanted Abraham to become aware of his grace toward the righteous. In talking with God, Abraham explored, but did not bargain with, God's mercy and justice. The direct relationship between the Abrahamic covenant and personal obedience is seen in 18:18-19. The blessings of that covenant would come by God's sovereign promise, but only for the particular people or groups that obeyed his commands.

Oriental etiquette has a strong emphasis on caring for the needs of strangers. Both Abraham and Lot proved that they were sensitive to these customs of hospitality, which were regarded as a sacred duty, since it was believed that guests were sent by God himself. The promises that God made to be fulfilled through Abraham included a blessing for all people, even those who were strangers to God's covenant (18:18). Because of this promise, Abraham's hospitality has reached out to strangers down through the centuries, even to believers today, through the work of his descendant, Jesus Christ.

According to oriental custom, a host was responsible for protecting his guests from harm, whatever the cost (19:4-8). Thus, Lot offered his daughters to the wicked men in order to protect his guests. The demands of hospitality explain, but do not justify, Lot's actions. Why did God have compassion on Lot (19:16)? Because "God had listened to Abraham's request and kept Lot safe" (19:29), which was in accordance with his covenant with Abraham. God had told Abraham, "All the families of the earth will be blessed through you" (Gen. 12:3), and Lot was no exception. However, Lot's lineage, known later as the Moabites and Ammonites, would become enemies of Israel (19:30-38).

20:1-18 ABRAHAM AND THE PHILISTINES

Abraham moved into the land of the Philistines where he again told Sarah to say that she was his sister and not his wife (cf. Abraham's similar deception in Egypt in 12:11-19). As a result, Sarah was taken into the king's house. Would Sarah be lost to a Philistine king? No. This event, as was true of the one in Egypt, shows the importance of preserving Sarah's as well as Abraham's great claim to God's promises. God was greater than any human pharaoh or king. Notice God's power over the event of childbearing (20:18). All of this account needs to be read in the full light of the promise of Isaac's

birth (17:21). Abraham should have waited for God's specific commands before following his own fleshly and logical options. As the people of Israel heard these stories, they would realize how secure they were as God's people. Nothing could stop his promised blessings of salvation and ultimate deliverance from taking place.

21:1-34 ISAAC IS BORN

God had said a son would be born to Abraham and Sarah (stressed three times in 21:1-2). Read this account in light of what Abraham had tried to do intentionally to achieve this promise through a son by Hagar, as well as what he had done unintentionally to block it by pawning Sarah off to Pharaoh and a Philistine king. According to custom, if a natural heir was born, the heir through the slave woman would lose the right of being chief inheritor (21:10-11). However, previous heirs were to be well treated. In the desert near Beersheba, God confirmed to Hagar that he would continue to care for Ishmael, the previous heir, and make of his descendants a great nation (21:17-18).

Abraham then settled near Beersheba, figuratively claiming the land God had promised him. The tree he planted (21:33) indicated to God his permanent residence there and his being at peace. Then Abraham worshiped God. The major migration of the Philistines (a group of "Sea Peoples") by boat from the Aegean Islands took place around 1168 B.C. The reference here to the Philistines (21:34), which is supported by archaeological discoveries, provides evidence of earlier movements of these people to Palestine.

22:1–26:35 God's Promises through Abraham's Son Isaac

22:1-24 GOD TESTS ABRAHAM'S FAITH

According to tradition, the mountain in the land of Moriah where God tested Abraham (22:1) is the hill upon which Solomon built the temple (2 Chron. 3:1). When Abraham had successfully passed the testing, God declared his promises to him (22:16-18). Was God's command that Abraham slay his son Isaac immoral? No, for God was testing Abraham's willingness to obey him completely, and he stopped him before he could actually kill Isaac. However, one day God would allow the sacrifice of his own Son for mankind's sins. God gave a special promise to Abraham (22:16-17) because of the combination of his obedience and faith (cf. 15:6).

23:1-20 ABRAHAM BURIES SARAH

After Sarah's death, Abraham just wanted to purchase a cave for her burial place (23:3-9), but Ephron would not sell his cave without the adjoining field. According to Hittite land laws, a land owner had to continue to pay taxes until he disposed of the entire property. It is very possible that Ephron insisted on selling the whole plot so he would not have to continue paying taxes. After bartering with Ephron over the price of the cave and field in a way typical of those in the Near East, Abraham gained a place to bury Sarah.

24:1–25:12 ABRAHAM FINDS A BRIDE FOR ISAAC

When Abraham's servant was told to get a wife for Isaac, he placed his hand under Abraham's thigh. This gesture accompanied the servant's solemn oath to return with a wife for Isaac. The area beneath the thigh was regarded as the seat of procreative powers and the placing of the servant's hand there pointed to the nature of this oath. It would be the means for gaining a wife for Isaac and making possible the birth of the next generation of Abraham's descendants; it also highlighted the importance of acquiring the proper wife, thus preserving the family line through which God's promises would be fulfilled.

The servant was sent to Mesopotamia (24:10), which refers to the land of Aram between the Tigris and Euphrates rivers. Isaac took a wife from among his relatives, not from among the Canaanites. There were to be no political marriage alliances in Abraham's family to secure the land God had promised (24:3). By arranging a marriage for his son that gained him nothing materially or politically, Abraham proved that he trusted God to give the land of Palestine to his descendants. Isaac then became Abraham's sole inheritor (25:1-12).

25:13-34 ISAAC AND ESAU

The life-style of Ishmael's descendants (25:12-18) is attested to by the words, "The clans descended from Ishmael camped close to one another" (25:18).

Isaac's oldest son, Esau, had a birthright that included the right of a double inheritance, the privilege of becoming head of the family, and the right of a special parental blessing (25:19-34; cf. 27:19, 36; Deut. 21:17). Ancient clay tablets found at Nuzi indicate it was legitimate to exchange one's birthright for something else. Esau's problem was his casual and unconcerned attitude toward the birthright (25:31-34; Heb. 12:16-17). It was not simply the question of his despising his place as the first-born. It was his indifference to the privilege of carrying on God's plan for world redemption through Abraham and his children. Esau did not care whether or not he was next in line for carrying on God's work of redemption to the world.

26:1-11 ISAAC AND ABIMELECH

When another famine occurred, God kept Isaac in the land rather than sending him to Egypt, in order to state his covenant to him. Isaac's being in Gerar set the atmosphere for his lie to the Philistines regarding Rebekah (26:7-11). He lied even though he had just been promised God's blessing and his

heir had already been born. This section's close similarities to Abraham's lie to Pharaoh is designed to show how Abraham's and Isaac's fears were equally groundless in light of God's promise. God would protect his chosen ones and fulfill his promises just as he had said. The fears of all God's people who follow after, as physical or spiritual descendants of Abraham, are equally groundless.

26:12-35 THE DISPUTES ABOUT WELLS

The disputes about the wells and their being stopped up amounted to an attempt by the Philistines to drive Isaac out of the land. This contributed to the whole drama of how God accomplished his promise for his people's possession of the land. Would Isaac, the promised heir, find no place to live in the Promised Land? God told him, "Do not be afraid" (26:24), and Isaac responded by calling upon the name of the Lord (26:25). The events surrounding the naming of Beersheba (26:26-33) are a confirmation of how God brings blessing from foreign peoples (Gen. 12:1-3). In contrast to all of Abraham's earlier efforts to make sure Isaac married a proper woman is a note concerning Isaac's concern about the wrong marriages of his son Esau (26:34-35).

27:1–36:43 God's Promises through Abraham's Grandson Jacob

Overview: The purpose of this section is to highlight the struggle between Jacob and Esau. It shows how the blessing would come to Jacob, and it also foreshadows the character of his descendants, the nation of Israel, whose name means, "one that struggles with God." Jacob (later named Israel) struggled at birth (25:22-26), for his birthright (25:27-34), in his deceptive grab for the blessing of the firstborn (27:1-46), and with God at the Jabbok River (32:1-32).

Who were the men who gained the birthright throughout the book of Genesis? Many times it was not the person expected to receive it. Much emphasis is placed on the reversal of birthrights from the older or oldest son to a younger one. Abraham, Isaac, Jacob and Joseph were all younger sons. Later on, two other younger sons would be chosen for God's blessings: David and Solomon.

Genesis 28–36 relates the births of each of Jacob's sons whose descendants would become the twelve tribes of Israel. The story would be of great interest to those who had recently come out of Egypt or to those who wanted the details of their heritage. But this story of origins is told with warts and all, because it ultimately is a story of how God brought redemption to his people. God is portrayed as perfect, but his agents are seen for what they really were—sinful, needy people trying to gain favor with God, even though at times it was for the wrong reasons.

Jacob's story tells of God's covenant that was given to him in the land, of God blessing him while he was working for Laban in Paddan Aram, and of his receiving a new name and new beginning as he reentered the Promised Land. Years earlier Jacob's grandfather, Abraham, had gone to Egypt, miracles had occurred there, and he had come out richer than he had gone in. Jacob was forced to go to Paddan Aram, he prospered during his stay there, and he left as a wealthy man who found God's favor upon his return to the Promised Land. For God's chosen people, even exile can be a time of preservation and renewed blessing.

27:1-45 GOD ALLOWS THE RIGHT MAN TO BE BLESSED: JACOB

In Isaac's plans to bless Esau, he was ignoring the plain word of God about which son should have supremacy (25:23). Isaac's blessing of Jacob, which was actually intended for Esau, pictured Jacob as master of his brothers (27:29; cf. 25:23). When Esau came in later and Isaac realized what had happened, he trembled because he saw the hand of God in what he had unknowingly done (27:33). The Nuzi tablets attest to the fact that an oral blessing was legally binding. Once given, the blessing could not be successfully contested (27:33). Afterward, Esau lamented loudly, hated Jacob, and made plans to kill him.

Jacob had highly valued the covenant blessing and had sought it eagerly, even though his methods were deceptive. God blessed him in spite of his sin, not because of it. The key actor in this story was God, not Jacob, Isaac or Esau. God was forging ahead with his redemptive plan. Since he was accomplishing his goals through real humans, his perfect plan was worked through sinful and error-ridden people. The long line of imperfect agents in God's redemptive plan forms a stark contrast to the single and perfect consummation of that plan—Jesus Christ.

27:46–36:43 JACOB SECURES THE PROMISE TO ABRAHAM

In the section 27:46–28:22, the covenant is reaffirmed to Abraham's grandson, Jacob. Isaac had given Jacob the blessing of Abraham's covenant (28:4), and then God confirmed that blessing to Jacob in a dream (28:10-17). The next morning Jacob made a vow to God (28:18-22) that anticipated his return to the Promised Land. Jacob could have been about seventy-seven years old as he served Laban for his daughter Rachel (29: 1-20). He married both Leah and Rachel (29:21-30), and with them and their two maidservants he fathered his twelve children (29:31–30:24). Then Jacob used deception to gain provisions for his household (30:25-43). Why was he blessed by God in spite of his deceptive methods? Jacob did not receive God's blessing because he deserved it, but because he was a descendant of Abraham, and a recipient of God's promise to Abraham.

Although Jacob married two wives (29:27), bigamy was an exception to God's original plan for marriage (2:24; Mal. 2:13-15). It is never condoned or condemned in Scripture, but it also seems to result in unhappy situations (1 Sam. 1:2-7). The mandrakes that Leah's son found (30:14) were herbs similar in size and shape to a small apple. They were thought in ancient times to stimulate physical desire and aid in conception. Rachel's motive for wanting them was for increased fertility; but while she got the mandrakes, Leah got another son (30:17). God was in control, and later he gave Rachel her first child, Joseph, according to his own perfect timing (30:22-24).

In his breeding methods Jacob sought to influence the color of the animal's offspring by placing peeled, white striped branches before the animals as they bred (30:37-43). These strange actions were apparently based on a God-given dream (31:10-13). Whether or not God told Jacob to actually use such methods, it was he who sovereignly caused the birth of the animals that would prosper Jacob and give him success (31:9).

After the Lord commanded Jacob to return to the Promised Land, he began his journey with his wives, livestock and other possessions (31:13-20). Before leaving, Rachel stole her father's "household gods" (31:19). These were small figures of female deities that probably were important to Rachel for two reasons: they were thought to guarantee fertility, and they symbolized inheritance rights. No doubt Rachel wanted to guarantee that she would have more children and to maintain Jacob's right to a portion of Laban's wealth. Jacob later buried these images at Shechem (35:2-4).

When Jacob reached the entrance to the Promised Land, he prayed at the Jabbok River (32:9-12). Note the revelation of God's character in this section. Struggling with God will bring victory when such struggling is done by means of prayer, earnestly and humbly seeking his favor. The name "Israel" means "one who struggles with God." That explains the inclusion of the dialogue of 32:26-29. Jacob was struggling for a blessing. Hosea 12:1-5, which refers to Jacob, should be read in this connection. Ever since his birth, Jacob had struggled with men to receive the birthright that would give him the blessings of the Abrahamic covenant. Here he was shown that in all his previous human efforts to gain the blessing through deception, his real enemy had been God. In Hosea 12:6 the nation of Israel was told to do the same thing as Jacob did here—prevail by prayer to God, not by looking for help from human sources. Jacob's struggle was a physical picture of his need for God, and many years later the nation had the same need. Jacob learned that as heir of the covenant promises, he had nothing to fear from humans (32:11). Wrestling with God for his blessings should release all believers from their fear of lesser mortals.

Jacob's safe arrival in Shechem (33:1-20) fulfilled God's promise to him given in 28:15. Jacob's daughter was violated by Shechem, the son of Hamor, the area's ruler. Afterward Hamor advised Jacob and his sons of how to establish a union with the land's residents and achieve peace and prosperity there. Jacob demanded that the men of Shechem be circumcised, thus identifying themselves with God's covenant people, before allowing intermarriage. But instead of seeking a peaceful way, Simeon and Levi used deception and physical violence for survival in the land, killing all the men of Shechem in revenge for Shechem's violation of their sister. Jacob rebuked them for their excessive action (34:1-31), and years later he judged them for it (49:5-7). The incident at Shechem stood against intermarriage with the residents of Canaan—something that God opposed for Jacob and his family. This incident also resulted in great fear of Jacob's family among the resident Canaanites (35:5). That fear also was a result of the family members' purifying themselves before God at Bethel, for God was their real protection against anyone who might harm them.

At Bethel, where years earlier Jacob had vowed to make God his God (28:21), God reconfirmed his covenant with him (35:1-15). See introductory map for Bethel. As the family traveled on, Jacob's last son, Benjamin, was born and Rachel died in childbirth. Reuben wrongfully used his father's concubine, which resulted in the forfeiture of his birthright as the firstborn son (49:3-4; cf. 1 Chron. 5:1).

The generations of Isaac's son Esau are listed in 36:2-43. Note how many times it is mentioned that Esau was also called Edom (36:1, 8, 9, 43). Esau was the ancestor of the Edomites, perpetual enemies of Israel throughout the Old Testament period (cf. Obadiah, which is a book of prophecy against Edom). This genealogy told the Israelites, who had left Egypt in the exodus, where their enemies came from.

37:1–50:26 God's Promises through Abraham's Great-Grandson Joseph

Overview: The section of 37:1–50:26 relates back to 15:13-16 and also prepares the reader for Israel's upcoming exodus from Egypt. It also emphasizes dreams, because when several of God's leaders were in bondage in foreign countries, God appeared to them by this means. See the parallels in the accounts of Abraham, Daniel, and the dreams of Joseph, Jesus' earthly stepfather. This section also shows how the seed of Israel was preserved (50:20) in spite of famine in the land. Although the ground was still cursed, God continued to protect his own people. Jacob was buried in the land, and Joseph would be also. Compare 49:26, where Jacob

blessed Joseph, with 37:7-11, where Joseph told about his dreams and his family bowing down before him. Although this section ends with a coffin, that fact is not bad. Joseph's command to take his coffin to the Promised Land represents the hope of God's future visit to the world (50:24) to make possible the salvation of mankind.

37:1-38 JOSEPH SOLD INTO SLAVERY

Joseph's special robe is variously interpreted as ornamented, varicolored, or long-sleeved. It designated Joseph as a favored son and was a garment that an overseer, not a worker, would wear. His exaltation by his father and the sharing of his dream of exaltation offended his family, but these facts were directly in line with what God had planned for him. Although the Ishmaelites and Midianites are interchangeable in this passage (cf. Judg. 8:22, 24), it is probable that Ishmael was their ancestor, whereas Midian was their land and place of origin.

38:1-30 JUDAH AND TAMAR

This story is designed to show the righteousness of Tamar and the negative attributes of Judah (compare 38:25-26 with 37:32-33). In 38:25-26, Tamar "sent this message" to Judah and Judah "recognized" the tokens she sent. In 37:32-33 Judah and his brothers "took" Joseph's bloodstained coat as a message to Jacob. Jacob "recognized" Joseph's coat and was thus deceived. This structure presents parallels involving the sight of personal items of clothing and the recognition of startling implications from them. Judah created a deception to trick Jacob into thinking Joseph was dead. Jacob's recognition of Joseph's bloody coat issued in his proclamation of the death of his son. Tamar created a deception to trick Judah. Judah was the cause of Jacob's deception in Genesis 37, and then he himself was the victim of deception in Genesis 38. Judah's recognition of his own seal, cord, and staff issued in his proclamation of the righteousness of Tamar and his own unrighteousness in not letting his son Shelah marry her. Meanwhile his great unrighteousness in selling Joseph into slavery awaited its exposure in Genesis 42:21-22 and 44:18-34.

Deuteronomy 25:5-6 commanded that a brother's offspring replace his dead brother, and that principle was in effect in Judah's day. Tamar may have been influenced by a Hittite law that held that when no brother-in-law existed to fulfill the levirite duty, the father-in-law was responsible. Note also the contrast of Judah's lusts with Joseph's purity in Egypt. Judah's son Onan sinned by refusing to perform his responsibility as a brother-in-law to father children by his brother's widow. He may have coveted the firstborn's property for himself (cf. Num. 27:8-11).

39:1–41:57 JOSEPH'S RISE, FALL AND RESTORATION

The Lord prospered Joseph and then allowed him to be thrown into prison, which was actually a light sentence for his alleged crime (39:1-23). The key phrase is "the Lord was with him" (39:21, 23). Again God worked through dreams—this time the dreams of Pharaoh's cupbearer and baker (40:1-22). The cupbearer did not remember Joseph (40:23), but God was always with him and did not forget.

Pharaoh's dreams (41:1-36) were interpreted by Joseph because God gave him the interpretations (41:16, 25; cf. 40:8). Joseph became prime minister of Egypt at age thirty (41:37-46). He received Pharaoh's signet ring by which he could transact affairs of the state in the name and with the authority of Pharaoh. Joseph was given a daughter of the priest of On for his wife. On (41:45, 50), which was located at the head of the Nile Delta, is the Hebrew name for Heliopolis, an early capital and principal center of sun worship in ancient Egypt. Joseph's rise to power saved Egypt from famine and allowed it to become a haven for famine relief, which was just what Jacob's family would need.

42:1–45:28 JOSEPH AND HIS BROTHERS

Joseph's dealings with his brothers were not motivated by his desire for vengeance. Rather, he was testing his brothers to determine if they had had a change of heart. His actions caused his brothers to reflect on their conduct of past years and to admit their guilt (42:21-22). Joseph's intentions are revealed in 42:9.

Divination by water, which Joseph told his steward to mention when finding his cup in Benjamin's sack (44:5), was a widespread practice in ancient times when precious gems or oil were put into the water and interpreted. It is highly unlikely that Joseph, to whom God had revealed so much regarding the interpretation of dreams, would practice divination, but the uniqueness of the cup gave his scheme an air of authenticity. Note the role of Judah in confessing the brothers' guilt and pleading to replace Benjamin as Joseph's slave (44:18-34). Joseph knew that God had allowed all that had happened to him in order to preserve and bring Jacob's family into Egypt (45:5, 7; cf. 15:13-14). He also knew God's covenant promise to Abraham to preserve his descendants in the chosen line.

Jacob's family was allowed to settle in Goshen (45:10) in the western delta of the Nile, the best watered and fertile land in Egypt. During the next 430 years, until the exodus, the family of Jacob grew into the great nation of Israel.

46:1–47:31 JACOB'S FAMILY COMES TO EGYPT

At Joseph's request, Jacob and his family moved to Egypt, where they were kept alive during the drought and where they would live for the next four hundred years. Jacob's request for burial in the Promised Land of Canaan (47:27-31) was honored. He was trusting God's covenant promise as well as what God had told him before leaving the Prom-

ised Land about making his family into a great nation in Egypt and then bringing them back (46:3-4; 48:21; cf. Exod. 3:7 and Matt. 22:32).

48:1–49:33 JACOB'S FINAL BLESSINGS AND PREDICTIONS

Jacob adopted the two sons of Joseph, Ephraim and Manasseh (48:1-22), who took their father's place and became tribal heads. Some believe that this means that Joseph then took the leadership position of the firstborn since after Jacob's blessing of his sons, he had double representation among the tribes. The Scriptures explain that Reuben's "birthright was given to the sons of his brother Joseph. For this reason, Reuben is not listed in the genealogy as the firstborn" (1 Chron. 5:1). Actually, the only "rights" that Joseph received were the "double portion" plus the blessings given to his sons. And although Joseph ruled over his brothers when they first went to Egypt because of his high position over the whole land, his descendants never assumed a leadership position over the later nation of Israel. God's covenant line of promise was continued through Judah, who was technically next in line for the birthright after it had been forfeited by Reuben, Simeon and Levi. And Judah was the royal line through which Christ, the promised One, came (49:8-10). After the book of Genesis ends, no tribe was singled out as that through which God's chosen line would continue until God told David, who was from the tribe of Judah, that he would establish the throne of his kingdom forever.

In Jacob's predictions regarding his twelve sons and their descendants (49:1-33), the exact meaning of the phrase "until the coming of the one to whom it belongs" (49:10) is uncertain. Traditional interpretation, both by Christian and Jewish scholars, is that it is a proper name for the coming Messiah. That view is in keeping with the context (cf. Rev. 5:5).

Jacob's charge to bury him in the Promised Land was an act of faith that one day God would allow his descendants to return and settle there (cf. 50:24-25; Heb. 11:22).

50:1-26 JOSEPH'S FINAL ACTS

After Joseph buried Jacob in the Promised Land (50:1-14), he subdued his brothers' fear that he might take revenge on them now that their father was dead (50:15-21) and exhorted them regarding God's faithfulness to Abraham and his descendants (50:22-24). He assured them that God would come to their family's aid and return them to the Promised Land. When that happened, they were to take Joseph's bones with them. No doubt Joseph had heard about and remembered what God had told Abraham regarding his descendants' spending four hundred years in a foreign country (cf. 15:13-14).

EXODUS

BASIC FACTS

HISTORICAL SETTING

Discovering the date of Israel's exodus from Egypt is a difficult task. Dates which have been put forth for the Exodus fall into two major periods, one in the fifteenth and the other in the thirteenth century B.C. (around 1446 B.C. and 1266 B.C. respectively). Scholars settle on one date or the other depending on how they evaluate information from two major sources: biblical data and archaeological discoveries.

Biblical Data

The Bible has two primary references to the Exodus that are accompanied by some kind of time frame to help with dating. The interpretive issue in deciding for an earlier or a later date for the Exodus centers on whether the numbers in these two passages should be taken literally or as symbolic and general time references. The first passage is in 1 Kings 6:1, where the Exodus is placed 480 years before the dedication of the temple, an event which took place in 966 B.C. Taken at face value, 480 plus 966 yields a date for the Exodus of 1446 B.C.

It appears, however, that the 480 years symbolically represent 12 generations. Those who take a fifteenth-century B.C. date for the Exodus calculate a generation at forty years each (12 x 40 = 480), so are able to maintain the date for the Exodus around 1446 B.C. For this view, the number 480 symbolizes 12 generations but also closely approximates 480 real years.

Those who hold a thirteenth-century B.C. date calculate a generation at 25 years each (12 x 25 = 300) and place the Exodus around 1266 B.C. They consider the 480 years a symbolic statement of time that differs from the actual historical record by around 180 years.

The second biblical passage is Judges 11:26, in which Jephthah, who lived around 1100 B.C., said the conquest of Palestine happened 300 years earlier. Adding 40 years for the wilderness wanderings puts the actual Exodus about 340 years prior. Counting back from 1100 B.C. the 340 years place the Exodus into the fifteenth century.

Those who take a thirteenth-century B.C. date conclude that Jephthah's figure of 300 years was only rough and general and not meant to be taken as a historically precise statement. The result is a date that is different from Jephthah's estimation by about 175 years, putting the Exodus at around 1266 B.C.

Archaeological Discoveries

On the archaeological side, one important find is an ancient record called the

Merneptah Stela, which notes that Pharaoh Merneptah encountered Israel in Palestine around 1220 B.C. Historically, then, the Exodus must be dated before 1220 B.C. at the latest.

A second archaeological find concerns the Egyptian city of Rameses (see introductory map). The reference to the city of Rameses in Exodus 1:11 may substantiate that Rameses II (1304–1238 B.C.) was the pharaoh of the Exodus. But those who hold to an earlier, fifteenth-century B.C. date believe that (1) the city may have been named for another Rameses or that (2) when Israel was in Egypt the city had a different name. After rebuilding the city, Rameses would then have renamed it in his own honor, and that new name found its way into the biblical text and replaced the older name current when Israel was in Egypt.

A third area of archaeology that is used to date the Exodus concerns certain destruction levels in ancient city ruins found in Israel. The question centers on who did the destroying and when. For example, Deborah and Barak destroyed the city of Hazor during the period of the Judges. A destruction level that has been uncovered by archaeologists and attributed to Deborah and Barak's attack contains pieces of pottery that must be dated no later than the late thirteenth century. If that is indeed the destruction caused by Deborah and Barak, then the Exodus had to have occurred much earlier than the date commonly given of around 1266 B.C.

Archaeological evidence from Jericho is also interpreted various ways, either to support an earlier or later date for the Exodus. John Garstang's excavations at the site of Jericho resulted in the discovery of a violent destruction which he dated around 1400 B.C. This destruction level coincides with the biblical date of the conquest. But a later archaeologist, Kathleen Kenyon, concluded that the destruction level was from a significantly later date.

Other scholars conclude that certain destruction levels at other archaeological sites dated in the thirteenth century show that Israel did not begin the conquest until the thirteenth century B.C. Those who hold to a fifteenth-century date conclude that those destructions were caused by another nation, for example Egypt, after Israel had already been in the land since 1406 B.C. Again, the question of who caused the destruction levels is debated.

A fourth area of archaeology and the date of the Exodus concerns the Amarna letters (around 1400–1366 B.C.). Those letters mention the Habiru, who invaded southern and central Palestine. Abdi-Hiba, governor of Jerusalem, wrote numerous letters to Pharaoh Akhnaton (1377–1358 B.C.) requesting Egyptian aid against the encroaching Habiru if the country was to be saved for Egypt. If the term "Habiru" either equates with or includes the Israelites, then that places the nation of Israel in Palestine and confirms a fifteenth-century date for the Exodus. However, not all scholars agree that "Habiru" can even refer to, much less equate with, the Hebrews.

Theology and History

Amazingly, the Bible does not name the pharaoh of the Exodus, and surviving Egyptian records do not mention Joseph, Moses, the Exodus or the pharaoh of that time. God clearly had no desire to tell who the pharaoh was and thereby frame the Exodus in a specific time. In that light, the use of biblical and archaeological data to date the Exodus must remain tentative. Indeed, the foundational date for the beginning of this whole chronology, the date for Abraham, is still legitimately debated. Also, the dates of the judges are far from certain, so a simple count backward from the relatively certain dates of David and Solomon is tentative at best. Depending on when Abraham and the judges are dated, the entire chronology for Israel's descent into and exodus out of Egypt can slide hundreds of years either way.

But the important issue concerns how the biblical text is interpreted and applied. No substantial difference in interpreting and applying the truths of Exodus results from adopting either an earlier or a later date. Knowing the exact date of the Exodus does not add to or diminish experiencing the truth of the Exodus, just as knowing the exact date of the crucifixion of Christ neither adds to nor diminishes the believer's experience of his exodus from the power of sin and death. Both the early and late views of the date of the Exodus give honor to the integrity of the biblical text. And both allow for full appreciation of the great truth of God's power to redeem his people from bondage.

Israel in Egypt

If Israel sojourned in Egypt 430 years (Exod. 12:40), and assuming an early date for the Exodus, Jacob's entrance into the land of Egypt would have taken place around 1876 B.C., during the reign of Sesostris III (1878–1841 B.C.). Joseph would have died under the reign of Amenemhet III around 1805 B.C. For the next two hundred years the Israelites lived in relative peace and prosperity in Egypt. They received favorable treatment under the Hyksos (foreign rulers), who ruled Egypt from 1730 to 1580 B.C., because they too were largely Semitic.

Assuming an early date for the Exodus, the setting of events in contemporary Egyptian history can be reconstructed as follows: Ahmoses (1580–1548 B.C.), the founder of the Eighteenth Dynasty who drove out the Hyksos from Egypt, was the pharaoh who did not know Joseph (1:8). Amenhotep I (1548–1528 B.C.) carried out oppressive measures against the Hebrews (1:22). Thutmoses I (1528–1508 B.C.) was the father of Hatshepsut, perhaps the lady who was Pharaoh's daughter and who rescued the baby Moses from the river. Moses was born around 1526 B.C. (2:2-5). Thutmoses II (1508–1504 B.C.) was the brother and husband of Hatshepsut (1504–1483 B.C.), who was also the daughter of Thutmoses I. Thutmoses III (1504–1448 B.C.) was the stepson of Hatshepsut and expanded the kingdom of Egypt. Amenhotep II (1448–1423 B.C.) was possibly the pharaoh of the Exodus (5:1-2). Thutmoses IV (1423–1410 B.C.), the next pharaoh of Egypt, was not the eldest son of Amenhotep II. In a dream it was revealed to him that he would be the next monarch of Egypt.

AUTHOR

For the question concerning the Pentateuch's authorship, see the *Author* section in the introduction to Genesis. The book of Exodus itself does not name its author, who is therefore anonymous. It is interesting to note that, though Moses was viewed as the figure behind the book of Exodus, in Exodus and throughout the Pentateuch, Moses is always referred to in the third person "he," not the first person "I." The Pentateuch unfolds its message through a biographical, not an autobiographical, perspective.

The traditional view concerning the authorship of Exodus is that it was written by Moses. This view is supported by the following considerations: (1) Joshua refers to the Mosaic authorship of the book of the law, which would have included much of Exodus (Josh. 8:34-35; cf. Exod. 24:3-4). (2) The book is closely connected with Genesis, which has traditionally been viewed as authored by Moses. (3) Moses names himself several times in connection with the Lord's command to write (Exod. 17:14; 24:4;

34:27), (4) Jesus ascribed texts from Exodus to Moses (see Mark 7:10, where Jesus quotes Exod. 20:12 and 21:17; and Mark 12:26, where he quotes Exod. 3:6). When Jesus said that Moses wrote of him, Jesus affirmed the conventional view of Moses being the author of Genesis through Deuteronomy (John 5:46). (5) The unity and literary construction of the work points to the Mosaic authorship of the whole book of Exodus.

Luke reflects the common tradition of putting the "law of the Lord" (in this case specifically referring to Exod. 13:2, 12 and Lev. 12:8) under the broad heading of "law of Moses" (Luke 2:23-24; see also Acts 13:39). Although referring to the Pentateuch by Moses' name does not mean that Moses wrote every word of these books, it does affirm him as the chief figure in the Pentateuch and as their primary human author. Any others who had a later part in editing Moses' work remain unnamed. Moses was viewed as the human transmitter of the laws of God and the chief literary figure behind the Pentateuch.

DATE

The book of Exodus contains a covenant given by God from Mount Sinai. The basic form of that covenant closely parallels secular covenants only current in the fifteenth to thirteenth centuries B.C., thereby dating the book's material to that time period. There is good reason to believe that the book itself was composed shortly after the events that it describes. Exodus was probably written shortly after the book of Genesis, during Israel's wilderness wanderings (1445–1406 B.C., assuming an early date for the exodus).

PURPOSE

The book of Exodus was designed to show how the Israelites got out of Egypt and how God came to dwell among them in the tabernacle. It formed the bridge from the story of Joseph in Egypt at the end of Genesis to the detailed laws of the Mosaic covenant in Leviticus.

Exodus was probably written during the forty years of Israel's wilderness wanderings. It therefore is not simply a bland historical record of the Exodus and God's giving of the law. Rather, it is a book that was originally written to an extremely stubborn, sinful, and complaining group of people. They had seen God's miraculous salvation, and yet they complained against him and quickly turned to serve other gods. The book of Exodus was written to remind them how great their salvation was and how divine the origin of their law and tabernacle. It was given to them to deepen their love for their Redeemer and warn them against further disobedience.

GEOGRAPHY AND ITS IMPORTANCE

Exodus twice moves geographically between city and wilderness. It begins in Egypt in the area of Goshen and the cities of Pithom and Raamses and then moves with Moses out into the wilderness of Midian. The Exodus narrative then returns with Moses to the cities of Egypt and, as the entire nation leaves Egypt, moves back into the wilderness and to the foot of Mount Sinai. The cities of Egypt are the places of bondage. The areas of wilderness are where God intimately meets with his people. Therefore the most important geographical place in Exodus is a little tent at the foot of Mount Sinai called the tabernacle, where God's glory came to dwell in awesome presence with his redeemed people.

Many places mentioned in the Exodus account have not been located with certainty. It is not known for sure where the sea was that God parted for Israel. Even the exact location of Mount Sinai and the wilderness Israel entered is debated. But the key geographical concept in the Exodus relates to Goshen being spared from the plagues while the rest of Egypt was not spared. This dividing line between God's plagues and his redemption became like a spiritual geographic line not limited to any one place. It moved out of Egypt with God's people, simultaneously separating them from and witnessing to the cursed world around them. See the introductory map.

Modern names and boundaries are shown in gray.
Copyright © 1986, 1988 by Tyndale House Publishers, Inc.

GUIDING CONCEPTS

THE EXODUS, THE LAW, AND THE TABERNACLE

First, note the following points made concerning the Exodus itself: (1) the unpreventable growth of Jacob's family until it became a large nation; (2) the preservation and growth of Israel's leader, Moses; (3) God's witness to and judgment of Egypt; and (4) Israel's miraculous deliverance from the Egyptians and her preservation in the wilderness.

Second, note these key events that took place during Israel's one-year stay at Mount Sinai: (1) the giving of the law; (2) Israel's doubts and disobedience right after seeing God's great salvation; and (3) the uncompromising balance between God's grace and judgment for his redeemed people. For example, read these passages to see how God's presence worked both to save and to judge: Exodus 2:24-25; 3:5-8; 4:22-23; 13:14-16; 19:19-22; 20:1-21; 24:1-11; 25:8; 29:45-46; 40:35.

Third, note the great detail surrounding the tabernacle's construction and the sacrificial aspects related to it. In the Bible, great detail means great importance. This was true in the description of the tabernacle, the place where humans would meet with God for forgiveness and worship. What might seem boring to the modern reader is, in reality, a painstakingly detailed literary effort to recreate the reality and importance of the earthly place where God would meet with humans. For another example of lengthy description and great importance, see the passage describing Ezekiel's temple (Ezek. 40:1–44:31).

TWO PLACES AND ONE PERSON
Exodus is a book about two places and one person. The places are Egypt and Sinai, and the person is Moses, who led Israel from one place to the other. By way of a one-year stay at the foot of Mount Sinai, Israel was brought to the goal of the Exodus: God coming to live among his people. Exodus should be viewed not only as a book about Israel's redemption from bondage but, in addition, as the nation's release so that they could experience a more intimate relationship with God.

A WILDERNESS TRAINING GROUND
In the book of Exodus, Israel was called out of a land with relative comforts to a barren wilderness. For the newly born nation, the wilderness was a severe and rough nursery. Although Israel was not born with the proverbial silver spoon in her mouth, she did come to life under the protection of a wise and gracious God. The One who called the world into being and hovered over the earth like a protective bird when it was formless and empty (Gen. 1) was also abiding over newborn Israel in her time of chaos and disobedience. God used the wilderness as a training ground for his chosen people.

BIBLE-WIDE CONCEPTS

FROM GENESIS TO EXODUS: THE LINK WITH ABRAHAM
In the book of Genesis God had revealed his greatness in creation, his holiness in response to sin, and his grace in recreating a fallen world. The central focus of that grace lay in God's promise to Abraham to create a *people* of God who would live in the *land* God provided and experience the fullness of his divine presence and *blessing*. Those three elements—people, land, and blessing—form the link between Genesis and Exodus.

CURSE
In Genesis 3, Adam's sin brought both a great curse and a great promise from God. The curse caused human beings to experience broken relationships with one another, the earth, and God. Genesis 3 also records God's promise of a future son of Adam who would crush the head of the serpent. The roots of this promise's fulfillment deepen in the book of Exodus, where God sets apart a special group of people through whom the Messiah would come and bring ultimate victory over Satan and the curse of sin and death.

BLESSING
In Genesis 12:2-3, God promised that Abraham's descendants would become a large nation that would claim the land of Canaan as a homeland and be the source of inter-national blessing. At the close of Genesis, the family of Jacob in Egypt remained opti-

mistic concerning the promise, though its fulfillment was still far off (see Gen. 15:13-14, where four hundred years of bondage were predicted).

At that time Abraham's descendants consisted of a family group of less than eighty, not a large nation by any means. Furthermore, they were living in Egypt, not in the land God had promised. And finally, though Joseph had made a start at being a local blessing to the Egyptians, the people of Jacob were nowhere near being the international blessing God had promised. In the Exodus, the people of Israel began a journey that would not only take them from bondage in Egypt but would also make them the source of great blessing for all mankind.

EXODUS

The events in Exodus narrow the gap in a stunning way between God's promise to Abraham and his fulfillment of that promise. The small family of Jacob grew into a large nation in Egypt, and was then redeemed out of that land. Israel was schooled by God in the desert, pointed toward the Promised Land, and brought into a new and more intimate relationship with God. At the end of the book of Exodus, Abraham's descendants had become a nation that was being led toward the land promised by God, and God's dwelling among them in the tabernacle set the scene for them to become an international blessing.

THE INTERNATIONAL SCOPE OF BLESSING AND CURSING

In Genesis 12:2-3, God had told Abraham that his line would be both a blessing and a curse to others. God's divine presence with Israel to bless and to curse other people is seen throughout Exodus as he cursed those who did not treat Israel kindly and blessed those who did. Israel indeed began to become the touchstone of God's blessing and cursing in the world. That focus would eventually narrow to one person, Jesus Christ, who would become the final watershed for God's blessings and curses.

The curse was carried out in judgments on the people of Egypt and Canaan. The Exodus from Egypt was the next major step in fulfilling what God had alluded to in Genesis 15:16 regarding his plan for the Amorites, the inhabitants of the Promised Land. At that time he had given them four hundred more years, but now their time was up and judgment was about to fall upon them. God also had a purpose for the Egyptians, a purpose foreshadowed in Genesis 12:14-20, where God had struck the house of an earlier pharaoh with plagues in order for him to release Abraham's wife, Sarah. God desired to reveal who he was to the Egyptians (Exod. 7:5) and to bring some of them out of their country with Israel (12:38). These things were also a foreshadowing of a final redemptive and successful move on God's part to win the Egyptians (Isa. 19:19-25). In Exodus, God's great international promise of worldwide redemption took a giant step forward, which is seen in God's *people*, moving toward God's *land* under the *blessing* of God's presence.

SALVATION AND LAW

The basic aspects of God's redemptive promises center on these two key concepts that stretch from Genesis to Revelation: redemption and direction. God redeems his people and then gives them direction as to how they should live. In the book of Exodus, redemption is seen in the Exodus from Egypt and the direction given Israel in the Mosaic covenant.

Actually, the theme of redemption and direction had already been established in Genesis. For example, see Genesis 18:19, where God's promise of blessing to Abraham was intertwined with Abraham's duty to teach his children the way of the Lord by doing righteousness and justice—the core descriptions of the law later to be given through Moses. In Exodus, the laws given at Mount Sinai are linked to God's eternal purpose for his recreation: to create a perfectly obedient people.

The Passover lamb of Exodus 12 saved from death Israel's firstborn males, who were symbolic of the nation as a whole (see "Israel is my firstborn son," Exod. 4:22). The death plague broke the yoke of bondage, and the death of the Passover lamb saved Israel from death. From that point on, the Passover pictured the core of God's redemption: deliverance from death and bondage. In the New Testament, the shadows of the Passover lamb find their substance in Christ, our Passover Lamb (1 Cor. 5:7), who saved all believers from eternal death and bondage to sin. That great exodus from death and sin will be finalized in the next great exodus for believers, which will be from this age into the eternal Promised Land of the new heavens and earth.

God's self-revelation under Moses and the greater Moses, Jesus, is designed both to save and to aid obedience. God's pattern, whether it be to Abraham, to Israel, or to the church, is to follow redemption with direction, and forgiveness with instruction.

WHEN GOD TOUCHES EARTH TO SAVE AND JUDGE

One last link of Exodus to future biblical events was God's appearance on Mount Sinai. He appeared in fire, smoke, thunder, lightning, and earthquake. All of those fireworks were due to what happens when a piece of cursed and finite earth is touched by the almighty and holy God. The fire-and-smoke appearance of God was similar to when he made his covenant with Abraham (Gen. 15:17). But the most striking similarity to the fireworks on Mount Sinai appears in the book of Revelation, as God's holy presence appears not just on one mountaintop but over the entire world. When this is fulfilled the earth will quake, burn, and eventually disintegrate as God's presence causes thunder, lightning, and earthquakes (compare Exod. 19:16, 18 with Rev. 6:4; 8:5; 11:19; 15:8; 16:18). Mount Sinai in Exodus is a small picture of what is ahead for the entire world when God comes to finalize his covenant of redemption and require the full application of his law.

NEEDS MET BY EXODUS

The families of Israel were suffering physically and emotionally in slavery. But then God dazzled them with miracles, overcame their slavemasters and led them out into the barren and foreign wilderness. God's redemption had taken his people from one difficult situation to another. Although subservient to cruel slavemasters in Egypt, the Israelites were home in a relatively comfortable and known setting. They may have been oppressed, but at least they knew what to expect each day. In the wilderness, God's people had to learn to cope with the unexpected and the unknown.

Without the comfort zone of their past home they had to rely solely upon God. Where would their food come from? Where were they going? God fed and God led. The masters of Egypt were gone and replaced by the great master and Creator. But the unknowns were too great for most of the adult Israelites. In their view, God as master was not trustworthy, and his provisions of food and direction on the journey were not acceptable. The book of Exodus brings answers to the following questions and problems faced by God's people as they struggled to leave behind their place of bondage and faced the uncertainties of the journey to the Promised Land:

- What happened to God's promise to Abraham that his children would become great (Gen. 15:16) and return to the Promised Land?
- How did Moses become such a great leader?
- How did Israel get out of Egypt?
- Why did God come to dwell in the tabernacle in the midst of the people of Israel?
- What did God expect of the Israelites after they were redeemed?
- What were the conditions for their fellowship with God?
- What did God do when they rebelled or failed?
- What were the major areas about which God's redeemed people griped and disbelieved?
- How strong was God's commitment to his people?

These questions are similar to those that believers, the redeemed people of God in Christ, ask today as they struggle to leave their pasts behind, to know and trust their Redeemer more deeply, and to maintain faith in the uncertainties of their journey through life. Exodus affirms God's desire to dwell intimately with believers of all ages, to replace their past bondage with present worship and service for him, and, even though they fail in their commitment to him, to confirm his unbreakable commitment to them.

OUTLINE OF EXODUS

  I. GOD'S PRESENCE FOR DELIVERANCE: SOCIAL, POLITICAL, AND SPIRITUAL (1:1–18:27)
   A. The Miracle of Preservation in Egypt (1:1–2:25)
   B. Moses and Aaron Commissioned as Mediators (3:1–4:26)
   C. The Miracle of Deliverance (4:27–13:16)
   D. Saved through the Red Sea (13:17–15:21)
   E. Preserved in the Wilderness (15:22–18:27)

 II. GOD'S PRESENCE FOR HOLINESS: THE COVENANT IS GIVEN AND RECONFIRMED (19:1–34:35)
   A. Divine and Human Separation Highlighted (19:1-25)
   B. The Covenant Presented by God: Legal Paragraphs (20:1–23:33)
   C. The Covenant Ratified (24:1-11)
   D. Laws Given for Tabernacle and Priests (24:12–31:18)
   E. The Covenant Broken and Restored (32:1–34:35)

III. GOD'S PRESENCE FOR FELLOWSHIP: GOD DWELLS IN ISRAEL (35:1–40:38)
   A. The Dwelling Place Constructed (35:1–40:16)
   B. God Begins Dwelling in the Tabernacle (40:17-38)

EXODUS NOTES

1:1–18:27 GOD'S PRESENCE FOR DELIVERANCE: SOCIAL, POLITICAL, AND SPIRITUAL

1:1–2:25 The Miracle of Preservation in Egypt

Overview: Exodus 1 reemphasizes three keys first stated and developed in Genesis as to how God planned to bring his salvation to the world. First, Exodus 1 echoes the original creation mandate to God's people that they be fruitful and multiply. Note the use of the term "multiplied" throughout Exodus 1 (1:7, 12, 20). In the beginning of Genesis, God created the earth and commanded the human and animal population to be fruitful and increase (Gen. 1:22, 28). That command was restated to Noah after the flood (Gen. 9:1, 7). In the beginning of the book of Exodus, the Israelites obeyed that command and became fruitful and multiplied until the land of Egypt was filled with them (Exod. 1:7).

Second, Exodus 1 takes a major step in showing what God meant when he promised that Abraham's line would multiply and be mighty. Besides being a clear reference back to the creation account of Genesis, that fruitfulness was a fulfillment of God's promise to Abraham's line through Isaac (Gen. 12:2; 17:6; 22:17; 26:24; 35:11).

Third, this section shows how the fear of the Lord was used to fulfill God's promise of blessing. Note "feared God" in Exodus 1:17, 21. This chapter shows why and how the little family of Jacob was able to become a mighty nation that threatened the political stability of ancient Egypt. Not only does this chapter look back to the key themes of Genesis, it also acts as a prologue to the key themes of Exodus that begin in Exodus 2.

Exodus 1 shows how God preserved and multiplied the children of Abraham for hundreds of years and specifically how male children were preserved by women who feared God. Exodus 2 shows the specific story of the preservation of one male baby, Moses. The chapter scans Moses' birth, preservation as a baby, childhood, his act of murder, his flight to the Sinai Desert, his marriage, and the birth of his first son. Moses moved from being a stranger in Egypt to becoming an alien in Sinai (2:22), from being a baby in Egypt to fathering a baby in the desert. Exodus 2 ends with the death of Pharaoh and God's hearing the cries of his people.

The pharaohs who ruled over the Israelites fall into two groups: (1) those who were in power during Joseph's day and soon after, who allowed the children of Abraham to prosper in peace; and (2) those who ruled later and did not know who Joseph was (1:8). Two such pharaohs are noted, though not by name: (1) the one who began the initial persecution and ruled during Moses' early life; and (2) the ruler at the time of Moses' return and the Exodus. It is during the reign of the latter that God began to take redemptive action in relieving his people's affliction and redeeming them out of bondage in Egypt and into his holy presence.

1:1-22 NATIONAL PRESERVATION

The Hebrews used the first words of the book of Exodus for its Hebrew title, which means, "the names of." The English Bible took the book's title from the Septuagint (Greek OT), which named the book according to its principal theme: the Exodus. A strong allusion exists here (1:7) to the creation account in Genesis 1 and the blessing God promised in Genesis 35:11. God had promised to make Jacob a great nation; here he is fulfilling that promise. The new king was probably Ahmoses (1:8; 1580–1548 B.C.), who drove out the Hyksos (the foreign rulers) and founded the Eighteenth Dynasty. Many scholars appeal to the reference to the city of Rameses (1:11) in arguing that Rameses II (1304–1238 B.C.) was the pharaoh of the Exodus. That would place the Exodus from Egypt at a later time than would be otherwise indicated by the biblical record. It may be that (1) the city was named for another Rameses; or (2) the name in the biblical text was updated from one of the site's earlier archaic names (Zoan, Tanis, Avaris). After rebuilding the city, Rameses renamed it in his own honor. For more on the use of the name of the city Rameses in dating the exodus, see the introductory section under *Historical Setting.*

The motivation behind the midwives' action (1:15-22) was that they feared God (1:17). The vigor of the Israelite women during the birth process is alluded to in 1:7. Evidently the midwives let the boys live (1:17), either by delaying their own arrival until after the births had taken place (1:19), or by lying to Pharaoh. At any rate, they were blessed because they feared the Lord and did not murder the male babies at birth. God showed his verdict on their actions by blessing them (1:20).

2:1-25 PERSONAL PRESERVATION: MOSES

Moses' parents, Amram and Jochebed (2:1-2; cf. 6:20), already had two children: Aaron, three years old (7:7), and Miriam, perhaps about seven years old. Pharaoh's daughter, who found Moses in the river (2:2-10), was probably Hatshepsut, who later ruled as the pharaoh (1504–1483 B.C.). Moses would have been raised in Thebes, the capital and center of Amun worship, where he was instructed in the wisdom of the Egyptians. The Exodus account does not dwell on Moses' childhood but moves directly from his being drawn out of the Nile to his act of murder at about the age of forty and his subsequent flight to the desert. The structure of this section shows how Moses was preserved twice from death—from drowning as an infant and then from death by execution near the age of forty.

Moses was almost forty when he fled from Pharaoh (2:15-25; cf. Acts 7:23). Midian was a desert land on the eastern fringe of the Sinai Peninsula. At that time Moses could not deliver Israel from Egypt, but he did deliver the daughters of Reuel, or Jethro, from some hostile shepherds (2:19). Later God would make Moses his chosen deliverer, but only at his own sovereignly appointed time. Moses married one of Jethro's daughters, and he named his first son Gershom, literally, "a stranger here" (2:22). His second son he named Eliezer, which means "God is my help" (18:3-4).

After spending forty years in the wilderness as a shepherd (2:23; cf. Acts 7:30), Moses was eighty years old when called by God to lead Israel. Four terms in 2:23-25 describe Israel's distress: "groaned," "cried out," "slavery," and "cries." Those terms of distress were matched by four terms describing God's personal activity on behalf of Israel that encapsulate the content of Exodus: "heard," "remembered," "looked down on," and "felt deep concern."

3:1–4:26 Moses and Aaron Commissioned as Mediators

Overview: In this section, God teaches Moses about his redemptive plans for Israel and commissions Moses and Aaron as his spokesmen before Pharaoh. Exodus 2 ended with God taking notice of Israel, and in Exodus 3 God begins to take action. Exodus 4 is structured around two questions from Moses concerning what to do if his hearers do not listen (4:1) and his inability to speak well (4:10, 13). The mountain where God spoke to Moses has two names: Horeb and Sinai (3:1; cf. 19:1; Deut. 4:10). Traditionally identified as Jebel Musa, it is 7,632 feet high and located in southern Sinai (see introductory map).

3:1-12 GOD ANNOUNCES HIS INTENTIONS TO SAVE ISRAEL

In 3:6 God implied that he remembered his covenant with Abraham. The four terms used in 2:23-25 for God's personal saving activity are restated or implied in 3:6-12, where God said Israel's cry had reached him and that he had seen, heard, and was concerned about his people. Those aspects of God's awareness of the Israelites' situation in slavery resulted in the great act found in 3:8—God had come down to rescue them.

3:13-22 GOD REVEALS HIS REDEMPTIVE NAME

Here God revealed the significance of his personal name, Yahweh (3:13-15). The name, probably

derived from the verb "to be," speaks of God as the self-existent One. God had promised that his presence would be with Moses (3:12). "I will be" (in this case, "with you") forms the basis for his name in 3:14. God is the One who is known by what he is. Throughout history God proclaims: I Am—the Creator; I Am—the Judge; I Am—the Covenant-keeping One; I Am—the Faithful One. And in Exodus, God was about to proclaim: I Am—the Redeemer.

God is who he is, known only by what he chooses to reveal about himself by his words or his actions. In Scripture God chose to reveal his character through his name and by what he said and did. That involved a progressive unfolding (cf. 20:1; Deut. 26:8-9; Judg. 2:12) as he was dynamic and active throughout biblical history. The name "Yahweh" is his memorial name to all generations (Exod. 3:14-15), and his name displays his character. God remembered his covenant, made long before with Abraham (2:24). There is nothing forgetful or arbitrary with regard to God's character. His consistency is the basis of all revelation and cements the continuity between the Old and New Testaments. That consistency also forms the basis of hope. The readers of Exodus from that time until the present can therefore wait for God to act again according to his promise.

Many Jewish people do not speak the divine name found in 3:14 but substitute instead the word "Lord." They often use Leviticus 24:16 and Exodus 20:7 as the background for God's name not being taken in vain. They believe they will avoid taking God's name in vain simply by never pronouncing it and by substituting another word, "Lord," for "Yahweh."

Moses' request for only three days to offer sacrifices to the Lord (3:18) was not an attempt to trick Pharaoh, but probably reflects oriental bargaining. His first request was quite conservative in order to give Pharaoh every reason to respond positively.

4:1-17 GOD GIVES MOSES SIGNS OF AUTHORITY

The signs of authority given to Moses by God were designed to cause the Israelites to believe what he said (4:5) and show them that God was present (4:12; cf. 3:13-15).

4:18-26 THE AUTHORITY OF THE COVENANT SIGN

This section concerns Moses' departure from the desert. Here God also illustrates his high view of the firstborn by saying what he would do to Pharaoh for harming God's firstborn, Israel (4:22-23), and by what God almost did to Moses because he had not obeyed God regarding his own firstborn son (4:24-26). The hardening of Pharaoh's heart (4:21) was not only a divine judgment on one who had already hardened his own heart against the Lord (cf. 7:13; 8:15) but was also God's way to glorify himself (9:15-16).

The circumcision of Moses' son, a command decreed by God (4:24-26; cf. Gen. 17:9-14), had been neglected by Moses, perhaps to accommodate Zipporah. For that failure, God was about to take Moses' life. God was being consistent with his promise to and demands of Abraham and his descendants in the chosen line. Moses was not the beginning of God's redemption. Rather, he was God's man to bring about the next great step in the redemption promised to Abraham.

4:27–13:16 The Miracle of Deliverance

Overview: This section contains a series of actions and reactions between Moses and Pharaoh. The sequence is peppered with the repetition of two key thoughts that God had already given to Moses in the desert: (1) God would fulfill without doubt his promise of deliverance (Exod. 3:8, 16-17; 6:8; 7:4); and (2) Pharaoh would not let deliverance happen except under great compulsion (3:19; 6:1; 7:3-4; 9:35; 10:9-11). All the forces of Egyptian might were against Israel's release from bondage, but God's might was working to break that bondage.

What God could have done in an instant (9:15-16), he did by degrees in order to detail his great power and Pharaoh's great defiance. That detail produced a record of God's power and grace as a continual warning to those who would resist him, and as a display of his faithfulness and ability to save those to whom he promises redemption (that is nowhere better stated than in 10:1-2). Note the key phrase and variations: "And you will know that I am the Lord" (6:7; 7:5, 17; 8:22; 9:15-16, 27; 10:2). The plagues of Egypt were to display the knowledge of God for the Egyptians, Israelites, and their future generations.

4:27–6:27 OPPORTUNITY FOR VOLUNTARY OBEDIENCE

The essence of this section is Israel's response to Moses' message: they believed and worshiped when they saw the signs (4:29-31). But God had more to teach them about how to continue to believe and worship, even when experiencing unpleasant circumstances. Note their immediate hostility and doubt (5:21), which were indicative of their upcoming response to difficulties in the wilderness.

Pharaoh's question about God and negative response to Moses' first request would soon be answered (5:1-4). Both he and future generations of Egyptians and Israelites would be shown who God was. His question, "Who is the Lord, that I should listen to him?" continues to be a question that troubles not only the unbeliever but, more pointedly, presents a continual challenge to the believer as well.

Moses' cry of dismay to God in 5:22-23 sums up the pain and frustration of people who on the one hand have the promise of God, but on the other hand have to suffer pain while waiting for its fulfillment (5:2-23). The person suffering unjustly is given a special challenge to hold onto God's promises in faith rather than to abandon hope because of difficulties and pain.

Previously the patriarchs had known God by the name "El Shaddai," which means, "God Almighty" (6:1-9), and the name "Yahweh" was also known (cf. Gen. 4:26), but its full significance was not known as it was now revealed to Moses (3:13-15). Here God clearly linked the approaching Exodus to a fulfillment of his promise to Abraham to bless the descendants of his chosen line and return the Israelites to the Promised Land, eventually blessing all the nations of the earth through them. Thus, the Exodus was a giant step toward fulfilling God's international mission for Israel. But, as 6:9 shows, personal pain and discouragement crowded out the Israelites' faith and hope in that great mission. Moses' protest that he could not speak well (6:10-13, 28-30) was mentioned both before and after the genealogies of his and Aaron's families. Thus, just prior to the formal inauguration of God's saving activity through Moses, his Levitical pedigree was given.

6:28–7:13 COUNTERFEIT MIRACLES

God gave Moses his full authority before Pharaoh, but he also hardened Pharaoh's heart (7:1-7). The reason for doing so is found in the latter part of 7:3—to multiply the signs and wonders of God in Egypt. The Exodus was, first of all, a display of God's power (7:3) and judgment (7:4), and only secondarily an act of redemption. In other words, the Exodus was essentially a statement concerning God, not humans. This event was to reveal God's glory first, and then secondarily bring about human redemption. That vision of God's redeeming glory would serve as the focus of the redeemed community's motivation to serve him. Later, when they ceased to appreciate God's redeeming glory, they stopped appreciating their own redemption and wandered off to follow their own interests.

How Pharaoh's wise men and sorcerers were able to counterfeit Moses' signs is not known (7:8-12). The text expresses no surprise at the magicians' abilities. But whatever the nature of their secret arts, the point of this event is the supremacy of the Lord's representative over the Egyptians. This was a small foreshadowing of God's devastating supremacy about to be shown in the final plagues.

7:14-25 THE DIVINE NILE

Because the Egyptians considered the Nile to be sacred, turning it into blood was an insult to their gods of the river—*Khnum* (guardian of the Nile sources) and *Hapi* (spirit of the Nile). This was also a judgment against another Nile river god, *Osiris* (god of the underworld), because the Egyptians believed that the Nile was his bloodstream.

8:1-15 SACRED FROGS

God had made Moses "seem like God" and Aaron as Moses' "prophet" to Pharaoh (7:1). At the Lord's command all that Moses told Aaron to do came to pass, and frogs appeared over the whole land of Egypt. In ancient Egypt, frogs were sacred and never intentionally killed, since they were regarded as deified representatives of the goddess *Heqt*. The Egyptians believed that *Heqt* assisted with fertility and was associated with childbirth. *Heqt's* popularity undoubtedly diminished as her devotees were tormented by the plague.

8:16-19 LICE

The dust becoming gnats was a judgment against the earth god, *Seth*. Pharaoh would not listen when his magicians acknowledged that this plague proved that God was at work (8:19). None of Pharaoh's magicians could duplicate this plague.

8:20-32 FLIES

Swarms of flies appeared in all the land of Egypt except Goshen, which God protected because the Israelites lived there. Besides being a great discomfort to the Egyptians, this and the next two plagues on livestock attacked Egypt's foremost goddess, *Hathor*, who was represented by the cow.

9:1-7 LIVESTOCK

The fifth plague destroyed the Egyptian livestock and was directed against *Ptah*, the god of Memphis, represented by the sacred Apis bull, and *Hathor*, the goddess of love, beauty, and joy, who was represented by the cow.

9:8-12 BOILS

The sixth plague of boils caused great suffering for all Egyptians. It continued the assault upon the gods of Egypt (9:9; cf. 12:12), in particular the gods represented by animals. Since ashes were used by Egyptian priests to bless the people, this plague ironically used a mode of blessing as a means for a curse.

9:13-35 HAIL AND FIRE

The plague of hail and fire, destroying Egyptian herds and crops, was an insult to *Isis*, the goddess of life, and *Seth*, the protector of the crops. This judgment also would have humiliated *Nut*, the sky goddess who was looked to for blessing, and *Serapis*, the god of fire and water. The purpose of the plague is noted in 9:14, 16. Note that some Egyptians already feared the word of the Lord (9:20).

10:1-20 LOCUSTS

The devastation of all green living things by the plague of locusts demonstrated the impotence of *Isis*, the goddess of life, and *Seth*, the protector of the crops.

10:21-29 DARKNESS

The plague of darkness that covered all the land of Egypt except Goshen was an insult to *Re*, or *Amun*, the sun-god and chief deity of Thebes. When this plague struck, Pharaoh offered his third compromise to Moses (10:24).

THE PLAGUES

Their Purpose. *The issue at stake throughout the plagues was that Pharaoh should recognize that God was supreme and therefore should be served, not ignored (see Pharaoh's response in 5:2). The issue in Pharaoh's mind hinged on the question of which was stronger, the Hebrew God or the gods of the Egyptians. Whenever his magicians duplicated a plague of God, Pharaoh's response was one of apathy and unconcern (7:23). He concluded that the God of the Hebrews was not so strong after all and could be ignored.*

The ten plagues of divine judgment upon Pharaoh and Egypt were supernatural events designed to: (1) authenticate God's messenger, Moses (4:21); (2) introduce Pharaoh to Israel's sovereign God (5:2; 7:17; 9:14); (3) demonstrate to the Egyptians the power of God (9:16; 14:4); (4) execute judgment on the gods of Egypt (12:12; Num. 33:4); and (5) witness to all the earth and to Israel's future generations the greatness of God (9:16; 10:2).

The plagues centered on the Nile as the focus of Egypt's religious idols. They covered a period from an unusually high flooding of the Nile river in July or August to the death of the firstborn around April of the next year. The recurring idea of all Egypt ("whole country," and "men and animals," 8:2, 17; 9:11, 19, 25; 10:22) builds to the climax of the death of the firstborn of both men and animals and the judgment of the gods of Egypt (12:12). Each plague was a progressively severe judgment not only on the gods of Egypt but on those who worshiped them as well.

Their Nature. *Anytime that God brings about changes in nature, he does it to remind mankind that he is the one and only Creator and that he does whatever he wants with his creation. These changes are usually negative in order to get the attention of people who are preoccupied with their lives of sin. Normally their attitude is the same as Pharaoh's: "Who is God that I should obey him?" Both the beginning and continuance of redemption are based on the believer's acknowledgment of God as the creator who is totally sovereign and powerful to save and to judge. Famines and droughts, plagues and fire, locusts and earthquakes from Genesis to Revelation all signaled the same problem: the Creator was trying to get the attention of some sinner.*

11:1-10 DEATH

The last plague, the death of the firstborn, was announced (11:1-8), followed by a summary statement of all the plagues (11:9-10). The focus of Exodus 12 shifts to the people of Israel and their preparation for the Passover.

12:1-28 THE PASSOVER

In Exodus 12:1-28 God gave Moses instructions for the Passover and told him of its significance. It would be observed at the beginning of what God established as the first month of Israel's calendar year (12:2; Nisan, March–April). The essence of the Passover is found in 12:12. God would (1) strike down all the firstborn, both human and animal; (2) execute judgments against all the gods of Egypt; and (3) pass over the houses of the Israelites. Thus, the Passover was not only a divine judgment on humanity and the unseen demonic world but also served as a divine redemption for believers. The Passover, which was preceded by seven days of purification (12:15), was a sacrifice that spared the offerers from God's plague of death (12:13, 27).

12:29-51 THE PLAGUES' EFFECTS

This section recounts the effects of the plague upon Egypt as well as Israel's departure. Since the Egyptians considered every Pharaoh to be divine, this final plague would constitute a judgment on the divine heir to the throne. It would also insult the Egyptian gods' responsibility for protecting the royal family.

The number of adult men of Israel participating in the Exodus was approximately 600,000 (12:37). Assuming that most were married and had children, a conservative estimate of Israel's total population at that time would be about 2,500,000. When Israel was later numbered before entering the Promised Land, the total number of men was approximately the same (Num. 26:51). Many liberal scholars reject these figures, arguing the impossibility of such a multitude surviving forty years in the wilderness of Sinai. But the Exodus was a supernatural event, making the total number of people delivered from Egypt and their survival in the wilderness a testimony to God's great power.

The Israelites lived in Egypt 430 years, most of them in bondage, from the time of Jacob's entrance into the land (1876 B.C.) until the Exodus (12:40-51). The four hundred years mentioned in Genesis 15:13 and Acts 7:6 is a round figure. Many people who were not Israelites left Egypt with the nation of Israel (12:38); and since other foreigners would attach themselves to Israel in the future, rules were given regarding how a foreigner could eat the Passover and celebrate God's redemption with Israel (12:43-51). The emphasis here is not only on who was entitled to eat the Passover, but also on how a stranger could become qualified to eat it. That emphasis is elaborated in 13:1-16, where the focus shifts to celebrating the Passover feast after Israel entered the Promised Land.

13:1-16 REDEMPTION OF THE FIRSTBORN

God's provision through establishing a sacrificial offering for the redemption of Israel's firstborn males (13:13) released the Israelites from God's claim on them. God later took the Levites as his own in place of all the firstborn males (Num. 3:12). The firstborn functioned as a symbol for all Israel (cf. Exod. 4:22), for the firstborn became the Lord's (13:11-16) as a symbol of the nation's collective redemption. The continual sacrifice of firstborn animals and the redemption of the firstborn Israelite males was a graphic way to perpetuate the memory of Israel's deliverance from Egypt. The Passover also functioned as a reminder of God's redemption (13:8-10) in order to motivate the believers to keep the covenant of Moses (cf. 20:2). The Passover had diverted God's wrath (12:13, 27).

The Passover also pictured the sacrifice of Christ, who is our Passover. Christ, the firstborn of a new creation, represents all believers before God through sacrifice and makes it possible for God to "pass over" our sins. Believers today are to celebrate the Feast of Unleavened Bread by living lives of purity and sincerity, not for just one week a year, but every day through Christ's fulfillment of Israel's Passover (1 Cor. 5:7). See the *Historical Setting* section for a discussion of the date of Israel's Exodus from Egypt.

13:17–15:21 Saved through the Red Sea

Exodus 13:17–15:21 records the first part of the three-month period from the exodus to Israel's arrival at Mount Sinai in the wilderness. This section is built around two acts of God: first, redemption from bondage—the Passover and the departure from Egypt; and second, God's provision in the wilderness—crossing through the Red Sea, manna, quails, water, defeating Amalek, and Jethro's confession of faith in God and his advice to Moses on running the camp.

In this section God honored himself by means of Israel's salvation through the Red Sea (14:21-22) and the destruction of the Egyptian army (14:23-28). These events caused the Israelites to fear the Lord and to trust him and his servant Moses (14:31). The psalm of praise and instruction that resulted from the Red Sea incident (15:1-21) has a threefold emphasis: (1) God is a warrior for his people (15:3); (2) God leads his people in lovingkindness (15:13); and (3) he brings them to his holy habitation and mountain of his inheritance (15:17). The journey from bondage to the promised inheritance would be long and dangerous, but God would be there to protect and care for them.

That period of danger and risk would become an example in both the Old and New Testaments. Redemption, whether achieved by means of the Passover or the Cross, involves a long and hard journey before the believer attains God's full promises.

Israel's first camping place had been at Succoth, a location just to the east of Pithom (12:37). They traveled next to Etham on the edge of the wilderness (13:20), a place somewhere to the southeast, not far from the northern tip of the Red Sea. The next camp at Pi Hahiroth (14:2) has not been identified. Most of these place names mentioned in the record of Israel's journey to Sinai have not been identified with certainty. (See the introductory map for a general idea of the route that Israel followed.) God led Israel by a circuitous route so that they would not have to face war immediately, which might cause them to lose their courage and return to Egypt (13:17). Later God would let his people experience war (13:17), but only after one year of teaching them his laws at Mount Sinai and coming into their midst in power and by fellowship through the tabernacle. The Red Sea (13:18) may be more literally translated Sea of Reeds, referring to a large body of water in the vicinity of the Bitter Lakes near the modern Suez Canal.

The key issues in the account of 14:1-31 are: (1) the Israelites' fear (14:10-12); (2) Pharaoh's desire to return Israel to his service (14:5); and (3) God's inexorable sovereignty in making himself known both to Egypt and to Israel as he accomplished his great acts through his servant Moses (14:4, 17-18, 30-31). Naturalistic explanations of the crossing through the sea, such as calling it a shallow sea or saying it was at ebb tide, simply do not satisfy the text or explain the impact of this event on Israel's theology and literature.

These key elements in the psalm sung by Israel in 15:1-21 form the core of God's future redemptive revelation: (1) the Lord who is strong has become Israel's salvation (15:2); (2) the Lord is a warrior (15:3); (3) he is incomparable: "Who else among the gods is like you, O Lord?" (15:11); (4) he would plant Israel in his inheritance (15:17); and (5) the Lord is an eternal king (15:18).

15:22–18:27 Preserved in the Wilderness

The Israelites' risky and dangerous journey to receive God's inheritance is emphasized as the focus shifts from their praise of God to their complaints about the lack of provisions and even about what God did supply when he gave them food. This period was designed to test the Israelites' opinions about God (15:25; 16:4). Their redemption from Egypt had been just the beginning. Heart-probing and faith-testing experiences were in God's design for them during their journey between Egypt

and the Promised Land. The tests of their hearts would center on the bitter water at Marah (15:22-26); the manna and quail (15:27–16:36); water (17:1-7); the battle with the Amalekites (17:8-16); and Jethro's great confession of faith in God and his advice to Moses on how to solve Israel's judicial problems (18:1-27).

The sweetened water at Marah was a sign of God's healing power for those who would obey him (15:26). See the introductory map for the approximate locations of Marah and Israel's next camp, Elim (15:27). Equal manna provisions for each person (16:18) and the Sabbath commandment (16:28-29) tested Israel's willingness to trust in God to supply their needs and to obey his commands.

The name given to the bread from heaven, "manna," means, "What is it?" Consider its looks (Exod. 16:14; Num. 11:7), its taste (Exod. 16:31; Num. 11:8), its preparation (Exod. 16:23; Num. 11:8), its source (Exod. 16:4, 15; John 6:32), its purpose (Deut. 8:3), and its uniqueness (Deut. 8:3). Manna is typical of Christ, the Bread of Life (John 6:33-35).

The people were not only thirsty, but they also doubted that God was even present with them (17:1-7). That is the heart of what it means to test the Lord. After all his great redemptive miracles, they still doubted that he was with them for their good. The key to Israel's victory over the Amalekites was God's power that was mediated through Moses, the sign of which was Moses' upraised hands (17:8-16).

The section in 18:1-27 concerns two main events: (1) Jethro's great confession of faith in God (18:10-12); and (2) his advice to Moses on how to administrate Israel judicially (18:13-26).

19:1–34:35 GOD'S PRESENCE FOR HOLINESS: THE COVENANT IS GIVEN AND RECONFIRMED

Overview: This large section, 19:1–34:35, is famous for two things: (1) the Ten Commandments and (2) Israel's idolatry with the golden calf. The following events are covered: God's descent upon Mount Sinai (19:1-25), God's giving the Ten Commandments (20:1-17), God's giving ordinances for worship and feasts (20:18–23:33), Moses and Israel's leaders eating with God on the mountain (24:1-11), Moses going up onto the mountain for forty days to receive instructions for the tabernacle's priests and offerings (24:12–31:18), the Israelites worshiping the golden calf, their punishment and repentance, Moses receiving assurance of God's presence (32:1–34:9), and another forty days for Moses on the mountain for receiving instructions concerning Israel's behavior after entering the Promised Land (34:10-28). See chart below.

19:1-25 Divine and Human Separation Highlighted

God, who had called Israel his firstborn son (Exod. 4:22) and had just redeemed the nation out of Egypt, then told the people to stay away from him or die. Why would God redeem his people only to keep them away from himself? The great God of the Exodus, who had been so lethal to the Egyptians, was just as much of a threat to Israel, for his holiness is nonpartisan. The only way God would be able to stop being so distant and dangerous to his people and come to dwell among them would be on the basis of the covenant he was about to make with them.

(vassals). These treaties, copies of which have been discovered and translated, followed a regular pattern and included the following elements that also are found in God's treaty with Israel:

(1) Historical preparation. The date was identified (19:1), the geographical setting given (19:2), and the activity cited of both the suzerain (God, 19:4) and the mediator of the covenant (Moses, 19:7).

(2) Preamble. God was identified as the great Suzerain, the author of the covenant (20:1).

(3) Historical prologue. A record was given of previous relations between the two parties involved (20:2). Past benefits of the suzerain were set forth to inspire gratitude and obedience on the part of the vassal people.

ISRAEL'S ONE-YEAR STAY AT SINAI

Approximate Dates	Biblical Dates and Events	References
FIRST YEAR		
June 1?	Third month, first year at Sinai	Exod. 19:1
June 3	God appears	Exod. 19:11, 20
June 6?	Law and sacrifice	Exod. 20:1–24:11
June 7-12	Moses waits to ascend	Exod. 24:12-16
June 12–July 22	Moses receives the law	Exod. 24:18–31:18
July 23	Golden-calf incident	Exod. 32:1-29
July 24	Moses intercedes for Israel	Exod. 32:30-35
? days	Moses outside the camp	Exod. 33:7-11
?	Moses spends forty days on Sinai	Exod. 34:4-29
?–March 30	Tabernacle built	Exod. 36–39
SECOND YEAR		
April 1	Tabernacle erected	Exod. 40:2
April 1-30?	Laws and rules given	Lev. 1–27; cf. Num. 1:1
April 1-12	Gifts given for offerings	Num. 7
April 14	Second Passover observed	Num. 9:3
May 1	Census taken for God's army	Num. 1:1-4
May 20	Departure from Sinai	Num. 10:11-12

20:1–23:33 The Covenant Presented by God: Legal Paragraphs

20:1-26 ANCIENT CONTRACT FORMS

The Ten Commandments do not begin with hoops for God's people to jump through but with a reminder of his redemptive acts of love (20:1, 6). That saving grace forms the context of and motivation for keeping any specific commandment. God designed the immediate context of the thunder and lightning to give the people visible signs that would help them fear him and continue to keep his commandments (20:20).

During this biblical period in history, international treaties were used to outline the relationship between a king (suzerain) and his subject people

(4) Stipulations or obligations. These were laid upon the vassal people by the suzerain. The basic stipulations gave a concise statement of the suzerain's will for his people (20:3-17). The detailed stipulations (20:18–23:33; 25:1–31:29) provided examples and applications.

(5) Provision for deposit and reading. A copy of the covenant would be placed in the sanctuary of the vassals and the suzerain (25:16, 21). From time to time there would be a public reading of the covenant terms to the people (Deut. 1–34; Josh. 24).

(6) Witnesses. Usually long lists of gods were called upon to witness the ratification of the covenant so that there would be legal witnesses to testify in case of default. Since there were no other

gods for Israel, the witnesses invoked were the heavens and earth (Deut. 4:26; 32:1).

(7) Cursings. Curses were called down upon those who would break the covenant (Deut. 27:15-26; 28:15-68) and blessings on those who remain loyal to it (Deut. 28:1-14).

(8) Ratification. The covenant was ratified by its acceptance by the people, the sacrifice and sprinkling of blood, and the eating and drinking of the covenant meal (Exod. 24). The covenant was then officially in force.

In studying the Mosaic Law it becomes clear that God used a contemporary cultural institution, a contract form, to communicate his will to his people. This treaty form would have been especially meaningful to the Israelites since they had been bound to their Egyptian overlords under similar arrangements. By employing this form, Israel's freedom from worldly authority as well as the nation's submission to the Lord are given particular emphasis.

The point of any such contract was to show how the king would care for his new people and what the people had to do to stay in the king's favor. It is extremely important to understand that God used a covenant form that stressed the personal relationships involved. God did not use an impersonal list of laws. Instead, he presented himself as the King who had already done so much for his people that they, in return, should have been gratefully willing to return service and love to him.

The prohibition of Exodus 20:26 was a warning against ritual nakedness, which at the time was an integral part of fertility cult worship.

21:1-36 RESTITUTION
The principle of restitution was applied to the issues of the worth of a servant, or slave (21:1-11) and death penalties for various acts (21:12-36). The key principle (21:13-25) is that justice demands equality of restitution, no more (which would be revenge) and no less (which would trivialize the seriousness of the offense). In the case of mothers and children, special laws were given to protect the helpless and innocent (21:22-25). If a man caused a woman to give birth prematurely but the infant was not harmed, then a simple fine was to be levied. If the child or mother was harmed, then the law of retaliation was applied. Punishment was restricted to that which was commensurate with the injury. In these verses God shows clear concern for protecting unborn children, a concern that people today would do well to heed. Surely the abortion of millions of unborn babies will fall under God's condemnation.

22:1-31 COMMUNITY LAWS
Restitution was required for both intentional and inadvertent breaches of trust (22:1-6). The section 22:18-31 covers various laws such as sorcery (22:18), afflicting the poor and foreigners (22:21-27) and offering of the firstborn son to God (22:29-31).

23:1-33 FEASTS
Some of the great feasts of Israel are presented here: the sabbatical year (23:10-13); and the three feasts of Unleavened Bread, Harvest, and Ingathering (23:14-17). The feasts were actually a time of humility and celebration before the Lord, not exclusively times to eat. The last sentence of 23:19 has been understood by Jewish people as a basis for separating meat and dairy products. But archaeological discoveries indicate that it was actually a warning against Canaanite cultic worship in which this ritual was practiced.

God promised that an angel would go before Israel and give the land of Canaan to them (23:20-33). The hornet (23:28) may be a figurative reference to the panic and terror that came upon the Canaanites as they anticipated the Israelite conquest (Josh. 2:9).

24:1-11 Covenant Ratified
Although Exodus 19 had presented a God who was virtually unapproachable on penalty of death, here several humans not only approached the mountain and saw a vision of God but also actually ate a communal meal in his presence. That meal celebrated the ratification of the Mosaic covenant. The people's response, which was a wise and sincere commitment to the covenant (24:3, 7), was pleasing in God's sight (Deut. 5:28-29).

24:12–31:18 Laws Given for Tabernacle and Priests
24:12-18 MOSES ON THE MOUNTAIN
The setting for the giving of the laws for the tabernacle and priests was the blazing mountaintop that

---

ILLUSTRATIONS OF CHRIST IN THE TABERNACLE

Table of Showbread	Christ, the Bread of Life (John 6:35, 48)
Golden Lampstand	Christ, the Light of the World (John 8:12; 9:5)
Inner Veil	Christ's broken body (Mark 15:38; Heb. 10:20)
Bronze Altar	Christ's perfect sacrifice (Heb. 9:14)
Incense Altar	Christ's intercessory prayer (Heb. 7:25)
Bronze Laver	Christ's blood that cleanses from sin (Rom. 5:9; 1 John 1:9)

enveloped Moses for forty days (24:17-18). For Israel that setting elevated the laws and gave them a visual portrayal of God's abiding glory. The laws of his glory were to be seen in that original light, not simply as good ideas from humans to follow.

The tabernacle served to remind Israel of God's presence among his people and prefigured the redemptive work of Christ who lived, or "tabernacled," among the human race (John 1:14). A *type* is an Old Testament illustration that, having its place and purpose in biblical history, is divinely appointed to foreshadow some New Testament truth. Many parts of the tabernacle are types of Christ (see chart below).

25:1-40 INTERIOR ARTICLES
Instructions were given for (1) collecting the peoples' contributions for the tabernacle (Exod. 25:1-9); (2) making the Ark of the Covenant (25:10-22), the place where God would meet with Moses (25:22); (3) making the table that would hold the bread of the presence (25:23-30); and (4) making the lampstand (25:31-40).

26:1-37 CURTAINS
Instructions were given for making (1) the tabernacle curtains and their supports (26:1-30); (2) the veil (26:31-35); and (3) the curtain, or screen, for the tabernacle doorway (26:36-37).

27:1-21 EXTERIOR ARTICLES
Instructions were given for making (1) the altar (27:1-8); and (2) the courtyard, or court, of the tabernacle (27:9-19); as well as for (3) the maintenance of the lamp (27:20-21).

28:1-43 PRIESTLY DRESS
Instructions for priestly garments included the preparation of (1) Aaron's clothing (28:1-5); (2) the ephod of gold (28:6-14) that he would wear to represent Israel before the Lord; (3) the breastpiece of judgment (28:15-30), to which were attached the Urim and Thummim (28:30), which would be used to determine God's will (28:30-31; cf. 1 Sam. 23:9-12); (4) the gold plate to be attached to his turban (28:36-38); and (5) the robes, turbans, tunics, sashes and other items for Aaron and his sons (28:31-43).

29:1-46 PRIESTLY DEDICATION
Instructions for dedicating and consecrating the priests included: (1) dressing and anointing them (29:1-9); and (2) making the sin, burnt and wave offerings that would purify them before the Lord (29:10-35). Other offerings were to be offered on a daily basis to consecrate the tabernacle (29:36-44). The beautiful point of all this was that God would dwell among Israel and that Israel would know him (29:45-46).

30:1-38 INCENSE AND SUPPORT
Instructions were given for: (1) making the altar of incense (30:1-10); (2) taking a census of Israel's eligible fighting men, which would bring financial support for the tabernacle services when each paid his half-shekel offering (30:11-16); (3) making the bronze basin, or laver (30:17-21); (4) preparing the special oil for anointing the priests and tabernacle and its utensils (30:22-33); and (5) making the special incense (30:34-38).

31:1-18 CRAFTSMEN
The men who made the tabernacle were filled with the Spirit of God (31:3). The first part of the law (Exod. 20–31) concludes with the commanded sign of observing the Sabbath (31:12-18).

32:1–34:35 The Covenant Broken and Restored

32:1-35 ISRAEL SPARED
The apparent reasons that God did not wipe out the nation for its worship of the golden calf were because of the negative witness such action would give to the Egyptians (32:12), as well as God's remembrance of his covenant with Abraham (32:13). But God's gracious act did not preclude his killing three thousand people who had gone out of control (32:25-29) or stopping Moses' continued intercession on the nation's behalf (32:30-35). The expression "blot me out" (32:32) was borrowed from the register that was kept of Israel's citizens. It means "Let me die an untimely death and no longer be listed among the living."

What made God angry with his enemies was their stubborn opposition to him (4:21; 8:15; 14:17). What made him angry regarding Israel was her unfaithfulness (33:3). That unfaithfulness would become the basis in the future for the prophets' continual remarks concerning Israel's having broken the Mosaic covenant. See 15:26 and note the close relationship between plagues and sickness in 1 Kings 8:37.

God's anger has different effects. In Exodus 19:4 God's judgments on Egypt worked for Israel's salvation. In Exodus 32 his anger worked to purify and discipline Israel. Thus, disaster for God's redeemed people is not a time for the loss of hope and faith, but rather, a time for growth through discipline.

Although 32:14 reads " the LORD withdrew his threat," in actual fact God does not change his mind or ways (32:14; cf. Mal. 3:6; James 1:17). Rather, this is a human expression that attributes human emotions to God, emphasizing the pain, sorrow and grief he experiences due to mankind's sin.

33:1-23 MOSES' FAVOR
The intimate way in which God related to Moses is seen in 33:7-11. This section describes the favor with which God viewed Moses, the critical issue of God's presence with Israel, and Moses' desire to know God even more intimately by seeing his glory (33:12-23). The tent mentioned in 33:7 was not the tabernacle, which was yet to be

completed, but a place where Moses could meet with God privately.

34:1-35 MOSES' VISION OF GOD
Moses not only received the renewed covenant (34:1, 27-28) but also glimpsed God's person more closely. The words of 34:6-7, describing God's loving and uncompromisingly holy character, have become one of the most often quoted Bible passages. The description of the veil (34:29-35) rounds out the events that had led up to Moses' intimate meeting with God. Moses' new vision of God's glory was a source of awe and fright (34:30) and also a confirmation of God's glory surrounding the words Moses brought to Israel. Compare 34:26 with 23:19.

35:1–40:38 GOD'S PRESENCE FOR FELLOWSHIP: GOD DWELLS IN ISRAEL
Overview: This section (35:1–40:38) builds to the climax of Exodus 40, where God came to dwell with his people. Long, detailed instructions were given concerning how to build the tabernacle and worship there. Although many details are listed, the section really centers on one major thing—how God can once again dwell among humans. All the details of the tabernacle merely stress that it was to be a holy residence because of its holy Resident. These numerous details climax at the end of the book, when God, once deadly to approach on the mountain, was able to dwell in the center of Israel's camp.

35:1–40:16 The Dwelling Place Constructed
35:1-35 OFFERINGS FROM THE HEART
The key word in 35:1-35 concerning offerings for the tabernacle is "willing" (35:22, 26). The people truly gave from a willing heart and a spirit stirred by God.

36:1-38 THE TABERNACLE IS CONSTRUCTED
The recounting of the people's heartfelt offerings overlaps with an account of the skill of the Spirit-filled workmen (36:4-6). The next section describes the construction of the inner tent curtains and outer covering (36:8-19); the boards, bases, and bars for supporting the curtains (36:20-34); and the curtain, or veil, to go in front of the Holy of Holies, as well as the curtain, or screen, for the entrance to the tent (36:35-38).

37:1–38:31 THE ARTICLES ARE BUILT
The workmen constructed the Ark of the Covenant (37:1-9); the table and its utensils (37:10-16); the lampstand (37:17-24); and the altar of incense, as well as preparing the oil and incense (37:25-29). They made the altar of burnt offering (38:1-7); the bronze basin, or laver, and its stand (38:8); and the tabernacle courtyard, or court (38:9-20). An account is also given of the material used in the tabernacle's construction (38:21-31).

39:1–40:16 THE TABERNACLE IS COMPLETED
A description is given of the preparation of the priestly garments, with special emphasis on the breastpiece (39:8-21). The entire construction project was concluded and summarized, ending with Moses' inspection and blessing (31:32-42). The tabernacle was erected almost one year after the Exodus from Egypt.

40:17-38 God Begins Dwelling in the Tabernacle
The instructions for setting up the tabernacle (40:1-16) were matched with Moses' obedience in carrying them out (40:17-33). Previously Moses had been able to enter his small tent of meeting outside the camp and observe God's partial glory (33:7-11). But not even Moses could enter this greater tent of meeting, a tent where God's full glory dwelt (40:35), for at that point God began to dwell with his people in a more intimate way. God was one step further away from the tragedy of man's fall into sin and one step closer to his future perfect dwelling among believers when his tabernacle will appear in the new heavens and earth (Rev. 21:3).

LEVITICUS

BASIC FACTS

HISTORICAL SETTING

The events recorded in the book took place at the foot of Mount Sinai. The time period goes from the setting up of the tabernacle to Israel's departure from Sinai about one month and twenty days later (cf. Exod. 40:17 with Num. 10:11). The people had been away from Egypt just one year when the events of this book took place. For a discussion of the date of Israel's exodus from Egypt, see the *Historical Setting* section to the book of Exodus.

AUTHOR

The author of Leviticus is not named. The Lord addressed Moses repeatedly throughout the book (1:1; 4:1; 6:1, 8, 19, 24; 7:22), making Moses the most likely person to have recorded these words. The Mosaic authorship of Leviticus is further supported by other evidence. The material in the book was revealed at Sinai, and it is highly probable that Moses would have recorded the revelations he received there from the Lord. The book follows and is closely linked with Exodus (Lev. 1:1), which was certainly authored by Moses. When Jesus called the laws concerning leprosy (Lev. 14:2-3) as those which Moses commanded (Matt. 8:4; Mark 1:44), he affirmed Moses as the one who first brought the words of Leviticus to Israel.

The third book of Moses is referred to in Jewish usage as "and he called," an English translation of the first Hebrew words in Leviticus 1:1. The Old Testament Greek translators gave it the name "The Levitical Book" because of its emphasis on priestly regulations for the tribe of Levi. The Latin Vulgate rendered the book's title "Leviticus," from which the English title is taken.

DATE

Modern criticism has questioned the antiquity of Leviticus, dating it in the period of 500–450 B.C. However, since the discovery of Ugaritic literature, some arguments against an early date are no longer valid. These arguments are based on a premise that the forms of ritual and sacrifice found in Leviticus were only developed late in Israel's history. But the finds at Ugarit show these forms were in existence 1,500 years before Christ. The terminology used at Ugarit in the fifteenth century B.C. is remarkably parallel to that of Leviticus. Terms such as burnt offering, whole burnt offering, trespass offering, and peace offering are found in Ugaritic literature.

Leviticus was probably written shortly after the book of Exodus was written during the wilderness wanderings. It records the words God spoke to Moses out of the tabernacle (1:1) during Israel's last two months at Mount Sinai.

PURPOSE

Leviticus gives the details of how a believer could live in the presence of God and enjoy his blessings. It is designed to clarify both what is and what is not pleasing to God. The largest part of the book is used to describe how sinful man can attain forgiveness and restoration after breaking one of God's laws.

GEOGRAPHY AND ITS IMPORTANCE

The Israelites were camped at Mount Sinai at the time the events and revelations of Leviticus took place. Wherever the exact location of Mount Sinai may be, the book of Leviticus locates its readers right outside of the tabernacle's front curtains and lets them listen to the voice of God telling his people what they must do now that he has come to dwell with them. The stark and threatening aspects of Israel's journey through the wilderness, already seen in Exodus and about to be seen in Numbers, fade into the background. Leviticus focuses on a vision of God's holiness—a vision that is true no matter where the people are located. See the introductory map.

GUIDING CONCEPTS

FELLOWSHIP WITH GOD

God said, "I will live among you, and I will not despise you. I will walk among you; I will be your God, and you will be my people" (Lev. 26:11-12). All the various rituals and laws in Leviticus have one main goal—to enable God and his children to have fellowship with each other. That fellowship would glorify God and graciously give blessing and joy to his people. Look for the following key concepts that made God's desires for fellowship with Israel possible: (1) holiness; (2) sacrifice; and (3) forgiveness. All the book's diverse aspects revolve around those three concepts.

BIBLE-WIDE CONCEPTS

BLESSING THROUGH OBEDIENCE

In Genesis 18:19 God had said that he had chosen Abraham "so that he will direct his sons and their families to keep the way of the Lord and do what is right and just. Then [God] will do for him all that [he has] promised." Notice the key words and phrases: "so that," "direct," "keep the way of the Lord," and "right and just." "So that" introduces the purpose for God having chosen Abraham. God chose Abraham *so that* he could "direct his children," *so that* God would bring about his promises. Thus the purpose for God choosing Abraham was twofold: (1) to get Abraham and his descendants to pass on God's laws (2) in order to bring in God's promises. "Direct" reveals the task for Abraham and his children: to instruct and teach family members. "Keep the way of the Lord" and "right and just" are two technical terms for God's laws and describe what was to be taught and passed on from generation to generation. Abraham's election and salvation by faith were accompanied by the necessary call to obeying God's laws. The way to experiencing God's blessings was through obedience to the way of the Lord. No one who lived like the devil could expect to experience the blessing of Abraham.

The way of the Lord, that is, God's commands of righteousness and justice, were known to Abraham. In fact, all mankind was under obligation to honor the morality that God required (Rom. 1:18-20, 32). But in the covenant with Moses some of the laws of God were specifically noted as conditions for fellowship with God (for example, see the change that took place under the Mosaic covenant reflected in Rom. 5:13-14). Exodus 20–31 outlines the major laws of relationship within the community of the redeemed. The last part of Exodus outlines the construction of the the tabernacle which served as the central way of access to God. Leviticus continues the giving of the Mosaic covenant from the tabernacle rather than from smoke-covered Mount Sinai, as was seen in Exodus.

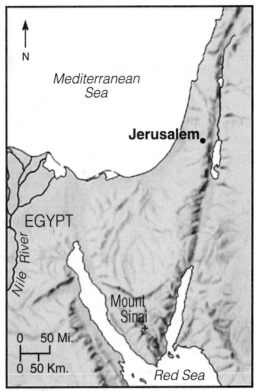

LAW AS A BLESSING OR A CURSE

Leviticus 26 contains a list of blessings and curses that would result if a person kept or ignored God's commandments. The most important thing to note when reading this list is that keeping the law would bring the promised blessings. In other words, the law told the Israelites how to be blessed by God. That is why David could say that he loved the law, that it was a light on his path, and that it was sweeter than honey. Paul also said that the law was holy, righteous, and good. The law is good because it reveals what God wants so that believers can please him.

The blessings and curses of the Mosaic covenant stem directly from the blessings and curses inherent in God's creation of the world. Adam and Eve were told that they would be blessed if they kept God's law concerning the tree of the knowledge of good and evil or cursed if they did not. Since they did not keep God's law they were cursed. All the smaller curses of the Mosaic law are but pale reflections of the greater curse upon the world resulting from Adam's disobedience. All the smaller blessings of the Mosaic law are but pale reflections of the greater blessing the world will ultimately experience based on Christ's obedience.

OBEDIENCE AS GRATITUDE FOR SALVATION

Abraham believed God, and God declared him to be righteous. From his initial and essential faith in God, Abraham was then required to keep the way of the Lord by acting righteously and justly, no longer in order to be counted as righteous but to consistently confirm his original faith in and love for God. His obedience was the only appropriate response to God's gracious promise and acts on his behalf. The same was true for Israel before the tabernacle of God. As a nation, Israel had placed its faith in God, believing and obeying his instructions for the Exodus from Egypt. Only God knew those individuals who from the heart had truly believed in him and had been counted righteous. All were taken through the sea and were provided with manna from heaven and water from the rock. But many showed a deficiency in their relationship with God since they were destroyed in the wilderness. (Reflecting on this incident, Paul relates it to the Christian life in 1 Cor. 10:1-6.) Leviticus continues the theme of obedience of the redeemed by focusing on the place where God and humans met.

THE ISSUE OF THE HOLY SEED

From Genesis through Revelation the key issue concerning who will receive God's redemption centers on who will say yes to God, both in heart and in life. God wanted a people who would give him devotion and obedience. He was preparing a race of people who could be blessed instead of cursed. Leviticus shows the major step God took on the journey from Eden to the new earth to help people enjoy his blessings. Israel, as God's holy people, would become equipped to be a worldwide witness so that "in Abraham" all the nations of the earth could be blessed (Gen. 12:3).

THE ISSUE OF LAND PROMISES

The wickedness of the Canaanites would cause God to destroy and replace them with the Israelites (see Gen. 15:16). Leviticus first focuses on the implications of the presence of the tabernacle among the Israelites and then focuses on the implications of Israel's presence in the Promised Land. The holy God would enable Israel to purge the Promised Land of its enemies. The Israelites would only remain in the land as long as they remained faithful to their Redeemer.

THE LEVITICAL OFFERINGS AND CHRIST

The offerings were the shadows of the reality and substance of Christ's sacrifice. Each offering pictured his perfect atonement and forgiveness. Believers today must consider the significance of the sacrifices for the Old Testament worshiper, the illustrative significance of sacrifice for the Christian, and the principles that may be applied to all believers. The sacrifices were predictive, expressing a need that they could not perfectly satisfy (Heb. 10:4); but the promised Redeemer they prefigured would fulfill and complete these sacrifices (Eph. 5:2; 1 Cor. 10:11; Heb. 9:14; see chart below).

THE OLD TESTAMENT SACRIFICES AND CHRIST

Burnt offering	Christ offered himself completely (Heb. 9:14) and without blemish (Heb.4:15) as a fragrant offering to God (Eph. 5:2).
Grain offering	Christ offered himself as spiritual food (John 6:33-58).
Peace offering	Christ proclaimed peace (Eph. 2:17), made peace (Col. 1:20), and is our peace (Eph. 2:14).
Sin offering	Christ took the believer's sin (John 1:29; 2 Cor. 5:21) and died in the sinner's place (Mark 10:45).
Guilt offering	Christ made compensation for the damage done by sin (2 Cor. 5:19).

NEEDS MET BY LEVITICUS

The book of Leviticus shows Israel during a very difficult time. They had been redeemed out of Egypt but now found themselves in the middle of the wilderness. They had already complained about God's provisions and fallen into idolatry during the golden calf incident. Any thoughts of a carefree life of freedom from Egyptian bondage had passed. God, who had redeemed them, now thundered and flashed over them from the top of Mount Sinai. God was so awesome and lethal that anyone who touched the mountain would die. For God's people, the grace of his redemption had been transformed into a vision of his terrifying holiness. And now that holy God dwelt among them in the tabernacle. The Israelites could only watch and wait to find out if their sinful nation could coexist with their holy God. The structure and content of Leviticus show that it was written to answer questions regarding the needs of the Israelite believers.

- What can be done about sins that are committed?
- How can God live so close and yet not destroy those who sin, even if it is inadvertently?
- How can the sinful people of Israel find forgiveness?
- How can the Israelites keep themselves clean before the Lord?
- Just how holy is the Lord and what does that mean for his people?

Believers ask these questions today. The redemption of believers from sin is wonderful, but, like Israel, they may find that God's uncompromising drive for holiness becomes overwhelming. The failures of sin can seem all too frequent and believers may wonder how God can exist with them without destroying them. But for God's redeemed people, then and now, Leviticus points the way to the balance between God's free redemption and uncompromising holiness. Sacrifice removes the guilt of sin. And only then, in the state of perfect forgiveness, can the believer have the grace and motivation to seek to be holy as God is holy.

OUTLINE OF LEVITICUS

I. REMAINING IN GOD'S PRESENCE (1:1–16:34)
   A. Guidelines for the Offerings (1:1–7:38)
   B. Mediator: Holiness of Priests (8:1–10:20)
   C. The Holiness of the People (11:1–15:35)
   D. Yearly Provision for National Holiness (16:1-34)

II. REMAINING IN GOD'S LAND (17:1–27:34)
   A. Avoidance of Egyptian and Canaanite Perversions (17:1–20:27)
   B. The Guardians of the Offerings (21:1–22:33)
   C. Rests: Reminders of God's Creator-Owner Sovereignty (23:1–25:55)
   D. Conditions for Remaining in Canaan (26:1-46)
   E. Appendix: Vows (27:1-34)

LEVITICUS NOTES

1:1–16:34 REMAINING
IN GOD'S PRESENCE

Overview: The section 1:1–16:34 focuses on the way Israel should relate to God in their midst. God moved from the awesome Mount Sinai, covered in lightning, thunder, and smoke, down into a tent in the very middle of the Israelites' camp. It moves from: (1) sacrifice (Lev. 1–7); to (2) priestly mediators (Lev. 8–10); to (3) removing all uncleanness that would defile the tabernacle (Lev. 11–16).

1:1–7:28 Guidelines for the Offerings

Overview: The first seven chapters of Leviticus introduce that which the Lord communicated to Moses from the doorway of the tabernacle. The subject matter immediately turns to offerings: "Whenever you present offerings to the Lord . . ." (1:2). The descriptions of the offerings presuppose a prior knowledge of their significance on the part of the Israelites. Terms such as burnt offering, whole burnt offering, trespass offering, and peace offering are found in extrabiblical writings contemporary with Leviticus. Therefore, the offerings themselves were not new for Israel. However, what was new was their incorporation into the religious life of God's covenant people. The offerings were designed to bring forgiveness to an individual or to the nation as a whole when they had broken the covenant with God or had sinned against other people.

The theological key to these first seven chapters is the concept of bringing an offering "to the Lord" (1:2) in order to be "accepted by the Lord" (1:3). The personal key is the repeated phrase of assured forgiveness (4:20, 26, 31, 35; 5:10, 13, 16, 18; 6:7). The Israelite who sacrificed for a particular sin would have the full assurance of being forgiven for that sin.

1:1-17 BURNT OFFERING

The burnt offering could be made with one of the following animals: a bull (1:1-9); a sheep or goat (1:10-13); or a bird (1:14-17). The literal meaning of the Hebrew word for burnt offering was "that which goes up," that is, what went up to God. The Hebrew word for "offering" (1:2; *qorban*) is derived from the Hebrew verb meaning "to draw near." Thus, an offering prepared the way for Israel to draw near to God. The laying of the offerer's hands on the sacrifice was a symbolic act of identification with the offering (1:4). It was just as if the worshiper was saying, "This animal represents me; its blood shall be shed in my behalf." The word "atonement" comes from the

---

THE OFFERINGS

. . . As Gifts. The purpose of the offerings was summed up in the word "gift." First, as with the giving of any gift, the recipient was the key figure in view. The offerings were gifts to God, given to him because he is the sovereign Lord and everyone owes all to him. From Cain and Abel onward, God's people have known to give back to him part of what he, as sovereign Creator, has given to them.

Second, the one who gave to God became deprived of some necessities of life. But though the person lost the gift, he gained a bond of grace and forgiveness with God. The altar became the place of mediation between God and humans. Third, some of the offerings were totally burned up on the altar, but that burning was not seen as the gift's destruction. The burning symbolized, through the rising of the heat and smoke, the gift's transference into God's invisible realm. These offerings were called in Hebrew "that which goes up," implying that the gift went up in the smoke into the realm of God. It also made the giving of the gift final—the offerer could not take it back. The burnt offering was, in that sense, the most perfect offering, for God received all of it.

. . . As Communion. Every offering signified an element of communion between God and the offerer that showed a certain degree of friendship and intimacy. The offerer ate a meal of renewed fellowship after he had been forgiven by God.

. . . As Forgiveness. Every offering was a means for receiving God's forgiveness. In one way or another the offerer had broken the covenant and stood unclean before the Lord. The offering was designed to reestablish a relationship with God by atoning for a particular sin. Sin put anyone in jeopardy with God, and the particular focus of offense throughout Leviticus was the defilement of the tabernacle, which was both God's dwelling place and the location of the covenant regulations (15:31; 20:3).

The offerings brought forgiveness for inadvertent sin (4:2, 13-14, 22, 27; 5:15) as well as conscious sin (5:1, 4; 6:1-7). No atonement was available for a defiant, high-handed sin (Num. 15:30-31), but see Numbers 16:46-48, where the offering of incense stopped the plague. For another example, David realized that no sacrifice was available for his sins of murder and adultery (2 Sam. 12:13); however, his true repentance did bring atonement for his sins. A resounding theme throughout the Old Testament was that the sacrifices were not mechanical. They could only bring forgiveness when accompanied by a sinner's contrite heart (cf. Pss. 4:4-5; 20:1-5; 40:6; 50:7-16; 51:14-19).

same Hebrew root as the noun meaning "ransom" or "ransom price." The verb form of this word means "to atone by offering a substitute." The image was of an aroma that was pleasing to God. Blood atonement was not the central feature of this offering. Rather, central were the cutting, washing, and arranging of the pieces of the offering on the altar and then the burning of them, by which was accomplished the actual sending of the gift up to God. This offering was often coupled with a sin, or peace, offering. The significance of this offering was that it called the offerer to complete surrender and dedication to God.

2:1-16 GRAIN OFFERING
The grain or cereal offering consisted either of portions of flour mixed with oil and incense (2:1-3), or baked or cooked offerings (2:4-10) prepared with no leaven but seasoned with salt (2:11-13), or roasted ripened heads of new grain (2:14-16). The salt signified the permanence and purity of the worshiper's devotion to God (2:13; cf. Num. 18:19). The grain offering was usually made along with a burnt offering (Num. 28:5, 12-13) and was always made with a peace, or fellowship, offering (Lev. 7:12-14). The giver shared in, offered, and dedicated the fruits of his personal labors to the Lord.

3:1-17 PEACE, OR FELLOWSHIP, OFFERING
The peace, or fellowship, offering was either an animal from the herds (3:1-5), or a lamb (3:6-11), or a goat (3:12-17). This offering was brought on the basis of the offerer's voluntary desire. The name of the offering does not indicate that the offerer would gain peace with God, but that he was celebrating the fact of the peace and wholeness brought about by his faith in God's redemption and covenant.

4:1-35 SIN OFFERING
The law covered unintentional sins committed by either the priests (4:1-12), the whole congregation of Israel (4:13-21), a leader (4:22-26), or a lay person (4:27-35). The kind of offering was suited to the rank of the offerer. The ritual included the laying on of hands with its significance of identifying the sacrifice with the sinner whose sins it would atone for.

5:1-19 GUILT OFFERING
The guilt offering, a specialized type of sin offering, was either a lamb or goat (5:1-6), or two birds (5:7-10), or fine flour (5:11-13). It covered offenses against the Lord's holy things (5:14-16) or any unintentional sin (5:17-18). Three types of offense required a guilt offering: (1) an offense against God's holy things (5:15-16); (2) an offense against God's commands (5:17-19); and (3) an offense against one's neighbor (6:1-7).

6:1-7:30 RESTITUTION
The section 6:1-7:30 covers restitution, which comprised a guilt offering plus twenty percent of the damage incurred (6:1-7). The reiteration of the various offerings that were described earlier focuses on the priest's specific duties in performing those offerings (burnt offerings, 6:8-13; grain offerings, 6:14-18; grain offerings at priests' anointings, 6:19-23; sin offerings, 6:24-30; guilt offerings, 7:1-10; peace, or fellowship, offerings, 7:11-36; and a final summary, 7:37-38).

These principles were to be learned from the offerings: (1) God demands that sins be paid for and acquitted (sin and guilt offerings, Rom. 8:1); (2) God delivers assurance of forgiveness (peace, or fellowship, offering, John 14:27); (3) God desires adoration (grain offering, Heb. 13:15); (4) God delights in acknowledgment of his lordship (burnt offering, Rom. 12:1).

8:1-10:20 Mediator: Holiness of Priests
Overview: Leviticus 1–7 focused on the offerings, whereas Leviticus 8–10 focuses on the priests who mediated the offerings. Two points are stressed: (1) the priests were qualified to mediate on the basis of a complicated and completely obedient process of purification (Lev. 8–9); and (2) they could be fatally disqualified by one act of disobedient imperfection (Lev. 10).

8:1-9:24 OBEDIENCE TO GOD'S COMMANDS
Every major section of Leviticus 8 ends with the phrase "as the Lord had commanded Moses," or variations of it (8:5, 13, 17, 21, 29). That obedience was continued by Aaron and his sons (8:36), who were ordained and dedicated in this chapter. The consecration offering (8:22), when literally translated from the Hebrew, means "filling," since "to fill the hands" was a technical term for ordaining someone to an office (cf. Exod. 32:29, where this word is translated "set apart"). The blood (Lev. 8:23) was placed on the priest's "ear" (because he was to heed God's words), on the "thumb of his right hand" (because he was to perform God's work), and on the "big toe of his right foot" (because he was to follow God's ways). The theme of God's commandments being carried out continues in Leviticus 9 (9:7, 21) in reference to the nation's dedication and purification. The main point of all this was that the people be given an opportunity to see the Lord's glory (9:6, 23).

10:1-20 NADAB AND ABIHU
The phrase "disobeyed the Lord" (10:1) bursts out in terrible contrast to the previously unbroken chain of "as the Lord had commanded" seen throughout Leviticus 8–9. The nature of the sin of Aaron's sons is not fully explained. Possibly they were stirred by the shouts of the people to present

an offering of incense. Yet they did it at an improper time (not at God's direction) and in an improper way (not prepared from the altar fire). The fire was called "different" since it was contrary to what was prescribed (Exod. 30:9). Whatever the particular reason behind Nadab and Abihu's actions, the point was that they did not treat God as holy (10:3). A possibility is raised in 10:9 that the sons were intoxicated.

Eleazar and Ithamar disobeyed when they burned up the portion of the sin offering that they should have eaten (10:16-20). Aaron explained to Moses that, in light of the judgment on Nadab and Abihu, they did not consider themselves sufficiently free from sin to deserve to eat the designated portion of the sin offering. Moses was satisfied with the explanation. Although an ordinance had been broken, the violation had been motivated by a desire to treat God as holy.

11:1–15:35 The Holiness of the People

Overview: Leviticus 11–15 focused on the daily life and purity of the people. While these rules may seem strange to believers today, the underlying point is very much a part of the Christian life (15:31). The people were to stay pure as defined by these rules so that they would not defile either God who had redeemed them or the place of his dwelling. For the Israelite it was God's saving act in the Exodus; for the Christian it is God's redemption in Christ.

11:1-23 CLEAN AND UNCLEAN CREATURES

The regulations of clean and unclean creatures (11:1-23) must be understood in light of the New Testament teaching in Acts 10:11-15; 11:9; 15:20, 29, and Mark 7:19. The criteria of clean and unclean were applied to animals, birds, water creatures, and insects. The principle of clean and unclean animals had been known since the Flood, because Noah knew those distinctions (Gen. 7:2). The explicit purpose for clean and unclean distinctions is found in relating Leviticus 11:43-45 to 20:22-26. The food distinctions were to be a witness of Israel's holiness to her God. Ethical, health, and aesthetic reasons have also been given for the distinction between clean and unclean foods. However, the point is that God has always had a right as the Creator to tell the people he has created what they can and cannot eat. See, for example, the stories of Adam and Eve (Gen. 1:29-30; 2:16-17) and Noah (Gen. 9:3-4). Obedience to these dietary laws brought a person into conformity with God's own holiness (Lev. 11:44). Even touching the carcass of a dead animal would make a person unclean (11:24-40). Dead animal carcasses, just as dead human bodies, were defiling since death is the result of sin (Gen. 2:17; Rom. 3:23).

11:24–15:33 CLEAN AND UNCLEAN HUMAN BEINGS

The law for cleansing from birth impurity (12:1-8) was observed by Mary after the birth of the Lord Jesus (Luke 2:22-24). The reason for the uncleanness of childbirth may be traced to the Fall and the curse pronounced immediately afterward. Pain and suffering were to accompany childbirth (Gen. 3:15), and death would ultimately follow (Gen. 2:17; 3:19). Consequently, everything connected with procreation (childbirth, menstruation, seminal emission) was treated as unclean, rendering a person unfit for a specified period of time to perform religious duties.

The laws concerning infectious skin diseases, including leprosy, in people, and mildew, in infected articles (13:1–14:57), were followed by a long section on the laws concerning what to do when a person or object was healed of such a disease (Lev. 14). Leprosy (Hansen's disease) was greatly feared by the Israelites, not only because of the physical damage done by the disease, but also because of the strict laws that isolated the leper from the rest of society. Leviticus 15 put forth the laws concerning male and female discharges and gave two examples for each. The point of this passage was to protect Israel from death (remember Nadab and Abihu) by teaching them how to avoid defiling the tabernacle (15:31), God's dwelling place among them.

16:1-34 Yearly Provision for National Holiness

Sitting squarely in the middle of the book is Leviticus 16, which describes how, once a year, all of Israel would stand in perfect forgiveness before the Lord. This chapter forms the climax to the sins, offerings and forgiveness described in Leviticus 1–15. The Day of Atonement was a yearly provision for national holiness. (For the meaning of "atonement," see 1:4.) Even after all the sacrifices the people and priests would have made throughout the year, they still needed cleansing. There was always the possibility that some unnoticed sin would defile the people, priests, or tabernacle (16:33). This special day called attention to the basic nature of God's forgiveness provided in the Mosaic covenant: it was limited to specific sins and would only be complete when the leaders or priests were obedient to all the Mosaic stipulations. The inadequacy of the priesthood was shown (16:1, 6, 13), as was the priest's need to bathe and change clothing (16:4, 24). The consciousness of sin's guilt, whether known or unknown, real or potential, was always present (Heb. 9:6-10).

The ritual offering of the "scapegoat" (Lev. 16:10) is described (16:20-22). Although it is debated whether the Hebrew term *azazel*, translated as "scapegoat" in 16:26, means "complete destruction" or "the goat that has gone away," what the ritual symbolized is clear: sin had been removed from Israel. The scapegoat is typical of Christ "who takes away the sins of the world" (John 1:29). "Fasting" (Lev. 16:31) is often associated with self-examination and prayer (cf. Ezra 8:21; Ps. 35:13; Isa. 58:3, 5) and speaks of true repentance. The Day of Atonement called attention to humanity's essential distance from God because of the curse's resultant impurities (Lev. 16:16). The nation was to humble itself (Exod. 10:3; Mic. 6:8). For one brief and holy day each year the entire nation would be cleansed from their sins (Lev. 16:30).

17:1–27:34 REMAINING IN GOD'S LAND
Overview: The section 17:1–27:34 emphasizes what Israel would have to do to remain in the Promised Land. They would remain there by avoiding the pagan practices in Egypt and Canaan (Lev. 17–20), by the priestly mediators of the sacrifices not committing any unclean acts (Lev. 21–22), and by the Israelites consistently honoring God's "Creator ownership" of the land by observing his ordained feasts and Sabbaths (Lev. 23–26). The book concludes by including even freewill vows in the conditions for covenant blessing.

17:1–20:27 Avoidance of Egyptian and Canaanite Perversions
Overview: Leviticus 1–16 centered on the lives of the people in relation to God's holy presence in the tabernacle. Leviticus 17–20 centers on the people in relation to the sinful practices that surrounded them in Egypt and would surround them in Canaan. The land, symbolizing God, was going to vomit out the Canaanites because they had defiled it. The land would do the same thing to the Israelites if they sinned in the same way.

17:1-16 THE ALTAR AND BLOOD
The altar in front of the tabernacle (17:1-9) was to be Israel's focus of true worship. God, the King, would brook no rival altars. The expression "cut off" (17:3-4) refers to the death penalty (Exod. 31:14). The "evil spirits" (17:7) possibly were worshiped in an orgiastic ceremony (cf. 2 Chron. 11:15). The blood sacrifice (17:10-16) reveals the nature of the atonement: it was graciously given (17:11b), not the result of human perfection. Because of its sacrificial purpose, blood was not to be eaten. This law taught respect for human life, which the blood represented.

God provided various means for forgiving the Israelites' sins: (1) presenting the blood of a sacrifice and eating its flesh (10:17); (2) intercession (Exod. 32:30); (3) offering incense (Num. 16:47); and (4) laying one's hands on an animal sacrifice (Lev. 16:21-22). Ransom was central to the idea of

atonement (cf. Exod. 21:30). The blood was effective because it represented life; if there is no blood, there is no life. The blood functioned as the symbol of life that ransomed the lives of God's people.

18:1–19:37 SEXUAL, CULTIC AND CIVIL SINS
Egyptian and Canaanite perversions were to be avoided (18:1-5). Specific examples of sexual perversion involved blood relatives (18:6-23). Such sins were the reason the land's inhabitants were about to be destroyed (18:24-30). This explains God's purpose for leaving Israel in Egypt for the four hundred years mentioned in Genesis 15:13. He had given these nations time to repent, but they had not done so. The religious and civil laws given to Israel, with the repetition of the words "I am the LORD," revealed a close interrelationship between the worship of God (19:2, 4, 12, 16, 18, 28, 30-32, 36-37) and God's maintenance of the Promised Land (19:9-10, 23, 29, 33).

20:1-27 PUNISHMENT FOR SINS
The theme of avoiding sin in the Promised Land continues in Leviticus 20. God has revealed the future of man in his Word, and seeking to know and control that future through mediums, spiritists or astrology is tantamount to unbelief and rebellion (20:6). "They are guilty of a capital offense" (20:9) meant that the law of blood revenge would not apply in this case. The offender would have to bear the guilt for his own death. This chapter rounds out the section on the Israelites avoiding pagan perversions so that the Promised Land would not vomit them out of it (20:22-23). It also stresses the reasons for dietary and religious separation (20:25-26).

21:1–22:33 The Guardians of the Offerings
Overview: Leviticus 21–22 describes the necessary wholeness and acceptability of the priests and offerings.

21:1-24 LONG-TERM QUALIFICATIONS
The long-term qualifications for the priests included: (1) rules regarding touching the dead, shaving, cutting the hair and body, and marriage (21:1-9); (2) specific rules for the high priest (21:10-15); and (3) rules for those with physical defects (21:16-24). All this was so that God's sanctuary would not be profaned (21:23). Cutting the hair, beard, and body were pagan practices that both the people and priests were to avoid (21:5; cf. 19:27-28).

22:1-33 SHORT-TERM DISQUALIFICATIONS
The short-term disqualifications for the priests involved: (1) uncleanness (22:1-9); (2) eating holy things (22:10-16); (3) defects in the offerings (22:17-25); and (4) imperfection of sacrificial animals (22:26-33). The command of 22:28 was to

guard against Israel's participation in Canaanite cultic worship (cf. Exod. 34:26).

23:1–25:55 Rests: Reminders of God's Creator-Owner Sovereignty

Overview: The section of 23:1–25:55 on Israel's feasts and sabbaths emphasizes God's Creator ownership of all he gives to his redeemed. It looks back to the perfection of Eden and forward to the perfect justice and ecology of the new earth. Leviticus 17–22 focused on Israel's relationship to the Promised Land, and that relationship continues here. The Israelites had to realize that the land was on temporary lease to them from God and was not their own possession; it was theirs only as long as they satisfied the requirements of their covenant with God. They had been redeemed from Egypt to become God's servants, not their own masters (25:55).

God's sacred assemblies for the Israelites were designed to instruct them in holiness, remind them of their covenant relationship with God, and provide them with opportunities for worship. Each feast and convocation looked back to a specific historical event in Israel's past and forward to an endtime event in her future (see chart below).

23:1–24:23 WEEKLY WORSHIP AND SABBATH HOLINESS

The purpose for these Sabbath rests was to remind the Israelites of God who had created them and owned them. Feasts were actually holy convocations appointed for specific times (23:2) to be observed by all Israelites wherever they were living (23:3). These were in contrast to some unholy feasts that had occurred in Israel's history (Exod. 32:5; 1 Sam. 30:16). The holy observances are described as follows: (1) the weekly Sabbath (Lev. 23:3); (2) Passover and the Feast of Unleavened Bread (23:4-8); (3) Firstfruits (23:9-14); (4) the Feast of Harvest, or Weeks, or Pentecost (23:15-21); (5) the Feast of Trumpets or Ingathering (23:22-25); (6) the Day of Atonement (23:26-32); and (7) the Feast of Tabernacles, or Booths (23:33-44).

The care of the lampstand (24:1-4) and the loaves of bread, or cakes (24:5-9), represented all of Israel in worship before the Lord. Blasphemy meant to demean and declare something cursed (24:10-23). Laying hands on the head of the offender represented the removal of the other Israelites from the blasphemy that they had heard (24:14). This is analogous to "washing one's hands" to remove guilt (Deut. 21:6). On the basis of Leviticus 24:16, Jews have traditionally refused to pronounce the name "Yahweh" and have substituted "Adonai" (Lord) to avoid the sin of blasphemy.

25:1-55 SPECIAL YEARS

The focus of the sabbatical year and the Year of Jubilee was on the Promised Land of Canaan (25:2). The purpose of the sabbatical year (25:1-7) was to concede that the basics of life are God's.

OLD TESTAMENT FEASTS AND THEIR SIGNIFICANCE

Sabbath	This looked back to the Creation and the Mosaic covenant (Exod. 20:11; 31:12-17) and forward to the believer's rest in Christ's finished work (Heb. 4:1-11).
Passover	This looked back to Israel's redemption from bondage in Egypt (*Pesach*, Exod. 12:1-30) and forward to the redemption from sin through Christ (1 Cor. 5:7).
Unleavened Bread	This looked back to Israel's separation from Egypt (*Matsah*, Exod. 13:1-10) and forward to the fellowship possible because of Christ (1 Cor. 5:7-8; 1 John 1:1-4).
Firstfruits	This looked back to the first harvest God gave Israel in the Promised Land (Lev. 23:10) and forward to the first resurrection harvest (1 Cor. 15:20, 23; 1 Thess. 4:13-18).
Feast of Weeks	Later known as Pentecost, this celebration looked back to the firstfruits of the grain harvest (*Shevuoth*, Lev. 23:16) and forward to God's first harvest of the redeemed in Christ (Acts 2).
Trumpets	This looked back to the beginning of the civil year (*Rosh Hashana*, Lev. 23:23-25; 25:9) and forward to the regathering of God's people (Ezek. 37:12-14; 1 Cor. 15:52).
Day of Atonement	This looked back to the need for cleansing from national sin (*Yom Kippur*, Lev. 16) and forward to Christ's atonement (Heb. 9:28) and Israel's repentance (Zech. 12:10–13:1).
Tabernacles, or Booths	This looked back to the wilderness wanderings (*Succoth*, Lev. 23:43) and forward to Israel's joy in Christ's kingdom (Zech. 14:16).

Failure to keep this year resulted in the seventy years of captivity in Babylon (2 Chron. 36:21). The word "jubilee" is from the Hebrew word *yobel*, or "ram's horn," which was blown to announce the fiftieth year. The Year of Jubilee (Lev. 25:8-55) again affirmed that the land was God's (25:23) and that the people were his (25:55). Since everything belonged to him, the liberation and restoration of this year were under his sovereign ownership. The Israelite who had sold himself into bondage was to be treated more as a hired servant than a slave. Six years was the maximum period an Israelite could be required to serve (Exod. 21:2).

26:1-46 Conditions for Remaining in Canaan

The pattern of Israel's blessing for obedience, discipline for disobedience, and restoration for repentance is presented. It was a pattern that would be repeated many times throughout Israel's history from this point on. Blessings and provision for remaining in the Promised Land (26:1-13) were described conditionally: "If you keep my laws and are careful to obey my commands . . ." (Lev. 26:3). See the situation forty years later as Moses gave similar words (Deut. 27–28). Conditional curses followed (Lev. 26:14-39): "If you do not listen to me or obey my commands . . ." (26:14). The repeated use of "seven times" (26:18, 21, 24, 28) stressed the necessity of keeping the sabbaths (26:34). After necessary punishment, God promised the equally necessary restoration of his own people (26:40-46), as he remembered his covenant with Abraham (26:42, 45).

27:1-34 Appendix: Vows

The appendix of Leviticus 27 brings even the freewill vows under the morality of the Mosaic legislation. There was no requirement to ever make a vow (Deut. 23:21-22), but if someone did, then it had to be kept. A "devoted" thing (Lev. 27:28) was devoted to God, as were the spoils of Jericho (Josh. 6:17). For God's redeemed people, holiness involved the large and the small, the external and the internal.

NUMBERS

BASIC FACTS

HISTORICAL SETTING

The historical events recorded in the book of Numbers began exactly one month after the completion of the tabernacle (Num. 1:1; Exod. 40:17). This book takes the reader through the nearly forty years of wilderness wanderings and ends its narrative on the plains of Moab near the Jordan River.

AUTHOR

Numbers 33:2 ascribes literary activity to Moses in relation to the material of the book, and it is stated repeatedly that God spoke these words to Moses (1:1; 2:1; 3:5, 14, 40). The Mosaic authorship of Numbers is supported by the following considerations: (1) The book is connected with the three previous books in which Mosaic authorship is confirmed; (2) Many references state the fact that God spoke these words to Moses (1:1; 2:1; 3:5), and it is most likely that Moses himself would have recorded this revelation; (3) The authorship of the record of Israel's journeys in the wilderness is ascribed to Moses (33:2), making it probable that the rest of Numbers was written by him as well; (4) The local color, authentic wilderness background, and antiquity of the material lend support to the Mosaic authorship of Numbers. A few editorial insertions, such as the enumeration of the Transjordan cities built by the offspring of Gad, Reuben, and Makir, son of Manasseh (32:33-35), were added subsequent to the time of Moses. For a fuller discussion of the authorship of the Pentateuch, see the introductory section for Genesis.

DATE

Numbers was written, or at least completed, after the death of Aaron (20:28), which took place on the first day of the fifth month of the fortieth year after the Exodus (33:38-39). Aaron died at the age of 123 (33:39), just a few months before Moses, who was 120 years old when he died (Deut. 34:7).

PURPOSE

The book of Numbers communicates that Israel was God's army and that God's people would take the Promised Land by means of military force, as God's instrument of judgment upon the wicked people living in the land of Canaan. It also shows that God's children may sin and be disciplined, but that his promises for blessing are ultimately unstoppable. The wilderness wanderings brought about a denial of God's blessings for those who had sinned, but not for the faithful.

GEOGRAPHY AND ITS IMPORTANCE

The book of Numbers begins at Mount Sinai as Israel prepares to take the Promised Land by military force. The book then tells why Israel moved twice to Kadesh-barnea. The first time at Kadesh-barnea, the nation disbelieved that God was a warrior strong enough to give them the land. As a result, God banished Israel to nearly forty years of waiting in the wilderness. The second time at Kadesh-barnea, after the completion of Israel's waiting period, the Israelites prepared to go around the east side of the Promised Land, heading north and arriving on the Plains of Moab, just across from Jericho. As that journey exposed Israel to the nations of Edom, Ammon, Bashan, and Moab, it also exposed Israel to her own weakness of faith and to God's great power and loyalty.

GUIDING CONCEPTS

A FORFEITED BLESSING

Numbers records how sin in a believer's life can prevent blessing. An entire generation sinned unto death and forfeited blessing as a result of the rebellion at Kadesh-barnea. The nation's full deliverance and inheritance of the land were delayed forty years because of their unbelief in God's provision and protection (Heb. 3:16-19). But because God was dealing with a redeemed people (Exod. 12; 1 Cor. 10:1-4), their unbelief resulted in their loss of blessing, not of salvation.

THE COMPLAINING OF THE REDEEMED

Israel's complaining is a major emphasis of Numbers. The people had only traveled three days' distance from Sinai when they began complaining (Num. 11:1-3; cf. 10:33). They complained about their diet of manna (11:4-6) and against the leadership provided by Moses and Aaron (12:1-2; 14:2, 36). Their complaining against God resulted in the judgment of death decreed on the first generation of Israelites in the wilderness (14:27-29). The people's constant grumbling was as bad as their refusal to enter the land (16:11, 41; 17:5, 10). By complaining against God they were break-

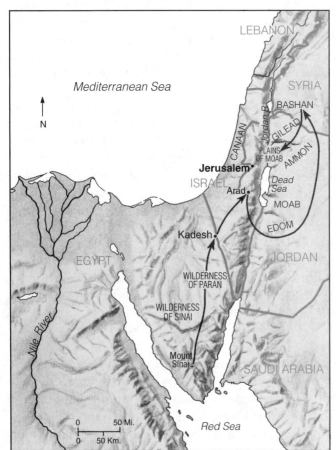

Modern names and boundaries are shown in gray. Copyright © 1986, 1988 by Tyndale House Publishers, Inc.

ing the covenant with their great King. The complaining about God's provision of food and drink must not overshadow for the reader of the book their more serious complaints against God's appointed leaders. Throughout Numbers, the people of Israel showed an attitude that was sometimes ambivalent, sometimes hostile, toward God's chosen leaders.

DIVINE JUDGMENT

The wrath of God, manifested in judgment against sin, is well illustrated in the book (11:1, 10, 33; 12:9-10). God's wrath is the natural expression of his holiness manifesting itself against the willful sin and rebellion of humans (1:53-54; 11:1, 10, 33; 12:9; 16:46; 18:5; 22:22-34; 25:3-4, 11; 32:10, 14). Numbers teaches that God's wrath may be stopped by an offering (16:46-48) or by intercession (14:11-20). While God's wrath is prominent in Numbers, it is revealed in the New Testament as well (Ananias and Sapphira, Acts 5:1-11; all mankind, Rom. 2:5-9; abusers of the Lord's table, 1 Cor. 11:28-30; unfaithful Christians, Heb. 10:30-31 and 12:29; and the unbelieving world, Rev. 6:15-17; 16:19; 19:15). Only faith in God's Son, who has satisfied God's wrath (Rom. 3:25; 1 John 2:2), can save the sinner from divine judgment.

THE ARMY OF GOD

Israel was forged into an army that was to carry out God's judgment upon the inhabitants of Canaan (Num. 1:3; 2:32). This judgment should always be read in the light of Genesis 15:16.

THE UNSTOPPABLE PROMISES OF GOD

Even in light of Israel's continual failures, Numbers shows that God's promises to Abraham were absolutely certain (Num. 15:1-2; 23:8, 20). See the chart below.

BIBLE-WIDE CONCEPTS

THREE MAJOR JOURNEYS

The first five books of the Bible present three major journeys undertaken by the people of Israel: (1) from Egypt to Mount Sinai (Exod. 12:37–19:2); (2) from Sinai to Kadesh-barnea (Num. 10–13); and (3) from Kadesh-barnea to the plains of Moab (Num. 15:1–21:35). Genesis presents a detailed prologue showing how humanity's hope for redemption was narrowed down to one small family that was driven to Egypt by famine. Exodus details the first great journey of this family as it leaves Egypt and travels to Mount Sinai.

Numbers tells of the second and third fateful journeys of Israel. The second is the

KEY EVENTS FROM THE EXODUS TO TRANSJORDAN

Exodus 12:41	Exodus from Egypt
Exodus 19:1	Arrival at Sinai
Exodus 40:17	Tabernacle erected
Numbers 1:2	Israel's first numbering
Numbers 13:23, 26	Arrival at Kadesh
Numbers 33:37-38	Departure from Kadesh (Aaron's death)
Deuteronomy 1:3	Moses' address to Israel
Joshua 4:19	Israel's crossing of the Jordan

great journey of salvation from Sinai to Kadesh. The third is the regrouping of Israel into God's holy army during the wilderness wanderings.

Deuteronomy functions as a hinge between Genesis through Numbers and the historical books of Joshua through 2 Kings. It sums up Israel's history and salvation to that point and provides the perspective through which the rest of Israel's history is to be viewed.

NUMBERS IN THE NEW TESTAMENT

The apostle Paul in 1 Corinthians used Israel's wilderness experience as an example of how believers can be disqualified because of disobedience. The chart below compares 1 Corinthians 10 with Israel's experience in the wilderness.

Note that both 1 Corinthians and Numbers are warnings for those in the covenant. The book of Hebrews also uses Israel's failures to encourage Christians not to make the same mistakes. But, above all, the book of Numbers takes its place in the Bible-wide concept of God's relentless commitment to keep his redemptive promises even in the light of his people's continual failures, whether under Moses or Christ.

NEEDS MET BY NUMBERS

God's people never learned. The book of Numbers shows both the old generation and the new one after it making the same mistakes. The book covers the time period in which hundreds of thousands of Israelites died after rebelling against the Lord. The Promised Land was so close, yet God kept the nation out for nearly forty years. The book spoke to the needs of those Israelites who had trouble holding on to their faith in God's great promises when they saw the tragedy of sin all around them. These questions probably bothered them:

- Why did an entire generation of God's people die in the wilderness?
- Had the sins of Israel voided God's great promises to Abraham and Moses?
- Why did God form the Israelite nation into an army on the march?
- What did God want believers to do as they experienced his discipline?

For the Christian, the book of Numbers is filled with bad examples which should be avoided. But it also presents a loud and clear message. It was written to show how prone God's people were to failure, how insistent God was that they be disciplined, and how equally persistent God was that his people get back up from the self-inflicted pain of their disobedience and move on toward God's promised blessings.

ISRAEL'S WILDERNESS EXPERIENCES IN THE NEW TESTAMENT

Exodus 32:4-6	1 Corinthians 10:7
Numbers 11:4	1 Corinthians 10:6
Numbers 16:41-49; 17:5, 10	1 Corinthians 10:10
Numbers 20:11	1 Corinthians 10:4
Numbers 21:5-6	1 Corinthians 10:9
Numbers 25:1-9	1 Corinthians 10:8
Numbers 26:65	1 Corinthians 10:5

OUTLINE OF NUMBERS

I. FROM SINAI TO KADESH (1:1–14:45)
   A. The Departure from Sinai (1:1–10:36)
   B. Complaint and Judgment: Blindness toward God's Provision (11:1-35)
   C. Complaint and Judgment: Blindness toward God's Prophet (12:1-16)
   D. Complaint and Judgment: Blindness toward God's Power (13:1–14:45)

II. ISRAEL'S WANDERINGS: DISINTEGRATION (15:1–19:22)
   A. Laws while in the Land (15:1-41)
   B. Complaint and Judgment: Blindness toward God's Priest (16:1–18:32)
   C. Cleansing after Touching Dead Bodies (19:1-22)

III. FROM KADESH TO MOAB: REGROUPING THE TROOPS (20:1–36:13)
   A. Complaint and Provision: Leaders Judged (20:1-29)
   B. Complaint and Judgment: Blindness toward God's Provision of Manna (21:1-35)
   C. God's Absolute and Sovereign Blessing of Israel Emphasized (22:1–24:25)
   D. Idolatry and Judgment: Blessing Lost through Human Irresponsibility (25:1-18)
   E. Second Census for War (26:1-65)
   F. Second Leader Commissioned (27:1-23)
   G. Continuity of Worship in the Land Emphasized (28:1–30:16)
   H. Transjordan Conquered (31:1–32:42)
   I. Review from Egypt to Canaan, with the Method for Dividing Canaan (33:1–36:13)

NUMBERS NOTES

1:1–14:45 FROM SINAI TO KADESH

Overview: Numbers 1–10 gives a series of dates that ranges from the day that the tabernacle was finished to the day that Israel broke camp (1:1; 7:1; 9:1, 15; 10:11). Throughout the book the stress is on doing everything exactly as God had commanded Moses (1:54; 2:34; 3:51; 4:49). The section 1:1–14:45 ends with the defeat of God's army by the Israelites' lack of faith in God's ability to beat their enemies. The nation lost the right to enter the Promised Land and had to wait for forty years to go in.

1:1–10:36 The Departure from Sinai

1:1 TITLE

The Hebrews called this book either "and he spoke" or "in the wilderness of," according to the words used in the first verse. The Septuagint translators gave it the title Numbers because of the prominence of the census figures in the book. This tradition was followed by the Latin Vulgate and English versions. Numbers begins with a chronological notice indicating that the numbering of the people took place just a year and one month after the Exodus from Egypt. Just one month had passed since the completion of the tabernacle (Exod. 40:17).

1:2-54 THE CENSUS

The army of God was counted and positioned around the tabernacle for military purposes (1:1-4). Israel had 603,550 men over twenty years of age (1:46). Including women and children, the figure would rise to an estimated 2 million. Many have doubted that such a large multitude of people could survive in the wilderness for 40 years. Yet God had used a supernatural event to deliver them from Egypt, and in the same way he sustained them in the desert by his divine power.

The census was clearly designed to count those who were to go out to war (1:3, 20, 22, 24, 26, 28, 30, 32, 34, 36, 38, 40, 42, 45). While God would prove himself lethal to the inhabitants of Canaan, he also would be lethal to any Israelite who profaned his tabernacle. Thus the Levites formed a protective shield around the tabernacle that was set up in the center of the camp (1:51, 53).

2:1-3:51 THE ARMY CAMP

The Israelites' way of obedience would be to act as God's army against the inhabitants of Canaan. They were encamped according to their twelve tribal groups around the tabernacle (2:1-34), with three tribes on each side. In addition, the Levites, who were not counted among the twelve tribes, were numbered and organized to camp around all four sides of the tabernacle (3:1-51). Of all the Israelites, they encamped closest to the tabernacle. The main reason for doing so was to protect the lay person from death due to inadvertently profaning the tabernacle (3:10). The Hebrew word translated "ordained" (3:3) literally means "to fill one's hand." Aaron's sons were entrusted with the authority and responsibility to officiate at the sacrificial altar. The rest of the Levites, that is, all the remaining descendants of the tribe of Levi, were appointed to serve the priests (who were descendants of Aaron, a Levite). Thus, all priests were Levites, but not all Levites were priests.

Because all the firstborn males of Israel had been saved from the death angel in the Egyptian plagues (Exod. 12), the firstborn male of every family was to be set apart to God (3:12-13). The Levites were appointed to act as substitutes before God in their place. The total of 22,000 Levites given in 3:39 is correct if the Greek Old Testament (Septuagint text) is followed in 3:28, where the figure is 8,300 instead of the 8,600 in the Hebrew text. The discrepancy in the Hebrew text is due to a scribal omission of one letter that makes the difference between a "three" and a "six." The priests performed the sacrificial rites while the other Levites assisted by taking care of the outward elements of the tabernacle and its furnishings (1:50). The families were those of Gershon (3:21-26), Kohath (3:27-32), and Merari (3:33-37). The ransom of the firstborn (3:13, 41, 44-51) had been established at the Passover (Exod. 4:22-23). The Lord made a one-for-one substitution of the 22,000 Levites for each firstborn male of Israel, of whom there were 22,273. For the additional 273 firstborn Israelites, an equivalent in redemption money was paid to the priests (3:39-51).

4:1–6:21 THE HOLINESS OF THE TABERNACLE

The Levites' duties are described (4:1-49). The holiness of the tabernacle was emphasized, with special reference to protecting from death the sons of Kohath, whose responsibility was to care for the sanctuary (4:17-20). Whereas in Numbers the families of Gershon, Kohath, and Merari were numbered according to all males a month in age or older, in Numbers 4 those who were from thirty to fifty years of age were numbered. These men, who would serve in the work of the tabernacle, totaled 8,580 (4:46-48). Numbers 3 tells the work that each family was to do while the tabernacle was set up, whereas Numbers 4 details how they were to take care of the tabernacle and its parts when the camp would move to another place.

In Numbers 5, a new element to the laws of infectious skin disease, including leprosy (cf. Lev. 13–14), was introduced. The camp of God was to be pure from persons inflicted with these diseases, as well as those who were unclean due to contact with dead bodies (Num. 5:1-4). Any personal guilt of one Israelite against another was ultimately a direct offense to God (5:6). The test of a wife's adultery (5:11-31) was to help avoid the kind of family strife that could shake the camp to its roots. The mixture that a wife suspected of adultery was to drink was not a lethal poison; the terrible results for guilt came from a direct curse of God (5:27-28). The ritual test for adultery illustrated the seriousness of this issue in the Israelite community. God provided this means of exposing the guilty and vindicating the innocent. The underlying principle was that God knows and judges sin. See Leviticus 20:10 for a man's penalty for adultery and Hosea 4:14 for an amplification.

The Nazirite vow (6:1-21) gave the lay person an opportunity to come near to the status of priests (cf. 6:7 with Lev. 21:1-3, 11). The word *Nazirite* (Num. 6:2) is derived from a Hebrew verb meaning "to separate." The Nazirite vow provided opportunity for a voluntary dedication (or separation) of oneself to God (6:18). The idea was that of separation for a special ministry to God. Abstinence from wine signified giving up life's luxuries (cf. Jer. 35:6-8),

---

THE ARRANGEMENT OF THE TRIBES AROUND THE TABERNACLE
In the camp of Israel the twelve tribes were arranged symmetrically around the tabernacle. The physical location of the tabernacle in Israel's camp visualized two truths that the people needed to hold in tension. First, God was to be at the physical and spiritual center of the nation's life. Second, because God was too holy to dwell directly with his people, he ordained a protective barrier of priests and Levites between him and the nation. The Israelites needed to be close to God, making him the center of their lives, while also recognizing that they were unworthy of his holy presence among them.

The camp illustrates circles of holiness. The outside world was excluded from Israel's camp, and thus, from close fellowship with God. The vast majority of God's chosen people were within the camp, the first circle of holiness. Only the priests and Levites were allowed into the next circle of holiness. The most exclusive circle was limited to the high priest. Once a year, he alone could enter into the Most Holy Place—the inner room of the tabernacle. But even though these degrees of holiness and priestly barriers are done away with for believers in Christ, they still need to balance their desire for God's intimate fellowship with an awesome respect for his holiness.

and the uncut hair signified presenting oneself to God intact and whole (cf. Exod. 20:25 for uncut stones and Deut. 15:19 for unshorn animals). The vow could be temporary (e.g., Paul, Acts 18:18; four men, Acts 21:23-28) or for life (Samson, Samuel, and John the Baptist).

6:22-27 THE AARONIC BLESSING
The great Aaronic blessing (Num. 6:22-27) is placed here as a conclusion to the covenant God had given from the thundering top of Mount Sinai and from the glorious tabernacle. God would bless and keep (i.e., take care of) the nation (cf. "care for" the garden in Gen. 2:15). He also would make his face shine on the Israelites and be gracious to them (cf. Exod. 34:6). The face of God's holiness that was to shine upon Israel could equal life or death, but God desired his blessings to fall upon those who were faithful so that they could experience peace (Num. 6:26) and wholeness in their relationship with their redeeming God.

7:1–8:26 THE DEDICATION OF THE TABERNACLE AND PRIESTS
The service of the tabernacle was completed in twelve days, during which the twelve tribes presented offerings (7:1-89) to be used for the dedication of the altar (7:84, 88), the special place where the Israelites could have their sins forgiven before God. These offerings were given after the tabernacle had been set up (7:1). The carts and oxen that were provided were used to transport the tabernacle and its fixtures when the Israelites were on the move. But the Ark of the Covenant was to be carried by the Kohathites on their shoulders (7:9).

The importance of the high priest was stressed (8:1-4), followed by a beautiful example of the Levites as "living sacrifices" (8:5-26). Regarding the Levites being presented as a special offering to do the Lord's work (8:11), see 1 Chronicles 23–26 and 2 Chronicles 17:8-9 and 19:8 for the varieties of priestly work assigned to them. The protection of Israel from violating God's holiness was again stressed (Num. 8:19). The age limits for Levitical service were twenty-five to fifty years (8:24-25). Numbers 4:3 gives a slightly different age period of thirty to fifty years. The five-year difference may have involved a training period before the official period of service began.

9:1-23 THE SECOND PASSOVER
The second Passover was observed fourteen days after the tabernacle was finished (9:1-14). A summary was given of the history of God's presence with the Israelites during their wanderings (9:15-23).

10:1-36 THE DEPARTURE FROM SINAI
After final instructions regarding trumpet blasts to be used for signals (10:1-10), the Israelites moved out of their camp for the first time since the tribes had been designated specific places to camp and the order in which they would travel (10:11-36). According to the Jewish Mishnah, the alarm for war was a succession of short blasts that made it distinct from a sustained blast that meant they should move from their camp (10:5). After eleven months at Mount Sinai (10:11; cf. Exod. 19:1), the cloud of God's glory lifted from the tabernacle and the people moved out. Moses' words were really a song that envisioned the Ark as God's warrior presence to fight against Israel's enemies (10:35-36). Israel was beginning a march that was to lead them into war against the inhabitants of the Promised Land.

11:1-35 Complaint and Judgment: Blindness toward God's Provision
Now the book moves into a series of complaints of the people and God's resultant judgments. Their first complaint was about their hardships, and they made it in God's hearing (11:1-3). This complaint was caused by their blindness toward God's provision. Moses called the place Taberah ("burning") because of the judgment God sent. Their second complaint (11:4-30) stemmed from their greed for food other than manna (11:4, 34; for more about manna cf. Exod. 16:31). The people wanted what was not provided by God's gracious presence (Num. 6:24-27). They fondly remembered the food of Egypt and wailed before God (11:4-10, 18-20). The seventy elders who helped Moses care for the people (Num. 11:16) were distinct from the rulers of thousands, hundreds, fifties, and tens who had been appointed earlier (Exod. 18:21-26). God met Moses' great emotional needs (11:10-15) by giving spiritual discernment to these leaders (11:16-30). Moses' prayer that the Lord would put his Spirit on all his people (11:29) would come true on the day of Pentecost. Perhaps the people's greedy craving indicated their unbelief in the adequacy of God's provision (11:33). The place was named Kibroth Hattaavah, meaning "the graves of greediness."

12:1-16 Complaint and Judgment: Blindness toward God's Prophet
The third complaint concerned Miriam and Aaron's blindness as to who was God's true prophet. In the Hebrew text the feminine ending on the verb "spoke" makes it clear that Miriam instigated the complaint and rebellion (12:1). Hence, she alone was judged with leprosy. To "spit in someone's face" (12:14) was a sign of shame imposed upon wrongdoers (Deut. 25:9; Isa. 50:6). Miriam and Aaron had confused Moses' function as God's spokesman (12:6) with his position as a believer before God. All Israel was equally favored before God in his saving grace. But God had different functions for different individuals. Humility in the Bible is one's appreciation of who he is in God's sight (12:3). Moses knew his place before God

according to God's standards, and he did not cease to call on God's graciousness in his prayer (12:13).

13:1–14:45 Complaint and Judgment: Blindness toward God's Power

The fourth complaint and judgment concerned the people's blindness to God's power to give Israel the Promised Land. Deuteronomy 1:22 indicates that God had yielded to the people's request that the land be searched out (Num. 13:2). In listing the spies, note that Moses had added the name of God to the name of Hoshea (meaning "salvation"), making his name Joshua (meaning "The Lord is salvation," 13:16). The spies brought back full and accurate knowledge concerning what Israel was up against (13:1-29), but they gave two conflicting reports. The spies who made the majority report only saw the giants (cf. Gen. 6:4), whereas Joshua and Caleb saw victory. The descendants of Anak, the giants, were noted for their great size and strength (13:28). They were described as being related to the Nephilim (13:33), who lived on the earth before and after the flood (Gen. 6:4). Using hyperbole (exaggeration for the sake of emphasis), the writer compares the Israelites to grasshoppers.

In the resulting rebellion the Israelites tried to appoint a new leader to take them back to Egypt (14:1-4) and attempted to stone the old leaders (14:5-10). From God's point of view, the purpose for sending in the spies was not to determine if the conquest was possible, but to show Israel what God was going to give his people. All of the Israelites' actions were actually a rebellion against the Lord himself, not their leaders (14:9, 11). God's destruction of the people was stopped by Moses' intercession for them (14:11-19), but a forty-year period of wandering in the desert was God's verdict against them (14:20-38), along with a great failure in battle (14:39-45). Figuring that at least 1,200,000 people were to die in the next thirty-seven and a half years means that there were approximately eighty-five funerals a day, seven per waking hour. This would be a continuous reminder to Israel of God's wrath and judgment on sin (14:29). Of course, large numbers of them died during a few days' time in the rebellion of Korah and the following day's plague, as well as those who died by the snakes or in the plague following the worship of Baal of Peor.

15:1–19:22 ISRAEL'S WANDERINGS: DISINTEGRATION

Overview: This section introduces the forty-year period of Israel's wanderings, beginning with a surprising reaffirmation of God's land promise and ending with a massive sacrifice to cleanse the nation from the death that had pervaded the wanderings. The events of 15:1–19:22 happened in the early part of the wanderings because the sacri-fice commanded in Numbers 19 was designed to cleanse the nation from the uncleanness caused by touching the many dead bodies of the first generation that was to die in the wilderness.

15:1-41 Laws While in the Land

Just after condemning the older Israelites to wander in the desert for forty years, God reaffirmed that the next generation of Israel would go into the land ("When you finally settle the land," 15:2, 18). That gave the nation a focus of hope in the wilderness. Their task was to remember God's great redemption (cf. 15:37-41 regarding tassels as a reminder). In spite of the Israelites' unbelief and unfaithfulness, God would eventually bring them into their inheritance (15:2). The word "brazenly" (15:30) literally reads, "with a high hand," such as a fist raised in defiance. There was no provision for atonement for such a sin. The offender would be put to death, "cut off from the community" (Exod. 31:14). The case of the wood gatherer showed that God regarded the intent to sin as being equivalent to the sin itself (15:32-36; cf. Matt. 5:21-28). The tassels, intended as a reminder to obey the law, came to be used hypocritically by the New Testament Pharisees (Num. 15:38-41; cf. Matt. 23:5).

16:1–18:32 Complaint and Judgment: Blindness toward God's Priest

16:1-50 THE BLINDNESS OF THE LEADERS AND PEOPLE

The fifth complaint concerned the people's blindness toward God's true priest, specifically the authority of the Aaronic line versus that of Korah (16:1-3, 6-7). The issue again was a confusion between the differing functions that God assigns to his leaders and the essential equality of every believer before God. While all were redeemed, not all could come into the holy places of God, at least not until Christ opened the way into God's Holy of Holies for all believers. The judgment that fell upon the rebels (16:28-35) caused the Israelites to make their sixth complaint the next day (16:41), and this again brought a plague. Throughout these complaints and judgments, Israel owed its continued existence to the gracious intercession of Moses (16:47-50).

17:1-13 GOD SIGNIFIES HIS PRIEST

God put to rest the matter of Aaron's authority as his chosen high priest by causing the sprouting of Aaron's rod (17:1-9). A rod symbolized a man's rule over his house, and the budding of the rod confirmed the divinely appointed spiritual leader, putting an end to the murmuring.

18:1-32 CLARIFICATION OF PRIESTLY AND LEVITICAL WORK

The people's response to Aaron's rod that budded (17:12-13) led to God's clarification of where the responsibility lay for the tabernacle service (18:1-

32). Note the key phrase "I give you" (18:12; cf. 18:19, 26). God provides for his own. The priests would guard the lay people, including the other Levites who were not priests, who would die if they committed an offense against the sanctuary (18:3, 5, 7, 22, 32).

19:1-22 Cleansing after Touching Dead Bodies

Death pervades the book, and here God provided a relatively quick and easy way to cleanse a person from defiling the tabernacle as the nation wandered in the desert and witnessed the deaths of the members of the first generation (19:13, 20). Because of the mass defilement by so many deaths during the wilderness wanderings, God instituted the red heifer ritual to make cleansing readily accessible from unavoidable contact with a dead body (cf. Lev. 11:24-47).

20:1–36:13 FROM KADESH TO MOAB: REGROUPING THE TROOPS

Overview: The events of section 20:1–36:13 take the reader to the fortieth year of Israel's wanderings. They were still complaining just like they had in the first year. There was no difference in the hearts of the people after the forty years of wandering, for they still were complaining as the old generation had done. But God relentlessly forged ahead to bring the nation to the border of the Promised Land.

20:1-29 Complaint and Provision: Leaders Judged

The seventh complaint concerned the need for water (cf. Exod. 15:22-26; 17:1-7). The account of Moses' disobedience when striking the rock at Meribah for water is similar to God's provision of water from a rock that is recorded in Exodus 17:1-7, but the settings, chronologies, and details distinguish the two incidents. Throughout Numbers there are recurring phrases regarding Moses' obedience according to the Lord's commands to him (1:54; 2:34; 3:51; 4:37, 49; 8:20; 9:5, 23; 10:13; 16:40; 20:9). They lead the reader to this one moment of Moses' disobedience. Moses was humble (12:3); that is, he did exactly what the Lord commanded him, except for this one instance.

Also, the long section of Numbers 15–18 had stressed the significance of God's authority behind the symbol of Aaron's rod, the very rod Moses used wrongly here to strike the rock. To disobey was to disbelieve (20:12), and to disbelieve was to dishonor God among the believers.

The rivalry that had existed between Jacob and Esau (Gen. 25:20-34) now developed between their descendants, Israel and Edom (Num. 20:14-21). Edom became a continual enemy of Israel (Gen. 36:l, 8; Obad. l-2l). The death of Aaron, the high priest, marked the end of an era and signified a new

beginning for the second generation of Israelites (20:22-29).

21:1-35 Complaint and Judgment: Blindness toward God's Provision of Manna

The Israelites' eighth complaint again concerned their blindness toward God's provision of manna. God's deliverance of them in battle (21:1-3) had no connection in their minds with being grateful for his provision. Again Moses interceded for the people by providing them a focal point, the bronze snake, at which they could look for life despite their being bitten by poisonous snakes (21:8-9). Jesus compared this event to what would happen to himself (John 3:14-15). The bronze snake was later used as an idol and had to be destroyed (2 Kings 18:4).

The itinerary of places where Israel camped while traveling to Moab (Num. 21:10-20) is given in more detail in 33:41-49. "The Book of the Wars of the Lord" (21:14) was an ancient collection of war songs used by Moses and other scribes as a source of information.

22:1–24:25 God's Absolute and Sovereign Blessing of Israel Emphasized

Overview: Numbers 22–25 emphasize God's absolute and sovereign blessing of Israel. God had promised Abraham that the one who cursed him would be cursed and the one who blessed him would be blessed. In the account of Balaam (see also 2 Pet. 2:15; Jude 1:10-11), it is obvious that when he was speaking for God, it was impossible for him to curse Israel.

22:1-41 BALAAM COMMISSIONED

Balak realized that God's blessing was upon Israel (Num. 22:5-6), and soon Balaam would realize this also (22:12, 20; 23:8; 24:9-10), but that did not stop either of them from trying to curse her. God's lethal opposition (22:31-33) was against Balaam's intention to curse instead of bless Israel. God was clearly open to Balaam's going to Balak, but only if he intended to bless Israel (22:20, 35). Balak's fear of Israel was expressed in 22:2-4. God did indeed intend to completely destroy the inhabitants of Canaan, for he wanted the land of Canaan as well as the Israelites to be devoted to himself. This rationale is revealed in Deuteronomy 7:1-6.

Who and what was Balaam? His name in the biblical text literally means "he who destroys the people," possibly a distortion of his original name, meaning "a divine brings forth." Balaam was from Pethor, located in northern Mesopotamia about twelve miles south of Carchemish, four hundred miles from Moab. While his identity has been debated, it appears that Balaam was a *baru* prophet, that is, a kind of diviner who looks at animals, birds, ants, and the livers of sacrificed animals to predict the future. He was hired by Balak, king of Moab, to curse Israel.

23:1–24:5 BALAAM'S PROPHECIES OF BLESSING

Balaam's prophecies are characterized by the repetition of the phrase "This was the prophecy Balaam delivered" (23:7, 18; 24:3, 15, 20-21, 23). The movement from one hill to another (23:27) shows the then-prevalent pagan view regarding local gods. Balak thought that perhaps Balaam could move to a place where God, whom he considered to be a local god who was only powerful in a specific locality, would not have the power to stop him from cursing Israel. The prophecies of Balaam, the pagan diviner, are masterpieces of Semitic poetry that reveal great truths concerning the relationship of God and Israel. Although Balaam was a wicked diviner, God spoke truth through him (22:35; 24:13). If God could speak through the mouth of a donkey, he also could speak through the mouth of Balaam. There were seven prophecies: 23:7-12; 23:18-24; 24:3-9; 24:15-19; 24:20; 24:21-22; 24:23-24. Balaam's continued blessings upon Israel (24:1-9) turned into his cursings against Balak, Moab, Edom, and other nations (24:10-25).

25:1-18 Idolatry and Judgment: Blessing Lost through Human Irresponsibility

Although Balaam could not bring a curse against Israel, the nation itself could bring a curse from within by its own disobedience. At this point Israel's sin consisted of idolatry with the Moabites. Balaam's counsel was behind this event (31:16). While camped in Moab, Israelites were enticed into sexual immorality with Moabite women, which resulted in their participating in the worship of Baal of Peor. Worship in the Baal cult involved dramatization of sexual acts intended to incite Baal to lust so that he would have sexual relations with Anath, the goddess of love and war, and thus fertilize the land.

The plague that followed the Israelites' sin killed 24,000 (25:9). When the apostle Paul mentioned this event in 1 Corinthians 10:18 he said that 23,000 had died. He did not include those who were executed by the judges (Num. 25:4-5). The Zadokites (25:10-13), who later replaced the priestly line because of the sin of Eli (1 Sam. 2:30-35), traced their descent through the priest Phinehas, who killed the Israelite man and the Midianite woman he had taken into his tent.

26:1-65 Second Census for War

The contrast is sharp between the terrible plague Israel had brought upon itself in Numbers 25 and the direct movement in Numbers 26 of renumbering the men of the nation who would fight to gain the Promised Land. Through all the Israelites' complaints and judgments, God's march toward

fulfilling his promises to them was relentless and certain. Divine judgments, plagues, slayings, and hardships accounted for the lack of Israel's population growth during the forty years in the wilderness (26:51; cf. 2:32).

27:1-23 Second Leader Commissioned

Israel's anticipation of inheriting the land was given specific focus when God established a legal requirement regarding family lines without male heirs (27:1-11). When God told Moses of his impending death, he also instructed him to commission Joshua as his successor (27:12-23). The "mountains east of the river" (27:12) refers to Mount Nebo (Deut. 32:49). (See Deuteronomy's introductory map for Mount Nebo's location.) "God of the spirits of all living things" (Num. 27:16) refers to God, who sustains the physical life of all creatures (cf. 16:22), and "sacred lots" (27:21) refers to the Urim and Thummim (Exod. 28:30).

28:1–30:16 Continuity of Worship in the Land Emphasized

Overview: The section 28:1–30:16 presents the instructions for feasts and vows from the perspective of Israel's being in the Promised Land. These three chapters, like Leviticus 23, record the annual events on the religious calendar. Here, however, the quantities of the offerings are given in anticipation of Israel's settlement in the land.

28:1–29:40 THE FEASTS OF ISRAEL

The focus here is on the daily offerings (28:1-8), specifically, those for the Sabbath (28:9-10); new months, or new year (28:11-15); the Passover (28:16-25); and the Feast of Firstfruits, or Weeks (28:26-31). The seventh month (29:1) contained the Feast of Trumpets (29:1-6), the Day of Atonement (29:7-11), and the Feast of Tabernacles, or Booths (29:12-40). See Leviticus 16 and 23:23-44 for more details.

30:1-16 THE AUTHORITY OF MEN OVER THEIR WIVES AND DAUGHTERS

Numbers 30 describes the various levels of responsibility and authority between men and their wives as well as fathers and daughters in the matter of vows. The vow's essence was a humbling of the person (30:13) before the Lord for service and therefore was highly sacred. The question of vows by a woman under the authority of a man was bound to arise and was answered here. The regulations concerning the discharge of vows upheld the sanctity of the promise (cf. Eccles. 5:4-5) while also recognizing the principle of subjection to authority in the home (Num. 30:3-5).

31:1–32:42 Transjordan Conquered

31:1-54 THE MIDIANITES DESTROYED

The Midianites, on Balaam's counsel (31:16), had successfully tempted Israel to idolatry (25:1-3).

Now, the destruction of the Midianites (31:1-24) brought an immense amount of wealth to Israel and to the tabernacle servants (31:25-54). Midian's destruction also secured the settlement of the Transjordan territories by the tribes of Reuben, Gad, and the half-tribe of Manasseh.

The war against Midian (31:3) was a holy war commanded by God to execute his vengeance (cf. 25:16-18). (See the introductory map in Exodus for Midian's location.) These executions (31:17-18) were designed to protect the Israelites from further defilement by involvement with the Midianites (cf. 25:1-3) and to prevent the propagation of the Midianite race. The young virgins were spared for marriage (Deut. 21:10-14) and slavery (Lev. 25:44-46). The gold accepted as a memorial (Num. 31:54) would serve as a reminder to Israel of the remarkable victory (31:49, 54).

32:1-42 THE SETTLEMENT EAST OF THE JORDAN
The text does not indicate that there were any problems with some of the Israelites settling in the land east of the Jordan (Transjordan). Other Scriptures give the specific boundaries of the land promised to Abraham, and the Transjordan area is included in the general area described (Gen. 15:18; Exod. 23:31; Num. 34:1-15; Deut. 1:7-8). The only problem that concerned Moses was the potential loss of the Transjordanian tribes in helping the rest of Israel to take the land west of the Jordan, but this problem was peacefully solved (Num. 32:17). The Transjordan territories of Sihon, Bashan, and Gilead (all in modern Jordan) were distributed among the tribes of Reuben, Gad, and the half-tribe of Manasseh (32:33-42). (See introductory map.)

33:1–36:13 Review from Egypt to Canaan, with the Method for Dividing Canaan
Overview: This final section of 33:1–36:13 gives a summary list of the wilderness wanderings (Num. 33), Canaan's boundaries and instructions for dividing the land (Num. 34), the locations of the Levitical cities and cities of refuge (Num. 35), and the maintenance of land portions allotted to each tribe (Num. 36). In spite of all the Israelites' failures recorded in this book, the people were now making detailed plans for entering the land as God had promised.

33:1-56 REVIEW OF THE JOURNEY
Numbers 33 begins by reviewing the Israelites' journey from Egypt to Moab (33:1-49) and ends with a pointed exhortation to them to carry out completely the destruction of the inhabitants of the land of Canaan (33:56). Listed are the encampments used during the thirty-seven and a half years of wilderness

wanderings (33:19-49). Few of these sites can be identified today. Instructions for the conquest were (1) to drive out the inhabitants, (2) to destroy everything connected with the false religions of Canaan, and (3) to divide the land among the tribes (33:52-54).

34:1-29 MEN APPOINTED TO DIVIDE CANAAN
The land's boundaries were given, and men were appointed who would later distribute it among the tribes (cf. Gen. 15:18).

35:1-34 PORTIONS FOR LEVITES AND CITIES OF REFUGE
Numbers 35 and 36 list God's commands given in the plains of Moab (35:1; 36:13) and provide specific instructions on how the land would be divided and maintained. Forty-eight cities were allocated for the Levites, who received no tribal territory. The Levitical cities were strategically located in order to allow their inhabitants an opportunity to provide a godly influence throughout the land. Six of the cities would serve as cities of refuge (35:9-34). Three of the six cities were located east of the Jordan River and the other three were located symmetrically on the west side. This made at least one of the six cities of refuge easily accessible to all locations in Israel. The cities of refuge served as places of refuge for those who killed someone unintentionally. According to the law, a murderer was to be put to death (Exod. 21:12, 14), but the cities of refuge provided protection from the blood avenger (kinsman of the slain) if the bloodshed was unintentional (Num. 35:11-12). Moses regulated the custom of blood vengeance by (1) distinguishing between accidental and deliberate homicide, (2) providing a place of refuge for the offender, (3) interposing the judicial judgment of the elders, and (4) stipulating that no one could be put to death on the testimony of just one witness. The purpose of the regulation was to avoid bloodshed that would defile the land in which God would live among the people of Israel (35:33-34).

36:1-13 MAINTENANCE OF PORTIONS THROUGH INHERITANCE
The book ends with a return to the question of keeping each tribe's land inheritance within that specific tribe (36:9). The concept of allotting portions of the land as special gifts of God to each tribe was very important, for it was one fruit of God's redemption from Egypt. Moses had ordered that daughters could inherit their father's property if there were no male heirs (27:1-11). Now, in order to preserve each tribe's inheritance, he decreed that such female heirs had to marry within their own tribes (36:8). If such female heirs chose to marry outside their own tribe, their inheritance would be forfeited.

DEUTERONOMY

BASIC FACTS

HISTORICAL SETTING

The journey from Egypt to Palestine, which might have taken less than two weeks, was lengthened to forty years because of Israel's disobedience. The restatement of the covenant, which included the law, for the new generation of Israel took place on the plains of Moab across the Jordan River from Jericho (Deut. 1:5; Num. 36:13). (See introductory map for Jericho's location.) This was followed by Moses' death and thirty days of mourning. The people, having received a new leader, a new high priest, and a new copy of the covenant, were ready to enter Canaan and conquer the Promised Land. Deuteronomy covers the period from the first of Shebat (a month corresponding to a time period in January and February; 1:3) to thirty days after Moses' death (34:8), a time period of about sixty days (Josh. 4:19).

AUTHOR

The Mosaic authorship is rejected by liberal critics who date the book to the time of Josiah, making its publication the basis of his great reformation (2 Kings 22–23). However, the Mosaic authorship of the book is supported by several evidences.

Deuteronomy 31:9 states explicitly, "Moses wrote down this law." His authorship is also referred to in 31:24. The Jews of Jesus' day held to the Mosaic authorship (Matt. 22:24; Mark 10:3-4; 12:19). Jesus refers to Deuteronomy 24:1-4 as the commandment of Moses (Matt. 19:8).

Only Deuteronomy 34 is demonstrably post-Mosaic because it records the account of Moses' death. That account may well have been written by Joshua in keeping with early Jewish tradition. The book's unity and authenticity as a Mosaic product are also confirmed by the conformity of its structure to that of the covenant treaty form of the fifteenth to thirteenth centuries B.C. For a fuller discussion of the authorship of the Pentateuch see the introductory section to Genesis.

DATE

The three sermons of Moses, which make up the majority of the book of Deuteronomy, were given just before his death and before Israel crossed over into the Promised Land under the leadership of Joshua. The date for the original writing of Deuteronomy would be nearly forty years after Israel's exodus from Egypt. The two major positions concerning the dating of the Exodus (around 1446 B.C. or 1266 B.C.) would date

Deuteronomy at around 1406 B.C. or 1226 B.C. respectively. See the introduction to Exodus for a discussion concerning the date of Israel's exodus from Egypt.

PURPOSE

The book of Deuteronomy was designed to present the link between the Israel of Egypt and the Israel of the Promised Land, between the giving of the law at Sinai and the application of that law in the Promised Land. It is a series of three sermons by Moses designed to remind the nation of the past and prepare them for the problems of the future.

GEOGRAPHY AND ITS IMPORTANCE

The book of Deuteronomy takes place on the east side of the Jordan River across from Jericho. With the sides of the Arabah Valley rising over one thousand feet on either side and the great city of Jericho in the distance, Moses recounted the long journey of Israel's patriarchs from Ur to Egypt and related it to their present need for obedience and faith. Moses' story of Israel's journey and his elaboration of God's laws prepared the nation to cross the Jordan River, conquer Jericho, and climb the western side of the Arabah Valley to take the Promised Land.

GUIDING CONCEPTS

RELATIONSHIP TO THE NEW TESTAMENT

This is one of the most widely quoted books in the Bible. The New Testament writers quote it over 80 times in 17 of the 27 New Testament books. Christ used it to confirm his messiahship, to summarize the law, and to refute the devil (Matt. 4:4, cf. Deut. 8:3; Matt. 4:7, cf. Deut. 6:16; Matt. 4:10, cf. Deut. 6:13). It is quoted 356 times in later Old Testament books as well, which points to the importance of its contents and significance of its truths.

STRUCTURE

Deuteronomy 1:5 explains that the book is an exposition of the covenant of God. The three addresses of Moses were designed not to give new laws but to deepen Israel's appreciation of the law's significance. The first five verses (1:1-5) are an editorial introduction to the whole book. The first address (1:6–4:43) retells the past great saving acts of God for Israel. Deuteronomy 4:44-49 is an introduction to the second address. The second address (5:1–28:68) explains the significance of the law of God. The third address (29:1–30:20) is a final summary explanation of the covenant's demands. The section 31:1–34:12 is the account of the last acts of Moses and his death.

OBEDIENCE

Numbers brought the people to the border of the land, and Deuteronomy prepared them for entering it by emphasizing the necessity of their obedience to the law of God. The motive and goal for following God in obedience was the promise of God's blessing. The standard of obedience was God's Word. The incentive to obedience was God's faithfulness, whereas the alternative to obedience was God's judgment. Deuteronomy called on Israel to fear God, to walk in his ways, to love him, to serve him, and to keep his commandments (10:12-13).

RELATIONSHIP

The most important feature of the Mosaic covenant was the bond of relationship between God and humanity. God's original promises to Abraham provided a continual backdrop to the book's message. Abraham was mentioned directly or indirectly in 1:8, 11, 21, 35; 6:10; 9:5, 27; 26:5; 29:13; 31:20; 32:17; and 34:1-4. The benefits promised were direct effects of God's love (1:11; 7:13). That divine love was the primary source of the covenant bond (4:37; 7:7-13; 10:12-19; 11:1, 13, 22; 13:3; 19:9; 30:6, 16). Above all, God desired that Israel would return his love from the heart as a genuine expression of gratitude and obedience.

That concept of love pervades the book and should eliminate any thoughts that the Mosaic covenant was intended to be an external and heartless conformity to God's law (4:7-9, 29, 39; 5:29; 6:5-6; 8:2, 5, 10-14, 17-18; 10:15-21; 11:13-15, 18; 26:16; 30:6; 32:46-47). It had been love all along—all the way back to Abraham. The concept of God's love clarified the fact that his relationship with his people under the covenant was one of love rather than legalism. No stronger statement in this regard exists in Deuteronomy than in 5:29. In light of that background, these words of Christ have an even more significant meaning for believers: "If you love me, obey my commandments" (John 14:15).

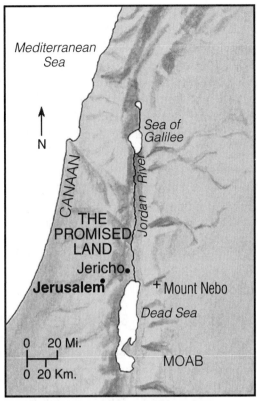

THE NEED FOR RENEWING THE COVENANT

The Mosaic convenant needed renewal, not because God had changed but because humans change. Each new generation had to commit itself to God in love and obedience. This renewal was made in 26:16-19 and would later be repeated at Mount Ebal and Mount Gerizim (27:4-8; cf. Josh. 23–24).

BIBLE-WIDE CONCEPTS

Deuteronomy gives a basic perspective by which to view the rest of the Bible, especially from Joshua through 2 Kings. It takes the foundational Abrahamic promises of *land, people,* and *blessing,* puts them within the framework of the Mosaic covenant, and looks ahead to the day when the fulfillment of those promises would burst out of the old covenant into the glory of the new covenant in Christ. Here are the basic pillars of God's redemptive work laid out in Deuteronomy.

Israel's redemption from Egypt was completely bound up with her obedience to God's commands (29:25). God's blessing and judgment of Israel were completely dependent on the nation's obedience or disobedience to his commands (4:25-26; 6:3, 13-15). Just as 5:31 was the basis for Israel's gaining the land and staying in it (cf. Josh. 1:2-8), Deuteronomy 28:15 explains why Israel might be cast out of the land (cf. 2 Kings 17:13-18). And Deuteronomy 4:29-31 and 30:2-10 reveal the way in which the exiled nation could once again be restored into God's promised blessings (cf. 1 Kings 11:36; 2 Kings 25:27-30). The keeping of God's commands was completely related to Israel's worship at the place that God alone had chosen (Deut. 12:5, 11, 13-14; 14:23-25; 16:2, 5-7). Eventually that place would be the temple in Jerusalem.

Although the reign of David was still far off, 17:14-20 gave instructions as to how the kings of Israel were to act. Actually, long before this Abraham had been promised that there would be a line of kings among his descendants (Gen. 17:6, 17), and this promise had been repeated to Jacob (Gen. 35:11). The word of the Lord is potent; no matter how much time might pass, it will be accomplished (Deut. 32:46-47). Phrases about God fulfilling his word and keeping his promises occur repeatedly throughout 1 and 2 Kings (see, for example, 1 Kings 2:27; 6:11-12; 8:20; 2 Kings 1:16-17; 2:22; cf. 3:12).

NEEDS MET BY DEUTERONOMY

Since the Exodus from Egypt, Israel had seen God save them through the Red Sea, supply food and safety for nearly forty years, come from the thundering top of Mount Sinai down into the relatively tiny tabernacle in the middle of the camp, and systematically destroy virtually all of the adult generation that had originally failed to enter the Promised Land. The redemption and vengeance of God stood in stark and possibly irreconcilable contrast. His holiness and grace could be seen by some as threats rather than as allies.

So, just before God's people entered the Promised Land, Deuteronomy taught that God's demands for holiness were driven by his character and that the essence of his character as expressed to his people was love. Did he redeem? It was because he loved. Did he discipline? It was because he loved. And through his redemption and discipline God showed himself to be absolutely holy. God wanted their hearts to stand in grateful remembrance of his past and present love. The book of Deuteronomy uncovers what had been implicit all along—the love of God—and meets some basic needs of God's people. The structure and content of Deuteronomy show that its author was answering questions like the following for the people of Israel:

- Why should Israel keep remembering things that God did so long ago?
- Why does God continue to love and care for the people of Israel?
- What is the appropriate response of God's people to his love?
- Can God's people expect the future to correct their past disobedience?
- Will the disobedience of Israel void God's promises to Abraham?
- What is the relationship between inner life and external behavior?

Christians ask similar questions today. All believers await entrance into the heavenly Promised Land. Meanwhile, Deuteronomy helps believers understand that dwelling with God now or in eternity involves holding together both his redemption and discipline. Deuteronomy encourages believers to remember how much they are loved by God and their original desperate need for that love. In this light, Deuteronomy asks that Christian service grow out of an honest love for God from the heart.

OUTLINE OF DEUTERONOMY

I. THE HISTORICAL BACKGROUND FOR THE COVENANT (1:1–4:43)
  A. From Sinai to Kadesh: The Old Generation (1:1-46)
  B. From Kadesh to the Plains of Moab: The New Generation (2:1–3:29)
  C. The Remembrance of God's Acts of Redemption (4:1-43)

II. BASIC STIPULATION OF THE COVENANT RELATIONSHIP: REMEMBER (4:44–11:32)
  A. The Ten Commandments Elaborated (4:44–5:33)
  B. Remember God in the Land: Redemption (6:1-25)
  C. Remember the Covenant with God: Avoiding Idolatry (7:1-26)
  D. Remember the Manna: Avoiding Self-Sufficiency (8:1-20)
  E. Remember Rebelliousness: Avoiding Self-Righteousness (9:1–10:22)
  F. Remember the Condition for Knowing God's Love: Obedience (11:1-32)

III. DETAILED STIPULATIONS OF THE COVENANT RELATIONSHIP (12:1–26:19)
  A. Fellowship and Diet (12:1–16:17)
  B. Persons in Leadership (16:18–18:22)
  C. Cities in the Land (19:1–20:20)
  D. Fresh Applications of the Moral Laws in the Land (21:1–26:19)

IV. GOD'S SOVEREIGNTY AND HUMAN RESPONSIBILITY IN BLESSING (27:1–30:20)
  A. Blessings and Curses (27:1–28:68)
  B. Banishment and Restoration (29:1–30:20)

V. CORRECTIVE PICTURES (31:1–32:52)

VI. THE FINAL BLESSING OF MOSES (33:1-29)

VII. THE DEATH OF MOSES (34:1-12)

DEUTERONOMY NOTES

1:1–4:43 THE HISTORICAL BACKGROUND FOR THE COVENANT
Overview: The first address of Moses functioned as a reminder of Israel's failures. It was not intended to browbeat the nation, but to provide a context that magnified the great grace and love involved in God's continued commitment to her.

1:1-46 From Sinai to Kadesh: The Old Generation

1:1 TITLE
The Hebrew title for the book, which literally means "these are the words" or "words," was taken from the opening line of 1:1. Later, the translators of the Greek Septuagint descriptively entitled the book "second law," from 17:18, which says, "copy these laws." It was then rendered in the Latin Vulgate as *Deuteronomium* and in the English versions as Deuteronomy. The English title, which comes from the Latin title meaning, "second law," reflects an incorrect understanding of the words in 17:18. They are best translated "copy of the law," rather than "second law," which suggests that the book of Deuteronomy contains something new and distinct from the Mosaic covenant given at Sinai.

1:2-5 INTRODUCTION

A short introduction (1:2-5) sets the tone for the first subject, Israel's history as they traveled from Sinai to Kadesh (1:2), as well as for that of the entire book, which is an exposition of God's covenant with Israel (1:5). Moses' explanation and application of the law to the second generation took place on the plains of Moab, in Transjordan, just east of Jericho and the Jordan River (1:5).

1:6-46 FROM SINAI TO KADESH

"Amorites" (1:7) was a general term for the inhabitants of Canaan (1:8). The promise to the patriarchs mentioned repeatedly in Deuteronomy (1:35; 4:31; 6:10, 18, 23, etc.) refers to the Abrahamic covenant (Gen. 12:1-3). The next step in fulfilling this promise was the occupation of the land. Some of Canaan's inhabitants were of extraordinary size. Og of Bashan was noted as having the first king-size bed, measuring more than thirteen feet long by six feet wide (Deut. 3:11).

The account of the trip from Sinai to the failure at Kadesh was punctuated with mentions of Israel's disputes (1:12) and the people's claim that God hated them (1:27). At that time Joshua was designated as the successor to Moses (1:37-38). The function of this four-chapter rehearsal of Israel's history was to heighten her anticipation of God's promises by taking to heart his past faithfulness. That faithfulness, coupled with his promise of future exaltation, was designed to bring about the present faithfulness of God's people.

2:1–3:29 From Kadesh to the Plains of Moab: The New Generation

In the journey from Kadesh to the plains of Moab, the Israelites saw the Lord's power as they defeated Sihon. The background to that and all their other victories was that the Lord had a pattern of dispossessing one nation of its land by means of another nation (2:20-23). That cut both ways for Israel. God would have them dispossess and utterly destroy the inhabitants of Canaan, but he could, and would, dispossess Israel of the Promised Land if she became unfaithful.

By Israel's defeat of Og (3:1-22), the way was cleared for the Transjordanian tribes to settle on the east side of the Jordan. The rest of the nation of Israel would soon cross the Jordan River and enter the Promised Land, but Moses would not enter it. He was only allowed to view the Promised Land from afar (3:23-29).

4:1-43 The Remembrance of God's Acts of Redemption

Moses urged the remembrance of God's acts of redemption (4:3, 9-10) and exhorted the nation to watch its behavior carefully (4:15, 23). Although Israel had been promised the title deed to the Promised Land (Gen. 13:15), only through obedience to the law would she actually possess the land and remain there (Deut. 4:1). Israel was warned by the reminder (4:3) of God's discipline of the disobedient in Numbers 25. The duty of remembering is stressed both positively and negatively throughout Deuteronomy (4:9; 5:15; 7:18; 8:2, 18; 9:7; 15:15). Forgetfulness opens the door to disobedience and failure. God is spirit, and true worship is after the pattern of his essential nature (4:15-19; cf. John 4:23-24). Exile from the Promised Land would be the ultimate discipline for breaking the covenant (Deut. 4:27; 28:41, 64; 29:22-28). God promised to be faithful to the covenant promises in spite of the disobedience of his people (4:31). Deuteronomy is comprised of the law (God's instruction), stipulations (exhortations or reminders), decrees (permanent rules of conduct), and laws (judgments, judicial decisions; 4:44-45). The core of the matter was God's absolutely unique love for Israel (4:32-40).

4:44–11:32 BASIC STIPULATION OF THE COVENANT RELATIONSHIP: REMEMBER

Overview: The basic theme of remembrance as the key to remaining faithful to God is continued throughout section 4:44–11:32. The emphasis was on a relationship from the heart that would breed allegiance to the God who loves, saves, and keeps.

4:44–5:33 The Ten Commandments Elaborated

The second address of Moses restated and explained the Ten Commandments. The basic stipulations of the covenant were reiterated (5:6-21; cf. Exod. 20:3-17). According to Mosaic law each person was responsible for his or her own sins, and they and their descendants after them would suffer consequences for those sins (Deut. 5:9). The innocent were not to be punished for the guilty (Deut. 24:16; Ezek. 18:4), yet the criminal acts of a father would affect the children. The parent would be judged for the sin, but the children would often suffer some of the consequences. The people of Israel's motivation to keep the Sabbath came from the remembrance of their redemption from Egypt (5:15). In Exodus 20:11, the motivation had been a remembrance of the creation Sabbath.

Although legally binding, the law was intended not to restrict life, but to lead to fullness of life (Deut. 5:33). Blessing would accompany obedience. The exclamation of God in 5:29 displayed the depth of his desire to bless and have fellowship with Israel.

6:1-25 Remember God in the Land: Redemption

Deuteronomy 6 literally went to the heart of what God desired for Israel in the Mosaic covenant: love from the heart (6:5-6; cf. 11:18-19). Here God asked Israel to put the commands on her heart for her own good (6:4-6). In the new covenant in Christ, God did that work himself and placed the law within the believer (Heb. 8:10; Phil. 2:12-13). The section 6:4-9 is known in Jewish tradition as the *Shema* (literally, "hear" or "listen") which declares the uniqueness and unity of God. This is emphasized by the words, "the Lord alone."

On the basis of 6:8, some pious Jews wear a phylactery, a small box containing portions of Scripture (cf. Matt. 23:5), on their forehead and forearm during prayer. Many Jewish homes have a *mezuzah*, a small scroll-shaped container, on the doorpost. The point is that the Israelite people were to learn the law and not forget the Lord (Deut. 6:10-12). The home was to serve as the center for religious education (6:20-25). In response to a child's inquiry, the great truths about God were to be taught. Israel was to remember her redemption (6:12) and not repeat the mistakes of the past in the wilderness (6:16). Jesus quoted 6:16 during his time of temptation in the wilderness (Matt. 4:7).

7:1-26 Remember the Covenant with God: Avoiding Idolatry

The command not to intermarry with the Canaanites (7:1-5) was designed to keep Israel as God's special possession. God did not give Israel blessings because she was a great nation but because he loved her and was keeping his promise to Abraham (7:8).

Because the Israelites were to be a separated people, God reminded them of their election as his own special possession from among the people of the earth (7:1-6). Sacred stones, or pillars, were upright stones associated with male deities (7:5). Asherah (or Asherim) poles were wooden symbols of the female deity Asherah. The reason for Israel's separation from the Canaanites lay in Israel's election and holiness (7:6). Association with other nations would lead the Israelites into idolatry.

Lest the Israelites should become proud of being in such a select and favored position, God went on to remind them of the nature of his love (7:7-8) and of their responsibility to him (7:9-11). Israel did not merit the blessing through obedience, but obedience was the means by which she was to maintain the covenant relationship that was God's established course and context for her blessing (7:12). God's love is an undeserved, selective affection by which he binds himself to his people and which results in the redemption of his people from bondage (7:17-26). Because God had demonstrated his love by the act of redemption, the redeemed were thus obligated to demonstrate their love for him in return. For comments on the "hornets" (7:20), see Exodus 23:28.

8:1-20 Remember the Manna: Avoiding Self-Sufficiency

The Israelites were to remember what happened to them in the wilderness (8:2, 11); specifically, they were to remember why God gave them the manna: to humble them (8:3, 16) and find out what was in their hearts concerning obedience (8:2-3). The provision of manna was intended to teach Israel that God's word was more essential to their existence than food. The essence of forgetting God is the failure to keep his commands (8:11). Pride is the danger of success (8:14), for there is always the temptation to think that what has been achieved is the result of human effort rather than the gift of God. Proud self-sufficiency would be the Israelites' undoing (8:17-19), causing them to become like the nations that were destroyed before them (8:20).

9:1–10:22 Remember Rebelliousness: Avoiding Self-Righteousness

Lest Israel become self-righteous (9:4), she was to remember her continual rebelliousness in the wilderness (9:7, 13, 22, 24, 27). Israel was entering the Promised Land due to the wickedness of the people of Canaan (9:4-5; see "sin of the Amorites," Gen. 15:16). Those Israelites who might be foolish enough to claim that the gift of the land was a result of their righteousness would be suffering from a case of religious amnesia (Deut. 9:4). Against the background of the fulfillment of God's promise to Abraham to make him a great nation, God reemphasized that the conditions of the covenant (1) had come from God's love (10:15), (2) were for the people's good (10:13), and (3) were to be obeyed from the heart (10:16).

The covenant's basic requirements were summarized (10:12-13). Note that fear of the Lord and love for him were not mutually exclusive concepts, for God expected his people to do both at the same time. The command "cleanse your sinful hearts" (10:16) was reminiscent of the Abrahamic covenant (Gen. 17:9-12), but it was used figuratively here for consecration to God (cf. Josh. 5:2-9). "Cling to" (Deut. 10:20) suggests an extremely close and intimate relationship with God.

11:1-32 Remember the Condition for Knowing God's Love: Obedience

Obedience (11:1, 13, 18, 22) to God's ways would bring the nation strength and victory (11:9). The Promised Land was under God's special care (11:12). The expression "flowing with milk and honey" (11:9) is a pastoral figure of abundance. The "rains in their proper seasons" softened the soil after the summer drought, enabling the farmer to plow and plant, and ensured a good harvest (11:14). If either of these failed, the crops would be sure to suffer.

12:1–26:19 DETAILED STIPULATIONS OF THE COVENANT RELATIONSHIP

Overview: In the section 12:1–26:19 detailed conditions for having a relationship with God are given—conditions that touch on all areas of human life. No area of life was left without a word, which revealed God's total concern for Israel. The purpose of the conditions was not that the people would center their attention on impersonal external rules for heartless obedience, but on a holy and loving relationship with God. Those conditions were summarized and applied in 26:18-19.

The Ten Commandments (5:6-21) formed the basis for the laws expounded in Deuteronomy 12–25. See the chart below.

12:1–16:17 Fellowship and Diet

12:1-32 FELLOWSHIP AT GOD'S PLACE

In contrast with the many places of pagan worship that had to be destroyed (12:1-4), Israel was to worship only at the place God would choose for her and where he would dwell; it would ultimately be Jerusalem (12:5, 11, 14). The place of sacrifice would indicate whether or not the true God was being served.

The command for the destruction of the Canaanite cultic centers (12:2-4) was designed both to punish the sinful inhabitants of Canaan (Lev. 18:25) and to protect the Israelites from false gods (Deut. 7:25-26). The centralization of Israel's worship was to prevent contaminating the worship of the Lord, Yahweh, with idolatrous practices (12:13-14).

13:1-18 IDOLATRY

Three possible means of seduction to idolatry were condemned: (1) a prophet (13:1-5); (2) a family member (13:6-11); and (3) wicked and worthless men (13:12-18). Note the repeated phrase "let us worship" (13:2, 6, 13). In Moses' day, treaties were made between kings and the subjects they had conquered (sometimes called suzerain-vassal treaties). In these ancient treaties, the king required his vassals (subject nations) to report any conspiracy, rebellion, or disloyalty and to take active measures against offenders. This obligation finds its counterpart in Deuteronomy 13.

14:1-29 DIET

God as the Creator and Redeemer has a right to dictate even what his people can eat. Here the conditions of what to eat (14:3-21) and where to eat (14:22-29) were established along with Israel's responsibility to be separate and holy to God. Shaving the head and lacerating the body, activities forbidden to the Israelites, were pagan cultic practices performed to secure favor from false gods (1 Kings 18:28). Regulations were repeated for clean and unclean foods (cf. Lev. 11:1-45 with Deut. 14:3-20) and the pagan practice of boiling a young goat in its mother's milk was again forbidden (cf. 14:21 with Exodus 23:19).

Each year Israel was to bring its tithes to Jerusalem to share with the Levites and priests (Deut. 14:22-27). Every third year, the people were to store the tithes in their own towns to share with the Levites and the needy (14:28-29). That third-year offering appears to replace the regular yearly tithe that was to be taken to Jerusalem ("the tithe of all your crops," 14:28). Some scholars see the third-year tithe to be in addition to the regular yearly tithe. Both the local and the centralized locations for the tithes met the general command to share the yearly tithes with the Levites and the priests throughout the land (Lev. 27:30-33; Num. 18:21-32).

15:1-23 SABBATICAL YEARS

Sabbatical years and the period immediately prior to them were to be full of generous acts by the Israelites in light of their redemption by God. The motivation for that generosity was to be their remembrance of being redeemed out of Egyptian slavery. It is debated whether the debt of 15:1-6 was to be canceled permanently or simply suspended for the year. Servitude could be rendered for the repayment of a debt (15:12-18). But the limit was six years unless the slave requested to become a lifelong servant.

THE TEN COMMANDMENTS IN DEUTERONOMY

Commandment	Text	Description
1-2	12:1-31	Worship
3	13:1–14:27	Name of God
4	14:28–16:17	Sabbath
5	16:18–18:22	Authority
6	19:1–22:8	Homicide
7	22:9–23:19	Adultery
8	23:20–24:7	Theft
9	24:8–25:4	False Charges
10	25:6-16	Coveting

16:1-17 FEASTS

Israel's three great feasts—the Passover ("Unleavened Bread," 16:1-8), the Festival of Harvest ("Pentecost," 16:9-12) and the Festival of Shelters ("Booths," 16:13-17)—were designed to keep fresh in the Israelites' minds the remembrance of their redemption by God (16:3, 12).

16:18–18:22 Persons in Leadership

16:18–17:20 LEADERSHIP DECISION-MAKING

All of the conditions of the law called for accurate judgment. The section 16:18–17:20 gives instructions for judgment that moved from judges and officials (16:18-22), to the people (17:1-7), to the priests (17:8-13), and ultimately, to the future king (17:14-20). Since the witnesses were to deliver the first lethal blows of a death sentence, this would tend to guard against possible perjury (17:7). The foundation for the establishment of the Israelite monarchy was laid (17:14-20; cf. Gen. 49:10; Num. 24:17; 1 Sam. 8–10). The survival of the kingly line (Deut. 17:18-20) would become a parallel theme to the survival of the nation as a whole. Kingly survival would become the backbone of the books of Kings and Chronicles and the foundation for Israel's messianic hope. Marriage into the royalty of foreign powers was used by pagan kings as a means of strengthening their treaties. But Israel's king was to depend on the Lord rather than on military strength, political alliances, or personal wealth, and he was not to take many wives, or his heart would be led astray from the Lord (17:16-20).

18:1-22 CARE FOR LEVITES

The Levites, who were to settle throughout the land, were to be cared for (18:1-8) by the other Israelites as they taught the people the conditions of the covenant. The occult flourished among the pagan inhabitants of Canaan, and the Israelites were warned against it (18:9-14).

Moses said that God would bring the nation a greater Prophet (18:15), that is, Jesus Christ (Acts 3:19-26). Every prophet that arose after Moses would share in an aspect of the hope for this greater Prophet. The word "prophet" (Deut. 18:15) means one who speaks for another (Exod. 7:1-2). The biblical prophet was one who spoke forth a message for God (Deut. 18:18; cf. Jer. 1:4-7).

19:1–20:20 Cities in the Land

Another aspect of God's judgment and mercy was found in the laws protecting those who unintentionally took a human life (19:1-21). The cities of refuge were given to allow a person time to gain a just trial.

Two factors stand out regarding the instructions for fighting against the cities of Canaan: (1) the God of the Exodus would be with the Israelites and fight for them (20:1, 4); and (2) anyone or anything that breathed in the cities of Canaan had to be completely destroyed, in contrast to only the men having to be killed in cities taken outside the land (20:10-18). Because Israel's success did not depend upon military power but God's presence, allowance was made for exemption from military service (20:5-9). During a military siege of a city it was customary in ancient times for an army to cut down the surrounding trees, both to destroy the enemy's land and to build siege equipment (20:19-20). This was prohibited in order to protect Israel's inheritance.

21:1–26:19 Fresh Applications of the Moral Laws in the Land

Overview: The section of 21:1–26:19 makes fresh applications of the moral laws given at Sinai to situations that would arise in the Promised Land. The themes of purging evil from the land and dealing with others in fairness and decency were based on the fact of God's holy presence with Israel (23:14).

21:1–22:11 CIVIL PURITY

These civil instructions were aimed solely at removing impurity and avoiding sin within the land: (1) atoning for the impurity of the guilt of innocent blood (21:1-9); (2) avoiding the mistreatment of captive women and maintaining the firstborn's rights (21:15-17); and (3) punishing rebellion and enforcing capital punishment (21:18-23). The public exposure of a corpse ("hanged on a tree") was a means of adding disgrace to an executed criminal.

In 21:15-17 it is debatable whether Moses was legislating for a man who had two wives (polygamy) or had had two wives in succession. Since the text can be translated "has had two wives," it is questionable whether polygamy was involved. Deviant sexual behavior, not clothing styles, was the object of concern in 22:5.

22:12-30 MORAL PURITY

The social laws (22:1-12) were followed by moral laws (22:13-30), the theme of which was to purge evil from the congregation of Israel (22:21-22, 24). The legislation of 22:13-19 was designed to protect a virgin against false allegations of unchastity.

23:1-25 PURITY IN THE ASSEMBLY

Instructions for the holiness of the assembly (23:1-3, 7-8) and the camp (23:13) were dictated by the presence of God in Israel's midst (23:14). The "assembly of the Lord" refers to the people of God gathered in his presence for worship. The exclusion of Moabites and Ammonites (23:3) from the assembly continued the standard set forth to Abraham: "I will bless those who bless you and curse those who curse you" (Gen. 12:3).

Self-emasculation was a heathen cultic practice performed to ingratiate a worshiper with the gods (23:1). "Male prostitute" is literally "dog" in

Hebrew (23:18). Money from unclean sources could not be brought to the house of God (23:18).

24:1–26:19 PURITY AND JUSTICE MOTIVATED BY GRATITUDE

The various topics covered in 24:1–26:19 hinge on the purity of the land (24:4), the remembrance of events that had occurred in the wilderness (24:9), and during the Exodus (24:18, 22). The legislation of 24:1-4 neither instituted nor condoned divorce but simply prohibited a particular type of remarriage after divorce. A man could not remarry his divorced wife if, in the meantime, she had had an intervening marriage. The precise meaning of "shameful" (24:1, literally, "a naked matter") is hotly debated by Jewish rabbis, and is uncertain. Apparently the legislation was designed to discourage divorce and prevent the establishment of an illicit union.

While loans were permitted (24:10-13), charging a fellow Israelite interest was forbidden (23:19-20). The "security" functioned as collateral to secure repayment of the loan (24:10-12). However, the borrower was not to be deprived of his means of livelihood (24:6) or cloak (24:13).

Deuteronomy 25:6 continues the theme of human compassion, decency, and fairness with laws regarding dignity in punishment (25:1-3); a proverb on wages for work (25:4); care for widows (25:5-10); indecency (25:11-12); accurate and honest weights and measures (25:13-16); and the command to destroy the Amalekites for their unfair war against Israel (25:17-19). The apostle Paul later appealed to 25:4 to support the principle that the worker was worthy of his hire (1 Cor. 9:9-11). The law of the levirate marriage (the word comes from the Latin *levir* which means "husband's brother") served as the essential background to Ruth's marriage to Boaz (Deut. 25:5-10; cf. Ruth 3–4).

The offering of firstfruits was to be made in connection with a confession of God as the Redeemer (from Abraham to the Exodus) and the Giver of the Promised Land (Deut. 26:4-11). The creedal confession of Hebrew history recalled God's mighty deeds in the Exodus and conquest (26:5-10). The second speech of Moses ended with the formal commitment of Israel to keep God's instructions (26:16-19).

27:1–30:20 GOD'S SOVEREIGNTY AND HUMAN RESPONSIBILITY IN BLESSING

Overview: The blessings and curses (27:1–28:68) presented the two ways that were open to the children of God. The way of blessing was open to all (29:1-29), and in the end God would perform great acts of purification and inner perfection to bind his children to himself permanently (30:1-20).

27:1–28:68 Blessings and Curses

In the section 27:1–28:68, fourteen verses describe the blessings (28:1-14) and sixty-six verses the curses

(27:15-26; 28:15-68). Clearly, the thrust was on warning the Israelites of what would happen when they disobeyed. Mount Ebal (3,083 feet high) and Mount Gerizim (2,890 feet high) are situated north and south, respectively, of Shechem (27:12-13). The slopes of these two mountains form a natural amphitheater suitable for the occasion. Israel's history of disobedience and divine discipline was anticipated (28:15-68). The cursing ended with the threat of a complete reversal of the Exodus, with Israel once again in captivity in Egypt (28:68). This threat became a prophecy of Israel's doom because it was a model of human sinfulness. Given the opportunity to know God, humans inevitably fail.

29:1–30:20 Banishment and Restoration

The third speech of Moses began by including all the future believers in Israel in the covenant's demands (29:14-15) and by referring again to the curses (29:22-28). There could only be one reason why Israel would fall into destruction—her disobedience (29:24-25); it would not be a failure of God's love. The way of blessing, however, was plain and open to all (29:29).

God's discipline of Israel would end when she returned to him with all her heart (30:2). This promise enlarged and confirmed the provisions in the Abrahamic covenant regarding the land (Gen. 12:1, 7; 13:12; 17:7-8). Although the people of Israel possessed the "title deed" to the Promised Land, their living in the land and enjoying its blessings would be dependent upon their obedience. Any future restoration to blessings in the land would be conditional on their repentance (Deut. 30:1-5). This concept was crucial in the messages of the prophets, including John the Baptist and Jesus (Matt. 3:2; 4:17). Obedience to the law was possible for a believing Israelite (Deut. 30:11-13). Love and loyalty to God would result in life and prosperity (30:15-20), whereas disobedience and desertion would result in death and adversity. God would perform an inner act of purification (30:6). Again, the accessibility of blessing was stressed (30:11-20).

31:1–32:52 CORRECTIVE PICTURES

The section 31:1–32:52 brings together two seemingly opposing concepts. On the one hand, Moses was told by God of Israel's certain failure (31:16-19) but ultimate restoration (32:36-43), and he composed a song about both events (32:1-44). On the other hand, he exhorted Israel to be faithful (32:44-47). Those concepts formed the backbone of all future prophetic addresses to the redeemed. Failure is bound to come, but believers are not to be the ones who live in failure. That Moses was the original author of the material in Deuteronomy is made clear by 31:9 (see also 31:24). Moses' song presented the entire span—past, present, and future—of Israel's history. Every time the Israelites sang it they would bear witness of their agreement to the terms and implications of their covenant relationship with God. The Hebrew term for "Israel" (32:15) is "Jeshurun," which means "the upright one." It is an honorific title or "pet name" for Israel. Although used in a positive context in 33:5, it is also used reproachfully in 32:15 to express the thought that Israel failed to meet God's ideal.

33:1-29 THE FINAL BLESSING OF MOSES
Although failure would come, ultimate restoration was always the final note to be sounded when God's redemption was in view. Moses' final blessing stressed the love of God (33:3) and the incomparability both of God (33:26) and of his redeemed people (33:29).

34:1-12 THE DEATH OF MOSES
God linked Moses' view of the Promised Land to his covenant with Abraham, Isaac, and Jacob (34:4) and then took Moses to be with himself (34:5). The book ends with the passing of Moses' authority to Joshua (34:9) and a final exclamation of Moses' greatness (34:10-12), a greatness only to be surpassed by the greater Prophet, Jesus Christ (18:15).

JOSHUA

BASIC FACTS

HISTORICAL SETTING

At the time of the conquest, Canaan was populated by a variety of people that included Hittites, Amorites, Canaanites, Perizzites, Hivites and Jebusites (Josh. 9:1). The Canaanites and Jebusites were native to the land. The Hittites were from Asia Minor to the north, while the Amorites were from the Arabian Desert, and the Hivites were from either the mountains of Seir (Gen. 36:20) or the mountains of Lebanon (Gen. 10:17; Judg. 3:3). Little is known of the origin of the Perizzites. Most of the inhabitants of Canaan lived in the lowlands rather than the hills, though there were important cities in the hill country, including Kiriath Arba, Jebus, Luz, and Shechem. Canaan had been dominated earlier by Egypt, but from 1400 B.C. Egypt's influence on the land of Canaan rapidly diminished.

The religions of Canaan were idolatrous and involved the worship of El, the supreme god of the Canaanite pantheon, and Baal, his son and successor. Astarte, Asherah, and Anath (who was a combination sister and spouse of Baal) were all patronesses of sex and war. They were worshipped by the people of Canaan. Canaanite religion was so perverted that God actually drove the people out of the land in judgment because of it (Gen. 15:16; Lev. 18:24-25; Deut. 9:4-5). Israel was commanded to have nothing to do with the wicked ways of the people of Canaan (Deut. 12:29-31).

AUTHOR

The central figure in the book is Joshua, who was appointed by God to bring the people of Israel into the Promised Land (Deut. 31:14, 23). In his early life Joshua distinguished himself in serving Moses (Exod. 17:9-13; 24:13). Moses had changed his name from Hoshea to Joshua (Num. 13:16). Joshua and Caleb had brought back the minority report after spying out the land (Num. 13:30; 14:6-9), and as a result they were spared the judgment against the unbelieving Israelites.

Although the book is anonymous, it is reasonable to conclude from the following evidences that it was written from eyewitness and personal accounts by Joshua himself. Intimate biographical details, which only Joshua himself could have known, are given from the very first chapter (Josh. 1:2-9). Joshua wrote his own farewell address that is recorded in 24:1-25. In Joshua 5:1, 6 the first person plural is used, which points to the record of an eyewitness who had participated in the events.

Evidence of later editorial work is seen by the inclusion of events that occurred after Joshua's death (24:29-31; 15:13, 17; 19:47). Taken together, this evidence points to the substantial composition of Joshua by the man after whom the book is named. The supplementary

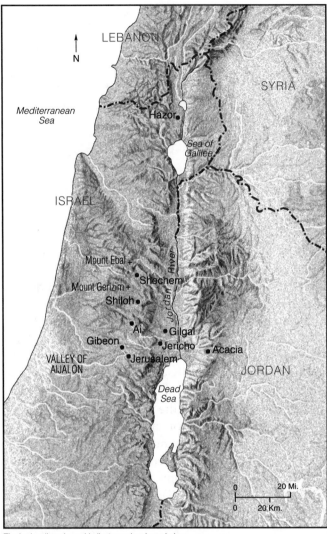

The broken lines (–·–·–·) indicate modern boundaries.
Copyright © 1986, 1988 by Tyndale House Publishers, Inc.

material recording events after Joshua's death may have been added by Eleazar the high priest, or perhaps by his son Phinehas.

DATE

The events of the book cover about thirty-one years from the beginning of the conquest (1406 B.C., taking an early date) to the death of Joshua around 1375 B.C. (24:29). While some hold to a late date for the book, there is evidence of an early date of composition. One argument in support of an early date for the book is that Canaanite cities are mentioned by their archaic names (15:9, 13, 49). The most direct evidence for an early date is that 13:4-6 and 19:28 indicate that Sidon was the most important city of Phoenicia. This indicates a date of writing before the twelfth century B.C., when Tyre began to grow in power, taking supremacy from Sidon.

If Joshua was about the age of Caleb, who was 40 years old at the time of the mission into Canaan, then he would have died about 1375 B.C. at 110 years of age (24:29). The book was written prior to the death of Joshua and most likely edited shortly thereafter.

PURPOSE

The purpose of Joshua was to show future readers that the Hebrews did ultimately conquer and occupy the Promised Land in accordance with God's divine purposes, demonstrating his faithfulness in keeping his covenant promises (Deut. 9:5).

GEOGRAPHY AND ITS IMPORTANCE

Israel's initial conquest of Palestine began with the taking of Jericho and the difficult climb up the west side of the Arabah Valley to conquer Ai. That first military campaign drove a wedge between the northern and southern regions of Palestine. Then, the campaign continued south to take Jerusalem and its surrounding regions. The last part of the initial conquest was to march north for a great victory at Hazor. Israel was able to take hold of the central mountain range of Palestine, which gave them control over the east-west passages throughout the land. But Israel balked at fighting the Philistines, who controlled the fertile coastal plains. The central, southern, and northern campaigns provided rugged geographical and human opposition to display how God was the great warrior for his people and to test Israel's faith in his abilities.

GUIDING CONCEPTS

THE FORMER PROPHETS

The books of Joshua, Judges, 1 and 2 Samuel, and 1 and 2 Kings are known as the former prophets. (The latter prophets are Isaiah, Jeremiah, Ezekiel, Daniel, and Hosea through Malachi.) The former and latter prophets differ not only in the general time they were written but also in their style and content. The former prophets use historical narrative to communicate their goal, while the latter prophets, in the main, use prophetic speeches. The former prophets can be placed together to form a continuous history of Israel from Joshua's conquest to the Babylonian captivity, while the latter prophets present detailed prophetic speeches with very little historical narrative to help locate them in time. The essential difference between the two groups is their style and content. But both groups use their special contents to achieve a common goal: the prophetic exhortation to the hearers to stop sinning and return to obeying God with grateful and awe-filled hearts.

The books of Joshua, Judges, Samuel, and Kings are not just books of history; they have been received by God's people throughout the ages as books of prophecy. But they are not prophecy in the sense of telling the future. Rather, they are prophecy in the sense of proclaiming God's truth to instruct, challenge, and encourage God's people. So, when these books are read, they should not be viewed as dry history. They were purposely constructed from a pastoral perspective to provide messages of help to meet the needs of God's people.

GOD'S FAITHFULNESS

The book of Joshua is the culmination of God's promise to give the Israelites their own land (Gen. 12:1; 17:8). It is the record of the conquest of the land that God had promised to bring about (Deut. 7:1-2), and thus it demonstrates God's faithfulness to his covenant with the patriarchs and the nation by settling the tribes in the Promised Land (Josh. 11:23; 21:43). Israel's victories were not attributed to her military skill and superiority, but to the power of God himself. While Joshua was Israel's leader and quite influential upon the spiritual lives of the people (24:31), the book makes it clear that the credit for the conquest belonged to God alone (3:10; 4:23-24; 5:13-14; 6:16; 21:44; 23:3, 9-10). The book emphasizes God's faithfulness in bringing about all that he had promised to do for the young nation of Israel.

God's covenant faithfulness also is seen in his provision of a leader to follow Moses. The man he selected had proven his faithfulness by encouraging Israel to be bold enough to enter the land in spite of its dangers (Num. 14:6-10, 29-30). Only Joshua and Caleb from the old generation were allowed to enter the land. God himself selected Joshua as the leader of his people (Num. 27:15-23; Deut. 31:23). Joshua's name in Hebrew means "God is salvation." That name in Greek is Jesus, the name given to the Lord because he would save his people (Matt. 1:21).

ISRAEL'S FAITHFULNESS
Central to the success of God's people was their obedience to the word of God, which, for them, was the law handed down by Moses. Both the leader, Joshua, and the people were to meditate on the law day and night in order for them to have success (Josh. 1:8; 8:32-35; 23:6-16; 24:26-27). Human effort alone was not able to bring victory. Only the blessing brought by obedience was the way to enter the fullness of God's promises.

GOD'S HOLINESS
God's holiness is seen in his command that Israel completely exterminate the inhabitants of Canaan (6:21; 8:26; Deut. 20:16). That judgment was the natural expression of God's holiness manifesting itself against sin and wickedness. God had long before promised that the inhabitants of Canaan were due for divine judgment—a prophecy fulfilled four hundred years later (Gen. 15:16; cf. Deut. 7:3-6). The moment of judgment had now come. As with all of God's promises, it never matters how much time elapses between his making of a promise and its fulfillment. His word of blessing or judgment will always be fulfilled. That aspect of God also relates to his own people. He shows no favorites and does not overlook the sins of his people. Israel was to have no other gods (Exod. 20:3; cf. Deut. 5:7, which restates Exod. 20:3). The holiness of God also is seen in his pronouncement of judgment upon the sin of Achan (Josh. 7:10-15).

BIBLE-WIDE CONCEPTS

PUTTING AN END TO SIN
Sin, Judgment, and Grace
The first Bible-wide contribution of Joshua concerns God's judgment on sin. Ever since the Garden of Eden, God had shown himself to be utterly against humanity's "no" to his desires. However, even in the face of his gracious long-suffering, human beings continued to deepen their commitment to do what they wanted instead of what he wanted. That unfortunate situation put God's reputation in jeopardy. Why did he not put an end to all the injustice and cruelty of humanity? If he really hated sin, why did he not stop it? Was he not strong enough? Or had he softened in his acceptance of sin? Did not the fact that he used sin to accomplish his own ends betray some kind of sinister compromise of his holiness? Those questions have been asked or implied by both rebellious and pious people throughout Bible times to the present.

These questions, besides assuming that God has to justify his actions to mortals, miss one key point that pervades Scripture from Genesis to Joshua and is cemented in the Noahic covenant: God desires people's salvation more than their damnation. The Noahic covenant teaches that God will put up with people's sin in order to give them time to repent. The length of time he does so indicates the depth of his grace. So far, it has been thousands and thousands of years. However, his time of grace for repentance will come to an end, and that is what was seen happening to the people of Canaan in the book of Joshua. They had been given four hundred years to repent, but they did not respond (Gen. 15:13-16). The time for judgment had arrived. Much earlier, the world before the Flood had been given 120 years to repent (Gen. 6:3) before its judgment came. Israel itself was given hundreds of years of opportunity in the Promised Land before the desolation of the land and the captivities of the people took place. Presently, the entire world has been given thousands of years, but its end will come at the Lord's return. And, individually, each person has been given a limited stretch of years on this earth to respond to God's ways.

Jericho and the Book of Revelation

In the nation's march around the city of Jericho, the imagery of the seven trumpets announcing God's presence enthroned above the Ark of the Covenant anticipated the seven cosmic trumpets of the book of Revelation that signal the mighty presence of God from the Ark of the Covenant in the heavenly temple (Rev. 8:2; 11:19). What was just one city in Joshua becomes the entire globe in the book of Revelation. The downfall of Jericho and the land of Canaan is simply one more picture of both God's grace and judgment. The time he gives for repentance shows his love. The flash of final judgment shows that he indeed has been in control. He does not overlook sin, and he is not too weak to judge. God's judgments are designed to show his inevitable evaluation of disobedience and evil, and in doing so he justifies both his holy character and his long-suffering compassion.

Judgment as Cleansing

God's judgment also paved the way for his people to receive their divine promises of redemption. The flood cleansed the earth for Noah's new, though unsuccessful, start. The death of the old generation of Israelites in the wilderness cleansed the nation for its new start in the land of Palestine. The destruction of the Canaanites cleansed the land for the holy tribes of Israel. And the destruction of the present heavens and earth will provide the final cleansing of the universe for the new and totally successful beginning for God's redeemed people.

A PROMISED LAND

What was so important about the particular plot of ground now called the Holy Land? We know that it was promised to Abraham. But there is something more important about it that stretches all the way back to the creation. God created the entire universe but began its human population on a small scale: two people in a small location called Eden. The people were told to multiply and spread over the whole earth and extend the perfection of the Garden of Eden worldwide. Likewise, the small band of Noah's family was to have another chance to provide worldwide blessing. In the same way, Israel was to start small and to extend God's blessings to the entire world. God has always had the entire world in view even though, at various times, he has started his plan for blessing the world with only a few people in a small location. Adam and Eve in Eden, Noah grounded on the mountains of Ararat, and the people of Israel in Palestine all represent new beginnings to God's plan for worldwide blessing.

So when God gave the land of Palestine to Israel, he simply gave another beginning with the goal of making possible a world right with God. The land was a down payment for a worldwide inheritance. That is what believers will see at the end of this age when there is a new start, this time in a new heavens and earth. The heavenly city of Revelation is described, in part, in terms taken from the Garden of Eden (Rev. 22:1-2). And God's rule and blessing will forever extend around the real Promised Land: heaven on earth.

What is so important about the Holy Land? It foreshadows the perfect rest yet to come. It points toward the holy perfection of which Palestine is just a shadow.

GOD THE WARRIOR

Certainly the main thrust of the book of Joshua teaches that God was the warrior who fought for Israel in order to give all that he had promised to the nation of Israel. But why did the promise have to come through bloody battle? Back in Genesis 15:13, God had told Abraham that after a period of four hundred years of captivity in a foreign land, Abraham's children would return to Palestine. The reason for the four-hundred-year delay was then given: "After four generations your descendants will return here to this land, when the sin of the Amorites has run its course" (Gen. 15:16). God had a plan, not made known to us, for the Amorites (Amorites is a general term used to describe all the inhabitants of Palestine). After that four-hundred-year period, Israel would return to take the land and, at that time, the sin of the inhabitants of Palestine would come to an end. Thus, Israel's return to the Promised Land was directly related to putting an end to the Canaanites' evil.

Israel's return would carry out God's judgment for iniquity (cf. Lev. 18:24-25). That explains why Israel's receipt of the land had to come through the divine warfare of judgment and also why Israel was not to take any of the spoils of the initial cities, which were holy to the Lord's judgment. The judgment was the Lord's; therefore, the battle was the Lord's (Josh. 1:2, 15; 10:14). Thus, the Lord described the land as a gift to Israel from him (1:2-3). The giving of the land was an accomplished fact from God's perspective of sovereignty and power even before the conquest began. Just as Abraham was instructed to rise up and walk through the Promised Land (Gen. 13:17), so Joshua could know that each step he took had been prepared for him by God (Josh. 1:3).

Because God was the warrior, Israel had hope for the future. God would give them rest (1:13-14; 22:4). That rest was, in part, anticipated in the days of Noah (Gen. 5:29). It was a rest that would give relief from the awful toils brought on by God's curse on Adam's sin. In this age, spiritual rest has been ushered in by Christ's death and resurrection, which allowed the Holy Spirit to enter the lives of believers in a new and intimate way. Ultimately, the promised rest will come in its fullness in the new heavens and earth. God will never forsake or leave those who trust in him (Josh. 1:5; Matt. 28:20).

NEEDS MET BY JOSHUA

Israel needed to know several important facts that the book of Joshua supplied. The nation had been disciplined for her past failures to enter the land, but God's promise was not voided by disobedience. Israel was now poised to enter the Promised Land. Moses was dead, but God would not leave the nation without a leader to bring them into God's promise. And once again, God brought his chosen people from one difficult situation to another. He took them from Egypt into the wilderness to test their hearts (Deut. 8:1-5), and he was about to test his people again.

The taking of the Promised Land would not be easy. Although God's people had to do the physical fighting, their spiritual battle was always to affirm the invisible presence of the Lord at their side and to obey him. Past failures were forgotten, Joshua was

God's leader, and God himself was always present for victory. The following questions allude to the major needs met by the book of Joshua.

- How did God prove his commitment to give Israel the Promised Land?
- If God was powerful enough to give his people victory, what were the reasons they failed from time to time?
- What kind of leader did God provide after Moses?
- What was God's chosen leader like and what was the key to his success?
- Why did God not give his people immediate and complete victory?
- Why did God let his people go through an ongoing process of battles and challenges?
- Why was the Mosaic covenant crucial to the success of God's people in gaining the Promised Land?

The book of Joshua provides answers to these important questions. It is not made up of dry historical facts; it is alive with the author's purpose to help God's people face the challenges of ongoing battle, remain true to God's salvation, and enjoy the rewards of their victories. Israel seemed to always be in one fight or another. The Israelites no doubt wished they could just stop having to struggle all the time. Even after their military takeover of the land, they would still have to struggle with the battles caused by personal and national sin. Christians may sometimes feel the same way. Will there never be a time to relax? Although Christians do not fight physical battles for the Promised Land, they fight the same spiritual fight as Israel of old. And like Israel, the redemption of believers today has not lifted them out of the struggles of the world. If anything, their redemption has more sharply defined the nature of the enemy, the locations of the battlefields, and the only powerful way to victory.

OUTLINE OF JOSHUA

I. CONQUERING THE LAND (1:1–12:24)
   A. The Central Campaign (1:1–10:28)
   B. The Southern Campaign (10:29-43)
   C. The Northern Campaign (11:1-23)
   D. The Review of the Conquest (12:1-24)

II. DIVIDING THE LAND (13:1–22:34)
   A. The Remaining Land (13:1-7)
   B. The Transjordan (13:8-33)
   C. Canaan (14:1–22:34)

III. EXHORTATION TO OBEDIENCE AND COVENANT REAFFIRMATION
    (23:1–24:33)

JOSHUA NOTES

1:1–12:24 CONQUERING THE LAND

Overview: Joshua 1–12 takes the reader from the crossing of the Jordan River to the destruction of Jericho, the failure at Ai, and the initial subduing of the north, south, and central portions of the Promised Land. The major themes are the saving power of God, the fierce opposition of the Canaanites, and the alternating fear and faith of the Israelites.

More specifically, Joshua 1–10 emphasizes: Joshua's God-given authority as the next leader in line after Moses (Josh. 1); the careful preparations for (Josh. 2) and actual taking of Jericho (Josh. 6), separated by a detailed section on the preparation of God's children to carry out his warfare by personal consecration and the crossing of the Jordan (Josh. 3–4), by their circumcision and the celebration of the Passover (Josh. 5). God would do the initial fighting, but his people were responsible to be pure before him. Joshua 7–8 details the people's first failure because of Achan's sin and the second victory as the nation purified itself and fought against Ai. Joshua 9 records Israel's mistake of making a covenant with the people of Gibeon, who were Canaanites who should have been destroyed. That covenant obligated Israel to protect Gibeon from its enemies, an obligation that resulted in Israel's great victory in the valley of Aijalon, where the sun and moon stood still (Josh. 10).

1:1–10:28 The Central Campaign

1:1-9 INTRODUCTION

Joshua 1:1-9 presents the following themes: (1) the giving of the land by God himself (cf. 1:11, 13, 15); (2) Joshua as the mediator of God's victory (1:5-6, 9); (3) the land as a promise to Abraham (1:6); and (4) the centrality of obedience to the conditions of Moses' covenant (1:7-8). Joshua's meditation on the word of God was to focus on obedience. From that obedience came the automatic presence of God to save.

God had promised this land to Abraham (1:3-4; cf. Gen. 15:18-21). It was a gift, but possession required Israel's corresponding military action. Divine sovereignty and human responsibility complement one another. Obedience (Josh. 1:7) enables a person to live according to God's divine order and thus enjoy God's best (cf. Deut. 30:15-20). The word "meditate" (Josh. 1:8) means to speak in an undertone, and it involves recitation as well as memorization.

1:10-18 THE LAND AS REST

Joshua 1:10-18 emphasizes that the giving of the land to Israel was equal to their receiving rest (1:13, 15), and the strength and courage of Joshua, Israel's leader, was to be based on his full obedience to the word of God. Joshua's obedience was immediate and exemplary, which was especially significant because the Jordan River was at flood stage (3:15), and crossing it would be especially difficult. The Transjordanian tribes are the focus in 1:12-18 (cf. 12:1-6).

2:1-24 JOSHUA AND CALEB SPY OUT THE LAND

The spies were sent out secretly, perhaps because of what the public report by the spies sent out by Moses had brought about (Num. 13–14). Rahab's confession acknowledged that God had given Israel the land. She requested a blessing that reflected belief in what God had said in Genesis 12:3, that is, that he would bless those who blessed Abraham's line. The report that the hearts of the Canaanites had melted (Josh. 2:11, 24) continued the response to God's defeat of kings Sihon and Og in Numbers 21:21-35. Attempts have been made since early times to represent Rahab as merely an innkeeper, but the Hebrew word confirms that she was a prostitute. Her house would have been a good place to spend the night unnoticed. Situated on the wall (Josh. 2:15), it allowed for the possibility, if necessary, of a secret escape by the spies.

But if God already had promised victory, why did Joshua choose to spy out the land? Joshua obviously discerned the need to exercise his human responsibility, understanding his part in accomplishing God's promised victory. But whatever was Joshua's specific reason, the point of the story lies in Rahab's confession of God's great power as well as his mercy. That confession earned Rahab a place in Scripture as one of the great people of faith (Matt. 1:5; Heb. 11:31). Rahab lied to protect the Israelite spies. Many have sought to justify her actions based on the situation, but that is unnecessary. What the New Testament commends here is her faith (Heb. 11:31), not the lie that she told. God could have protected the spies even if she had told the truth. Rahab's confession was much like that made earlier by Moses (Deut. 4:39).

3:1-17 THE CROSSING OF THE JORDAN

The Ark led the way into the Jordan River (Josh. 3:1-4), remained in the middle while the nation crossed (3:17), and was the sign of the presence of the God of heaven (3:11). A distance of a thousand yards (2,000 cubits) was to be kept between the people and the Ark (3:3). The people were consecrated (3:5), and the great crossing was God's way of exalting Joshua before the nation (3:7). The crossing of the Jordan River was as significant for these Israelites as the crossing of the Red Sea had been for their parents. The Jordan River was blocked by a landslide in A.D. 1267 for sixteen hours, and again in 1927 for twenty-one hours. However, the mention that the river was at flood stage at the time of Israel's crossing and that the people crossed on dry ground suggests a miraculous event (cf. 5:1). The crossing of the Jordan River took place in the spring of the year at the time of the barley harvest (3:15). That was a difficult time to ford the Jordan River due to the flooding that always resulted from the spring run of the melting snow on Mount Hermon. This miraculous event would fortify the Israelites' faith for the struggles that lay ahead of them (3:10). Joshua was exalted because God showed his presence with him.

4:1-24 MEMORIAL STONES FROM THE CROSSING

The stones that were set up both in the middle of the Jordan River and on the other side were to serve as future reminders that Israel had once been in the middle of the river and that God had taken them over to the other side (4:9, 20). The date (4:19) was probably Nisan (March–April) 10, 1406 B.C. Gilgal was the first Israelite camp in Canaan. While the exact location is uncertain, many have identified it with Khirbet el-Mefjer, two and one-half miles northeast of Jericho (see introductory map). The crossing of the Jordan River is paralleled with the crossing of the Red Sea (4:23). It was a sign of God's might designed to help the people to remember and reverence God forever (4:24).

5:1-15 THE ABRAHAMIC COVENANT IS HONORED

The response of the Canaanites (5:1) to Israel's crossing of the Jordan River was linked to 4:24: "so that all the nations of the earth might know." The circumcision of the male Israelites was their last link to "the shame of [their] slavery in Egypt," that is, their ties to the journey out of Egypt to Canaan (5:9). The rite of circumcision, the sign of the Abrahamic covenant (Gen. 17:9-14), was not observed during the forty years of Israel's wilderness wanderings. Joshua renewed the rite, which was symbolic of the obedience promised by the second generation (Josh. 1:17). The Israelites' observance of the Passover in the land and their eating of food in the Promised Land broke their last tie with the Exodus from Egypt. The manna ceased (5:12). As the Lord had appeared to Moses (Exod. 3), so he appeared to Joshua. Where the army of God was, in this case in front of Jericho, that place was holy (Josh. 5:13-15).

6:1-27 JERICHO IS DESTROYED

The message God gave to Joshua in 5:13-14 was elaborated (6:1-5). Jericho, one of the oldest fortified cities in the ancient Near East, was west of the Jordan River and six miles north of the Dead Sea. The key phrase is "I [the Lord] have given you Jericho" (6:2), which was shouted in 6:16 as Israel

actually took the city. The instructions for the conquest reveal that the city was to be overthrown by God's power, not military might. Rams' horns were generally used for religious, not military, festivals (cf. Exod. 19:16, 19; and Lev. 23:24; 25:9), while silver trumpets were used for announcing wars (Num. 10:2-10). Thus, the use of rams' horns shows that the taking of Jericho fell under the heading of a religious rather than a military activity.

The city was given by God through his judgment and was to be returned as an offering to him. Therefore, no human being was to receive any of the city's goods, for what was taken was to be God's exclusive property. Anything that could not be burned was to be placed in the sanctuary. The battle needed to be fought for two reasons: (1) sin needed to be punished; and (2) Israel's purity needed to be maintained (Deut. 9:5; Lev. 18:24-30). Israel was engaged in a holy war. It was no ordinary kind of battle, and it will occur only once more—at the second coming of the Lord.

The purpose of the seven rams' horns before the Ark was to announce the presence of the King of the universe. That announcement was made once each day for six days. The seventh day brought the perfection of God's judgment on Jericho and his promise of giving the city to Israel. To take anything from the city would bring a curse on the nation (Josh. 6:18). Achan would soon violate that command (7:1). The fall of Jericho is a capsule picture of God's judgment. Everything was destroyed, and any material objects that could not be burned were holy to the Lord.

The promise of redemption for Rahab and her family came about because she had hidden the messengers of Israel (6:22-25). In the sovereignty of God, Rahab was spared (6:25) and became the great-great-grandmother of David (Ruth 4:21) and an ancestor of Christ (Matt. 1:5-6). Jericho was to remain ruined as a picture of God's attitude toward sin. The curse for rebuilding Jericho (Josh. 6:26) was fulfilled a long time later during the reign of Ahab (1 Kings 16:34).

7:1-26 THE SIN OF ACHAN

There is considerable debate regarding the location of Ai (see introductory map). The traditional identification, et-Tell, was not occupied at the time of the conquest. The defeat of Israel at Ai caused Joshua to question why God brought his people into the land only to let them be defeated. Joshua mistakenly thought the problem was with God. The sin of Achan illustrates how one person can influence the fate of the entire nation. The ban on taking anything from Jericho had been violated, and the entire nation suffered the consequences of defeat.

The Israelites began to wonder why God had let them down (Josh. 7:7). But the whole story of Achan's judgment was designed to show Israel that the problem was with them, not with God. Stones with markings indicating yes and no were cast like dice. God used this procedure to make his will known (Prov. 16:33). Achan's confession was to give glory to God by showing what the problem was (Josh. 7:19). In view of the prohibition against executing children for the sins of their parents (Deut. 24:16), it may be assumed that Achan's children were accomplices. However, the point of the story goes beyond who did and did not sin. Thirty-six innocent men suffered death in the first battle against Ai because of Achan's sin (Josh. 7:5).

This judgment on the house of Achan was a severe first-time lesson for the nation and takes its place in a line of similar actions by God throughout Scripture. There was the severe first-time lesson of the fall of Adam (Gen. 3); the flood (Gen. 6–8); the judgment on the worship of the golden calf (Exod. 32); the wilderness wanderings (Num. 14); and the deaths of Ananias and Sapphira (Acts 5). Surely someone else took things that were holy to God. Surely someone else worshiped an idol. Surely someone else lied to the church about his giving. But God makes his points in severe first-time lessons and then moves on in patience and grace. He desires that his people will learn their lessons without having to undergo catastrophic destruction every time they disobey.

8:1-35 AI IS DESTROYED

With purity restored and through clever military tactics, Israel was able to defeat Ai. God reconfirmed his promise of giving the land (Josh. 8:1) and the Israelites reconfirmed their commitment to him after their victory. They went to Mount Ebal and Mount Gerizim and reconfirmed the covenant God had made with them at Sinai (8:30-35). That fulfilled God's commands given in Deuteronomy 11:26-30 and 27:11-14. The covenant-renewal ceremony, begun on the plains of Moab (Deut. 12:26), was to be concluded in Canaan (Deut. 27:2-8). Shechem, situated between Mount Ebal and Mount Gerizim, was probably subjugated by Joshua at this time (cf. Josh. 11:19).

9:1-27 A COVENANT WITH THE CANAANITES

Gibeon is located at el-Jib, six miles northwest of Jerusalem (see introductory map). The Gibeonites deceived Israel into making a treaty with them. They must have known that Israel was permitted to make peace with the people who lived in far-off cities, but not with those from cities in the Promised Land. The Gibeonites' confession (9:24-25) showed that the nations rightly understood the great power of God on Israel's behalf. A covenant with the Canaanites flew in the face of God's command to destroy all of them. Israel's leaders failed to ask for the Lord's counsel (9:14) and relied instead upon their own ability to discern what was

right. Thus, they violated God's commands in Exodus 23:32; 34:12 and Deuteronomy 7:2. Much later, this covenant with the Gibeonites was violated by King Saul, with devastating results (2 Sam. 21:1-6). The judgment mentioned in Joshua 9:27 may have had an evangelistic intent. It would expose the Gibeonites to God's continual revelation as displayed at the tabernacle.

10:1-28 GOD HONORS THE COVENANT WITH THE CANAANITES

Israel's alliance with Gibeon resulted in the nation having to fight to defend Gibeon against the coalition of five Canaanite kings. The march from Gilgal to Gibeon was twenty-four miles. God clearly promised Israel the victory (10:8, 19, 25) and even gave them a miraculous extension of daylight to finish the battle (10:12-14). The key to this section and to the conquest of the Promised Land as a whole is seen in 10:14: "The Lord fought for Israel!"

There are three basic interpretations of Joshua's long day: (1) Poetic interpretation: The story is poetry and not to be taken literally. The sun only seemed to stand still because of the weariness of the soldiers and the heat of the battle. (2) Total-eclipse view: On the basis of Babylonian astronomical texts, the words "stand still" (10:12) are rendered "became dark" or "eclipsed." (3) The prolongation-of-light view: The passage is taken literally to mean that Joshua was miraculously allowed to complete the battle before darkness set in. That may have taken place as a result of a passing comet (a theory of Velikovsky), the tilting of the earth's axis, or the refraction of the sun's rays on a local level. The Book of Jashar (10:13) may have been a history of Israel's wars in which some important events and great men were commemorated poetically (cf. 2 Sam. 1:18).

Joshua followed the custom of ancient conquerers to impress his army captains with the significance of this victory (Josh. 10:24). Putting their feet on the necks of the kings symbolized the complete subjection of the enemy. (Cf. 10:27 with Deuteronomy 21:22-23.)

10:29-43 The Southern Campaign

This next section surveys the southern conquest. Israel had first driven a wedge between the north and south of Canaan, thus destroying the Canaanites' ability for unified opposition. Again, God fought for the nation (10:42). The purpose of Israel's initial campaigns through the middle of the land of Canaan and then the southern and northern parts was to make a preliminary conquest of the entire land. Not all of the land was taken, and some areas had to be retaken later (15:13-17). But these initial raids of the entire nation knocked out the key military centers and prepared the way for each tribe to go in and finish the conquest within its own apportioned area.

11:1-23 The Northern Campaign

A survey of the northern campaign is given in 11:1-15. Hazor was a very large and strategic Canaanite city located about ten miles north of the Sea of Galilee. North of Galilee, near Mount Merom, many kings assembled to make a last-ditch effort to stop Israel's conquest. Merom, noted for its large spring, was situated about seven miles southwest of Hazor. Again God made it clear that it was his battle and that victory was assured (11:6). Joshua was commanded to hamstring the horses, which disabled the animals for military activity by cutting the back sinews of the hind leg. They could still pull a plow but could not be used in battle. The remark to burn the cities (11:13) refers to the northern campaign. Both Jericho and Ai were also burned (6:24; 8:19).

The key phrase for defining the nature of this conquest is in 11:15 and 20. This all happened in complete obedience to the Lord's commands through Moses to Joshua. The entire campaign is summarized in 11:16-23, ending with the note that the "descendants of Anak" were destroyed (11:21-22). The Anakites were the giants who brought so much fear to Israel earlier when the nation failed to have faith in God's ability to bring them into the land (cf. Num. 13:33, where the sons of Anak are also called Nephilim). The Nephilim were fearsome, but they always had to be viewed by Israel as being under God's power. Even though they were strong, there were Nephilim who had been destroyed in the flood (Gen.6:4), others who were killed in the conquest (Josh. 11:21-22), and Goliath who was killed later by David (1 Sam. 17:45-51). All of the people of Canaan, with the exception of the Gibeonites, were hardened by God, like Pharaoh, so that God might show his wrath against sin and his mercy to his chosen people.

The conquest of Canaan and the division of the land took about seven years to complete. Caleb was forty years old when Moses sent spies the first time into the land, and he was eighty-five at the time of Joshua's division of the land (Josh. 14:7-10). The final division of the land took place six or seven years after Israel entered the land. Joshua took the whole land, as God had promised (1:2-5), but that did not mean that the work was all done. While the military strength of the inhabitants of Canaan had been broken, much of the land was still not occupied (13:2-6). It would be the responsibility of the individual tribes to subjugate and occupy their designated territories.

12:1-24 The Review of the Conquest

The entire initial conquest was summarized by noting the Transjordan victories (12:1-6), then those of southern (12:8-16) and northern Canaan (12:17-24). The only information regarding how

long these campaigns took is in 11:18. It was a period of about five years (cf. 14:10).

13:1–22:34 DIVIDING THE LAND

Overview: The section of 13:1–22:34 narrates the division of the land by highlighting Israel's failures and faith in finalizing the conquest (13:1–19:51). Even at the end of Joshua's life, not all of Canaan had been taken from the former inhabitants of that land (23:4-5). After the twelve tribes were allotted their lands, the cities for refuge and for the Levites were assigned (20:1–21:45). The building of an altar by the Transjordanian tribes in Canaan nearly brought about a civil war (22:1-34). The book concludes with the last addresses of Joshua, which include a plea for faithfulness (23:1-16) and a witness to Israel's reaffirmation of the covenant (24:1-34).

13:1-7 The Remaining Land

Joshua 13 begins at the end of Joshua's life (13:1). The initial campaigns by the entire nation of Israel were in the past, and each tribe still had much work to do in trusting the Lord for complete victory. Much land remained to be captured. Joshua apportioned the Transjordan lands (13:2-33) and then the lands within Canaan (14:1–19:51). The detailed description of the tribal boundaries may seem very uninteresting to the contemporary reader, but these records served as the title deed for Israel's inheritance in the land. The tribes would have been extremely interested in these accurate and detailed boundary descriptions. Detailed descriptions of God's physical blessings of promise and redemption can be just as meaningful as descriptions of his spiritual blessings.

13:8-33 The Transjordan

The Transjordan lands, located east of the Jordan River, were apportioned to the two and a half tribes in the way that Moses had divided them (13:8, 15, 24, 29, 32; 14:5). The lands within Canaan were apportioned to the remaining tribes by the priest Eleazar, Joshua, and the heads of the households of the tribes (14:1).

14:1–22:34 Canaan

14:1–19:51 LAND FOR THE TWELVE TRIBES

The land was divided among the twelve tribes by lot (14:2; Num. 34:16-29) and according to need, which was determined by the size of each tribe (Num. 26:54-56). The general location was determined by the casting of lots, while the amount of territory given depended upon the tribe's size. Joshua 14:7-10 records information that makes it possible to calculate the conquest's duration. Caleb was forty years old at the time of the Exodus and was eighty-five after forty years in the wilderness and the five years of the conquest. Caleb received as his personal inheritance the city of Hebron, known earlier as the city of Arba (15:13). Joseph's sons, Manasseh and Ephraim (16:4), took his place as tribal heads among the tribes of Israel (Gen. 48:5). Gezer (Josh. 16:10), a strategic fortress city on the coastal plain, did not come under full Israelite control until the days of Solomon (1 Kings 9:16). Shiloh (Josh. 18:1), located in the hill country of Ephraim twenty miles north of Jerusalem, was to serve as Israel's political and religious center for the next three hundred years.

In fulfillment of Jacob's prophetic judgment (Gen. 49:5-7), the tribe of Simeon received no land inheritance of its own (Josh. 19:1-9). But Simeon did inherit seventeen cities within the large tribal territory of Judah. Some of the Simeonites later migrated north (2 Chron. 15:9; 34:6). Dan's allotment was very vulnerable to the Philistine menace (Josh. 19:40-48), and a remnant of the tribe later migrated north to Leshem (Laish), which they captured and renamed Dan (Judg. 18).

Throughout this long section describing the division of the land among the twelve tribes, notes of both faith and fear were sounded: Caleb's faith and resulting conquest (Josh. 14:11-15; 15:13-19); Judah's inability to drive out the Jebusites (15:63); Ephraim's inability to drive out the Canaanites in Gezer (16:10); Manasseh's inability to drive out the Canaanites (17:11-13); Ephraim and Manasseh's fear of the Canaanites (17:14-18); and the procrastination of seven tribes in taking their lands (18:2-3).

20:1-9 CITIES OF REFUGE

After the land was divided, cities of refuge were established, as Moses had instructed (20:1-9; Num. 35:9-34, Deut. 4:41-43; 19:1-3). Three were located east and three west of the Jordan River. See the accompanying chart.

The cities of refuge were to give protection from revenge to someone who accidentally killed a person (cf. Deut. 19:1-13; 21:1-9; Num. 35:9-29). This concept went back to the Noahic covenant (Gen. 9) and the prohibition against murder. The person who had accidentally killed someone had to stay in the city where he had fled until the death of the current high priest (Num. 35:25-28).

21:1-45 CITIES FOR THE LEVITES

Yet another fulfillment of God's commands through Moses was the allotting of the cities for the

Levites (Josh. 21:2-3). Those forty-eight cities were selected in locations that would make it possible for the Levites to provide a spiritual influence throughout all of the twelve tribes of Israel. The presence of those cities was also a reminder of the true inheritance of the Levites, and all of Israel as well: the Lord himself (13:33).

22:1-34 THE TRANSJORDAN ALTAR

Before returning across the Jordan River to their own lands, the Transjordanian tribes built a copy of the altar of sacrifice (22:10). The rest of the Israelites perceived their act to be one of idolatry (22:17) as well as a potential bringer of God's anger (22:18). The erection of the altar appeared to be a violation of the law of Deuteronomy 12:13-14 that required a central sanctuary. But the Transjordanian tribes explained that the altar was only a symbol to unify worship and was never to be used for sacrifices. The rest of the Israelites accepted that explanation (Josh. 22:26-29) and a civil war was avoided (22:33). Such a war would have been in accordance with Deuteronomy 13:12-18, which required the Israelites to destroy an apostate city.

23:1–24:33 EXHORTATION TO OBEDIENCE AND COVENANT REAFFIRMATION

An address was given by Joshua near the end of his life (Josh. 23). He commended Israel to have faith in God's ability to drive out the rest of the nations still remaining in the land (23:1-5) and to faithfulness in serving God alone (23:6-11). Like Moses, Joshua emphasized the curses of the covenant that would fall upon the disobedient (23:12-16; cf. Lev. 23:14-33; Deut. 28:15-68). He ended this message by noting God's unfailing consistency. God would bless obedience and punish disobedience.

Joshua's final address to Israel (Josh. 24) took place at Shechem. It was a formal renewal of the covenant that God had made with Israel through Moses. The preamble of his address rehearsed God's faithful election of Israel (24:1-2). The historical section told of God's redemption in detail (24:3-13). The next section called upon Israel to witness and reconfirm her allegiance to God's covenant (24:14-24). The final section tells about Joshua writing and storing the renewed covenant in the "Book of the Law of God" as a witness to the events of that day (24:25-28).

THE CITIES OF REFUGE

West	East
Kedesh in Galilee	Bezer in Reuben
Shechem in Ephraim	Ramoth in Gilead
Hebron in Judah	Golan in Bashan

Some scholars have suggested that the hornets of 24:12 were the sacred symbol of the pharaohs and that the Egyptians had softened up the people of Canaan by fighting against them shortly before Israel's conquest. But God's sending of the hornets was still a future event on the eve of the conquest (Deut. 7:20). See the comments on Exodus 23:28 for another suggestion. The words "You are not able to serve the Lord" (Josh. 24:19) were intended to impress the Israelites with the weight of the responsibility before them. The statement "He will not forgive" was not a general rule (cf. 1 John 1:9), but it is to be understood in the context of certain divine judgment for denying God (Josh. 24:20; cf. Num. 15:30).

Joshua ordered the tribes to convene at Shechem (Josh. 24:1; cf. Deut. 27:4-8, 12-26) for a public reading of the covenant's terms and a renewal of the covenant relationship. Joshua 24:1-28 follows the outline of the ancient treaties between a king and his subjects (cf. Exod. 19–24). See the chart below.

The conclusion of the book of Joshua rounded out the key themes of the books of Genesis through Deuteronomy. Joshua, Moses' successor, died. Joseph's bones found their final resting place in the Promised Land. And Eleazar, a son of Aaron, died. After many years, God had brought Abraham's descendants to the land that he had promised them. The years of wandering had come to a close and the era of the judges was about to begin.

JOSHUA 24 AS A VASSAL TREATY

24:1-2	The Preamble
24:2-13	The Historical Prologue
24:14-25	The Covenant Stipulations
24:26-27	The Deposit of the Covenant

JUDGES

BASIC FACTS

HISTORICAL SETTING

Most of Israel's oppressors of this period were local enemies near the borders of Canaan, for during this time in world history, the large powers of the ancient Near East were not engaged in active domination of Palestine. Egypt's rulers after Amenhotep III were weaker and no longer interested in the control of Palestine. Mitanni, of northern Mesopotamia, was curtailed in strength due to the rise in power of the Hittites under Shuppiluliumas. Assyria and Babylon, farther to the east, did not play a significant role in Palestine at this time. The foreign oppressors that successively attacked Israel were the Mesopotamians, the Moabites, the Canaanites, the Midianites, the Ammonites and, most seriously of all, the Philistines.

AUTHOR

There is no clear indication in the book as to the identity of the author. According to tradition, Samuel was the author, although this tradition is difficult to substantiate. It is known that Samuel was a writer (1 Sam. 10:25), and he may have authored the book. The evidence concerning the date of writing (see below) would indicate that, at least, Judges was written by a contemporary of Samuel. The final editing of the book was completed during the monarchies of David and Solomon.

DATE

The following internal evidences point to an early origin of Judges, sometime during the monarchies of David and Solomon: (1) Judges 1:21 indicates that the Jebusites were still living in Jerusalem at the date of writing. This shows an ongoing Jebusite presence such as is noted in 2 Samuel 24:16, where David purchased the temple site from Araunah the Jebusite. (2) Judges 1:29 declares that the Canaanites were still living in Gezer, which indicates a date of composition prior to when the city was captured by Pharaoh and given as a dowry to his daughter, Solomon's wife (1 Kings 9:16). (3) Judges 3:3 indicates that Sidon, rather than Tyre, was the chief city of Phoenicia, which points to a date of writing around 1040 B.C., prior to Tyre's rise in influence. (4) The reference to the absence of a king in Israel (Judg. 17:6; 18:1; 21:25) implies composition in the early monarchy while the blessings and benefits of the monarchy were in the forefront of the people's minds.

The book of Judges presents a problem of chronology. If all of the terms of office of the judges are totaled, they equal 410 years. However, 1 Kings 6:1 states that only 480 years elapsed between the Exodus and Solomon's fourth year, when he began to build the

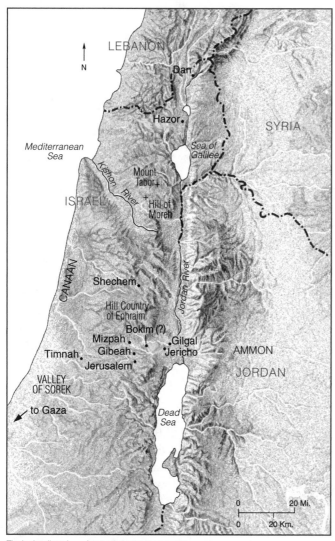

The broken lines (—·—·) indicate modern boundaries.
Copyright © 1986, 1988 by Tyndale House Publishers, Inc.

temple. That leaves only 70 years for the wilderness wanderings, the conquest, the reign of Saul, the reign of David, and four years of Solomon's rule—all of which in reality total 145 years. The 410 year total for the events of Judges is, therefore, about 75 years too long.

The solution to this problem is that many of the careers of the judges overlapped. The judges ruled in their particular separated areas of Israel and could well have given leadership at the same time (Judg. 10:1-5). Judges 10:7ff. implies that Jephthah, who was occupied with the Ammonites to the east of the Jordan River, and Samson, who was concerned with the Philistines on the west, were contemporaries. The period of the judges, then, covers about 325 years from the death of Joshua (around 1375 B.C.) to the anointing of Saul as king of Israel (1050 B.C.).

PURPOSE

The book of Judges was designed to show the bridge between Joshua's conquest and David's monarchy. It shows God's protection of the faithful in Israel and how basic religious and governmental problems were solved by God's anointed king. The book corrects and encourages God's people by (1) showing how bad it was when there was no king to unite and deliver all of Israel; and (2) how good it was now that God had provided a single king bound to God by the Davidic covenant.

GEOGRAPHY AND ITS IMPORTANCE

The book of Judges shows how God allowed enemies from the surrounding regions to defeat the Israelites if they stopped obeying him. Moab to the southeast, Hazor to the north, Midian to the northeast, Ammon to the east, and the Philistines to the west all captured parts of Israel. The nation was being militarily eaten away by the consequences of her sin. The defeats had driven Israel farther up into the central mountain range. The ability of the Israelites to expand down onto the fertile plains and defeat the enemy was directly related to their willingness to change from sin to obedience and to trust God for help.

GUIDING CONCEPTS

JUDGES AS ONE OF THE FORMER PROPHETS

Judges is one of the books of the former prophets (Joshua, Judges, 1 and 2 Samuel, 1 and 2 Kings). For a discussion of the differences between the former and latter prophets, see the introduction to Joshua under *Guiding Concepts*. The book might be viewed as just a series of stories or a history of failures in Israel. But the book should be seen as prophecy—not prophecy that tells the future, but prophecy that exhorts God's people to live better lives and not to repeat the mistakes of the past. No book in the Bible is just history, for all history in the Bible is seen as illustrative of spiritual truth, especially of God's sovereignty over history to bring his salvation to the human race.

The Holy Spirit was given for specific tasks throughout the book (Judg. 3:10; 6:34; 11:29; 13:25; 14:6, 19; 15:14). This relation to the Spirit links back to Deuteronomy 34:9 and Numbers 11:17, 25, 29; 27:18-23. Victory was the mark of the presence of the Spirit. The anointing of the Spirit would eventually focus on the anointed king of Israel in the line of David (2 Sam. 7:12-16) and be fulfilled in the Anointed One, the Messiah Jesus (Matt. 3:16-17; Luke 4:17-21).

THE ILLUSTRATION OF THREE PROBLEMS

The book was designed to illustrate three problems: (1) incomplete conquest; (2) unfaithfulness to God's covenant; and (3) civil chaos.

Incomplete conquest

After the general conquest, there were still Canaanites in the Esdraelon and Aijalon valleys. Their foreign presence had driven wedges that divided Israel into northern, central, and southern sections, and almost totally destroyed Israel's ability to act as a unified whole. Full cooperation between the Israelites was not easy because Israel was not united. That situation was an almost identical reversal of Joshua's strategy during the initial conquest when he first drove a wedge into the center of Canaan and then took the north and south.

Unfaithfulness to God's covenant

The book mentions the sin of the people a number of times (2:11; 3:7-8, 12; 4:1; 6:1; 10:6; 13:1). After such disobedience, war was usually the test for faithfulness and God's means for reminding the people of their responsibilities under the covenant (cf. 2:20-23 and Deut. 8:2; 13:3).

Civil chaos

The problem of civil chaos is noted in the phrase "the people did whatever seemed right in their own eyes," which is linked to the phrase "in those days Israel had no king." These phrases sum up the situation in Israel (Judg. 17:6; 18:1; 19:1; 21:25) and expose two sides to a common problem—the problem of civil chaos. It was the king who would solve the problem of the people doing whatever they wanted. The king would bring an end to the civil and military defeats that came from the people's unfaithfulness to God's covenant.

The king would unite the nation civilly, politically, and religiously. The historical time for that perspective of kingship can only be placed within the reigns of David and Solomon and the framework of the Davidic covenant made in 2 Samuel 7. Although the book covers events that happened before a king arrived in Israel, it was clearly written after a king had begun to rule in Israel. The book looked back to the preking time to show how bad that period had been. This would encourage the readers not to make the same mistakes and it would encourage them to appreciate their present king and to look forward to the fullness of blessing that God would bring through his greater King to come.

TITLE

The Hebrew title of the book is translated as Judges. The name relates to the deliverers of the tribes of Israel following the conquest and until the time that a king ruled in Israel. The book's name makes one think of a law court with a presiding judge, but legal decision was only a part of what the judges in the book of Judges did. The judges were also military leaders, a fact supported by Judges 2:14 and 4:5. The judges also had a special empowering by God to accomplish their civil and military tasks.

BIBLE-WIDE CONCEPTS

THE NEED FOR A LEADER

Judges shows that God's people desperately needed a Spirit-anointed leader. Each time they fell into defeat, God provided a person of his choosing to bring about release. The people who were anointed by God as redeemers and judges throughout this book pointed forward to a time when God would choose his leaders from the single line of Davidic kings under the Davidic covenant's promises (cf. 2 Sam. 7). And that line of Davidic kings pointed to one single Redeemer, Jesus the Messiah. That great King would become the perfect Mediator and Deliverer for mankind; he would be the One who would fulfill the deepest of their needs.

The record of human failure stretches from Genesis to Revelation, but the contribution of Judges is that while repeating the cycle of sin, it also leaves hope for the faithful that God will provide leaders to deliver his people. Judges also emphasizes the power of repentance and the faithfulness of God. Each time God's people repented of their sin, God was faithful to forgive and restore.

PRESSURES FOR CULTURAL CONFORMITY

Judges also contributes to the understanding of how contemporary culture and other religions can bring immense pressure upon the people of God. The battle is with the world system that pressures believers, successfully at times, to reject God. The book of Judges emphasizes that a key problem for Israel was forgetting God's great acts of the past, especially the Exodus from Egypt. The Passover and all of Israel's feasts were designed to keep the people remembering God's great redemptive acts. When they forgot what God had done in the past, they inevitably excluded God from their present. As the Exodus was to the Jew, so the Cross is to the Christian. The faith of believers continually calls them to remember God's great act at the Cross. To forget that would be to loosen their moorings in forgiveness and to compromise their faith through legalistic or lawless living.

NEEDS MET BY JUDGES

The period of Israel's history from Joshua to King David was rough indeed. The Israelites forgot many truths about their past relationship to God through Moses and Joshua. The events of the great exodus from Egypt dimmed, and the religious, cultural, and military pressures of the surrounding countries burned brightly. By the time the book of Judges was written, Israel already had a king, probably David or Solomon, and needed to be reminded of what life was like without a God-anointed leader at the helm. The content and structure of Judges show that its author was answering questions like the following for the people of Israel:

- What are the reasons Israel is defeated so often?
- How can the Israelites end the severe discipline for their disobedience?
- How can the Israelites change their destructive patterns of behavior?
- Why is it good for Israel to have a king?
- What has happened to the covenant since Moses and Joshua died?
- Is God still enforcing his covenant?
- Is God still rewarding and blessing obedience to his regulations and laws?

These questions are not unlike those that Christians are asking today. The "great exodus" provided for believers by Christ's death on the cross took place a long time ago. The pressures of life can be great, but this book reminds all believers, then and now, to appreciate how great it is to have the King of kings in charge of their lives. Cycles of destructive behavior can only be broken by submission to the gracious rule of our Lord and King.

OUTLINE OF JUDGES

I. TWO PROBLEMS NOTED (1:1–3:6)
   A. Incomplete Conquest (1:1-36)
   B. Covenant Unfaithfulness (2:1–3:6)

II. THE PROBLEMS ILLUSTRATED (3:7–16:31)
   A. Othniel (3:7-11)
   B. Ehud (3:12-30)
   C. Shamgar (3:31)
   D. Deborah and Barak (4:1–5:31)
   E. Gideon (6:1–8:32)
   F. Abimelech (8:33–9:57)
   G. Jephthah (10:6–12:7)
   H. Ibzan, Elon, and Abdon (12:8-15)
   I. Samson (13:1–16:31)

III. A THIRD PROBLEM ILLUSTRATED: DOING RIGHT IN ONE'S OWN EYES
   (17:1–21:25)
   A. The Migration of the Tribe of Dan (17:1–18:31)
   B. The Events in the Tribe of Benjamin (19:1–21:25)

JUDGES NOTES

1:1–3:6 TWO PROBLEMS NOTED

Overview: The section of 1:1–3:6 takes the reader from the Israelites' partial victory to their pervasive failures in receiving the Promised Land and ends with their weeping before God (1:1–2:5). Judah and Simeon (1:1-7) had some major victories after the death of Joshua. There were links to Caleb, hero of the wanderings and conquest with Joshua (1:12-15), the family of Moses' father-in-law (1:16), and the sons of Joseph (1:22-29). But victory was only partial (1:27-35). The migration of the tribe of Dan into the hills (1:34) was a preparation for the Danites being mentioned later on in the book (17:1–18:31).

The Lord appeared to the Israelites (2:1-5) and explained why they had not driven out all the Canaanites. They had made covenants with the people of the land whose foreign gods would snare them (2:3). That set up the problems of the book of Judges and also pointed to their solutions: Israel would need a king to help the nation keep covenant faithfulness and provide military might that God would support. There is a flashback in 2:6-10 to the end of Joshua's life noting what happened after his death: Israel as a whole ceased to know God and his acts (2:10).

Judges 2:20-23 continues what was first stated in 2:1-5. Israel did not choose to follow in the ways of Joshua. In order to test Israel's desire to obey God, Joshua did not drive out their Canaanite enemies for them. This is similar to God's testing of Israel in the wilderness to see if they would obey him (Deut. 8:2-3) and to his testing of Jesus in the wilderness (Jesus quoted from Deut. 8:3 in Matt. 4:4). The rough times experienced by the Israelites were designed to expose where their hearts really were when it came to loving God. This is also true of difficulties experienced by believers today. A list of the nations God left in Canaan to test Israel is given in 3:1-6. Again, the purpose of testing was defined (3:4).

1:1-36 Incomplete Conquest

After the death of Joshua, Judah was singled out as having the Lord's presence for victory (1:2). The strength of the Canaanites had been shattered by Joshua during the conquest, but it was the responsi-bility of the tribes to complete the work and flush out remaining pockets of resistance. The law of retaliation (Lev. 24:17-21) was applied to Adoni-Bezek (Judg. 1:6-7). He was receiving the treatment he had given others.

The Israelites captured the heights but could not occupy the valleys, which were controlled by the Canaanites with their iron-reinforced chariots (1:19), or fully take Jerusalem (1:21). Two Canaanite worship centers, Beth Shemesh ("house of Sun") and Beth Anath ("house of Anath"), were allowed to remain (1:33). Anath, the sister and consort of Baal, was a goddess of fertility. That failure to completely drive out the Canaanites constituted disobedience to God's clear command (Exod. 23:33).

2:1–3:6 Covenant Unfaithfulness

In light of the military and religious compromises of Judges 1, the Lord appeared and condemned Israel for her disobedience (2:1-5). Israel's failure to obey God's instructions (Exod. 23:32; 34:12-13) encouraged idolatry and intermarriage with nonbelieving Canaanites (Judg. 2:11-13, 17, 19; 3:5-6; cf. Deut. 7:3; Exod. 34:15-16). When Israel lost a battle, the question that was inevitably asked was "Why?" God had promised Israel the land, but the blessing of full occupation was to be given only on the condition that Israel lived in obedience. Any failure was due to a problem with Israel, not God.

The place they named "Weepers" is "Bokim" in Hebrew (Judg. 2:5). Subsequent history reveals that the Israelites lamented the consequences of their disobedience but did nothing about the cause of their judgment. The parents had not passed on the knowledge of the Lord to their children (2:10).

Baal (2:13) was the son and successor of El, the supreme god of the Canaanite pantheon. Baal, whose name meant "lord," was a fertility god whose domain was the sky. The worship of Baal involved sexual rituals thought to bring productivity to the people and the land. Astarte, or Ashtaroth, was the female counterpart to Baal. She served as a goddess of fertility and war.

The giving over of Israel into her enemies' hands (2:14) was in keeping with the curse of the cove-

ISRAEL'S CYCLE OF SIN AND RESTORATION

Relapse	Israel did evil in the sight of the Lord	3:7
Ruin	God sold them into foreign domination	3:8
Repentance	Israel cried out to the Lord	3:9
Restoration	Deliverance was given through a judge	3:9-10
Rest	The land had peace	3:11
Relapse	Israel returned to evil after the judge's death	3:12

nant (Deut. 28:25), which was still in force even though Moses and Joshua were dead.

The judges functioned as Spirit-empowered deliverers (Judg. 2:16). During times of peace they arbitrated disputes and made decisions regarding judgments. During times of war they led the Israelite army in victory against its enemies.

Israel's cycles of apostasy (2:16-19) always began with a *relapse* into sin, followed by *ruin* and servitude to a foreign power. After crying out to God in *repentance*, the nation would be *restored* through a judge and enjoy a period of *rest*. This cycle, repeated throughout the book of Judges, formed the pattern for Israel's bondage and deliverance. The chart, *Israel's Cycle of Sin and Restoration*, furnishes an example of this often repeated sequence (Judges 3:7-12).

There was clearly a relationship between the living presence of the judge and the people's ability to remain faithful to God. It was as if the people were kept by the judge's spiritual power and leadership.

The presence of the enemy in the land (2:22–3:2) was to test the Israelites' faith in God and their obedience to his commands (2:22; 3:1, 4), as well as to teach them the art of warfare (3:2). God knew the hardness of their hearts. He wanted them to realize their errors and get back to living according to God's way.

3:7–16:31 THE PROBLEMS ILLUSTRATED

Overview: The chart, *Israel's Oppressors and Deliverers*, lists the leaders mentioned in this section of Judges. Although thirteen judges are mentioned, seven receive specific emphasis in illustrating the repeated cycle of sin, repentance, and deliverance. Those seven judges are related to seven episodes that are introduced with the concept of Israel doing evil in the sight of the Lord (3:7; 3:12; 4:1; 6:1; 8:33-34; 10:6; 13:1), and they should receive the most emphasis in studying the book. No specific enemy

was mentioned in relation to the minor judges (Tola, Jair, Ibzan, Elon, and Abdon). Instead, their prosperity before the Lord was established by noting their large families and many donkeys. For each judge, power for deliverance and prosperity marked them off as God's chosen leaders. Concepts like God raising up a judge, or deliverer (3:9, 15; 11:29), the deliverer saving Israel (3:31), and God being present with each judge in a special way (6:16, 34) show that these people point to the great Deliverer, Jesus Christ.

3:7-11 Othniel

Aram, or Mesopotamia (3:8), means "the land between the rivers" and refers to the region of the Tigris and Euphrates rivers. The Hebrew means "Aram of the rivers" and refers to the Aramean territory centered at Damascus. Othniel was Caleb's son-in-law (1:13; cf. Josh. 15:15-17).

The Holy Spirit came upon Othniel (Judg. 3:10), Gideon (6:34), Jephthah (11:29), and Samson (13:25). The Spirit served (1) to empower those judges for their appointed tasks of deliverance, (2) to show that victory came from God's power, and (3) to point toward the future anointed king of Israel and, through him, to the perfect King of kings, Jesus.

3:12-30 Ehud

The Moabites (3:12) were the incestuous offspring of Lot and his oldest daughter (Gen. 19:37). They occupied a territory in Transjordan east of the Dead Sea. Moab was behind the evil of Balak and Balaam (Num. 22–24) and the Midianite idolatry (Num. 25). Jericho (3:13) means the "the City of Palms" in Hebrew. This whole episode is a reminder of the initial conquest of Jericho by Joshua (3:28). Ehud (3:16) was the cloak-and-dagger judge. His message for King Eglon was fatal. The entire story was designed to delight the reader with its intrigue, misunderstandings, and perfect timing.

ISRAEL'S OPPRESSORS AND DELIVERERS

Oppressor	Deliverer	Reference
Mesopotamian	Othniel	3:7-11
Moabite	Ehud	3:12-30
Philistine	Shamgar	3:31
Canaanite	Deborah	4:1–5:31
Midianite	Gideon	6:1–8:32
Civil war	Abimelech	8:33–9:57
Unknown	Tola	10:1-2
Unknown	Jair	10:3-5
Ammonite	Jephthah	10:6–12:7
Unknown	Ibzan	12:8-10
Unknown	Elon	12:11-12
Unknown	Abdon	12:13-15
Philistine	Samson	13:1–16:31

3:31 Shamgar

An oxgoad was a stout stick, often bronze-tipped, used to guide and impel oxen at work (3:31). Shamgar also saved Israel, though the enemy was not mentioned.

4:1–5:31 Deborah and Barak

Joshua had conquered Hazor (Josh. 11:1-15), but the Canaanites rebuilt the city. Jabin was apparently a dynastic title applied to each successive Canaanite king (Josh. 11:1), not a personal name. Deborah (Judg. 4:4) was a prophetess, wife, and mother (4:4; 5:7). Before directing Barak in the defeat of the Canaanites, she served as a judge in settling civil disputes (4:5). The Kishon River (4:13) is a seasonal river that flows northwest through the Jezreel Valley (see introductory map). During the battle, a rainstorm filled the riverbed (5:4), immobilizing the Canaanites' chariots.

Jael's deception and treacherous murder of Sisera need not be justified (4:21). God clearly said the honor of victory would go to a woman (4:9). Israel's victory over Jabin and the Canaanites was commemorated poetically (5:1-31). The key to the meaning of this passage is found in 5:31.

6:1–8:32 Gideon

The story about Gideon shows that not all Israelites had forgotten what God had done for them in the past (2:10). Gideon knew the God of the Exodus (6:13) and wondered why God had ceased doing miracles. Readers today can look back and realize that God's miracles were not happening in Israel at that time because of the sins of the people. But his miracles would appear through his anointed leaders, as Gideon was about to personally discover.

The Midianites (6:1) were descendants of Abraham through Keturah, his second wife (Gen. 25:2). They were a seminomadic desert people who lived south and southeast of Canaan. They had worked together with Moab in the days of Moses to bring Israel into idolatry (Num. 22–25). The Amalekites (Judg. 6:3) were descendants of Esau (Gen. 36:16). They were a nomadic desert tribe that moved about in the northern Sinai and the Negev.

Asherah (Judg. 6:25) was the chief consort of El in Canaanite mythology and served as a mother goddess. (For comments on Baal, see Judg. 2:13.) By his exploits, Gideon acquired a new name, Jerub-Baal (6:32), meaning "let Baal defend himself."

Gideon's fleece (6:36-40) should not serve as a pattern to believers for determining the will of God. God's directive already had been given, and victory had been promised (6:14, 16, 36). Gideon had difficulty believing what God told him and was testing God to find out if he meant what he said (6:16-17). This account shows how God often works patiently through people like Gideon—people with little faith.

The troops were reduced (7:2) to prevent Israel from boasting in victory instead of giving God the glory he deserved. Gideon's victory was followed by tragic failure (8:27-30). He fashioned a golden ephod that became an object of worship (8:27), and he also acquired many wives who gave birth to his seventy sons (8:30). Gideon rightly understood that God alone was to be King over the nation (8:23). Surprisingly, Gideon named one of his sons Abimelech, which means "my father is king." That son, who was born of Gideon's concubine, would become ruler of the nation by murdering all but one of his brothers.

8:33–9:57 Abimelech

The judges demonstrated the great things that God could do for Israel through his anointed leaders. This story, by contrast, reveals the evils that could come to Israel through wicked leadership—in this case, the leadership of Abimelech. This story reveals the importance of following God's own Spirit-anointed leaders.

Baal-Berith (8:33) means "Baal of the covenant," whose shrine was at Shechem (9:1-4). The Israelites forgot that God was the only God of the covenant.

Jotham's fable proclaimed from Mount Gerizim (9:7-21) revealed the true character of Abimelech, Gideon's worthless son. The ignoble death of Abimelech (9:50-57) at Thebez, ten miles northeast of Shechem, illustrates the principle of divine retribution (9:56-57). An upper millstone (9:53) was the large upper stone that was moved back and forth on a larger stone when grinding corn. It was about ten inches long and easily gripped.

Tola in Ephraim and Jair in Gilead (10:1-5) probably served contemporaneously. The Hebrew word translated "after" or "followed" can also be translated as "with" (10:3).

10:6–12:7 Jephthah

The story of Jephthah begins once again with Israel's sin and its resulting oppression causing the nation to cry out to God. God's mercy caused him to lift the nation out of its misery (10:16). He delivered the Israelites through his servant Jephthah, a man who, like Gideon, remembered God's great acts in the Exodus and conquest (11:12-27). The thrust of Jephthah's message was "What God gives remains given!" And Jephthah acted on that belief.

The Israelites worshiped (10:6) the gods of Canaan (Baal and Ashtoreth), Aram (Hadad and Rimmon), Sidon (Baal Melqaret), Moab (Chemosh), Ammon (Molech), and Philistia (Baal-zebub and Dagon). The Ammonites (10:7) were the descendants of the incestuous relationship between Lot and his youngest daughter (Gen. 19:38). They occupied the Transjordan territory north of Moab. Jephthah attempted unsuccessfully to negotiate a settlement with the Ammonites (Judg. 11:12-28)

The three hundred years mentioned in 11:26 is an important figure in calculating the date of the Exodus. Jephthah's judgeship began at about 1096 B.C. Three hundred years earlier would be the approximate date of Joshua's conquest (around 1406 B.C.). The forty years in the wilderness prior to the conquest would put the Exodus at 1446 B.C.

Jephthah's rash vow (11:30-31) is the subject of considerable debate. Two common views on how Jephthah fulfilled his vow are: (1) he offered his daughter as a burnt sacrifice, or (2) he devoted his daughter to a life of service at the tabernacle. The most straightforward rendering of the Hebrew text suggests that his daughter died as a burnt sacrifice. But if this is so, why did the daughter bewail her virginity (11:37) rather than her impending death? Neither view is without problems, although the first view is preferred since it is supported by the most straightforward rendering of the text.

Because of certain dialectical changes in the Hebrew language, the Ephraimites could not pronounce "sh" but said "s" when forced to say Shibboleth (12:4-6).

12:8-15 Ibzan, Elon, and Abdon
The mention of large families and many donkeys implies wealth and prosperity from the hand of God. The enemies and events relating to these three judges are not specifically mentioned.

13:1–16:31 Samson
Overview: The story of Samson is comprised of the announcement of his birth and call as a lifelong Nazirite (13:1-23), his ill-fated marriage (13:24–14:20), and his revenge (15:1-20). In addition to Samson's wife, the story ends with the mention of two more women, a prostitute (16:1-3) and Delilah (16:4-31). All three of the women in Samson's life were Philistines, the arch-enemies of Israel in the land of Canaan. Samson illustrates the uneasy and ultimately fatal alliance that the Israelites had with one of the nations that they should have destroyed when they entered the Promised Land. This Spirit-filled leader, a man with great potential, inspired great victory, but, paradoxically, he also suffered great defeat because of his own foolishness. The great, though limited, victory that Samson did attain was the goal toward which every king of Israel would strive, but a goal which Jesus alone would attain.

13:1-23 SAMSON'S BIRTH ANNOUNCED, THE NAZIRITE VOW EXPLAINED
Samson was to be a Nazirite to God from the womb (13:5). Accordingly, he was not to drink wine, cut his hair, or touch a dead body (cf. Num. 6:1-6). Manoah's response (Judg. 13:21) indicates that he viewed the angel of the Lord as actually an appearance of God himself.

Samson was set apart by God to begin the deliver-ance of the Israelites from the Philistines (13:1, 5). The Philistines were Indo-Europeans from the Aegean Islands who migrated eastward under the pressure of the Dorian Greeks. The main invasion took place around 1168 B.C. They were repulsed by the Egyptians and eventually settled on Israel's southern coastal plain. They controlled the coastal plain north to Mount Carmel and the Jezreel Valley to the Jordan River.

13:24-16:31 SAMSON'S STRUGGLES
Zorah and Eshtaol (13:25) are situated in the Sorek Valley that pierces the hill country about fifteen miles west of Jerusalem. Timnah (14:1) is about four miles west of Zorah, Samson's hometown. In helping himself to the tasty treat of honey (14:8-9), Samson violated his Nazirite vow that prohibited contact with a dead body. Samson carried the massive Gaza gate forty miles uphill to Hebron (16:3). (See the introductory map for the location of Samson's deeds.) He had so much potential, but it was wasted in his pursuit of pleasure.

Dagon (16:23) was the chief god of the Philistines. He was probably a fertility deity associated with grain production, the prominent agricultural pursuit in the Philistine territory.

The Philistine temple discovered at Tel Qasile illustrates the situation in which Samson found himself (16:26). The roof of the main hall was supported by two pillars close enough together for a large man to grasp both of them. Even though Samson judged Israel for twenty years and caused the Philistines a great deal of trouble and humiliation (16:30-31), he failed to remove the Philistine threat from the nation.

17:1–21:25 A THIRD PROBLEM ILLUSTRATED: DOING RIGHT IN ONE'S OWN EYES
Overview: Judges 1–16 illustrates the problems of an incomplete conquest and covenant unfaithfulness. Judges 17–21 illustrates the problem of civil chaos. That problem is highlighted by the repeated phrase "the people did whatever seemed right in their own eyes" (17:6; 21:25). But that problem is linked to another repeated phrase: "In those days Israel had no king" (17:6; 18:1; 19:1; 21:25). When there was a king in Israel, civil order and peace were enforced. The book of Judges showed its readers how bad it was before God ordained a king in order to help them realize how good conditions were under the king. Acceptance of the leadership of God's anointed king foreshadowed mankind's hope for a future ruler, the King of kings, Jesus.

17:1–18:31 The Migration of the Tribe of Dan
The idolatry of Micah and the migration of the tribe of Dan must be placed early in the period of the

judges because Joshua 19:47 mentions this move and Joshua was written while Rahab was still alive (Josh. 6:25). Without a king, extensive religious apostasy like that of Micah took place in Israel (Judg. 17:6-13). The period of the judges was a time of loose morals, openness to many different gods and religions, and political chaos.

Bethlehem (17:7) was not one of the cities designated for the Levites (Josh. 21:9-42). The absurdity of Micah's situation (Judg. 17:13) is emphasized by the fact that he anticipated God's blessing because he had a genuine Levite to serve in his idolatrous shrine.

The powerful Philistines had not permitted the Danites to occupy the coastal plain (18:1), forcing them up into the mountains. Cramped between Judah and Philistia, the tribe of Dan searched for a new territory. Micah's gods (18:26) were not worth fighting over, for he could always make some more. Laish, far to the north, was captured and renamed Dan (18:29). (See introductory map for Dan's location.) From that time on, Dan was a center for idolatrous worship (1 Kings 12:29).

Some ancient versions read "Gershom, the son of Moses" (Judg. 18:30). Thus, the priests at Dan were descendants of Moses, not Aaron. The editorial note "until the time of the captivity of the land" refers to the later conquest of Galilee by Tiglath Pileser III in 733 B.C. (2 Kings 15:29). This comment shows that editorial changes were made in the book of Judges after the time of the Assyrian conquest.

19:1–21:25 The Events in the Tribe of Benjamin

The section of 19:1–21:25 outlines a civil war among the sons of Israel. The perversions at Gibeah (19:1-30) led to civil war and the destruction of many of the males of the tribe of Benjamin (20:1-48). The section ends with a strange scheme to allow the remaining males of Benjamin to find wives from among the Israelites (21:1-25).

A concubine (19:1) was a secondary wife, often acquired by purchase or as a war captive. In antiquity, when a marriage produced no heir, a barren wife would present a slave concubine to her husband to produce offspring. Although the practice was not condoned, the concubines were

protected under the Mosaic law (Exod. 21:7-11). Since concubines were expensive to maintain, they were considered to be a sign of wealth and status.

Jebus (Judg. 19:10) is the Canaanite city that later became Jerusalem. Gibeah (19:12), located four miles north of Jerusalem, became Israel's capital in Saul's time. The moral intentions of the men of Gibeah (19:22) match those of the men of Sodom (Gen. 19:5). According to Oriental custom (Judg. 19:23-24), a host had to protect his guests from harm, whatever the cost. The demands of hospitality and the low status of women in this period of apostasy help to explain this horrendous proposal.

The dismemberment and distribution of the concubine's body to the twelve tribes (19:29) constituted a warning concerning the nation's deep immorality as well as a challenge to make things right.

The two military defeats of Israel by Benjamin drove Israel to prayer and fasting in an earnest attempt to discern God's will (20:26). The rock of Rimmon was about four miles east of Bethel (20:45). The Israelites soon regretted their rash oath concerning Benjamin (21:1, 7, 18).

Jabesh Gilead (21:8), an Israelite city in Transjordan, was to be punished for failing to participate in the discipline of Benjamin. Years later, King Saul, a Benjamite, would rescue this city from the Ammonites (1 Sam. 11:8-11). As a result, the inhabitants of this city would show great bravery by coming to Beth Shan and removing the bodies of Saul and his sons from the city gate and burying them (1 Sam. 31:11-13).

Since the daughters of Shiloh were taken rather than given, the Israelites did not consider themselves in violation of their rash oath (21:19-23). Shiloh was situated in the hill country of Ephraim about twenty miles north of Jerusalem.

Moral decisions in the period of the judges were made on the basis of whatever seemed to suit the situation, not on God's unchanging character. The result was political, moral, and religious chaos. This situation was partially remedied through the Davidic kings and has been perfectly remedied through the Son of David, Jesus the Messiah.

RUTH

BASIC FACTS

HISTORICAL SETTING
The events of the book happened sometime during the period of the judges (1375–1050 B.C.) according to Ruth 1:1. Judges 21:25 is the key to the historical setting of the book: "In those days Israel had no king, so the people did whatever seemed right in their own eyes."

The period of the judges was a time of political, religious, and moral chaos. The political chaos is seen in the cycles of apostasy that resulted in oppression by foreign powers. The religious chaos is seen in the person of Micah, who set up his own house priest instead of going to Shiloh to worship (Judg. 17). The moral chaos is illustrated in the perversions recorded in Judges 19. The book of Ruth must be seen in contrast with the book of Judges. The book of Ruth is an oasis of fidelity in a time of idolatry, sin, and infidelity.

AUTHOR
According to rabbinic tradition, Samuel was the author of the book of Ruth. While this is possible, it is unlikely since the concluding genealogy implies that David was well known at the time the book was written. The book is anonymous and the author is unknown.

DATE
The book of Ruth appears to have been written during David's reign (1010–970 B.C.). It could not have been written earlier than the time of King David since he is mentioned by name (Ruth 4:22), unless the genealogy was added later. Had the book been written later than the time of David, the name of his famous son Solomon probably would have been listed in the record of Ruth's descendants.

PURPOSE
The book's historical purpose was to relate an episode in David's ancestry that accounted for the introduction of non-Israelite blood into his family line. The theological purpose is to show the place of the spirit of the law over the letter of the law, illustrating that the exception to the law is based on faith and loyalty to God.

GEOGRAPHY AND ITS IMPORTANCE

The distance from the mountains of Moab to the city of Bethlehem is around forty miles as the crow flies. But on the ground the trip involved a descent and ascent of over four thousand feet. The journey of Naomi and her daughter-in-law Ruth first involved descending from Moab into the Arabah Valley, a descent of over four thousand feet from the valley's eastern rim to its floor, the lowest spot on the earth, 1,300 feet below sea level. Then the pair had to cross the thirteen miles of dry valley floor, ascend over four thousand feet up the valley's western side and make their way through the wilderness of Judea to the little village of Bethlehem. But the journey of that obscure pair of widows prepared the foundation of both a geographical and a spiritual bridge between the Gentile nation of Moab and God's nation of Israel. Ruth became a great-grandmother of King David and part of the family line leading to Jesus the Messiah. In David, and perfectly under Christ, Jews and Gentiles are unified, and when Christ's kingdom is completed, all nations will live at peace.

GUIDING CONCEPTS

THE SOVEREIGNTY OF GOD

God's sovereignty is so obvious in the book of Ruth that the author uses subtle irony when he writes that "as it happened, she found herself working in a field that belonged to Boaz" (2:3). It was within God's sovereign plan and purposes that Ruth would return to Bethlehem with Naomi, that Ruth would come to the field of Boaz, that Boaz was a near relative, that the nearest kinsman would be unwilling to redeem, and that Ruth would become the great-grandmother of David and be an important link in the genealogy of Jesus Christ (Matt. 1:1-17).

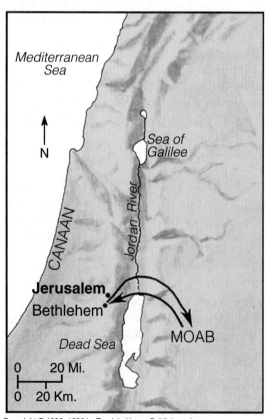

THE KINSMAN-REDEEMER

The qualifications and functions of the kinsman-redeemer are illustrated in the person of Boaz, who is typical of the Lord Jesus Christ. The kinsman-redeemer had to be a blood relative to have the right of redemption, even as Christ was a blood relative of man through the Virgin Birth (John 1:14; Phil. 2:5-8; Heb. 2:14-18). The kinsman-redeemer had to have the resources to purchase the forfeited inheritance, even as Christ had the resource of his own precious blood (1 Pet. 1:18-19). The kinsman-redeemer also had to have the resolve to redeem, even as Christ laid down his life of his own volition (Mark 10:45; John 10:15-18). The book of Ruth is one of the most instructive Old Testament books concerning the redemptive work of Christ.

PRAYER
The book records the prayers of Naomi (Ruth 1:9; 2:19-20), Boaz (2:4, 12; 3:10), and the people of Israel (2:4; 4:11-12, 14-15). God answered those prayers, giving Ruth rest and a fine son, and giving Boaz great blessing.

BIBLE-WIDE CONCEPTS

DAVIDIC COVENANT
The book of Ruth serves as an important background to the covenant God made with David in 2 Samuel 7. Some historical parallels are as follows: famine forced Elimelech to go to Moab, just as Israel had been forced to go to Egypt in the time of Joseph; Ruth aligned herself with Naomi and the true God and went to Canaan (1:15-16; 2:12), just as the mixed multitude had aligned itself with Israel when they left Egypt for Canaan. Rahab, the prostitute from Jericho, was married to Salmon and gave birth to Boaz. Boaz's mother was a Canaanite and his wife was a Moabite. What pervaded the international lineage of David and, ultimately, Jesus Christ, was the universal promise to Abraham: salvation by faith in God, no matter what one's race.

ABRAHAMIC COVENANT
The book contributes to the overall message of the Bible: the promise of worldwide redemption. The source of that redemption is God's promises to Abraham. He was promised a land, offspring, and blessing from God. Abraham also was promised to be a blessing to all the nations of the earth (Gen. 12:1-3). Although God started with an ethnic group from Abraham, he intended to include all ethnic groups in Abraham's blessings.

The book of Ruth contributes to the Abrahamic promise in two ways: (1) the background of David, to whom the kingdom was promised, is given and, more to the point, (2) the Gentile element in the great promises to David is noted. Ruth was from Moab, a nation of Gentiles, not Israel.

THE SPIRIT OF THE LAW
The book of Ruth shows the place of the spirit of the law over the letter of the law. The spirit of the law is seen in the action of Boaz, who went beyond the letter of the law, which said that the widows and foreigners could glean in the fields (Lev. 19:9-10). Boaz not only invited Ruth to glean among the sheaves, but he also required his workers to drop grain for her (Ruth 2:15-16). The spirit of the law also is seen in the ancestry of David. The law said that no Moabite nor any of his descendants, even to the tenth generation, could enter the assembly of God (Deut. 23:3). However, David was the third-generation descendant of Ruth, and yet he became king of Israel, built an altar, and sacrificed to God (2 Sam. 24:25). While God's moral law must never be violated, the book of Ruth illustrates a legitimate exception to the ceremonial law when it is based on faith and loyal love for God.

NEEDS MET BY RUTH

The Bible gives little detail of King David's birth or childhood. It picks up his life's story just before Samuel anointed him as king. But there was one part of David's background that held a special importance for God's people: his great-grandparents. The importance was in the Moabite background of Ruth, David's great-grandmother. Also important was the time in which she lived—the frequently corrupt period of the judges, when there was no king and everyone did what was right in his own eyes, not God's. God wanted his people to know that his promises to Abraham concerning making a great nation were not ethnically limited.

The great nation God had in mind included both Jews and Gentiles. The entrance into that nation was by faith, not physical birth. Israelites could not claim a right to God's Abrahamic promises of blessing simply because they were Jewish. They needed faith and obedience to God. Likewise, even a Gentile from the despised Moabite nation could be honored by God on the basis of allegiance to God. When Israel was in the splendid period of King David's rule, God caused the book of Ruth to be written to remind the nation of how anyone stood before God: by faith and obedience alone. The structure and content of Ruth show that its author was answering questions like these for his readers:

- Is it true that King David had a Moabite among his ancestors?
- What is God's attitude toward receiving Gentiles, especially Moabites, into the nation of Israel?
- Were conditions all bad during the time of the judges?
- Which is more important, faith in God or a pure family lineage?

For the Christian, knowing that Ruth was of Moabite descent and that the way to God's blessings was equally accessible to all ethnic groups by faith is just as potent now as it was in King David's day. Throughout time, God's people have had a way of forgetting the simple truth that they stand before God in his grace alone, not in their own self-righteousness, ethnic background, or social standing. Through its beauty and simplicity, the book of Ruth reminds believers again of that single and critical truth.

OUTLINE OF RUTH

I. NAOMI RETURNS TO BETHLEHEM WITH HER DAUGHTER-IN-LAW RUTH (1:1-22)

II. BOAZ CARES FOR RUTH DURING THE BARLEY HARVEST (2:1-23)

III. RUTH UPHOLDS THE LAW BY SEEKING BOAZ AS HER KINSMAN-REDEEMER (3:1-18)

IV. BOAZ MARRIES RUTH: THEY BECOME GREAT-GRANDPARENTS OF DAVID (4:1-22)

RUTH NOTES

1:1-22 NAOMI RETURNS TO BETHLEHEM AS A WIDOW WITH HER DAUGHTER-IN-LAW RUTH

The book of Ruth is named after the principal character of the narrative, Ruth, a Moabitess who, after the death of her husband, journeyed to Bethlehem with her widowed mother-in-law. The four major scenes in this dramatic story take place outdoors—on the road (Ruth 1:7-18), in the field (2:8-16), at the threshing floor (3:6-13), and at the gate (4:1-12). The lawless period of the judges (Judg. 21:25) provides the setting for the book of Ruth. Famine in a land of marginal rainfall is not uncommon, but for Israel it was a sign of God's judgment (Lev. 26:3-4, 19-20; Deut. 28:12, 23-24). The names of the children (Ruth 1:2)—Mahlon, meaning "sickly," and Kilion, meaning "failing"—reflect the circumstances in Judah resulting from famine.

Marriage to Moabite women (1:4) was a drastic step, for it banned ten generations of one's descendants from participation in Israel's worship (Deut. 23:3). Naomi referred (Ruth 1:11) to levirate marriage (cf. Deut. 25:5-10), which required a man to marry the childless widow of his deceased brother. The purpose of this institution was to preserve the family name and property. Naomi recognized God's chastening in her life (Ruth 1:20), and when she returned from Moab she asked not to be called Naomi, meaning "pleasant," but Mara, meaning "bitter." Barley (1:22) was harvested in the early spring (March–April).

2:1-23 BOAZ CARES FOR RUTH DURING THE BARLEY HARVEST

Ruth was qualified to glean (2:2) from the fields after the harvest because she was a widow and a stranger (Lev. 19:9-10; Deut. 24:19). "As it happened" (Ruth 2:3) she came upon the field of Boaz. God's sovereign hand is clearly seen in leading Ruth to the field of this kinsman. Such God-honoring greetings (2:4) would have been very unusual during this period of the judges. The book of Ruth is an oasis of fidelity in a time of Israel's idolatry, sin, and infidelity.

The poetic imagery "under whose wings" (2:12) depicts the shelter and protection that God provides (cf. Matt. 23:37). Ruth had found a place of refuge in Israel's God. The kindnesses of Boaz (Ruth 2:14-16) went far beyond what the law required. An ephah (2:17) was approximately the same amount as a bushel, which was an astounding amount for a day's gleaning.

Naomi disclosed that Boaz was a near kinsman or family redeemer (2:20). As such, he could be expected to function as a protector of family rights, protecting property (Lev. 25:25) and persons (Deut. 25:5-10).

3:1-18 RUTH UPHOLDS THE LAW BY SEEKING BOAZ AS HER KINSMAN-REDEEMER

The threshing floor (Ruth 3:2) was a hard surface where the grain was trampled by animals in order to break the kernels from the stalks of grain. Winnowing involved separating the grain from the tiny broken pieces of the stalk (the chaff) after threshing. The mixture was tossed into the air, and the evening breeze would blow the lighter material away from the grain.

Boaz was going to sleep at the threshing floor to protect his grain (3:4). The uncovering of the feet of Boaz (3:7) was a symbol of Ruth's submission; it alerted her kinsman-redeemer to the fact that she sought his protection. In light of the culture and the high moral character of Ruth and Boaz, there was nothing improper about this procedure. The words "spread the corner of your covering" (3:9) functioned as a marriage proposal that Boaz was only too happy to consider. The word "covering" is the translation of the same Hebrew word that in 2:12 refers to the "wings" of God. Boaz took precaution against scandal (3:14), which showed that he already was functioning as Ruth's protector.

4:1-22 BOAZ MARRIES RUTH: THEY BECOME GREAT-GRANDPARENTS OF DAVID

The town gate (4:1) customarily served as a meeting place where legal transactions were authorized and judicial decisions were made. The offer of the opportunity to purchase Elimelech's land at first looked attractive to the nearest kinsman-redeemer (4:4). He assumed that this was the limit of his obligation. But then he refused to purchase it because he did not want to invest in property that would not ultimately be his (4:6). He also may have hoped to inherit this property and avoid paying for it (Num. 27:9).

By removing his sandal (Ruth 4:8), a symbol of land possession, the nearest kinsman permanently renounced his claim on the property. The marriage of Ruth to Boaz (4:10) was similar to a levirate marriage. But due to the fact that Boaz was the brother of Elimelech (4:3) rather than Mahlon, it differed slightly from the law of Deuteronomy 25:5-10. The reference to Judah and Tamar (Ruth 4:12) recalled a situation in which the levirate responsibility was not honored (Gen. 38). Obed (Ruth 4:17), Naomi's legal grandson, was the child of Mahlon according to Jewish law (4:10) and the child of Boaz by actual paternity (4:12). Boaz and Ruth became King David's great-grandparents (4:21-22).

1 & 2 SAMUEL

BASIC FACTS

HISTORICAL SETTING

The religious scene

The nation of Israel was at a religious low point. Even the priesthood was corrupt (1 Sam. 2:12-17). Samuel's sons, who served as judges, were dishonest and corrupt (8:1-3), and the people of Israel refused to listen to the voice of their prophet Samuel (8:19). Yet in the midst of that corruption, there was a remnant of righteous people who were faithfully worshiping and sacrificing to the Lord at Shiloh (1:3).

The ark of the covenant was at Shiloh (4:4), but it was taken from there to the battle of Ebenezer, where it was captured by the Philistines (4:11). The ark was later returned to Beth-shemesh (6:19) and then to Kiriath-jearim (7:1). Eventually it was brought to Jerusalem by David twenty years later (2 Sam. 6). (See introductory map.)

The political scene

Politically, the book begins with the last judge, Samuel. The people of Israel refused to listen to Samuel and insisted on having a king to rule over them (8:19). Samuel anointed Saul as Israel's first king (10:1), and he later anointed David (16:6-13). Gibeah was Saul's fortress and capital (10:26; 15:34). David reigned approximately seven years in Hebron before he moved his capital to Jerusalem after being appointed king over all of Israel (2 Sam. 5:3-5). At that time Israel began to move into its greatest religious, social, political, and military period.

The international setting during the united monarchy of David and Solomon was one of transition. The great empires of the ancient world were in a state of weakness that allowed Israel to develop nationally without external restraint. Assyria was in decline, and the Hittites of Asia Minor had passed into insignificance. Egypt was weak and involved in internal conflict.

The Philistines, having recently migrated from the Aegean Islands and Asia Minor under the pressure of the Dorian Greeks (around 1168 B.C.), constituted Israel's main threat. They had a monopoly on the manufacture and use of iron tools and weapons, which gave them a decided military and economic advantage and kept Israel on the defensive (1 Sam. 13:19-22).

The threat of the Philistines was an impetus to the nation to unite under the leadership of Samuel, Saul, and David. The weakness of the great international powers made possible the expansion of the kingdom under David until Israel reached its peak of military and political power.

AUTHOR

The author of 1 and 2 Samuel is not known. According to Jewish tradition, Samuel, Nathan, and Gad all had a part in the recording of the events of the book of Samuel. This theory is suggested by 1 Chronicles 29:29.

DATE

Parts of the book were written after Samuel died (1 Sam. 25:1; 28:13-20) and even after the division of Solomon's kingdom (see 1 Sam. 27:6, where the phrase "kings of Judah" implies the post-Solomonic division of the southern kingdom of Judah from the northern kingdom of Israel). The fall of Samaria in 722 B.C. is not mentioned, so it is reasonable to date the book somewhere between 931 and 722 B.C. The events cover the time from the ministry of Eli to the close of David's reign. Taking 931 B.C. as the date of the division of the kingdom after Solomon, the dates for Israel's first three kings are as follows: Saul reigned forty years (Acts 13:21) (1050–1010 B.C.); David reigned forty years (2 Sam. 5:4) (1010–970 B.C.); and Solomon reigned forty years (1 Kings 11:42) (970–931 B.C.).

Samuel's date of birth may be determined by the fact that he had sons old enough to be judges in Beersheba (1 Sam. 8:1-2) before Saul began to reign in 1050 B.C. That places Samuel's birth around 1100 B.C., just prior to the outbreak of Ammonite and Philistine oppression and the birth of Samson.

PURPOSE

The historical purpose of the book of Samuel was to provide an official account of Samuel's ministry as well as of the rise and development of the monarchy and the kingdom of Israel from the days of Saul through most of the reign of David. The theological purpose was to show God's sovereignty over the theocratic kingdom as he set up, deposed, and commanded the rulers of Israel. The heart of that sovereignty was God's commitment to his people through the covenant he made with King David (2 Sam. 7). That covenant is so crucial to understanding the message of 1 and 2 Samuel that its basic aspects are presented in the *Bible-Wide Concepts* section rather than being covered later in comments on 2 Samuel 7.

GEOGRAPHY AND ITS IMPORTANCE

The books of 1 and 2 Samuel were originally one unbroken book. Taken in its original unity, the book of Samuel begins with the ark at Shiloh and ends with the purchase of the temple site in Jerusalem. The geographical movement from Shiloh to Jerusalem demonstrates the bookwide struggle to get two things into their proper place in Jerusalem—the ark and the king. Both the ark and the king were key ingredients for establishing God's rule over the nation. The ark represented the center of the temple and its priestly duties. The king had a special father-son relationship with God and became the director of the entire nation's prosperity or defeat. The enemies of Israel only had military victory when the people of Israel were experiencing spiritual defeat. In the book of Samuel, four surrounding nations were at war with Israel: the Philistines to the west, the Ammonites to the east, the Moabites and Edomites to the southeast, and the Amalekites to the south.

GUIDING CONCEPTS

THE ORIGINAL UNITY OF FIRST AND SECOND SAMUEL

The books of 1 and 2 Samuel are included in the former prophets. (See the discussion of the significance of the former prophets in the introduction to Joshua.) The main point is that the books are not dry ancient history. They are full of pointedly arranged stories designed to cause readers to think about making their lives more pleasing to God.

The two books of Samuel were originally inspired as one book. The same was true of the books of Kings. Later, the translators of the Greek Old Testament combined the books of Samuel and Kings into a complete history of the kings of Israel. The translators divided each book into two parts. The four parts were called Reigns A, B, C, and D.

Those who translated the Bible into Latin kept the four-part division of the Greek Old Testament but called the first two parts 1 and 2 Samuel and the third and fourth parts 1 and 2 Kings. These divisions have been used in the English translations as well. (See the chart below.)

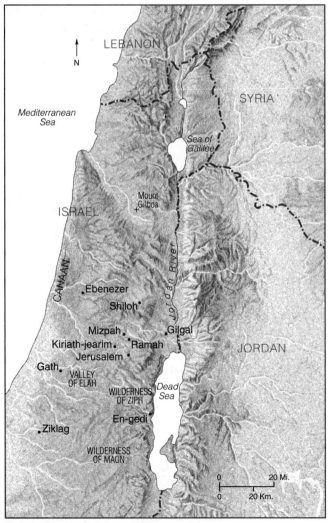

The broken lines (— ·— ·) indicate modern boundaries.
Copyright © 1986, 1988 by Tyndale House Publishers, Inc.

Why is all this important? The original unity of Samuel is vital to maintain for understanding the original and God-given message of the book. The importance of this will become clear after looking at the book's structure. This *Concise Bible Commentary* will present all of these books in light of their original unity. Thus, the books of 1 and 2 Samuel will be viewed as a single unit.

THE STRUCTURE OF SAMUEL

Although God's great covenant with David and its implications pervade 1 and 2 Samuel both in content and structure, the narrative of the book begins with the prophet Samuel. Samuel did not simply function as a transitional figure between the judges and the kings. He also functioned as the prophetic voice God used to announce his views regarding Israel's desires for a king. Then, after God had endorsed the monarchy,

Samuel served as the wise spokesman from God who anointed the first two kings. The aborted reign of Saul, the first king anointed by Samuel, was not simply a mistake. The reign of Saul revealed what God demanded of Israel's kings and his attitude toward rebellion; it illustrated what it meant to have God's loving-kindness withdrawn. Because of the special covenant that God later made with David, the second king anointed by Samuel, God's loving-kindness would never depart from David's line.

SAMUEL AND KINGS IN THE EARLY TRANSLATIONS

Original	Greek Old Testament	Latin and English
	Reigns A ——<	1 Samuel
Samuel —————		
	Reigns B ——->>	2 Samuel
	Reigns C ——->>	1 Kings
Kings —————		
	Reigns D ——->>	2 Kings

The reign of David showed how God's demands for obedience were placed within a gracious commitment to continue with David's line even though it would fall into gross sin. Although the book of Samuel is superficially about the kings of Israel, at its heart it is about a God who was more concerned about bringing in the rule of the Messiah-King than about taking away his loving-kindness from dynasty after failed dynasty. The end of the book of Samuel (2 Sam. 21–24; remember, it was originally one book) reveals the centrality of the Davidic covenant to the content and structure of the book. The author arranged the material to show the reality of human failure, while also recognizing the glory of God's promises to David:

National Judgment: Saul's Sin, David's Entreaty (2 Sam. 21:1-14)
   Military Victory through Mighty Men (2 Sam. 21:15-22)
      Song of Praise for the Davidic Covenant: Past Victory (2 Sam. 22:1-51)
      Song of Praise for the Davidic Covenant: Future Security (2 Sam. 23:1-7)
   Military Victory through Mighty Men (2 Sam. 23:8-39)
National Judgment: David's Sin, David's Entreaty (2 Sam. 24:1-25)

The above structure shows the perspective and basic themes of the book of Samuel: (1) When the king obeyed, God blessed the land; (2) God's covenant with David brought military peace and security; (3) The Davidic covenant brought to remembrance God's blessing in the past and provided hope for the future.

BIBLE-WIDE CONCEPTS

KINGSHIP IN ISRAEL

From Genesis on, God had promised to bring about a kingly rule in Israel. Kings would come from the line of Abraham (Gen. 17:6, 16; 35:11). Judah would have the scepter of rule (Gen. 49:10). The entire nation was to be a kingdom of priests (Exod. 19:6). A scepter would arise from Israel to defeat her enemies (Num. 24:7, 17). The king would be of God's choosing and subject to his rules (Deut. 17:14-20). Gideon argued that the

Lord, not a king, should rule over Israel (Judg. 8:22-23). While a king would indeed arise in Israel, these quoted texts present an ambivalent attitude toward kingship. It was seen as something that would happen, but also as a thing that could have some negative consequences for the nation.

THE DAVIDIC COVENANT

Abrahamic promise

Second Samuel 7:12-16 records the Davidic covenant, which amplifies and confirms the seed promises of the Abrahamic covenant (Gen. 12:1-3). Abraham was promised a land, a nation, a divine blessing, and an international influence for good (Gen. 12:1-3). The Davidic covenant took up the nation and blessing aspects and focused them on one individual—the king of Israel. The Davidic covenant promised David an eternal house, an eternal throne, and an eternal kingdom, guaranteeing that the right to rule over Israel would always belong to one of David's descendants (cf. Luke 1:31-33).

Mosaic Law and the temple

The king would become the catalyst for maintaining the temple worship, keeping the Mosaic covenant's laws, and guiding the nation into personal and international blessings. As the king went, so went the nation. Under a good king, there was good for the nation. But history shows that most of the kings were bad and ultimately led the nation away from God's blessings. Only Jesus, the Son of David, would be the One to bring God's people into a reign of perfect obedience and blessing.

The house of God

Just before God announced that he would make a covenant, David offered to build God a house. The tabernacle still housed the ark of the covenant, and David wanted to have a more splendid structure for Israel's worship (2 Sam. 7:1-3). God made a counteroffer to build a house for David, a royal house with a lineage that would go on forever (2 Sam. 7:4-17). The seed of Abraham now had a new focus: the royal line of David. The role of Israel among the nations also was refocused. The king would now be the mediator between Israel and the nations.

Permanent loving-kindness

Without a doubt the heart of the book's purpose is to illustrate the greatness of God's promises made to David in the Davidic covenant. That was accomplished by showing the difference between King Saul and King David. The covenant with David said that God would not take away his loving-kindness as he had taken it away from Saul (2 Sam. 7:15). God's loving-kindness in that case was equivalent to his gracious presence that enabled Saul or David to be king, God's anointed leader. God took his loving-kindness away from Saul, but he would not do so with David's royal line.

The most important section of the Davidic covenant is in 2 Samuel 7:14-15. David's son would be a son of God (7:14). God and the king would have a special relationship of father-son intimacy. If the son committed sin, he would be disciplined by his heavenly Father. But God's loving-kindness would never depart (2 Sam. 7:15).

This permanent loving-kindness is the seal of God's commitment to David's line and its ultimate victorious kingdom. Saul forms the contrast as one who lost God's loving-kindness regarding kingship. God withdrew his loving-kindness, the special anointing of his Spirit for kingship, from Saul because of his sin. That would not be the case with David's line. Even though David and his descendants would sin, God would still be committed to them on the basis of his promise (2 Sam. 7:14). In contrast to God's relationship with Saul, the book of Samuel shows how the relationship mediated by the Davidic covenant was powerful and enduring and continued even despite David's sins. Although David's descendants might sin, resulting in severe discipline, God's loving-kindness would never depart.

Why was David allowed to be king even though his sins far outstripped those of Saul? Because God was committed to bringing in a Ruler for Israel and the world through his promises to David, not on the basis that any son of David was sinless (2 Sam. 7:14). Only one Son of David would be sinless—Jesus the King, to whom all the Davidic promises pointed. All the others would, in one way or another, fall prey to human failure.

The hope for the Messiah

The book of Samuel illustrates the source of messianic hope for a King to rule the world. Saul was not all bad, and David was not all good. The point of the book is that God alone is good and powerful enough to bring in the universal rule of Jesus, the King of his own choosing. David recognized that eternal and wonderful gift of promise as he praised God in 2 Samuel 7:18-29. The promise was for more than a line of kings. It was for a worldwide outpouring of blessing mediated by a future King of Israel. That great promise was fulfilled in Jesus the Messiah, the anointed King, not only of Israel, but of the whole world.

NEEDS MET BY SAMUEL

When the book of Samuel was written, God's anointed king had brought God's people great pleasure and great pain. The exhilarating first part of David's reign brought military victories and civil prosperity. The last part of David's reign brought defeat and civil war. The king had sinned greatly and everything seemed to be falling apart. What had happened to those great divine promises of a line of godly kings ruling forever in might and peace? The book of Samuel was written to explain the origins of God's chosen kings and also to show where the real potency lay in keeping those kings on the throne—in the sovereign covenant between God and David, not in the perfections or imperfections of the human kings. The book of Samuel answers a number of important questions for the children of Israel who were under the rule of David and Solomon.

- What was the history of God's work from the judges to the kings?
- Why did Israel need a king?
- Was it a bad thing for Israel to want a king in the first place?
- How committed was God to David and his lineage?
- What was God's ultimate goal in preserving the line of David?
- Would God someday reject David for his sin just as he had rejected Saul?
- In what way was the king a mediator for the entire nation?

The book of Samuel shows how deeply committed God was to the idea of kingship. God proved his commitment by maintaining a long series of earthly kings from Saul, eventually stretching to Jehoiachin. That mixed line of success and failure framed the goal of all earthly kingship—the ultimate coming of Jesus the King. The kings of Israel failed, but Jesus was perfect. The kings lost the link of mediation between their subjects and God, but Jesus brought the perfect mediation of king and priest combined. For Israel, as the king went, so went the people. The same is true now for all who are the people of the King of kings.

OUTLINE OF SAMUEL

I. GOD PROVIDES A SON TO LEAD ISRAEL (1 SAMUEL 1:1–2:11)
   A. Samuel Is Born and Dedicated (1:1-28)
   B. Hannah's Prayer (2:1-11)

II. GOD JUDGES RELIGIOUS GREED AND SUPERSTITION (2:12–7:17)
   A. Offerings Eaten in Greed (2:12-17)
   B. Judgment Predicted on Eli's Sons (2:18–3:12)
   C. Superstition Rejected (4:1–6:18)
   D. True Religion Restored (6:19–7:17)

III. GOD CHOOSES HIS KINGS (8:1–31:13)
   A. Saul (8:1–15:35)
   B. David (16:1–31:13)

IV. DAVID GROWS STRONGER (2 SAMUEL 1:1–10:19)
   A. Lament for the House of Saul (1:1-27)
   B. Conflict with the House of Saul (2:1–4:12)
   C. Establishment of the House of David (5:1–10:19)

V. DAVID'S HOUSEHOLD EVIL (11:1–20:26)
   A. Adultery and Murder (11:1–12:31)
   B. Revenge (13:1-39)
   C. Insurrection in David's Kingdom (14:1–20:26)

VI. DAVID AS A MEDIATOR AND PRESERVER (21:1–24:25)
   A. National Judgment: Saul's Sin, David's Entreaty (21:1-14)
   B. Military Victory through Mighty Men (21:15-22)
   C. Song of Praise for the Davidic Covenant: Past Victory (22:1-51)
   D. Song of Praise for the Davidic Covenant: Future Security (23:1-7)
   E. Military Victory through Mighty Men (23:8-39)
   F. National Judgment: David's Sin, David's Entreaty (24:1-25)

FIRST SAMUEL NOTES

1:1–2:11 GOD PROVIDES A SON TO LEAD ISRAEL

Overview: The climax of the section 1 Samuel 1:1–2:11 is Hannah's prayer of exaltation in 2:1-11, where she praises God for his care for the lowly, his judgment on the proud, and his blessings on his king. The focus from the outset is on Samuel's relationship to God's future work through his kings. In Scripture, God often displayed his new works of redemption by choosing women to bear children in a miraculous way: Sarah (Gen. 21:1-2), Rachel (Gen. 30:22-23), Manoah's wife (Judg. 13:2-3), Hannah (1 Sam. 1:19-20; 2:21), Elizabeth (Luke 1:13), and Mary (Luke 1:26-31). God showed that nothing stops his purposes, not even barren wombs, and that he is the source of these promised sons, seen most perfectly in the virgin conception of Jesus. In the birth of Samuel God provided a leader and intercessor for Israel.

1:1-28 Samuel is Born and Dedicated

Ramathaim Zuphim (meaning "the heights of the Zuphite") is the longer name for "Ramah" (1:1, 19), located about five miles north of Jerusalem. Elkanah lived in Ephraim, but he was a Levite by lineage (1 Chron. 6:26, 33). Although polygamy (1:2) was practiced in the biblical period, it was at variance with God's original plan for marriage (Gen. 2:24) and never resulted in a happy homelife (1 Sam. 1:6). Shiloh (1:3) was the location of the tabernacle (Josh. 18:1). "Lord Almighty" (1 Sam. 1:11; 17:45) is a military designation referring to God as the One who commands the armies of Israel and the angelic armies of heaven (1 Kings. 22:19). The term emphasizes God's sovereignty and omnipotence.

Hannah promised (1 Sam. 1:11) that her son would be dedicated to lifelong Levitical service (Num. 4:3; 8:24-26) and would be a lifelong Nazirite (Num. 6:2-6). The son's name, Samuel (meaning "name of God" or perhaps "heard of God," 1 Sam. 1:20), served as a continual reminder of God's mercy toward those who call upon his name. Hebrew children were normally weaned at two to three years of age (1:23). The words "giving him" (1 Sam. 1:28) literally mean "made him over to"; they speak of an irrevocable giving up of the child to the Lord.

2:1-11 Hannah's Prayer

Hannah's prayer was a psalm of praise about the incomparability of God. Based on his greatness, there should be no arrogance (2:3) but rather humility. Humility is submission to God's ways. Notice the upcoming bad example of Saul as he insists on his own way rather than listening to God. Humility is the essential quality for God's servants, seen most perfectly in the humble Son of Man, Jesus. The king would be the instrument of judgment against all evil.

The Hebrew word for "grave" (2:6) refers to the dark, shadowy, silent place of the dead. Both the righteous and the wicked will go there at death (Gen. 37:35; Ps. 9:17).

2:12–7:17 GOD JUDGES RELIGIOUS GREED AND SUPERSTITION

2:12-17 Offerings Eaten in Greed

Why were Eli's sons not immediately judged? Nadab and Abihu sinned at the tabernacle and were instantly judged (Lev. 10:1-11). God's delay of his judgment upon Eli's sons provides a longer example of God's sovereign plans to show himself holy whether by instant or delayed judgment (see

1 Sam. 2:25). To despise the offering was to make the wrong use of it and actually to despise the Lord (cf. Deut. 31:20). They despised the link of sacrifice between God and the human race. They knew what the food was for, but they did with it as they pleased. Their immorality approached the immorality of the rituals of pagan cultic prostitution (1 Sam. 2:22).

Samuel's faithfulness contrasts with the unfaithfulness of Hophni and Phinehas. As priests, Eli's sons knew about God, but they did not know him in a personal way. Their disobedience would lead to their deaths (2:25).

2:18–3:12 Judgment Predicted on Eli's Sons

A tunic (2:18) was a close-fitting, sleeveless vest that extended to the hips and was worn almost exclusively by priests, especially when officiating before the altar (Exod. 28:6-14; 1 Sam. 2:28).

The prophecy of 2:35-36 indicates that God intended to transfer the high priesthood back to the line of Eleazar in the person of Zadok, the faithful priest of David during Absalom's revolt (1 Kings 2:26-27, 35).

The initial meeting between the Lord and Samuel was to give Samuel the prophecy of the death of Eli's sons (1 Sam. 3:1-18). A summary statement confirmed God's presence with Samuel and his renewed presence at Shiloh (3:19-21). "One end of the land to the other" (3:20), a distance of about 150 miles, became an expression denoting the northern and southern extremities of the Israelite nation.

4:1–6:18 Superstition Rejected

4:1-22 THE ARK IS TAKEN AND ELI'S SONS ARE JUDGED

The Israelites treated the ark of the covenant like a goodluck charm. They did not pray to find out why they had been defeated, as Joshua had done at Ai (Josh. 7:6-11). They assumed the problem was with the Lord, not themselves (1 Sam. 4:3). The Philistines, on the other hand, simply plucked up their courage, entered the battle, and emerged victorious with the ark. Aphek (4:1; NT "Antipatris") was a strategic Canaanite city on the coastal plain northeast of modern Tel-Aviv. It controlled the travel route that passed between the headwaters of the Yarkon River and the hill country of Ephraim.

The child born to Phinehas's wife was named Ichabod (4:21), meaning "no glory," for the loss of the ark meant the absence of glory in Israel (4:22). Archaeological excavations at Shiloh indicate that the city was destroyed around 1050 B.C., perhaps by the Philistines after they captured the ark (cf. Jer. 7:12-14). (See the introductory map for Shiloh's location.)

5:1-12 THE LORD GOD TREATED AS ONE GOD AMONG MANY

The Philistines treated the God of Israel as one god among many (1 Sam. 5:1–6:18). Ashdod (5:1) was a Philistine city located on the Mediterranean seacoast about twenty-two miles south of Joppa. There was a close relationship between Dagon (5:2) and Baal. In ancient literature, Baal is sometimes referred to as "the son of Dagon," Philistia's fertility deity. The Hebrew word translated "tumors" (5:6) is derived from the verb "to swell" and may refer to boils. In view of the rats that ravaged the land (6:5), these sores may have been symptomatic of bubonic plague.

Why did the ark not help Israel when she had it? Why did it hurt the Philistines after they defeated Israel? Because God had two messages to deliver. To Israel, God was saying that he was to be treated as holy. Disobedience had resulted in the absence of his power to deliver. To the Philistines, God was proving his awesome character—a character unique and far above those of their imaginary gods. In both cases, the ark proved to be the sign of God's presence, either to bless or to judge. Moving the ark from city to city was the Philistines' attempt to see if they could find a place where God would not be powerful. It was similar to Balak's movement from mountain to mountain to try to move out of the area of God's power (Num. 23:13, 27). However, God was powerful everywhere and thus proved that he was not just one god among many.

Gath (1 Sam. 5:8), another of the five Philistine cities (6:17), was located twelve miles southeast of Ashdod. Ekron (5:10), probably located at Tell Miqne, was six miles north of Gath (see introductory map).

6:1-18 THE RETURN OF THE ARK

The fact that the ark returned to Israel in the unattended ox cart showed the Philistines that the plagues they experienced were not by chance (6:9) but from the Lord. The Philistines believed in sympathetic magic, that is, the removal of evil or disaster via models of their sores (6:4-5). By sending away the golden models, they hoped to remove the disease from their land. These expensive articles also served as a sacrifice, intended to placate the angry God of Israel.

6:19–7:17 True Religion Restored

6:19-21 RESTORED THE HARD WAY

The return of the ark began a restoration of true religion in Israel. The first step in this restoration was taken the hard way at Beth-shemesh (6:19-21). God showed the Israelites that he was still holy and powerful enough to judge those whose curiosity and irreverence caused them to peek into the ark (6:19). Apparently this was a violation of Numbers 4:20.

The question of 6:20 cuts both ways. God's holiness applies both to believers and unbelievers. God is consistent and therein lies the believer's security and way of blessing. There is never a context for irreverence.

The ark was a spiritual work (Exod. 35:30-31; 31:3) and was built by a person gifted spiritually and artistically by God (37:1-9). It was the place where God met with his people (25:22). See 2 Samuel 6:6-11 for a reminder, twenty years later, of God's holiness.

7:1-17 RESTORED BY THE WAY OF OBEDIENCE

The second step in the restoration of true religion in Israel was taken by following the way of obedience. Guarding the ark (1 Sam. 7:1) meant protecting it from theft and protecting the Israelites from potentially fatal curiosity. As a result of their obedience, the nation moved from repentance (7:6) to victorious battle. Samuel gathered Israel for a prayer meeting at Mizpah, seven miles north of Jerusalem (see introductory map). Having won the victory on their knees, they went out and won the battle. The image of victory is overlaid with the image of Samuel offering a burnt sacrifice during the actual battle (7:10). The stone (7:12) was named Ebenezer, meaning "stone of help," as a memorial of God's deliverance of his people (see introductory map for Ebenezer's location). Amorites (7:14) is a general term for the original inhabitants of Canaan (Gen. 15:16; Josh. 7:7).

8:1–31:13 GOD CHOOSES HIS KINGS

8:1–15:35 Saul

Overview: The background for this section is found in Deuteronomy 17:14-20. In 1 Samuel 8 the surface reason for wanting a king was the failure of Samuel's sons to judge rightly (8:5). God had always provided a leader for his people—from Moses, to tribal leaders and judges, to Samuel. The difference in having a king as a leader was one of style, in this case, conformity to the nations around them (8:5). And therein lay the problem. The real reason was the people's rejection of the invisible God as their King (8:7). They wanted an earthly king to fight their battles for them, just as if God did not already do that.

First Samuel 8–15 focuses on Saul's reign as king. The people insisted on having a king even though Samuel told them a king would oppress them (8:17-19). The selection and anointing of Saul as king took place against the background of his journey to find his father's lost donkeys (9:3; 10:16). But the heart of this section can be seen in God's gracious choice of Saul as king, contrasted with Saul's less than satisfactory response to the honor God had bestowed upon him.

The Lord clearly chose Saul (9:15-17; 10:24).

Saul had an initial victory over the Ammonites (11:1-13) that ended with a renewal of the kingdom celebration at Gilgal (11:14-15). Samuel spoke pointed remarks to the people concerning their wrong desire to have a king and, in spite of that desire, he also emphasized God's unceasing commitment to Israel (12:1-25). Saul disobeyed the Lord by not waiting for Samuel to offer the sacrifice (13:1-4). Then Saul acted foolishly concerning Jonathan and was contradicted by the people (14:1-52). Saul's second act of disobedience, concerning the spoils taken from the Amalekites, brought the final split with Samuel as well as God's regret for making Saul king (15:1-35).

But why did God allow this "false start" with Saul rather than going straight to David in the first place? This section on Saul prepares the reader for the reign of David in four significant ways: (1) The people's desire for a king was a mistake, but it was a mistake through which God would deliver his promised blessings. (2) Kingship would, on a human level, ultimately fail. (3) The choice of Israel's kings was up to God alone. (4) The nation's well-being was dependent on the obedience of the king. The failure of Saul's rule prepares the reader for the success of David's. However, David's success was based on God's covenant with him, not his obedience.

8:1-22 ISRAEL'S REQUEST FOR A KING

The people's request for a king showed that they thought their problem was an organizational one. They failed to recognize that their basic problem was one of sin. Samuel, like Eli, may have been too involved in his ministry to deal with his family, and God was dishonored as a result (8:3). Conformity to the ways of unbelievers (8:5, 20) was displeasing to the Lord and indicative of spiritual decline. God intended for Israel to ultimately have a king, but he was not pleased with their self-centered motivation. Nevertheless, he allowed the people to have their desire.

9:1–13:23 SAUL'S FIRST FAILURE AS KING

9:1–10:16 Saul is anointed and endued with the Spirit of God.
The term "seer" (9:9, from "to see") points to the receptive aspect—a servant of God's ability to perceive God's will. The term "prophet" points to the seer's ability to communicate. The place of worship and sacrifice was located on a hill or artificial platform (9:12). The custom of worshiping at high places was essentially Canaanite (Deut. 12:2-5), but Israel used such facilities to worship God before the construction of the temple. For example, Solomon worshiped at the high place at Gibeon (1 Kings 3:4).

Anointing involved a consecration or a setting apart for service (10:1). It was a religious act that established a special relationship between God and the king who served as his representative and ruler over the people. Before any engagement with the Philistines, Saul was to meet Samuel at Gilgal, where Samuel would offer sacrifices of burnt offerings and fellowship offerings to God (10:8). Saul did not obey Samuel's orders (13:8-14). Casting lots to answer questions is also seen in Joshua 7:14 where the phrase "the Lord will point out the guilty clan" refers to casting lots to select the clan of God's choice (cf. 1 Sam. 10:20-22; 28:16 where casting lots is also implied). The Bible describes, but does not command, the practice of casting lots. In the Old Testament, casting lots seems to have been primarily connected with priestly ministry and the use of the Urim and Thummim. For a New Testament setting for drawing lots, see Acts 1:26. Saul's hometown of Gibeah, three miles north of Jerusalem, became the first capital of the Israelite monarchy (10:26).

10:17–11:15 Saul is publicly confirmed as king.
Jabesh-gilead (11:1), east of the Jordan River in the territory of Manasseh, was under siege by Nahash, whose name means "snake." The morning watch, which was just before dawn, (11:11) was the last of the night watches (Lam. 2:19; Judg. 7:19; Exod. 14:24-27; Mark 6:48). They attacked while the Ammonites were still asleep. Barak (12:11) is also known as Bedan (NASB; KJV) which may be a scribal error for the name Barak of Judges 4–5 or possibly Abdon (Judg. 12:13, 15).

12:1-25 Samuel's farewell address.
Samuel focused on the essentials in his farewell speech. He got to the heart of the nation's problem in desiring to have a king. They had forgotten God, the One who had delivered them throughout all of their history (12:1-12). To emphasize the severity of asking for a king, God sent thunder and rain (12:18-19). In spite of the people's mistake, if they and the king would obey the conditions of the Mosaic covenant, then God would remain with them. The king himself would not be the solution to Israel's problems, because he would not be above the conditions of the Mosaic covenant. For both king and people the way to blessing remained the same: obedience to God (12:24-25). God's love and faithfulness had not changed.

13:1-23 The disobedience of Saul.
Saul's disobedience is related in 13:1-23, which presents the first of three foolish acts of Saul. Here he disobeyed God's orders for sacrifice. In 1 Samuel 15 he disobeyed God's order for not keeping any spoils of war. Between those two failures, in 1 Samuel 14, he put the nation under a foolish oath. These three actions form a contrast with the great and wise first acts of David and Solomon, the kings to come.

There is an obvious textual difficulty in 13:1. Originally it probably read "Saul was one and [thirty or forty?] years old when he began to reign, and when he had reigned two years over Israel, . . ." The age of Saul in this passage is impossible to know for sure since the various ancient texts disagree. The figure of 3,000 chariots in 13:5 is given as 30,000 in some translations (cf. NASB and KJV), a number which is excessively large (13:5). Some versions of the Greek and Syriac Old Testament read 3,000.

The events of 10:8–13:8 cannot be compressed into seven days. The agreement had been made two years earlier that, prior to any engagement with the Philistines, Saul would meet Samuel at Gilgal for sacrifice and worship. Samuel's delay was a test of Saul's faith and obedience. The Philistine monopoly on iron and metal-working craftsmen (13:19-23) continued until the time of David (1 Chron. 22:3).

14:1-52 SAUL'S FOOLISH ORDER
Here "ephod" is used instead of "the Ark of God" (1 Sam. 14:18), perhaps in light of the statement in 1 Samuel 7:2. Beth-aven (14:23; meaning, "house of evil") is a purposeful corruption of the name Bethel (meaning, "house of God"; cf. 1 Kings 12:26-33). On eating meat with the blood (1 Sam. 14:33), see Leviticus 17:10-14. Saul expanded his kingdom to the south (Edom), east (Moab and Ammon), north (Zobah), and west (Philistia).

15:1-35 SAUL'S DISQUALIFYING FAILURE
The Amalekites (15:2) fought against Israel at Rephidim (Exod. 17:8-13) and were placed under divine judgment by the Lord (Deut. 25:19). Note Saul's pious reasons for his disobedience in 1 Samuel 15:13, 20-21. God began to show how Saul, through his disobedience, was rejected from the kingship, preparing the way for David's anointing.

This sequence of Saul's rejection is the first feature of the "Dynastic Defense," which runs from 1 Samuel 15 through 2 Samuel 8 and outlines the reasons why the rule of David, the new king, was legitimate. Such a defense would be especially important in the case of a king like David, who founded a new dynasty and could have been charged with usurping the throne. The features of this defense included: (1) the disqualification of the preceding ruler (1 Sam. 15); (2) the ability of the successor to lead and rule as demonstrated by his military achievements (1 Sam. 17); (3) the new king's leniency on political foes (1 Sam. 24, 26); (4) the king's interest in religious matters (2 Sam. 6–7); and (5) the record of kingdom expansion as evidence of divine blessing (2 Sam. 8).

In 15:11 God does not change his mind (cf. 15:29; James 1:17). Rather, God's regret is an expression of sorrow over Saul's sinful rebellion (cf. Gen. 6:6). The "Glory of Israel" (1 Sam. 15:29) is a unique term for God, emphasizing his constancy and endurance.

16:1–31:13 David
Overview: This long section was designed to show how God preserved David from attempts on his life by Saul and foreign leaders and how faithful David was in trusting God to vindicate and avenge the wrong that was done to him. That faith contrasts with Saul's self-assertive reliance on his own wisdom and military might. The essence of what God wanted from a king was a patient trust in God's own power and timing. David absolutely resisted taking the throne by his own scheming or according to his own schedule. He waited for the Lord even at the cost of exile, hardship, and personal loss. David is a fine example of the righteous sufferer who patiently waits for exaltation in God's own time. As such, he is a type of Jesus, the perfect righteous Sufferer. In this light, read Philippians 2:1-18.

16:1-23 ANOINTED AT BETHLEHEM, BROUGHT BEFORE SAUL
David was anointed by Samuel, and he played the harp to soothe Saul's torment. The Lord did not suggest deception (1 Sam. 16:2), but he gave Samuel official sacrificial business to do in Bethlehem. While there, Samuel would be able to anoint David. Saul's mental torment (16:14) may refer to demonic attack or influence. Perhaps God appointed a demon to torment Saul in order to drive the king to repentance. David's appointment as Saul's armor-bearer (16:21) probably took place after he killed Goliath, but it is recorded here because it fits with the theme of his entrance into royal service. The physical anointing with oil was symbolic of the anointing with the Holy Spirit (16:3, 6-7, 12-13). This activity of the Spirit for leadership was seen in the events of Numbers 11:24-30 and throughout the book of Judges. Here the anointing is specifically for kingship and symbolizes God's special enablement of David to be king. The spiritual presence of God for the king was the essence of the love spoken of in 2 Samuel 7:15, the love that departed from Saul.

17:1–18:9 THE VICTORY OVER GOLIATH
Goliath's taunting was a new low for the nation of Israel. One man blocked the entire army of God, an army that had seen entire nations run before it in fear. The Israelites viewed the situation only in human terms, much like their forefathers had viewed with fear and faithlessness the giants in the land (Num. 13:26–14:10). Goliath was 9 feet, 9 inches tall and wore a coat of armor weighing 125 pounds; his bronze javelin weighed 17 pounds (1 Sam. 17:4-5). But the heart of this story is David's confession in 17:45-47. Outward physical appearances were nothing when compared with the power of the unseen God. David relied not on

Saul's armor but on his own proven abilities (17:39-40). Above all, he remembered what was truly important (17:45). The victory would become a witness to the world of who God was. David's conquest over Goliath revealed the power that one faithful man could possess—the man with the kind of heart God looked for (13:14; 16:7). In 17:55-58 Saul knew David from his contact in the court (16:18-23), but he needed to know his father's name to reward the family for the victory (17:25).

When Saul became David's enemy and began his initial persecution of him, David escaped two attempts on his life. Saul is described in the terms of pure jealousy (18:1-9). Note the mentions of what Saul was thinking (18:11, 17, 21). His jealousy issued in his making two attempts to murder David: first by hurling his spear at him (18:11), and then by requesting David to kill one hundred Philistines (18:25). Note the gradual growth of Saul's hatred for David (18:9, 12, 15, 29).

19:1-24 FOUR LIFESAVING EVENTS FOR DAVID
Jonathan successfully interceded with Saul for David (19:1-7). But later David again escaped Saul's spear when it was thrown at him (19:8-10). Then Michal helped David in his escape from Saul's plan for his assassination (19:11-17). The Holy Spirit prevented four attempts by Saul and his men to kill David from succeeding (19:18-24). The Spirit controlled the words and actions of Saul and his men, who spoke God's words instead of doing evil deeds. This section shows that the split between David and Saul was all caused by Saul, for David wanted peace within Israel.

20:1-42 SAUL'S HATRED SOLIDIFIES
Jonathan told David that he would find out Saul's feelings about him at the New Moon Festival (20:12-13). This was a sacrificial meal that had both religious and civil significance (Num. 10:10; 28:11-15). The peace between David and Jonathan contrasts with Saul's hostility. From this point on David was a fugitive and outcast with regard to the royal court.

21:1-22:23 THE TRAGEDY AT NOB
David went to Nob, a priestly community located just one mile north of Jerusalem. He planned to meet there with his band of men (cf. Matt. 12:3). David and his men ate the consecrated bread, or showbread, which was reserved for the priests (Exod. 25:30). Psalms 34 and 56 have their background in this encounter.

The priests at Nob were slain because Saul thought they had conspired with David against him (1 Sam. 22:12-19). While their deaths (22:17-19) were a partial fulfillment of the prophesied judgment on Eli's house (2:27-36), Saul was nevertheless responsible for this condemnable act. The cave of Adullam (22:1) may have been the background

of Psalms 57 and 142. The "stronghold" (Hebrew, *mesudah*) (1 Sam. 22:5) is probably a reference to Masada, the mountain fortress that towers 1,320 feet above the Dead Sea. On 22:9, see Psalm 52:1.

23:1-29 TWO TOWNS BETRAY DAVID
The Lord delivered David from Saul at Keilah, and David fled to the wilderness where he was delivered again from Saul. Keilah (23:1) was situated near the border of Philistine territory, about three miles south of Adullam. The hill country of Ziph (23:14) surrounds the city of Ziph, about four miles southeast of Jerusalem (see introductory map). Arabah (23:24) means "wasteland." Jeshimon means "desert" or "waste" and refers to the desolate wilderness southeast of Hebron.

24:1-26:25 THREE "SPARINGS"
The section of 24:1-26:25 focuses on three events in which people's lives were spared.

First, David spared Saul's life (24:1-22). Note David's care for the Lord's anointed (24:5, 10; cf. 26:9, 11, 23; 29:1-11). That was leading up to Saul's death in 31:1-13. When Saul died, his death was in no way connected to David. This section also contains two prophecies of David's kingdom by Saul (24:20; 26:25).

Second, David was spared from performing an act of rash vengeance against Nabal by the wisdom of Abigail (25:1-44). Abigail stopped David and thus protected him from possible retaliation by Nabal's relatives. God cares for his own, keeping them "secure in his treasure pouch" (25:29). David's growing number of wives (25:43-44) marked the beginning of his royal harem, which was in violation of Deuteronomy 17:17.

Third, David again spared Saul (1 Sam. 26:1-25; cf. 26:9, 11, 23). When David spared Saul's life in the camp, Saul again foretold David's future victory. En Gedi (24:1), a lovely freshwater oasis surrounded by desert, was located on the western shore of the Dead Sea. David's experience in the cave (24:3) may have provided the background for Psalms 57 and 142. David trusted God to remove Saul from the kingship rather than taking matters into his own hands (1 Sam. 24:10). David expresses concern that to be driven from the land of Israel would be the equivalent of abandoning the worship of the true God (26:19). Whether Saul was sincere or not in confessing that he had sinned (26:21), David recognized the king's mental instability and declined the invitation.

27:1-31:13 DAVID'S EXILE AMONG THE PHILISTINES
David pretended to be loyal to the Philistines (27:1-12), but he deceived them by destroying their cities. Gath (27:2), a Philistine city (6:17), was situated twelve miles east of Ashdod. Ziklag (27:6) was situated on the Philistine coastal plain about fifteen miles northwest of Beersheba (see introductory

map). The sixteen months (27:7) David spent in enemy territory prepared him for later Philistine wars by acquainting him with the geography of Philistia. The "south of Judah" (27:10) refers to the dry country at the southern end of Israel.

Saul sought a word from God regarding his battle against the Philistines (28:1-25). In 1 Samuel 28–31 the focus of the narrative shifts back and forth between David and Saul. David is presented as the victorious and anointed one, while Saul is the failing and rejected one.

The results of Saul's visiting the medium at Endor were to affirm David as king and to confirm Saul's death (28:7-19). The removal of mediums and psychics was in keeping with the law (28:3; cf. Exod. 22:18; Lev. 19:31; Deut. 18:9-13). The Philistines were camped in the Valley of Jezreel at Shunem, a city located at the foot of the Hill of Moreh, while the Israelites were camped five miles to the south at Mount Gilboa (see introductory map). For Urim see the discussion on Exodus 28:30. The term "medium" (1 Sam. 28:7) literally means "a mistress of a ghost." Mediums consult the dead to determine the future. This medium practiced her forbidden profession at Endor, located between the Hill of Moreh and Mount Tabor.

Is the appearance of Samuel to be interpreted as a psychological experience, demonic impersonation, trickery, or genuine? The text says it was Samuel, and the message was clearly from God (28:16-19). Perhaps this event is akin to the appearance of Moses and Elijah on the Mount of Transfiguration (Matt. 17:3).

God delivered David from the dilemma of having to fight Israel or being slain by the Philistines for treason. David was spared from fighting God's anointed (1 Sam. 29:1-11). He defeated the Amalekites and showed justice to his troops. The Amalekite attack was a further consequence of Saul's failure to carry out God's command (15:2-3, 10-19). David's generosity (30:26-31) won him the support of the citizens of Judah who were later to name him king (2 Sam. 2:1-4).

Saul and his sons were killed in battle (1 Sam. 31:1-13). Their bodies were taken to Beth-shan, located at the junction of the Jezreel and Jordan valleys, and were hung on the wall by the city square (cf. 2 Sam. 21:12). The men of Jabesh Gilead had not forgotten Saul's kindness to them in the past (1 Sam. 11:1-11). They removed their bodies and gave them an honorable burial.

SECOND SAMUEL NOTES

1:1–10:19 DAVID GROWS STRONGER
Overview: The many events of this section make two central points: (1) David committed no deceit or treachery to gain his kingdom. He acted with compassion and justice. That forms a stark contrast with other people such as Joab, Rechab, and Baanah, who committed murder for revenge or favor with the king. (2) God blessed David with loyal subjects and military victory. All of that provided the context for the establishment of God's covenant with David in 2 Samuel 7. David dealt with attempts to overthrow his rule, defeated the Philistines, secured a place for the ark, and finally was given an eternal covenant of blessing.

1:1-27 Lament for the House of Saul
1:1-16 THE AMALEKITE'S STORY
The Amalekite's story was a fabrication (see the true account in 1 Sam. 31:4-5). He must have come across Saul's body on the battlefield and taken his crown and bracelet to substantiate the lie. The event highlighted what has been proved throughout 1 Samuel—that David honored the Lord and in no way would harm Saul, the Lord's anointed.

1:17-27 DAVID'S LAMENT FOR SAUL AND JONATHAN
The Book of Jashar (1:18) is also mentioned in

Joshua 10:13 and appears to have contained poetry about Israel's military heroes. The Book of Jashar itself has not been found. Presumably, the original readers of the book of Samuel had access to the Book of Jashar, which was used to give support to the facts in Samuel. The facts of Samuel were well supported by other contemporary documents. Although the contemporary support for Samuel, the Book of Jashar, has disappeared, the book of God's choice and revelation remains.

How could David speak so well of Saul after all that Saul had done to him? David viewed Saul from the standpoint of all the good that Saul had accomplished in Israel and of his previously high position before the Lord. David left judgment up to God and gave honor where it was due. The word "hills" (2 Sam. 1:19) refers to Mount Gilboa (cf. 1 Sam. 31:8). The key phrase "How the mighty heroes have fallen" (2 Sam. 1:25, 27) expresses the burden of the lament.

2:1–4:12 Conflict with the House of Saul
2:1-32 ABNER AND JOAB'S FIRST CONFLICT
David settled in at Hebron, but Abner, Saul's commander of Israel's army, led a military attempt to make Saul's son Ish-Bosheth king of the northern part of Israel. That led to an initial defeat of Abner's forces by Joab, David's commander. Abner,

with the tribe of Benjamin's support, retreated after killing Joab's brother. Benjamin was the tribe to which Saul belonged. This functions as an example of the resistance David encountered to his becoming king over all Israel; it is summarized in 3:1.

Hebron (2:1), located in the Judean hills nineteen miles south of Jerusalem (see introductory map), served as David's capital during the first seven and a half years of his reign (2:11). The name Ishbosheth (2:8) means "man of shame." This is a deliberate twisting of the original name Eshbaal (meaning "Baal lives") in light of his demise. The contest between champions (2:12-17) on behalf of the opposing armies took place at Gibeon (el-Jib), six miles north of Jerusalem. The pool with its steps has been excavated and can be seen today.

3:1-39 JOAB MURDERS ABNER
David's marriage to the daughter of Talmai (3:3), king of Geshur, probably sealed an alliance between the two kings. Marriage alliances between royal houses as a means of concluding treaties and cementing relationships between nations were common in the ancient Near East. But David's multiple marriages violated Israelite law (Deut. 7:3; 17:17). The kings of Israel were to depend on God for help, not on alliances with foreign rulers.

Abner vowed to help make David king over all Israel (2 Sam. 3:9-10) and began by making unifying speeches before the Benjamites and David's subjects in Hebron (3:17-19). Abner was slain in Hebron, a city of refuge (Josh. 20:7), where not even a blood avenger could slay a murderer without a trial (2 Sam. 3:22-27; cf. Num. 35:22-25). The death of Abner is presented in such a way as to confirm again that David did not resort to murder to gain the kingdom (2 Sam. 3:28, 37).

4:1-12 DAVID JUSTLY ELIMINATES HIS OPPOSITION
The reference to Mephibosheth (4:4), a living descendant of Saul, lays the foundation for 2 Samuel 9. Ishbosheth was "innocent" (4:11) in that he was not guilty of any wicked deed or crime. He had merely assumed the throne upon Saul's death at the encouragement of Abner. Again, David was shown to be righteous and fair as he built his kingdom by justice, not treachery.

5:1–10:19 Establishing the House of David

5:1-25 DAVID WINS JERUSALEM AND DEFEATS THE PHILISTINES
The several references to the Lord's appointment of David confirm the central reason for his success (3:18; 5:2, 10, 12). David became king of the entire nation (5:1-5) and captured Jerusalem (5:6-10). Zion (5:7), the Jebusite fortress, became David's capital, the City of David. The city had steep cliffs on three sides, a good water supply, and was on the

north-south travel route. The fortress (5:9), or Millo (NASB and KJV, from the Hebrew, "to fill"), was a mound or terrace that served as a foundation for a building. In 5:10 the secret of David's success is revealed: God's presence with him. Again, the multiplication of David's wives (5:13) was a direct violation of Deuteronomy 17:17.

God gave David two initial victories over the Philistines. The valley of Rephaim (5:18) penetrated the hill country from the coastal plain to the west, giving strategic access to Jerusalem. Baal-perazim (5:20) is literally translated "the Lord of breaking forth." The image is that of floodwaters breaking through a dam just as David's troops broke through the Philistine assault.

6:1-23 DAVID RETURNS THE ARK TO JERUSALEM
The ark was to be carried by the sons of Kohath (Num. 3:30-31), not placed on a cart or vehicle, and it was not to be touched (Num. 4:15). The violation cost Uzzah his life and again reminded Israel that no matter how long ago God had said something, he still meant it (2 Sam. 6:3-7). That was the basis both of their fear of God and of their confidence in his consistency.

The term "danced" (6:14) literally means "whirled around." It served as an exuberant expression of worship and praise (Ps. 149:3). For comments on "ephod," see 1 Samuel 2:18. The words "exposed himself" (2 Sam. 6:20) are a derogatory reference to David's wearing an ephod. Normally, a longer robe was worn under the ephod (Exod. 28:31-35). Without the longer robe, more of David's body was exposed. However, the problem was with Michal's hard heart toward the Lord that resulted in her sarcastic and untrue criticism, not with any inappropriateness with David's dress.

7:1-29 A HOUSE FOR GOD AND A HOUSE FOR DAVID
Second Samuel 7 revolves around one main idea: the concept of "house." David wanted to build God a *house*—the temple. God made a covenant to build the *house* of royal lineage for David. The emphasis is on what God already had done and would do in the future for David (note the "I will" statements in 7:9, 10, 11, 12, 13, 14). The heart of the covenant was the promise of God's loving-kindness that would never depart. Saul's experience had illustrated what it meant for God to remove his loving-kindness (7:15).

David was not allowed to build the temple (7:5) because he had waged wars and shed blood (1 Chron. 22:8; 28:3). David wanted to build God a house, but God told him that he would build a house or dynasty that would be a royal dynasty for him (2 Sam. 7:11-13). The promise God made to David, known as the Davidic covenant (Ps. 89:20-

37), was built upon the promise God made to Abraham regarding a future nation (Gen. 12:2). God promised David an eternal house, throne, and kingdom (2 Sam. 7:16). David's house or dynasty would always be the royal line and would continue forever. The right to rule on the throne would always belong to David's seed. Finally, the right to a literal kingdom or dominion would never be taken from David's posterity. The rule of David's dynasty was interrupted with the Babylonian exile, but the right to rule was never rescinded. The ultimate fulfillment of this promise will be realized in Jesus Christ (Luke 1:31-33; see the fuller discussion of the Davidic covenant in the introductory section).

David's response of praise to this great covenant revolved around three aspects of God's grace: (1) God's favor at the present time (2 Sam. 7:18-21); (2) God's work in the past (7:22-24); and (3) God's promise for the future (7:25-29).

8:1-18 DAVID SECURES PEACE FROM EXTERNAL ENEMIES
David's list of defeated enemies (the Philistines, 8:1; the Moabites, 8:2; Zobah, 8:3-4; the Arameans, or Syrians, 8:5-8) led to a summary statement of his rule: it was unified, just, and righteous (8:15). The chief city was Metheg Ammah, or Gath (8:1; 1 Chron. 18:1). (See the introductory map for Gath's location.) David either spared the young Moabites whose height was approximately one cord and executed the adults whose height was two cords, or he selected one of three rows of soldiers to be spared execution (2 Sam. 8:2). Zobah (8:3) was an Aramean kingdom north of Damascus. In 8:4 the Greek version reads 1,000 chariots and 7,000 horsemen or charioteers (see 1 Chron. 18:4). The term "Syrians" for "Arameans" (8:5, KJV) is not correct since Syria did not exist as a political entity until the Greek period. The Hebrew reads "Aram" and the people were Arameans. This territory was in the region of Damascus. The reference in 8:13 to Edom rather than to the Syrians (KJV) is probably correct (Ps. 60:1; 1 Chron. 18:12).

9:1-13 DAVID'S KINDNESS TO THE MEMORY OF JONATHAN
The expression "a dead dog" (2 Sam. 9:8) refers to someone contemptible and useless. David provided the necessities of life for Mephibosheth (9:10), but he had to make provision for the maintenance of his own family and servants.

10:1-19 DAVID DEFEATS THE AMMONITES AND THE ARAMEANS
This is a mighty example of David's strength in battle and forms the contrast to David's upcoming great failure in 2 Samuel 11. The shaving (10:4) was regarded as a form of grave humiliation and indignity. The 700 charioteers (10:18) is probably a scribal error in transmission for 7,000 (cf. 1 Chron. 19:18).

11:1–20:26 DAVID'S HOUSEHOLD EVIL
11:1–12:31 Adultery and Murder
11:1-27 THE SIN
The deadly result of David's actions regarding Bathsheba and Uriah is found in 2 Samuel 11:27, "the Lord was very displeased with what David had done" or his act "was evil in the Lord's sight," the very phrase found throughout the book of Judges to describe the beginning of God's judgments (Judg. 2:11; 3:7, 12; 4:1; 6:1).

Most Oriental homes had an enclosed courtyard that was regarded as part of the house. But the interior of Bathsheba's courtyard could be seen from David's palace roof (2 Sam. 11:2), which was at a higher elevation on Mount Zion. David saw, he inquired, and then he yielded to temptation (11:2-5). This same progression of sin is revealed in James 1:14-15. David's lust gave birth to sin, which resulted in judgment. The words "She had just completed the purification rites" (2 Sam. 11:4) reflect the requirements of the Mosaic Law (Lev. 15:18). The expression "relax" used by David in speaking to Uriah (2 Sam. 11:8) meant that David wished for him to spend some time at home. While David had succeeded in concealing his sin from the general public, the omniscient God knew of the whole evil affair (11:27).

12:1-31 THE CONVICTION AND REPENTANCE
This event illustrates the power of the Davidic covenant. God would indeed punish David's disobedience, but his loving-kindness would never be taken away (7:14-15). The chapter describes the indictment of David and the births of two sons: one who died and the other who was beloved by the Lord, Solomon (12:24). Nathan brought the words of God's condemnation of David's sin (12:1-4) and his love for David's son (12:25).

These predictions of discipline (12:9-11) were fulfilled in the violent deaths of Amnon (13:28-29) and Absalom (18:15), and Absalom's public appropriation of David's royal concubines (16:22). David's confession was immediate, as was God's gracious forgiveness (12:13). The fuller expression of David's confession is found in Psalm 51.

Many people use 12:23 to support the view that infants and children who die are taken to heaven. However, the verse is not speaking of the question of an afterlife, but of the inevitability of death. The child could not return to life and activity, but David would someday join his son in death. David expected to go to Sheol, the place of the righteous and unrighteous dead (Ps. 16:10; 6:4-5). Although the Bible does not reveal what happens to an infant that dies, the holy and righteous God can be trusted to do what is right. The name Jedidiah (2 Sam. 12:25, meaning "beloved of the Lord") marked Solomon as the successor to David's throne.

God's continued blessing on David's military might was reconfirmed in 12:26-31. Rabbah (12:29, modern Amman), located in Transjordan at the border of the desert, was the capital of Ammon. It was later rebuilt and renamed Philadelphia. There are two views regarding David's treatment of the Ammonites (12:31). He either imposed hard labor or cruel death on the captives. The latter view would be more in accordance with 1 Chronicles 20:3 (NASB; cf. KJV), which says David "cut them with saws and with sharp instruments and with axes." That punishment was in accordance with Ammonite ways (1 Sam. 11:2; Amos 1:13) and was probably limited to those who resisted David.

13:1-39 Revenge
This story concerns Amnon's lust for and rape of Tamar (2 Sam. 13:1-14), Absalom's two-year-long grudge that resulted in revenge (13:15-29), and the initial exile of Absalom and David's longing for him. But why are these depressing stories recorded in Scripture? They are a direct fulfillment of God's punishment for David's sin with Bathsheba as spoken through Nathan the prophet (12:10-11). Like David, Amnon had a moment of sexual incontinence. Like David, Absalom resorted to murder. David was furious, but he took no action because he had been guilty of similar sins (13:21). In the same way Absalom was full of hatred but had no communication with Amnon (13:22).

Levitical law prohibited marriage to one's brother or sister (Lev. 18:11). Perhaps Tamar made the suggestion of marriage in the hope that there would be a chance for her to escape (2 Sam. 13:13). The Jewish Talmud assumes that Tamar was of illegitimate birth and therefore the two could have been married. Baal-hazor (13:23), located at the highest point in the mountains of Ephraim at 3,333 feet, is fifteen miles north of Jerusalem. The territory of Geshur (13:38) extends along the eastern shore of the Sea of Galilee and the northern bank of the Yarmuk River.

14:1–20:26 Insurrection in David's Kingdom
14:1-33 DAVID CALLS FOR ABSALOM'S RETURN
The woman from Tekoa (14:1-20) used the same technique as Nathan did in 2 Samuel 12 in order to convict David of his guilt. The technique was effective because it was easier for David to see sin in others than it was to see it in himself. The self-righteousness that covers personal sin in ourselves inevitably wants to see the same kind of sin punished in others. The unfolding of God's punishment for David's sin continued.

Three men were consumed by interpersonal conflicts and their uncontrolled personal lust: (1) Amnon wanted, got, and hated; (2) Absalom hated, murdered, wanted to see his father, David, deceived, and was murdered; and (3) David longed for his son but would not see him. All of this created an awful state of family strife.

Tekoa (14:2), the hometown of the prophet Amos, was located five miles south of Bethlehem. David's unwillingness to completely forgive and restore Absalom (14:23-24) bore bitter fruit in the heart of his son (cf. 2 Sam. 15–18).

15:1-37 DAVID FLEES FROM ABSALOM
While in Hebron, Absalom accomplished a military coup, causing David to flee east out of Jerusalem. David saw himself as expendable and under the sovereign will of God (15:25-26; 16:12). David also was not without his own plans (15:34). Some translations (NASB, KJV) have the figure "forty" (15:7), which is probably a scribal error and should read "four," as do the Septuagint, Syriac, and Josephus. David fled, fearing for his personal safety and seeking to avoid an attack on Jerusalem (15:14). The brook Kidron (15:23) separates the Mount of Olives from the temple mount.

16:1-23 ABSALOM SECURES JERUSALEM
Two remnants of Saul's old regime, Mephibosheth (16:1-4) and Shimei (16:5-14), begin the section of 16:1-23. Absalom's taking David's harem (16:20-23) fulfilled the judgments prophesied in 12:11-12. In ancient times the seizure of the royal harem demonstrated possession of the throne (16:21-22; cf. 3:7). This public spectacle was the greatest possible insult to David.

17:1-29 GOD PROTECTS DAVID
In case the reader wonders what God's attitude toward Absalom was at this point, 17:14 provides the answer. God had someone other than Absalom in mind for the next king after David. God gave David time to escape by thwarting the counsel of Ahithophel (17:14). En-rogel (17:17) is a spring situated a short distance south of the junction of the Kidron and Hinnom valleys, not far from Jerusalem. Ahithophel (17:23) committed suicide because (1) he was humiliated by Absalom's rejection of his advice, and (2) he could foresee Absalom's defeat and knew that he would then be accountable to David for his disloyalty. Mahanaim (17:24), situated in Transjordan, was Ishbosheth's former capital (2:8). (See the introductory map for the location of Mahanaim.)

18:1-33 DAVID DEFEATS ABSALOM
With the tragic words of 18:33, the prophecy that the sword would not depart from David's house took on terrible proportions. The forest of Ephraim (18:6) was north of the Jabbok River in Transjordan. Because of the rugged nature of the terrain, the pursuit through the forest resulted in more deaths than the battle (18:8). The tradition that

Absalom was caught by his hair comes from Josephus, but it makes sense in light of 14:26. The coming of a band of men would signify a defeat to those waiting in the city, but the coming of one man signified a victory (18:26-27).

19:1-43 DAVID REESTABLISHES HIS RULE

Second Samuel 19 shows the return of David as he dealt with military unity by ending his mourning for Absalom (19:1-8) and by attaching Amasa to his army (19:9-15). The two remnants of Saul's regime that affected David as he left the city were dealt with again upon his return (19:16-30). Barzillai, the man who had supported David during his exile, was honored (19:31-43).

Joab warned that David's disposition was affecting the morale and loyalty of the people (19:7). David would be in deep trouble if he did not express appreciation for those who had fought for him. David replaced Joab with Amasa (19:13) to secure the allegiance of the rebel army (17:25) and to discipline Joab for slaying Absalom. The expression "Israel" (19:20) refers to Ephraim (the offspring of Joseph's son), which, as a large tribe, was representative of the ten northern tribes. For 19:24-30, compare Mephibosheth's story with Ziba's (16:1-4). Did Mephibosheth or Ziba lie? Apparently David could not decide and gave both a share of the inheritance.

20:1-26 SHEBA

Again a split occurred between Israel and Judah under Sheba's rebellion. The slogan "you men of Israel, let's all go home" (20:1) meant "Let's go home and from there we will offer resistance." A kiss on the cheek (20:9) was a customary oriental greeting. Joab committed another murder of David's ally Amasa (20:9-10). Abel-beth-maacah (20:14) was about twenty-five miles north of the Sea of Galilee in the Hula Valley. The "loyal city" (20:19) refers to Abel-beth-maacah, which was a prominent city or capital of the region. The forced labor (20:24) was one of the evils of kingship promised by Samuel (1 Sam. 8:11-16).

The defeat of Sheba's civil war marked the end of the various attempts to overthrow or divide up David's kingdom listed in the book of Samuel. It continues the report of God's judgment on David's sins of adultery and murder, yet it also recounts

God's grace, which is seen in the preservation of David's kingdom and in God not removing his loving-kindness as he had done with King Saul. Although David suffered discipline, he still ended up secure and victorious (2 Sam. 20:23-26).

21:1–24:25 DAVID AS A MEDIATOR AND PRESERVER

Second Samuel 21–24 forms one beautifully constructed literary unit. The chart below the arrangement of its content.

The Davidic covenant was at the heart and source of all of David's victories for the nation. Military victory only came about through God's covenanted support to establish David securely in the land (2 Sam. 7:9-10). The framework for this section begins and ends with two national judgments. The first (2 Sam. 21) was caused by Saul breaking the covenant with the Gibeonites, which was established under Joshua (Josh. 9:16-21). The last (2 Sam. 24) was caused by David's sin in counting the members of his armies. Both instances concluded with the Lord answering the prayers of Israel: "God ended the famine in the land of Israel" (21:14) and "the Lord answered his prayer" (24:25).

How was God moved and by whose entreaty? In 2 Samuel 21 it was on the basis of doing what the king had commanded (21:14). In 2 Samuel 24 God was moved through the king's priestly intercession. The message was clear: the king was the mediator between God and the nation. When he obeyed, God was moved to bless the people and the land. But the source and power of that blessing were in the covenant God had made with David.

Both books of Samuel need to be interpreted in the light of this concluding section. It reveals God's original intentions for the kingship in Israel: God alone was to be King. It explains the abortive reign of Saul: an example of what it means to have God take his loving-kindness away from the king. It also explains the ups and downs of David's rule: discipline with the rods of men (2 Sam. 7:14) but with love from God that never departs (7:15).

The great covenant with David points to the King of kings, God's Son. Every human king showed himself to be more or less imperfect. Originally, God alone was to be King. And he accomplished

OUTLINE OF 2 SAMUEL 21–24

National Judgment: Saul's Act (21:1-14)
   Military Victory through Mighty Men (21:15-22)
      Song of Praise for the Davidic Covenant: Past Victory (22:1-51)
      Song of Praise for the Davidic Covenant: Future Security (23:1-7)
   Military Victory through Mighty Men (23:8-39)
National Judgment: David's Act (24:1-25)

that through Jesus, who was both his incarnate Son and the Son of David. Through Jesus' mediation and obedience believers may all experience the nondeparting love of God (cf. 2 Sam. 7:15 with 2 Cor. 6:18).

21:1-14 National Judgment: Saul's Sin, David's Entreaty

Saul violated the treaty Joshua had made four hundred years earlier with the Gibeonites (Josh. 9:3-27). In light of Deuteronomy 24:16 and Ezekiel 18:1-4, 14-17, it is probable that the seven sons (2 Sam. 21:6) were directly implicated in the attack upon the Gibeonites. Since Michal died childless (6:23), it is likely that the reference (21:8) is to Merab, the wife of Adriel (1 Sam. 18:19). Rizpah (2 Samuel 21:10-11) remained by the dead bodies from the time of the barley harvest in April to the early rains of October (cf. Deut. 21:23). When David was told what she had done, he took the bones of Saul and Jonathan from the citizens of Jabesh Gilead and buried them, as well as the bones of those who had been recently killed (2 Sam. 21:11-14).

21:15-22 Military Victory through Mighty Men

The spear of Ishbi-benob (21:16) weighed about eight pounds. The "light of Israel" was David, whose life and actions served as a bright light for the nation (21:17). Here, the slaying of Goliath was attributed to Elhanan (21:19), in contradiction to 1 Samuel 17:50. The parallel account in 1 Chronicles 20:5 indicates that Elhanan killed "the brother of Goliath."

22:1-51 Song of Praise for the Davidic Covenant: Past Victory

This hymn of praise (2 Sam. 22:1-51) is almost identical to Psalm 18. The "Lord's promises" (22:31) is used in Scripture as an image of divine power.

23:1-7 Song of Praise for the Davidic Covenant: Future Security

The "last words of David" (23:1) were probably his last formal utterance. The basis of his hope was the everlasting covenant (23:5).

23:8-39 Military Victory through Mighty Men

According to 1 Chronicles 11:10, these mighty men (2 Sam. 23:8-39) helped David to become king. The "thirty-seven" (23:39) included the three (23:8-12), Abishai and Benaiah (23:18-23), the thirty-one (23:24-39) and David's commander, Joab (23:37).

24:1-25 National Judgment: David's Sin, David's Entreaty

While Satan actually instigated the pride and rebellion that led to the numbering of the people (1 Chron. 21:1), God was using Satan to accomplish his plan (2 Sam. 24:1; cf. Gen. 50:20). Why was the numbering of the people wrong (2 Sam. 24:10)? Josephus speculated that David forgot to collect the half-shekel temple tax when he took the census (Exod. 30:12-13). Perhaps he had been commanded not to number the people but did so anyway. Perhaps the numbering was evidence of a lack of faith. David may have been trusting in his own resources rather than in the Lord. The exact reason is not important. The text simply asserts that it was wrong for him to do so.

David insisted on buying the threshing floor because he did not want to give the Lord something that had cost him nothing (2 Sam. 24:24). He believed in sacrificial giving (cf. 2 Cor. 8:1-3). The threshing floor that David purchased (2 Sam. 24:24) is identified in 2 Chronicles 3:1 as Mount Moriah. Traditionally this is understood to be the mountain in the land of Moriah where Abraham offered Isaac (Gen. 22:2), and it would soon be the site of Solomon's temple.

Religious, military, and civil unity was achieved under the king in Israel (2 Sam. 20:23-26). Those were the three continual problems that the Israelites had struggled with in the book of Judges. The book of Samuel shows that God's man on the throne could make significant intercession for the nation to bring about God's rule in Israel. All of this was a temporal and imperfect vision of the rule to be brought in by the perfect Son of David, Jesus the Messiah.

1 & 2 KINGS

BASIC FACTS

HISTORICAL SETTING

The books of Kings begin where the books of Samuel left off, with the death of David and the coronation of his son Solomon. The books then cover the histories of the united kingdom and the divided kingdoms, leading up to the fall of the northern kingdom, Israel, to Assyria in 722 B.C. and the later fall of Judah to Babylon in 586 B.C. Throughout the books, Syria, Assyria, and Babylon are the great political threats to God's people.

AUTHOR

The author of these books is unknown. Jeremiah has been named as author by some scholars because portions of his prophecy appear in 2 Kings 24–25 (cf. Jer. 39–42; 52 with 2 Kings 24–25). But the common consensus admits that the author(s) cannot be identified with any certainty.

DATE

The books cover the events during the time period between 970 and 586 B.C. They end with the elevation of King Jehoiachin in Babylon during the Babylonian captivity. Whatever the exact date of writing, the events recorded end in the middle of the Babylonian exile.

PURPOSE

The books are designed to explain why God's people fell into such great destruction and captivity. They show the people's consistent disobedience contrasted with God's consistent faithfulness to his words of blessing and discipline. God was faithful to his promises to David. But in light of the failures of David and Solomon, the great figures in the books of Kings are the prophets Elijah and Elisha. The prophets came in to rebuke sin and encourage a return to faithfulness.

GEOGRAPHY AND ITS IMPORTANCE

The books of 1 and 2 Kings were originally one unbroken book. The book was written while Israel was still in captivity, cut off from her homeland. Geographically, the single book of Kings begins in Jerusalem and ends in Babylon. This movement from Jerusalem to Babylon involves the split of God's people into two nations, north and south;

the split of God's rule through kings into two lines, David's line and a series of dynasties in the north; and then the final destruction of first the northern and then the southern half of God's nation. The split of the kingdom into north and south resulted in several capital cities (Jerusalem in the south; Shechem, and later, Tirzah and Samaria in the north) and three centers of worship (Jerusalem in the south; Dan and Bethel in the north). By the end of the book of Kings, a small number of God's people had fled back to Egypt and most had been taken as captives to Babylon.

GUIDING CONCEPTS

THE FUNCTION OF THE PROPHETS

The book of Kings is part of the collection of books known as the former prophets (Joshua, Judges, Samuel, Kings). For a discussion concerning the former prophets see the *Guiding Concepts* section for Joshua. These books, when taken together with the

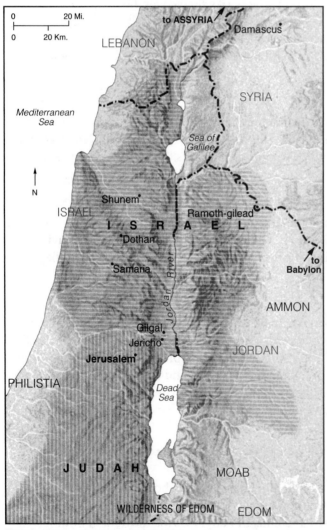

The broken lines (— ·— ·) indicate modern boundaries.
Copyright © 1986, 1988 by Tyndale House Publishers, Inc.

book of Deuteronomy, form a beautiful history of God's relationship with his people. This means that the book of Kings is not merely a book of dry history. Rather, it is a book designed to bring a prophetic word of exhortation and encouragement to God's people in the midst of their failure and discipline for their sins. Throughout the book of Kings, great emphasis is placed on the certainty of the fulfillment of God's prophetic words of blessing and warning. No matter how long ago God had spoken a word, the certainty of its fulfillment remained in full force forever. That cut both ways to provide both security and warning to God's people, as God's words confirmed the potency of his covenants through Abraham, Moses, and David.

THE UNITY OF FIRST AND SECOND KINGS

The two books of Kings were inspired by God as one

unified whole. Therefore, they can only be properly understood by studying them as a single unit. For example, the exaltation of King Jehoiachin by the king of Babylon in the last chapter of 2 Kings is the positive end toward which both 1 and 2 Kings are headed. Furthermore, 2 Kings 17:7-23 is the key to understanding the structure of 1 Kings and illustrates why Israel and Judah fell into captivity. Also, without the lesson taught in 2 Kings 17, Solomon's great speech at the dedication of the temple in 1 Kings 8 cannot be set into its proper context. This *Concise Bible Commentary* approaches 1 and 2 Kings as a single interpretive whole.

THE PERSPECTIVE OF THE BOOK

The end of 2 Kings gives a perspective for viewing the entire work. The last act described in the book of 2 Kings is the elevation of Jehoiachin out of prison and into the king of Babylon's court. That event occurred a little past halfway through the seventy-year period of exile. The best that could be said when the book was written was that the king of Judah had been released from prison; it was a sign that God's favor through the Davidic covenant was still operative, even during Israel's exile. Therefore, the book of Kings was written from the perspective of being in the Babylonian exile, a time when failure still stung and release was still far off.

That exilic viewpoint was designed to make sure the exiles stopped blaming God for their defeats and instead confessed their own responsibility for failure. It also was geared to providing the only ray of hope possible in the middle of exile: God's unswerving faithfulness to David, even through the past reigns of faithless kings. Just as God's promise of discipline for sin was certain, so also was his promise of blessing. It was up to the people of God to decide if they would repent from their careless attitude toward God during the captivity and faithfully wait for his promised restoration of David's royal line.

KEY SPEECHES IN THE BOOK OF KINGS

Several key speeches enable readers to understand and apply the message of 1 and 2 Kings: (1) The temple as the location of both present and future hope (1 Kings 8:12-61); (2) Prophecy of the divided kingdom (1 Kings 11:31-39); (3) Reasons for the Assyrian captivity of Israel (2 Kings 17). Second Kings 17 is the key chapter for revealing the purpose and perspective of the book of Kings; and (4) Reasons for the Babylonian captivity of Judah (2 Kings 21:10-15; cf. 24:1-4).

THE EVALUATIONS OF THE KINGS

Throughout 1 and 2 Kings, the description of each king's reign includes a moral evaluation. The northern kings all were given bad evaluations and are compared to Jeroboam I, who led the northern kingdom into idolatry (cf. 1 Kings 11:28-29; 14:16; 15:26, 30, 34; 16:2, 13, 26; 21:22; 2 Kings 3:3; 10:29, 31; 13:2, 6, 11; 14:24; 15:9, 18, 24, 28; 17:21; 21:10-16; there is a fulfillment of 1 Kings 13:1-3 in 2 Kings 23:15; note also 2 Kings 23:26-27). A phrase like the one in Judges occurs throughout the book of Kings: "did evil in the Lord's sight" (1 Kings 11:6; 14:22; 15:26, 34; 16:19, 25, 30; 21:20, 25; 22:52; 2 Kings 3:2; 8:18, 27; 13:2, 11; 14:24; 15:9, 18, 24, 28; 17:2, 17; 21:2, 6, 15-16, 20; 23:32; 24:9, 19). The evil done by the Israelites is described in 1 Kings 14:23-24 and 2 Kings 16:3; 17:7-12; 21:6 (cf. Deut. 12:2-3, 31). The central focus of obedience was true worship at the Jerusalem temple. The focus of disobedience involved other places of worship, even under the guise of worshiping the true God of Israel.

BIBLE-WIDE CONCEPTS

THE FOCUS ON THE DAVIDIC COVENANT

Another key concept is found in the phrases "David and his descendants" and "David's sake" (some selected verses are 1 Kings 2:33, 45; 8:66; 11:12-13, 32, 34, 36, 39; 15:4-5; 2 Kings 8:19; 19:34; 20:6). The rebellions of the various kings only served as a contrast to highlight God's faithfulness to his covenant with David.

THE PERSPECTIVE OF THE EXODUS FROM EGYPT

The past acts of God's love were firmly rooted in the Exodus from Egypt. The Exodus was to Israel what the Cross is to the Christian: the focus of God's love and power to break the bondage of evil. All of Israel's subsequent rebellions were viewed as sadly contradictory to the original salvation and purity brought about by the Exodus. The book of Kings continually refers to that great redemptive event. The temple's construction (1 Kings 6:1) and dedication (8:9, 16, 21, 51, 53; 9:9) were linked back to the Exodus. Even the apostate Jeroboam I used the Exodus to encourage the worship of his false gods (12:28). Israel's failure to love God from the Exodus on is given as the primary reason for the Assyrian and Babylonian captivities (2 Kings 17:7, 36; 21:15). And the reason for those captivities already had been prophesied by God long before in Deuteronomy 29:24-25.

NEEDS MET BY FIRST AND SECOND KINGS

The book of Kings presents the history of Israel from David's final years to about half-way through the Babylonian captivity. The perspective given is one that recognized God's divine promise despite human failure. Israel had received the great promises of God to Abraham, Moses, and David. Israel had also lost its temple and land and was now cast off into captivity. The book of Kings shows how the Babylonian captivity did not mean the end of God's promises to Abraham and David and that the reason for the sad state of God's people was not due to God's failure but to their own. The structure and content of Kings show that its author was answering questions like the following for his readers.

- Is God in control of Israel and the nations around it? (For the answer to that question see the following passages: 1 Kings 2:27; 6:11-12; 8:20, 56; 12:15; 13:1, 2, 5, 9, 16-18, 20-26, 32; 14:17-18; 15:29; 16:12, 34; 17:16, 24; 18:31, 36; 20:35-36; 2 Kings 2:22; 4:44; 7:1, 16; 9:36; 10:10, 17; 14:25; 15:12; 23:16-17; 24:2.)
- Why is Israel in such trouble if God is in control? (For the answer, see Deut. 28:9; Josh. 1:8; 2 Kings 17:13.)
- In light of Israel's past failures, is there is any hope for a future with God? (See 1 Kings 8:28-30; 11:36; 2 Kings 23:25; 25:27-30.)

Christians today may find themselves in the middle of God's discipline, much like the Israelites found themselves in captivity. But that pain of discipline should not be taken as if God has voided all his promises. Believers first need to realize that the pain of discipline is due to their own failure, not God's. Then, the discipline should be seen as a clear confirmation that they are still his children, still under his disciplining care, and still participating in the hope of his promises. Discipline should result in a confession of failures, a reaffirmation of commitment to obedience, and hope for future restoration.

OUTLINE OF FIRST AND SECOND KINGS

I. OBEDIENCE: THE UNITED KINGDOM (1 KINGS 1:1–11:43)
   A. The Kingdom Is Established (1:1–2:46)
   B. Kingdom Blessings from Obedience (3:1–10:29)
   C. Foundations of Chastisement (11:1-43)

II. CHASTISEMENT: THE DIVIDED KINGDOM (1 KINGS 12:1—2 KINGS 17:41)
   A. Jeroboam's Lost Opportunity (1 Kings 12:1–14:20)
   B. The Lamp of David in Jerusalem (1 Kings 14:21–15:24)
   C. The Prophetic Word Certified against Covenant Unfaithfulness (1 Kings 15:25—
      2 Kings 10:36)
   D. Covenant Blessing from Obedience (2 Kings 11:1–14:29)
   E. Chastisement Confirmed and Explained (2 Kings 15:1–17:41)

III. PRESERVATION: THE SOLITARY KINGDOM (2 KINGS 18:1–25:30)
   A. Reform: Babylon Introduced (18:1–20:21)
   B. Irrevocable Chastisement: Manasseh and Amon (21:1-26)
   C. Reform in the Shadow of Judgment: Josiah (22:1–23:30)
   D. Chastisement Confirmed (23:31–25:26)
   E. Preservation of the Davidic Kingship: Jehoiachin Restored (25:27-30)

FIRST KINGS NOTES

1:1–11:43 OBEDIENCE: THE UNITED KINGDOM

Overview: First Kings 1–11 shows how Solomon overcame various threats to his reign, built the temple, and became the object of international respect. The key phrase is "he was firmly established on the throne" (1 Kings 2:12), a fulfillment of the promise in 2 Samuel 7:12. The lovingkindness of the Davidic covenant was confirmed for Solomon (1 Kings 3:6) and illustrated in his great wisdom to rule with justice (3:28). First Kings 4 shows Israel at its greatest height and describes its greatness in the terms of the Abrahamic promise of land (cf. 4:21 with Gen. 15:18). First Kings 5–10 details the temple's completion and the kingdom's impact on the nations. First Kings 11 shows the split in the kingdom brought on by Solomon's sins. The great amount of detail used to describe the religious and international successes of Solomon's rule illustrates to the suffering exiles how great all of their lives could be when the king obeyed God, and why blessing could so quickly turn to destruction

when the king rebelled. It also presents a picture of the hope for the future restored kingdom of David when God will once again establish the Son of David on the throne in Israel.

1:1–2:46 The Kingdom Is Established

1:1-53 LEADERSHIP IN CRISIS

First Kings 1–2 tells of struggles through which Solomon had to pass in order to be placed securely on the throne (2:46). Solomon ruled forty years (970–931 B.C.). The word "nurse" (1:2) refers to someone who is in an intimate relationship with another person. The fact that David did not have intimate sexual relations with Abishag (1:4) is recorded to demonstrate that she was not David's concubine and to explain how it could thus occur to Adonijah to ask that she become his wife (2:17; cf. Deut. 22:30).

   Three statements about David (1 Kings 1:1; 2:1; 2:10) show the king's weakness and his openness to a military takeover. Adonijah's first rebellion took place because the king was ill. His second rebellion concerned taking David's virgin for his own wife (1:4). Adonijah (1:5), David's fourth but oldest surviving son (cf. 2 Sam. 3:2-4), regarded himself as next in line for the throne. Usually the king's oldest living son would reign, but Solomon had been promised the throne (1 Kings 1:13, 17, 30). Solomon had been singled out in 2 Samuel 12:24-25 as the one loved by the Lord (cf. 1 Chron. 22:6-10). Adonijah was either unaware of David's vow to make Solomon king, or he chose to ignore it. En-rogel (1 Kings 1:9), a spring marking the boundary between Judah and Benjamin (Josh. 18:16), is located near Jerusalem, just south of the junction of the Kidron and Hinnom valleys.

When his supporters dispersed (1 Kings 1:49-50), Adonijah took refuge at the tabernacle, which was at Gibeon (1 Chron. 16:39). Taking hold of the horns of the altar was a means of claiming refuge from an avenger (cf. Exod. 21:14). Adonijah was placed under severe conditions (1 Kings 1:52) and house arrest (1:53), forcing him to retire from public life.

2:1-12 THE CHARGE TO SOLOMON
David's charge to Solomon (2:1-4) echoed God's exhortation to Joshua (Josh. 1:6-7). Obedience was the key to success (1 Kings 2:4). The promise (2:4) referred to the covenant God had made with David (2 Sam. 7:12-16). "The City of David" refers to Zion, or Jerusalem, where David established his capital (1 Kings 2:10).

2:13-46 OLD BUSINESS CONCLUDED
Appropriating the royal harem of a deposed king was a recognized method of laying claim to the throne (2:22). This was Adonijah's second attempt to take the kingdom away from Solomon. Solomon understood Adonijah's request as an attempt to usurp his kingship (2:17), although Bathsheba naively believed the request to be merely motivated by love. She may not have regarded Abishag as a concubine since David had not known her intimately (1:4). Abiathar's dismissal from his position as priest (2:27) fulfilled the judgment on the house of Eli made in 1 Samuel 2:30-36. Abiathar, the last of Eli's descendants to serve as a priest, was replaced by Zadok (1 Kings 2:35), who had remained faithful to the house of David.

Shimei forfeited his life (2:46) by violating the conditions of his confinement (2:36-38). The judgments on Adonijah and Shimei cleared the way for the secure establishment of Solomon's reign (2:12, 46).

3:1–10:29 Kingdom Blessings from Obedience
3:1–4:34 WISDOM: THE HEART OF BLESSING
3:1-28 Solomon asks for wisdom.
The cornerstone of Solomon's foreign policy was his use of international marriage to conclude treaties and cement relationships (3:1). His treaty with Egypt was unique, for it is the only instance in

history where the daughter of a pharaoh was given to a foreign ruler. Egypt was friendly toward Israel at that point, but it would not be so later. Also, the potential for Solomon to fall into idolatry due to the influence of his non-Israelite wives was great (cf. 11:2). The high places (3:2) were elevated platforms, usually set on a hill, used by the Canaanites for worship. They were to be destroyed at the time of the conquest (Num. 33:52). The Israelites adapted the high place at Gibeon as a place to worship God after the destruction of the tabernacle at Shiloh (Jer. 7:12) and before the construction of the temple at Jerusalem (1 Chron. 16:39).

Solomon's "understanding mind" (1 Kings 3:9) was literally a hearing heart, that is, one that was quick to listen and obey. Such obedience was the central issue of kingship in God's kingdom—knowing the difference between good and evil and obeying God. Solomon's decision in the case of the two prostitutes (3:16-28) illustrates the wisdom that God gave him. Wisdom is the practical and successful application of God's truth to life's situations. See Proverbs 2:6-22 for a description of wisdom and its benefits. The result of Solomon's wisdom was national respect by the people of the king for his wisdom and justice (1 Kings 3:28).

4:1-28 National blessing.
The national blessings of Solomon's rule clustered around Abrahamic themes: the numerous people of Israel (4:20; cf. Gen. 22:17); the boundaries of the land (1 Kings 4:21; cf. Gen. 15:18); the peace and prosperity (1 Kings 4:22-25; cf. Gen. 22:17; Mic. 4:4). Seeking to minimize tribal rivalry, Solomon reorganized the kingdom into twelve administrative districts that cut across old tribal boundaries (1 Kings 4:1-19). Although Solomon received tribute from lands as far north as the Euphrates (4:21), he did not possess these territories, nor did they fall under his permanent jurisdiction. "Each family had its own home and garden" (4:25) is an image of security and contentment (cf. Mic. 4:4). The number of 4,000 stalls for chariot horses (1 Kings 4:26; cf. 2 Chron. 9:25) is given as 40,000 in some translations (NASB and KJV). That figure is exceptionally large and probably represents a scribal error in the transmission of the Hebrew text.

4:29-34 The fame of Solomon's wisdom.
Solomon was known internationally for his wisdom. Many of Solomon's proverbs (4:32) are recorded in the book of Proverbs. The best of his 1,005 songs is preserved as "The Song of Songs." Solomon's wisdom links back to Adam's insight into nature when he named the animals of God's original creation (4:34). God's original command for people to rule the earth came with their ability to understand how the earth works. The ability to name the plants and animals and to discuss the

world of nature shows an important element of dominion and wisdom at work.

5:1–7:51 THE TEMPLE IS CONSTRUCTED
The temple was the earthly focus of the kingdom and the symbol of God's presence in Israel. Solomon and Hiram, king of Tyre, entered into an economic alliance (5:11). Hiram provided materials and skilled craftsmen to build the temple in return for Israel's wheat and oil. The Phoenicians were great shipbuilders and merchants, but their land was lacking in agricultural productivity (cf. Acts 12:20). The slave status for the Israelites (1 Kings 5:13), although apparently only a temporary measure (cf. 9:22), must have been a bitter pill for the freeborn Israelites to swallow.

The 1 Kings 6:1 text is important in determining the date of the Exodus. The construction of the temple began 480 years after the Exodus, in the fourth year of Solomon's reign. If the division of the Israelite monarchy took place in 931 B.C., as is generally accepted, then the fourth year of Solomon's forty-year reign would have been in 966 B.C. The addition of 480 years to 966 B.C. makes the biblical date of the Exodus 1446 B.C. Some scholars argue that 480 is symbolic in that it is representative of twelve forty-year generations. But the historical nature of the text and specific chronological notes (fourth year, second month) support a literal, non-symbolic view of the Kings text.

However, the literary point of this look back to the Exodus was to remind the readers, who were suffering in the Exile, of the great redemptive reference point of the temple. Its source was in God's great promises made so many years earlier in Egypt and at Mount Sinai. Solomon took seven years to build the temple (6:38), but thirteen years to build his own palace (7:1). The measurements of the temple were 90 by 30 by 45 feet, which made the temple twice the size of the tabernacle.

The Huram referred to in 7:13 was not Hiram, the king of Tyre (5:1), but a skillful worker in bronze (7:14). Jakin means "he shall establish," and Boaz means "in it is strength" (7:21). The dimensions of the bronze Sea, used for ritual cleansing (7:23), have raised questions about the accuracy of the original text of Scripture. According to the mathematical formula, a circle's circumference is equal to pi multiplied by that circle's diameter. The difficulty is that, according to this formula, the diameter should have been 14.3 feet instead of 15 feet (10 cubits). Possible answers to this problem are that the cast bronze Sea may have been several inches thick, or perhaps it had an outer lip that provided the extra inches necessary for the full 15-foot diameter.

8:1-66 THE DEDICATION OF THE TEMPLE
The dedication of the temple took place in the month of Ethanim (8:1-2, later known as "Tishri,"

which falls somewhere in September–October). It was held eleven months after its completion (6:38), perhaps to coincide with the beginning of the new year. The feast of dedication held from the eighth through the fourteenth days of the month was immediately followed by the Feast of Tabernacles held from the fifteenth through the twenty-first days. The curtain of the tabernacle (2 Chron. 3:14) appears to have been a slight distance inside the entrance of the Most Holy Place so that the poles used to carry the ark were visible from the Holy Place. The cloud (1 Kings 8:10), symbolizing God's presence, was not mentioned again until Ezekiel's vision of its departure (Ezek. 9:3; 10:4; 11:23). Repentance (1 Kings 8:46-50) was set forth as the basis for forgiveness and the restoration of blessing after the people's disobedience and failure (cf. Deut. 30:1-10).

God had kept his covenant of loving-kindness with David (1 Kings 8:22-26). But that meant the nation was still responsible to obey him and his commandments. The main part of the dedication stated the conditions for restoration if the people sinned. The temple was the place where God would hear and forgive his repentant people (8:27-53). Note the pattern of "if" or "when" (8:31, 33, 35, 37, 42, 44, 46-48) coupled with "hear" and "forgive" (8:32, 34, 36, 39, 43, 45, 49-50). Note especially 8:46-53 regarding captivity. Here the purpose is given for all the details surrounding the dedication of the temple. The temple would be the only place where God would hear and forgive.

Those in exile would read this section and know what their duty was: to repent and pray to God. The basis of their hope was the two covenants that framed this dedication: the Davidic (8:23-26) and the Mosaic (8:56-61). At the heart of the temple was the Most Holy Place, and at the heart of that room was a copy of the Mosaic covenant that formed the basis for Israel's relationship with God.

9:1-9 THE DAVIDIC COVENANT PASSES TO SOLOMON
The Lord appeared to Solomon a second time (9:2) and reconfirmed the Davidic covenant. God's two appearances to Solomon showed the grace of God that Solomon ultimately abused (11:9). God said that if the king obeyed, all would go well; but if he did not, then adversity would come upon the people and they would be driven from the land (9:6-9). This would be a clear reminder for the exiles in Babylon, hearing the content of this book for the first time, as to why they were there. The key concepts of land, throne, temple, and Egypt were repeated (9:4-9).

9:10-28 CIVIL AND MILITARY PROJECTS
Hiram, king of Tyre, had sent 120 talents of gold to assist in financing Solomon's vast building project (9:14). With his treasury depleted, Solomon tried to pay his obligations by giving Hiram twenty towns in

Galilee (9:11), but Hiram called them "Cabul" (9:13), meaning "as good as nothing." The term "Millo" (9:15), meaning "supporting terraces," is derived from a word that means "to fill," hence, "a mound," and refers to rock terraces used as foundations for buildings in Jerusalem. The exact location is uncertain. Other building projects were noted (9:10-28). With the completion of the temple, Solomon was able to consolidate the worship of God in Jerusalem (9:25) and away from the pagan high places (3:1-2).

10:1-13 INTERNATIONAL GLORY
First Kings 10 demonstrates the fulfillment of God's promise that Solomon would be extremely wealthy and uniquely honored (3:10-14). The queen of Sheba's praise (10:1-13) reflected a fulfillment of God's promise to Abraham that all the nations would be blessed through his descendants (Gen. 12:3; 1 Kings 10:24). Sheba is identified with the southern part of the Arabian Peninsula. Note the use of gold (1 Kings 10:14-22). To get an estimate of Solomon's yearly revenue, multiply 800,000 ounces (25 tons) by the present price of gold. Acquiring large numbers of horses (10:26-28) constituted a violation of the covenant regulations for the king (Deut. 17:16). Solomon was to trust in the Lord, not in military might (cf. Isa. 31:1-3).

10:14-29 GLORIES AND BLESSINGS SUMMARIZED
The summary of Solomon's international glory (1 Kings 10:23-29) describes the highest point Israel had reached in experiencing the blessings promised to Abraham, Moses, and David, and it forms a stark contrast with the next chapter. The purpose of the book of Kings was not to glory in the past kingdom but to teach why Israel had lost it all in exile and what her hope was for the future.

11:1-43 Foundations of Chastisement
11:1-8 SOLOMON'S IDOLATRY
Solomon, who had a discerning or understanding mind (3:9), let his love for women (11:1-2) turn his heart away from God, a fact that is repeated three times in 11:2-4. By marrying foreign wives, he broke the law of Moses. Solomon used marriage alliances to secure treaties with Egypt, Moab, Ammon, Edom, Sidon, and the Hittites. This multiplying of wives and alliances with foreign powers violated the covenant (Exod. 34:12; Deut. 17:16-17) and led to Solomon's ruin. No clear reason is given why he did this, but 1 Kings 11:4 links his idolatry with his old age.

Ashtoreth (11:5) was a fertility deity, the Canaanite counterpart of the Babylonian Ishtar; Molech was a chief god of the Ammonites; and Chemosh (11:7) was a deity of the Moabites to whom children were sacrificed (cf. 2 Kings 3:26-27). Worship of Molech also involved the ritual burning of children (Lev. 18:21). The Mount of Olives (1 Kings 11:7) is the mountain

from which the Lord ascended to heaven, and to which he will return. In Solomon's day it was dotted with pagan altars.

11:9-43 GOD OUTLINES HIS JUDGMENT
God brought disciplinary judgment on Solomon by dividing the kingdom (11:11-13) and raising up adversaries (11:14-28). Ten tribes were promised to Jeroboam (11:30-33), and one was promised to Rehoboam. That totaled eleven tribes, but the cloak was torn into twelve pieces. Technically, Rehoboam was promised the one tribe, Judah, but the tribe of Benjamin was allied with Judah (cf. 12:21). Jeroboam received the other ten tribes, including Simeon, a tribe that appears to have migrated north (2 Chron. 15:9; 34:6). Through all this discipline, God was faithful to his covenant with David. His loving-kindness would never depart, even in judgment (1 Kings 11:13, 32, 34, 36, 38-39; cf. also Gen. 22:16-18; 26:3-5 for the source of this love in Abraham's covenant). Three men arose to carry out God's judgment: Hadad the Edomite (from the south, 1 Kings 11:14); Rezon of Aram (to the north, 11:23); and Jeroboam of Israel (in Israel's midst, 11:26).

1 KINGS 12:1—2 KINGS 17:41 CHASTISEMENT: THE DIVIDED KINGDOM
Overview: The divided monarchy (931–722 B.C.) can be divided into four major periods: (1) The Period of Conflict between Israel and Judah (1 Kings 12:1–16:28), 931–875 B.C. (2) The Period of Alliance between Israel and Judah (1 Kings 16:29—2 Kings 11:16), 874–835 B.C. (3) The Period of Independence for Israel and Judah (2 Kings 11:17–15:38), 835–740 B.C. and (4) The Period of Assyrian Domination (2 Kings 16–17), 740–722 B.C.

The first period of the divided monarchy was characterized by military conflict between Israel and Judah until the border was finally established between Mizpah and Bethel (1 Kings 15:21-22). (See the introductory map.) This section extends from the original split between the north (Israel) and south (Judah) to the time when the north was taken captive to Assyria.

The stress throughout is on the fulfillment of God's words of warning concerning rebellion. No matter how long before he had spoken a word, what he had foretold would always happen. That fact was necessary to stress to the exiles in Babylon so that they would understand why they were there. God had not failed; on the contrary, Israel had. But just as God was true to his words of warning, so he would also be faithful to his words of promise and restoration.

12:1–14:20 Jeroboam's Lost Opportunity
12:1-24 JEROBOAM CONFIRMED AS KING
Jeroboam became king due to the foolishness of Rehoboam (12:12-14). But the point of this section is

to show how the word of God was fulfilled through human events (12:15). Jeroboam was acting according to the will of God, and 1 Kings 12–14 shows how he lost his own opportunity to rule Israel. Discipline with scorpions (12:11) refers to the use of whips with barbed hooks tied to the leather thongs.　.

12:25–13:34 GOD'S WORD AGAINST JEROBOAM CONFIRMED

Jeroboam (931–910 B.C.) established a substitute religion of golden calf worship (12:28), a substitute priesthood that was not of the tribe of Levi (12:31), and a substitute feast that was held just one month after the Festival of Shelters (12:32). By doing that, Jeroboam set out to stop the ten tribes of the nation of Israel from returning to the nation of Judah, the "dynasty of David" (12:26-27). In other words, he purposely set out to defeat the clear-cut promise God had made to David (2 Sam. 7). Images of calves (1 Kings 12:28) were associated with Canaanite fertility rituals. Both El and Baal were frequently likened to bulls.

The test of the man of God illustrates the severe consequences of disobedience to divine revelation (13:1-34). The old (false) prophet deceived the man of God into being disobedient to God's original and clear direction. What prompted this deception is not revealed in the text. But the message for the reader is clear: not even the one who delivers the prophecy is above keeping its conditions. When God says something, he means it.

The word of God concerning Josiah was spoken in 13:2. The fatal judgment for the prophet's disobedience confirmed the potency and certainty of the prophecy (13:23-32). This prophecy would be fulfilled years later in 2 Kings 23:15-16. The pattern of the word of God being spoken and then confirmed occurs throughout the book of Kings. It was a pattern that needed to be repeated for those who had been taken into exile.

14:1-20 JUDGMENT ON JEROBOAM IS EXECUTED

As is true throughout the book of Kings, David was the model for a good king (1 Kings 14:8). David was set forth as the ideal servant to whom all other kings were compared (cf. 15:3). Just as David's heart for God secured blessing for Judah, so Jeroboam's disobedience secured destruction for the northern kingdom. The terrible disgrace of having their dead bodies eaten by wild animals (14:11) was one of the cursings of disobedience (Deut. 28:26). The ultimate disgrace for Jeroboam's disobedience was the Assyrian captivity (1 Kings 14:15). God's word of judgment (14:12) was confirmed in 14:18 by the phrase "as the Lord had promised." This is the first promise (14:15) of the Assyrian captivity (722 B.C.) resulting from the northern kingdom's disobedience to the covenant

(cf. Deut. 28:63-64). The Jewish nation of Israel fell into captivity because of her disobedience, not because of God's lack of faithfulness.

14:21–15:24 The Lamp of David in Jerusalem

14:21-31 REHOBOAM

Rehoboam of Judah (931–913 B.C.) was just as apostate as Jeroboam. His idolatrous activities constituted a return to the Canaanite religion. According to his royal records, Shishak, king of Egypt (1 Kings 14:25), identified with Sheshonak I (945–924 B.C.), captured 150 cities in Palestine. This pharaoh may have been the father-in-law of Solomon (cf. 3:1).

15:1-8 ABIJAH

The reign of Abijam (913–911 B.C.) functioned as an example of God's covenant-keeping acts in history. He was unfaithful, but God was faithful to his covenant with David (15:4-5). Abijam fashioned his life after the ungodly example of his father, Rehoboam. God preserved the dynasty of Abijam for the sake of his promise to David (2 Sam. 7:12-16).

15:9-24 ASA

Asa's conformity to the heart of David (15:11) removed all idolatry in the land, even that of his own mother. Asa (911–870 B.C.) was the first great religious reformer in Judah. God blessed him with a reign of forty-one years. Ben-hadad (15:18), king of Aram, was the first of three Aramean rulers to bear this name (2 Kings 6:24; 13:24). The name means "son of [the god] Hadad" and probably served as a dynastic title.

1 Kings 15:25—2 Kings 10:36 The Prophetic Word Certified against Covenant Unfaithfulness

15:25–16:7 NADAB AND BAASHA

Nadab of Israel (910–909 B.C.; 1 Kings 15:25-28) succeeded his father Jeroboam (15:26) to the throne and continued in his evil ways. Baasha of Israel (909–886 B.C.; 15:28–16:7) killed Nadab and became king in his place. That murder fulfilled the word of God concerning the household of Jeroboam (14:10). Again, the resounding point made throughout the book is that when God says something, it happens. His words of judgment are as certain as his words of blessing. The entire section from 1 Kings 15:25 through 2 Kings 10:36 shows how God's prophetic words against covenant unfaithfulness were fulfilled. Baasha also was like Jeroboam and suffered a similar fate (1 Kings 16:2-7).

16:8-20 ELAH AND ZIMRI

Elah of Israel (886–885 B.C.; 16:8-14) had an alcohol problem. He was overthrown by a military leader, Zimri, in order to fulfill God's word of judgment against Baasha (16:12). Zimri of Israel (885 B.C.; 16:9-20) reigned just one week. When the report of his conspiracy reached the army, Omri was declared king; as a result, Zimri burned the palace at Tirzah over his own head.

16:21-34 THE DYNASTY OF OMRI IS INTRODUCED

Omri of Israel (885–874 B.C.; 16:21-28) disputed with Tibni for the throne and became king after a four-year struggle. He was best known for founding a new capital at Samaria on a three hundred-foot-high hill overlooking an important valley in the heart of the northern kingdom. Omri's conquest of Moab was recorded by Mesha on the famous Moabite Stone.

The dynasty of Omri spans from 1 Kings 16:21 through 2 Kings 10:17. Its most famous king was Ahab of Israel (874–853 B.C.; 1 Kings 16:29–22:40), who succeeded Omri and became a powerful but very wicked king. Ahab's wife, Jezebel (16:31), tried to make Baal worship the official religion of the royal court. Her name originally meant "my divine father is a prince," a fitting name for the daughter of a pagan king. But the biblical writer has dropped one letter so that the name means "unexalted," a mockery of the evil queen. Like Baal, Asherah (16:33) was a prominent fertility deity in the Canaanite religion. She was the chief goddess of Tyre, a city of Phoenicia, the homeland of Jezebel.

The reference in 16:34 is to child sacrifice at the groundbreaking ceremony for the rebuilding of Jericho (cf. Josh. 6:26). The word of God, spoken long before in the days of Joshua, was still potent in the days of Ahab. No amount of time could diminish the power of God's promises and warnings. The power of the warnings explains the pain of God's discipline. The power of God's promise gives hope and motivation for repentance. That held true for Israel in captivity as it does for people today in the bondage of their own personal exiles.

17:1-24 ELIJAH IS PRESERVED OUTSIDE OF THE LAND

Lack of rain (1 Kings 17:1) was one of the curses of the covenant that would result from disobedience (Deut. 28:23-24). Zarephath (1 Kings 17:9) was situated between Tyre and Sidon, the very center of the Baal cult. There Elijah would demonstrate God's power to provide flour, oil, and rain—blessings customarily attributed to Baal. Also, this section emphasizes that God can protect the faithful—in this case, Elijah and the widow—even when outside of the land of Israel. This would be a powerful lesson to the Israelites in captivity in Babylon that God can bless his faithful people anywhere. The point of the resurrection of the widow's son was found in the widow's response to the miracle (17:24). The prophet's word was truth, even though the king and other Israelites did not believe it.

18:1-46 GOD'S WORD THROUGH ELIJAH IS CONFIRMED

The Obadiah of the minor prophets was not the same man as this protector of the godly (18:3). Ahab's comment that Elijah had caused the famine (18:17) sums up the lessons of the book of Kings. The people had to learn that it was not the prophets who had troubled the land. Rather, it was their own sins that had brought on the judgment of the Exile.

Mount Carmel (18:20), a 1,742-foot-high promontory jutting in a northwest direction into the Mediterranean Sea, was thought by the Canaanites to be a dwelling of the gods. On this mountain, Elijah confronted the Baal cult. Elijah's mockery attributed basic bodily necessities to Baal (18:27). Elijah was saying that Baal could not respond to his worshipers because he had gone to the toilet. The point of this display is summed up in 18:36, where Elijah acknowledged that the God of Abraham was behind all that he had done. God's people always had trouble believing that God was speaking through his prophets. The people gave the proper, though temporary, response in 18:39.

Elijah ran to Jezreel (18:46), Ahab's camp, to report the victory of God and encourage popular opinion against Jezebel. Note the confession in 18:39. God's control of the rain was a direct attack upon Baal's supposed power.

19:1-21 GOD'S FAITHFULNESS TO THE REMNANT

The section of 19:1–22:40 shows how the prophets' words against Ahab were confirmed. The "afraid" of 19:3 may be translated "and he saw." If Elijah had been afraid, he could have just fled to Judah and the safety Jehoshaphat could provide. What did he see and why did he flee to Sinai? It appears that Elijah realized that he would be no more successful at ending Israel's apostasy than the prophets who had preceded him had been (19:4). He mistakenly thought he was the last faithful person left (18:22, 36; 19:4, 10, 14). That observation led to his discouragement and deep despair.

He fled to Sinai, the source of Israel's covenant through Moses, to recapture the original vision for the nation. There, at Mount Sinai, Elijah understood that the kingdom of God was hidden and easily missed, like God's still, small voice. However, the kingdom was potent and fully under God's sovereign plan. That idea of the hidden and powerful nature of the kingdom was taken up again in the parables of Jesus (Matt. 13) and in his role as the humiliated Son of Man. In 2 Kings, the Elisha narrative reveals more of the hidden and preserved faithful remnant.

The first two parts of Elijah's threefold commission (1 Kings 19:15-16) were carried out by Elijah's disciple Elisha. Elisha anointed Hazael and Jehu. So what did God mean by saying that Elijah would anoint those two (19:15-16)? Elijah passed his authority on to Elisha, and in that sense he anointed Jehu and Hazael. That is the beginning of the concept of Elijah as a type, as is seen later, for example, in John the Baptist (Matt. 17:10-12). Special prophets of God came as Elijah did, that is, in Elijah's spirit and power.

The cloak (1 Kings 19:19) was an outer garment of distinction worn by prominent individuals, especially prophets. Putting the cloak on Elisha was a symbolic act indicating that Elijah's office and authority were to be inherited by Elisha.

20:1-34 A PROPHET'S WORD OF VICTORY IS CONFIRMED

Ben-hadad stationed his army around Ahab's city, Samaria (20:1-21). *Aram* (20:1) is the correct Hebrew term. The people were the Arameans. The King James Version translates "Aram" as "Syria," but Syria did not exist as a political entity until the intertestamental period.

The next two battles provided lessons about God's character. The first battle (20:13-21) taught about God's greatness on Israel's behalf. The second (20:22-34) taught about God's greatness to Israel in contrast to the Arameans' limited concept of God's power (20:28). God gave Israel victory both at Samaria in the mountains and at Aphek in the plain to show that, unlike the localized gods of Canaan, God ruled all territories and regions. Ahab received two proofs of God's greatness.

20:35–22:40 THREE PROPHETS' WORDS OF JUDGMENT ARE CONFIRMED

The story of 20:35-36 again emphasized the necessity of honoring the word of God. At issue was honoring God who gave the message, not passing judgment on the message's seeming insignificance. The judgment prophesied in 20:42 was fulfilled in 22:29-38 (cf. also 21:19).

21:1-29 Ahab's Murder of Naboth.
Ahab was sullen and angry (cf. 20:43 and 21:4). On the basis of the biblical laws of inheritance, Naboth had refused to give Ahab his land (cf. Lev. 25:23-28; Num. 36:7). Ahab's murder of Naboth led to an extremely negative evaluation of his reign (1 Kings 21:25-26). However, even Ahab was able to repent (21:27-29) and, because of his humility, he

received God's kindness. That would have carried the clear message to the readers in exile that no one was beyond receiving God's favor if he would simply humble himself before God.

22:1-40 Micaiah and the Death of Ahab.
Ahab's attitude was one of hatred toward the true prophets of God (22:8). Ahab called Elijah his enemy in 21:20. Far from being Ahab's enemies, the prophets of God were attempting to save the nation's life. That fact would be clear later to those who would read these words in exile and mourn over their repeated animosity toward God's spokesmen in the past.

Ramoth-gilead (22:3) was an important frontier town east of the Jordan River in the territory of Gad (see introductory map). Micaiah, the name of the true prophet, means "Who is like Yahweh?" (22:7-28). God is sovereign over the good and evil spirits, that is, angels and demons (22:20-23). He allowed the deceiving spirit of the false prophets to lead Ahab into battle and to his death. This is a clear example of why the nation went into exile— because God judged their idolatry and social sins by allowing them to believe false prophets. Essentially, the false prophets told sinners that they were really all right before God and that there was no need for repentance from sin. The people's belief in that contradiction of God's clearly revealed laws— the contradiction that had been made by the false prophets—would result in fitting judgment.

22:41-50 JEHOSHAPHAT INTRODUCED

Jehoshaphat (873–848 B.C.) was a spiritual reformer, but not without fault (22:43). His greatest failure was allowing his son, Jehoram, to marry Athaliah, the daughter of Ahab and Jezebel (cf. 2 Kings 8:16-18). The period of conflict between Israel and Judah ended when Jehoshaphat made peace with Ahab (1 Kings 22:44). The treaty was sealed by the marriage of Athaliah to Jehoram (2 Kings 8:16-18, 26-27).

1 KINGS 22:51—2 KINGS 1:18 AHAZIAH'S JUDGMENT IS CONFIRMED

Ahaziah, the son of Ahab, of Israel (853–852 B.C.), followed in the wicked ways of his father (1 Kings 22:51-53). The division between 1 and 2 Kings at 1 Kings 22:53, which splits the account of Ahaziah's reign in half, is the result of later editing.

SECOND KINGS NOTES

Second Kings 1 affirms that when God says something will happen, it does; in this case it was the death of Ahaziah (1:4, 17). The chapter also affirms the divine authority granted to the true prophet of God. Note the two "if" sentences (1:10, 12) followed by the proof: "let fire come down from heaven" (1:10, 12). Elijah called fire from heaven

against the false prophets of Baal (1 Kings 18:36-38). But in this case it represented judgment against the Israelites.

Baal-zebub (2 Kings 1:3) means "Baal of the fly," a mocking alteration of the god's true name, "Baal the prince." The leather belt (1:8) was a belt used to bind garments about one's body. The soldiers

(1:10) were participating in the king's rebellion against Elijah, God's representative, and thus were subjected to divine judgment. Joram of Israel (852–841 B.C.) was the son of Ahab of Israel. He succeeded his brother to the throne because Ahaziah had no son. He was wicked, but not to the extent of Ahab and Jezebel (3:2-3).

2:1-25 POWER IN ELISHA'S WORDS
The travel from Bethel (2:3) to Jericho (2:5) was punctuated with prophecies of Elijah's departure. The travel back from Jericho (2:18-21) to Bethel (2:23-24) proved Elisha's power. The central section is a reminder of God's parting of the waters at creation, at the Red Sea, and at the entrance into the land of Israel. It shows how Elisha received the power. The double portion was the inheritance of the firstborn or heir (Deut. 21:17). Elisha was requesting that he might be the heir or successor of Elijah, which was indeed God's will (1 Kings 19:16). Like Enoch (Gen. 5:24), Elijah was translated to heaven without dying. He departed by a whirlwind or windstorm. Such a storm was often used as a visual symbol of God's presence (Job 38:1; 40:6; Ezek. 1:4; Zech. 9:14).

The group of boys (2 Kings 2:23-24) were not children but young men who could be held morally accountable for their actions (cf. 1 Sam. 16:11; 1 Kings 3:7; Jer. 1:6-7). Not only were their words disrespectful, but they also constituted a challenge to Elisha's divinely appointed ministry. Their judgment was in keeping with the curses pronounced in the Mosaic law against those who were disobedient (Deut. 28:26).

3:1-27 WORDS OF VICTORY OVER MOAB
Second Kings 3 records how Israel campaigned with Judah and Edom against rebellious Moab (3:4-7). Kir-hareseth (3:25) is identified with Kerak on the Transjordan highlands, east of the Dead Sea. With his capital under siege, Mesha sacrificed his oldest son to Chemosh in a final desperate attempt to induce the god to give him victory (3:27). The "anger against Israel" may have been the Lord's anger because the siege resulted in human sacrifice, or the anger of the Moabites, who were challenged to rally against Israel. The three kings of Israel, Judah, and Edom were victorious.

4:1–6:7 THE POWER OF ELISHA
Second Kings 4:1–6:7 begins a long section in which the prophet's words against the house of Omri are confirmed (4:1–10:17). Second Kings 4 shows the blessings that came to those who aligned themselves with the true prophets of God. The wife of a deceased prophet received a miracle of oil (4:1-7). A woman who provided food and a room for Elisha received her dead son back by resurrection (4:8-37). The poisonous food of the sons of the prophets was transformed into good food (4:38-44).

The blessings that came from people aligning themselves with the true prophets of God continued. Naaman was blessed (5:1-27). The lesson he learned, and that the reader should learn, is repeated in 5:8, 15, and 18. The healing of Naaman, the Aramean army captain, demonstrated God's lordship over the whole earth and showed his mercy on an obedient Gentile. Here the Abrahamic covenant (Gen. 12:1-3) was being fulfilled as Israel was bringing blessing to the Gentiles. Although expressing faith in God (2 Kings 5:17), Naaman still held to the view that no god could be worshiped properly except in his own land. Therefore, Naaman wanted two loads of earth from the land of Israel so he could worship the God of Israel on his own soil. "Rimmon," also known as Hadad Rimmon (5:18; Zech. 12:11), referred to the supreme deity of the Arameans.

Again, the blessings of the prophets continued. The sons of the prophets were given their lost ax head (6:1-7). The recovery of the ax head reveals that God is concerned even with small things and helps his faithful ones with such matters. Elisha's miraculous ministry in this section demonstrates that there is no need that God cannot meet when it comes to loving his faithful ones.

6:8–7:20 THE POWER OF GOD TO DELIVER FROM SYRIA
Dothan (6:13), where Joseph had found his brothers (Gen. 37:13-17), was located thirteen miles north of Samaria in a broad valley leading into the Jezreel Valley (see introductory map). Elisha taught love for one's enemies (2 Kings 6:22; cf. Matt. 5:43-45). This is the second Ben-hadad mentioned in 1 and 2 Kings (2 Kings 6:24. The horror of cannibalism (6:29) was one of the curses that would result from disobedience to the covenant (Deut. 28:53).

God gave Elisha power to deliver Israel from Syria once in 2 Kings 6:8-23 and again in 6:24–7:20. That kind of military victory could have been Israel's continually if she had just listened to God's warnings through his prophets.

The doubt of the officer in charge of guarding the gate of Samaria brought God's judgment upon him (7:2, 17-20), but Elisha's word was confirmed (7:16). The prediction of a return to reasonable prices and available commodities took place in the midst of a siege-induced famine (6:25). The point being made for the readers of this book who were in exile was that God would do the impossible, but only the faithful would experience those blessings.

8:1-6 THE WOMAN FROM SHUNEM IS PRESERVED
The story of the woman from Shunem (8:1-6) again stressed the blessings of God on his faithful people, not only while within the land, but also while outside of the land of Israel. (See the introductory

map for Shunem's location.) This would be a message of encouragement to the faithful believers who were exiled to places far from their homeland.

8:7-15 HAZAEL BECOMES KING OF SYRIA
Hazael was a high officer in the court of Ben-hadad II who killed his master and became one of the most powerful kings of Aram (or Syria). Why did Elisha command Hazael to lie to Ben-hadad when the Lord had shown the prophet that the king would die (8:10)? Actually, Elisha predicted that Ben-hadad's illness itself would not be fatal. However, Ben-hadad would die, but at the hand of Hazael. Hazael, in 8:11, was gazing at Elisha the prophet, lost in his thoughts of how he might take the throne from the ailing Ben-hadad.

8:16-24 PRESERVATION FOR JUDAH
Jehoram, the son of Jehoshaphat of Judah (853–841 B.C.), walked in the evil ways of the kings of Israel, for he had married Athaliah, Ahab's daughter (8:16-24). God disciplined him with the loss of territory, but God preserved the throne of Judah because of his promise to David (8:19; 2 Sam. 7:12-16).

8:25–10:17 THE HOUSE OF AHAB IS DESTROYED
Ahaziah, the son of Jehoram of Judah (841 B.C.), appears to have been strongly influenced by his mother, Athaliah, and thus followed the wicked example of the northern kings of Israel (2 Kings 8:25-29). Joram (8:28-29; whose name is sometimes spelled Jehoram) refers to the king of Israel, the son of Ahab (8:16). This king of Israel is to be distinguished from the king of Judah with the same name.

Jehu, the commander of Israel's army, brought the wicked dynasty of Omri to an end and became the next king of Israel (841–814 B.C.; 9:1-37). His rule was the most bloody of any king of Israel. The divine commission to destroy the house of Ahab (9:7-8) constituted God's retribution on Jezebel's sins and fulfilled the promised judgment on Ahab's son (1 Kings 21:19, 29). After Jehu was proclaimed king (2 Kings 9:13), he began his bloody purge that included the murder of Joram, king of Israel (9:14-26); Ahaziah, king of Judah (9:27-29); and Jezebel (9:30-37).

The power of God's word spoken through Elijah continued as Jehu judged Ahab's sons (10:1-11; note especially 10:10, 17). He extended his judgment to the supporters of Ahab (10:11), the relatives of Ahaziah (10:12-14) and of Ahab (10:17), and the prophets of Baal (10:18-28). But his zeal for the Lord was misguided (10:16). He overstepped the commission given him by the Lord (9:7-10). "Just as the Lord had promised through Elijah" (10:17) refers to 1 Kings 21:19.

The pattern throughout the book of Kings is to show that every evil will be judged according to the word of God spoken through his prophets. The seventy-year Babylonian exile was simply the consistent culmination of God's righteous judgments upon Israel's disobedience.

10:18-36 JEHU IS CHASTENED
God chastened Jehu (2 Kings 10:29-36) through the Arameans, and the northern kingdom lost all of its Transjordan territories to Hazael. The records of Shalmaneser III also indicate that Jehu was forced to pay heavy tribute to the Assyrians.

11:1–14:29 Covenant Blessing from Obedience
11:1–12:21 THE RETURN OF THE PEOPLE TO THE COVENANT
11:1-20 Joash spared
The section of 11:1–14:29 shows the blessings that came to Judah when the king returned to keeping the Mosaic covenant. Athaliah of Judah (841–835 B.C.) usurped the throne when Ahaziah, her husband, was slain by Jehu. She immediately sought to revive the Baal cult in Judah (11:18) that her mother, Jezebel, had so successfully introduced in Israel. Even though Athaliah tried to wipe out all of David's offspring, God preserved one royal son according to his covenant with David.

The period of alliance between Israel and Judah was brought to an end by the murder of Ahaziah by Jehu (9:27-29) and the killing of Athaliah by the captains of Judah (11:13-16). Then both of the two kingdoms entered a period of independence, power, and prosperity. The latter part of this period was considered the "Golden Age" for Israel and Judah.

12:1-21 Joash reigns
Joash, also known as Jehoash, the son of Ahaziah, reigned next in Judah (835–796 B.C.). He was brought to the throne as a lad of seven by Jehoiada the priest. The early years of the king's reign, when he ruled under the influence and guidance of Jehoiada, were marked by spiritual reform. But this did not continue after Jehoiada's death (2 Chron. 24:17-22). As soon as the temple was restored (12:4-16), its wealth was given to Hazael, the king of Aram (or Syria), to keep him from attacking Jerusalem (12:17-18).

13:1–14:29 GOD'S FAITHFULNESS TO THE ABRAHAMIC COVENANT
13:1-9 Jehoahaz
Second Kings 13–14 clearly shows all the weaknesses of the kings of Judah and Israel. Jehoahaz of Israel (814–798 B.C.) succeeded his father, Jehu, to the throne. His days were characterized by continual Aramean oppression (13:22). His glimmer of faith (13:4) was answered by victory. The unnamed deliverer (13:5) may refer to the Assyrian emperor Adad-nirari (810–783 B.C.) who attacked Damascus in 806 B.C., thus weakening the Arameans.

13:10-25 Joash
Jehoash of Israel (798–782 B.C.), another evil king, defeated Hazael and recovered Israel's territory that had been taken by the Arameans. Throughout the book of Kings, the reasons why God preserved the nation are clearly ascribed to his faithfulness to his covenant with David. In 13:23 the foundational reason for God's faithfulness is given: the covenant with Abraham.

The little story of 13:20-21 continues the theme of the power of God through his prophets. In this case, even the bones of Elisha were powerful enough to raise the dead.

14:1-22 Amaziah
Amaziah of Judah (796–767 B.C.) improved on the record of his father, Joash, but failed to remove the tempting pagan high places from the land. Beth Shemesh (14:11), a city in the Judean foothills, is located at the head of the Sorek Valley, about fifteen miles southwest of Jerusalem.

14:23-29 Jeroboam II
Jeroboam II of Israel (793–753 B.C.), although an evil king, was noted for his great expansion of the northern kingdom. He recovered Damascus and Hamath (14:28) for Israel and extended Israel's border as far south as the Sea of the Arabah, that is, the Dead Sea (14:25). The prophet Jonah (14:25), who fled the Lord's commission to preach at Nineveh, lived at Gath Hepher in Galilee (cf. Josh. 19:13) during the reign of Jeroboam II.

15:1–17:61 Chastisement Confirmed

15:1-7 UZZIAH
The section of 15:1–17:41 confirms and explains the ultimate judgment upon Israel. Uzziah (Azariah) of Judah (791–739 B.C.) was known for his great building projects and strong military power. He expanded the southern kingdom east, west, and south. In the end, he succumbed to pride and had to live out his days under God's judgment as a leper.

15:8-12 ZECHARIAH
Zechariah of Israel (753 B.C.) was the fourth and last ruler of Jehu's dynasty. Again, the stress was on the fulfillment of God's word (15:12; cf. 10:30).

15:13-15 SHALLUM
During the Assyrian threat against Israel, Shallum of Israel (752 B.C.) ruled for just one month before being overthrown by Menahem. That was the beginning of the end for the northern kingdom. In just thirty years Israel would fall to the Assyrians.

15:16-22 MENAHEM
Menahem of Israel (752–742 B.C.) was a wicked king whose depravity can be illustrated by his dealings with the rebellious city of Tappuah ("Tiphsah" in Hebrew; 15:16). Tiglath-pileser ("Pul" in

Hebrew), the king of Assyria (15:19), was probably Tiglath-pileser III (754–727 B.C.), who assumed the name of a great king of the past when he ascended to the throne of Assyria. Under the leadership of Tiglath-pileser, the kingdom of Assyria became a great empire that eventually swallowed up the petty kingdoms of Aram and Israel. At this time, both Judah and Israel began to enter a period of Assyrian domination (2 Kings 16–21). Menahem paid tribute to Assyria (15:19-20). In doing so he retained his throne but became an Assyrian vassal.

15:23-26 PEKAHIAH
Pekahiah of Israel (742–740 B.C.) ruled only two years before being overthrown by Pekah.

15:27-31 PEKAH
Pekah of Israel (740–732 B.C.) and Rezin of Damascus, the Aramean king, formed an alliance to resist Assyria. Ahaz, king of Judah, refused to join their anti-Assyrian alliance and was attacked by Pekah and Rezin (Isa. 7:1-7). Against the warnings of the prophet Isaiah, Ahaz called upon Assyria for help. Tiglath-pileser responded with three devastating campaigns against Israel and Damascus (734–732 B.C.). In 733 B.C. Assyria captured northern Israel (2 Kings 15:29) and exiled the population. The days of the northern kingdom were numbered.

15:32-38 JOTHAM
During the Assyrian threat against the southern kingdom, Jotham of Judah (750–731 B.C.) was a good king whose concern for the things of God was evidenced by his rebuilding of the upper gate of the temple (cf. 2 Chron. 27:3).

16:1-20 AHAZ
Ahaz of Judah (743–715 B.C.) was a wicked king who was faced with Assyrian domination. He chose to submit to Assyria rather than join the anti-Assyrian coalition of Rezin and Pekah (16:7). The phrase "sacrificing his own son in the fire" (16:3) refers to the sacrifice of Ahaz's son to Molech, a Canaanite god of Ammonite origin. Damascus was captured by Assyria in 732 B.C. (16:9). Ahaz usurped the function of the priests by offering sacrifices himself upon an altar built to resemble the Assyrian altar at Damascus (16:11-13).

17:1-61 HOSHEA
Israel was taken into Assyrian captivity. Hoshea (732–722 B.C.), the last king of Israel, began his rule as an Assyrian vassal paying annual tribute to Tiglath-pileser III and his successor, Shalmaneser V (727–722 B.C.). Then, in league with Egypt, he revolted (17:4). After three years of siege, Samaria was captured. Sargon II (722–705 B.C.) succeeded Shalmaneser and claimed the victory. He then exiled Israel's inhabitants to distant regions of the Assyrian Empire.

17:7-41 Chastisement Explained

While 17:1-6 provides the political reason for Israel's captivity, 17:7-41 provides the religious explanation. Israel's sins against the God who had redeemed them from Egypt are described in 17:7-12. God had warned Israel through his prophets (17:13-18). First Kings 1–16 described that warning in detail. Why? In order to convince the exiled captives that their continual disobedience, not God's lack of interest, had caused their downfall. They had not departed from the sins instituted by Jeroboam (17:21). God's prophetic word of judgment was sure (17:23).

The Samaritans of the first century A.D. (John 4) had their origins in the mixture of ethnic backgrounds and worship institutions described here (2 Kings 17:24-41). Again, the Exodus from Egypt and the Mosaic covenant were the focus of obedience and the measure for disobedience (17:36-38).

18:1–25:30 PRESERVATION: THE SOLITARY KINGDOM

Overview: The rest of 2 Kings describes the history of the solitary kingdom of Judah, which was subject to three foreign powers during this period: Assyria (2 Kings 18–21), Egypt (2 Kings 22–23), and Babylon (2 Kings 24–25). This section stresses that God is faithful to the slightest show of repentance and to his great covenant with David. Although this section appears to continue the judgment of Judah's sins on into the Babylonian captivity, it is actually an upbeat description of how God preserved the kingly line promised to David. When the northern kingdom, Israel, ended with the Assyrian captivity, the southern kingdom, Judah, continued to have a son of David as king. Even though the physical kingdom was destroyed and the people had no religious or political independence, God was still faithful to keep a son of David alive to return and reign someday according to his promise.

18:1–20:21 Reform: Babylon Introduced

18:1-37 THE NORTHERN KINGDOM FALLS AND JERUSALEM IS ATTACKED

Hezekiah of Judah (728–686 B.C.) was one of the most godly descendants of David to sit on the throne of Judah. He began his reign with a revival of orthodox religion. The bronze serpent made by Moses in the wilderness (Num. 21:8-9) had become an object of worship (2 Kings 18:4). Its name, "Nehushtan," sounds like the Hebrew terms for "snake," "bronze," and "unclean thing."

Hezekiah did not rebel against Assyria (18:7) until after the death of Sargon II (705 B.C.), who had captured Samaria. In 701 B.C. Sennacherib, king of Assyria (705–681 B.C.), invaded Judah; he captured forty-six cities and besieged Jerusalem. In his own annals he wrote of Hezekiah, "Himself I

made a prisoner in Jerusalem, his royal residence, like a bird in a cage." Lachish (18:14), about seventeen miles west of Hebron, guards an important valley that gives access to the hill country of Judah. While Sennacherib was besieging the city, Hezekiah submitted to Assyria and met the demand for tribute (18:14-16). Sensing that Hezekiah could not stand up to him, Sennacherib decided to go ahead with the capture of Jerusalem. The meaning of the Hebrew word translated "field commander" (18:17) is uncertain. The title implied a position of high-level leadership. This leader was an official emissary and spokesman for Sennacherib. The Rabshakeh (most likely a title, not a name) threatened Hezekiah so that he would surrender (18:17-25). For God's perspective on Judah's tendency to rely on Egypt for deliverance (18:21), see Isaiah 30:1-2 and 31:1-3.

Addressing the Judeans, the Rabshakeh promised peace and prosperity in return for their submission to Assyria (2 Kings 18:27-36). He threatened the people of Israel with proud rhetorical questions (18:33-35).

19:1-37 GOD SPARES JERUSALEM FOR HIS NAME'S SAKE

The key to 2 Kings 19 is in verses 4 and 34. God repulsed Assyria from Jerusalem because Assyria had blasphemed against the Holy One of Israel and because God was faithful to his covenant with David. The tearing of one's clothes and putting on rough sackcloth (19:1) was a traditional sign of grief and mourning. Isaiah encouraged Hezekiah with a promise of deliverance from the Assyrian menace (19:7).

Some scholars believe that 2 Kings 18:17–19:37 refers to a later Assyrian campaign (around 688 B.C.), based on the reference to Tirhakah (19:9), who ascended the throne of Egypt in 690 or 689 B.C. However, Tirhakah was twenty years old at the time of this campaign and appears to have been summoned by his brother, the king, to lead the campaign into Judah. He assumed a responsible role in this endeavor, although he was only the crown prince at the time. But since he later became king, the application of the title of king in telling the story is appropriate.

Hoping to avoid fighting on two fronts at the same time, that is, against both Judah and Egypt, Sennacherib sent a letter to Hezekiah demanding his submission (19:10). Hezekiah prayed that Judah's divine deliverance from Sennacherib would testify to Yahweh's uniqueness as the one true God (19:19). God said that he would preserve Judah and enable the people to prosper in their land (19:30). God accomplished the deliverance (19:34) for the sake of his own glory and his covenant faithfulness to David (cf. 2 Sam. 7:12-16).

Esarhaddon (681–669 B.C.) succeeded his father to the throne of Assyria (19:36-37).

20:1-21 HEZEKIAH'S LIFE IS EXTENDED

It is generally held that Hezekiah's illness and recovery took place before Sennacherib's attack since the promise of deliverance from the Assyrians (20:6) would not have been necessary if Sennacherib's army had already been destroyed. The miraculous retreat of the shadow on the steps (20:10-11) was probably a local miracle accomplished by the refraction of light rather than a reversal of the earth's rotation. The foolish and unnecessary display of Jerusalem's wealth (20:13) whetted the appetites of the Babylonians, who later brought their troops against Jerusalem. The pool and the tunnel (20:20) are further described in 2 Chronicles 32:30. Hezekiah built the tunnel to carry water from the Gihon spring, outside the city walls, to the pool of Siloam, which was within the protective defenses of Jerusalem. The Siloam inscription, discovered in the tunnel, indicates that the workers cut from opposite ends and met in the middle.

21:1-26 Irrevocable Chastisement: Manasseh and Amon

Second Kings 21 outlines the basis of the irrevocable chastisement that would fall on Judah. Manasseh of Judah (697–642 B.C.) was one of the most wicked kings to rule the southern kingdom. His apostasy actually exceeded the conditions of the Canaanites who had lived in the land of Israel before the conquest (21:9). Second Chronicles 33:10-13 records that he later repented of this evil, but he could not change the ways of the people. Like Ahaz (2 Kings 16:3), Manasseh practiced child sacrifice (21:6). Manasseh's son, Amon (642–640 B.C.; 21:19-26), followed the evil ways that his father had practiced before his change of heart. The end of God's patience and the extent of Judah's rebellion from the day the Israelites were taken out of Egypt are clearly shown (21:10-15).

22:1–23:30 Reform in the Shadow of Judgment: Josiah

Josiah (640–609 B.C.) brought reform in the very shadow of judgment. Because of his humility before God, he was spared from seeing Judah's downfall (22:11, 19-20). This reform was in the light of certain destruction (22:15-17). The exiles reading this would be encouraged that reform of any sort, even after discipline, would be received with favor by God. Josiah, Judah's greatest reformer, was compared with David (22:2) and noted for his unprecedented obedience (23:25). His first step in reform was to repair the Jerusalem temple, which had been neglected during the fifty-seven years of the reigns of Manasseh and Amon.

The eighteenth year of Josiah (22:3) would have been 622 B.C. Just four years earlier (626 B.C.), the city of Babylon had rebelled and begun a destructive campaign against Assyria. In 612 B.C. the Babylonian and Median armies captured Nineveh, Assyria's capital. Assyria's last stronghold, Haran, fell to Babylon in 610 B.C. Both Egypt and Babylon were interested in ruling Judah. Egypt would have the first opportunity to do so.

Some scholars have suggested that the Book of the Law (22:8) was Deuteronomy, written by a pious scribe and planted in the temple area so that it might be discovered and accepted as Mosaic. The manuscript may well have been Deuteronomy, since it contained both the curses of disobedience as well as positive instruction, but there is no reason to suggest that it was a fabrication. Studies in form criticism have done much to confirm the authenticity of Deuteronomy and its Mosaic authorship.

Jeremiah was the son of Hilkiah the priest (22:14). Jeremiah, who had begun his prophetic ministry just five years earlier, in the thirteenth year of Josiah's reign (2 Kings 22:3; cf. Jer. 1:2), was not mentioned. This is not unusual, for he would not have gained a widespread reputation as a prophet by this time.

The first half of 2 Kings 23 describes Josiah's reformation. The act of 23:16 fulfilled the prophecy of 1 Kings 13:2. Although the prophecy had been spoken long before, God was in control to bring about his word of judgment and blessing.

The record of reform provides a stark commentary on the idolatry and apostasy that characterized the reigns of Manasseh and Amon. Topheth (2 Kings 23:10) literally means "place of burning" and refers to the altar hearth of Molech, a god to whom children were sacrificed by burning. With Assyria on the decline, Josiah was able to assert his influence even into Samaria (23:15-20).

Josiah lost his life at Megiddo when he went out to confront Pharaoh Neco of Egypt (23:29). Pharaoh Neco probably felt threatened by the rapid Assyrian demise in the face of aggressive Babylon. No doubt he sought to equalize the balance of power by rushing to the aid of Assyria's Asshuruballit, who was attempting to recapture Haran in 609 B.C. Assuming that any friend of Assyria was an enemy of Judah, Josiah tried to stop the Egyptian advance. He lost his life in the attempt, but he was spared the sadness of witnessing Judah's destruction.

23:31–25:26 Chastisement Confirmed

23:31-35 JEHOAHAZ

Jehoahaz of Judah (609 B.C.) was the first of Josiah's three sons to rule Judah. But his reign lasted only three months. When Pharaoh Neco returned from his campaign against Babylon, Jehoahaz was deposed and imprisoned. Judah fell under Egyptian domination.

23:36–24:7 JEHOIAKIM

Jehoiakim of Judah (609–597 B.C.) paid tribute to Egypt in order to keep his throne. The change of his name from Eliakim (23:34) was in keeping with a sovereign's privilege in dealing with a vassal ruler. In the fourth year of Jehoiakim's reign, 605 B.C., the Babylonians defeated the Egyptian army at Carchemish (Jer. 46:2) and became the new world power. Nebuchadnezzar (605–562 B.C.) moved quickly to secure his newly won territory of Judah. He proceeded to Jerusalem and took some of the royal family, along with many temple vessels, back to Babylon (Dan. 1:1). This is considered the first deportation to Babylon (605 B.C.).

24:8-17 JEHOIACHIN

Jehoiachin (597 B.C.), son of Jehoiakim, ruled only three months before Jerusalem was attacked by Nebuchadnezzar. This resulted in the second deportation of Judah to Babylon (2 Kings 24:14). Jehoiachin was also known as Coniah (Jer. 22:28, NASB and KJV) and Jeconiah (Matt. 1:12, NIV and KJV).

24:17–25:7 ZEDEKIAH

Zedekiah (597–586 B.C.), Josiah's third son, was installed as a puppet ruler by Nebuchadnezzar and reigned eleven years. After that period of submission to Babylon, Zedekiah decided to revolt (24:18-21; cf. 2 Chron. 36:13).

25:8-26 THE FINAL DEPORTATION TO BABYLON

Nebuchadnezzar began his final attack on Jerusalem in December of 588 B.C. After eighteen months of siege, the city walls were breached (July 586 B.C.). Then there was a third deportation of Judeans from their homeland. The three deportations of Judah are summarized in the chart below.

Riblah (2 Kings 25:20), located about sixty miles north of Damascus, was the staging ground for Nebuchadnezzar's attack against Judah. Nebuchadnezzar appointed Gedaliah to govern Judah as a province of Babylon (25:22). Mizpah (25:23), usually identified with the site of Tell en-Nasbeh, located about eight miles north of Jerusalem, served as Gedaliah's residence and the administrative center for Judah. Jeremiah was kidnapped and taken to Egypt with the rebels (25:25-26; cf. Jer. 43:6-7).

25:27-30 Preservation of the Davidic Kingship: Jehoiachin Restored

The release of Jehoiachin in 560 B.C. by the king of Babylon (2 Kings 25:27) was evidence that the line of David was still under God's protective care (cf. 2 Sam. 7:12-16). The elevation of a king in captivity may not seem like much of an achievement, but to the captives it would be certain proof that God had not forgotten his people or his promises. That proof would encourage his people to get their lives squared away in order to honor God and prepare for his future acts of release and redemption.

THE THREE DEPORTATIONS OF JUDAH

First Deportation	Daniel 1:1	605 B.C.
Second Deportation	2 Kings 24:14-15	597 B.C.
Third Deportation	2 Kings 25:11	586 B.C.

---

1 & 2 CHRONICLES

BASIC FACTS

HISTORICAL SETTING

The books of 1 and 2 Chronicles cover the history from the first man, Adam, to the restoration of Israel from the Babylonian captivity (around 538 B.C.). Originally a single book, it was completed sometime after the Jews' return to Palestine during the difficult times when they tried to reestablish their nation and religion after the catastrophe of the Babylonian captivity. Babylon had fallen and Persia ruled that empire.

AUTHOR

The author of Chronicles is unknown. Since Ezra was a priest and scribe during the time it was probably written, he has often been accepted as the most likely candidate for the author. This is further substantiated by the fact that the book of Ezra begins exactly the way Chronicles ends.

DATE

If Ezra wrote Chronicles, it would put the date of writing around 457 B.C. The time period re-created in the book, no matter who the original author was, is the positive time of reconstruction after Israel had returned from captivity in Babylon.

PURPOSE

The book of Chronicles was designed to encourage the Jews who had returned to rebuild their nation and continue in faithfulness to God. Punishment for sins was in the past, and their future held the fulfillment of the bright promises God had made to Abraham and David.

GEOGRAPHY AND ITS IMPORTANCE

The book of Chronicles begins geographically at Hebron and ends with the Persian king Cyrus's decree for Israel to return from exile to her own land. Although the book begins at Hebron, it quickly moves to David capturing and settling Jerusalem. The focus from that point on is the temple. After the split of Israel into northern and southern kingdoms, the focus is still on good kings like Josiah and Hezekiah and their temple reforms. Even at the end of the book, when Cyrus allowed Israel to return to her land, the central purpose was to restore the temple (2 Chron. 36:23). The book of

Chronicles has one geographic focus, the temple at Jerusalem, and one corresponding thematic focus, encouraging faithfulness in the worship of God.

GUIDING CONCEPTS

THE ORIGINAL UNITY OF FIRST AND SECOND CHRONICLES

The books of 1 and 2 Chronicles were inspired as one book. The translators of the Greek Old Testament (the Septuagint) split the book into two parts. They named the books "The Things Left Out" because they thought Chronicles simply filled in the gaps of events that had been left out of the books of Samuel and Kings. But Chronicles is much more than material that fills in gaps. Although there is some new material in Chronicles, large sections of the book are a nearly verbatim repetition from Kings. In fact, nearly half of Chronicles is almost verbatim repetition from the books of Samuel and Kings. If the purpose of Chronicles was to fill in gaps, why would there be the massive amounts of repetition? Obviously its purpose was not to fill in gaps, and its repetition serves as the key to understanding its real purpose.

Actually, Chronicles was designed to build a foundation by repeating God's greatest past redemptive acts on Israel's behalf. Then, upon that foundation, the writer of Chronicles gives a message of encouragement for Israel's future after the Babylonian captivity, a future which would be built upon the ruins of her past sins and upon the power of God's unchanging promises.

THE END OF SECOND CHRONICLES

The end of the book of Chronicles takes the reader to the first year of Cyrus, king of Persia (538 B.C.). Cyrus allowed the Israelites to return to their homeland, and that is the note upon which the book ends. The last verse (2 Chron. 36:23)

The broken lines (— ·— ·) indicate modern boundaries.
Copyright © 1986, 1988 by Tyndale House Publishers, Inc.

is a positive call to all Jews to return to the land of God's promises. The thrust was for them to be optimistic about the future. God's disciplining punishment was past. It was now the time for them to regroup and to rebuild what had been destroyed. God had been faithful to his promises, and now the Jews were once more to receive their part in his blessings of redemption.

Chronicles was designed to retell Israel's history by emphasizing the actions that brought God's blessing. Those actions were to be models for Israel after she returned to the land. The time for chastisement and dwelling on failure was past. The book of Kings already had struck the notes of failure and its consequent judgment. Chronicles emphasizes the positive past as a basis for a positive future. Israel was to learn from the past and strive for a God-honoring future.

THE TEMPLE AS THE FOCUS OF A POSITIVE PERSPECTIVE

Chronicles has a clear focus on how the kings' righteous actions supported the pure worship of God at the temple. The temple was where the Mosaic covenant resided in the Most Holy Place. It was the place where God met with human beings to hear their prayers and forgive their sins. Chronicles emphasizes the proper treatment of the temple in order to encourage the same honor on the part of those who returned from the Exile to rebuild the temple.

Once the story moves past David and Solomon, the bad points of the kings are mentioned, but nothing is written about the northern kingdom of Israel except as its kings came into contact with the kings of Judah. The focus is all on Judah—the good things that happened during the reigns of David and Solomon and the bad events that occurred after them. The emphasis is on the wonderful period of the unified kingdom when David and Solomon were obedient to God and maintained worship in the way that God desired. That was where the readers' minds were to dwell.

THE STRUCTURE OF CHRONICLES

Genealogies	1 Chron. 1–9
Saul	1 Chron. 10
David (nineteen chapters)	1 Chron. 11–29
Military support unified	1 Chron. 11–12
Ark, temple, and Davidic covenant	1 Chron. 13–17
Military victories and support	1 Chron. 18–20
Plans and offerings for the temple	1 Chron. 21–29
Solomon (nine chapters)	2 Chron. 1–9
Building and dedication of the temple	2 Chron. 1–7
Activites, wealth, and power	2 Chron. 8–9
Rehoboam	2 Chron. 10–12
Abijah	2 Chron. 13
Asa	2 Chron. 14–16
Jehoshaphat	2 Chron. 17–20
Jehoram through Ahaz	2 Chron. 21–28
Hezekiah	2 Chron. 29–32
Manasseh	2 Chron. 33
Josiah	2 Chron. 34–35
Captivity and release	2 Chron. 36

STRUCTURE

The emphasis of the book of Chronicles can be seen in the chart on the previous page.

Most of the content of Chronicles is about David and Solomon (28 out of 65 chapters), especially their work on the temple and Israel's worship there (21 out of 28 chapters). The focus is on the great work on the temple by the two great men of God, David and Solomon. That emphasis was needed to encourage the Israelites who had returned from the Exile to work on rebuilding the temple and restoring the city of Jerusalem (see the books of Haggai and Zechariah).

BIBLE-WIDE CONCEPTS

THE COVENANT SUCCESSES OF DAVID AND SOLOMON

The book of Chronicles emphasizes the good deeds of David and Solomon. While the book of Kings showed how the sins of the kings brought about the captivity, the book of Chronicles shows how the kings' obedience brought blessing. The sins of David and Solomon are either not mentioned or are minimized. When the book of Chronicles covers the life of David, it does not mention the sad episodes of his adultery with Bathsheba and murder of Uriah, of Amnon's violation of Tamar, or of Absalom's rebellion. In telling of Solomon's life, no mention is made of Adonijah's problems, of Solomon's punishment of David's enemies, or of his polygamy and idolatry. The Jews had read of those problems in the book of Kings. The book of Chronicles leaves them out to emphasize a positive perspective for rebuilding the kingdom. The book recounts examples of God's commitment to the covenant blessings that he had promised to Abraham, Moses, and David.

NEEDS MET BY 1 & 2 CHRONICLES

Chronicles ends with the people of Israel being called to return to their homeland. But it leads up to that happy moment by rehearsing the successes and failures of Israel's past. At the moment of their release from God's discipline, God's people needed a reminder of what had made them successful and what had led to their disastrous failures. The emphasis is clearly on repeating in the future what had made them successful in the past. The book of Chronicles answered questions like the following for the Israelites who had returned from the Babylonian exile to rebuild the kingdom in Israel.

- How can the people of Israel go on with their lives after such a great destruction of their homeland and seventy years of exile?
- Can the future be as great in any way as the outstanding moments of Israel's history?
- How can what happens "after" the captivity be anything like what happened "before" the captivity when the two periods are separated by a time of awful discipline?
- Has Israel's original hope for future redemption been completely destroyed by her terrible sin and long period of discipline?
- Can the Israelites still hope in the promises that God made to Abraham, Moses, and David?

The prophetic point of Chronicles is that God's people can count on God's promises even after a time of discipline for failure. He proved his commitment to Israel and the Davidic kingship by bringing Israel from exile back to the Promised Land. He has brought all believers into the age of the fulfillment of all his promises through Jesus Christ. The Christian must learn from the past what makes for success or for failure. Recovering from discipline involves leaving the negatives of the past behind and focusing on the positive actions that bring obedience and blessing.

OUTLINE OF 1 & 2 CHRONICLES

I. ESTABLISHING THE HOLY CITY (1 CHRONICLES 1:1—2 CHRONICLES 9:31)
   A. Legitimizing the Nation's Ancestry (1 Chron. 1:1–9:1)
   B. David: The Legitimate King (1 Chron. 9:2–29:30)
   C. Solomon: The Legitimate Heir (2 Chron. 1:1–9:31)

II. MAINTAINING THE HOLY CITY (2 CHRONICLES 10:1–36:23)
   A. Preservation of Lineage (10:1–23:21)
   B. Restoration to the Land (24:1–36:23)

1 CHRONICLES NOTES

1 CHRON. 1:1—2 CHRON. 9:31
ESTABLISHING THE HOLY CITY
1:1–9:1 Legitimizing the Nation's Ancestry
Overview: First Chronicles 1–9 records genealogies that trace the development of the human race from Adam to David. The purpose was to define the place of God's chosen people in world history and to show the origins of the Davidic line through which the Messiah would come. While these genealogies are not very interesting to today's reader, they were of great value and importance to the returned exiles.

Genealogies trace one's lineage in order to legitimize one's background. These genealogies trace, in incomplete form, all the tribes of Israel back to Abraham and a line from Abraham all the way back to Adam. But only two family lines have unbroken genealogies extending through the Babylonian exile: those of David and Eleazar. That is, only the royal and priestly lines are emphasized. That emphasis shows the purpose of the genealogies: to legitimize the ancestry of the royal and priestly lines of the kingdom. The other lines are sketchy and do not form an unbroken line through the postexilic period.

The genealogies also have a set structure by which the reader can more fully understand their purpose: (1) the genealogy leading up to Israel (1 Chron. 1); (2) the genealogies of Judah, Levi and Benjamin (1 Chron. 2–8); and (3) the genealogy of postexilic Israel (1 Chron. 9).

The function of this structure is to show the continuity of the postexilic nation with respect to all of Israel's history. After the destruction of the nation and seventy years of captivity, the Israelites needed to regroup and reorient themselves to their nation's history and its purpose for existence. The genealogies rehearse both the history and the purpose of the line of Israel.

In 1 Chronicles 1 the important people are listed last, while in 2:1–8:40 the important tribes of Israel are listed first. The genealogy of 1:1-54 goes as far as the offspring of Israel (1:34; 2:1), and that of 2:1–8:40 works its way down from the most important offspring of Israel, the royal line of David (2:1–4:23), to the privileged but ill-fated tribe of Benjamin, of King Saul's family (8:29-40).

In 2:1 the tribes are introduced in this order: (1) Reuben, (2) Simeon, (3) Levi, (4) Judah, (5) Issachar, (6) Zebulun, (7) Dan, (8) Joseph, (9) Benjamin, (10) Naphtali, (11) Gad, (12) Asher. But the tribes' actual genealogies are listed in the order presented in the chart on the next page.

1:1-54 ADAM THROUGH ISAAC
In 1 Chronicles 1 the most important people are listed last. For example, the families of Noah's sons (1:4) are listed in the order of Japheth (1:5-7), Ham (1:8-16), and then Shem (1:17-27), the line through which Abraham came. In the line of Abraham (1:28), Ishmael is listed first (1:29-33) and then Isaac (1:34). When the sons of Isaac are named (1:34), Esau is first (1:35-54) and then, as the most important, Israel (2:1–9:44).

First Chronicles 1:1-4 provides a condensed version of the genealogy of Genesis 5. Gaps in ancient genealogies were not regarded as inaccuracies because the purpose of a genealogy was not to provide a step-by-step historical chronology but to trace a family line to its chief ancestor. First Chronicles 1:5-27 reproduces, except for minor variations in spelling, the genealogy of Genesis 10. Abram's name (1 Chron. 1:27, meaning, "exalted father") was changed to Abraham (meaning, "father of a multitude"; cf. Gen. 17:5). Jacob (1 Chron. 1:34) is referred to here by his new name, Israel (meaning, "he who strives with God"), which he received after his night of wrestling with the Lord. Then the descendants of Esau, who was the ancestor of the Edomites, are given (1:35-54).

2:1–9:1 JACOB'S SONS
2:1–4:23 Judah
Bathshua (2:3) literally means "daughter of Shua," as in Genesis 38:2. Achan (1 Chron. 2:7) is the Achan of Josh. 7:1. According to 1 Samuel 16:10-

11, Jesse had eight sons, David being the youngest. One apparently died in childhood and thus was omitted from the genealogy (1 Chron. 2:13). Bezalel (2:20) was the chief architect of the tabernacle (Exod. 31:2).

The content of 1 Chronicles 2:4–4:1 centers on the line of David, which came from Hezron (2:9) through Ram (2:10), and its structure is as follows:

I. INTRODUCTION: SONS OF JUDAH (JERAHMEEL, RAM, CALEB) (2:3-9)
   A. Line of Ram: David (2:10-17)

II. LINE OF CALEB (2:18-24)

III. LINE OF JERAHMEEL (2:25-41)
   A. Supplement to Caleb (2:42-55)
   B. Supplement to David (3:1-24)

IV. CONCLUSION: SONS OF JUDAH (4:1)

The line of David is traced down to the grandsons of Zerubbabel after the return from Babylon.

THE LISTINGS OF TRIBAL GENEALOGIES IN CHRONICLES

Group One
- Judah (2:1–4:23): Judah was the house of the Davidic covenant, which was promised an unending royal reign. Clearly, the first major emphasis of Chronicles is on the past and future of the Davidic hope for the king.
- Simeon (4:24-43): Simeon was grouped with Judah off and on throughout its history (cf. Josh. 19:1; Judg. 1:3, 17). After the single kingdom split into the north (Israel) and the south (Judah), the tribe of Simeon apparently migrated into the northern kingdom (cf. 2 Chron. 15:9). However, the faithful of that tribe returned to Judah as 2 Chronicles 15:9 shows.

Group Two
- Reuben (5:1-10): Reuben was Israel's firstborn. Gad and the half-tribe of Manasseh are grouped with Reuben because they all settled across the Jordan River to the east of the other ten tribes.
- Gad (5:11-22).
- The half-tribe of Manasseh (5:23-26).

Group Three
- Levi (6:1-81): Levi was the great tribe of priests and ministers for the temple worship. The second major emphasis of Chronicles is the establishment of the proper orders for worship at God's holy temple.

Group Four
- Issachar (7:1-5): The rest of the tribes north of Judah are listed, but Dan and Zebulun are not mentioned.
- Benjamin (7:6-12): Benjamin, King Saul's tribe, is mentioned twice, both at the beginning and the end of this section.
- Naphtali (7:13).
- The other half-tribe of Manasseh (7:14-19).
- Ephraim (7:20-29).
- Asher (7:30-40).
- Benjamin (8:1-40).

First Chronicles 3 traces the line from David to the restoration from exile. Bathsheba (3:5) was another name for Bathshua. Of those mentioned in 1 Chronicles 4, only Perez was a son of Judah. But the term "sons" is used loosely in the Hebrew language and can refer to grandsons or, even more broadly, to descendants. For the descendants of Simeon (4:24-43) and their territory, see Joshua 19:1-8.

5:1-26 The Transjordan tribes.
Although Reuben (5:1) was the firstborn and had the right of double inheritance (Deut. 21:17), he lost this privileged position due to his uncontrolled passions (Gen. 35:22; 49:3-4). Tiglath-pileser (1 Chron. 5:6) was the king of Assyria, who subjugated northern Israel in 733 B.C. (2 Kings 15:29). The descendants of Gad are listed (1 Chron. 5:11-17), as are the wars of the Transjordan tribes (5:18-22). The Exile (5:22) refers to the Assyrian captivity of 722 B.C. The descendants of Manasseh are given in 5:23-24. Pul (5:26) is probably the original name of Tiglath-pileser (see the note on 2 Kings 15:19).

provided in 7:6-12, tracing the ancestry of Saul (cf. 8:33), Israel's first king. The phrase "skilled warriors" is repeated (8:40) with reference to the tribe of Benjamin. David would sin by wanting to number those mighty men of war rather than trusting in God to provide the victory no matter what the number of warriors (1 Chron. 21). The contents of 8:29-38 are repeated nearly verbatim in 9:35-44. "The Book of the Kings of Israel" (9:1) is not a reference to the canonical book of Kings, but to a royal court record that is now lost. The verse (9:1) functions as an end to the preexilic listing of families and prepares the reader for the list of postexilic returnees that is given next.

9:2–29:30 David: The Legitimate King
Overview: First Chronicles 1–8 focused on the line of David, the ministers at the temple, and the surrounding tribes full of mighty men of valor to fight for the kingdom. In 1 Chronicles 9–29, which includes the rest of the book, the interest centers on David and his line of kings. More space is devoted

---

THE SONS OF LEVI

6:2-15	Kohath's line: Especially Aaron and Moses
6:16-30	Two Cycles of the Three Sons of Levi
6:31-48	David's Temple Musicians
6:49-53	Kohath's Line: Aaron's Sons
6:54-81	Kohath's Line: Settlements

6:1-81 Levi
First Chronicles 6 revolves around the temple service inaugurated by David and Solomon. The three sons of Levi—Gershon, Kohath, and Merari—are mentioned (6:1). The structure of chapter 6 is outlined in the above chart, *The Sons of Levi.*

The emphasis is on the priestly line from Aaron on. That would legitimize the priestly line, which was beginning anew, and its mediatorial work at the postexilic temple in Jerusalem. This section would have been of special interest to Ezra, the probable author of Chronicles, who was himself a priest.

7:1–9:1 The Remaining Tribes
Listed in this section are the descendants of Issachar (7:1-5), Benjamin (7:6-12), Naphtali (7:13), Manasseh (7:14-19), Ephraim (7:20-29), and Asher (7:30-40). One key to the emphasis is the repetition of the phrase "men available for military service" with reference to the first two and the last tribes mentioned in 1 Chronicles 7 (Issachar, 7:2, 5; Benjamin, 7:7, 9, 11; Asher, 7:40, "skilled warriors"). Ephraim was the tribe of Joshua (7:27). Manasseh and Ephraim are listed together because they were the sons of Joseph (7:29).

First Chronicles 8 supplements the information

to David than to any other ruler. He is set forth as the founder of the royal dynasty in Judah and as an example of a successful ruler for those who returned from exile to pick up the pieces of the earthly kingdom of God.

9:2-34 THE POPULATION OF JERUSALEM
The section of 9:2-34 gives the family names of those who returned to live in Jerusalem after the exile. First Chronicles 9 quotes extensively from Nehemiah 11, which lists the initial repopulation of Jerusalem. The purpose is to show the continuity with the original and God-ordained ministry of worship (1 Chron. 9:22). Just as it had been under David and Solomon, so it could be once again.

9:35-44 SAUL'S ANCESTRY
The members of the family of Saul (9:35-44) lived in Gibeon and Jerusalem. These verses, repeated from 8:29-38, serve to introduce Saul's fall in battle, which, in turn, prepared the way for David's ascent to the throne. Unlike the book of Kings, there is no interest here in the details of Saul's rise and fall as king.

10:1-14 SAUL'S REMOVAL
The story of Saul's death (1010 B.C.) is not told just to repeat the historical record (cf. 1 Sam. 31).

Rather, the author has a definite moralistic emphasis. An important lesson is to be learned by the restored population of Israel (cf. 1 Chron. 10:13-14). Those verses assume a familiarity with the accounts in 1 Samuel and simply present a succinct summary of all that was wrong with Saul's rule as well as giving a warning to any future king.

This particular temple of Dagon (10:10), the chief god of the Philistines, was located in Beth-shan (1 Sam. 31:10). Archaeologists have uncovered a large temple at the site.

11:1-3 DAVID ANOINTED

The section of 1 Chronicles 11:1–12:40 shows how there was total support for God's legitimate king. David ruled over Judah from 1010 to 970 B.C. Key phrases used throughout the reigns of David and Solomon were "all Israel," "all the people of Israel," "all the Israelites," "all the political leaders of Israel," "the entire community of Israel," and "all the tribes of Israel" (11:1, 4, 10; 12:38; 13:5; 15:3, 28; 19:17; 23:2; 29:23, 26; 2 Chron. 1:2; 5:6; 7:8). David's and Solomon's reigns had complete support from all of Israel, unlike the later times of the divided kingdom when the north and south fought against each other in civil war. David reigned for his first seven and a half years at Hebron, located in the hill country about twenty-five miles south of Jerusalem (see introductory map).

11:4-9 JERUSALEM CAPTURED

The capture of the Jebusite fortress (1 Chron. 11:4-7) gave David a strategic site for his capital. Its central location (actually in Benjamite territory) would help David secure the loyalties of the northern tribes. Jerusalem, also known as Jebus (11:4), became Zion, the City of David (11:5). The Millo (11:8, or "the supporting terraces," NASB and KJV), meaning "filling up," was a rock terrace probably used as a building's foundation. The exact location is uncertain. The author was very interested to point out the basis for David's success: the Lord was with him (e.g., 11:9). Again, the spiritual aspect of the nation's history is highlighted.

11:10–12:40 MIGHTY MEN WHO SUPPORTED DAVID

David's mighty men and their feats (11:10-47) provided security and support for the kingdom. Mighty men figured largely in the events of 1 Chronicles 11:10-47 and also in 2 Samuel 21:15-22; 23:8-39. The cave of Adullam (1 Chron. 11:15) is located about seventeen miles southwest of Jerusalem in the vicinity of the city that bears the name. The Rephaim is a branch of the Sorek Valley which provides access to Jerusalem from the Philistine coastal plain.

The repeated phrase "warriors" or "brave warriors" (12:1, 8, 21) is connected with a list of warriors from the twelve tribes (12:23-38) to show the original and growing support for God's king, David. The entire nation was of one mind to make David king (12:38). Ziklag (12:1) was a Philistine city in the east Negev that David used as the base for various raids (1 Sam. 27:6-11). The warriors came to David at Hebron to help him establish his throne over all Israel. The total number of warriors was about 350,000. The mention of past joy (1 Chron. 12:40) was to kindle afresh a similar joy for restored Israel.

13:1-14 THE FIRST ATTEMPT TO RETURN THE ARK TO JERUSALEM

The author was very much interested in Israel's worship and religious institutions. He went to considerable length to show David's high regard for the ark of the covenant, as evidenced by his bringing it up to Jerusalem. The ark (13:5) had remained at Kiriath Jearim (modern Abu-Ghosh), about ten miles east of Jerusalem, since it had been recovered from the Philistines in the days of Samuel (1 Sam. 7:1-2). "One end of the country to the other" (1 Chron. 13:5) refers to "the Shihor River of Egypt" (KJV), which is identified with the Wadi el 'Arish and served as the southern boundary of the Israelite territory. Lebo Hamath, or the entrance of Hamath, was the northern border and probably was located between the Lebanon and Anti-Lebanon mountains at about the same latitude as the island of Cyprus.

The ark was to be carried on poles, not transported on a cart, and it was not to be touched. The judgment on Uzzah (13:10) may seem severe, but God's holiness was at stake (cf. Num. 4:15). The author did not want any similar matters of ritual and procedure to be ignored by the returnees from Babylon for whom he was writing.

14:1-17 ENEMIES SUBDUED

First Chronicles 14 moves from David's kingdom being highly exalted (14:2) to the fame and fear of David spreading to all the nations, which was a sober reminder of what God would do again through his Davidic king to come. It was up to the fledgling nation to once again believe God's promises and work obediently to restore the kingdom. The king's marrying multiple wives (14:3) was a violation of Deuteronomy 17:17. David's example led the way for Solomon's excesses in this area. The valley of Rephaim (1 Chron. 14:9) gave the Philistines direct access to Jerusalem from the coastal plain. Baal-perazim (14:11) literally means "the lord of breaking forth." David's troops broke through the Philistine offensive as raging waters might break through a dam. Gibeon (14:16) is in the hill country just north of Jerusalem, while Gezer is on the northwestern edge of the Shephelah, or foothills.

15:1–16:3 THE ARK IS SUCCESSFULLY BROUGHT TO JERUSALEM

The emphasis on the great joy in Israel (12:40) continues (15:16, 25; 16:4). Having learned from his previous bad experience (13:7-10), David instructed that the ark be transported properly (15:2). David was the first Israelite to give significant recognition to the place of music in worship (15:16-24), the purpose of which was to "sing joyful songs to the accompaniment of lyres, harps, and cymbals" (15:16). For a note on the "tunic" (15:27), see 1 Samuel 2:18.

16:4-43 REJOICING AND THE CARE OF THE ARK

The central thrust here is David's function in assigning Asaph to praise the Lord in poetry and song (16:7, 37). At the heart of 1 Chronicles 16 is an example of such praise (16:8-36), which is a compilation of Psalms 105:1-15 and 106:1, 47-48. For more on the burnt and peace offerings (1 Chron. 16:1), see Leviticus 1–3. The expression "song of thanksgiving" (1 Chron. 16:7) literally means "to give public acknowledgment." That is the essence of biblical praise—a public declaration of God's greatness (his attributes) and his goodness (his actions). This song of thanksgiving rehearses the great elements of Israel's faith and hope: seeking the Lord (16:8-11), remembering his past deeds (16:12-14), remembering his covenant with Abraham (16:15-22), and praising him as Creator and coming Judge of all the nations (16:23-36). It would take the eyes of encouraged faith to believe in such a future for the small band of returned Jews. Zadok (16:39) was the priest who remained faithful to David in the time of Absalom's revolt. The ark was now in Jerusalem, but the tabernacle stood at the worship center at Gibeon.

17:1-27 GOD'S HOUSE FOR DAVID

David was concerned because he had a lovely home in Jerusalem, while the ark was in a mere tent. David wanted to build God a house, but instead the Lord declared that he would build a house for David (17:10). Here the word "house" (17:10) is used in the sense of royal house, family, or dynasty. The Davidic covenant (17:11-14; cf. 2 Sam. 7:14-29) amplifies and confirms the promise God gave Abraham in Genesis 12:1-3 about his future long line of descendants.

One surprising aspect of God's promise to Abraham was the mention that kings would also be part of his line (Gen. 17:6, 16; 35:11). That promise of kings was made specific in the Davidic covenant. The royal line of Israel's kings was an original part of the wonderful promise that God made to Abraham. Here God promises David that he will have a son (the Messiah) who will sit on his throne and rule his kingdom forever (1 Chron. 17:11-14). This promise would serve as a tremendous encouragement to the struggling people of restored Israel.

18:1–20:8 WARS: ENEMIES SUBDUED

God promised David that his enemies would be subdued (1 Chron. 17:10). The subduing of various enemies of Israel is described (18:1). Further proof is given of God's loving-kindness upon David (18:13). David was the first king to deal adequately with the Philistine menace. The record of David's conquests to the west, east, north, and south was designed to show the newly restored nation how God blesses those who love and serve him as David did.

Moab (18:2) was located in Transjordan, east of the Dead Sea. Zobah (18:3) was probably located somewhere northeast of Damascus. Modern Hama, located on the Orontes River, is identified with ancient Hamath (18:3). The Valley of Salt (18:12) is probably a reference to the Rift Valley, which is south of the Dead Sea. To the southeast of the sea lies the territory of Edom. Ahimelech (18:16; cf. 2 Sam. 8:17) is incorrectly given as Abimelech in some translations (NASB and KJV).

First Chronicles 19 gives a further illustration of how God, through his covenant with David, subdued all his enemies (cf. 17:10). The territory of the Ammonites (19:1) was located in Transjordan, northeast of the Dead Sea. Such treatment as that described in 19:4 would be regarded as a grave insult. The thirty-eight tons of silver (19:6) would approximate 1,200,000 ounces. Medeba (19:7), located about twenty miles southwest of modern Amman, the capital of Jordan, is the location of the famous sixth-century Medeba Mosaic Map. "Arameans" (19:10) is incorrectly given as "Syrians" in the King James Version.

First Chronicles 20 covers the time of David's sins concerning Bathsheba and her husband, Uriah. However, 1 Chronicles does not mention them because its aim is to present the best of Israel's history in order to build the best kind of future. This rounds out the story of 1 Chronicles 19 concerning the Ammonites. Rabbah (20:1), the capital of the Ammonites, is identified with present-day Amman. For David's treatment of the Ammonites (20:3), see the note on 2 Samuel 12:31. Gezer (1 Chron. 20:4) is located on the northwestern edge of the Shephelah about twenty-two miles west of Jerusalem. The giants were among the original inhabitants of Canaan (cf. Gen. 15:18-21 and Num. 13:28, 33). Gath (1 Chron. 20:6), one of the five Philistine cities, was located on the coastal plain south of Ekron.

21:1-30 CENSUS AND PLAGUE

It is easy to miss the fact that this section of 1 Chronicles gives details about the significance of

God's covenant with David (cf. 17:3-27). The essence of that covenant was that God would subdue Israel's enemies and build a royal house of kings for David. First Chronicles 18–20 illustrates God's promise to subdue David's enemies (17:10). But that was simply to provide the security for Israel to build and worship at God's house, which David desired to build (17:1-2; cf. 22:18-19).

First Chronicles 21 again takes up the theme of building a house for God and shows the surprising and tragic circumstances through which the temple's location was selected. Satan, as Israel's ultimate enemy, was behind the numbering of Israel's armies (21:1-8). David's prayer of intercession (21:8-17) was accepted, and he was commanded to provide an intercessory offering (21:18-27). The king's intercession for the nation was emphasized as a key element of the Davidic covenant (cf. 2 Sam. 21:14; 24:25).

When God responded to David's prayers by sending fire from heaven upon his altar, David realized that Jerusalem was where God's temple and altar should be (1 Chron. 21:28-30). Fire from heaven was a sign of God's presence; such affirmation had previously appeared at these key junctures in God's redemptive history: at the altar before the tabernacle with Moses and Aaron (Lev. 9:24); with Gideon's offering (Judg. 6:21); with Elijah's offering on Mount Carmel (1 Kings 18:38); and with Solomon as God reaffirmed his choice of the temple site (2 Chron. 7:1).

For Satan's involvement (1 Chron. 21:1), see the note on 2 Samuel 24:1. But David took responsibility (1 Chron. 21:8, 17). He was taking a census to find out how many men he had for his army (cf. 27:1-23), which was an insult to God's already proven ability to deliver Israel from all her enemies and a misuse of the mighty men God had given to David. David (21:7) appears to have been trusting in his own resources rather than in God's (see the note on 2 Sam. 24:10).

"Beersheba to Dan" (1 Chron. 21:2) is a reference to the traditionally southern and northern extremities of the Israelite territory. The figures of 1,100,000 and 470,000 found in 21:5 are given as 800,000 and 500,000 for Israel and Judah, respectively, in 2 Samuel 24:9. It may be that the figure for Israel in 1 Samuel does not include the nearly 300,000 men listed in 1 Chronicles 27. The figure for Judah in 1 Samuel 24:9 may not include the 30,000 of 2 Samuel 6:1. It is also possible that the figures in Chronicles have been rounded off.

The punishment options (1 Chron. 21:12) were of an increasing severity with a decreasing duration. Araunah (21:15) is also translated Ornan (NASB and KJV; cf. 2 Sam. 24:16). David adhered to the principle of sacrificial giving (1 Chron. 21:24). He knew that the value of a gift that he offered to God would be measured by his own degree of sacrifice (Luke 21:1-4). The total purchase price of 600 pieces of gold, about 300 ounces (1 Chron. 21:25), covered the cost of the threshing floor and oxen and also included the surrounding area. This was where Solomon later built the temple. Although Solomon built the temple (cf. 17:11-12), it was David who had the vision for the project (22:5) and made arrangements for implementing its construction.

22:1-19 THE CHARGE TO SOLOMON
The theme of the temple's construction is here continued. David's wars and bloodshed disqualified him from the privilege of building God's temple (22:8-9), but they also were used by God to fulfill his promise of subduing Israel's enemies (cf. 22:18 with 17:10). The task of building the temple was reserved for Solomon, whose reign was characterized by peace. The resources set aside for the project included about 120 million ounces of gold and 1.2 billion ounces of silver.

23:1–24:31 TEMPLE ORDERS FOR PRIESTS
See 1 Kings 1 for more details about Solomon's turbulent ascent to the throne (1 Chron. 23:1). David's great administration and his organization of the temple ministry are described in 1 Chronicles 23–27. The army and civil administrators (1 Chron. 27) were supports for leading the nation in its mission to worship God and to be a living witness to his greatness. Assignments were given to the various priestly families, and the Levites were divided into twenty-four divisions, each of which would minister at the temple two weeks out of the year. David appears to have lowered the age requirement of those entering into Levitical service (23:3, 24; cf. Num. 4:3; 8:24). Zacharias, father of John the Baptist, was of the priesthood of Abijah (1 Chron. 24:10; cf. Luke 1:5) and was ministering in the temple when he received the angelic announcement that he was soon to be a father.

The organization of the temple personnel from Aaron's descendants and the rest of the sons of Levi was completed (1 Chron. 24:1-31). These lists are a reminder of the care that David took in organizing the temple worship. This probably encouraged the same care on the part of the returnees from the exile.

25:1-31 TEMPLE ORDERS FOR MUSICIANS
First Chronicles 25 reflects one of the great high points in the history of worship. Here David appointed temple musicians to lead the worship through music. The word "proclaim God's messages" (25:1) suggests some musical proclamations of divine revelation that came as expressions of praise and worship (cf. 1 Sam. 10:5; 2 Kings

3:15-16). Words and music that edified the hearers were the heart of biblical praise and worship.

26:1-32 TEMPLE ORDERS FOR GATEKEEPERS AND TREASURERS
The gatekeepers (1 Chron. 26:1-19) were appointed to guard the temple and prevent unauthorized persons from entering it. The courtyard (26:18) probably refers to a colonnade or open chamber on the west side of the temple area. The Levites were responsible for the temple's treasures and dedicated offerings (26:20-28). Certain officers and judges were given responsibility for those matters relating to the temple that had to be dealt with outside Jerusalem (for example, hewing timber and quarrying stones; 26:29-32).

27:1-43 TEMPLE ORDERS FOR MILITARY HEADS
David organized his army into twelve divisions of 24,000 men, each of which served one month out of the year (27:1-15). David organized the tribes by placing certain leaders over them (27:16-24). It is not known why Gad and Asher were missing. David had a number of overseers and counselors to assist him in his administrative responsibilities (27:25-34).

28:1–29:30 COVENANT AFFIRMATION
In light of the selection of the temple site and the preparations for its building and use (1 Chron. 21–27), 1 Chronicles 28–29 contains a speech by David to his assembled nation. The speech centers on praise to God for his covenant with David (28:4-7), the passing on of the temple plans to Solomon (28:11-19), and the authority to command the builders (28:20-21). The ark of the covenant is likened to a footstool for God (28:2), who was enthroned above the cherubim (1 Chron. 13:6).

Although David was the appointed ruler, he recognized that God was the supreme King over Israel (28:5). A conditional aspect of God's covenant is reflected in 28:7-8. Such conditionality can only refer to individual and personal invalidation of covenant benefits. The promise, confirmed by God's oath, would be continued even though individual participation might be delayed or forfeited. In such cases, the promises would be passed on to the heirs. The cherubim (28:18) over the ark of the covenant were likened to God's chariot (cf. Ps. 18:10). The temple plans were not David's own but were the result of divine revelation (1 Chron. 28:19).

The key to understanding the significance of the offerings of David (29:1-5) and the people (29:6-9) can be found in the words, "in addition to" (29:3), "willingly," and "freely" (29:6, 9, 17). The atmosphere was one of rejoicing (29:9) and joy (29:22). The message for the newly returned Jews was to adopt the same gladness and purity of heart in their work on the new temple. The offering of David (29:4) amounted to about 3.6 million ounces of gold and 8.4 million ounces of silver. The precious metals (29:7) amounted to over 6 million ounces of gold and 12 million ounces of silver.

The first coronation of Solomon (29:22; cf. 1 Kings 1:32-40; 1 Chron. 23:1) was in response to Adonijah's attempt to usurp the throne. Here Solomon's kingship was confirmed and publicly acknowledged. Zadok was confirmed as high priest as a result of Abiathar's disloyalty (1 Kings 1:5-8). Again, the phrase "all Israel" (1 Chron. 29:23, 26) was applied to both Solomon and David to show the original unity and support of both the northern and southern tribes of Israel. Special emphasis was given to the officials and the mighty men (29:24), the political and military powers. None of the writings mentioned in 29:29 have been preserved.

SECOND CHRONICLES NOTES

1:1–9:31 Solomon: The Legitimate Heir
Overview: Second Chronicles 1–9 is devoted to Solomon's reign as king. Very little information is given here that is not found in 1 Kings. The writer's religious focus is evidenced by the attention given to the temple and the instructions for worship.

1:1-17 SOLOMON'S KINGDOM POWER
God established Solomon's kingdom (2 Chron. 1:1) as he had promised (cf. 1 Chron. 28:7). For "all Israel" (2 Chron. 1:2) see the usage throughout 1 Chronicles, for example, 29:23, 26. Solomon carried on the unified rule over all Israel. It was a unity that was maintained by those who returned from the Exile. Solomon initiated a massive dedication of the king and nation to God (1:1-6). On that basis, the thrust of 1:7-17 is to show how Solomon's great wealth and international power came to him from God because he asked for wisdom (1:7-12).

The tabernacle (1:3) was situated at Gibeon, about six miles northwest of Jerusalem. For a description of the bronze altar (1:5), compare Exodus 27:1-8. In acquiring so many horses (2 Chron. 1:14-16), Solomon violated a specific prohibition given by God (Deut. 17:16). The king was to depend on the Lord, not his own military might. Cilicia (2 Chron. 1:16) was a region of southeast Asia Minor. Solomon paid about 240 ounces of silver for the chariots and about 60 ounces of silver for his horses (1:17). Presumably he made a good profit through his horse and chariot trade.

2:1-18 THE PLANS AND PURPOSE OF THE TEMPLE

Solomon decided to build a temple for God (2:1), and then he started to build (3:1). Plans were laid out for collecting the raw materials to be used in the building of the temple (2:1-18). The temple was to be a place for the name of the Lord (2:1) and a place to burn sacrifices to him (2:6); it was to be a place to worship and to remember the name of God (cf. 6:11, 22-24, 34-39, 41).

Hiram (2:3) sometimes appears as Huram and it is sometimes translated as such (NASB and KJV). Almug (2:8) is thought by some to be red sandalwood. Huram-abi (2:13) was a half-Israelite whose mother was of the tribe of Dan, but she appears to have lived in the territory of Naphtali (cf. 1 Kings 7:13-14). Joppa (2 Chron. 2:16), Jerusalem's closest Mediterranean seaport, was situated about thirty-five miles to the northwest.

3:1–5:1 THE TEMPLE IS COMPLETED

The golden walls of the temple's inner rooms, the sculptured cherubim overlaid with gold, the woven curtain, and the porch of the temple are described (3:1-17). Mount Moriah (3:1), where the temple was built, is believed to be the mountain in the land of Moriah where Abraham offered Isaac (Gen. 22:2). Solomon began to build the temple in the spring (April–May) of 966 B.C. The location of Parvaim (3:6) is uncertain, although some have suggested Arabia or Yemen. Twenty-three tons of pure gold (3:8) is approximately 736,000 ounces. For the names of the pillars (3:17), see the note on 1 Kings 7:21.

The emphasis is on the altar (2 Chron. 4:1-6)— the place where Israel's sins were forgiven through sacrifice—and on the golden lampstands (4:7). The other items in the temple are only mentioned briefly. Here it is recorded that the Sea could hold about 16,500 gallons of water (4:5). First Kings 7:26 mentions only 11,000 gallons of water. Perhaps the 16,500 gallons included the amount held by the smaller basins (4:6).

5:2-14 GOD'S GLORY FILLS THE TEMPLE

Upon the completion of the temple, the ark was brought up from Jerusalem, the City of David, also known as Zion, to the temple mount, just to the north. Two key elements were present. First, the response of the people was summed up by the musicians: they praised and glorified God for his goodness and lovingkindness (5:13), the words that sum up all of God's character, kind covenants and acts of redemption. Second, the temple, like the tabernacle (Exod. 40:34-35), was filled with the glory of God (2 Chron. 5:14). That showed that God's presence and blessing were with the temple just as they had been with the tabernacle before it. The temple's size and ornamentation did not deter-

mine God's presence, but the ark with its binding covenant did.

The feast of dedication (5:3), held in the seventh month (September–October), was followed by the Festival of Shelters (see the note on 1 Kings 8:2). Apparently Aaron's staff and the jar of manna (Heb. 9:4; cf. Exod. 16:33-34; Num. 17:10) had been lost by this time (2 Chron. 5:10).

6:1-42 SOLOMON'S PRAYER OF DEDICATION

The relationship between the Mosaic and Davidic covenants is clearly presented. The temple and Solomon were fulfillments of the promise that God had made to David in 2 Samuel 7 (2 Chron. 6:9-10). As God's chosen man, Solomon placed the ark, which contained the Mosaic covenant (6:11), at Jerusalem, God's chosen place (6:6). On the basis of the Mosaic covenant, the king mediated between God and the people. That mediation found its ultimate fulfillment in the mediation of God's perfect Son of David, Jesus the Messiah.

The word "name" appears throughout 2 Chronicles 6 and refers to God's reputation or attributes that were focused upon the temple and all that it signified (6:7-8, 10, 20, 24, 26, 33-34, 38). Solomon's prayer of dedication (6:12-42) acknowledged God's covenant commitment to David (6:14-17) and solicited forgiveness and restoration when the nation would fall into sin. The pattern throughout this section is "if/when . . . then" and covers various problem situations and their remedy of remembering God, praying to him in the temple, and hoping in his remembrance and covenant forgiveness. That same instruction and hope applied to the returned exiles.

7:1-22 THE DEDICATION FEAST AND WARNINGS FOR DISOBEDIENCE

After Solomon prayed, fire from heaven consumed the burnt offering and sacrifices (7:1). The three other times in the Old Testament when God showed his approval by sending fire from heaven were: when Gideon presented an offering (Judg. 6:20-21), the sacrifice of Elijah on Mount Carmel (1 Kings 18:38), and when David built the first altar on the threshing floor of Araunah, or Ornan (1 Chron. 21:26; on 2 Chron. 7:9, see the note on 1 Kings 8:2). All Israel supported Solomon, observed the feast, and had great joy in God (2 Chron. 7:8).

God answered Solomon's dedicatory prayer by promising mercy and forgiveness on the basis of repentance (7:13-15), a new addition to what was given in 1 Kings 9:3-5, and the covenant with David (2 Chron. 7:17-22). This promise provided the theological foundation for the preaching of the Old Testament prophets in calling Israel to repentance and for the key role of the ruling son of David in preserving the nation from disaster. That role of preservation was perfected in the great Son of David, Jesus, whose perfect rule assures perfect peace and salvation.

8:1-18 SUMMARY OF SOLOMON'S PROJECTS
Solomon's great building projects were interspersed with the assurance that the temple was run exactly as the king commanded (8:15). Hamath-zobah (8:3) has not been specifically identified, but it was probably located somewhere northeast of Damascus. Tadmor (8:4), later known as Palmyra, is an oasis in the Syrian desert located halfway between Damascus and the Euphrates River. For Hamath (8:4), see 1 Chronicles 18:3. Upper Beth-horon and Lower Beth-horon (2 Chron. 8:5), situated on a strategic route into the hill country from the coastal plain, were located ten and twelve miles, respectively, northwest of Jerusalem. Baalath (8:6), of the tribe of Dan (Josh. 19:44), was situated at the edge of the coastal plain. Ezion-geber (2 Chron. 8:17), at the north end of the Gulf of Aqaba, was the port for Solomon's Red Sea fleet of ships (1 Kings 9:26). Elath (2 Chron. 8:17) was apparently located nearby, although some scholars have suggested that Elath and Ezion-geber were one and the same. Ophir (8:18) was situated along the Red Sea in southern Arabia, in the area of today's Yemen.

9:1-31 SOLOMON'S INTERNATIONAL WEALTH
There are two special aspects to the description of the greatness of Solomon in 9:1-31. First, the queen of Sheba rightly saw God's blessing behind all the impressive riches of the kingdom (9:8). Second, the longer descriptions of the greatness of the kingdom show the fulfillment of God's promises to both Solomon (regarding greater fame and riches than all kings, 9:22: cf. 1:11-12) and Abraham (regarding the boundaries of the land, 9:26; cf. Gen. 15:18). That was as close as Israel would come to the fulfillment of the Abrahamic and Davidic promises this side of the Millennium.

Sheba (2 Chron. 9:1) was located in southern Arabia, in the vicinity of today's Yemen. The 9,000 pounds of gold (9:9) amount to about 144,000 ounces. The 25 tons (9:13) are about 800,000 ounces.

10:1–36:23 MAINTAINING THE HOLY CITY
Overview: The rest of 2 Chronicles (10–36) records the history of the kings of Judah, highlighting their spiritual successes and failures. The success of each king was measured by his faithfulness to God and the Mosaic covenant. This history was intended to instruct Israel's restoration community in the importance of obeying God so they might enjoy his blessings and avoid divine chastening.

10:1–23:21 Preservation of Lineage
10:1–12:16 REHOBOAM
The kingdom divided (10:1-19) under Rehoboam (931–913 B.C.). The division caused a tragic change in the meaning of the term "all Israel." Whereas all of Israel, that is, all the twelve tribes from both the northern and the southern parts of Israel, came to make Rehoboam king of the nation (10:1), the ten northern tribes, who from that time onward became known as Israel, departed in rebellion (10:16-19). "Let's go home home, Israel" (10:16) was a call for the northern tribes to disassociate themselves from the dynasty of David, represented by Rehoboam, and thus declare independence from Judah. Adoniram (10:18) is also spelled Hadoram (NASB and KJV) or Adoram (1 Kings 12:18; NASB and KJV).

After his initial mistake of refusing to heed the advice of the elders (2 Chron. 10:3-16), Rehoboam began to rule wisely (11:1-23). Because the purpose of the book of Chronicles was to encourage the restored tribes toward unity and obedience, the unified aspects of the divided nation were emphasized. For example, the southern tribes of Judah and Benjamin drew the faithful from out of the north (11:3, 13–14). And in 12:1 "all Israel" refers just to the southern tribes under the Davidic king, Rehoboam.

A unique historical contribution of 2 Chronicles is the list of cities that Rehoboam fortified in anticipation of Shishak's invasion (11:5-12; cf. 12:1-4). Those cities were located at strategic points to the west, south, and east of the hill country of Judah. Jeroboam made goat idols (11:15) that were fashioned after the idols of Canaan that bore the image of the goat. For more on the calf idols that he made (11:15), see the note on 1 Kings 12:28-29. Absalom's one daughter, called Maacah here (2 Chron. 11:20), was also named Tamar (2 Sam. 14:27). The Hebrew term for "daughter" may also mean "granddaughter" (cf. 1 Kings 15:2). (For the king's marriage regulations, 11:21; cf. Deut. 17:17.)

Rehoboam was humbled (2 Chron. 12:1-16) when Shishak, the king of Egypt (12:2), attacked Judah in 925 B.C. Inscriptions at Karnak list the cities that Shishak conquered. He was aided by Libyan (Lubim) and Cushite (Ethiopian) forces. His other allies, the Sukkites (Sukkim), were another tribe of people apparently from Africa but not presently identified. The lesson of 12:8 would have special meaning for those who had just returned from seventy years of captivity in Babylon. Note the threefold use of the term "humbled" (12:7, 12) in connection with the conditions of 7:14. In or out of the land, a person's humble heart might not do away with all the negative consequences of his failure, but it would bring God's kindness and blessing.

13:1–16:14 ABIJAH TO ASA
13:1–14:1 Abijah
Abijah (913–911 B.C.) gave an address that was a reinforcement and reminder of the authority given to the ruling son of David on the basis of the Davidic covenant (13:5, 8). On that basis, God gave Abijah the victory over Jeroboam (13:15). That example (13:18) would have been an encouragement for the citizens of Israel's restoration community. Mount Zemaraim (13:4) was located in southern Ephraim, about thirteen miles north of Jerusalem. Like David and Solomon, Abijah violated the marriage law for the king (13:21; cf. Deut. 17:17).

14:2-15 Asa
Asa (911–870 B.C.) cried to God for help in war (14:11-12), as his father, Abijah, had done (13:14-15), and was victorious. But later (16:1-14) he relied on help from Aram (or Syria), not God (16:7). Mareshah (14:10), situated halfway between Jerusalem and Gaza, was one of Rehoboam's fortresses (11:8). Gerar (14:13) was situated about nine miles northeast of Gaza.

15:1-19 Prophetic Encouragement
Prophetic encouragement was given to Asa. A genuine response to the word of the Lord brought repentance, cleansing, and blessing. Again, the defections from the northern tribes to Judah were noted (15:9). Seeking God with all their heart brought rest (15:15; cf. also 14:6). Asherah (15:16) was a Canaanite fertility goddess. A problem of chronology appears in 15:19–16:1 because Baasha died before Asa's thirty-sixth year. The numbers thirty-fifth and thirty-sixth probably reflect a copyist's misreading of the numbers fifteenth and sixteenth.

16:1-14 Asa Relies on Aram
Asa's spiritual life had gone sour. Instead of responding positively to the word of God, he became angry (16:10). The result was further divine discipline (16:12). The fire (16:14) refers to the burning of spices (cf. Jer. 34:5), not cremation.

17:1–21:3 JEHOSHAPHAT
17:1-19 Jehoshaphat's Strength
Three key aspects of Jehoshaphat's rule (873–848 B.C.) were noted. First, he equipped the fortified cities (17:2, 12), as Solomon (8:5) and Rehoboam (11:5) had done. Second, the Lord established his kingdom (17:5) as he had done for David (1 Chron. 14:2) and Solomon (2 Chron. 1:1). And third, Jehoshaphat sent out officials to teach the ways of God to the Israelites (17:5-9; cf. 19:4). "Images of Baal" (17:3) refers to the local varieties of idols used in Baal worship (cf. Num. 25:3; Josh. 11:17; Judg. 9:4; 2 Kings 1:2).

18:1-34 Jehoshaphat's Alliance with Ahab
To seal the alliance (18:1), Ahab's daughter Athaliah was given in marriage to Jehoshaphat's son Jehoram (cf. 2 Kings 8:16-18). Ramoth-gilead (2 Chron. 18:2) was located east of the Jordan River, about thirty miles southeast of the Sea of Galilee. God commissioned a demonic spirit (18:20-22) to induce the false prophets of Ahab to lie. While God does not initiate evil, in the exercise of his sovereignty he can use even the actions of evil instruments to accomplish his purposes. The contrast is between the faithless King Ahab (18:6-7) and the faithful King Jehoshaphat (18:31).

19:1-11 Jehoshaphat's Justice
Jehoshaphat's fourth great aspect is noted: his insistence on justice (19:8-9). Beersheba (19:4) is located at the center of the Negev, about twenty-six miles southwest of Hebron. The usual division between the administration of things of the Lord and of the king is noted (19:11; see, for example, the lists of temple workers, things of the Lord, mighty men, and things of the king in 1 Chron. 11:10–12:40; 15:1–16:43).

20:1–21:3 Victory over Moab and Ammon
Again Jehoshaphat turned to the Lord in the time of war, but the emphasis was on God as the warrior for Israel (see especially the Spirit-inspired words of Jahaziel in 20:14-17). The great prayer of Jehoshaphat repeated the believer's confidence in the God of the initial conquest of Israel (20:7-8), the dedication of the temple (20:9; cf. 6:22-39), and the victories in the journey from Egypt to Canaan (20:10). The victory brought rest on all sides, a concept based on the Davidic covenant, and noted for David (1 Chron. 17:9-10; 18:1; 19:19; 22:8; 23:25), Solomon (1 Chron. 22:9; 2 Chron. 1:1), and Asa (14:7; 15:15).

Some Hebrew texts read "Aram" rather than "Edom" (20:2), but Edom harmonizes better with 20:22-23, which mentions Mount Seir (Edom). The invasion came from the east. En Gedi was situated along the western shore of the Dead Sea, about thirty miles south of Jericho. Undoubtedly the author included 20:4 to be an encouragement and a challenge to the restoration community. The wilderness of Tekoa (20:20) was located east of Tekoa, about five miles southeast of Bethlehem. The Hebrew name for the Valley of Blessing (20:26) is Beracah, which means "blessing." The exact location of Tarshish, mentioned in 20:36 (NASB and KJV) is uncertain. It may have been situated in southern Spain or perhaps on the island of Sardinia. For Ezion-geber (20:36), see the note on 8:17.

21:4–23:21 JEHORAM AND ATHALIAH
21:4-20 Jehoram
The military security won by Jehoshaphat was lost by the disobedience of Jehoram (853–841 B.C.). God preserved the nation because of his promise to

David (21:7), but he let Edom (21:8), the Philistines, and the Arabs (20:16) invade Israel. The Davidic promise continued even though the particular king was rejected (21:20), a clear example of God's loving-kindness that would never depart (cf. 1 Chron. 17:13). Libnah (2 Chron. 21:10) was a Philistine city located about twenty-five miles southwest of Jerusalem. The expression "to give themselves to pagan gods" (21:11) has its background in the Canaanite fertility cult in which sexual immorality was practiced. It refers to the spiritual unfaithfulness of the Israelites toward God as they pursued other gods. Elijah had ascended to heaven by this time (21:12). The letter had been written by Elijah but was delivered by another prophet. For the significance of "did not build a great fire" (21:19), see the note on 16:14.

22:1–23:21 Athaliah
The evil from the house of Ahab, the king of the northern tribes, continued. His grandson Ahaziah (841 B.C.) was judged for his disobedience (22:1-9). Then Ahab's daughter Athaliah (841–835 B.C.) killed all of the royal line of David but one, Joash, who took the throne six years later (22:10-12). The house of David shriveled down to but one heir. Joash's preservation illustrated once again God's absolute faithfulness to his promises to David that he would always have an heir to the throne of the kingdom.

Joash (835–796 B.C.) was anointed king through the political and military plans of the high priest Jehoiada (23:1-21). The basis for his action was the Davidic covenant (23:3). Athaliah's death (23:12-15) cleared the way for the reestablishment of the Mosaic law and the Davidic celebration of God's redemption (23:18). The covenant (23:11) refers to a copy of the Mosaic law.

24:1–36:23 Restoration to the Land
24:1–28:27 JOASH TO AHAZ
24:1-27 Joash
Joash's chief triumph was his effort to restore the temple under the high priest Jehoiada's oversight (24:1-14). After Jehoiada's death, Joash dropped God for idols and killed Jehoiada's son Zechariah (24:15-22). (Jesus referred to the stoning of Zechariah in Matthew 23:35.) Through it all, God showed his kindness by sending prophets to warn the king and people to return to loving God.

25:1-28 Amaziah
The same pattern occurred during the reign of another king, Amaziah (796–767 B.C.): having the kingdom firmly in hand (2 Chron. 25:3), gaining great victory (25:11-12), worshiping idols (25:14-15), and then losing his military security (25:22-24) and, eventually, his life (25:27). God wanted

Amaziah to trust in him for the victory, not in his own military might (cf. Deut. 17:16).

The Valley of Salt (2 Chron. 25:11) is that section of the Rift Valley located at the south end of the Dead Sea. Seir (25:14) is another name for Edom. To the record of Kings, Chronicles adds this account of Amaziah's defection. He worshiped the gods of the defeated enemy. Beth-shemesh (25:23) was located about fifteen miles west of Jerusalem. Lachish (25:27) was about twenty-five miles southwest of Jerusalem.

26:1-23 Uzziah
The key phrase for Uzziah (791–739 B.C.), as well as for all the kings of Judah and the returned exiles, is found in the last part of 26:5: "as long as the King sought the Lord, God gave him success." Uzziah's downfall was his pride in his kingdom's military strength (25:16; cf. Prov. 16:18), which led him to want to function as a priest in addition to being king (2 Chron. 26:18). That was Saul's problem as well (1 Sam. 13:8-9; cf. Exod. 30:7-8). But only One could be both priest and king, Jesus the Messiah and High Priest of the Christian faith. Uzziah, like Jehoram (2 Chron. 21:20), was not buried in the tombs of the kings (26:23).

Elath (26:2) was an important seaport located at the north end of the Gulf of Aqaba. The Zechariah of 26:5 is not a reference to Zechariah the postexilic prophet. Gur (26:7) has not been identified. The "machines" (26:15; also translated "engines") refer to catapults.

27:1-9 Jotham
As with many other good kings, Jotham's positive contributions (750–731 B.C.) included building fortresses and temple renovation (27:3-4). The moral for his life (27:6) was a direct message to the little band of returned exiles. The silver (27:5) amounted to about 120,000 ounces.

28:1-27 Ahaz
Judah suffered terrible defeats by Aram (28:5), by the northern tribes of Israel (28:6-8), and by Assyria (28:20-21) because of the sins of Ahaz (743–715 B.C.). Yet Ahaz went on to do even worse (28:22-27). He showed a misconception common among God's people, that is, that defeat at the hands of another nation meant that the god of that nation was stronger than the God of Israel (28:23). Instead, the lesson of the book of Chronicles was that the defeat of God's people meant that there was a problem with their faithfulness, not with God's power. During Ahaz's reign the northern tribes were taken away into the Assyrian captivity, but Chronicles does not even mention that. Its focus is on Judah alone and her faith, faithlessness, and ultimate release from the Babylonian captivity.

For "sacrificing his own sons in the fire" (28:3), see the note on 2 Kings 16:3. For more on Tiglath-pileser (2 Chron. 28:20; also spelled "Tilgath Pilneser"), see the note on 2 Kings 15:19.

29:1–35:27 HEZEKIAH TO JOSIAH

29:1–32:33 Hezekiah

Hezekiah (728–686 B.C.) repaired the temple and, unlike Ahaz before him, understood that the true reason for Israel's defeats was the king's unfaithfulness (29:1-11). He cleansed the temple (29:12-19), consecrated the people, and reestablished David's orders for the praise and worship of God in the temple service (29:20-36). Again there were joy and worship in the nation (29:30, 36) as a result of the restoration of the temple worship (29:35). The "courtyard east of the temple" (29:4) refers to the open space east of the temple area.

A great Passover celebration was held (30:1-27). There were some Israelites (30:1) living in the north who had not been taken captive by the Assyrians in 722 B.C. with the rest of the northern tribes (cf. 30:10-11). Note the phrases "at the king's command" (30:6), "all Israel" (30:1), "throughout all Israel" (30:5), "the Israelites" (31:1), and "strong desire to unite" (30:12). Those were reminders of the golden days of David and Solomon when the king's command was pleasing to God and coincided with his commands, and the unified nation supported the king with one heart.

Hezekiah's Passover prayer (30:18-20) illustrated the ultimate triumph of inner heart obedience over external legal details. In this exceptional case, Hezekiah's attitude was accepted by God even though external rituals were not followed. That great purity of heart extended the celebration another week (30:23) and marked a return to the greatness of Solomon's reign (30:26). The additional seven days of celebration coincided with the Festival of Unleavened Bread.

Hezekiah destroyed idolatry and increased the offerings (31:1-21). The people supported the king and destroyed idols in Judah, Benjamin, Ephraim, and Manasseh (31:1). Then Hezekiah established the divisions of the temple ministers and saw to their proper support through tithes. The summary of 30:20-21 rounds out the description begun in 29:2 of how Hezekiah did right in accordance with the ways of his father, David. The thrust of this entire section was to encourage the returned Jews to restore the temple and its worship with all their hearts. The sacred stones, or pillars, and the Asherah poles (31:1), represented the Canaanite fertility deities (cf. the note on Deut. 7:5). Late spring (2 Chron. 31:7), or the third month, is Sivan (May–June), and early autumn, the seventh month, is Tishri (September–October).

The acts of faithfulness were directly linked to Assyria's attack on Judah (32:1-33). Usually such attacks were due to the king's disobedience, but this attack functioned as a vehicle to display the essence of Israel's faith in the presence of the God of heaven and earth (32:7; cf. 2 Kings 6:16). Sennacherib's speech asked the key questions that probed the heart of Israel's understanding of why she succeeded or failed: (1) "What are you trusting in?" (32:10); and (2) Would a defeat in Israel be due to the fact that her God, Yahweh, was inferior? (32:13-14). Hezekiah's prayer brought about an indisputable answer from the true God (32:20-23). Hezekiah's prideful end was downplayed (32:24-26) in order to emphasize his God-given wealth and devotion (32:29, 32).

For "Millo" (32:5) see the note on 1 Kings 9:15. For Sennacherib's attack (2 Chron. 32:9), see the notes on 2 Kings 18:1-37. For Hezekiah's water tunnel (32:30), see the note on 2 Kings 20:20.

33:1-25 Manasseh and Amon

Manasseh (697–642 B.C.) brought Judah back to the spiritual darkness that existed in the land before Joshua conquered it (33:2). It was as if all the good done from the time of Joshua through the time of Hezekiah had been undone (33:9). Incredibly, the nation's worst king humbled himself in the Assyrian exile, was heard by God, and was returned to the land (33:10-13). Manasseh had the longest reign, was the worst king of Judah, and was the most brilliant example of restoration from the Exile on the basis of his having a tender and humble heart before God. The key to restoration is a person's humility of heart when convicted of sin, no matter how great the sin. That was a lesson for the returned Jews and the people of God from then on. The valley of the son of Hinnom (33:6) was the L-shaped valley that is situated west and south of Jerusalem. Amon (642–640 B.C.) functioned as an example of one who did not humble himself before God (33:23).

34:1-35:27 Josiah

The account of Josiah's reign (640–609 B.C.) can be divided into his eight years of rule (34:3) followed by his four years of seeking the Lord (34:3). Those years were followed by a nationwide six-year purging of idolatry (34:3-7) and a subsequent cleansing and rebuilding of the temple (34:8-13). Josiah's response to finding the Law of Moses (34:14; cf. 2 Kings 22:8-13) resulted in the prophetic speeches by Hilkiah the high priest and Huldah the prophetess that stated why the nation would fall (34:21, 25) and why Josiah's reign would be spared destruction (34:26-28). Even in the shadow of certain destruction, it was important to do right before God. The tension between undergoing consequences for past sins and at the same time maintaining obedience to God was something that the returned exiles had to endure and learn from.

Second Chronicles 35 ties together the key

elements of Israel's faith: obedience according to David, Solomon (35:4), and Moses (35:6), all mediated according to the command of the present king, Josiah (35:16). Hezekiah's Passover celebration was linked to the time of Solomon (30:26), while Josiah's Passover looked back to the time of Samuel (35:18). The ark, which apparently was removed from the temple during the apostasy of Amon or Manasseh, was returned to the temple (35:3). For a discussion of Josiah's intentions in fighting the king of Egypt (35:20), see the note on 2 Kings 23:29. Megiddo (35:22) was a fortress city in the Jezreel Valley that guarded an important pass through Mount Carmel to the coastal plain.

36:1-21 JEHOAHAZ TO ZEDEKIAH
The four last kings of Judah were listed quickly; the last three all did evil in the sight of God: Jehoahaz (36:1-4; 609 B.C.); Jehoiakim (36:4-8; 609–597 B.C.); Jehoiachin (36:9-10; 597 B.C.); and Zedekiah (36:11-21; 597–586 B.C.). Nebuchadnezzar's first invasion of Jerusalem was in 605 B.C. when Jehoiakim was king. In his second invasion and deportation of the Israelites (36:10), the king and ten thousand Jews were taken into captivity. Even after all that horror, Zedekiah still did not soften his heart before God (36:13). God's compassion was seen in his continual

warnings (36:15); his wrath was shown in the destruction of Jerusalem (36:16). For a note on Nebuchadnezzar's attack and siege (36:17-18), see the notes on 2 Kings 25:1. The third deportation to Babylon took place after the destruction of Jerusalem in 586 B.C. (2 Chron. 36:20).

The writer explains that the deportation was divine discipline for neglect of the sabbatical year (36:21; cf. Lev. 25:4; 26:34-35). That was another important lesson the writer wanted to emphasize for the newly returned Jews. They had just come out of that discipline and needed to be reminded of its cause and purpose.

36:22-23 THE DECREE OF CYRUS
Cyrus captured the city of Babylon in 539 B.C., and his first official year as king was 538 B.C. The reference to Jeremiah's prophecy (2 Chron. 36:21; cf. Jer. 25:12-13; 29:10) indicates that God was in control from the very beginning. After seventy years of discipline, God prepared the way for the Jews to return to their land. His promises to Abraham, Moses, and David were certain. The book ends with upbeat words of release and restoration. The return of the exiles was, in effect, a second exodus—not from Egypt, but from Babylon. The nation reentered the land with a chance to start again.

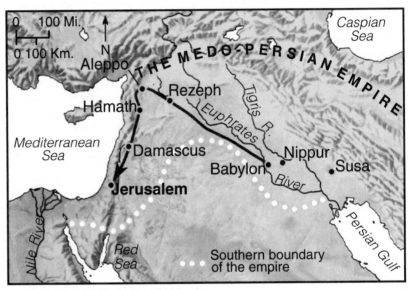

EZRA

BASIC FACTS

HISTORICAL SETTING
Jewish exiles first returned from the Babylonian captivity under Zerubbabel in about 538 B.C. The date of Ezra's return to Jerusalem is a matter of some scholarly debate, but the biblical evidence points to 458 B.C., the seventh year of Artaxerxes (464–424 B.C.). Over sixty years separate the first part of the book (Ezra 1–6) and last part (Ezra 7–10). During Ezra's time Greece was in its golden age, Athens flourished, and Socrates was a young adult.

AUTHOR
Ezra, the priest and scribe, is the commonly accepted author of the book of Ezra. He probably had a part in editing the two books of Chronicles and Nehemiah as well.

DATE
The book of Ezra was written in the period after Israel's Babylonian captivity, sometime after Ezra returned to Jerusalem. The book mentions several specific dates that help the reader understand its structure and emphasis. For these dates, see the chart on page 192.

This overview of the dates and their events introduces the two main issues of the book: (1) the overcoming of attempts to stop the restoration of the temple, and (2) the overcoming of attempts to reintroduce foreign marriages of a kind that would introduce idolatry, the very reason for Israel's past downfall and her captivity in Babylon.

PURPOSE
The book of Ezra was designed to show how God supported those who returned from the captivity and to encourage faithfulness in regard to the hard task of rebuilding the nation.

GEOGRAPHY AND ITS IMPORTANCE

The return of Israel to her land, followed by the special returns of Ezra and Nehemiah, were made under the rule of the Medo-Persian Empire. God placed Israel under a long period of foreign rule by Assyria, Babylon, Persia, Greece, and Rome before he sent his Messiah to redeem the nation. Israel's exit from Babylon mirrored her exodus from Egypt and repeated the geographical and spiritual pattern of movement from bondage to release, from foreign captivity to captivity to God.

GUIDING CONCEPTS

FORM AND CONTENT

Three decrees
The book centers on three decrees that would result in the prosperity of Jerusalem and the Jewish people: (1) that of Cyrus (1:1), (2) that of Darius (6:8), and (3) that of Artaxerxes (7:11). In 6:14 the three decrees are seen in close unity, even though they relate to separate matters that occurred over a long period of time.

Two returns
The two returns of the Jews from the Babylonian captivity were made during the reign of Cyrus (539 B.C.), with Sheshbazzar as the leader, and during the reign of Artaxerxes (458 B.C.), with Ezra as the leader.

Two tasks
The two tasks of the people of Israel in the book were to rebuild the temple (6:15) and to obey the law concerning marriages and the purity of worship of God alone (7:10).

Form
The book focuses on the activities and leadership of two men: Sheshbazzar, the prince, and Ezra, the priest. (See the chart below.)

All of these events are seen in the light of Jeremiah's prophecy of restoration (1:1; cf. Jer. 29:1-14). According to Jeremiah, the nation was to settle down in Babylon and expect seventy years of captivity. After that, God promised that his plans to rebuild the nation and return his people to the land of Israel would come about. The book of Ezra focuses upon and describes that period of promised relocation and reconstruction as the period of a renewed building of the temple and teaching of the Law for the nation of Israel.

THE PROBLEM WITH FOREIGN WIVES
Why was it so bad for the Jews to marry foreign women? First of all, the Law had prohibited marrying women of the Canaanite nations (cf. Exod. 23:31-33; 34:12-16; Deut. 7:1-4). Second, during Israel's history, foreign wives had always brought idolatry into the nation of Israel. Solomon's problems in this area are noted in 1 Kings 11:1-8. The postexilic community needed to avoid a relapse into the idolatry that brought about their downfall.

BIBLE-WIDE CONCEPTS

PROMISE OF RESTORATION

The geographic promise
God gave the newly created earth to Adam, the newly dried earth to Noah, and the land of Canaan to Abraham, Moses, and the nation of Israel. That land of Israel was an

---

THE WORK OF SHESHBAZZAR AND EZRA

Event	Sheshbazzar	Ezra
Release and Travel	1:1–2:70	7:1–8:34
Return and Worship	3:1-7	8:35-36
Task of Rebuilding	3:8–6:22	9:1–10:44
	Davidic Line	Aaronic Line
	Builder of the Temple	Teacher of the People

---

essential part of God's promise to the Jewish nation. But what happened to the promise of land when the nation of Israel was exiled during the Babylonian captivity? It remained firm and sure. Ezra showed his readers that the Israelites would be restored to the land that always had and would be theirs. And that promise looks forward ultimately to the new heavens and earth where the land promised will extend around the globe to all nations.

The Davidic promise

God had promised an eternal line of kingly rule through the Davidic covenant. What had the Exile done to that promise? Both Sheshbazzar and Zerubbabel were members of David's royal line (see the genealogy of 1 Chron. 3:18-19 where some scholars iden-

---

SPECIFIC DATES MENTIONED IN EZRA

1:1	The first year of Cyrus's reign (539–530 B.C.)	The time of Cyrus's decree to allow the Jews to return to Jerusalem.
4:5	Darius I (522–486 B.C.)	The temple's rebuilding was frustrated from the reign of Cyrus until the reign of Darius (Cambyses, 530–522 B.C., is not mentioned).
4:6	Xerxes I (486–464 B.C.)	He was the Ahasuerus of Esther's day and received an accusation against the returned Jews.
4:7	Artaxerxes I (464–423 B.C.)	This was Ezra's time. Artaxerxes I issued a decree to stop the work of rebuilding the city of Jerusalem.
6:15	Sixth year of Darius (516 B.C.)	The temple's rebuilding was completed. Note that this date goes back in time to the reign of Darius, mentioned in 4:5. It is out of chronological sequence to include the later work stoppages noted during the reigns of Xerxes (Ahasuerus) amd Artaxerxes (4:6-7) and also to end the discussion of the stoppages happily with the completion of the second temple. Chronologically, the attacks on the efforts to rebuild Jerusalem continued long after the temple was restored. But the writer wanted to end the discussion of the frustrated rebuilding efforts and move on to the even more important point of the book: the purification of God's people.
7:7	The seventh year of Artaxerxes I (458 B.C.)	Ezra 7 has much to say about the seventh year. It was the year in which Ezra returned to Jerusalem and reformed the marriage practices of some of the Jewish returnees.
7:8	The fifth month, first day	Ezra arrived in Jerusalem under Artaxerxes' good decree.
8:31	The first month, twelfth day	This reflects back on the day that Ezra left to return to Jerusalem.
10:9	The ninth month, twentieth day	The people assembled to hear Ezra read the Law.
10:16	The tenth month, first day	Ezra began to investigate the Israelite men who had married foreign wives.
10:17	First month, the first day of the next year (457 B.C.)	Ezra finished the investigation, and the Israelite men were separated from their foreign wives.

tify Shenazzar as Sheshbazzar). Other scholars believe Shenazzar to be an uncle of
Sheshbazzar. The Davidic line was still in place and leading the return from exile. But
how would that rule be fully reestablished? Under the domination of Persia, then
Greece and Rome, Israel would wait for God's answer to that question. When Jesus the
King finally came, he inaugurated a new kind of rule from heaven at the right hand of
God. But he will come again and fully establish the Davidic rule promised so long ago.

The Mosaic promise

After the Babylonian exile, were the people of Israel still bound by the Mosaic covenant
as they had been before it took place? From Ezra's viewpoint, the Law was still as binding as ever. The keeping of it was still the way to receive divine blessing. The breaking
of it, in the case of intermarriage, was still the way to destruction. The Law's firmness
and continuity stretched into the life of Jesus, the Prophet who was greater than Moses.
In the Sermon on the Mount (Matt. 5–7), Jesus said he came to uphold and fulfill the
Mosaic law, and in his death he annulled Moses' covenant and replaced it with a
deeper law and a more binding covenant that was sealed by his blood. But for those
Israelites who were living in Ezra's time, the Mosaic covenant still held out its blessings
and curses. People have always been and always will be responsible to obey God's
desires, from the beginning of time in the Garden of Eden, to the coming glories of
God's future kingdom.

NEEDS MET BY EZRA

The people of God returned to their land but they were still under the domination of
Persia and under military threat from the surrounding peoples. Where was the great
glory of the days of Solomon? Where was the powerful presence of God? The days of
glory had to be patiently awaited and the power of God was present, but hidden, and
had to be seen through the eyes of faith. God's promises and presence still remained.
In that light, the returned exiles failed and succeeded in several ways. Their experiences
were written down so that future readers would have a proper and realistic perspective
on just what Israel's restoration from the captivity did and did not mean. These are
some of the questions that the exiles probably asked and that the book of Ezra
answers.

- What will God's promised restoration of Israel from the captivity be like?
- What are the problems that the people of Israel will face upon return?
- Has God's discipline through the Exile made Israel immune to further sin and
  failure?
- Has God's restoration of the people of Israel to the Promised Land made them
  immune to external attacks?
- Are God's preexilic promises to Abraham, Moses, and David still in force?
- What good did the Exile really do for Israel?

As the book of Ezra provided answers to these questions, it enabled God's people to
move on under his guidance with their eyes wide open both to the greatness of his
power to accomplish his promises and to the greatness of their own power to derail
their blessings through their disobedience. The good news was that God had redeemed

them from captivity and brought them back to their land. The bad news was that they were still the same old people; they were still weak and needed God's grace to keep them from sin. In Christ we share similar good and bad news and enjoy the same wonderful grace.

OUTLINE OF EZRA

I. RECONSTRUCTION OF THE PLACE OF THE COVENANT (1:1–6:22)
   A. Release: The Divine Stirring of Cyrus (1:1–2:70)
   B. Reconstruction of the Temple (3:1–6:22)

II. RESTORATION OF THE PRACTICE OF THE COVENANT (7:1–10:44)
   A. Release (7:1–8:34)
   B. Restoration of Covenant Purity (9:1–10:44)

EZRA NOTES

1:1–6:22 RECONSTRUCTION OF THE PLACE OF THE COVENANT

1:1–2:70 Release: The Divine Stirring of Cyrus

Overview: The return of the Jews from the Exile (1:1) was in accord with Jeremiah's prophecy (Jer. 29). The joy of return was to be matched with human response, as seen throughout the book in key phrases like "return" and "returned" (Ezra 1:3, 5, 11; 2:1), "assisted," "helped" and "honoring" (1:6; 6:22; 7:28), God's gift of the law, and the "gracious hand of the Lord" (7:6, 9), and "vowed" (10:19). Ezra 2 lists the men of Israel (2:2-35), priests and Levites (2:36-42), servants (2:43-58), and unregistered people (2:59-63) who came back from the captivity.

1:1-4 THE DECREE OF CYRUS

Cyrus, the king of Anshan, a region in eastern Elam and part of the area populated by the Persian tribes, defeated the king of Media and welded the Median and Persian empires into a dual monarchy called Medo-Persia. In 539 B.C. he captured Babylon, bringing the Babylonian Empire to a close. Cyrus's proclamation (1:2-4) fulfilled Jeremiah's prophecy of restoration after seventy years of captivity in Babylon (Jer. 25:1-18; 29:10). As many as 160 years earlier, Isaiah had named Cyrus as God's chosen instrument to liberate the Jews (Isa. 44:28–45:7,13). Cyrus's accession year was 539 B.C., making 538 B.C. his first official year on the throne.

Although Cyrus acknowledged the Lord (Ezra 1:2), on the Cyrus Cylinder he ascribed his victories to Marduk, the god of Babylon. Scripture clearly states that Cyrus was an unbeliever (Isa. 45:4). The purpose of the Jews' return to Jerusalem from Bab-ylon (Ezra 1:3) was to give them an opportunity to rebuild God's temple that Nebuchadnezzar had destroyed in 586 B.C.

1:5-11 ENCOURAGEMENT FOR THE RETURN

The Jewish historian Josephus (*Antiquities,* 11.8) reported that many of the Jews did not want to leave Babylon (1:5-6) because of their many possessions. Cyrus decreed that the Jews who were returning be given a portion of the treasure that Nebuchadnezzar had taken from the Jerusalem temple (1:7); Darius I apparently returned the rest (6:5).

There are three views regarding the identity of Sheshbazzar (1:8), whom Cyrus appointed as the governor (5:14). (1) Sheshbazzar was just another name for Zerubbabel. (2) Sheshbazzar was the officially appointed leader, and Zerubbabel was the popular but unofficial leader. (3) They were both leaders, but they led at different times, Sheshbazzar preceding Zerubbabel. Both men were called "governor of Judah" and were associated with laying the temple's foundation (Ezra 5:16; Zech. 4:9), but only Zerubbabel was associated with its completion (Hag. 1:12; Zech. 4:9). Possibly Sheshbazzar died soon after the Jews' return to Jerusalem and was succeeded by Zerubbabel. Although 5,400 items were returned (1:11), only 2,499 of the more important ones are specifically listed (1:9-10).

2:1-67 THOSE WHO RETURNED

The list of the Jews who returned included men (2:2-35), priests (2:36-39), Levites (2:40-42), servants to the temple and to Solomon (2:43-58), unregistered families (2:59-63), and the totals (2:64-67). The same list with some variation (due to scribal errors or problems with the transmission of numbers) appears in Nehemiah 7:6-73. "Nehemiah" (Ezra 2:2) does not refer to Jerusalem's famous wall builder. While biblical genealogies (2:61-63) may seem boring and unimportant to readers today, these verses show why they were so essential for the Jews of ancient times. The actual number (2:64) by count was 42,360. They apparently arrived in Jerusalem at the ruined temple site in 537 B.C. (2:68).

2:68-70 THE FREEWILL OFFERING
Note the principle of giving (2:69; cf. 2 Cor. 8:3). The Israelites gave willingly and out of their ability, from hearts committed to God's revealed will.

3:1–6:22 Reconstruction of the Temple
Overview: There were two responses to the completion of the temple's foundation (Ezra 3:10). First, there was a mixed reaction among the Jews of joy for the present reconstruction and tears for the loss of past glory (3:11-13). Second, the enemies of Israel stopped the Jews from doing further work until the reign of Darius (6:14). That prepares the reader for the last part of the book, where another enemy appeared to threaten the fragile existence of the returned people of Israel: the Israelites were prone to marriages with foreigners, which would only result in the acceptance of idolatrous practices. In 4:1-3 Israel's leaders excluded foreigners from working on the temple, yet, at the end of the book, some Jews had married foreigners.

3:1-7 SEVENTH-MONTH ACTIVITIES
The seventh month, or "early autumn" (3:1), was Tishri (September–October). It was noted for its three religious convocations: the Festival of Trumpets (on the first of the month), the Day of Atonement (on the tenth of the month), and the Festival of Shelters (during the fifteenth to the twentieth days of the month; cf. Lev. 23:1-36).

3:8-13 THE FOUNDATION IS LAID
The second month, or "midspring" (Ezra 3:8), was Iyyar (April–May). The temple's foundation (3:10) was laid in 536 B.C. The great practice of praising God's loving-kindness, so prevalent in the Psalms before the Exile, was begun once again (3:11).

4:1-24 FOREIGNERS ARE EXCLUDED
Ezra 4 records the opposition to the temple's construction that took place from 536 B.C. to the days of Artaxerxes (around 446 B.C.). Esar-haddon (4:2; 681–669 B.C.), son of Sennacherib, had brought foreigners to the land of Israel after expelling the Jews of the northern tribes to Assyria. They worshiped the God of Israel as well as many other gods (2 Kings 17:41). The opposition recorded here (4:4; 536 B.C.) was not unique. Ezra went on to cite two other examples of opposition in later history: (1) the opposition in the days of Xerxes I, also known as Ahasuerus (4:6), and (2) the opposition

in the days of Artaxerxes (4:7-23). Xerxes I, or Ahasuerus (4:6; 486–464 B.C.), ruled Persia during the days of Esther (cf. Esther 1:1). Artaxerxes (Ezra 4:7; 464–424 B.C.) ruled Persia during the days of Nehemiah.

The enemies of the Jews wrote to Artaxerxes, asking that he not permit Jerusalem to be rebuilt (4:11-16). Ezra 4:8–6:18 was originally written in Aramaic, which served as the international language at the time of the Persian Empire. The word "except" (4:21) is crucial in the king's reply. In a few short years Artaxerxes would grant Nehemiah's request to rebuild Jerusalem (Neh. 2). With Ezra 4:24 the parenthesis of 4:6-23 is complete. Ezra 4:24 is a statement concerning the cessation of the temple's construction in 536 B.C. That cessation continued until 520 B.C., the second year of the reign of Darius (522–486 B.C.).

5:1-5 THE ROLE OF THE PROPHETS IN OPPOSITION
The ministry of the prophets Haggai and Zechariah (5:1) is further detailed in the books that bear their names. When once again challenged as to their right to build the temple (5:3-5), the Jews continued their work while the matter was investigated by Tattenai.

5:6–6:12 THE LETTER TO AND DECREE FROM DARIUS I
In Ecbatana (6:2), a summer residence of the Persian kings located about two hundred miles south of the Caspian Sea, an official memorandum containing details of Cyrus's original decree was discovered (6:3-5). Darius must have stunned Tattenai by strengthening the original decree of Cyrus (6:8-11). This was no idle threat (6:11). Herodotus reports that Darius impaled three thousand Babylonians after he put down a rebellion in their capital city. He then destroyed the walls and gates of Babylon, something Cyrus had not done.

6:13-22 THE TEMPLE IS COMPLETED
Credit also was given to a later ruler, Artaxerxes (6:14; 464–424 B.C.), who helped in the maintenance of the temple (7:15-21). The work was completed on March 12, 515 B.C., twenty-one years after the foundation had been laid (6:13-22). Again, the stress on the nation's purity (6:21) contrasts with the upcoming impurity of mixed marriages. The reference to the "king of Assyria" (6:22) is unexpected but not unusual. Obviously, Darius was meant. A similar expression is used in Nehemiah 9:32 to refer to Assyrian, Babylonian, and Persian kings. Since the Persians ruled former Assyrian territories, it could be said that Darius was king of Assyria, just as Cyrus claimed the title "king of Babylon."

7:1–10:44 RESTORATION OF THE PRACTICE OF THE COVENANT

Overview: Ezra's words in Ezra 7:10 echo Deuteronomy 33:10. The hand of God was upon Ezra (Ezra 7:14, 23, 25) as he made preparations to return to Israel. As God had worked in Cyrus (1:1), he also worked in Artaxerxes (7:27). The problem of purity is met with Ezra's great confession (9:5-15) and careful correction (10:1-44).

7:1–8:34 Release

7:1-28 THE DECREE OF ARTAXERXES I

Almost sixty years separate the events recorded in Ezra 6 and Ezra 7. During this period (515–458 B.C.), the events of the book of Esther took place in Susa (see introductory map). Ezra's family line (7:1-5) was traced back to Aaron, Israel's first high priest. At one time a "scribe" (7:6) was little more than a secretary, but later the office increased in importance. The scribe, or teacher, became a preserver and interpreter of the Law. Ezra's desire to teach displayed the heart of a biblical philosophy of education (7:10). The order is significant. A person cannot practice what he has not thoroughly studied; and he should not teach principles he has not carefully applied. Perhaps Ezra was using some of the extra funds in an attempt to rebuild Jerusalem's walls (7:18; cf. 4:12). "Temple servant" (7:24) literally means "one who is given" and refers to those dedicated to the temple service as assistants to the Levites.

8:1-20 THOSE WHO RETURNED

A shortage of Levites (8:15-19) would have greatly inhibited the program Ezra wanted to implement, so he sent out a last-minute appeal for reinforcements. As a result, 38 Levites and 220 temple servants responded to his appeal.

8:21-36 THE JOURNEY: SAFE DELIVERANCE OF THE OFFERING

Ezra took precautionary measures with regard to money matters (8:24-30), as did Paul with the money he collected and handled (cf. 2 Cor. 8:20-21). God gave Ezra and the exiles traveling safety during the four months of their nine hundred-mile journey (8:31).

9:1–10:44 Restoration of Covenant Purity

9:1-15 EZRA'S CONFESSION

Ezra had been in Jerusalem about four and a half months when the officials brought to his attention the problem of mixed marriages. Deuteronomy 7:1-5 had forbidden the intermarriage of Israelites with unbelieving foreigners and warned of the idolatrous consequences of such a practice. If this continued, the Jews would soon lose their national identity and could end up in exile once again. Ezra displayed the customary signs of grief, evidence of his intense concern (Ezra 9:3-4). He did not stand apart from his people and condemn them, but he identified himself with them in their guilt and interceded on their behalf (9:5-15). The "remnant" (9:8; "peg," NASB, and "nail," KJV) probably refers to the Israelites who had returned from the Exile. As a tent peg secures a tent, so the returned exiles secured Israel's national existence.

10:1-44 THE HOLY RACE IS PURIFIED

Shecaniah offered Ezra a suggestion as to how to deal with the matter of intermarriage: separation of the marriage partners (10:2-4). Since the normal Hebrew word for "divorce" is not used, it is uncertain whether remarriage was intended or allowed. The words "obey the law of God" (10:3) probably referred to Deuteronomy 7:1-5, a text condemning mixed marriages with unbelievers. The people agreed to follow Shechaniah's suggestion. It took three months to complete the investigations and carry out the divorce proceedings. Seventeen priests, ten Levites, and eighty-four laymen (other versions list eighty-six due to a different textual reading of 10:38) were found guilty and put away their foreign wives (Ezra 10:18-43).

This sad incident (10:44) is not included in Ezra to provide a biblical basis for divorce. Rather, it illustrates the great tragedy of marital breakup. Any attempt to make application of this unusual situation by Christians seeking to divorce an unbelieving spouse would be prohibited by Paul's words in 1 Corinthians 7:12-13. It is a picture of the need for purity among God's people.

NEHEMIAH

BASIC FACTS

HISTORICAL SETTING

In 539 B.C. Cyrus, king of Persia, destroyed the Babylonian Empire and released the Israelites from captivity. Nehemiah continues the story of Israel's reconstruction after the captivity. The book begins its record of events around thirteen years after the period of Ezra's temple reforms, and it shows how Jerusalem was finally rebuilt and repopulated. The events recorded in the book of Nehemiah span the reigns of five Persian kings: Cyrus, 559–530 B.C.; Cambyses, 530–522 B.C.; Darius I, 522–486 B.C.; Xerxes I, 486–465 B.C.; and Artaxerxes I, 464–423 B.C.

AUTHOR

Nehemiah was a Jewish servant to the king of Persia. Although it is difficult to know for certain who wrote the book in its final form, it is clearly based on Nehemiah's first-hand memoirs.

DATE

Nehemiah came to Jerusalem in 445 B.C. For the general conditions of those times, see the book of Ezra, Haggai 2:1-10, and Zechariah 2:6-13. The book of Nehemiah presents a chronology that clearly shows the emphasis and point of the book. (See chart on the following page.)

The dedication of the wall was done after Nehemiah returned from his trip to Babylon (13:4, 6). After his return, he purified the temple service and dedicated the wall. The exact date cannot be known.

The events of Nehemiah 13 happened before those of Nehemiah 12, while Nehemiah was away in Babylon. Nehemiah wrote about those events last because he wanted to emphasize the sins of the Jewish leaders and how he corrected them.

PURPOSE

The book of Nehemiah was designed to round out the story of the postexilic reconstruction of the nation of Israel. It shows God's support for the rebuilding through faithful men like Nehemiah who had to fight against hostile enemies and unfaithful Israelites.

GEOGRAPHY AND ITS IMPORTANCE

Jerusalem was a symbol either of God's blessing or of his curse. Because the time of his anger was past, Nehemiah wanted the city to reflect the new time of God's blessing. That would only happen when the walls and gates were repaired and the city repopulated. As the city's destruction had conformed to the people's sinfulness, the city's restoration would reflect the people's repentance and God's restored blessing.

GUIDING CONCEPTS

REPROACH

At the beginning of the book, Nehemiah was very concerned about the disgrace that Jerusalem was still under. The words "disgrace" and "mocked" are repeated (1:3; 2:17; 4:4; 5:9). They reflect more than a tragic state of disrepair; they also reflect an attitude of God, which was why Nehemiah was so disturbed. The words were used by the prophets to describe what God would do to Jerusalem because of its people's sins (cf. Jer. 23:40; 24:9; 29:18; 44:8, 12; Lam. 5:1; Ezek. 5:14-15). The reproach was grounded in God's judgment upon his sinful people.

It was terrible for the city of Jerusalem to look as if it still was under disgrace. The temple had been rebuilt for more than seventy-five years, and God had given his blessing, release, and restoration to the people of Israel. For the city to appear as if it was still under God's judgment was to insult God and to demean the dignity of his restored people. The reproach was not just a landscaping and construction problem. Rather, it involved the theological implications of judgment upon sinful people. Although the nation of Israel could not conquer the entire land again, it could make all the necessary efforts to show that the city of God's presence was rebuilt, inhabited, and prosperous.

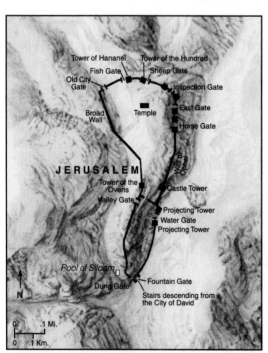

Copyright © 1986, 1988 by Tyndale House Publishers, Inc.

PURIFICATION

Nehemiah was concerned that the Israelites should obey the law of Moses so that the nation would be pure in God's sight (Neh. 1:5, 7-9; 5:7, 9; 7:2; 8:2, 9, 12, 17; 9:3; 10:28-29; 13:1-3). Passages like Leviticus 26:33 and Deuteronomy 23:3-5 lay behind Nehemiah's efforts. The specific areas in need of purification were the temple service, the observance of the Sabbath, and the observance of laws against usury (Neh. 5:7; 12:30, 45; 13:3, 9, 22, 30).

BIBLE-WIDE CONCEPTS

THE CITY AND TEMPLE OF GOD

Throughout the history recorded in Scripture, God designated special starting places in which his people could grow in their commission to rule the world and fellowship with him. Those places included the garden called Eden, the land of Palestine promised to Abraham's offspring, and at the heart of that land, the city of Jerusalem. At the center of the city, the temple was the place of fellowship between God and his people based on their obedience to the Mosaic covenant that rested in the Most Holy Place. For hundreds of years the peace or unrest of that city was the barometer of God's blessing or curse upon the entire land and people of God. But Jerusalem came to an abrupt end when destroyed by Babylon and lay in ruins for over seventy years. Those ruins were a sign of God's judgment on his people's sin. Even when Ezra and Nehemiah had done what they could to remove the reproach of the city's ruins, God's city and people awaited the full restoration of Jerusalem as the center of God's blessing.

The restored temple and city would only survive and be blessed when populated by people with restored obedience. Because God's blessing is always related to his personal presence, the restoration of Jerusalem by Nehemiah is a foreshadowing of the ultimate restoration of the city by God's own creative hand. The heavenly Jerusalem will descend from heaven and God will openly dwell among humanity. The temple, which was only a small building in the original city, will be replaced with the infinite presence of God himself (Rev. 21:3). The new Jerusalem will come from heaven prepared by God himself (Rev. 21:2). And the population of that city will live in perfect obedience and happiness (Rev. 21:3-27).

THE REMOVAL OF SIN'S REPROACH

Nehemiah saw the ruined city as a sign of God's reproach and disgrace (1:3; 2:17) for the nation's sins. He saw it as his responsibility to help remove that disgrace in light of the promises of the Mosaic covenant. Even after the Babylonian exile that covenant was still in force. Abraham's people were bound by God's covenant with Israel to love and obey God's commands from the heart. Nehemiah's task of exhorting people to remove the reproach of their sin is similar to the exhortations of Paul and others found throughout the New Testament to put away the patterns of the old ways of life that brought God's condemnation. The time for judgment was past, and it was time to put away the things of the past.

That human and divine cooperation in removing the signs of past judgment is also

---

THE CHRONOLOGY OF NEHEMIAH

Reference	Text Marker	Date
1:1	Twentieth year of Artaxerxes	445–444 B.C.
2:1	Twentieth year of Artaxerxes	445–444 B.C.
5:14	Nehemiah governs twelve years	456–444 B.C.
6:15	Twenty-fifth day, sixth month	444 B.C.
7:73	Seventh month	444 B.C.
8:2	First day	444 B.C.
8:13-18	Second through the eighth days	444 B.C.
9:1	Twenty-fourth day	444 B.C.
12:27–13:3	The dedication of the wall	444 B.C.

based on God's promises to Abraham. Two key elements of God's promises to Abraham were still in force in balancing human and divine responsibility. First, the world still had ill-will toward Israel ("[God will] curse those who curse you" Gen. 12:3; see also the hostility between the seed of the woman and the seed of the serpent in Gen. 3:15). The world was openly hostile to God's people succeeding in spiritual maturity and obedience. Second, God's people still had to obey and pass along the way of the Lord to following generations (see God's description of Abraham and his line's task in Gen. 18:19). That meant obeying the commands of the Mosaic covenant. Israel had to keep separate from the world in holiness and purity, the chief example in this book being when Nehemiah kept foreigners from working on Jerusalem and from marrying Israelites. The chief example in the New Testament is separation from sin and avoidance of being yoked together with unbelievers and thereby adopting their ungodly perspectives on life.

NEEDS MET BY NEHEMIAH

The book of Nehemiah gives a realistic picture of postexilic life. The nation's strengths and liabilities were still the same. Obedience would bring national and personal stability, while disobedience would put the nation in a state of jeopardy like that which existed before the exile. The task was to live in the light of God's presence and promises even though the earthly fulfillment of those promises was hidden in the future. The Israelites, who had recently returned from the Exile, may have been asking questions like these.

- Does God still expect the people of Israel to keep the old Mosaic Law now that they have been released from exile?
- Why was it so bad that Jerusalem lay in relative ruins for nearly one hundred years after the return of the first Jews from the captivity?
- Has the captivity made the Jewish nation any less prone to social and civil evils?
- Is God still willing to stand behind Jewish resistance to the hostility of surrounding nations?

The people of Nehemiah's day and believers today need to have a realistic picture of where the nation of Israel stood in relation to other nations and God. As Israel recovered from the discipline for her sins she needed to be strong in two areas: faith and patience. Faith inspires believers to believe in God and in his ability to do what he promises. Faith keeps them working hard to recover and to avoid repeating the failures of the past. Patience keeps believers from losing heart during the time spent waiting for God to fulfill his promises.

OUTLINE OF NEHEMIAH

I. RELEASE (1:1–2:8)
   A. Reproach of the Remnant Noted (1:1-3)
   B. Petition for Remembering the Covenant (1:4-11)
   C. First Step in Remembrance Granted (2:1-8)

II. REMOVAL OF REPROACH IN THE FACE OF OPPOSITION (2:9–6:19)
    A. Opposition: Secret Survey (2:9-16)
    B. Work Commenced (2:17–3:32)
    C. Opposition: Work in Warfare (4:1-23)
    D. Opposition: Internal Reproach (5:1-19)
    E. Opposition: Wall Completed (6:1-19)

III. RESTORATION OF COVENANT PURITY (7:1–13:31)
    A. Population of Jerusalem: Protection and Increase (7:1-73)
    B. Care for the House of God: Seventh-Month Activities (8:1–10:39)
    C. Population of Jerusalem: Increase (11:1–12:26)
    D. Purity Restored: Dedication of the Wall (12:27–13:31)

NEHEMIAH NOTES

1:1–2:8 RELEASE
Overview: God is seen as being behind the scenes but powerfully causing Nehemiah's success in leaving Babylon (1:11) and getting the wall rebuilt (2:20; 4:9-10, 15). The great detail presented in Nehemiah 3 makes the rebuilding process graphic and also memorializes those brave individuals as models for later generations. The opponents of Israel's return were seen as enemies of God and under his judgment (4:4-5; 6:14).

1:1-3 Reproach of the Remnant Noted
The name "Nehemiah" means "comfort of Yahweh." The book contains Nehemiah's personal memoirs of the rebuilding of Jerusalem. The month of Kislev, or "autumn" (1:1), falls within the months of November–December, and the twentieth year (of the Persian king Artaxerxes) was 445 B.C. Susa, destroyed after the rise of Babylon, was later rebuilt and became the winter residence of Darius and his successors. The condition of Jerusalem mentioned in 1:3 reflects Artaxerxes' decision to stop the rebuilding of the city until an investigation could be completed. The work was stopped by force of arms (Ezra 4:21-23). Nehemiah prayed for his people and the situation in Jerusalem for four months (Neh. 1:1; 2:1).

1:4-11 Petition for Remembering the Covenant
Nehemiah's prayer (1:5-11) was a model of adoration (1:5), confession (1:6-7), and petition (1:8-11). He pleaded God's character. Note the place of Leviticus 26:33 in the prayer. As the king's "cupbearer" (Neh. 1:11), he held a position of great responsibility and influence in the Persian court. Not only did he drink first of the king's wine to guard against poisoning, but he also kept accounts and exercised other administrative responsibilities.

Only a person of exceptional trustworthiness would be given such a post.

2:1-8 First Step in Remembrance Granted
The date was Nisan (March–April), or "spring" (2:1), of 445 B.C., Artaxerxes' twentieth year (464–424 B.C.). Although Nisan is the first month on the Jewish calendar, Artaxerxes' official year began in the month of Tishri (September–October). The date of the decree to rebuild Jerusalem is important prophetically, for it serves as the beginning point of the seventy weeks of Daniel 9:24-27. Nehemiah was fearful when the king noticed his sad face (Neh. 2:2), for he knew that sadness might suggest that he was dissatisfied with the king and was plotting against him. Nehemiah probably agreed to return to Susa soon after rebuilding Jerusalem's wall (2:6), but the time that he spent in Jerusalem eventually extended to twelve years (5:14). Nehemiah attributed his success to God's intervention and blessing (2:8).

2:9–6:19 REMOVAL OF REPROACH IN THE FACE OF OPPOSITION
2:9-16 Opposition: Secret Survey
Artaxerxes' decision (2:4-8) constituted a reversal of his own royal policy (Ezra 4:21). Sanballat was the governor of Samaria, north of Judah, and Tobiah was a Persian official having authority in Ammon, east of the Jordan River (Neh. 2:10). They probably learned of Nehemiah's mission through official correspondence and became opponents of the new governor. The distance from Susa to Jerusalem was approximately nine hundred miles, and travel between the two cities would have taken about four months (see the note on Ezra 8:31). Nehemiah surveyed Jerusalem at night in order to keep his plans secret until he could ascertain the magnitude

of the task (Neh. 2:12). Nehemiah left from the Valley Gate, on the east side of the city, and traveled south toward the Fountain Gate (2:13-15). It is not known if he completed the circuit around the walls or turned back because of the rubble. (See the introductory map for locations on the Jerusalem wall during Nehemiah's day.)

2:17–3:32 Work Commenced

Geshem (2:19), a powerful Arab chieftain, joined in opposing Nehemiah's work. But in the midst of opposition and persecution, Nehemiah remained confident in the God of the impossible (2:20; cf. Luke 1:37; Phil. 4:13).

Nehemiah described the repair of the walls with their ten gates and four defensive towers (Neh. 3). Beginning with the Sheep Gate at the northeast corner of the city, he moved in a counterclockwise direction, describing the work. All classes participated in the project, including priests (3:1), goldsmiths and perfumers (3:8), rulers and women (3:12), Levites (3:17), and merchants (3:32). In directing this project, Nehemiah demonstrated his administrative and organizational skills.

4:1-23 Opposition: Work in Warfare

Because the earlier efforts of Sanballat and his allies were insufficient to stop the work on the walls, they intensified their opposition. The rhetorical questions of 4:2 implied that the Jews could not expect to complete the project of rebuilding the walls. Nehemiah prayed for God to bring judgment on those enemies who were persecuting his people (4:4-5). The theological basis for this request was the Lord's promise to Abraham (Gen. 12:3), when God said, "I will bless those who bless you and curse those who curse you." Nehemiah was simply praying that the Lord would do as he had promised. Nehemiah prayed that their enemies' guilt would not go unpunished. Ridicule was overcome by the people's determination (4:6). Their enemies' conspiracy was overcome by their prayer and preparedness (4:9). Their despair was overcome by Nehemiah's encouragement (4:13-14) and their preparedness for attack (4:17). In summary, the opposition was overcome by faith, "our God will fight for us" (4:20), and hard work, "guard duty at night as well as work during the day" (4:22). Even when washing or drinking, the workers were prepared to fight (4:23).

5:1-19 Opposition: Internal Reproach

According to the Jewish law, an Israelite was prohibited from charging interest on loans to poor fellow Israelites. An outcry arose among the oppressed people because this law was being neglected (Neh. 5:1-5). Usury was the loaning of money at excessive rates of interest (5:7; cf. Exod.

22:25 and Lev. 25:36). Nehemiah demanded that the practice of usury cease and that confiscated property be returned (Neh. 5:10-11). If calculated on a monthly basis, the interest would have amounted to 12 percent per year. Nehemiah served his first term as governor of Judah from the twentieth to the thirty-second year of Artaxerxes, or 445–432 B.C. As a man of integrity, Nehemiah did not use his position of authority for self-enrichment (5:15). Instead, he provided hospitality for 150 Jews and officials who had no place to live in Jerusalem. Nehemiah's memoirs may have been a votive offering, presented to the Lord in the temple (5:19; cf. 13:14, 22, 31).

6:1-19 Opposition: Wall Completed

Continued opposition to the building of the wall consisted of three plots against Nehemiah. First, the enemy tried to lure Nehemiah away from Jerusalem where he could be kidnapped or put to death (6:2). Ono was a village situated about twenty miles northwest of Jerusalem. Second, Nehemiah was accused of rebelling against Persian rule (6:5-6). Third, they tried to lure Nehemiah into breaking the Jewish law by entering the temple (6:10-13); a privilege reserved only for priests (Num. 1:51; 18:7). Although Josephus records that the building program took two years and four months (*Antiquities* 11.179), the Hebrew text indicates that the wall was completed with God's help in just fifty-two days on October 2, 445 B.C. (Neh. 6:15). Tobiah, Nehemiah's enemy, sought to infiltrate Jewish ranks by marrying into the family of a Jewish noble, Shecaniah (6:17-18). His son also followed this pattern.

7:1–13:31 RESTORATION OF COVENANT PURITY

Overview: The heart of this book is the covenant renewal where the people recommitted themselves to keeping the law and maintaining the temple (Neh. 7–10). Nehemiah 11 narrates the repopulating of Jerusalem, the purpose of which was to remove the reproach from the city. The temple had been rebuilt, and Jerusalem's wall had been rebuilt. When the city's emptiness was filled, Nehemiah recorded the dedication of the city's wall, the symbol of the final removal of reproach and the commencement of religious and civil life on the preexilic order under David and Solomon (12:45-46). Finally, Nehemiah 13 shows the correction of impurities in the nation that were cleansed upon Nehemiah's return to Jerusalem and just before the dedication of the wall.

7:1-73 Population of Jerusalem: Protection and Increase

Although Jerusalem had been rebuilt, its inhabitants were few (7:4). For several generations the Jews had avoided making their home in the city that had no wall. The rest of Nehemiah 7 provides a register of the Jews who had returned to Jerusalem with Sheshbazzar and Zerubbabel in 537 B.C. The list is almost identical to that found in Ezra 2. Apparently, Nehemiah wanted to make sure that those repopulating Jerusalem were of pure Jewish ancestry, and the record served to this end. Many attempts have been made to account for the numerical differences between this list and the one found in Ezra 2. Perhaps Ezra 2 was merely an estimate that was later revised and preserved here. The Nehemiah named in Nehemiah 7:7 was not Nehemiah the wall builder.

8:1–10:39 Care for the House of God: Seventh-Month Activities

8:1-12 LAW AND MOURNING

The first day of the seventh month, October 8 (8:1), may provide a literary link between the events of Ezra 3:1-4 (the Festival of Shelters) and the events of Nehemiah 8. Nehemiah appeared to be reminding the reader of that great gathering with the hopes that a comparison would be made with the gathering spoken of in Nehemiah 8. The Water Gate (8:1) was in the east wall of the city and gave access to the Spring of Gihon. The first day of the seventh month was the day set aside to observe the Festival of Trumpets (8:2; Num. 29:1). That feast was a time to humble their souls and confess their sins of arrogance before God. Out of respect for the word of God, the people stood when it was being read (Neh. 8:5). Since many of the returned exiles had forgotten their Hebrew, the Levites translated the Scripture from Hebrew into Aramaic so that the Jews could understand the message (8:8).

8:13-18 THE FEAST OF TABERNACLES, OR BOOTHS

Reading the Law (8:14), the Jews were reminded of the Lord's instructions to celebrate the Festival of Shelters (Lev. 23:39-43). The Festival of Shelters had not been kept with such enthusiasm since the entry of the Israelites into Canaan (Neh. 8:17).

9:1–10:39 CONFESSION AND DESIRE FOR RESTORATION

After the Festival of Shelters, the people gathered to hear the Word of the Lord, confess their sins, and commit themselves to keeping the stipulations of the covenant. The prayer of 9:4-37 could well be used to trace Israel's religious history. It covers the covenants with Abraham and Moses, national rebellion, God's compassion, the period of the Judges, the Exile and the captivity, and the present state of the returned nation. Wearing "sackcloth" (9:1) was a common expression of grief and sadness. God used the Holy Spirit to communicate his revelation to the prophets (9:30; cf. 2 Pet. 1:21).

Nehemiah recorded the names of the civic and religious leaders who signed the covenant renewal document (Neh. 10). Mosaic legislation required the payment of one-fifth of an ounce of silver (Exod. 30:11-16), but Nehemiah apparently reduced it in light of economic conditions (Neh. 10:32). The obligations agreed upon (10:29-39) may be summarized in their final words: "We promise together not to neglect the Temple of our God" (10:39).

11:1–12:26 Population of Jerusalem: Increase

11:1-24 THE REGISTER OF CITY DWELLERS

Nehemiah used two procedures to encourage the resettlement of Jerusalem: he cast lots (11:1), and he asked for volunteers (11:2). Casting lots was a means of determining God's will prior to the permanent, indwelling ministry of the Spirit (cf. Prov. 16:33). Nehemiah listed the various heads of families living in Jerusalem (Neh. 11:4-24). A similar list with some differences appears in 1 Chronicles 9:2-34.

11:25-36 DWELLERS IN THE LAND

A very helpful list (Neh. 11:25-36) was given of postexilic Jewish communities in the areas formerly known as Judah and Benjamin.

12:1-26 PRIESTS

Nehemiah provided a list of the priests and Levites, the spiritual leaders who were living in Jerusalem (12:26).

12:27–13:31 Purity Restored: Dedication of the Wall

12:27–13:3 THE DAY OF DEDICATION

The historical narrative now continues in 12:27–13:3 from 11:2. Nehemiah described the dedication of the wall, which followed the covenant renewal of Nehemiah 10. Two great choirs (12:31-42) led by Ezra and Nehemiah mounted the city wall at the Valley Gate and proceeded in opposite directions to a meeting point in the temple area. Like David, Nehemiah took great care in the administration of the Levitical temple ministry. He appointed personnel and saw to it that foreigners were excluded from the assembly (13:3; cf. Deut. 23:3-5).

13:4-29 EXAMPLES OF PURIFICATION

Nehemiah served as governor of Judah for twelve years before returning to Persia to report to Artaxerxes in 432 B.C. It is not known how long he stayed away from Jerusalem, but it was long enough for the people to begin to neglect tithing (Neh. 13:10-14) and the Sabbath laws (13:15-22), and to become involved once again in mixed marriages with unbelievers (13:23-29). In Nehemiah's absence, Malachi preached and rebuked the people for these failures.

When Nehemiah returned to Jerusalem, he corrected these abuses. His reforms in Jerusalem during the early days of his second governorship are recorded in 13:30-31.

The thirty-second year of Artaxerxes (13:6) was 432 B.C. Artaxerxes was referred to as the king of Babylon just as Cyrus, who conquered and ruled the territory of Babylon, once claimed this title. Mixed marriages with unbelievers (13:23) had been a problem for Ezra about twenty-five years earlier (Ezra 9) and remained a thorny problem.

13:30-31 SUMMARY AND PETITION

Nehemiah concluded his memoirs with a summary of his contributions to the nation's spiritual welfare. He would be remembered as a gifted administrator and devoted servant of God. The book does not end with the happy dedication of the wall but with the prior and unhappy sins of the people that were corrected by God's faithful man, Nehemiah. The reader comes away recognizing the threat of personal sin, yet also having the hope that God will continue to provide faithful leaders such as Nehemiah.

ESTHER

BASIC FACTS

HISTORICAL SETTING

Esther's family was one of many Israelite families that chose to remain in Persia rather than return to Israel. The Jews first returned to Palestine in 536 B.C. Ezra and Nehemiah returned to Jerusalem in 475 B.C. and 444 B.C., respectively. Esther lived in the period of King Xerxes I, also identified as Ahasuerus (486–465 B.C.). Her story took place after Ezra's temple reforms and before Nehemiah's rebuilding of Jerusalem's wall. Just as Israel was striving to live once again in God's land, the political forces of Persia were about to try to destroy God's people.

AUTHOR

The author of the book of Esther remains unknown, although tradition has asserted that Mordecai wrote the book.

DATE

The story took place in 484 B.C., the third year of the reign of the Persian king Xerxes I, known elsewhere in Scripture as Ahasuerus. The temple had been built under Zerubbabel's leadership in 516 B.C. Ezra and Nehemiah would not arrive in Israel for more than twenty-five years. God's promise to return the nation to its land had been accomplished, but the Israelites' full restoration flickered like a candle in the wind. Enemies surrounded them.

PURPOSE

The purpose of the book of Esther was to give the origin of the feast of Purim, which was a time of both lamentation and celebration. The story was written to give a context for all the emotional elements of the feast.

GEOGRAPHY AND ITS IMPORTANCE

The key relationship of geography to theme in Esther concerns what happens to God's people who live outside the Promised Land. God shows that he blesses his people wherever they live. The power is not in the Promised Land itself. It is God who controls all lands and spreads the power of his promises to Abraham and Moses around the earth. It was Esther, living far from Israel in Ahasuerus's palace at Susa, who was used to save all the Jews, in and out of the Promised Land.

GUIDING CONCEPTS

LITERARY STYLE

Esther was written in a style that is more interested in plot and action than in character and personality. The reader sees the characters' actions but rarely sees deeply into why they acted or how they felt. The book's emphasis is on decisions that issue action.

Esther also follows the classic form of comedy. It begins with the main characters in prosperity, moves them into potentially tragic events, and concludes with a quick rise to a happy ending. In addition, the book contains several elements of good dramatic writing such as suspense (5:2; 8:3-4), irony (6:1-6, 12; 7:10), passion (1:12; 2:1; 2:17; 3:6; 4:1), and plot conflict (6:1-10).

THE TWO LETTERS AT THE END OF THE BOOK

Two letters, one from Mordecai (9:20-28) and one from Esther (9:29-32), made the feast of Purim part of Israel's religious life. Mordecai wrote and told of all these events. The feast's celebration confirmed God's desire to keep Israel alive.

RELIGIOUS PERSPECTIVE

Is the book secular just because it does not mention God by name? No. Fasting would include prayer (4:16). Mordecai refused to worship Haman (3:5). Certainly those events show a religious perspective. But the broader Bible-wide concepts confirm the deep religious perspective of Israel's history and promise.

BIBLE-WIDE CONCEPTS

THE PRESERVATION OF ISRAEL

This book reminded the people of Israel of God's promises to preserve them. God had promised Abraham that his line would become a great nation and that he would be with Abraham to bless or curse the people of the world according to how they treated Abra-

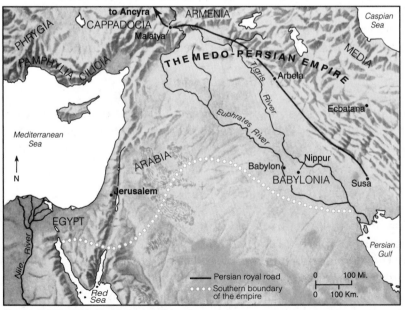

Copyright © 1986, 1988 by Tyndale House Publishers, Inc.

ham and his family (Gen. 12:1-3). Egypt had been a place of both bondage and preservation for Israel. Like Egypt, Babylon served as a place of bondage for Israel, but it was also a place of preservation for the nation and a staging ground for Israel's return to the Promised Land.

The book was designed to be appreciated best by those who understood God's past revelation to Israel in Scripture. The king's edict would bring destruction to all the Jews who lived within the Persian provinces (3:14), which included the land of Israel. All the returned Jews could have been exterminated. Also, just as God's miraculous works before the Israelites' exodus from Egypt caused many non-Jews to join God's people, so what he accomplished through Esther caused many Persians to become Jewish, that is, believers in the Jewish religion (8:17; 9:27).

ISRAEL AND HER ENEMIES
Finally, the book reflects an old conflict between Israel and the Amalekites. Mordecai was a descendant of Kish, of the line of King Saul (2:5). Haman was a descendant of Agag (3:1), king of the ancient Amalekites. For the story of the conflict between these two family lines, read 1 Samuel 15:7-9, 32-33. For Israel's prior conflicts with the Amalekites, read Exodus 17:8-13 and Deuteronomy 25:17-19. Israel's enemies always tried to exterminate them, but God's promise to Abraham was always in force to preserve them. The book of Esther serves as another confirmation that God would always uphold his promise of preservation.

NEEDS MET BY ESTHER

With all of God's promises and power, he allowed his people to undergo some very harrowing experiences. His redeemed people were never immune to Satan's attempts to mar or destroy what was holy and good. In Esther, the nation of Israel came close to extermination. But the book does not explain why God allowed the nation to come to the brink of annihilation. It simply shows two Jews, Mordecai and Esther, being courageous and true to their heritage. And through them, the nation escaped yet another attempt on its life. The book answers some difficult questions that arise from the nation of Israel's troubled existence during captivity and exile. The structure and content of Esther show that its author was probably answering questions like these.

- Has God left Israel to the mercy of the nations who hate them and have power over them?
- God has restored Israel to the Promised Land, but does that mean the Jews have the fullness of God's promises to Abraham?
- Why do Jews celebrate a feast (Purim) related to their escape from extermination and how was God involved in their deliverance?
- Did Israel's failure cause God to annul his promises for their redemption?

Like Israel, Christians may at times feel like their recovery from past failures is being blocked by their present bad circumstances. Why does God not make things less difficult? Why do believers seem to move from one crisis to another? A book like Esther helps believers understand that, though they may not find out why things happen the way they do, they can know that their task is to affirm their heritage and God's presence and sovereignty. The believer's task is to be strong and do what is right no matter what situation he faces. The triune God has not left his people alone. The Father, his Son, who died at the hands of world hatred, and his Spirit, who grieves and groans over the broken creation, are all there to uphold believers. Amidst a world of hatred, God's hidden presence and promises stand firm.

OUTLINE OF ESTHER

I. ESTHER ATTAINS ROYALTY (1:1–2:23)
 A. A Queen Lost (1:1-22)
 B. A Queen Found (2:1-18)
 C. A Favor Earned: Assassination Plot (2:19-23)

II. "SUCH A TIME AS THIS" (3:1–9:19)
 A. Problem: Jewish Insubordination (3:1-6)
 B. Edict: Jewish Annihilation (3:7–8:2)
 C. Edict: Jewish Preservation (8:3–9:19)

III. THE FORMULATION OF THE FEAST OF PURIM (9:20-22)

IV. THE GREATNESS OF MORDECAI (10:1-3)

ESTHER NOTES

1:1–2:23 ESTHER ATTAINS ROYALTY
Overview: Esther 1 describes the problem created when Vashti disobeyed the king. All the men of the kingdom feared that their wives, following the example of Vashti, would also disobey them, so they advised a harsh and immediate punishment. That event made clear the great wrath that could result when the king was disobeyed. Esther would have to overcome her fear of the king's wrath when she boldly entered his presence without being summoned in order to save her people from sure destruction.

1:1-22 A Queen Lost
1:1-9 BANQUET: GLORY AND PLANNING
The story of Esther is set in the rule of Xerxes I, known in other sources as Ahasuerus (486–464 B.C.). The number of provinces varied as the empire's boundaries were extended or adjusted (cf. Dan. 6:1-2). For Susa (1:2), see the note on Nehemiah 1:1. The year was 483 B.C. According to the Greek historian Herodotus, the king laid plans for his unsuccessful campaign against Greece during these festivities. The king customarily pledged his guests to drink a certain amount, but at this banquet they could drink as much or as little as they liked (Esther 1:8). Persian queens usually ate at the king's table, but on this occasion the men and women dined separately.

1:10-12 PROBLEM: FEMALE INSUBORDINATION
The reason for Vashti's refusal is not given in the text. Herodotus notes that she feared for her dignity

in the midst of such a drunken group. But the Jewish Talmud suggests that modesty was the issue, indicating that the king called Vashti to appear dressed "only with the royal crown."

1:13-22 EDICT: FEMALE SUBMISSION
The king's counselors were concerned that Vashti's refusal would set a pattern for other Persian wives (1:16-17). The king's decree required that the husband rule the home and that his native tongue be used by his family. The decree was sent throughout the Persian Empire, which boasted an efficient postal system (1:22). By using a relay system of riders on horseback, messages sent from Susa could reach Sardis, a distance of 1,200 miles, in less than a week!

2:1-18 A Queen Found
2:1-4 PROBLEM: NEED FOR A QUEEN
A three-year gap separates the events of Esther 1 and 2. During this period Xerxes I campaigned against Greece and was defeated at Salamis (480 B.C.). Upon his return he set out to find a replacement for Vashti.

2:5-18 EDICT: FINDING A QUEEN
Mordecai's great-grandfather, Kish (2:5), had been one of the exiles taken to Babylon with King Jehoiachin in 597 B.C. Hadassah (2:7) means "myrtle." Her Persian name, Esther, means "star." Esther was "placed" into the custody of Hegai (2:8). This was an involuntary decision. Why did Esther not reveal that she was a Jewess (2:10)? Perhaps she feared for her safety or did not want to prejudice the

king against her. The women who entered the contest became members of the king's harem (2:8, 14). As concubines they were wives of secondary rank and regarded as the legal chattel of the king. Esther became queen of Persia in "early winter" (2:16-17), the month of Tebeth (December–January) of 479 B.C.

2:19-23 A Favor Earned: Assassination Plot

Esther 2:19 refers to another occasion when Xerxes I added to his harem, after Esther had been made queen. Although not rewarded, Mordecai's kindness was recorded in the royal chronicle (2:21-23). God's sovereignty is shown as the details of the narrative begin to fit together.

3:1–9:19 "SUCH A TIME AS THIS"

Overview: The section of 3:1–9:19 presents the plot to kill all Jews in the Persian Empire and the beginning of Esther's plan to avert the disaster. The irony of timing brought together the king's remembrance of Mordecai's favor and Haman's pride. The result was the reversal of Haman's intended evil. Haman was hanged and Mordecai was honored. The edict for the Jews' extermination was reversed.

3:1-6 Problem: Jewish Insubordination

The events of Esther 3 occurred more than four years after Esther's coronation as queen. Haman, the "enemy of the Jews" (3:10), was descended from Agag, whom Saul had spared and Samuel had killed (1 Sam. 15:8, 33). This would make him an Amalekite, a traditional enemy of the Jews. To bow before a Persian ruler was regarded as paying homage to a divine being (Esther 3:2). Mordecai refused to bow before Haman or any human ruler. But killing Mordecai would not solve Haman's problem, for all pious Jews would refuse to bow before a mere man (3:5-6); thus, he determined to destroy all the Jews throughout Persia.

3:7–8:2 Edict: Jewish Annihilation

3:7-15 EDICT ELICITED

The date was April, 474 B.C. Haman cast the lot (Hebrew, *pur*) to determine the most propitious time to carry out his plot against the Jews. The lot fell on the twelfth month, Adar (February–March). Financial incentives persuaded the king to accept Haman's proposal. Xerxes I entrusted the signet ring to Haman to validate the document. The king did not even bother to read the decree, which was signed on April 17. It would become effective on March 7, 473 B.C. (3:12-13).

4:1–8:2 TWO REVELATIONS FOR XERXES

Shocked by the decree, Mordecai displayed the traditional signs of mourning (4:1). His message, revealed to Hathach (4:6-7), disclosed that Esther

was a Jewess ("her people," 4:8). To protect the king's life, Persian law prohibited anyone from entering his inner court without invitation (4:11). As a Jewess, Esther the queen was subject to Haman's death edict (4:13). Mordecai was convinced that God would somehow intervene and save the Jewish people from extinction (4:14). Perhaps his conviction rested on God's promise in Jeremiah 31:36-37. Mordecai suggested the possibility that God may have brought Esther to her position as queen for the very purpose of intervening in behalf of her people. Esther's words, "If I must die, I am willing to die," expressed her submission to do God's will no matter what the cost (4:16; cf. Luke 1:37).

In the context of the "three days" (Esther 4:16), the expression "three days later" (5:1) reflects the Jewish view of time that regarded a part of any day as the whole. Following Oriental custom, Esther did not make her request known immediately (5:4). She either lost courage or sensed that the time was not right to bring her petition before the king (5:7-8). Providentially, that delay allowed for the king's sleepless night and began the sequence of events leading to Haman's humiliation.

In Esther 6 God's sovereign hand is seen working through seemingly insignificant events. Haman was a living illustration of Proverbs 16:18: "Pride goes before destruction, and haughtiness before a fall." Haman's wife, Zeresh, and his advisers interpreted the turn of events in which Mordecai, a Jew, was honored as a bad omen (6:13). Perhaps they knew something of God's promise to judge those who would harm his Jewish people (Gen. 12:3; Zech. 2:8-9).

At last Esther identified herself as a Jewess (Esther 7:3). The word "sold" (7:4) reflected Haman's promise of silver for the king's treasury (3:9). Haman appeared to have been prostrating himself before the reclining queen, perhaps clasping her feet (cf. 2 Kings 4:27) as he begged for his life (Esther 7:8). Xerxes I interpreted this as a physical assault on Esther. As a condemned prisoner, Haman's face was "covered" (7:8) in preparation for his execution.

8:3–9:19 Edict: Jewish Preservation

8:3-17 ESTHER'S PETITION AND THE KING'S RESPONSE

Esther petitioned the king to revoke Haman's decree and prevent the impending calamity on the Jewish people. Since, according to the law of the Medes and the Persians, Haman's edict could not be repealed (cf. 1:19), Xerxes gave Mordecai authority to enact a counteredict that would allow the Jews to protect themselves against the attack that already had been authorized (8:7-8). Mordecai's decree was written on June 25, about two months after the first edict (8:9). That gave the Jews eight months to prepare to defend themselves against attack. The counteredict was intended to discourage Persians from taking advantage of Haman's decree (8:11). The date set by Mordecai's decree was the same as that of Haman's, March 7, 473 B.C. (8:12). This is the only occurrence of the expression "became Jews" (8:17) in the Old Testament.

9:1-19 THE JEWS DEFEND THEMSELVES
The killing of the sons of Haman would not be justified unless they had shared in their father's plot or were among those who had attacked the Jews (9:12-14; cf. Deut. 24:16; Ezek. 18:4). The repeated fact that the Jews "took no plunder" (Esther 9:15-16) indicates that their actions were in self-defense and not motivated by the prospect of gain. The hanging of Haman's sons involved the public exposure of their bodies to shame the offenders and deter further attacks (9:13). Esther apparently learned of a plot against the Jews in Susa that was to be carried out on the following day, so she asked the king for an exten-

sion of the decree (9:12-16). March 7 and 8 were designated for the Jews' rejoicing over deliverance from enemy persecution (9:17).

9:20-22 THE FORMULATION OF THE FEAST OF PURIM
The salvation of the Jews involved a massive and successful effort of self-protection. The institution of the feast of Purim was made by the means of two letters, and the book concludes with its major thrust throughout: the welfare of the whole nation of Israel. The name of the feast of Purim is taken from the word for "lot" (Hebrew, *pur*) (9:26); *purim* is the plural form. The celebration of Purim was designed to keep alive the memory of this providential deliverance (9:28).

10:1-3 THE GREATNESS OF MORDECAI
It is not known how long Mordecai held office, but historical records indicate that by 465 B.C. another ruler had taken his place.

JOB

BASIC FACTS

HISTORICAL SETTING

The book of Job shows what life was like for people well before the coming of Moses and the Mosaic covenant. Job, rather than a priest, performed his own sacrifices (42:8) and lived in an age that was similar to that of the patriarchs (42:16). The location of the land of Uz (1:1), where Job lived, is difficult to know for sure. That it was situated somewhere southeast of Palestine is one prominent viewpoint. Although the precise date when Job lived and the location of his home are unknown, this is not important to unlocking the book's timeless message.

AUTHOR

The book of Job is without a named author. Theories of authorship range from Job himself (date unknown), to Moses (around 1440 B.C.), to Solomon or someone of his time (around 950 B.C.), to an unknown writer who lived around 200 B.C. Jewish tradition has suggested that Moses either found or wrote the book. But again, knowing who wrote the book would do little to aid in understanding the significance of its message.

DATE

The events of the book are best set during the general time of Abraham, Isaac, and Jacob (around 2000 to 1800 B.C.). The date of writing is not known.

PURPOSE

Is the purpose of the book to show that suffering is a sign of God's displeasure? No, for if it were, what could be said about the suffering of Abel, Uriah the Hittite, Naboth, the prophets, Christ, or the Christian martyrs? The book's beginning clearly answers no to the question of whether Job was sinful. There is a kind of human suffering that is not a result of God's displeasure over sin. The option of suffering for reasons other than personal sin remains open.

Is the purpose of the book to solve the problem of suffering? No solution is given for that problem in the book of Job, and to look for a solution to it will only warp a reader's interpretation. The answer to why God allows suffering in the world remains unanswered. The book teaches that during the times when believers suffer innocently, their relationship with God can still remain unbroken. God has neither forsaken them, nor is he angry with them. Job never lost his integrity (2:3, 9-10; 27:5; 31:6), and therefore he never lost his good relationship with God. After all, that was the very heart of the test in the first place—to see if Job would abandon God if God took away his material and physical blessings. Job's faith in God did not waver. He just needed to learn that some of his expectations of God, such as getting instant answers to his questions, would not be immediately or necessarily fulfilled.

The book of Job reveals the truth that believers should continue trusting in God even when undeserved suffering occurs in their lives. Believers often suffer like Job without knowing why. They need to learn to admit that God has better control of their lives as the Creator than they do themselves. Also, there are some things about nature and suffering that believers are just not meant to know. Most important, if what believers know about the person of God is not motivation enough to keep them worshiping him, then they have forgotten that they are only finite mortals. The book of Job probes the hearts of believers, uncovering the reasons why they follow God. Do believers follow God because of the benefits he gives or out of a deep love and sacrificial reverence for God?

Satan was taught a lesson: the nature and person of God himself should be enough to motivate human devotion. Job's so-called comforters were taught a lesson: not all suffering is due to personal sin. Job was taught a lesson: if a person knows he is innocent but still suffers, then he must not accuse God of injustice but continue to believe in God's presence and trust in his ability to do the best for everyone concerned.

GUIDING CONCEPTS

THE PROSE INTRODUCTION AND CONCLUSION
The book's introduction (1:1–2:13) and conclusion (42:7-17) are written in prose. All of the contents between these verses, with the exception of the small prose section in 32:1-6, are written as poetry. So the book's beginning and end are set off from the majority of the book by their different literary form, creating brackets within which the poetry sections are to be understood.

The prose introduction clearly gives the reason for Job's suffering: it reveals that Job loved God for God's sake alone and not for the things that God could give him. Job's suffering was in no way due to his personal sin.

The book's prose conclusion clearly affirms that Job was right and that his friends were wrong. In fact, Job had to offer a sacrifice for his friends' sins. Also, Job received replacements for all the material things that he had lost. Job was totally affirmed for speaking what was right concerning God. That perspective of Job's innocent suffering presented at the beginning and end of the book is crucial for understanding the positions brought out in its central section.

THE CENTRAL POETIC SECTION
The ideas of God and five very fallible human beings dominate the book's central section. It is a poetic section designed to capture the reader's emotions as well as his intellect. The contents revolve around one question: Why is Job suffering? Job, his three friends, and Elihu all gave their best answers to this question. but the irony of the book is in the fact that the readers already know why, for they have already been given the reason in Job 1–2.

As readers study the intricate arguments regarding why Job was suffering, they should become increasingly aware that somehow all the speakers were missing the point. For Job was suffering because Satan incited God to ruin him without cause (2:3), and the human debaters all were on the wrong track.

Job felt wronged and wanted an answer for his unjust suffering. Job's three friends had made up their minds that he was suffering because of his sin. Moreover, Elihu asserted that Job not only had sinned, but if he did not get an answer right away, there was more that God wanted him to learn. All the human participants wrongly assumed that finding the cause of a person's suffering would provide the key to his coping with his suffering. Job's friends were sure that the cause was sin, and that is the cause usually sought by believers. Neither job nor his friends would ever have guessed the real cause of his suffering (2:3). nor would they have guessed that knowing the cause would have been of little help in successfully making it through the time of suffering.

The pursuit of the idea that sin is always the cause for suffering has continued into the present time. Some interpreters try to convict Job of committing a sin *during* his suffering because the first chapters of the book make it clear that Job had committed no blatant sin *before* his suffering. For example, some claim that Job's sin resulted from his having said that God had wronged him (19:6 and similar passages). But that position is based on the assumption that Job must have sinned in some way in order to justify his suffering as understandable punishment from God. But the book clearly does not allow the reader to assume that sin was the cause for Job's suffering. Its message comes from another, more surprising, direction.

THE MESSAGE OF THE BOOK
The way to cope with suffering is not in finding the cause of that suffering. Job never did find out why he had suffered, or at least the book of Job does not say that he did. The way for believers to cope with suffering is not in finding out why they are suffering, but in finding out who God is. Job was eventually affirmed as blameless, but not until he had understood the point that simply knowing that he was innocent was not the way to cope with suffering. A profound knowlege of God as the Creator and Sustainer of the universe was all that God offered and all that Job needed.

Yes, Job was indeed innocent. Yes, God is righteous in his dealings with the world. But in Job's day, as well as today, personal innocence and divine justice are not what believers really need to stay true to God and to be assured of his presence during times of deep and undeserved suffering. Like Job, believers may not receive answers to their questions of innocence and justice. But what they need is a deeper, firsthand vision of who God is.

So the book of Job is not about why the righteous person suffers or about how suffering itself leads to a deeper view of God. It is ultimately about how believers can go on trusting God even when some of their most urgent questions are not answered. It is about how they can know the unseen God is with them and for them even when their lives are being crushed to pieces. It is about how they can continue trusting in God while living in a cursed world.

SOME ASSUMPTIONS ABOUT HOW LIFE WORKS
The characters in the book make several observations about life as well as several assumptions about why those observations are true.

Observations about life

(1) Some people are righteous and prosper. (2) Some people are unrighteous and suffer. (3) Some people are unrighteous and prosper. (4) Some people are righteous and suffer.

Assumptions about life

(1) Some people are righteous because they believe that will cause them to prosper (the view of Satan). (2) The unrighteous sufferer deserves to suffer because he has sinned (the common view of all the human characters in the book of Job). (3) The unrighteous person who prospers now will be judged in the afterlife (the argument of Job). (4) The idea of a righteous sufferer is an impossibility, for the righteous God would only bring suffering upon the sinner (the argument of Job's so-called comforters and Elihu). (5) Suffering does happen to the righteous, but if it does God owes the sufferer an immediate explanation (the argument of Job).

Conclusions about life

The book concludes by recognizing that Job had not been righteous just because he thought God would make him prosper, as Satan had accused. Job had been righteous for the proper motives. Job's assertion that he deserved a reason from God for his suffering was shown to be false, for he never received an explanation of why he was suffering. His assumption that he deserved an explanation was corrected to another conclusion: that he, like all people, was excluded from a certain area of God's knowledge. The crisis for Job was whether knowing much about God would suffice when he could not know everything about God.

The same is true for believers today. If they successfully weather the crisis they are undergoing by trusting in God, they will be able to continue on in life and in their faith in God. Without that trust in God their faith will not grow. They will live by the potentially devastating assumption that God owes them something that he has clearly stated no human being will receive in this life.

PRINCIPLES FOR APPLICATION

Do not generalize about the message of the book of Job. There is no concern in the book about the problem of evil. God sovereignly hid (Job 1–2) and upheld his righteous ethical and created order (Job 38–42). The book does not teach believers principles to follow for carefully choosing their mates or that God will double their blessings after a time of suffering.

It is especially true that the book does not teach that religious insight only comes after suffering. Job's insight about God did not come as the result of his suffering, for he was still as blind to the cause of his suffering after it had ended as he had been before and during it. Also, the book does not try to idealize suffering as a way to deeper spirituality. Job did not find God firsthand in his suffering because that would imply all believers need that type of awful experience in order to come to God. But the very point of wisdom literature is to help the reader not to have to experience that kind of pain in order to learn the insights given.

The book teaches that God must be appreciated by believers even in their suffering. Creation reveals God's power, not his righteousness. And that revelation shows that God is so much greater and wiser than anything created, including the human race, that no one has a legitimate excuse not to worship him.

The book encourages believers to be open to surprises in life and to avoid having closed minds about how life operates. The minds of Job's so-called comforters were closed to the possibility of the wicked prospering and the righteous suffering. Job's mind was closed to the reality of what his own function was within God's great scheme. The book asserts that God is upholding the moral order of life. In Job's case what God was doing was hidden, but Job was obligated to worship him nonetheless.

BIBLE-WIDE CONCEPTS

THE PROBLEM OF EVIL

Although the book itself does not answer why God has allowed evil, the question inevitably arises in the reader's mind. However, the book does provide insight: not into why there is evil, but into how a believer can cope with it. For Job, his way of coping was to accept his limitations. He did not know why he was suffering, nor could he do anything to find out. He might have wanted more knowledge and power. But if he was to find any peace, he had to accept the limitations God had placed on him. Such is man's limitation concerning evil. Job never knew why he was suffering at the hands of evil, but his way of going on in life was to accept his ignorance in the light of what he did know about God.

From the time of Genesis on, God and Satan have been in conflict. That conflict is pictured in the Bible as the conflict between the offspring of the serpent and the offspring of the woman (Gen. 3:15). Cain killed righteous Abel, righteous Lot suffered in Sodom, and King David suffered unjust persecution, as did many prophets of Israel. The Son of God suffered unjustly to bring redemption to the world.

The point is that the conflict between God and Satan has many dimensions, some known to believers and some known only to God in the hiddenness of heaven. The book of Job teaches that the righteous person will allow God to carry out his own purposes in the awful conflict with Satan. God does not have to share those purposes with the human race. Ultimately he will publicly expose, defeat, and condemn Satan to an eternity of damnation. But until then God must be trusted to have victory secure, even though believers cannot always know all the details of the process.

THE RIGHTEOUS SUFFERER

The book of Job reveals a biblical teaching concerning questions that the person who suffers without a sinful cause might have. The fact that people suffered innocently destroyed the serene philosophy that assumed that wrong was always punished and right always rewarded. What actually happens is that wrong is often rewarded while right is punished, at least in this age. A history deformed by sin slinks between the creation of the old heaven and earth and the future creation of the new heaven and earth. How will a person who seeks after God fare in such a world? Will he somehow escape the deformities of unfairness and injustice?

The book of Job takes its place in the Bible by answering no. Until God's new creation begins, the righteous person will be vulnerable to injustice and suffering. Like Abel, Lot, David, the prophets, and Jesus, today's follower of God suffers. But the book of Job teaches that such suffering in no way means that God has abandoned the sufferer or voided his future eternal blessings.

JOB AS WISDOM LITERATURE

The book of Job is a type of wisdom literature that asks the hard questions of life. Proverbs makes profound statements about how the world works and how people can enjoy prosperity and avoid foolishness, but books like Ecclesiastes and Job probe into the gray areas, where answers are not easily found.

NEEDS MET BY JOB

Although the date of the book of Job is uncertain, it is clear that it was written for God's people who needed to understand how to cope with the injustices of life. The book attempts to correct the tendency among God's people to blame God for their pain whether by mild insinuation or by blatant attack. It also corrects the error of many to blame personal sin for all the sufferings that people experience. Pain brings hurt and hurt brings anger. But when the pain is undeserved, a believer may feel that he is suffering unjustly. It is easy to begin thinking that somehow God is not dealing fairly with his people. The book confronts head-on the issue of how believers should cope with unjust suffering. These are some of the difficult questions asked and answered in the book of Job:

- When a believer is hurting, does that always mean he is being punished for something he has done wrong?
- When a believer is hurting, does that mean he is suffering for someone else's sins?
- If a believer is innocent and still hurting, does that mean he is being wronged?
- How could God really be concerned about innocent people and yet allow them to suffer?
- If believers have to go on suffering in this broken world, can they really go on affirming God's goodness and trustworthiness?
- Will a believer hurt less if he can find out why he is suffering?

The book of Job meets the believer's need for a perspective on how to cope with undeserved suffering. Much of life's pain is not deserved. People do not deserve to hit their thumbs with a hammer or to break a leg while skiing. They do not deserve to be hit by careless drivers or to be laid off from their jobs. Many bad things happen to people because they live in a cursed world, not because God is out to get them. When he wants a person's attention, God does use fatherly discipline. But the book of Job makes it clear that there are additional reasons for human suffering other than just the narrow perspective of deserved discipline. Job opens up the more profound yet less black-and-white experience of unjust suffering—an experience chosen by the Lord Jesus and into which he beckons all believers to follow. The book of Job meets the believer's need to know how to face the challenge of unjust suffering with honest cries to God and absolute confidence in his sovereignty and goodness.

OUTLINE OF JOB

I. THE MOTIVE FOR ALLEGIANCE TO GOD (1:1–2:10)
   A. Character: Righteous and Blessed (1:1-5)
   B. Conflict: Righteous Because Blessed (1:6–2:10)

II. THE QUEST FOR THE CONDITIONS FOR DIVINE PRESENCE (2:11–42:17)
   A. Establishing the Reality of Job's Righteousness (2:11–14:22)
   B. Establishing the Reality of God's Justice (15:1–21:34)
   C. Establishing the Reality of Earthly Moral Government (22:1–25:6)
   D. Integrating God's Power and Wisdom with Innocent Suffering (26:1–31:40)
   E. The Teaching Ministry of Chastisement: Elihu (32:1–37:24)
   F. The Answer to Implied Injustice: God Speaks (38:1–42:6)
   G. The Answer to Implied Sin (42:7-17)

JOB NOTES

1:1–2:10 THE MOTIVE FOR ALLEGIANCE TO GOD
Overview: The book's two essential issues of character and conflict are exposed. Job's character was righteous, and he was blessed by God (1:1-5). But Satan caused conflict by contending that Job was being righteous because he knew he would be blessed as a result (1:6–2:10). The external and personal attacks of Satan confirmed Job's blameless integrity (1:22; 2:3, 10). The perfection of God's character alone was motive enough for Job's devotion to him.

1:1-5 Character: Righteous and Blessed
Job 1:1 is essential to an understanding of Job's suffering. Was it the result of sin? Not according to the clear statement found here and repeated by God in 1:8 and 2:3. Job was no mere formalist, for he recognized that sin was not only exhibited in wrong activities and deeds but could also be expressed as an attitude of the heart (1:5).

1:6–2:10 Conflict: Righteous Because Blessed
1:6-22 THE FIRST ATTACK
The Hebrew word translated "curse" in English (1:11; 2:9) is literally the word for "blessed." But the writer was unwilling to use the Hebrew word for "curse" with reference to God. So he wrote the word for "bless," knowing that the Hebrew reader would understand from the context that the opposite was intended. The word translated "angels" (1:6; cf. 38:7) is used elsewhere for "sons of God" (Gen. 6:2). Satan (Job 1:6), whose name means "adversary," was among the angels who appeared in heaven before God. Satan's access to heaven will be terminated during the tribulation (Rev. 12:9).

To begin the process of conflict between Satan and Job, God called attention to Job as an example of genuine faith and piety (Job 1:8). Satan suggested that Job was good because God had been good to him, had always "protected" (1:10) him, and that Job served God only for the benefits he received. Satan argued that if God took away Job's possessions, his devotion would evaporate. It is encouraging to know that Satan is subject to God's sovereign control and brings trial to the lives of believers only by divine permission (1:12).

The Sabeans (1:15) were a powerful and wealthy people who lived in what is today southern Arabia. The fire of God was probably lightning (1:16). The Chaldeans mentioned in 1:17 were a regional group of nomadic marauders, not to be confused with the later Chaldeans who founded the Babylonian Empire.

Job exhibited the traditional signs of mourning (1:20; cf. Gen. 37:34; Jer. 7:29). He lost his possessions, but not his faith. Although tested through a most difficult trial, Job's piety was proven genuine (Job 1:22).

2:1-10 THE SECOND ATTACK
The words "harm him without cause" (2:3) indicate that there was no sin in Job's life that God was judging. The expression "skin for skin" (2:4) suggests that a person will give some skin from his hands to save the skin on his nose. Satan was suggesting that Job was willing to lose all his possessions in order to escape with his life. The precise nature of Job's disease (2:7) has not been determined medically. The symptoms included enflamed boils (2:7), intense itching (2:8), worms in the open flesh (7:5), feverish nightmares (7:14),

bad breath (19:17), pain in the bones (30:17), fever, and blackening of the skin (30:30).

Job did not call his wife a "godless woman" (2:10), but he suggested that she was speaking like one. Job knew that she, too, was distraught after losing their children and possessions. He did not condemn her but encouraged and instructed her.

2:11–42:17 THE QUEST FOR THE CONDITIONS FOR DIVINE PRESENCE

Overview: The large section of 2:11–42:17 elaborates two basic assumptions: First, Job assumed that he deserved an answer from God as to why he was suffering for no cause. Second, Job's comforters assumed that Job was hiding his sins and was implying that the problem was with God and not with himself. If Job was righteous for God's sake alone, would God alone be enough for him? Job's statemate of faith was: "If I've not sinned, then the problem is with God." But Job would learn the other option: "I must take my finite place under God's infinite wisdom and sovereignty."

Readers of the book of Job already know why God let Job suffer—for no cause (2:3). So throughout this long exposition it is clear that Job was right and the others were wrong. Why does God want believers to listen to these long and mistaken arguments? To teach them that no matter how elaborate and flowery the argument, sin is not always the cause behind someone's suffering. A believer's first deep-seated and instinctive response to suffering is to wonder what he or others did wrong. That response is at times dead wrong. The long exposure in this section to impressive yet wrong assertions of sin is designed to hammer home their inadequacy.

As time passes, the reader also wonders if God will tell Job about what had happened earlier between him and Satan. Will God put an end to Job's pain and tell him that he indeed is righteous and that the situation started in heaven? The longer this section stretches out, the more pressing the need becomes for an answer from God. Surely God will affirm Job as blameless and Satan as the culprit.

But God's long-awaited reply goes in a completely unexpected and surprising direction. He says nothing about Job's righteousness or Satan's attacks. Instead, he asserts his power and sovereignty over creation. That authority provides the ultimate context for Job's assessment of what God owes him and what his next move should be. It also provides the key to a believer's next move when faced with undeserved suffering.

2:11–14:22 Establishing the Reality of Job's Righteousness

2:11–3:26 WHY THE RIGHTEOUS SUFFER

The locations of the homes of Job's friends (2:11) cannot be identified with any certainty. Teman,

associated with Eliphaz, was a town or tribe in Edom (cf. Jer. 49:7). Seven days (Job 2:13) was the usual time for mourning the dead (cf. Gen. 50:10; 1 Sam. 31:13). Job lamented life and blessed death in Job 3. But he did not curse God as Satan had anticipated, and he never did so later. The text moves from historical narrative (Job 1–2) to poetry (3:1–42:6), where imagery and figures of speech abound. Job viewed his conception as the beginning of his life (the Hebrew word for "conceived" is used in 3:3). The "sea monster" (3:8), also known as Leviathan, was the dragon monster that Baal is said to have killed in an ancient mythical story. Job wished that this monster had swallowed up the sun on the day of his birth so that his birthday had never dawned. Job, of course, knew that the stories of Leviathan were myths, but he referred to them in the same poetic way someone might refer to Santa Claus today in connection with Christmas giving. This is borrowed imagery, not borrowed theology.

Job lamented the fact that he had not been still-born (3:16). Job asserted that all of his life had been a big waste. Why had God let him get so far in life and then taken everything away?

4:1–5:27 ELIPHAZ'S CONCLUSION: JOB HAS SINNED

The cycles of talk between Job and his friends begin in Job 4:1–5:27. The first cycle in Job 4–14 forms a complete pattern of Job responding to each of the three friends. The next two cycles are not so complete, indicating a progressive breakdown of ideas and arguments.

Eliphaz (4:1), the first of Job's three friends to speak, argued on the basis of personal experience (4:8) and his mystical vision (4:12-21) that calamity was the lot of sinners, not saints. His thesis, and that of his colleagues, was that suffering was always an immediate result of sin. However, though sin certainly brings trouble, not all trouble results from sin (cf. John 9:1-3). The truth that those who sow evil also reap it (Job 4:8) is reflected in Proverbs 22:8. But Eliphaz sought to make a universal dogma out of a general observation. He expected the negative answer, "No," to his questions (Job 4:17; cf. Rom. 3:23). The phrase "charged some of them with folly" (Job 4:18) must be a reference to Satan and the fallen angels (cf. Rev. 12:4, 7-9).

Eliphaz suggested that Job's children had sinned (Job 5:4). He had a high view of God as being sovereign, righteous, and just (5:9-16). According to him, Job should have recognized God's discipline in his life and repented (5:17).

6:1–7:21 JOB'S RESPONSE: GIVE ME ONE EXAMPLE

In his reponse to Eliphaz (Job 6–7), Job argued that any sin he might have committed was far outweighed by the calamity he had suffered. He said there was no need for complaint when all was going well (6:5) and that food and salt go together (6:6) just as trouble and wailing do. Job wanted to be killed (6:9), the very thing that God would not allow Satan to do to him. Job told his friends to illustrate his sins concretely (6:14-30). A seasonal brook (6:15) is a river that flows in the winter when it rains but dries up in the summer heat. Job's friends were compared to such a stream.

"Those who die will not come back" (7:9) refers to the "grave," a place sometimes translated as "sheol" (NASB), a transliteration of the Hebrew word referring to the place of the dead. Some scholars believe that this may be the point where Job broke his good record of not sinning and did sin by complaining against God (7:11-21). He asked why, if he had sinned, God had not pardoned him (7:21), and he suggested that God had better do something before it was too late.

8:1-22 BILDAD
Bildad the Shuhite argued on the basis of tradition, presenting views that past generations had searched out and taught (8:8). Although he did not openly accuse Job of sin, he questioned his integrity because of his extensive suffering (8:6). In the end, he advised Job to seek God and be restored (8:5-7). Like Eliphaz (5:4), Bildad suggested that Job's children might have sinned (8:4). Bildad presented three illustrations of the godless man: he was like the papyrus plant that withered without water (8:11-13); his home and possessions were brushed aside like a spider's web (8:14); and like a quick-growing plant, he was uprooted (8:16-18).

But Bildad missed the key option in suffering, which is that the good person may be suffering for reasons known only to God. Notice the irony in 8:20. Despite all these accusations by his friends, Job never let go of his integrity (1:1, 8, 22; 2:3).

9:1-10:22 JOB
Job acknowledged that God was too powerful and great for any person to oppose or question (9:1-12). Underlying his comments was this unspoken question: Was God, perhaps, a cruel perfectionist? The Bear, Orion, and the Pleiades are constellations (9:9). "Him" (9:13) refers to the sea monster, the mythical Leviathan (cf. 3:8; another name for the Leviathan is "Rahab"). According to one myth, Rahab and her confederates made an assault on heaven, but they were thwarted. Job was actually saying, "If God overthrew the rebellious supernatural powers, what chance do I have before him?" One may think that here Job spoke wrongly about God (9:23), for is it true that God really "laughs when a plague suddenly kills the innocent"? But the meaning of the word "laughs" must be understood in the context of 9:23-24, where Job was speaking of times of calamity or when wicked

persons were in power. God destroys both the guiltless and the wicked in military or natural disasters (9:22), and in that sense he does mock the despair of the innocent. Innocence is no plea against suffering in this world. That sentiment is of one piece with the teaching of Ecclesiastes, which shows that being either good or bad is no guarantee of prosperity in this life because death mocks everyone.

Job sought a mediator to listen to both sides and arbitrate a fair decision (9:33). What a difference the incarnation of Jesus has made for believers (cf. 1 Tim. 2:5). In the absence of a mediator to represent him, Job made a direct appeal to God in an attempt to understand why God appeared to be against him (10:1-8). Job reflected on God's personal involvement in the formation of his body in the womb (10:9-12). He then repeated the theme of Job 3, lamenting his life (10:18-19).

11:1-20 ZOPHAR
Zophar, the rationalist, appealed to a common-sense application of orthodox but impersonal theology in dealing with Job's suffering (11:7-12). He suggested that Job was guilty and should repent (11:11, 14-15), and he also implied that Job was getting only a portion of the punishment he deserved (11:6). The proverb he used in 11:12 was intended to stress Job's stupidity for not seeing things as clearly as he did. The implication was that if Job had God's wisdom, he would see how bad he really was.

12:1-14:22 JOB
Job concluded the first round of talks with a lengthy discourse in response to Zophar and his friends (12:1-14:22). He calculated that bringing his case before God might result in his death, but he was willing to risk it (13:14-15) because his hope in God was all that he had left. His words were a significant expression of his faith in the midst of trial. Job demanded to know the precise charges against him (13:23). He believed that a tree has more hope than man; for if a tree is cut down, it will sprout again (14:7). Job longed for a resurrection hope beyond the grave, (14:13-14), for such hope would help him endure his present suffering. But rather than providing Job with hope, God had eroded what little hope he had (14:18-19).

In this first airing of the debaters' views, several mistakes were made and argued for on both sides. The friends mistakenly argued that Job had sinned, while Job mistakenly argued that he should be given a reason for his suffering.

15:1-21:34 Establishing the Reality of God's Justice
Overview: The section of 15:1-21:34 is the second cycle of exchanges between Job and his friends. It was a tug-of-war to establish the reality of God's

justice. The friends argued that only evil people were punished. But Job proved that good people also suffered, so he asked where a person's hope was for being good (15:1–17:16). Again the friends argued that evil was punished and good was rewarded. But once more Job asserted that good people suffer, concluding that their only hope was related to life after death (18:1–19:29).

Then the friends changed their approach and admitted that evil people might prosper, but their prosperity would exist for only a brief time. But Job replied that some evil people prospered for a long time (20:1–21:34).

15:1–17:16 BOTH GOOD AND EVIL PEOPLE ARE PUNISHED: WHERE IS HOPE?
15:1-35 Eliphaz
Eliphaz suggested that Job's guilt caused his long defense (15:1-16); a defense that would be unnecessary if Job was truly innocent. He continued to appeal to what he knew ("from my own experience") as the basis for his instruction to Job (15:17), declaring again that the wicked, not the righteous, suffer (15:20; cf. 15:25). He even described the destruction of the wicked in vivid detail (15:29-35).

16:1–17:16 Job
In 16:3 Job returned the remark made by Eliphaz in 15:2. Beginning to view God as an enemy, Job compared him to an animal that had hunted him down (16:9), a lion that had him by the neck (16:12), an archer shooting at him (16:13), and a warrior breaching a stronghold (16:14). Placing his hope in a heavenly advocate (16:19; cf. 19:25), with courtroom imagery Job appealed for God to pledge himself to appear in his behalf to prove his innocence (17:3-5). In despair, Job saw the grave as his only hope of relief from suffering (17:13-16).

18:1–19:29 BOTH GOOD AND EVIL PEOPLE ARE PUNISHED: HOPE IS AFTER DEATH
18:1-21 Bildad
Bildad, the traditionalist, expounds the fate of the wicked.

19:1-29 Job
Even if Job's suffering would turn out to be the result of some sin, the three friends had not yet identified his failure (19:4). They had spoken in generalities, not specifics. Here, for the sake of argument, Job overstepped the line of appropriate discussion regarding God (19:6). He presented the startling accusation of God doing wrong as the only possible conclusion in light of the contradiction between his friends' accusations and his own known innocence. He used a logical "if . . . then" conclusion about God, but it was an attack upon his accusers, not an article of faith from his own heart.

The writing of his words in a book was one of Job's desires that was realized (19:23). Earlier he had wished for a mediator (9:33), and later he expressed hope in a heavenly advocate (16:19-21). Here the idea was perfected (19:25). Although without hope in this life, he knew that God would vindicate him. The word "Redeemer" refers to a kinsman-redeemer (cf. Ruth 2:1), whose responsibility it was to redeem and restore a relative who had become a slave or had lost his property. Job's hope was ultimately realized in Christ (1 Tim. 2:5; Heb. 7:25). Job expressed his belief in a bodily resurrection (Job 19:26-27). After death ("after my body has decayed") he was certain that he would see God with his eyes.

20:1–21:34 EVIL PEOPLE PROSPER BRIEFLY; EVIL PEOPLE PROSPER FOR A LONG TIME!
20:1-29 Zophar
Zophar referred (20:3) to Job's sarcasm in 12:1-5. Responding to Job's earlier statement in 12:6 that the wicked do prosper, Zophar countered that their prosperity was brief (20:4-11; cf. 20:21). A wildfire (20:26) refers to one kindled by God rather than man, perhaps by lightning (cf. 1:16).

21:1-34 Job
Job continued to respond by pointing out the fallacy of his friends' analysis, for the wicked do indeed prosper (21:8-13). He highlighted the identical temporal destiny of the good and the wicked (21:23-26); both end up in the grave. Job meant that the wicked are spared or reserved in the day of calamity and delivered in safety from the day of wrath (21:30).

22:1–25:6 Establishing the Reality of Earthly Moral Government
22:1-30 ELIPHAZ
The section of 22:1-30 continues the debaters' intellectual struggle to establish the reality of earthly moral government. They all continued to have their own brands of problems with the idea that someone who had not sinned could suffer so badly. That idea seemed to go against their basic understanding of how God managed things in the world. Eliphaz argued that since God would not punish a man for his piety, Job must be guilty of great sin (22:4-5). Then he cataloged Job's supposed sins (22:6-9). But such wrongdoing was denied by Job (29:12-20), as well as by the author of the book (1:1) and by God himself (1:8). Eliphaz did not tell the truth about Job. Why? Because he was so hung up on suffering only being caused by sin. That narrow view made for his black-and-white approach to life, an approach that denied all the complexity and ambiguity of life brought about by the fall of Adam. In the end of the book God would bring this view

under divine judgment in need of sacrifice by the righteous Job.

Clothing (22:6), usually an outer garment, could be taken as a pledge of the repayment of a loan, but it was not to be kept overnight (Exod. 22:25-27). Although Eliphaz was sure Job was not innocent, he declared that God would pardon Job if he would repent and be cleansed of his wrong (Job 22:30).

23:1–24:25 JOB
Responding to Eliphaz, Job insisted on his innocence (23:1-17). He wondered why God did not at least appoint certain days to hear cases and pronounce judgment on those who practiced violence and oppression (24:2-17). In 24:18-20 Job seems to admit that evil men do suffer under God's judgment. Either Job had modified his previous analysis, now admitting that the wicked do sometimes come under judgment, or he was quoting the view of his friends. Translations that follow the second alternative insert the words: "You [Job's friends] say . . ." at the beginning of 24:18 (RSV). A third alternative is to assign 24:18-20 to Zophar as it seems to echo his earlier speeches.

25:1-6 BILDAD
Bildad avoided Job's challenge (24:25) to prove him wrong, but he tried to bring Job to his knees before God's power and holiness (25:1-6).

26:1–31:40 Integrating God's Power and Wisdom with Innocent Suffering
Overview: The section of 26:1–31:40 presents Job's best attempt at uniting the power and wisdom of God with his own experience of innocent suffering. It was a three-part effort (26:1-14; 27:1–28:28; 29:1–31:40). Job clearly asserted God's power (26:1-14). Then he asserted his own righteousness and God's great wisdom (27:1–28:28). Job ended this address by declaring that he was open to justified punishment for any sin of his that might be revealed to him (31:1-40).

26:1-14 ASSERTION OF GOD'S POWER
For "great sea monster" (or "Leviathan," 26:12), see the note on 3:8. Job insisted that when a person had described God's wisdom and power to the best of his ability, he had just scratched the surface. There was infinitely more that could be said.

27:1–28:28 ASSERTION OF JOB'S RIGHTEOUSNESS AND GOD'S WISDOM
Some scholars suggest that Job 27 contains Zophar's speech. But the reference in 27:1 to Job being the speaker is clear. Zophar apparently dropped out of the dialogue after he last spoke in 20:1-29 and no more is heard from him.

In 27:13-23 Job appears to have modified his earlier position by admitting that the wicked would not enjoy their prosperity (27:14) and that it would

not be their final destiny (27:19). But he held firm to his opinion that the wicked prosper for a season.

The heat of the debate was past, and Job reflected on the wisdom of God, where he was certain the answer to his dilemma had to be found. While man is able to mine the treasures hidden in the ground (28:1-11), wisdom cannot be found so easily. The major theme of the wisdom books (Job, Proverbs, Ecclesiastes, Song of Songs) is introduced: "the fear of the Lord" (28:28). This concept is the beginning point and the fundamental lesson in one's search for wisdom (Prov. 1:7). The parallel phrase, "to forsake evil is real understanding" (28:28), explains how the fear of the Lord may be practically applied.

29:1–31:40 JOB'S BEST SYNTHETIC EFFORT
Job listed God's past blessings to him (29:1-25). Producing evidence against the accusations of his friends, Job testified to his own kindness in helping the afflicted in the past (29:12-20).

Job lamented that while he used to be respected and appreciated for his kindnesses, he had become the object of taunts (30:1, 9). His "garment" (30:18) probably referred to his skin; his body had been disfigured as a result of his disease.

Job was open to justified punishment for any revealed sin that he might have committed (31:1-40). Job 31 is a high point in the ethical teaching of the Old Testament. Note the emphasis on a person's heart attitude, not just the outward observance of his good deeds. Job denied any private sins of his heart (31:1-8). In 31:10 he was really saying, "If I have sinned, may I die and my widow become another man's wife." He appealed for God to answer his claim of innocence (31:35), and he said he was willing to be punished if found guilty (31:38-40).

32:1–37:24 The Teaching Ministry of Chastisement: Elihu
Overview: The message of Elihu emphasizes two central points. First, God can teach, but he will not be forced into doing anything (32:1–35:16). And second, God will eventually inform mankind of its evil, but they must wait for him (36:1–37:24). Critical scholars believe that this is a later addition by a scribe who felt that Job's friends had overlooked some important points. However, the section fits well with the book's argument and provides a transition between the words of Job's friends and those of God. Elihu had a broader view of suffering and suggested that God might have intended to teach Job something (33:16; 35:11; 36:22).

32:1–35:16 GOD CAN TEACH BUT WILL NOT BE COERCED
Elihu was sure he could solve the problem that Job's friends had failed to solve (32:1-22). His words "they had condemned God by their inability to answer Job's arguments" (32:3) appear to reflect

the author's evaluation of the comments made by Job's friends. Elihu said wisdom was not the exclusive possession of the aged (32:8-9), for the young could be wise if they knew that they should seek wisdom from the Lord.

Elihu maintained that God is able to keep people from sin and teach them about it (33:1-33). He told Job that he, too, was just a man, so Job should have nothing to fear from his words (33:6-7). He quoted Job's declarations of innocence, which also were indictments against God (33:9-11). He rightly declared that Job was out of line in making such statements about God (33:12). This is a key concept (33:13), especially in light of Job's experience, for God does not always reveal the reasons for his actions. In spite of man's perplexity, he must trust God to do what is right. Elihu recognized that God might use suffering and dying to turn people from their wicked ways and lead them to repentance (33:26).

In 34:1-37 Elihu argued that God is not unjust, for evil is ultimately punished. He summed up Job's complaint: God perverts justice (34:5-6), and righteousness does not pay (34:9). The first complaint was answered by Elihu in Job 34 and the second in Job 35. Elihu spoke for the wise who, having considered the evidence, would also condemn Job (34:34-37). Like Job's friends, he assumed that Job had sinned, but he was especially concerned about Job's rebellious attitude over the perplexity of his suffering (34:37).

In 35:1-16 Elihu dealt with the question of whether God was obligated to answer Job's request. He said human vice or virtue cannot bring any advantage to the transcendent God, so people cannot expect immediate recompense (35:6-7).

36:1–37:24 GOD WILL INFORM OF EVIL: WAIT FOR HIM
Elihu urged Job to let God teach him (36:1-33). He said that suffering was not inconsistent with divine justice, for God used it for constructive purposes— to teach people and lead them to repentance (36:10). Warning Job against turning aside to evil by developing a rebellious and critical attitude as a result of his affliction (36:21), Elihu exhorted him to transform his complaint into praise (36:24-33).

In 37:1-24 Elihu expounded on the power and justice of God. He described the greatness of God the Creator that is beyond full human comprehension (37:14-15). Since God is infinitely great, he must be infinitely just (37:23). "God's breath" is a poetic expression for the wind (37:10). In ancient times, mirrors were made of molded, polished metal (37:18).

38:1–42:6 The Answer to Implied Injustice: God Speaks
Overview: God provided his own answer to Job's implication of divine injustice by proclaiming his

knowledge of and ability in the creation and maintenance of the earth and heavens (38:1-38) and in his sovereignty over the animal kingdom (38:39–39:30). In conclusion, he measured the power required for any who would try to challenge him (40:1–41:34). The major point was that if God controls the intricate orders of creation, which Job could only dimly understand, surely Job could trust him to order his life even though God's doings were beyond his human comprehension. Amazingly, God never mentioned the problem of suffering. In response, Job declared his newly found insight and took the only logical next step: to stop challenging God and be quiet (42:1-6). Note the sarcasm in this section (38:3, 5, 21; 40:7).

38:1–39:30 CREATION KNOWLEDGE AND ABILITY
The "whirlwind" (38:1) represents a theophany, which is an appearance of God in visible form (cf. Ezek. 1:4, 28). In Job 38:4 and the following verses God is likened to a master builder or architect, and his creation is poetically described. Throughout this section God draws attention to his unsearchable wisdom, power, and sovereignty in order to impress Job with the immensity of Job's own ignorance and lack of power. The stars that are visible on the horizon in the early morning are Venus and Mercury (38:7). The angels, or the "sons of God," rejoiced as they witnessed creation (38:7; cf. 1:6). The constellations of Pleiades, Orion, and the Bear are mentioned again (38:31-32; cf. 9:9).

The point was that Job had to see God in relation to the world; this is also true of believers today. Job's problem was not sin; it was his inability to realize his own limited place in the world in relation to God. The way for Job to receive release from his mental turmoil was not by obtaining justice; it was by becoming aware of and accepting his proper place.

40:1–41:34 REQUIRED POWER TO CHALLENGE GOD
The illustrations of God's sovereignty and power had shown Job that he should not have found fault with God. Instead, he had to submit to God even though he did not completely understand his ways. This had been the major flaw in Job's response to suffering. The link between God's power over creation and his ability to make right judgments was made in 40:8. Job had called into question the righteousness of God's actions. The "crocodile" (41:1) referred to the dragon monster that was so prominent in ancient mythology and was known as an enemy of the created order. While he was untamable by man, for God he was a mere plaything (41:5). The word translated "hippopotamus" in the NLT (40:15) is "behemoth" in Hebrew. "Behemoth" is the plural form of the Hebrew word for beast, which suggests that it was an animal of great size and strength. It is debated as to

what specific beast was meant—an elephant, hippopotamus, or rhinoceros. Such a beast was beyond man's control, but it was under God's power.

42:1-6 JOB'S INSIGHT INTO HIS PROPER POSITION

Job's suffering in and of itself brought him no new awareness of God. In fact, it brought him into a foolish position of challenging God's actions. Only God's self-revelation deepened Job's relationship with him. He had known about God, but the pain of his suffering and the folly of his challenge provided the context into which God brought a revelation that opened up for Job a deeper and more personal experience with God. Having seen God as he was, Job humbly repented before him, not because of a sin committed before his suffering, but due to his critical and judgmental attitude toward God that he had allowed to develop during his suffering. Job never deserted or cursed God. Actually, the very intensity and focus of his complaints toward God showed his insistence and faith that God alone was the source of his past, present, and future hope for life. His complaint was confirmation, not denial, of his faithfulness and integrity toward God. No greater passage than 13:15-16 can be found in the book to confirm that truth.

42:7-17 The Answer to Implied Sin

42:7-9 THE FRIENDS' ERROR

The end of the book provides a clear answer to the implication that Job's suffering was caused by sin. The friends, not Job, were condemned (42:7-9).

42:10-17 THE RESTORED FRUITS OF RIGHTEOUSNESS

After Job and his friends were evaluated by the Lord, Job's normal fruits of righteousness were restored (42:10-17). The view of Job's friends—that suffering is always a result of sin—had been proven wrong by God's spoken words. Job was not condemned because he had spoken rightly. He acquired twice as many animals as he had originally owned but the same number of children. Job fully recovered from his affliction and lived out his life in good health.

PSALMS

HISTORICAL SETTING
The general historical setting for the singing and reciting of psalms was the temple in Jerusalem, designed by David and built by Solomon. But though most of the psalms share this general focus of temple worship, the specific historical backgrounds and settings for each of the 150 psalms are quite diverse. The writing of the psalms grew out of specific concerns and events that spanned the time period from the Exodus (Ps. 90) to the Babylonian captivity (Ps. 137).

AUTHOR
The majority of the authors represented in the book of Psalms were associated with the temple. David headed the group that included various temple musicians who contributed other psalms. A large number of the psalms are anonymous. (See the section regarding the book's structure.)

DATE
The earliest psalm (probably Ps. 90) was probably written by Moses shortly after the Israelites left their bondage in Egypt (around 1446 B.C.). The latest psalm (probably Ps. 137) was written sometime during the Babylonian captivity (586–538 B.C.). All 150 psalms were collected into manuscripts sometime before the second century B.C. Manuscripts from this time period were recently discovered near the Dead Sea, showing that by then the collection of psalms was already complete in its present form.

PURPOSE
The book of Psalms was designed to aid in the worship of God by supplying poetic examples of life's ups and downs. Each event or struggle represented in the Psalms is punctuated with the triumph and peace that can only be found through heartfelt praise to God. See *Background of the Use of the Psalms, Lament in the Psalms,* and *Praise in the Psalms* for more detail concerning the original and present purposes of the psalms.

GUIDING CONCEPTS

THE BACKGROUND OF THE USE OF PSALMS
The book of Psalms is the Bible's own hymnal. Its contents are psalms that were used to praise God for personal and national wonders of redemption. Sometimes psalms

grew out of a psalmist's private experience of despair, and sometimes from Israel's national suffering as a result of military defeat. Some psalms were composed by temple priests and professional musicians, and others were written by the kings of Israel. But in the collection of psalms as it now exists, the psalms center around the temple of God in Jerusalem, as a brief survey of the background of the psalms will show.

King David was the first to organize the musicians in the temple and to incorporate psalms into Israel's temple worship. The psalms were designed to be sung as joyful songs (1 Chron. 15:16), to praise the Lord (1 Chron. 23:5, 30), and actually to prophesy through the words and music (1 Chron. 25:1, 3). The psalms were not just songs of praise; they were also statements of prophecy, not only in the telling of the future, but especially in exhorting and comforting God's people to remain true to him through all the pressures of life that might cause them to fall away. David organized the temple's composers and musicians and became the catalyst for Israel's great tradition of psalms. See 1 Chronicles 16:7-36 (which quotes Ps. 105:1-15), where David first assigned and organized the singing of psalms at the temple.

Throughout the Old Testament, David and his musician Asaph are viewed as the originators of the temple's songs of praise. King Solomon used the psalms during the dedication of the temple (2 Chron. 5:7-14). Jehoshaphat encouraged his armies through an exhortation of psalms (2 Chron. 20:20-21). Hezekiah used the psalms of David and Asaph (2 Chron. 29:30). During the great Passover of Josiah, the psalms of David were used (2 Chron. 35:15). Even after the return of Israel from the Babylonian captivity, Zerubbabel celebrated the rebuilding of the foundation of the temple with psalms according to the directions of King David (Ezra 3:10-11). And when the rebuilt wall of Jerusalem was dedicated, Nehemiah had the priests sing psalms according to the command of David and his son Solomon (Neh. 12:27-29; 45-46).

HOW PSALMS COMMUNICATE THEIR MEANING

Although the psalms are poetry, they do not deliver their message through rhyming words. They get their point across by laying out a thought one way and then immediately following it with a parallel thought that takes the first thought a step further. It is this interplay between parallel thoughts that forms the individual bricks that add up to the meaning of each psalm. In order to understand the psalms, the reader must avoid seeing the sentences of each psalm as independent wholes and recognize the relationships between parallel lines and sentences.

Sometimes a parallel sentence does little more than say the same thing as the first sentence using slightly different words (e.g., Ps. 146:2). But be sure to grasp the contribution of those "slightly different words." For example, in the case of Psalm 146:2, the addition of the repeated word "my" deepens and personalizes the content of the first line.

Sometimes a parallel sentence repeats the same thought as the first, but does so by stating the opposite or the negative side of what was said in the first line. That opposite side drives home the truth of the first line by contrast and usually functions to provide the reader with an understanding of what could happen if the words of the first line are not taken seriously. For example, see Psalm 1:6.

Sometimes a parallel sentence simply illustrates the first line. Actually, each pair of parallel sentences in the psalms has its own unique relationship. It is up to the reader to seek out and enjoy the wonderful variety that God has woven into his book of poetry.

But, above all, the psalms communicate their meaning by speaking to the reader's emotions and feelings as well as his mind. And the reader who wants to know what a psalm means will have to open up his heart as well as his mind.

THE STRUCTURE OF THE BOOK OF PSALMS

The collection of 150 psalms in the book of Psalms contains five benedictions that mark off five sections (Pss. 41:13; 72:19-20; 89:52; 106:48; Ps. 150 is a doxology in its entirety). And each of the five collections is grouped around the psalms written by a specific author.

THE FIRST COLLECTION: PSALMS 1–41

David	37
Unknown author(s)	4

This first collection contains twenty-one psalms that lament life's problems and eleven that are purely praise psalms. Lament predominates, for nearly all of David's songs in this collection relate to his suffering at the hands of his enemies. Psalms 1 and 2, two of the four anonymous psalms in this section, serve as an introduction for all five collections in the book of Psalms.

THE SECOND COLLECTION: PSALMS 42–72

David	18
Descendants of Korah	7
Asaph	1
Solomon	1
Unknown author(s)	4

This second collection centers around psalms written by David and the sons of Korah. Again, lament predominates in this section. All seven of the psalms written by the sons of Korah in this collection are included in the section of Psalms 42–49 (Ps. 43 is anonymous). Then, after a psalm of Asaph (Ps. 50), comes the Davidic group. David authored all the psalms in the section of Psalms 51–71 except for two anonymous psalms (Pss. 67; 71). The second collection ends with a final psalm from Solomon (Ps. 72).

The Davidic group is characterized by titles or superscriptions that note the wars and trials that inspired his writings (see Pss. 51; 52; 54; 56; 57; 59; 60; 63; and 70). In the first collection such superscriptions are found with Psalms 3; 18; 30; 34; and 38. The one remaining superscription of this type is not found until Psalm 142 in the fifth collection.

THE THIRD COLLECTION: PSALMS 73–89

Asaph	11
David	1
Descendants of Korah	4
Heman	1
Ethan	1

Again lament predominates in the third collection. The Asaph group appears first (Pss. 73–83). The last section of this collection includes four psalms by the sons of Korah and one each by David, Heman, and Ethan.

THE FOURTH COLLECTION: PSALMS 90–106
Moses   1
David   2
Unknown author(s)   14

Among the psalms of the fourth collection, praise and the kingship of God are the predominant themes. This section, made up for the most part by anonymous psalms, is opened by what is thought to be the oldest of the psalms (Ps. 90), written by Moses soon after the Israelites made their exodus from Egyptian bondage.

THE FIFTH COLLECTION: PSALMS 107–150
David   15
Solomon   1
Unknown author(s)   28

The fifth collection of psalms exhibits a decided emphasis on wisdom psalms and the events of the postexilic period (for example, see Ps. 137). Psalms 120–134 help the reader visualize a pilgrim's ascent to the city of Jerusalem and the temple mountain. Psalms 146–150 are the hallelujah psalms, which form a resounding and essential conclusion to all five books.

It appears that David's psalms were originally collected into two separate groups, the collections perhaps being made at quite different times. These can be seen in collections one and two. Then a group of psalms, the third collection, that consists mostly of the psalms of Asaph, who was David's chief musician, was collected. The fourth and fifth collections contain mostly anonymous works. Possibly many of those psalms were thought to be by David and so were eventually collected together. Those collections emphasize special love for the city of Jerusalem and for praising God simply on the basis of who he is. In most of the psalms this praise is given to God, not by people in prosperity, but by those who suffered the difficulties of human pain.

LAMENT IN THE PSALMS

Why are so many of the psalms, especially those of David, full of the complaints and laments of God's people? Psalms of lament actually form the largest number of psalms. Why are not all of the songs focused on praising God for his great redemption? First of all, the psalms, like the rest of Scripture, express many of the realities of life, and those realities include pain and lament. Like the books of Job and Ecclesiastes, the book of Psalms shows God's people struggling, not only with the black-and-white issues of life, but also with the gray. These psalms show God's people doing right yet still suffering at the hands of powerful but lawless people. That is the context for all the encouragement given to believers to wait through the difficult times for God's deliverance. The idea is not to ignore evil; rather, it means that believers should do all they can and then wait for God to act.

Second, all psalms that begin by lamenting over the pain and injustice of life always end their lament with praise to God. So why does God take his people through all the pain? Because God wants his people to watch the psalmists time after time show trust *during* the trials of life. It is one thing to praise God when the pain has gone. But it is more profound to praise him when the pain is still present. The kind of complaint and lament found in the psalms is not faithless carping against God. On the contrary, it is actually an expression of ultimate faith in him to remedy the bad situation.

The lament psalms all follow a rather standard format. The following sections describe two basic patterns of lament. These patterns follow the work of Claus Westermann (*Praise and Lament in the Psalms,* John Knox Press, 1981).

An Individual's Lament: Psalms 6; 13; 22; 102; 142

This type of psalm is basically a petition or supplication based on the situation of someone in distress. Frequently the distress is described in detail and with picturesque vividness. The basic format of the lament involves:

1. An address and introductory cry for help and/or turning to God.

2. The actual lament, which summarizes the individual's problems, his external foes, and addresses God directly.

3. A confession of trust, which follows the lament and usually begins with "but." At this point the author has changed from complaining to confessing his ultimate trust in God's salvation.

4. A request for God to be favorable (with such words as "look" and "hear") and to intervene (with words like "help," "save," and "rescue").

5. A presentation of various reasons that should motivate God to intervene.

6. A statement by the writer of his assurance of being heard.

7. A conclusion that sometimes includes a double wish: blessing for those who love God, and cursing for those who do not.

8. A conclusion that sometimes features the author vowing to make a public confession of praise and promising to tell others what God has done if God should choose to intervene. This is not bargaining with God, with the psalmist saying, "If you save me, I'll praise you." Rather, the spirit of the vow is, "When you answer and save me, it will only be right that I answer you with public praise." The essence of truly biblical praise is the confession in public of who God is, what he has done, and how dependent his people are on him.

9. A conclusion that sometimes includes a word of praise to God after the petition has been answered.

In some psalms the "confession of trust" is so dominant that a distinctive subcategory appears—the song of trust (see Pss. 4; 11; 16; 23; 62; 63; and 131).

A National Lament: Psalms 74; 79; 80

The psalm of national lament or lament of the people is very similar to the individual's lament and can contain all or some of the same characteristics. The major difference between the two is that the national lament concerns the suffering and distress of the whole community rather than that of a single individual.

PRAISE IN THE PSALMS

Even in the psalms of lament, expressing praise to God for who he is and for what he has done is of major concern. But other psalms were designed to allow for even more emphasis on praise and less on the painful experiences of life.

Psalms of Individual Declarative Praise: Psalms 18; 30; 40

Psalms of individual declarative praise are often more specific than the psalms that report how God has met the needs of the community. This praise is offered by an individual worshiper rather than a group. A psalm of individual declarative praise will usually feature:

1. A proclamation of praise.
2. An introductory summary.
3. A statement looking back to the time of need.
4. A report on God's deliverance.
5. A vow of praise to God (a promise to tell others what God has done).
6. Praise of God's mighty acts.

Psalms of National Declarative Praise: Psalms 124; 129

This kind of psalm reports that God has acted and met a specific need of the community. Three basic features of this kind of psalm are: (1) recognizing that God should be praised because he has acted on the nation's behalf, (2) praising God as a direct response to a specific act that has just occurred, and (3) praising God in a joyful manner. A psalm of national declarative praise usually includes:

1. An exhortation to praise God.
2. An introductory summary (God's deeds and praise declared).
3. A statement looking back to the time of need.
4. Praise to God.
5. A report on God's intervention.

Psalms of Descriptive Praise: Psalms 36; 105; 113; 117; 135; 136; 146

Descriptive praise is a public confession or acknowledgment of God's greatness or goodness. This praise does not necessarily arise out of a historical situation, but there remains at the core of such praise an experience in the history of the people with God. Declarative praise often passes into descriptive praise as the psalmist reflects on a unique occurrence in history and speaks of God's majesty and grace. These psalms feature the following characteristics:

1. An imperative call to praise God
2. Reasons for praise:
    a. God is great
       i. As the Creator
       ii. As the Lord of history
    b. God is good
       i. He saves
       ii. He preserves

Although many other categories of the psalms are set forth in various commentaries, they generally are related to the content of the particular psalm rather than its structure.

SPECIAL VARIATIONS ON LAMENT AND PRAISE IN PSALMS
Alphabetical Psalms: 9; 25; 34; 37; 111; 112; 119; 145
In alphabetical psalms the initial letters of successive lines form the Hebrew alphabet or some part of it. This literary pattern was an aid for the Israelites in memorizing these psalms.

Creation Psalms: 8; 33; 104; 148
The creation of the physical universe is the central theme of the creation psalms. God's glory and power are demonstrated in these psalms by describing the unspeakable wonders of his creation.

Exodus Psalms: 44; 66; 68; 74; 77; 78; 80; 81; 95; 105; 106; 114; 135; 136
The theme of Israel's deliverance from Egyptian bondage is a central theme of the exodus psalms. God's greatness is demonstrated in these psalms by describing the numerous miracles performed to bring about freedom for the Israelites. The crossing of the Red Sea, perhaps one of the most spectacular miracles, is a prominent feature.

Imprecatory Psalms: 7; 35; 58; 59; 69; 83; 109; 137; 139
Imprecatory psalms are psalms in which a prayer for judgment (an imprecation) on the psalmist's enemies is a leading feature of the psalm. These psalms have their theological basis in the Abrahamic covenant, which said that curses would come upon Israel's enemies.

Penitential Psalms: 6; 32; 38; 51; 102; 130; 143
The key feature of the penitential psalms is the psalmist's penitence over his own sins and failures. He acknowledges his guilt before the Lord and recognizes his need for divine favor and forgiveness.

Pilgrim Psalms: 120–134
The pilgrim psalms or "Songs of Ascent" were probably sung by the Jewish pilgrims going up to Jerusalem to celebrate the three major festivals of the year (Deut. 16:16). The psalms were sung as they ascended into the hill country to worship in Jerusalem. The pilgrim psalms praise God for his choice of Jerusalem as his holy city.

Royal Psalms: 47; 93; 96–99
The royal or enthronement psalms extol God's choice of his king, David. These psalms ultimately emphasize the kingship of God and explain the establishment of God's rule through the Davidic covenant and its kings from David on to the promised Messiah, Jesus. God's universal rule is mediated through the earthly Davidic line, and the earthly and heavenly aspects of God's rule come together perfectly through the past, present, and future rule of Jesus the Messiah. The psalmist recognizes that God is reigning on the throne and repeatedly declares, "God is King!" These psalms are basically psalms of descriptive praise, which are expanded and modified by the theme of God's kingship.

Didactic Psalms: 14; 15; 24; 50; 52; 53; 75; 78; 81; 95; 105
The didactic psalms form a category of psalms that has the common purpose of teaching truth through a variety of forms. The wisdom psalms form a major subgroup of the didactic psalms and express the thought patterns and themes of the Wisdom Literature (Pss. 1, 37, 49, 73, 91, 112, 128, 133, 139).

Torah Psalms: 19; 119
Torah psalms express the psalmist's praise for the Torah, the "instruction" of God. In these psalms the Word of God is glorified and exalted. Torah psalms also can be

described as hymns to the law, mentioned under a series of synonyms: law, statutes, words, testimonies, judgments, precepts, commandments, and promises.

Messianic Psalms: 2; 8; 16; 22; 41; 45; 69; 72; 89; 102; 109–110; 118; 132

The messianic psalms are those that predict aspects of the person and work of Jesus Christ. While skeptics have questioned the validity of such a category of psalms, Christ explicitly declared in Luke 24:44 that the psalms speak of him. Jesus quoted Psalm 22:1 as he hung on the cross (Matt. 27:46), thus demonstrating its messianic significance.

BIBLE-WIDE CONCEPTS

LAMENT OVER PERSONAL AND WORLD EVIL

Feelings of pain and grief over the horrible acts of human beings have been around for nearly as long as people themselves. Shame and fear gripped Adam and Eve, and Abel's blood cried out from the ground. Mankind's wickedness made God sorry that he had made them (Gen. 6:6). From those early cries of people suffering from pain and grief grew the tradition of the psalms. At the end of the Bible, in Revelation 6:10 the souls of the martyred saints cry out the lament concerning how long God had waited to avenge their deaths. The psalmists put into words and music their experiences of the joys and sorrows of life.

The laments of life, which stretch from Genesis through Revelation, have two aspects. First, biblical lament presupposes the ideal of good while a person is experiencing evil. The person laments because he knows and also desires God's ways in a world that is shot through with evil. Second, biblical lament reinforces the absolute truth of the world's cursed and bent nature that was brought about by the curse of God in Genesis 3. Those two aspects form a continuous line from the blood of Abel, through the blood of Christ, to the blood of the martyrs of the Great Tribulation. From a biblical perspective, the cry of the faithful sufferer is the cry of one committed to God's ways while living in a world under Satan's power. That lament will only cease when God's curse is removed in the new heavens and earth.

HOPE FOR THE COMING OF THE MESSIAH

The great lament of the righteous sufferer in the book of Psalms usually gives rise to the sufferer's burning desire for God's justice to be placed upon the one inflicting the pain. Pain moves the person to hope for a deliverer. The psalms emphasize God's absolute sovereignty over this world that has gone awry. God will come and set the record straight. From the fear of Adam and Eve to the cry of the last martyr, mankind has looked with hope for a redeemer. Throughout the psalms God confirms that a deliverer will come, and he will specifically come as a King after the line of David. The psalms forge the link of a divine Deliverer with the prior promise of the Davidic covenant and the future promise of redemption through the greater Son of David, Jesus the King.

THE TEMPLE AS THE CENTER FOR WORSHIP

The temple of Jerusalem and the psalms were closely related. In the temple was the ark of the covenant, which contained the covenant that God had made with Moses. That covenant was the means through which human beings reached upward in hope of redemption while God reached downward to fulfill that hope. It is no wonder that the 150 songs, which celebrate that wonderful redemptive relationship, have been collected in the book of Psalms in the Bible. Although the temple was destroyed, the songs of redemption continued to be remembered and sung by the Israelites. And today in the church, which is the temple of the living God, those same songs still continue to express the pain, joy, and hope of all believers. In the future new age, when the tabernacle of God will come to dwell fully among God's people, they will continue to sing these songs and, no doubt, even greater songs.

NEEDS MET BY THE PSALMS

There is one common link between the many diverse situations and needs of the people of God represented in the 150 psalms. Each psalm was written because something good had just happened—an act or insight that was directly the result of God's character or actions. The writer wanted the listeners to experience what had happened as a context for a mutual praise of God. Throughout their history, God's people needed reminders and experiences of his matchless character, redeeming actions, and just judgments. The psalms met that need for both reminder and experience. As reminders, the psalms present detailed teaching concerning God's laws and history. As experience, the psalms stir the emotions as the pain of life is transformed by the grace of God's character and only a few of the questions that believers with needs ask as they read and recite the psalms:

- Can God ever forget believers when they are suffering?
- Do believers need to be reminded about God's control over everything?
- Is God ever going to make things right?
- What are some good things that could be said when God answers prayer?
- Have other believers ever felt the way I do about life and God?

The Christian stands in a long line of those who, though being a heavenly people, still experience the pain of living in a fallen world. In that pain a believer needs the same reminder and experience of God's love and redemption that was needed by Moses, David, Ezra, Matthew, or Paul—exactly what the psalms have offered God's people of all generations. The psalms provide concrete illustrations of how God turns the strain and pain of life into food for devotion and praise to God. And that praise was ultimately to be shared with others. Although many of the incidents represented in the book of Psalms originated in private experience, they had to find their way into open sharing with God's people. Praise, like God's redemption and glory, is not to remain private or hidden. The situations of believers today may differ from those experienced by the psalmists, but the needs are the same—to have sanity in stress, to know deliverance from evil, to be able to express gratitude for redemption, and to find profound delight in God's incomparable character.

OUTLINE OF PSALMS

I. COLLECTION ONE (PSALMS 1–41)
II. COLLECTION TWO (PSALMS 42–72)
III. COLLECTION THREE (PSALMS 73–89)
IV. COLLECTION FOUR (PSALMS 90–106)
V. COLLECTION FIVE (PSALMS 107–150)

PSALMS NOTES

PSALMS 1–41 COLLECTION ONE
Psalm 1
Two Ways of Life
A wisdom psalm

Psalm 1 gives a simple but comprehensive description of the state of the world's beginning from the time of God's curse upon Adam's sin. The godly seed of the woman is always confronted with the ways of the ungodly seed of Satan, the serpent, or snake. The entire world is on the way to the Last Judgment, but the righteous person will stand and be approved (1:6) by God. "The joys" (1:1) can be literally rendered "happy." The verbs "follow," "stand," and "join" (1:1) describe the successive steps of a person's involvement with evil. The Hebrew word translated "think" (1:2) can also be used for the growling of a lion over its prey. This suggests that thinking, or meditation, is a vocal, not just a mental, activity. The biblical concept of meditation involves a thoughtful and reflective recitation of the Word of God. Wisdom psalms are noted for contrasting the ways of the righteous with the ways of the wicked. This psalm presents two contrasting ways of life and the two contrasting destinies that go along with them. This contrast sets the context for all the psalms that follow. What is "good" in a person's life is not relative to personal pain or pleasure. It is relative only to what God thinks about that life.

Psalm 2
The Messiah's Ultimate Victory
A messianic psalm of David (see Acts 4:25-26)

In Psalm 2 the "anointed one" is the King in the Davidic line. He is the Son of God in the sense of 2 Samuel 7:14, "I will be his father, and he will be my son." This reference to the Son of God and Son of David found its fulfillment in the only begotten Son of God and greatest Son of David, Jesus, the anointed King of kings. Psalm 1 begins with joy (1:1), and Psalm 2 ends with joy (2:12). These first two psalms form the introduction to all the rest of the psalms and set the context of blessing and judgment, involving loving obedience (1:2), rebellion (1:4; 2:2), and devoted worship of God and his Son (2:11-12). The king of Israel was anointed with oil as part of a religious consecration (2:2), and he became known as "God's Anointed." The Hebrew word translated "anointed" literally means "Messiah." David's experience described in this psalm would be ultimately fulfilled in Christ. Jesus, the Messiah, will reign as King in Jerusalem during the Millennium (2:6; Isa. 2:3). The New Testament links the words "Today I have become your Father" (2:7) with Christ's resurrection (cf. Acts 13:33-34; Rom. 1:4; Heb. 1:5; 5:5).

Psalm 3
A Morning Prayer of Trust in God
An individual's lament

As the chosen king of God, David waited for God to make right the wrong things that had been done against him. The king's patient waiting resulted in blessing for the people (3:8). Similarly, Christ's waiting for God's vindication has issued in his perfect blessing and salvation for all believers. Note the superscription to Psalm 3: "A psalm of David, regarding the time David fled from his son Absalom." Thirteen psalms (3; 7; 18; 34; 51; 52; 54; 56; 57; 59; 60; 63; and 142) have similar superscriptions that provide the historical settings out of which these psalms were composed. It is hazardous to attempt to reconstruct the historical settings of the other psalms where no such indication is given as to the historical occasion for which they were written. The background of Psalm 3 is Absalom's revolt (cf. 2 Sam. 15). The word "Interlude" (Ps. 3:2; Hebrew "Selah"), which occurs seventy-one times in the book of Psalms, was probably a musical notation that signaled a change of musical accompaniment.

Psalm 4
An Evening Prayer of Trust in God
A song of trust

Psalm 4 expresses the frustration of the godly king who is waiting, in the middle of criticism (4:2, 6), for God to reveal his righteousness. For all faithful believers, God alone brings peace and gladness in a world of contradictory evil (4:7). The words of the superscription, "For the choir director: A psalm of David, to be accompanied by stringed instruments" (4:1), appear in fifty-five psalms and indicate that this psalm was to be set to music and sung in public worship in praise of God. "Proper sacrifices" (4:5) refer to those sacrifices brought by a believer with a pure motive and sincere heart (cf. Mic. 6:6-8). "Let the smile of your face shine on us, Lord" (4:6) is an expression from the priestly benediction (cf. Num. 6:25-26), that means "show favor."

Psalm 5
A Morning Prayer for Protection
An individual's lament

Requests for God to hear (Ps. 5:1), answer (4:1), or stop delaying (6:3) are found throughout the psalms. They are not disrespectful commands; rather, they are poignant cries of a suffering faithful believer going to his only possible source of hope. The first half of Psalm 5 speaks of prayer in the temple, while the latter half asks for judgment on enemies and blessings on the faithful. "Unfailing love" (5:7) is one of God's attributes revealed in Exodus 34:6-7. The root meaning of the Hebrew word brings to mind the loyalty epitomized in the stork, a symbol of motherhood. It can be rendered "loyal love" or "covenant loyalty." That love is embodied in God's loving-kindness to David and his family line of descendants through the Davidic covenant (2 Sam. 7:15). In Psalm 5:10 the imprecation, or the prayer for God to judge (see "Imprecatory psalms" mentioned previously), David petitioned God to punish the wicked and thus vindicate his own righteousness. Such prayers were grounded on God's promise to "curse" those who persecuted Abraham's descendants (cf. Gen. 12:3).

Psalm 6
A Prayer for Physical Deliverance
An individual's lament, a penitential psalm

The king was being persecuted by his enemies (6:7), enemies who were fighting against God's anointed king. Assurance of relief (6:10) came only after the time of suffering. During that time, the assurance of being heard by God was sufficient for the king to remain faithful. In 6:5 David was simply saying that only the people who are living have an opportunity to give public praise to God on earth. The grave refers to the place of the dead. The phrase "Go away, all you who do evil" in 6:8 was quoted by Jesus in condemnation of superficial religion (cf. Matt. 7:23). God had heard and answered David's prayer (6:8-9)!

Psalm 7
A Prayer for Justice
An individual's lament, an imprecatory psalm

David could take refuge in God because he was righteous. That was his defense and stabilizing foundation (7:8-10) when he was attacked by his enemies, which in this case was one of his Israelite brothers. The word translated "me" (7:2) could also be rendered "my life." In 7:9-11 David prayed an imprecation (see "Imprecatory psalms" above), asking God to punish the wicked and preserve the righteous (cf. Gen. 12:3). The word "thank" (7:17) could be better rendered "give public acknowledgment," referring to praise in which God's greatness and his goodness, his attributes, and his actions are declared publicly.

Psalm 8
God's Glory Revealed in Creation
A creation psalm, a messianic psalm

The majesty of God comes not only from his greatness displayed in creation but also in his crowning of lowly humanity with majesty. That bestowal of majesty was perfected in the perfect divine majesty of the incarnate Son of God. The "stringed instrument" (Hebrew "gittith") in the superscription of Psalm 8 is an obscure musical term, perhaps referring to an instrument or tune from Gath. The psalmist's lofty view of man reflects the fact that man was created in God's image (8:5;

cf. Gen. 1:27). In Hebrews 2:6-8 the concept is applied to Christ in his incarnation.

Psalm 9
Praise for God's Judgment
A psalm of individual declarative praise

The present reign of evil against God will be resolved in God's last judgment. In the meantime, his faithful followers worship him in the present and trust in his victory that will occur in the future. The focus on the nations (Ps. 9:5, 8, 15, 17, 19-20) shows the original global intentions of God's rule through his chosen line of David. God, who is the avenger of blood, will not overlook deeds of violence (9:12). The words "Quiet Interlude" (9:16) provide directions for a musical interlude. The grave (9:17) is the place of the dead.

Psalm 10
A Prayer against the Wicked
An individual's lament

In light of the predominance of world evil, the writer asked why God seemed far away (10:1). People were saying God was dead (10:4), that God isn't watching (10:11), and that God would not judge (10:13). However, God had heard the request and would act, but the righteous had to wait for him (10:16-18) to purify the world (10:15). In some Hebrew manuscripts and ancient versions Psalms 9 and 10 are joined as one. In the Hebrew text, they form a partial alphabetic acrostic. This is an imprecation against the wicked (10:15; see "Imprecatory psalms" mentioned previously).

Psalm 11
God, the Refuge of the Righteous
A song of trust

The conflicts of this age are tests of character. The righteous will find rest and see the face of God (11:7), whereas the unrighteous will be judged in terms descriptive of the great tribulation and the lake of fire (11:6). The psalmist's friends advised him to "fly" while there was a chance (11:1). Like a building, society rests on "foundations" (11:3). If the foundation is undermined, the building will soon collapse. "Watches" (11:4) implies the image of eyes and is a powerful anthropomorphism (attributing human features to God) referring to God's careful scrutiny of mankind.

Psalm 12
The Prayer of a Faithful Believer
An individual's lament

As the godly people disappeared (12:1), David asserted his belief that God was in control and would protect the faithful believers for their ultimate safety and relief (12:5). The psalm was written by David to be set to music and sung in public worship (see the superscription of Ps. 12). The "faithful" person (12:1) is loyal to God and upright in character. The phrase "purified seven times" (12:6) indicates that the silver was completely pure.

Psalm 13
A Prayer for Help from God
An individual's lament

Aside from desiring survival for his own sake, David did not want his enemies to overcome him because he was God's chosen king. Again, God's love shown in the Davidic covenant was David's security (13:5). His four repetitions of the rhetorical question "How long?" reveal the depths of his despair (13:1-2).

Psalm 14
The Folly and Wickedness of Mankind
An individual's lament, a didactic psalm

The fool mentioned in Psalm 14 was David's fellow Israelite who in practice really was an agnostic. For although he knew that God existed, his words and his practical life denied that God was powerful enough to act. After quoting 14:1-3 in his letter to the Roman church in the New Testament (Rom. 3:10-12), the apostle Paul concluded that all mankind is corrupt, having fallen short of God's standard of righteousness (Rom. 3:23). Despite his despair over the wickedness of evildoers, David joyfully anticipated the blessings of the messianic kingdom, which would bring an end to the reign of evil (14:7; cf. Isa. 2:2-4; 4:2-6).

Psalm 15
The Character of a Faithful Believer
A didactic psalm

The essence of David's rhetorical question in Psalm 15:1 is, "What kind of person may enjoy fellowship with God?" The matter of lending money without charging "interest" is related to the Old Testament prohibition of charging excessive rates of interest or charging interest on loans to the poor (15:5; cf. Lev. 25:35-46; Deut. 24:10-13). This prohibition does not relate to receiving modest interest on bank deposits today.

Psalm 16
The Joy of Trusting God
A song of trust, a messianic psalm

The "sacrifices" (16:4) referred either to sacrifices offered to idols or drink offerings made by those whose hands were bloodstained. In the New Testament Peter quoted 16:8-11 in Acts 2:25-28, commenting that David was speaking prophetically of the resurrection of Christ (Acts 2:31). Using the language of hyperbole to express his resurrection hope for faithful believers, David predicted what would literally be fulfilled in the life of Christ (Ps. 16:10); for Jesus, God's "Holy One," underwent no bodily decay in the grave (cf. Acts 13:35).

Psalm 17
Prayer for the Vindication of the Righteous
An individual's lament

David was not making a claim for sinless perfection in Psalm 17:1 (cf. 51:3). Rather, he was presenting himself as a man of integrity, free from deceit (17:3). The "apple of your eye" (17:8) is a reference to the eye's precious and delicate pupil, which must be carefully protected. The wicked enjoy temporal prosperity or "earthly gain" (17:14), but the righteous who "rise" in the resurrection to life (cf. John 5:28-29) will enjoy the presence of God forever (Ps. 17:15).

Psalm 18
Praise for God's Deliverance
A psalm of individual declarative praise

Psalm 18, also found in 2 Samuel 22, celebrated the Lord's deliverance of David from Saul and the securing of David's kingdom. That victory was a brief and miniature picture of what the final victory of David's great Son, Jesus, will be at the end of the age. Until then, momentary victory, though soon swallowed up by conflicts and defeats, gives believers a basis for their hope in the future and final victory. Psalm 18:7-15 contains the language of theophany, that is, the language describing an appearance of God. Here God is depicted as revealing himself through the upheavals of nature. In 18:20-24 David was not claiming to be sinless; he was simply recalling how he had obeyed God, particularly with regard to his dealings with Saul (cf. 1 Sam. 24:10-12). David viewed God's deliverance and blessing as rewards for his obedience in this area. God will act appropriately with every person whether he intentionally chooses evil or good (18:25-27). With God's help, David had completely overcome his enemies and made them his servants (18:43-45; cf. 2 Sam. 8). In the New Testament Paul quoted Psalm 18:49 (Rom. 15:9) with reference to Gentile worship of the Messiah. The hope of the world centers on David's line of descendants and all those who align themselves with it (Ps. 18:49-50).

Psalm 19
Praise of God's Revelation
A Torah psalm

The great themes of creation (19:1-6), the law (19:7-11), and the fear of God (19:9) are linked together here as the motivation for man's verbal and heartfelt devotion to God (19:14). Without words or voices, the beauty and wonder of creation shouts, "God, the Creator, exists!" In 19:7-9 David provided a sixfold description of the law, God's special revelation. The various synonyms emphasize different aspects of God's word. The "law," in Hebrew, "Torah," is God's instruction to his people; the "decrees" are a witness to God's truth;

the "commandments" are divine directions for man to follow; the "commands" are God's orders or imperatives; "reverence for the Lord" is the reverence that God's word fosters; and the "laws" are God's decisions. "Deliberate sins" (19:13) are those sins done knowingly and willfully (cf. Num. 15:30-31).

Psalm 20
A Prayer for Victory
A royal psalm

The repeated use of "may . . ." throughout Psalm 20 makes this psalm a confident wish for the reader or hearer to be helped by God. David promised to lead others in a song of praise when the help came from the Lord (20:5). For "Interlude" (20:3), see the note for Psalm 3:2. In David's time there was often the temptation to trust in military might (20:7; "armies" and "weapons") rather than in God (cf. Isa. 31:1; Deut. 17:16). David, a mere earthly monarch, recognized that God is the true King and Deliverer.

Psalm 21
Thanksgiving for Victory
A royal psalm

The first half of Psalm 21 is a beautiful description of how God had blessed the king. The victories foretold in the second half were based on the loving-kindness of God found in the Davidic covenant (2 Sam. 7:14-15). The king was the mediator of God's victories over the enemies. This is most fully seen in the victory of Christ over sin, death, and the nations at his first and second comings. "Him" (Ps. 21:3) refers to David, the king (cf. the superscription of Ps. 21). In 21:7-12 the nation expressed its wishes for the king.

Psalm 22
Triumph through Suffering
An individual's lament, a messianic psalm

Psalm 22 shows the tension David felt while knowing that God was totally powerful to help him at the same time that he was experiencing what appeared to be the absence of God's presence to help. The faithful person may cry out in great pain and yet affirm God's goodness and ultimate deliverance (22:3, 8, 10, 22). Jesus quoted the first part of 22:1 while he was dying on the cross (Matt. 27:46), acknowledging his sense of abandonment by the Father as he bore on his own person the sin of mankind. The imagery of Psalm 22:3 represents Israel's praise serving as a throne of glory for God. The "worm" (22:6) serves as an illustration of humiliation, one being trodden underfoot with contempt. For the fulfillment of 22:7 in Christ's suffering, see Matthew 27:39; and for Psalm 22:8, see Matthew 27:43. In Psalm 22:14-16 David prophetically described the crucifixion, for it was

a means of execution that was not known until Roman times. The suffering that David described by using hyperboles was literally experienced by Christ. For the piercing of Christ's body foretold in 22:16, see John 20:25. For the fulfillment regarding his clothing in Psalm 22:18, see Matthew 27:35. David prayed for deliverance from death (Ps. 22:19-21), while Christ's deliverance was accomplished by his resurrection from the dead. For 22:22, see Hebrews 2:12. David predicted the universal worship of God during the millennial kingdom (Ps. 22:27-31; cf. Zech. 8:20-23; 14:6-11).

Psalm 23
The Divine Shepherd
A song of trust

Psalm 23 is a psalm of praise deeply rooted in God's covenant promise to David. See God's promise to build a house for David and provide him with permanent loving-kindness in 2 Samuel 7:11-16. In a pastoral community the "shepherd" would be recognized as an illustration of one who serves as a leader, companion, guide, and provider (Ps. 23:1). In the ancient Near East, the term was frequently applied to the king (cf. Ezek. 34:1-23). The shepherd used the "rod" as a weapon of defense to drive off beasts of prey, and the "staff" to lean upon as well as to guide straying sheep (Ps 23:4). The Hebrew words translated "the dark valley of death" (23:4) are better translated "valley of deep darkness."

Psalm 24
Greeting the King of Glory
A psalm of descriptive praise, a messianic psalm

Psalm 24 moves from God as Creator, to the holy requirements for mortals to be in his presence, to a jubilant welcome for God to enter into his temple. For a question and answer similar to the one in 24:3, see Psalm 15. Jacob is an example of one who sought God (24:6; cf. Gen. 32:30). In Psalm 24:7-10 the gates were exhorted to look up and welcome God, the King of glory, as he entered the walled city of Jerusalem. The historical context may have been the transference of the ark of the covenant from the house of Obed-Edom to Jerusalem (2 Sam. 6:10-17).

Psalm 25
A Prayer for Help and Pardon
An individual's lament, an alphabetical psalm

The king of Israel prayed for his own forgiveness and ended with a prayer of mediation for the entire nation. The "name" (25:11) refers to God's reputation. David was actually praying, "In keeping with your reputation for grace and compassion, forgive my sin."

Psalm 26
A Prayer for Vindication and Protection
An individual's lament

The king of Israel sought personal vindication

from God because of his purity and trust (26:1). "Cross-examine" (26:2) literally means "judge" or "administer justice." Here David claimed to have conducted himself according to God's laws with sincerity of purpose, not sinless perfection. David did some bad things, but he was a good man, "a man after his [God's] own heart" (1 Sam. 13:14). The "tabernacle" (Ps. 26:8) was where the ark of the covenant was kept (2 Sam. 6:17). David prayed that God would discriminate between him and the wicked so that he would not be taken into judgment with them (Ps. 26:9).

Psalm 27
A Song of Trust
An individual's lament

Light is a figure often used in Scripture to refer to God (27:1; cf. John 8:12; 9:5; 1 John 1:5), since it dispels darkness and brightens life. Again David's great desire surfaced to dwell in the "house of the Lord," that is, the tabernacle, which represented God's presence (27:4). David wanted to be with God and to do his will (27:11). His obedience assured him of God's presence, and that formed the basis of his requests for deliverance from his enemies and the stamina to wait for God (27:14). The tone of the psalm changes in 27:7 from that of explicit trust in God to a tone of lament for the hostile circumstances the psalmist was experiencing. David's comment, "Even if my father and mother abandon me" (27:10), should be understood as conditional, not as something that actually had happened. He was pointing out that God's care is even more constant than that of parents. "Wait" (27:14) carries the sense of trust (cf. Isa. 40:31).

Psalm 28
An Answered Prayer
An individual's lament

In the face of evil, David prayed for his own deliverance and that of his people (28:1-2, 9). The king mediated for God's people, praying that God would not be unresponsive, that is, "silent" to his appeal, lest his life be endangered (28:1). The "holy sanctuary" (28:2) refers to the tabernacle (cf. 2 Sam. 6:17). The community of Israel was regarded as God's "possession" (28:9; cf. Deut. 4:20).

Psalm 29
The Voice of God in the Storm
A psalm of descriptive praise

God, who is sovereign over nature's storms, is also the God of Israel's redemption (29:11). The link between God as Creator and as Savior is made strongly throughout the Old Testament. The "angels" (29:1) were invoked to acknowledge God's majesty and sovereignty over nature. David described an "epiphany," that is, an appearance of God, in the storm (Ps. 29:9). Seven times the "voice of the Lord" moved the elements of nature (29:3-9). Reflecting on the Lord's sovereignty over creation, David recalled the flood of Noah's day (29:10; cf. Gen. 6–8).

Psalm 30
Praise for Healing
A psalm of individual declarative praise

Psalm 30 speaks of a time of restoration for David (30:2) after a close brush with death (30:3) due to his prideful and self-sufficient attitude (30:6). It was a time of joy after suffering discipline. The superscription indicates that the psalm was composed for the "dedication of the temple," a reference to either David's palace (2 Sam. 5:11) or perhaps the house of Obed-Edom, where the ark of the covenant remained for three months before being brought up to Jerusalem (2 Sam. 6:10-11). Some scholars suggest that this refers to the dedication of the temple site after the outbreak of pestilence (2 Sam. 24:15-25). God delivered David from near death, for the pit was the grave, the place of the dead (Ps. 30:31). Some scholars hold that 30:6-7 refers to David's pride, which led him to number the people (2 Sam. 24:1-14). If David died, there would be no further opportunity for him to praise God on earth (Ps. 30:9; cf. Ps. 6:4-5).

Psalm 31
A Prayer for Deliverance
An individual's lament

David's hope for God's covenant love forms the backbone of Psalm 31 (see 31:7, 16, 21). David committed his life to God (31:5). These words were quoted by Jesus on the cross (Luke 23:46) and by Stephen just before being stoned (Acts 7:59). In Psalm 31:9-13 David expressed his distress in exaggerated language for the sake of emphasis. Then in 31:17-18 he prayed for God's judgment on his persecutors in keeping with his promises in Genesis 12:3 and 2 Samuel 7.

Psalm 32
The Blessing of Forgiveness
A psalm of individual declarative praise

The covenant of God with Israel demanded a believer's careful attention to the confession of his sins. In Psalm 32, King David described his struggle with personal sin and his movement to confession and forgiveness. So wonderful is that forgiveness that the psalm ends with instructions about how others may have the same blessing. The word "joy" (32:1) can be literally translated "happy." David described God's chastening prior to his confession (32:4). God responded with an admonition in light of David's experience (32:5). The reader is reminded that God will watch over the paths of those in danger of straying (32:8).

Psalm 33
Praise to the Creator and Sustainer
A psalm of descriptive praise, a creation psalm

Creation (33:6-9) is an illustration of God's love (33:5), which forms the basis of hope (33:18, 22). Psalm 33:6-7 is a poetic reflection on Genesis 1–2. The proper attitude to have in relationship to God the Creator is one of holy reverence and awe (33:9). God's sovereignty extends beyond creation to the rule of nations (33:10). For "the Lord watches over those who fear him" (33:18); see Psalm 32:8.

Psalm 34
Praise and Instruction
A psalm of individual declarative praise, an alphabetical psalm

Psalm 34:19 reveals a major theme of Psalm 34 and of all the psalms. Here the tension of suffering unjustly is balanced with the confidence of ultimate vindication. The superscription relates Psalm 34 to the incident of David's pretending to be insane in 1 Samuel 21:11-15. The Philistine king's name was "Achish," but he is referred to here by his dynastic title "Abimelech," meaning "my father is king." God's reputation is magnified by those who publicly acknowledge his goodness and greatness (Ps. 34:3). Psalm 34:5 is probably a generalization based on David's experience and could be rendered, "People look to him [God] and . . . their faces are never shamed." David was giving a general principle that people who look in faith to God for help will ultimately not suffer shame. David's bones not being broken (34:20) was ultimately realized by Jesus in his crucifixion (cf. John 19:36).

Psalm 35
A Plea for Vindication
An individual's lament, an imprecatory psalm

The key concepts of Psalm 35 are suffering without cause (35:7, 19) and praying for God to arise and provide salvation (35:2, 17, 22-23). The word "oppose" (35:1) is a legal term that suggests a courtroom setting where David, the defendant, called on God, his Advocate, to defend him against accusers. "Let me hear you say" (35:3) was his request for an encouraging message from God. In keeping with God's promises in Genesis 12:3 and 2 Samuel 7:9-11, David prayed that God would judge those who were persecuting him (35:4-8). David promised to give public acknowledgment, or praise, of God's goodness when the deliverance was accomplished (35:18).

Psalm 36
The Loyal Love of God
A psalm of descriptive praise

Sinfulness lurks in the heart of the wicked, inciting rebellion against God (36:1). The love of God refers to his loyal love or covenant loyalty (36:5).

The attribute of God's love (36:5-12) is highlighted against the contrasting ways of the wicked (36:1-4). The "shadow of your wings" (36:7), picturing a hen with her chicks, is a beautiful figure of protection and refuge.

Psalm 37
The Problem of Evil
A wisdom psalm, an aphabetical psalm

David warned against being agitated or anxious about God's apparent inconsistency in letting evildoers triumph, for their prosperity is short-lived (37:1-2). Beginning with 37:1, every other verse begins with successive letters of the Hebrew alphabet. The word "delight" (37:4) speaks of "exquisite" joy. When believers delight in the Lord, his desires become their desires. Then their prayers are answered as they do his will. The statement of 37:19 regarding God's provision is characteristic of the Bible's Wisdom Literature; it is not a universal promise but a general statement that God will care for his own. In the present age believers may suffer the grief of poverty and starvation. But this passage looks to God's ideal for his people—an ideal that will only be realized in the new heavens and earth. The message of the psalm is summarized in 37:22. The psalmist's testimony in 37:25 is not a promise or a doctrine and cannot be taken as a universal truth.

Psalm 38
A Prayer of the Penitent
An individual's lament, a penitential psalm

Psalm 38 clearly shows how righteous persons view their own sin within the broader context of their lives. David's sins were many (38:4), but he could say he followed what was good (38:20). The fact that David was a man after God's own heart illustrates that the righteous person is not sinless but is always eager to correct his errors. In contrast, the wicked person is content to stay in his sins. According to the superscription, this psalm of David was designed as a "remembrance." This indicates that it was to be recited in connection with the "token portion" of the grain offering (cf. Lev. 2:2, 9, 16; 5:12). David recognized God's hand of discipline on his life. The particular sin is not identified, but it was probably different from that of Psalm 51. Like one who could not hear or speak, David would make no defense or try to justify himself (38:13-14).

Psalm 39
A Prayer of the Afflicted
An individual's lament

In a time of discipline, David wanted to get a better perspective on the shortness and relative insignificance of his life. Only one thing mattered: hope in God. "Jeduthun" (in the superscription of Ps. 39) was one of the choir directors appointed by David to lead in public worship (cf. 1 Chron. 16:41). At first David suffered in silence (Ps. 39:1-2). Breaking his silence, he asked God to help him understand and accept the brevity of life (39:3-4). He asked God to turn away his gaze of wrath so that he might enjoy the time that was left him on earth (39:13).

Psalm 40
Praise and Prayer
A song of trust (40:1-11), an individual's lament (40:12-17), a messianic psalm

God always wanted his law to get into people's hearts so that it would become their instinctive response (40:8). In the new covenant, made through the death of Christ, he fulfills that desire (cf. Jer. 31:33 and Ezek. 36:26-27). For David, his own sins (Ps. 40:12) and the attacks from others simply thrust his hope more securely upon God's loving-kindness (40:11). Consistent with the prophets, David acknowledged that God was not pleased with sacrifice only but wanted a heart of faith and obedience (40:6; cf. Hos. 6:6; Mic. 6:6-8). Hebrews 10:5-7 quotes Psalm 40:6-8 with reference to Christ's obedience on the cross. Psalm 40:13-17 reappears separately as Psalm 70.

Psalm 41
Thanksgiving and Complaint
An individual's lament

David was suffering from a case of physical illness brought about because of sin (41:4). The king's enemies had taken advantage of the situation (41:5-6). But David's integrity and his essential willingness to correct his mistakes and seek after God would be honored by God (41:12). "He gives them prosperity" (41:2) recalls the thought of Matthew 5:7. Jesus quoted Psalm 41:9 in connection with his betrayal by Judas (John 13:18). Psalm 41:13 was not a part of the psalm originally, but it was added as a concluding doxology to the first collection or book of Psalms (Pss. 1–41).

PSALMS 42–72 COLLECTION TWO
Psalm 42
Thirsting for God
An individual's lament

In Psalm 42 the psalmist's enemies had a twice-repeated response to his suffering, "Where is this God of yours?" The psalmist's crisis of faith was only resolved by his realization of God's power and his own faith in eventual restoration. This *maskil*, or contemplative poem, was either written or sung by the sons of Korah, descendants of the noted rebel (cf. Num. 16–17; 26:11). These are words of introspection (Ps. 42:5). The 9,200-foot Mount Hermon (42:6) is situated about thirty-five miles northeast

of the Sea of Galilee. The location of Mount Mizar (which means "littleness") has not been identified.

Psalm 43
A Prayer for Vindication and Restoration
An individual's lament

Several Hebrew manuscripts combine Psalms 43 and 42. This fact as well as the refrain (43:5), which is repeated from 42:11, suggest that the two psalms were originally one composition.

Psalm 44
A Prayer for National Deliverance
A national lament, an exodus psalm

Psalm 44 presents a case where the writer, like Job, was suffering, but not as a result of committing any sin. He did not know why he was suffering; he had not forgotten God (44:17). For no cause of sin within themselves, the people were as sheep about to be slaughtered (44:22). The psalm's superscription is similar to the one for Psalm 42. Psalm 44:3 contains the great truth of Israel's victorious conquest of Canaan (cf. Josh. 10:42). "Your people" (Ps. 44:4) refers to the tribes of Israel, of which Jacob was the forefather. God, as it were, had sold his people into captivity, but he had derived no profit from the transaction (44:12). In 44:17-22 the people were lamenting that God's discipline had not been consistent with their own faithfulness to him. The apostle Paul quoted 44:22 in Romans 8:36 in describing the believers' experience in this unbelieving world.

Psalm 45
The Marriage of the King
A royal psalm, a messianic psalm

Psalm 45, a *maskil*, or contemplative poem, is a "love song" or wedding song. The "king" (45:1) has been identified by scholars as either Solomon, Ahab, or the Messiah King. The latter view seems to be supported by 45:6-7. The historical king in view was probably Solomon, but Christ may be the ultimate fulfillment. In such a case, the people of God would be the bride (45:9). On the basis of 45:12, it has been suggested that the king was Ahab, bridegroom of Jezebel, whom the "princes of Tyre will shower" with gifts.

Psalm 46
God, a Mighty Fortress
A song of trust

Psalm 46 is an affirmation that God indeed will be exalted in the world. That fact forms the core of the believer's trust and ability to relax in the trials of this age (46:10). The superscription makes it apparent that the psalm was to be sung by soprano voices. The "city of our God" refers to Zion (46:4; cf. 48:2). For "Lord Almighty" (46:11), see the note on 1 Samuel 1:3. God determines the destinies of the nations; therefore, believers are to depend on him rather than on political striving (46:10).

Psalm 47
God, the King of the Earth
A royal psalm

God is seen in Psalm 47 as a king ascending his throne on his coronation day. But his throne, unlike that of any earthly ruler, is above all the world. The "descendants of Korah" (in the superscription) were descended from the man who rebelled against Moses (cf. Num. 16–17; 26:11). King David appointed them poets and musicians in the temple (cf. 1 Chron. 6:13-17). The theme of God's kingship is the major characteristic of the royal psalms, which look forward to God's reign on earth during Christ's millennial kingdom. God's kingship is absolute; he reigns over all creation.

Psalm 48 Zion, the City of the King
A psalm of descriptive praise

The "city of our God" (48:1) refers to Zion, site of the Jerusalem temple mount. In Canaanite legend, Zaphon, or "north," was where the gods reportedly dwelled (cf. Isa. 14:13). The implication is that Zion is where Yahweh, the true God, dwells. The ships of Tarshish (48:7; cf. Jonah 1:3) were noted for their size and voyaging capabilities.

Psalm 49
The Fate of the Wealthy Wicked
A wisdom psalm

Psalm 49 gives a believer's perspective for coping with enemies. The wicked will not gain eternal life (49:9). Although they may have power, it will only be during this life. This perspective demands a firm persuasion that this earthly life is extremely fleeting and will be replaced with eternal life or death (49:14-15). For the superscription, compare that of Psalm 42. The redemption and extension of a person's life cannot be bought from God (49:7). No amount of money can buy life when God has decreed one's death. Like the dumb beasts, even the wealthy must perish (49:12). While those wealthy persons who rely on their money will perish, those who trust in the Lord will be preserved from premature death ("the power of death," 49:15). There is no sin in being rich (49:16-20). But when one glories in material prosperity and forgets about God, then his life is little more than an animal's existence.

Psalm 50
The Nature of True Worship
A didactic psalm

Psalm 50 indicts the people who give superficial lip service to God while their hearts are actually opposing him (50:16-17). This is a psalm of Asaph, a famous and skilled musician David had appointed chief of the Levites who provided music at the ceremony held when the ark of the covenant was brought back to Jerusalem (1 Chron. 16:4-6). The expression "faithful people" (Ps. 50:5) refers to those with whom God was in a covenant relationship, that is, the believing Israelites. On 50:8-9, see Hosea 6:6; Micah 6:6-8; and Isaiah 1:11-15 for similar condemnations of empty ritual in worship. God's keeping "silent" (50:21) in response to the misdeeds of the wicked was wrongly interpreted by some as a reflection of God's own character, an indication of his approval.

Psalm 51
A Sinner's Prayer for Pardon
A penitential psalm

There was only one acceptable act to restore David after his adultery and murder—having a broken spirit and contrite heart (51:17). David's contrition was genuine; therefore he was accepted by God. The historical setting of Psalm 51 is found in 2 Samuel 11–12. David's confession of sin (2 Sam. 12:13) is expanded here. He made his appeal on the basis of God's "unfailing love" and "great compassion" (Ps. 51:1). David sinned against Bathsheba and Uriah, but all sin is ultimately an offense against God (51:4; cf. Gen. 39:9). In Psalm 51:5 David was not suggesting that his conception or birth involved acts of sin. Rather, he traced his own sin nature to his very beginning, that is, his conception. David prayed in accordance with the covenant that God had made with him (Ps. 51:11). God's loving-kindness would never depart, even in severe discipline (cf. 2 Sam. 7:14-15). The "Spirit" (Ps. 51:11) is here seen as the symbol of David's anointing as king, not in the sense of David's redemption. David's "shedding blood" (51:14) was due to his murder of Uriah.

Psalm 52
The Judgment on the Wicked
An individual's lament, a didactic psalm

Psalm 52 is a *maskil*, or contemplative poem, that has its setting in 1 Samuel 21:1–22:19 where Doeg reported David's visit with Ahimelech the priest to Saul. The words "in the house of God" (Ps. 52:8) may begin a new sentence. The wicked is torn away from his own home (52:5), but the righteous is always welcome in God's house.

Psalm 53
The Folly and Wickedness of Men
An individual's lament, a didactic psalm

Psalm 53, which is almost identical to Psalm 14, is a contemplative poem (a *maskil*) with an obscure melody indicator (*mahalath*). Paul quotes 53:1-3 in Romans 3:10-12 to show that all mankind is guilty of sin. Psalm 53:5 may refer to the occasion of deliverance that provided the impetus for the reworking of Psalm 14.

Psalm 54
A Prayer for Deliverance
An individual's lament

Psalm 54, a *maskil*, or contemplative poem, has its historical setting in 1 Samuel 23:19-29, where the Ziphites revealed David's hiding place to Saul. In 54:5 David trusted God to right the wrong done rather than taking matters into his own hands.

Psalm 55
Betrayal by a Friend
An individual's lament

While most psalms speak of life's problems, Psalm 55 highlights the betrayal by a most trusted and intimate friend (55:12-13) as the cause of pain. When David asked God to bring confusion to his enemies (55:9), he may have had the tower of Babel in mind (cf. Gen. 11). He prayed that God would judge his enemies, bringing an end to their lives as he had done with Korah and his followers (55:15; cf. Num. 16:30-32). The grave refers to the place of the dead. Psalm 55:22 contains the major lesson of the psalm.

Psalm 56
A Plea for Deliverance
An individual's lament

Although trampled by men, David trusted in God and would fulfill his vows to praise him for deliverance. The tune title in the psalm's superscription refers to the community of Israel ("A dove") in a distant land. The historical setting is 1 Samuel 21:10-15, which records David's feigned insanity at Gath (cf. the superscription of Ps. 34). God knew David's every hurt and was intimately concerned (56:8). For vows (56:12), see Ecclesiastes 5:4-5 and Numbers 30:2. For thank offerings, see Leviticus 7:11-18.

Psalm 57
A Prayer for Protection
An individual's lament

A key focus in Psalm 57 is the steadfastness of David's heart to praise God in the middle of his problems (57:7). The tune or melody indicator in the superscription appears also in the superscriptions of Psalms 57–59 and 75. The historical setting for Psalm 57 is probably the cave of Adullam (1 Sam. 22:1) or possibly the cave at Engedi (1 Sam. 24:1-7). Either David was actually fighting lions (57:4), or he was making free use of hyperbole, that is, exaggeration for the sake of emphasis.

Psalm 58
A Protest against Injustice
An individual's lament

The great tension for the righteous person is watching injustice go on and on without seeing God move in to right it. The heart of Psalm 58 is found in what the righteous do when God finally rewards and judges (58:10-11). A biblical view of man's depravity from his earliest beginning is reflected in 58:3-5 (cf. 51:5). This fallen moral state shared by all humanity can be traced to Adam (Rom. 5:12).

Psalm 59
A Prayer for Rescue
An individual's lament

The historical setting for Psalm 59 is found in 1 Samuel 19:11-12. Like that of Psalm 58:6-9, the imprecation of 59:11-15 was motivated by a desire to teach people about God, specifically, "Then the whole world will know that God reigns in Israel" (59:13). God is sovereign, even over the wicked.

Psalm 60
A Prayer for National Crisis
A national lament

The historical setting is that of 2 Samuel 8 (also 1 Chron. 18) where David was fighting in the north with Aram Naharaim (Mesopotamia) and Aram Zobah (near Damascus) and was attacked in the south by Edom. Joab met the attack and achieved a great victory. God had given a "banner" (Ps. 60:4) as a rallying point for the people. God assured his people that he still was maintaining his sovereignty over the tribes of Israel (60:6-7). The other nations were regarded as mere servants of God (60:8). Moab and Edom were in the lands east of the Jordan River. Philistia was in Israel along the Mediterranean coast. Reliance upon God's strength is the key to success (60:12; cf. Phil. 4:13).

Psalm 61
A Prayer for Restoration
An individual's lament

The king sought refuge in his God. God's refuge and protection were illustrated by four figures: a high rock, a strong tower, a tent, and sheltering wings (61:2-4). In 61:6-7 David recalled God's promise given to him in 2 Samuel 7:16 of an everlasting lineage and kingdom.

Psalm 62
God, the Believer's Only Refuge
A song of trust

The heart of Psalm 62 is in its combination of God's power and loving-kindness (62:11-12) for judging human behavior. The meaning of "Jeduthun" in the superscription is disputed, but it may refer to one of the choir directors appointed by David (1 Chron. 16:41). David viewed God as his only real security and refuge (Ps. 62:2). Regardless of status or position, the wicked will be found wanting in the Day of Judgment (62:9).

Psalm 63
A Thirsting Soul Satisfied in God
A song of trust

David's faith pierced through life's problems to a deep enjoyment of God's loving-kindness (63:3).

The superscription places the historical setting of the psalm at David's time in the wilderness of Judah, possibly during Absalom's revolt (2 Sam. 15:23, 28). The "sanctuary" (Ps. 63:2) refers not to the temple but the temporary tent for the ark of the covenant (2 Sam. 6:17). The "king" (Ps. 63:11) is a reference to David.

Psalm 64
A Prayer for Deliverance
An individual's lament

What David's enemies intended to do to their victim, God would do to them (64:7; cf. Gal. 6:7). God's judgment on the wicked elicits, from both psalmist and reader alike, a healthy recognition of his holiness and high standards (Ps. 64:9; cf. Acts 5:11).

Psalm 65
A Hymn of Thanksgiving
A psalm of descriptive praise

After a brief mention of personal sin and forgiveness, David described God's righteousness in terms of nature and harvest. Zion (65:1) refers to Jerusalem. The "rivers of God" (65:9) refer to God's provision of rain. The "bountiful harvest" (65:11) was due to the abundance of rain along the paths where God had, as it were, walked.

Psalm 66
A Song of Deliverance
A psalm of national declarative praise (66:1-12), a psalm of individual declarative praise (66:13-20), an exodus psalm

God's saving of the nation Israel through the Exodus became a pattern or type to remind the people of Israel of God's continual desire to save them. The psalmist recalled the great events of the Exodus, crossing the Red Sea (Exod. 14–15) and the Jordan River (Josh. 4). For "burnt offerings" (Ps. 66:13), see Leviticus 1. This psalm reminds the reader that sinful attitudes of the heart block effective prayer (Ps. 66:18).

Psalm 67
A Call for Universal Praise to God
A psalm of national declarative praise

Psalm 67:1 is based on the priestly blessing of Numbers 6:24-26. The psalmist prayed for God's blessing for the purpose of causing all peoples to know (Ps. 67:2) and fear him (see 67:7).

Psalm 68
The Triumph of God
A psalm of national declarative praise, an exodus psalm, a messianic psalm

God is described as ascending to his throne in Jerusalem as King over all the nations and receiving gifts of honor from all (68:18, 29). This psalm contains a variety of designations for God: *Elohim,*

translated "God" (68:1); *Yah,* an abbreviation for Yahweh, translated "Lord" (68:4); *El-Shaddai,* translated "Almighty" (68:14); *Yahweh,* translated "Lord" (68:16); *Yah Elohim,* translated "Lord God" (68:18); and *Adonai,* translated "Lord" (68:19). The reference in 68:7-14 is to the Israelite exodus from Egypt to Canaan. The rebellious were those who because of disobedience and unbelief had died in the wilderness. "Zalmon" (68:14) is a hill near Shechem. The "mountains of Bashan" (68:15) is probably a reference to the 9,200-foot Mount Hermon. In a figurative sense, loftier peaks look with envy at Mount Zion, the mountain chosen by God as the place where he is to be worshiped (68:16). Paul quotes 68:18 in Ephesians 4:8 with reference to Christ's person and work. The "wild animals lurking in the reeds" (Ps. 68:30) refers to the hippopotamus, which represented Egypt, one of Israel's enemies.

Psalm 69
A Prayer for Retribution
An individual's lament, an imprecatory psalm, a messianic psalm

Psalm 69 gives a clear explanation of why so often good people are unjustly attacked. The attackers are really reproaching God by hating his faithful followers (69:9). David experienced hatred (69:4), but Jesus endured hatred in a more complete measure (see John 15:25; cf. Ps. 69:8 with John 7:3-5). The disciples linked Psalm 69:9 with Jesus' temple cleansing (see John 2:17). Matthew linked Psalm 69:21 with Jesus' suffering at Golgotha (Matt. 27:34). Jesus may have been alluding to Psalm 69:25 in Matthew 23:38. Peter quoted it with reference to Judas (Acts 1:20). The "Book of Life" (Ps. 69:28) refers to the registry of the living. David was praying for the premature death of the wicked so that they might be distinguished from the righteous.

Psalm 70
A Prayer for God's Help
An individual's lament

Nearly identical to Psalm 40:13-17, Psalm 70 is designated in the superscription to "bring us to the Lord's remembrance"and was apparently used in connection with the token part of the grain offering (cf. Lev. 2:2, 9, 16).

Psalm 71
The Prayer of an Experienced Saint
An individual's lament

Psalm 71 is an expression of trust based on the psalmist's long walk of fellowship with God. The expression "from my mother's womb" (71:6) may be understood to refer to God as a gracious benefactor. Although it may seem that God is far away, he has promised never to abandon or forsake his own (71:12; cf. Heb. 13:5). The psalmist, who viewed himself as good as dead, expressed confidence in God's power to restore him (Ps. 71:20).

Psalm 72
A Prayer for the King
A royal psalm, a messianic psalm

These key things, desired by God from David and the line of kings descended from him, are stressed in Psalm 72: justice in the king's rule (72:2-4), the king's rule over the entire kingdom (72:8), and peace in the land and the fullness of harvest under the king's rule (72:16). Solomon, who was the writer of this psalm, also may have written Psalm 127. The "king" (72:1) refers historically to Solomon, but the expansive nature of the prayer (72:8, 11, 17) suggests that the prophetic reference looks to Christ in his kingdom to come. Universal worship of Christ by kings and nations will be characteristic of the messianic kingdom (72:11; cf. Zech. 14:9). The editorial note of Psalm 72:20 indicates that at one time this psalm concluded a collection of Davidic prayers. Psalm 72 serves as a conclusion to the second collection of psalms.

PSALMS 73–89 COLLECTION THREE
Psalm 73
The Prosperity of the Wicked
A wisdom psalm

Psalm 73 is a frank confession by the writer of his being jealous of bad people who were prospering. But in the case of the wicked, their end explains the futility of their lives. They often prosper when alive, but death ends their prosperity. On the other hand, even when righteous people suffer trouble, their lives are full of God's goodness (73:1). Asaph (see the superscription and the note on Ps. 50) authored Psalms 73–83. Psalm 73 falls in the category of Wisdom Literature, which is noted for its use of generalization (73:3-5). Obviously there are exceptions to the psalmist's description of the wicked. But, from a temporal perspective, they often do prosper, or at least seem to do so. The wicked "boast against the very heavens" (73:9), that is, they blaspheme God. Their conduct tends to have a corrupting influence on God's people (73:10). Often believers turn to the wicked and drink deeply of their sayings, philosophies, and values. Who has not wondered if serving God is really worth the personal deprivation and discipline (73:13-14)? In 73:15-17 the psalmist provides a divine perspective on his thoughts expressed in 73:3-14.

Psalm 74
The Prayer of a Devastated Nation
A national lament, an exodus psalm

The author, Asaph, probably does not refer to the contemporary of David but to one of his descendants. In lament psalms, the psalmist often expressed himself in terms of what he felt rather than what he actually believed theologically. The "ruins" (74:3) refer to the temple, which was completely devastated by the Babylonian attack. For the burning of the sanctuary (74:7), see 2 Kings 25:8-9 and 2 Chronicles 36:18-19. "All the places where God was worshiped" (74:8) refers not to synagogues, which developed during the Babylonian captivity, but perhaps to places of prayer and private devotion. "Leviathan" (74:14) refers to a dragon monster that figures prominently as an enemy of the created order in ancient Babylonian mythology. The psalmist used this poetic image to emphasize God's power over his creation. "Your doves" (74:19) is a figure that likens Israel to a defenseless bird. In 74:20 the psalmist reminded God of the covenant promises made to Abraham (cf. Gen. 12:1-3).

Psalm 75
God Judges with Equity
A psalm of national declarative praise, a didactic psalm

Psalm 75 gives the key to how the righteous cope with seemingly unjudged evil in the world. God has set a time to judge (75:2). Although that time is known only to him and may be near or far, its fact is certain and forms the basis for hope and warning. The psalm's melody indicator "To the tune of 'Do Not Destroy'" in the superscription also is seen in Psalms 57–59. God is absolutely sovereign. As the cup of wine may bring stumbling, so the cup of God's wrath will bring destruction (75:8; cf. Isa. 51:17).

Psalm 76
A Song of Victory
A psalm of descriptive praise

God's great deliverance of Jerusalem from its surrounding enemies is a sign that he saves the humble (76:9). The defeat did not take place in Jerusalem, but the city served as God's headquarters. This psalm repeats the concept of fear (76:7-8, 11-12) as the context for praise and worship (76:11-12).

Psalm 77
Comfort through Remembering God's Works
An individual's lament (77:1-9), a psalm of national praise (77:13-20), an exodus psalm

Psalm 77 clearly shows one important aspect of comfort: believers remembering God's past acts of love when they are in the middle of difficult times. "Jeduthun" in the superscription is a disputed term appearing also in the superscriptions of Psalms 39 and 62. Thoughts about God disturbed the psalmist (77:3). How could he keep faith when God seemed to have rejected him (77:7-9)? But remembering God's great deeds in the past gave him faith and

encouragement for his present struggles (77:11-15).
In 77:16-20 the psalmist praised God for his deliverance of Israel at the time of the Exodus.

Psalm 78
Israel's Failures and God's Grace
A didactic psalm, an exodus psalm,
a messianic psalm

The purpose of Psalm 78 was to pass along the old stories of God's judgment and redemption to future generations (78:3-4). It does that by recounting both the great redemptive acts of God in the Exodus from Egypt and the forgetfulness and failures of Israel along the way. The story ends with God's grace prevailing in establishing his temple and his Davidic king in Jerusalem. Matthew quoted 78:2 in Matthew 13:35 to show that Jesus' speaking in parables fulfilled prophecy. The reference in Psalm 78:9 is not to a specific battle but to a history of Israel's unfaithfulness in relationship to the things of God (cf. Judg. 1:29). Baal Shem Tov, founder of the Hassidic movement in eighteenth-century Poland, said, "Forgetfulness leads to exile, while remembrance is the secret of redemption." This man could very well have learned this lesson from 78:11. The "food of angels" (78:25) refers to manna, the "bread from heaven" (78:24). The deaths of some Israelites led others to question how they had offended God (78:34). God's people were to learn from the mistakes of those who had gone before them.

Psalm 79
Lament over the Destruction of Jerusalem
A national lament, an imprecatory psalm

Psalm 79's prayer for judgment on the psalmist's enemies was based on God's promise in Genesis 12:1-3 to bring judgment on those who cursed Israel. The cry for God's vengeance upon the enemies of his people was motivated in part by the desire to answer those who asked, "Where is their God?" (79:10). Another motivation for God to deliver his people came from their promise to praise him (79:13).

Psalm 80
A Prayer for Rescue from Calamity
A national lament, an exodus psalm

The "cherubim" (80:1) refers to the figures, representing spiritual beings, on the ark of the covenant (Exod. 25:22). The "vine" (Ps. 80:8) is Israel, the nation that sprouted in Egypt but was planted and took root in Canaan. The vine, Israel, expanded toward the Mediterranean Sea and the Euphrates River (80:11; cf. 80:12 with Isa. 5:5.) Psalm 80:17 is not a reference to Jesus the Messiah but to the people God's right hand planted (cf. 80:15), that is, Israel.

Psalm 81
God's Goodness and Israel's Waywardness
A didactic psalm, an exodus psalm

Psalm 81 presents a common pattern in the psalms, that is, the use of the Exodus as a motivation for present faithfulness. The ram's horn was blown on the first day of the seventh month (80:3; cf. Num. 29:1). The "New Moon" refers to the fifteenth day of the seventh month when the celebration of the Festival of Shelters began. The incidents that took place at Meribah (Ps. 81:7) are recorded in Exodus 17:1-7 and Numbers 20:1-13. The psalmist's moving unexpectedly from the usage of the third to the second person (Ps. 81:8) was not uncommon in Hebrew writings.

Psalm 82
Judgment on the Unjust Judges
A national lament

Psalm 82 is a poetic presentation of the justice demanded in the law of God handed down at Mount Sinai. The term "gods" (82:6) was used in this context to describe those who were to "preside over" or "judge" others (82:1); these were men who had been given authority on earth to represent God's interests and enforce his law. Jesus used this verse in John 10:34 to defend his use of the title "Son of God" (John 10:35-36).

Psalm 83
A Prayer for Judgment on the Nations
An individual's lament, an imprecatory psalm,
an exodus psalm

The harsh judgment of God that the psalmist demanded here (83:13-15) was ultimately for redemptive ends (83:16). In 83:6-8 the noteworthy enemies of Israel were identified. Two great victories, by Gideon over the Midianites (Judg. 7), and by Deborah and Barak over the Canaanites (Judg. 4–5) were recalled in Psalm 83:9. Oreb and Zeeb (Ps. 83:11) were Midianite princes (Judg. 7:25), and Zebah and Zalmunna were kings of Midian (Judg. 8:5-21). In Psalm 83:16, 18 the strong imprecation against Israel's enemies had an evangelistic purpose. God's judgment was, and still is today, designed to cause the wicked to "submit to" him and recognize that he alone is the "Most High" over all the earth.

Psalm 84
The Delight of Fellowship with God
A psalm of descriptive praise

For the "descendants of Korah," see the note on Psalm 42. How "happy" are those who spend their lives in God's service! (84:4). The idea in 84:6 is that God turns weeping into blessing. To "be a gatekeeper" at God's house (84:10) expresses an attitude of worship and service.

Psalm 85
A Prayer for Restoration
A national lament

As usual, behind the desire for physical blessings is the more profound desire to experience the love, faithfulness, righteousness, and peace of a relationship with God (85:10-11). In 85:9-13 the psalmist described the millennial kingdom, during which God's "glory" will be exhibited in Israel in the person of Christ.

Psalm 86
A Prayer for Deliverance
An individual's lament

David trusted in the great revelation of God given so long ago to Moses in Exodus 34:6 (Ps. 86:5, 13). The Hebrew word translated as "devoted" (86:2) can also be translated "loyal" and refers to one who is faithful to his covenant relationship with God. In 86:11 David prayed that his heart would be totally focused on God's awesome reputation ("truth"), not distracted by other interests or desires.

Psalm 87
A Song of Zion
A psalm of descriptive praise

Jerusalem has received the great blessing of God's presence. The Hebrew word for "Egypt" (87:4) is "Rahab," another name for Leviathan, the dragon monster mentioned frequently in ancient Babylonian mythology as an enemy of the created order. The psalmist was saying that the powerful enemies that once warred against Israel will one day bow the knee to God (Phil. 2:10-11). The future kingdom will be characterized as a time of great joy and celebration (Ps. 87:7).

Psalm 88
The Distress of Unanswered Prayer
An individual's lament

Psalm 88 is one of the bleakest psalms. No answer is given or hope specified. But, at least, the writer was still praying and clinging to God. The psalm is a contemplative poem. "Heman the Ezrahite" was apparently one of the directors of the temple music. The "pit" (88:6) refers to the place of the dead. The point of 88:10 was that if God did not intervene, it would be too late; the psalmist would be dead.

Psalm 89
God's Covenant with David
A messianic psalm

The central fact of Psalm 89 is the permanent love that God gave to David in his covenant (89:28, 33). That permanence formed the foundation for the king's hope for restoration from personal sin and the ultimate preservation of the kingdom from its enemies (89:35-37). The psalm is a contemplative

poem. The identity of Ethan is unknown. The theme of Psalm 89 is the Davidic covenant, the promise that God made to David in 2 Samuel 7:12-16. For "sea monster" (89:10), see the note on Psalm 87:4. "Tabor" and "Hermon" (89:12) are prominent mountains in Israel. The two men mentioned in 89:19 may refer to Gad and Nathan (1 Sam. 22:5; 2 Sam. 12:1), although some manuscripts are written in the singular, alluding to Nathan, the key figure in the historical context (2 Sam. 7). Psalm 89:25 is a reference to promised dominion, from the Mediterranean Sea to the Euphrates and Tigris rivers. The covenant promise to David and his dynasty is eternal (89:28-29), unconditional (89:30-34), and permanent (89:35-37). In 89:38-39 David lamented that his immediate experience did not seem to match what God had promised. Psalm 89:52 serves as the conclusion to the third book of the Psalter.

PSALMS 90–106 COLLECTION FOUR
Psalm 90
God's Eternity and Man's Brevity
A national lament

Psalm 90 is the oldest psalm and was authored by Moses. The return to "dust" (90:3) is part of the curse resulting from Adam's sin (Gen. 3:19). God's perspective is different than man's. A thousand years is but an instant in the context of eternity (Ps. 90:4). This verse is applied by Peter in 2 Peter 3:8. Realizing the brevity of life, the reader is reminded to make decisions that reflect wisdom (Ps. 90:12). The prayer is for God to return his expressions of grace instead of wrath and discipline (90:13). To confirm the works of one's hands (90:17) is to provide blessing that matches inward righteousness.

Psalm 91
Security in the Lord
A wisdom psalm

The deliverance of God is promised for the one who loves and knows him (91:14). The "shadow of the Almighty" (91:1) suggests the image of a mother bird protecting her little ones under her wings (91:4). God will protect his own against danger and attack (91:5-7). Psalm 91:10 should not be taken as a personal promise for protection from every evil circumstance. It is a general principle, seen in the Wisdom Literature of the Bible, that the righteous will be spared unnecessary and avoidable difficulties. Satan quoted Psalm 91:11-12 in the context of Christ's temptation (see Matt. 4:6; Luke 4:10-11).

Psalm 92
Praise for God's Goodness
A psalm of individual declarative praise

Meditation on the great works and deep thoughts of God is the way to avoid sin and deepen wisdom (92:5-6). Psalm 92 was designated for use on the

Sabbath day (cf. Exod. 20:8; Deut. 5:12). The fool lacks spiritual perception (Ps. 92:6).

Psalm 93
The Reign of God
A royal psalm

God reigns presently as sovereign Creator of the universe (Ps. 103:19), but his reign will one day be culminated when Christ takes his throne on earth. So Psalm 93 is prophetic as well as descriptive of present reality. The "oceans" (93:3) refer figuratively to the enemy nations surrounding Israel.

Psalm 94
The Appeal to a Just Judge
A national lament

The Lord who has created the ear and the eye hears and sees all. In that light, the one who listens to him is blessed and will find support in God's love (94:18). Compare 94:14 with Hebrews 13:5. Like Habakkuk, the psalmist questioned how a righteous God can use an evil or wicked instrument to accomplish his purposes (94:20). The answer is found in the principle of divine retribution (94:23).

Psalm 95
A Call to Worship
A psalm of descriptive praise, an exodus psalm, a didactic psalm

God as Creator (Ps. 95:1-5) is the foundation for worship and softness of heart. The test of 95:7-11 is quoted in Hebrews 3:7-11 as a warning against unbelief. The wilderness wanderings were used to remind the readers of the importance of obedience (Ps. 95:8). For the historical situation, see Exodus 17:1-7. The unbelieving generation of Israelites forfeited the "rest" and blessing they could have enjoyed in Canaan (Ps. 95:11).

Psalm 96
A Call to Praise the Righteous Judge
A royal psalm

The major idea here is the coming of the Lord to judge the world. Psalm 96 is reproduced almost verbatim in 1 Chronicles 16:23-33, where it was said to have been composed when David brought the ark of the covenant to Jerusalem. While the Lord reigns in a sovereign sense today (Ps. 96:10), one day Christ's kingdom rule on earth will culminate the fulfillment of this prophecy (96:13). During the age of the kingdom, the curse on earth that resulted from man's sin will be removed (96:12). When peace and harmony return to the natural realm, even the the trees will "rustle with praise."

Psalm 97
The Kingship of God
A royal psalm

For a note on "The Lord is king" (97:1), see Psalm 96:10. In 97:2-6 language reminiscent of that used during God's self-revelation at Sinai is used to emphasize his awesome presence. The psalmist was not implying that the heathen idols were true gods (97:7). Rather, assuming the polytheistic viewpoint of the ancient world, he indicated that all so-called gods must bow before the one true God (cf. 97:9; 1 Cor. 8:4-6). Sharing God's attitude regarding evil is an essential characteristic of those who sincerely acknowledge his rule (97:10; cf. Prov. 8:13). The end notes of Psalm 97 are to hate evil and to be glad in the Lord (97:10, 12).

Psalm 98
Praise of God, the Judge
A royal psalm

Psalm 98 shows the two pillars, past and future, that enable hope and faithfulness in the present: God's past redemption and his future coming to judge. The psalmist's testimony (98:3) is similar to the promise of Isaiah 52:10. God has demonstrated his saving power in the great deliverances of the past. This mighty demonstration of his salvation was culminated at the cross. For Psalm 98:7-8, see the note on Psalm 96:12. God the Savior is also God the Judge (98:9). His second coming will be marked by his judgment of the nations (cf. Joel 3:13-17).

Psalm 99
Holy Is God
A royal psalm

The double-edged nature of God seen in his forgiving yet exacting ways (Ps. 99:8) forms the basis for worship. The truth that God reigns (99:1) means that the present, with its good and evil, is perfectly and fully under God's control and is being brought to its final end of judgment and reward (cf. 96:10). The word "holy" (99:3) basically means "separate." When used with reference to God, it means that God is separate from all that is contrary to his nature, from that which is common or unclean. Derived from the concept of "separation" is that of moral or ethical purity.

Psalm 100
An Exhortation to Worship
A psalm of descriptive praise

God's goodness, evidenced by his love and his faithfulness (100:5), is the theme of Psalm 100.

Psalm 101
Vows of a King
A royal psalm

David showed himself as the king after God's heart, eliminating evil and encouraging faithfulness. While David tried to apply these ethical standards to himself, they will be ultimately fulfilled by the Messiah in his kingdom (101:2-5). Each morning the king will administer justice, keeping Israel and Jerusalem ("the city") morally clean (101:8).

Psalm 102
An Afflicted Man's Prayer for Himself and Zion
An individual's lament, a penitential psalm, a messianic psalm

The superscription of Psalm 102 reveals the life setting of the psalmist—a time of affliction and distress. The references to the condition of Jerusalem suggest the time period of the captivity. In 102:3-5 the psalmist used exaggeration for the sake of emphasis to reveal the extent of his distress. He anticipated a time when God would extend his compassion to Jerusalem (102:13). One such expression of divine compassion was when God raised up Cyrus to decree the return of the Jews (Ezra 1:1-4). Psalm 102:13 suggests that God's compassion on Jerusalem will be ultimately realized in the messianic kingdom when the peoples and nations gather to serve him (102:22).

Psalm 103
The Great Benefits of a Gracious God
A psalm of descriptive praise

God's love (103:8, quoting Exod. 34:6) is demonstrated through his forgiveness (Ps. 103:8, 10, 12). For "holy" (103:1), see the note on Psalm 99:3. In the Hebrew parallelism of this verse, the term "diseases" (103:3) is a figurative reference to the sickness of sin. The "fear" of God (103:11) refers to reverential awe and respect that are exhibited in turning from evil and pursuing God's will (cf. Job 28:28; Ps. 111:10). Since east and west are at opposite points on the compass, they never meet (103:12). God's dominion extends to all of his creation (103:19).

Psalm 104
The Greatness of God the Creator
A creation psalm

Psalm 104 is a poetic reflection on Genesis 1–2. Here poetic imagery is used to describe God's heavenly abode. The "floods of water" (Ps. 104:6) refer to the moisture in the atmosphere (see Gen. 1:7, "the waters above"). Psalm 104:4 is quoted in Hebrews 1:7 with reference to the ministries of angels. Psalm 104:6 is not a reference to the world flood (Gen. 6), but to the separation of sea and dry land on the third day (Gen. 1:9-10). Leviathan (Ps. 104:26) is the dragon monster prominent in ancient Babylonian mythology as an enemy of the created order; see the note on it in Job 3:8.

Psalm 105
The Faithfulness of God in Israel's History
A psalm of descriptive praise, an exodus psalm, a didactic psalm

Psalm 105 sums up the immediate implication of God's prior covenant with Abraham and his great redemption of Israel from Egypt under Moses.

God desired to have a people who would obey and praise him (105:45). For God's covenant with Abraham, see Genesis 12:1-3. The covenant was confirmed with Isaac (Gen. 26:2-4) and Jacob (Gen. 28:13-15; 35:11-12). The fact that God remembered his promise to Abraham (Ps. 105:42) provides the key to understanding all the blessings that God has bestowed on Israel. God was being faithful to the Abrahamic promise (Gen. 12:1-3; 15:18-21).

Psalm 106
Confession of National Sin
A national lament, an exodus psalm

The future glory of Israel (Ps. 106:5) is viewed through her past failures under Moses up into the Babylonian captivity. That view provides the basis for repentance and hope. The words "Praise the Lord" (106:1) are literally in Hebrew "hallelujah," which can be translated "Give a shout of praise for God." "Your heritage" (106:5) refers to the inheritance of Israel (33:12). For the rebellious attitude of Israel by the Red Sea (106:7), see Exodus 14:11-12. For Psalm 106:17, see Numbers 16:1-35; for Psalm 106:19, see Exodus 32:1-4; for Psalm 106:28, see Numbers 25:1-9. The nation was not deserving of God's compassion, but he extended it anyway (Ps. 106:44). Psalm 106:48 serves as a doxology for the fourth section of the book of Psalms (Pss. 90–106).

PSALMS 107–150 COLLECTION FIVE
Psalm 107
God's Deliverance in a Time of Trouble
A psalm of individual declarative praise

The "love" of God is Psalm 107's main theme (cf. 107:1, 8, 15, 21, 31, 43). The psalm illustrates God's gracious care and intervention for his own by several illustrations. Being lost in the desert, experiencing captivity, suffering from illness due to personal sin, sea storms, and agricultural drought are all opportunities for people to call on God and to see his loving-kindness in action. Similar imagery to 107:10 appears in Isaiah 42:7, describing the conditions of the exiles in Babylon.

Psalm 108
Praise and Prayer for Victory
An individual's lament

Psalm 108:1-5 corresponds with Psalm 57:7-11. The exact words of Psalm 108:7-12 also appear in Psalm 60:6-11.

Psalm 109
A Prayer for Retribution
An individual's lament, an imprecatory psalm

The root problem of David's enemies was that they did not reflect the loving-kindness of their God (109:16). In 109:6-20, David's prayer for retribution is based on God's promise in Genesis 12:1-3 to "curse" those who "curse" Abraham's descendants and also upon the Davidic covenant of 2 Samuel 7. Compare Psalm 109:25 with 22:7. The mockery of Christ (Matt. 27:39; Mark 15:29) was a fulfillment of these verses.

Psalm 110
The Messianic King-Priest
A messianic psalm

Psalm 110 pointed toward another King who would be above David; this King, Jesus the Messiah, would stand between David and God the Father. This psalm is an important Old Testament passage for the book of Hebrews (Heb. 1:3, 13; 5:6; 7:17, 21; 10:13). Psalm 110 was also a crucial Old Testament passage for Peter on the Day of Pentecost for showing that the greater Son of David, Jesus, had to ascend to the right hand of God (Acts 2:34-36). Jesus used Psalm 110:1 to prove his deity to the questioning Pharisees (Matt. 22:41-45). The "LORD" refers to God the Father, while "my Lord" refers to the second person of the Trinity, Jesus the Son (110:1). The rule of Christ will be culminated in the millennial kingdom (110:2). God's believing people will rally around the Messiah in recognition of his lordship and rule (110:3). The metaphor "the morning dew" (110:3) refers to the freshness and vitality of those who will serve God. Like Melchizedek (Gen. 14:18), Christ holds both offices of king and priest (Heb. 7:1-28). The battle scene described in Psalm 110:5-6 will take place at Christ's second coming (Zech. 14:1-15; Rev. 19:11-21).

Psalm 111
The Praise of God's Goodness
A psalm of descriptive praise, an alphabetical psalm

The goodness of the Lord is here focused on his support of his people by providing food and redemptive covenant promises (Ps. 111:5-6). "Reverence for the Lord" (111:10) is the major theme of the Bible's books of Wisdom Literature (cf. Job 28:28; Prov. 1:7; 9:10; Eccles. 12:13).

Psalm 112
The Happy Man
A wisdom psalm, an alphabetical psalm

Psalm 112 gives insight into the strength often seen in the suffering children of God. Because they know they are doing right before God, their hearts are steadfast and without fear (112:7-8). The Hebrew parallelism likens to "fear the Lord" with delighting in God's commands (112:1). The righteous will look with satisfaction upon the defeat of the wicked (112:8), who will see the triumph of the righteous and be dismayed (112:10).

Psalm 113
The Unique Greatness of God
A psalm of declarative praise

Psalms 113–118 are called the "Hallel" or "praise" psalms and are sung by Jewish families during their celebration of the Passover. Psalm 113:5 asks who is like God in order to give believers the perspective they need when, in their eyes, troubles get too big and God seems too small. "From east to west" (113:3) means in all lands. God is exalted (transcendent), but this does not preclude his concern for the welfare of his creatures (113:5-6). Hannah (1 Sam. 1:1–2:10) illustrates the truth of Psalm 113:9.

Psalm 114
The Wonder of the Exodus
A psalm of descriptive praise, an exodus psalm

In Psalm 114 the Exodus is recreated with a few bold strokes to motivate holy fear and worship. Technically, the sanctuary (tabernacle or temple) was located in the land of Benjamin (Josh. 18:16), but in time it became associated with the tribe of Judah because the Judean kings ruled from Jerusalem (Ps. 114:2). Psalm 114:3 is a reference to the events of the Exodus, crossing the Red Sea (Exod. 14) and the Jordan River (Josh. 3). Psalm 114:4 is a reference to the quaking of Mount Sinai (Exod. 19:18). And Psalm 114:8 is a reference to God's provision of water in the wilderness (Exod. 17:1-7).

Psalm 115
A Prayer for God to Honor His Name
A national lament

The nations mocked Israel concerning the perceived absence of her God. In that light the writer prayed for God to glorify his name (Ps 115:1). Compare 115:4-8 with Isaiah 44:9-20. Psalm 115:17 is not intended as a theological commentary on the afterlife. The point is simply that when God's people are dead they are not present to praise the Lord on earth.

Psalm 116
Thanksgiving for Deliverance from Death
A psalm of individual declarative praise

Compare Psalm 116:3-4 with 18:4-6. The second line of 116:11 could be rendered "the whole of man is deceptive." Thus, man is unreliable. The "cup symbolizing his salvation" (116:13) alludes to the drink offering (Exod. 29:40-41; Num. 28:7). For "promises" (116:18), see Numbers 30 and Ecclesiastes 5:4-5.

Psalm 117
A Shout of Praise
A psalm of descriptive praise

God's love and faithfulness brings to remembrance his covenant loyalty and reflects the revelation of God's character to Moses in Exodus 34:6.

Psalm 118
Thanksgiving for Deliverance
A psalm of individual declarative praise,
a messianic psalm

This is the last of the "Hallel" or "praise" psalms (Ps. 113–118), which were sung at the Passover. This was probably the hymn sung by Jesus and the disciples in the Upper Room before they departed for the Mount of Olives (see Matt. 26:30). He will "look in triumph" (Ps. 118:7) on God's judgment on the wicked. Jesus quoted 118:22-23 with reference to his being rejected by his own Jewish people (Matt. 21:42-44; Mark 12:10-11). They also were quoted by Peter (see Acts 4:11; 1 Peter 2:7). See also Isaiah 28:16. The people called out these words of praise (Ps. 118:25-26) at Christ's royal entry into Jerusalem (cf. Matt. 21:9; Mark 11:9-10; Luke 19:38).

Psalm 119
The Law of the Lord
A Torah psalm, an alphabetical psalm

Psalm 119 consists of twenty-two stanzas corresponding successively to the letters in the Hebrew alphabet. The eight verses of each stanza all begin with the same letter. This pattern is maintained throughout the psalm until the alphabet is complete. The often-used term "law" has the idea of teaching, direction, or instruction. The law is the gracious revelation of what God wants in order for believers to have fellowship with him. It reveals who he is in holiness and justice. The wicked are insensitive to the ethical ideals set forth in the law (119:70). A "wineskin in the smoke" (119:83) is an image representing someone who has become dried, shriveled, and of little use. Man's knowledge of earthly matters is limited, but God's word is extensive and comprehensive in scope and application (119:96). The "grateful thanks" (119:108) of the psalmist's mouth is a true sacrifice of praise (Heb. 13:15). In this context, the expression "seven times" (119:164) is used poetically to mean "many times" or "frequently." Praise should be part of a regular pattern for living.

Psalm 120
Prayer for Help against a Slanderer
An individual's lament, a pilgrim psalm

Psalm 120 shows the discomfort of a righteous person in the middle of people of ungodly speech. The superscription "A song for the ascent to Jerusalem" is found attached to Psalms 120–134. The term "ascent" suggests that these psalms were sung as the Jews went up to Jerusalem for worship at the three annual pilgrim feasts (Deut. 16:16). God's judgment on the slanderer is likened to sharp arrows and glowing coals (Ps. 120:4). Meshech (120:5; cf. Gen. 10:2) and Kedar (Gen. 25:13) were mountain and desert tribes, respectively, dwelling outside the land of Israel. The slander had made the psalmist feel as though he lived in hostile surroundings.

Psalm 121
God, the Keeper of Israel
A psalm of individual declarative praise,
a pilgrim psalm

Psalm 121 asserts the absolute and ultimate safety of the child of God. The essence is found in 121:7, where God is praised as the one who protects his people from evil. For "A song for the ascent," see Psalm 120. The "mountains" (121:1) may refer to those that surround Zion (cf. 125:2). The expression "as you come and go" (121:8) refers to all of one's affairs and undertakings.

Psalm 122
Prayer for the Prosperity of Jerusalem
A psalm of individual declarative praise,
a pilgrim psalm

The blessings of the house of the Lord in Jerusalem begin and end this psalm (122:1, 9) and frame the central thrust of the psalm (122:2-8) which concerns the house of David (122:5). The key prayer for the peace of Jerusalem (repeated three times in 122:5-8) is for the benefit of those who love the city (122:6), that is, for those committed to the God of Israel and his statutes—the Law of Moses (122:4-5).

Psalm 123
Looking to the Lord
A national lament, a pilgrim psalm

Note the images of dependency used in 123:2 to help the reader visualize his dependency on God. The "hand" is that which supplies the need. The scorn and contempt by the proud were more than the psalmist could bear (123:4), and hence this prayer.

Psalm 124
Help in the Name of the Lord
A psalm of national declarative praise,
a pilgrim psalm

Psalm 124:8 contains a major theme expressed by all the psalms. Help and deliverance are based on the reputation and power of God, the Creator.

Psalm 125
The Security of God's People
A national lament, a pilgrim psalm

Note the comparison of the righteous person to a mountain (125:1). Usually God is pictured that way. The mountains literally surround Jerusalem (125:2). To the north is Mount Moriah (2,425 feet high); to the east, the Mount of Olives (2,700 feet high); to the west, the Western Hill (2,550 feet high); and to the south, the so-called Mount of Evil Counsel where the local United Nations Headquarters is presently located.

Psalm 126
A Prayer for Full Restoration
*A psalm of national declarative praise,
a pilgrim psalm*

The first group of exiled Jews returned to Jerusalem under the decree of Cyrus in 537 B.C. (Ezra 1:1-4). The psalmist prayed for a restoration blessing that was forfeited with captivity to the same degree that the dry riverbeds in the southern desert ("streams," Ps. 126:4) are filled to overflowing with the winter rain. The metaphor of harvest in 126:5-6 is used to illustrate the results of the prayerful efforts of the exiles to reestablish themselves in the land.

Psalm 127
Prosperity Comes from the Lord
A wisdom psalm, a pilgrim psalm

This is the second of Solomon's two recorded psalms (cf. Ps. 72). Man's labor is in vain unless God is in it (127:2). The last line suggests that God will provide for his own, even during times of sleep. Hence, those who know God can be free from anxiety. Those with large families can have confidence in the face of personal threat or public criticism because of the support and encouragement of their offspring (127:5). The "city gates" (127:5) was the place for settling legal disputes in ancient times (see Ruth 4:1ff.).

Psalm 128
The Blessing of Revering God
A wisdom psalm, a pilgrim psalm

The wife is likened to a "fruitful vine" (128:3) bringing the blessing of progeny. Because of the presence of the temple in "Zion," God was viewed as residing there (128:5). Thus the blessings from God come from Zion.

Psalm 129
God Delivers His People
*A psalm of national declarative praise,
a pilgrim psalm*

Persecuted Israel is likened to a scourged man with welts on his back like the deep "furrows" made by a plow in a field (129:3). Grass often grows on the tops of flat roofed houses (129:6), but with little soil, it withers quickly under the hot sun.

Psalm 130
Hope in God's Forgiving Love
*An individual's lament, a penitential psalm,
a pilgrim psalm*

God's pardon of sin is designed to turn man's heart toward him in reverence (130:4). The repetition of identical lines (130:6) is used here for emphasis, expressing urgency.

Psalm 131
The Virtue of Humility
A song of trust, a pilgrim psalm

The imagery "small child is quiet with its mother" (131:2) suggests one who is happy and secure, having gone through the difficult weaning process. Such is the psalmist's condition after being weaned from a desire for status.

Psalm 132
A Prayer for Blessing on the Sanctuary
A royal psalm, a messianic psalm, a pilgrim psalm

David's desire to build God a temple (Ps. 132:2-5) is reflected in 2 Samuel 7:1-7. "Ephrathah" (132:6), also known as Ephrath, is another name for Bethlehem (Gen. 35:19), but may be used here for the district in which Kiriath Jearim was located where the ark of the covenant was kept for twenty years (1 Sam. 7:1-2). The "king you chose for your people" (132:10) refers to the future kings of the Davidic dynasty. God's promise to David and his descendants (132:11-12; see 2 Sam. 7:12-16) was unconditional, yet participation in the benefits of this promise could be forfeited by disobedience ("if," Ps. 132:12). In such cases, the promise would be passed on to the next ruler. The promises of 132:15-17 will ultimately be fulfilled in Christ in the messianic kingdom.

Psalm 133
The Praise of Brotherly Unity
A wisdom psalm, a pilgrim psalm

Brotherly unity (133:1) is compared with three progressively powerful images: (1) oil on the head and beard; (2) dew on Mount Hermon; and (3) the bestowal of God's blessings on Mount Zion, that is, Jerusalem. Unity is a blessing that has its source in God himself. The oil on Aaron's head and beard refers to Leviticus 8:12 and Aaron's anointing with oil to begin the great ministry of atonement in the tabernacle. The blessing of God's people living in unity is like the oil of blessing being poured not only over the high priest Aaron but also over the entire city of Jerusalem. Moist, Mediterranean air blown inland to the foothills of Mount Hermon (9,200 feet high) results in a very heavy dew fall in the area mentioned (133:3). This represented the abundant blessing of unity that God would bring to Jerusalem.

Psalm 134
An Exhortation to Bless the Lord
A psalm of descriptive praise, a pilgrim psalm

Those who served at the temple throughout the night received a blessing. This psalm forms a benediction for the Songs of Ascent (Pss. 120–134). The biblical concept of "bless" (134:3) includes the good things God gives including his presence with his people.

Psalm 135
Praise of God's Greatness
A psalm of descriptive praise, an exodus psalm

God should be praised for his election of Israel (Ps. 135:4) and her redemption out of Egypt.

Compare 135:7 with Jeremiah 10:13 and 51:16. For Israel's victories over Sihon and Og (135:11), see Numbers 21:21-35.

Psalm 136
Praise for God's Loyal Love
A psalm of descriptive praise, an exodus psalm

Psalm 136 exalts the Lord for the many expressions of his loving-kindness. That aspect of God's character is rooted in Exodus 34:6 and God's redemption of Israel out of Egypt. The psalm was probably used antiphonally in temple worship, with the refrain being sung by the Levites or the congregation.

Psalm 137
The Song of the Exiles
A national lament, an imprecatory psalm

The "rivers of Babylon" were the irrigation canals that channeled water from the Tigris and Euphrates rivers (cf. Jer. 51:13; Ezek. 1:1). The Edomites were the descendants of Esau, Jacob's brother (137:7; cf. Gen. 36:8). Instead of showing kindness to their Israelite kinsmen, they called for Jerusalem's destruction. Some link Edom's crimes against Jerusalem with the judgment pronounced against them in Obadiah 1:11-14. The law of retaliation (Lev. 24:17-21) is applied in Psalm 137:8-9. Such crimes had been perpetrated against Israelite children (cf. 2 Kings 8:12; Hos. 10:14), and the Babylonians were guilty of them (cf. Jer. 51:24 with Isa. 13:16). This shocking imprecation is ultimately grounded on God's promise in Genesis 12:3.

Psalm 138
Great Is God's Glory
A psalm of individual declarative praise

The pagan "gods" (138:1) or idols were mocked by the psalmist's praise of the true God. The "promises" (138:2) refer to a specific answer to prayer. God's answer had surpassed all that David had previously understood his reputation ("name") to signify. Although God is glorious and greatly exalted, he is concerned for the "humble," those who truly love and reverence him (138:5-6).

Psalm 139
A Devout Contemplation of God
An individual's lament, an imprecatory psalm, a wisdom psalm

David praised God for his knowledge (139:1-6), omnipresence (139:7-12), and his plan for all of his days (139:13-16). On that basis David praised God and asked for his judgment upon the wicked and upon himself as well (139:23-24). Psalm 139:13-15 makes a strong biblical statement concerning God's involvement in the development of life within the womb. Psalm 139:16 reveals God's prior knowledge of each individual life before birth (cf. Eph. 1:11). In Psalm 139:19-

20, on the basis of God's promise to Abraham (Gen. 12:3), David prayed for God's judgment on the wicked and murderers.

Psalm 140
A Prayer for Protection
An individual's lament

As a protective helmet, God protects his own from the wicked enemy (140:7). David prayed that the evil plans of the wicked would recoil and entangle them (140:9). The "burning coals" (140:10) may allude to God's judgment of Sodom and Gomorrah (Gen. 19:24).

Psalm 141
A Prayer for Protection
An individual's lament

Before David prayed for protection from his enemies, he prayed for protection from his own evil potential (141:1-4). For the use of incense in the tabernacle (141:2), see Exodus 30:8. For the evening offering, see Exodus 29:39-41. The "delicacies" (141:4) of the wicked are the fruits of their ungodly practices. Psalm 141:6-7 are variously interpreted. The wicked will be overthrown (141:6), but not without great cost to the righteous (141:7).

Psalm 142
A Prayer for Help
An individual's lament

The historical setting of this contemplative poem (*maskil*) was probably either the cave of Adullam (1 Sam. 22:1-5) or the cave at En-gedi (1 Sam. 24:1-7). The Lord told the Levites, who had no territorial inheritance, that he was their inheritance in the land of Israel (Ps. 142:5; cf. Num. 18:20). God was David's possession and provision. David's "prison" (142:7) was probably the cave where he was hiding from Saul.

Psalm 143
A Prayer for Deliverance
An individual's lament, a penitential psalm

David prayed for inner strength to do God's will (143:10) and outer protection from his enemies. "Firm footing" (143:10) was used figuratively for conditions free from obstructions resulting in peace and prosperity. The imprecation of 143:12 was based on God's promise in Genesis 12:3.

Psalm 144
A Prayer for Rescue and Prosperity
A royal psalm

Compare Psalm 144:3 with 8:4. In 144:5-8 David prayed for God's divine intervention whereby the forces of nature were enlisted as allies with God's people (cf. Josh. 10:10-11; Judg. 5:20-21). Psalm 144:12-15 depicts the happy estate resulting from God's presence and protection.

Psalm 145
Glory to God
A psalm of declarative praise,
an alphabetical psalm

Psalm 145 forms an alphabetical acrostic with each verse beginning with a successive letter of the Hebrew alphabet. The Hebrew letter *nun* is missing, but it appears in a Hebrew text from Qumran. The great revelation of Exodus 34:6 forms the core of and foundation for David's faith. The "faithful followers" (145:10) refer to those who exercise covenant loyalty in their relationship with God and man.

Psalm 146
Praise of God's Power
A psalm of descriptive praise

The Lord was praised for his justice and provisions. He had shown himself to conform to his own laws. The five psalms that conclude the psalter all begin and end with "Praise the Lord." For 146:8, see Matthew 20:29-34 and John 9:1-7.

Psalm 147
Praise of God's Goodness
A psalm of descriptive praise

Psalm 147 moves its focus in three broad strokes from the stars to the afflicted, from all of nature to those persons who fear God, and from all the nations to Israel's special favor. Hundreds of billions of stars are known to exist in the Milky Way galaxy, which is regarded as but a speck in the star clusters of the known universe (147:4). Man depends upon physical strength for victory and accomplishment, but such things are not a factor in God's dealings (147:10). In ancient times, the "bars" of city gates would be strengthened against attack (147:13). God has done this for his people. He did something unique and special with Israel when he entrusted them with his special revelation ("his principles and laws," 147:19-20).

Psalm 148
All Creation Invoked to Praise God
A psalm of descriptive praise, a creation psalm

From nature to humanity, all are commanded to praise God. The term "armies of heaven" (148:2) refers to numerous heavenly beings.

Psalm 149
Praise for Victory
A psalm of descriptive praise

For "the faithful" (149:1, 5), see the note on Psalm 145:10. Psalm 149:6-9 anticipates the subjection of the nations under Christ's rule during the messianic kingdom (see Ps. 2:8).

Psalm 150
A Universal Call to Praise
A psalm of descriptive praise

The writers of the psalms recognized the importance of music as an instrument for praise. The listing of the various instruments (150:3-5) suggests that all resourses at one's disposal are to be called upon to exalt the great name of God. Praise is the essence of the redeemed person's life. It shows continual appreciation for the redemption God gives believers and continual appreciation of their frailty and need for God's strength. It shows continual appreciation of his desires to right the world.

PROVERBS

BASIC FACTS

HISTORICAL SETTING
The courts of Solomon (Prov. 1:1) and Hezekiah (25:1), two of Israel's greatest kings, provide the historical setting for the book of Proverbs. The proverbs illustrate the wisdom that was desired by God for the kings of his Davidic line.

AUTHOR
The book of Proverbs includes material from several authors. Solomon, as God's chosen king of Israel, is the primary source for the wise sayings in this book. Other lesser authors are "the wise" (22:17), Agur (30:1), and Lemuel (31:1).

DATE
The book was originally composed in the days of Solomon (971–931 B.C.; see 1:1) and then completed in the days of Hezekiah (between 715 and 686 B.C.; see 25:1).

PURPOSE
The book of Proverbs was designed to help believers deepen their healthy fear of God and to apply that fear to the varied events of daily life. The proverbs graphically described these events as opportunities for making wise or foolish choices that could bring either blessing or disaster. But the book of Proverbs was not collected and compiled simply to give a long checklist of various items for successful living. Its purpose was to strengthen the confidence of believers in God's ultimate control over the world to help them take responsibility for their actions and accept the consequences of wrongdoing.

The book probes deeply into how people's thoughts affect their actions. The book divides thoughts and acts into two major categories, each one based on either true or false understandings of God's involvement in the world. The foolish act as if God does not exist. The wise conduct themselves in the full realization that God exists and that actions have unavoidable consequences, good or bad. Thus, the book's main purpose is to correct the worldviews of readers—to turn them away from foolish fantasies (see, for example, 12:11; 28:19) and back to the fear of God (1:7). Then the various wise actions described in the book will result from that inner awe and respect for God.

In summary, the purpose of the book of Proverbs is to save people from the realm of darkness and death caused by error and ignorance. It is also to save them in order that they might enter the realm of life as God originally intended.

GUIDING CONCEPTS

THE VIEWPOINT OF PROVERBS

The book of Proverbs uses pithy and vivid statements to equip the godly person for
life (3:17-18). It strives to instill values as well as motivate behavior (1:3). It was very
important for every Jewish son to learn a trade, usually one passed from father to son.
Proverbs paints the picture of a son being groomed to take over after the father is gone,
especially in the skills of daily life. It uses poetry in order to present truth to the heart as
well as to the mind. Overall, there is no consistent grouping of the individual proverbs
by topic. There is no need for a closely knit argument. Each day normal human experience brings many diverse topics to deal with. Proverbs matches life on the busy streets.

Proverbs speaks from the experience of age. It is as if wise and gentle people were
sharing their years of experience with the younger generation. Proverbs probes the
works of creation, seeing in it God's power to order the world he made. It is international in its scope because it recognizes that the entire world, not just a single nation,
is under God, who created all things. The way in which he created the world to operate
is beneficial for everyone. This universal perspective is different from that of the rest of
the Old Testament, which emphasizes the relationship of Israel to God under the
Mosaic covenant. The Old Testament generally has a national focus; Proverbs has a
focus that is international.

THE COURT OF SOLOMON

Solomon had asked for and received great wisdom (1 Kings 3:9). He also was the one
God spoke of in 2 Samuel 7:14, the one who, as king of Israel under the Davidic covenant, would have a special father-son relationship with God. The wisdom of Solomon,
as described in 1 Kings 4:29-34, related to everything from trees to animals, birds, and
fish. Solomon's wisdom did not pertain only to godly matters. The wisdom God gave
him was insight into how the entire world operated, on the vegetable, animal, and
mineral levels. And, as is true in his proverbs, that wisdom also related to how God
intended the home, the body, the business, and the community to best operate. True
wisdom looks at the world and finds out how things work the best. It is very practical.

BIBLE-WIDE CONCEPTS

PROVERBS AND CREATION

Wisdom is much more than a skill. It is actually God's underlying plan and thought for
the universe. Proverbs 8:22-31 links wisdom with the very blueprint of creation. Wisdom
is God's detailed plan of how his creation was designed to operate. "The fear of the
Lord" is the foundation of wisdom, for it connects people with God's original plan not
only for creation but for their lives. A wise person follows that original plan as best he
can so that his life will reflect order and not chaos.

God is sovereign over his creation and knows the heart of every man or woman
(15:3, 11; 16:2). He rewards good and evil (12:2; 22:22-23). His control does away
with an impersonal view of how life works. God is the personal sustainer of the universe. It is up to the wise person to ground his life not in high ethical or social norms
but in the personal God who controls the world. From that relationship, which the
Bible calls "the fear of the Lord," will then issue the particular ethics and behavior that

match God's original intentions for creation. Only there will life be found (12:28; 13:9; 19:16).

But that wisdom does not come easily. It is a decision of faith to accept the revealed order and rule of God (1:23; 3:5-6; 4:7). Each person is responsible to search for it (2:2-5; 25:2; 28:12-28; 30:5-6). It is available to all people—from wise leaders to the farmer in his field (Isa. 28:23-29).

These words of wisdom often come in the form of commands (e.g., 1:8; 2:1; 3:1; 4:4; 6:23; 13:13; 28:4). They stand on the same level as Moses' commands and are to be bound on the tablet of the heart (3:3; cf. Deut. 6:8; 11:18). They are fulfilled and perfected in Jesus, the Son of God, the personified wisdom of God (Col. 2:1-3) and the upholder of creation (Col. 1:16).

NEEDS MET BY PROVERBS

The first readers of the book of Proverbs were not just people who enjoyed a special relationship with God. They were people called upon to reinvigorate God's original plan for humanity to have dominion over the earth and to make God an important part of every aspect of life. That original creation mandate for humanity allowed for no split between secular and sacred. From tilling the ground to fellowshiping with God, everything was of one noble and God-oriented whole. So, for the Israelite, religion stretched far beyond the tabernacle into the field, street, business, and home. All areas of life were to reflect God's designs for success. Proverbs extended the commands of the law into wise words to guide a person into godly living in all areas of his daily life. Questions like the following are answered in the book of Proverbs.

- What does God have to say about the parts of life that do not seem to be directly related to religion?
- How can a person become truly wise?
- Does God bring the consequences of a person's actions upon him immediately or do the consequences take awhile to appear?
- What makes a choice foolish or wise?
- How can a person avoid doing what so many of his friends are doing?
- If consequences of sin are not always immediate, where can a person find the stability to continue making wise choices?
- How long can a person get away with making foolish choices?
- What may motivate a person to keep trying to make wise choices?

The book of Proverbs portrays the situations of life as they really are, not the way people might wish them to be. Unfortunately, it is all too easy for people to live in a world of their own creation. The atheist creates a world that has no God. The disobedient believer creates a world in which God somehow winks at personal sins. The one who spends more than he earns creates an imaginary world in which bankruptcy somehow never finds him. The one who overeats and underexercises lives in a fantasy world in which heart attacks always happen to someone else.

But in the real world, the world of Proverbs, the norm is that bad actions have bad consequences—perhaps not immediately, but inevitably. In the real world overspending leads to financial problems, overeating leads to health problems, immorality leads to personal and family problems, and dishonesty leads to exposure and ruin. Such a world is not pretty. But most people would rather have reality over fantasy. Only through that reality can the book of Proverbs reveal the ultimate reality that is the ground of all wisdom: the fear of God.

OUTLINE OF PROVERBS

PROVERBS NOTES*

1:1-7 INTRODUCTION
The reference to Solomon (1:1) does not mean that he wrote the whole book (24:23; 30:1; 31:1), but that he was the major and most illustrious contributor. The purpose of the book of Proverbs (1:2-4) is to bring to the reader an understanding of true "wisdom" and inspire him to allow it to guide his decisions and conduct (see Job 28:28). To exercise "wisdom" (1:2) means to order one's affairs according to God's righteous guidelines and thus avoid unnecessary difficulties in life. The word "discipline" contains the idea of training by word (24:32) or deed (23:13). In view are wise dealings (1:3) that lead to successful living; "right" is right behavior; "just" is the application of righteousness in making the right decision; and "fair" is moral integrity. Wisdom will give prudence to the naive or simpleminded, the person susceptible to being misled (1:4). The person without experience will learn how to avoid the pitfalls of life.

Proverbs will benefit both the wise and the simple (1:5-6). The wise will be able to navigate around life's hidden reefs with care. The "proverb" (in Hebrew, *mashal*) is simply a method of teaching by means of comparison. The theme of the proverbs is that the "fear of the Lord" (1:7) is the first lesson in the pursuit of wisdom. To "fear" God means acknowledging his standards and reverently submitting to his will. Numerous applications of the "fear of the Lord" are presented by the wisdom

writers (see Job 28:28; Eccles. 12:13; Ps. 111:10; Prov. 2:5; 8:13; 9:10). Solomon wanted to emphasize that wisdom is not acquired by some mechanical formula but comes through a right relationship with God. The "fool" is the mentally naive and morally irresponsible person who has little regard for God's guidelines ("wisdom") and discipline.

1:8–9:18 THE PARENTS' VIEW OF LIFE
Overview: The first nine chapters give the parents' view of life and prepare the reader for Solomon's words in 10:1–22:16. They form a foundation for wisdom that is worldwide in its application. It is not simply "religious wisdom," but it is applicable in all aspects of the world and people's personal lives. The mood in the book is like that seen in a loving father's hands on his son's shoulders. The mother also has a high position of honor as a teacher in the book of Proverbs (1:8; 4:3; 6:20; 10:1), a characteristic uncommon in literature of the ancient Near East.

These chapters were written by the overall editor of the book and were written in a royal setting in the court of the king. Although these chapters are anonymous, the rest of the book's contents have named authors. This editorial introduction sets the perspective and interpretive tone for the rest of the book. The first major and following section of Proverbs contains discourses on wisdom. Here Solomon taught by contrast, comparing the ways of the wise with those of the foolish.

*The substance of some of the notes for Proverbs was also published in the Ryrie Study Bible.

1:8-33 The Father's Call to Wisdom

The individual proverbs had their original setting in the home where the wise parent addressed his "child" concerning practical lessons in life (1:8-9). The word "listen" (1:8) means "to pay attention to and put into practice."

Sin is attractive (1:10-14) but deadly (1:15-19). The sinner may gain the world at the cost of his own soul (Mark 8:36). The grave (1:12) is the place of the dead, while wisdom is seen as a rejected street creature (1:20-33), who is not in the temple but out in life's everyday routine. Wisdom is personified as a godly woman inviting all to come and learn from her teaching, but the majority refuse to listen.

2:1-22 Wisdom's Benefits

The father spoke again as a wise master teacher, describing the benefits of pursuing wisdom. The concept that God is the ultimate source of wisdom makes Israel's Wisdom Literature unique (2:6). True wisdom is God-given, not merely the result of human effort or ability (cf. 1 Kings 3:9-12; James 1:5). Wisdom will deliver one from the ways of evil men (2:10-15) and adulterous women (2:16-19). The adulteress is referred to as a wayward woman in that she is outside the circle of a man's proper relationships (2:16).

3:1-35 Wisdom's Security

Wisdom not only protects one from evil, it also promises many earthly rewards (3:1-18). The word "seek" (3:6) means to "know." In all of the activities and pursuits of life, God must be kept central. The word "direct" means to clear obstructions enabling one to reach the appointed goal. The "tree of life" (3:18; cf. Gen. 2:9; Rev. 2:7) is a metaphor for a "source of life." Wisdom played a dynamic part in the creation of the universe (3:19-20), so it can have a significant part in ordering the affairs of each person's life.

4:1-27 Exhortation to Grasp Wisdom

Wisdom provides many benefits for anyone who will follow its direction (4:1-27). It is seen as the way or path (4:11) upon which people are to journey through life. The first step for a person in acquiring wisdom is to make up his mind that he really wants it and is willing to subject his own ideas and desires to God's revealed will (4:7). The two conflicting ways of the wicked and the righteous is a common theme of the wisdom writers (4:18-19). The "full light of day" (4:18) refers to noontime, when the sun is directly overhead. The "heart" (4:23) refers to one's inner being or mind.

5:1-23 Marital Fidelity

The exercise of wisdom will help guard a person against the temptations of adultery. The wisdom of marital fidelity is contrasted with its foolish and dishonoring alternative (5:7-23). The figurative language in 5:15 refers to marital intercourse. The "springs" of 5:16 refer to one's offspring or children.

6:1-35 Debt and Adultery

To "co-sign" (6:1) means to take responsibility for another person's loan; so if the borrower defaults, the cosigner has to pay the obligation. The wise teacher warned his son to avoid such financial folly. The proverbs are based on general observations about life. Job recognized that there are exceptions to this general prediction concerning the destiny of the wicked (Job 12:6). The proverbial expression "six . . . seven" (Prov. 6:16) means that the list, though specific, is not exhaustive (30:15, 18). The seventh commandment, "Do not commit adultery" (Exod. 20:14), is the theme of Proverbs 6:20-35. With adultery there is no possible means of giving back to the rightful spouse what has been taken (6:35).

7:1-27 Description of a Son's Downfall

The words "precious possession" (7:2) are used to emphasize how precious the teachings of God's word should be in the lives of his people. The theme of this section, the folly of yielding to the enticements of a harlot, is introduced in 7:5. Here the warnings against adultery were dramatized as the teacher described how a young fool succumbed to the temptations of an adulteress. Having offered sacrifices, she had a good supply of meat on hand to share with her guest (7:14; cf. Lev. 7:15).

8:1-36 Wisdom and Creation

Wisdom is personified and exalted by proclaiming her excellences. She is a guide offered to every person (Prov. 8:1-11) as the key to all success (8:12-21). The careful application of God's guidelines for living will generally result in a more favorable economic situation, but financial prosperity must always be kept in proper perspective (8:19).

Wisdom's eternal character is shown in 8:22-31 and ultimately points to Christ, in whom is found "all the treasures of wisdom" (Col. 2:3; cf. Phil. 2:3-11; 1 Cor. 1:24; Jer. 9:23-24). Christ, who is wisdom incarnate, is the ultimate wise man. Wisdom is pictured as an architect at God's side at creation (8:30). "Listen" (8:32) means to both hear and obey.

9:1-18 Wisdom and Foolishness Personified

The rival invitations of wisdom (9:1-6) and folly (9:13-18) serve to conclude this section. The "seven pillars" (9:1) signify an ideally constructed house. Mixed wine (9:2, 5) refers to wine flavored with spices (Song of Songs 8:2). The theme of the book is repeated (1:7) in this concluding section (9:10). Like a harlot, folly promotes the attractiveness of what is forbidden (9:17). "Stolen water" and "food eaten in secret" (9:17) may be figures of illicit intercourse (see 5:15-20; 30:20).

10:1–22:16 THE PROVERBS OF SOLOMON, PART ONE

Overview: Here Solomon presents 375 of the over 3,000 proverbs he wrote (1 Kings 4:32). Proverbs are short sayings taken from everyday life that are intended to serve as practical guidelines for successful living. These proverbs are general principles that may have exceptions. They are not intended as personal promises or meant to apply in unusual or exceptional situations. This is not a problem with their inerrancy, but a matter of understanding the nature of proverbs and the contexts in which they do apply.

10:1-32 The Security of the Wise

Violent, vicious language flows from the mouth of the wicked (10:6). The proverbs confirm the general principle that a person reaps what he sows (10:16). When one's prosperity comes as a blessing from the Lord, there is freedom from the usual anxieties and trouble accompanying the accumulation of wealth (10:22).

11:1-31 Wisdom's Blessing in Society

The term "wise leadership" (11:14) literally means "steering," or wise direction on the course of life. The word "discretion" (11:22) can be literally translated "taste" and refers to moral perception. For "trees that bear life" (11:30), see 3:18. Spiritual salvation is not in view here but rather the winning of others to the ways of wisdom.

12:1-28 Security and Diligence in Work

"Discipline" (12:1) is training by word or deed. For an example of such a "worthy wife" (12:4), see 31:10-31. The mouth of the upright will deliver the innocent from undeserved judgment (12:6). Better to be of humble circumstances and have something to eat than to have an honored position and be hungry (12:9). The wicked covets the possessions of others in order to stabilize his own position (12:12). But the righteous man works for what he has and enjoys the joy and security of earning one's due. "Quick-tempered" (12:16) means angry. A prudent man knows when to speak and when to remain quiet (12:23). The lazy man neglects essential responsibilities (12:27). An allusion to the immortality of the one who knows God is found in 12:28.

13:1-25 Wisdom's Gains and Life's Injustices

The "light" (13:9) serves here as a symbol of joy and prosperity (cf. Esther 8:16). Proverbs 13:21 is a general principle, but there are exceptions, as in the case of Job.

14:1-35 Wisdom and Earthly Power

There is always a price for growth and accomplishment (14:4). The prudent man does not walk blindly but carefully considers his steps and chooses his way (14:8). There is a way that seems to be ethically correct, but it leads to destruction (14:12). Wisdom generally does result in greater economic stability because financial entanglements (6:1-5) are avoided (14:24). The "life-giving fountain"(14:27) is a source of spiritual vitality. The righteous have an eternal hope in contrast to the wicked, who can expect only humiliation and judgment (14:32). The fool boasts of what little knowledge he has, while the wise man avoids making a display of himself (14:33).

15:1-33 Wisdom in Heart and Speech

"Death and Destruction" (15:11; "Sheol and Abaddon," NASB; "Hell and destruction," KJV) both refer to the place of the dead, the grave. "Abaddon" is a Greek word from which "destruction" is rendered. "Sheol" is a Hebrew word meaning "place of the dead." "A cheerful look" (15:30) refers to the sparkle seen in the eyes of one who has received good news.

16:1-33 The Sovereignty of God over Life's Events

"Commit" (16:3) literally means "roll." It calls the reader to roll his burdens onto the Lord's shoulders; they are not too great for him. Atonement for man's sin is the result of God's love and faithfulness (16:6). A reverence for God and an appreciation of his power to judge motivate a person to turn from temptation. The expression "speaks with divine wisdom" (16:10) points to the finality and authority of the king's words. The "gentle rain" (16:15) falls just before harvest, assuring that there will be an abundant crop. A "life-giving fountain" (16:22) is a metaphor for a source of spiritual vitality. The expressions "with narrowed eyes" and "without a word" (16:30) refer to a nonverbal expression of malice; much evil can be communicated through body language. Lot casting was a means of determining the will of God (16:33). Although the casting of lots appears to be by chance, the decision is ultimately from the Lord.

17:1-28 Avoiding Injustice and Quarreling

A bribe can be used to secure a profitable business deal, but the practice is clearly condemned (17:8; cf. 17:23). Forgiveness preserves friendship unless someone takes advantage of such graciousness by repeating the offense (17:9). The fool thinks wisdom can be bought with a price (17:16). For "co-sign" (17:18), see Proverbs 6:1-5. Wisdom is readily accessible, but the foolish are preoccupied with other interests (17:24).

18:1-24 Consequences of Good and Bad Decisions

A "bubbling brook" (18:4) refers to the teaching of the wise that is crystal clear, that is, easily understood. The "name of the Lord" (18:10) speaks of God's true character and reputation. The word "gift" (18:16) is a more neutral term than "bribe" and refers to an innocent courtesy (cf. 1 Sam. 17:18). The "gate locked with iron bars" (18:19) refers to barriers in friendly relations. In the selection of friends, quality counts more than quantity (18:24).

19:1-29 Contrasts of Wealth and Wisdom

The fool blames the Lord for the disasters he brings upon himself (19:3). A comfortable living situation tends to reinforce the careless ways of a fool (19:10). Proverbs 19:16 speaks of temporal punishment, for example, premature death, not eternal judgment (cf. Deut. 30:15-20). The neglect of child discipline results in premature death for a disobedient or rebellious child (19:18; cf. Exod. 21:15). A simpleton needs to visualize or experience the consequences of folly but a wise man will correct his conduct simply in response to a reproof (Prov. 19:25).

20:1-30 Discernment of Inner Motives

The words "in the right season" (20:4) reflect the custom in ancient Israel of planting the winter wheat in the fall. The intentions of a man's heart may be hidden, but the wise person is able to penetrate below the surface and know the inner thoughts (20:5). Compare 20:7 with Exodus 20:5-6. The answer implied by the context is "nobody" (Prov. 20:9; cf. Rom. 3:10-18). In ancient times a garment was often used as collateral against a loan (20:16; cf. Exod. 22:25-27). "Stolen bread" (Prov. 20:17) implies dishonest gain. The "lamp" (20:20) is a symbol for a person's life (cf. 13:9; 24:20; 2 Sam. 21:17). Compare Proverbs 20:25 with Ecclesiastes 5:4-5. Physical discipline may have very beneficial results in purging evil and correcting conduct (Prov. 20:30).

21:1-31 God's Sovereignty and Justice

The "Righteous One" is probably a reference to God (21:12). Proverbs 21:14 reflects a fact of experience, but it does not promote bribery. The "bold front" (21:29) is an expression of defiance.

22:1–24:34 GENERAL COLLECTIONS OF PROVERBS

Overview: The next section contains the "words of the wise" (22:17). Here the pattern returns to that of chapters 1–9, using proverbial discourses.

22:1-29 Wealth and Poverty

The words "to choose the right path" (22:6) literally translate "according to his way," that is, the child's habits and interests. The proverb teaches the duty of reinforcing a child's interests and abilities during the early years of life. The last line of 22:16 appears to refer to bribery, which fails to accomplish its purpose. For 22:26 see the note on 17:18. The reference "you" is to the harsh creditor (22:27).

23:1-35 Self-Control and Discipline

The expression "put a knife to your throat" (23:2) refers to restraining one's appetite. A delicious meal may be provided with an ulterior motive. Like 23:1-3, the warning is against being deceived by an insincere host (23:4-8). For the "boundary markers" (23:10), see Deuteronomy 19:14. The "Redeemer" (Prov. 23:11) refers to the near kinsman, like Boaz who served as family protector for Ruth and Naomi (cf. Lev. 25:25-28 and Ruth 3:9). The term may also be used of God (Isa. 41:14). The words "won't die" (23:13) infer that having learned obedience through parental discipline, the child will not die as an adult as a penalty for a crime. The expression "save them from death" (Prov. 23:14) means "prevent an untimely death." The "deep pit" and "treacherous" (23:27) have sexual associations, but they focus primarily on the inescapable doom of those who fall into the harlot's clutches. The image here is of a sailor who falls in a drunken stupor into the sea or goes to sleep in a precarious crow's nest at the top of a ship's mast (23:34).

24:1-34 Avoiding Envy of Successful but Evil People

Members of society have a responsibility to be informed concerning those whose lives are in danger (Prov. 24:11-12). Ignorance is no excuse for one's neglect of vital issues. The "light" (24:20) of the wicked refers to their short-lived joy and prosperity. The words "associate with rebels" (24:21) refer in this context to a desire to alter or oppose recognized civil authority. The proverbs speak with high regard of the truth, an "honest reply" (24:26).

25:1–29:27 THE PROVERBS OF SOLOMON, PART TWO

Overview: In this section more of Solomon's proverbs are presented. They have been "copied" by an editorial committee of Hezekiah's men. The word means "to remove" and indicates that these proverbs were extracted from other Solomonic materials and incorporated into Proverbs during the reign of King Hezekiah (715–686 B.C.).

25:1-28 Self-Control in Speech

The proverbs highlight the difficulty of understanding the ways and decisions of a ruler (25:3). The proverb warns against striving after personal honor (25:6). It is acceptable to receive honor, but not to seek it. These proverbs speak of the caution necessary in bringing charges against someone (25:9). The reference in 25:11 appears to be to gold and silver sculptures. Although the illustration is obscure, the message is clear. "Refreshing as of snow" (25:13) refers to cold ice water from the mountain snow. Kindness extended to an enemy will incite him to shame and bring reward to the benefactor (25:21-22).

26:1-28 The Power of Words for Good or Evil

Observations about fools comprise the contents of 26:1-12. A curse without a cause will never be effective (26:2). While it is unwise to argue with a fool (26:4), there may be times when a sound reproof is appropriate (26:5). The rest of Proverbs 26 contains observations about lazy people (26:13-16) and scoundrels (26:17-28).

27:1-27 Friendship and Foresight

Compare 27:1 with James 4:13-16. "Hidden love" (27:5) does not demonstrate its existence by ministering a needed reproof. Love often demands reproof of the object of that love. Wealth and what wealth can buy never really satisfy, but such possessions look attractive to those who have so little (27:7). The value of a close friend in contrast to a relative who lacks interest in one's concerns is highlighted in 27:10. A good pupil will enhance the reputation of a teacher against his critics (27:11). For "Death and Destruction" (27:20), see the note on 15:11. A man's response to praise serves as a test of his true character (27:21). This treatise on pastoral life provides a balance between physical labor and trusting in God's sufficiency (27:23-27).

28:1-28 The Security of Obedience to the Law

A wise ruler can bring stability during a time of national upheaval. The poor oppressing the poor is as absurd as rain washing away crops instead of watering them (28:3). One's attitude toward the law reflects one's standing in relationship with the wicked (28:4). "Charging interest" (28:8) refers to charging excessive rates of interest, a practice forbidden by Israelite law (Lev. 25:36). For Proverbs 28:9, see Psalm 66:18. The words "cover over their sins" (Prov. 28:13) mean "refuses to admit his guilt" (Ps. 32:5). In this context, "tender conscience" (Prov. 28:14) refers to sin and its consequences. Proverbs 28:17 refers to the pursuit of a murderer by the blood avenger (Num. 35:19). Some people will violate justice for the smallest bribe (Prov. 28:21).

29:1-27 Wisdom and Justice

Scorners delight in stirring people to controversy, but the wise seek to minimize nonessential differences (29:8). Some of God's blessings are enjoyed by both the oppressor and the poor (29:13; cf.

Matt. 5:45). Without prophetic revelation ("divine guidance") from God, people are unrestrained and will fall under divine judgment (Prov. 29:18). The thought may be that a pampered slave will begin to act like an heir, conducting himself as though he were free from a servant's obligations (29:21).

30:1-33 THE WORDS OF AGUR

The author of Proverbs 30 is said to be Agur (meaning "gatherer"), son of Jakeh. Early rabbis and church fathers identified Solomon as the "gatherer" of wisdom. There is no certainty as to the author's identification. Although he had a high view of God, Agur did not pretend to have mastered wisdom and theology (30:3). Man is not able to fully comprehend the ways of an infinite God (30:4). Compare 30:6 with Revelation 22:18. In Proverbs 30:7-9 Agur prays for honesty and for circumstances that will not cause that character to deviate. In 30:11-14 four types of wicked men are highlighted: the disrespectful, the hypocrite, the proud, and the greedy. The proverbs that count (see "three . . . four" in 30:15, 18, 21, 29) illustrate the process of the wise person going through life making lists of observations about wise and foolish events. The first number "three" makes the basic emphasis. The additional number on the list "four" heightens the emphasis and suggests that more examples could be added. As in all proverbs, the readers are being probed to add their own observations to the list. One of the curses for violating the covenant was that the body would be left unburied for the birds to feed on (30:17; cf. Deut. 28:26). The exhortation is to self-restraint in light of the certain consequences of foolish behavior (30:32-33).

31:1-9 THE WORDS OF LEMUEL

This section and perhaps the verses that follow (31:10-31) are attributed to King Lemuel. Some have identified Lemuel (his name meaning "belonging to God") with Solomon, but that is simply speculation. Like Samuel (cf. 1 Sam. 1:11), Lemuel was born in response to his mother's vows (Prov. 31:2). Proverbs 31:6-7 does not advocate intoxication, but it simply reflects the medicinal use of wine in ancient times, much like a tranquilizer would be prescribed today. The phrase "those who cannot speak" (31:8) is used figuratively for the defenseless, those unable to plead their own cause.

31:10-31 POEM TO AN EXCELLENT WIFE

These verses describe an ideal woman who is both a challenge and an encouragement for women to strive in their own lives for such qualities as are exemplified here. The verses form an acrostic or alphabetical poem, with each verse beginning with successive letters of the Hebrew alphabet. The term translated "virtuous" (31:10) refers elsewhere to strength, ability, efficiency, wealth, and valor. She works late into the night (31:18). Earlier, the book noted that an understanding wife is from the Lord (19:14). Here, that gift from God is described in detail. The key to the character of this worthy woman is found in the fact that she "fears the Lord" (31:30; cf. 1:7). The book begins and ends by focusing on this motivating concept.

ECCLESIASTES

BASIC FACTS

HISTORICAL SETTING

The historical setting for the book of Ecclesiastes was the reign of Solomon
(970–931 B.C.), the grandest in Israel's history. At its highest point it was the envy
of all the surrounding kingdoms. Israel was also at the high point of its blessings
under God's great Abrahamic, Davidic, and Mosaic promises.

AUTHOR

Solomon, king of Israel, was the author. Some scholars have argued on the basis of the
unusual language in the book that another unknown author wrote the book at a much
later date.

DATE

The book of Ecclesiastes was written somewhere during the last period of Solomon's
reign of forty years (970–931 B.C.). Some have argued for a date as late as 400 B.C. on
the basis of the unusual language in the work. But the linguistic arguments for a late
date have been undermined by discoveries of fourteenth-century B.C. Ugaritic tablets
that show linguistic similarities with Ecclesiastes.

PURPOSE

The book of Ecclesiastes was designed to make people wise and happy. It makes them
wise by showing the futility of building their hopes on the material and social goods of
this world. It makes them happy by showing how, within the context of fearing God,
they can fully enjoy the goods of this world.

GUIDING CONCEPTS

THE PERSPECTIVE OF THE WRITER

Even during the wonderful and prosperous time of Solomon's reign there was still
injustice. Did not innocent children die of disease? Did not some masters abuse their
servants? Did not some wrongs go unpunished? Even during Solomon's great reign,
the effects of the curse of God in Eden were still in ugly force. The effect of the curse on
man and nature was not reversed. People still sinned.

Because people continued to sin, people continued to die. And death is at the heart
of mankind's feelings of despair and futility (see Rom. 8; 1 Cor. 15). The writer of

Ecclesiastes wanted his readers to see how seriously they should take living in a fallen world. For those who have lived since Christ's coming, death, and resurrection, this realistic perspective should help them to see the importance and necessity of Christ's death. What some might call pessimism and fatalism in the book, the writer calls realism. It is a realism bred from looking deeply into both the darkness of a cursed creation and into the sunlight of God's sovereignty.

Ecclesiastes is part of a wisdom tradition in Israel that took a long hard look at all sides of reality, not just at the sugarplum fantasy life that believers can all too easily create for themselves. The writer looked at a world where wrongs went unpunished, children died, and cheaters won. Then he asked how someone could live in it. The writer's answer may not be easy to accept, but it is true to reality.

KEY PHRASES

Several key phrases are repeated throughout the book and give the reader insight into its primary truths.

"Everything Is Meaningless"

However the Hebrew word translated "meaningless" is rendered, its main idea is futility. Life is not ultimately meaningless, but it is futile because what people often start out to do escapes them in the end. People hope for long life, happiness, and health. But they cannot count on any of those. By repeating that life is meaningless (see, for example, 1:2, 14; 2:1, 11, 15, 17, 19, 23, 26) the writer stressed the reality of this age—death puts an end to all earthly projects, noble or otherwise. A companion phrase is "chasing the wind" (1:14; 2:11, 17, 26; 4:4, etc.). Life is not worthless or meaningless; it is just unpredictable, often unfair, and always ends in death. The book's wisdom seeks to show how to find meaning and worth in such a bent world.

"Under the Sun"

The phrase "under the sun" sets the interpretive context of the book (1:9, 14; 2:17, etc.). It deals with issues under the sun, that is, on the earth—the place of human work, frustration, and hope.

The writer also reveals the thought processes in coming to his conclusions in phrases like "I realize," "I saw," "I have noticed" (1:17; 2:14; 5:18), and "I said to myself" (see 2:1, 15; 3:17; see also 1:13, 17; 2:3; 7:25; 8:9, 16; 9:1). Because of the book's depressing nature, the reader might think that the writer presents merely human reflection, apart from God's revelation. But that is not true. The author reflects upon life in full view of God's teaching concerning the human condition due to Adam's sin and concerning God's commands for human obedience.

"Enjoy"

The writer asks the reader eat, drink, and enjoy the good of life (for example, 2:24; 3:12-13, 22; 5:18-19; 8:15; 9:7, 9). That is not a fatalistic leap into decadence. Rather, it comes as God-given insight into how people are to work and live in a cursed and fallen world. Difficult? Yes. Frustrating? Yes. But people are to rejoice in the good that comes their way. Note 3:22 and 8:15 in this regard. God's eternal work abides, and that is the focus of the believer's hope. For now, in this life, people are not to put their hope or faith in human works, but they can and should enjoy them.

"Fear God"

The reader might think that the writer's admonition to "fear God" in 12:13 is the final conclusion of the book. But actually it is the perspective of the entire work (cf. 3:14; 5:7; 7:18; 8:12-13). It pervades the book and produces the insight into how to keep going on and finding joy in such a disappointing world. It creates a balance for enjoying the good and appreciating the bad without falling into either decadence or pessimism. Reverence for God (3:13; 5:1-7) and submission (12:13-14) grow out of fearing God. The fear of God keeps believers from giving up when evil strikes or diving into excess when they strike it rich. Faith is not found just at the end of the book; it is the book's whole perspective.

BIBLE-WIDE CONCEPTS

THE CURSE AND DEATH

The book of Ecclesiastes uses several themes that can be found from Genesis through Revelation. God's curse upon creation because of Adam's sin has bent the world against God's original Sabbath goodness and against humanity's hope for justice and satisfaction. Things do not work out the way they should. Death ends all the earthly joys of home, family, and business, and it is the same for people who are both good and bad. This does not seem fair. And, in the short run, it is not. Ecclesiastes describes in graphic and realistic detail what life has been like since Adam sinned. It portrays the devastation of the consequences of sin that stretch from Genesis through Revelation. Death takes everyone.

GOD'S SOVEREIGNTY AND JUSTICE

Also, Ecclesiastes speaks to the great issue of taking life as God deals it out, trusting in his wisdom and sovereignty. It asks the reader to trust that God will ultimately right all wrongs and reward all good. God has not revealed to mortal men all of his reasons for the way things are. People are kept in the dark about some very important issues. Ecclesiastes probes how God's people feel about those patches of darkness. Will they reject God and live for today? Or will they find in the darkness the clue to God's sovereignty and their humility? Throughout Scripture believers are told to take what God in his goodness gives to them. God keeps his secrets throughout the Bible. It is the wise person who accepts his limited knowledge and fears God, whether in the time of Adam, Abraham, Solomon, Isaiah, Christ, or the present.

NEEDS MET BY ECCLESIASTES

Ecclesiastes was written to people who needed to know that God's plans for his children included a full range of the world's experiences. Even under the great blessings of Solomon's early reign life was still hard. It was peppered with injustice; it was inexorably sliding downward into death. God did not innoculate his people against either life's pain and injustice or its pleasure and joy. Above all, God did not prevent his people from running into the inevitable wall of death—the dismantling of what they had sought to build and hang onto in this life. The book met the needs of God's people to be able both to accept the ultimate futility of life and, within that perspective, to have the presence of mind to please God and fully enjoy the good things of life. Ecclesiastes responds to difficult questions asked by people in Solomon's day and by people of today as well.

- Since all people are going to die anyway, what difference does it make in how they live?
- Why be good if the good and bad go down in death together?
- Why be good if it is no guarantee of being rich and successful in this life?
- How can people put their lives in the broader context of eternity rather than just living as if there were no tomorrow?
- How can people honestly face up to death and still have a positive outlook on life?
- How can people hold God's redemptive promises together while living in such a bent world?

One of the mysteries of the Christian faith is the unjust murder of God's Son on the cross. The perfect Son experienced suffering and pain along with joy and pleasure on this earth before he was taken up into heaven. The Christian is called to follow that pattern of suffering *now* and exaltation to heaven *later*. But being a child of God and yet suffering the wrongs of this world can create a great challenge to the Christian faith. But Ecclesiastes reveals a bigger picture: an understanding of life that sees beyond present moments of pain or pleasure. It points toward ultimate physical death and the subsequent evaluation of people by God. It reminds believers that even though their sins are forgiven and they have a place in the new heavens and earth, they must still cope with the daily problems of this age. They must make joyful and responsible choices that come, not from fleshly abandon, but from the fear of God.

OUTLINE OF ECCLESIASTES

I. PROPOSITION: LIFE IS FULL OF UNFULFILLED ASPIRATIONS (1:1-18)
   A. Statement: Life Is Futile (1:1-2)
   B. Summary Support: Nature Goes on, but People Come and Go (1:3-18)

II. ADVANTAGE SOUGHT (2:1-7:29)
   A. Attempts at Having Control over Life (2:1-26)
   B. Attempts at Understanding the Whole Plan of Life (3:1-22)
   C. Attempts to Find Advantages in Life (4:1-7:29)

III. WHERE ADVANTAGE CAN BE FOUND AND UNDERSTOOD (8:1-12:14)
   A. The Benefits of Wisdom and Fear of God (8:1-9:1)
   B. The Impact of Death (9:2-12)
   C. The Benefits of Wisdom (9:13-11:6)
   D. The Impact of Judgment (11:7-12:8)
   E. Conclusion: Fear the Lord (12:9-14)

ECCLESIASTES NOTES

1:1-18 PROPOSITION: LIFE IS FULL OF UNFULFILLED ASPIRATIONS

1:1-2 Statement: Life Is Futile

The word "Teacher" (1:1) is translated from the Hebrew term *Qohelet* and refers to one who convenes and speaks at an assembly. In the context of this book, the assembly is not a general congregation but a gathering of the wise (Jer. 18:18). The phrase "King David's son, who ruled in Jerusalem" (1:1) supports the Jewish tradition that Solomon wrote the book. The theme of futility is developed in 1:3-11 and continues throughout the book (1:2). It accords with Paul's words in Romans 8:20-22 that all creation is subject to futility because of sin (Gen. 3:17-18).

1:3-18 Summary Support: Nature Goes On, but People Come and Go

The word "get" (1:3) is a commercial term meaning "surplus" on a balance sheet. The author asks, "Is there any guarantee of positive benefit or reward for a person's work?" The endless cycles of nature illustrate the monotonous futility of much of life on earth (1:4-11). The words "under the sun" (1:14) are a figure of speech that means "upon the earth" where man dwells under the sun. The expression "chasing the wind" speaks of futile activity (1:14). Solomon was convinced that the works of people on earth were permeated with futility and paradoxes that cannot be resolved. Solomon's great wisdom simply enabled him to see more clearly the frustrating futility of life (1:18).

2:1–7:29 ADVANTAGE SOUGHT

2:1-26 Attempts at Having Control over Life

2:1-11 EXPERIENCE OF PLEASURE

Solomon's unlimited resources enabled him to conduct a great experiment to search for meaning in life (2:1-11). He sought fulfillment in indulgence (2:1-3), achievements (2:4-6), possessions (2:7-8), and fame (2:9), but none of these brought meaning or satisfaction.

2:12-23 KNOWLEDGE OF INEVITABLE DEATH

Solomon was convinced that anyone trying his experiences would come up with the same conclusion (2:12). Death is the "same fate" that befalls both the wise and the fool (2:14). Solomon despaired over leaving the results of his labor to his heir (2:18-20) and over the lack of gratifying or lasting reward for his work.

2:24-26 CONCLUSION: ENJOY GOD'S GIFTS

Having contemplated the utter futility of life, Solomon presented his divinely inspired solution: Rather than chafe under frustration and futility, enjoy to the fullest the life God has given (2:24).

This advice is repeated six times (3:12-13; 3:22; 5:18-19; 8:15; 9:7-9). Solomon's wise counsel was quite different from the Epicurean philosophy "Let us eat, drink, and be merry, for tomorrow we die." Solomon's solution to life's futility was balanced in the book's conclusion by the warning that one's life must be regulated by an awareness of coming judgment (12:14). Those who know God, the Creator, should enjoy life most (2:25). There is no real enjoyment of life apart from him.

3:1-22 Attempts at Understanding the Whole Plan of Life

3:1-8 THE OBSERVABLE PLAN

The words of 3:1 suggest a "divinely ordained" time, not just an appropriate time (Eph. 1:11). God has entrusted governmental authority with responsibility to carry out capital punishment in the case of murder (3:3; Gen. 9:6). The word "hate" (Eccles. 3:8) does not always suggest hostility or malice, for it can be an expression speaking of an appropriate attitude toward evil (Luke 14:26).

3:9-22 THE HIDDEN PLAN

There is beauty, yet mystery, to God's design (Eccles. 3:11). God gives people an eternal perspective ("planted eternity in the human heart") to see beyond the futility of this life "under the sun." Yet he has not revealed all of life's mysteries. The words "nothing better" (3:12) emphasize by understatement. The intended sense is "the best thing." As in 3:1, the reader is reminded that God ordained the continual cycles of life (3:15). Both human beings and animals face a common fate: death and the return to dust (3:19-22). But humans must also face judgment. Ecclesiastes 3:21, which should read as an affirmation rather than a question, reveals a distinction between human beings and animals (cf. 12:14).

4:1–7:29 Attempts to Find Advantages in Life

4:1-16 FIVE AREAS OF OBSERVATION

Oppression makes death look more attractive than life (4:1-3). Rest and work must be kept in proper balance (4:5-6). The futility of excessive work without need or purpose is highlighted in 4:8. There is strength in numbers (4:12). The instability and uncertainty of political support is emphasized in 4:14-16. Fickle crowds soon forget their favored rulers and replace them with others.

5:1–6:12 THE FEAR OF GOD AND RICHES

The words "keep your ears open and your mouth shut" (5:1) mean "be careful." The "mindless offerings" refer to unworthy worship, mere religious externalism that exhibits no reverence for God. As preoccupation with one's work makes for many dreams, so excessive words are characteristic of the prayer of a fool (5:3). The "messenger" (5:6) refers to the Levitical priest who would receive what was vowed. The "dreaming all the time" (5:7) seems to reflect a preoccupation with one's work (cf. 5:3).

Often there is corruption at every level, with oppressors being subject to the same treatment by those higher up (5:8). For the fourth time Solomon presented his answer to the frustration and futility of life (5:18). A better translation of 5:18 is "Furthermore, as for every man to whom God has given riches and wealth and has empowered to eat from them and to receive his reward and rejoice in his labor—this is the gift of God." This verse indicates that a capacity to enjoy one's possessions is itself one of God's gifts to man (see 6:2). A long life without satisfaction and enjoyment is futile (6:6). Man is neither able to control his earthly destiny (6:10) nor able to know his future (6:12). The context relates this truth to the futility of pursuing riches.

7:1-29 DEATH OBSERVED

Solomon offered a series of proverbial sayings concerning wisdom and folly (7:1-14). Visiting a home stricken by tragedy serves as a reminder of the brevity of life and the need for wisdom (7:2). Sorrow may have a beneficial effect, tempering mirth by life's realities (7:3). Wisdom is undoubtedly superior to wealth, but Solomon acknowledged that wealth with wisdom is better than wisdom alone (7:11). God is sovereign over all the circumstances of a person's life—both prosperity and adversity (7:13-14; cf. Eph. 1:11). In 7:15–8:15 Solomon reflected on the advantages and limitations of wisdom.

The polarity in Ecclesiastes, which reproduces the true character of this world, is reflected in 7:16. Exaggerated, superficial righteousness is to no avail. Solomon counsels that those who truly fear God should hold fast to wisdom and righteousness (7:18). Even Solomon's wisdom (1 Kings 3:12, 16-28) was insufficient to enable him to comprehend all the mysteries of life (7:23). A wise and upright man or woman is a rare find indeed (7:28-29).

8:1–12:14 WHERE ADVANTAGE CAN BE FOUND AND UNDERSTOOD

8:1–9:1 The Benefits of Wisdom and Fear of God

No one understands a situation or problem like a wise person (8:1). His wisdom "lights up" his countenance as he deals wisely with others. "Vowed before God" (8:2) means the oath of allegiance made in God's name to a ruler at the time of coronation (2 Kings 11:17). Wisdom and authority have limits, even for a king like Solomon (Eccles. 8:6-8). Solomon observed that life did not always operate by the cause and effect, reward-for-good

and punishment-for-bad principle of retribution (8:10-14). For the fifth time, Solomon commended the enjoyment of life as the only means of coping with life's perplexities (8:15). Although believers long to understand the intricate details of God's plan, even their most diligent efforts will not remove the mystery (8:17). Whether life's circumstances are happy ("love") or unhappy ("hatred"), there is consolation in knowing that God is in control (i.e., everything is "in God's hand," 9:1).

9:2-12 The Impact of Death
9:2-6 DEATH TREATS EVERYONE THE SAME
Death is no respecter of persons (9:2). One fate (death) awaits both the wicked and the righteous. Solomon conceded that the living have an advantage over the dead (9:4), for the dead have no further opportunities to secure reward for their life's labors (9:4-6).

9:7-12 ENJOY LIFE
Solomon once again (the sixth time) commended the enjoyment of life (9:7-10). White garments were customarily worn at a festival (9:8). Solomon was saying, "Don't wait for tomorrow's festival to find relief from today's frustrations. Enjoy life now; live each day as a celebration." Solomon added a new dimension to his advice—taking hold of a present opportunity (9:10). Life is not just a party; it is an opportunity to serve God and mankind. The fact that such opportunities are limited to life on earth makes it imperative that no day be wasted. There is no guarantee of reward for life's endeavors (9:11-12). A person's success and life span are not guaranteed by his ability or health.

9:13–11:6 The Benefits of Wisdom
9:13-10:4 WISDOM IMPRESSES OTHER PEOPLE
In 9:13–11:6 Solomon presented another series of proverbs on wisdom and folly (cf. 7:1-14). A confident and calm composure may dispel a king's anger (10:4).

10:5–11:6 BOLDNESS IN LIVING IN THE PRESENT
Successful living starts with the practical application of God's wisdom (10:10). Lacking discipline, the fool wastes his energies and is unable to accomplish even the most basic tasks (10:15). The attitude of the undisciplined princes mentioned in 10:16 is expressed in 10:19. In this context, "a little bird" (10:20) is a poetic expression referring to a disclosure by some unknown source.

Some active response to life's opportunities is necessary, even when success is not guaranteed (11:2). Many of life's circumstances are outside the sphere of man's influence or control (11:3). Uncertainty in life sometimes makes people overly cautious with the result that nothing gets done

(11:4). The theme of God's mysterious ways is repeated once again (11:5; cf. 3:11; 7:14; 8:17).

11:7–12:8 The Impact of Judgment

11:7-10 ENJOY LIFE
God's gift of life ("light") should be fully enjoyed, especially in view of the fact that it will eventually terminate with death ("dark days"; 11:7-8). Once again, Solomon exhorted the reader to enjoy life (11:9-10). There is no suggestion of embracing sinful pleasures in his words, "Do everything you want to do." The last line of 11:9 would curb any tendency toward excess.

12:1-8 LIVE CORRECTLY
Solomon exhorted his readers to remember God before they were overtaken by old age and poor health (12:1-7). Old age is described as a gathering storm (12:2) and as an old man (12:5). "Even the chirping of birds will wake you up" (12:4) describes one's inability to sleep; being "afraid of heights" (12:5) is difficulty in descending stairs. The phrase "the silver cord of life snaps" (12:6) means loss of life support; "golden bowl is broken" is the crash of death; "water jar is smashed" is the loss of fragile life; "pulley is broken at the well" means that the apparatus for sustaining life is ruined.

The body returns to dust, but the spirit returns to God for judgment (12:7; cf. John 5:28-29). The original thesis is repeated (12:8; cf. 1:2).

12:9-14 Conclusion: Fear the Lord
Solomon affirmed that his writings were upright and true (12:10). The words of Ecclesiastes have a divine source (12:11). They come from "a Shepherd" (God). The parallel relationship between the words "fear God" and "obey his commandments" reveals that the fear of the Lord is observed and proved by obeying God's word (12:13). The words "duty of every person" imply that wisdom is what the lives of human beings are really all about. The reminder regarding final accountability before God serves to curb any improper application of the counsel to enjoy life (12:14).

SONG OF SONGS

BASIC FACTS

HISTORICAL SETTING

This book gives the dialogue of a king, his wife, and her friends in the king's harem. The man and woman described their love for each other, while the friends praised the woman's beauty and favored place before the king. The reader hears about the beauty of love from several directions. The particular setting was the harem of King Solomon.

AUTHOR

The book itself names Solomon as the chief figure throughout (1:1, 5; 3:7, 9, 11; 8:11-12). Although Solomon's direct authorship has been debated, the text of the book affirms Solomon or someone in his immediate court as the writer. Some scholars believe that the song was written long after Solomon's days but attributed to his style as a writer of wisdom literature. They allege that certain words in the song come from later Persian and Greek times, making the possible composition or final editing of the work around the time of the Babylonian exile. In this case, the reference to Solomon in 1:1 is translated, "This is Solomon's song of songs." Although the final editing of the book may have been done around the time of the Exile (around 587 B.C.), the book's wisdom and its description of the unity and luxury of the kingdom fit well with Solomon's reign and his own abilities as an author.

DATE

Solomonic authorship places the date during his reign (970–930 B.C.). It may have gone through a final editing process around the time of Judah's exile (around 587 B.C.).

PURPOSE

As in many of the psalms, the reader of the Song of Songs is not directly addressed. He is simply told what two lovers (Solomon and his bride) said and is thus drawn into their relationship. But what kind of application of this relationship are readers to make to their own lives? The purpose of the book was twofold. First, through its splendid poetry, God affirms the goodness of sexual love. Second, the repeated passages of warning (2:7; 3:5; 8:4) command the listener to set love within its proper context of marriage. Like the Bible's other books that express the wisdom and poetry of Israel, the Song of Songs instructs and inspires concerning the beauties and proper contexts of physical love.

GUIDING CONCEPTS

SOME APPROACHES TO INTERPRETING THE BOOK

Throughout history people have interpreted this book from various and quite different perspectives. Some interpreters view the book as a straightforward love song or collection of several love songs that speak of the beauties of human sexual love within the context of marriage. Other interpreters either exclude or diminish the erotic aspects in order to find a more symbolic purpose for the book. In this view, the man and woman are symbols of God and his people. The love of the man is compared to the love of God for Israel or to the love of Christ for his church.

Other interpreters have viewed the book as a collection of love or wedding songs, a dramatic script or a reflection of pagan fertility rites made over into acceptable Jewish theology. But the literal thrust of praising the love between a man and a woman, in this case, king Solomon and one of his wives, is the simplest and most straightforward way to interpret the book.

The symbolic approach to the book is deeply rooted in early Jewish and then Christian interpretations and essentially grows out of a discomfort with viewing a book of the Bible as so completely dedicated to the joys of the human sexual relationship. But the book in and of itself gives no clue that it is to be taken in a symbolic way. It presents itself as a literal poem extolling marital love. Thus, the book must first be seen as primarily instructive on the level of human sexual fulfillment. Another dimension to appreciate may then be explored when the book is placed into its Bible-wide context. Then the king and his love for his bride may secondarily take on a symbolic representation of God and his love for his people.

THE SHEPHERD

Some interpreters conclude that the figures of the shepherd and of Solomon are two different characters. Thus, Solomon becomes the villain who is trying to take the lady into his harem, away from her true love, the shepherd. Others view the shepherd and Solomon to be the same figure. Solomon was in casual dress when he visited his northern property, part of which was the vineyard of the Shulammite (6:13). That she first saw Solomon in shepherd's attire accounts for the kingly and shepherdly descriptions of him throughout the song.

DIALOGUE

One powerful feature of this song is the way the man and woman describe their love for each other in the second person: "What a lovely filly you are, my beloved one" (1:9). That allows the reader to feel that he is being let into a very intimate relationship, much like reading someone else's love letter. Why this style? First, because it drives the sensualness and beauty of physical love deep into the reader's consciousness. Second, as the word of God, it provides a definition of love by which people can judge their own love relationships, and it leads them to consider the vitality and sanctity of those relationships. Another powerful feature is the repeated command, issued to the other members of Solomon's harem, to keep love within its proper context (2:7; 3:5; 8:4).

BIBLE-WIDE CONCEPTS

HUMAN LOVE

Ever since Adam first saw Eve, human love at its best has been the driving force for populating the earth and bringing man and woman into a fulfilled relationship of marriage in light of God's original creation order. Although Scripture also describes numerous negative examples of human lust at its worst, the Song of Songs takes its place in reinforcing what God really intended from the beginning. That this song concerns Solomon's wedding is especially significant. Here, the son of David, anointed over Israel as king according to the Davidic covenant, was about to take his bride. To have seen the king so passionately and appropriately in love with his bride would have been an encouragement to his people that he was strong, virile, and caring. But that leads the reader on to the divine dimension involved in the anointed king of Israel.

DIVINE LOVE

To see the greater Son of David, Jesus the anointed King, behind the figure of Solomon is inescapable. Whereas the Jewish interpretation viewed the Song of Songs as an expression of God's love for Israel, the Christian interpretation put it within the frame of Christ's love for the church. But the symbolism is best established on the basis of the Davidic covenant, which always looked forward to the fullness of God's rule through his anointed King. Israel's king was always a visible representative for God in his love and sovereignty over his people. On human and divine levels, the Song of Songs shows the beauties of physical and spiritual love—of a man for his wife and of God for his people.

NEEDS MET BY THE SONG OF SONGS

Throughout Scripture, poetry is part of God's word because it can draw a person's emotions, as well as his mind, into the subject at hand. With the Song of Songs, the subject is erotic love. The point is to sanctify it and put it in its biblical context. In this case it is the context of the divinely anointed king of Israel. The following are some questions that were undoubtedly asked in Solomon's day. These same questions are often asked by people today as well.

- Are strong erotic feelings appropriate for godly people?
- What does God say about physical love?

God has created humanity with virtually insatiable sexual drives. But, as with the rest of the passions instilled at the original creation, sexual passion has been grossly perverted and distorted by Satan's schemes and the acts of sinful people. The Song of Songs breaks into the sexual madness that so often surrounds believers today with a graphic description of God's blessing on erotic love. But that description also clearly sets the confines of such love within marriage. The Song of Songs gives the person desiring to marry a beautiful goal to await. It gives the married person encouragement to seek similar mutual sexual fulfillment. It gives the immoral person a glimpse of the beauty God offers in place of degrading sexual counterfeits. It gives all believers a physical symbol of God's own spiritual love for them in Christ.

OUTLINE OF THE SONG OF SONGS

I. TITLE (1:1)

II. IN THE KING'S CHAMBERS: THE BRIDE DESCRIBES HERSELF AND HOW SHE FEELS ABOUT HER FIANCÉ (1:2–2:7)

III. THE KING INVITES HIS BRIDE FOR A SPRINGTIME TRIP; THE BRIDE DREAMS OF LOSING THE KING (2:8–3:5)

IV. SOLOMON DESCRIBES HIS BRIDE (3:6–5:1)

V. THE BRIDE DESCRIBES HER HUSBAND (5:2–6:3)

VI. THE KING DESCRIBES HIS WIFE (6:4–7:9)

VII. THE DESIRES OF THE WOMAN (7:10–8:4)

VIII. THE POWER OF LOVE AND THE REWARDS OF PURITY (8:5-14)

SONG OF SONGS NOTES

1:1 TITLE
The words "song of songs" are a translation of the Hebrew superlative that could be rendered "most excellent of songs." Of the 1,005 songs Solomon wrote (1 Kings 4:32), this one was regarded as the very best.

1:2–2:7 IN THE KING'S CHAMBERS: THE BRIDE DESCRIBES HERSELF AND HOW SHE FEELS ABOUT HER FIANCÉ
The Shulammite spoke of Solomon (1:1-4). The word "Shulammite" means a "maid of Shulam" (6:13). The Hebrew word for "love" (1:2) here refers to sexual love. The "young women" (1:3) were the young ladies of the court, the "women of Jerusalem" (1:5). The Hebrew word for "love" in 1:3 refers to a love growing out of the will, similar to the Greek *agapé*. The word may sometimes include sexual love, but it is not limited to that. The daughters of Jerusalem spoke of Solomon (1:4).

The Shulammite spoke about herself (1:5-6) to Solomon (1:7). Her complexion had been darkened ("tanned," 1:5) from working in the "hot sun" (1:6). The "tents of Kedar" (1:5) were made of black goat's hair. The family background of the Shulammite is revealed in the fact that she had two older brothers who forced her to work in their vineyard. As a result, she was unable to care for her own vineyard, a figurative reference to her own physical being. Solomon may have been on a hunting trip when he first encountered the Shulammite, who evidently mistook him for a shepherd (1:7). This verse is used by some interpreters in support of the "shepherd hypothesis," which posits that the cast of the book consists of three persons: (1) the shepherd; (2) the lady who loves the shepherd; and (3) Solomon, who tries to win her away from the shepherd.

Solomon spoke to the Shulammite (1:8-11). The word "beloved" refers to a beloved companion (1:9, 15; 2:2, 10, 13). The "filly" is an image of strength, form, and beauty (1:9; cf. 1 Kings 4:26). The Shulammite spoke about Solomon (1:12-14). The "bouquet of flowers" (1:14) refer to a fragrant yellow and white flower that grew at Engedi, an oasis on the west shore of the Dead Sea. Solomon spoke to the Shulammite (1:15), and she responded to his love (1:16-17).

She reflected on her appearance, expressing her own lack of self-esteem (2:1). The "rose" (lit., "crocus") was a humble meadow flower. Solomon talked to the Shulammite, elevating her sense of self-worth (2:2). She replied to Solomon telling of her contentment and delight in his love (2:3-6), and she also expressed her desire for sexual intimacies. The Hebrew word translated "embrace" is used in a sexual sense and may be rendered "fondle" (2:6; cf. Prov. 5:20).

The Shulammite addressed the young virgins of the royal court concerning the importance of remaining chaste prior to marriage (Song of Songs 2:7). The words "awaken love" can better be rendered "arouse the sexual expression of love," while "until the time is right" can better be translated "until it pleases," that is, "until it is with the right person within the bounds of marriage." This warning against premarital sexual arousal appears three times (2:7; 3:5; 8:4).

2:8–3:5 THE KING INVITES HIS BRIDE FOR A SPRINGTIME TRIP; THE BRIDE DREAMS OF LOSING THE KING
The Shulammite talked about Solomon, recalling his marriage proposal (2:8-13). Then he spoke to her (2:14). The word "dove" (2:14) is a term of endearment. The Shulammite, in mentioning their relationship, resolved to prevent any distraction ("foxes") from spoiling it (2:15). She spoke again of her relationship with Solomon (2:16-17). The

"rugged mountains" (2:17) can be translated from the Hebrew as "mountains of cleavage."

The Shulammite dreamed of seeking and then finding Solomon (3:1-5). She sensed a critical need for Solomon's companionship in the early days of their marriage. The warning against arousing sexual love prematurely was set against the background of the difficulties of marital adjustment (cf. 2:7).

3:6–5:1 SOLOMON DESCRIBES HIS BRIDE

The daughters of Jerusalem described the bridal procession to Jerusalem (3:6-10). Solomon's "carriage" was a chair set on poles and enclosed by a small canopy. It would have been carried by the king's servants. Solomon's mother was Bathsheba (1 Kings 1:11).

Solomon described the beauty of his bride (Song of Songs 4:1-5) in imaginative and highly poetic imagery. The Shulammite (cf. 2:17) interrupted the praise of Solomon anticipating the consummation of her marriage (4:6). In the meantime, she would spend time in Solomon's royal garden, where imported myrrh and frankincense grow. These fragrant trees were not native to any part of Israel. Solomon's marriage proposal and praise for his bride is given in 4:7-15. Solomon invited the Shulammite to leave her homeland, the mountains of Lebanon, and go with him to Jerusalem. The "garden" imagery (4:12) is used to refer to the Shulammite's physical body, which she had saved exclusively ("private") for her future husband, Solomon. The "spring that no one else can drink from" and "fountain of my own" (4:12) are poetic figures for virginity (cf. Prov. 5:15-18). The Shulammite invited Solomon to consummate their marriage (Song of Songs 4:16). The imagery of eating and drinking was used as a euphemism for the sexual delights of marriage. After the marriage had been consummated (5:1), the lovers were instructed to enjoy their love fully.

5:2–6:3 THE BRIDE DESCRIBES HER HUSBAND

The Shulammite dreamed of refusing Solomon (5:2-7). After rejecting his late-night advances, she had sought help from the daughters of Jerusalem in finding him. After they ask her for a description of Solomon, she responded by describing her beloved in highly figurative poetic language (5:10-16). The daughters of Jerusalem then asked her where to look for Solomon (6:1). The Shulammite directed them to look in the king's garden (6:2-3).

6:4–7:9 THE KING DESCRIBES HIS WIFE

Solomon described the Shulammite as he and his bride were reunited (6:4-9). Tirzah was the capital of

the northern kingdom until Omri built a new capital at Samaria (1 Kings 14:17). Solomon eventually had seven hundred wives and three hundred concubines (1 Kings 11:3), but evidently he viewed the Shulammite as unique, possibly the only wife he truly loved. The daughters of Jerusalem praised the Shulammite's beauty (6:10). Verse 6:10 may reflect the praise of the Shulammite's beauty by the daughters of Jerusalem. Because of the response in 6:13, verses 6:11-12 may reflect the Shulammite's words rather than her lover's. Royalty came upon the Shulammite suddenly, before she had a chance to realize what was happening (6:12). The daughters asked to gaze upon the Shulammite's beauty (6:13). Solomon questioned, "Why do you [the daughters of Jerusalem] gaze so intently at this young woman of Shulam, as she moves so gracefully between two lines of dancers?" When Solomon spoke to the Shulammite, extolling her beauty (7:1-9), she responded to his expressions of love (7:9-10).

7:10–8:4 THE DESIRES OF THE WOMAN

The Shulammite asked Solomon to take her on a kind of marriage enrichment retreat in the country (7:10-13). In ancient times "man-drakes" (7:13), small apple-like herbs, were thought to stimulate sexual desire and aid in conception.

The Shulammite expressed her desire for a closer relationship with Solomon (8:1-4). Once again (cf. 2:7; 3:5), the request for sexual intimacies was followed by a warning to avoid the premature arousal of sexual love.

8:5-14 THE POWER OF LOVE AND THE REWARDS OF PURITY

The villagers raised the question of 8:5 as they saw Solomon and the Shulammite approaching. Solomon recalled his courtship and spoke words of love to her (8:5-7). Genuine love can only be given, never bought. The last line of 8:7 is best translated "his offer would be utterly despised." The Shulammite's brothers spoke regarding the proper care of her young, immature sister (8:8), recognizing two possible situations (8:9). If she was "chaste," her chastity would be honored; but if she was "promiscuous," measures would be taken to protect her from the sexual advances of young men. The Shulammite reflected on her own virtue and submission to Solomon in marriage (8:10-12). She spoke of her physical body as "my own vineyard" (8:12; cf. 1:6), which she had surrendered to Solomon in marriage. The "two hundred pieces of silver" were for her brothers, who had a part in encouraging her own chastity (8:12). When Solomon requested that she sing him a song (8:13), she responded in song, inviting him to enjoy her as she had promised (8:14; cf. 7:12).

ISAIAH

HISTORICAL SETTING

Throughout Isaiah's life Assyria presented a great threat to God's people. In 853 B.C. Assyria came into direct conflict with Ahab of Israel. In 745 B.C. Menahem of Israel paid tribute money to Tiglath-pileser III. Two kings later, Hoshea rebelled against Assyria. That brought about the destruction and deportation of the northern kingdom of Israel (722 B.C.). Isaiah prophesied before and after the downfall of the northern kingdom of Israel and successfully warned the southern kingdom, Judah, to avoid the same fate by returning to God. Under Hezekiah, the nation repented and was saved from destruction by the Assyrians (701 B.C.). Although the threat of Assyria was diminished, the greater threat of the rising nation of Babylonia loomed in the future. Although Isaiah predicted the Babylonian captivity, he also proclaimed the future restoration of the nation to the glory of God.

The book of Isaiah is centered around three key historical events. The first is the coalition between Syria and Ephraim in the days of Ahaz (Isa. 7–12; cf. 2 Kings 16:5-9). The second is the fall of the northern kingdom of Samaria (722 B.C.; Isa. 28:1ff.). The third is the invasion of Judea by Sennacherib in 701 B.C. (Isa. 36–39).

AUTHOR

The book presents itself as the words of Isaiah the prophet, who ministered from around 740 to 700 B.C. Many scholars believe the book is divided between two authors—Isaiah, who wrote Isaiah 1–39, and another prophet who lived some two hundred years later (Isa. 40–66). To be sure, Isaiah 40–66 are quite different in content and mood from Isaiah 1–39. But that difference is due to Isaiah's looking beyond the eighth century B.C. to the time of the Babylonian captivity, and beyond, to the time of the new heavens and earth.

DATE

Isaiah's call came in the year of Uzziah's death (740 B.C.). Isaiah noted three kings under whom he ministered: Jotham of Judah (750–732 B.C.; who was coregent with Uzziah), Ahaz of Israel (735–716 B.C.), and Hezekiah of Judah (716–687 B.C.). The composition of Isaiah may be placed sometime after 701 B.C. and before the prophet's death.

PURPOSE

Isaiah related prophecies predicting inescapable judgment for the world and highlighted the comfort offered to the righteous remnant. The Anointed One of God would be the leader of God's restored world. The catalysts for God's actions of judgment and restoration were his holiness (Isa. 6) and his loving-kindness (Isa. 63:7). The message was that God's victory would come through a time of humiliation for his people and for his Servant. Exaltation would come after humiliation. That message was designed to encourage repentance by looking to past and future judgments and to the future blessings for service in times of suffering.

GEOGRAPHY AND ITS IMPORTANCE

The geographical scope of Isaiah moves from the land of Israel, to the nations of the world, to the destruction and re-creation of the entire earth. The central focus moves from the immediate threat of Assyria to the future conquests of Babylonia and Persia. Israel is attacked, taken captive to foreign lands, and restored to her homeland. These geographical cycles—of captivity and restoration, and destruction and creation—ultimately reflect the great spiritual cycles of sin and forgiveness, offense and reconciliation.

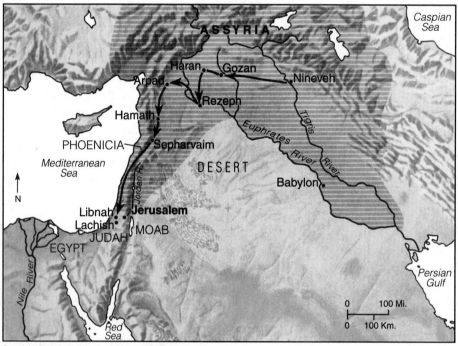

GUIDING CONCEPTS

THE STRUCTURE OF ISAIAH
Dates

Several dates are given in the book of Isaiah that mark off its structure and highlight its message. The book's first verse mentions several kings and also functions as a summary title for the entire prophecy. The dates of those kings began in 792 B.C. (Uzziah) and ended in 687 B.C. (Hezekiah). Isaiah 1–5 is devoted to Israel's condemnation and reflects no specific date. Isaiah 6 is dated around 740 B.C., the year Uzziah died. Isaiah

7–12 is dated in the days of Ahaz, around 735 B.C. (7:1). Isaiah 13–66 mentions the specific dates of the death of Ahaz (14:28; 715 B.C.), the arrival of the commander under Sargon III at Ashdod (20:1; 711 B.C.), the fourteenth year of Hezekiah's reign (36:1; 701 B.C.), and the year Sennacherib died (37:38; 681 B.C.). Isaiah 13–66 falls within the general time period of King Hezekiah's reign (716–687 B.C.).

Judgment

The primary foci of the book are judgment (Isa. 1–39) and comfort (Isa. 40–66). Isaiah 1–39 punctuates each specific judgment section with incredible announcements of God's worldwide judgment and the restoration of his people. See the accompanying chart, *Judgment and Restoration.*

First, judgment was announced upon Israel (Isa. 1–12) for her broken covenant (1:1-31) and her pride (Isa. 2–6). But Israel would be exalted through chastisement because God would be with her (Isa. 7–12). The focus was on the faithless alliance of Ahaz with Assyria. Second, judgment was announced upon the nations (Isa. 13–27). Specific nations were named, but the section ends with God reigning supreme over all (27:13). Third, judgment was again announced upon Israel for her trust in foreign alliances with Egypt (Isa. 28–35) and Hezekiah's foolish boasting to the Babylonians (Isa. 36–39). In Isaiah 1–39 judgment fell upon the nations for their mistreatment of Israel and upon Israel for her inappropriate trust in them, especially in Assyria, Egypt, and Babylonia. The three centers of Israel's misplaced trust were the three centers of her most cruel captivities. Isaiah 36–39 forms a transition from Assyrian to Babylonian concerns.

Comfort

Isaiah 40–66 is divided into three sections, each ending with similar phrases (48:22; 57:21; 66:24). The first section (40:1–48:22) emphasizes ultimate deliverance from Babylonia through the incomparable greatness of God. The second section (49:1–57:21) describes the servant of God, Israel, in her worldwide calling. Her leadership is rebuked (Isa. 56) and invitations to salvation are given (Isa. 51). The third section (58:1–66:24) provides the conditions for seeing the future glory of God. Israel is divided into the faithful and faithless. The faithful remnant cries out for deliverance (63:7–64:12), receives an answer from God (65:1-25), and learns about those who will be excluded from the new creation (66:1-24).

BIBLE-WIDE CONCEPTS

THE EXODUS AND ISAIAH

Exodus themes and the exiles

Isaiah frequently linked the Babylonian and Egyptian captivities together. The Egyptian

JUDGMENT AND RESTORATION

	Specific Judgment	Worldwide Judgment and Restoration
On Israel	Isaiah 2–10	Isaiah 11–12
On the Nations	Isaiah 13–23	Isaiah 24–27
On Israel's Alliance with Egypt	Isaiah 28–33	Isaiah 34–35
On Israel's Boasting to Babylon	Isaiah 36–39	

bondage had both preserved and oppressed Israel. The same was true of Israel's captivity in Babylon. God had released Israel from Egypt in a mighty display of his love and power. The same applied to Israel's release from Babylon. Israel was released from Egypt to claim her Promised Land. Israel was released from Babylon to regather and reclaim her inheritance of land and redemptive promises. The tension between bondage and release would be repeated again as Christ released believers from the bondage of personal sin, and it will occur for the final time as the new heavens and earth are released into the new creation. Jeremiah saw a future time when Israel would not refer to the Exodus but to the restoration from the Captivity as the most recent and great act of God's salvation (Jer. 16:14-15).

The Exodus in Isaiah
The "exodus and release" theme pervades Isaiah's prophecy (10:24-27; 11:16; 19:24-25; 27:12-13; 30:1-3; 31:1; 36:6; 43:3; 45:14; 48:20-21; 52:4-6; 66:2, 22-23). For a nation entering captivity, the question of God's power over the gods of Assyria and Babylonia was a burning issue (21:9; 48:20-21), but God had already shown himself to be the victor over the gods of Egypt at the Exodus.

The Exodus and Creation
Creation and redemption are closely intertwined in Scripture. Isaiah described Israel's past and future redemption in view of God being her Creator. Read carefully the following passages: Isaiah 43:1-7, 15-21; 51:12-16; 63:7-14 (cf. also 42:5-7; 44:21-28; 48:13; 45:18). Neither creation nor exodus were simply onetime events. They were continuous models of God's ability to bring freedom out of bondage and order out of chaos. Paul described Christianity in terms of the creation (2 Cor. 5:16-17), the exodus Passover (1 Cor. 5:7-8), and the wilderness wanderings (1 Cor. 10:1-4).

As Creator, God can judge evil by returning the earth to its pre-creation formlessness and void (Isa. 24:1-6; cf. Gen. 6–8). He is also always present and powerful to re-create both his people and a new universe (Isa. 51:16). That creative power became the basis for the redemption of his people and the commission of them to a worldwide mission of witness (45:18-25). The remnant was preserved through the destruction and re-creation process, and the world was exhorted to join in that preservation and redemption.

THE HOPE FOR A DIVINE KING
Isaiah's prophecy deepened and broadened God's promise that a Davidic king would rule forever. The promises to David looked toward a Davidic Ruler who, contrary to worldly standards, would come to a throne of international proportions through suffering and humiliation. Isaiah called this Ruler the Branch, Servant, and Shoot (4:2; 11:1; 42:1; 52:13–53:12). That Davidic branch found its fulfillment in Jesus, the King of Israel. His humiliation brought the forgiveness of sins to all believers. His exaltation assured their eternal future in his presence. The combination of first the Servant's humiliation and second his exaltation also became the pattern for his followers. Jesus taught that a time of humble service and suffering comes before the time of the servant's exaltation and reward (Matt. 10:24-39; 24:9-13, 30-31; Mark 8:31-38; John 15:18-25).

THE FULFILLMENT OF ABRAHAMIC BLESSINGS
Isaiah described the fulfillment of God's promises to Abraham. The Abrahamic themes of *land, seed,* and *blessing* are found throughout the book (29:22; 41:8-11; 51:1-3;

63:16). All these promises look back to the original and perfect creation and ahead to the perfection of the new heavens and earth.

Israel's possession, or nonpossession, of the land promised to Abraham became a barometer for measuring their obedience. When discipline was needed, God used the hostility of and even captivity by other nations to bring about Israel's repentance, a punishment about which Moses and Solomon, among others, had repeatedly warned (Deut. 32:1-47; 1 Kings 8:33-34, 46-51; 9:6-9). Israel's disobedience resulted in God allowing hostile nations to succeed in their attacks and exile his people from the Promised Land. But God had also promised to protect Abraham and his descendants, blessing those who blessed them and cursing those who cursed them (Gen. 12:3). This promise of Israel's preservation pervades Isaiah (34:8; 35:4), while the enemies of Israel are cursed in judgment. In fact, the only way a curse could be brought upon God's people was for them to bring it upon themselves by their own rebellion against God.

God's judgment upon Israel's enemies is described in great detail (cf., for example, Isa. 12) and finds its completion in the gruesome judgments of the book of Revelation. Hostility against God's righteous people found its origin in Satan in Genesis 3. This hostility will find its end in Satan's judgment at the end of the age when Satan comes out in full force against God's people (Rev. 12:1-17). But God will defeat all of Satan's hostile nations, and then the promises to Abraham, which were always with a view to "all the families of the earth" (Gen. 12:3), will be fulfilled when the Promised Land of God's blessing is fully realized in the new heavens and earth (Isa. 65:17, 25; 66:1-24; Rev. 21:1–22:6). Then the themes of creation and redemption will perfectly merge. The Promised Land will be global and perfect, populated by the redeemed who will be perfect in soul and in body.

NEEDS MET BY ISAIAH

The original readers of the book of Isaiah lived in an Israel that had recently lost its northern half to Assyrian captivity (722 B.C.) and whose southern half, including the holy city of Jerusalem, was escaping a similar fate only by God's grace and the rare obedience of a few of Judah's kings. Through Isaiah, God told his people of all the painful discipline and beautiful salvation he had in store. He exposed how his people tended to forget their call to be holy and blame God when being disciplined for their own sins. Because of their present and impending judgment, God showed his people how to maintain hope for salvation in the middle of painful judgment. Even though righteous people like Ezekiel and Daniel would have to undergo war and captivity, God's people were not to lose heart, become bitter, or give up seeking to fear God.

The book of Isaiah is of massive scope and proportions and therefore covers a multitude of topics and needs. At its heart is an announcement of judgment, a call to repentance, and a message of hope after suffering a time of humiliation. These central themes give answers to questions that God's people were asking in Isaiah's day.

- Why is the nation of Israel suffering military and economic trouble?
- Why is God angry at Israel—what did they do?
- Why is God allowing wicked foreign nations to attack Israel and get away with it?
- If God is punishing the people of Israel for their sins, is there any hope for the future?

- How can any good come out of Israel's personal and national humiliation?
- What can be done to escape God's terrible judgment?
- What do the people of Israel need to do to repent and turn from their sins?

Readers may find the long descriptions of Israel's and other nations' judgments repetitive and without any apparent Christian application. But the very length of the book of Isaiah is a large part of its point. Why did God tell in such detail that his people were forgetful and sinful, that their enemies would be destroyed, and that a glorious future lay ahead? God went to great lengths to remind his people of these things because they were so forgetful. He described at great length the ultimate defeat of Israel's enemies because his people tended to fear the forces of world evil and wondered if they would win out in the end. Because believers in Isaiah's day (like today) tended to forget what a bright future was in store for them, and especially how that future hope was to encourage and direct them into present joy and obedience, God described the future blessings in great detail. The long book of Isaiah meets three continuing needs of all believers: to be reminded of (1) God's past acts of redemption for them, (2) his present abilities to protect them from evil, and (3) his future plans for their complete blessing and his fully revealed glory.

OUTLINE OF ISAIAH

I. INESCAPABLE JUDGMENT AND HOPE FOR ISRAEL (1:1–12:6)
   A. God's Lawsuit against Judah (1:1-31)
   B. God's Exaltation over the Proud (2:1–6:13)
   C. Restoration through Chastisement: Judgment on Ahaz (7:1–12:6)

II. GLOBAL JUDGMENT: MOTIVATION FOR REPENTANCE (13:1–27:13)
   A. Babylon (13:1–14:27)
   B. Nations Surrounding Israel (14:28–17:14)
   C. Ethiopia and Egypt (18:1–20:6)
   D. Four Symbolic Titles of Judgment (21:1–22:25)
   E. Tyre (23:1–18)
   F. Global Response after Global Judgment (24:1–27:13)

III. BOOK OF WOES: FOREIGN ALLIANCES CONTINUED (28:1–35:10)
   A. Samaria and Jerusalem: Fall and Comfort (28:1-29)
   B. Ariel: Fall and Comfort (29:1-24)
   C. Results of Egyptian Alliance: Part One (30:1-33)
   D. Results of Egyptian Alliance: Part Two (31:1–32:30)
   E. Deliverance and Glory of Jerusalem (33:1-24)
   F. Finale of Judgment (34:1–35:10)

IV. TWO SIGNS OF DELIVERANCE (36:1–39:8)
   A. Assyrian Threats: The Faith of Hezekiah (36:1–37:38)
   B. Babylonian Overtones (38:1–39:8)

V. CYCLES OF COMFORT AFTER CAPTIVITY (40:1–66:24)
   A. God Contrasted with Idols (40:1–48:22)
   B. The Servant's Humiliation and Exaltation (49:1–57:21)
   C. Israel: The Faithful and the Faithless (58:1–66:24)

ISAIAH NOTES

1:1–12:6 INESCAPABLE JUDGMENT AND HOPE FOR ISRAEL

1:1-31 God's Lawsuit against Judah

Overview: Isaiah 1 is an introductory message containing the themes of the entire book: the sinfulness of Israel, the tender appeals of God, certain judgment, and promised blessings of restoration. All the promises for Judah and Jerusalem can be found in summary form in the first chapter of Isaiah.

1:1 AUTHOR, DATE, ADDRESSEES

Isaiah prophesied during the reigns of four different kings, and he addressed the problems and people of those reigns. Uzziah (791–739 B.C.), also known as Azariah, was a good king. Jotham (750–731 B.C.) was also a good king. Ahaz (743–715 B.C.) was wicked and idolatrous. Hezekiah (728–686 B.C.) was a godly king and a religious reformer.

1:2-31 THE COMPLAINT IS DEVELOPED

Isaiah is first presented in his role as a prosecuting attorney in behalf of God, indicting the sinful nation for breaking the law of the Mosaic covenant (1:2-3). The "heavens" and "earth" were called upon as "witnesses" against the covenant breakers (cf. Deut. 4:26; 30:19). Five terms are used for sin in 1:4 to describe the sinful condition of the people of Judah. "Sinful" means "to miss the mark"; "guilt" is "to bend or twist aside"; "evil" are those who "do harm and injury"; "corrupt" means "to ruin, to destroy"; and "despised" means "to be estranged or to revolt." The title "the Holy One of Israel," which is almost unique to Isaiah, appears twenty-four times in the book.

The sickness described here is a metaphor for sin (1:5-6). God had disciplined the nation, but the people had not repented and been healed. During Isaiah's lifetime, the land of Judah was devastated by foreign armies that God used to discipline his people (1:7-9).

In 1:11-15, God was not rejecting the Levitical blood sacrifices. He only rejected the religious hypocrisy that usually went along with them. Many brought sacrifices to God, but their worship was merely external and they lacked sincere love for God (cf. 1 Sam. 15:22; Jer. 7:21-23; Hos. 6:6; Amos 5:21-24). The "new moon" (1:13) was a minor religious festival celebrating the appearance of a new moon (cf. 1 Chron. 23:31). Isaiah was not suggesting salvation by works (1:16). He simply emphasized the Lord's promise to cleanse those who come to him by faith and through the appointed way of sacrifice (Isa. 1:18; cf. Lev. 4:20).

The orphan and the widow were regarded as the defenseless in Israelite society (1:17; cf. Deut. 10:18; 24:19). There was a lament over the moral decline of God's people (Isa. 1:21-23). The "watered-down wine" (1:22) is probably a reference to wheat beer.

The "therefore" (1:24) refers to all that has preceded, principally the description of the nation's sinful condition. After disciplinary judgment (1:25) comes restoration (1:26). Isaiah carries the reader from history to eschatology, predicting kingdom blessing for the redeemed (1:27) and future judgment for the wicked (1:28-31).

2:1–6:13 God's Exaltation over the Proud

Overview: Isaiah 2:1 presents a clear break from Isaiah 1. Isaiah 2:1–6:13 forms the second subsection and shows the inevitable process leading up to God's international sovereignty (cf. the last phrase in 2:11 and 2:17). The link between Isaiah 1 and Isaiah 2–6 is God's exaltation over the proud (1:2, 4, 20, 31 and, for example, 2:11-17). The heart of 2:1–6:13 is God's specific criticism against his people (3:13–4:6). They were crushing the poor (3:13-15). The results of God's judgment upon his people would be final purification (4:2-6). Isaiah 2:1–4:6 presents a unified thought concerning what will happen in "the last days" (2:2, 20; 3:6-7, 18; 4:2). Esteemed people will be humbled, and God's glory will be exalted.

Isaiah 5 presents the imagery of a vineyard, Israel, that has worthless produce. That judgment and purification are compatible is confirmed in the following vision of God in the temple, purifying Isaiah's lips (6:1-13) in preparation for him to take his prophetic message to Israel. Isaiah's lips were burned unto purification (6:1-7), and the nation itself would endure a burning toward the same end (6:8-13). For God's people, judgment was not for destruction but for purification.

2:1–5:30 GOD'S INTERNATIONAL PROMINENCE IN THE LAST DAYS

2:1-22 A Call to International Repentance

These verses are nearly identical with Micah 4:1-5 and describe the blessings of the future messianic, or kingdom, era. The "last days" (2:2) is a reference to the messianic era when Jesus will return to rule his kingdom (cf. Hos. 3:5). Jerusalem will serve as the center for government, and both Gentiles and Jews will go there to worship Jesus the Messiah. The return to peace will involve a reversal of the prophecy of Joel 3:10. The "people of Israel" (Isa. 2:5) refers to the nation Israel, which descended from Jacob. "In that day" (2:12) is a reference to the day of the Lord, the major theme of Joel and Zephaniah.

3:1-12 Judgment Elaborated

Woe was pronounced for rebellion against God's presence. Judgments on Judah and Jerusalem included famine, drought (3:1), the removal of national leadership (3:4), and poverty (3:6).

3:13–4:6 God's Contention
War would so greatly destroy Israel's male population that women would resort to polygamy or husband-sharing to avoid the reproach of childlessness (4:1). The glories of the messianic kingdom were anticipated in 4:2-6. The "branch" (4:2; lit., "sprout") is a reference to the Messiah (cf. Jer. 23:5), who would grow like a sprout from the fallen "tree" of David (6:13; cf. Luke 1:32-33). The "cloud throughout the day" (4:5) and "clouds of fire at night" recalled God's deliverance and protection at the time of the Exodus.

5:1-30 Vineyard Imagery
Woes were pronounced on worthless deeds. The nation of Israel was portrayed under the figure of a vineyard (5:7; cf. Jer. 12:10; Ps. 80:8-13). The destruction of the vineyard illustrated the judgment to come upon Israel for the nation's disobedience to the Mosaic covenant. Standing in judgment over his people, the Lord pronounced seven exclamatory woes. God condemned selfish greed (5:8-10), dissipation (5:11-17), skepticism (5:18-19), perverted standards (5:20), proud self-sufficiency (5:21), alcoholic excess (5:22), and the perversion of justice (5:23). The "signal" (5:26) is a military banner that served as a gathering point for the nations (that is, Assyria and Babylonia).

6:1-13 JUDGMENT AND PRESERVATION AUTHENTICATE GOD'S MESSAGE
King Uzziah's death in 739 B.C. marked the end of a great period of expansion and prosperity for Judah. "Seraphim" (6:2), literally, "burning ones," are angelic creatures. Here their ministry focused on the worship of God. God was described as thrice holy, a superlative meaning that his holiness is beyond human expression. The theme of God's holiness pervaded Isaiah's prophetic ministry. Isaiah's lips were cleansed in preparation for the commencement of his prophetic ministry. Isaiah's ministry was divinely intended to harden the hearts

of the people (6:9-10). This heartbreaking assignment rested on God's decision to judge the nation. Jesus quoted this text in Matthew 13:14-15, and Paul used it in Acts 28:26-27. The judgment would continue until Judah's removal from the land by the exile. The nation of Israel in exile was portrayed as a fallen and burned tree. But after seventy years in captivity, a "tenth" of the people would return (6:13). And there would be life in the roots of the stump from which the Messiah ("the holy seed") would "grow again".

7:1–12:6 Restoration through Chastisement: Judgment on Ahaz
Overview: Isaiah 7–12 shows how God would bring about restoration through his chastisement of Israel. He used a series of signs that referred first to the contemporary nation and, second, to times beyond his own. Isaiah in 8:18 clearly referred to himself and his children as signs (see chart below).

Isaiah 7–12 was spoken in the context of the coalition by Ahaz against Judah. It stresses that a remnant of the nation will return (7:3). Immanuel ("God with us") is the sign of judgment and of salvation in "that day" (7:18, 20-21, 23; 10:5-34). That day of God is composed of at least two elements: (1) judgment on Israel on the basis of the Mosaic covenant; (2) restoration of Israel around the throne of David by judging Israel's enemies and by restoring Israel's kings on the basis of the Davidic covenant.

7:1-25 THE SIGN OF THE INFANT IMMANUEL
During the reign of Ahaz (743–715 B.C.) Judah was attacked by Pekah (king of Israel) and Rezin (king of Damascus) for refusing to stand against Assyria's aggression under Tiglath-pileser III (745–727 B.C.). The name "Shear-jashub" (7:3) means "a remnant shall return" (that is, from captivity). Judgment on the northern kingdom ("Ephraim") was to come within sixty-five years. Actually, the capital, Samaria,

---

ISAIAH'S SIGNS AND THEIR SIGNIFICANCE

Sign	First reference	Second reference
Shear-jashub "A remnant shall return" (7:3)	Return from the Babylonian exile	The regathering of Israel in the end times
Immanuel "God with us" (7:14)	God's presence to judge and save in the time of Ahaz	Jesus at his first and second comings
Maher-shalal-hash-baz "Swift is the booty; speedy is the prey" (8:3)	Fall of Israel to Babylon	Fall of the world at the Second Coming
Isaiah "God is salvation"	Salvation of the remnant through Babylonian captivity	The final salvation of the remnant (11:4, 11, 16; 12:2)

fell within eleven years in 722 B.C. The Lord commanded Ahaz to ask for a supernatural sign that God would accomplish the deliverance promised (7:11). Ahaz had already made up his mind to appeal to Assyria for help rather than trusting God.

The sign of the "virgin" (7:14) has been variously interpreted. Some interpreters suggest that the prophecy was completely fulfilled in Isaiah's day. Others recognize a fulfillment in the virgin-born Son of Mary (Matt. 1:23). A third position recognizes some kind of fulfillment in the time of Isaiah with a final culmination in the virgin birth of Jesus. Isaiah 8 suggests a fulfillment in Isaiah's day through his wife (8:3, 8, 10, 18). This was probably Isaiah's second wife, and hence a virgin. Matthew recognized that the prophecy had its most complete realization in the birth of Christ. The name "Immanuel" means "God with us" (8:8, 10).

The "curds and honey" (7:15) reflect a diet of natural foods, the only foods available after the agricultural economy had been destroyed (cf. 7:21-23). Before the virgin-born child reached the age of moral perception, judgment would come upon the land of Pekah and Rezin (7:4, 16). That took place during the campaigns of Tiglath-pileser III in 733 and 732 B.C., respectively. The "king of Assyria" (7:17) refers to Tiglath-pileser III. The devastation of Judah (7:20-23) took place during Sennacherib's 701 B.C. campaign (cf. Isa. 36–37).

8:1-4 THE SIGN OF THE TABLET AND SON
"Maher-shalal-hash-baz," the name of Isaiah's second son, means "swift is the booty, speedy is the prey." This son was a symbol of upcoming judgment by the troops of Babylonia.

8:5-10:4 IMMINENT JUDGMENT IN IMMANUEL'S LAND
While Assyria would do its best to destroy Judah, the nation would be spared because of the promise of God's presence (Isa. 8:10; for "Immanuel," see 7:14). Darkness and gloom characterized Galilee in Isaiah's day because of the Assyrian crisis (9:1-2; cf. 2 Kings 15:29). But this would be dispelled by the radiant "light" of the Messiah who would one day shine in Galilee (cf. quote in Matt. 4:15-16). The battle of Midian (Isa. 9:4) was fought by Gideon (Judg. 7–8). Four names were used to describe the coming Immanuel (Isa. 9:6). Each reflects the office of deity and humanity. "Wonderful Counselor" means an extraordinary (godlike) advisor; "Mighty God" means a heroic God; "Everlasting Father" means an everlasting overseer; and "Prince of Peace" means a captain who secures spiritual peace and tranquillity. His government will continue because it rests on the unconditional covenant God made with David (2 Sam. 7:12-16; cf. Luke 1:32-33). The section of Isaiah 9:8–10:4 reflects the doom about to befall the northern kingdom for its

failure to respond to God's discipline. The key phrase "But even then the Lord's anger will not be satisfied. His fist is still poised to strike" (9:12, 17, 21; 10:4) was repeated four times.

10:5-12:6 RESTORATION IN THE LIGHT OF ASSYRIA'S DESTRUCTION
10:5-19 The Time for Assyria's Downfall
Assyria was simply the instrument that God used to judge his people (cf. 10:15). Assyria boasted of the cities north of Judah that it had conquered.

10:20–12:6 Further Implications for Judah's Restoration
The "remnant" referred to the small portion of Israel that would survive the captivity (6:13). They would return to the Lord (10:21) and to the land of Israel (10:22). Isaiah 10:28-32 graphically described the Assyrian advances through Judah toward Jerusalem in preparation for the 701 B.C. siege (cf. 36:1-2). The "shoot" (11:1) that would spring from Jesse (David's father) was the messianic King (4:2; 6:13; 7:14; 8:8, 10; 9:6-7; 11:1-5; 42:1-4; 52:13–53:12; Jer. 23:5). The three pairs of gifts bestowed by the Spirit are intellectual, administrative, and spiritual. Isaiah proclaimed the harmony and peace that will characterize the kingdom as all creation is liberated from the curse resulting from man's fall (Isa. 11:6-9; cf. Gen. 3; Rom. 8:19-22; Rev. 22:3). The "second" (Isa. 11:11) time refers to a regathering of the Jewish people following the tribulation (Matt. 24:15-20, 31). This song of praise (Isa. 12:1) will be sung on that day when the Jews are regathered from among the nations as a believing people. "Isaiah" (meaning "God is salvation") as a sign (8:18) is fulfilled when these events occur.

13:1–27:13 GLOBAL JUDGMENT: MOTIVATION FOR REPENTANCE
Overview: The section of 13:1–23:18, like 2:1, begins with a new heading (13:1). It is a further elaboration of Isaiah 1–12, especially of having God present with his people to judge and rule. The day of God's judgment and rule was elaborated (8:9-10; 13:6, 9-13). In Isaiah 13–23 Isaiah spoke prophecies of judgment on several foreign nations. The point was this: Since the other nations were held accountable for violations of social justice based on the law of conscience (Rom. 2:14), Israel certainly could not expect to escape God's judgment. The greater the light of revelation, the greater the responsibility. The basic topical structure of this section is laid out thus: Babylon (13:1–14:27); Israel's neighbors (14:28–17:14); Ethiopia and Egypt (18:1–20:6); four symbols of judgment (21:1–22:25); and Tyre (23:1-18). The section ends with the international response after God's international judgment (24:1–27:13). The God of Israel alone reigns supreme.

13:1–14:27 Babylon
13:1-22 BABYLON'S DESTRUCTION DESCRIBED
The first oracle concerned Babylon, which served as God's instrument of judgment against Judah in 701 and 586 B.C. In 13:4 the "army" refers to the Medo-Persian troops of Cyrus, who conquered Babylon in 539 B.C. The "Lord's time" (13:6) is a term that can be used historically for God's judgment on a people or place, including Israel. The term is also used for that eschatological period when God will deal out wrath (the tribulation) and blessing (the messianic kingdom). Sometimes when a historical day of the Lord was being described, the writer included some references to future end-time judgment and blessing. The events described in 13:10-13 go beyond the historical judgment on Babylon in 539 B.C. and suggest the end-time judgments of the Tribulation. Strabo, the first century geographer, wrote of Babylon, "A great desert is the great city" (13:19-22).

14:1-27 ISRAEL'S TAUNT AGAINST BABYLON
When Israel returned to her land, enjoying peace and blessing (14:1-3), a taunt song would be sung against the tyrant, "the king of Babylon" (14:4). The deceased tyrant's reception into Sheol, the place of the dead, was described (14:9-11). Instead of being honored as other great kings, this tyrant would receive only dishonor. The words "fallen from heaven" (14:12) figuratively describe the tyrant's loss of political prestige. The words "shining star, son of the morning" can be literally translated "shining one." The Vulgate rendered it by the Latin term "lucifer," meaning "light-bringing." Eventually the Latin word "lucifer" came to be identified as a name for Satan. There is very little evidence to commend this view. Certainly the judgments described in 14:16-21 have not happened to Satan.

Like many proud kings of the ancient Near East, the "king of Babylon" sought divine position and privilege (14:13-15). But such would not be his. Instead, he would be subject to degradation and humiliation (14:16-21). The oracle against Assyria (14:24-27) was fulfilled in Assyria's destruction recorded in 37:21-38.

14:28–17:14 Nations Surrounding Israel
14:28-32 ORACLE AGAINST PHILISTIA
The prophetic oracle against Philistia was dated in the year of King Ahaz's death (715 B.C.). They sought to resist Assyria, but Isaiah predicted their demise (14:30).

15:1–16:14 ORACLE AGAINST MOAB
Moab's judgment, probably by Assyria, was described as swift and complete. Having arrived in Edom, the Moabite refugees appealed to Judah for political asylum. Moab's request was denied because of the nation's pride (16:6).

17:1-14 ORACLE AGAINST DAMASCUS
This oracle was not only against Damascus; it was also spoken against the northern kingdom of Israel. Damascus was the capital of Aram, which Tiglath-pileser III captured for Assyria in 732 B.C. "Asherah poles" (17:8) were wooden pillars representing the Canaanite fertility goddess.

18:1–20:6 Ethiopia and Egypt
18:1-7 ORACLE AGAINST ETHIOPIA
Ethiopia, located south of Egypt, ruled Egypt from 715 to 663 B.C. and pursued an anti-Assyrian foreign policy like Judah's.

19:1–20:6 ORACLE AGAINST EGYPT
Egypt, involved in an anti-Assyrian conspiracy with Judah (cf. 2 Kings 18:21, 24), was conquered by Esarhaddon in 669 B.C. His son Ashurbanipal gained control of all of Egypt in 663 B.C. Egypt was regarded as a haven from famine in time of drought because its water came from the Nile, with its source in the mountain highlands of Africa (19:5-10). For the "waters" of Egypt to dry up would be regarded as a great natural calamity. The "year" (20:1) was 712 B.C., when Tartan, Sargon's general, captured Ashdod, which was situated east of Jerusalem on Israel's coastal plain. Isaiah's scanty attire (2:2) suggested the situation of a prisoner or a person in exile, which was the destiny of Egypt and Ethiopia.

21:1–22:25 Four Symbolic Titles of Judgment
21:1-10 ORACLE AGAINST BABYLON: WILDERNESS OF THE SEA
In cuneiform inscriptions, south Babylonia is called the "land of the sea" because of its proximity to the Persian Gulf. Elam and Media (21:2) are the Persian territories to the north and east of Babylon. See Daniel 5 for the details of this feast. The city of Babylon fell to Cyrus in 539 B.C.

21:11-12 ORACLE AGAINST EDOM: SILENCE
The Hebrew name for "Edom" (21:11) is "Dumah" (21:11), which means "silence" or "stillness," a wordplay that foretells its destruction.

21:13-17 ORACLE AGAINST ARABIA
Cuneiform inscriptions reveal that Arabian rulers paid tribute to Assyrian kings Tiglath-pileser III and Sargon II.

22:1-25 ORACLE AGAINST JERUSALEM: VALLEY OF VISION
The oracle related to the 701 B.C. siege of Jerusalem by Sennacherib. The work of Hezekiah in securing Jerusalem's water supply in anticipation of the Assyrian siege was reflected in 22:11 (cf. 2 Chron. 32:3-4, 30). Shebna (22:15) was a powerful pro-Egyptian politician in the reign of Hezekiah (cf. 2 Kings 18:18). Eliakim became Shebna's replace-

ment (cf. 2 Kings 18:18). The "key" (Isa. 22:22) served as symbol of authority that a steward had over a house (cf. Matt. 16:19).

23:1-18 Oracle against Tyre
Tyre was noted as one of the finest port cities of Phoenicia. For "Tarshish," see Jonah 1:3. The "Babylonians" (23:13) was used synonymously with "Chaldeans." A dynasty of Chaldeans ruled the land of Babylonia. For "seventy" years (23:15), from Nebuchadnezzar's conquest until the fall of Babylon, Tyre lapsed into poverty and insignificance.

24:1–27:13 Global Response after Global Judgment
Overview: The section of 24:1–27:13 forms the finale to Isaiah 13–23, as Isaiah 12 was to Isaiah 7–11. It is a great hymn to God's holiness. This is the essence of God's dealing with all of his enemies. Isaiah 27 revived the vineyard imagery (cf. Isa. 5), only this time the vineyard was under the eternal protection of God.

24:1-23 Destruction Ends in God's Reign
The coming tribulation judgment will affect the whole earth and all classes of people. Sin is the basis of God's judgment. The "everlasting covenant" (24:5) must refer to the moral law of God revealed in his word and written in man's heart (cf. Rom. 2:14-15). This period of world devastation (Isa. 24:17-22) is also known as the "time of trouble for my people Israel" (Jer. 30:7). The sun and moon will darken in preparation for the full revelation of the Messiah's glorious kingdom (cf. Rev. 21:23).

25:1-12 SONG OF DELIVERANCE: A GREAT BANQUET
The "cities" (25:2) may be a reference to Babylon, which was representative of unbelieving opposition to God. The kingdom age (25:6) was likened to a great banquet (cf. Matt. 22:1-14). Isaiah 25:8 is quoted in 1 Corinthians 15:54 and Revelation 21:4. There will be no physical death during the kingdom age.

26:1-21 ISRAEL BROUGHT BACK FROM THE DEAD
The song of praise in Isaiah 26 will be sung by the redeemed as they enjoy the blessings of the messianic kingdom. The dead tyrants of 26:13 could no longer trouble or threaten Israel. The comments on their destruction in 26:14 do not deny the doctrine of the universal resurrection (cf. 26:19; Rev. 20:11-15).

27:1-13 SONG OF THE PROTECTED VINEYARD
"Leviathan" (27:1; cf. Job 3:8) is a figurative reference to the enemies or opposition of God. For "Asherah" (Isa. 27:9), see the comment on 17:8. The "brook of Egypt" (27:12) refers to the Wadi

el-Arish, the main geographical barrier between Israel and Egypt.

28:1–35:10 BOOK OF WOES: FOREIGN ALLIANCES CONTINUED
Overview: The section of 28:1–35:10 contains five woes on Israel and the nations (28:1; 29:1, 15; 30:1; 31:1). God used Assyria (28:11 and 33:19 bracket this section) to judge Israel for her alliances with Egypt. The key verse is 35:4. Isaiah 28–33 contains prophecies to Samaria, and Isaiah 34–35 is the international finale to God's judgment.

28:1-29 Samaria and Jerusalem: Fall and Comfort
Ephraim was the chief tribe of the northern kingdom of Israel. As the people mocked Isaiah's prophecy as nonsense (28:9-10), so they would get their fill of the nonsensical language of the Assyrians (28:11). Paul used 28:11 in 1 Corinthians 14:21 to demonstrate the purpose of tongues as a sign of God's judgment on unbelieving Jews. Instead of trusting in shaking alliances (28:15), God's people were to rely on the firm Cornerstone, the Messiah (cf. Ps. 118:22; Rom. 9:33; 10:11; 1 Pet. 2:6). For the historical background of "Mount Perazim" (28:21), see 2 Samuel 5:17-25. God works in many different ways to accomplish his purposes (Isa. 28:23-29).

29:1-24 Ariel: Fall and Comfort
Ariel (lit., "[altar] hearth of God") referred to Jerusalem, the place of sacrifice. The attack of Sennacherib in 701 B.C. was prophesied. This condemnation of Israel's empty formalism (29:13-14) is quoted by Jesus in Mark 7:6-7. The secret negotiations with Egypt (cf. Isa. 31:1; 36:9) were no secret to God. Paul used the illustration of the potter in a lesson on the sovereignty of God (Rom. 9:20-21). Isaiah portrayed the blessings of the Messianic kingdom (Isa. 29:17-24).

30:1-33 Results of Egyptian Alliance: Part One
30:1-17 DESTRUCTION FOR RELIANCE ON EGYPT
This section reflects the existence of a pro-Egyptian party in Hezekiah's court. God warned that true deliverance was not to be found in Egypt but in the security of his own person. Zoan (better known today as Tanis) is located in the northeast region of the Nile Delta. Hanes (known today as Ahnas) is located west of the Nile about fifty-five miles south of Memphis.

30:18-33 COMFORT
To encourage the people, Isaiah described the glories of the messianic kingdom. The destruction of Assyria (30:31) served to foreshadow the eschatological Day of the Lord. Topheth (30:33; lit.,

"place of burning"), was where human sacrifices were carried out in the Hinnom Valley located southwest of Jerusalem (2 Kings 23:10).

31:1–32:30 Results of Egyptian Alliance: Part Two

31:1-9 DESTRUCTION
Isaiah contrasted the futility of human resources with the security of divine protection. See 37:36 for the destruction of the Assyrian army. The "generals" (31:9) referred to the protective fortress of Assyria (cf. 33:16), perhaps Nineveh.

32:1-8 COMFORT
Isaiah described the righteous rule of the messianic king (7:14; 9:6; 11:1).

32:9-20 APPENDIX: WOMEN OF JERUSALEM
The "women who lie around in lazy ease" were the frivolous women of Jerusalem who would soon experience Assyria's wrath. In 32:15-20 Isaiah promised the blessings of the Spirit during the righteous kingdom of the Messiah.

33:1-24 Deliverance and Glory of Jerusalem
The Assyrians, "who have destroyed everything" (33:1), were warned of coming divine judgment (37:36-38). Isaiah described the response of the sinners in Jerusalem to God's judgment on Assyria (33:13-16). The glories of the messianic kingdom were previewed (33:17-24). The Assyrian official who counted out the captives, weighed out the tribute, and considered the city towers in preparation for siege was referred to in 33:18.

34:1–35:10 Finale of Judgment

34:1-17 THE CERTAINTY OF APOCALYPTIC DESTRUCTION
The end-time judgments of the Day of the Lord were described in detail. "Edom" (34:5), representative of the world powers that have opposed Israel, would be utterly destroyed. "Bozrah" (34:6) was the capital of Edom. The "night creatures" (34:14; lit., "Lilith") were noted in ancient mythology as night demons that frequented desolate places. The imagery was used here to illustrate the total desolation of the heathen lands. The "book of the Lord" (34:16) referred to Isaiah's prophecies. All would be fulfilled.

35:1-10 THE JOY OF THE RANSOMED
The judgments of the Tribulation (Isa. 34) prepared the way for the blessings of the messianic kingdom. These prophecies will be fulfilled at the Messiah's coming as God lifts the curse from his creation.

36:1–39:8 TWO SIGNS OF DELIVERANCE
Overview: This section is arranged topically rather than chronologically. Isaiah 36 and 37 showed the fulfillment of the prophecies concerning the coming Assyrian attack on Jerusalem. Isaiah 38 and 39 revealed Hezekiah's dealings with Babylon and prepared the way for the chapters of consolation for the exiles in the Babylonian captivity. Chronologically, the events were arranged as follows: (1) Hezekiah's illness, healing, and God's promise of deliverance from Assyria (38:1-6); (2) the visit by the Babylonian embassy and Isaiah's rebuke of Hezekiah's foolish conduct (39:1-8); and (3) the siege of Jerusalem by Sennacherib in 701 B.C. (Isa. 36–37).

This section on Hezekiah stands in contrast to the previous section on Ahaz (Isa. 7–35). God gave Ahaz a sign of deliverance from Assyria, but Ahaz rejected it. Hezekiah accepted God's ways and was accepted by him (37:3-4). In Isaiah 7–35 the threat of Assyria and prophecies of future judgment predominated. In Isaiah 40–66, Babylon loomed as a new threat, but even so, prophecies of future comfort were emphasized. Isaiah 36–39 functioned as a good example of faith that would lead to promises of ultimate restoration.

36:1–37:38 Assyrian Threats: The Faith of Hezekiah

36:1–37:7 THE FIRST THREAT
The "fourteenth" (36:1) year of Hezekiah corresponds with 701 B.C. Sennacherib reported in his royal annals that he had captured forty-six cities in his assault on Judah. The title of "personal representative" (36:2) implied a position of high-level leadership. This leader was an official emissary and spokesman for Sennacherib. Aramaic (36:11), a Semitic dialect similar to Hebrew, was the diplomatic and commercial language of the ancient Near East. Tearing one's clothes and wearing "sackcloth" was a sign of mourning and distress (37:1). The reference to a newborn "child" (37:3) was a metaphor suggesting a critical moment when special help would be needed.

37:8-38 THE DEATH OF SENNACHERIB
Libnah (37:8) is situated in the Elah Valley about twenty miles west of Bethlehem. Lachish is located about ten miles south of Libnah. Tirhakah (37:9) was not the reigning king in 701 B.C. but later succeeded his brother to this office. The "Assyrian representative" (37:8) cited historical evidence that the gods had been unable to protect the cities of Mesopotamia and Aram from Assyrian conquest (37:12-13).

God promised that Jerusalem would be spared (37:30-33). Although agricultural pursuits would be interrupted by the siege, normal conditions would return to the land within three years. Herodotus, a first-century Greek historian, recorded that a plague of field mice entered the camp and gnawed the weapons of the soldiers, making them defenseless (37:36). Ararat (37:38) is a mountain-

ous region of eastern Turkey. Esarhaddon ruled
Assyria from 680 to 669 B.C.

38:1–39:8 Babylonian Overtones

38:1-22 THE EXTENSION OF HEZEKIAH'S LIFE

The miracle was probably a local phenomenon
rather than a total reversal of the earth's rotation. In
death, one is cut off from the public assembly, the
historical context for "praise" (38:18) (public
acknowledgment of God's great works and deeds).

39:1-8 HEZEKIAH'S FOOLISHNESS
BEFORE THE BABYLONIANS

The words "Soon after this" (39:1) link Hezekiah's
foolishness with his illness and recovery, before
Assyria's attack on Jerusalem. Merodach-Baladan
(721–709 B.C.) reigned over the city of Babylon
for periods during the reigns of Sargon II and
Sennacherib. The prophecy of 39:6 would be
realized in the days of the Babylonian king
Nebuchadnezzar (cf. Dan. 1:2; 2 Kings 24–25).

40:1–66:24 CYCLES OF COMFORT
AFTER CAPTIVITY

Overview: The section of 40:1–66:24 contains three
cycles of comfort (Isa. 40–48; 49–57; 58–66). The
first describes the incomparability of God and Israel
as contrasted with idols and idolaters (40:1–48:22).
The second shows how God's Servant, the promised
Messiah, in his humiliation and exaltation, will bring
Israel to its worldwide calling (49:1–57:21). The
third divides Israel into two groups for eternal
reward: the faithless and the faithful in a final invitation to repentance (58:1–66:24).

Many scholars believe that Isaiah 40–66 was
written by a different author and refer to this
section as "Deutero-Isaiah." Their main problem
has to do with accepting the possibility of predictive prophecy. Isaiah lived during the Assyrian
period, and the prophecies of Isaiah 40–66 assume
a prophetic viewpoint. Isaiah wrote as if the Babylonian exile (586 B.C.) had already taken place. If
the reader can accept the possibility that Isaiah
could look into the future by divinely inspired
prophecy, there is no real problem with him
authoring both sections of the book.

40:1–48:22 God Contrasted with Idols

Overview: The words in 40:1–48:22 brought
comfort by focusing on the greatness of God (40:1-
31), the introduction of his Servant (42:1–43:13),
and then a lengthy description of the destruction of
Babylon (43:14–48:22).

40:1-31 GOD AS DELIVERER OF HIS PEOPLE

The prophets of Israel, Isaiah in particular, were
exhorted to speak words of consolation to God's
people in the Babylonian exile. A herald
announced the coming of God among his people
(40:3). The "voice" (40:3) was revealed by the New

Testament to be that of John the Baptist (Matt. 3:3),
the introducer of Jesus, the Messiah. The divine
plan of the Messiah's coming depended on God,
not man (40:6-8). This plan is as certain as his
word, which stands forever.

Isaiah 40:12-26 demonstrated the awesome
power of God. Nothing could hinder God's coming
to the people of Judah. He is incomparably greater
than any foe! "Who has measured off the heavens
with his fingers" (40:12) refers to a "span," which
is the distance between the thumb and little finger,
about nine inches. The "circle" (40:22) of the earth
referred to the sky that appeared to be a canopy.
Biblical cosmology describes the universe as it
appears, not with detailed, scientific exactness. To
the people of Judah, weary from exile, God promised that he had not lost sight of them in Babylon
(40:27). God promised his unfailing strength to
those who would "wait" patiently in him (40:31).

41:1-29 THE INCOMPARABLE POWER
AND KNOWLEDGE OF GOD

The "lands beyond the sea" (41:1) served as a
figure referring to the people of the Mediterranean
world. The one aroused "from the east" (41:2)
referred to Cyrus, king of Anshan, who inherited
the kingdom of the Medes (550 B.C.) and captured
Babylon (539 B.C.) to found the Persian Empire.
Although Cyrus was an unbeliever, he was called
to do God's righteous will (cf. 45:1-5). In 41:8-9
the believers of Israel were addressed as God's
"servant." The term also was used of Isaiah (20:3)
and the Messiah (49:5). The context is the key to
determining who was being referred to by the term
"servant." The "mountains" (41:15) referred to
mountain-like shrines (called "ziggurats") that
were used for idolatrous worship. God addressed
the pagan idols, challenging them to prove their
worth (41:21-24). They were asked to predict a
near prophecy ("long ago") or a distant prophecy
("what the future holds").

42:1–43:13 THE INTRODUCTION
OF THE SERVANT

The first of four great Servant Songs was presented
in 42:1-9. The "servant" is identified by Matthew
12:18-20 as Jesus, the Messiah. The establishment
of a just order ("justice") was a key theme in the
song (42:1, 3-4). The servant is the instrument by
which a new "covenant" will be effected (cf. Jer.
31:31-34; Ezek. 36:25-28; Heb. 8:6-13). For the
opening of blind eyes (42:7), see John 9:1-7. The
song of praise in 42:10-17 glorified God for his
future (tribulation) triumph over the wicked.
"Kedar" (42:11), the second son of Ishmael (Gen.
25:13), occupied the desert east of Transjordan. The
"servant" (Isa. 42:19) nation (Israel) was rebuked
for its lethargic spiritual state (for being "blind"
and "deaf"). In spite of Israel's unfaithfulness, God

promised to restore the nation from exile (43:1-7). The return from Babylon may serve as a precursor of the Jews' return to Israel after the Tribulation (Matt. 24:31).

43:14–44:5 BABYLON DESTROYED, ISRAEL RESTORED

Isaiah predicted that God was going to overthrow Babylon (43:14). The "ancestors" (43:27) probably referred to Jacob (cf. Hos. 12:3). The nation "servant" Israel was addressed (44:1). The pouring out of God's Spirit speaks of Israel's spiritual revival as a believing people of God (44:3; cf. Joel 2:28; Ezek. 39:29).

44:6-23 GOD VERSUS THE GODS OF THE NATIONS

The foolishness of idolatry is illustrated by the man who used part of a log to make a "god" and the other part as fuel for his fire.

44:24–45:25 GOD USES CYRUS FOR ISRAEL'S RESTORATION

Cyrus, king of Persia, conquered Babylon and decreed the return of the Jews to their homeland (Ezra 1:1-4). Cyrus was called God's anointed (45:1-5; lit., "messiah"). As he freed the Jews from bondage to the Babylonians, so Jesus, the divine Messiah, delivers all who will believe in him from their penalty of sin. The words "you did not know me" (45:4) make it clear that Cyrus was an unbeliever. He spoke about God in political ways (Ezra 1:2-4), but he did not know him personally. The words "bad times" (Isa. 45:7) were a strong statement concerning God's sovereignty over all events (Eph. 1:11). God raised up Cyrus to accomplish his purposes in restoring the Jews and rebuilding Jerusalem (cf. Phil. 2:10 with Isa. 45:23).

46:1-13 GOD DESTROYS BABEL'S GODS

Isaiah 46 illustrated the superiority of God over the gods of Babylon. "Bel" was the Babylonian equivalent to Baal. "Nebo," the son of Marduk, was the god of writing and education. The "bird of prey" (46:11) was a reference to Cyrus (41:2).

47:1-15 GOD DESTROYS BABYLON

The prophecy of 47:1-15 was of Babylon's destruction, which was fulfilled when Cyrus captured the city in 539 B.C. (Dan. 5). Babylon's failure was uncovered in 47:6. God had used the nation to discipline his people, but they went beyond reasonable punishment and showed no "mercy" (Zech. 1:16). The sorcerers of Babylon were challenged to do the impossible—to avert the disaster that would befall the city (47:12-15).

48:1-22 GOD DELIVERS ISRAEL FROM BABYLON

Isaiah 48 summarizes the message of Isaiah 40–47, reiterating Israel's promised deliverance through Cyrus (48:14-15). The best support in the Old

Testament for the doctrine of the Trinity may be provided in 48:16. The Father ("Sovereign Lord") sent the Son ("me") and the Holy Spirit ("his Spirit"). Isaiah 40–66 closes with a solemn statement concerning the wicked (cf. 57:21; 66:24).

49:1–57:21 The Servant's Humiliation and Exaltation

Overview: The section of 49:1–57:21 shows how God uses his Servant's humiliation and exaltation to bring Israel to its worldwide calling. The historical perspective is from the time period after the return from Babylon. The Servant attested to the glory of God (Isa. 49) and his message (Isa. 50) and invited the righteous remnant in Israel to hear and receive God's blessings once his wrath had passed (51:1–52:12). The Servant himself would be exalted, but only after undergoing intense, but redemptive, humiliation (52:13–53:12). After that profound insight into God's redemption plan follows a four-part invitation to accept such a costly salvation (54:1-17; 55:1-13; 56:1-8; 56:9–57:21).

49:1-26 THE SELF-ATTESTATION OF THE SERVANT

The second Servant Song was presented (cf. 42:1-9). Rejected by his own people (49:4), the Messiah would bring salvation to the Gentiles (49:5-6) and restore Israel to God (49:5). His mouth was likened to a sharpened "sword," a reference to the Messiah's speaking ministry (49:2; cf. Heb. 4:12). The name "Israel" was applied to the Messiah, the One who fulfilled God's expectation for his people (49:3). The Messiah appeared to have labored "to no purpose" to bring God's people to himself, but his work will eventually be rewarded (49:4). The Messiah was given literally as a "token and pledge to Israel" (49:8; cf. Gen. 12:1-3). One of the strongest statements in Scripture regarding God's faithfulness to his people is found in 49:15-16.

50:1-11 THE SERVANT'S FAITHFULNESS

Because of her sins, God divorced and sold Israel to her enemies (50:1). But those terms are descriptive of Israel's discipline only. God never broke his commitment to the relationship he had with Israel. The nation was temporarily rejected because of sin (cf. Jer. 31:35-37). The third Servant Song was presented (Isa. 50:4-9; cf. 42:1-9 and 49:1-13). Here it is revealed how the Servant learned through his own rejection to comfort the weary and discouraged. The phrase "Sovereign Lord" occurs four times and may be better translated "My Master God." It emphasized that the Servant had a Master (God) to whom he submitted and in whom he found help. The "words of wisdom" (50:4) was a reference to his speaking or prophetic ministry. The followers of the Servant were called upon to trust in God, who would bring judgment upon the disobedient (50:10-11).

51:1-23 INVITATION TO SALVATION AFTER WRATH

God encouraged the righteous remnant ("all who hope for deliverence") by promising deliverance from Babylon and future blessings for his people. "Dragon of the Nile" (51:9) is another reference to the mythical dragon monster, Leviathan (27:1), that was at odds with God and his created order.

52:1-12 JERUSALEM RELEASED FROM CAPTIVITY

Zion (God's people) was called upon to throw off the stupor of God's judgment ("Wake up") in preparation for the blessings of God's future kingdom reign (52:1). The "good news" for the exiles was that they could return to their homeland (52:7). Isaiah linked this historical message with a message about the end times: "The God of Israel reigns!" (52:7). While Christ reigns presently at the right hand of God the Father through the work of the Spirit on the earth, he will one day return visibly to rule his kingdom on earth. Paul used this verse in Romans 10:15 of the messengers who herald the "good news" of salvation in Christ. The message was addressed to the Jews in Babylon, who would have to choose between economic security in Babylon and the hazards and hardships of returning to Judah (see note on Ezra 1:5).

52:13–53:12 THE EXALTATION OF THE SERVANT

Isaiah presented the fourth Servant Song, predicting that the Servant would die in the place of the guilty in order to satisfy God's judgment on sin. Early Jewish interpretation of this passage understood the "servant" (52:13) to refer to the Messiah. This also was the interpretation by the early church (cf. Acts 8:30-35). Not until the twelfth century was it suggested that the "servant" of Isaiah 53 was the nation of Israel. But the nation of Israel has not suffered innocently (53:9) or willingly (53:7). Nor did Israel's suffering provide substitutionary atonement (53:5).

The Messiah's resurrection, ascension, and exaltation were predicted in 52:13. For the disfigurement of Christ, see Matthew 27:28-31. The word "startle" (Isa. 52:15) is the translation of the Hebrew word for "ceremonial cleansing." The Messiah's death would effect a spiritual cleansing potentially applicable even for the Gentiles ("nations").

Redeemed Israel spoke in retrospect and explained why they rejected the Messiah, Jesus (53:1-3). The Messiah bore the consequences of Israel's sin although they did not realize it at the time. Sin is pictured here in terms of its results or consequences in people's lives—sickness and pain. Matthew used this text with reference to Jesus' healing ministry (see note on Matt. 8:17). The emphasis in 53:5 is on substitution. What Christ suffered, he suffered for believers ("our sins," "peace," and

"healed"). The figure of straying sheep was used to describe the spiritual apostasy of Israel and all people (53:6; cf. Rom. 3:23). The Messiah Servant suffered willingly and silently (cf. Matt. 26:63; 27:11-14; Luke 23:9). The unjust judicial proceedings Christ was subjected to were reflected in 53:8. The Jewish Sanhedrin violated their own laws by (1) convening at the house of Caiaphas rather than the regular meeting place, (2) meeting at night rather than during the day, (3) convening on the eve of a Sabbath and a festival, (4) pronouncing the judgment the same day as the trial, and (5) ignoring the formalities allowing for the possibility of acquittal in cases involving a capital sentence. Although condemned with wicked criminals (the two thieves), Christ was buried in the tomb of a rich man (cf. Matt. 27:57-60).

The Servant Song concluded with God's promise to exalt his Servant because he did the Father's will in dying as a guilt offering (53:10-12; cf. Phil. 2:9-11). The "heirs" was a reference to Christ's spiritual progeny who would trust in his redemptive work. Because of Christ's suffering, many would be justified (cf. Rom. 5:1,18).

54:1-17 JERUSALEM: RESTORED AS A WIFE

Israel was exhorted to "break forth into loud and joyful song" (54:1) for her punishment was past. Now the nation could anticipate blessing and prosperity. Israel's rejection was necessary because of sin, but it was temporary because of God's covenant promise. See Genesis 9:11 with reference to Isaiah 54:9. These verses await their complete fulfillment in the messianic kingdom (Isa. 54:11-17).

55:1-13 INVITATION TO TASTE SALVATION

God offered salvation to all who would respond, whether Jew or Gentile. The word "thirsty" is used throughout Scripture as a metaphor for spiritual longing (cf. Ps. 42:1; John 4:14). The "everlasting covenant" (Isa. 55:3) or new covenant (Jer. 31:31) is associated with the Davidic covenant of 2 Samuel 7:12-16 ("unfailing love that I promised to David," Isa. 55:3). Both are unconditional and are founded on God's promise to Abraham (Gen. 12:1-3). God's prophetic "word" will most certainly be fulfilled, for it rests on the character of his own person (55:11; 40:8).

56:1-8 COVENANT UNION FOR OUTCASTS

God emphasized that the Gentiles who believed (56:3) would not be excluded from his blessing (56:7). The inclusion of Gentiles in God's plan for world blessing is seen in Genesis 12:3; Amos 9:12; Acts 15:16-18; Romans 4:9-16; Galatians 3:7-9; and Ephesians 2:11-19; 3:4-6.

56:9–57:21 ISRAEL'S LEADERSHIP IS REBUKED

In contrast to the righteous, the wicked face certain condemnation and judgment. Isaiah used picturesque language to describe the prophets of Israel (Isa. 56:10). They were likened to blind "watchmen" and "watchdogs" that could not bark. Isaiah suggested a positive view of death in that it removed a righteous person (like Josiah in 2 Kings 23) from the evil of the day (Isa. 57:2-8). God is willing to provide deliverance from judgment for those who are truly humble and repentant (57:15; cf. 2 Pet. 3:9). The second section of Isaiah 40–66 concludes with a statement of God's judgment on the wicked (Isa. 57:21; cf. 48:22).

58:1–66:24 Israel: The faithful and the faithless

Overview: In 58:1–66:24 Israel is divided into the faithful and the faithless to clarify the conditions for entering into God's future glory. It forms a final invitation and comfort. The heart of this section is the remnant's prayer for deliverance (63:7–64:12) and God's answer (65:1-25). The book ends by showing who will be excluded from the blessings of the new heavens and earth (66:1-24).

58:1-14 TRUE AND FALSE WORSHIP

Hand ritual (like fasting) without genuine heart righteousness (expressed by deeds of kindness) is unacceptable to God (cf. Matt. 23:13-36). The "Sabbath" was designed by God to be a day for turning aside from routine work to rest and be spiritually refreshed (Isa. 58:13). It was to be a day to "delight" in the Lord.

59:1-21 SIN'S PARTITION JUDGED

Isaiah 59 reveals the gospel in the Old Testament: "All have sinned" (Rom. 3:23; cf. Isa. 59:2). "The wages of sin" (Rom. 6:23; cf. Isa. 59:10). "But God showed his great love for us by sending Christ to die for us while we were still sinners" (Rom. 5:8; cf. Isa. 59:16). The "one Mediator" is Christ (1 Tim. 2:5). When Christ returns, he will judge the wicked and redeem his people, Israel, "those in Israel who have turned from their sins" (Isa. 59:20).

60:1-22 LIGHT AND GLORY UPON JERUSALEM

Isaiah 60 reveals that Israel can anticipate a glorious future and significant ministry in the messianic kingdom. The "darkness" that "will cover all the nations of the earth" (60:2) refers to the tribulation period that will precede Christ's return (cf. Matt. 24:29). In the messianic kingdom Israel will fulfill its destiny as a "light" to the nations (cf. Zech. 8:20-23). The "wealth of many lands" (Isa. 60:5) will come to Israel when the Gentiles (60:6-9) gather at Jerusalem to worship the messianic King (cf. Zech. 8:20-22; Hag. 2:7-9). The "sanctuary" (Isa. 60:13) refers to the messianic temple (cf. Ezek. 40–42). In contrast to Israel's national experience in history, Isaiah revealed the kingdom blessings the nation could anticipate (Isa. 60:15-22). The

promise of land (Deut. 30:1-5) was once again affirmed.

61:1-11 THE SERVANT'S GLORY AND VENGEANCE

Isaiah 61 revealed that the Messiah, who ministered salvation at his first coming, will minister comfort for redeemed Israel at his second coming. Jesus read and applied 61:1-2 to his own ministry when he preached in the synagogue at Nazareth (Luke 4:16-21). Jesus did not quote 61:2-3 in the synagogue at Nazareth because they will be fulfilled at his second coming. In the kingdom, redeemed Israel will realize its destiny to be a priestly nation (Exod. 19:6).

62:1-12 JERUSALEM'S INTERNATIONAL GLORY

In the messianic kingdom, redeemed Israel will be vindicated, honored, and protected. While Israel experienced separation from God because of her sin (Isa. 50:1), a day is coming when the believing nation will be fully restored as Yahweh's bride (cf. 54:4-10). "Bride of God" (62:4) is a translation of the familiar Hebrew term *Beulah*, which means "married." What a contrast there is between Jerusalem's "watchmen" in the kingdom and those of Isaiah's day (62:6; cf. 56:10).

63:1-6 EDOM: IMAGE OF INTERNATIONAL VENGEANCE

At the Messiah's coming, he will execute his wrathful judgment on the unbelieving enemies of his people. Edom, territory located southeast of Israel, was representative of Israel's enemies. Bozrah was the capital of Edom. The picture presented by the prophet was of a divine warrior returning from judgment. His garments were red from the blood of those he had judged. The imagery is precisely that of Revelation 14:18-20 and 19:3.

63:7–64:12 THE REMNANT'S PRAISE AND PLEA

Redeemed Israel acknowledged God's past mercies (Isa. 63:7-14) and prayed for him to deal kindly with his repentant people. The phrase "divided the sea" (63:12) is an allusion to one of the great miracles of the Exodus, the parting of the Red Sea (Exod. 14:16). Even though "Abraham" and "Jacob" might disown their descendants because of their sin, certainly God, "our Father," cannot deny his own children (Isa. 63:16; cf. 2 Tim. 2:13).

Paul quoted Isaiah 64:4 in 1 Corinthians 2:9 with reference to the heavenly glories awaiting the believer in Christ. Israel's unworthiness for God's mercy was highlighted. The appeal for forgiveness and restoration was based totally on God's grace (Isa. 64:5-12).

65:1-25 GOD'S ANSWER TO THE REMNANT'S PLEA

God declared that he would judge the wicked and preserve the righteous. Although Israel rejected God, he remained faithful in calling his people to repentance. The words "looking for me" (65:1) are an expression referring to public worship. Idolatry (65:3), eating forbidden food (65:4), and spiritual pride (65:5) were among the sins of the Israelites of Isaiah's day. The words "go out among the graves" (65:4) may refer to consulting with the dead (cf. 1 Sam. 28:3-25). The "Valley of Achor" (65:10) was where Achan was judged for his sin (Josh. 7:24). The point is, even places of past judgment will be blessed when God redeems his people. "Fate and Destiny" (65:11) refer to Gad (the Aramaean god of luck) and Meni (the god of destiny). The future blessings anticipated by God's people were described in 65:17-25. The "new heavens" and "new earth" (66:22) are a unique contribution by Isaiah to biblical eschatology. This theme was picked up by Peter (2 Pet. 3:13) and John (Rev. 21:1). After the dissolution of the present heavens and earth, which have been cursed by sin and judgment, God will create new heavens and a new earth as the physical context for the eternal state for believers. The curse on the earth that came as a result of Adam's fall (Gen. 3:17-19) will be reversed in the eternal state (Rev. 22:3).

66:1-24 EXCLUSIONS FROM THE NEW HEAVENS AND EARTH

The future blessings of the redeemed were further described. Isaiah 66:2 revealed the kind of person that God truly delights in (cf. Mic. 6:8). Religious hypocrisy was strongly condemned (Isa. 66:3). God is never pleased with hand ritual apart from heart righteousness. Isaiah 66:7-9 anticipated the spiritual rebirth of the nation of Israel, an event to coincide with the second coming of the Messiah (cf. Zech. 12:10–13:1; Rom. 11:26). The blessings and prosperity of the messianic kingdom (Isa. 66:10-14) were set in contrast with a vivid description of the judgment to be anticipated at the Lord's coming (66:15-17; cf. 2 Thess. 1:7-9). During the time of the messianic kingdom, believers among the Gentile nations will gather in Jerusalem to worship the Messiah with believing Jews (Isa. 66:18-20). Isaiah's grand prophecy concluded with a description of the eternal state (66:22-23; cf. Rev. 21:1–22:5) and a final announcement of the certain divine judgment of the wicked (Isa. 66:24; cf. Rev. 20:15-20). The joy of the redeemed was contrasted with the pain of the damned, all of which glorifies the compassion and justice of God.

JEREMIAH

BASIC FACTS

HISTORICAL SETTING
During Jeremiah's time, Egypt was involved in two decisive battles with Babylonia. The first was in 609 B.C. (cf. 2 Chron. 35:20-25). The second, in 605 B.C., saw Egypt broken in defeat (cf. 2 Chron. 36:1-6; Jer. 46:1-26). Assyria, in its attempt to block the rise of Babylonia, had unsuccessfully sided with Egypt. Babylonia was now strong and on the rise ultimately to defeat both Egypt and Assyria.

AUTHOR
The book of Jeremiah was written by the prophet Jeremiah. When his first volume of prophecies was destroyed by King Jehoiakim (Jer. 36:22-23), Jeremiah dictated the original prophecies as well as additional messages (36:32) to his secretary, Baruch.

DATE
The book begins by listing the kings under whom Jeremiah prophesied (1:2-3): Josiah (640–609 B.C.), Jehoiakim (609–597 B.C.), and Zedekiah (597–586 B.C.). Two other kings of this period, Jehoahaz (609 B.C.) and Jehoiachin (597 B.C.), are not mentioned in this first list of Jeremiah's kings. The thirteenth year of Josiah's reign (628 B.C.) was during a period when he had been aggressively seeking God since his eighth year (cf. 2 Chron. 34:3). In the eighteenth year of Josiah's reign he brought about one of Israel's greatest reforms. The fourth year of the reign of Jehoiakim (1:3; 606 B.C.) as king is mentioned in 36:32, in which he burned Jeremiah's scroll of prophecy. The fourth year of Zedekiah (27:1; 28:1; 51:59; 594 B.C.) was a year of great tragedy and upheaval as the nation drew closer to its final collapse.

PURPOSE
The book was designed to show the exiles the reasons for their captivity. They were not in Babylon because God had forgotten his promises to Israel but because Israel had been unfaithful to him. The book also taught the captives to wait patiently for the seventy years to elapse and not to seek a quick release through military or political means by trusting in other nations for deliverance. Finally, the book encouraged the captives that after their bondage there would come a time of restoration and renewal under the new covenant.

GEOGRAPHY AND ITS IMPORTANCE

Nebuchadnezzar's troops first destroyed the major cities to the north and south of Jerusalem. Then, without the support of her surrounding cities, Jerusalem also fell after a long siege. Jerusalem's destruction marked the end of the settlement of Palestine that began with Joshua's great defeat of Jericho. Early in Jeremiah's ministry, he predicted the coming exile of Judah in Babylon. And later during the Babylonian captivity, Jeremiah wrote that Israel would one day be restored to her land. The concept of getting back home was strong and deep for God's people. But Jeremiah placed geographical restoration squarely within a larger spiritual restoration. To "get home" physically demanded getting home in a spiritual sense, a sense described in the miracles of Jeremiah's new covenant. The physical captivity in Babylon reflected a spiritual bondage to sin and its consequences. The promise of geographical restoration to the Promised Land reflected an inner spiritual restoration. It was outward evidence of inner forgiveness and the indwelling of the Holy Spirit.

GUIDING CONCEPTS

JEREMIAH THE MAN

The book of Jeremiah provides numerous insights into the private and public life of Jeremiah the prophet. He originally came from the town of Anathoth, just north of Jerusalem (1:1; 11:21-23; 29:27; 32:7-9). Jeremiah revealed his feelings about his call (1:4-10). He gave up any hope of having a normal family life (16:1-13). His ministry was continually surrounded by hostility from his neighbors (11:21-23; 12:6) and his professional peers (5:31; 26:1-6). His life was threatened (26:24). He was publicly humiliated (20:1-6) and put in a hole in the ground (38:6-13). Throughout his trials, Jeremiah was honest and transparent. He freely shared his feelings and at the same time always maintained a vital trust in God (14:17-18; 15:15-23; 18:20; 20:7-18; 32:1-44; 38:1-13). Why did God give so much personal information about this prophet?

The descriptions of Jeremiah's personal feelings and troubles were not included just to make a good story but also to provide a personal context in which the prophetic message could be received. The inclusion of Jeremiah's feelings shows that God's prophets were not gloom-and-doom machines cranking out tirades against sinners. Rather, God's spokesmen were just as human as their audiences, and their sometimes harsh messages sprang from hearts broken by the rampant sin that surrounded them and from a desire to establish hope in God's wonderful promises of blessing.

But this picture of the prophet's heart being broken for God's people is a reflection of the pain in God's own heart. Thus, Jeremiah's pain and striving with the nation is a human reflection of God's divine and genuine pain as he strives to correct and bless his hard-hearted people. This genuine involvement of God with the pain of his sin-blasted creation is consummately seen in the agony of his Son on the cross. Jeremiah's personal life was revealed so that believers may be reminded to receive his harsh words of prophetic rebuke within the personal context of God's loving concern for their best.

THE ARRANGEMENT OF THE BOOK'S CONTENTS
The long book of Jeremiah, unlike the majority of the other prophets, is not arranged in chronological order. Stories and prophecies from various periods in Jeremiah's life are arranged together. Messages of hope or destruction, personal stories from Jeremiah's life, and historical events appear side by side. Some scholars account for this apparent lack of usual order in arrangement by noting the process leading up to the writing of the book.

Jeremiah had prophesied for twenty years before God told him to write his messages down. Thus the first compilation of Jeremiah contained some kind of listing ("all my messages"; 36:2) or summary version of twenty years of warning and encouraging the nation. But when King Jehoiakim heard the prophecy, he burned the scroll section by section (36:22-23), showed no fear of God, and sought to arrest Jeremiah. Jeremiah then rewrote the original prophecy and added even more to it (36:32). Thus, some scholars believe the turbulent times surrounding the writing of Jeremiah account for the book's seeming lack of order.

The book does have an overall progression and order, however. It begins with the beginning of Jeremiah's ministry (1:1-19), then encourages God's people to repent (2:1–45:5), shows God's absolute rule over the nations (cf. this aspect of Jeremiah's call in 1:10), and concludes by describing not only the fall of Jerusalem but also the elevation of David's son, Jehoiachin, in captivity. This clearly shows that the book was purposely designed to contribute to the ongoing development of God's promises to Abraham's children. They had been told by Moses in Deuteronomy that disobedience would bring destruction. But they also had been told of God's promises to Abraham to bring in a large nation and universal blessing and of God's promises to David to always have one of his sons ruling on the throne of Israel. Jeremiah's structure shows how the prophecies of destruction were accomplished without destroying the promises of Davidic rule that would someday be perfectly fulfilled in the Messiah.

BLESSINGS LOST AND GAINED
Jeremiah 1–29 and 34–52 outline the loss of Israel's blessings under the Mosaic covenant. Israel lost her throne, her land, her temple, and a good number of her inhabitants because she had violated the conditions of the covenant. But at the heart of the book (Jer. 30–33) is a promised remedy for Israel's covenant violations: a new covenant. Israel, under that new covenant, would have the law placed in her heart so that she would never again lose God's blessings.

BIBLE-WIDE CONCEPTS

LINKS TO KINGS, CHRONICLES, AND EZRA
Jeremiah, like 1 and 2 Kings, presents a detailed description of the failures that led to the destruction of Jerusalem. See, for example, Jeremiah 52 and 2 Kings 24–25.

Jeremiah has an even closer relationship to the book of Kings, for both end with the elevation of Jehoiachin in captivity (2 Kings 25:27-30; Jer. 52:31-34). Jeremiah presents a midexilic perspective, like 1 and 2 Kings. The most optimistic way the authors of these books could end their books was to show that the anointed son of David, Jehoiachin, was still under the Davidic promise of God, even while he was in captivity.

However, Jeremiah also contains a link to the even more positive ending of 1 and 2 Chronicles, where Cyrus, the Persian king, released Israel from captivity. The writer of Chronicles calls the words of Cyrus a fulfillment of Jeremiah's prophecy. Jeremiah 29:10-14 clearly prophesied a seventy-year captivity, after which God would release his people. Ezra 1:1 begins the account of the return of the Jews to the land with the words from Cyrus's decree (2 Chron. 36:22) and names that return as a fulfillment of Jeremiah's prophecy. Thus Jeremiah presents a clear link between Israel's chastisement and her restoration.

THE NEW COVENANT

A second exodus

In the first exodus God's people were led out from Egypt's captivity and into a relationship with God based on the covenant given to Moses. The captivity in Babylon also was followed by an exodus that led to a new relationship through a new covenant. Jeremiah spoke of the release from Babylon as a second exodus (Jer. 16:14-15; 23:7-8). That pattern of bondage, release, and relationship will be fulfilled at the end of this age when God brings complete release from the bondage of sin and death and allows the creation to enter into an unhindered relationship with him. That will be the third and final exodus from bondage to freedom. Jeremiah 31 speaks of Israel's inability to keep the Mosaic covenant (31:32), thus excluding her from the blessings of Abraham. But the new covenant would bring with it the ability to keep God's ways, thus opening up unhindered participation in the fullness of God's promises to Abraham concerning the land, the nation, and God's presence.

The time of Israel's restoration

Jeremiah described Israel's restoration as a time of release from captivity, victory over hostile nations' attacks, and the establishment of God's perfect rule through the fulfillment of Abrahamic and Davidic promises. Jeremiah described this time as if the release, victory, and rule would happen one right after the other and soon after the captivity took place. However, as Daniel found out, the release from Babylon and the full restoration of Israel's promises were separated by seventy weeks of years (Dan. 9:24-27). And as Jesus noted, the future time of full restoration is known only to God (Matt. 24:36).

Certainty, not chronological closeness, was the point of linking release, victory, and rule together. Although actually separated by thousands of years, the promised releases from oppression, victories over the nations, and the establishment of God's perfect rule will certainly happen. The actual time frame is secondary to God's people basing their present hope on a certain future. Knowing the certainty, not the date, is what provides a foundation for present repentance and hope. God's people tended to take God's threats or promises seriously only after it was too late. They put off making important decisions if they thought the deadline was far off. Jeremiah's point of present urgency would have been lost if he had told Israel that the events of victory and rule were thousands of years away. He presented future events as inevitable and certain, with present consequences for decisions of repentance and commitment, no matter how far in the future the fulfillment of the prophecies might be.

THE PLACE OF THE GENTILES

God's word to Abraham was that the nations would be blessed in him (Gen. 12:3). But how were the Gentiles related to Israel's blessing? Jeremiah spoke of a time when God's blessing would be international, for both Jew and Gentile. At that time all the nations would be obedient to the Lord (Jer. 3:16-18) and find their blessing in him (4:2). Jews and Gentiles are equal when it comes to God's evaluation of their hearts (9:25-26). All the nations of Jeremiah's day were subject to exile and, if they had responded in obedience to God, they would have been given his restoration (12:14-17; 25:29-31).

That accountability of the Gentiles before God went back to God's claim as Creator. The covenant with Abraham included all the people of the world. The covenant with Moses focused on the Jewish nation as an evangelistic witness to all the nations concerning God's salvation. The new covenant broke down all ethnic barriers between Jews and Gentiles, while maintaining the centrality of the seed of Abraham and of David through the promised Messiah (i.e., Jesus). The international blessing inherent in the promises to Abraham (Gen. 12:3) was no longer mediated by the priests in the Jerusalem temple but by the Son at the Father's right hand. Earthly ethnic and religious distinctions were done away with.

COVENANT PROMISES

God's promises were not frustrated by Israel's disobedience (31:35-37). His promises, though delayed from a human standpoint, would be fulfilled. God's words to Jacob (30:3, 7, 10) and David (30:9) were still in force, even in the light of Israel's disobedience and disastrous captivity. Paul (2 Cor. 3) and the writer to Hebrews (Heb. 8-10) explained what Jesus meant when he spoke of the new covenant in his blood (Luke 22:20). Indeed, the name "New Testament" shows that the entire New Testament is an exposition of the new covenant's meaning and implications. Jeremiah 31 begins an explanation of the new covenant that will be completed by the New Testament books.

NEEDS MET BY JEREMIAH

Jeremiah originally spoke to people who lived before and just after the downfall of Jerusalem to the Babylonians. But the book was finally composed after the middle of the seventy years of captivity, as its ending shows. Why would these people need to read about the past events of Israel's downfall? First, they needed to see God's heart of pain and compassion reflected through Jeremiah's own life and words. God cared about them, even in their rebellion and self-earned discipline. Second, God had not forgotten his promises to Abraham and David. The captivity in Babylon was a painful but temporary part of God's path to ultimate blessing. The hearers of the book of Jeremiah were challenged both to accept their discipline and to take hope in God's love and faithfulness to his promises. The book of Jeremiah answered some of the Israelites' hard, but necessary, questions.

- What hope remains for Israel after her destruction and captivity?
- Are God's covenant promises through Abraham and David still in force?
- Can God's people run away and escape God's judgment?
- How can a new covenant be any better than the covenants God has already made with Abraham, Moses, and David?

The Christian reader of Jeremiah must hold together two interesting concepts. First, the new covenant about which Jeremiah spoke has been inaugurated in Christ. The New Testament is devoted to explaining the implications of the new covenant for the believer. That covenant brings a more effective and intimate relationship with God than the one offered through Moses. Second, Christian readers must try to understand how they are to relate to the words of warning and potential disaster facing the nation of Israel. Do words of potential judgment for disobedience relate to believers who are participants in the new covenant? Are Jeremiah's words without present application, or is Israel to be viewed as a type of the church and her judgments somehow spiritualized into personal disciplines for the Christian?

The answer lies in realizing that the historical specifics unique to Israel at the time of her captivity are secondary to God's continuing attitude toward sin in his people. He hates any sin in his people's lives. The chronological dates of the captivity and of future restoration are also secondary to God's desire that his people take seriously their call to love him and pass his desires on to others, no matter how far in the future judgment or blessing may be. Jeremiah meets the needs of believers today by warning that God will bring discipline for their rebellion just as he did for Israel's. But believers can be assured that during the times of discipline, God's heart hurts for them and remains committed to their ultimate restoration in his promised blessings. To participate in his new covenant in Christ is to remain subject both to his discipline and to his inevitable blessing.

OUTLINE OF JEREMIAH

I. INTRODUCTION: END-TIME WORDS OF WARNING (1:1-19)
   A. The Times (1:1-3)
   B. The Commission (1:4-19)

II. ACCUSATION: COVENANT UNFAITHFULNESS (2:1-6:30)
   A. The Initial Confrontation (2:1-37)
   B. God's Desire for Repentance and Reason for Discipline (3:1-6:30)

III. COVENANT RENEWAL AND CHASTISEMENTS (7:1-19:13)
   A. Understanding in Chastisement (7:1-10:25)
   B. Covenant Recall (11:1-19:13)

IV. GOING OVER THE LEADERS' HEADS TO THE PEOPLE (19:14-29:32)
   A. Priestly Opposition (19:14-20:18)
   B. Kingly Reproach (21:1-22:30)
   C. Prophetic Hostility (23:1-29:32)

V. NEW COVENANT RESTORATION (30:1-33:26)
   A. Promise of Discernment in the End (30:1-31:40)

JEREMIAH NOTES

1:1-19 INTRODUCTION: END-TIME WORDS OF WARNING

Overview: After a short historical prologue (1:1-3), Jeremiah's commission sets forth the thrust of the book (1:4-19). He was known personally by God from before his birth, and God's word through him was to be certain. His appointment for building up and destroying nations (1:10) is related to the various themes used throughout the book. The book of Jeremiah describes Israel's downfall and restoration and concludes with a long section that shows God's ultimate rule over all the nations (46:1–51:64). The very end of the book reaffirms God's promises to build up Israel by the elevation of King Jehoiachin, the son of David, while still in exile.

1:1-3 The Times

Jeremiah, whose name means "Yahweh establishes," was of the priestly family residing at Anathoth (modern Anata), located about three miles north of Jerusalem. Although Jeremiah was the author, the "prophecies" were recorded by Baruch, the prophet's amanuensis (36:4, 32). The thirteenth year of Josiah (640–609 B.C.) was 627 B.C. Jeremiah continued his ministry in Jerusalem through the reigns of the last kings of Judah and until the exile to Babylon had begun in 586 B.C.

1:4-19 The Commission

In 1:4-10 two key thoughts dominated Jeremiah's commissioning as a prophet: (1) his divine appointment (1:5), and (2) the provision of God's word (1:7, 9). The word "young" (1:6) was used to denote a person from the age of infancy to early manhood. The words "I knew you" (1:5) speak of God's intimate awareness and purposeful affection. While yet in his mother's womb, Jeremiah was set apart by God for his prophetic ministry. Jeremiah's mission was described in terms of judgment and edification (1:10). The four synonyms used for destruction, in comparison to the two used for building up, indicate that the prophet's message was to be predominately one of warning about Judah's coming judgment.

In Israel, the almond tree is the first tree to blossom, and thus it announces the coming of spring (1:11-12). As spring always follows the blossoming of the almond, so prophetic fulfillment would follow Jeremiah's predictions. The boiling pot (1:13-16) was tilted from the north, the direction from which Babylon's invasion would come (3:18). Soon the scalding contents, the Babylonian invaders, would flow south over Israel.

Getting "dressed" involved tucking the end of a man's long outer robe into his belt in preparation

for walking or working (1:17). The command signified a readiness for work, and for Jeremiah it meant
the work of preaching. The prophet had to expect
opposition (cf. John 15:18-25), but he would not
be overcome by it (1:18-19; cf. Rom. 8:31-39).

2:1–6:30 ACCUSATION: COVENANT UNFAITHFULNESS

Overview: The section of Jeremiah 2:1–6:30 was
God's initial confrontation with the nation. It
progressed on the basis of the following themes: The
Israelites loved God at the first, but they soon
stopped loving him (2:2-3); God asked what wrong
he had done to them (2:5). He then asked why they
were on the roads to Assyria and Egypt (2:18). The
implied answer was that, even though he had disciplined them in the past, they had not responded
(2:30). The nations' leaders, pictured here as shepherds, were corrupt but would be replaced with
others who would be men after God's own heart
(3:15). And all Israelites needed a heart cleansing
(4:4). Because of Israel's sin, God's future judgment
was pictured as the earth returning to formlessness
and void (4:23-26). But that would not be a
complete destruction (5:18). Finally, the prophets
and priests gave the people false words of peace and
were condemned for their deceit (6:13-14; cf. 14:13-
16). These condemnations and promises in the first
chapters form a foundation for all the themes introduced and developed throughout the book.

2:1-37 The Initial Confrontation

God's love for Israel (2:1-37) contrasts with the
apostasy of the nation. The figures of bride and
bridegroom (2:2-3) depict the relationship between
God and Israel during the nation's early life after
the Exodus ("through the barren wilderness").
Although God had been faithful to Israel, the
people were unfaithful to him (2:5-8). They
forsook the Lord (2:5-6) and defiled the land (2:7).
The leaders (priests, teachers, rulers, and prophets)
led the way to apostasy. The result was that the
Lord had a case against Israel for violating the
Mosaic covenant (2:9). The words "bring my case"
denoted the activity of making an accusation or a
complaint. "Kedar" (2:10) referred to Arabia.

There are two kinds of water sources in Israel—
springs with "living" or fresh water, and cisterns
(small reservoirs) with stale or stagnant water. The
metaphor of water sources (2:13) graphically illustrated Israel's apostasy. Jeremiah 2:15 apparently
referred to the destruction of the northern kingdom
in 722 B.C. by Assyria. Jeremiah 2:16 probably
referred to the killing of Josiah by the Egyptians (cf.
2 Kings 23:29). Memphis (near modern Cairo) was
the ancient capital of Lower Egypt. Tahpanhes
was on the eastern border of the Nile Delta
commanding the road to Israel.

For 2:21, see the vineyard imagery in Isaiah 5:1-7
and Psalm 80:8-13. The apostate nation was likened
to a wild donkey in heat whose desire was so great
that any mate that wanted her could have her without effort (2:24). Judah should not have expected to
find help through an alliance with Egypt (2:36). The
reference to "Assyria" recalled Ahaz's attempt to
secure help from Assyria when the nation was threatened by Pekah (2 Kings 16:5-18).

3:1–6:30 God's Desire for Repentance and Reason for Discipline

3:1-5 RETURNING ADULTERESS

Deuteronomy 24:1-4 provides the legal background
for 3:1. The law prohibited a man from remarrying
his former wife if in the meantime she had been
married to another man. This law was referred to in
order to illustrate defiled Israel's condition resulting from apostasy (3:2-3).

3:6–6:30 REPENTANCE AND DESTRUCTION

Israel's punishment should have caused Judah to
repent, but she didn't (3:10). The comment in 3:10
sheds light on the Lord's view of Josiah's reform
(3:6), which appears to have been superficial. In
3:12–4:4 God addressed the northern kingdom
("Israel," 3:12) in exile in order to set forth a warning for Judah, the southern kingdom, to repent.
Jeremiah spoke of a future day when both kingdoms would be regathered to the land by the Shepherd after God's own heart (3:15-18). In that future
kingdom, the believing nation would not miss the
ark of the covenant because her attention would be
focused on the "throne of the Lord" (3:17). Israel's
repentance and confession of sin were an example
for Judah (3:22-25). But God demanded that the
repentance had to be sincere (4:1-2). He looked for
evidence of repentance, which can be found in the
fruit of true faith. The application was made for
Judah and Jerusalem (4:3-4). Only genuine repentance could avert judgment. The sign of circumcision was an outward witness of an inward, spiritual
reality. The command "Cleanse your minds and
hearts" (4:4) spoke figuratively of the need to separate oneself from sin and reconsecrate oneself to
God.

Jeremiah announced coming destruction from the
north (4:5-31). Babylon was likened to a "lion"
seeking prey (4:7), a "burning wind" (4:11), and a
threatening "storm wind" (4:13). The words "empty
and formless" (4:23) were used in Genesis 1:2 to
describe the earth before the six days of God's
creative work. The strong metaphor suggested that
the earth would be reduced to its state before the
Creation (4:24-26).

Jeremiah 5 gives the reason for God's judgment
on Judah. The essence of the answer is found in
5:18-19. The people had forsaken God and had
served other gods. Jeremiah was instructed to

search the streets of Jerusalem for one righteous man because God promised to pardon Judah if just one such person could be found (5:1; cf. Gen. 18:22-23). However, a complete destruction of Judah was decreed (Jer. 5:10). For the imagery of the vine (5:10), see Isaiah 5:1-7 and John 15:1-11. In spite of Israel's apostasy, God promised not to destroy the nation completely (Jer. 5:18). The basis of this encouragement was God's unconditional commitment to keeping his promise (Gen. 12:1-3; 2 Sam. 7:12-16). Both "Israel" (the northern kingdom) and "Judah" (the southern kingdom) were exceedingly wicked and deserving of divine discipline (5:20-31).

In Jeremiah 6 the prophet predicted the inevitable and imminent destruction of unrepentant Jerusalem (6:6), a prophecy fulfilled in the 586 B.C. destruction of the city by the Babylonians. The "people of Benjamin" (6:1) were exhorted to flee from Jerusalem because of its impending judgment. Tekoa (6:1) was situated on the edge of the Judean wilderness, twelve miles south of Jerusalem. Beth-hakkerem (6:1) has been identified with Ramat Rahel, located two miles south of Jerusalem.

The phrase "enemy shepherds" (6:3) was used figuratively to refer to the enemy kings and flocks of invaders (cf. 12:10) coming to feed on Judah. The "watchmen" were the prophets (6:17; cf. Ezek. 3:17), who were supposed to rebuke the nation's sins and warn the people of coming disaster. Costly but superficial sacrifices could not please God (6:20). Ancient "Sheba" (6:20) was located in the southern Arabian Peninsula in the vicinity of modern Yemen. To arouse the nation from its apathy, the approaching Babylonian enemy was described in terrifying terms (6:22-26). A "tester" (6:27) tested the quality of a metal to determine its value.

7:1–19:13 COVENANT RENEWAL AND CHASTISEMENTS

Overview: The people were to understand why they were going to be disciplined so severely (7:1–10:25). From the temple's gates (7:2) Jeremiah criticized Israel's false hope in the temple building (7:4). He urged them to remember what had happened at Shiloh and why it had happened (7:8-15). He drove them to search for true heart-level service to God rather than depend on the false security of an external and legalistic religion (9:23-24). He is God the Creator, not a false god of human imagination (Jer. 10). The command for heart-level obedience would be fulfilled in the new covenant mentioned in Jeremiah 31. The punishment of the nation was done in full light of the future promises of blessing and restoration.

The nation's sins were so great that God told Jeremiah not to pray for the people's deliverance (7:16; 11:14; 14:11). The potential still remained

for international blessing for the nations who learned the ways of God through the ways of his people (12:14-17). The prophecy foretelling the Babylonian captivity (Jer. 13) was followed by a list of sins and judgments (14:1–19:13), including drought (14:1–15:21), military judgment, and Sabbath breaking (17:1-27). This section ended with the mention of the potter's rights (18:1-23) over the pot's destruction (19:1-13).

7:1–10:25 Understanding in Chastisement

7:1-34 UNDERSTAND SHILOH'S JUDGMENT

In Jeremiah's "temple sermon," which he delivered at the gate of the temple, he warned that the people could not expect to be delivered from attack simply because of the presence of the temple in Jerusalem (7:4). They were reminded of God's past judgment on Shiloh (7:12), where the tabernacle had been set up. What had happened at Shiloh could also happen to Jerusalem. The theme of Jeremiah's temple sermon was presented in 7:3. Jesus quoted 7:11 in Mark 11:17; cf. Luke 19:46. Shiloh (7:12), located about twenty miles north of Jerusalem, was the location of the tabernacle in the time of the judges (Josh. 18:1). The city was destroyed by the Philistines around 1050 B.C. The "Queen of Heaven" (Jer. 7:18) referred to the heathen fertility goddess Astarte, known in Babylon as Ishtar (cf. 44:17).

With stinging sarcasm, God rebuked the people whose sacrifices meant nothing as expressions of genuine worship (7:21-22). Obedience, not ritual, had been God's overriding concern when he instituted the sacrifices at Sinai (1 Sam. 15:22; Hos. 6:6). "Topheth" (Jer. 7:31) probably meant "fireplace." "Hinnom" (6:31) referred to the L-shaped valley situated west and south of Jerusalem where the heathen custom of child sacrifice was practiced (cf. 2 Kings 16:3; 21:6).

8:1–10:25 UNDERSTAND WISDOM VERSUS FOOLISHNESS

The desecration of graves was practiced as a supreme insult to the dead (Jer. 8:1-2; cf. Deut. 21:22-23). The Lord warned that Judah's stubborn apostasy was the sure way to national ruin (Jer. 8:4-17). Jeremiah lamented the iniquity of Zion (8:18–9:22). The "medicine" (8:22) referred to a resin used for healing purposes. Gilead (8:22), a region east of the Jordan River, was famous for its balm from early times (cf. Gen. 37:25). Jeremiah 9:16 was the prophet's first mention of Judah's dispersion from the land. It was the ultimate judgment on the nation for violating the stipulations of the covenant (cf. Lev. 26:33; Deut. 28:64). The "mourners" (Jer. 9:17) were professional and hired mourners (cf. Matt. 9:23).

Jeremiah 10 set forth the greatness of God, the Creator and Sustainer of the universe, contrasted with impotent idols. For "Tarshish" (10:9), see the note on Jonah 1:3. The location of "Uphaz" (10:9) is unknown. Jeremiah 10:11 was written in Aramaic, a Semitic language similar to Hebrew and the common language of the people in exile. The Lord instructed the people, "pack your bag" for the trip into exile (10:17). The land was likened to a tent that had been pulled down and destroyed (10:20). The "shepherds" (10:21) is a figurative reference to the leaders of the nation.

11:1–19:13 Covenant Recall
11:1–13:27 THE CALL TO OBEDIENCE
11:1-23 Impending Curses
In 11:1-5 the prophet called the people into remembrance of the Mosaic covenant, which God had instituted with his people at Sinai. The covenant promised blessings for obedience and curses for disobedience (Deut. 28–30). Because the Israelites had violated the covenant, they would receive the judgments that God had promised (11:10-11). A plot against Jeremiah's life by the men of his hometown, Anathoth, was reflected in 11:18-23. They wanted to kill him and thus silence his message (11:19).

12:1-17 Times of Judgment and Compassion
Reflecting on his own sufferings, Jeremiah wrestled with the age-old question of why the wicked prosper (12:6). God responded, "The worst is yet to come!" The Lord described the judgment coming on Judah with such certainty that he spoke as if it had already occurred (12:7-13). The "evil nations" (12:14) were nations neighboring Judah (Aram, Moab, and Ammon) that would share her fate of exile from the land.

13:1-27 Waistband: Obedience
The "linen belt" was used in ancient times to brace a man's hip joints for prolonged periods of exertion and to hold up his robe for greater freedom in walking and work. The Euphrates River is 350 to 400 miles northeast of the land of Judah (13:4). Some scholars suggest that the text refers not to the Euphrates but to the village of Parah, located about three miles from Jeremiah's hometown. The two names are almost identical in the Hebrew. Just as the waistband was ruined by the waters of the Euphrates, in the same way the Lord would also destroy Jerusalem and Judah because of their sin (13:7).

The filled wine jugs symbolized the fact that God would fill the people with confusion, as when men are drunk (13:12-14). Their drunkenness would lead to their destruction. The prophet was instructed to address King Jehoiachin and the queen mother, Nehushta (13:18; cf. 2 Kings 24:8). Those "marching down from the north" were the Babylonians (13:20). The stark metaphor of 13:26 was taken from the public shaming of a harlot. The "adultery" (13:27)

referred to the peoples' idolatrous worship that frequently involved cultic prostitution.

14:1–19:13 THE LIST OF CURSES
14:1–15:21 Drought
The drought that came upon Judah was one of the curses of disobedience spoken of in the Mosaic covenant (14:1-6; cf. Deut. 28:24; Lev. 26:19). Jeremiah prayed twice (Jer. 14:7-9, 19-22) that the Lord would spare Judah the promised judgment, but twice he was told that the prayers for the nation were futile (14:10-12; 15:1-9). Nothing could alter the judgment for which the nation was destined. Jeremiah also appealed to God's covenant promise (Gen. 12:1-3) as a theological basis for his sparing the nation (Jer. 14:21).

Moses (15:1; cf. Exod. 32:11-14) and Samuel (1 Sam. 7:5-9; 12:19-25) were noted as great prayer warriors who had prayed in behalf of the nation. For Manasseh's sin (Jer. 15:4), see 2 Kings 23:26; 24:3. The winnowing process was a means of separating wheat from chaff (Jer. 15:7). Grain was tossed into the air, and the wind blew the lighter chaff away while the grain's kernels fell at the feet of the winnower.

Jeremiah experienced both despair and strengthening by the Lord (15:10-21). In Jeremiah's day the hardest iron came from regions in the north (15:12). Certainly Judah's "iron" had no chance to break the stronger "iron" of Babylonia. In the depths of his despair, Jeremiah charged God with deception (15:18). Like a brook that dries up in the summer when it is most needed, so God had seemingly failed him.

16:1-21 Military Judgment and Restoration
The life of Jeremiah was to illustrate his message to Judah of her coming judgment. He was prohibited from marrying (16:1-4), mourning (16:5-7), and feasting (16:8-9). The expression "offer a meal" (16:7) referred to the custom of providing a meal for mourners after the funeral (2 Sam. 3:35). The "cup of wine to console" may have referred to a similar custom. Although God would exile the people, he promised to restore them later to their homeland (16:13-15; cf. Deut. 30:1-10). The thought of 16:13 regarding the captivity was continued in 16:16. Like "fishermen" and "hunters," the Babylonians would capture and destroy the Judeans.

17:1-27 Sabbath Breaking
The sin of the nation and the consequent judgment were once again highlighted. Indelible sin meant inevitable judgment. The "Asherah" (17:2) referred to the Canaanite fertility goddess whose image was set up on hills and in sacred groves of trees. Compare Psalm 1 with Jeremiah 17:7-8. Jeremiah saw the Sabbath as a test case for obedience (17:19-27). The observance of the Sabbath was the prereq-

uisite for the return of national glory and prosperity. The "Negev" (17:26) is the dry region located just south of Judah, centering around Beersheba.

18:1–19:13 The Land as a Reproach
Just as the potter had control over the clay on his wheel, the Lord was sovereign over the nations of the earth—to build them up or to destroy them. The potter's "wheel" (18:3) consisted of two flat, circular stones connected by a vertical axis. The potter turned the lower stone with his feet, which caused the upper "wheel" to revolve. The rhetorical questions in 18:14 sought a negative answer. The point was that while nature pursues its God-directed course unchanged, the nation had unnaturally changed its course by turning from God. In response to his enemies' plot against his life, Jeremiah prayed that God would bring upon them the curses of the covenant (18:18-23; cf. Deut. 28:15-68). The theological basis for this prayer is found in God's promise in Genesis 12:3.

In Jeremiah 19 the breaking of the potter's jar illustrated the calamity that was soon to come upon Judah and Jerusalem (19:3). The "valley of the son of Hinnom" (19:2) is identical with the valley of Ben (the son) Hinnom. See the note on 7:31. The "blood of innocent children" (19:4) referred to the children who were sacrificed in heathen ceremonies in the Hinnom Valley. The "drink offerings" (19:13) were sacrifices or offerings of wine (cf. Num. 15:4-5).

19:14–29:32 GOING OVER THE LEADERS' HEADS TO THE PEOPLE

Overview: Jeremiah was beaten and imprisoned by the priests (Jer. 19:14–20:18). He then reproached King Zedekiah for his sinful leadership (21:1–24:10). The shepherd theme (12:10; 23:1) reappeared. At this point in the book, the time shifts backward to the fourth year of Jehoiakim and his twenty-three-year rebellion against God (25:1-38; cf. 25:3-4, 12-14). Moving back farther to events during the first year of Jehoiakim's reign (26:1-24), the author records Jeremiah's escape from the king's death sentence. The next scene moves ahead to the fourth year of Zedekiah (28:1). There, Zedekiah was warned to submit to Nebuchadnezzar (27:1-22), and Hananiah received a death sentence from Jeremiah for his false prophecy (28:1-17). But prophets also were lying to the Israelite exiles in Babylon, promising a quick release. In response, Jeremiah wrote his famous letter to the exiles in which he clearly told them to settle in for a seventy-year stay (29:1-32).

19:14–20:18 Priestly Opposition
Jeremiah 20 records the response of the religious establishment to Jeremiah's message of coming judgment on Judah and Jerusalem. "Pashhur"

(20:1) ranked next to the high priest in authority and had charge of the temple area. His position may have been identical with the "captain of the Temple guard" (Acts 4:1). Jeremiah gave Pashhur a new name, "The Man Who Lives in Terror" (Hebrew "Magor-missabib," meaning "terror on every side"), symbolic of the coming judgment on Jerusalem by the Babylonians. In 20:7-18 is found one of Jeremiah's most revealing confessions. His prayer illustrates the personal cost of faithfully declaring God's word (20:8).

21:1–22:30 Kingly Reproach
The prophecy recorded in Jeremiah 21 took place in the reign of Zedekiah (597–586 B.C.), the last king of Judah. He was urged to submit to Nebuchadnezzar in light of the certainty of Jerusalem's fall (21:10). The words "we are safe on our mountain" (21:13) were a reference to Jerusalem's inhabitants.

There are two possible interpretations of Jeremiah 22: (1) It is a prophecy concerning judgment on Shallum, Jehoiakim, and Coniah (or Jehoiachin); or (2) it is a prophecy of judgment on Zedekiah (21:1, 3; 22:1, 6, 10, 30), illustrated by the divine judgment that fell on his three predecessors. According to the second view, there was no curse on the line of Coniah (22:24-30) because Jeremiah was referring to Zedekiah. The fact that Matthew did not recognize a curse on Jehoiachin (Matt. 1:11) lends support to this interpretation.

In Jeremiah 22:1-9 the prophet addressed Zedekiah, the reigning "king of Judah" (22:1). Shallum (or Jehoahaz) took the throne after Josiah's death but reigned only three months (2 Kings 23:31-34). In 22:13-23 Jehoiakim (609–597 B.C.) succeeded Shallum. This wicked king received a donkey's burial, which actually was no burial at all (Jer. 22:18-19; 2 Kings 24:6). Coniah (Jer. 22:24-28), also called Jehoiachin and Jeconiah, reigned only three months before Nebuchadezzer captured Jerusalem in 597 B.C. and exiled ten thousand Judeans (2 Kings 24:8-16). Coniah was imprisoned in Babylon but later released (2 Kings 25:27-30). The book of Jeremiah ends by recounting the event of Coniah's release (52:28-34).

In 22:29-30 Jeremiah concluded his oracle with an application that went back to Jehoiachin ("this man, Jehoiachin" 22:30), the addressee of Jeremiah 22:24-30. The word "childless" referred to the fact that Jehoiachin's sons were slain by Nebuchadnezzar before he was exiled to Babylon. None of his children sat on the throne of David.

23:1–29:32 Prophetic Hostility
23:1-40 THE RESULTANT REPROACH
Jeremiah describes the coming of the Messiah, the righteous King. The "shepherds" referred to the wicked rulers of Judah (10:21). The term "Branch"

(23:5) is a messianic title (cf. Isa. 11:1; Zech. 3:8; 6:12) and indicated that the Messiah would be a fresh sprout from the stump of a felled tree, that is, the seemingly dead line of David. The religious leaders, that is, the false prophets and apostate priests, were condemned (Jer. 23:9-40). The Hebrew term translated "prophecy" (23:33) was a standard term for a message received by divine revelation. The misuse of this term by the false prophets and apostate priests brought it into disrepute (23:36).

24:1-10 THE REPROACH OF ZEDEKIAH AND HIS OFFICIALS
Jeremiah's vision of 24:1-10 took place after the captivity of Jehoiachin in 597 B.C. The "good figs" were Judeans removed from the land, whereas the "bad figs" were those, like Zedekiah, who remained.

25:1-38 THE FOURTH YEAR OF JEHOIAKIM
The duration of the Babylonian captivity was revealed. The "fourth year of Jehoiakim's reign" was 605 B.C. The "seventy" years (25:12) can be calculated from either 605 B.C. or 586 B.C. It is probably best to figure the period from 605 B.C., since that was the date of the prophecy. The conclusion of the period was 536 B.C. (including both 605 and 586 B.C. in the seventy years), when the returned Jewish exiles began rebuilding the Jerusalem temple (Ezra 3:1-6). Judgments would come on apostate Israel and the nations that had oppressed God's people (Jer. 25:15-38). The universal extent of that judgment (25:30-31) suggests that the verses referred all the way ahead to the future end-time tribulation events.

26:1-24 THE FIRST YEAR OF JEHOIAKIM
Jeremiah 26 records the circumstances surrounding Jeremiah's preaching of the temple sermon (7:1–8:3). For "Shiloh" (26:6), see the note on 7:12. Micah's prophecy of judgment against Jerusalem and the temple (Mic. 3:12) was recalled as evidence against putting Jeremiah to death (Jer. 26:8, 18). But the ultimate reason that Jeremiah was spared death was because of God's promise (26:24; cf. 1:18-19).

27:1–28:17 THE FOURTH YEAR OF ZEDEKIAH
27:1-22 Submission to Nebuchadnezzar
Zedekiah (597–586 B.C.) was placed on the throne by Nebuchadnezzar and was the last king of Judah. Although at first Zedekiah submitted to Babylonian rule, he later conspired with neighboring kings to overthrow Babylon. Jeremiah sought to correct the notion that such an overthrow was possible (27:12), urging submission rather than rebellion. The "yoke" and "leather thongs" (27:2) were symbolic of Judah's certain subjection by Babylon. The "gold utensils taken from my Temple" (27:16) had been taken by Nebuchadnezzar when he sacked Jerusalem in 597 B.C. (2 Kings 24:13). Usually a conqueror took a defeated nation's idols as a symbolic gesture of victory. But since the Jewish faith tolerated no idols, the temple vessels were taken instead. The promise of Jeremiah 27:22 was fulfilled in 537 B.C. when Sheshbazzar led the first group of exiles back to Jerusalem (Ezra 1:7-11).

28:1-17 False Hananiah
Hananiah, a false prophet, broke Jeremiah's "yoke" (Jer. 27:2) and predicted that Babylon would fall and the exiles would return within two years (cf. 25:11). In 28:1 it seems unusual to call the fourth year of Zedekiah the "early" part of his reign. But according to Jewish practice, the reign was divided into halves—the beginning and the end. The beginning was simply the first half of his reign. The word "Amen!" (28:6) means "may it be confirmed." Jeremiah wished such a prophecy could be true. About two months elapsed between Hananiah's false prophecy and his death (cf. 28:1).

29:1-32 FALSE PROPHETS IN BABYLON
Jeremiah 29 records Jeremiah's letter written to the Judean exiles who had been taken to Babylon in 597 B.C. (2 Kings 24:10-17). Once again (29:10; cf. 25:11), a seventy-year captivity was anticipated. But a return to the land of Israel was also promised (cf. Deut. 30:1-5). The punishment of Zedekiah and Ahab was like that experienced by Daniel's three friends (Dan. 3:20). Only, for these two false prophets, there was no deliverance. Instead, they became an object lesson of the Lord's wrath (Jer. 29:23). Jeremiah's letter (29:24-28) provoked opposition from Shemaiah, a Judean leader in Babylon who called for the Jerusalem temple's authorities ("Zephaniah" the priest, and "other priests") to rebuke Jeremiah for his prophecies.

30:1–33:22 NEW COVENANT RESTORATION
Overview: The section of 30:1–33:22 is the central section on the restoration of God's people (30:3). It begins with the certainty of God's promise to David (30:9) and ends with an explosion of covenant promises that will be as certain as the covenant for day and night (33:25): the covenants with David (33:15-17, 26), Moses (33:18), and Abraham (33:26). God explained that Israel would understand his discipline and his loving-kindness in the latter days (30:24). Jeremiah 31 elaborates on the time of restoration and understanding. The shepherd theme reappears (31:10), but unlike the hostile shepherds of the past, this Shepherd will be the Lord himself. Note the appearance of the section divider, "The time will come" (31:27, 31, 38; 33:14). Jeremiah 32, in the tenth year of Zedekiah, describes not only the downfall of Jerusalem but also the promise of restoration.

30:1–31:40 Promise of Discernment in the End

30:1–31:26 RESTORED FORTUNES: LAND

If Jeremiah 30–31 was written at the same time as Jeremiah 32–33, then the year was 587 B.C., and Jerusalem was under Nebuchadnezzar's siege (32:1). Jeremiah was in prison while famine and pestilence raged in Jerusalem and the Babylonians were at the city's gates. This was Judah's darkest hour, and the people were in need of hope and comfort. Jeremiah announced that the nation of Israel would be preserved, restored, and given a new covenant. The "time of trouble for my people Israel" (30:7) refers to the coming tribulation during which the people of Israel will suffer intense persecution (Matt. 24:9-22). "That day" (Jer. 30:8) is the day of the Messiah's return to judge his enemies and deliver the believing remnant of Israel from the antichrist's persecution (cf. Zech. 14:1-4).

After the Tribulation (30:12-17), God will bring healing to the seemingly incurable wounds received by Israel as the result of her sin and God's divine judgment. The healing will be both physical (restoration to prosperity) and spiritual (restoration of blessing). In the Messiah's kingdom, Jerusalem will be reestablished as the center of rightful rule and true worship. The "ruler" (30:21) is the Messiah. The often-repeated phrase of 30:22 (cf. Exod. 6:7; Jer. 32:38; Ezek. 36:28; Hos. 2:23; Zech. 13:9) expresses God's covenantal intention for his people.

During a time of future blessing the faithful of both Israel (Jer. 31:1-22) and Judah (31:23-26) will be gathered from their dispersion into the Land of Promise. Ramah (31:15), the home of Samuel (1 Sam. 7:17), was located about five miles north of Jerusalem. It was there that the captives were gathered before being taken to Babylon (40:1). In this poetic figure, Rachel, the mother of Joseph and Benjamin, is portrayed as weeping for her descendants going into exile. Matthew saw fulfillment of this verse in Herod's slaughter of the children in Bethlehem (Matt. 2:17-18). The meaning of the prophecy "Israel will embrace her God" (31:22) points to Israel's return to God; Israel will encompass or cling to the Lord.

31:27-30 BUILD AND PLANT: INDIVIDUAL ACCOUNTABILITY

The words of Jeremiah 31:28 are based on the commission given to Jeremiah in 1:10.

31:31-37 THE NEW COVENANT

The section of 31:31-37 is the central Old Testament passage on the new covenant (quoted in Heb. 8:6-13). Because Israel had failed to keep the old covenant (the contractual obligation begun at Mount Sinai), God promised that he would institute a new and better one. This promise amplified and confirmed the blessing promise of the Abrahamic covenant (Gen. 12:3). It was unconditional ("I will"), everlasting (Ezek. 37:6), and promised regeneration and the forgiveness of sin (31:33-34) through faith in Christ, based on his sacrificial death for sins (1 Cor. 11:25; Heb. 7:22; 8:6-13).

The repeated words "says the Lord" (31:31-34) divide the promise into its major sections. The first section, "The day will come" (31:31), makes the promise certain for a future time. The second section (31:31-32) stresses that the new covenant will not be like the old covenant that people broke. The implication is that something will happen to keep people from breaking the new covenant. The third section (31:33) announces the new covenant. The fourth section (31:33-34) shows in what way the covenant is new. It puts the law of God in a new place—the heart (cf. 24:7; 29:13; 32:40). That results in a universal relationship with and knowledge of God. The fifth section (31:34) gives the reason ("for") why the new covenant can happen. The iniquity and sin of God's people will be forgiven and forgotten.

The new covenant was a renewed covenant that replaced the shadow of the Mosaic covenant with the substance of Christ's sacrifice and heavenly mediation. It was made with the same people of God, the children of Abraham by faith. It contained the same law of God (cf. Deut. 6:6-7; 10:12; 30:6) but placed it in the heart. It promised a saving relationship with the same God (cf. Exod. 34:6-7 and 2 Cor. 6:16). And it offered complete forgiveness (cf. Exod. 34:6-7; Lev. 4:20; Num. 14:18; Deut. 5:9-10). The new covenant took up the elements of the Mosaic covenant but expanded and deepened them into fulfillment. The permanence of the cycles of nature (31:35-36) illustrated the certainty of God's preservation of the Hebrew people.

31:38-40 THE CITY IS REBUILT

The "Tower of Hananel" was located along the north wall of ancient Jerusalem. The "Corner Gate" was probably situated at the northwest corner of the wall. The locations of "Gareb" and "Goah" are unknown. The "graveyard and ash dump in the valley" referred to the Hinnom (7:31). The brook "Kidron" separated the temple mount from the Mount of Olives. The "Horse Gate" was in the east wall of the city.

32:1-44 A Picture of Restoration

Jeremiah's purchase of a field near Jerusalem demonstrated the prophet's faith in God's promise of restoration. The "tenth" year of Zedekiah (32:1) was 587 B.C. Jerusalem was under siege and Jeremiah was in prison, having been incarcerated by Zedekiah for prophesying the fall of Jerusalem. The transaction in 32:7 was based on the law of redemption (cf. Lev. 25:25, 32-34).

Jeremiah's purchase of the field (32:10) took on greater significance when it was realized that it had already fallen to the Babylonians. The purchase was Jeremiah's expression of faith that God would one day restore Israel to the land as he had promised (32:15). Baruch (32:13) was Jeremiah's scribe, or secretary, who wrote much of the book under the prophet's direction (cf. 36:27-28). The "siege ramps" (32:24) were earthen ramps built against the city walls by the invaders. The ramps provided access to the weaker, upper sections of the walls. The L-shaped Ben Hinnom Valley lies west and south of Jerusalem. Molech was the god of the Ammonites whose worship included child sacrifice.

33:1-26 Certainty of Restoration
Jeremiah 33 continues the theme of restoration that was introduced in Jeremiah 30. Here Jeremiah predicted restoration to the land (33:1-9), restoration to prosperity (33:10-13), and restoration of the Davidic throne (33:14-26). These prophecies related to Israel's future. The "Branch on King David's throne" is a messianic title (23:5-6; cf. Isa. 4:2; 11:1-5; Zech. 3:8; 6:12). Jesus, the Messiah, will sit on David's throne and rule his kingdom (cf. 2 Sam. 7:12-16; Luke 1:32-33). "My covenant with David" (Jer. 33:21) referred to God's promise in 2 Samuel 7:12-16. It was as certain as the ordinances of heaven.

34:1–45:5 COVENANT CHASTISEMENT CONFIRMED: SUBMIT OR DIE!
Overview: The section of Jeremiah 34:1–45:5 is a section of contrasts. The Babylonian captivity mirrored the nation's captivity of its own people in slavery (34:1-22). The Rechabites' obedience to their ancestral father stood in stark contrast to Israel's disobedience to her heavenly Father (35:1-19). God commanded that a scroll be written so that its hearers might repent and release God's forgiveness (36:3). But the king's officials feared the king, and the king did not fear God. Instead, he burned the scroll that was designed to avert destruction and bring about God's blessing (36:1-32).

The section of 37:1–45:5 revolved around Israel's hope in Egypt versus her hope in God. Zedekiah received no help from Egypt (38:1-28) or from trying to escape from Jerusalem (39:1-18). The Jews who remained after the downfall of Jerusalem were commanded to stay in Israel (40:1-16) and definitely not go down to Egypt (42:1-22). But they murdered Gedaliah (41:1-18) and chose flight into Egypt (42:1-22). From Egypt, Jeremiah predicted destruction by Babylon (43:1-13) due to the Jews' idolatry (44:1-30). There was painful irony to see Israel returning to Egypt, the place of her original bondage and redemption. A short prophecy of Jeremiah 45 serves as a summary of

Jeremiah's prophecies and concludes the broad section of Jeremiah 1–45.

34:1-22 Siege: Submit to Babylon
The events of Jeremiah 34 illustrate the depths to which the king and people of Jeremiah's day had plunged. While Jerusalem was under attack (34:6-7), Jeremiah delivered a message from God to King Zedekiah (34:1-2) and the people (34:8-22). The fate of Zedekiah (34:4) was recorded in 2 Kings 25:5-7. Lachish (34:7) was a fortress city located twenty-three miles southwest of Jerusalem. Azekah (34:7) was located eleven miles north of Lachish (see introductory map). Both cities are well known from the "Lachish Letters," which were written in Hebrew at the time of Nebuchadnezzar's invasion of Judah and discovered in 1935. Letter IV reads, "We are watching for the signals of Lachish . . . for we no longer can see the signals of Azekah."

Perhaps to gain God's favor, Zedekiah induced the people to promise to emancipate their Hebrew slaves, who according to the law were supposed to be given their freedom after six years (34:8-10; cf. Exod. 21:1-6; Deut. 15:12-18). When the Babylonian siege lifted temporarily due to the approach of the Egyptian army (Jer. 37:6-11), the pledge was broken and the slaves were returned to servitude. When ancient covenants were ratified, an animal was sacrificed, and those participating in the agreement walked between the parts (34:18). By this they were saying, "So may I be [that is, dead] if I break this covenant" (cf. Gen. 15:9-17).

35:1–36:32 Kingly Lack of Submission
35:1-19 RECABITE OBEDIENCE
The Recabites were descendants of a nomadic tribe of Kenites who had joined with the Israelites when the Babylonians invaded the land (Jer. 35:11). They were followers of Jehonadab, the son of Recab (2 Kings 10:15-16, 23), who sought to maintain the desert ideal by avoiding the "corruptions" of city life, such as farming, wine, and houses. The Recabites were obedient to their dead ancestor in contrast to the Judeans who had disobeyed their living God.

36:1-32 DISOBEDIENCE IN THE DAVIDIC LINE
Jeremiah 36 recorded the contempt of Jehoiakim for the word of God. The "scroll" (36:2), which was made of papyrus or vellum, would be used to record Jeremiah's prophecies from 627 B.C. until the "fourth year that Jehoiakim son of Josiah was king" (36:1), or 605 B.C. For "Baruch" (36:4), see the note on 32:12. The date was December 604 B.C. The probable reason for the "fasting" (36:9) was the increased threat of a Babylonian invasion of Judah. The "winterized part of the palace" (36:22) may have referred to a warmer, more sheltered room of the palace. No historical record was provided about the details of Jehoiakim's death (36:30; cf. 2 Kings

24:6). This judgment was one of the curses of disobedience specified in the covenant (Deut. 28:26).

37:1–39:10 Zedekiah's End

37:1-21 NO HELP FROM PHARAOH
During a brief lifting of the Babylonian siege due to the advance of the Egyptians (Jer. 37:5), Jeremiah sought to leave Jerusalem to attend to some family property (37:12). Apparently he was charged with desertion (37:13) and imprisoned underground (37:15-16). The "dungeon cell" (37:16) was probably an empty cistern, an underground water reservoir. Pharaoh Hophra (44:30), ruler of Egypt (589–570 B.C.), may have encouraged Zedekiah to revolt and then come to his aid.

38:1–39:10 NO HELP IN FLIGHT
The term "official" (38:7) or "eunuch" (NASB and KJV) originally referred to one who cared for the king's harem (cf. "the women," 38:22). Later the term was used of a trusted officer or palace official. The fall and destruction of Jerusalem are described in greater detail in Jeremiah 52. After eighteen months of siege, the walls of Jerusalem were breached on the ninth of Tammuz (our June–July) in 586 B.C. (39:1-2). One month later the city was burned (cf. 52:12-13). Some have equated "Nergal-sharezer" (39:3) with Neriglissar, who succeeded Nebuchadnezzar's son (560–556 B.C.). For 39:10, see Jeremiah 24:8-10.

39:11–44:30 Gedaliah's End

39:11–43:7 MURDER AND FLIGHT TO EGYPT
At Ramah (40:1), situated five miles north of Jerusalem, the Judeans were gathered in preparation for deportation. In the absence of a Judean king, Gedaliah was appointed governor of Judah (40:5; cf. 2 Kings 25:22-24). Mizpah (now Tell en-Nasbeh) was located eight miles north of Jerusalem. It became the administrative center during Gedaliah's short governorship (Jer. 40:6).

Why was Gedaliah assassinated (41:1-2)? It may have been that Ishmael, a member of the royal family, was jealous for the throne. Or perhaps Gedaliah was viewed as a traitor for assuming a post under the appointment of the Babylonians. The men demonstrated extreme signs of mourning at his death (41:5). "Geruth-kimham" meant the lodging place of Kimham, the son of Barzillai, who exhibited such kindness to David (41:17; cf. 2 Sam. 17:27-29; 19:31-39).

Afraid to stay in Judah after the murder of Gedaliah (Jer. 42:1–43:7), the people who were on the way to Egypt (41:17) stopped to ask Jeremiah to ask God what they should do (42:1-3). The answer came from God that they should stay in the land and not go to Egypt (42:19), but they decided to go to Egypt anyway, forcing Jeremiah to go with

them (43:1-7). For Tahpanhes (43:7), see the note on 2:16.

43:8–44:30 NO HELP IN EGYPT
Jeremiah's prediction of the Babylonian conquest of Egypt was fulfilled in 568 B.C. by Nebuchadnezzar during the reign of Pharaoh Ahmosis II (43:8-13). Heliopolis ("city of the sun"), or "temple of the sun" (43:13), located near modern Cairo, was a worship center for the sun-god Ra. The "sacred pillars" (43:13) were tall, tapered granite shafts used by the Egyptians as monuments.

Jeremiah warned the Jews in Egypt of the consequences of idolatry (44:1-10). For Tahpanhes, see the note on 2:16. Migdol (44:1) was located near the northeast boundary of Egypt. Memphis (44:1), still in existence today, is located about fifteen miles south of modern Cairo. In Upper Egypt (44:1) some Jews established a military colony at Yeb (Elephantine). Rejecting the words of Jeremiah, the Jews declared their allegiance to the "Queen of Heaven" (44:17), a reference to the heathen fertility deity known in Canaan as Astarte (the Babylonian Ishtar). The downfall of Pharaoh Hophra (588–569 B.C.) would serve to confirm God's word through Jeremiah (44:29-30). He was assassinated by a former government official Amasis, also known as Ahmoses II (569–526 B.C.).

45:1-5 Summary
The brief message of Jeremiah in 45:1-5 to his scribe, Baruch, was dictated in the fourth year of Jehoiakim, or 605 B.C. Baruch's reward was his physical preservation. He would suffer with the Judeans, but his life would be spared.

46:1–51:64 GOD'S RULE OVER THE NATIONS
Overview: In the middle of all the gloom of Jeremiah 1–45, Jeremiah 30–33 stood out as a bright light of God's ultimate restoration of Israel to be over the nations. In Jeremiah 46–51 are collected several prophecies against foreign nations that reinforced that ultimate restoration. The nations' hostile attitudes toward Israel are summed up in 50:7, 11 and 51:24, 49. The judgment was a direct reflection of God's promise to Abraham to curse those who cursed Israel (Gen. 12:3). Jeremiah was ordained a "spokesman to the world" (Jer. 1:5). The nations prophesied against were Egypt (46:1-28), Philistia (47:1-7), Moab (48:1-47), Ammon (49:1-6), Edom (49:7-22), Damascus (49:23-27), Hazor (49:28-33), Elam (49:34-39), and Babylonia (50:1–51:64). Egypt and Babylonia begin and end the list as the two nations that had held Israel in bondage. Babylonia received the most space concerning judgment. The relation of this list to Israel's hope was found in 46:28; 50:33-34; 51:5.

God also had gracious plans for many of the hostile nations (48:47; 49:6, 39).

46:1-28 Egypt

The defeat of Egypt at the battle of Carchemish in 605 B.C. gave Babylonia dominion over the land of Israel. "Ethiopia" (46:9) referred to the region south of Egypt (the Upper Nile region). "Libya" referred to the northern coast of Africa. The Lydians were inhabitants of Asia Minor, and the Egyptians employed them as mercenaries. For the medicine, or "ointment," of Gilead (46:11), see the note on Jeremiah 8:22. For locations of cities in 46:14, see the note on 44:1. Mount Tabor (46:18) is located in the Jezreel Valley. Mount Carmel reaches its peak on the Mediterranean coast near modern Haifa. Thebes (46:25) is located about four hundred miles up the Nile from Cairo. Amon was the chief deity worshiped there.

47:1-7 Philistia

The Philistines migrated from the Aegean Islands under pressure from the Dorian Greeks around 1168 B.C. They were repulsed from the Delta of Egypt and settled on the southern coastal plain of Israel. The name Palestine is derived from Philistine. The reference in 47:1 was to Pharaoh Neco's campaign in 609 B.C. when he went to the aid of Assyria against Babylonia (2 Kings 23:29). The "flood . . . from the north" (47:2) referred to the invasion by Babylonia. Tyre and Sidon were Phoenician cities. Caphtor referred to Crete, one of the Mediterranean islands from which the Philistines came (Amos 9:7). Gaza and Ashkelon (47:5) were two of Philistia's five principal cities located on the Mediterranean coast of Philistia to the southwest of Israel.

48:1-47 Moab

The Moabites were the descendants of the incestuous union of Lot and his eldest daughter (Gen. 19:30-38). They occupied the region east of the Dead Sea between the Arnon and Zered rivers. The background of the prophetic judgments may have been the attack mentioned in 2 Kings 24:2. Chemosh (48:7) was the chief deity of the Moabites (Num. 21:29; 2 Kings 23:13). Like the undisturbed lees, Moab had not yet gone into exile. Dibon (48:18), famous for the discovery of the Moabite Stone, was located north of the Arnon, thirteen miles east of the Dead Sea. The land of Moab (48:42) was inhabited by the Nabateans in the first century B.C. and later by the Arabs.

49:1-6 Ammon

The Ammonites were the descendants of the incestuous union of Lot and his youngest daughter (Gen. 19:30-38). They occupied the desert region north of Moab. Molech was the chief deity of Ammon (1 Kings 11:5). Rabbah, the capital of Ammon, was located at the site of modern Amman, the capital of Jordan.

49:7-22 Edom

The Edomites were the descendants of Esau, Jacob's twin brother (Gen. 25:21-25; 36:8). They lived in the desert region south of the Dead Sea. Teman was a city in Edom thought to be located about three miles east of Petra. Dedan was a tribe of traders descended from Abraham and Keturah (Gen. 25:1-3) dwelling southeast of Edom. Bozrah was a fortified city in Edom located about thirty miles north of Petra.

49:23-27 Damascus

Damascus, the capital of the Aramaeans (Syria), survives as a major city today and is located about 130 miles north of Jerusalem. Hamath was located on the Orontes River about 110 miles north of Damascus. Arpad was situated about 20 miles northwest of Aleppo.

49:28-33 Hazor

Jeremiah 49:28-33 is related to Nebuchadnezzar's attempt to bring certain regions of the Syrian desert under Babylonian control (599 B.C.). Kedar was the son of Ishmael (Gen. 25:13). The Hazor mentioned here was a desert area, not the city in northern Israel.

49:34-39 Elam

Elam was a region of Mesopotamia located just north of the Persian Gulf. Elam was overrun by Nebuchadnezzar in the winter of 596 B.C. This nation, as a part of the Medo-Persian Empire, later overthrew Babylonian rule (cf. Isa. 21:2; Dan. 8:2).

50:1–51:64 Babylon's Scroll of Destruction

Babylon, located in central Mesopotamia on the Euphrates, was the capital of the Babylonian Empire. The term "Babylonians" referred to the ruling dynasty of Babylon but was used synonymously with the term "Chaldeans." Bel (50:2) was the Babylonian equivalent of the Canaanite Baal. Marduk was the chief god of Babylon. The nation (50:3) that rose against Babylon was Persia under the leadership of Cyrus. He came from Media, "north" of Babylon, and captured the city in 539 B.C. (cf. Dan. 5). In 514 B.C. Darius Hystaspes put down a revolt in Babylon and partially destroyed the city walls (50:13). In 478 B.C. Xerxes destroyed Babylon's walls and temples. The names Merathaim (50:21; "double rebellion") and Pekod ("visitation") were a play on the names of actual places in southern Babylonia. The Jerusalem temple was destroyed and burned by the Babylonians (50:28; cf. 2 Kings 25:9). The reference in 50:44 is to Cyrus,

God's instrument of judgment against Babylon (cf. Isa. 45:1-5).

Leb Kamai means in Hebrew "the heart of those who rise against me." It is a cryptic reference to "Babylonia" (51:1). The fall of Babylon was seen to be so certain in the mind of the prophet that it was described in the past tense (51:8). The Medes lived east of the Tigris River and south of the Caspian Sea (51:11). Cyrus, who overthrew Babylon, was of Median descent. He succeeded in uniting the Medes and the Persians into one empire.

Jeremiah 51:20-23 referred to Cyrus (cf. 50:44). The "armies of Ararat, Minni, and Ashkenaz" (51:27) referred to regions north of Babylon that were conquered by the Medes and became a part of Cyrus's empire. The "river" (51:36) may refer to the moat that surrounded the city of Babylon or possibly a reservoir. Seraiah was the brother of Baruch (51:59; cf. 32:12). As quartermaster he was responsible for the king's accommodations during travel.

52:1-34 FROM JERUSALEM'S FALL TO THE ELEVATION OF JEHOIACHIN

The book of Jeremiah's prophecies ends with a summary from Jerusalem's fall to the elevation of Jehoiachin (52:1-34). That gave further encouragement that God had not abandoned his promises to King David. God's loving-kindness still remained. In the closing chapter (Jer. 52), Jeremiah presented the fate of Jerusalem, Zedekiah, and Jehoiachin. The material here is nearly identical to that of 2 Kings 24:18–25:30. This historical appendix was added to show how Jeremiah's message of judgment was fulfilled and to remind the reader of the continuing power of the Davidic covenant. The siege of Jerusalem began in the winter of 587 B.C. and continued until midsummer of the next year (586 B.C.) when the conquest was completed. Riblah (52:9), located thirty-five miles northeast of Baalbek, was the site of the Babylonian military headquarters (2 Kings 25:6, 20-21).

The first deportation to Babylon occurred in 605 B.C., during which choice young men were taken to be servants in the Babylonian court (2 Kings 24:1; Dan. 1:1). A second deportation took place in 597 B.C. and involved around 10,000 Judeans (2 Kings 24:12-16). The count of 3,023 exiles (Jer. 52:28) was probably the number of adult males. A third deportation (2 Kings 25:8-21) took place in 586 B.C. in connection with the destruction of Jerusalem and the burning of the temple (Jer. 52:29). After the assassination of Gedaliah, the governor appointed by Babylon (52:30; cf. 40:7–41:18), the people feared further retaliation from the Babylonians and fled to Egypt. The release of Jehoiachin from prison in 560 B.C. suggested to the exiled Jews that God had not forgotten his people. He was preserving the Davidic line even in exile, and his promises for the future were certain.

LAMENTATIONS

BASIC FACTS

HISTORICAL SETTING
The setting of Lamentations was the destruction of Jerusalem by the armies of Babylon under Nebuchadnezzar.

AUTHOR
The author has traditionally been named as Jeremiah, but the work itself does not name the author. However, it gives all the appearance of an eyewitness report.

DATE
The eyewitness quality and charged emotionalism of the work suggest a date of writing shortly after Jerusalem's destruction in 586 B.C.

PURPOSE
The book clearly shows why Jerusalem was destroyed: Judah's prophets, priests, and people had sinned (1:8; 2:14; 4:13-14) and had broken God's commandments given in the Mosaic covenant long before (1:18; 2:6-17). But at the heart of the book is a confession of trust in God's "unfailing love" and "mercies" (3:22). Although the terrible destruction of Jerusalem was due to Israel's sin (1:8), God's love still provided a glimmer of future hope. The purpose of the book was to express lament for the destruction of Jerusalem and to provide a platform for moving on in life. That platform was repentance (3:39-40) based on trust in God's unceasing love (3:22-23). Lamentations 5, the last chapter, sums up the thrust of the book. God would remember Israel's reproach (5:1) and restore the nation (5:21-22).

GUIDING CONCEPTS

Lamentations is a collection of five poems, each comprising a chapter in the English versions. The major concepts developed are the destruction of Jerusalem and the temple (1:1, 10; 2:1, 6-7), famine (1:11), cries for judgment on Israel's destroyers (1:21-22; 3:64-66; 4:21-22), and the tragic irresponsibility of her prophets and priests (2:13-14; 4:13-14).

BIBLE-WIDE CONCEPTS

The book related back to the promises of God to Abraham and Moses. In the Mosaic covenant, exile from the land was a promised consequence of sin. Lamentations showed that nearly one thousand years after the covenant had been made, it was still in force. Also, God's promise of unceasing love (3:22-23) reached back to the revelation of God to Moses at Sinai (Exod. 34:6) and the covenant with David (2 Sam. 7:14-15). It was that long-standing promise of permanent love that gave the writer of Lamentations hope. Finally, the desires for the judgment of Israel's enemies had their source in the promise to Abraham that all who cursed Israel would be cursed by God (Gen. 12:3).

NEEDS MET BY LAMENTATIONS

Lamentations takes the particular event of Jerusalem's downfall and shapes it into a timeless cry of anyone of God's children who suffers—for his own or for others' sins. The core confession of trust in God's love, even in the most tragic of situations (3:32-33), forms the center of the book's answers to these questions regarding the Israelites' life needs.

- Why has the nation of Israel's life fallen apart (1:8)?
- Why was God not on the side of Israel, his chosen people (4:12)?
- What should be Israel's next step (3:39-40)?
- What could possibly provide the security for any hope for the future (3:32-33)?

Jeremiah's agony over Jerusalem's destruction mirrors God's own pain over disciplining his children (3:31-33). The reason for discipline is the sin of God's children. The application of discipline comes from God's love and holiness. The purpose of reading about the past act of God's judgment on Jerusalem is hopefully to avert the need for God disciplining believers today in a similar way (3:40). In the flurry of present activities it is easy to forget that God exists and still demands holy living. Reading about the great judgment on God's holy city of Jerusalem should remind believers that as temples of God's Holy Spirit they also are not immune to God's severe discipline should they fall into sin. The book also serves as an example of how to mourn for sins and cry to God. Grief and pain are to be expressed, not denied or kept within. Lamentations gives believers something to identify with when they experience discipline. God's anger toward sin is real. But it is the anger of a loving father who will deal out pain if it is necessary to mature his children. And believers can always say, with Jeremiah, the "punishment will end" (4:22).

OUTLINE OF LAMENTATIONS

A. MOURNING AND CRYING FOR VENGEANCE (1:1-22)
B. THE NEGLIGENCE OF THE PROPHETS (2:1-22)
C. CALL FOR REPENTANCE (3:1-66)
D. THE NEGLIGENCE OF THE PRIESTS AND PROPHETS (4:1-22)
E. THE REMNANT PRAYS FOR RESTORATION (5:1-22)

LAMENTATIONS NOTES

1:1-22 MOURNING AND CRYING FOR VENGEANCE

The author used poetry packed with strong and vivid imagery to lament the condition of Jerusalem, the city of Zion. The nation's "lovers" (1:2) were the neighboring countries with whom Judah tried to form alliances against Babylon—Egypt, Edom, Moab, Ammon, Tyre, and Sidon. The roads, once full of worshipers traveling to Jerusalem, were deserted (1:4). Like Zedekiah, Israel's leadership fled from Jerusalem (1:6; cf. Jer. 39:4-7). The siege conditions in Jerusalem were reflected in 1:11, when people exchanged their precious treasures for food. The figures of "fire" (meaning "total destruction") and a "trap" (that is, "captivity") describe the calamities that befell Jerusalem (1:13). "Allies" (1:19) comes from the same Hebrew word that was translated "lovers" in 1:2. The author prayed that God would bring about "the day" of Babylon's judgment (1:21; cf. Jer. 50–51).

2:1-22 THE NEGLIGENCE OF THE PROPHETS

The author reflected on the fact that Zion's sorrows had come as a judgment from the Lord. The conditions described in Lamentations 2:11-12 reflect the famine, which was one of the accompaniments of siege warfare. The false prophets had predicted a return to peace and prosperity (2:14; cf. Jer. 14:13). Jeering and scoffing were ancient gestures of malicious joy and contempt (Lam. 2:15). In ancient times the night was divided into three four-hour periods (2:19). The writer suggested that the people awaken at the beginning of each of these periods ("during the night") so they could continue weeping. Cannibalism was one of the horrors experienced by the starving Judeans in Jerusalem during the Babylonian siege (2:20). This was one of the judgments God promised for disobedience (Deut. 28:53).

3:1-66 CALL FOR REPENTANCE

The author reflected on his personal experiences of affliction during his prophetic ministry (Lam. 3:1-18). He then received encouragement and consolation by reflecting on God's faithfulness (3:21-29). He used the imagery of hyperbole, that is, exaggeration for the sake of emphasis. The words "unfailing love" (3:22) are translated from a Hebrew term related to the Hebrew word for

"stork," suggesting a mother's love and faithfulness. It can be translated "loyal love" or "covenant loyalty." Burying "face down in the dust" (3:29) was an Oriental expression of submission. In 3:37-38 is a strong statement of God's sovereignty over all circumstances (cf. Eccles. 7:14; Rom. 8:28; Eph. 1:11). The writer referred to his own imprisonment in the "pit" (Lam. 3:53; cf. Jer. 38:6). The expression "This is the end" (3:54) means "I was as good as dead." In 3:64-66 the author did not take personal vengeance on his persecutors, but left retribution to the Lord (cf. Rom. 12:19).

4:1-22 THE NEGLIGENCE OF THE PRIESTS AND PROPHETS

Jeremiah reflected on the horrors of Jerusalem's suffering during the Babylonian siege. Those "who once lived in palaces" (Lam. 4:5) were the wealthy. No one helped Sodom (4:6). For cannibalism (4:10), see the note on 2:20. After their true character was recognized, the false prophets and wicked priests were condemned as "defiled" like lepers (4:15; cf. Lev. 13:45-46). The "nations that could offer no help at all" (Lam. 4:17) refers to Egypt, with whom Zedekiah attempted to form an alliance against Babylon (cf. Jer. 37:7). Edom (Lam. 4:21), whose people were descendants of Esau, Judah's neighbor to the southeast, was warned of God's judgment for her part in the sufferings of the Judeans, the descendants of Jacob. "Uz" (4:21), situated in the territory of Edom, was the home of Job (cf. Job. 1:1).

5:1-22 THE REMNANT PRAYS FOR RESTORATION

Jeremiah confessed the sins of the nation, recounting the calamities, and then petitioned God for restoration. The reference to Assyria (5:6) is a bit confusing unless one understands that Babylonia was meant. The Babylonian Empire had inherited the territory that had once been Assyria. For a similar usage, see Ezra 6:22. In 5:13 is a reference to the forced labor imposed upon the Judeans by their conquerors. According to Jewish custom, the request of 5:21 is repeated at the conclusion of the book in order to avoid ending on an unpleasant note. But history has shown that God had certainly not rejected his people (Rom. 11:1-5).

EZEKIEL

BASIC FACTS

HISTORICAL SETTING
The book of Ezekiel records prophecies and events that took place during the early part of the Babylonian captivity. Ezekiel was probably taken captive to Babylon in 597 B.C. From Babylon he wrote of Jerusalem's final downfall in 586 B.C. and prophesied the future glories that God had in store for his people.

AUTHOR
The author was the priest (1:3) and prophet Ezekiel. He lived in Jerusalem at the same time as Jeremiah. Ezekiel was probably taken captive to Babylon in 597 B.C. and may have personally known Daniel, who had been taken to Babylon during the earlier deportation of 605 B.C. The book shows a uniform style throughout, indicating the work of a single author.

DATE
Ezekiel began to prophesy in 593 B.C., the fifth year of Jehoiachin's captivity (1:2). The last dated message is from 573 B.C. (29:17). The compilation of the complete book may be dated shortly after 573 B.C.

PURPOSE
At this point in history, the people of the northern kingdom had been in exile for over a century (since 722 B.C.), and the people of the southern kingdom (Judah) had already suffered two of their three exiles to Babylon (in 605 and 597 B.C.). Jerusalem had not yet been destroyed, and the exiled Jews would naturally have had great hopes that Jerusalem might somehow survive. But God had clearly spoken otherwise. Their false hopes kept God's people from facing the truth: their own sins would soon bring about the destruction of their city and nation (586 B.C.). Ezekiel's prophecy was designed to place the responsibility for Jerusalem's downfall squarely on the shoulders of the Jews. But the prophecy's message also provided comfort for the Jews after the destruction of Jerusalem by graphically presenting the prediction of a restored Jerusalem, temple, and land.

GEOGRAPHY AND ITS IMPORTANCE

Two geographical images control the themes of Ezekiel: the mobile presence of God and the new temple. First, God was described as being mobile, moving about on beautiful wheels. The temple remained in Jerusalem, but God was not restricted to the temple. His presence moved all over the earth, and thus moved freely between Jerusalem and the captives in Babylon. Second, though the temple was destroyed, God would rebuild it, and Ezekiel described that

new temple in graphic terms. Ezekiel called the captives to purify themselves and develop their relationship with God while exiled in Babylon. Then they would be ready to return to Jerusalem and worship in his purified and rebuilt temple. The idea is similar to the woman at the Samaritan well in Jesus' day who debated about worshiping God at Samaria or at Jerusalem (John 4). Jesus replied that the issue was spirit and truth, not the geographical location of worship.

Believers will all worship at the new temple in the heavenly Jerusalem, but first they must be ready to worship and obey God wherever they are in this present world. The geography of Ezekiel follows the presence of God as it departs from the old temple, exhorts the exiles in Babylon, and then returns to dwell forever in the new temple.

GUIDING CONCEPTS

CHRONOLOGY AND CONTENT

Ezekiel consistently gave precise dates for each of his major prophecies. Those dates were in chronological order, with minor exceptions.

   This overview covers the major sections and messages of Ezekiel: the commission of Ezekiel; the events surrounding the departure of the glory of God from the temple; the failure of Israel's leadership; and the destruction of Israel and her enemies. Then after thirteen years came the prophecy of the return of God's glory and the restoration of the temple. The book takes the readers from the time when the glory departed to when the glory returned.

LINKS TO KING JEHOIACHIN

Ezekiel's prophecy can be linked to the years of King Jehoiachin's exile. The date in 1:2, the fifth year of the king's exile, becomes the book's chronological starting point. Zedekiah, the king ruling in Jerusalem while Ezekiel prophesied in Babylon, was not seen as the legitimate ruler because he was set in place by Nebuchadnezzar as a "puppet" ruler. Jeremiah had already made it clear that the nation was destined for seventy years of captivity (cf. Jer. 25). No one in Jerusalem could change that fact. Jehoiachin, living in Babylonian exile, was the focus of Israel's national hope. Second Kings 25:27-30 records that about halfway through the captivity, Jehoiachin was released from prison and elevated to a high position under the Babylonian king. Thus, in Jehoiachin's elevation in exile, Israel's hopes for the temple and Davidic throne were kept alive.

BIBLE-WIDE CONCEPTS

THE PURPOSE OF DISCIPLINE
Although part of Judah's people had been taken captive to Babylon, many of the Jews were still in Jerusalem, causing some to falsely believe that complete destruction of the nation would not take place. The captives' minds were still in Jerusalem and not on God's purpose for them in captivity. They wanted to escape God's discipline, but God wanted them to stay and learn vital lessons from it. The recurring phrase that the Jews heard from God in Babylon, "You will know that I am the Lord" (7:4, 27; 11:10; 34:27; 36:11, 38; 37:6, 13, 28; 38:23; 39:22, 28), had also been spoken to Israel when God took her out of Egypt. The Exodus itself and the judgments on Egypt revealed to Israel (Exod. 6:7) and to the Egyptians (Exod. 7:5, 17; 9:14) who God is and provided graphic instruction and encouragement for Israel (Exod. 10:1-2). In Ezekiel the phrase functions in a similar way. Israel would know that God is the Lord first by means of judgment, and later, by restoration.

THE DWELLING PLACES OF GOD'S GLORY
The book of Ezekiel begins with the departure of God's glory from the temple and ends with the return of God's glory. The prophet wanted to tell his readers the reasons for and implications of God's presence and absence. In the beginning, God's presence rested upon the perfectly created earth. At Sinai he filled the tabernacle with his glory (Exod. 40:34-38); and later, Solomon's temple also was filled with God's presence (1 Kings 8:10-11). In the future, the entire new earth will be God's temple, filled with his unhindered presence (Rev. 21:3). God has always come to dwell with humans on the basis of his saving grace. But man's sin and stubborn refusal to repent caused the

THE CHRONOLOGY OF EZEKIEL

Passage	Ezekiel's Date Year / Month / Day			Julian Date B.C.	Content
1:2	5	4	5	July 31, 593	Commission and message of Ezekiel
8:1	6	6	5	Sept. 17, 592	God's glory departs from the temple; don't trust in a brief exile
20:1	7	5	10	Aug. 9, 591	False trust in leadership
24:1	9	10	10	Jan. 15, 588	Jerusalem and her enemies will be destroyed
26:1	11	(10)	1	Feb. 12, 586	Tyre destroyed
29:1	10	10	12	Jan. 7, 587	Egypt cannot save
29:17	27	1	1	Apr. 26, 571	Egypt cannot save
30:20	11	1	7	Apr. 29, 587	Egypt cannot save
31:1	11	3	1	June 21, 587	Egypt destroyed
32:1	12	12	1	Mar. 3, 585	Egypt destroyed
32:17	12	(12)	15	Mar. 17, 585	Egypt destroyed
33:21	12	10	5	Jan. 19, 586	Jerusalem destroyed
40:1	25	1	10	Apr. 20, 573	Prophecy of the new temple and God's returned glory

removal of God's holy presence. Ezekiel spoke of a future time when God would make believers perfect in obedience so that his presence could abide with them forever (11:19-20; 36:25-35). Place those passages together with Jeremiah 31:31-34 to gain a fuller understanding of God's promised new covenant. That covenant was also referred to as a covenant of peace (34:25-31; 37:26).

THE LEADERSHIP OF KING AND PRIEST
God would again establish the rule of David's throne. In the section on leadership (Ezek. 20–23), God said he would put a rightful heir on the throne (21:27). The Davidic covenant was still in force. Also, in the section on restoration (Ezek. 34), God promised the return of good shepherds (34:11-31) for the nation. At their head would be one shepherd, David (34:23-24; 37:24). That figure of David looked to an earthly son of David on the throne and also to the greater Son of David, Jesus the Messiah.

THE SEED OF ABRAHAM
Although, from a human standpoint, Israel would be lost in captivity, God promised that the seed of Abraham would always survive and would someday be restored. The vision of the dry bones (Ezek. 37) affirmed that God would keep his promise to Abraham.

NEEDS MET BY EZEKIEL

The original hearers of Ezekiel's message needed to understand that the temple, Jerusalem, and the land of Palestine (the "Promised Land") were not good luck charms against the consequences of personal sin. The buildings and land only gained worth and power from God's presence. When Israel lost her temple, holy city, and land, she blamed God and thought that he had abandoned her forever. Ezekiel met the people's need both to accept responsibility for their own sins and not to give up hope in God's ultimate restoration and forgiveness. They needed to place their faith in God, not in things, and let that personal relationship turn them from sin to obedience. Some special needs are met by the book of Ezekiel, needs that are only felt when believers are under the heavy hand of God's discipline. The content and structure of Ezekiel show that the exiled Jews were probably asking questions like these.

- Should Israel worry more about their suffering under God's discipline than about hearing what God had to teach them through it?
- Is the temple so sacred that God would never destroy it, no matter how bad his people might be?
- Is the temple a kind of national security blanket for Israel?
- If God actually does destroy the temple, does that mean he has also destroyed all his other promises to his people?
- What does the future hold for Israel's hopes of a good king, a temple, and the presence of God?

The point of the vision of God's glory in Ezekiel 1 and 8–10 was to show the exiled Israelites that God's presence was not restricted to the temple or to the land of Israel. God was in Israel, Babylon, and everywhere. All that counted was obedience to his laws, not a superstitious clinging to his temple or land. In fact, he had even more incredible plans for a new temple in a renewed land (Ezek. 36–48). But, in the present or future, in the Promised Land or in temporary exile in a foreign land, believers were to enjoy the presence of God available through obedience, and trust in God for a better future.

The book of Ezekiel encourages believers to avoid putting anything in the place of a vital relationship with the living God. They are to repent, turn from idols, and renounce their detestable practices (14:6). Ezekiel presents a vision to lift the heads of believers from the present works of God through his people, beautiful though they may be, to see an incredibly glorious future. Ezekiel encourages believers to live with the vision of a new earth in their minds, with God alone reigning in their hearts, and with a commitment to responsible obedience in the present world.

OUTLINE OF EZEKIEL

I. JUDGMENT: GOD'S GLORY AND MAN'S REBELLION (1:1–7:27)
   A. Ezekiel's Commission: Bound and Loosed for Judgment (1:1–3:27)
   B. Object Lessons of Jerusalem's Destruction (4:1–7:27)

II. THE VACANT TEMPLE: DEPARTED GLORY (8:1–39:29)
   A. Do Not Trust in the Temple Being Preserved (8:1–11:25)
   B. Do Not Trust in a Brief Exile (12:1–19:14)
   C. Do Not Trust the Leaders for Deliverance (20:1–23:49)
   D. Do Not Trust Other Nations for Deliverance (24:1–33:20)
   E. Jerusalem Falls: Now Is the Time for Hope and Rest (33:21–39:29)

III. THE OCCUPIED TEMPLE: RETURNED GLORY (40:1–48:35)
   A. The Setting: A City and a Guide (40:1-4)
   B. The Temple Described (40:5–42:20)
   C. The Temple Occupied: God's Holiness (43:1-9)
   D. Temple Obligations: Humans' Holiness (43:10–46:24)
   E. The New Land (47:1–48:35)

EZEKIEL NOTES

1:1–7:27 JUDGMENT: GOD'S GLORY AND MAN'S REBELLION

1:1–3:27 Ezekiel's Commission: Bound and Loosed for Judgment
Overview: God was pictured in 1:26-28 as riding a throne on a platform with wheels, showing that his presence was not limited to the temple in Jerusalem. His presence is mobile, able to go anywhere for blessing or for judgment. He could be with the remnant left in Jerusalem or with those in Babylonian exile. The splendor of God in judgment and restoration was a vision that was continually behind all the words of this book. The watchman theme (3:17) would appear again in 33:7-9. Note

the theme of a "rebel " (2:5-6, 8; 3:9, 26-27). Ezekiel's eating of the scroll (3:3) was in contrast with Israel's refusal to hear and apply the words of God (3:7-8).

1:1-28 GOD APPEARS IN HIS GLORY
1:1-3 The Setting
The "thirtieth year" (1:1) referred to Ezekiel's age, the age at which Old Testament priests began their ministries (cf. Num. 4:3, 23-30). The "Kebar River" (1:1) was one of the navigable canals branching from the Euphrates, which flowed southeast from Babylon. The "fifth year" (1:2) from King Jehoiachin's exile (597 B.C.) would have been 593 B.C. The name "Ezekiel" means "God strengthens."

1:4-28 The Vision Is Described
Interpreters often become so engrossed in guessing the meaning of the details of this vision that they overlook its major significance. It was a vision of the glory of the Lord (1:1, 28). The vision left Ezekiel with an abiding sense of God's glory, which was often reflected in his prophetic ministry (3:23; 8:4; 10:4; 11:22). Whatever Ezekiel saw, he was limited in his ability to describe it. He used the Hebrew words translated "like" and "appearance" to describe what was completely beyond his earthly experience.

The "four living beings" (1:5) were later identified by Ezekiel as "cherubim" (10:20), an order of angels sometimes associated with the worship of God (cf. Gen. 3:24; Exod. 25:18-22). The singular was *cherub* and perhaps related to the Akkadian root meaning "to bless, praise, adore." The spirit (1:12) was identified in 1:20 as the "spirit of the four living beings," not the Holy Spirit. The chrysolite (1:16), literally, "tarshish," is a stone perhaps like topaz. Over the heads of the living creatures was a "surface" that served as a platform for the "throne" (1:26). Comparison of 1:26-27 with Revelation 1:13-18 suggests that the one sitting on the throne was Christ.

2:1–3:27 GOD COMMISSIONS EZEKIEL

2:1-7 The Target Group Is Described
Ezekiel recorded his call and commissioning. The expression "son of man" (2:1, 3, 6, 8; 3:1, 3-4, 10, 17, 25; etc.) is used ninety-three times in this book and simply meant "mortal man," in contrast with the majestic God. See the note on Daniel 7:13 for a contrasting usage of the term. The "briers" (2:6), "thorns," and "scorpions" suggested the difficulty of Ezekiel's ministry.

2:8–3:3 Ezekiel Eats the Scroll
Contrary to usual practice, this scroll was written on both sides, front and back (2:10). Another scroll written on both sides is found in the seven-sealed judgment scroll of Revelation 5:1. The writing on both sides suggested an extensive and detailed message. The eating of the scroll (3:1-3) suggested the assimilation of the message (cf. Rev. 10:8-11). In spite of the message of judgment, the scroll was "sweet as honey" (3:3) because it was the word of God (cf. Ps. 19:10).

3:4-15 Ezekiel Is Sent to the Exiles
To meet the challenge of a difficult ministry, God made Ezekiel as hardened as Israel's heart (3:8). The phrase "the Spirit lifted me up" (3:12) should not be understood as physical removal, but as an expression for prophetic vision (cf. 8:3; 11:1, 24). Telabib (3:15), whose location is uncertain, was the major settlement of the exiles in Babylon. The words "bitterness" and "turmoil" (3:14) suggested Ezekiel's awareness of impending judgment.

3:16-27 Ezekiel's Watchman Ministry
The work of the "watchman" (3:17) was depicted in 2 Samuel 18:24-27 and 2 Kings 9:17-20. Ezekiel's job was to warn the nation, both the wicked and the righteous (3:18-21), of impending divine judgment. While each group was responsible for its own actions, Ezekiel was accountable to present the warning. Some have found support in 3:20 for the view that the believer ("good") can turn from God and die an eternal death, that is, lose his or her salvation. However, the context is that of the Mosaic covenant where physical (not spiritual) life and death were in view (Deut. 30:15-20). The "ropes" (3:25) suggested some physical restraint and possibly the rejection of Ezekiel's ministry. Ezekiel remained unable to speak except when the Lord opened his mouth to proclaim his word. This situation continued for seven and a half years until the fall of Jerusalem (cf. 33:22).

4:1–7:27 Object Lessons of Jerusalem's Destruction

Overview: Throughout Ezekiel's declarations of judgment on Judah and Jerusalem, he used a number of symbolic actions or revelatory signs that caused the people to ask what he meant (12:9; 24:19; 37:18) and gave him an opportunity to explain their significance and drive home the application. The process of judgment described in Ezekiel 4 and throughout the book was linked by the forty years of 4:6 and the explicit statement of 20:34-36. The refining process of the wilderness wanderings was to purify the nation before the conquest of the Promised Land under Joshua. Similarly, God's punishment of Israel in war and captivity was designed to achieve the same end.

The cause of the Babylonian captivity was Israel's defilement of God's sanctuary (5:11). After God's wrath the nation would know that he had spoken (5:13; cf. also 6:7, 13-14; 7:4, 9, 27). That would confirm God's ability to enforce his covenant laws (6:9-10) and complete his covenant promises. For example, God hid his face from Israel in 7:22 and uncovered his face in 39:29.

4:1-17 JERUSALEM BESIEGED: THE CLAY TABLET

The sign of the "brick" (4:1) depicted Jerusalem's coming siege and fall. The "iron griddle" (4:3) is thought to represent (1) the severity of the siege, (2) the barrier of sin between God and the people, or (3) God's protection of Ezekiel as he pronounced judgment. The sign of the prophet's posture depicted the duration of Jerusalem's punishment (4:4-8). The total of 430 days was based upon the past years of Israel's iniquity and corresponded to the years of coming judgment. Because all numbering in the book is dated from the captivity of Jehoiachin (597 B.C.), the 430 could be subtracted from 597 to give 167 B.C. (the year of the Maccabean revolt) as the end of the period of judgment. The sign of the famine portrayed the suffering and deprivation of siege conditions (4:9-17). This procedure was not only repulsive but polluting (cf. Deut. 23:12-14). The point was that Israel would soon be eating the unclean food of the foreign nations in exile.

5:1-17 JERUSALEM'S INHABITANTS: THE HAIR AND REPROACH

The signs of the "sword," "razor" (5:1), and dividing of the shaved hair portrayed the coming destruction of the people by fire, sword, and scattering in exile. The preservation of a few hairs in the edge of Ezekiel's robe suggested that a remnant would be spared. This is stated more explicitly in 6:8-9; 7:16-18. The "regulations" referred to the stipulations of the covenant (5:6). Disobedience resulted in the curses of the covenant rather than its blessings (cf. Deut. 28:15-68). The horror of cannibalism became a historical fact as recorded by Jeremiah (see the note on Lam. 2:20).

6:1-14 MOUNTAINS OF ISRAEL: HIGH PLACES DESTROYED

The "mountains" (6:2) referred to the hilltop shrines where Canaanite cultic worship was practiced (6:3-4; cf. Jer. 3:6). Certain "valleys" were also used for the worship of Molech (cf. Jer. 7:31-32). The phrase "you will know that I am the Lord" (6:7) was repeated sixty-eight times in the book of Ezekiel. God's judgment had an evangelistic purpose: God would prove to his own people and all the nations of the world that he is truly God. God seasoned judgment with grace by the promise to preserve a remnant (6:8; cf. Isa. 6:13). Clapping (6:11) was sometimes an expression of joyous praise (cf. Ps. 47:1), but here it referred to remorse and derision over Judah's sin and judgment.

7:1-27 THE NATION'S END

Ezekiel described the imminent and complete destruction of Judah (7:5, 9). Neither the buyer nor the seller should have rejoiced over a good transaction because of the coming disaster. The coming captivity would make it impossible for the seller to regain his property in the Year of Jubilee (Lev. 25:10-12) because he would not be in the land. God's "treasured land" (7:22) referred to the Jerusalem temple. The sign of the "chains" (7:23) portrayed the coming captivity in Babylon. The calamity of the captivity would leave the Judeans without spiritual leadership, instruction, and counsel (7:26).

8:1–39:29 THE VACANT TEMPLE: DEPARTED GLORY

8:1–11:25 Do Not Trust in the Temple Being Preserved

Overview: The section of 8:1–11:25 showed what God would do to Jerusalem and why. This was

preparation for his message to the exiles. Ezekiel 1–7 describes the judgment in general. Ezekiel 8–39 goes into the specifics. Ezekiel's vision of Jerusalem was designed to cut through any sentimental or romanticizing thoughts about why God should spare the holy city. In reality, it was a place of rank paganism. Because of that, the exiles were not to think that the temple would, at all costs, be preserved. Note the repetition of "even greater sins" (8:6, 13, 15) with reference to Jerusalem's idolatry. The faithful of the city were to be marked (9:4, 6) for salvation, but none was found. All were candidates for death (9:8).

As God's glory departed (Ezek. 9–10), God answered Ezekiel's twice-repeated question concerning the survival of the remnant (9:8; 11:13). The temple might fall and Jerusalem might be razed, but God himself would be the captives' sanctuary (11:16). That is exactly how the book ends (48:35). The new hearts of flesh and spirit would enable the redeemed to follow God and keep his laws (11:19-20). That promise would be a tremendous comfort to the captives. The true temple had always been God himself. And his people could dwell in that temple anywhere on earth.

8:1-4 EZEKIEL IS TAKEN IN A VISION TO JERUSALEM

The date was September 17, 592 B.C., fourteen months after Ezekiel's first vision (1:1-2). Although Ezekiel was in Babylon, he was transported to Jerusalem by prophetic vision so that he might report to the exiles why God had to bring such severe judgment on the city. The "idol" (8:3) was an idolatrous image, perhaps the Canaanite goddess Asherah (cf. 2 Chron. 33:7, 15), which provoked God to jealous anger.

8:5–9:11 THE GLORY MOVES TO THE THRESHOLD

The seventy elders had become involved in idolatry because they believed that God had abandoned the nation. Tammuz (8:14) was the ancient Babylonian god of vegetation and lover of Ishtar, whose death at the time of the summer heat was mourned annually and whose resurrection was celebrated in the spring. In the inner court of the temple, an area restricted to the priests, Ezekiel observed the worship of Shamash, the sun-god of the Babylonians (8:16). The expression "thumbing their noses" (8:17) referred to some obscure or obscene practice, perhaps connected with the worship of the sun. The "six men" were probably angels (9:2). A "writer's case" (9:2) would contain pens, ink, and a knife for cutting the parchment of papyrus. This marked the beginning of the departure of the glory of the Lord from Jerusalem (9:3). It first left the Most Holy Place, where it had dwelt over the cherubim (see the note on 1:5) mounted on top of the ark of the covenant. It then proceeded to the threshold of the temple, to the east gate (10:19), and finally to the Mount of Olives, east of the city (11:23). The "mark" on the righteous was intended for their protection throughout the forthcoming judgment (9:4; cf. Gen. 4:15; Rev. 7:3).

10:1–11:21 EAST GATE EVENTS

The central truth of Ezekiel 10 is that the judgment to fall on Jerusalem was from the hand of God (10:2, 6-8). The "wheels" (10:2) were described in 1:15-21. The "city" (10:2) referred to Jerusalem. The "glowing coals" (10:2) suggested the manner of Jerusalem's destruction in 586 B.C., that is, by burning. For "chrysolite" (10:9), see the note on 1:16. One of the four faces was described as that of an "ox" (10:14). Since cherubs were angelic beings with a basic animal form and wings, the ox could be regarded as the form of a cherub. Ezekiel linked the cherubim with the "living beings" he saw in 1:5 at the Kebar River (10:22).

The leaders of Jerusalem argued that as the pot protects the meat from the fire, so the walls of Jerusalem would protect the people from judgment (11:3). Ezekiel denied that they would find such protection in the doomed city (11:11). The death of Pelatiah, one of the leaders of the people, was a striking confirmation of Ezekiel's message of judgment (11:13). This led the prophet to intercede for the remnant. God reaffirmed his promise of Deuteronomy 30:1-4 to regather his people to their land after their exile (11:14-17). The promise of a new heart and a new spirit described by Ezekiel were part of what Jeremiah called the new covenant (11:19-20; cf. Jer. 31:31-40).

11:22-25 THE GLORY DEPARTS TO THE EAST MOUNTAIN

After his vision of Jerusalem had ended, Ezekiel reported what he had seen to the community of exiles in Babylonia (11:24).

12:1–19:14 Do Not Trust in a Brief Exile

Overview: The false prophets were mentioned in 12:24-25 and elaborated upon in Ezekiel 13–14. In Ezekiel 13 the false prophets were condemned for predicting Jerusalem's survival. In Ezekiel 14, those who fell prey to the false prophets were described. They had set up idols in their hearts (14:3-7). As the false prophet was, so would be the one who listened to him (14:10). All of God's judgment in this regard sought to recapture his people's hearts (14:5), to bring them into a more intimate relationship with him (14:11, 23). But only personal repentance could allow this to occur; great people of the past could not help (14:12-20), and distant relatives (14:18) could not be blamed for Israel's downfall.

The purpose of Ezekiel 15–16 was to contrast the people's great sinfulness and rebellion with God's

great forgiveness (16:63). And the purpose of that great forgiveness was to make his people ashamed and humbled before him, and lead them to repentance. The last part of this book, Ezekiel 40–48, greatly detailed God's forgiveness and covenant of peace. Therefore, the function of the entire book was to impact the reader with the glory of God's forgiveness so that he would become humble now and not risk the dangers of God's judgment.

Ezekiel 17 describes Zedekiah's attempt to use Egypt's help to defend Israel against Babylon. That prepared the reader for the lengthy section concerning Egypt's destruction (Ezek. 29–32). Rather than blaming their fathers, the Israelites were to change their lives (18:21, 24-25, 30-31). This section ends with a formal lament for the leaders of Israel.

12:1-28 IMMINENT DESTRUCTION

12:1-16 Exile of the Prince of Jerusalem
The sign of the baggage ("pack whatever you can carry on your back," 12:3) portrayed the coming siege of Jerusalem and exile of the inhabitants (12:11). The "wall" (12:5) was probably the wall of Ezekiel's house. The message of 12:10 concerned both the people of Jerusalem ("people of Israel") and Zedekiah, Judah's last king. Although taken captive, Zedekiah never saw the land of Babylon (12:13), for he was blinded by his captors (2 Kings 25:1-7).

12:17-28 Picture of Fear: Eating and Trembling
The sign of trembling (12:18) portrayed the distressing conditions of Jerusalem during the Babylonian invasion, siege, and resulting captivity. Encouraged by the false prophets, the people thought the prophecies of judgment would never be fulfilled, or that they would be fulfilled in the distant future (12:22, 27).

13:1–14:11 TRUE AND FALSE PROPHETS

13:1-23 False Prophecies of Peace
The false prophets who promised peace when there was no peace were denounced (13:2-16). "Jackals" (13:4) were noted for being mischievous, deceptive, and destructive. The false prophets merely whitewashed the insecure walls of the nation instead of strengthening them (13:10-16). Such walls could never withstand the storms of God's judgment. The false prophetesses spoke their own messages, instead of God's, and practiced sorcery (13:17-23; cf. Lev. 19:26). The exact nature and purpose of the "charms" and "veils" (13:18) are unknown.

14:1-11 True Prophecy: Idols in Their Hearts
The "leaders" (14:1) were supposed to be the spiritual leaders of the nation, but they had "set up idols in their hearts" (14:3).

14:12–18:32 ESCAPE FROM JUDGMENT BY REPENTANCE

14:12-23 The Coming Judgment Is Inescapable
The exiles implied that they could rely on their forefathers: Noah, Daniel, and Job. God declared

that judgment on the wicked was not going to be averted by the righteousness of a few. Some scholars have identified "Daniel" with "Dani'el" of the Ugaritic legend discovered in the Ras Shamra Tablets (around 1400 B.C.). But the immoral character of the legendary Dani'el (a participant in drunkenness, cursing, and murder) makes such a view very unlikely. The "survivors" (14:22), a wicked remnant, would be sent to Babylon to show the righteous in exile that God's judgment on Jerusalem was neither excessive nor arbitrary.

15:1-8 Once Burned, but Not Twice
The parable of the unproductive vine showed that Jerusalem, God's vine (Ps. 80:8-12; Isa. 5:1-7), was no longer good for anything but burning.

16:1-63 The Abominations of Israel Are Made Known
The allegory of the adulterous wife forcefully depicted the history of God's dealings with Israel and her response to him. The place of Jerusalem's origin—in Canaan, the land of the Amorites and Hittites—was emphasized (16:3; cf. Gen. 10:15-19; 15:16; Num. 13:29; Josh. 5:1). The rubbing with salt (16:4) was intended to cleanse the skin and strengthen the body. The spreading of the "cloak" (16:8) over Jerusalem symbolized God's marriage with his people (cf. Ruth 3:9). The "covenant" (16:8) may have referred to the Mosaic covenant or possibly the marriage contract between God and Jerusalem. Jerusalem "looked like a queen" (16:13) serving as capital of the united kingdom under David and Solomon.

The image of the "prostitute" (16:15) was often used by the prophets to depict the unfaithfulness of God's people. Since Canaanite worship often included acts of cultic prostitution, the figure of speech was most appropriate. Child sacrifice was one of the horrors of pagan worship (16:20-21; cf. Jer. 7:30-32). Unlike other prostitutes who were paid for their favors, Jerusalem paid others to engage in her illicit activities (16:33-34).

The tribute money was the price of consorting with foreign powers. Jerusalem's corruption was highlighted by comparing her with two wicked "sisters," the cities of Samaria and Sodom (16:46). Jerusalem's wickedness exceeded both (16:48). God promised restoration on the basis of Deuteronomy 30:1-10 (cf. 16:53). If God could restore devastated Sodom, then he would have no trouble restoring Jerusalem. God would remember his "covenant" (the Abrahamic covenant of Gen. 12:1-3) and establish an "everlasting covenant" (16:60; cf. the "new covenant" of Jer. 31:31-34).

17:1-24 Can Israel Rely on Egypt?
Ezekiel 17 is both a riddle and an allegory. As a riddle, it needs to be explained; and as an allegory, it makes several points of comparison. The "great eagle" (17:3) is identified in 17:12 as the king of

Babylon, Nebuchadnezzar (605–562 B.C.), who exiled Jehoiachin and other nobles in 597 B.C. (cf. 2 Kings 24:10-12). The second "great eagle" (17:7) is identified in 17:15-17 as the king of Egypt, Pharaoh Hophra (589–570 B.C.), to whom Zedekiah looked for help in his rebellion against Nebuchadnezzar.

The features of the allegory are explained in 17:11-21. After the exile of Jehoiachin to Babylon (17:12), Zedekiah was placed on the throne as a vassal of Nebuchadnezzar (17:13). He was obedient at first, but then he rebelled, looking to Egypt for help to overthrow the Babylonian yoke (17:15). Zedekiah was exiled to Babylon (17:20) and his troops slain (17:21). The parable of the "cedar" (17:22-24), representative of the house of David, is a messianic prophecy regarding the preservation of David's dynasty (2 Sam. 7:12-16) in spite of the judgment on Jehoiachin and Zedekiah. The "shoot" (Ezek. 17:22) referred to the Messiah (cf. Isa. 11:1; Jer. 23:5), and the "high and lofty mountain" (Ezek. 17:22) was Zion (cf. 20:40).

18:1-18 Individual Responsibility for Repentance
The exiles were accepting the view reflected in the popular proverb that they were suffering the consequences of the sins of their forefathers. Ezekiel declared the principle of individual responsibility for sin ("The person who sins will be the one who dies," 18:4) and expounded it through the chapter. For an understanding of the "pledge" (18:7), see Exodus 22:26. Loans to fellow Israelites were to be without interest (Ezek. 18:8; cf. Exod. 22:25). Eternal life is always secured by grace through faith (Ezek. 18:9; cf. Gen. 15:6; Eph. 2:8). The promise "will surely live" (Ezek. 18:9) referred to physical salvation—deliverance from the curses of the covenant (cf. Deut. 28:15-68).

18:19-32 The Principle Is Summarized
Each person was responsible for his or her own actions. The Israelites were not accountable for the sins of the previous generation. God's ways are just because he deals with people according to their present condition rather than their family history (Ezek. 18:25-29).

19:1-14 LAMENTATION FOR THE PRINCES
The "lioness" (19:2) represented Judah (cf. Gen. 49:9), and the "cubs" (Ezek. 19:3) represented two of her kings. The first of the "cubs" was Jehoahaz, who was taken captive to Egypt by Pharaoh Neco in 609 B.C. (cf. 2 Kings 23:30-34). Judah's next ruler, Jehoiakim, was passed by, and the second of the "cubs" may be identified with Jehoiachin, who was taken to Babylon in 597 B.C. (cf. 2 Kings 24:8-16). The destruction of Judah was likened to the removal of a "vine" (Ezek. 19:10-12). Judah's removal took place in 586 B.C. The "branches" referred to the office of king.

20:1–23:49 Do Not Trust the Leaders for Deliverance

Overview: Behind God's past restraint (20:9, 14, 22) and present judgment (20:44) was the witness of his name to the nations. The section of 20:1–23:49 condemned the sins of the prophets, priests, princes, and people. The Babylonian captivity was compared with Israel's past wilderness wanderings (20:36). The purpose of both was to judge and purify the children of God.

20:1-44 THE IDOLATROUS LEADERS

The oracles of Ezekiel 20 were given just before the fall of Jerusalem. Here Ezekiel described in literal terms the history of Israel's rebellion, which was figuratively portrayed in Ezekiel 16. The leaders had continually rebelled against God; therefore, he refused to answer them when they came to "ask" of him (20:3). What had been true in the past (20:5-29) was true in the present (20:30-32). The people persisted in idolatry and false worship. God's dealings with the nation described in these verses appear to be referring to the future tribulation period (20:33-44; cf. Zech. 13:8-9). Then, as a purged and purified people, they will be united with their Messiah and restored to his land (Ezek. 20:40-42).

20:45–21:32 CERTAIN JUDGMENT ON LEADERS

The passage of 20:45–21:32 concerned the southern region of Judah. The sign of the sharpened sword (21:3), a symbol of divine judgment, indicated that Judah's destruction was imminent (21:1-17). The sanctuary (21:2) denoted the various buildings that together comprised the Jerusalem temple. Compare Ezekiel's mourning (21:12) to Jeremiah 31:19. The intensity of the judgment was indicated by the words "take the sword and brandish it twice, even three times" (21:14), which was perhaps a reference to the three deportations of people to Babylon in 605, 597, and 586 B.C. The sign of Nebuchadnezzar's sword identified the king of Babylon as God's agent of judgment (21:18-27). Rabbah (21:20) was the capital of Ammon, the country east of Israel across the Jordan River.

Divination (21:21) was the art of knowing or foretelling the unknown apart from God's way of prophetic revelation. Among the ways this was done in ancient times included shaking "arrows" from a "quiver" and examining the "liver" of a sacrificed animal. The "prince of Israel" (21:25) referred to King Zedekiah. Israel would have no king until the Messiah came (21:27; cf. Gen. 49:10). The restoration of Jehoiachin to the throne (cf. 2 Kings 25:27-30) was only a temporary measure. Nebuchadnezzar postponed but did not give up his plans to attack Ammon (Ezek. 21:28-32).

22:1–23:49 IDOLATRIES REHEARSED

22:1-31 Cause the City to Know Its Abominations

The purpose of Ezekiel 22 was to make sure that Jerusalem understood "why" judgment was coming. The essence of her sin is found in 22:12, "They never even think of me and my commands, says the Sovereign Lord." "Scatter you among the nations" (22:15) was the ultimate curse of the covenant (cf. Deut. 28:41, 63-64). The sign of the smelting furnace was designed to show the intent of God's judgment (22:17-22). He did not want to destroy his people but desired rather to remove her impurities (her sin) as raw ore must be smelted to remove the dross.

23:1-49 Political and Religious Prostitution

As he had done in Ezekiel 16, the prophet used an allegory in Ezekiel 23 to depict the adulterous character of God's people. However, in Ezekiel 16 the emphasis was upon Israel's spiritual adultery (idolatry), while in Ezekiel 23 the emphasis was upon the nation's political adultery (alliances with Egypt, Assyria, and Babylon). The nation's unfaithfulness began in her youth, even while Israel was still in Egypt. The name "Oholah" (23:4) means "tent woman" and referred to Samaria, representing the northern kingdom. The name "Oholibah" means "My tent is in her" (a reference to the "tabernacle" or temple in Judah) and referred to Jerusalem, representing the southern kingdom. Jerusalem was condemned for alliances with Assyria (by Ahaz, 2 Kings 16:7), Babylon (by Hezekiah, 2 Kings 20:12-15), and Egypt (by Zedekiah, Jer. 2:18; 37:7). "Pekod and Shoa and Koa" (Ezek. 23:23) were tribal groups east of the Tigris River within the Babylonian Empire.

A punishment causing physical deformity was often practiced on a convicted adulteress in Egypt and Babylon (23:25). Jerusalem would experience the same judgment as Samaria (23:32; "You will drink from the same cup of terror as your sister")— the judgment of death that was due the adulteress (23:47; cf. Deut. 22:21-22).

24:1–33:20 Do Not Trust Other Nations for Deliverance

Overview: God is the Judge of all the nations, not just Jerusalem. In Ezekiel 24:1–33:20 the foreign nations were accountable to God on the basis of general revelation and the law of conscience. If they were accountable, how much more accountable were the Judeans, who had been entrusted with the very word of God? This section describes the beginning of the siege of Jerusalem (Ezek. 24) and then shows how happy Israel's surrounding nations were about Israel's imminent destruction. In that light, much is written concerning the judgment on those nations. God's judgment on these nations reflects the background of the Abrahamic covenant (28:26; cf. Gen. 12:3).

As a mighty political and trade center, Tyre received much attention (Ezek. 26:1–28:26). Egypt received much prophecy because of its own pride and Israel's mistaken notion that Egypt could defeat Babylon and save Israel (29:1–33:20). However, like Assyria, Egypt too would fall to Babylon (31:1–32:32).

24:1–25:17 JERUSALEM AND NEAR NATIONS DESTROYED
24:1-27 No Mourning over the Destruction of Jerusalem
The long prophesied attack and siege of Jerusalem began in December of 588 B.C. ("On January 15, during the ninth year" 24:1) and culminated with the destruction of the city in June and July of 586 B.C. The parable of the cooking pot depicted God's judgment on Jerusalem (24:3-14). The cooking pot (Jerusalem) would boil its contents (the people), and then the empty pot would itself be burned up.

The death of Ezekiel's wife was a sign designed to portray the loss of God's blessing for Jerusalem (24:15-24). The "dearest treasure" (24:16) referred to Ezekiel's wife. The same expression was used in 24:21 to refer to the Jerusalem temple. As Ezekiel was forbidden the customary mourning practices with regard to his wife's death, the people were not to mourn God's judgment on Jerusalem, for it was just (24:22-23). On the day the fall of Jerusalem was reported to Ezekiel, his tongue would no longer be dumb (cf. 3:25-27), and he would be free to speak messages of hope and consolation (24:27).

25:1-17 Judgment on Jerusalem's Neighbors
The Ammonites (25:2) were descendants of the incestuous relationship between Lot and his younger daughter (Gen. 19:36-38). Rabbah (25:5), later known as Philadelphia, was the chief city of Ammon. The Moabites were the descendants of the incestuous relationship between Lot and his eldest daughter (25:8-11; cf. Gen. 19:36-38). Seir is another name for Edom (cf. Gen. 36:8), the land of the descendants of Esau. Josephus recorded that Nebuchadnezzar attacked and subjugated the regions of Ammon and Moab five years after the destruction of Jerusalem (*Antiquities*, 10.9.7). Edom, the region of the descendants of Esau (25:12-14; cf. Gen. 36:8), was overrun first by the Nabateans and later by the Maccabeans during the intertestamental period. For Edom's sins, see Jeremiah 49:7-22 and Obadiah 1:10-14. Most of the Philistines migrated from the Aegean Islands to the southern coast of Israel around the twelfth century B.C. (25:15-17). They were a powerful and aggressive people and were Israel's greatest threat at the beginning of the monarchy. For more on the judg-

ment of the Philistines (25:16), see Isaiah 14:29-32 and Zephaniah 2:5.

26:1–28:26 TYRE DESTROYED
26:1-21 The Oracle of Judgment
Ezekiel 26–28 contains judgments against Tyre. Tyre was a Phoenician seaport which had been allied with Israel during the reigns of David and Solomon, but the allies later drifted apart (cf. Joel 3:4-8; Amos 1:9-10). The city was well known for its merchant fleet and commerce. Much of the imagery describing its fall was related to its commercial importance. The "twelfth year" (26:1) was 586 B.C. Nebuchadnezzar besieged Tyre for thirteen years and destroyed the city on the coast, but not the island fortress. Alexander the Great took the fortress in 332 B.C. by building a causeway from the rubble of the city out to the island. Although rebuilt during the Roman period, Tyre was once again destroyed during the Crusades.

27:1-36 Lamentation for Tyre: Mighty Ship
Senir (27:5) was another name for Mount Hermon. Lebanon is the mountain range north of Galilee. Bashan (27:6) referred to the Transjordan hills northeast of Galilee. Elishah (27:7) probably referred to the island of Cyprus. Sidon (27:8) is another Phoenician seaport north of Tyre. Arvad was the most northerly Phoenician town. It was situated on a rocky island directly opposite the island of Cyprus. Gebal (27:9), later known as Byblos, was a Phoenician city just north of modern Beirut. Tyre was depicted as a great merchant vessel that was completely destroyed by an "eastern gale" (27:26), apparently a reference to Nebuchadnezzar. The ruined Tyre was described and lamented (27:26-36) under the image of a sailing ship.

28:1-26 The Ruler of Tyre Is Condemned
While Ezekiel 27 focused on the destruction of the city of Tyre, Ezekiel 28 emphasized the fall and destruction of the leader of Tyre, King Ithobaal II. Following the church fathers, many have suggested that this text describes the person and work of Satan. But some of these verses could not be applied to Satan (cf. 28:18-19). The most natural way to understand this poetical passage is as a satirical attack on the pagan king of Tyre. Many of the images used in the passage were taken from the religious background of Tyre. The patron deity of the city was Baal Melqart ("Baal, king of the city"). Apparently Ithobaal appropriated divine honors ("I am a god," 28:2). To call a king a god was common at that time.

Ezekiel predicted the king's humiliation and demise with poetic language and terms that could be understood by the people of his day who would have been familiar with the religion of Tyre. For "Daniel" (28:3), see the note on 14:14. Like many rulers of his day, this king claimed deity ("I am a god," 28:2), but he was only a man. The prophet lamented the destruction of the king of Tyre (28:11-19). The phrase "perfection of wisdom and beauty" (28:12) was taken from the city's proud boast in 27:3. The name Eden (28:13; cf. Gen. 2:8) was again used in 36:35 to describe a place that was like Eden in vegetation and beauty.

The king viewed himself as the "mighty angelic guardian" (28:14) of the sacred sanctuary of Baal Melqart. The king was "blameless" (28:15) until he became guilty of pride and commercial transgressions. His sin took place in the commercial "trade" area (28:18), something that could not be said of Satan. Sidon, located twenty miles north of Tyre, was subjugated by Nebuchadnezzar when Tyre was defeated (28:20-26; cf. Jer. 27:3, 6). See the note on 26:3-14 for Nebuchadnezzar's siege of Tyre.

29:1–33:20 EGYPT DESTROYED

29:1-16 Initial Condemnation: Pride
The prophecies against Egypt were delivered in January of 586 B.C., about seven months before the fall of Jerusalem. The "king of Egypt" (29:3) at this time was Pharaoh Hophra (588–569 B.C.). Judgment fell on Egypt around 570 B.C., when the country was conquered by Nebuchadnezzar (29:8). Migdol (29:10) was located on the northeast border of Egypt. Egypt was restored to independence around 530 B.C. after the conquest of Babylon by Cyrus (539 B.C.).

29:17–30:19 Two Oracles: Egypt's Destruction
This was Ezekiel's last dated prophecy (570 B.C.). The prophecy of Egypt's fall was fulfilled in Nebuchadnezzar's campaign against Egypt (30:1-19), around 570 B.C. Here the term "day of the Lord" (30:3) was used of the time of Egypt's fall and destruction. The expression may also refer to the future eschatological "day of the Lord." "Lydia" (30:5) is thought to refer to the Ludites (Gen. 10:13; "Ludim," NASB and KJV). The Ludim were probably an otherwise unknown African nation. Some have identified the Ludim with the Lydians of Asia Minor. "Libya" is literally "Chub," a people that has not been identified. For "Migdol to Aswan" (30:6), see 29:10. Ezekiel named the principal cities of Egypt existing in the sixth century B.C. that were destined for destruction (30:13-18).

30:20-26 A Sign of Complete Defeat
The date was 586 B.C., about three months before the fall of Jerusalem. The reference was to Pharaoh Hophra (cf. 29:3).

31:1-18 Egypt compared with Assyria
The allegory of the cedar of Lebanon in Ezekiel 31 depicted the pride and fall of Assyria as a warning to Egypt. The date was 586 B.C., just one month before Jerusalem's fall. Assyria, the great Mesopotamian power to the north, ruled the

ancient Near East from 860 to 612 B.C. The figurative descent into the "grave," the place of the dead, was used to depict the humiliation of Babylon (31:15-17; cf. Isa. 14:15), Tyre (Ezek. 26:20), and Egypt (32:18).

32:1-16 Lamentation for Pharaoh
Ezekiel lamented the destruction of Pharaoh Hophra and Egypt (cf. 29:8). The date was March 3, 585 B.C., one year and seven months after the fall of Jerusalem (32:1).

32:17-32 Lamentation for the Multitude of Egypt
This prophecy was given just two weeks after that of 32:1. "Elam" (32:24) referred to a region of southeast Mesopotamia just north of the Persian Gulf. "Meshech and Tubal" were descendants of Japheth (32:26; cf. Gen. 10:2), who occupied a mountainous area of Asia south of the Black Sea. "Edom," the descendants of Esau (32:29; cf. Gen. 36:8), occupied a region southeast of the Dead Sea.

33:1-20 The Watchman Theme Is Repeated
Ezekiel 33 is a transitional chapter. The message, delivered in February–March of 585 B.C., echoed Ezekiel's commissioning as a watchman. The exiles recognized their own sin and iniquity and questioned what they should do next. God's ways had not changed, and he commanded them to repent (33:11; cf. Deut. 30:15-20).

33:21–39:29 Jerusalem Falls: Now Is the Time for Hope and Rest

Overview: This section examined the accusation that God was not doing right (33:17, 20). This accusation was made by people with hearts that were committed to doing their own evil, no matter what God said (33:31-32). They laid a false claim on the promise to Abraham (33:24). Once Jerusalem had fallen (33:21), God moved on to tell of restoration and peace. The central concepts of Ezekiel 35–39 are found in 34:25-31. The evil shepherds (34:2, 7) would be replaced by the one good shepherd (34:23, 25, 27).

A central concern throughout this section was the vindication of God's holy name (36:21). Ezekiel 37 functions as an illustration of the restoration spoken of in 36:16-38. The covenant of peace was tested for the last time (Ezek. 38–39). While Israel had been regathered, she would undergo one last attempt to displace her from the land.

33:21-33 A FINAL CLAIM FOR DELIVERANCE
The report of Jerusalem's fall was received by the Jews in Babylon January 8, 585 B.C., about a year and a half after the event. Some manuscripts, however, read the "eleventh" month which allowed for six months rather than eighteen for the news to travel to Babylon. With the fall of Jerusalem, Ezekiel's tongue was loosed to begin a ministry of comfort and encouragement (24:25-27). Enjoy-

ment of the land was conditioned on obedience to the covenant.

34:1-31 CASE ANSWERED: DESTROYED BUT FINALLY RESTORED

Ezekiel 34 is an indictment against the wicked leaders of Israel under the figure of "shepherds" (34:2), a common metaphor for kings and rulers. God was Israel's true Shepherd in contrast to the false ones Israel had previously followed (cf. Ps. 23:1; John 10:1-18). God himself would shepherd his people ("sheep"), restoring them to their land after a period of persecution and scattering (34:13). The image changed, and the designations "sheep" and "goats" were used to refer to the leaders of the people, who took advantage of their privileged positions to enrich themselves at the expense of the people (34:17). "My servant David" referred to David's greater Son, the Messiah (34:23-24; cf. Isa. 9:6-7; Jer. 23:5-6). David's name was being used typically as the one who realized the promises given to David in 2 Samuel 7:12-16. The "covenant of peace" (34:25) was associated with but not identical to the new covenant (34:25-31; cf. Jer. 31:31-34). The provisions included the physical blessings of the messianic kingdom.

35:1–36:15 TWO MOUNTAINS: ONE FALLEN, ONE RESTORED

This prophecy against Edom or "Mount Seir" (cf. Gen. 36:8-9) elaborated the judgment pronounced in 25:12-14. Ezekiel 36 contains the most comprehensive description of God's plan of redemption found in this book. "Israel's mountains" (36:1) were representative of all of Israel's land. Restored Israel would be productive (36:8-9), populated (36:10-11), and peaceful (36:13-15).

36:16–37:28 GOD'S HOLY NAME AND ISRAEL'S RENEWAL

36:16–37:14 The Holy Name Vindicated
The restoration promised was the second (36:24; cf. Isa. 11:11), or final, return to the land by the Jews after the Tribulation's scattering. This return is based on the provisions of Deuteronomy 30:1-10. Ezekiel did not use the expression "new covenant" in this passage (36:25-28), but the provisions are identical with those of the new covenant described in Jeremiah 31:31-34. The remnant of Israel will be gathered back to their land as a believing, redeemed people (Ezek. 36:28; cf. Matt. 24:31).

The vision of the dry bones illustrated how the restoration of the nation (Ezek. 36:24) will be accomplished. There were two stages in the resurrection of the dry bones (37:7-10). As Ezekiel prophesied over the bones, they came together and formed human beings, but without the breath of life. Ezekiel prophesied again and "breath" came into them and they came to life (37:9-10). In the interpretation of the vision it was revealed that

Israel would first be brought to national life and restored to the land (37:12), and then the Lord would give the nation spiritual life (37:14). The first stage may have taken place on May 14, 1948, when Israel once again became a nation after a two thousand-year eclipse. The "graves" (37:12) may have been a reference to the foreign countries of Israel's captivities or were simply a reference to Israel's lost hope (similar to the "dry bones").

37:15-17 Unification under One King: the Hand of God
The union of the two sticks, "Israel" and "Judah," represented the reuniting of the northern and southern kingdoms into one nation (37:22). "My servant David" (37:24) was a reference to the messianic king, Jesus (cf. 34:23-24). For the "covenant of peace" (37:26), see 34:25-31.

38:1–39:29 THE LAST TEST OF THE COVENANT OF PEACE

38:1-23 Gog Defeated: God Magnified
Ezekiel 38–39 described the invasion and the destruction of a great northern power, "Gog." One of the major interpretive problems of the book, especially this section, is where in history to put the invasion spoken of here. There are four main views: (1) during the church age, probably at its close; (2) during the Tribulation, after the Rapture; (3) after the Second Coming, just before the beginning of the Millennium; (4) after the millennial reign of Christ. Another possibility is a dual fulfillment during the Tribulation (Rev. 19:17-19) and after the Millennium (Rev. 20:7-10).

There has been considerable discussion over the five names mentioned in these verses (38:2-6). "Gog" is the leader of the land of Magog, a name not found outside the Bible. This land is north of Israel (38:15; 39:2). "Meshech" and "Tubal" (38:2) have been identified as Phrygia and Cappadocia. "Gomer" (38:6) referred to the Cimmerians, tribes settled along the Danube and Rhine that later formed the Germanic peoples. "Beth-togarmah" referred to the Armenians.

The invasion was scheduled for the "distant future" (38:8), an eschatological designation, when Israel is restored to the land and living in security. "Sheba and Dedan" (38:13) refer to Arab peoples. "Tarshish" is also mentioned in Jonah 1:3. God is sovereign over all events (Ezek. 38:16; cf. Eph. 1:11), including the invasion of Gog. He will use this wicked nation to discipline his own people (cf. Zech. 13:8-9). The instrument of judgment ("Gog") will then be judged by God (38:17-23). Ezekiel then provided a more detailed and vivid account of the disaster that will befall Gog's armies (39:1-16).

39:1-29 Gog Defeated: Results Elaborated
The birds and beasts eating of the bodies of the slain was one of the curses of God's covenant with Israel

(cf. Deut. 28:26), and here it is visited upon Israel's enemies. The burning of the weapons of war for "seven" years (Ezek. 39:9) is problematic if interpreted literally. The number "seven" may be used symbolically to represent the complete destruction of military weapons. "Gog's Hordes" (39:11) literally means "the multitude of Gog." Cleansing will be required because bloodshed defiles the land (39:14; cf. Num. 35:33-34). "Hamonah" (39:16) literally means "multitude." The bird supper may correspond with the events recorded in Revelation 19:17-19 or those of Revelation 20:8-9, or perhaps both. The full and final restoration of Israel, both physically and spiritually, will take place after the Tribulation and Second Coming (Ezek. 39:25-29; Zech. 12:10–13:1; Matt. 24:31).

40:1–48:35 THE OCCUPIED TEMPLE: RETURNED GLORY

Overview: There are differences of opinion among scholars regarding the interpretation of the description of Ezekiel's temple. Some interpreters believe it to be the postexilic temple built during the time of Zerubbabel. But there are too many differences between this glorious temple and the temple built after the Exile. Others believe that it describes the kingdom of God in its heavenly state. This equates Ezekiel 40–48 with Revelation 21–22. Others see a figurative description of the present church age. Another view is to see a future temple during a period called the Millennium. Other prophets confirm that there will be a literal, physical temple in the messianic age (Isa. 60:13; Jer. 33:17-18; Joel 3:18; Hag. 2:7; Zech. 6:12; 14:20).

The exact time and nature implied by the vision, however, is secondary to its main point. It is a graphic portrayal that underscores the absolute certainty of the future restoration of Israel and her friends. Ezekiel did not have the benefits of television or motion pictures by which he could visualize the certain message of restoration. His finely detailed and elaborate brick-by-brick description of the new city and temple achieves a similar end: affirmation of future hope. That future hope was to form the basis for present repentance (43:10-11) and obedience to God.

God waited fourteen years after the fall of Jerusalem before he gave this vision (40:1). He started by giving the setting and a guide (40:1-4). Then he described the temple (40:5–42:20). The phrase "I could see" (40:5) marks the two sections of the vision so far: the two descriptions of the temple and God's returning glory. The movement is from the outside to the inside of the temple.

The temple is occupied by God (43:1-9). The east gate events are a direct link to the earlier vision of the sins of Jerusalem and the departure of God's glory (10:18-19). The human obligations of order

and faithfulness are still the same (43:10–44:31). The new land is ruled by a prince who provides for the temple worship and feasts (45:1-24). As in the original conquest of the land under Joshua, the land is described and then divided for the twelve tribes (47:1–48:35). The book even ends like the book of Joshua, with the land allotments and a farewell address.

40:1-4 The Setting: A City and a Guide
The vision of Ezekiel's temple was received in the fifteenth year of Jehoiachin's exile, or 573 B.C. It was the tenth of Nisan (March–April), the day when Jewish families began to prepare for the Passover. The "man" (40:3) was apparently an angel who showed Ezekiel the temple. The "tape" was for longer measurements, and the "rod" for shorter measurements.

40:5–42:20 The Temple Described
40:5-47 THE WALL, GATES, AND INNER COURT
This "wall" surrounding the temple court was not to be confused with the wall that surrounded the entire temple region (42:15-20). The "descendants of Zadok" (40:46) were descendants of the priest who had been faithful to David and Solomon at the time of Adonijah's attempt on the throne (cf. 1 Kings 1:8; 2:35). The "courtyard" (40:47) refers to the inner courtyard of the temple. The "altar" refers to the altar for sacrifice (43:13-17).

40:48–41:26 THE TEMPLE
Unlike the tabernacle or the Jerusalem temple, there is no ark or any furniture found in its Most Holy Place. The purpose of this separate building (41:12) is unknown. It has been suggested that it was to be used for the disposal of refuse from the sacrifices. This "altar made of wood" (41:22) was not the altar for sacrifice, but it corresponds to the altar of incense in the tabernacle.

42:1-20 PRIESTS' CHAMBERS AND OVERALL MEASUREMENTS
The large "wall" (42:20) was different from that in 40:5; it enclosed the whole temple complex, separating it from the rest of the land.

43:1-9 The Temple Occupied: God's Holiness
The same "glory of the God of Israel" (43:2) that Ezekiel had seen departing from Jerusalem (11:22-23) now returns to fill the temple (43:4-5).

43:10–46:24 Temple Obligations: Humans' Holiness
43:10–44:3 THE PROCLAMATION OF HOLINESS
The altar of burnt offerings was designed for use in worship in the Messiah's kingdom (43:13-27). The existence of this altar is the major objection to a literal view of the millennial temple. How can sacri-

fices be offered if Christ's redemptive work is finished (cf. Heb. 10:3-14)? But it should be noted that Ezekiel was not alone in mentioning animal sacrifice during the time of Israel's restoration (cf. Jer. 33:15-18). The Old Testament sacrifices did not have redemptive power in and of themselves (Heb. 10:4), and neither will these sacrifices. Yet the Old Testament sacrifices did point to Christ, the One who would fully and finally deal with sin. And so the millennial sacrifices will point back to the death of Christ in commemoration or remembrance of the perfect sacrifice and salvation that he accomplished at Calvary.

The closure of the East Gate is often linked to the present closure of the East Gate in modern-day Jerusalem (44:1-3). But the closure spoken of here is yet future and will take place during the restored kingdom. Who is the "prince" (44:3)? He has been identified as the Messiah. However, this prince must offer a sin offering (46:12) and will have sons (46:16). Others have identified him with David. But the texts used (34:23-24; 37:24) speak of the Messiah, not the historical David. Thus, the prince is probably a future individual who will serve as a ruler or messianic representative in the kingdom.

44:4–45:8 CARE IN WORSHIP AND LAND PORTIONS
The Levites who were unfaithful during the periods of Israel's history (cf. 1 Kings 2:26-35) will not be able to offer sacrifices (44:13), but they will perform duties in the outer court of the temple (44:14). For the "priests of the family of Zadok" (44:15), see 40:46.

The temple was situated in the middle of a sacred territory measuring about eight square miles, surrounded by the priests' houses (45:1-8).

45:9–46:24 THE WORSHIP OFFERED BY THE PRINCE
An "ephah" (45:11) was a dry measure equal to

two-thirds of a bushel. A "bath" was a liquid measure equal to about six gallons. In 45:25 Ezekiel was referring to the Feast of Tabernacles (cf. Deut. 16:13-15; Zech. 14:16-19). For the "days of new moon celebrations" (46:1), note 2 Kings 4:23; Isaiah 66:23; Amos 8:5.

47:1–48:35 The New Land
47:1-12 THE RIVER
The main point in 47:1-12 is that the land will be restored and blessed with prosperity as the curse of sin is lifted (cf. Rev. 22:3). The river flowing from the temple eastward toward the Dead Sea will bring healing to the parched desert land. This river is similar to but not identical with that found in Revelation 22:1-2. It is symbolic of the blessings that will flow from God's presence in the sanctuary to the land.

47:13–48:35 DIVISIONS FOR THE TRIBES
The northern boundary will run from the "Mediterranean" (47:15) north of Tyre to a point near Damascus. The eastern boundary will run along the Jordan River Valley to the "Dead Sea" (47:18). The southern boundary will run from a point south of the Dead Sea to the "brook of Egypt" 47:19, the Wadi [of Egypt]. The western boundary will run along the coast of the Mediterranean. The "foreigners" (47:22-23) is a reference to Gentile believers who will live in the land and share in the blessings of the Messiah's kingdom.

Ezekiel provided another description of the land and its divisions (48:8-22; cf. 45:1-8). "Joseph" (48:32) was representative of Ephraim and Manasseh, Joseph's two sons. Jerusalem shall be known as "The Lord Is There," a promise of God's abiding presence among his people (48:35). The book ends like the book of Joshua. The Promised Land is given to the cleansed and faithful people of God.

DANIEL

HISTORICAL SETTING
The three deportations of Judah to Babylon
The first deportation of Judah, the southern kingdom, to Babylon was in 605 B.C., during which Daniel was taken as a young man to Babylon (Dan. 1:1). In 597 B.C., after Daniel had been in Babylon for eight years, a second deportation occurred (cf. 2 Kings 24:11-16). In 586 B.C. the third deportation occurred (cf. 2 Kings 25:1-21), and the city of Jerusalem was destroyed. By that time, Daniel had been in captivity for seventeen years.

The return of the Jews to Jerusalem
In 538 B.C. the Persian king, Cyrus, allowed the Jews to return to Israel (cf. Ezra 1:1-4). Daniel's last dated prophecy was made in the third year of Cyrus (Dan. 10:1), around two years after Zerubbabel's return to Palestine. Throughout the entire span of Israel's captivity, Daniel spoke to Israel and influenced her for good. Some captives thought that God had cast Israel aside (Jer. 33:24), but God's work through Daniel in exile showed that he was still present, powerful, and willing to forgive his people.

AUTHOR
The book itself makes the claim to have been written by Daniel, who prophesied for nearly seventy years throughout the Babylonian captivity (Dan. 7:1). He was taken into captivity in the deportation of 605 B.C., maintained a brilliant testimony before his captors, and was blessed with divine revelations of the immediate and far future. Because of the predictive element in the book, some scholars date the book about four

---

THE CHRONOLOGY OF DANIEL

Reference	Date	Event
1:1	605 B.C.	Third year of Jehoiakim
1:21	539 B.C.	First year of Cyrus
2:1	604 B.C.	Second year of Nebuchadnezzar
5:1	539 B.C.	Last year of Belshazzar
5:31	539 B.C.	Darius the Mede
7:1	553 B.C.	First year of Belshazzar
8:1	551 B.C.	Third year of Belshazzar
9:1	539 B.C.	First year of Darius
10:1	537 B.C.	Third year of Cyrus

---

hundred years after the captivity, during the persecution by Antiochus Epiphanes (176–164 B.C.). But the practice of using an ancient hero's name for a book written by someone else does not have enough support here or with any other book in Scripture.

DATE

The writing of the book probably took place soon after the latest date mentioned in the book (10:1), that is, around 536 B.C. The explicit dates in the book cover a time period of approximately sixty-eight years. They were purposely listed to link up with the great kings and movements in Israel's captivity and Babylon's fall under Persia. The issue of international sovereignty was central. The book of Daniel showed that the rise and fall of kingdoms, even secular kingdoms, was in God's hands. See the accompanying chart for a list of dates and events mentioned in Daniel.

PURPOSE

The book of Daniel was designed to encourage the Israelites to live holy lives before God in order to maintain a good witness to those who held them captive in Babylonia.

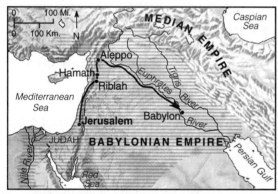

Copyright © 1986, 1988 by Tyndale House Publishers, Inc.

It did this by three means: First, it showed the examples of Daniel and his friends risking their lives to remain faithful to God. Second, it showed how God was totally in control of their present circumstances to care for and preserve his faithful people. Third, it showed the extent of that control through visions of the future, building present faithfulness upon future hope for restoration and fulfillment of God's promises.

GEOGRAPHY AND ITS IMPORTANCE

Daniel had been taken captive from Jerusalem to Babylon. Many years later, while he was still cut off from his homeland, Daniel received visions of Israel going through a long period of domination by the foreign nations of Babylon, Persia, Greece, and the Roman Empire. But Daniel also saw that those geographical and national shifts of power were under the sovereign control of God who would ultimately unify the world under his rule.

GUIDING CONCEPTS

DREAMS AND VISIONS

When one looks at the order of the dreams and visions in the book of Daniel and puts them together with their dates, an even clearer picture of the book's purpose emerges. Three of the visions found in the book of Daniel were dated at the beginning of the reigns of each of the three kings mentioned in the book: (1) Nebuchadnezzar (Dan. 2:1-49); (2) Belshazzar (7:1-28); and (3) Darius (9:1-27). But a look at the section that was originally set off in the Aramaic language (Dan. 2–7) reveals the heart of the book's message. See the accompanying chart, *Dreams and Visions in Daniel.*

The Aramaic section consists of six dreams and the events surrounding those dreams. The beginning and ending dreams in this section (2:4–7:28) consist of two four-part visions that visualize events spanning the course of history. The second and second to last dreams relate two acts of deliverance: from the fiery furnace and the lions' den. The middle two dreams recount God's humbling of two great rulers of Babylon: Nebuchadnezzar, the one who destroyed Jerusalem; and Belshazzar, the last king to rule Babylon before being conquered by the Persian king, Cyrus.

This is how the arrangement looks when grouped by the content of each vision:

1. The Four-Part Statue (2:1-49).
2. The Golden Image: Deliverance from the Furnace (3:1-30).
3. The Tree: Nebuchadnezzar Humbled (4:1-37).
4. The Wall: Belshazzar Humbled (5:1-31).
5. The Edict against Prayer: Deliverance from Lions (6:1-28).
6. The Four Beasts (7:1-28).

The section of Daniel 2–7 was written in a language understood internationally at that time, Aramaic. This was important as it contained truth concerning the Gentile nations. Its content was framed at the beginning and the end with a description of international rule from the present on into the dark future (the two four-part visions). Then, the next level told of two great acts of God's power and mercy to the Jews in captivity (deliverance from the furnace and the lions). But at the heart of the book, two great rulers were humbled and dethroned by God, proving that God alone was sovereign over the international scene. That was the message needed by the captives and the newly returned Jews.

The sequence of visions in this section answered the question of what life would be like for the Jewish nation. It would be under continual domination by the Gentile powers. But an end would come and God would reign. Until then, the book assured the readers, God was in total control of any and all international powers. The book gave a balanced perspective to the present and hope for the future by showing that God was sovereign.

DREAMS AND VISIONS IN DANIEL

Section One (originally written in Aramaic, not Hebrew)

2:1-49	Four-part statue	Nebuchadnezzar's dream (604 B.C.)
3:1-30	Golden Image	Deliverance of the three Hebrews
4:1-37	Tree	Dream of Nebuchadnezzar's humbling
5:1-31	Writing on Wall	Prediction of Belshazzar's end (539 B.C.)
6:1-28	Edict against Prayer	Deliverance of Daniel (539 B.C.)
7:1-28	Four Beasts	Dream: General (553 B.C.)

Section Two (the Aramaic section ends, the Hebrew section begins)

8:1-27	Ram and Goat	Dream: Specific (551 B.C.)
9:1-27	Seventy Weeks	Dream: General (539 B.C.)
10:1–12:13	End-Time Conflicts	Dream: Specific (537 B.C.)

The rest of the book (Dan. 8–12) was written in the Hebrew language to the Jewish people and was a sequence of general and specific visions that elaborated on the visions of the four-part statue (Dan. 2) and the four beasts (Dan. 7).

THE ENDINGS OF THREE VISIONS

The four-part statue vision (2:1-49) ends with the eternal kingdom being established. The vision of the four beasts (7:1-28) ends with the eternal kingdom being established for the saints of the highest One (7:14, 18, 22, 27). The vision of the seventy weeks (9:1-27) ends with complete destruction of the enemy and complete victory, purification, and honor for God's people (9:24). Throughout, God shows his power to rule over hostile forces and bring in his kingdom. That is why the specific events in Daniel 9–12 were so necessary for God's people to hear as they faced that awful time of chastisement and the prospect of an indefinite period of Gentile domination stretching into the future.

BIBLE-WIDE CONCEPTS

THE RELATIONSHIP TO JEREMIAH

Jeremiah 25:11-12 and 29:10 first announced that the Babylonian captivity would last seventy years. Jeremiah 34:13-14 linked the captivity to Israel's lack of observing the seventh-year Sabbaths (cf. 2 Chron. 36:21). The number seventy symbolized the seventy seventh-year Sabbath rests that Israel had not kept. That added up to a 490-year period stretching back into Israel's disobedient history. So, when Daniel was meditating over the seventy years of captivity, he was also meditating over a 490-year period of disobedience. And that seventy-times-seven framework was exactly what God used in the vision of the seventy weeks in Daniel 9. He presented a series of seventy weeks, but of years, not days. The number 490 was already on Daniel's mind. Thus the six aspects (9:24) of purifying at the end of the seventieth week were similar to the function of the seventy years of Israel's captivity.

MIRACLES AND WORLD RULERS

Israel would be dominated by a number of international rulers before the end of Daniel's seventieth week. Israel, the northern kingdom, had earlier suffered under Assyrian domination; Babylon was the present power; and Persia, Greece, and Rome would soon follow, one after the other. Daniel's message was that God would allow those nations a time of international dominance. But eventually he would destroy all national attempts at world rule and replace them with his own worldwide reign.

God had allowed periods of increased miracles at great junctures in history. Those periods stand out clearly: Moses and the exodus from Egypt; Elijah and Elisha; Daniel and the exile; and the time of Christ and the apostles. At times of great new developments God also supplied the faithful with visible proof of his omnipotence. But the faithful also needed proof of his control of the future. The dreams and visions of the future were given to show that God not only had power over the present but he also had knowledge and control of the future. The Lord used Daniel to confirm the end of the age and the certain fact of his future return (cf. Matt. 24:15).

NEEDS MET BY DANIEL

Daniel wrote during Israel's captivity in Babylon, a time of great physical and spiritual loss for the nation. To those who cared, it seemed as if all of God's promises had been permanently broken. There was no temple or land, and no son of David was ruling over God's people. Perhaps the gods of Babylon were stonger than the God of Israel. Perhaps the Israelites should just forget their past and go along with Babylon and its cultural and religious ways. But the book of Daniel affirmed that it was Israel's sin, not God's weakness or lack of care, that brought about captivity. Israel's call to do God's will and prepare for his wonderful future was still in force. Far from conforming to the religion of Babylon, Israel was to conform to God's holiness. His people might be in or out of the Promised Land or in present or future times of trouble, but neither the place nor the problem was to affect the commitment of the people of Israel to their all-powerful and ever-present God. They were probably struggling with thoughts and questions much like these.

- Many of the Israelites thought the kingdom would come after the seventy years of captivity, but Daniel said they had 490 more years to wait. How could God be in control of that?
- If Israel is going to have to wait for deliverance, what is their task in the meantime?
- What possible purposes could God have in letting things go on and on, rather than bringing this age to an end quickly?
- Since Israel is under the godless domination of world rulers, is God still powerful and present to help?

The book of Daniel meets some needs that believers face today—needs born from having to wait for God's victory and not having all the answers. First, modern believers, like Israel, have the great challenge of waiting for God's promises for a better future without losing their hope and desire to please God in the present. Daniel's seventy years of captivity stretched into 490 years until the Messiah would come. And for believers today, the years of waiting for the Messiah's return now approach two thousand. For some believers, their desire to be faithful is inversely proportional to how long it will be before Christ returns. Because the date of his return seems so far in the future, they feel no need to work on the project of personal holiness day by day. But Daniel's words about the distant future were to encourage and sober believers to recognize the powerful hope they actually have. Although Daniel does not diminish the pain and depression of living so long in a sinful world, neither does he allow believers to give up walking with God. On the contrary, the evil of the world that stretches into the future is to be a showcase for the purity and goodness of the faithful.

Second, like Israel in captivity, believers today have the problem of living with and learning from the consequences of their own or others' sins. Daniel's greatest pain is expressed not over the sins of unbelievers, but of believers. Daniel speaks to believers of all ages as those who, like Israel, have suffered discipline for their disobedience yet still are prone to be faithless. But far from browbeating, he shows them how lovingly God preserves them through world evil to the end when they will be fully restored and unbelievers will be judged. The vision of God's present sovereignty and creation's ultimate rest is the fire God sought to light in hearts needing stability and purity. The world and its evil will run its course. But the task of all believers, like Daniel's, is to shine as pure witnesses to the world of God's call to redemption.

OUTLINE OF DANIEL

I. DANIEL BECOMES ESTABLISHED IN THE COURT OF NEBUCHADNEZZAR (1:1-21)
   A. Taken to Babylon (1:1-7)
   B. Daniel Refuses to Be Defiled (1:8-16)
   C. God Grants Knowledge and Understanding (1:17-21)

II. THE TIMES OF THE NATIONS (ARAMAIC SECTION 2:1–7:28)
   A. The Four-Part Statue (2:1-49)
   B. The Golden Image: Deliverance from the Furnace (3:1-30)
   C. The Tree: Nebuchadnezzar Humbled (4:1-37)
   D. The Writing on the Wall: Belshazzar Humbled (5:1-30)
   E. The Edict against Prayer: Deliverance from the Lions (5:31–6:28)
   F. The Four Beasts (7:1-28)

III. THE NATIONS' IMPACT ON ISRAEL (8:1–12:13)
   A. Ram and Goat: Holiness Defiled and Restored (8:1-27)
   B. Seventy Weeks: Holiness Defiled and Restored (9:1-27)
   C. End-Time Conflicts: From Cyrus to the End of the Age (10:1–12:13)

DANIEL NOTES

1:1-21 DANIEL BECOMES ESTABLISHED IN THE COURT OF NEBUCHADNEZZAR

Overview: Daniel 1 shows the pure character of Daniel and his friends. They understood that the Babylonian captivity was for the purification, not the destruction, of God's people. The chapter also emphasizes what God, in his sovereignty, gave to his people. God gave Jehoiakim into the hands of the Babylonians (Dan. 1:2), showing how Daniel came into captivity. God gave Daniel favor and sympathy from the Babylonians (1:9), showing a fulfillment of Solomon's prayer for captives in 1 Kings 8:50. God gave Daniel and his friends knowledge and understanding (Dan. 1:17), setting the foundation for the revelations to come. These men proved the purity of their character. All the visions and interpretations that are seen throughout this book should be viewed as the gifts of God as he had compassion on his people in bondage.

1:1-7 Taken to Babylon

In 626 B.C. Nabopolassar (626–605 B.C.) became the king of the city of Babylon and began a campaign to overthrow the Assyrian yoke. In 612 B.C. Nineveh was captured, and in 610 B.C. Haran,

the last Assyrian stronghold, was conquered. Concerned by Babylon's rapid rise to power, Egypt intervened and gained control of Israel for a brief period. But Egyptian sovereignty was lost when Babylon defeated Egypt at Carchemish in 605 B.C. Babylon became the new world power, and Nebuchadnezzar (605–562 B.C.) moved quickly to secure his newly won territory.

The "third" year of Jehoiakim (605 B.C.) reflects the Babylonian custom of designating the first year of rule as the accession year. Thus, the "third" year (Dan. 1:1) coincides with the "fourth" year of Jehoiakim as reflected in the more common method of reckoning (cf. Jer. 46:2). Jehoiakim (609–597 B.C.) submitted to Babylon and became a vassal king. The appropriation of the temple's vessels reflects the practice of a conqueror placing the gods of the vanquished enemy in his own sanctuary. This gesture claimed victory for the Babylonian gods. Babylonia (1:2) is also called Shinar (NASB) (see NIV footnote; cf. Gen. 10:10; 11:2).

The siege against Jerusalem in 605 B.C. resulted in the deportation of some of the royal family and nobles, including Daniel and his three friends. Ashpenaz was the chief of the "palace officials"

(Dan. 1:3), literally, "eunuchs." While the term was originally used of those who tended to the king's harem, it came to have a general usage for a trusted advisor of the king.

Nabopolassar, the first king of Babylon, was of Chaldean (Kaldu) descent. The term was later applied to the land of Babylonia (i.e., Chaldea) and its inhabitants. Daniel and his friends were given names that honored the Babylonian deities: Bel (Babylonian for the Semitic Baal), Aku (the moon god), and Nebo (son of Bel). Their Hebrew and Babylonian names had these meanings: Daniel ("God is my judge") was changed to Belteshazzar ("May Bel protect his life"); Hananiah ("Yahweh is gracious") was changed to Shadrach ("command of Aku"); Mishael ("Who is what God is?") was changed to Meshach ("Who is what Aku is?"); Azariah ("Yahweh helps") was changed to Abednego ("servant of Nebo").

1:8-16 Daniel Refuses to Be Defiled

The problem with the palace food was that it would not have been prepared according to the Mosaic Law (cf. Lev. 17:10); it may have included unclean meat (cf. Lev. 11); and it may have been dedicated to Babylonian deities (cf. Exod. 34:15). Actually, all food in Babylon was considered unclean by the Hebrews (cf. Ezek. 4:13; Hos. 9:3-4). But the point is that the men were submissive to their captors in everything except those things that would lead to disobedience to God. They would not be defiled.

1:17-21 God Grants Knowledge and Understanding

The words "ten times better" (Dan. 1:20) are probably hyperbole (i.e., exaggeration for emphasis). Daniel 1:21 does not indicate that Daniel's ministry concluded in the first year of Cyrus (10:1; 538 B.C.). Rather, his ministry continued through the Babylonian and into the Persian period.

2:1–7:28 THE TIMES OF THE NATIONS (ARAMAIC SECTION)

Overview: The section of Daniel 2:1–7:28 was written in Aramaic, the language used by the Jews in Babylon, instead of Hebrew (cf. Ezra 4:7). Daniel 2, 3, and 4 all start with Nebuchadnezzar and end with his praise to God. Getting the identification and interpretation of the dream was a matter of life

and death (Dan. 2:17-18). The prayer was for God's compassion (cf. 1 Kings 8:50). Daniel's praise (Dan. 2:19-23) forms the background to all of the actions in the book. God is totally sovereign over times and kings (2:21), and he is the only true source of revelations (2:22). The dreams and visions throughout the book are reflections of God's sovereign control. The three confessions of Nebuchadnezzar (2:46-49; 3:28-30; 4:34-37) confirm God's sovereignty and trustworthiness. God is above all gods and kings (2:47), is able to deliver (3:29), and humbles the proud (4:37).

Nebuchadnezzar, the greatest Babylonian king, had his pride humbled in Daniel 4. Belshazzar, Babylonia's last king, was humbled in Daniel 5. Daniel 6 is about Daniel's deliverance from the lions; it matches up with Daniel 3 and the deliverance of Shadrach, Meshach, and Abednego from the fiery furnace. Darius's praise of God (6:26-27) matches the three praises of Nebuchadnezzar (2:46-49; 3:28-30; 4:34-37). Again, God shows compassion to his captive people through the deeds of their Babylonian captors (6:28; cf. 3:30). The purpose of this section is to detail God's plans to give the kingdom to the people of God through a long process of international ups and downs (7:27).

2:1-49 The Four-Part Statue

2:1-13 MAGICIANS UNABLE TO INTERPRET THE DREAM

The "second" year of Nebuchadnezzar (2:1; 603 B.C.) was actually the third year of Daniel's training. The first year (605 B.C.) would have been Nebuchadnezzar's accession year. Four classes of wise men were identified (2:2): "magicians" were sacred writers or scholars; "enchanters" were sacred priests; "sorcerers" were those who practiced sorcery or incantations; "astrologers" or "Chaldeans" referred to a priestly class in the Babylonian religion.

It is clear that Nebuchadnezzar did not forget the dream (2:5) but required that the dream be revealed in order to validate the interpretation (cf. 2:9). How else could he have known that the interpretation was valid and that his wise men were not deceiving him?

2:14-49 DANIEL RECEIVES AND INTERPRETS THE VISION

The petition led to God's answer and Daniel's praise. Prophetically, Israel has two ages: (1) the present

---

NEBUCHADNEZZAR'S IMAGE AND ITS SIGNIFICANCE

2:36-38	Gold head	Nebuchadnezzar—Babylon
2:39	Silver chest and arms	Persia
2:39	Bronze abdomen and thighs	Greece
2:40	Iron legs	Rome
2:41-43	Iron and clay feet	Divided Roman Empire
2:44-45	The rock cut out of a mountain	The Messiah's kingdom

---

age—the age of promise, and (2) the age to come—the messianic age when the covenant promises will be fulfilled (2:28). Daniel's vision concerned the "future" (2:28), the time from Daniel's day to the establishment of God's kingdom.

From the head downward, the image was made of materials that were of decreasing value but of increasing strength, until the feet (2:31-35), where weakness and deterioration set in. Interpreters vary in identifying the parts of the figure with ancient kingdoms (2:36-45). The commonly accepted view that fits best with the context of the book (cf. Dan. 7–8) is presented in the accompanying chart.

The "rock" (2:45) image is used often in the Old Testament to refer to the Messiah (cf. Ps. 118:22; Isa. 28:16; Zech. 3:9). It becomes one of the most important figures used for Christ throughout the New Testament (cf. Matt. 21:42; Acts 4:11; Rom. 9:33; 1 Pet. 2:6-8).

3:1-30 The Golden Image: Deliverance from the Furnace

3:1-7 THE SETTING
The image was ninety feet high and nine feet wide (Dan. 3:1). Dura was a city six miles south of Babylon. Archaeologists have discovered a large platform forty-five feet square and twenty feet high that may have served as the pedestal for Nebuchadnezzar's image. The "princes" (3:2-3) were chief ruling officials over the provinces in Babylon. The furnace (3:6) may have been a brick kiln used for firing bricks. Several such furnaces have been excavated outside the site of ancient Babylon.

3:8-27 THE DELIVERANCE
The three Jews believed that God was able to deliver them, but they did not presume to know his will (3:17-18). Even in the face of possible martyrdom, they refused to participate in idolatry (3:18). Their confidence may have been based on Isaiah 43:1-2. The "seven times" (Dan. 3:19) was a proverbial expression (cf. Prov. 24:16). The point was to exclude the possibility of supernatural intervention. The Talmud identifies the one "like a divine being" (Dan. 3:25) as the angel Gabriel. Christians usually identify the figure as the preincarnate Christ.

3:28-30 NEBUCHADNEZZAR'S RESPONSE
Nebuchadnezzar's decree served as the climax of this story. It provided for the recognition of Judaism and protection for its followers.

4:1-37 The Tree: Nebuchadnezzar Humbled

4:1-18 THE DREAM
Chronologically, Daniel 4:1-3 belongs at the end of Daniel 4 because the words grew out of Nebuchadnezzar's experiences. This story has an introduction (4:1-3) and conclusion (4:34-37). Nebuchadnezzar must have realized that the dream had special

significance for him because he was alarmed by it (4:5). See the note on 2:2 regarding the various wise men (4:6). Daniel's late arrival allowed for the incompetence of the king's wise men to be clearly demonstrated and gave Daniel's interpretation greater impact (4:8). Daniel's Babylonian name, "Belteshazzar," means "may Bel protect his life." The expression "the spirit of the holy gods" (4:8) suggests that Nebuchadnezzar was coming to a realization that Daniel's God was different, and more powerful, than his own.

The expression "messenger" (4:13) referred to an observing angel. The purpose of the "iron and bronze" (4:15) is unclear. It may suggest that the stump was to be preserved in order that it might grow again. The pronoun "him" (4:15) indicates that the tree represented a person. The "seven periods of time" (4:16) are time periods of uncertain duration. Following the Septuagint, most scholars interpret them to be "years." Daniel 4:17 reveals the major theme of the book—the sovereignty of God.

4:19-27 EVANGELISTIC INTERPRETATION
Through his experience, Nebuchadnezzar (4:20-22) was to learn that the Lord is the ultimate Sovereign and that he delegates dominion so that man cannot take the glory or credit. Daniel counseled the king to repent in order to avoid God's judgment (4:27).

4:28-37 THE KING IS RESTORED
Nebuchadnezzar had every reason to take pride in Babylon. The building of this famous city, with its hanging gardens, massive walls, and many temples, was one of his greatest accomplishments. However he failed to acknowledge that none of this would have been possible apart from God's sovereign will. Nebuchadnezzar suffered from a known form of mental illness called "zoanthropy," which is the delusion that one has become an animal. Nebuchadnezzar learned his lesson concerning God's judgment on pride. Many believe that he was genuinely converted and became a believer in God.

5:1-30 The Writing on the Wall: Belshazzar Humbled

5:1-12 THE WRITING: THE DEMAND FOR DANIEL
Daniel 5 records the downfall of Babylonia and the rise of Persia in fulfillment of the second part of Nebuchadnezzar's vision (2:39). This forms an abrupt shift to the end of Nebuchadnezzar's kingdom. Note the link of 5:2 to 1:2. The year was 539 B.C., and Babylon was surrounded by the armies of Cyrus. Daniel was probably eighty years old at this time, having been taken captive from Jerusalem in 605 B.C. Until recently, the existence of "Belshazzar" as king of Babylon was in question, and thus, the historical credibility of the book of Daniel was also in question. But the discovery of the Nabonidus

Chronicle has confirmed that Belshazzar was the eldest son and coregent of Nabonidus, reigning with his father from 553 to 539 B.C. Nabonidus was in charge of the military, and Belshazzar was in charge of the administration of the empire. The "gold and silver cups" (5:2) were part of the temple's treasure taken from Jerusalem by Nebuchadnezzar in 605 B.C. (cf. 1:2).

The Hebrew word translated "predecessor" (5:2) can be used of ancestors, which was true in this case. In 5:4 Belshazzar was saying in effect, "What god is great enough to do us any harm? We even conquered the people of Israel, and their God." The "third highest ruler" (5:7) was the ruler after Nabonidus and Belshazzar. The "queen" (5:10) was Nitocris, the wife of Nabonidus and mother of Belshazzar.

5:13-30 INTERPRETATION AND FULFILLMENT
The Aramaic words have been transliterated into English: *Mene, Mene, Tekel,* and *Upharsin* (5:25). God gave Daniel the ability to declare the meaning of this cryptic message: *Mene* meant "numbered": God had numbered the days of the kingdom; the repetition of *Mene* was for emphasis. *Tekel* meant "weighed": God had weighed the king in the balances and found him deficient. *Peres* meant "divided": God had divided the kingdom and given it to the Medes and the Persians. *Upharsin* meant "divided": the plural noun form of *Peres,* the plural being used for emphasis.

Daniel became the "third" ruler, along with Nabonidus and Belshazzar (5:29). Ancient historians Herodotus and Zenophon reported that Cyrus had his soldiers divert the Euphrates River, which ran under the walls and through the city. The army then used the river channel to enter and capture Babylon without a fight (5:30; 539 B.C.).

5:31–6:28 The Edict against Prayer: Deliverance from the Lions
5:31–6:9 THE EDICT SIGNED
There are differences of opinion among scholars as to the identity of "Darius the Mede" (5:31). The two major views identify him with (1) Gubaru, whom Cyrus appointed governor over Babylon immediately after taking the city, or (2) Cyrus the Persian (cf. 6:28). Daniel 6 contains one of the most familiar stories in the Old Testament, that of Daniel in the lions' den. "Darius" (6:1) may have been Cyrus or Gubaru (cf. 5:31). For "prince" (6:1), see the note on 3:2-3. The laws of the Medes and Persians were irrevocable (6:8; cf. Esther 1:19; 8:8).

6:10-28 DANIEL DELIVERED FROM THE LIONS
Daniel 6:10 reflects Hebrew prayer habits in the biblical period. The faithful Hebrews faced Jerusalem (cf. 1 Kings 8:41-43; Tobit 3:11), got on their knees (cf. 1 Kings 8:54; Ezra 9:5; Ps. 95:6), and

prayed three times a day (Ps. 55:17). The words of Darius may have indicated true faith or mere hope (cf. Dan. 6:16, with 3:15-17; and cf. 6:26-27 with 2:20-23; 3:28-29; 4:33-35; and cf. 6:28 with 3:30). The "angel" (6:22) may be the same person who was with the three young men in the furnace (cf. 3:25), possibly the preincarnate Christ. Persian law (6:24), in contrast to the Mosaic code (cf. Deut. 24:16; Jer. 31:29), required the punishment of the criminals' families along with the offenders. Some scholars translate Daniel 6:28 as "Daniel prospered during the reign of Darius, that is, the reign of Cyrus the Persian," identifying Darius and Cyrus as the same person (see NLT footnote). Cyrus ruled Persia from 539 to 530 B.C.

7:1-28 The Four Beasts
7:1-14 THE DREAM
Chronologically, Daniel 7 follows Daniel 4. It deals with the Babylonian rather than the Persian period. Thematically, however, it builds on the revelation of Nebuchadnezzar's vision in Daniel 2 and forms the ending bracket to the section of Daniel 2–7.

The "first year of King Belshazzar's reign" (7:1) was 553 B.C., when he began to serve as coregent with his father, Nabonidus (556–539 B.C.). The "four huge beasts" (7:3) compare with the "four" major parts of Nebuchadnezzar's image (cf. 7:17, 2:31-45). The gate of Babylon was decorated with images of winged lions (7:4). The "lion" and "eagle" were both used in Jeremiah 49:19-22 to refer to Nebuchadnezzar, king of Babylon.

Medo-Persia, which succeeded Babylon, was a lopsided coalition like the lopsided bear (Dan. 7:5). Greece, under the leadership of Alexander the Great, conquered Persia in 331 B.C. The "four wings" on the swift leopard (7:6) suggested the speed of Alexander's conquest, and the "four heads," the division of the empire among his generals after his death: (1) Egypt and Palestine were given to Ptolemy; (2) the area of Phrygia to the Indus River was given to Seleucus; (3) Thrace and Bithynia were put under Lysimachus; and (4) Macedonia was given to Cassander. Rome (7:7-8) succeeded Greece with the coming of Pompey to Palestine in 63 B.C.

The little horn (7:8) is the subject of further revelation in 7:24-25. The "Ancient One" (7:9) is a reference to God the Father (cf. 7:13). The one "who looked like a man" (7:13) was distinguished from the "Ancient One" (God the Father) and received a "kingdom" (7:14). This would suggest that he was identified with the coming Messiah and would someday be revealed as the preincarnate Christ (cf. 2 Sam. 7:12-16; Luke 1:32-33).

7:15-28 THE DREAM INTERPRETED
The interpretation of Daniel's vision is first given in summary form (Dan. 7:17-18) and then in further

detail (7:19-27). Daniel was particularly interested in the fourth beast and the boastful little horn (7:8). The fourth beast was actually a "world power" that would be powerful enough to dominate the whole earth (7:23). The "ten horns" (7:24) of the beast (7:7) were identified as ten kings who were contemporaneous with the fourth kingdom. Out of this group would arise the little horn (7:8) who would gain control of the fourth kingdom. His character and activities identify him with the Antichrist of the tribulation period (cf. Rev. 13:1-10). If the word "time" (Dan. 7:25) may be translated "year," the period "time, times, and half a time" would then refer to three and a half years.

8:1–12:13 THE NATIONS' IMPACT ON ISRAEL

Overview: Daniel 8–12 details the future for God's people. Daniel 2–7 detailed the future for the Gentile powers. God was sovereign over the Gentile kingdoms. Daniel 8–12 shows that he is also sovereign to bring ultimate victory to his people. The pattern in this section is to move from the oppression of God's people to their final victory. The explanation of the vision of the ram, goat, and horns in Daniel 8 ended with God's total victory for his people (8:25). Daniel's prayer in Daniel 9 reflected Solomon's prayer long before at the dedication of the temple. It was a prayer that confessed the reason for the captivity in Babylon (9:12-13), petitioned for the end of God's anger toward Jerusalem (9:16), and requested God's compassion, hearing, and forgiveness (cf. 1 Kings 8:30, 34, 36, 39, 43, 45; and especially 8:49-50). God's response to that prayer was the decree of seventy weeks. A period of oppression would end with the complete destruction of the anti-God forces (Dan. 9:27). Jerusalem, once defiled, would have her holiness restored. The great suffering involved here was to instruct the captives that not all suffering under God's sovereignty was due to divine punishment, as was the captivity in Babylon. Much conflict would come from human sources.

Daniel 10 revealed that another and related conflict was in the angelic realm. The subject was what would happen to the people of God in the latter days (10:14). But more space was given to the subject of the struggle to bring the message. Angelic conflict and angelic strength for Israel were stressed. The details of the content of the prophecy of the future were meant to be obscure (12:9). But the overall point was crystal clear: God is absolutely for his people's complete victory and would bring it about.

Daniel 11 continues the speech of the angel and specific details about the kingdoms to come. It concludes with the end of the "despicable man" (11:21, 45). In the various descriptions of the future, note the difference between human attempts to bring in the end (11:14, 27, 35) and the real end of the age and the establishment of the kingdom of God (12:1-3). God's people would suffer, but ultimate victory was certain.

8:1-27 Ram and Goat: Holiness Defiled and Restored

8:1-14 THE DREAM

In Daniel 8, Daniel returned to the Hebrew language (cf. 2:4) because these chapters relate to the history and destiny of Israel. Daniel 8 provides the details concerning the second and third kingdoms, Medo-Persia and Greece. The "third year" (8:1) would be around 551 B.C., when Cyrus established a joint state of Medes and Persians. Elam (8:2) was a province located about 230 miles east of Babylon. Susa was the ancient capital of the Elamite Empire and later became one of the capitals of Persia.

The "ram" (8:3) is identified in 8:20 with Medo-Persia (the lopsided bear of 7:5). The "goat" (8:5) is identified in 8:21 with Greece, and the "large horn" (8:5) symbolizes the empire's first king, Alexander the Great. The destruction of the "large horn" (8:8) was realized with Alexander's death in Babylon (323 B.C.) at the age of thirty-three. The small horn (8:9) is not to be identified with the little horn of 7:8, for this horn arose out of the Greek Empire, while the previous one arose out of the Roman Empire. The little horn should be identified with Antiochus IV Epiphanes (175–164 B.C.), who sought to unify Greek rule through the Hellenization of the empire. He sought to extend his rule south toward Palestine, and he persecuted the Jewish people there.

Antiochus went to Jerusalem and converted the temple into a shrine dedicated to Zeus (8:10-12). On December 16, 167 B.C., he had a sow (an unclean animal according to God's law) sacrificed on the sacred altar, and "daily sacrifices" at the temple (8:11) by the Jews ceased. This defilement interrupted sacrifice for 2,300 evenings and mornings, a reference to the evening and morning offering (8:14). The period, then, was just a little over three years, from 167 to 164 B.C., when the temple sacrifices were reinstated by the Maccabeans.

8:15-27 THE INTERPRETATION

"Gabriel" (8:16) is one of the two angels mentioned by name in the Bible. He has often served God by relaying important messages (cf. Luke 1:19, 26). Daniel 8:23-26 provides further detail regarding the person and work of Antiochus IV Ephipanes (cf. 1 Maccabees 1–6).

9:1-27 Seventy Sevens: Holiness Defiled and Restored

9:1-19 THE PRAYER OF DANIEL

As Daniel 2 and 7 outlined God's prophetic program for the Gentile nations, so Daniel 9 revealed God's prophetic program for Israel. The "first year of the reign of Darius" (9:1) was 538 B.C. He actually took the throne in 539 B.C. Daniel had been studying Jeremiah 25:11 and 29:10 regarding God's promise to restore the Judeans to their homeland after seventy years of captivity (Dan. 9:2). Daniel realized that the period was almost complete (605–539 B.C., sixty-six years of seventy had passed). He wondered how God would bring about the restoration and what would follow.

Daniel is an example of a man of prayer (9:3-19; 2:19-23; 6:10). The "time of the evening sacrifice" would be about 3:00 P.M. (9:21; cf. Exod. 29:39). The "seventy sets of sevens" (Dan. 9:24) may be weeks of "years." The prophecy would then concern seventy seven-year periods, or 490 years. Daniel 9:24 outlines and summarizes the program for this period.

9:20-27 SEVENTY WEEKS FOR RESTORATION

The seventy weeks begin with the "command" to "rebuild Jerusalem" (9:25), which was issued by Artaxerxes for Nehemiah (cf. Neh. 2:1-8). The date was March 5, 444 B.C. The seventy weeks are divided into three periods: During the first (7 weeks, or 49 years), Jerusalem was rebuilt. The second (62 weeks, or 434 years) concludes with the coming of the Messiah at his royal entry, March 30, A.D. 33. The third (one week, or seven years) is still in the future and is possibly to be identified with the tribulation period.

After the sixty-nine weeks (the 62 + 7), the Messiah would be "killed" (Dan. 9:26), an apparent reference to his crucifixion, and "the city and the Temple" of Jerusalem would be destroyed. The "armies" (9:26) were the Roman people, who destroyed Jerusalem and the temple in A.D. 70. There is evidence of a gap between the 69th and 70th week, for what is predicted in 9:27 has not yet taken place. The "ruler" (9:26) is the Antichrist, who will rise out of what may possibly be a revived type of the Roman Empire (7:8, 24-26). In the middle of the "one set of seven" (9:27), or "week," he will take control of the Jewish temple and put a stop to worship, demanding that *he* be worshiped (cf. Matt. 24:15; 2 Thess. 2:4). But he will be destroyed at Christ's second coming (cf. Rev. 19:11, 20-21).

10:1–12:13 End-Time Conflicts: From Cyrus to the End of the Age

10:1–11:1 THE GLORIOUS DELIVERER OF THE VISION

In Daniel 9, the prophet was praying as a result of reading Jeremiah. In Daniel 10, he was praying during the season of the Passover (the fourteenth day of the first month) and the Feast of Unleavened Bread (the fifteenth to the twenty-first days of the first month). The "third year of the reign of King Cyrus" (10:1) was 536 B.C. Daniel had been in Bab-

ylon approximately seventy years. The "man dressed in linen" (10:5) has been identified as either the preincarnate Christ (cf. Rev. 1:12-20) or an angelic messenger (Dan. 10:11). The messenger mentioned here had a human appearance (10:18) and was an associate of Michael (10:13). He may have been Gabriel (cf. 8:16; 9:21). The "prince of the kingdom of Persia" (10:13) was apparently a supernatural figure who tried to oppose God's plan. Michael (the name means "Who is like God?") is one of two angels specifically named in Scripture. He is designated "archangel" (10:13; cf. Jude 1:9). These verses (10:13, 20–11:1) provide some insight into the believers' spiritual warfare (cf. Eph. 6:12). The revelation concerns "the future" (Dan. 10:14; cf. 2:28), from the period of Daniel's day until the inauguration of Christ's kingdom.

11:2–12:4 THE VISION OF THE END

The four kings to follow Cyrus included: Cambyses (530–522 B.C.), Pseudo-Smerdis (an imposter), Darius I (522–486 B.C.), and Xerxes I (486–464 B.C.). The "mighty king" (11:3) referred to Alexander the Great (334–323 B.C), who conquered the Persian Empire. The section of 11:5-20 reveals the warfare that would take place between two of the four generals that inherited Alexander's empire— Seleucus, who ruled Syria, and Ptolemy, who ruled Egypt. These generals fought against one another and used Palestine as their battlefield. The primary purpose of this section was to provide background for Antiochus IV Epiphanes.

Antiochus IV Epiphanes (175–163 B.C.) encouraged the worship of himself in the form of the Olympian Zeus (11:21-35). His name Epiphanes meant "the manifest god," but his enemies perverted it to "Epimanes" ("madman"). This section further elaborates what was revealed about him in 8:9-14. In 170 B.C. Antiochus invaded Egypt and besieged Alexandria (11:25). An insurrection in Jerusalem forced Antiochus to withdraw (11:28). He went to Jerusalem and plundered the temple (1 Macc. 1:20-29). Returning to Egypt in 168 B.C., he was confronted by a Roman commander who forced him to withdraw (Dan. 11:29-30). Bitter about this turn of events, he took out his hostilities on Jerusalem (1 Macc. 1:29-67).

The "western coastlands" (Dan. 11:30) referred to Cyprus. On December 16, 167 B.C., Antiochus desecrated the Jerusalem temple by dedicating it to the worship of Zeus (11:31). The Maccabees resisted Antiochus and eventually cleansed the temple (December 14, 164 B.C.), but many Jews lost their lives during this awful period (11:32-35). In 11:36–12:3 the focus shifts to the prophetic future, from the Antiochus of history to the Antichrist of the end time (7:8). The king of 11:36 was distinguished from "the king of the North" (11:40) and therefore could not have been Antiochus. The "gods of his ancestors" (11:37) may have referred to religion in general or his personal religious heritage (11:37-38). His "god" (11:38) would be military might and power. The "god beloved of women" (11:37) has been variously interpreted to refer to human love, a desire for peace, or the messianic hope. Daniel 11:40-45 revealed the end-time campaign of Armageddon (cf. Rev. 16:16). The ultimate conclusion will be the Antichrist's destruction at Christ's second coming (Dan. 11:45; cf. Rev. 19:11-21). The "glorious land" (Dan. 11:41) referred to Palestine. The "holy mountain" (11:45) referred to Jerusalem.

For "Michael" (12:1), see the note on 10:13. The "time of anguish" (12:1) is the Tribulation (cf. Matt. 24:9-26). Those "rescued" (Dan. 12:1) are the faithful believers who will respond to Christ at his second coming (cf. Zech. 12:10–13:1) and be spared judgment. Two kinds of resurrection were recognized—one to life and one to judgment (cf. John 5:28-29). The "book" (Dan. 12:4) of Daniel's prophecies was to be sealed up or preserved intact until the period to which they applied came about.

12:5-13 FINAL WORDS TO DANIEL

In answer to the question in 12:6, it was revealed that the period of oppression under the Antichrist's dominion would be "time, times and half a time" (12:7), or three and a half years (cf. 7:25). This period coincides with the last three and a half years of the Tribulation. The "sacrilegious object that causes desecration" (12:11) referred to the Antichrist (cf. Matt. 24:15), who will abolish Jewish sacrifice and take a position in the temple, demanding the worship due only to God (2 Thess. 2:3-8). The 1,290 days is three and a half years plus thirty days. That period will bring some aspect of the tribulation judgments to a complete conclusion. The 1,335 days (Dan. 12:12) is three and a half years plus seventy-five days. Some unspecified blessing will be realized for believers who endure to that time, perhaps the beginning of Christ's kingdom reign. Daniel's death ("rest") will culminate in resurrection ("rise") so he can share in the glory of Christ's kingdom (12:13). The book encourages purity while believers wait for the end of this age and the beginning of the next.

HOSEA

HISTORICAL SETTING

Hosea began his ministry in Israel during the prosperous reign of Jeroboam II (cf.
2 Kings 14:25, 28). After Jeroboam's death, anarchy and confusion ensued. Four of the
last six kings of Israel were assassinated. Internationally, Assyria was in the ascendency
and moving west toward Palestine. The kingdom of Israel was at a spiritual low point
during Hosea's ministry. The priests were leading the people into sin (Hos. 4:6-9; 6:9);
idolatry and temple prostitution were rampant (4:11-14); and drunkenness and adultery were characteristic of the kings (7:3-5). Amos and possibly Jonah were Hosea's
contemporaries in Israel while Isaiah and Micah were his contemporaries in Judah.
Hosea and Amos prophesied during the closing years of the northern kingdom of
Israel, even as Jeremiah prophesied during the last years of the southern kingdom
of Judah.

AUTHOR

The book begins by attributing the prophecies to Hosea, the son of Beeri (1:1). Even
liberal critics have attributed most of this prophecy to the historical prophet Hosea.
The author is not mentioned outside this book, and little is known about him. He was
probably a citizen of the northern kingdom and exercised his prophetic office there. He
wrote with familiarity of the circumstances and the topography of the north (5:1; 6:8-
9; 12:12; 14:6).

DATE

Hosea began his prophetic work in the reign of Israel's king Jeroboam II (793–753
B.C.). Because the fall of Samaria was not mentioned by Hosea, it is probable that
he completed his ministry before 722 B.C. His book may be regarded as containing
messages delivered over a period of about thirty years, from 755 to 725 B.C. The
prophecy was probably committed to writing around 725 B.C.

PURPOSE

The book of Hosea was designed to convince the Israelites that they needed to repent
and to turn to their long-suffering God so that judgment might be averted. They
needed to know that God loved them in spite of their unfaithfulness.

GUIDING CONCEPTS

TITLE

The prophecy was named after its author, Hosea, whose name means "salvation" or "deliverance." The name of the prophet was the same as that of the last king of the northern kingdom, Hoshea. In order to keep the two names separate, the English Bible always spells the name of the prophet without the second "h," that is, Hosea.

GOD'S COMPASSION AND CONTENTION

God's loving-kindness was expressed in the terms of the relationships between father and child (11:1) or husband and wife (2:19). But God's compassion also made room for the chastisement of his disobedient people. Those who disobeyed had to be judged (as in a court of law) and God's complaint against them took the form of a lawsuit (4:1; 6:7; 8:1; 12:2). They would be punished according to their fulfillment of God's covenant requirements.

But the chastisement of God's people took place within the context of God's unchanging commitment. His goal through discipline was his people's perfection, never his people's eternal destruction. Through his unfailing love, God desired to inspire a similar love in his people. Hosea emphasized that the essence of God's kingdom was a relationship of response to God's love.

STRUCTURE

The book of Hosea is structured around a movement between passages declaring punishment and passages declaring healing for God's people. Hosea 14:4 lays out the program for the entire book: "Then I will heal you of your idolatry and faithlessness, and my love will know no bounds, for my anger will be gone forever!" To compare passages of apostasy and healing in Hosea, see the accompanying chart.

Although God's discipline for sin may have gotten the attention of his children, it was his love and healing that caused them to repent and return to him. In Hosea, God's lawsuit was completely surrounded by his loyal love.

BIBLE-WIDE CONCEPTS

The priority of God's love over his judgment in the book of Hosea can be seen in how the New Testament writers quoted from the book. Hosea was perfect for expressing how God loved his people even while they were still sinners. The following passages from Hosea are quoted in the New Testament: Hosea 1:10 in Romans 9:26; Hosea 2:23 in Romans 9:25; Hosea 6:6 in Matthew 9:13 and 12:7; Hosea 11:1 in Matthew 2:15; and Hosea 13:14 in 1 Corinthians 15:55.

God's compassion for his people had its source in his character. The classic and

---

APOSTASY AND HEALING IN HOSEA

Apostasy	1:1-9; 3:1-3; 4:1–5:15; 6:4-11; 7:1–11:7; 11:12–13:13; 13:15-16
Healing	1:10–2:23; 3:4-5; 6:1-3; 6:11; 11:8-11; 13:14; 14:1-9

often-quoted passages on his compassion are Exodus 33:19 and 34:5-16. God's sovereign goodness would restore Israel under Davidic leadership (Hos. 1:11; 3:5) and as a whole nation (2:23). The promises to Abraham would be fulfilled. Compare Genesis 22:17 with Hosea 1:10; 2:23; and Genesis 18:19 with Hosea 2:19.

The future Assyrian captivity (8:9; 9:3; 10:6; 11:5, 11; 12:1; 14:3) that God had planned for his people of the northern kingdom was compared and contrasted with the past bondage of Israel in Egypt (2:15; 8:13; 9:3, 6; 11:1, 11; 12:1, 9, 13; 13:4). God's restoration of Israel from Assyrian (and Babylonian) captivity was seen as another saving event, similar to the great exodus from Egypt under Moses.

NEEDS MET BY HOSEA

When God's people suffered, they instinctively asked God why. Hosea wanted to know how Israel's pain, caused by pagan nations, squared with what he knew about God's holiness and love for his people. Why would God allow them to suffer so much? Hosea's audience needed to know that their problems were caused by their own spiritual adultery. The pain of discipline through military defeat had long before been promised in the Law of Moses should the covenant be broken. But the readers' deepest need was to know that the pain was just a step along the way of God's efforts, not to destroy, but to get his people to respond to his love. God stood as the faithful and loving husband. His people stood condemned as unfaithful. But they needed to know that the combination of God's discipline and love was his call to return to him. This book clearly revealed to the people of Israel the goal of and motivation behind God's punishment. The content and structure of Hosea's prophecy show that the Israelites were probably asking questions like the following. Hosea gave them very clear answers.

- Why is the nation of Israel being punished? (Because they have broken God's covenant relationship.)
- Does God now hate his chosen people? (No. He is punishing them because he loves them.)
- Have God's people lost the promises God made to them? (No. He was punishing them so that he could gain their repentance and restore them in the future.)

God's people continually have to struggle with living in a cursed world. In addition, believers have to struggle with their own tendencies to disobey God. And, like Israel, Christians may experience God's painful discipline. During the times of discipline, they need to hear Hosea's message that God's love should be motivation enough to keep them faithful. It was the believers, not God, who broke the bond of faithfulness to such a degree that only the pain of discipline would be sufficient to bring them back. To the question of why, believers receive a twofold answer. The pain was caused by their sin but was motivated by God's loving desire to restore their original relationship of love and obedience. The pain is designed not to make believers run away from God but back to him.

OUTLINE OF HOSEA

I. INTRODUCTION: AUTHOR AND DATE (1:1)

II. HUMAN UNFAITHFULNESS AND GOD'S LOYAL LOVE (1:2–3:5)
   A. God's First Address: Take a Wife (1:2–2:23)
   B. God's Second Address: Love an Adulteress (3:1-5)

III. ISRAEL'S PROSECUTION OVER HER BROKEN VOWS (4:1–13:16)
   A. The Threefold Complaint of God (4:1-3)
   B. The Complaint Elaborated (4:4–13:16)

IV. GOD'S APPEAL OF LOYAL LOVE (14:1-9)

HOSEA NOTES

1:1 INTRODUCTION: AUTHOR AND DATE
"Hosea" means "salvation." Hosea ministered under the reigns of the following kings: Uzziah, or Azariah (791–739 B.C.), Jotham (750–731 B.C.), Ahaz (743–715 B.C.), Hezekiah (728–686 B.C.), and Jeroboam II (793–753 B.C.).

1:2–3:5 HUMAN UNFAITHFULNESS AND GOD'S LOYAL LOVE
1:2–2:23 God's First Address: Take a Wife
1:2-9 THREE CHILDREN AS PICTURES OF JUDGMENT
The prophet's marriage and children were symbolic of the deteriorating relationship between God and his people due to Israel's waywardness. The expression "marry a prostitute" (1:2) is interpreted to mean that Gomer had an inclination toward harlotry that developed after her marriage, or that she was a harlot when she married Hosea. The latter view is probably more in keeping with Israel's history of idolatry from the beginning (cf. Josh. 24:14; Ezek. 23:8; Amos 5:25-26).

The name "Jezreel" (Hos. 1:4) means "God sows," and in this context it referred to the sowing of God's judgment. Jezreel was also a geographical place name used for the broad valley of Esdraelon that separated the hills of Samaria from Galilee. The sins committed by Jehu, king of Israel (841–814 B.C.), in the Valley of Jezreel (cf. 2 Kings 9:11–10:36) would be punished. Jehu's dynasty came to an end in 753 B.C. with the slaying of King Zechariah (cf. 2 Kings 15:8-12). The "end" of the northern kingdom of Israel came in the Assyrian conquest of Samaria in 722 B.C. The expression "put an end" (Hos. 1:5) referred to utter defeat (cf. Ps. 46:9).

The name "Lo-ruhamah" (Hos. 1:6) means "not pitied," signifying that the northern kingdom of

Israel could not expect mercy or compassion from the Lord. The Lord's compassion on Judah, in contrast to Israel, was demonstrated in Judah's miraculous deliverance from the Assyrian siege in 701 B.C. (Hos. 1:7; cf. 2 Kings 19:34-37). The name "Lo-ammi" (Hos. 1:9) means "not my people." This name represented a reversal of the terms of the covenant that God had made with his people (cf. Lev. 26:9-12). This rejection would not be permanent, in light of the unconditional promise of the Abrahamic covenant (cf. Gen. 12:1-3).

1:10–2:23 THREE CHILDREN AS PICTURES OF RESTORATION
Immediately following his words of judgment, Hosea proclaimed a message of hope. He summarized the restoration in the terms of the Abrahamic promise (Hos. 1:10-11), then he gave the details of restoration in 2:1-23. Here God promised physical and spiritual blessing for Israel. The names of Hosea's children, which were previously symbolic of judgment, were changed to symbols of hope. "Ammi" means "my people," and "Ruhamah" means "pitied."

The metaphor of marital separation was used to depict the relationship between God and Israel due to the nation's apostasy. As harlotry undermined marriage, so sin and apostasy separated the people of Israel from their God. The Nuzi Tablets attest to the fact that public exposure of an adulterous wife was common in the culture of the ancient Near East (Hos. 2:3; cf. Ezek. 16:37-38). The "lovers" (Hos. 2:5) of the people were the Canaanite gods, Baal and Asherah, whom they credited with providing the necessities of life.

Hosea described the coming judgment on Israel's unfaithfulness (2:6-13). For "stip her naked" (2:10), see the note on 2:3. Once again Hosea turned from prophecies of judgment to promises of blessing (2:14-23). The logic ("But then," 2:14) was found only in the unceasing love of God for his people. The "Valley of Trouble" (2:15), where Achan died (Josh. 7:26), would become a "gateway of hope." Judgment would lead the way to blessing. Affection was implied in "my husband," while rule was implied in "my master" (Hos. 2:16). The "covenant" (2:18) was simply a divine ordinance that brought harmony to all creation. The words of 2:19-20 are traditionally recited by Jews when they put on their phylacteries (cf. Deut. 6:8). The words "unfailing love" (Hos. 2:19), or loyal love, reflects a central theme in Hosea of God's unceasing love (covenant loyalty) for his people.

The blessings of God's unhindered reign were described (2:21-23). The land that was once made desolate by God's judgment would bring forth grain, wine, and oil. The names once associated with judgment were now associated with blessing: "My people," "plant," and "love."

3:1-5 God's Second Address: Love an Adulteress

Hosea 3 records one of the greatest expressions of God's unceasing love found anywhere in the Bible. It reveals the apostasy of God's people, Israel, and their future repentance and restoration. Although Gomer had been unfaithful, God commanded Hosea to take her back as a wife and love her again. Hosea modeled the alternative to divorce for marital unfaithfulness. The "choice gifts" (3:1) were a reference to idol sacrifices. The price of a slave during the Old Testament period was thirty shekels, but Gomer was worth only half that (3:2; cf. Exod. 21:32). Hosea paid part of the price in grain.

Hosea 3:4 depicted the present condition of Israel—neither idolatrous nor enjoying fellowship with God. The messianic era, the "last days," when God will be reunited with his repentant and believing people ,was described in Hosea 3:5. "David's descendant, their king" referred to the Messiah (cf. Ezek. 34:23-24).

4:1–13:16 ISRAEL'S PROSECUTION OVER HER BROKEN VOWS

4:1-3 The Threefold Complaint of God
In Hosea 4–13 the prophet gave the details of what was set forth through the illustration of his marriage to Gomer in Hosea 1–3. In 4:1-3 Hosea represented the Lord as a prosecuting attorney bringing an indictment ("a lawsuit") against the people for their violation of the covenant's stipulations.

4:4–13:16 The Complaint Elaborated
4:4–6:3 NO KNOWLEDGE OF GOD
4:4-19 The Sins of Israel
The term "mother" (4:5) was used with reference to the nation. Prostitution (4:11-15) was used as an image of spiritual unfaithfulness. The people were

unfaithful to God by turning from him to worship idols. The content of 4:14 is an enigma. Why wouldn't God punish the adulterous daughters? Perhaps because the men were the worse offenders. "Gilgal" and "Beth-aven" (4:15) were centers of false worship. "Beth-aven" ("house of iniquity") was Hosea's name for Bethel ("house of God").

5:1-15 Priests and Kings Condemned
The priests and kings were condemned for ensnaring the people with false worship. "Mizpah" (5:1) was located in Gilead, east of the Jordan River (cf. Gen. 31:49). Several biblical cities bore the name "Tabor" (Hos. 5:1). "Their false religion will devour them" (5:7) meant that in a very short time (a month) they would be judged. "Gibeah" and "Ramah" (5:8) were cities located on hills in the central territory of Benjamin. They would serve as good places from which to sound an alarm.

The "great king" (Hos. 5:13) was probably a reference to Tiglath Pileser III, to whom Ahab appealed for help against the attacks of Rezin and Pekah (cf. 2 Kings 16:7-9). The Lord's withdrawal from Israel's presence (Hos. 5:15) may have referred to the Babylonian exile or possibly the future tribulation.

6:1-11 Exhortation to Return to the Lord
Note the words "a short time" (6:2).
6:4–10:15 NO LOYAL LOVE FOR GOD
6:4-11 The Covenant Transgressed
The "love" (6:4) referred to the covenant loyalty. Hosea did not deny the validity of sacrifice offered in the right spirit, but he declared that mere sacrificial ritual meant nothing apart from a person's heart righteousness (6:6; cf. 1 Sam. 15:22). "Adam" (Hos. 6:7), literally, "man," may have referred to Adam's disobedience to God's command in the garden, or mankind's disobedience in general. "Shechem" (6:9), located about thirty-two miles north of Jerusalem, was the site of the covenant renewal ceremony when the Israelites entered Canaan (cf. Deut. 27:11-14; Josh. 8:30-35).

7:1-16 False Trust in the Nations
"Samaria" (Hos. 7:1), the capital of the northern kingdom (also called "Ephraim"), was used here to refer to the whole country. Only eight of the seventeen kings of Israel died natural deaths (7:7). The other nine were murdered by their successors. Ephraim had joined in alliances with other nations (7:11), and she came out like a "half-baked cake" (7:8).

8:1–9:17 Ultimate Captivity among the Nations
Israel's enemy, Assyria, was likened to an eagle swooping down upon its prey to attack (8:1). The reasons for God's judgment were recorded (8:1-14). The "calf" idol (8:5) referred to the golden calf worship established by Jeroboam (cf. 1 Kings 12:28-29). The worship of idols would result not in feast

but in famine, which was God's judgment on disobedience (Hos. 8:7). The "burden of the great king"
(8:10) referred to the tribute imposed upon Israel by
the king of Assyria. "Go back down to Egypt" (8:13)
is a figurative reference to Israel being carried into
Assyria. God would reverse the Exodus and send
Israel back into captivity.

Because of their spiritual harlotry (9:1-3), the
Israelites would be rejected from God's land. They
would return to bondage, or "Egypt" (9:3). Unable
to offer the firstfruits of harvest in the Jerusalem
temple (Exod. 22:29; 23:19; Lev. 23:10-12), their
food would be considered "unclean" (Hos. 9:3).
The reference to "Egypt" as a gathering place (9:6)
may have alluded to the migration of the Judeans
after the assassination of Gedaliah (2 Kings 25:26).
"Memphis," situated on the Nile just south of
Cairo, was regarded as an important burial center.

The "depraved" actions (9:9) of Gibeah was an
allusion to the atrocity recorded in Judges 19:22-
30. Israel's past apostasy was illustrated from the
incident at Baal Peor (Hos. 9:10-14; cf. Num. 25).
Israel's present apostasy was illustrated by what
was going on at Gilgal, an important site in
Israel's history (cf. 1 Sam. 11:15) that had become
a center for idolatrous worship (Hos. 4:15; 12:11).

10:1-15 Sinful Independence from God As King
"We have no king" (10:3) meant that there was no
king worthy of the title. "Beth-aven" (10:5) referred
to Bethel (see the note on 4:15). The words of the
last part of 10:8 appear in Revelation 6:16. From the
days of the abuse of the Levite's concubine at Gibeah
(Hos. 10:9; cf. Judg. 19:22-30), Israel had had a
history of sin and immorality. Hosea issued a last-
minute call to repentance (Hos. 10:12). "Shalman"
(10:14) was probably a reference to Shalmaneser V
(cf. 2 Kings 17:3). "Beth-arbel" (Hos. 10:14) was a
town located east of the Jordan River in Gilead.

11:1-11 THE TRIUMPH OF LOYAL LOVE: THE SON ISRAEL
Israel's waywardness and God's unceasing love for
the nation were emphasized (11:1). The deliverance of Israel from Egypt was likened to God's care
for a son. The calling "out of Egypt" (11:1) was a
reference to Israel's exodus. This text was used by
Matthew (Matt. 2:15) with reference to Jesus' return
to Israel after being taken to Egypt by Joseph and
Mary. On the basis of the solidarity of the Jewish
people, what was vital in the nation's corporate
experience found its ultimate fulfillment in the
Messiah, Jesus.

"The more I" (Hos. 11:2; that is, God through the
prophets) "called to him" (Israel), the more persistent was Israel's idolatry. "Admah" and "Zeboiim"

(11:8) were towns destroyed with Sodom and
Gomorrah (cf. Deut. 29:23). Hosea looked to a day
of restoration when the "lion" (Hos. 11:10; cf. Rev.
5:5) would roar and his dispersed people would
return from the east and west to resettle in Israel
(cf. Matt. 24:31; Deut. 30:1-10).

11:12–13:16 NO TRUTH: THE SON'S HISTORY IS RECALLED
11:12–12:14 Return to the God of the Exodus
Israel played one nation against another, to her own
destruction (Hos. 12:1). "Jacob" (12:2) was used
here with reference to his descendants, the tribes of
Israel. For these incidents in the life of Jacob (12:3-
4), see Genesis 25:26 and 32:24-28. Hosea reflected
on the past deliverance of Jacob from Esau when he
fled to Aram (12:12; cf. Gen. 29) and Israel's deliverance from Egypt by "a prophet" (12:13), that is,
Moses (cf. Exod. 1–14). Failing to respond to God's
grace, Israel would have to bear the consequences of
sin ("payment," Hos. 12:14).

13:1-16 Destruction and Restoration
Because Israel had forgotten God their Savior
(13:6), the Lord would be to them like a devouring
beast (13:7-8). "Kiss the calf idols" (13:2) referred
to Israel's worship of the golden calves. The allusion (13:10) was to the Israelites' earlier demand
for a king so that they might be like other nations
and protected from their enemies (1 Sam. 8:20).
Israel, "like a child who resists being born" (Hos.
13:13), unwisely delayed responding to God's
discipline.

In spite of Israel's disobedience, God made a
gracious promise (13:14). Paul quoted part of this
verse in 1 Corinthians 15:55. The Assyrians were
noted for terrible atrocities (Hos. 13:16). For example, Ashurnasirpal (883–859 B.C.) boasted of burning men and maidens alive, cutting off the hands
and feet of his captives, and putting out their eyes.

14:1-9 GOD'S APPEAL OF LOYAL LOVE
The prophet issued a final call to repentance and
promised pardon and gracious restoration (14:1-2).
The people promised that they would no longer
turn to Assyria (14:3; cf. 2 Kings 16:7-9), Egyptian
warhorses (Hos. 14:3; cf. 1 Kings 10:28), or idols
(cf. Jer. 10:1-10) for help. God's promise of pardon
and blessing (Hos. 14:5-7) will be realized in the
messianic kingdom. Believing Israel will enjoy such
blessing then that those associated with them will
also greatly benefit (cf. Gen. 12:3). God looked
with favor upon Ephraim's renunciation of idolatry
(Hos. 14:8). God's final words were an exhortation
to see the heart of true wisdom and the justice of
God (14:9).

JOEL

HISTORICAL SETTING
The exact historical setting for Joel's prophecy is not known. One possibility is that he prophesied to the southern kingdom of Judah while Joash served as king. Joash began his reign (835–796 B.C.) when he was a boy, after having been hidden in the temple by Jehosheba to protect him from the murder of the royal offspring instigated by Athaliah as she usurped the throne (cf. 2 Kings 11:1-3). Joash was crowned king at the age of seven by his high priest and advisor, Jehoiada (cf. 2 Kings 11:21–12:2). A devastating locust swarm invaded Judah sometime early in the reign of the young king. That great catastrophe sounded the alarm for a call to repentance in view of a greater judgment to come, the Day of the Lord. If Joel prophesied during the reign of Joash, the ministry of the prophet Elisha was going on at the same time in Israel to the north.

AUTHOR
The author of the book was Joel, the son of Pethuel. Nothing is known about the author's circumstances in life except that he lived and prophesied in Judah and Jerusalem (Joel 1:9; 2:15-17, 23, 32; 3:1).

DATE
Scholars suggest possible dates for Joel's ministry ranging from the reign of Joash (835–796 B.C.) to after the Babylonian captivity sometime in the sixth century B.C. Joel, whose name means "Yahweh is God," lived and prophesied in Judah and Jerusalem (1:9; 2:15-17, 23, 32; 3:1). The book does not mention any reigning king or otherwise datable event. It appears that Amos borrowed from Joel (cf. Joel 3:16 with Amos 1:2; Joel 3:18 with Amos 9:13). This would put Joel before 760 B.C. Also, the position of the book between Hosea and Amos in the Hebrew canon suggests a preexilic date.

PURPOSE
The book of Joel was designed to call the nation to repentance on the basis of the calamity of the locust plague, a token of the more devastating judgment of the coming Day of the Lord. The prophecy was also intended to comfort the nation with promises of future salvation and prosperity in the Day of the Lord, a day of deliverance for Israel and destruction for her foes.

GUIDING CONCEPTS

JUDGMENT AND BLESSING

This book was to be told and retold throughout generations (Joel 1:3) in order to keep its message before the people of God. In view were two locust plagues: one in Israel's past, the other in the future. The locust attack had destroyed the crops of the land and linked back to the promised punishment for disobeying God (1 Kings 8:37-40). The future plague was equated with the Day of the Lord and pictured the army of God coming to destroy his foes (Joel 2:1). The link between the past and future plagues was that both were gracious calls from God for human repentance (2:32).

Some Israelites only saw the redemptive aspect of the Day of the Lord, when God would come to save his people. But they missed its other aspect in which the people of God would experience judgment (cf. Amos 5:18-20). They cheered judgment on their enemies but denied judgment would ever be leveled against themselves.

But even in discipline God would be faithful to preserve the nation (2:32; 3:1, 16). He would also judge the nations for their past acts of injustice toward Israel (3:2). Joel asked his readers to think about the future in light of the past. The future would only escalate and perfect the partial judgment seen in the past attack of locusts. Therefore, the readers were to call upon God so that they would be spared from his wrath.

BIBLE-WIDE CONCEPTS

LOCUSTS AS CURSES FOR COVENANT DISOBEDIENCE

God chose Jerusalem to be the earthly location of his presence (3:16, 21). His people were to keep the laws of the Mosaic covenant and enjoy the blessing of his presence. If they obeyed, God promised his care and provision. If they disobeyed, they could expect his curses. When Solomon dedicated the temple, he mentioned locusts as an example of one such curse (cf. 1 Kings 8:37). Before that, the Mosaic covenant had also spoken of locusts as a curse on covenant disobedience (cf. Deut. 28:38). The locust curse was one of many signs and wonders from God (Joel 2:30; cf. Deut. 28:46).

THE DAY OF THE LORD

The Day of the Lord was first a time of judgment for Israel, and then for the nations. It was a time when God would rule. It would be a terrible day, and Joel asked who could endure it (Joel 2:11). His answer is found in 2:12, 32. The function of the locusts and other signs and wonders was to cause the people to repent. They were acts of a gracious God reaching out to his people.

Joel spoke of a time when the Spirit would be poured out on all humanity for prophecy (2:28), and great cosmic signs and wonders would come about (2:30-31). The prophecies and signs were intended to motivate people to call on the Lord's name (2:32). Peter, in Acts 2, showed how today's believers are participating in that time of the Spirit, even though they still await the completion of all the listed signs and wonders. Paul also used Joel 2:32 to confirm how God saves those who call upon him (cf. Rom. 10:12-14).

NEEDS MET BY JOEL

Joel's audience needed to be reminded of several things. First, they needed to learn that for God's chosen people, painful judgment was yet one more gracious call of God for repentance and restoration. Second, they needed to be reminded of their sin, which had become a way of life. As a first step toward that end, they needed to picture their disobedience not in the context of their limited setting in time but within the grand panorama of God's past and future judgments on sin. In that context they were to ask themselves if their sins were worth their shunning God's love and risking his judgment.

Getting this broad past and future perspective did not come easily. Israel needed to be reminded that the past locust plague, devastating though it was, was only a small taste of the greater future judgment of God. Past judgments were previews of even greater future judgment. It was too easy for the people simply to think that when the locust plague was past, there was no more judgment to worry about. They forgot that God's judgments are not like the days on a calendar to be torn off and forgotten. God's past judgment defines his future judgment, and both are brought into the present by the prophet to show God's never-changing attitude toward sin.

The issue was not, Is judgment here right now? The issue was, Is God here and what is his attitude toward sin? The people who wanted a relationship with God would repent in response to this last question. The one who would rather sin and gamble with God's judgment would not repent. The structure and content of Joel show that the Israelites were asking questions like the following.

- The locust plague was bad enough; what will the Day of the Lord be like?
- If Israel must participate in the Day of the Lord, how can they know that they will survive it?
- Why is it necessary to suffer under all this judgment before God can come to dwell with his people forever?

Like Israel in Joel's day, believers today also need a broad perspective to show them that the past judgment of God against sin was evidenced in the cross and that future judgment will come at the end of the age. Until then, believers are to live in full remembrance of God's hatred toward sin, which cost his Son great suffering and will cost unbelievers an eternity of anguish. How much does God hate sin and want people to return to him? Enough to take the life of his dear Son, to bring judgment upon the world at the end of the age, and to proclaim eternal rewards for the faithful or suffering for the faithless. The judgments on the cross and in eternity are not to be seen only as far in the past and far into the future without present implications. They are to be seen as God's present call to people to repent and live with him in holy fellowship. The book of Joel teaches its readers to be mindful of both the past and future judgments now, and encourages them to fill the present with God's presence and live to please him.

OUTLINE OF JOEL

I. SUMMONS TO HEAR AND TRANSMIT (1:1-3)

II. LOCUSTS AS GOD'S JUDGMENT AND CALL TO REPENTANCE (1:4–2:17)
  A. The Certainty of Destruction (1:4)
  B. Commands for Mourning (1:5-20)

JOEL NOTES

1:1-3 SUMMONS TO HEAR AND TRANSMIT

In Joel 1 the prophet described the devastating effect of the locust plague on the country of Judah. Here Joel reminded the people of the serious nature of the unprecedented calamity and made it the basis for an appeal for national mourning and repentance. The name "Joel" means "Yahweh is God." The rhetorical question (1:2-3) suggests a negative answer.

1:4–2:17 LOCUSTS AS GOD'S JUDGMENT AND CALL TO REPENTANCE

1:4 The Certainty of Destruction

Joel described dramatically and poetically how swarm after swarm of locusts had diminished the potential harvest to nothing. The four different terms used for locusts were probably poetic synonyms rather than four distinct kinds of locusts or stages of locust development. Locust plagues were one of the curses of the covenant for disobedience (cf. Deut. 28:38, 42).

1:5-20 Commands for Mourning

1:5-7 WINE DRINKERS: LOCUSTS

With serrated jaws rasping from side to side, adult locusts consume daily their body weight in food. It is estimated that a single swarm can eat in one day what forty thousand people eat in one year. They are able to live four days without feeding, surviving on stored fat. Locust swarms have been known to blanket two thousand square miles, stripping vegetation, fouling the air with their excrement, and triggering epidemics as they die and rot. Branches (1:7) stripped of bark by the rasping teeth of the locusts were left splintered and ghostly white. The "grain" or "wine" offerings (1:9) could not be offered because the locusts had destroyed the crops.

1:8-12 SONS OF MEN: DROUGHT

The nation, priests, and people were called to mourn the desolation of the land. The nation was likened to a young woman who was widowed on her wedding day. The Judeans had anticipated the joy of harvest (cf. Isa. 9:3; Ps. 4:7), but now because of the disaster, the "joy has dried up" (Joel 1:12).

1:13-20 NATIONAL ASSEMBLY AT THE HOUSE OF GOD

Joel reminded the leaders that repentance was the prerequisite to restoration of God's provision (1:13-14; cf. Deut. 30:1-5; 2 Chron. 7:14) and called the nation to repentance. The "day of the Lord" (Joel 1:15) referred to a time of judgment and deliverance either in the past or in the future. Joel viewed the locust plague as a historical day of judgment that served as a premonition of an even greater future Day of the Lord. Apparently drought followed the locust plague and contributed to the desolation of the land (1:17). Even the animals suffered from the drought and "cry out" (1:20) for a renewal of God's provision (cf. Rom. 8:22).

2:1-11 The Day of the Lord: Who Can Endure It?

Joel returned to the words of 1:15, "the day of the Lord." Here he used the illustration of the locust plague to turn the minds of the Judeans to a far worse judgment yet ahead. The "trumpet" (2:1, lit., "shophar"), or ram's horn, was used in ancient times to signal a military alarm (cf. Jer. 6:17; Amos 3:6). The darkness caused by the locust swarms was used as imagery for the judgment of the Day of the Lord (Joel 2:2). Darkness in Scripture is often a figure for misery, distress, and judgment (cf. Isa. 8:22; 60:2; Jer. 13:16). The "mighty army" that invaded Judah were clearly the locusts (cf. Joel 2:11). They were mentioned as a warning of even greater future judgment. Joel described the locusts and their destruction of the land in vivid, poetic terms (2:3-11). Hyperbole (that is, exaggeration for emphasis) was used to elicit images of greater judgment in the minds of the people (2:10).

2:12-17 Command to Repent

Having warned of the nearness of the approaching Day of the Lord (2:1), Joel called the nation to repentance. The character of God, revealed to Moses in Exodus 34:6, was repeated here (Joel 2:13) as a basis for an appeal for repentance. According to the Jewish Mishnah, newlyweds were excused from reciting daily prayers on their wedding day, but not in such a time of spiritual emergency (2:16).

2:18-27 FUTURE REMOVAL OF THE SAINTS' REPROACH

2:18-20 Removal of the Northerners

Joel 2:18 is also translated, "Then the Lord was zealous . . . and had pity. . . ." In response to the people's repentance, God promised restoration (2:19). The "no longer" (2:19) may have been a promise of deliverance from another wave of locusts, or perhaps it looked forward to a time when Israel would enjoy the blessings of God's future kingdom. The "armies from the north" (2:20) probably referred to the army of locusts that served as the illustration of judgment in 2:1-11.

2:21-27 Restoration of the Locust Years

The "autumn" and "spring" rains (2:23) fall in the early autumn and early spring, respectively. The autumn rains serve to soften the soil for planting winter wheat. The spring rains cause the ripe grain to swell and ensure a good harvest.

2:28–3:21 FUTURE RESTORATION OF ISRAEL

2:28-29 The Spirit Poured Out

Joel described spiritual blessings that God promised to bestow on his people at a future time (2:28-29). The passage was quoted by Peter in Acts 2:17-21 on the Day of Pentecost to explain the outpouring of the Holy Spirit. "After" (Joel 2:28) indicated that the spiritual blessings of 2:28-32 would follow sometime after the physical blessings of 2:21-27. The expression "pour out" (2:28) is a metaphor for abundance (cf. Prov. 1:23) and was mentioned twice for emphasis. The ministries of the Spirit promised here were fulfilled at Pentecost (cf. Acts 11:28; 21:9; 2 Cor. 12:1-4; Rev. 1:1-3).

2:30-31 Wonders Displayed

The heavenly signs promised (Joel 2:30) will take place before the "great and terrible" Day of the Lord (2:31), apparently the period of the most severe judgment (cf. Rev. 16). The kinds of judgments mentioned here also appear in the context of end-time judgment (cf. Rev. 6:12; 8:7-8, 12; 9:18).

2:32–3:21 Survivors Called

2:32 THE PROMISE OF DELIVERANCE
Joel promised that those who repented ("anyone who calls on the name of the Lord") would be delivered. Zechariah 14:1-5 describes this end-time situation as involving a remnant of Jews who repent and believe in the Messiah at his second coming.

3:1-16 THE PLACE OF DELIVERANCE
Just as the Lord had brought judgment on Judah through the locust plague, he promised judgment on the foreign nations for their mistreatment of Judah (Joel 3:2). The time of this judgment is the second coming of Christ (cf. Zech. 14:1-3; Matt. 25:31-46) and God's restoration of Israel will take place at the same time (cf. Matt. 24:31). "Jehoshaphat" (Joel 3:2) literally means "Yahweh judges" and the location of the valley of that name has not been identified with certainty. The basis of God's judgment was the Gentile nations' treatment of the Israelite people (3:2-8). From his experience with Gentile oppression in his own day, Joel listed the kinds of things that the Gentiles will be accountable for—crimes against the land (3:2), the people (3:3, 6), and the temple (3:5).

Some scholars have argued that the mention of the "Greeks" (3:6) supports a postexilic date for Joel. However, Greek people were known to be in Assyria by the time of Sargon II (722–705 B.C.). They also were known to be in Egypt before 1300 B.C. With a touch of sarcasm, God called the nations to prepare for the judgment that is to take place at the Messiah's second advent (3:9-12; cf. Rev. 19:11-15). The nations' weapons will be insufficient to stand against God (Joel 3:10); thus, their "plowshares" should be fashioned into "swords," and their "pruning hooks" into "spears" (3:10). This exhortation is later reversed in Isaiah 2:4 and Micah 4:3. The "warriors" referred to angels (Joel 3:11; cf. Mark 8:38; Rev. 19:14).

The "valley of decision" (Joel 3:14) was another name for the "Valley of Jehoshaphat" (3:2). The nations will not be making their decision, but God will be making his, which will be a verdict of "guilty."

3:17-21 THE RESULTS OF DELIVERANCE
After the judgment on the nations, Judah will enjoy the fulfillment of God's promises to them. Joel concluded the prophecy with a description of the conditions that will exist in the messianic age. An abundance of "wine" (3:18) is representative of the joy that will overflow during the messianic age. Jesus was giving an insight into his person and work when he produced an abundance of wine at the wedding at Cana (John 2:1-11). The "valley of acacias" (Joel 3:18), literally, "Valley of Shittim," was the location of the last Israelite encampment before they entered Canaan (cf. Num. 25:1; Josh. 3:1). "Egypt" and "Edom" (Joel 3:19) were representative of the Gentile nations that have been judged by the Lord. They were set in contrast with Judah, which will be blessed by the presence of the Lord (3:21).

AMOS

HISTORICAL SETTING
Amos prophesied at a time when the southern kingdom of Judah under Uzziah and the northern kingdom of Israel under Jeroboam II were at the height of their prosperity. The northern kingdom's expansion caused it to become the largest and most influential country along the eastern Mediterranean seacoast. Uzziah had expanded the southern kingdom west to the Philistine territory (cf. 2 Chron. 26:6), south into the Negev (cf. 2 Chron. 26:10), and into the territory of the Arabians and Meunites (cf. 2 Chron. 26:7). During this period the relationship between Judah and Israel was peaceful, and both kingdoms enjoyed peace and prosperity that had not been equaled since the reign of Solomon. Assyria was no present threat to Israel, but Amos as well as Isaiah saw that that nation would be the instrument of God's impending judgment on his rebellious people (Amos 5:27; 7:11, 16-17; cf. Isa. 10:5).

AUTHOR
The prophet Amos, whose name means "burden," lived in Tekoa (Amos 1:1), a village five miles southeast of Bethlehem in the hill country of Judah. His occupation was that of a shepherd (1:1) and gardener (taking care of sycamore fig trees) (7:14). Thus he lived in the southern kingdom of Judah but prophesied in the northern kingdom of Israel.

DATE
The prophecy can be dated by the reference in 1:1 to kings Uzziah (791–739 B.C.) and Jeroboam II (793–753 B.C.). A probable date of composition would be around 760 B.C.

PURPOSE
The book of Amos was designed to pronounce judgment against the northern kingdom's social injustices, moral degeneracy, and spiritual apostasy. Amos intended to show the nation's accountability to comply with the covenant's obligations, both in letter and spirit. The prophet insisted that the external practice of religious rituals, divorced from right ethical conduct in society, was unacceptable to God.

GUIDING CONCEPTS

REPEATED PHRASES
An earthquake figured largely in the book (cf. 1:1; 8:8; 9:1, 5). The phrase "This is what the Lord says" signals the start of each new section (1:3, 6, 9, 11, 13; 2:1, 4, 6) in Amos

1–2. Also note the "So I will" pattern (1:4, etc.). There are three short hymns in 4:13; 5:8-9; and 9:5-6. There is a threefold repetition of "Listen" (3:1; 4:1; 5:1).

The repeated phrase "But still you wouldn't return to me" shows the intended result of God's discipline (4:6, 8-11). Any pain God caused was designed to bring the people back to himself. There is a cause and effect relationship repeated throughout Amos 5–6 by the use of "therefore" (5:13, 16, 27; 6:7). Evidently God's people would only admit to the "light" aspect of the Day of the Lord, that is, his redemption (5:18). However, they needed to understand the corrective aspects of the Day of the Lord: judgment first for all, and only then redemption for those who repent.

BIBLE-WIDE CONCEPTS

In 9:8-15, reference was made to the restoration of the fallen tent of David and the blessings to come for all the Gentiles. The goal of reaching the Gentiles explains the list of offending nations at the beginning of the book. They were listed not only as recipients of God's judgment but also because, like Israel, their faithful remnants would receive God's salvation. The Davidic hope of Israel was also the hope of the nations. The implications of this truth were not fully realized until after Christ's resurrection. The apostles and early Christians struggled with how the Gentiles fit into God's plan of salvation (cf. Acts 15).

The original Christian community, primarily composed of Jews, had to accept that the line of David, always so centrally a Jewish hope, was in reality a blessing and hope for the entire world. To substantiate that fact, James quoted Amos 9:8-15 in the Jerusalem council (Acts 15:16-18) that debated whether Gentiles had to follow the rituals of the Mosaic Law, or if they could be saved on the basis of faith in the Messiah (Jesus) alone. Like the promises to Abraham (Gen. 12:1-3), the promises of God to David begin with Israel but inevitably extend to all races because these promises are based on faithfulness to God. In fact, at times God had to bypass blessing the vast majority of the Jewish nation.

At the beginning of the Christian witness in Jerusalem, Stephen quoted Amos 5:25-27 when referring to the Jews' own long history of rebelling against God, who graciously came to dwell with them in the tabernacle. Israel constantly rejected God's prophets. Throughout Scripture God's people, whether under Moses or Christ, could never get away with replacing obedience with claims of religious status based on race, history, or land. See also Acts 7:42-43 regarding Amos 5:25-27.

NEEDS MET BY AMOS

Amos's audience had two problems needing correction: arrogance and despair. First, some of Amos's hearers were arrogant because they thought their religious heritage exempted them from God's judgment. Because they were Jewish, lived in the holy land, and had the temple, they concluded that God would indeed judge the world but certainly never punish them. In their view, the Day of the Lord was light for them and darkness for the world. They were condemning sin in unbelievers but were blind to their own gross offenses against God.

Second, others of Amos's hearers were in despair. They felt that Jewish disobedience had completely wrecked any hope for the fulfillment of God's promises to Abraham and David. If the arrogant were blind to God's comprehensive judgment, the despairing group was blind to God's unbreakable loyalty. His loyalty to his promises could never be broken by human disloyalty. Thus, the book of Amos met basic needs for two quite different groups of people: those who thought their sins would not be judged by God, and those who thought their failures had destroyed all hope for the fulfillment of God's promises. The content and structure of Amos show that the Israelites were struggling with questions like these.

- Are the people of Israel somehow exempt from God's judgment because they are God's people?
- Will the Day of the Lord be a day of judgment for everyone except God's people?
- Have all of Israel's failures voided God's promises to Abraham and David?

Arrogance and despair are also found within the Christian community. Christians may think that because they are in Christ, they are immune to God's disciplining judgment. Or they may think that their failures have cut them off from God's love. Amos asserts that neither one of these positions is true because neither one is true to God's character. He remains holy, and his forgiveness of sins in Christ does not do away with his absolute demand that believers live holy lives. But at the same time God remains loyal to his people, and acts of disobedience can never void his promises in Christ. Amos meets the needs of believers, for rebuke when they snobbishly presume on God's grace, and for encouragement when they foolishly forget God's loyalty.

OUTLINE OF AMOS

I. INTRODUCTION: AUTHOR, DATE, ADDRESSES (1:1-2)

II. INTERNATIONAL CONDEMNATION: VIOLATION OF BROTHERHOOD (1:3–2:16)
   A. The Nations Surrounding Israel Condemned (1:3–2:3)
   B. Israel Condemned (2:4-16)

III. THE ULTIMATE SOURCE OF CONDEMNATION: GOD'S CHARACTER (3:1–6:14)
   A. Certainty of Destruction (3:1-15)
   B. Correction Disregarded (4:1-13)
   C. The Dirge Resulting from Sinful Violations (5:1–6:14)

IV. THE END OF OPPORTUNITY: VISIONS OF FINAL JUDGMENT (7:1–8:3)
   A. Times of Opportunity (7:1-6)
   B. The End of Opportunity (7:7–8:3)

V. WHEN GOD SWEARS NOT TO FORGET (8:4–9:15)
   A. Destruction Detailed (8:4–9:8)
   B. Restoration of the Faithful Kernel (9:9-15)

AMOS NOTES

1:1-2 INTRODUCTION: AUTHOR, DATE, ADDRESSES

Tekoa was located in Judah about twelve miles south of Jerusalem. Amos prophesied around 760 B.C. in the days of Uzziah (791–739 B.C.) and Jeroboam II (793–753 B.C.). The earthquake, referred to two centuries later by Zechariah (Zech. 14:4-5), is said by Josephus to have occurred in connection with Uzziah's sin (cf. 2 Chron. 26:16). Zion is a synonym for Jerusalem. Carmel, the mountain range separating Samaria from the Jezreel Valley, was noted for luxuriant vegetation (Song 7:5; Isa. 35:2). If Carmel "withers" under God's judgment, how great will be the desolation elsewhere where conditions are normally less favorable?

1:3–2:16 INTERNATIONAL CONDEMNATION: VIOLATION OF BROTHERHOOD

Overview: Although the book of Amos is full of flashes of God's judgment, it, like all the books of the prophets, was also a call to repentance (Amos 5:4). Amos 1–2 records the prophecies against the foreign nations. Since the other nations were to be punished for breaches of the law of social justice (1:3, 6, 11; cf. Rom. 2:14), so Israel could not escape. As the list of foreign nations about to be punished grew, so would the glee of the Israelite readers. But Amos went on to expose Israel's mistake, that is, their conception that the Day of the Lord would not touch them. Amos told the readers that the coming Day of the Lord would not be a day of light but one of darkness, both for the Gentile nations and for the people of God (Amos 5:18). The list moved directly from the nations to Judah (2:4) and Israel (2:6).

1:3–2:3 The Nations Surrounding Israel Condemned

1:3-10 DAMASCUS, GAZA, AND TYRE

The phrase "again and again" (1:3) indicated that the list was not exhaustive. The threshing of "Gilead" (1:3) in Transjordan involved driving heavy threshing sledges with iron spikes over their fallen enemies. "Hazael" (1:4; cf. 2 Kings 8:7-15) ruled Aram at the time of Amos. "Ben-hadad" (2 Kings 13:3, 25) was his son and successor.

The prophecy was fulfilled when Tiglath Pileser III captured Damascus in 732 B.C. and exiled its inhabitants (Amos 1:5; cf. 2 Kings 16:9). The "valley of Aven" (Amos 1:5) referred to the Beka Valley in Lebanon. Kir was a province of Mesopotamia from which the Arameans came (cf. 9:7). Gaza (1:6) was one of the major Philistine cities on the southern coastal plain of Judah (cf. 1 Sam. 6:17). It fell to Tiglath Pileser III of Assyria in 734 B.C. Ashdod, Ashkelon, and Ekron (Amos 1:8) were major cities of Philistia (cf. 1 Sam.

6:17). Tyre (Amos 1:9) was a great trade center and port in Phoenicia. The merchants of Tyre were guilty of Israelite slave trade with Edom. The "treaty of brotherhood" (1:9) was between Hiram, king of Tyre, and David and Solomon (cf. 1 Kings 5:1-12). Tyre was besieged by Nebuchadnezzar (Amos 1:10) for thirteen years (585–573 B.C.) and was eventually destroyed by Alexander the Great in 332 B.C.

1:11–2:3 EDOM, AMMON, AND MOAB

Enmity between Edom and Israel can be traced back to the strife between Esau and Jacob, from whom the two nations descended (1:11). Teman (1:12) was a district of Edom, and Bozrah was the chief city. Judgment fell on Edom when the Hasmonean priest John Hyrcanus (135–104 B.C.) conquered the region around 120 B.C., compelling all its inhabitants to adopt Judaism.

The Ammonites descended from Lot's incestuous relationship with his youngest daughter (1:13; cf. Gen. 19:36-38). They occupied Transjordan territory north of Moab. The atrocities mentioned here were perpetuated for the purpose of territorial expansion (cf. 2 Kings 8:12). Rabbah (Amos 1:14), later known as Philadelphia, was the capital of Ammon. The Ammonites were subjugated by Tiglath Pileser III (745–727 B.C.) and by Sennacherib (705–681 B.C.).

The Moabites descended from Lot's incestuous relationship with his eldest daughter (2:1; cf. Gen. 19:36-37). They occupied the land east of the Dead Sea, south of Ammon. Kerioth (Amos 2:2) was one of Moab's prominent cities (cf. Jer. 48:24). Judgment fell on Moab when Nebuchadnezzar completely subjugated the region (cf. Jer. 48:46-47; Josephus, *Antiquities* 10.9.7).

2:4-16 Israel Condemned

While the other nations were punished for sins against the laws of nature and conscience, Judah was judged for sinning against the revealed will of God (Amos 2:4). Land-hungry creditors begrudged the poor even the "dust" that they cast on their heads as mourners (2:7). The statement "Both father and son sleep with the same woman" (2:7) referred to father and son having sexual relations with the same temple prostitute. Garments taken as security for loans were to be returned before sunset, not kept overnight (2:8; cf. Exod. 22:26-27). The "Amorite" (Amos 2:9) was a name often used to designate the people of Canaan generally (cf. Deut. 1:20). They forced the Nazirites to drink wine in violation of their vow (Amos 2:12; cf. Num. 6:1-21).

3:1–6:14 THE ULTIMATE SOURCE OF CONDEMNATION: GOD'S CHARACTER

Overview: Each of Amos's three sermons began with the call "Listen" (3:1; 4:1; 5:1). Amos 4 recounted how all the judgments that God had sent to Israel had not caused them to repent (4:6, 8-11) and ended with a "therefore" of final judgment (4:12). God desired to give them life (5:4, 14-15), but their sins would eventually carry them into exile (5:27). Amos 6 brought criticism on Israel's arrogance and lack of grief (6:6) over their spiritual ruin.

3:1-15 Certainty of Destruction
Because God had taken the Israelites into a special relationship with himself, he would hold them accountable for the unique privilege of having him as their loving and disciplining Father (3:1-2). Amos made an appeal to the law of cause and effect to prove that no calamity came upon Jerusalem except by God's sovereign determination (3:6). Philistia and Egypt (3:9) were representative of heathen nations that had witnessed Israel's iniquity, and they would witness against Israel before God.

The judgment on the northern kingdom (3:11-15) was fulfilled in 722 B.C. after a three-year siege and capture of Samaria by the Assyrians (cf. 2 Kings 17:1-6). Bethel (Amos 3:14), an idolatrous worship center, would be desecrated (1 Kings 12:32). The "horns of the altar" were a place of refuge (Amos 3:14; cf. Exod. 21:14; 1 Kings 1:50), but even this refuge would be denied Israel in her day of judgment. The "palaces filled with ivory" (Amos 3:15) referred to houses with ivory inlays in wooden panels and revealed the vast wealth and waste in Israel. Many of these ivory inlays have been found in the excavation of Samaria.

4:1-13 Correction Disregarded
Amos began his second sermon by addressing the women of Samaria who were likened to the well-fed cows of "Bashan," a territory noted for its luxuriant pastures and fat cattle (cf. Deut. 32:14). Assyrian reliefs sometimes depict captives being pulled along with a rope fastened to a ring in the lip (cf. 2 Chron. 33:11). With biting sarcasm, Amos rebuked the false worship of the Israelites (Amos 4:4-5). Bethel and Gilgal (4:4) were singled out because they had once been such sacred places (cf. Gen. 35:1-16; Josh. 5:1-9) but had been perverted. God brought disciplinary judgment (the curses of the Mosaic covenant) on the people, but they were unresponsive to his chastening (Amos 4:6-11). The phrase "But still you wouldn't return to me" (4:6; etc.) was repeated five times.

5:1–6:14 The Dirge Resulting from Sinful Violations

5:1-27 A CALL TO SEEK THE LORD
Amos's closing sermon called the nation to repentance and restated the outcome of the nation's moral and religious apostasy. The emphasis was a call to seek the Lord (5:4, 6, 14). The past tense ("Fallen," 5:2) indicates that the fall of Israel was so certain that it could be viewed as already having taken place. In 5:4-17

Amos called the people to repentance with the words "seek God and live" (5:4, 6, 14). "Bitter pill" (5:7) is a reference to a bitter, poisonous herb (cf. Deut. 29:18; Jer. 9:15). Those who were responsible to administer justice produced bitter injustice. "Pleiades and Orion" (Amos 5:8) were constellations (cf. Job 9:9; 38:31). Speaking out against injustice may not have been in his best interests, but Amos considered it necessary (Amos 5:13). The "people who remain" (5:15) referred to the faithful of Israel with whom the Old Testament prophecies would be fulfilled (cf. Isa. 6:13; 11:11; Mic. 2:12; 4:7).

In Amos 5:18-20 the prophet noted that some people were looking forward to the coming Day of the Lord, believing that God would deliver and vindicate Israel. Amos corrected that view, showing that the judgment of the Day of the Lord was inescapable. Although the Israelites worshiped God during their forty years in the wilderness, they also served idols (5:26). "Sakkuth" is the Assyrian god of war. "Kaiwan" may have been the Babylonian name of this same war deity. The prophecy of 5:27 was fulfilled in 722 B.C. (cf. 2 Kings 17:1-6).

6:1-14 THE WOE OF ISRAEL'S SINS
The great cities of Mesopotamia, Calneh, and Hamath (Amos 6:2) declined, lost their independence, and were annexed to Assyria. Certainly Israel could not expect to escape judgment. In 6:8-11 Amos predicted the siege and destruction of Samaria ("the city," 6:8). In the midst of such divine judgment, the name of God was not to be used, for to call upon him after such apostasy would be sheer hypocrisy and would invite further judgment. Israel's perversion of justice was contrary to the natural order of things (6:12)—like expecting horses to run on rocks or oxen to plow on rocks.

Lo-debar and Karnaim (6:13) were cities in Transjordan (cf. Gen. 14:5; 2 Sam. 9:4) which Jeroboam II may have captured when he restored the boundaries of Israel (cf. 2 Kings 14:25). Hamath (Amos 6:14) was located in the extreme north of Israel, and the Arabah is located in the south. The enemy would overrun the whole land.

7:1–8:3 THE END OF OPPORTUNITY: VISIONS OF FINAL JUDGMENT
Overview: God showed that he could graciously avert further disaster on the land (7:3, 6). But his offer of grace met with no repentance, so the last three visions revealed certain destruction. Amos 8–9 presented a discussion of God's rights as Creator to judge Israel (cf. especially 8:7-9; 9:5-6). The formula "The Sovereign Lord showed me" introduced the first four of the five visions (7:1, 4, 7; 8:1).

7:1-6 Times of Opportunity
The first judgment envisioned was a locust plague (7:1; cf. Deut. 28:38). The words "the Lord relented"

(Amos 7:3) referred to God changing his method of dealing with sinful creatures. While his attitude toward sin remained the same (7:4; cf. 1 Sam. 15:29; James 1:17), he could change his method of dealing with it, showing mercy in response to his people's repentance. The second vision (Amos 7:4-6) was of a consuming fire about to destroy both the land and the sea ("the depths of the sea," 7:4).

7:7–8:3 The End of Opportunity

The third vision was of a plumb line (7:7-9), an instrument designed to measure whether or not a wall was vertical. Just as a tilted wall would have to be removed, so the nation of Israel would have to be judged. The judgment on Jeroboam II's dynasty was fulfilled with his son Zechariah's assassination by Shallum (2 Kings 15:8-10).

Amaziah (Amos 7:10-17), the priest of the apostate worship center at Bethel, accused Amos of being a conspirator against Jeroboam II and ordered him to return to Judah (7:12). Amos was a farmer until God called him to a prophetic ministry (7:14). A small incision in the "fig trees" was necessary to make them ripen properly. The fourth vision (8:1-3) was of a basket of summer fruit. As the gathering of summer fruit marked the end of the harvest, so Israel had come to the end of her national existence.

8:4–9:15 WHEN GOD SWEARS NOT TO FORGET

8:4–9:8 Destruction Detailed

The section of 8:4–9:8 stressed God's sovereignty as the Creator. He has intimate knowledge and power to judge and to restore. The people of Israel were glad when the Sabbaths and religious festivals concluded so that they could get on with their crooked business practices. The practice of swearing in the name of the gods was referred to in 8:14 (cf. Deut. 6:13; Josh. 23:7). Such deities would be powerless to help in the coming calamity.

The fifth vision depicted the Lord at the altar of an idolatrous shrine, possibly at Bethel (Amos 9:1), about to execute judgment (9:1-8). No matter where the people fled, they would not escape God's wrath (9:2-4). "Carmel" (9:3) referred to the mountain range separating Samaria from the valley of Jezreel. Since God is sovereign over the migrations of nations, Israel could not appeal to her deliverance from Egypt as evidence of divine privilege and exemption from the consequences of sin (9:7). The fifth vision (9:1) began with "I saw" (cf. also 7:1, 4, 7; 8:1).

9:9-15 Restoration of the Faithful Kernel

The end of the book turned to restoration of the faithful remnant, the "kernel" (9:9), of God's faithful people. A promise of restoration and blessing concluded the prophecy. "The fallen kingdom of David" (9:11) referred to the Davidic dynasty, which God promised to restore (cf. 2 Sam. 7:12-16; Luke 1:32-33; and especially Acts 15:16-18). Edom (Amos 9:12) was representative of the Gentile nations that will have a part in the Messiah's kingdom. James appealed to Amos 9:11-12 in Acts 15:16-18 to argue for including believing Gentiles in the church. The kingdom of the Messiah will be characterized by prosperity and security for the people of God (Amos 9:13-15).

OBADIAH

BASIC FACTS

HISTORICAL SETTING

Accepting an early date of 845 B.C. for Obadiah places its writing during the reign of Jehoram (853–841 B.C.). During this time the Edomites expressed their hatred for Israel (cf. 2 Kings 8:20-22; 2 Chron. 21:8-10), and Israel also experienced some major invasions by the Philistines and Arabs (cf. 2 Chron. 21:16-17; Joel 3:3-6).

AUTHOR

Obadiah means "servant of Yahweh." Beyond his name, nothing is known of the life of this prophet.

DATE

The book of Obadiah describes judgment on Edom for its hostilities against Israel. The two most commonly accepted dates for the Edomite hostility described in Obadiah are 845 B.C., during the reign of Jehoram (2 Chron. 21:8-10, 16-17), and 586 B.C., after the destruction of Jerusalem in which the Edomites rejoiced (Ps. 137:7; Lam. 4:21; Ezek. 25:12). Obadiah seemed to be describing a situation that stopped short of the severe Edomite activities of 586 B.C. Thus, the more probable date of composition is during the reign of Jehoram (853–841 B.C.) after Edom revolted against Judah (cf. 2 Kings 8:20-22; 2 Chron. 21:8-17).

Support for the early date of Obadiah is also found in observing that both Amos (760 B.C.) and Jeremiah (627 B.C.) showed an acquaintance with the book. Compare Obadiah 1:4 with Amos 9:2; Obadiah 1:14 with Amos 1:6; Obadiah 1:19 with Amos 9:12; and Obadiah 1:1-6 with Jeremiah 49:7-16. Thus, a very probable date for Obadiah is around 845 B.C., near the end of Jehoram's reign.

PURPOSE

The book of Obadiah was designed to show God's covenant faithfulness to Israel, not to gloat in Israel's ultimate victory over her arch rival, Edom. God showed that he held sovereign rule over all the nations. The book brought comfort to Israel during a low time, and the Lord promised restoration after deep humiliation. Edom was shown as a representative entity of the ungodly powers of this world that threatened the people of God. God would judge Edom's pride and humiliation of Israel (Obad. 1:10-14).

GUIDING CONCEPTS

KEY THEMES

Some of the key themes in this short book are the sovereignty of God (1:2, 8, 15, 21), the causes of Edom's self-deception (1:3, 7-9), and the reason for Edom's approaching downfall (1:10). The Day of the Lord was in view in various passages (1:11-15, 16-18). The book encouraged the remnant of believers (1:17, 19-21) by making firm the promise of restoration to the land. Obadiah taught that judgment and the Day of the Lord were the necessary means to establishing the kingdom. There was constant interplay between the images of two mountains, "Mount Zion" representing the nation of Israel, and "the mountains of Edom" representing the nation of Edom (1:3, 8-9, 16-17, 19, 21).

BIBLE-WIDE CONCEPTS

JACOB AND ESAU

Throughout the Old Testament there had been conflict between the family lines of Jacob and Esau. Those brothers each fathered a nation; Jacob fathered the nation of Israel, and Esau's descendants became the nation of Edom (cf. Gen. 27:29, 39-40; 36:8; Num. 20:14-21). Edom was ultimately destroyed in A.D. 70 by the Romans. The problem addressed in Obadiah was how the kingdom (Obad. 1:21) of the Lord could be regained. God would repay the evil done against Israel by Edom. That was a fulfillment of the covenant of Genesis 12:3—God would curse those who cursed Israel. The promise to Abraham is still in effect (Obad. 1:10, 15; cf. Gen. 27:29). Abraham's land will be restored (Obad. 1:17, 19-20), and all the nations will be judged (1:15).

THE EDOMITES AND CHRIST

Even in the New Testament times strife between the Hebrews and Edomites continued in the Jews' hatred for King Herod who was of Idumean (Edomite) descent. Herod tried to kill the ultimate Representative of Israel, Christ (Matt. 2:1-18). The judgment that would come upon the Edomites because of their cruelty and lack of compassion toward the descendants of Jacob was described in many Old Testament prophecies (cf. Isa. 34:5-15; Jer. 49:7-22; Lam. 4:21-22; Ezek. 25:12-14; Amos 1:11-12).

NEEDS MET BY OBADIAH

The military and cultural wars between Israel and Edom had stretched on for centuries, and, at the time of Obadiah's prophecy, Israel seemed to be on the losing side. God's people needed to know two things: victory was certain and it was for God's glory alone. The book ends with its main point: the kingdom will be the Lord's. The people of God needed to see their present unfortunate circumstances in the light of their future victory. This perspective would not lessen the pain of the present, but it would provide hope and faith: two things necessary for keeping God's people faithful to him. The book of Obadiah met many long-standing needs of the people of God. During this time of difficulty, the people of Israel were probably asking questions like these.

- Will God let Israel's enemies go on harming them forever?
- When will God put an end to Israel's age-old rivalry with Edom?
- Is Israel still being protected by God's promise to Abraham?

The problems between Israel and Edom were not simply minor ancient skirmishes between two little nations. Edom represents all nations (1:15) in two ways: pride against God and hostility against God's people. This pride and hostility took its most ugly form in Christ's crucifixion and received its most destructive blow in Christ's resurrection. From this point on, believers may read the book of Obadiah as a confirmation of God's ultimate rule over the nations. The present aggravation of believers over the pain and injustice of the world needs to be viewed through God's promises. Obadiah should give believers hope during times of suffering and revive their faith in God's certain future. At the same time it calls them to avoid acting with the same arrogance and hostility as God's enemies.

OUTLINE OF OBADIAH

I. GOD'S PROCESS OF CUTTING DOWN EDOM (1:1-9)
   A. Judgment by the Nations (1:1)
   B. Inner Deception: Not Knowing God (1:2-6)
   C. Outer Deception: The Removal of Insight (1:7-9)

II. THE CAUSE AND EFFECT IN EDOM'S DESTRUCTION (1:10-14)
   A. Reason for Judgment (1:10-11)
   B. Warning Not to Repeat Disobedience (1:12-14)

III. THE PURPOSE OF EDOM'S JUDGMENT: RESTORATION OF THE KINGDOM (1:15-21)
   A. International Recompense for Past Deeds (1:15-16)
   B. Jacob's Place in the Recompense of Edom (1:17-18)
   C. The Possession of the Kingdom (1:19-21)

OBADIAH NOTES

1:1-9 GOD'S PROCESS OF CUTTING DOWN EDOM

1:1 Judgment by the Nations

The prophet's name, "Obadiah," meaning "servant of the Lord," was quite a common name in the Old Testament. Nothing is known about this particular Obadiah except that he appears to have lived in the southern kingdom of Judah. "Edom" (1:1), meaning "red," was the name given to Esau when he sold his birthright to his brother Jacob for some reddish soup (cf. Gen. 25:30). The land of Edom was located in a mountainous area southeast of the Dead Sea.

1:2-6 Inner Deception: Not Knowing God

Edom deceived herself (repeated twice in 1:3) by means of her arrogance. She dreamed up an unreal world in which she could never be brought down (1:3). The word "rock" (lit., "sela") probably referred to Petra, an important commercial center of Edom. The city was surrounded by high mountains and could be entered only by a narrow ravine. Although seemingly inaccessible in her secure mountain fortress, Edom was not outside the range of God's judgment. The completeness of Edom's approaching destruction was illustrated by referring to the pattern of thieves and harvesters who had to leave something behind (1:5). By contrast, the plunderers of Edom would leave nothing. Trade routes passing through Edom enabled the people to acquire great wealth. But such "treasure" would be plundered (1:6).

1:7-9 Outer Deception: The Removal of Insight

Edom's prideful inner deception results in her being deceived by the surrounding nations (1:7). Her self-deception made her blind and foolishly susceptible to being deceived by others. Historically, Edom was renowned for her wisdom. Access to international trade routes enabled the Edomites to acquire wisdom from abroad. Thus, Obadiah's statement that they would be deceived contained a tone of sarcasm. Teman (1:9; cf. Job. 2:11), an important city of Edom, was located about five miles northeast of Petra.

1:10-14 THE CAUSE AND EFFECT IN EDOM'S DESTRUCTION

1:10-11 Reason for Judgment

Obadiah explained the reason for Edom's coming destruction. The major scholarly debate over this section relates to the historical circumstances of Edom's sin against Judah. Many scholars would place it in connection with the 586 B.C. destruction of Jerusalem. However, Obadiah made no mention of the Babylonians, Nebuchadnezzar, the deportation, or the burning of the Jerusalem temple. The more probable historical situation was the attack on Jerusalem during the reign of Jehoram (2 Chron. 21:8-10, 16-17), which the Edomites applauded. "Israel" (Obad. 1:10, Hebrew "your brother Jacob") referred here to the Israelites and reminded the people of the brotherly relationship between Esau and his brother Jacob. The Hasmonean leader John Hyrcanus (135–104 B.C.) forced the people of Edom to adopt Judaism or be killed. Edom, known later as Idumea, was attacked and devastated by Simon ben Gioras during the Jewish War (A.D. 66–70). Josephus reported that the land was totally destroyed.

1:12-14 Warning Not to Repeat Disobedience

Obadiah described the actions of the Edomites as if he were viewing an instant playback. The eight imperatives (1:12-14) described what the Edomites actually did while Jerusalem was being destroyed. The Edomites took up positions around the city where they could prevent the escape of the Jewish fugitives and turn them over to the enemy (1:14).

1:15-21 THE PURPOSE OF EDOM'S JUDGMENT: RESTORATION OF THE KINGDOM

1:15-16 International Recompense for Past Deeds

Obadiah described the "day" of the Lord (1:15) as drawing near. This expression was used to describe both the judgment and blessing that Edom would experience historically and the future judgment and blessing that will be experienced in the final Day of the Lord. Obadiah appeared to blend both elements to show that what Edom would experience historically would be the fate of all godless nations in the future. The words "godless nations" (not just Edom) indicate that the prophet had a future judgment in view.

1:17-18 Jacob's Place in the Recompense of Edom

Whereas nations like Edom could expect only judgment, the righteous, like the faithful of Israel, awaited restoration and blessing. "Israel" (1:18), representative of the wicked nations that persecuted God's people, would be totally destroyed, in keeping with the promise of Genesis 12:3.

1:19-21 The Possession of the Kingdom

Obadiah described the full extent of Israel's restoration to the land. The "Negev" (Obad. 1:19) referred to the southern, dry region centering around Beersheba. The "foothills" referred to the low hills between the Philistine coastal plain and the hill country of Judea. Ephraim and Samaria (1:19) referred to the territories of the northern kingdom. Benjamin was located just north of Judah. Gilead was in Transjordan, southeast of the Sea of Galilee. Zarephath (1:20) was located in Phoenicia. Sepharad is of uncertain location. Recent scholarship suggests that it was identical with Sardis of Asia Minor. The "deliverers" (1:21) who ascended Mount Zion (Jerusalem) probably referred to returned exiles (1:17). They may have been appointed to help in the Lord Messiah's kingdom rule. At that time the kingdom was not the Lord's (1:21); it was in the hands of sinful leaders and followers. But someday it would be fully under the Lord's rule (1:21).

JONAH

BASIC FACTS

HISTORICAL SETTING
Jonah ministered under Jeroboam II (793–753 B.C.). Nineveh, the greatest city of the Assyrian Empire, had already begun to take tribute from Israel as early as 841 B.C.; thus Jonah was called to go to the dominant city of Israel's enemy nation. Assyria would continue to have supremacy until its destruction by Babylonia in 612 B.C.

AUTHOR
Jonah was only mentioned once elsewhere in Old Testament Scripture (2 Kings 14:25). No other facts about Jonah are known, except the name of his father (Jon. 1:1) and his birthplace (2 Kings 14:25).

DATE
Jonah ministered during the reign of Jeroboam II, who ruled from 793 to 753 B.C. If the Jonah mentioned in 2 Kings 14:25 was the author of this book, then the date of writing was around 760 B.C.

PURPOSE
The book of Jonah was designed to convict the readers of their selfishness and bigotry concerning the spread of God's message of salvation to all ethnic groups. It contrasted the great unbiased compassion of God with the miserly and inbred self-interest of Jonah and his provincial religion.

GEOGRAPHY AND ITS IMPORTANCE

Jonah wanted to flee to Tarshish because it was in the opposite direction from Nineveh. The great geographical distance between Tarshish and Nineveh matched Jonah's emotional distance from the spiritually needy people in Nineveh. God loved and wanted to save Nineveh, but Jonah did not want God to have mercy on Israel's great enemy. In the middle of the great fish Jonah received God's mercy and praised God for his salvation. But when Jonah arrived in the middle of Nineveh, his heart was far away from the people and God's love for them.

GUIDING CONCEPTS

STRUCTURE

The book of Jonah is not a typical prophetic address. It is a very personal story about the prophet's disgust at thinking that God might forgive a group of non-Israelite pagans. The book was structured around two commands for Jonah to go to

Copyright © 1986, 1988 by Tyndale House Publishers, Inc.

Nineveh (1:2; 3:2). Those two commands support two interpretive points. First, God confirmed the calling of Jonah, and the nation of Israel along with him, to be evangelistic lights to the nations. Jonah had to wrestle with his own choice of confessing or denying God's love for the nations. Second, God confirmed his own unchanging desire for the redemption of the world outside of Israel. At the structural center of the book is Jonah's psalm of praise (2:1-9). This psalm provides the book with a basic theological viewpoint ("salvation comes from the Lord," 2:9). That viewpoint resulted in conflict for Jonah but redemption for the sailors on Jonah's "getaway" ship and for the people of Nineveh.

The content of the book was organized in a layered manner.

1:1-3 Jonah's Unexplained Disobedience
1:4-16 God Saves the Sailors
1:17–2:10 God Saves Jonah
3:1-10 God Saves Nineveh
4:1-11 Jonah's Disobedience Explained and Challenged

Note the relationships between the first and last parts, and the second and fourth parts of the outline above. Part three (1:17–2:10) was at the very heart of the book and was framed between the layers of God's salvation of the sailors on the "getaway" boat and the people of Nineveh. The outer layers formed a book-wide frame of Jonah's disobedience. The questions of 4:4 and 4:9 pointed the way to the book's message and application. If God was so willing to save sailors, Jonah, and Nineveh, why was Jonah so angry?

MESSAGE

Why did Jonah not delight in telling Nineveh of its possible destruction (1:2)? Jonah's disobedience was not explained until 4:2, where he quoted Exodus 34:6. He knew that if the people of Nineveh repented, God would forgive them. And that galled him. God's final questions to Jonah were questions for the readers as well (Jon. 4:9). The message of impending judgment had one major purpose: to get people to repent and avoid judgment. Only a sour person like Jonah would get angry because God had forgiven someone else.

BIBLE-WIDE CONCEPTS

God's universal rule and offer of redemption were mentioned throughout the Old Testament (cf. Gen. 9:27; 12:3; Lev. 19:33-34; 1 Sam. 2:10; Isa. 2:2; Joel 2:28-32). God greatly desired for all the people in Nineveh to come to know him. Jonah's quote of Exodus 34:6 in 4:2 showed that God's compassion extended worldwide, not just to the Jews under the Mosaic covenant. But Jonah did not want to accept the worldwide perspective of the Abrahamic covenant, in which all nations would be blessed. Compassion (Exod. 34:6) is of the very character of God; therefore, it is universal, not bound by ethnic and geographic limits.

The Lord used the book of Jonah as a prophetic sign of the future redemption in Christ for both Jew and Gentile (cf. Matt. 12:39-41; Luke 11:29-32). It looked forward to Christ's redemptive work that would offer peace and salvation to all people.

NEEDS MET BY JONAH

Israel needed to know that God did not play favorites. His grace extended equally to all who asked for it, and his judgment fell on all who disobeyed—and that included Israel. Simply being born into Israel played no part in receiving God's grace or avoiding his judgment. The deciding factor was faith and obedience, not ethnic or religious background. That leveling of everyone before God cleared the way for Israel to understand that her world mission was redemption, not condemnation.

Jonah and his hearers needed to stop giving their racial and cultural hatred a religious stamp of approval. Their personal hatred for cruel and ungodly nations like Assyria did not give them the right to withhold the message of God's grace and rejoice when God's judgment fell. On the contrary, a pagan nation's impending doom should have filled their hearts with compassion, causing them to rush to share God's grace and possibly avert the judgment. Israel needed to replace her judgmental heart with one full of compassion for the lost world. The book of Jonah pointed the way to a less narrow and ethnic view of religion. The structure and content of Jonah show that the Israelites were probably asking questions like these.

- Why should anyone go to tell foreign enemies about how to avoid God's judgment?
- What is the relationship between Israel's salvation and the world's possible damnation?
- What is the relationship between the desire of Israel to receive compassion and her desire for the world to receive it?

When one person causes another person pain, not only pain is felt, but anger as well. Continued hurt only increases both the pain and anger. Jonah (and his nation) lived with the constant cruel oppression of Assyria, and it was easy for his anger to grow right along with his nation's pain. When people are hurt and angry they tend to fight back with the best weapons they have at their disposal. In Jonah's case it was his supposed ability to affect the eternal destiny of his enemies. What better weapon than to be able to let someone go to hell? But the Bible calls believers to take their hurts before God and to replace their hate with compassion. Christ is the supreme example of one exhibiting compassion in a situation where most people would show hate. He had all the best reasons to hate the human race in all their selfishness, sin, and offensive ways. He had the power to let them just slide off into a deserved hell. But his anger against sin was replaced with compassion for the lost, and he suffered the sins and insults of mankind in order to bring them the message of redemption. The book of Jonah makes it clear that though there are indeed things in life to hate, a believer's anger is never to eclipse his compassion and call to share God's grace.

OUTLINE OF JONAH

I. THE FIRST COMMISSIONING: GOD'S LONG-SUFFERING TOWARD JONAH (1:1–2:10)
   A. Jonah's Unexplained Disobedience (1:1-3)
   B. God Saves the Sailors (1:4-16)
   C. God Saves Jonah (1:17–2:10)

II. THE SECOND COMMISSIONING: GOD'S LONG-SUFFERING TOWARD NINEVEH (3:1–4:11)
   A. God Saves Nineveh (3:1-10)
   B. Jonah's Disobedience Explained and Challenged (4:1-11)

JONAH NOTES

1:1–2:10 THE FIRST COMMISSIONING: GOD'S LONG-SUFFERING TOWARD JONAH

1:1-3 Jonah's Unexplained Disobedience

The name "Jonah" (1:1) means "dove." Second Kings 14:25 records that he lived and ministered during the reign of Israel's King Jeroboam II (793–753 B.C.). The historicity of the prophet was confirmed by Jesus (Matt. 12:39-41; Luke 11:29-32). Nineveh was located just east of the Tigris River in northern Mesopotamia (see introductory map). Although Nineveh was the largest Assyrian city in the time of Jonah, it was not the capital. At the time of Jonah's visit, the capital was at Calah, about twenty-five miles to the southeast. Nineveh, the last capital of the Assyrian Empire, was destroyed by the Babylonian and Median armies in 612 B.C.

The city was surrounded by a wall seven and three quarters miles in length. The "great city" had an area sufficient to house a population of 120,000 (1:2; 4:11). It is probable that the whole district administered by Nineveh encompassed a very wide area, including the surrounding lesser cities and villages. Thus "three days" would be necessary to reach the city center from the outlying suburbs (3:3). The Hebrew language does not distinguish between the metropolis itself and the general region. Tarshish (1:3), according to the Greek historian Herodotus, was a mining and smelting center in southern Spain. An inscription found in A.D. 1773 suggests that Tarshish might have been located on the island of Sardinia.

1:4-16 God Saves the Sailors

1:4-9 JONAH'S CONFESSION

The sovereignty of God was evidenced throughout the book of Jonah. God "flung a powerful wind" (1:4) and "arranged for a great fish" (1:17), a "leafy plant" (4:6), and a "scorching east wind" (4:8). Lot casting (1:7) was a means of determining the will of God (cf. Josh. 7:16; 1 Sam. 10:20-24; Prov. 16:33; Acts 1:23-26).

1:10-16 THE SAILORS' CONFESSION

Jonah's response can be interpreted in at least two ways: (1) he would rather die than obey God, or (2) he recognized his worthiness of death and was willing to endure this punishment. The sailors prayed that in throwing Jonah overboard, they would not be held guilty for his death (1:14).

1:17–2:10 God Saves Jonah

Jesus compared his own impending death and resurrection with Jonah's "three days and three nights" in the fish (1:17; cf. Matt. 12:39-40; 16:4; Luke 11:29-30). The time periods were essentially the same, and both ended with a surprise—Jonah delivered and Jesus resurrected. Jonah was probably near drowning (2:3, 5-6) as he sank to the bottom of the sea. He viewed the fish as salvation from death and a sign that God would bring him safely back to Jerusalem.

Jonah prayed "from inside the fish" (Jon. 2:1) and recorded his prayer and recollections subsequent to his release and his ministry at Nineveh. The "world of the dead" (2:2) literally reads "the belly of Sheol," referring to the grave as a devouring monster that had swallowed Jonah. Jonah thought of himself as good as dead. There is no evidence to suggest that he actually died and was resurrected like Christ. The primary point of similarity between the experience of Jonah and Jesus was the time element—"three days and three nights" (1:17) and being in a grave (2:2).

Although he had sinned, Jonah knew that God would forgive him, and he looked with anticipation to worshiping in Jerusalem ("your holy Temple") again (2:4). Jonah promised to praise God for the deliverance he anticipated by faith (2:9). The fish obeyed God more readily than Jonah had (2:10)!

3:1–4:11 THE SECOND COMMISSIONING: GOD'S LONG-SUFFERING TOWARD NINEVEH

3:1-10 God Saves Nineveh

3:1-4 JONAH'S WITNESS

God gave Jonah a second chance, as he did John Mark (Acts 13:13; 2 Tim. 4:11). The city of Nineveh was large but smaller than the language may seem to imply. The "city so large" (Jon. 3:2) probably referred to "greater Nineveh," including the lesser cities and villages situated nearby. The "three days" (3:3) would have been necessary to completely traverse the metropolis, including its outlying suburbs.

The moral corruption and wickedness of the city and people were attested to by the prophet Nahum. Jonah came to Nineveh either during the reign of Adadmirari III (810–783 B.C.), Shalmaneser IV (782–773 B.C.), Ashur-dan III (772–755 B.C.), or Ashurnirari V (754–745 B.C.). If his appearance is put within the reign of Ashur-dan III, then the plagues recorded in Assyrian annals in 765 and 759 B.C., and the total eclipse of 763 B.C., may have been regarded as portents of divine wrath that prepared the city for Jonah's message. During this period Assyria was experiencing weakness and degeneration caused by the rising menace of the Urartu peoples, internal dissension within Assyria itself, and a succession of weak rulers. This turn of events for the empire also may have prepared the city of Nineveh to respond to Jonah's call to repentance. The Hebrew word for "destruction" (3:10) expresses the idea of complete devastation (cf. Gen. 19:25).

3:5-10 NINEVEH'S CONFESSION

An eclipse on June 15, 763 B.C., may have been taken as a warning of impending disaster and helped to kindle a repentant spirit among the people of Nineveh (Jon. 3:5). The "king of Nineveh" (3:6) was probably Ashur-dan III (772–755 B.C.). Sitting in dust or "ashes" was a sign of mourning (3:6; cf. Job 2:8; Mic. 1:10). While God's character does not change (cf. 1 Sam. 15:29; James 1:17), he may show mercy instead of wrath in response to man's genuine repentance.

4:1-11 Jonah's Disobedience Explained and Challenged

4:1-4 JONAH'S ANGER OVER GOD'S SAVING CHARACTER

Jonah explained why he fled his commission (Jon. 4:2). He had proper doctrine (cf. Exod. 34:6), but he did not share God's love for the lost. While he had been forgiven, he did not want to accept the fact that non-Israelites would be forgiven too.

4:5-11 JONAH'S ANGER COMPARED WITH GOD' COMPASSION

Jonah apparently thought the Ninevites might fall back into sin and that God might judge Nineveh after all, so he went outside the city to watch what would happen (Jon. 4:5). It has been suggested that the "leafy plant" or vine (4:6) was the quick-growing castor oil plant that can grow to about eight feet in height during its growing season. The "east wind" (4:8) is known for its excessive heat and dryness (cf. Ps. 103:16; Isa. 27:8; Jer. 4:11).

In Jonah 4:9-11 God explained his compassion on Nineveh by making an analogy with Jonah's concern for the plant. If Jonah was concerned about a mere plant that grew up on its own without the care of a gardener, how much more compassion might God extend to the people of Nineveh whom he had loved and labored to bring to repentance? The 120,000 people (4:11) may have referred to literal children or mature people who were like children in terms of their spiritual perception.

MICAH

HISTORICAL SETTING

Micah ministered in the period surrounding the destruction of the northern kingdom of Israel (722 B.C.) by Assyria. That destruction also terrorized the inhabitants of the southern kingdom of Judah. Micah warned the people of both the north and the south to change their ways. The quotation of Micah 3:12 in Jeremiah 26:18-19 indicates that Micah's warnings were taken seriously and made a contribution to the reform that took place under Hezekiah. Micah prophesied contemporaneously with Hosea and Amos in the northern kingdom and Isaiah in Jerusalem in the southern kingdom.

AUTHOR

Micah was the only prophet whose writing ministry was directed to both the northern and southern kingdoms (Mic. 1:1). Although his father's name was not given, Micah's name (meaning, "Who is like the Lord?") indicates that his parents were pious and faithful worshipers of God. Although Micah 1–3 is accepted by most scholars as written by Micah the prophet, Micah 4–5 is believed by some to have been added during the Exile, and Micah 6:1–7:6 is viewed as a later anonymous prophecy from the period of King Manasseh. However, the repeated expression "listen" (1:2; 3:1; 6:1) and the book-wide pattern of alternating sections of judgment and salvation (see the section below on structure) support the unity of the book and in no way undermine Micah as the single author.

DATE

Micah's prophecies began at least a decade before the fall of Samaria in 722 B.C. (cf. 1:6). He prophesied during the reigns of Jotham (750–731 B.C.), Ahaz (743–715 B.C.), and Hezekiah (728–686 B.C.). Micah's prophetic ministry in writing can be dated between 735 and 700 B.C.

PURPOSE

The book of Micah was designed to encourage repentance by threats of judgment and promises of the ultimate triumph of God's promises to Abraham and to King David.

GUIDING CONCEPTS

STRUCTURE

Note the repetition of "listen" (1:2; 3:1; 6:1). The book is structured in layers of judgment (1:2–2:11; 3:1-12; 6:1–7:6) and salvation (2:12-13; 4:1–5:15; 7:7-20). In his prophecies, Micah balanced God's judgment with the reality of his love.

BIBLE-WIDE CONCEPTS

Jesus used Micah 7:6 to support how he came not to bring peace, but a sword (cf. Matt. 10:34-39). The central problem in both Micah's and Jesus' time was the same: a lack of commitment to God (cf. Mic. 6:7-8 with Matt. 10:31-33). The coming of the messianic kingdom involved judgment first, then peace. And that judgment and turbulence involved a potential crisis of family allegiance versus trust in God (Mic. 7:6).

The priests and scribes quoted Micah 5:2 to show Herod where the promised King of Israel would be born (Matt. 2:6). The coming of the promised King includes all the concepts of land, blessing, and rule promised from Abraham, through Moses, to David. The last verse of Micah grounds all of his hopes and fears in God's loving-kindness to Abraham (Mic. 7:20). That great promise describes the essence of God's character: God will show "faithfulness" and "love" (7:20; cf. John 1:17).

NEEDS MET BY MICAH

Micah's hearers faced certain destruction and captivity because they had stubbornly refused to stop their private and public sins. Because of that, the Assyrians would soon come and destroy the northern half of God's nation. To the rebellious, Micah offered the way to repent and return to God. But a small group had remained faithful to God. And to that group Micah brought special words of encouragement. He told them that the nation's sin had not voided God's promises to Abraham and that there was a way for them to get through the time of discipline and pain.

It was hard for the faithful to have to suffer the punishment brought on by the unfaithful. Good and bad alike lost their land, homes, and lives. Micah explained that the nation as a whole would suffer discipline, but only temporarily. Beyond lay a future of restoration and peace. Micah's task was to strengthen that future hope in the face of a present that threatened to dismantle all hope. His intention was not to make the present pain of sin's consequences go away. It was to get the people to the point where, when the discipline ended, they could receive future blessings either by the repentance of the unfaithful or by strengthening the hope and endurance of the faithful. The book of Micah called God's people to stop sinning and encouraged them to persevere druing the period of God's discipline. The content and structure of Micah show that the Israelites were probably asking questions like these.

- How long will God let the injustice of Israel's leaders go on?
- What future hope will there be when the entire nation of Israel is torn apart by exile?
- What are God's people supposed to do in the light of certain judgment?
- Have the great promises to Abraham been voided by the sins of Israel?

The problems faced by God's people in Micah's day continue today. Christians face living in a society where leaders are corrupt and do not do right by those they are supposed to serve. Many of God's people face the potential economic or military collapse of their nations and wonder how they can live through an uncertain future. But Micah speaks now as he did long ago. Although people today indeed will have to live with the consequences of their sins and the sins of others, God's promises of future blessing are still secure. The task for the present is to increase obedience and readiness to glorify God now and to receive his blessings in the future.

OUTLINE OF MICAH

I. INTRODUCTION (1:1)

II. REBELLION PUNISHED (1:2–2:13)
    A. God's Witness (1:2)
    B. Destruction upon the Nation (1:3-7)
    C. Captivity Promised (1:8-16)
    D. Woe Speech: Injustice to the Family of God (2:1-11)
    E. Divine Headship Restored (2:12-13)

III. LEADERSHIP CORRECTED (3:1–5:15)
    A. Leadership Condemned (3:1-12)
    B. The Kingdom Restored (4:1-8)
    C. Babylon and the Day of God (4:9-13)
    D. The Rule of One Who Is Peace (5:1-15)

IV. REBELLION PUNISHED (6:1–7:20)
    A. God's Lawsuit (6:1-16)
    B. Woe Speech: Injustice to the Family (7:1-6)
    C. God's Rule Restored: Abrahamic Promise (7:7-20)

MICAH NOTES

1:1 INTRODUCTION
Micah 1–2 formed Micah's first message. The name "Micah" means "Who is like Yahweh?" The city of "Moresheth" was located in the vicinity of "Gath" (cf. 1:14) about six miles northeast of Lachish. Micah carried out his ministry during the reigns of Jotham (750–731 B.C.), Ahaz (743–715 B.C.), and Hezekiah (728–686 B.C.). His message concerned both the northern ("Samaria") and southern ("Jerusalem") kingdoms.

1:2–2:13 REBELLION PUNISHED
1:2 God's Witness
Using the imagery of a law court with the divine Judge, witnesses, and the accused, Micah announced God's judgment.

1:3-7 Destruction upon the Nation
The "high places" referred to the centers of idolatrous worship in Samaria and Jerusalem (1:3).

Samaria was ravaged by the Assyrians in 722 B.C. (cf. 2 Kings 17:1-6). The "money earned by her prostitution" (Mic. 1:7) referred to payment given to a temple prostitute. The treasures of Samaria would be used by the Assyrians in worshiping their gods.

1:8-16 Captivity Promised
Going barefoot (1:8; cf. 2 Sam. 15:30) and without one's outer cloak ("naked," 1:8; cf. Isa. 20:2-4) were traditional signs of mourning. Micah singled out for mourning a number of towns situated in the Shephelah, a ridge of hills located between the hill country of Judea and the lowlands descending to the Mediterranean Sea (Mic. 1:10-15). Although it is difficult to detect in the English text, Micah employed a play on words suggesting a symbolic significance in many of the names. Knowing the

meaning of the Hebrew names helps in appreciating the puns employed by Micah. Beth-leaphrah (1:10) means "house of dust." Shaphir (1:11) means "beauty-town." Zaanan (1:11) means "going out." Maroth (1:12) means "bitterness." Aczib (1:14) means "deception." Mareshah (1:15) means "possession." Adullam (1:15) means "retreat" or "refuge." The shaving of the head (1:16, "bald") was apparently also a mourning custom (cf. Isa. 3:24; Amos 8:10; see also Deut. 14:1).

2:1-11 Woe Speech: Injustice to the Family of God

Micah revealed the reason for the coming judgment. To set "boundaries" (Mic. 2:5) is a reference to doing a survey with a view to distributing land. No survey would be necessary because the people would be exiled. The words "Don't prophesy" (2:6) were apparently spoken by those who opposed Micah's ministry. Micah quoted the wicked who doubted that God would allow a calamity such as exile. But the prophet pointed out that God cares for those who obey him. The place filled "with sin and ruined" (2:10) was reminiscent of Leviticus 18:25-28. With biting sarcasm, Micah declared that the people would rather listen to a lying windbag than a true prophet of God (Mic. 2:11).

2:12-13 Divine Headship Restored

Having announced severe judgment, Micah provided a word of encouragement regarding the regathering of dispersed Israel to their land (cf. Deut. 30:1-10). The one who "will break out" (2:13), who clears the obstacles for this return, is probably the messianic King.

3:1–5:15 LEADERSHIP CORRECTED

3:1-12 Leadership Condemned

Micah 3–5 formed Micah's second message. The Lord as supreme head (2:13) addressed the heads of Israel (3:1). The image of the holy mountain linked Micah 3 and Micah 4 (cf. 3:12 and 4:1). "Justice" is the key word in Micah 3. While the corrupt national leaders abhorred justice, God delighted in it. Using the figure of a defenseless flock, Micah portrayed the violence carried out against the people (3:2-3). The false prophets predicted "peace" to make the people happy and to make sure that the people would pay them generously (3:5).

Micah's qualifications to speak for God included the presence of the Holy Spirit, a sense of justice, and courage to denounce and expose sin (3:8). Micah was the first of the prophets to threaten Judah with the annihilation of its capital and the destruction of the temple (3:12). This prophecy made such an impression that it was quoted by the elders in defense of Jeremiah a century later (cf. Jer. 26:18).

4:1-8 The Kingdom Restored

There were great contrasts between nations that desired to worship God (Mic. 4:2) and those that desired to destroy Israel (4:11). The fall of Jerusalem in 586 B.C. merged with the image of the final Day of the Lord (4:12-13).

The prophecy of 4:1-3, concerning the messianic era, is nearly identical to that found in Isaiah 2:2-4. The same revelation may have been granted to both prophets about the same time. This prophecy constituted a reversal of the prophecy given by Joel in the context of anticipated judgment (cf. Joel 3:10). Micah's day was contrasted with the messianic era in Micah 4:5. Israel's future recognition of God was to prompt true worship now. The "citadel of God's people" (4:8) was a poetic synonym for Jerusalem, likening the city to a tower from which a shepherd watched his sheep.

4:9-13 Babylon and the Day of God

Dispersion and captivity in Babylon (4:10) were two of the sufferings that had to precede Israel's restoration and blessing. Both the exile and the return from captivity were predicted (4:10; cf. Ezra 1:1-4). In Micah 4:11-13 the prophet moved to the distant future, describing the gathering of the nations around Jerusalem for judgment (cf. Joel 3:1-16). At that time, God will give Israel victory over all her enemies (Mic. 4:13).

5:1-15 The Rule of One Who Is Peace

A promised ruler would come to Israel and have international dominion (5:4, 6, 15). Israel would be purged first, then the nations (5:12-15). In 5:1 Micah referred back to the thought of 4:9. At the time of Babylon's invasion, Zedekiah ("king to lead you") was smitten and humiliated (cf. 2 Kings 25:6-7). In contrast to the smitten king (Mic. 5:1), a great ruler (5:2) would come for God's people. Ephrathah (5:2, meaning "fruitful") was an ancient name for Bethlehem (cf. Gen. 35:19; Ruth 4:11). This additional name served to distinguish Bethlehem of Judah from Bethlehem of Zebulun (cf. Josh. 19:15). The last sentence of 5:2 affirmed the existence of this messianic Ruler before his birth (cf. John 1:1). Micah 5:2 provided the answer to the Magi's question in Matthew 2:1-6. The solution to the leadership problem will be a perfect Ruler of the Davidic line.

The "woman" (Mic. 5:3) referred to the Virgin Mary (cf. Isa. 7:14). As the good shepherd, Christ will care for the needs of his flock (Mic. 5:4; cf. John 10:1-18). "Peace" (Mic. 5:5-6) summed up what the Messiah would mean for Israel and the world. The Assyrian foe of Micah's day was representative of the enemies of Israel that God would enable his people to overcome. Nimrod, the son of Cush, founded a kingdom in Babylonia that later extended to Assyria (cf. Gen. 10:8-12). Micah revealed God's dealings with Israel's remnant, which will be purged, purified, and converted (Mic. 5:7-15). Military weapons will be unnecessary in the messianic age (5:10-11; cf. Isa. 2:4).

6:1–7:20 REBELLION PUNISHED
6:1-16 God's Lawsuit
Micah 6–7 formed Micah's third message. Just as the mountains, hills, and earth were invoked as witnesses to the ratification of Israel's covenant (cf. Deut. 4:26; 32:1), so they were called upon as witnesses of the covenant violations (Mic. 6:1-2). The Lord led Israel from Egypt, provided national leadership, and delivered the people from their enemies (6:4-5). God's gracious dealings with his people in the past should have resulted in their love and obedience. For "Balak" and "Balaam" (6:5), see Numbers 22–24. The rhetorical questions (Mic. 6:6-7) imply a negative answer. What does the Lord desire of his people? No matter how great the sacrifice made, the sacrifice alone is insufficient to satisfy God's requirements for justice. God's demand (6:8) links ethics with piety, duty toward people with duty toward God. He wants believers' hearts to be pure and requires that they prove their purity through their actions (cf. Deut. 6:5-6; 10:12).

In Micah 6:9-16 the prophet set forth the sinfulness of Jerusalem (6:9-12) and described her coming judgment (6:13-16). The laws of "King Omri" and example "of wicked King Ahab" (6:16) referred to the unbridled wickedness, oppression, and idolatry that characterized the reigns of these two kings (cf. 1 Kings 16:25-26, 29-33; 18:4; 21:25).

7:1-6 Woe Speech: Injustice to the Family
In 7:1-6 Micah lamented the iniquity of the nation. Like an orchard or vineyard devoid of fruit after harvest, there were no godly or righteous people left in Judah.

7:7-20 God's Rule Restored: Abrahamic Promise
The "enemies" (7:8) that threatened Judah were either Assyrians or Babylonians. In 7:11-17 the Lord promised the restoration of his people. Micah predicted a reversal of all exiles, allowing the Jewish people to return to their land (cf. Matt. 24:31). Bashan and Gilead (7:14) were northern Transjordan territories.

In Micah 7:18-20, encouraged by the revelation of God's ultimate deliverance of his people, the prophet broke forth in praise of God's mercy and forgiveness. Note how 7:18-20 relates to Jeremiah 31:34 and the forgiving of iniquities. The Jews joined these verses to the book of Jonah for reading in the synagogue on the afternoon of the Day of Atonement. All that God did for his people by way of forgiveness, compassion, and loyal love was based on his promise to Abraham (7:20; cf. Gen. 12:1-3). Micah affirmed that godly leadership would be restored.

NAHUM

HISTORICAL SETTING

The events surrounding the book of Nahum took place before 612 B.C., when Nineveh
was destroyed by the Babylonian and Median armies. Assyria was still dominant in the
west (1:12-13; 2:12-13; 3:1-4). Nahum probably prophesied during the long reign of
wicked Manasseh (697–642 B.C.). Ashurbanipal, king of Assyria, placed Manasseh on
the throne of Judah as one of his vassals who assisted in his campaign against Egypt.
Manasseh introduced into Judah the official Assyrian religious cult and many other pagan
practices (cf. 2 Kings 21:1-18; 2 Chron. 33:1-9). Assyria had extended its dominion into
Palestine and Egypt and dominated the international scene of the ancient Near East.
Ashurbanipal was especially noted for the ruthless cruelty and atrocities that he brought
upon the victims of his campaigns. Through Nahum, the Lord judged and condemned
Nineveh's power and oppression (1:1-15), despite its seeming invulnerability.

AUTHOR

The book is titled as "a vision to Nahum" (1:1). Nothing is known about Nahum
except that he was a native of Elkosh, the location of which has not been determined
with certainty. The prophet's name means "comfort" or "consolation," which probably
related to his message of comfort to Judah from the threats of Assyrian oppression.

DATE

The reference to the capture of "Thebes" (3:8) by the Assyrians in 663 B.C. reveals the
earliest possible date for the writing of the book. As Egypt was plundered by Assyria
(3:8-9; cf. Isa. 20:1-6), so Assyria would be plundered by the Babylonians. The destruction of Nineveh by the Babylonian and Median armies took place in 612 B.C. Nahum
1:12-13; 2:12-13; and 3:1-4 suggest that Assyria, whose power began to decline rapidly
after the death of Ashurbanipal (660–633 B.C.), was still dominant in the west. Therefore, the probable date of Nahum's prophetic ministry and the composition of the
book was around 650 B.C. while Nineveh was still in its glory.

PURPOSE

The book of Nahum was designed to console Judah by its announcement of coming
judgment on her enemy, Nineveh. Nahum warned concerning God's wrath toward
persistent wickedness and vindicated God's holiness in the eyes of the heathen empire
of Assyria. The book demonstrated that the God of Israel, the nation that the Assyrians

had despised, was in fact the sovereign Controller of the destiny of all nations. Even the greatest of world powers had to submit to his sovereign will and justice.

GUIDING CONCEPTS

The main themes of the book of Nahum can be found in its revelation of God as the Avenger (1:2) and the Restorer (2:2). Nineveh's military campaigns were viewed as direct assaults upon God (1:9, 11) and as the vehicles of God's punishment of Israel (1:12). Therefore, God would judge Nineveh for its assaults and would put an end to his discipline of Israel. Note the emphasis on "his power is great" (1:3). Nahum is primarily a book of judgment, but it also reveals the consistency of God's loving-kindness.

BIBLE-WIDE CONCEPTS

GOD'S JEALOUSY AND PATIENCE
Exodus 34:6-7 provided the background for God's jealousy, wrath, and slowness to anger (Nah. 1:2-3). The Hebrew word translated "jealous" (1:2) is used throughout the Old Testament and is sometimes translated "zealous" (cf. Exod. 20:5; Isa. 9:7; 59:16-21; Joel 2:18). The words of Exodus 34:6-7 were spoken to Moses at Sinai and became a two-edged sword of protection and punishment for Israel and the nations.

CITIES AND THE RULE OF GOD
Several cities were singled out for destruction by God in the Bible: Babel (Gen. 11:1-9), Sodom and Gomorrah (Gen. 19), Jericho (Josh. 6), Nineveh (Nahum), and Babylon (Babel), which will be destroyed in the end times (Rev. 18:21). These cities were destroyed because they epitomized all that was against the rule of God. Even Jerusalem was destroyed when it rebelled against God. But a city could also express God's reign and, like the new Jerusalem, be full of his glory and blessing. And even Nineveh had been spared judgment at one time when its people repented (cf. Jonah).

NEEDS MET BY NAHUM

The Assyrian atrocities against the Jewish nation put God's people in a complex psychological bind. Assyria had cut off the northern tribes from Israel and was known for her fierce and merciless destruction. Although the people of Israel's own sin had brought judgment upon them, God had used a gross pagan nation as his instrument of discipline. What did that mean for Assyria? Was that nation ever going to be punished for what it did to Israel? And how could God's people endure such difficult times where God's judgment on Israel's enemies seemed not to exist? Nahum showed that Nineveh was indeed God's enemy and would eventually be judged. The more difficult question of how to endure the times of pain and discipline was also answered by Nahum. God was good, was a refuge, and never lost track of those who sought him for protection (1:7). The structure and content of Nahum show that the Israelites under Nineveh's sword were asking questions like the following.

- Does God care that Nineveh has done such damage to Israel and the rest of the world?
- Is God for or against Nineveh (2:13; 3:5)?
- Will God ever stop Israel's oppression and restore it to its former glory (1:15)?

Nineveh is not just an ancient city, long since destroyed for equally ancient reasons. It stands as an illustration of God's enemies throughout the ages (1:3-5). With this in mind, the book of Nahum provides a very sensitive balance for God's people in tough times. The book helps believers walk a balance between rejoicing when God's enemies get what they deserve, avoiding a self-righteous arrogance that brings the same judgment, and finding encouragement in bad times to hope in the future. Nahum's message of certain judgment at the end of a period of grace has been fully amplified in this time between the cross of Christ and his return to judge and reward. Believers need to know not only that God will indeed punish the guilty (1:3) but also that his wrath is slow in coming in order to allow time for many to find their refuge in him (1:7).

OUTLINE OF NAHUM

I. PATIENCE AND POWER: GOD'S CHARACTER FOCUSED ON NINEVEH (1:1-15)
   A. Introduction (1:1)
   B. The Power of God in Wrath toward His Enemies (1:2-8)
   C. The Destruction of Nineveh's Evil Plots against God (1:9-14)
   D. What Nineveh's Cutting Off Means for Judah (1:15)

II. GOD'S ATTACK ON NINEVEH DESCRIBED (2:1-13)
   A. Jacob Restored by God's Attack (2:1-2)
   B. The Attack Described: Horror and Completeness (2:3-12)
   C. The Destroyer Delivers the Sentence (2:13)

III. THE CAUSE AND CERTAINTY OF NINEVEH'S CAPTIVITY (3:1-19)
   A. Woe Speech: International Corruption (3:1-7)
   B. Certain Captivity: God Shows No Partiality (3:8-19)

NAHUM NOTES

1:1-15 PATIENCE AND POWER: GOD'S CHARACTER FOCUSED ON NINEVEH

1:1 Introduction
Nineveh was the last capital of the Assyrian Empire. The prophet's name, "Nahum," means "comfort" or "consolation," probably reinforcing his message of comfort to Judah from the threats of Assyria. The location of "Elkosh" (1:1) has not been determined with certainty.

1:2-8 The Power of God in Wrath toward His Enemies
In Hebrew, Nahum 1:2-8 forms an alphabetic acrostic. The theme of this poem was the certainty and severity of God's judgment on the enemies of his people. Bashan, Carmel, and Lebanon (1:4) were places known for their lush fertility (cf. Amos 1:2; 4:1; Ezek. 31:16). The rhetorical questions in Nahum 1:6 imply the answer "No one." Divine wrath is not indiscriminate (1:7). The Lord is inherently good and a stronghold for the righteous who seek refuge in his person. God promised to make an end of Nineveh (1:8, "sweeps away"). The Greek historian Ctesias recounted that the overthrow of Nineveh took place at a time of great flooding that swept away the city's gates and the foundations of the king's palace.

1:9-14 The Destruction of Nineveh's Evil Plots against God

God would not have to raise up a nation against Nineveh "twice" (1:9) for the city would never rise to power again. The words "scheming against the Lord" (1:9) have been taken to refer to either Assyria's Sennacherib (705–681 B.C.) or the reigning king, Sinsharrishkun (623–612 B.C.). The extinction of the king's dynasty was fulfilled in the suicide of Sennacherib's great-grandson, Saracus, in the last days of the Assyrian Empire (1:14). Sennacherib's death took place in the "temple" (2 Kings 19:37) of his god, Nisroch.

1:15 What Nineveh's Cutting Off Means for Judah

The "good news" (Nah. 1:15) in this context was Judah's deliverance from the threat of Assyria, which coincided with the fall of Nineveh in 612 B.C. The Judeans were called upon to celebrate their "festivals" (1:15), which were interrupted by the Assyrian invasion (cf. Deut. 16:16), and pay their "vows" (1:15; cf. Eccles. 5:4, 5) made during times of distress. This text is almost identical with Isaiah 52:7, which speaks of deliverance from Babylon.

2:1-13 GOD'S ATTACK ON NINEVEH DESCRIBED

2:1-2 Jacob Restored by God's Attack

Nahum 2 described the destruction of Nineveh. The "enemy armies" (2:1) was a reference to the combined armies of the Medes and Babylonians, who would conquer Nineveh in 612 B.C. "Israel" (Nah. 2:2) denotes the northern kingdom.

2:3-12 The Attack Described: Horror and Completeness

"Red" (2:3) was the favorite color of the fighting men of Media. Both their shields and cloaks were dyed crimson. The "glittering chariots" (2:3) may have referred to metal plating or to sharp scythes projecting from the axle hubs. The "defenses" (2:5; lit., "covering") was a framework of wood covered with leather. It provided protection for the soldiers who worked the battering ram against the city walls.

Unusually high flooding at the time of Nineveh's fall resulted in the destruction of the king's palace (2:6). The city of Nineveh was captured and sacked for her treasures (2:7-10). Nineveh had been like a "reservoir" of water (2:8), a trade center where people would gather. The taunt song of 2:11-12 depicted the overthrow of the once-proud city of Nineveh. Nineveh was pictured as a den of "lions" (2:11), symbolizing the city's power, pride, and fearlessness.

2:13 The Destroyer Delivers the Sentence

With the fall of Nineveh, the Assyrian "messengers," or royal emissaries like Rabshakeh (cf. 2 Kings 19:23), would no longer be heard demanding tribute from subject kingdoms.

3:1-19 THE CAUSE AND CERTAINTY OF NINEVEH'S CAPTIVITY

3:1-7 Woe Speech: International Corruption

Nahum concluded with a statement on the reason for Nineveh's destruction. Nineveh was called a "city of murder and lies" (Nah. 3:1), alluding to the bloody and ruthless Assyrian military activities. Shalmaneser III boasted that he used the bodies of the slain to span the Orontes River before there was a bridge. One of the most vivid battle scenes in all of Hebrew literature is described in 3:1-7. Nineveh was likened to a harlot, a favorite metaphor of the biblical prophets. Nineveh's "shame" (3:5) consisted of treachery against other peoples and nations. The exposure of one's nakedness (3:5) was a great humiliation and often served as the punishment for adultery (cf. Ezek. 16:37-41).

3:8-19 Certain Captivity: God Shows No Partiality

In Nahum 3:8-15 the prophet provided Nineveh with a historical illustration of No Amon (lit., "the city of Amon"), later known as Thebes. The city was the capital of Upper Egypt during the time of the new kingdom (1580–1085 B.C.). It was situated on the Nile and was noted for its fine temples, royal palaces, and great strength. In many ways it was much like Nineveh. Yet it fell to the Assyrians in 663 B.C., and Nineveh too would fall. Thebes had powerful alliances with the neighboring nations of the Ethiopians to the south, "Put "(3:9), identified with Somalia, and "Libya," probably a reference to Libya in North Africa. The cruelties mentioned in 3:10 were customary in ancient warfare (cf. 2 Kings 8:12; Ps. 137:7-9).

A similar fate ("And you") was to overtake Nineveh (Nah. 3:11-19). The people of Nineveh would be like "women" (3:13), that is, unprepared militarily to defend the city. With a note of satire, Nahum invited the city to prepare for siege (3:14). The "shepherd" (3:18) refers to the leaders of the Assyrian Empire who were dead ("stood still," Ps. 76:6). Nineveh was destroyed in 612 B.C. and disappeared from history until the rediscovery of the site by British excavators in A.D. 1846.

HABAKKUK

HISTORICAL SETTING

The people of Israel had persisted in telling God no, even though for hundreds of years he had been asking them to obey. Now God was using two giant world powers to discipline his people. The great nation of Assyria had already lopped off the northern half of the nation in 722 B.C., and God was bringing the greater nation of Babylon down to finish the job by destroying the southern half. In 605 B.C. Babylonia had just destroyed the Egyptian armies that had marched north of Israel to try to stop the southward advance of the Babylonians. Although the exact setting of Habakkuk's ministry is uncertain, he probably ministered in the times of kings Josiah, Jehoahaz, and Jehoiakim (640–597 B.C.).

AUTHOR

The name "Habakkuk" means "embrace" or "embracer." Little is known about the author except that he lived and ministered during the last days of the southern king-dom of Judah just before the first Babylonian attack on Jerusalem in 605 B.C.

DATE

The book of Habakkuk has been dated by conservative scholars in the reigns of Manasseh (697–642 B.C.), Josiah (640–609 B.C.), and Jehoiakim (609–597 B.C.). The only clear historical reference in the book is in Habakkuk 1:6, probably referring to the Chaldeans as an actual threat to Judah in 605 B.C. The ministry of Habakkuk and the composition of the book both took place early in the reign of Jehoiakim, probably around 607–606 B.C.

PURPOSE

The book of Habakkuk provided comfort and hope during one of the darkest periods of Israel's history, a time during which she suffered the deserved punishment for her sins.

GUIDING CONCEPTS

QUESTION-AND-ANSWER STYLE

The book of Habakkuk was written in the form of a question and answer session between Habakkuk and God. The questions of Habakkuk were similar to those asked by most honest seekers of God who see evil that has gone unpunished. These questions reveal to the reader much of the book's content and the direction of its application. The book begins like a lament psalm: "How long?" "I cry" (1:2-3). Then Habakkuk asked another set of questions concerning God's silence in the face of evil (1:13-14). Although God would eventually judge evil, the answer to the questions of "How long?" and "Does he care?" was given in 2:4. The righteous were called to wait and be faithful, even when some questions could not be answered immediately.

BIBLE-WIDE CONCEPTS

This book has been quoted by several New Testament authors. Habakkuk 2:4 was quoted in Romans 1:17, Galatians 3:11, and Hebrews 10:38. Habakkuk 1:5 was quoted in Acts 13:40-41, where the judgment of God on Israel by using the Babylonians was used to illustrate the judgment that God would bring on the world in the Day of the Lord.

Habakkuk saw violence among his people (1:2; cf. Gen. 6:11; Job 19:7; Jer. 20:8; Ezek. 45:9) that resulted in neglect of the law (Hab. 1:4). The prophet longed for judgment (1:12) in order to find restoration. The process of judgment followed by restoration found in the book of Habakkuk is central to the entire Bible's teaching of the purpose of judgment on this side of the grave. God judges his people to cause them to repent so that he can restore them.

NEEDS MET BY HABAKKUK

Habakkuk wanted God to end the rampant sin in the nation of Israel. But he faced another crisis when he found out that God was going to use the godless nation of Babylonia to put an end to that sin. Habakkuk spoke to people who desired purity and who also were experiencing God's judgment. The content and structure of Habakkuk's prophecy show that he was answering questions like the following for the people of Israel.

- How long will it be before God will judge sin?
- How can God use a pagan nation to judge and purify his people?
- What are God's people supposed to do during the time of judgment?

Two elements of Habakkuk continue to puzzle and encourage believers today. The first concerns their desire for God to put an end to evil. Believers may think that God is not doing anything about the evil that surrounds them. The second area concerns the conflict that believers have with the means God chooses to punish sin. They may think he is waiting too long or not using the proper methods.

Modern Christians may wonder exactly why Habakkuk had a problem with Babylon being God's instrument of discipline for Israel. From Moses on, God had spoken about military defeat and captivity in a foreign land as the way he would bring discipline to his disobedient people. By what other means could Habakkuk have expected God to bring discipline? Perhaps he expected either plague or drought as more acceptable ways for God to bring discipline. At any rate, Habakkuk could not conceive of a holy God using unholy people to destroy Jerusalem and bring Israel into captivity.

God's holiness is not diminished by his working his will through good and evil alike. On the one hand, it may appear that God is not doing anything about evil. On the other hand, Habakkuk encourages his readers to believe that God, in his own way and time, is doing something about evil and that they must persist in hope and faithful obedience. Habakkuk teaches that even in discipline God is a faithful friend who will enable those who trust in him to bear the pain and come out purified.

OUTLINE OF HABAKKUK

I. LAMENT OF HABAKKUK: WAITING FOR GOD TO SAVE (1:1-4)

II. GOD'S INSTRUMENT OF SALVATION: EXTERNAL FORCE (1:5-11)
   A. God's Answer (1:5-6)
   B. The Chaldeans Described (1:7-11)

III. HABAKKUK'S QUESTION: HOW LONG WILL EVIL BE ALLOWED TO CONTINUE? (1:12–2:1)
   A. Habakkuk's Perplexity (1:12-13)
   B. The Enemy Described (1:14–2:1)

IV. GOD'S RESPONSE: SALVATION OF THE RIGHTEOUS AND CERTAINTY OF JUDGMENT (2:2-20)
   A. Certainty of Judgment (2:2-3)
   B. The Destruction of the Proud "Home Builder" (2:4-20)

V. HABAKKUK'S RESPONSE (3:1-19)
   A. Introduction (3:1)
   B. Twofold Response to the Revelation in Habakkuk 1–2 (3:2-19)

HABAKKUK NOTES

1:1-4 LAMENT OF HABAKKUK: WAITING FOR GOD TO SAVE
Habakkuk was perplexed over Judah's unpunished wickedness. He asked, "Why does evil triumph?" "Why doesn't God intervene?" Habakkuk reflected on Judah's wickedness. "How," Habakkuk wondered, "can a holy God look upon such sin with complacency?" The Hebrew word translated "paralyzed" (1:4) literally means "chilled," or "numbed."

1:5-11 GOD'S INSTRUMENT OF SALVATION: EXTERNAL FORCE
1:5-6 God's Answer
The Lord answered Habakkuk's question (cf. 1:2-4) by informing him that Judah would be judged by God through the Babylonians. The Babylonians ("Kaldu" in the Assyrian annals) were a Semitic people of southern Babylonia. When Nabo-

polassar, a native Chaldean governor, took the Babylonian throne in 626 B.C., he inaugurated a dynasty that made the "Chaldean" name famous. The word is used in the Bible as a virtual synonym for "Babylonian."

1:7-11 The Chaldeans Described
The Chaldeans or Babylonians were described as a fierce and terrifying people. They were a law unto themselves and were known for taking conquered peoples into captivity. The words "pile ramps of earth" (1:10) refer to the practice of placing earth against a city's wall so that the siege equipment could batter down the weaker upper sections. Although the Chaldeans were God's instrument to punish the Judeans, they were held accountable for their excessive violence against Judah (1:11; cf. Zech. 1:15). Divine sovereignty does not annul human responsibility.

1:12–2:1 HABAKKUK'S QUESTION: HOW LONG WILL EVIL BE ALLOWED TO CONTINUE?

1:12-13 Habakkuk's Perplexity

Habakkuk expressed his perplexity that God could use such a wicked instrument as the Chaldeans to punish a people more righteous than they. How could this be consistent with God's holy character? The words "is your plan in all of this to wipe us out? Surely not!" (Hab. 1:12) must be grounded on Habakkuk's confidence in God's unchangable purposes (cf. Gen. 12:1-3; 2 Sam. 7:12-16). Because God is too pure to regard iniquity, how could he look with apparent favor on the treacherous Chaldeans?

1:14–2:1 The Enemy Described

In Habakkuk 1:14-17 the prophet described the Chaldeans as fishermen who used every means ("hooks" and "nets") to capture the helpless Hebrews ("fish," 1:14). "Worship their nets" (1:16) may have referred to sacrifices to their weapons of war as was practiced by the Scythians, who offered a yearly sacrifice to a curved sword, the symbol of the war god Ares. Like a watchman on a city wall, Habakkuk waited patiently for God's reply or correction (2:1).

2:2-20 GOD'S RESPONSE: SALVATION OF THE RIGHTEOUS AND CERTAINTY OF JUDGMENT

2:2-3 Certainty of Judgment

In response to Habakkuk's perplexity, the Lord set forth the principle of divine recompense. Habakkuk 2:2 may have referred to announcing the message or to living obediently in response to the divine revelation. Three assurances were given that the promise of God would certainly come to pass (2:3).

2:4-20 The Destruction of the Proud "Home Builder"

2:4-5 THE BASIC INSIGHT

The "proud" (2:4) referred to the Chaldeans whose arrogance had already been alluded to (1:10-11). Such were destined for destruction. The "righteous" (2:4) referred to the godly of Judah in contrast to the proud and wicked Chaldeans. The "righteous" shall "live," that is, "prosper and be blessed." The words "by their faith" referred to the godly person's deep reliance upon God.

The New Testament quoted this reference (2:4) three times (cf. Rom. 1:17; Gal. 3:11; Heb. 10:38). Habakkuk emphasized that the righteous man would live. Paul emphasized that the righteous man would live by faith. Habakkuk 2:5 was a transitional verse in which the Chaldeans were further described. "Death" (2:5) was a reference to the grave, the place of the dead.

2:6-8 THE OPPRESSORS BECOME THE OPPRESSED

Habakkuk concluded this section of the book with a taunt song against the Chaldean oppressor. Five woes were pronounced. In the first woe, the victims of injustice ("all their captives," 2:6) were to take up a taunt song against the wicked Chaldeans.

2:9-11 THE HOUSE CRIES FOR VENGEANCE

In the second woe, destruction is predicted for all those who gained power and wealth unjustly. "Putting your families beyond the reach of danger" (2:9) was to build a seemingly secure and invulnerable home (cf. Obad. 1:4).

2:12-14 DESTRUCTION DISPLAYS GOD'S GLORY

In the third woe, punishment is promised for the unjust and God's glory is foreseen. The "glory of the Lord" spoken of in Habakkuk 2:14 was prophetic and looked to the messianic kingdom for fulfillment. This prophecy is found five times in the Old Testament (cf. Num. 14:21; Ps. 72:19; Isa. 6:3; 11:9).

2:15-17 DRINKING FROM GOD'S CUP OF WRATH

In the fourth woe, disaster was predicted for those who did shameless deeds. "You cut down the forests of Lebanon" (Hab. 2:17) referred to the destruction of trees and cattle in the mountainous region north of Galilee (cf. Isa. 14:7-8).

2:18-20 POWERLESS NATIONAL GODS

In the fifth woe, the makers of idols were called to account. In contrast with the impotent idols, the Lord of heaven was about to execute judgment. The earth was to keep silent—a hushed expectancy of imminent judgment (cf. Zeph. 1:7; Zech. 2:13; Rev. 8:1).

3:1-19 HABAKKUK'S RESPONSE

3:1 Introduction

The response of 3:1 was a model for the proper view of the nation's downfall. Habakkuk concluded with a prayer that would be set to music and was to be used in worship (cf. 3:19). In 3:1, the Hebrew adds the term "according to shigionoth," which was a musical signal that indicated its usage as a song and may have indicated more specifically that it was "an irregular or wandering song."

3:2-19 Twofold Response to the Revelation in Habakkuk 1–2

3:2 REQUEST FOR WRATH AND MERCY

Habakkuk prayed that God would put into effect his program of judgment on Judah and then on Babylon. But he asked that in executing judgment, God would temper his wrath with mercy. The word "mercy" (3:2; lit., "womb") refers to a motherly sense of compassion and pity.

3:3-15 GOD'S WAR FOR HIS PEOPLE'S SALVATION

Habakkuk 3:3-15 described an appearance of God to the prophet. God approached from "Paran" (northwest of Mount Sinai) and Edom. Cushan (3:7) was a neighbor of Midian in the Sinai Peninsula.

The rhetorical questions of 3:8 ask whether or not God was angry at his creation. The implied answer is "No, this is the exercise of his wrath against the wicked nations." As the prophet prayed (3:2), the Lord remembered mercy (3:13). He went forth as a divine warrior to deliver his people. This forms an answer to Habakkuk's opening question in 1:2.

3:16-19 DESCRIPTION OF THE FRUIT OF FAITH

The "people who invade us" (3:16) referred to the Chaldeans who invaded Judah in 605 B.C. after Nebuchadnezzar defeated Egypt at the battle of Carchemish. In 3:17-19 Habakkuk expressed his quiet trust in the Lord's sovereign purposes. Although judgment would come to Judah (3:17), Habakkuk determined to rejoice in the Lord (3:18), for the One who led his people into trial would enable them to bear it (3:19).

ZEPHANIAH

BASIC FACTS

HISTORICAL SETTING
The spiritual condition of the kingdom of Judah progressively worsened from the death of Hezekiah (728–686 B.C.) until the reign of Josiah (612 B.C.). Josiah was the greatest of the reformers of Judah. In 627 B.C. he began religious reform in Judah and Jerusalem (cf. 2 Chron. 34:3). This great era of reform was influenced by the ministries of the prophets Zephaniah, Jeremiah, and Nahum. During this period Judah was free from foreign intervention but was facing a rapid Babylonian expansion. The prophecy of Zephaniah was an announcement of judgment on Judah in particular and the world in general. It is most probable that the threat of the Babylonian invasion provided the political background for the prophecy.

AUTHOR
Zephaniah's ancestry was traced back four generations to show the prophet's relationship with Hezekiah, who was inferred to be King Hezekiah of Judah (Zeph. 1:1). Therefore, Zephaniah was a prophet of royal blood and a distant relative of Josiah, the king under whose reign he prophesied. Zephaniah apparently lived in Jerusalem (1:4, 10-11) and may have been influential in stirring Josiah to his reforms (cf. 2 Chron. 34:1-7). The prophet's contemporaries included Nahum and Jeremiah.

DATE
Zephaniah ministered in the days of Josiah (640–609 B.C.). The moral and religious conditions described by Zephaniah (1:3-6, 8-9, 12; 3:1-7) indicate that the prophecy was given before Josiah's reforms while the spiritual condition of Judah was still low as a result of the evil reigns of Manasseh and Amon. The book should be dated between 640 and 621 B.C.

PURPOSE
The book of Zephaniah was designed to warn of the impending universal judgment of the Day of the Lord and to call the remnant of God's people to repent (2:3) and be protected.

GUIDING CONCEPTS

THE DAY OF THE LORD
Zephaniah has much to say about the Day of the Lord (1:7-8, 10, 12, 14, 18; 2:2; 3:8, 11, 16, 20). The message elaborated on the judgment that would take place as well as

the purifying and redeeming effect the Day of the Lord would have on the righteous remnant (1:4; 2:7, 9; 3:9, 12-13, 19-20). Until that time of restoration, Zephaniah gave several explicit commands to the remnant (1:7; 2:1, 3; 3:8, 14).

BIBLE-WIDE CONCEPTS

The message began with images that reached back to the flood of Noah's day (1:2-3). Compare the same terms in 1:2-3 with Genesis 6:7. The focus was on Judah, but the message related to a global judgment (Zeph. 1:2).

The words "humble" (2:3; 3:12) and "humbly" (2:3) described those who would survive the coming judgment (cf. Hab. 3:2; Matt. 3:7). Those descriptions were taken up by Jesus as he described those who are blessed (Matt. 5:3, 5). Another phrase concerning the lame and the outcast (Zeph. 3:19) had its significance expanded as Jesus healed those who were both physically and spiritually lame or outcast. That humble remnant is a group that suffers, either justly or unjustly, but comes out at the end as faithful and committed to God's ways.

The nations (2:4) were again drawn within God's plans for Israel. God told Abraham that he would bless those who blessed Israel and curse those who cursed Israel. In 2:8, 10, God carried out that promise. All nations would bring homage to the God of Israel as a result of his acts of judgment (2:11; cf. Phil. 2:9-11). Jesus expanded the teachings of the Day of the Lord in his Olivet discourse (Matt. 24:1–25:46; Luke 21:10-36). The nations functioned as a witness of God's wrath and restoration (Zeph. 3:9).

NEEDS MET BY ZEPHANIAH

Zephaniah's audience was about to experience the most severe judgment in Israel's history. It was too late to avert it and there was no way out. At this point, even repentance could not stop national destruction. But when God's holiness finally caused his long-suffering to end and his judgment to begin, his people always seemed to misunderstand what was going on. The judgment came as a shock, even though the prophets had warned of it for years. So, before judgment fell, Zephaniah's hearers needed to understand the cause of and purpose for their judgment. Zephaniah helped the people of Israel to understand why they were about to be judged (for their own personal sin), what the purpose was (personal purity), and what it implied about the character of God (that he was holy and loving). The fears of the righteous people of God were addressed in full view of the coming Day of the Lord. The content and structure of Zephaniah's prophecy show that he answered questions like the following for the people of Israel.

- If the Day of the Lord is coming soon can the judgment still be avoided?
- What will happen to the people who are righteous?
- What will happen to God's enemies?

Unlike the people of Zephaniah's day, believers today have no certain word that their nation is going to be destroyed by God's judgment. But they do know that his condemnation of Israel's sins falls equally on any present nation's sins. Believers also know that the Day of the Lord still lies ahead for the just and unjust alike. And for God's people, Zephaniah's calls to repentance and assertion of the purifying effect of the Day of the Lord are as pointed today as they were in his own time. Believers need to respond to the pictures of God's jealousy, vengeance, and holiness with humility and consistent commitment.

OUTLINE OF ZEPHANIAH

I. SENTENCE AND ACCUSATION: TOTAL DESTRUCTION (1:1-6)

II. THE DAY OF GOD: IMMINENT (1:7-18)
   A. Focus on Jerusalem's Inhabitants (1:7-13)
   B. Focus on International Destruction (1:14-18)

III. GATHER AND SEEK: ALL THE HUMBLE OF THE LAND (2:1-15)
   A. Plea for Repentance (2:1-3)
   B. Repent in the Light of International Devastation (2:4-15)

IV. WOE SPEECH: WAIT THROUGH DESTRUCTION FOR RESTORATION (3:1-20)
   A. Unheeded Admonitions (3:1-7)
   B. Words for the Faithful Remnant (3:8-20)

ZEPHANIAH NOTES

1:1-6 SENTENCE AND ACCUSATION: TOTAL DESTRUCTION

The name "Zephaniah" means "Yahweh hides" or "hidden of Yahweh," and suggests that God hides or protects those who belong to him. The prophecy began with a declaration of universal judgment (Zeph. 1:2-3). This judgment was virtually a reversal of God's work at the creation of the world. The word "rubble" (1:3) is used elsewhere to describe idols (cf. Ezek. 14:3). Zephaniah set forth the reason for God's judgment on Judah (Zeph. 1:4-6). Baal was the Canaanite god of fertility whose worship involved sexual rites. The worship of heavenly bodies (forbidden by Deut. 4:19; 17:3) was practiced by the Assyrians and Babylonians and became common among the idolaters of Judah (Jer. 19:13; Ezek. 8:16). "Molech" (1:5) was the chief deity of the Ammonites (see 1 Kings 11:5).

1:7-18 THE DAY OF GOD: IMMINENT

1:7-13 Focus on Jerusalem's Inhabitants

The "day of the Lord" is that period during which God will deal with his people through judgment or deliverance. The "day of the Lord" can refer to an event in past history or future prophecy. Here Zephaniah used it to refer to the coming "slaughter" (Zeph. 1:7) of Judah to the army of Babylon. Those who follow "pagan customs" (1:8) were the

wealthy rulers who had taken the customs and values of pagans. Zephaniah 1:10 pictured the Babylonian enemy coming into the city from the north and occupying the prominent positions of the city ("the surrounding hills"). The "Fish Gate" was in the northern wall (cf. Neh. 3:3; 12:39), which gave access to the "Mishneh section" (2 Kings 22:14). The "market area" (Zeph. 1:11) is thought to have been a section of Jerusalem possibly located in the Tyropoean Valley. The expression "indifferent" people (1:12) referred to those who were self-satisfied and apathetic in regard to their character or circumstances.

1:14-18 Focus on International Destruction

The Babylonian attack on Jerusalem was a portent of the universal judgment ("the whole land," 1:18) that the eschatological Day of the Lord will bring. Compare this description of judgment with the description in 2 Peter 3:10.

2:1-15 GATHER AND SEEK: ALL THE HUMBLE OF THE LAND

2:1-3 Plea for Repentance

Judah, the "shameless nation," was called to repent and thus escape God's wrath. The appointed "time" (2:2) referred to the divinely determined judgment on Judah by the Babylonians (Zeph. 1:8-13). The

Hebrew word used in the expression "Perhaps even yet the Lord will protect you" (2:3) is a close synonym to the Hebrew word that forms the prophet's name, Zephaniah, "Hidden of Yahweh."

2:4-15 Repent in the Light of International Devastation

2:4-7 PHILISTINE DESTRUCTION BRINGS JUDAH'S RESTORATION

Zephaniah focused on the historical Day of the Lord that was experienced by the Gentile nations that had persecuted God's people. Philistia was one of the Gentile nations in line for God's judgment. The Philistines migrated from the Aegean Islands and Asia Minor under the pressure of the Dorian Greeks. Repulsed by Egypt, these people settled on the coastal plains of Israel and became a formidable enemy.

Gaza, Ashkelon, Ashdod, and Ekron were all major Philistine cities (cf. 1 Sam. 6:17). They were subdued by Nebuchadnezzar in 586 B.C. The Kerethites ("Philistines," Zeph. 2:5) were a subgroup of the Philistines that came from Crete (cf. Amos 9:7). A remnant of Judah would inherit the Philistine coastal plain after the return from exile (Zeph. 2:7). Ultimate fulfillment of these prophecies would be realized in the messianic kingdom.

2:8-10 MOAB AND AMMON DESTROYED BY THE REMNANT

The nations of Moab and Ammon had long been enemies of the Israelites, and they too would suffer judgment. Moab and Ammon were treated together because they were both located east of Judah and shared a common ancestor, Lot (cf. Gen. 19:36-38). The "salt pits" (Zeph. 2:9) referred to evaporation pits into which Dead Sea water was channeled for the purpose of extracting salt.

2:11 TRANSITION VERSE: GOD DOES ALL THIS

To destroy "all the gods" referred to the pagan idols being deprived of sacrifices by which they were thought to be fed.

2:12-15 ETHIOPIA AND ASSYRIA DESTROYED

2:12 Judgment on Ethiopia

Since Ethiopia (Cush) ruled Egypt from about 720 to 654 B.C. and its fortunes were bound up with those of Egypt, it is probable that the reference to the "Ethiopians" was a general reference to Egypt and its allies. The prophecy may have been fulfilled with Nebuchadnezzar's punitive invasion of Egypt in 568 B.C.

2:13-15 Judgment on Assyria

The destruction of Assyria and its capital, Nineveh (2:13), was given fuller treatment in the prophecy of Nahum. Nineveh fell to the combined forces of the Babylonians and the Medes in 612 B.C.

3:1-20 WOE SPEECH: WAIT THROUGH DESTRUCTION FOR RESTORATION

3:1-7 Unheeded Admonitions

Despite the fact that Jerusalem was special in God's plan for man's redemption, her people would suffer judgment because they would not repent of their sin. Although the city was not mentioned by name, it is quite apparent from the context that Jerusalem, the capital of the southern kingdom, was meant. Four classes of national leaders were singled out for condemnation (3:3-4).

3:8-20 Words for the Faithful Remnant

3:8-13 CLEANSED OF REBELLION WITHIN

Zephaniah announced the universal judgment on the nations in the eschatological Day of the Lord. Contextually, it seems that this judgment will be realized during the future Tribulation and Christ's second advent. The destruction of "all the earth" by "fire" may suggest the purging of the heavens and earth (cf. 2 Pet. 3:10-13). The phrase "purify the lips" (Zeph. 3:9) does not mean that they will worship God with the Hebrew language, but with lips uncontaminated by the mention of idols. God's people Israel will become this spiritual people when they see their Messiah and repent (cf. Zech. 12:10–13:1).

3:14-20 CLEANSED FROM ALL ENEMIES

In Zephaniah 3:15-17 the Lord is pictured with his people as a present King (3:15), a protective warrior (3:16-17), and a rejoicing bridegroom (3:17).

HAGGAI

HISTORICAL SETTING

In 539 B.C. Babylon fell to the armies of Persia, and soon afterward (538 B.C.) Cyrus gave permission to the Jews to return to their homeland and renew their worship of God in Jerusalem (Ezra 1:1-4). In 537 B.C. a group of Jews returned under the leadership of the prince of Judah, Sheshbazzar (Ezra 1:8). The foundation of the temple was laid during the second year of their return (Ezra 3:8-13; 536 B.C.), but the builders soon met with opposition. The Samaritans to the north requested to participate in the temple's construction, but they were refused by Zerubbabel and the leaders of the people (Ezra 4:1-3). The Samaritans then discouraged the builders through false counselors (Ezra 4:4-5) and the temple's construction was halted (Ezra 4:24).

It was not until the second year of Darius I that Haggai and Zechariah appeared and encouraged the people to rise up and rebuild the temple (Ezra 5:1-2; 520 B.C.). The work again met with opposition (Ezra 5:3), but the opposition was overcome by the decree of Darius (Ezra 6:8-12) and the temple was completed in 515 B.C. (Ezra 6:13-22).

Haggai ministered during a period characterized by spiritual indifference. The people of Judah were procrastinating concerning their religious duties (Hag. 1:2) and were occupied with their personal interests (1:4, 9). Because of this sinful attitude the people were not experiencing God's blessing (1:6, 10-11). Although they were engaging in some degree of worship, their sacrifices were regarded as unclean because of their sinful attitude (2:14). Haggai exhorted the Jews of that day to observe their spiritual priorities if they were to enjoy material prosperity and divine blessing.

AUTHOR

Haggai was the first of the three postexilic prophets. His ministry to the Jews of Jerusalem is referred to in Ezra 5:1-2 and 6:14. Both Haggai and his contemporary, Zechariah, had great influence in encouraging the Jews to rebuild the temple. Haggai was probably born in Babylon and returned to Judah with the first contingent of Jews under Sheshbazzar (Ezra 5:14) in 537 B.C.

DATE

The book of Haggai may be dated in the reign of Darius, who ruled Persia from 522 to 486 B.C. Haggai's first message was delivered on the first of Elul (August–September) in the second year of Darius (520 B.C.). The last of the four messages came on the twenty-fourth of Kislev (November–December) in the same year. All four messages were given within a period of about four months during the year 520 B.C.

PURPOSE

The book of Haggai was designed to stimulate the lethargic leaders and people of Judah to recognize their spiritual responsibilities and rebuild the temple. Renewed devotion to God would overcome the problems of drought and economic depression.

GUIDING CONCEPTS

STRUCTURE

Several dates given in the book of Haggai (1:1, 15; 2:1, 10, 20) keep the reader's attention focused on the contemporary historical context and the rebuilding of the temple. The prophetic message called the people to consider their ways (1:5, 7). God also made several statements about himself: "I am with you" (1:13; 2:4-5), "I will again shake" (2:6-7), "I will bring peace" (2:9), and "I will treat you [Zerubbabel] like a signet ring" (2:23). The means of moving from judgment to blessing was by showing obedience to the king, priest, and people. And that call to obedience (1:12) is placed between the sections on judgment (1:1-11) and blessing (2:1-23).

Portions of the book also parallel each other (cf. 1:1-15 with 2:10-19, concerning poor crops; God shaking the nations to bring wealth for the temple [2:1-9]; and glory for the ruler [2:20-23]). Note the repetition of "Zerubbabel," "Joshua," and "remnant" or "people in the land" (1:12, 14; 2:2, 4). Haggai tried to encourage the postexilic people with promises for the present and future.

BIBLE-WIDE CONCEPTS

THE REMNANT

Haggai spoke to the remnant that had returned from exile. It was a living fulfillment of Isaiah's son Shear-Jashub, whose name meant "a remnant shall return" (cf. Isa. 6:11-13; 7:3; 10:21; 11:11). Although God had fulfilled his promise of return, the nation was still obligated to obey him. The true nature of the release from captivity was a return to God, not simply to a land (Hag. 2:17; cf. Amos 4:9). Restoration did not do away with the need for obedience or for a relationship with God.

PRESENCE AND SPIRIT

God's phrase "I am with you" finds its greater fulfillment in Matthew 28:20 and Revelation 21:3. The powers of the heavens will be shaken in the Day of the Lord (Hag. 2:6; cf. Matt. 24:29; Luke 21:26; Heb. 12:26).

"Sparked the enthusiasm of" (Hag. 1:14) takes its place in the Bible-wide presentation of God stirring up people's spirits to do his will (cf. Exod. 36:1-2; 1 Chron 5:26; 2 Chron. 21:16; 36:22; Ezra 1:5).

ENRICHING GOD'S PEOPLE

The first part of Haggai 2 took place during the seventh month (Hag. 2:1-9). For Israel that month contained the Feast of Trumpets on the first day, the Day of Atonement on the tenth day, and the Feast of Tabernacles from the fifteenth to the twenty-third day.

The Feast of Tabernacles celebrated Israel's Exodus from egypt and God's tender care for them in the wilderness. During the Feast of Tabernacles (the twenty-first day, 2:1) the Lord paralleled Israel's present postexilic state with Israel when she first came out of Egypt (2:5-6). As God had shaken Egypt and given wealth to his people (cf. Exod. 12:35-36), so he would also shake the world to restore Israel and her king to great prosperity.

THE HOPE FOR A KING FROM DAVID'S LINE
Clearly, the hope for a king in David's line ends the book (Hag. 2:20-23). The king will sit with international authority (cf. Jer. 22:24, for the king as God's signet ring). The shaking of the heavens and earth spoken of here was the foundation for later theological developments such as the role of the Spirit in stirring up his people to action (Hag. 1:12-15); the greater glory for the temple (2:1-9); a great blessing because of the renewed temple (2:10-19); and a greater king on the throne (2:20-23).

NEEDS MET BY HAGGAI

Haggai's hearers needed to understand the cause and effect relationship between their sin and their problems like drought, national economic depression, and personal lack of money. They had problems because they put their own interests before God's. They needed to understand the high priority of commitment to rebuilding God's temple. And all of that was in the face of not having learned God's intended lessons from the discipline of seventy years of captivity in Babylon. True, they no longer had a problem with worshiping pagan idols. But they simply moved on to another form of idolatry—putting personal comfort over advancing the kingdom of God. Once again, the slow coming of God's promises became a potential trap for discouragement and diversion of their commitment to God. They needed to understand that no matter how long God took to fulfill all his promises, they had to remain sharp in their obedience. The structure and content of Haggai's prophecy show that the people of Israel were probably struggling with questions like these.

- Why do those of God's people who returned from exile not have enough food and money?
- Is rebuilding a temple, which will be much less beautiful than Solomon's temple, really that important now that God's people are back from exile?
- Is the small rebuilt temple all that Israel has to show for the great promises that God made to Abraham, Moses, and David?
- Why doesn't Israel's restoration look as great as the prophets made it out to be?
- Will there be another, greater restoration sometime in the future?

Christians today are not faced with rebuilding God's temple after a period of seventy years of captivity. The lands and economies of modern believers are not experiencing drought and depression because they have not rebuilt God's city and temple. But in Haggai the hearers were encouraged to rebuild the temple, small though it was compared to Solomon's temple, as a sign of their commitment to the law of God and to his greater future temple. The people's present commitment to God was a token of their faith in and hope for the future final and glorious presence of God on earth. God's presence with his people was typified by the temple but realized in the real presence of God in Christ and in his Spirit. For the Christian, Haggai's mention of agricultural or financial troubles being remedied by commitment to God's temple do not need to be spiritualized into modern economic principles of success. The issue for God's people then and now is commitment to God's manner of presence—in the temple back then and in the Holy Spirit now.

OUTLINE OF HAGGAI

I. THE FIRST MESSAGE: AN EXHORTATION TO REBUILD (1:1-15)
    A. A Call to Consider: Rationale for Rebuilding (1:1-11)
    B. Building Commenced: Stirred up by the Spirit (1:12-15)

II. ASSURANCE IN REBUILDING (2:1-23)
    A. The Second Message: Wealth for the New Temple (2:1-9)
    B. The Third Message: Prosperity for the Land (2:10-19)
    C. The Fourth Message: Prominence for the Ruler (2:20-23)

HAGGAI NOTES

1:1-15 THE FIRST MESSAGE: AN EXHORTATION TO REBUILD

1:1-11 A Call to Consider: Rationale for Rebuilding

1:1-2 THE FACT OF PROCRASTINATION
The "second year" (1:1) of Darius (522–486 B.C.) corresponds with 520 B.C. The name "Haggai" means "festal" or "my feast," suggesting that he may have been born on some festal occasion. "Zerubbabel" apparently succeeded Sheshbazzar as governor of Judah (see the note on Ezra 1:8). Joshua, known by the name "Jeshua" in Ezra and Nehemiah, was the son of Jehozadak, who was high priest at the time of the Babylonian invasion (cf. 1 Chron. 6:15). The foundation of the temple was laid in 536 B.C. (cf. Ezra 3:1-10), but for fifteen years the people procrastinated, being content with just a foundation and altar.

1:3-4 QUESTIONS OF MOTIVATION
The first message was an exhortation to rebuild. Instead of focusing on the priority of the temple, the people were busy building their own "luxurious" homes (Hag. 1:4). Good things had crowded out the best. They had allowed concern for their own comfort to get in the way of doing the work God had for them to do.

1:5-6 CONSIDER: YOU DO NOT HAVE ENOUGH
The exhortation "Consider how things are going for you!" (1:5) suggests that the people were to reflect on their activities and the results that would come about because of those activities. The fruitless expenditures and disappointed expectations seen in Haggai 1:6 reflected the chastening of the Lord.

1:7-11 CONSIDER: THE REASON FOR YOUR LACK
The meager harvest was traced to the neglect of the temple (1:9). Drought and famine were instruments of God's wrath that were intended to turn his people back to himself (1:10-11; cf. Lev. 26:19-20).

1:12-15 Building Commenced: Stirred up by the Spirit
The people responded wholeheartedly to Haggai's exhortation. The "remnant of God's people" (1:12) was a reference to those who had returned to Judah from the Babylonian captivity (cf. Isa. 6:11-13; 7:3; 10:21; 11:11). Twenty-three days had passed since the message (Hag. 1:2-11) was declared by Haggai. Note the repetition of the words "Zerubbabel," "Joshua," and "remnant" or "people in the land" (1:12, 14; 2:2, 4). The future was great for the obedient prince, priest, and purified people. The Lord stirred up the spirits of Zerubbabel, Joshua, and the remnant (1:14). This stirring up of Israel's leaders ends a section that began with 1:1, when Haggai first brought them the "message" from the Lord (cf. also Exod. 36:1-2; 1 Chron. 5:26; 2 Chron. 21:16; 36:22; Ezra 1:5).

2:1-23 ASSURANCE IN REBUILDING

2:1-9 The Second Message: Wealth for the New Temple

The second message (2:1-9) was a word of encouragement to the remnant of Israel. The date of the second message was October 17. This was a busy day in a busy month on the Jewish religious calendar. The Festival of Trumpets was observed on the first day, the Day of Atonement on the tenth day, and the Festival of Shelters on the fifteenth through twenty-first days.

There were those among the community of the returned exiles who had seen the Jerusalem temple before its destruction by the Babylonians (Hag. 2:3). They compared the past glories of Solomon's temple with the present realities of the restoration temple and became quite discouraged. According to Jewish tradition, missing from the second temple were: the ark of the covenant, the Urim and Thummim, the holy fire, the Shekinah, and the Holy Spirit (Babylonian Talmud, Yoma 21b).

The people were reflecting on what was missing, not on what they had. Haggai encouraged the people with a promise of God's personal presence. The shaking of the "heavens" and the "nations" (Hag. 2:6-7) probably referred to God's future intervention into the affairs of men whereby he would overthrow earthly kingdoms in preparation for the establishment of the messianic kingdom. These words were quoted by the writer of Hebrews (Heb. 12:26-27) in connection with Christ's second advent.

The rabbis and church fathers have taken the well-known translation "the treasures of all the nations" to refer to the Messiah (Hag. 2:7). The "future glory of this Temple" (2:9) may refer to the second temple refurbished by Herod the Great, or to the messianic temple (cf. Ezek. 40–43). The promise of "peace" (2:9; cf. Isa. 9:6-7) would suggest the messianic interpretation.

2:10-19 The Third Message: Prosperity for the Land

The third message (2:10-19), a promise of blessing and restoration, was on December 18. Haggai used an illustration to explain the absence of God's blessing in past years (Hag. 2:11-14). Holiness could not be transmitted by mere contact with holy things. However, defilement could be transmitted by personal contact (cf. Num. 19:11-13). The application is in Haggai 2:14. Judah's disobedience brought defilement and rendered even sacrificial worship unacceptable. The words "this people" (2:14) referred to the Judeans and contain a note of censure.

In 2:15-19 Haggai compared the past problems with the future possibilities. The Hebrew term for the words "from now on" (2:15) is better translated "backward." Haggai wanted the people to look back to past chastening (2:16-17) before they began to obey and rebuild the temple ("lay the foundation of the Lord's Temple," 2:15). In 2:19 Haggai looked to God's future blessing of the repentant people.

2:20-23 The Fourth Message: Prominence for the Ruler

The fourth message, a messianic prophecy, looked forward to a righteous ruler who would bring peace and prosperity to Israel. This message was given on the same day as the third message. The Persian Empire was quite unstable at this time. What was the future of Israel in this insecure situation? God promised to overthrow and destroy the Gentile world powers and preserve Israel. The "signet ring" (2:23) was used to make the mark of its owner on a document or clay tablet. It reflected authority and was to be guarded and preserved. God promised that Zerubbabel would be his signet, or representative authority to the people. The promise related primarily to Zerubbabel's dynasty. His family line would be honored and preserved, and through Zerubbabel's lineage would come Jesus the Messiah (cf. Matt. 1:12; Luke 3:27).

ZECHARIAH

HISTORICAL SETTING

The Jews had returned from captivity in Babylon to their homeland in 537 B.C. The temple's foundations had been laid in 536 B.C. (Ezra 3:10), but the construction had ceased because of opposition from the Samaritans (cf. Ezra 4:1-5). For sixteen years the temple building was neglected by the selfish returned exiles who did not recognize their spiritual priorities (cf. Hag. 1:4). Throughout the ministries of Haggai and Zechariah the people were encouraged to rise up and rebuild the temple (cf. Ezra 5:1-2).

The prophet saw Greece as a menace to the Persian Empire, and the prophecy fits well into Zechariah's day. From 520 B.C. onward the Greeks of Asia Minor were a continual source of trouble for Darius, and in 500 B.C. the great Ionian revolt occurred. By 490 B.C. Darius had stamped out the Ionian uprising, but the Persians were later defeated at Marathon (490 B.C.) and Salamis (480 B.C.). This was a time of insecurity in the Persian Empire.

AUTHOR

Zechariah was the grandson of Iddo, who was one of the heads of the priestly families that returned to Judah after the Exile (cf. Neh. 12:4). A contemporary with Haggai, he was influential in encouraging the people of Judah to rise up and rebuild the temple (cf. Ezra 5:1-2; 6:14). Zechariah seemed to have succeeded his grandfather, Iddo, as head of the priestly family (Neh. 12:12-16), from which it may be inferred that his father, Berekiah (Zech. 1:1), died before he was able to succeed to the priesthood. Zechariah is generally considered to have been a young man when he received the visions of Zechariah 1–7 (cf. 2:4). He entered his prophetic ministry two months after Haggai concluded his first oracle.

Some believe that Zechariah 9–14 was not original to Zechariah and contains anonymous prophecies from a later period. These arguments are based on what some see as different styles and vocabularies. However, the prophetic end-time thrust of this section, and a time period of about twenty years between the giving of the two main sections of the book, may well account for such differences. It was accepted early as part of Zechariah's prophecy, since no Hebrew manuscripts have been discovered with this section of Zechariah missing.

DATE

Zechariah began his ministry in the second year of Darius (522–486 B.C.) in 520 B.C. His last dated prophecy (7:1) was two years later on the fourth day of Kislev

(November–December) in 518 B.C. The latter chapters of the prophecy (Zech. 9–14) appear to have been composed sometime later, possibly around 500 B.C., in view of the reference to Greece (9:13). The book of Zechariah was thus composed between 520 and 500 B.C.

PURPOSE

The book of Zechariah was designed to provide a detailed picture of God's future dealings with his chosen people. Zechariah 1–8 demanded the ethical responsibility of the people, while Zechariah 9–14 moved on to revive the hopes of the obedient. The believers needed to turn from their sins. The book comforted and encouraged the remnant by revealing future glories, the overthrow of Israel's enemies, and the universal reign of the Messiah. They had undergone an immense amount of suffering, but if they expected future blessings from God they would have to reform their civil and religious practices.

GUIDING CONCEPTS

The two major concepts that controlled the book were the necessity of a functioning temple and the return of the people's hearts and actions to the conditions of the Mosaic covenant. All the various visions of hope and judgment were centered on those two concepts. Zechariah 1–8 contains a series of visions designed to encourage personal repentance and reconstruction of the temple. Zechariah 9–14 moved away from the specifics of Zechariah's day and looked to the furious struggles of the end times. Evil did its worst but, in the end, God remained the victorious King.

BIBLE-WIDE CONCEPTS

Zechariah taught a great deal concerning the first and second comings of the Messiah. He referred to the Messiah as God's servant (3:8), the Branch, the stone (3:9), and the shepherd (13:7). Concerning the first coming of Christ, Zechariah prophesied his entrance into Jerusalem on a colt (9:9), his rejection by Israel (11:1-17), his betrayal for thirty pieces of silver (11:12-13), the piercing of his hands and feet (12:10), and his work on the cross (13:1).

Concerning the Messiah's second coming, Zechariah prophesied the conversion of Israel (13:1-9), the destruction of Israel's enemies by the Messiah (14:3, 12-15), the restoration of Jerusalem (14:8-11, 16-21), and the reign of the promised Messiah from Zion (14:9). The prophecy of Zechariah contains one of the most outstanding passages in the Old Testament concerning the removal of sin and imputation of righteousness (3:1-5).

NEEDS MET BY ZECHARIAH

In Zechariah's day, even though the Jews had been restored from captivity they were still under foreign domination. The promises of God's unhindered worldwide reign seemed as far off as ever. Added to that, God's people were still entrenched in sin as if the lessons of captivity had never been learned. Zechariah encouraged his hearers to return to the Lord by giving graphic descriptions of God's future end-time judgments. God's people had lost their will to consistently obey because they had lost sight of God's absolute control and presence. Just because they could not see stupendous evidences of God's presence did not mean he was absent or was not running history exactly as he wanted. As Zechariah affirmed God's complete present control, he also affirmed God's ability to judge or reward those in the present. God's control over history meant moral accountability. The returned nation of Israel had a long list of promises for great prosperity. But those promises seemed very far off, if still in effect at all. Zechariah presented a rather full picture of what lay ahead for Israel in order to confirm the promises and to comfort God's people. The content and structure of Zechariah show that the people of Israel were probably struggling with questions like these.

- What will happen to the priesthood and the line of David?
- Will Israel ever be able to overcome her enemies?
- Because God has returned his people to their land, are they now immune to God's judgment?
- Will the people of Israel ever be the kind of people God wants them to be?

Two of the greatest strains on faith are tough present circumstances and the long time it takes before God's promises are fulfilled. When it seems that God is not actively present in history, it is easy to think he will neither hold his people accountable for their sins nor reward them for their faithfulness. In such a situation their faithfulness tends to collapse and sin tends to increase. Zechariah works to combine the great past acts of God and graphic descriptions of his future judgments and rewards into a package that fills the present with a sense of God's complete control. With this perspective believers can move through this time of waiting, no matter how long ahead it stretches, with a firm sense of God's control and presence to judge and reward.

OUTLINE OF ZECHARIAH

I. CALL TO REPENTANCE: DO NOT BE LIKE YOUR FATHERS (1:1-6)

II. EIGHT VISIONS: GOD'S PROTECTION OF HIS HOUSE (1:7–6:15)
   A. The Temple Built and Enemies Punished (1:7-21)
   B. The Temple Built: Enemies Punished and Leaders Accepted (2:1–4:14)
   C. A Rival Temple Built and Enemies Punished (5:1–6:8)
   D. Returnees Encouraged: The Branch Builds the Temple (6:9-15)

III. THE POSTEXILIC MIND-SET: SADNESS TURNED TO JOY (7:1–8:23)
   A. The Setting: The Question about Fasting (7:1-3)
   B. Motivation and Rebellion Exposed (7:4-14)
   C. Words of Assurance (8:1-17)
   D. Questions Answered and Illustrated (8:18-23)

IV. TWO BURDENS (9:1–14:21)
   A. Against Nations and Leadership: The Victorious Flock (9:1–11:17)
   B. Israel's Victory through Mourning (12:1–14:21)

ZECHARIAH NOTES

1:1-6 CALL TO REPENTANCE: DO NOT BE LIKE YOUR FATHERS

The date was "midautumn" (Marchesvan, "the eighth month," which falls in October–November), 520 B.C., "the second year of King Darius's" (1:1). The name "Zechariah" means "Yahweh remembers." The words "your ancestors" (1:2) referred to the forefathers of the present generation. Their sins resulted in the Babylonian exile. The words "Return to me" (1:3) speak of repentance, that is, a change of attitude resulting in a change of conduct. And Zechariah said, "Repentance is the prerequisite for enjoying God's blessing." The "earlier prophets" (1:4) were those who lived before the Exile and warned of coming judgment. Zechariah warned that life is short, and it is perilous to pass up the opportunity to repent when it is available.

1:7–6:15 EIGHT VISIONS: GOD'S PROTECTION OF HIS HOUSE

1:7-21 The Temple Built and Enemies Punished

1:7-17 THE WORLDWIDE PATROL: NATIONS AT EASE

Note the following pattern in Zechariah's visions: (1) "I saw"; (2) "What does this mean?" (3) An explanation given by the interpreting angel.

In the vision of the red horse's rider among the myrtle trees (1:7-17) God promised to bless Israel by showing compassion and rebuilding Jerusalem. The date of this vision was February 15 (1:7), 519 B.C., three months after the call to repentance (1:1-6). In 1:8-12 there were four participants in the vision: Zechariah, the rider on the red horse, the interpreting angel, and the angel of the Lord (1:11). Myrtle is an evergreen tree, once very common in the vicinity of Jerusalem (Neh. 8:15). Early in his rule, Darius had trouble with rebellion in parts of his empire. Now all was quiet and peaceful.

The "seventy years" (Zech. 1:12) referred to the period the temple had lain in ruins (586–516 B.C.). The question was, How much longer would Israel be under Gentile domination? God promised to rebuild Jerusalem and the temple (1:16). Jerusalem's election ("again . . . choose Jerusalem") was emphasized prominently in Zechariah (1:17; cf. 2:12; 3:2).

1:18-21 FOUR HORNS AND FOUR CRAFTSMEN

Zechariah was given a vision of four horns and four craftsmen (1:18-21) in which God promised to destroy Israel's enemies. The horn was an image of invincible strength (cf. Dan. 8:5-8). The "horns" (Zech. 1:18) that persecuted Israel and Judah were Assyria, Babylon, Medo-Persia, and Greece. The "blacksmiths" (1:20) would destroy the "horns"

(1:21). Babylon destroyed Assyria, Medo-Persia destroyed Babylon, Greece destroyed Medo-Persia, and Greece was succeeded by the Roman Empire.

2:1–4:14 The Temple Built: Enemies Punished and Leaders Accepted

2:1-13 PROTECTION: NO WALLS NEEDED

The vision of a surveyor with a measuring line (2:1-13) gave the remnant hope that Jerusalem would be restored and rebuilt. The "measuring line" (2:1) was a surveyor's tool. The measuring of Jerusalem was with a view to rebuilding the city. God promised his protection, a "wall of fire" (2:5; cf. Exod. 13:22). Those who had not yet returned to Judah from Babylon were urged to do so. The "north" (Zech. 2:6) was the direction of travel routes between Israel and Babylon, although Babylon was located directly east of Israel. In 2:9 God promised to protect his people (cf. Gen. 12:3). Zechariah 2:10-12 appears to have its fulfillment in the messianic kingdom ("I will live among you," 2:11).

3:1-10 PRIEST ACCEPTED

Zechariah's vision of the cleansing of Joshua the high priest (3:1-10) led the way to the cleansing of the whole nation. The nation was to be cleansed spiritually by the promised Messiah. The scene of this vision was a heavenly courtroom where Joshua, the representative of the people of Judah, was standing before the "angel of the Lord" while being accused by Satan. The "stick that has been snatched from a fire" (3:2) referred to Judah, delivered from the "fire" of the Babylonian captivity. The "filthy" clothing (3:3) symbolized the pollution of sin that needed to be removed (cf. Isa. 4:4).

The cleansing of Joshua (Zech. 3:4-5) symbolized the removal of the guilt of sin ("I have taken away your sins," 3:4) and the imputation of God's righteousness ("fine new clothes," 3:4). Joshua was recommissioned and promised God's blessing for obedience (3:7). In 3:8-9 the Messiah was depicted as a servant (cf. Isa. 53:11), a Branch (cf. Isa. 4:2), and a stone (cf. Ps. 118:22; Isa. 28:16). The word "facets" (Zech. 3:9) is translated "eyes" in Hebrew and may also be translated "springs" or "fountains," which symbolized the spiritual cleansing of the people by the Messiah (cf. 3:4). The image of sitting under a person's vine and fig tree (3:10) was an image of peace and tranquility and spoke of the messianic kingdom (cf. Micah 4:4).

4:1-14 TEMPLE COMPLETED

The vision of the gold lampstand and two olive trees (4:1-14) pointed to the rebuilding of the temple. This rebuilding would take place by God's enablement. In Zechariah 4:2-3 the prophet saw a lampstand with seven lights, each having seven channels (or "spouts"). The "olive trees" provided the supply of oil for the lamps through "gold tubes" (4:11-12). The key message of the vision is contained in 4:6. The rebuilding of the temple would be accomplished by the ministry of God's Spirit. The "mountain" (4:7) referred to mountainous opposition or obstacles. The "seven lamps" (4:2, 10) are identified as "the eyes of the Lord." The "two olive branches" (4:12) were identified as "two anointed ones" (4:14), representative of the political and religious offices in Israel: king and priest. Many identify the "two" with Joshua, the high priest, and Zerubbabel, the governor.

5:1–6:8 A Rival Temple Built and Enemies Punished

5:1-4 SCROLL: UNIVERSAL JUDGMENT
Zechariah's vision of the flying scroll (5:1-4) indicated that there would be severe judgment on those who neglected the law. The "scroll" was the size of a billboard, thirty by fifteen feet (5:2; twenty by ten cubits, NASB and KJV; a "cubit" was a unit of measure equivalent to eighteen inches). The scroll, containing the curses of disobedience (cf. Deut. 28:15-68), signified that lawbreakers would be judged. God's judgment was sure, penetrating, and severe.

5:5-11 EPHAH: THE RIVAL IDOL IN SHINAR
The vision of the woman in a measuring basket (5:5-11) was a prophecy of hope that sin and wickedness would be removed from Israel. The "basket for measuring" (5:6; "ephah," NASB and KJV) was a unit of dry measure estimated at around two-thirds of a bushel, or almost four and a half gallons. This ephah basket may have been larger since it contained a woman (5:7). The woman in the basket ("Wickedness") was a personification of sin (5:8).

6:1-8 WORLDWIDE PATROL: UNIVERSAL JUDGMENT
The vision of the four chariots (6:1-8) foretold the divine judgment that would fall upon the Gentile nations. The chariot and teams represented four divine agents of judgment. The "four spirits of heaven" (6:5) referred to heavenly messengers or agents. As a result of their activity, God's wrath was appeased (6:8). Victory in the turbulent "north" (6:8) suggested that there was victory over every foe.

6:9-15 Returnees Encouraged: The Branch Builds the Temple
The Messiah will be crowned as High Priest and King. The "exiled" (6:10) referred to the new arrivals from Babylon, who brought gifts of silver and gold (6:11) to help the restoration community. The Hebrew word translated "crown" (6:11) is literally "crowns" and could refer to an ornate or double crown. The "Branch" (6:12) was a reference to the

Messiah (cf. 3:8-9) who would build "the Temple of the Lord," the millennial temple (cf. Hag. 2:6-9; Ezek. 40–43). In the Messiah the two offices of king and priest will be united in one Person (Zech. 6:13; cf. John 1:49; Heb. 3:1). The expression "from distant lands" referred to Gentiles (Zech. 6:15; cf. Eph. 2:13).

7:1–8:23 THE POSTEXILIC MIND-SET: SADNESS TURNED TO JOY

7:1-3 The Setting: The Question about Fasting
The date was December 7, the "fourth year" (7:1), or 518 B.C. Bethel (7:2) was located about twelve miles north of Jerusalem. The people of Bethel sent a delegation to inquire of the priests in Jerusalem. The question was (7:3), "Should we continue to mourn and fast each summer on the anniversary of the Temple's destruction, as we have done for so many years?"

7:4-14 Motivation and Rebellion Exposed
Zechariah exposed the selfish motives of the people in their self-righteous fasting. The fast during the "autumn" lamented the slaying of Gedaliah (cf. 2 Kings 25:25). Zechariah's prophecies were in continuity with those prophets who preceded him (7:7). The "Negev," meaning "south," referred to the desert area in southern Judah centering around Beersheba. The "foothills of Judah" referred to the Shephelah, a low ridge of hills between the hill country of Judah and the coastal plain. The "they" (7:11) referred to the disobedient Judeans living in the land before the Babylonian exile (cf. 7:14).

8:1-17 Words of Assurance
In 8:1-8 the prophet turned from the subject of Judah's desolation to speak of her future restoration. God's return to "Zion" (8:3; Jerusalem) provided the theological basis for the blessings that would follow. This regathering of the God's people (8:7) corresponds with the idea of regathering in Matthew 24:31. The foundation of the temple was laid in 536 B.C. (Ezra 3:7-13).

8:18-23 Questions Answered and Illustrated
The former fasts would become feasts as a result of God's blessing on his obedient people. The fast of "early summer" (Zech. 8:19) commemorated the breach of Jerusalem's walls (cf. Jer. 39:2); the fast of "midsummer" (Zech. 8:19) commemorated the temple's destruction (cf. 2 Kings 25:8-9); the fast of "autumn" commemorated the slaying of Gedaliah (cf. 2 Kings 25:25); and the fast of "winter" commemorated the beginning of Nebuchadnezzar's siege (2 Kings 25:1). The expression "to ask the Lord" (8:21) meant to sacrifice to God and worship him. In 8:22-23 Zechariah anticipated a time when

Gentiles would seek to worship God in Jerusalem. Gentiles would be included among the people of God by faith (cf. Eph. 2:13-19).

9:1–14:21 TWO BURDENS
9:1–11:17 Against Nations and Leadership: the Victorious Flock
9:1-10 THE COMING KING: DOMINION AND PEACE

Zechariah's oracle concerning the Gentile nations and Israel (Zech. 9:1-8) looks forward to God's judgment of Israel's enemies. There has been much scholarly debate regarding the text of 9:1-8. Scholars disagree about which historical circumstances were the subject of the prophecy's predictions. Most identify the contents of this section with Alexander the Great's campaign through Palestine (332–331 B.C.). Others have argued that it refers to a military campaign during the time of Josiah, Tiglath Pileser III, Sargon, or the Maccabees. The difficulty is that no one historical setting really answers to all the details of the situation described in these verses. More recently, it has been suggested that the section was set in the literary form of a "divine warrior hymn," a poem that describes a warrior-god's battle and the establishment of peace. In this view, no specific historical situation lies at the background. Rather, the poem presents God's intervention among the nations with a view to the establishment of the ideal that Yahweh had promised Israel.

"Aram" (9:1) was situated north of Hamath on the Orontes River southwest of Aleppo. Damascus, located sixty miles northeast of the Sea of Galilee, was the capital of Aram. Hamath (9:2) was named in some texts to represent the northern limits of the Promised Land (cf. Num. 13:21; Josh. 13:5). Tyre and Sidon were important port cities located in Phoenicia on the Mediterranean coast. Ashkelon, Gaza, Ekron, and Ashdod (9:5-6) were Philistine cities located on the coastal plain south of Joppa (cf. 1 Sam. 6:17). Having subjugated the nations, Yahweh returned as a victorious warrior to his temple (Zech. 9:8, "my Temple").

In 9:9-10 the first coming of Christ was set against the background of God's victory march (9:1-8). This prophecy was fulfilled when Jesus rode into Jerusalem on the colt of a donkey (cf. Matt. 21:2-7; John 12:12-15). A donkey was not regarded as a lowly creature in the ancient Near East, but rather as a king's mount. The inauguration of the Messiah's reign at his second coming was described in 9:10. During his future reign, instruments of warfare will be destroyed and universal peace established.

9:11-17 VICTORY AND RESTORATION

Zechariah 9:11-17 spoke of the release of captives ("prisoners") in exile. They were exhorted to return to Jerusalem ("the place of safety," 9:12). God was depicted as fashioning Judah and Ephraim into a bow and arrow, which would be used against Greece. The appearance of Greece (9:13; lit., "Javan") has led many scholars to date this section of Zechariah at a much later time. However, the term is used elsewhere for nations on the edge of civilization (cf. Gen. 20:2, 4; Isa. 66:19), which appears to be the usage here. The appearance of God (Zech. 9:14) was patterned after Israel's experience with God at Sinai, revealing God's sovereignty and power to protect his own.

The victory banquet of God's people in celebration of his victory over the nations and securing Zion was recorded in 9:15. The people would be filled with drink like a sacrificial basin and filled with meat like the corners of a sacrificial altar. God would shepherd and provide for his restored and repentant people.

10:1-11:3 LEADERSHIP CONDEMNED: RETURN FROM EXILE

The prophet described how God would restore his people to their land. The unifying theme of the section of 10:1–11:3 is the restoration of the Jewish people by divine power. The "gods" (10:2) were household idols (cf. Gen. 31:19), which led the people to their own destruction. The term "shepherd" (Zech. 10:2) is a figure for a leader or king. The metaphors in Zechariah 10:4-5 reflected the strength, stability, and victory that God would impart to his people, Judah (10:6). God's scattered people would be regathered to the land from worldwide dispersion (10:8-12). Assyria (10:10) referred to the region of northern Mesopotamia. Gilead was the Transjordan territory southeast of the Sea of Galilee. Lebanon referred to the region north of Galilee. God would overcome any obstacles or impediments, like "the sea" or "the Nile" (10:11), to Israel's return.

Zechariah 11 prophesied the rejection of the good shepherd of God's flock and his replacement by a worthless shepherd who would bring them ruin. Zechariah 11:1-3 depicted the devastation of the land of Israel due to the people's rejection of the Messiah, the good shepherd (11:4-17; cf. Matt. 23:37-39). The judgment was probably fulfilled in the A.D. 70 destruction of Jerusalem by the Romans. The dominant image of this passage was the wailing that would express the horror of Israel's devastation.

11:4-17 LEADERSHIP REJECTED

Zechariah revealed the destiny of the shepherd and the flock. The flock was said to be "intended for slaughter" (Zech. 11:7), destined for judgment. As shepherds carried implements to guide and protect the sheep (Ps. 23:4), so Zechariah carried two staffs. Their names suggest that he wanted the flock to enjoy God's "Favor" and experience national unity

("Union"). At least forty different conjectures have been offered as to the identity of the three shepherds whom Zechariah deposed (Zech. 11:8). Such speculation is unnecessary. These shepherds, whoever they were, did not share the true shepherd's vision and were removed from leadership.

The breaking of the staff "Favor" was symbolic of the termination of God's gracious dealings with his people (11:10). Then judgment was inevitable. The "covenant" referred not to the Abrahamic (Gen. 12:1-3) or Davidic covenants (2 Sam. 7:12-16), but to one made with the Gentile nations ("all the nations") on Israel's behalf. Zechariah, taking the role of the messianic shepherd, requested his wages for service rendered (Zech. 11:12-13). The "thirty pieces of silver" (11:12) was the price of an injured slave (cf. Exod. 21:32) and was the price paid to Judas for the betrayal of Jesus (cf. Matt. 26:14-15).

The rejection of the good shepherd meant that the national unity Zechariah had hoped for would not be achieved at this time (Zech. 11:14). In 11:15-17 the rejection of the good shepherd resulted in a leadership vacuum that would be filled by a wicked shepherd who would actually destroy the flock. A comparison of this shepherd with the sinister figure of Daniel 7:25 and 11:36-39 indicates that he represented the antichrist (2 Thess. 2:1-12; Rev. 13:1-10).

12:1–14:21 Israel's Victory through Mourning

12:1-9 NATIONS DESTROYED

Zechariah looked to the future day of Israel's deliverance from her enemies when the Gentile nations would be destroyed. The end-time setting is the campaign of Armageddon (Rev. 16:16) when the nations will come against Jerusalem (cf. Zech. 14:2). When the nations are gathered against Jerusalem, the Messiah will return and execute judgment on the Gentile powers so that he may rule the nations himself (12:4-9). Judah was likened to a "brazier" (12:6), a clay vessel used to carry hot coals for the purpose of building a fire. The "sheaves" referred to the grain that was cut, bound, and left standing in the field to dry. The Lord, the Messiah, would be the agent of judgment on the enemy and the agent of deliverance (12:8) for his people.

12:10–13:1 GRACE POURED OUT: ISRAEL MOURNS

In 12:10–13:6 Zechariah described Israel's spiritual deliverance. At the time of Christ's second coming, the remnant of Israel, which will have survived the tribulation judgments, will repent and believe in Jesus, the Messiah whom they "pierced" (12:10). The expression "a spirit of grace" (12:10) referred to the work of the Spirit in Israel's conversion. The "mourning of Hadad-rimmon" (12:11) may have referred to a place noted for some intense lamenta-

tion, or to the combined names of the vegetation gods "Hadad" and "Rimmon." The "valley of Megiddo" (12:11) referred to the plain that Megiddo controlled, the Jezreel Valley.

Zechariah 12:12-14 emphasizes the universal aspect of mourning for the Messiah, the royal family ("family of David," 12:12), the priestly family ("family of Levi," 12:13), and all citizens ("the surviving families," 12:14). Shimei was Levi's grandson (cf. Num. 3:18, 21).

The "fountain to cleanse" (Zech. 13:1) speaks of the cleansing from the impurity of sin that Christ made available at the cross. At the time of Christ's second coming, the remnant of Israel ("dynasty of David") will appropriate that provision and be saved (Rom. 11:26).

13:2-6 FALSE PROPHETS EXPOSED

Zechariah announced that a day was coming when false prophets would be purged from the land along with idolatry and demonic influence. The execution of the false prophet was based on the Mosaic Law (Zech. 13:3; cf. Deut. 13:5; 18:20). The "prophet's clothes" (Zech. 13:4; "hairy robe," NASB), that the false prophets would want to avoid, had been worn by Elijah (2 Kings 1:8) and seems to have been the distinctive attire of the prophets. The "scars" (Zech. 13:6) appeared to betray the profession of an ecstatic prophet who had slashed himself on the back and breast to gain the attention and blessing of his god (cf. 1 Kings 18:28).

13:7-9 SHEPHERD STRUCK: REMNANT PRESERVED

In 13:7-9, Zechariah resumed the shepherd motif and returned to the theme of the Messiah's rejection. The Lord commanded the sword to strike the Messiah shepherd. This indicates that the death of Christ was no mere accident but had been divinely determined (cf. Acts 2:23). The shepherd's death resulted in the scattering of his flock (cf. Matt. 26:31; Mark 14:27). The scattered flock would face great judgment (the Tribulation), which only one-third of the people would survive (cf. Matt. 24:15-22). The remnant that survived would be purged, purified, and reestablished in a covenant relationship with God (cf. Hos. 2:23; Rom. 11:26-27).

14:1-21 JERUSALEM DIVIDES THE SPOIL: FEAST OF BOOTHS KEPT

In Zechariah 14:1-5 the prophet described the events associated with the second coming of the Messiah at the end of the campaign of Armageddon (Rev. 16:16). Just before the Messiah's return, the unbelieving Gentile nations will gather at Jerusalem to besiege and destroy the city (Zech. 12:2). Christ's return to Jerusalem will turn what seems an unavoidable defeat into victory (14:4-9). Christ will return to the Mount of Olives, the very mountain from which he ascended (Acts 1:10-11). The splitting of the Mount of Olives will provide a way of escape for the besieged and defeated people in Jerusalem. The site of "Azal" (Zech. 14:5) has not been identified but must be somewhere in the desert east of Jerusalem. According to Josephus, the "earthquake" (14:5) occurred when Uzziah went into the temple to offer incense (cf. 2 Chron. 26:16-21).

Cosmic upheaval is associated with the Second Coming (Zech. 14:6-7). The glory of the Messiah's kingdom will be preceded by the darkness of the Tribulation (Joel 2:30-32). In Zechariah 14:8-11 the prophet described the culmination of the prophetic promise of a kingdom in which Israel's Messiah will rule on David's throne (cf. 2 Sam. 7:12-16; Luke 1:31-33). "Life-giving waters" (Zech. 14:8) was a reference to flowing water as opposed to stagnant water. Certain topographical changes will take place in the environs of Jerusalem to accomodate the messianic temple (14:10). "Geba" was situated six miles northeast of Jerusalem. "Rimmon" was about thirty-five miles southwest of Jerusalem.

While the surrounding terrain will be leveled, Jerusalem itself will be elevated so that the city will dominate the land (14:10; cf. Isa. 2:2; Mic. 4:1). "The Benjamin Gate" (Zech. 14:10) probably referred to a gate in the northern wall of the city. The "old gate" has not been identified. The "Corner Gate" probably marked the northwest limit of Jerusalem. The "Tower of Hananel" was a defensive fortification on the northern wall.

Zechariah 14:12-15 elaborates on the content of 12:4-9 and 14:3, providing further details of how God will fight against and destroy those nations that attack Jerusalem. In 14:16-21 Zechariah concluded with a description of worship in the Messiah's kingdom. The "Festival of Shelters" (14:16) referred to the fall feast of ingathering that commemorated the wilderness experience of Israel (cf. Lev. 23:33-43). In the messianic kingdom, the people of Judah and Jerusalem will be holy, as a priestly nation. The words "SET APART AS HOLY TO THE LORD" (Zech. 14:20) were inscribed on the gold headband of the high priest (cf. Exod. 28:36). The "traders" (Zech. 14:21) referred to the merchants who frequented the courts with their wares (cf. Neh. 13:19-22; Matt. 21:12; John 2:14). In the kingdom, there will be no distinction between the sacred and the secular. The bells, pots, and people all will be "HOLY TO THE LORD."

MALACHI

BASIC FACTS

HISTORICAL SETTING

In the thirty-second year of Artaxerxes (432 B.C.), Nehemiah left Jerusalem to visit the king in Babylon (Neh. 13:6). Some time after the visit he returned to Jerusalem and initiated the temple, Sabbath, and marriage reforms (Neh. 13:4-31). A Persian governor was apparently in authority during Nehemiah's absence (Mal. 1:8). Such a ruler would not have been in office during Nehemiah's governorship of 444–432 B.C. or his governorship following his visit to Babylon.

There is close agreement between the sins that Malachi denounced and those that Nehemiah sought to correct. Both books refer to the problems of priestly laxity (Mal. 1:6–2:9; Neh. 13:4-9, 29), the neglect of tithes (Mal. 3:7-12; Neh. 13:10-13), and intermarriage with foreign women (Mal. 2:10-16; Neh. 13:23-28).

Malachi prophesied about seventy-five years after the temple had been completed in 515 B.C.. The Jews had been home from exile for around one hundred years. Although they were cured of idolatry, they had lost the enthusiasm over the return and reestablishment of proper worship. Nehemiah had brought reform and revival (Neh. 10:28-39), but the people had again succumbed to religious indifference and moral laxity.

Having suffered plague and famine (Mal. 3:11), the people had begun to doubt God's love (1:2). They questioned his justice (2:17) and the benefit of obeying his commandments (3:14-15). The priesthood was corrupt (1:6; 2:1-9), and the Levitical offerings were unacceptable for sacrifice (1:8-10). The people were neglecting their responsibility of tithing (3:7-9) and were wearying God with their hypocrisy (2:17). They were even involved in the scandal of mixed marriage and divorce (2:10-16), activities condemned by the Mosaic law. It was such a wayward people that the Lord through the prophet Malachi called to repentance and obedience and warned of future judgment.

AUTHOR

The name Malachi means "my messenger." Because of this, some scholars have taken the name Malachi to simply be a generic name and regard the prophecy as anonymous. However, the writings of the prophets were never anonymous works. Nothing is recorded concerning the prophet's background or circumstances, but Talmudic tradition includes him as a member of the "Great Synagogue" with Haggai and Zechariah. This shows that he was considered an individual prophet at an early date, making it likely that "Malachi" was a personal name and not a generic one.

DATE

While the book of Malachi is not dated, scholars are in agreement that internal evidence indicates it is postexilic. The book must be dated after the ministry of Haggai and Zechariah, for the temple had been built and Levitical worship was in effect (Mal. 1:6-10; 2:1-3; 3:1, 10). While some have dated the prophecy just before the reform that was instigated by Ezra following his return in 458 B.C., a date of around 432 B.C. has much to commend it. It was probably during Nehemiah's absence between his first and second governorships that the corruption and abuses developed. It is reasonable to assume that Malachi protested those abuses prior to Nehemiah's return and reform, and hence a very probable date for the composition of the book is around 432–431 B.C.

PURPOSE

The book of Malachi was designed to restore the Jewish people to a right relationship with God by exposing the causes of their spiritual deterioration and setting forth the steps through which the community could be renewed. Malachi presented God's case against Israel as well as his promises for blessing.

GUIDING CONCEPTS

The argument of the people with the Lord pervades the entire book: "says the LORD"; "But you ask" (1:2, 6, 11-12, 13-14; 2:14, 17; 3:7, 13). The last chapter of Malachi resounds with the key themes of the Old Testament: the fear of the Lord (4:1); the remembrance of the law (4:4); blessings and curses (2:2; 4:6); Moses, Elijah, and the Lord (4:4-5).

The general failure of God's people dominates until the messenger of God comes to chastise and the Lord himself comes to judge and preserve the remnant. Worship of God will then be a global event (1:11, 14).

BIBLE-WIDE CONCEPTS

Malachi made an important contribution to Old Testament theology in his statements regarding the Lord's love for Israel as demonstrated by his choice of Jacob over Esau (1:2-5). The book is also instructive concerning the Day of the Lord (3:2, 17; 4:1, 3, 5). In announcing that day's approach, he pointed to the fact that it will be both a day of judgment (3:2; 4:1) and of deliverance (3:3, 4, 6, 16-18; 4:2-3). Malachi concluded his prophecy with a promise of the coming of the Messiah's forerunner, Elijah (John the Baptist), before the "great and dreadful day of the Lord" (Mal. 4:5; cf. Matt. 17:10-13; Mark 9:11-13). See also Matthew 3:1-3; 11:10, 14; and Luke 1:17.

NEEDS MET BY MALACHI

The last book of the Old Testament portrays God's people still struggling to understand God and what he desires from them. They still did not understand the reasons for their problems. Throughout the book of Malachi the people ask why they are having prob-lems even though God had been telling them why for centuries. Continually, God's people showed an amazing stamina and ability to deny their own sin and seek other reasons for their problems—blaming either God or others. Malachi sought to break through their denial of personal responsibility for their problems and called them to return to God. They also needed to be encouraged to work hard at building the focal point of God's presence, the temple. More than just a building for ritual, it was a gauge of the quality of their fellowship with the living God. The questions posed by God's people throughout the book provide the clearest indication of the needs the book was intended to meet.

- How has God shown love to his people (1:2)?
- How have the people of Israel defiled God (1:7)?
- Why is the Lord not answering the prayers of his people (2:13-14)?
- Why is God not doing something about injustice (2:17)?
- How have God's people robbed God (3:8)?
- What have the people said that has been against God (3:13-14)?
- God also asked a crucial question: Who can endure the day of the Lord's coming (3:2)? (This question was answered in 4:1-2.)

When, like Israel, believers suffer the consequences of their disobedience, it is easy for them to doubt God's love. The self-centered definition of God's love held by many believers coupled with their denial of their own evil makes them prime candidates for the exhortations of Malachi. Believers need to lift their heads above their own limited problems and see the great love of God in Christ. And they need to find the answers to why they are being disciplined and how they have offended God through a clear acceptance of their own part in disobedience. Malachi shows believers how denial of their sins furthers their discomfort, but admittance of their offenses opens the way for forgiveness and renewed fellowship with God. This will prepare believers for that eventual meeting with God face-to-face.

OUTLINE OF MALACHI

I. GOD'S LOVE QUESTIONED (1:1-5)
   A. Title (1:1)
   B. The Question of Past and Future Acts of Love Answered (1:2-5)

II. CORRUPT PRIESTHOOD: GOD'S NAME DEFILED (1:6–2:16)
   A. Defiled Offerings: What King Would Receive Them? (1:6-14)
   B. Defiled Covenant (2:1-16)

III. THE SONS OF LEVI PURIFIED (2:17–4:3)
   A. The Calls for Divine Accountability (2:17)
   B. The Divine Response (3:1–4:3)

IV. COVENANT OBEDIENCE RESTORED TO THE RIGHTEOUS REMNANT (4:4-6)

MALACHI NOTES

1:1-5 GOD'S LOVE QUESTIONED
1:1 Title
The name "Malachi" means "my messenger," an appropriate designation for a prophet of God.

1:2-5 The Question of Past and Future Acts of Love Answered
Malachi used questions and answers as a literary device to develop the message. The pattern is as follows: (1) an assertion or charge was made by God (a statement); (2) an objection in the form of a question was asked from the perspective of the people (a challenge); (3) a refutation of the objection was made by God (defense). In each section, the prophet dealt with a problem. This section dealt with the problem of the people doubting or denying God's love for them. The Lord's love for Israel was demonstrated by his choice of Jacob over Esau (Gen. 25:23) and by his severe dealings with Edom, the descendants of Esau (cf. Obadiah). During the intertestamental period, John Hyrcanus (135–104 B.C.) forced the people of Edom to adopt Judaism or be killed (Mal. 1:4). Edom, later known as Idumea, was attacked and devastated by Simon ben Gioras during the Jewish War (A.D. 66–70). Josephus reported that the land was totally destroyed. Malachi anticipated that God's people would one day acknowledge his greatness and his love (1:5).

1:6–2:16 CORRUPT PRIESTHOOD: GOD'S NAME DEFILED
1:6-14 Defiled Offerings: What King Would Receive Them?
1:6-12 QUALITY: BLIND, CRIPPLED, AND DISEASED
The problem in 1:6-12 was the failure of the priests to truly honor God. God's "name" (1:6) represents his character or reputation. The meat placed on God's altar was defiled by the disobedience of the people (1:8; cf. Hag. 2:12-14). They vowed to give God their best (cf. Eccles. 5:4-5), but when it came time to pay, they gave unworthy offerings—crippled and diseased animals. "From morning till night" (Mal. 1:11) was a reference to the entire world, from east to west, over which God would rule. The offerings that God anticipated would be given in the true worship of the future kingdom (cf. Ezek. 40–44).

1:13-14 INNER ATTITUDE: TIRESOME
The curses were based on the provisions in the Mosaic covenant for curses and blessings—curses for disobedience (Mal. 1:14; cf. Deut. 28:15-68) and blessings for obedience (Deut. 28:1-14).

2:1-16 Defiled Covenant
2:1-3 ADDRESS AND CURSE
Malachi spoke regarding the priests who had the responsibility to instruct God's people (Mal. 2:7; cf. Lev. 10:8-11; Deut. 33:10). They had failed in that sacred trust. For the curses of the covenant, see Deuteronomy 27:15-26 and 28:15-68.

2:4-16 COVENANT CONTINUED: TRUE AND FALSE MESSENGERS CONTRASTED
2:4-9 True Messenger: Levi
The "covenant with the Levites" referred to God's provision for the priesthood in Levi and his descendants (Num. 1:50). In Malachi 2:5-7 the prophet contrasted the ideal priest, represented by the name "Levi," the chief ancestor of the priests, with the ungodly priests of his day.

2:10-16 False Messengers
The intermarriage of the Judeans with unbelieving heathen women was a continual problem in the restoration community (Ezra 9–10; cf. Neh. 13:23-29). The rhetorical question "Are we not all children of the same Father?" (Mal. 2:10) was intended to be answered yes. In one sense, God is the Father of all, since he is the Creator. "Women who worship idols" (Mal. 2:11) referred to "an idolatrous woman." Throughout 2:13-16 the Lord identified "divorce" as a breaking of faith. In order to marry the idolatrous pagan women, the Judean men were divorcing their wives. In light of their treacherous dealings with their spouses (Mal. 2:14), God had no regard for their offerings.

Note that God "witnessed" the marriage union, and that such a union is a covenant relationship ("vows"), not something liable to be broken with God's approval (2:14). The emphasis is clear: "Remain true to the wife of your youth." The "coat" (2:16) was often used to symbolize the moral coverings of a person's actions (see, e.g., Zech. 3:3-4).

2:17–4:3 THE SONS OF LEVI PURIFIED
2:17 The Calls for Divine Accountability
The problem in Malachi 2:17–3:5 was the cynical unbelief that "wearied" God, that is, nearly exhausted his patience. The Judeans doubted God's justice.

3:1–4:3 The Divine Response
3:1-6 JUDGMENT: THE MESSENGER PURIFIES
The "messenger" (3:1) was identified by Jesus as John the Baptist (Matt. 11:10, 14), who served as Christ's forerunner, inviting people to repent and believe in him. The "Lord" and the "messenger of the [new] covenant" (3:1; cf. Matt. 26:28) referred

to Jesus. Malachi focused on the second coming of Christ, which will purge and purify both the priests and the people in preparation for the messianic kingdom. The "blazing fire that refines" (3:2) referred to a smelter's fire, used to purify ore. The "strong soap" was for cleaning. Since God is unchanging in his covenant relationship with Israel (Gen. 12:1-3), he will not completely destroy them (Mal. 3:6).

3:7-15 EXHORTATION: THE WAY OF REPENTANCE

The problem in 3:7-12 was the people's departure from God as reflected by their neglect of tithes and offerings. Two annual tithes were required according to Israelite law—one for the Levites (Lev. 27:30; Num. 18:21), and one to be used in worship at the annual feasts in Jerusalem (Deut. 14:22). A tithe was required every three years to provide for the needs of the poor (Deut. 14:28-29). There is debate as to whether this tithe for the poor was in addition to or served as a substitute for the tithe used in worship.

The New Testament pattern for tithing is proportionate giving—a person is to give "in relation to what you have earned" (1 Cor. 16:2). Certainly a tithe should be given proportionate to one's wealth, but not all proportionate giving is a tithe.

The anticipation of blessing for obedience to God's command to tithe was based on the Mosaic covenant, which promised blessings for obedience and curses for disobedience (Mal. 3:10; cf. Deut. 28:15-68). Generally, God will meet the needs of his own people (Ps. 34:9-10; Phil. 4:19), but that is not an unconditional guarantee. There certainly were and are exceptions. Yet, where God chooses not to provide physically, he gives sufficient grace to go without (2 Cor. 12:9).

The problem in 3:14-15 was that the people were guilty of arrogant words against God. They were saying, "There is no prophet who is serving God," and "God is not concerned about justice." God responded by showing that he did distinguish between the wicked and the righteous. The righteous would be blessed, and the wicked would be judged.

3:16–4:3 PRESERVATION: GOD-FEARERS SPARED

This section emphasizes the blessings that come to those who fear God, a concept repeated several times (3:16; 4:2; cf. also in 1:14; 2:2; and 3:5). The "scroll of remembrance" (3:16) was a figure derived from the custom of recording names of public benefactors (cf. Esther 6:1-2) so that they might be rewarded. God referred to the righteous remnant of his people as his "special treasure" (Mal. 3:17). Malachi anticipated a Day of the Lord (4:1; cf. 4:5) as a day of judgment on the wicked. The "Sun of Righteousness" (4:2) was a strong poetic image for a righteousness on the scale of the sun's brightness.

4:4-6 COVENANT OBEDIENCE RESTORED TO THE RIGHTEOUS REMNANT

The Old Testament concludes with an exhortation to remember the "law," God's "instructions", and to anticipate the coming of "Elijah." The "great and dreadful day of the Lord" (Mal. 4:5) referred to the most severe period of God's judgment that will come just before the second coming of Christ. Before that time, Elijah would come to call people to repentance and reunite disintegrating families, turning people's hearts to God. For the fulfillment of the promise concerning the coming of Elijah, see Matthew 3:1-3; 11:10, 14; 17:10-12; Luke 1:17; and John 1:21.

MATTHEW

BASIC FACTS

HISTORICAL SETTING

The historical setting for the book of Matthew was the life of Jesus and the period of his resurrection ministry that continued for forty days after his resurrection (Acts 1:3). Like the other synoptic Gospels (Mark and Luke), Matthew focused on the Galilean ministry of Jesus.

AUTHOR

The Gospel of Matthew is anonymous, but from a very early period the author has been identified as Matthew (Levi), the Galilean tax collector who became one of Jesus' disciples. The tradition of Matthean authorship can be found in the writings of Papias, Eusebius, and Origen. Matthew, originally named Levi, was the son of Alphaeus (cf. Mark 2:14). He worked at a tax collection station in Capernaum (Matt. 9:9), a city in the territory of Herod Antipas. Matthew promptly responded to Jesus' call and became one of only three writing apostles.

DATE

Scholars are divided as to whether Matthew or Mark was written first. Early tradition suggested that Matthew's Gospel account was the first written. Eusebius quoted Clement of Alexandria (A.D. 144–200) as saying that the Gospels with the genealogies (Matthew and Luke) were written first (*Historia Ecclesiastica*, 6.14). Recent scholarship has tended to place Mark first, with Matthew quoting 601 of Mark's 678 verses. But whether Matthew wrote his Gospel before Mark or not, the date of Matthew's account must have been prior to the destruction of Jerusalem in A.D. 70 because there was no hint in Matthew's record that Jerusalem was in ruins. The prophecies concerning Jerusalem's destruction clearly indicated that the event would still take place in the future (23:37-38; 24:1-2).

The word "still" (27:8; 28:15) indicated a period of years from the time of the events referred to and the writing of the Gospel account, but a period of twenty years would certainly satisfy the time lapse indicated in these passages. The account would probably not have been written before the first dispersion of the Jewish Christians under the persecution of Herod Agrippa I in A.D. 44 (Acts 12:1-7). Before that time the apostles would have been present with the Christians in Jerusalem and would have been able to impart authoritative teaching. The Gospel of Matthew was probably written around A.D. 50 to meet the needs of the Jewish Christians in Judea and those dispersed around the Roman Empire.

PURPOSE

Matthew desired his readers to understand that Jesus was the fulfillment of God's promises to Abraham, Israel's greatest patriarch, and to David, Israel's greatest king (1:1). The Gospel of Matthew was designed to convince its readers that Jesus of Nazareth was the promised Messiah of Old Testament prophecy. The book was also intended to reveal that the messianic kingdom was not fully realized in Jesus' day, but its fulfillment awaits his glorious return. Until then, Jesus the Messiah reigns in full authority over the earth as he seeks to make disciples around the world.

GEOGRAPHY AND ITS IMPORTANCE

Matthew used the geography of Israel's past to show how Jesus alone could be Israel's and the world's hope for the future. Matthew used the image of a sunrise dawning upon the Gentiles and foreigners in Galilee to introduce Jesus' ministry. Galilee is

The broken lines (– ·· – ··) indicate modern boundaries.
Copyright © 1986, 1988 by Tyndale House Publishers, Inc.

called Galilee of the foreigners (Matt. 4:15) because it had often been overtaken by hostile foreign enemies and in Christ's day was a mix of Jewish and Gentile inhabitants. The book focuses on Jesus' ministry in Galilee and ends with his resurrection appearance there and his promise to be forever present with those who believe in him. Galilee of the foreigners is where Jew and Greek met with Jesus, the greater son of David who will bring kingly rule, and the greater son of Abraham who will bring universal blessing to all nations of the world.

In addition to the Gentile thrust of Jesus' ministry in Galilee, Matthew saw many correspondences between the places in Jesus' life and Israel's past history. The geography involved in Jesus' birth in Bethlehem overlays Israel's past history of King David's birth. The killing of the babies in the Bethlehem area revived the horrors of Israel's captivity in Babylon. Jesus' trip to Egypt and return to Israel retraced Israel's ancient descent into and exodus from Egyptian bondage. Jesus' wandering in the Judean wilderness for forty days followed the pattern of Israel's forty-year wilderness wanderings. Jesus' sermon from the mountain (Matt. 5–7) and his glorious appearance on the mountain (Matt. 17) linked back to Moses' declaration of God's laws and the radiance of his face. But the correspondence between where Jesus and Israel went was designed to show what kind of man Jesus was. In all the places where Israel failed, Jesus was perfectly obedient and powerful. Circumstances and geography combine to reveal Jesus' perfect authority.

GUIDING CONCEPTS

OLD TESTAMENT QUOTATIONS

Jesus used Old Testament Scripture to emphasize key Old Testament concepts as he proclaimed the gospel and instructed his disciples. Matthew quoted Old Testament Scripture to show how it was fulfilled by the life of Jesus (1:22-23; 2:15, 17-18, 23; 4:13-16; 8:17; 12:17-21; 13:35; 21:4-5; 27:9-10). Matthew's purpose was to illustrate the sure fulfillment and power of God's covenant word and to identify Jesus as God's Messiah. What God had begun with Abraham, Moses, and David, he fulfilled in Jesus. The pattern of quoting Old Testament Scripture was set down by Jesus himself in 26:54-56. The Old Testament truths that were brought to their fulfillment in the life of Jesus revealed the redemptive heart of a loving God manifested through his Son.

COMPASSION

Compassion (sometimes translated "loyalty" or "loving-kindness") was an important concept taken up by Jesus from the Old Testament Scriptures. The central passage on the Lord's compassion in the Old Testament is Exodus 34:6-7 (cf. Deut. 30:1-6, 19-20). Jesus revealed God's compassion through everything he did while calling his followers to do the same. He required mercy and compassion from his followers and pointed to the key Old Testament passage of Hosea 6:6: "I want you to be merciful; I don't want your sacrifices" (cf. Matt. 5:7; 9:13, 27, 36; 12:7; 14:14; 15:22, 32; 17:15; 18:27, 33; 20:30-31, 34; 23:23). The kind of compassion taught by Jesus was not just a feeling. It was an act (9:13) that reflected the bringing of God's salvation to the world. The righteous remnant was to show compassion while they waited for God to judge and restore the world.

STUMBLING

"Stumbling" or "falling away" or "taking offense" was the opposite of having faith in Jesus. Matthew presented the majority of the "stumbling" sayings that appear in the New Testament. He was concerned to show his readers how to avoid falling away from, or stumbling over, the claims and person of Jesus Christ (5:29-30; 11:6; 13:21, 41, 57; 15:12; 16:23; 17:27; 18:6-9; 24:10; 26:31-33). Matthew desired to convince people of Jesus' messianic identity so they would not reject him and his message of the kingdom. The essence of stumbling (16:23) was part of a satanic trap to block the spread of God's redemption in Jesus the Messiah. Satan first sought to cause Jesus to stumble (cf. 4:1-11) and after failing to do this, set out to cause people to reject Jesus' claims to messiahship by any means possible.

AUTHORITY

The authority about which Matthew spoke was not just Jesus' physical power to do miracles. Jesus' authority was also shown in his power to command and expect obedience (7:28-29; 8:8-9; 9:6-8; 10:1; 21:23-24, 27; 28:18). The book of Matthew ends with the words of Jesus the Messiah's eternal claim to authority ringing loud and clear (28:18-20).

IDENTITY

The people mentioned in the book of Matthew had various opinions about who Jesus was (8:27; 9:14; 11:3; 14:1-2, 33; 16:13-16). That difference of opinion concerning his identity was used to make several points in the book. Outsiders never seemed to fully realize that Jesus was the Messiah. His disciples may have realized the truth about Jesus' Messiahship, but they still struggled with understanding the deeper truths of his identity, such as the predictions of his death on the cross. The question of Jesus' identity demanded that the honest disciple come to understand the heart of God's plan for world redemption through the suffering and sacrifice of his own Son. The closer Jesus' followers came to knowing who Jesus was, the closer they were to understanding the depth of God's compassionate and redemptive heart.

PRESENCE

Matthew began and ended his book by teaching about the presence of God in Jesus Christ. At the beginning of the book, the baby Jesus was named "Immanuel" (1:23), which means "God is with us." At the end, he was the crucified and risen Lord of heaven and earth, present with his people "even to the end of the age" (28:18-20). All that Jesus did and said between these accounts expanded and deepened the readers' understanding of their own responsibilities to obey the God who was eternally present with them. In this way, the concepts of God's authority and eternal presence were brought together.

BIBLE-WIDE CONCEPTS

Matthew is the first book in the New Testament canon. As such, it provides a bridge between the Old and New Testaments. This bridge was built on deep prophetic and theological foundations. Matthew showed continuity with the Old Testament in several ways. In his book, Matthew showed how Jesus fulfilled the promises that God had made to Abraham, Moses, and David to restore the divine presence with Israel. He developed profound links between the life of Jesus and the history of Israel (1:1–4:16). He showed how Jesus fulfilled the demands of the law and how he founded the Messianic community of the faithful (4:17–16:20). Jesus was the greater Joshua who would save his people from their sins. He was Immanuel, the God who was present with his people to judge and to save. These themes, that can be seen in both Old and New Testaments, will be expanded in the following notes.

NEEDS MET BY MATTHEW

The original readers of Matthew's Gospel had a great need for assurance that God was still with them. In the past, God's people had clung to that assurance throughout centuries of captivity and persecution. But believers in Jesus as the Messiah faced harsh criticism from the Jewish religious establishment that asserted that God could not possibly be with what they called a new and heretical sect. Matthew's reply was that God had indeed made himself present in the man from Nazareth called Jesus. For those who disbelieved, Matthew's Gospel provided extensive Old Testament proof that the man Jesus was also the Son of God, the Messiah. For those who believed, Matthew affirmed that, though absent physically, Jesus was spiritually and powerfully present until the end of the age. God had not abandoned his people. The suffering his people experienced was a sign, not of being abandoned by God, but of faithfully following in the steps of their suffering Savior.

Jesus' presence met a second need for the original readers. Along with comfort, Jesus presented a challenge to faith. As the prophet greater than Moses and the king greater than David, Jesus elaborated God's law and demanded self-sacrificing obedience. Like Israel of old, the new Israel of the church was prone to stumbling and lapses of faith and obedience. The presence of Jesus cut two ways for his church. It was both a comfort in hard times and a challenge to more consistent faithfulness. Matthew wrote to a community that needed help with its own faith and with its mission to witness to others. The structure and content of Matthew's Gospel reveal that he was answering questions like the following for his readers.

- Is Jesus the Messiah?
- If he is, how does he fit into Old Testament prophecy?
- What has happened to God's promises to Abraham, Moses, and David?
- Why did Jesus act in an unexpectedly quiet and humble way? (I thought the Messiah would come and break the power that Rome held over Israel.)
- If believers are really children of God, why are they being treated so badly? (I thought that when the Messiah came all would be well for those who believed in him.)
- Exactly where is this kingdom he came to bring about?
- How much longer will believers have to wait before the kingdom finally comes?
- What are believers in Jesus the Messiah supposed to be doing while they wait?

If the original readers of Matthew needed to be assured that God was with them, believers today need that assurance even more. When Matthew wrote his Gospel, Jesus had only been physically gone a few decades, whereas now he has been gone nearly two hundred decades. Matthew helps today's readers understand what Jesus' spiritual presence means for them today.

First, Matthew meets the need of believers to know how Jesus fits into the Old Testament promises. Many in Jesus' day and today believe that Jesus had no right to claim Old Testament roots and that he was just a religious zealot or imposter without God's prophetic authority. By showing that Jesus was indeed the one prophesied by the Old Testament, Matthew assures believers that God did not change his mind between the Old and the New Testaments. He did not abandon all he had promised before the appearance of Jesus. God's great promises to Abraham, Moses, and David have not been replaced with a new set of promises in Christ. In Jesus these great promises and laws were elaborated and deepened, not abrogated. Because Jesus came to fulfill, not destroy, God's Old Testament promises and laws, Matthew records many of Jesus' speeches that elaborate and apply God's Old Testament laws for Christ's disciples. Thus the religion of Jesus was not new and rootless. It was the perfection of God's will for obedience and redemption that reached from the first day of creation, to Moses on Mount Sinai, to David in Jerusalem, to Jesus resurrected and glorified in Galilee.

Second, Matthew explains Jesus' quiet and humble ways. Early in his ministry, people wondered why, if Jesus really was the promised Messiah, he lived life in such a quiet and humble way. Matthew shows how Jesus' humble life was the very vehicle for bringing world redemption. The time of Christ was the time for redemption, not judgment and destruction. Throughout his Gospel Matthew explains how Jesus' sufferings and sacrifices set a pattern for the cross-bearing ministry of all who follow him. Although believers do not know when Jesus will return, they do know what he wants them to do while they wait. The time of waiting is the time for selfless ministry to the world, not for a selfish attempt to reign and be served. The Gospel of Matthew helps to show how, like Jesus, the believers' time of glory and reigning must come only after a time of humble redemptive service to the world. Jesus' life brought salvation for the world. The humble works of believers today will serve to witness to that great redemption in Christ.

OUTLINE OF MATTHEW

I. CREDENTIALS AND CONTINUITY: JESUS FULFILLS OLD TESTAMENT PROPHECIES REGARDING THE MESSIAH (1:1–4:16)
   A. The Background and Birth of Jesus (1:1-25)
   B. Jesus in Egypt: Bondage and Exodus (2:1-23)
   C. John the Baptist Is Presented (3:1-12)
   D. Jesus Is Baptized (3:13-17)
   E. Jesus Is Tempted: Identity with Israel's Testing (4:1-11)
   F. The Location of Jesus' Ministry: Light Dawns on the Gentiles (4:12-16)

II. MESSIANIC IDENTITY: FULL AUTHORITY AS SERVANT AND SON OF GOD TO INAUGURATE HIS NEW COMMUNITY (4:17–16:20)
   A. The Community Is Called (4:17-25)
   B. Authority of Words: The Fulfilled Law (5:1–7:29)
   C. Authority and True Cleanness (8:1–11:1)
   D. The Question of Faith and Further Revelation about the Kingdom (11:2–13:58)
   E. Faith and True Cleanness: Controversies concerning Eating Bread with Unwashed Hands (14:1–16:12)
   F. Identity to the Community Supernaturally Revealed: Authority to Bind and Loose (16:13-20)

III. MESSIANIC DESTINY: FULL AUTHORITY TO COMMISSION AND PRESIDE OVER HIS NEW COMMUNITY (16:21–28:20)
   A. The Son and the Cross: The Stumbling Block of Self-Preservation (16:21–17:23)
   B. Sonship and Privilege in the New Community (17:24–18:35)
   C. Obedience and Privilege in the Kingdom (19:1–20:16)
   D. The Purpose of the Son's Coming: A Ransom (20:17-34)
   E. The Servant and Son Is Praised: Triumphal Entry (21:1-11)

F. Jesus Redefines Temple Functions (21:12-17)
G. The Fig Tree Cursed: a Faith Lesson in the Context of Rejection (21:18-22)
H. The Past Disobedience to God's Messengers (21:23–23:39)
I. The Final Evaluation of Obedience (24:1–25:46)
J. A Passion Prediction and Plot (26:1-5)
K. Betrayal and Arrest (26:6-56)
L. The Passion Narrative: Guilt and Identity (26:57–27:56)
M. Burial and Resurrection (27:57–28:15)
N. Commission to the Community: Identity, Authority, and Presence (28:16-20)

MATTHEW NOTES

1:1–4:16 CREDENTIALS AND CONTINUITY: JESUS FULFILLS OLD TESTAMENT PROPHECIES REGARDING THE MESSIAH

Overview: The record of the background and birth of Jesus in the book of Matthew revealed Jesus' links to the promises and prophecies of the Old Testament (1:1-25). The cornerstone of this section was the genealogy of Jesus, which included both Abraham and David. Although Jesus was a son of David, the most prominent of Jewish kings, his links to Abraham were also stressed. Abraham was named to lay the foundation for Jesus' being the one who would bring salvation to all the nations (cf. Gen. 12:3). This emphasis on international salvation also explains the presence of Gentile women in Jesus' genealogy, and the book's thrust to include all nations in the messianic kingdom. Drawing an ethnic circle around God's salvation, whether done by the disciples or the Jewish religious leaders, is soundly condemned by the power of God's universal promises to Abraham.

The reader cannot claim that the Davidic aspects of the genealogy were stressed simply because David was mentioned first (1:1). If Jesus was a son of David, he was also a son of Abraham. The element of Jesus' genealogy that was stressed was the Abrahamic element. The genealogy established Jesus' role as a son of David and highlighted the inclusion of the Gentiles in salvation history stemming from God's promises to Abraham. Note the Gentile elements in the genealogy (Tamar, 1:3; Rahab, 1:5; Ruth, 1:5; Uriah's wife, Bathsheba, 1:6). The genealogy showed that God sovereignly brought his salvation into the world through a long and complicated history. Jesus, the son of Abraham and David, brought together the Abrahamic (Gen. 12:1-3) and Davidic (2 Sam. 7:16-19) covenants. That union had international (Abrahamic) and royal (Davidic) implications for God's saving work through Israel.

The most important point of the birth story was the establishment of Jesus' divine sonship (1:18-25). Joseph's negative response to the news of Mary's pregnancy was corrected by divine revelation. Joseph became the first model of a faithful disciple who listened to and obeyed God's heavenly messages (1:18-21). From that point on, Matthew showed that Jesus' life paralleled Israel's history. Just as the nation of Israel had done many centuries earlier, Jesus was taken into and out of Egypt (1:15). His absence from Palestine was compared to the time of Israel's captivity in Babylon (2:18). He suffered temptations in the wilderness like Israel (4:4, 7, 10). He was the light promised both to Israel and the Gentiles (4:15-16). But whereas Israel often failed in her role as witness to God's redemption, Jesus proved himself to be all that Israel was not. He perfectly fulfilled the destiny that God had planned for Israel by mediating God's work of redemption for the whole world.

1:1-25 The Background and Birth of Jesus

Matthew began his Gospel with Jesus' genealogy, centering on two ancestors with whom God enacted major covenants: (1) Abraham (Gen. 12:1-3) and (2) David (2 Sam. 7:12-16). The genealogy demonstrated Jesus' legal right to the throne of David. Matthew apparently did not consider Jehoiachin as cursed (1:11; cf. Jer. 22:28-30). The prophet Jeremiah had questioned whether Jehoiachin was "a discarded, broken dish" (Jer. 22:28). The two verses that followed this description (Jer. 22:29-30) cursed Israel's king and stated that "none of his children will ever sit on the throne of David." If the curse in these two verses referred to Jehoiachin, one of Jesus' ancestors, the curse against Jehoiachin's descendants and Jesus' messiahship would be contradictory. But this is not a problem, for Jeremiah 22:28 referred to Jehoiachin, while Jeremiah 22:29-30 referred back to Zedekiah, the one to whom Jeremiah was addressing his words. The curse was on Zedekiah, not

Jehoiachin. With the words "O earth, earth, earth" (Jer. 22:29), Jeremiah started a new section and renewed his words to Zedekiah.

Although Jesus was the legal son of Joseph, the words "mother of" (1:16) indicated that he was the physical son of Mary (cf. 1:18). The number "fourteen" (1:17) was used as a memory device. There are gaps in this genealogy (cf. 1 Chron. 3:10-16), but its purpose was to show the relationship between Jesus and his important ancestors, not to record a complete family history.

A betrothal ("engaged," 1:18) was enacted by the payment of a bride's price and coming to a binding agreement regarding a future marriage. During the six to twelve month betrothal, the future husband would prepare a home for his bride. Betrothal was much more binding than modern engagements. A formal divorce (1:19) was necessary to break such a contract.

The name "Jesus" (1:21), a Greek form of the Hebrew name "Joshua," means "salvation is of God." His name revealed the redemptive nature of his ministry. Matthew saw the fulfillment of Isaiah's prophecy (Isa. 7:14) in the birth of Jesus to the virgin Mary (1:23). The virgin birth of Jesus testified to his uniqueness and sinlessness. Without a human father he inherited no sin nature from Adam. The baby was given two names: "Jesus" (1:21) and "Immanuel" (1:23). The first, "Jesus," revealed his mission, to "save his people from their sins." The second, "Immanuel," revealed who he was in that redemptive mission, "God is with us" to save and also to judge. Matthew confirmed the presence of God at the beginning (1:23) and at the end (28:20) of his Gospel.

Since King Herod the Great (2:1) died in the spring of 4 B.C., the birth of Jesus took place sometime before that date, perhaps during the winter of 5 or 4 B.C. (1:25). The present Christian Era, beginning in A.D. 1, should have had its beginning four or five years earlier. The dating followed today was based on the somewhat inaccurate calculations of Dionysius Exiguus (c. A.D. 496–540).

2:1-23 Jesus in Egypt: Bondage and Exodus

Overview: Matthew showed how Jesus was the Messiah by his identification with the experiences of the people of Israel in the Old Testament record. Jesus was presented as the one who fulfilled the role that God had intended the rebellious nation of Israel to play. Jesus' sojourn in Egypt was compared to the bondage that had been experienced by the people of Israel in that same land. Jesus was presented as the perfect Israelite in bondage (2:13-14) and in exodus (2:15). During the birth narrative (1:18-25), the historical setting of the events recorded was unclear. But at the coming of the

Magi and the subsequent escape to Egypt (2:1-18), the surrounding world of Herod's evil reign came sharply into focus.

2:1-12 THE MAGI VISIT

"King Herod" (2:1) was a descendant of the Edomites, who were commonly called Idumeans in Jesus' day (cf. Gen. 36:8; Obad. 1). Herod had ruled as governor of Galilee from 47–37 B.C. He was then promoted to rule as king over all Palestine from 37 to 4 B.C. He became famous for building cities, fortresses, and temples throughout the land but was generally opposed by the people because of his Edomite ancestry. The magi, or "wise men" (2:1), were originally a priestly tribe in the Persian Empire. As astronomers, they may have learned of the Jewish messianic expectation and understood the significance of the appearance of the star (cf. Num. 24:17). The magi often held positions of considerable political influence in Persia. In 40 B.C. Jewish rebels and the Persians had joined together to push the Romans and Herod, their puppet king, out of Palestine. But in 37 B.C. Herod came back with the Romans and again took control of Jerusalem. Ever since, the Jews had shown a continual desire to overthrow Herod. In this historical context it was not surprising that Herod was disturbed and reacted with great violence when the magi came in pomp from Persia, supported with cavalry for safety, looking for the new "king of the Jews" (2:2).

The past and current high priests made up the council of "leading priests" (2:4). According to Old Testament custom the high priest officiated until he died, but the Roman authorities did not follow this system and appointed new high priests at their own discretion. The "teachers of religious law" (2:4; "scribes," NASB and KJV), originally copiers of the Scriptures, were regarded as experts in Jewish law. The "newborn king of the Jews" (2:2) was assumed also to be the Messiah.

The "prophet" (2:5) who foresaw the birth of the Messiah in Bethlehem was Micah (cf. Mic. 5:2). Bethlehem (2:8), the birthplace of King David, was located just five miles south of Jerusalem. By the time the magi had arrived, Joseph had moved his family from the stable to a "house" (2:11; cf. Luke 2:39). According to the Luke account, the family of Joseph had returned to Nazareth, then back to Bethlehem before leaving for Egypt. God spoke through dreams (2:12) as he actively protected his Son from the deadly designs of Herod. The magi's gifts of gold, incense, and myrrh were worthy of a king.

2:13-15 BONDAGE IN EGYPT: THE SON IS CALLED OUT

Note the importance of dreams (2:13) in the early life of Jesus and in the Old Testament for Joseph in Egypt (Gen. 40–41) and Daniel in Babylon (Dan. 2–12). Matthew saw Joseph and his family's departure for Egypt as prophetically significant in the life of Jesus (2:15; cf. Hos. 11:1). The prophecy of Hosea 11:1 originally made reference to Israel's exodus from Egypt. Matthew saw a parallel relationship between the experiences of Jesus and Israel, and he understood by the Holy Spirit's inspiration that Hosea's prophecy applied to both.

Israel's great exodus from Egypt, so vital for the nation's corporate and redemptive experience, found its ultimate fulfillment in Jesus the Messiah. Israel was loved by God as a youth and was released from Egypt. Jesus was loved by God as a youth and released from Egypt. Matthew linked Jesus' experience in Egypt with the bondage, exodus, and preservation experienced by Israel during the Egyptian and Babylonian captivities. Jesus brought a fullness and completion to these earlier events in Israel's history.

2:16-18 PRESERVATION IN BABYLONIAN EXILE: RACHEL WEEPING

Quoting from Jeremiah 31:15, Matthew viewed the Babylonian exile and Herod's murder of the baby boys as part of the same broad picture of persecution and suffering experienced by God's people. In the original historical context, Jeremiah spoke of the "mourning and weeping unrestrained" by Israelite mothers whose children had been taken in the Babylonian exile. But that exile was a prelude to a brighter future through divine preservation in a foreign land and later restoration to Israel. Rachel (2:18) was the favorite wife of Jacob and was representative of the mothers of Israel who were weeping for their lost children. In Jeremiah 31 all the children of Israel are pictured under the image of Ephraim, who is called God's "oldest child" (Jer. 31:9; see also Jer. 31:6, 18, 20; Exod. 4:22). This figurative son was taken into captivity amidst great pain and death. The figure of Ephraim's sonship is fulfilled in God's unique son, Jesus, who was taken down into Egypt amidst the suffering of his people. But despite the suffering of his descendants, Ephraim was Joseph's favored son who was favored and blessed by his grandfather Jacob (cf. Gen. 48:14-20).

2:19-23 HUMBLE REMNANT: THE SON CALLED A NAZARENE

Archelaus (2:22; 4 B.C.–A.D. 6) was a cruel and oppressive ruler. Complaints against him by both Jews and Samaritans resulted in his banishment by Augustus Caesar. Matthew viewed Jesus' residence in Nazareth as prophetically significant (2:23). Nazareth was a despised town because of its association with Sepphoris, the Roman capital of Galilee, situated just four miles to the north. Matthew related the name "Nazareth" to the messianic title in Isaiah 11:1 (Heb. *netzer*, meaning "branch," "sprout," or "shoot"). Matthew's mention of the city of Nazareth combined the concepts of lowliness and the wordplay on a messianic title.

3:1-12 John the Baptist Is Presented

The "Judean wilderness" (3:1) was a barren desert region west of the Dead Sea. John's message was "Turn from your sins and turn to God, because the Kingdom of Heaven is near" (3:1-2). For years, people had been saying the kingdom of heaven was coming. John announced that it was at hand. John was identified as the one who would "Prepare a pathway for the Lord's coming" (3:3; cf. Isa. 40:3). See the context of Matthew's quote in the book of Isaiah (Isa. 40:1-11). John the Baptist came as a prelude to the messianic age. John's appearance (3:4) was similar to that of Elijah (2 Kings 1:8) and this was the only explicit connection made between John the Baptist and Elijah in the Matthew account. John was in the wilderness to "prepare a pathway for the Lord's coming." He had to be sought out (3:5) because his ministry was to a separated people who were willing to come away from society to confess their sins.

John's message had a twofold thrust (3:2). First, he wanted people to repent and be saved. This directed listeners to acknowledge their guilt (3:6) and change the attitudes of their hearts. Second, his end-time message, "the Kingdom of Heaven is near," had to do with the fulfillment of God's promise to David of a messianic kingdom (2 Sam. 7:12-16). Through his ministry, John the Baptist became the "voice shouting in the wilderness" (3:3) foreseen in Isaiah 40:3. He came as the messianic forerunner, the one sent ahead to announce the Messiah's coming.

The "coming judgment" (3:7) was related to the coming of the messianic kingdom. According to Josephus, the "Pharisees" (3:7) were "a body of Jews with the reputation of excelling the rest of their nation in the observances of religion, and as exact exponents of the laws." They were middle-class Jews, primarily associated with the synagogue. The "Sadducees" (3:7) were the priestly aristocracy associated with the Jewish temple. Unlike the Pharisees, they did not believe in the bodily resurrection, since they did not believe this doctrine was taught in the Mosaic Scriptures. They did not accept anything except the Mosaic Scriptures (Genesis, Exodus, Leviticus, Numbers, and Deuteronomy) as authoritative.

The expression "brood of snakes" (3:7) characterized the religious leaders as evil and deceitful. These leaders had misunderstood the significance of the original international scope of the Abrahamic covenant. John the Baptist anticipated judgment on the unrepentant and corrupt Jewish religious establishment (3:10; cf. 23:37-38; John 15:1-2, 6). John the Baptist's mission was to call Israel to repent and be changed at the level of the heart and character, not on the level of outward religious ritual.

The word "baptized" (3:11) was a transliteration of the Greek word *baptizo,* meaning "to dip" or "to immerse." The Greek root *bapto* was used by those in the dye trade to describe the "dipping" of cloth. As a result of this "dipping," the cloth would be identified with a new color. The word was used here of a religious act of baptism that would result in one becoming identified as a follower of John and his movement. The baptism "with the Holy Spirit and with fire" (3:11) foreseen by John suggested the work of Christ at Pentecost (Acts 2) and the final judgment (3:12; 13:40-42). The "winnowing fork" (3:12) was an instrument used for tossing threshed grain into the air to separate the wheat from the broken bits of straw (chaff). In the judgment, God would separate the repentant (grain) from the unrepentant (chaff) (cf. 25:31-46).

3:13-17 Jesus Is Baptized

John misunderstood Jesus' intentions at his baptism. John understood baptism to represent an act of repentance, and thus, protested Jesus' baptism. But Jesus did not come to repent of sin. He came to identify with his people in righteous alignment with God's purposes. He came to "do everything that is right" (3:15) by identifying himself with the righteous remnant of God's chosen people—the people he had come to represent and save (cf. 12:18-21). The righteousness Jesus sought to fulfill included God's plans and demands for his people and John the Baptist. It also included Jesus' identification with the righteous remnant in Israel.

God's announcement (3:17) was the first of three times when God spoke from heaven regarding his Son (cf. 17:5; John 12:28). There were two titles given here: (1) "Son" (cf. Exod. 4:22, where God spoke of the nation of Israel as his son) and (2) "beloved" (cf. Gen. 22:2, where Abraham called his only son, Isaac, "beloved"). Jesus was both the Messiah and the representative of the covenant people before God. That representation would become the basis for the mediating role he would take in God's ongoing work of redemption.

4:1-11 Jesus Is Tempted: Identity with Israel's Testing

Satan's intent in the temptations was to cause Jesus to sin by taking shortcuts to the accomplishment of his kingdom purposes. God's purpose was to demonstrate Jesus' sinlessness (cf. 2 Cor. 5:21; Heb. 4:15) through his obedience to the Father's will. Jesus responded to the temptations by quoting Scripture (Matt. 4:4, cf. Deut. 8:3; Matt. 4:7, cf. Deut. 6:16; and Matt. 4:10, cf. Deut. 6:13) and refusing to fall into sin.

During Jesus' temptations in the wilderness, he quoted from the Old Testament Scriptures connected with Israel's own wilderness experience. But where Israel had failed to obey God during its wilderness experience, Jesus succeeded in perfect obedience during his. God was "fully pleased" (Matt. 3:17) with Jesus' righteousness (3:15). His baptism and subsequent temptation in the wilderness was compared to Israel's passing through the Red Sea into the wilderness. Israel was tested for forty years and Jesus for forty days.

The first temptation (4:3-4) was with regard to food. It was a test of Jesus' dependence on and trust in the Father to provide for everyday needs. In his defense against Satan, Jesus quoted from Deuteronomy 8:1-3, where Moses was reminding the people of Israel of God's provision of manna in the wilderness. Satan was tempting Jesus to make his own manna and not trust in God's provision. In Deuteronomy 8, the people were reminded that the purpose of manna was to test the heart's devotion to God. The Israelites had to depend on God's provision since there was no other food supply available. This first temptation was intended to thwart Jesus' dependence upon his Father by causing him to use his own resources to meet his need. The words of Satan, "the Devil" (Matt. 4:3), could be translated, "Since you are the Son of God."

The second temptation (4:5-7) was with regard to safety. Satan hoped to tempt Jesus into trying or testing the power and ability of God. This would have been a rash self-assertion to prove a point that did not need proving. Such an act would have shown a lack of faith in the power of the Father. Compare the commandment "Do not test the Lord your God" (4:7; Deut. 6:16) with the time Israel put the Lord to the test in the wilderness because they were angry and lacked faith (Exod. 17:1-7). This test would prove whether or not God was with the nation of Israel in the Sinai wilderness or with Jesus in the Judean wilderness. But the people of Israel and Jesus needed no such proof. To test God again would prove only a lack of faith. Thus, this second temptation tested Jesus' faith in God's presence and control over life's events. The "highest point" (4:5) referred to the southeast corner of the temple that overlooked the deep Kidron Valley. The second temptation was intended to cause Jesus to put God to the test by placing himself in a precarious situation that would require divine intervention (4:6).

The third temptation (4:8-9) was with regard to power and wealth. It was a temptation to short-circuit God's plan for salvation that required the redemptive suffering of Jesus. Satan offered Jesus immediate glory and riches, while God's plan would take Jesus down a road of suffering and death. Jesus quoted Deuteronomy 6:13 in his defense against Satan. In Deuteronomy 6:10-15, Moses had warned the people of Israel as they entered the Promised Land to avoid the temptation to fall into idolatry. He warned Israel not to forget that God had given them all that they owned in the Promised Land. Similarly, Jesus had to avoid the temptation to embrace riches and forget God. Jesus was offered all of this world's kingdoms under Satan's authority (cf. John 12:30-32; Eph. 2:1-2) for just one little act of worship. But such sin would have disqualified Jesus as God's means of redemption to the world.

During his own wilderness experience, Jesus, the perfect Israelite, was identified with his people in the wilderness of Sinai. All his quotations of Old Testament Scripture reflected similar temptations experienced by the nation of Israel in the wilderness. But where Israel had failed, Jesus succeeded. Jesus' use of the Old Testament pointed to his temptations being the fulfillment and summation of Israel's wilderness temptations. Jesus, who would represent the people as a perfect sacrifice, had proved worthy of the task by conquering the temptations that had overcome Israel centuries before. Jesus banished Satan and as a result enjoyed God's provision (4:10-11).

4:12-16 The Location of Jesus' Ministry: Light Dawns on the Gentiles
Jesus identified with the nation of Israel through his ancestry and birth, as well as through his parallel experiences. The events of Jesus' youth summed up the major events of Israel's history. His temptations paralleled Israel's failures in the wilderness. He further identified with Israel by the locale of his ministry. But his work of salvation would not be for Israel alone. He also came to bring light to the Gentiles (4:12-16). Leaving Nazareth, he moved directly into the territory of Herod Antipas, the one who had imprisoned John the Baptist (4:12-13). For more on John the Baptist's arrest and execution (4:12), see Matthew 14:1-12.

"Zebulun and Naphtali" (4:13) were Israelite tribes that occupied the region of Galilee. Luke recorded that after his rejection, Jesus left Nazareth and settled in Capernaum, a fishing village and tax collection station along the northwest shore of the Sea of Galilee. Matthew did not mention Jesus' one-year Judean ministry noted in John 1–3.

The location of Zebulun and Naphtali related to the Old Testament prophecy of Isaiah (4:14-16; cf. Isa. 9:1-7). Although Galilee was occupied by the descendants of these tribes, a variety of Gentile people groups lived in the area as well. Jesus was beginning a major new movement; he was bringing a new light to the Gentiles. Matthew saw in Jesus' arrival in Galilee a fulfillment of Isaiah 9:1-2. A new era had dawned for a region that once lay in spiritual darkness. Jesus' ministry had started with Israel but would extend to all the nations.

4:17–16:20 MESSIANIC IDENTITY: FULL AUTHORITY AS SERVANT AND SON OF GOD TO INAUGURATE HIS NEW COMMUNITY
Overview: This section of the book of Matthew (4:17–16:20) is introduced by the phrase "From then on" (4:17). The events of this section elaborate the meaning of the simple message: "Turn from your sins and turn to God, because the Kingdom of Heaven is near" (4:17). The phrase "from then on" also introduces the final major section of the book (cf. 16:21). In that section, the passion or suffering of Jesus will be the primary focus.

The kingdom proclaimed by Jesus would come at God's own time and in God's own way. In section 4:17–16:20, that "time" and "way" were greatly illuminated and defined by the Lord's words and actions. The problem of man's sin was especially significant for the coming of the kingdom (cf. Isa. 51:1-8; 62:1-2; Dan. 9:24). Jesus' new covenant was based on a complete forgiveness of sins (cf. Jer. 31:33). The very name "Jesus" meant that he would save his people from their sins (Matt. 1:21). Therefore, whether people rejected or accepted Jesus, his death as the substitute for mankind's punishment was indispensable. The resolution of the sin problem was the only way to open the "gates" to the kingdom of God. The cross and the kingdom were inseparably linked.

This section presents four major events in the life of Jesus: (1) the calling of his new community of disciples (4:18-22); (2) the authority of his words in fulfillment of the law (5:1–7:29); (3) the authority of his deeds as his identity is questioned (8:1–16:12); and (4) the revelation of his identity, supernaturally revealed to his community of disciples, along with his gift of authority to "lock" and "open" (16:13-20).

4:17-25 The Community Is Called
Jesus' message was precisely the same as John the Baptist's (4:17; cf. 3:2). Jesus started where John left off, but he would soon go far beyond all that John had said and done (cf., for example, 4:23-25; 5:1–7:29). The call of the first disciples in 4:18-22 chronologically follows the events of John 1:35-51. This was not the first contact that these men had had with Jesus. They had heard John the Baptist identify him as the Lamb of God and had traveled with Jesus to Cana where they had seen his first miracle (John 2:1-11). But now at Jesus' invitation, they left their fishing to become fishers of men by proclaiming the gospel. The gospel was the "good news" of forgiveness for those who would repent and align themselves with the righteous remnant (cf. Isa. 1:19-20; 25:6-9; 51:1-8; Mal. 4:1-2).

Jesus was teaching in the synagogues (Matt. 4:23; cf. Luke 4:16-22), announcing the kingdom (cf.

Matt. 4:17), and authenticating his message by miracles (12:28; cf. John 20:30-31). The stress on healing was leading up to the Matthew 8:17 quote of Isaiah 53:4. Healing was a picture or outward sign of a greater restoration based on the forgiveness of sins (Matt. 9:6). Many interesting things happened during this part of Jesus' ministry, but Matthew rushed through the events to give the reader a sense of the general impact and growing ministry of Jesus.

"Ten Towns" (4:25, Greek "Decapolis") was a Gentile district east of the Jordan River known for its splendid Greek cities. This section (4:17-25) gave a quick summary of Jesus' teaching, preaching, and healing ministries as a contextual background for Jesus' well-known Sermon on the Mount in the following chapters (Matt. 5-7).

5:1-7:29 Authority of Words: The Fulfilled Law

Overview: Matthew 5-7 is commonly called the Sermon on the Mount. In it Jesus gave his definition of true righteousness. These chapters reveal the nature of true righteousness (Matt. 5), the question of rewards and which master should be served to receive those rewards (Matt. 6), and repentance as an individual responsibility and choice (Matt. 7). Some of the key elements reflected problems with the religious leaders (6:2, 5, 7, 16), questions about the nature and application of the Mosaic Law (5:17, 20, 48), and questions about the means of entering the kingdom of heaven (7:20-23).

The Sermon on the Mount served as an extended example of Jesus' preaching of repentance and the kingdom of God (cf. 4:17). He proclaimed the kingdom in order to inspire repentance in his listeners. He desired that his listeners might turn away from sinful attitudes and deeds in order to bring about a change in their standing before God. He wanted to lead people away from their fallible human wills so that they might follow the infallible will of God. The sermon gave descriptions of and demands for potential and aspiring kingdom dwellers.

The sermon was spoken to a curious multitude who had responded with interest to Jesus' message and miracles. They knew that righteousness was required for entrance into God's kingdom (cf. Ps. 24:3-6). But they wondered if the righteousness of their Pharisaic practices was sufficient for entrance into the kingdom. Jesus delivered the theme of his message in Matthew 5:20 where he said, "unless you obey God better than the teachers of religious law and the Pharisees do, you can't enter the Kingdom of Heaven at all!" The righteousness necessary for entering the kingdom was to be found through faith in Christ (6:33). The blessed people (5:1-12) were those that were closely related to the kingdom of God. When the kingdom came, it would be theirs.

5:1-12 EIGHT CHARACTERISTICS OF KINGDOM DWELLERS

The Beatitudes (5:1-12) revealed eight characteristics that should be true of the righteous remnant in the promised kingdom. The truths implied in these characteristics all reflect pervasive themes in the Old Testament. They revealed to the listeners what the lives of people in the process of repentance should be like and caused them to reflect upon their own character in relation to the character of God. The Beatitudes were built upon an *if/then* logic, and hidden in each Beatitude was an *if/then* relationship. For example, the first Beatitude says in essence, "*If* you realize you are in need of God, *then* you will receive the kingdom of God" (5:3). The Beatitudes both demand and describe. They *demand* good character as they *describe* the "blessed" results of following the demands of kingdom living.

The attitudes of realizing a "need" for God, "mourning," and "gentle and lowly" all draw upon Old Testament themes and underscore the need for human responsibility and the work of divine grace. The basic element demanded by all the Beatitudes was a right relationship with God. The Beatitudes were intended to inspire Matthew's readers to think about the character of the repentant person so that they also could follow the path of repentance.

Matthew 5:3-16 should be seen as one single unit of thought. The word "blessed" ("blesses," 5:3; etc.) literally means "happy." For "realize their need for him" (5:3) see Psalms 40:17; 69:29-30, 33-34; and Isaiah 57:15; 61:1; 66:2, 5. This characteristic describes the inner attitude of a person when confronted with the holy God and his demands. Realizing a "need for" God means admitting that no one can have spiritual wealth in and of themselves— that all are dependent on God alone for spiritual salvation and daily grace. Such a person aligns with God's will, even against the desires of his own.

For the attitude of "mourning" ("mourn," Matt. 5:4), see Isaiah 1:17, 23; 2:11, 17; 61:2. The afflicted were often seen as God's favorites in contrast with the powerful. This mourning was a reaction to seeing all that God had demanded for the kingdom and then seeing how far all of mankind had fallen short.

For the attitude of "meekness" ("gentle and lowly," Matt. 5:5) read Psalm 37:7-11 and Isaiah 57:15. Having the quality of "meekness" would result in possession of the new heavens and new earth (cf. Isa. 66; Rev. 21-22). The Beatitudes and the Sermon on the Mount as a whole continually looked forward to the time of judgment and reward in the end times.

To be "hungry and thirsty for justice" (Matt. 5:6) was to seek to live life as God intended for it to be lived. Concepts drawn from Old Testament Wisdom Literature were being applied here (cf. Prov. 8:22-

36). For "hearts are pure" (Matt. 5:8), see what it meant under the old covenant (Deut. 6) as well as under the new covenant (Jer. 31; Ezek. 36).

Those "who work for peace" (Matt. 5:9) will be called "children of God." They will be heirs to God's kingdom of which "peace" will be an important characteristic (cf. Isa. 9:6-7; 66:12-13; Mic. 4:3). Note the emphasis in 5:3, 4, 9, 10. In each of these verses, an implied contrast was being made between those who would be blessed in the age to come and the religious leaders of Jesus' day.

Those "persecuted because they live for God" (5:10) would also be heirs to the kingdom. This relates back to 5:3 regarding the kingdom and to 5:6 regarding righteousness. The idea of this verse carried a bit of irony. These people were being persecuted because they were hungry and thirsty for righteousness. But their persecutors would be the religious leaders of Israel, the ones who claimed to strictly follow the way of righteousness.

Jesus made a personal elaboration (5:11-12) of the comments in 5:10. He would become the cause for the persecution of the righteous ("because you are my followers," 5:11). The people who desired to be among the "blessed" of the kingdom would not find their time on earth easy. Matthew wrote for people who faced a time of persecution prior to the establishment of the kingdom. There was a parallel drawn in 5:12 with the prophets of the past who had suffered for the sake of righteousness.

5:13-16 TWO FUNCTIONS OF BLESSED PEOPLE

Those who had repented and suffered for righteousness were linked to the prophets of old (Matt. 5:12). The message that God called them to proclaim was the message of the gospel to all the world (28:19-20). The fact that believers were to be like "salt" (5:13) communicated the prophetic function of living righteous lives and calling others to repentance. It meant having an impact for God and not being ineffectual. Salt, by its very nature, flavors and preserves everything that it comes in contact with. If it did not do these things, then it would not be salt. Salt, a valuable commodity in the dry Middle East, was used in the biblical period for barter. In fact the word "salary" comes from the Latin *salarius* ("salt"). A person lacking integrity might have mixed white sand with the salt and then had more for trade. But salt mixed with sand lost some of its salty quality and became useless.

The fact that believers were to be like "light" (5:14-16) emphasized the aspect of visibility. As light attracts people and dispels darkness, so believers were to illumine the way to Jesus the Messiah, the true source of light. The doing of good works was a form of that light. Good works would inspire others to believe in and glorify God. Putting light "on a stand" and letting "shine for all" (5:15) looked

ahead to the final commission to go into all the world (28:19).

5:17-48 THE FULFILLED LAW: DIVINE PERFECTION

Jesus gave five examples of the fulfillment of the law. He corrected a possible misunderstanding concerning the purpose of his coming (5:17-20). He did not come to abolish the law (5:17). But he did come to demand perfection (cf. 5:48). Jesus had just spoken of good works (5:16), and he, like the prophets of old, demanded the same holy character and acts of obedience. He brought no new way of living in God's kingdom. He simply expanded and deepened God's longstanding desire for his creation's obedience and holiness. He started with the Pharisees' standard of righteousness: obedience to the law. But he applied that law not only to the external deeds that a person might do, but also to the attitudes and thoughts in the depths of a person's heart. Fulfilled law is no longer the law imposed upon a person from the outside, but that which is written on the heart and becomes an integral part of that person (cf. 5:22, 28, 32, 34, 39, 44). If the law becomes internalized, obedience becomes instinctive and pleasant, not something a person is forced to do. Throughout the Sermon on the Mount, Jesus called his hearers to move from external obedience to an obedience motivated by the law written upon the heart (5:22, 28, 32, 34, 39, 44; 6:19-24).

The word "fulfill" (5:17) meant "to clarify" the true meaning of the law as a way to walk or a way of life. It also meant "to complete," the opposite of "to abolish" (5:17). The "smallest detail" (5:18) of the Hebrew alphabet is the *yod*, about the size of an apostrophe. Notice the consequences if a person "breaks the smallest commandment" (5:19) or teaches "others to do the same." Jesus was teaching full and complete obedience to all the law.

True believers were to exhibit a righteousness surpassing that of the Pharisees (5:20). Righteousness equals the tally sheet of kept commands. The religious leaders of the day served as the foil in Jesus' sermon. What righteousness could they possibly have lacked? Five examples of how the Pharisees failed to fulfill the law were given in 5:21-28: (1) murder and anger 5:21-26; (2) adultery and lust 5:27-32; (3) vows and simplicity (5:33-37; cf. Lev. 19:12; Num. 30:2); (4) revenge and nonresistance (Matt. 5:38-42); and (5) loving enemies (5:43-48).

The words "You have heard" (5:21) referred not to the teaching of Moses but to the imbalanced Pharisaic interpretation of the law. The word translated "hell" (Gehenna, 5:22)) referred literally to the L-shaped Hinnom Valley, south and west of Jerusalem. Child sacrifices had once been offered there (cf. Jer. 7:31), but it had become in Jesus' time an unclean rubbish heap noted for its continual burning. It became a metaphor for the place of eternal punishment.

Jesus' words specifically condemned lust as a form of adultery (Matt. 5:28). In 5:29-30 Jesus used hyperbole (exaggeration for the sake of emphasis), which was a common biblical means of making a strong point. While Jesus did not intend physical maiming, he did emphasize the seriousness of the sin and its consequences.

Jesus referred to the faulty Pharisaic interpretation of Moses' teaching on divorce (5:31; cf. Deut. 24:1-4). Jesus condemned divorce for any reason except for marital unfaithfulness (Matt. 5:32). This has been interpreted to refer to adultery, unfaithfulness during betrothal (cf. 1:19), or incestuous marriage (cf. Lev. 18:6-18). This exception to the permanence of marriage appears only in Matthew (cf. Mark 10:2-12; Luke 16:18). Jesus said that one who divorces a spouse contributes to the adultery that may result in the following remarriage. He added that in many cases marriage to a divorced person constitutes adultery since divorce did not dissolve the "one-flesh" covenant relationship of the original marriage.

The Old Testament strongly condemned false oaths (cf. Exod. 20:7; Lev. 19:12), but the rabbis made hair-splitting distinctions between oaths that had to be fulfilled and those that did not (Matt. 5:33). The "law of retaliation" (Exod. 21:24) was not designed to encourage retaliation but to limit it with a view to justice (Matt. 5:38). The Phariees mistook this as an encouragement for revenge. The Old Testament had taught love for one's neighbor (Lev. 19:18), and the principle of hatred for one's enemies was a Pharisaic perversion (Matt. 5:43). Passages like Deuteronomy 23:3-4 were not excuses to hate one's enemies but needed to be interpreted in context. Deuteronomy 23:7-8 goes on to require the acceptance of Edomites and Egyptians. The issue was holiness in God's assembly, not a generic excuse to hate anyone who was offensive. The essential teaching for dealing with the problem of enemies was reliance upon God's, not man's, justice. For Matthew 5:40, compare 1 Corinthians 6:7. These acts of nonresistance motivated by unselfish love would clearly represent the shining good works that were to characterize the kingdom of heaven (Matt. 5:16).

God was the model for the characteristics of righteousness spoken of in the Sermon on the Mount. Believers were being asked to do what was humanly impossible. They were to do what God did: love their enemies—the very thing God did for mankind through the incarnation of his Son. This passage was not talking about ethical perfection (5:4). Rather, it was commanding believers to be as consistent and generous toward people as God is (causing rain and sun). The law of Christ freed believers from having a provincial attitude toward other people, toward the extent of God's love, and toward the intent of the Law. In 5:21-48 Jesus

rejected the Pharisaic interpretation of the Law as superficial. He emphasized inner conformity to the spirit of the law rather than mere outward conformity to the letter of the law. The true requirements of the Law were highlighted to convict listeners of their need to turn to Jesus, the one true source of righteousness.

6:1-34 REWARDS: SINGULAR MASTERY

Matthew 5 dealt with righteousness and God's demands. The subject in Matthew 6 turns to that which motivates most people to performance: rewards. The subjects covered were prayer, fasting, and the giving of alms. Because none of these three practices were demanded by the Law, there was a greater tendency to boast about doing them. Jesus rejected the common practice among the Pharisees of parading their piety to be noticed by men, and he condemned doing good works for personal glory.

6:2-4 Alms

Jesus struck at the heart of Pharisaic hypocrisy when he condemned the Pharisees for the way they performed their acts of prayer, fasting, and the giving of alms—the pillars of Jewish piety (cf. Tobit 12:8). To announce by "blowing trumpets" (6:2) was possibly a reference to the noisy manner in which offerings were tossed into the thirteen trumpet-shaped chests in the temple. The gifts given "in secret" (6:4) may have been a reference to the "Chamber of Secrets" in the temple where, according to the Mishnah, the devout gave their gifts in secret.

6:5-15 Prayer

The "door" (6:6) probably referred to the storeroom door. In most first-century Jewish homes, it was the only room that had a door. The "people of other religions" (6:7) were mentioned as people who prayed endlessly for fear that their gods might not hear them. But God does not need to be informed when prayers are being said. He already knows. Prayer should consist of a humble, yet confident, conversation with God.

The "Lord's Prayer" (Matt. 6:9-13) was clearly a model for the disciples to follow, not an exact formula to recite in each prayer. In the parallel passage in Luke 11:2-4, the words vary, but the pattern remains the same. The Bible teaches that God does not tempt man to sin (Matt. 6:13; cf. James 1:13-14). The words of Matthew 6:13 meant "Do not allow us to succumb to temptation." Prayer should align the will of the person praying with God's will ("your will be done," 6:10). It calls the believer to realize that God is the source of all blessing and that his creation is in need of his sustaining hand.

6:16-18 Fasting

Only one fast was required by the Mosaic Law, the Day of Atonement (Lev. 16:29-34), but many other fast days developed in Jewish tradition (cf. Zech. 8:19). Jesus advised his followers to go about their business on a fast day as they would on any other, so that only God would know of their sacrificial deed.

6:19-24 *Treasures Evidence Heart Attachment*
In Matthew 6:1-8 the focus was on the choice between receiving rewards from men or from God. In 6:19-34 the focus is on the choice between the treasures of earth or the treasures of heaven. Notice the reason for God being concerned about where believers hoard their treasures (6:21). God wants the hearts of his followers to be permanently with him, not captured by the things of earth that will soon disappear.

Impaired vision affects a person's whole body (6:22-23), and similar damaging consequences result from an obsession with money (6:24). The eye illuminates the body and gives it the ability to see the world around it. Without the aid of sight, it is easy to get lost or be deceived. Similarly, when a person lives for money, he is blinded to the truth about life and can be easily led astray. For such a person, dark and light are difficult to distinguish. True vision can only be found by serving God alone, the true master.

6:25-34 *The Avoidance of Anxiety*
Along with the Pharisees' concern for material gain came the problem of anxiety (6:25). The command "don't worry" was repeated three times (6:25, 31, 34) for emphasis. When God is the master of a person's life, that person has no need to be anxious about his physical needs. This does not mean that believers should refuse to work and expect God to provide for them. The fulfillment of human responsibility is necessary (like the bird that is fed only by seeking the food that has been provided). God will meet the needs of those who responsibly seek to obey him. With the problem of daily provision solved, believers are free to seek more important things in life, such as the kingdom of heaven (6:33).

In Matthew 5 the Father was presented as the model for perfect righteousness (5:21-48). Therefore, God the Father was the one to please with obedience and to seek after, not the hypocritical Jewish leaders (Matt. 6). In Matthew 7 a starting place for curing hypocrisy (for effecting true repentance) was presented; it called believers and any person who might judge other people to purify their own lives first before trying to change others (7:1-27; especially 7:5).

7:1-29 REPENTANCE: RESPONSIBLE INDIVIDUAL CHOICE
For the godly leader, personal inner reform must always precede the teaching of others. Jesus condemned the hypocritical judgments commonly made by the Pharisees. He called leaders to judge with humble discernment, not prideful criticism

(7:1-5). See 2 Samuel 12:1-7 for an example of how King David found it easy to judge someone else while he had a giant log in his own eye. The tendency for most people working for reform is to start by condemning others. Jesus reminded people to judge themselves before criticizing others because missing their own faults would leave them condemned. Jesus was not against people correcting and evaluating each other. On the contrary, he supported criticism that was done with humility and love (cf. Matt. 7:5). It is important to distinguish between judging self-righteously and discerning sin with proper humility (cf. Matt. 18:15; Gal. 6:1).

Jesus ended this section on avoiding self-righteous criticism with a warning to beware of false disciples (Matt. 7:6, "unholy people," "swine"). The section on throwing pearls (7:6) immediately followed Jesus' command to see clearly and without hypocrisy. Such clear sight was necessary for those who followed Jesus. He wanted them to be able to discriminate between the holy and unholy in order to give what was appropriate to where it was needed. The two illustrations of unholy people and pigs were not designed to insult the very people God came to save. Figuratively, were not all people unholy like pigs? Jesus taught here that when someone seeks to take the speck out of another's eye (7:5), he needs to have the wisdom to discern the specific situation and to bring the appropriate remedy. It is not appropriate, for example, to feed dogs the holy food used in the temple. Nor is it appropriate to trick pigs by giving them pearls instead of real food. The link between the two illustrations is the inappropriateness of the remedy for the need. The holy food was for the priests, not unholy people, and pearls are for jewelry, not for angering hungry pigs. It is doubtful that Jesus was calling any particular religious or secular group of people unholy or swine. He and his disciples shared God's holy truth with Jews, Gentiles, men and women alike. Some received his word and some responded to it with murderous anger. Jesus was not teaching to withhold God's truth from unworthy people. He was teaching his followers to be as wise and effective as possible while ministering the gospel.

Jesus concluded the Sermon on the Mount by offering entrance to the kingdom to those who would act on his words (7:7-27). The present imperatives could be translated in a continuous sense— "keep on asking," "keep on looking," and "keep on knocking" (7:7). This section also served as a warning ("Beware," 7:15) against false doctrines and ungodly living. To show how crucial this warning was, Jesus placed it in the context of the end times; it was important to act immediately, for the end was near ("hell," 7:13; "life," 7:14; "fire," 7:19; "on judgment day," 7:22; "Go away," 7:23; "it will fall with a mighty crash," 7:27). Jesus compared life's way, which could lead either into the kingdom or into destruction, to two roads (7:13-14), two trees (7:15-23), and two houses (7:24-27).

In his sermon, Jesus stressed the importance of doing God's will, that is, keeping his commandments within the covenant bond. Jesus illustrated the doing of God's will or the doing of its opposite by such concepts as good and bad "fruits" (7:16-20), or phrases like, "obey my Father" (7:21); "the things you did were unauthorized," (7:23); and "obeys me" (7:24). This was the application section of the Sermon on the Mount. The "narrow gate" (7:13) was the way of faith in Jesus Christ (inward righteousness). The wide gate was the way of Pharisaism (outward righteousness). The words of Jesus in this section reflected the blessings and curses given in Deuteronomy 11:26-29.

The false prophets (professing disciples) would be identified by their fruits—their deeds as well as their doctrines (Matt. 7:15-23). It would be practice, not mere profession, that would reflect a genuine relationship with God. This was an expansion of John the Baptist's message. Jesus was warning against false or hypocritical obedience (7:21).

The story of the two houses (7:24-27) illustrated the importance of practicing the wise words of Jesus. The common biblical motif of comparing the practices of wisdom and foolishness was employed in these verses. See Deuteronomy 30:19-20 on the blessings or curses that result from either listening to or ignoring the wise counsel of God.

After Jesus had completed the Sermon on the Mount, the audience was amazed at his authority (Matt. 7:28-29). In contrast with the scribes, who simply quoted the rabbinic interpretations of the law, Jesus spoke in a manner that reflected his intrinsic authority as the Son of God. Their response of awe and amazement should be the response of people today. Jesus spoke many other times in Matthew, but this was the only address with an audience response noted (11:1; 13:53; 19:1-2; 26:1-2).

8:1–11:1 Authority and True Cleanness

Overview: There are three guiding concepts found in this section: (1) the source of authority; (2) the source of cleanness; and (3) the source of revelation. In this section Jesus illustrated with his own life the principles given in the Sermon on the Mount.

8:1-34 AUTHORITY OVER ILLNESS AND DEMONS

The significant points to note in the section of 8:1-34 are the authority of Jesus over sin and suffering and the Gentile aspects of his ministry.

8:1-4 The Healing of a Leper

Lepers were regarded as unclean on the basis of Old Testament Levitical law (8:3; cf. Lev. 13:45-46). The

removal of sickness was one of the great blessings anticipated in the kingdom (Matt. 8:4; cf. Isa. 33:24). The purpose of this miracle was not only to cure the leper but to alert the Jewish religious establishment in Jerusalem that there was someone in Galilee exhibiting messianic credentials. The religious leaders in Jerusalem were notified and began an investigation of Jesus (cf. Matt. 9:1-8).

8:5-13 A Centurion's Faith

The centurion, or "Roman officer" (8:5), was an officer in the Roman army who was in charge of one hundred men (a "century"), though by Jesus' time the actual number of men had dropped to eighty. They were responsible for training their men, leading them into battle, keeping track of military equipment, posting guards, and making inspections.

Why were only Abraham, Isaac, and Jacob mentioned as those who would be in the kingdom and not Moses and David (8:11-12)? Because the Gentile, not the Jewish, inclusion into God's salvation was being stressed. Indeed, the sons of the kingdom had to be obedient, and their very sonship was a privilege, not a guarantee. Any obedient person would ultimately be included in the kingdom promised by Jesus without respect to his ethnic background.

Those who "come from all over the world" (8:11) was a reference to the Gentiles. The teachings of Jesus reflected the universal aspect of the Abrahamic covenant (Gen. 12:1-3). "Those for whom the Kingdom was prepared" (Matt. 8:12) was a reference to Jews who thought they would gain access to God's kingdom simply because they were descendants of Abraham. It is personal faith that enables one to appropriate the Messiah's promised benefits and blessings (8:13).

8:14-17 The Healing of Peter's Mother-in-Law

In Matthew 8:17, Matthew quoted from Isaiah 53:4. Diseases, griefs, and iniquities were seen as interrelated in the Old Testament. The root cause of all sickness and suffering was sin. By removing the effects of sin, that is, sickness, Jesus was demonstrating his ability to deal with the ultimate cause—sin itself.

The healings pointed forward to the work of Jesus on the cross by beginning the conquest of sin's effects (cf. Matt. 27:27-31 with Isa. 53:4-5). Matthew quoted from Isaiah 53 to show that in Jesus' works of physical healing and bringing forgiveness for sin, he was fulfilling the visible signs that the prophets attributed to the promised Messiah. The event recorded in Matthew 9:6 carried the concept of Jesus' forgiving sin further, though Matthew did not elaborate or theologize upon Jesus' substitutionary death. The work of theology was left for the apostle Paul.

8:18-22 The Focus and Priority of Discipleship

This is a departure saying and includes the first occurrence in Matthew of the phrase, "Son of Man."

Jesus' use of the term went against the common messianic concepts of the day, including the Messianic concept of militant Judaism. Jesus did not first come to reign victorious or destroy the military might of Rome. Where would Jesus take his followers in the political, military, or religious terms of the world (8:20)? Nowhere. Jesus cautioned the disciples to evaluate their reason for following him. He wanted to make sure that they knew that glory and conquest would only come after they had suffered humiliation in the eyes of the world.

The term "Son of Man" (8:20) was used thirty-two times in Matthew by Jesus to refer to himself. As used by Jesus, the term drew on the implications of its use in Daniel 7:13 (for more on the "Son of Man," see the guiding concepts for the Gospel of Mark). In Matthew 8:22 Jesus was saying, "let the spiritually dead bury the physically dead." There was no greater priority than following the Author of life.

8:23-27 The Obedient Storm: What Kind of Man Is This?
The "lake" (8:23) was a reference to the fresh water Sea of Galilee, situated about 680 feet below sea level. The Mediterranean winds often rush through the valleys of Galilee and swoop down into the basin of the Sea of Galilee causing strong tempests. The audience's response was noted in 8:27. Jesus's authority was demonstrated by his power over nature, and his calming of the storm also gave support to his claim to authority over sin and death (cf. 9:4-7).

8:28-34 Jesus Rejected in Gentile Territory
The "land of the Gadarenes" (8:28) was the region of Gadara, a city located six miles southeast of the Sea of Galilee (see introductory map). Mark and Luke located the miracle in connection with the better known, but more distant, city of Gerasa (cf. Mark 5:1; Luke 8:26). In destroying the swine, the demons may have wanted to discredit Jesus by causing people to associate him with the loss of material possessions (Matt. 8:32-34).

9:1-13 AUTHORITY OVER SIN
Jesus' "own town" (9:1) was Capernaum (cf. 4:13) (see introductory map). The background for this incident was in the previous chapter (8:4). The Pharisees and teachers of the law (9:3; cf. Luke 5:17, 21) had come from Jerusalem to investigate Jesus' ministry. The miracle was intended to validate Jesus' divine and Messianic authority before the officials of Israel (Matt. 9:6).

Matthew was a tax collector who collaborated with the Roman government to raise taxes from the Jewish people (9:9). Tax collectors were classed with harlots and thieves by their fellow Jews and were excluded from Jewish religious activities. In 9:13 Jesus quoted from Hosea 6:6, contrasting his own attitude toward ministry with that of the Pharisees.

Jesus' authority over sin related directly to the condition and needs of humanity. It would not have been enough if he had just had authority over nature and demons. Authority over sin was the significant aspect of Jesus' miracles. Miracles were signs (Matt. 9:6) that pointed to something even greater. An important key to understanding the significance of Jesus' miracles is that they were signs of salvation. They verified the claims of Jesus: "I will prove" (9:6). They were linked to the Son of Man and his authority on earth. Matthew's quote of Hosea 6:6 in Matthew 9:13 brought judgment against the false religious ritual of the Pharisees and teachers of the law. It required that they match, as God does, their character with their deeds. God's desire to save the lost was the controlling force in Jesus' ministry to sinners.

9:14-17 WINESKINS: JESUS' IDENTITY IS CLARIFIED FOR JOHN THE BAPTIST
In the light of Jesus' rejection by the Gentiles of Gadara (8:28-34), the hostility of the religious leaders, the meekness shown by Jesus (9:1-8), and his eating with those who were ritually unclean, John began to wonder whether Jesus was the Messiah. Why was he away in Galilee rather than in Jerusalem? Using the illustration of wineskins, Jesus told John's disciples not to try to make the new conform to old preconceptions and traditions.

John's disciples were fasting because John had been imprisoned by Herod Antipas (9:14; cf. 4:12; 14:1-3). The Pharisees fasted in accordance with Levitical commandment and Jewish tradition (cf. Lev. 16:29-34; Zech. 8:19). Jesus explained that it would be inappropriate to fast while the Messiah ("the groom") was present with his disciples (Matt. 9:15). Jesus did not intend to patch up Pharisaic Judaism but to initiate a vital new way of life through faith in his own person (9:16-17).

9:18-34 TWO CONCLUSIONS CONCERNING JESUS' AUTHORITY: PRAISE AND BLASPHEMY
This collection of miracles was, in part, preparatory for the section of 9:35–11:6 and in particular would serve to allay John the Baptist's doubts about the identity of Jesus (11:2-6). The four miracles mentioned in this section made Jesus famous throughout the land (9:26, 31). Two daughters were healed in this passage (9:18, 22). The "fringe" (9:20) that the sick woman touched may have been a reference to the tassels worn at the edge of Jewish garments to remind them to follow God's laws (cf. Num. 15:37-40). The healing of the ruler's daughter (9:23-26) was the first of three resurrection miracles that demonstrated Jesus' authority to give life and resurrect the dead (cf. John 5:25-29).

The blind men appealed to Jesus as the Messiah, the "Son of David" (Matt. 9:27). Jesus' instruction "Don't tell anyone about this" (9:30) was intended to prevent increased opposition and a premature crisis in his ministry. The accusation made by the

Pharisees that Jesus was empowered by demons (9:34) was repeated in 12:24.

10:1-4 THE RECIPIENTS OF THE AUTHORITY

Jesus shared his identity and authority with the community as they witnessed in a hostile world (9:35–11:1). The question of who Jesus was pervades this section (10:18, 22, 25, 32, 40). Persecution had already been predicted in 5:10-12. Note the contextual link of Matthew 10:25 with 9:34. The term "apostle" means one who is a special representative, in this case of Jesus the Messiah. The concept of "apostle" may have developed from the authorized representatives who were sent out in behalf of the Jewish religious establishment to render decisions and make pronouncements in the synagogues of the dispersion. So too, the twelve disciples were sent with Jesus' message and authority. The Zealots (10:4) were members of an extremist political party that sought the overthrow of Rome by force.

10:5-33 PERSEVERANCE IN PERSECUTION: WITNESS

The disciples were to go only to the "lost sheep" of Israel (Matt. 10:5-6). Israel was to be the key to world evangelism. Jesus began his work of evangelism with the Jews, the children of Abraham. Then, after his resurrection, he commanded them to make disciples around the world.

Jesus' comments on the persecution of his followers moved from the sufferings of his contemporaries to the persecution that would take place in the end times. The words of 10:9-10 suggest that the disciples anticipated that the mission was going to be short. The disciples were not to waste time raising support for this ministry. Their work would be limited to a time of crisis and extremity. The underlying principle, however, is timeless: God cares for those who seek to serve him.

The Lord's message in 10:16-39 was given in the form of an Old Testament prophetic discourse. It blended together prophecies of times that were both near and distant. Jesus offered hope for the persecuted disciple (10:22-23). The sermon was built on the principle of 10:24. Just as Jesus, their master, would suffer, his followers were to expect suffering—lest any be tempted to stumble over the cross and persecution. The "prince of demons" (10:25) is known as "Beelzebub" in the Greek and literally means "lord of flies," an Israelite term of mockery for the Philistine deity (cf. 2 Kings 1:2). Later the term became an epithet for Satan (cf. Matt. 9:34; 12:24). Confidence in confession was linked to confidence in God's sovereign care and intimate knowledge of his people (10:29-31).

10:34-39 PERSEVERANCE IN PERSECUTION: CROSS-BEARING

The "sword" (10:34) was a symbol of division and separation. Commitment to the Lord would bring about a division between Jesus' followers and the world. Jesus showed his disciples that acceptance of their own personal crosses was the way to finding life (10:39). "Take up your cross" (10:38) was also a battle cry for certain of the Zealots as they sacrificed themselves in the battle to overcome Rome. The "cross" (10:38) was an instrument of execution perfected by the Romans. Here it was used as a symbol of one's willingness to identify with Jesus and endure the pain of rejection and persecution.

10:40-42 REWARDS FOR RECEIVING CHRIST'S PROPHETS

The persecuted disciples needed to know that God was behind them (10:40). They were of the same status as the Old Testament prophets (10:41); the rewards of the people who would receive them can be compared to the rewards received by the widow of Zarephath who served Elijah (1 Kings 17:7-24). Eternal rewards would be given to all who served those of God's family, including the poor and needy, as if Jesus himself had been served (cf. Matt. 25:34-46). A summary statement in 11:1 links the preceding discourse to the narrative that follows.

11:2–13:58 The Question of Faith and Further Revelation about the Kingdom

11:2-6 JOHN THE BAPTIST QUESTIONS JESUS' MESSIAHSHIP

John had been imprisoned by Herod Antipas at Machaerus, a fortress east of the Dead Sea (11:2). The phrase "the Messiah we've been waiting for" (11:3; lit., "coming one") was a Messianic designation (cf. Ps. 118:26). Jesus intended that John's disciples would report to John (Matt. 11:5) that he was fulfilling the Messianic expectations revealed by Isaiah 35:5-6 and 61:1.

John the Baptist's questions and doubts were promoted by Jesus' works that apparently did not fit John's preconceptions of what the Messiah would be like (Matt. 11:2). Jesus gave his answer to John's question in 11:4-6, affirming his messianic identity. In his answer, Jesus showed how his actions fulfilled Isaiah's Old Testament prophecies concerning the Messiah (cf. 11:5 with Isa. 35:5-6 and 61:1 regarding the poor). Jesus pointed to his works as evidence of his Messianic identity. If this was so, what works did Jesus perform that caused John to question his identity as the Messiah? John probably questioned Jesus' identity because he failed to connect Jesus' works with the prophecies of the Old Testament. Even though John had been confronted with messianic acts, he was still asking if Jesus was the Messiah. He also had probably been influenced by the popular notion of the day that expected the Messiah to come as a victorious and mighty king, not as a carpenter's son who spent his time serving the poor and needy. John was about to be "offended" (11:6), or stumble, because of his presuppositions about how Jesus was supposed to behave or speak. Although Jesus had not measured up to John's expectations, Jesus' actions did not need to change; John's perceptions did.

11:7-24 JESUS QUESTIONS AND WARNS THE MULTITUDES CONCERNING THEIR EXPECTATIONS OF JOHN AND HIMSELF

The rhetorical questions of 11:7-8 anticipated negative answers. Jesus indicated (11:10) that the ministry of John the Baptist was the prophetic fulfillment of Malachi 3:1 and 4:5. John the Baptist fulfilled Malachi's expectation of the coming of "Elijah" (11:14; cf. Mal. 4:5) by coming in "the spirit and power of Elijah" (cf. Luke 1:17). The truth of Matthew 11:12 was illustrated by the imprisonment of John the Baptist and the hostility and rejection aimed at Jesus.

The woes (Matt. 11:20-24) showed the great responsibility that would fall on those who heard the gospel and rejected it. Korazin (11:21) was located about two miles north of the Sea of Galilee. Bethsaida (Bethsaida-Julias) was located just east of where the Jordan River enters the Dead Sea. Tyre and Sidon were located in Phoenicia, on the Mediterranean coast north of Galilee. Capernaum (11:23) was located on the northwest shore of the Sea of Galilee. Sodom was probably located in the Rift Valley in the vicinity of the south end of the Dead Sea. (For the above locations, see introductory map.)

11:25-30 JESUS INVITES REPENTANCE AND UNVEILS HIS CHARACTER

Jesus revealed his relationship with God the Father, thus showing how the character of the Father was revealed in him and how he, as the Son, represented the Father's sovereign authority (11:27). This revelation provided a foundation for Jesus' authoritative teaching ministry represented in the parables of Matthew 13. There are Old Testament allusions throughout this section. The "childlike" (11:25) were the humble and repentant listeners. To such listeners Jesus revealed the Father and taught the lessons of discipleship. Matthew 11:27 revealed the sovereignty of the Son of God, both in his relationship with the Father and his revealing the Father to mankind. But the gentle and humble way in which Jesus the Messiah chose to come would cause many to stumble. The "yoke" (11:29) of the Jewish people was heavy under the laws and traditions of the Pharisees. Jesus offered an easy yoke because he would carry the load (cf. Jer. 6:16). The concept of "rest" (11:29) points forward to the discussion of the Sabbath rest in Matthew 12.

12:1-14 THE CONTROVERSY OVER THE SABBATH

The Sabbath had been designated the sign of the Mosaic covenant (Exod. 31:13-17). That the Sabbath observance had become superficial and external was evidenced by the Pharisees' condemnation of Jesus' disciples.

In the section of Matthew 12:1-14, Jesus applied the principle of Hosea 6:6 to the Sabbath laws (Matt. 12:7). Jesus showed the Pharisees that the Sabbath was a day for mercy and rest, not for adding extra burdens to the lives of the people. Eating grain while passing through fields was permitted by Old Testament law (12:1; cf. Deut. 23:25). The fourth commandment (Exod. 20:8-11) set the Sabbath (the seventh day) apart as a day to reflect on God's work of creation and delight in the Lord (Isa. 58:13-14). This was an example of what Jesus meant in saying that his yoke was easy (Matt. 11:29). This passage compared the heavy burdens imposed by the Pharisees with the light burdens given by the Lord.

In 12:3-5 Jesus cited two examples where greater priorities took precedence over the Levitical law: (1) David's eating of the "holy bread" (1 Sam. 21:1-6) and (2) the priest's labor on the Sabbath (Lev. 24:8). As in Matthew 9:13, Jesus (12:7) once again cited Hosea 6:6. A heart of mercy and compassion would recognize that meeting a person's needs was more important than following every ritual element of Sabbath observance.

Jesus further illustrated the importance of doing acts of mercy before practicing religious ritual by healing a man with a shriveled hand on the Sabbath (Matt. 12:9-14). The Jewish religious leaders reacted by meeting to plan Jesus' death (12:14). This was the first indication that the religious leaders would plan to kill their Messiah.

12:15-21 THE REASON FOR SECRECY: VICTORY AND GENTILE HOPE

The withdrawal of Jesus from the mainstream of Jewish society in section 12:15-21 came as a result of the death plots against him (cf. 12:14). Jesus' secrecy fulfilled the prophecy about him (12:17-21) recorded in Isaiah 42:1-4. The purpose was to extend salvation to the Gentiles (Matt. 12:18, 21). This Gentile extension showed that the Jewish mission of Matthew 10 was only a first step in bringing the message of the kingdom to the world. The narrower Jewish mission of Matthew 10 was, in Matthew 12, expanded to include all nations. Jesus' love and care for the poor and sick (12:15) also illustrated the broadly inclusive nature of the kingdom.

12:22-45 THE KEY TO OBTAINING FURTHER REVELATION: OBEDIENCE TO THE WILL OF GOD

The section of 12:22-45 centered on the agent of revelation: the Holy Spirit. The Pharisees attempted to destroy the people's growing belief in Jesus as they debated his identity (12:22-37). Jesus was accused by the religious leaders of doing his miracles by the power of Satan (12:24). They were attributing the works of the Holy Spirit to Satan rather than to God. Jesus identified that as speaking "against the Holy Spirit" (12:31), a sin that would not be forgiven.

There were Jewish exorcists who claimed to have the authority to cast out demons (12:27; cf. Acts 19:13-20). Whether they actually had this power is uncertain. But since they were regarded as having this authority from God, it would be inconsistent to attribute Jesus' miracles of exorcism to Satan. The unforgivable sin may be defined as knowingly attributing the works of the Holy Spirit to Satan (Matt. 12:31). This was tantamount to final rejection of the Holy Spirit's testimony concerning the person of Jesus Christ.

In the section of 12:38-45, two examples of Gentile faith (12:41-42) were contrasted with the Jewish leaders' unbelief and desire for a sign (12:38). Jesus referred to the prophet Jonah's mission to the Gentiles of Nineveh to reveal the breadth of the salvation he offered and the unbelief of his chosen people, the Jews. See the notes concerning the purpose of the book of Jonah and on Jonah 4:10-11 regarding compassion. No further attesting miracles were promised the Jews except the "sign of the prophet Jonah" (12:39-40; cf. 16:4), which would be represented by the resurrection of Jesus from the grave. Jonah's three-day experience in the great fish was typical of Jesus' experience in the grave. Both Jonah and Jesus suffered what appeared to be tragic and final deaths, but instead, they both experienced miraculous deliverances. The point of comparison, the "three days and three nights," does not actually require that Jesus spend seventy-two hours in the grave. According to Jewish reckoning, any part of a day was regarded as the whole. Jesus spent parts of three days in the grave (Friday, Saturday, and Sunday), which met the requirement from the viewpoint of first century Jewish culture. The "evil spirit" (Matt. 12:43) was a reference to a demon.

12:46-50 FURTHER REVELATION TO THE FAITHFUL

In 12:46-50 Jesus revealed that those who obeyed his Father were the people truly related to him. Obedience to the faith was what established a spiritual relationship with Jesus the Messiah. Note the link of 12:50 with 13:55-56. The religious leaders saw and understood only Jesus' earthly relations and failed completely to understand his relationship to God the Father.

13:1-52 THE OBEDIENT RECEIVE MORE REVELATION: THE PARABLES

Matthew 13 contains a series of parables, true-to-life stories that teach spiritual truth. The Greek word "stories" (13:3), or "parables," suggests the idea of comparison. Parables often place two concepts, one known, the other unknown, side by side for comparison. They use the known concept, like the work of a farmer planting seed (13:3-9), to explain a central truth about the less familiar concept, like the way people receive the word of God concerning the kingdom of heaven (13:18-23). Although parables are fictitious stories, they present content and situations that are true-to-life. Parables contain wisdom elements, making them, in some ways, much like the Old Testament proverbs. They show how the truth being taught relates to the hearer, who, but for keen and obedient hearing, might well miss the parable's personal implications (13:9, 43: cf. 2 Samuel 12:1-7).

Here are some basic principles for interpreting the parables: (1) Knowing the original setting in which the parable was given is important for understanding its intended meaning. The known must be understood to make the transference to the realm of the unknown. (2) The central problem of the parable must be discovered. The parables were designed to deal with a particular problem or question. This can usually be discovered from the immediate context or related verses. (3) The central truth of the parable must be determined. Most of the parables focus on one central truth. Even those that have multiple points of comparison are usually designed to answer one question.

Why did Jesus teach in parables (Matt. 13:10-23)? There were two major purposes: (1) to reveal truth to the receptive (13:11-12) and (2) to conceal truth from the unresponsive—those who rejected Jesus (13:13-15). Jesus quoted Isaiah 6:9-10, originally written to describe the hardhearted Jews of preexilic Israel, to describe the unbelieving Jews of his own day. In addition, Jesus' use of parables fulfilled prophecy, for Psalm 78:2 predicted that the Messiah would teach by this means (Matt. 13:34-35).

Jesus used parables to explain to his hearers what would happen in the kingdom as a result of the leaders' blasphemy and rejection of him (cf. 12:22-45). They also explained why some rejected God's Messiah. The parable of the soils (13:1-8) explained much in this regard. This parable made it clear that the people's rejection of Jesus was not because his preaching was unsuccessful. The problem was with the unresponsive minds and hearts of his hearers, not with the truth or power of the speaker. The hearts of many who listened to the parables of Jesus were like the hardened path (13:4), the rocky soil (13:5-6), or the thorny ground (13:7). But others would be like the good soil, and through them the kingdom of God would grow (13:8).

The "secrets of the Kingdom of Heaven" (13:11) revealed by the parables were those things that had not previously been known but were then being revealed. The kingdom of God had certainly been previously known and had been anticipated throughout the Old Testament. The "secrets" of the kingdom were that it was revealed but rejected, that it was present but small and hidden like the mustard seed or the leaven, and that its members were the humble and poor, not the powerful and wealthy.

The key to receiving more revelation was revealed in 13:12. But what is it believers can have or not have? The concepts of "having" and "not having" are defined in 13:13-17 as closely related to seeing, hearing, understanding, and turning from sin. The audience of the parables ("the people," 13:10; "them," 13:11, 13-14) saw and heard but did not understand or perceive (13:14) or turn from their sins (13:15). The disciples had open hearts toward God and a basic understanding of Christ to which Jesus would add more and more understanding. The others had "hardened" (13:15) hearts and would lose the value of whatever meager knowledge of God they already had. Self-righteous people think they have something before God, but in God's eyes they have nothing. Matthew used the prophet Isaiah's words describing the willful rebellion of Israel (Isa. 6:9-10) to explain Jesus' use of parables to hide truth from the ungodly (Matt. 13:14-15). This would become a form of judgment upon the unrepentant. The call to "understand" (Matt. 13:19, 51) was a theme that Matthew used throughout his Gospel.

Note Isaiah 6:12-13 and the prophecy of the holy seed in the stump. Matthew 13:14-16 is a quotation of Isaiah 6:9-10 that scolds God's people for their hardness of heart and speaks of the time of their punishment. In the same Isaiah context, Isaiah 6:11-12 goes on to answer the question of how long the punishment would continue. Isaiah 6:13 then shows how the restoration of God's people comes about. The image of the shattered stump that sends forth a new shoot and springs back to life represents the spiritual process that unfolds in Matthew. Amidst the shattered stump of hard hearts and spiritual blindness, the "holy seed" begins to bring forth spiritual life and vitality.

The "weeds" (13:24-30) were weeds that appeared quite similar to wheat when immature, but were of an inferior quality. When full grown, they could be distinguished from the wheat and

removed before harvest. These weeds or tares were sometimes used for chicken feed. Later Jesus explained that the parable of the weeds or tares was a revelation of what would happen at the last judgment (Matt. 13:36-43).

The "mustard seed" (13:31-32) was the smallest of the garden seeds used by first century Jewish farmers. The mustard seed was often referred to in the Jewish Mishnah as an illustration of something quite small. Like the mustard seed, the kingdom would begin very small, but would grow to become a resting place for the godly. The "yeast" (13:33) functioned in a manner similar to the yeast used in modern times, causing dough to rise. It revealed the kingdom's hidden power to pervade and reshape the world. Like yeast, the kingdom, though hidden to the eye, would work its way through the whole world (the lump of dough) powerfully and completely. In 13:34-35 Matthew showed how Jesus' use of parables fulfilled the prophecy of Psalm 78:2. Jesus was seen as one of the Old Testament prophets speaking to a dull and rebellious people.

In the next set of parables, Jesus described the value of the kingdom in terms of treasure and pearls (13:44-46) and how opposition to the kingdom would be judged (13:47-50). The kingdom was seen as so valuable that it was worth all that the seeker owned.

The parable of the fishing net (13:47-50), like that of the weeds, revealed events of judgment and reward that would take place in the future. Jesus used the well-known activity of fishing to show that God would separate the worthy and unworthy in his kingdom (cf. Matt. 25:31-46). The following two verses (13:51-52) revealed what a disciple of the kingdom was called to do. The disciple was to be perceptive and listen to God's words. Then he was to relate the old to the new, that is, the work of Jesus to the revelation already given in the Old Testament.

Jesus' rejection at Nazareth (13:53-58) by his relatives and neighbors was a clear example of those who would be "offended" and reject Jesus (cf. 11:6). They were unable to accept Jesus' offer of

---

the new treasures along with the old (13:52). Note the link of 13:55-56 with 12:50. Those who had been closest to Jesus when he was a child rejected him. It was not the closeness of human relationship that proved one's relationship to Jesus, it was obedience to the will of his Father.

14:1–16:12 Faith and True Cleanness: Controversies concerning Eating Bread with Unwashed Hands

Overview: The entire section of 14:1–16:12 is concerned with eating. Two guiding concepts found in this section are (1) the juxtaposition of the physical with the spiritual, and (2) Jesus' elaboration of Deuteronomy 8:3. This important section has been summarized in the accompanying chart.

Jesus taught that when it concerned such items as food, shelter, and safety, the faith of his people should be automatic. He showed that his followers needed to be tuned into the more important concerns of his kingdom. The disciples were hung up on the mundane concern for bread. Though they had two well-known opinions concerning the meaning of leaven (bread and teaching), they chose to understand his teaching on the mundane level of bread and missed what he was really trying to tell them. They failed to receive Jesus' words from a faith perspective and almost missed his warning about the unclean teachings of the Pharisees.

14:1-12 IDENTITY: IS JESUS JOHN THE BAPTIST?
When Herod Antipas heard of Jesus, he feared that he was John the Baptist come back from the dead. At an earlier time, Herod had ordered that John be beheaded. Herod's confusion about the identity of Jesus showed the people's confusion about what God was doing through his great men. This set the background for the discussion regarding the identity of Jesus in Matthew 16. When his father (King Herod the Great) died, Herod Antipas received the title "tetrarch" ("ruler of a fourth part") and the authority to rule over Galilee and Perea (4 B.C.–A.D. 39). Herod Antipas, who was married to the daughter of a Nabatean king, fell in love with his brother Philip's wife, Herodias, who was also his niece (14:4). Herod Antipas divorced his wife and married Herodias in violation of the Mosaic Laws concerning incestuous marriages (Lev. 18:6-18). John condemned this marriage as "illegal," and as a result was killed in A.D. 31 or 32 (Matt. 14:10).

14:13–15:39 THE WILDERNESS LESSON OF FAITH IS ELABORATED
14:13-21 Five Thousand Are Fed
The feeding of the five thousand took place at a lonely or deserted place on the northeast shore of the Sea of Galilee near Bethsaida (cf. Luke 9:10). This miracle is the only one of Jesus' thirty-six recorded miracles that appears in all four Gospels. Jesus' withdrawal from the crowds was probably

due to Herod's interest in him (cf. Matt. 14:2). The news of his deeds had spread to the king's palace (14:13). Although Jesus had sought solitude, he looked with compassion on the multitude that had followed him. His miracles of healing and feeding would serve as illustrations to teach his disciples (16:5-12), and at that point, comments on the significance of the feeding would be given. Note the progression of events in 14:14, 16, 18, 21.

14:22-33 Walking on Water: God's Son Worshiped
The disciples responded to this sign of Jesus' power by worshiping him (14:33; cf. 28:17). The night was divided into four periods: 6:00 to 9:00 P.M., 9:00 to 12:00 P.M., 12:00 to 3:00 A.M., and 3:00 to 6:00 A.M. The "fourth watch" ("three o'clock in the morning," 14:25) was between 3:00 and 6:00 A.M. If the disciples had started out around sunset (14:22-23), they had been rowing for about nine hours.

14:34-36 Healings from the Cloak: The Messiah Recognized
Gennesaret (14:34) was a fertile plain on the northwest shore of the Sea of Galilee. The Sea of Galilee was sometimes referred to as the Lake of Gennesaret (cf. Luke 5:1) (see introductory map). The people brought their sick to Jesus, showing their recognition of the promised Messiah.

15:1-20 Confusion about the Clean and Unclean
Jesus sought to make clear to his disciples that true purity and faith began with the heart, not with external rituals. The "age-old traditions" (Matt. 15:2) was a reference to the *Halachah* or the "law of custom." This tradition was regarded by the Pharisees as equally binding as the written law. The "law of custom" called for ritual hand cleansing before eating. Neglect of this custom brought defilement. The Mishnah states, "Bread eaten with unwashed hands was as if it had been filth." This law is an example of the heavy burdens imposed by the Pharisees. The Pharisees' criticism of Jesus and his disciples was ironic in that the feeding of the multitude came from the absolutely pure hands of God's Son.

The professed commitment of the Pharisees to God and his law was used by them to avoid the parental obligations demanded by the law (15:4-5; cf. Exod. 20:12). Jesus used the sixth commandment (Exod. 20:12), which was the first one that applied to man's relationships with his fellowmen, because it exposed one of the Pharisees' sins.

In Matthew 15:7-9 Jesus identified the Pharisees with the hypocrites of Isaiah 29:13. Isaiah himself had contrasted a false religion of the lips with a true religion of the heart. Even in Isaiah's day, most of the Jews had worshiped vainly on the basis of human traditions. The Pharisees vividly exemplified the "what you say and do" (Matt. 15:11) type of impurity. Jesus taught that people were not defiled by ceremonial uncleanness but by moral impurity that issued from the heart (15:11). He sought to drive home the importance of honoring God in heartfelt sincerity. See 15:10, 16 regarding Jesus' desire to bring about true understanding among his hearers (cf. 13:51; 16:6, 9, 12).

In the section of 15:12-20 Jesus made clear the source of true impurity—the heart. The distinction between ethical impurity (purity of heart) and ritual impurity (purity in terms of law and tradition) was also further clarified (15:15-20). Jesus showed that a lack of understanding could indicate a problem with the purity of one's heart (15:19).

15:21-28 The Canaanite Woman: An Impure Person
Tyre and Sidon (15:21) were located in Phoenicia, a Mediterranean coastal region north of Galilee (see introductory map). Why did Jesus make this woman beg? Was she asking for a Messianic blessing ("Son of David," 15:22)? Jesus' silence raised a response from his disciples: "send her away" (15:23). They responded with the assumption that the benefits brought by Jesus were exclusively for the Jews and thus failed to respond with compassion. Jesus' statement "I was sent only to help the people of Israel" (15:24) seems to support the disciples' request to send her away. Yet Jesus intended to meet her need. In 15:24 he was simply clarifying the scope of his commission; he had been sent only to Israel. Jesus clarified the priorities that exist in any household (15:25-26). Children were always fed as a priority before the pets of the household. Jesus did not intend to insult the woman by calling her a dog; rather, he used a form of the word dog that meant "pet."

After clearly enunciating the priority that the Israelites took in his ministry, Jesus went on to teach the disciples and the woman that the Gentiles would also see benefits from his presence. Her claim to blessing was through the Abrahamic covenant, which promised that all nations would be blessed through Israel (cf. Gen. 12:3). After making his point about priority in the messianic ministry, Jesus healed her. The location, Tyre and Sidon, might have influenced Jesus' actions. Jesus waited until it was crystal clear that the woman would participate by faith in the blessing he would give her. For other examples of Jesus healing Gentiles, see Matthew 4:24; 8:5-13, 28-34.

15:29-39 Healings Glorify God and
Four Thousand Are Fed
Matthew was painting a picture of the Lord's compassion by recounting his works of healing and the second feeding of a multitude (15:32; cf. 14:14). Magadan (15:39) was located on the southern end of the plain of Gennesaret (see introductory map). It was probably identical with Magdala (modern Migdol). See the comment on Dalmanutha in the notes on Mark 8:10.

16:1-12 CONCLUSION: BEWARE OF UNCLEAN TEACHING
16:1-4 Magadan: Leaders Seek a Sign
The power of a sign is not in its display, but in that to which it points. Jesus presented an analogy based on the ability of the Pharisees and Sadducees to forecast the weather (Matt. 16:3). They could predict the weather but could not "read the obvious signs of the times." The signs of the times were his miracles of healing that authenticated him as the Messiah. The "sign of the prophet Jonah" (16:4) referred to the resurrection of Jesus (cf. 12:39-40).

16:5-12 Leaven: Watch Out for False Teaching
Until this point Matthew had not revealed to the reader the significance of the feedings. In these verses Matthew presented the key to understanding the life setting of the feedings and applications that could be made concerning them. The feedings revealed the sustaining power of God for his people in the wilderness of life. They were signs to encourage the people's faith in Jesus as the physical and spiritual sustainer of mankind. In his discussion of the feedings, Jesus warned his disciples to beware of a kind of leaven other than that used in bread. Jesus warned his disciples concerning the teachings of the Pharisees and Sadducees that, like leaven, had permeated and distorted the belief system of the whole nation (16:12).

16:13-20 Identity to the Community Supernaturally Revealed: Authority to Bind and Loose
The previous section (14:1–16:12) was started and immediately followed by accounts in which people sought to understand who Jesus really was. In 14:1-12 Herod believed Jesus to be John the Baptist returned from the dead (14:2). In 16:13-20 Jesus was confessed by Peter to be the Christ (Messiah), the true Son of God. Peter's confession stands at the heart of Matthew's Gospel. Did the disciples know who Jesus was? The range of opinions given (16:13-14) shows that though all viewed him as special, many did not view Jesus as a truly unique individual, the Son of God. But Peter's confession revealed that Jesus was a unique individual (16:15-17). And Jesus affirmed that confession as a supernatural revelation from the Father (16:17). Furthermore, the confession of Jesus as the Messiah intimated that Jesus had a direct revelatory link with the Father as the "Son of God" (cf. 11:25; 13:11). The words "human being" (16:17) should probably be taken in this context to refer to natural reason. The knowledge reflected in Peter's confession was based on special revelation.

This was not the first time Peter realized who Jesus was (cf. 14:33). The disciples had been convinced that Jesus was the Messiah at least since the events recorded in Matthew 10 took place. But until this point the disciples had thought of the Messiah as a powerful and victorious king who would deliver them from Roman oppression. This was Jesus' time to redefine his identity as the Messiah. As the Messiah, Jesus would not free his people from Roman oppression. Rather he would follow his destiny of building his church and going through death to resurrection. Understanding his identity as the Messiah had been the disciples' first step. The idea of the Messiah's destiny to suffer on the cross and be raised from the dead would be much more difficult for them to grasp.

Caesarea Philippi (16:13) was in northern Galilee near the foot of Mount Hermon (see introductory map). Philip, Herod's son who ruled this district (4 B.C.–A.D. 34), rebuilt the ancient pagan worship center of Paneion and named it after Caesar Augustus. It was called Caesarea Philippi to distinguish it from Caesarea on the Mediterranean seacoast. Some thought Jesus was John the Baptist risen from the dead (16:14; cf. 14:2), Elijah (cf. Mal. 4:5), Jeremiah (cf. 2 Macc. 2:4-8), or simply one of God's many prophets.

In Matthew 16:18-19 Jesus commissioned Peter to be the foundation of a new community. It was inconceivable to have a Messiah without his special community. The word "church" (16:18) simply means "the assembly of those called out." The "powers of hell" (16:18) was a figure of speech that referred to death. Even death would not prevail against this special community. What would the Messianic community be like? The community that Jesus revealed would be different from anything his disciples had ever imagined.

The name "Peter" (16:18) is simply the masculine form of the Greek word for "rock." Peter's name revealed his function in the Messiah's new community; he was to be a foundation. Jesus made a wordplay on Peter's name. Peter (*Petros* in Greek) means "a movable rock or stone." The word translated "rock" (*petra* in Greek) means "an immovable rock formation or rock mass." Scholars have debated whether the "rock" was a reference to Peter himself, Jesus, Peter's confession, or the truth of Peter's confession—that Jesus was the divine Messiah.

The "keys" (16:19) were a symbol of authority to open or close doors (cf. Isa. 22:22). "Lock" and "open" (Matt. 16:19) were terms used by the rabbis to describe what they permitted or prohibited, that is, declared lawful or unlawful. By judicial pronouncement they would lock or open someone with respect to a particular law. The authority given Peter was later given the other apostles (18:18). They pronounced people loosed from the consequences of sin on the basis of repentance, and bound to sin's consequences (judgment) without repentance. What was the point of locking and opening? It was related to allowing entrance into the kingdom of God and was given in contrast to the Pharisees' rules for kingdom entry.

16:21–28:20 MESSIANIC DESTINY: FULL AUTHORITY TO COMMISSION AND PRESIDE OVER HIS NEW COMMUNITY

16:21–17:23 The Son and the Cross: The Stumbling Block of Self-Preservation

16:21-28 TWO CROSSES: JESUS' AND THE DISCIPLES'

Jesus made the first specific prediction of his death and resurrection in 16:21-28. The key elements of the passion predictions were that Jesus would go to Jerusalem, suffer, die, and be raised from the dead. That plan was not immediately acceptable to the disciples. The essence of the "dangerous trap" (16:23) was the placing of human interests and plans over God's plans for world redemption. Peter was expressing the desire of Satan, to keep Jesus from his work of redemptive suffering on the cross. But Peter was really trying to preserve himself when he said, "Heaven forbid, Lord" (16:22). Peter, along with the other disciples, was looking for glory in the new kingdom and had no desire to participate in suffering and self-denial (16:24-25). The opposite option to following the natural human inclination of self-preservation was to follow Jesus and carry his cross (16:24). The self-denial demanded of those who would follow Jesus went against the disciples' natural inclinations. And what was natural to them as human beings, as is true so often, was also contrary to God's purposes. Peter, like the other disciples, would have to learn that he "must put aside [his] selfish ambition" (16:24) in order to "keep" his life (16:25). For to deny self would be to follow Jesus' pattern (the way to life) rather than Satan's (the way to death).

Jesus revealed the perils of following the path of self-preservation (16:25-27). Jesus exposed the selfish and materialistic attitudes (16:26) that motivated Peter to rebuke him. Peter probably dreamed of a place of glory in the messianic kingdom, and the death of the Messiah did not fit into his vision of glory. This desire for power and material wealth was at the heart of his desire for self-preservation. But Jesus revealed that the final evaluation by God would bring all deeds and motivations to light (16:27). The motivation of rewards and punishment was given to provide an eternal perspective to the self-denial demanded in 16:24-26. The divine call to carry the cross and the natural human revulsion to that call was the basis for the community instructions that followed. People tend naturally to avoid the self-denial demanded by the cross. The following instructions were designed to solve the problem. Jesus spoke of the two major aspects of his second coming: glory and judgment (16:27; cf. Ps. 62:12).

Jesus promised his followers that the kingdom would soon come (Matt. 16:28). After revealing to his followers the agonies they would face, Jesus, having just spoken of recompense and final judgment, offered a vision of his coming in the kingdom. Matthew 16 laid down the two foundations of the Christian faith: the Cross and the Second Coming.

17:1-13 THE TRANSFIGURATION

The greater the impact made by the discussion of Jesus' taking up his cross (16:21), the greater the readers' appreciation of what the transfiguration (17:1-8) had to do with their taking up the cross and following him. The words of 16:28 suggested that the transfiguration (17:1-8) would provide a foretaste of the Messiah's kingdom glory. That foretaste would greatly encourage those who would soon suffer persecution for their faith. Its purpose was to reveal the breadth of God's kingdom and Jesus' position within it. Jesus "shone like the sun" (17:2; cf. Exod. 24:1, 16; 34:29-35). Moses and Elijah were the surrounding figures who functioned to show how much superior Jesus the Messiah was (Matt. 17:5). Jesus was the fulfillment of the law (represented by Moses) and the prophets (represented by Elijah), especially with regards to his work as the suffering Messiah.

This event became a confirmation of Jesus Christ's divinity and a commission for the disciples. It made it clear to the disciples that Jesus' words were God's words. God's statement "Listen to him!" (17:5) implied "Because this Son is mine and beloved, you had better listen to him." Therefore, if the Son spoke of a cross for himself and his disciples (16:21-24), his disciples would have to accept that. But the disciples continued to struggle with Jesus' command to take up the cross, as can be seen throughout the rest of the book of Matthew. The glory seen in the transfiguration was to help the disciples dispel doubts about Jesus' call to self-denial.

The "high mountain" (17:1) probably was a reference to Mount Hermon (9,200 feet high), although the traditional site was Mount Tabor (1,843 feet high). Peter and John both mentioned this experience in their later writings (2 Pet. 1:16-18; John 1:14). According to Luke 9:31, Moses and Elijah were talking with Jesus about his departure, that is, his death and ascension to the right hand of God (Matt. 17:3). Peter wanted to build the three tabernacles (temporary shelters) to celebrate the Festival of Shelters (cf. Lev. 23:33-44), which would be observed in the kingdom (cf. Zech. 14:16). He had the right idea but was off on his timing. Relate Zechariah 14:16-19 to Peter's desire to set up booths for Jesus, Moses, and Elijah. This was the second time God spoke from heaven about his Son (Matt. 17:5; cf. 3:17; John 12:28).

The disciples discussed with Jesus the teaching that Elijah would appear before the coming of the Messiah (Matt. 17:9-13). In answer to the disciples' question about the coming of Elijah, Jesus affirmed the temporal sequence of Malachi 4:5-6 that Elijah would come first (Matt. 17:11). He also revealed that the prophecy of Elijah's coming had already been fulfilled (17:12). The disciples understood Jesus to be referring to John the Baptist (17:13), who fulfilled the prophecy in an unexpected way. John the Baptist had come in the spirit and power of Elijah (cf. Luke 1:17; John 1:19-27), and his coming was set against the background of Malachi 4:5-6. The suffering of Jesus and John were linked together (cf. Matt. 14:1-12; 17:9, 12).

The vision of the transfiguration looked forward to the time after Jesus' resurrection (17:9). But Jesus the Messiah's lifetime on earth would be spent in suffering and humility (16:21; 17:12), not glory. The prelude to the kingdom's coming was the suffering of Jesus and John the Baptist. After their suffering was complete, the time of restoration would begin (17:11).

17:14-21 THE EPILEPTIC BOY: LITTLE FAITH DURING JESUS' ABSENCE

This little story moves powerfully to its climax in 17:20, "Nothing would be impossible." The immediate problem was the inability of the disciples to heal in Jesus' absence. Jesus had been up on the mountain, like Moses had been away from his people on Mount Sinai. When the disciples failed to heal the boy, Jesus pointed to their lack of faith as the problem. But Jesus did not demand an extraordinarily large amount of faith; he described the amount of faith he had in mind. It was the size of a mustard seed—very small and quite attainable by all his disciples. But faith is not a physical quantity, so the essence of Jesus' response is that success comes not from the amount of a believer's faith but from the fact that he has even the smallest amount of true faith and wholly relies upon the power of God. The words of 17:21 are not found in many important Greek manuscripts.

17:22-23 A SECOND PASSION PREDICTION

Even with a second mention of his resurrection, the disciples were still grieved. Their grief masked their inability to accept and understand Jesus' mission as a suffering Savior and their own mission to follow in his footsteps. Peter could not accept Jesus' death in Matthew 16:21-23. In Matthew 20:17-19, the only recorded response to Jesus' third passion prediction was the disciples' quarrel about who would be the greatest in the kingdom (Matt. 20:20-27). They had replaced acceptance of Jesus' death with a self-centered striving for status.

17:24–18:35 Sonship and Privilege in the New Community

17:24-27 THE PRIORITY OF MINISTRY: THE TEMPLE TAX

In his conflict with the collectors of the temple tax, Jesus avoided causing even these religious leaders to be angry with him (17:27). His decisions were always ministry oriented. Here Jesus taught by his example that though sonship has privileges, those privileges should be given up in order to offer redemption to others. Capernaum (17:24; cf. 4:13) was located on the northwest shore of the Sea of Galilee. The question asked by the tax collectors (17:24) dealt with the payment of the annual half-shekel temple tax (cf. Exod. 30:11-15). Two drachmas were the Greek equivalent to the Jewish half-shekel. The "coin" (Matt. 17:27) was the equivalent of two half-shekels and provided sufficient payment for both Jesus and Peter.

18:1-6 GREATNESS AND GOD'S INTENTIONS

If the sons of the kingdom had to give up their rights to minister to others (17:27), Peter asked, "Which of us is the greatest?" (18:1). Why should the sons give up rights for strangers? The disciples could not accept the fact that sonship and servanthood were compatible. Jesus revealed the heart of the matter in 18:3-4. The disciples needed to become like little children, humble and dependent on the power of God. Humility, a proper and biblical evaluation of self, would be the mark of true greatness in God's kingdom. The "millstone" (18:6) was a heavy disk-shaped stone used for grinding grain. The "little ones" (18:10) was probably a figurative reference to believers, young or old (cf. 18:6). Matthew was continuing the use of the "child" metaphor used earlier (18:2, 5).

18:7-14 CAUSES OF STUMBLING AND THE PARABLE OF THE LOST SHEEP

Jesus made it clear (18:7-9) that impediments to following him in righteous humility had to be overcome and destroyed. This included the punishment of any person that might cause another to stumble (18:7; cf. 18:15-20). But the point being made by these words of admonition was not that Jesus desired to exclude people from the kingdom. In the following section (18:10-14) Jesus told the parable of the lost sheep. In this story Jesus showed that his goal was to bring salvation, even to the sheep that ran away (8:14), at the price of great personal sacrifice. The point behind avoiding all stumbling blocks that might deter a person from humbly following Jesus, and the point of this parable, was that Jesus desired that all might be saved.

18:15-20 DEALING WITH A SINFUL BROTHER

In 18:15-17 Jesus outlined four steps for dealing with a believing brother who is embroiled in sin: (1) Personal confrontation of the sinner (18:15); (2) Private conference with witnesses in order to verify both sides of the argument (18:16); (3) Public announcement to the church (18:17); and (4) Exclusion from fellowship (18:17). At each step, even after step four, opportunity was provided for repentance and restoration. This section on judgment and discipline is followed by one of the great passages on forgiveness (18:21-35). The ultimate purpose of church discipline was restoration and forgiveness.

The "two or three witnesses" (18:16; cf. Deut. 19:15) would serve to confirm the evidence and either strengthen the reproof or invalidate the accusation. A "pagan or a corrupt tax collector" (Matt. 18:17) served as a metaphor for unbelievers. For "prohibit" and "allow" (18:18), see the notes on 16:19. The "two" (18:19-20) do not constitute a "church." In this context "two or three" referred to those who were gathered for prayer regarding a matter of church discipline.

The power to "prohibit" and "allow" (18:18) was granted by Jesus in connection with decisions concerning community purity and discipline. Notice that the power to "prohibit" and "allow" in the similar verse of Matthew 16:19 ("lock" and "open") was given with respect to entrance into the community of Christ.

18:21-35 THE PARABLE OF THE UNFORGIVING SERVANT

Note how in 18:21, Peter still seemed to be thinking of the discussion in 18:15. He wondered how many times he should forgive someone who was offending him. The rabbis believed that they were required to forgive another person only three times (18:21-22). Peter doubled it and added one more for good measure. But Jesus demanded that his followers give unlimited forgiveness (18:22). Jesus' followers are to forgive others since they themselves have been forgiven of a debt they could never repay. Compassion or "pity" (18:27) lies at the root of forgiveness (cf. 18:33). The Lord's compassionate desire to feed (14:14; 15:32) and to heal (20:34) was a manifestation of his even deeper compassionate desire to forgive (18:27). In 18:33 Jesus pointed his disciples to the divine pattern: be perfect in forgiveness as the Father is perfect (cf. Matt. 5:43-48).

19:1–20:16 Obedience and Privilege in the Kingdom

19:1-12 GOD MUST RULE OVER MAN'S WANDERING DESIRES: DIVORCE

"The area east of the Jordan" (19:1) referred to the district east of the Jordan known as Perea, ruled by Herod Antipas (see introductory map). In the first century A.D., there were two prominent views on the subject of divorce and remarriage among the Jews (19:3). Rabbi Shammai taught that divorce was allowed only on the grounds of adultery. Rabbi

Hillel taught that divorce for any reason was permitted. Both viewed remarriage as permitted after legitimate divorce.

The Pharisees used the problem of divorce to test Jesus. They pitted God's prohibition of divorce against Moses' allowance of it, as if the latter superseded the former. Jesus pointed out that the Mosaic permission for divorce was also of divine origin and served only to highlight the hardness of human hearts, then and now, in not being able to live according to God's will for marriage.

In 19:4-6 Jesus demonstrated from Genesis 1:27 and 2:24 that divorce was alien to God's original plan for marriage. He concluded by rejecting both the liberal and conservative views of his day with the words of Matthew 19:6. The question of Moses' teaching on divorce (Deut. 24:1-4) was answered by pointing to the hardhearted attitude that necessitated it, and that the Mosaic permission was not in keeping with God's plan as it had been "originally intended" (Matt. 19:7-8). For "adultery" (19:9), compare the note on Matthew 5:32.

The words of 19:10-12 related to those who had been divorced or had divorced in the case of immorality. Jesus' rather strict teaching led the disciples to conclude that it was "better not to marry" in the first place (19:10). The term "eunuch" (19:12) was used metaphorically here of those who were not married. Some never married because of physical limitations, others because they were never asked. Then there were those who "renounced marriage" or "made themselves eunuchs" for the sake of the Messiah's kingdom. The disciples thought the option to the strict rules of marriage was a life of singleness. But Jesus' point was that remaining single for any reason, whether because of physical defects, personal choice, or by divorce, needed the gracious help of God (19:11). People were not to use a return to single life as a way to get out of a marriage. God wanted people who were married to submit to his rules for love and purity within the marriage bond.

19:13-15 GOD CALLS THE LITTLE CHILDREN

Immediately following his discussion of marriage, divorce, and the single life, which revealed that people often try to get out of certain commandments, Jesus returned to the subject of children and their important place in the kingdom of heaven. Jesus taught that the humble submission found in innocent children was required both in marriage (19:3-12) and in obtaining eternal life (19:16-22). The problem of people failing to follow Jesus and the law with humble obedience links back to the discussion in 17:22–18:35.

19:16-22 RICHES AND PRIVILEGE

A rich young man asked Jesus how he might gain eternal life (19:16). Jesus' reply demanded that the man focus on God and his word (19:17). All he needed to know was already there. But Jesus demanded that the man not only follow external laws but also work for inner change and submission to himself as God's Messiah (19:20-22). External conformity alone has never been pleasing to God; a contrite heart has always pleased him. The point of 19:21-22 was to probe into and identify the objects of the young man's inner commitment. He failed the test of true commitment to God because he was materialistically minded (19:22; cf. 6:24). Jesus demanded that the man give away his riches, which stood as a stumbling block between him and true righteousness (cf. 18:7-9). God must be the object of a person's ultimate commitment; riches must take the backseat (19:16-29).

19:23-29 REWARDS FOR OBEDIENCE: TRUE RICHES

Salvation cannot be bought (19:23-26). For a camel to pass through the eye of a sewing needle is impossible, just as it is impossible for someone who is unwilling to make material sacrifice to follow Jesus and enter his kingdom (19:24; cf. Luke 18:25). Jesus showed that in the kingdom of heaven there was no room for misplaced priorities or disobedience. Humble submission to the Father's will was a necessity. He wanted his disciples to demonstrate the surpassing righteousness he spoke of in the Sermon on the Mount (Matt. 5–7). Peter wondered if those who denied themselves for the sake of Jesus would ever receive a reward (19:27). Jesus made it clear that riches would only be given to his followers after the kingdom was fully realized (19:28-30). The "Kingdom" (19:28) referred to the future renewal of Israel's kingdom (cf. Acts 3:19-21). The parable of the workers in the vineyard (Matt. 20:1-16) would more fully develop Jesus' answer to Peter's question in 19:27.

19:30–20:16 NO SPECIAL PRIVILEGE: THE FIRST MAY BE LAST

The assertion that "many who seem to be important now will be the least important then, and those who are considered least here will be the greatest then" (19:30) was illustrated by Jesus' parable of the workers in the vineyard (20:1-16). The context for this parable was a discussion of the rewards that would be given in the future day of "the Kingdom" (19:28). In the parable, people grumbled over equal pay for less work (20:11). Jesus was revealing the leveling character of God's justice. The eternal life promised to Jesus' followers would be a reward given equally to those who had followed him a long time and to those who had known him only a short time (cf. 20:14-15). This would quell the tendency of man to seek preeminence. The parable of 20:1-16 served to illustrate the point of 19:30—that the first would be last, and the last first (cf. 20:16). A "daily wage" (20:2) is a Greek *denarius*.

20:17-34 The Purpose of the Son's Coming: a Ransom

20:17-19 ANOTHER PASSION PREDICTION: GENTILES

This prediction added the new element of Jesus being delivered to the Gentiles (20:19). It also made the first specific mention of his mode of death by crucifixion, a Roman method of execution. Jesus' prediction of humble suffering contrasted with the attitude of the disciples who desired positions of authority in the new kingdom (20:25). Their desire for power and position became clear as they neared Jerusalem, and their hope for the establishment of Jesus' kingdom over all the Gentiles was at its height.

20:20-28 THE MODEL OF THE SON OF MAN: TRUE GREATNESS IS REDEMPTIVE SERVICE

The rest of the disciples were indignant at the request of James and John's mother (20:24) because they also wanted the best positions in the kingdom. The disciples had completely misunderstood the nature of the kingdom that Jesus would bring. It would not be like the Gentile kingdoms in which rulers "lord it over" the people they rule (20:25). The disciples were not to be like the Gentiles, but like Jesus Christ. Jesus, in predicting his passion, desired to teach submission and humility to his disciples. The "cup" (20:22) referred to Jesus' impending suffering and death. James later drank the "cup" (cf. Acts 12:2). Jesus gave his life a ransom "for" (Matt. 20:28, "in the place of") many. These words by Jesus clearly taught the doctrine of the substitutionary atonement.

20:29-34 THE SON SERVES: JERICHO BLIND MEN HEALED

Matthew's account mentioned two blind men, while Mark 10:46-52 and Luke 18:35-43 mention only Bartimaeus, the more prominent of the two. Luke said that the miracle took place as they entered Jericho (Luke 18:35), while Matthew indicated that the miracle took place as they left (Matt. 20:29). Apparently the miracle took place as they left the old city of Jericho (Old Testament) and were nearing the newer city of Jericho (New Testament); the sites of these two towns lie about a half a mile apart. The expression "Son of David" (20:30) was a messianic title (cf. 2 Sam. 7:11-16; Isa. 9:7).

21:1-11 The Servant and Son Is Praised: Triumphal Entry

Bethphage (Matt. 21:1) was a village in the vicinity of the Mount of Olives about a half a mile east of Jerusalem. The donkey was the mount of royalty in the biblical period (21:2). The Zechariah passage (21:5; cf. Zech. 9:9) concerned God's great offer of salvation and restoration for Israel. Jesus rode the young colt of a donkey in fulfillment of Zechariah's prophecy. Jesus came in a gentle manner, not as a warrior on a war horse. "Branches" (Matt. 21:8; cf. John 12:13) were associated with rejoicing (cf. Lev. 23:40), and later with expressions of triumph or victory (1 Macc. 13:51). The passage surrounding Psalm 118:26, quoted by the crowds in Matthew 21:9, also concerned God's restoration of Israel through his chosen messenger (cf. Ps. 118:22-29). "Praise God" (21:9), a Hebrew imperative, means "save now." The crowd identified Jesus as "the prophet from Nazareth in Galilee" (Matt. 21:10-11).

21:12-17 Jesus Redefines Temple Functions

These debates between Jesus and the religious leaders achieved several ends. They revealed the false arguments being made against Jesus for what they were and his true identity was recognized. He was the Messiah, "the Son of David" (21:15). Jesus' words and deeds in the temple also served to teach his followers about true religion. The book of Matthew, as a whole, built to this confrontation between Jesus and the Jewish leaders with their distorted form of religion. The conclusion of this confrontation recognized the authority of Jesus the Messiah. These debates also provided an inspirational model of boldness in opposition to false religion.

In the context of Jesus driving the money changers from the temple (21:12-13), read Isaiah 56:6-8 and Jeremiah 7:8-11. Jesus redirected the minds and hearts of the people to God in prayer (Matt. 21:12-13) and praise (21:14-17). Read the entire verse of Psalm 8:2 to understand what Jesus intended in Matthew 21:16. The words of the psalm speak of praise and strength to confound his enemies. Also, the "child" image is found throughout Matthew's Gospel (cf. Matt. 11:25-30; 18:1-6; 19:13-15).

21:18-22 The Fig Tree Cursed: a Faith Lesson in the Context of Rejection

The cursing of the fig tree was a lesson in the relationship between faith and prayer (21:21). Jesus demonstrated to his disciples the power that was available to them through prayer. The foliage on the fig tree indicated that there should have been some early, small figs, but there were none. Jesus judged the tree for its false profession and its unfruitfulness (cf. John 15:6). This was Jesus' only destructive miracle.

21:23–23:39 The Past Disobedience to God's Messengers

21:23-27 JESUS AND JOHN THE BAPTIST: THE WAY OF RIGHTEOUSNESS

The debate concerning Jesus' authority was just a smoke screen used by the Jewish religious leaders to avoid obedience (21:23-27). The three parables that follow this debate (21:28–22:14) were designed to deal with this challenge to his authority (cf. 21:23).

21:28-32 THE PARABLE OF TWO SONS

In this parable Jesus showed the difference between professions of faith and the practice of faith. Jesus required that his followers do, not just agree with, the will of the Father. The "tax collectors" and "prostitutes" (21:31) functioned as examples of those who had truly repented, and Jesus sought to motivate the Jewish leaders to repentance by citing their example. Deeds, not words alone, were necessary to make a person acceptable to God.

21:33-46 THE PARABLE OF THE REJECTED SON

The kingdom was not cancelled, rather it was taken away from the proud Jewish leaders and would be given to a repentant people (21:43) who would produce the fruit of righteousness (cf. Zech. 12:10–13:1; Rom. 11:26-27). The present generation was under judgment based on their rejection of Jesus the Messiah (cf. Matt. 23:38). Psalm 118, quoted in Matthew 21:42 (Ps. 118:22-23), was also quoted in 21:9. Matthew 21 was built around Jesus' fulfillment of the prophetic words of Psalm 118 (cf. Matt. 21:9, 13, 16, 42; 23:39). The people who would lose the kingdom were those who thought they had it (21:43). The nation that would bear fruit would be composed of anyone who did the will of God (cf. 21:31). The response of hatred by the Jewish leaders toward Jesus was restrained by fear of the crowds (21:45-46).

22:1-14 THE PARABLE OF THE MARRIAGE FEAST

This parable elaborated on the idea that few are chosen to be a part of the kingdom (22:14; cf. 21:43). The historical context reflected in the parable was the rejection of God's messengers throughout Israel's history (cf. 21:33-39). It revealed qualifications necessary for a person to be called to the feast of God's kingdom. Many Jews had been invited to the banquet but showed themselves to be unworthy (22:8). Others (Gentiles) were then invited, but even among this group was found a fool who was not prepared to accept the invitation and enter the feast. The second invitation, like the first, required that the person invited be worthy of the invitation.

Following these parables, a number of debates occurred with the scheming Jewish leaders. The leaders had already been shown to be deficient regarding their understanding of the Scriptures (21:16, 42) and to be excluded from the kingdom due to their lack of faith (22:15, 23, 31-32). Now, exposed as people without faith, they debate with Jesus.

22:15-46 JESUS DEALS WITH HIS OPPOSITION AND ANSWERS POLITICAL, DOCTRINAL, AND RELIGIOUS QUESTIONS

22:15-22 Paying Taxes to Caesar

The Pharisees marveled at Jesus' response to their question concerning payment of the Roman poll tax (Matt. 22:15-22). Instead of becoming flustered, Jesus called them to reevaluate their own priorities. The "supporters of Herod" (22:16), or "Herodians," are usually identified as political supporters of the Herodian dynasty, but the dynasty of Herod had not been ruling in Judah since the expulsion of Archelaus in A.D. 6. When Herod became king in 37 B.C., he adopted the policy of selecting his own high priest. The "Herodians" mentioned here were probably descendants of the family of Boethus, whom Herod had selected as his high priest. The question involved the legitimacy of the Roman government in Palestine (22:17). Everyone would agree that a legitimate government has a right to tax its citizens. But the question behind the issue was "Is the Roman government legitimate?" This was an attempt by the Jewish leaders to make Jesus say something against the Roman government that would result in his arrest. But the Jewish leaders also knew that if Jesus defended the Roman poll tax, he would alienate his Jewish followers. Jesus avoided the two-way trap by acknowledging two legitimate spheres of authority—governmental and religious—both of which needed to be recognized (22:21).

22:23-33 Marriage and the Resurrection

Jesus' response to the question of the Sadducees about marriage in the resurrection astonished his listeners (22:23-24). Jesus saw through the falsity of their question, realizing that the Sadducees did not even believe in the resurrection of the dead as the Pharisees did. For more on the Sadducees (22:23), see the note on 3:7. The question of 22:24 was based on the law of levirate marriage (cf. Deut. 25:5-10). The Sadducees referred to this provision to demonstrate the absurdity of belief in the resurrection. Jesus produced evidence for the resurrection from the Pentateuch (Exod. 3:6), which the Sadducees recognized as their sole source for authoritative teaching (Matt. 22:32).

22:34-40 The Greatest Commandment

The Pharisees questioned Jesus concerning the greatest of the commandments (22:34-40). They had reduced the law to 365 negative and 248 positive commandments (22:36). Because it was difficult to know them all, a priority list was needed. The Pharisees' question related to the debates common among them over which commandments were "heavy" (most important) and which ones were "light" (less important). What commandment was at the top of Jesus' list? Jesus quoted Deuteronomy 6:5 and Leviticus 19:18 in answer to their question. What was startling was Jesus' connection of the command to love one's neighbor (Lev. 19:18) with the command to love God (Deut. 6:5). He made the command to love one's neighbor equally heavy with the command to love God, showing that the two were closely connected.

22:41-46 The Identity of the Messiah

After Jesus asked the question concerning whose son the Messiah was, no one else dared question him (Matt. 22:41-46). The Messiah would in their thinking be a human son, the "son of David" (22:42; cf. Ps. 110:1). But Jesus revealed that the Messiah would be not only David's son; he would also be David's Lord (Matt. 22:45). Jesus quoted Psalm 110:1 in Matthew 22:44. The only way David would call his descendant "Lord" (22:45) would be if his descendant, the Messiah, was divine.

23:1-36 WOES ON THE LEADERS: UNCLEAN AND WITHOUT THE LAW

This scathing denunciation of the scribes and Pharisees arose out of the incidents described in the preceding chapters. The religious leaders of Israel were presented as professional hypocrites. By saying "the official interpreters of the Scriptures" (23:2), Jesus was implying that the Pharisees were assuming Mosaic authority for their petty laws and traditions. The "prayer boxes" (23:5, also known as "phylacteries") were small boxes containing portions of Scripture (cf. Exod. 13:2-10; Deut. 6:4-9) that were strapped on the forehead and fore-arm during prayer (cf. Exod. 13:9, 16; Deut. 11:18). The "tassels" (Matt. 23:5; cf. Deut. 22:12) served as reminders to keep the law.

The term "Rabbi" (Matt. 23:7), from the Hebrew *rab* (meaning "great"), was a reverential form of address and title of respect. Note the threefold use of "for" in 23:8-10. Jesus called the Pharisees to give up their religion of human deeds and short-lived glory (23:5-7) and to seek God in humble repentance. Humility (23:12) was the key concept in Matthew 21–23.

Jesus gave seven woes (23:13-36). For tithing (23:23), see Deuteronomy 14:22-29. The leaders did not understand the true meaning of the law. They debated the outer and inner cleanness of utensils while the law really was concerned with people and their moral purity (Matt. 23:25-26). "Whitewashed tombs" (23:27) were clean on the outside but were full of hidden death and decay. Inner purity (23:27-28) was demanded in order to escape destruction (23:29-36).

The identity of the Zechariah who was murdered (23:5) cannot be known with certainty. In Old Testament Scripture, "Zechariah son of Berekiah" refers to the prophet Zechariah (Zech. 1:1). But nowhere else in Scripture is there an indication that he was killed. The prophet Zechariah was also called "son of Iddo" (Ezra 6:14) after his grandfather's name. In 2 Chronicles 24:20-22 a Zechariah, son of Jehoiada, was murdered in the way described by Jesus. If this Zechariah is the one Jesus had in mind, then the use of father's and grandfather's names, seen in the references to the Old

Testament prophet Zechariah, may also be reflected in Matthew 23:35. If this were true, then Jesus would have referred to Zechariah through his grandfather's name, Berekiah, while 2 Chronicles refers to him through his father's name, Jehoiada. Second Chronicles was the last book in the canon of Hebrew Scripture. The murder of "righteous Abel" (23:35) recorded in Genesis, and Zechariah's death recorded in 2 Chronicles, the last book of the Hebrew Bible, show how God's faithful followers have been persecuted throughout biblical history (cf. 23:37).

23:37-39 SUMMARY: CRY OF LONGING AND JUDGMENT

Jesus longed to be reconciled with his people, the Jews. Jesus had longed to restore the blessings on his people, but the key to unlocking those blessings was their own desire to ask. Jesus had asked two blind men what they wanted him to do for them (Matt. 20:32). Jesus was willing to restore the nation, but the nation did not want it from him ("you wouldn't let me," 23:37). Notice how Psalm 118 was used throughout Matthew 21–23; see Matthew 21:9 (cf. Ps. 118:25), Matthew 21:42-43 (cf. Ps. 118:22-23), and Matthew 23:37-39 (cf. Ps. 118:26). The "house" (Matt. 23:38) referred to the Jerusalem temple. Jesus concluded his comments by looking forward to his second coming when the Jewish people would welcome him and call him blessed (23:39; cf. Zech. 12:10–13:1).

24:1–25:46 The Final Evaluation of Obedience

Overview: With all Jesus had said about the errors of the Jewish leaders, one might wonder if he had any concern for the Jewish nation. This was answered in Matthew 24–25. The end-time perspective of this passage followed from the "comes" in 23:39 and the hypocrites' resistance to God's ways. Matthew 24:1–25:26 functioned in a number of different ways. It gave (1) warnings against being misled (24:4-5, 11, 24); (2) encouragement to be diligent and faithful (24:6, 10, 12-13, 23, 26); and (3) insight into the essence of obedience exemplified by love (24:12, 14; 25:40, 45). These chapters revealed the loving heart of Jesus arming his followers for the potential problems to be faced in his absence. The Olivet Discourse was a loving, warmhearted prophetic departure saying and took its place with the other departure sayings of the Bible (cf. Moses, Deut. 31–32; Joshua, Josh. 23–24; and Paul, Acts 16:13-36). The background of the Olivet Discourse was Jesus' announcement recorded in Matthew 23:37-39. Jesus had hinted of his second coming and the judgment that would come against Jerusalem. The disciples needed some clarification on these two matters.

24:1-31 THE DESTRUCTION OF JERUSALEM PREDICTED: SIGNS OF THE END TIMES

24:1-3 *Questions Concerning the Future*

The "Mount of Olives" (24:3) is a long north-south ridge that lies just east of Jerusalem. The disciples had two basic questions on their minds (24:3): (1) When would the temple be destroyed? (2) What would be the sign of Jesus' second coming that would coincide with the end of this age? The first question had to do with the destruction of Jerusalem in A.D. 70 and was answered in Luke 21:20-24. The second question concerned the end of the age as it related to Israel's prophetic history.

Jesus' prediction of the destruction of Jerusalem (24:1-2) brought to mind their question "When will all this take place?" (24:3). The content of the Olivet discourse illustrated and reflected the content of Matthew's Gospel as a whole. It revealed how those with the character traits of the Beatitudes, especially salt and light in persecution, would live in relationship with others and the end to which they would come. Jesus expected his followers to live out the command "Love your neighbor as yourself" (Matt. 22:39) as the observable, tangible proof of love for God (24:45-51). The sermon gave to the disciples comfort and assurance for a ministry in a time of great conflict (25:40, 45).

The disciples' question concerning Jesus' return (24:3) showed that they had not yet come to grips with his departure, suffering, and resurrection. Jesus had mentioned his coming in 23:39. As a result the disciples then ask when that will be and what it will look like.

24:4-14 *The Correction to Potential Misleading*

Note the "time" words used in Matthew 24–25 (cf. 24:15, 23, 29, 33). Jesus warned his disciples to beware of the false teachers that would come (24:4). Why did Jesus not directly answer their questions concerning the future? Because he had another purpose. He wanted to help them avoid falling away from doing his will while he was gone (24:45-46). The "beginning of the horrors to come" (24:8) was a technical phrase for the end times. The events described in 24:4-14 did not paint a picture of the very end (cf. 24:6, 8). Jesus encouraged endurance through a long time of persecution to continue preaching the gospel (24:9-14). Persecution of Jesus' followers links back to 5:11. Jesus' response in 24:14 more directly related to the disciples' question about the end times (24:3). The disciples were looking for the end. Jesus wanted them to look at what they were to do until the end arrived: witness for him (cf. Acts 1:6-8). That was the reason for this age of trial and persecution. Jesus defined "love" as the opposite of "sin" (24:12). In this sermon, Jesus was dealing with the disciples' motive for asking when the end would come (24:3). They were looking forward to the coming of the kingdom, in which they hoped to receive great glory as the disciples of the Messiah. Jesus continually redirected their thoughts to their present responsibilities to witness for him in a world that was hostile to their message.

24:15-22 *The Signs of the End*

The events described in 24:1-14 were not the end. The greatest tribulation would come later (24:15-22). 24:15 was a conclusion based on the warning against being misled (24:4). The "sacrilegious object that causes desecration" (24:15) referred to the antichrist (cf. Dan. 9:27; 2 Thess. 2:4). If the Tribulation continued indefinitely, all living things would be exterminated (Matt. 24:22). To prevent such extermination, the period would be "shortened."

24:23-28 *The Unmistakable Return*

During times of great tribulation, one would naturally look for relief. This would be the attraction of the false messiahs. The content of 24:27 was Jesus' first specific answer to the question concerning the signs of his return (24:3). The middle part of this section (24:24-26) showed Jesus' concern that his disciples not be deceived.

24:29-31 *The Son Comes*

Jesus quoted Isaiah 13:10 and 34:4 in Matthew 24:29. Note the context of these verses in the book of Isaiah. Jesus continued the answer to his disciples' question concerning the end times (Matt. 24:3) in 24:29-31 (cf. 24:36). Matthew 24:29-31 stressed the point made in 24:27 and emphasized Jesus' concern for those who would suffer. Jesus feared that their suffering would open them up to possible deception by false messiahs. Thus, he made it clear that his coming would be unmistakable, accompanied by great glory, angels, and a loud trumpet call (24:30-31). The desire for relief by the elect would be great, but Jesus left them with a message of comfort (24:31, "gather together his chosen ones"; cf. 24:4, 22, 24).

24:32–25:46 EXHORTATIONS TO FAITHFULNESS IN ABSENCE: PARABLES OF READINESS

24:32-36 *The Fig Tree: Certainty, but in Ignorance of the Exact Time*

The parable of the fig tree related to the cursing of the fig tree in 21:18-22. The word "generation" (24:34) probably referred to the generation that would experience the period of tribulation (24:4-28). The encouragement implicit in the passage was that they would not be totally destroyed before Jesus returned. Compare Matthew 24:30 with Daniel 7:13, and Matthew 24:31 with Isaiah 27:13. Matthew 24:36 gave the complete answer to 24:3 (cf. also 24:37; 25:46). Jesus' words "No one knows the day or the hour" (24:36) answered the disciples' question in 24:3 and set the stage for the need of endurance (24:13) during Jesus' absence (24:36–25:46).

24:37-44 Noah: Remain Alert and Ready
Just as the people of Noah's day were not ready for the impending judgment, the people in the end times would be blind and unprepared. Note that "swept" (24:39) and "taken" (24:40-41) referred to being taken in judgment, not to being taken to be with God in heaven. People did not understand (24:39) the signs of the times and the coming judgment. They continued on eating, drinking, marrying (24:38), working, and grinding (24:40-41) without insight into their impending doom.

24:45-51 Evil and Faithful Slaves
This parable examined the perils of long-term responsibility. All followers of Jesus have been put "in charge" as faithful slaves. The words "a while" (24:48; cf. 25:5, 19) gave the key to understanding the message Jesus was trying to get across in this section. Jesus was preparing his disciples for what would turn out to be a long absence. Jesus expected his followers to live according to the law of love (cf. 22:37-39; 25:31-46) and always be ready no matter how long he might wait to return.

25:1-13 The Parable of the Ten Virgins
The parable of the ten virgins taught about the proper preparation necessary to enter the kingdom. Only those who were prepared to serve the Messiah (25:1, "the bridegroom") would enter in. The groom's delay in coming caused some to be unready (25:5). Again, the length of the wait for the Messiah's return and the need to be ready no matter how long he might take was emphasized.

25:14-30 Laziness with the Master's Entrusted Possessions
In this parable the concept of reward was central (25:21, 23; cf. 24:47). The parable of the three servants spoke of the rewards that would be given to those entering the kingdom on the basis of their faithfulness to God-given opportunity for service. Those who failed to use their gifts and opportunities for service would suffer judgment (25:28-30).

25:31-46 True Obedience Defined: Love for the King's Brothers
This passage elaborated the concept in 25:26 that not only blatant acts of evil would reap judgment. The failure to do the will of the Father and to use his gifts for the sake of others would also bring judgment. It also described the gathering and evaluation of the elect (25:32; cf. 24:31). The subjects of judgment would be people from all the nations. The separation of the sheep and goats depicted the judgment on the Gentile nations that would precede the inauguration of the kingdom and determine who would enter. The basis for entrance was faith, evidenced by works

of kindness (25:35-39). No unbelievers ("goats") would be permitted to enter.

The two commands in 25:34, 41 brought some surprises (cf. 25:37, 44) for both the saved and the unsaved. For each group Jesus stressed the way they treated their fellow brothers and sisters (cf. 22:39). He had already defined who they were in 12:48-50. He placed great emphasis on community life in the gospel ministry. Jesus taught that the rewards of the kingdom were based on the good deeds performed for others. Showing love toward others would prove love for God (cf. 22:37-40; 1 John 4:7-8). Love for Jesus' family rounded out the concept of "the Kingdom of Heaven is theirs" of the Beatitudes (Matt. 5) and summed up all the character traits desired by Jesus for his followers: gentleness, humility, compassion, and obedience.

26:1-5 A Passion Prediction and Plot
Jesus' resurrection was not mentioned as it was in the other predictions of his death (cf. 16:21; 20:17-19). In this passage, Jesus focused on his impending death. Passover was a Jewish feast that commemorated God's deliverance of his people from Egypt (Exod. 12:1-30). It was observed annually on the fourteenth day of Nisan (Lev. 23:5), March–April, and was followed by the seven-day Feast of Unleavened Bread (Lev. 23:6-8) and the celebration of Firstfruits (Lev. 23:10-14). Caiaphas (26:3) served as high priest from A.D. 18 to 36, when his father-in-law, Annas (cf. John 18:13), was removed from the office.

26:6-56 Betrayal and Arrest
26:6-13 BURIAL PREPARATIONS: ONE PERSON LISTENED TO HIS PREDICTIONS
The apostle John identified the "woman" (Matt. 26:7) as Mary, the sister of Martha and Lazarus (cf. John 12:3). Jesus said that she had done a good deed toward him (26:10; cf. 25:40, 45). The merit of what this woman did for Jesus (Matt. 26:12-13) had to do with the fact that she knew what she was doing. The disciples were slow to believe that Jesus was going to die. Mary believed the words of Jesus and proved her belief by making preparations for his burial (26:12) at great personal sacrifice.

26:14-16 JUDAS'S PLOTTING
Judas's decision was influenced by Satan (cf. Luke 22:3) and motivated by a desire for financial gain (Matt. 26:15). Apparently Judas did not believe that Jesus was fulfilling the messianic role.

26:17-29 PASSOVER KEPT: COVENANT SYMBOLIZED
The "Festival of Unleavened Bread" (26:17) was so closely associated with the Passover that the term was used to designate the Passover season. Preparations for the Passover included: selection of a lamb (the tenth day of Nisan); burning all leaven (noon,

the fourteenth day of Nisan); sacrifice of the lamb (1:30–2:30 P.M., the fourteenth day of Nisan); and the roasting of the lamb on a spit in preparation for the Passover supper. It was common in ancient Israel to recline propped up on one's elbow on cushions around a table (26:20).

The forgiveness of sins was linked to the breaking of Jesus' body and the shedding of his blood (26:26-29). The sacrifice of Jesus, memorialized in this Passover supper, would be the means of man's forgiveness in the new covenant. Jesus used the elements of the Passover meal to provide a memorial of his body and blood (26:26-29). The "covenant" (26:28) referred to the new covenant (cf. Jer. 31:31-34; Ezek. 36:25-28) that was inaugurated by Jesus' death (Heb. 8:6). Jesus implied that he would soon be absent (26:29; cf. the absence in 24:48; 25:5, 19).

26:30-56 ARREST IN GETHSEMANE
26:30-35 Jesus Predicts the Disciples' Falling Away
The "hymn" (26:30) was probably Psalm 118, the last of the *hallel* psalms (Ps. 113–118) that were sung at Passover. Compare Jesus' prediction of the disciples' "falling away" (26:31) with the concept of endurance that he taught in Matthew 24–25. Jesus used Zechariah's prophecy of God's shepherd being struck and his sheep scattered (Zech. 13:7) to describe what would happen to himself and the disciples, his sheep (Matt. 26:31). The word "desert" (26:31, 33) is nearly synonymous with "deny" (26:34). Galilee (26:32) will again become significant (cf. 28:7, 10, 16; see also 4:15-16).

26:36-46 Jesus' Prayer for Deliverance: Strengthening the Flesh
Jesus' prayer in Gethsemane and the agony he experienced as he submitted to the will of his Father became a model for his disciples. Jesus prayed to aid his weak flesh in doing what his Father and his own spirit so willingly desired. Submission to God's will (Matt. 26:39, 44) was central to Jesus' prayer and should be the heart of prayer for all of his followers. Although Jesus always submitted to his Father's will, he kept asking for deliverance just as he had taught his followers to do (cf. 7:7). The name "Gethsemane" (26:36) means "oil press." This olive grove was located, according to tradition, at the foot of the eastern slope of the Mount of Olives.

26:47-56 Jesus Is Arrested: Flesh Strengthened to Obey God's Word
One of the disciples tried to stop Jesus' arrest, and they all were confused about why Jesus would allow such a thing to happen. John identified Peter as the one responsible for this defensive action (26:51; cf. John 18:10). They still did not understand Jesus' role as the suffering Messiah. Jesus' disciples were not willing to face up to God's plan that had been revealed through his prophets (Matt. 26:54, 56).

These verses reveal the nature of true discipleship and the problem of "deserting" or being "offended" because of Jesus' mission of suffering on the cross.

26:57–27:56 The Passion Narrative: Guilt and Identity
26:57–27:26 THE TRIALS: TWO CONTRADICTORY VERDICTS
Jesus was brought before the religious court of the Jews and then the civil court of Rome. The civil trial was necessary because the Jewish leaders did not have authority to execute the death penalty (John 18:31). His religious trial was before Annas (John 18:12-14), Caiaphas (Matt. 26:57), and then before the Sanhedrin (Mark 15:1). His civil trial was before Pilate, the Roman governor (Matt. 27:2), Herod Antipas (Luke 23:6-12), and once again before Pilate (Matt. 27:15-26).

The leaders brought false testimony against Jesus (26:57-68). Jesus' silence (26:63) was in fulfillment of Isaiah 53:7. Jesus combined Daniel 7:13 and Psalm 110:1 in his defense (Matt. 26:64). Tearing one's clothing (26:65) was a traditional sign of grief or mourning. Peter denied Jesus, just as had been predicted (26:69-75; cf. 26:31-35). Peter's Galilean accent suggested that he may have been one of Jesus' disciples (26:73).

The witnesses to Jesus' innocence came from surprising sources, Judas (27:3-10) and Pilate (27:11-26). Following the expulsion of Herod's son Archelaus from Judea in A.D. 6, Judea became a Roman Imperial Province governed by a Roman prefect (27:2). Pontius Pilate served as prefect from A.D. 26 to 36. He normally lived in Caesarea but stayed in Jerusalem during Jewish festivals to keep order. Pilate was staying in the "headquarters" (John 18:28), probably the Antonia Fortress, located just north of the temple area. The Jews did not have the authority to execute capital punishment, though they took it anyway several times (for example, cf. Acts 7:58). The message sent to Pilate from his wife while he was judging Jesus further attested his innocence (Matt. 27:19).

Judas's death fulfilled the prophecy of Zechariah 11:12-13. The "potter's field" (Matt. 27:7) was a section of property apparently used by the potters of Jerusalem to dig for clay. It was known in Acts 1:19 as "Akeldama," meaning "field of blood." In Matthew 27:9-10 Matthew quoted Zechariah 11:12-13 and alluded to Jeremiah 19:1-4 and 32:6-9. Composite quotations were often assigned to the more prominent author, in this case Jeremiah.

The Roman scourge, or whip, consisted of a short wooden handle to which several leather thongs were attached (Matt. 27:26). To the ends of the thongs were attached bits of lead, brass, or sharp bones. Josephus told of a man whose ribs were laid bare by scourging.

27:27-56 THE CRUCIFIXION

27:27-44 *The Mockers of Jesus*

Matthew connected those who insulted Jesus while he was on the cross with the fulfillment of Old Testament Scripture (cf. Isa. 53:3, 7). All the mocking was thematically similar. The mockers expected that if Jesus was the Messiah, he would be able to get off the cross. They were questioning his ability to fulfill the Messianic role that he claimed to be fulfilling. But the problem was not with Jesus' ability. It was with the people's conception of what the Messiah's role was. What looked to the unenlightened like a humiliating disaster was really the powerful work of God fulfilling his promise of redemption.

For more on the "headquarters" (27:27), see the note on 27:2. Simon (27:32) was from Cyrene, the capital of Cyrenaica, a Roman province located in North Africa. The name "Golgotha" (27:33) is Aramaic for "Skull Hill." The "gall" (27:34) was a bitter, and perhaps poisonous, herb. It has been suggested that this drink was given to the condemned to lessen the pain of crucifixion. The dividing of Jesus' clothes (27:35) was in fulfillment of Psalm 22:18.

27:45-56 *The Believers in Jesus, the Son of God*

"Until three o'clock" (Matt. 27:45) was from noon until 3:00 P.M. The words *"Eloi, Eloi, lema sabachthani"* (27:46) are Aramaic for "My God, My God, why have you forsaken me?" They were quoted from Psalm 22:1. Some in the crowd mistook *"Eloi"* for "Elijah" (27:47). The "curtain," or veil (27:51), separated the Holy Place from the Most Holy Place. According to Josephus it was ninety feet high. The tearing of the veil had great significance, for after the work of Jesus Christ the mediator was complete, the veil was no longer necessary to separate man from the holiness of God (cf. Heb. 10:19-20). Some people were raised through Christ's death and resurrection (Matt. 27:52; cf. 1 Cor. 15:20-23). Like Lazarus, they died again, but their resurrection marked off the dynamic witness of God's approval for his Son at this moment.

27:57–28:15 Burial and Resurrection

27:57-66 BURIAL AND SECURITY

Joseph was from Arimathea, a town of uncertain location (Matt. 27:57). He secured permission to bury Jesus in his own tomb. Jesus' burial in the tomb of a rich man took place in accordance with messianic prophecy (27:60; cf. Isa. 53:9). The securing of the grave with a sealed entrance and guards was an attempt to thwart the fulfillment of Jesus' prediction of his resurrection (Matt. 27:62-66). This was yet one more attempt to thwart God's work through Jesus. Such attempts to block the will of God had been seen earlier in Herod's murder of the babies in Bethlehem (2:13-18), the temptation of Jesus in the wilderness (4:1-11), and Peter's denial that Jesus should die (16:21-23). But nothing would stop the fulfillment of God's plan.

28:1-15 RESURRECTION AND BRIBERY

The resurrection of Jesus was the sign of Jonah (cf. 12:39-40), the last public sign to the Jews that Jesus was who he claimed to be (28:6). The disciples were commanded to return to Galilee (28:7, 10). That command was delivered by an angel and by Jesus himself. Jesus appeared five times on resurrection day: (1) to Mary Magdalene (Matt. 28:1; Mark 16:9-11; John 20:11-18), (2) to the other women (Matt. 28:8-10), (3) to Simon Peter (Luke 24:33-35; 1 Cor. 15:5), (4) to the two disciples (Mark 16:12-13; Luke 24:13-32), and (5) to the eleven apostles (Matt. 28:16-20; Mark 16:14; Luke 24:36-49; John 20:19-25).

28:16-20 Commission to the Community: Identity, Authority, and Presence

As was true throughout Matthew's Gospel, even at the end some doubted Jesus' identity (Matt. 28:17). They doubted whether he was one whom they should worship. But to their doubts Jesus gave the proclamation of his authority and his presence (28:18-20). Matthew 28:19 could be translated, "As you are going, make disciples. . . ." The imperative was "make disciples." The "going" was assumed. This ministry extended to "all the nations," which was in keeping with the universal prospect of blessing in the Abrahamic covenant (cf. Gen. 12:2-3). The ministries to accompany making disciples included "baptizing" (identifying believers with a local assembly) and "teaching" (laying the foundation for application). Jesus would fulfill his name "Immanuel," meaning "God with us," by being present with his people through the work of the Holy Spirit "even to the end of the age" (28:20; cf. Acts 1:1-8; 2:1-4).

MARK

HISTORICAL SETTING
The Gospel of Mark makes no reference to the birth of Jesus or his early ministry in Judea (cf. John 2:13–4:3). The record begins with the commencement of Jesus' public ministry at his baptism, which most likely took place in the summer or autumn of A.D. 29. Mark records the ministry of Jesus in Galilee (Mark 1:14–9:50), Perea (10:1-52), and Judea (11:1–13:37). The Gospel continues the record of Jesus' life to include his death and resurrection.

AUTHOR
Mark's Gospel is anonymous, but the testimony of the early church fathers, including Irenaeus, Clement of Alexandria, Origen, and Jerome, indicates that John Mark was the author of the work. John Mark was the son of a certain Mary in Jerusalem (Acts 12:12) and the cousin of Barnabas (Col. 4:10). His home was Jerusalem, and he may have witnessed some of the events of the life of Jesus. He may possibly have been the young man referred to in Mark 14:51.

Mark accompanied Paul and Barnabas from Jerusalem to Antioch and set out with them on their first missionary journey (Acts 12:25; 13:5). Upon reaching Perga, Mark returned home to Jerusalem (Acts 13:13). He later accompanied Barnabas on a missionary journey to Cyprus (Acts 15:37-39). Mark was probably in Rome with Peter before Peter's death (1 Pet. 5:13). Later he was with Paul at Rome (Col. 4:10; Philem. 23-24). While Mark had experienced an initial failure in his early ministry, he later proved himself a valuable servant of Jesus. Paul desired his presence in Rome during the final days of his second imprisonment (2 Tim. 4:11).

According to tradition, Mark was in Rome serving as Peter's interpreter before his death. Tradition also records that Mark ministered in Alexandria, founded a church there, and became its first bishop.

DATE
There is no explicit statement in the book of Mark as to its date or origin. Mark was undoubtedly written before A.D. 70 because there is no reference to the destruction of Jerusalem. Clement of Alexandria mentions that the Gospels with the genealogies were written first, so Mark would have been written after Matthew and Luke, sometime after A.D. 60.

Many scholars believe that Mark was written around A.D. 50 and was used by

Matthew and Luke in writing their Gospels. The thesis of the priority of Mark is based in large part on the theory that the Gospel writers were dependent on each other.

PURPOSE

The book of Mark was designed to present the person and works of Jesus as God's servant and Son attested by his mighty works. The abundance of miracles in the book is a key to discerning its purpose. While Mark records no more miracles than the other Gospel writers, he does have a greater concentration of miracles. Those mighty works authenticate the person of Jesus as a servant (10:45) and as the Son of God. This would create the kind of holy fear in the early believers that would cause them to obey his will and share his Good News.

GEOGRAPHY AND ITS IMPORTANCE

Mark begins geographically in the wilderness and ends at the empty tomb. At the center of the book is the revelation at Caesarea Philippi (Mark 8:27-38) of the deity of Jesus and his destiny to die on the cross. Isolated places like the wilderness, the stormy Sea of Galilee, open country, or a quiet early morning graveyard become the contexts for Jesus' followers to come to grips with how Jesus' destiny is intricately bound up with their own.

GUIDING CONCEPTS

WILDERNESS

Mark mentions the wilderness many times in the early chapters of his Gospel (1:3, 4, 12-13, 45; 6:31, 35). The wilderness was a place that was in many ways opposite to the city; it was a place where one would go out to meet God's prophet (1:5; cf. 1:38). It was the place of beasts (1:13) and loneliness (1:35; 6:31; cf. Matt. 14:13; Luke 4:42). The wilderness was the place of Jesus' testing and the stage for his initial victory over Satan. Mark, unlike Matthew, does not recall Israel's earlier experiences in the wilderness and thus compare and identify the Hebrew nation with Jesus. For Mark, the wilderness was a place set apart from the rebellious society of Israel, where the true seeker could hear the voice of God and seek to follow him. It was the place where the gospel had its beginnings (see his use of Isa. 40:3 in Mark 1:3) and the place to seek God in repentance (1:2; cf. Mal. 3:1).

IMMEDIATELY

Mark used the Greek word for "immediately," translated variously as "at once," "without delay," "just then," "just as," "quickly," "immediately," or "as soon as" far more than the other Gospel writers (Matthew, six times; Luke, one time; John, three times; Mark, forty-two times; for example, see Mark 1:12, 18, 20, 23, 28, 42-43; 2:8; 4:5, 15-17, 29; 5:29-30, 42; 6:25, 45, 50, 54; 7:25; 9:15, 24; 10:52; 11:2; 14:43, 45, 72). Mark used the word in the contexts of miracles, narrative, and the words of Jesus to show the reader that the time to repent and follow Jesus was right then. Jesus moved with immediacy, not because he was in a rush, but because the time to act was "now," and not a moment was to be lost in indecision and delay. The repetition of the word "immediately" drives the urgency of repentance home to the readers of Mark's Gospel.

FEAR

Mark used the concept of fear throughout his Gospel to teach the believers the proper response to the gospel of Jesus the Messiah (cf. 4:41; 5:15, 33, 36; 6:20, 50; 9:32; 10:32; 11:18, 32; 12:12; 16:8). Many hold that originally Mark's Gospel ended at 16:8 and that the present verses after that were added at a later time. If Mark ended his work at 16:8, then he purposely wanted to end with the concept of fear. While he certainly knew the rest of the gospel story, he wanted to stop there in order to drive home the absolute astonishment and fear that comprehension of Jesus' resurrection should cause. As disciples, believers are to reflect on that astonishment and fear to see if they have truly comprehended the meaning of the resurrection. The disciple fears, not because of possible punishment, but because of astonishment, awe, and respect in the presence of God's great redemptive act in Jesus Christ.

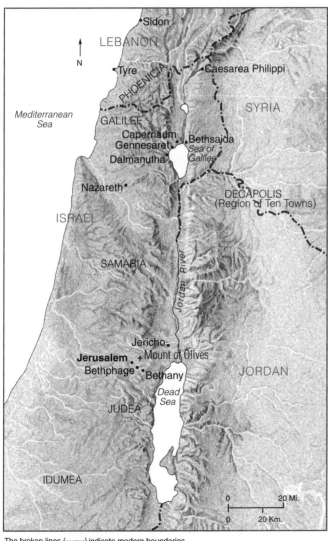

The broken lines (—·—·) indicate modern boundaries.
Copyright © 1986, 1988 by Tyndale House Publishers, Inc.

INCOMPREHENSION

Mark also wanted to show what the disciples did and did not understand about Jesus. That would help the believers see their own blind spots when it came to believing and following Jesus (4:12-13, 41; cf. Matt. 13:13-15, 19, 23, 51). Matthew focused on the end of the disciples' process of enlightenment. But Mark showed the disciples in the middle of the process, before the light of understanding had dawned on them (Mark 6:52; cf. Matt. 14:22-32). With the problems of physical and spiritual blindness in mind, compare Mark 8:17, 21 with Matthew 16:12. Note how both Matthew (Matt. 13:14-15) and Mark (Mark 4:12) use Isaiah 6:9.

Mark highlighted three of the disciples' misunderstandings about Jesus' nature and mission that became obvious after each of Jesus' three predictions of his death and resurrection (Mark 8:27-31; 9:30-32; 10:32-34). Mark's recording of the blindness of the disciples followed immediately after each prediction (8:32-33; 9:33-34; 10:35-37). Each time Jesus predicted his death, the disciples became concerned with other things, such as their desires for personal greatness or fear for their own lives. They could not seem to comprehend the significance of Jesus' death and resurrection. That was why, at the end of the book, Mark left his readers with the event of Jesus' resurrection; an event that demanded a reaction of utter astonishment, fear, and silence. The readers of Mark's Gospel, like the disciples, were called to pause and let this amazing revelation sink in.

THE REASON FOR JESUS' SECRECY

Mark 8:27-33 is the pivotal section of the book. The disciples had little trouble comprehending that Jesus was the Messiah, the Son of God (8:27-30). His identity was relatively easily grasped. But the challenge for the disciples, then and now, was to come to grips with the role that the Messiah would play during his time on earth. Jesus' role included death on a cross and a subsequent resurrection from the dead (8:31-33).

Jesus often moved about in secrecy or asked his followers not to talk about him (4:10-11; 5:43; 7:24; 8:30; 9:9, 30). Jesus proclaimed the gospel openly, but when he met with hardhearted resistance, he often revealed truth in parables that were difficult to understand. He shared fuller explanations and insights into the kingdom only with those who believed in him (4:11, 34). He unsuccessfully tried to keep his presence a secret (7:24, 36). He told several people not to tell anyone about him (5:43; 8:30; 9:9). Jesus' secrecy was an attempt on his part to clear the way for special teaching to his disciples (9:30-31). Jesus' amazing acts of raising the dead, healings, and feeding of thousands were certainly not geared to keeping a low profile. But Jesus had a twofold mission: to build a solid group of disciples and to move on to his goal of Jerusalem and the cross. He had no desire to build his own kingdom among the people of Galilee. Perhaps Matthew 12:18-21, quoting Isaiah 42:1-4, is the best explanation of Jesus' secrecy. His gentle teaching marked the men and women who would be his disciples, and his quiet ways allowed him to bring justice to victory through his death and resurrection. He was moving toward the cross and avoided the kind of public presence that would be more suitable to building an earthly kingdom then and there.

In part, Jesus' secrecy was explained in 8:27-33. His identity was being hidden from unbelievers who refused to hear him. His destiny was also partially hidden from the believing disciples, but his destiny to die was revealed to them that they might seek to understand its significance. The unveiling of the secret of Jesus' identity as the Messiah paved the way for the unveiling of the mystery of his destiny to die on the cross. The death of Jesus, which Peter so adamantly rejected (8:32-33), the church was called on to embrace. The church needed to comprehend the mystery of Jesus' destiny on the cross and in his resurrection. The cross became the model for earthly Christian experience; the resurrection became the basis for Christian hope.

BIBLE-WIDE CONCEPTS

THE SON OF MAN

The disciples quickly recognized Jesus' identity as the Messiah (8:27-30) but found it hard to understand the implications of his suffering (8:31-33). They needed to understand what Jesus meant when he called himself the "Son of Man." In Jesus' day the phrase was not commonly used as a title, and in Mark, only Jesus used the phrase with reference to himself. Therefore, Jesus' use of the phrase was unusual and worthy of close attention. It was Jesus' own unique way of naming himself.

Jesus referred to himself as the Son of Man in each of his passion predictions. The Old Testament background for the phrase can be found in Psalms 8:4; 80:17; Ezekiel 4:1; and Daniel 7:13. Jesus used the term in three different contexts. First, he used it in connection with his claim to authority in the forgiveness of sins (Mark 2:10) and his authority over the Sabbath (2:28). These were the only times Jesus used the title "Son of Man" before he used it in Mark 8 in connection with the revelation of his destiny of suffering.

Second, the title "Son of Man" was used by Jesus to reveal the fact of his incarnational limitation and humbling. Jesus the Messiah would not seek personal greatness, and he thus chose a title that would not bring him exaltation. "Son of Man" revealed the nature of God as savior and the bringer of atonement for sin through suffering and self-sacrifice (Mark 10:45). He called himself the "Son of Man" in each of his passion predictions (8:31; 9:31; 10:33). In addition, the phrase was used when Jesus further discussed his betrayal (14:21, 41), suffering (9:31), and resurrection (9:9). The suffering of the "Son of Man" would come in submission to God's will. He let God make the claim for his messiahship. That was done first through humiliation as the "Son of Man," and then through exaltation as the "Son of God" (Phil. 2). God in his voice from heaven approved Jesus at his baptism and transfiguration. The practical application of the entire book rests on one word: "even" (10:45, "For *even* I, the Son of Man . . ."). *Even* Jesus did not come to be served, but to serve. Should not believers follow in the same role of humble, and if necessary, suffering service?

Third, Jesus also used the phrase "Son of Man" with reference to his exaltation and return (8:38; 13:26; 14:62). He would reign exalted and would return, but only after the time of his suffering and humiliation. Mark laid out this same pattern of suffering before exaltation as the model for Jesus' followers. They would first have to humble themselves to be servants in bringing God's redemption to the world. That would involve varying degrees of suffering. Only then could they expect to share in Jesus' resurrection and exaltation. Jesus' first coming is the model for the present age of ministry. The glory of his second coming will belong to believers forever in the next age.

The phrase "Son of Man" was what Jesus used to explain his ministry. Because there were many ideas of how God would send his Messiah, Jesus used a phrase to describe himself that no one would recognize. Therefore, no one could read their presuppositions about how Jesus should act into the title. "Messiah" and "Son of God" brought up images of a conquering and reigning king. "Lord" as a title also only contained ideas of power, victory, and divinity. But "Son of Man" carried no clear content. Although some people in Jesus' day knew of Daniel's prophecy of a "Son of Man" who would be given the kingdom (Dan. 7:13), they were also used to hearing the phrase "son of man" used simply as a way of referring to someone as being human (as in Ezekiel 2:1; 3:1; 4:1; 31:2; 33:2; 34:2). In addition, Jesus brought new content to what the people were expecting from God's chosen Messiah. This is why the crowds were not clear as to what Jesus meant by applying the phrase to himself (see, for example, John 12:34). Jesus poured into this phrase the concepts of servanthood, suffering, and ultimate resurrection.

Jesus was indeed Lord, Messiah, and God, but the power and model of his mission as ransom payment for the world was summed up in the title "Son of Man." The church is to follow that model and not try to be great before the time when God will exalt all who are faithful.

NEEDS MET BY MARK

Mark wanted to help his readers come to grips with the difficult issues of belief in Jesus. Belief brought persecution, and that persecution would give rise to many hard questions about the purpose and benefits of believing in Jesus. Mark showed how the pain of persecution was closely linked to the cross of Christ. Faith in the cross of Jesus Christ also demanded the believer's own daily experience of the cross. Mark outlined major reasons why the disciples had difficulty in comprehending how their own lives were to conform to the humiliation and pain of Christ's cross. The days during which Mark wrote were very dangerous, and he helped his readers understand the seriousness of their faith in Jesus and the holy fear it demanded. Finally, Mark envisioned sharing in Christ's future exaltation and freedom from pain and suffering. But Mark always wanted his readers to keep the order straight: humble service in this age, glorious exaltation in the next. Mark met some basic needs for those who believed and yet struggled with embracing the full message of the gospel. The structure and content of Mark's Gospel show that he was answering questions like the following for his readers.

- What is required of believers beyond their initial belief in Jesus as Savior and God's Son?
- What encouragement can believers find in suffering for the sake of Christ?
- Why is it so hard for believers to accept their destiny of bearing the cross?
- What kind of life are believers called to in Jesus the Messiah's resurrection?

There are many things believers are afraid of today, but Mark speaks most effectively about a fear believers actually need. Mark wanted to replace the tendency of believers to live selfishly with a holy fear of God that would cause them to act and speak under the influence of Christ's astounding resurrection. Mark wrote to a Christian community that needed to understand that following Christ was a difficult and challenging task. It brought a great salvation but also stood against the natural desire of people to live selfishly. Status seeking and luxury building were to be weeded out of their lives and replaced with an aggressive commitment to bringing God's redemption to the world. Mark revealed the struggle the disciples had with giving up their desire for mortal greatness, a struggle shared by believers today. They were not immune to fear, misunderstanding, and status seeking. Like believers today, the disciples had trouble understanding and accepting the suffering that resulted from following their great Savior.

OUTLINE OF MARK

I. THE PROPHETIC FOUNDATION: JOHN THE BAPTIST (1:1-15)
  A. Title: Here Begins the Good News about Jesus the Messiah (1:1)
  B. The Prophetic Foundation: John the Baptist (1:2-15)

II. THE FOUNDATION OF POWER: ITS IMPLICATION FOR THE IDENTITY OF
JESUS (1:16–8:30)
A. The First Impact of Power (1:16-39)
B. Jesus Explains the Significance of His Acts of Power (1:40–3:6)
C. The Obedient Are Initiated into Power and Mystery (3:7–4:34)
D. Extreme Power for Extreme Cases (4:35–6:6)
E. Progressive Enlightenment: From Physical to Spiritual Reality (6:6–8:30)

III. THE FOUNDATION OF SUFFERING: ITS IMPLICATION FOR THE DISCIPLES'
SUBMISSION (8:31–16:20)
A. The Way to Jerusalem: The Struggles of Self-Denial (8:31–10:52)
B. Victory over Anti-Christian Delusion (11:1–13:37)
C. Betrayal and Arrest: The Disciples' Defeat by Flesh Unprepared by Prayer (14:1-52)
D. The Trial (14:53–15:15)
E. The Crucifixion and Burial (15:16-47)
F. Resurrection Events (16:1-20)

MARK NOTES

1:1-15 THE PROPHETIC FOUNDATION: JOHN THE BAPTIST

1:1 Title: Here Begins the Good News about Jesus the Messiah

The gospel is the "good news" concerning Jesus Christ. The title gives shape and direction to the book by setting forth the beginning components of the timeless Christian message. Mark began his book by giving believers in every generation the first principles of the gospel. He used the words "good news" more than any other Gospel writer (cf. 1:1, 14-15; 8:35; 10:29; 14:9; 16:15). Matthew used it in 4:23; 9:35; 24:14; 26:13. The Greek noun translated "good news" was not used in either Luke or John. Luke used the verb form "preach the gospel" twenty-five times, but Matthew used it only once; Mark and John did not use the verb form at all.

1:2-15 The Prophetic Foundation: John the Baptist

1:2-11 JOHN THE BAPTIST IS INTRODUCED
The coming of John the Baptist (1:2-3) was in fulfillment of Isaiah 40:3 and Malachi 3:1. John was contrasted with the one "who is far greater" (Mark 1:7) who would follow after him. John's baptism (1:4) signified repentance from sin on the part of the one baptized. This was done with a view to the redemption that would come through God's Messiah and his shed blood. The traditional site of John's ministry was on the Jordan River about eight miles southeast of Jericho. Locusts (1:6) were clean insects and could be eaten (cf. Lev. 11:22). Wild honey (1:6) was plentiful in Israel (Judg. 14:8; 1 Sam. 14:25). The baptism with the Holy Spirit

(Mark 1:8) took place at Pentecost (Acts 1:5; 2:33). This was the first of three times that God spoke words in affirmation of his Son from heaven (Mark 1:11; cf. 9:7; John 12:28).

1:12-15 THE TEMPTATION OF JESUS
Jesus was severely tempted (Mark 1:13), yet he did not yield to sin (Heb. 4:15). John's arrest and imprisonment (Mark 1:14) is recorded in Matthew 14:1-12 and Mark 6:17-29. The events recorded in John 1:19–4:54 took place before John the Baptist's arrest. For Mark 1:15, see the comments on the kingdom of God in the notes on Matthew 3:2. The words "Turn from your sins" (1:15) are also translated as "repent" (NIV), which means "to change one's mind" and assumes a consequent change in one's behavior. The word "believe" (1:15) means to "trust" or "rely upon."

1:16–8:30 THE FOUNDATION OF POWER: ITS IMPLICATION FOR THE IDENTITY OF JESUS

1:16-39 The First Impact of Power

This section traces Jesus' work from his first impact in calling fishermen to follow him and healing needy people, demon possessed, and sick, to his expanded ministry to all Galilee (1:38). This was not the first encounter Simon and Andrew had had with Jesus (1:16; cf. John 1:35-42). Capernaum (Mark 1:21), situated on the northwest shore of the Sea of Galilee, was an important tax collection station on the caravan route to Damascus. This was the home of Peter, Andrew, James, and John. Jesus relocated in Capernaum after his rejection from

Nazareth (Matt. 9:1; Mark 2:1). The "teachers of religious law" (1:22) debated the opinions and interpretations of leading rabbis, depending on secondhand tradition. Jesus did not need to refer to such authorities to authenticate his words.

1:40–3:6 Jesus Explains the Significance of His Acts of Power

This section stresses the importance of healings (leper and paralytic) for revealing the purpose of Jesus' coming (for sinners and humanity). For the laws regarding leprosy (1:40), see Leviticus 13–14. The miracle (1:40-42) was intended by Jesus to alert the Jewish establishment of his miraculous ministry in Galilee. For this reason, Jesus instructed the healed man to go straight to Jerusalem (1:44) rather than taking time to tell his story locally. The term "Son of Man" (2:10) is used fourteen times in Mark by Jesus to refer to himself. This strongly messianic term appears to be derived from Daniel 7:13 (see comments in the introductory notes). Levi (Mark 2:14), another name for "Matthew," was a tax collector in Capernaum, an important city for the collection of customs from caravans traveling north and south. The Baptist's disciples were fasting because John had been imprisoned by Herod Antipas (2:18). The Pharisees fasted according to Levitical commandment and Jewish tradition (cf. Lev. 16:29-34; Zech. 8:19). For a discussion of the Sabbath (Mark 2:23), see the notes on Matthew 12:2. For David's actions (Mark 2:25), see 1 Samuel 21:1-6. Jesus' point in Mark 3:4 was that refusing to do good was itself evil. For a note on the Pharisees (3:6), see Matthew 3:7. For a note on the Herodians, see Matthew 22:16.

3:7–4:34 The Obedient Are Initiated into Power and Mystery

3:7-35 POWER AND PARABLES OF OBEDIENCE

The secret of the kingdom was explained to the intimate group of obedient followers (Mark 3:7-35). The author put stress on how obedient people receive the mysteries of God. Idumea (3:8; from the Hebrew "Edom") refers to the region south of Judea, in the vicinity of the Negev and extending as far north as Hebron (see introductory map). For other lists of the apostles (3:16-19), see Matthew 10:1-4; Luke 6:13-16; and Acts 1:13. For an explanation of the term "Zealot," see the note on Matthew 10:4.

4:1-34 THE SECRET OF KINGDOM GROWTH: FERTILE SOIL

The secret of the kingdom of God (Mark 4:11) was how the Messiah could come and be rejected and how the kingdom could be present but hidden in seed form (4:26, 31). The parables ("stories," 4:2) are true to life stories that teach spiritual truth by comparison. The realm of the known is used to teach something in the realm of the unknown. For a further discussion on parables, see the notes on Matthew 13:3, 10-17. The pagan mystery religions had teachings that only the initiated insiders were taught. So too, the secrets of the kingdom of God were revealed only to Jesus' followers, but nondisciples heard only the parables without the explanations (Mark 4:11). For the mustard seed (4:31), see the note on Matthew 13:31-32.

4:35–6:6 Extreme Power for Extreme Cases

4:35-41 POWER OVER NATURE AND DEMONS

This event was designed to show the disciples more about Jesus' identity. The disciples' fear revealed their lack of faith and understanding as to Jesus' true identity (4:40). At the time of this event, the disciples were not yet ready to be taught. They were still astounded that Jesus could stop a storm. Their question, "Who is this?" carries its own answer. They were in the presence of God and understanding this fact would be the key to solving their problems of fear and faithlessness. He was to be the only object of their faith and he was sufficient to deliver them from fear. The "other side" (4:35) referred to the opposite side of the Sea of Galilee, a fresh water lake situated in Galilee about 680 feet below sea level. The valleys to the west allow the Mediterranean winds to funnel down on the sea, raising great tempests on the otherwise calm sea.

5:1-20 POWER OVER NUMEROUS DEMONS: DECAPOLIS PROCLAMATION

The "land of the Gerasenes" (5:1) referred to the district of the well-known Greek city of Geresa, located about thirty miles southeast of the Sea of Galilee. The city apparently shared water and commerce rights on the Sea of Galilee with other cities of the Decapolis. Matthew 8:28 referred to the lesser known city of Gadara, which, having a sizable Jewish population, would be more familiar to his Jewish readers. A "legion" (Mark 5:9) in the Roman army consisted of about 5,300 men. The man was possessed by a host of demons. "Ten Towns" (5:20, Greek "Decapolis") was a reference to a Gentile district east of the Jordan River known for its splendid Greek cities (see introductory map). The cities may have originally been ten (*deca*) in number, although their number varied from time to time. One of these cities, Scythopolis, lay west of the Jordan.

5:21-43 THE POWER OF FAITH

Jesus clarified the relation between his power and the woman's faith. She was not healed impersonally, but upon the meeting of her personal faith with Jesus' personal power. This stands in great contrast to the pagan concepts of impersonal divine power. The continual hemorrhage (5:25) would have rendered the woman perpetually unclean (cf. Lev. 15:25-27), unable to participate in temple worship. The language Jesus spoke (Mark 5:41) was Aramaic, a Semitic language like Hebrew, which was the common tongue of the Jewish people in the first century A.D.

6:1-6 THE POWER OF UNBELIEF
Although he had been born in Bethlehem, Jesus' "hometown" was Nazareth, the city in which he was raised (6:1) (see introductory map). Mark 6:3 tells of other children that were born to Joseph and Mary. Jesus had four half brothers and two half sisters. James became a leader in the Jerusalem church and authored the epistle of James. Judas, or Jude, wrote the epistle that bears his name.

6:6–8:30 Progressive Enlightenment: From Physical to Spiritual Reality
6:6-29 MISSION TO THE MULTITUDES: THE HOSTILE CONTEXT
After traveling through Gentile territory, Jews would shake the dust from their sandals and garments lest they contaminate the land of Israel. Here the act was to be done in protest against those who rejected Jesus the Messiah's messengers (6:11). King Herod (6:14) was a reference to Herod Antipas who ruled over Galilee and Perea (4 B.C.–A.D. 39). Herod Antipas divorced his wife and married his brother Philip's wife, who was also Antipas's niece (6:17-18). John condemned this incestuous marriage as unlawful (cf. Lev. 18:6-18). According to Josephus (*Antiquities*, 18.5.4), the dancing daughter of Herodias was named Salome (Mark 6:22). To save face with his guests, Herod Antipas kept his oath even though it was rash and wicked (6:26).

6:30-56 MISSION TO THE MULTITUDES: THE HIDDEN SOURCE OF SUSTENANCE
6:30-44 The Symbol of Bread
The feeding of the five thousand was not immediately explained by Mark. It was simply narrated. It was not until 7:52 that Mark revealed that the feeding was a symbol of Jesus' great power and divine nature. To stop with amazement at the feeding without taking to heart its implications for the one who did the feeding would be to make the same mistake as the disciples. The "shepherd" (6:34) was a common metaphor in the ancient Near East for a leader (cf. Ezek. 34:1-23) and has Messianic implications (cf. John 10:11-16). The "small fortune" (6:37) is translated as "200 denarii" in Greek. *Denarii*, the plural of *denarius*, which was a silver coin that amounted to approximately one day's wage in the New Testament period. The number "five thousand" (6:44) did not include the large number of women and children who were also present.

6:45-52 The Implications of the Symbol of Bread
Bethsaida (6:45), also known as Bethsaida-Julias, was a double site with a fishing village on the shore of the Sea of Galilee about one and a half miles south of the fortified city. It was located just east of the Jordan near the northeast shore of the Sea of Galilee (see introductory map). "About three o'clock in the morning" (6:48) is "about the fourth watch of the night" in Greek, and referred to the time between 3:00 and 6:00 A.M. The words "He started to go past them" (6:48) suggest that Jesus intended to "pass by" to give the disciples an opportunity to confess their need.

The disciples should have received insight from the feeding of the five thousand (6:44; cf. 6:52) that Jesus had full power over nature. Jesus was powerful, just as God was powerful. He was not just a miracle worker. Mark was dealing with the problem of fear and how believers should cope with it. The disciples understood the details of the feeding but only saw it as a marvel with no significance regarding who Jesus was. This reveals the parabolic nature of some of Jesus' acts. The apostle John called these miracles "signs." Jesus' miracles were signs that pointed away from the dazzle of the act to its significance: God was present to save those who would believe. The disciples' problem of hardheartedness was also shared by those who did not understand the parables (4:11-12).

6:53-56 The Recognition of Power
In contrast with the disciples' hard hearts and lack of understanding about Jesus' power (6:52), these people recognized Jesus and his power (6:54) and sought his healing. They even understood that his power was so great that just touching his clothing would bring healing (6:56). Gennesaret (6:53) was the plain located on the northwest shore of the Sea of Galilee southwest of Capernaum (see introductory map).

7:1-23 THE HIDDEN SOURCE OF UNCLEANNESS: THE HEART
For a note on the Pharisees (7:1), see Matthew 3:7. The "teachers of religious law" (7:1; "scribes," NASB and KJV) were originally copiers of the Scriptures who became regarded as experts in Jewish law. The "ancient traditions" (7:3) was a reference to the oral tradition of the Pharisees which amplified and applied the biblical law. Included were detailed specifications for such procedures as ritual cleansing before meals. The issue was Jewish ceremony, not personal hygiene. The Pharisees regarded bread eaten with unwashed hands as if it were filth (7:5). In 7:6-7 Jesus quotes from Isaiah 29:13. "What I could have given to you" (Mark 7:11) refers to a "gift," which is translated as "Corban" in Greek. "Corban" is the transliteration of a Hebrew word that means "offering." The word was used to refer to that which had been dedicated to God and withdrawn from secular use. The custom was used by the Pharisees as a means of avoiding parental obligations. Legal

loopholes allowed for these funds required of children to support ageing parents to be returned for personal use. Mark 7:16 is absent in several important Greek manuscripts.

7:24–8:30 THE SYMBOL OF BREAD: THE HIDDEN SOURCE OF SALVATION

7:24-30 Bread Crumbs As Salvation for a Gentile
Tyre (7:24) was located in Phoenicia, about twenty-five miles north of Ptolemais (Old Testament Acco) (see introductory map). The designation "Syrian Phoenicia" (7:26) indicates that the woman was of Phoenician stock and resided in the Roman province of Syria. Matthew referred to her as Canaanite, based on the name of the people that once occupied Israel and Phoenicia. For "dogs" (7:27), see the note on Matthew 15:26. Once she understood that her relationship to Jesus could be only received by faith, Jesus granted her request.

7:31-37 Hearing and Speaking Restored
For why Jesus commanded the crowds to be quiet (7:36), see the discussion concerning "The Reason for Jesus' Secrecy" in the Guiding Concepts section. However, the real emphasis in 7:36-37 was not on Jesus' desire for silence,but on the crowd's overwhelming excitement over Jesus' power to heal. The pattern of an awesome miracle followed by a command for silence and a rapid spreading of the word about Jesus stands in stark contrast with the situation at the end of the book where after Jesus' greatest miracle, his resurrection, the women were so awestricken they could, for a time, say nothing. It is easy to spread the word about Jesus' great miracles. It is much more difficult for believers to take to heart who they should be in light of who Jesus is. Such a recognition of personal responsibility takes a period of silent awestricken meditation. Sidon (7:31) was located in Phoenicia, about twenty-five miles north of Tyre (see introductory map). For "Ten Towns" (7:31), see the note on 5:20.

8:1-9 The Source of Sustenance Questioned
The disciples had still not gained insight from the time Jesus fed five thousand people. Their question in 8:4 shows the same blindness toward Jesus' power as they had in 6:51-52. They still did not consistently realize who Jesus was and what he was able to do for them. Jesus was the answer to all their spiritual and physical needs, but they blindly lamented the absence of a local bakery.

8:10-21 Hard Hearts Hide Spiritual Insight
Crossing from the eastern shore of the Sea of Galilee, Jesus came to the district of "Dalmanutha," a Syriac word that literally means "of the harbor" (see introductory map). Jesus' encounter with the Pharisees (8:11-13) took place at Magadan (Matt. 15:39) in the vicinity of the harbor. The leaders sought a sign from Jesus that would prove he was

the Messiah (Mark 8:11). "Yeast" (8:15; "leaven," NASB and KJV) was noted for its characteristic of permeating and influencing the dough in contact with it. The "yeast of the Pharisees and of Herod" referred to their false understanding of who Jesus was—a false understanding that was permeating the nation and leading many astray. The "yeast of the Pharisees and of Herod" brought doubt to those listening to Jesus' claims to be the Son of Man. Herod thought Jesus was John the Baptist risen from the dead (6:14-16). The religious leaders only wanted to test him and argue with him. Jesus took the time to warn against the "yeast of the Pharisees and of Herod" (8:14-21). Note the significance of Jesus' statement regarding unseeing eyes and unhearing ears. The disciples were capable of being just as blind as Herod or the Pharisees.

In 8:17-21 the fuller significance of the two miraculous feedings and why the leftover baskets of bread were counted is explained. Jesus requested that the leftover baskets of bread be counted to show the disciples his more-than-adequate ability to provide for physical needs. They would later learn that spiritual things, not bread, should be their focus. But this section ends with an unanswered question (8:21). The disciples were to understand that when it came to physical things, Jesus could do whatever he wished. He could feed thousands, walk on water, and bring instant health. But the disciples continued to be stuck on the physical level. Jesus wanted them to think on a spiritual level. Their thoughts dwelt on the problem of having no bread (8:16). They should have known Jesus could make all the bread he wanted and that his real concern was with providing for their spiritual needs. The question of 8:21 becomes a direct question to Mark's readers. Will they continue to misunderstand Jesus' absolute power to provide them with daily bread? Will they continue to worry about physical needs and be blind to the deeper life of spirit and insight into God's ways?

8:22-26 Progressive Healing: Sight Restored
Jesus healed this man in two stages because he wanted to illustrate, through this physical healing, the progressive way in which his disciples' spiritual blindness could be healed. Spiritual insight did not come instantly, as illustrated by the disciples' problems in comprehending who Jesus was and what role he would play. For Bethsaida (8:22), see the note on 6:45. Caesarea Philippi (8:27), built by Herod Philip in honor of Caesar Augustus, was located near the foot of Mount Hermon about twenty-five miles north of the Sea of Galilee (see introductory map).

8:27-30 The First Step in Seeing Clearly: Jesus Is the Messiah
The conversation recorded in Mark 8:27-30 clearly reveals Jesus' identity as God's Messiah.

8:31–16:20 THE FOUNDATION OF SUFFERING: ITS IMPLICATION FOR THE DISCIPLES' SUBMISSION

8:31–10:52 The Way to Jerusalem: The Struggles of Self-Denial

8:31–9:13 THE PASSION AND SELF-PRESERVATION: NEGATION OF SUFFERING

8:31-38 Two Rebukes
In this section, contrary to the plans and hopes of the disciples, Jesus makes it clear that he, as God's Son, will go to the cross. The conversation recorded in Mark 8:27-30 clearly revealed his identity. The events recorded in Mark 8:31-38 showed the disciples the mystery of Jesus' impending suffering and death. The disciples had expected the Messiah to come as a conquering king, not a sacrificial lamb, and as a result could not comprehend Jesus' predictions. The unveiling of the secret of Jesus' identity paved the way for the unveiling of the mystery of his destiny. The destiny of suffering that Peter rejected in his rebuke of Jesus, the church would be called upon to embrace. The church needs to comprehend and participate in the mystery of Jesus' destiny of suffering. The law of the cross prevails. The task is to realize that God's ultimate good does not necessarily guarantee comfort and easy living for all believers. Jesus' death on the cross was painful for him, but good for the world. That model of the cross bringing personal pain but corporate good is also the model of Christian experience (8:34). Peter could handle Jesus being the Messiah. But he rejected the Messiah's destiny of going to the cross. Why? Because Peter was worried that he might have to follow Jesus to the cross. That was why Jesus spoke also of the cross his disciples would have to bear (8:34). In not accepting all of Jesus' gospel, his followers were in danger of keeping him at a distance and not listening to or understanding him.

9:1-8 The Transfiguration: His Coming Certified
The words recorded in 9:1 suggested that the transfiguration of Jesus (9:2-9) was a foretaste of the kingdom glory promised in the future. Luke 9:28 says "about eight days." Mark's "six days" (Mark 9:2) include the last part of the first day and the beginning of the eighth. According to Jewish chronological reckoning, any part of the day would be regarded as the whole. The "mountain" was probably 9,200 foot-high Mount Hermon. Peter's "shrines" (9:5) were probably intended for celebrating the Festival of Shelters—the feast that would be celebrated in God's kingdom (Zech. 14:16).

9:9-13 The Transfiguration's Lesson: Suffering Must Precede Resurrection
Jesus wanted the vision of his glory to be kept until after his resurrection. Before then, the focus was on his suffering. For comments on the promise of Elijah's coming, see Matthew 17:10-13.

9:14-29 PRAYERLESS EXERCISE OF POWER
The disciples learn that Jesus' works were done by prayerful connection with the Father, not by some kind of magic or force of will.

9:30-50 THE PASSION AND SELF-EXALTATION: NO EXCLUSIVISM
This was the second time that Jesus predicted his death (Mark 9:31; cf. 8:31). The "millstone" (9:42) was a large disc-shaped stone used for grinding corn. Some background on "salt" (9:50) is helpful in the interpretation of this trilogy. Salt was used in ancient times as a preservative for meats and as a means of payment. The soldier who was "not worth his salt" had not earned his "salary" (a word derived from the Latin word for "salt"). Salt was sometimes diluted by the addition of white sand, which made it "unsalty." Such salt was cast on the roadbeds to inhibit the growth of weeds.

10:1-31 SUBMISSION TO THE DIVINE POWER IN SALVATION

10:1-12 Submission to God's Joining: Hard Hearts Condemned
The phrase "east of the Jordan River" (10:1) referred to Perea, a territory ruled by Herod Antipas. For the first century views on divorce, see the note on Matthew 19:3. For what Moses said about "divorce" (Mark 10:3), see the note on Deuteronomy 24:1-4. Jesus said in this passage that divorce and remarriage constituted adultery (Mark 10:11-12). See the note on Matthew 19:10-12 for a further discussion on this topic.

10:13-16 Submission to God's Requirements for the Kingdom
The disciples tried to keep the young children away from Jesus, but Jesus condemned their rebuking of the children who desired to come to him. The little children formed a contrast with the religious leaders who resisted God's plan for marriage (10:1-10) and with the rich man who would not trade earthly wealth for heavenly treasure (10:17-23). The little children came to Jesus and willingly received his embrace, touch, and blessing (10:16). Receiving the kingdom like little children (10:15) involves believers allowing themselves to have this kind of intimate and warm relationship with Jesus. The willing and trusting relationships exhibited by children are key ingredients in receiving the kingdom. The children also represented humble and servant-oriented lives (9:35-37). Prior to the obedience involved in keeping God's marriage laws or giving wealth to the poor must come the initial childlike trust and relationship with Jesus.

10:17-31 The Impossibility of Saving One's Self
In Mark 10:18 Jesus was asking, "Why do you call me 'good' when you don't recognize my deity?" For a camel to pass through the "eye of a needle" (10:25), that is, a sewing needle, is impossible, just

as it is impossible for one who is unwilling to make material sacrifices to follow Jesus and enter his kingdom.

10:32-52 THE PASSION AND SELF-EXALTATION: THE CORRECTIVE OF SERVANTHOOD

Jesus' third and final death announcement was the most precise (10:33-34). The prediction indicated that Jesus was sovereign over circumstances, not the victim of chance. The words "in your glorious Kingdom" (10:37) referred to the Messiah's future kingdom. The "cup" and "baptism" (10:39) were figures of speech referring to Jesus' sorrow and suffering, which James and John would share. James was executed by Herod Agrippa (Acts 12:2) and John exiled on the island of Patmos (Rev. 1:9). For the apparent discrepancy in this account (Mark 10:46-52) with Matthew and Luke, see the note on Matthew 20:29-34.

11:1–13:37 Victory over Anti-Christian Delusion

11:1-11 THE PUBLIC ENTRANCE INTO JERUSALEM

"Bethphage" and "Bethany" (Mark 11:1) were villages in the vicinity of the Mount of Olives about a half-mile east of Jerusalem (see introductory map). The words "Praise God" (11:9) are a transliteration of a Hebrew word that means "save now."

11:12-26 THE CONSTANT OBJECT OF FAITH

The "kingdom of our ancestor David" (11:10) was a reference to the kingdom that God had promised David's descendant would inherit (2 Sam. 7:12-16; Luke 1:32-33). "Merchants and their customers" (Mark 11:15) were buying and selling in the outer court (Court of the Gentiles) of the temple. In 11:17 Jesus quoted Isaiah 56:7 and Jeremiah 7:11. Mark 11:26 is absent from many early manuscripts but does appear in Matthew 6:15. Many scholars believe it was added to Mark's Gospel at a later time from the Matthew account.

11:27–12:44 DEBATES WITH DISOBEDIENT LEADERS

In Mark 12:1 Jesus quoted from Isaiah 5:2. Jesus was the "cornerstone" (Mark 12:10) that the "builders," the leaders of the nation, rejected (Ps. 118:22-23). For the Pharisees (Mark 12:13), see the note on Matthew 3:7. For the Herodians, see the comments on Matthew 22:16. The two sects were at opposite ends of the theological spectrum but had teamed up to trap Jesus with a political question. Everyone acknowledged that a legitimate government had the right to tax its subjects (Mark 12:14). The ultimate question was, "Is the Roman government legitimate?" For "Roman coin" (12:15), or *denarius,* see the note on 6:37. For more on the Sadducees (12:18), see the notes on Matthew 3:7. The question of Mark 12:23 was based on the law of levirate

marriage (cf. Deut. 25:5-10). The Sadducees referred to this provision to demonstrate the absurdity of belief in the resurrection. In Mark 12:26 Jesus produced evidence for the resurrection from the Pentateuch (Exod. 3:6), which the Sadducees recognized as their sole source for authoritative teaching. In Mark 12:36 Jesus quoted from David's Psalm 110:1.

The only possible answer to Jesus' question in Mark 12:37 was that David's descendant ("son") was a divine ("Lord") Messiah. The "collection box" (12:41) was in the temple in the Court of the Women. Located there were thirteen large brass receptacles with trumpet-shaped mouths. Nine were for sacrifice-tribute money, and four were for free-will offerings. The "pennies" (12:42) were worth very little but represented all the woman owned.

13:1-37 VICTORY IN JESUS' ABSENCE: PERSEVERANCE

The purpose of this sermon was to encourage and protect the disciples during Jesus' absence. It was a sermon designed to promote faith and obedience during a time of distress. It was the longest discourse in Mark, and it was the only extended speech of Jesus or anyone else recorded in Mark's Gospel. It functioned as a bridge between the public ministry of Jesus and the events of his passion. It was also a farewell discourse following the biblical pattern (cf. Gen. 49; Deut. 33; Josh. 23; and Acts 20:17-35).

The "Mount of Olives" (Mark 13:3) is a long north-south ridge that lies just east of Jerusalem. The two basic questions in 13:4 were: (1) "When will the temple be destroyed?" and (2) "When will these 'end of the age' events be fulfilled?" The discourse focused on answering the second question. The message covered the events leading up to the time of the end (13:5-13), the preservation of the faithful through the time of the judgments (13:14-27), and the concluding encouragements to perseverance (13:28-37).

There were nineteen commands given in 13:5-37. Note phrases like "watch out" and "stay alert" (13:9, 23, 33). Note that the things Jesus described always related back to 13:4 (13:5-8, 9-12, 14, 23, 24-27). The purpose was to show that believers were not to be disturbed by preliminary signs or to confuse them with the end of the age. Jesus' comments in Mark 13:32-37 were the real answer to the disciples' questions, not a mere afterthought. Jesus makes it clear that no one knows the time of his return and calls all his followers to stay faithful while awaiting this glorious event.

The time references used by Jesus speak of those who will be alive whenever the predicted events should happen (see the idea of "when" in 13:11, 14, 29). These were words of concern, love, and compassion that had been sparked by the disciples' desire for a sign. Jesus first gave an exhortation and then followed it with the reasons for the warning (see "for" in 13:19, 22, 35).

The reference to the "synagogues" (13:9), Jewish meeting places for prayer and Scripture reading, reflected the Jewish setting of this discourse. The "sacrilegious object that causes desecration" (13:14) was a reference to the antichrist (Dan. 9:27; 2 Thess. 2:4).

14:1-52 Betrayal and Arrest: The Disciples' Defeat by Flesh Unprepared by Prayer

14:1-11 MURDER PLOTS

The "Passover" (Mark 14:1) was one of the three annual festivals that the Jews attended in Jerusalem (Deut. 16:16). It commemorated the deliverance of Israel from Egypt (Exod. 12) and how God "passed over" the Israelite houses where the blood of the lamb had been applied. This feast on the fourteenth day of Nisan was followed by the Festival of Unleavened Bread (Nisan, days fifteen through twenty-one). The woman (Mark 14:3) was Mary of Bethany (cf. John 12:3). The costly perfume (Mark 14:3-5) was worth the equivalent of three hundred days' wages.

14:12-25 THE PASSOVER

This room "upstairs" (14:15) was apparently in the home of Mary, the mother of John Mark (cf. Luke 22:12; Acts 1:13-15; 12:12). The "covenant" (Mark 14:24) was a reference to the new covenant mentioned in Jeremiah 31:31-34, which Jesus brought into fruition by shedding his blood on the cross (Heb. 8:6-13).

14:26-52 THE ARREST

The name "Gethsemane" (Mark 14:32) means "oil press." This olive grove was traditionally thought to be located across the Kidron from the Eastern Gate of Jerusalem at the foot of the Mount of Olives. The "betrayer" (14:42) was a reference to Judas (14:43). All had promised loyalty, but all left him and fled (14:50). One wonders why such an insignificant incident would be included in the Gospel unless the young man was Mark, the writer (14:51-52). The incident may have been included to authenticate him as an eyewitness. The word "naked" (14:52) may simply mean "without an outer garment."

14:53–15:15 The Trial

14:53-65 CONDEMNED BY THE JEWS AS THE MESSIAH

The accusation made against Jesus in Mark 14:58 used a perversion of Jesus' teaching concerning his bodily resurrection as evidence against him (cf. John 2:19-21).

14:66-72 DENIED BY PETER

The Galileans spoke Aramaic with a noticeable accent, which is how Peter's association with Jesus and his disciples was revealed (14:70). Jesus had predicted Peter's denial in 14:27-31. He had also spoken of his ongoing relationship with the disciples afterward in Galilee (14:28). Peter's denial was tragic, but not fatal to his relationship with Christ. Throughout their time with Jesus, the disciples misunderstood the nature of his mission. They struggled most with Jesus' humility and suffering and with his demand that they follow him down the path toward a cross. Peter had earlier denied the place of the cross in Jesus' life (8:31-38), and at this point he denied his own part in taking on the sufferings of Jesus. The striving of the disciples for greatness (9:33-37) resulted in their rejection of the lowliness associated with Jesus as he turned his way toward the cross.

15:1-15 CONDEMNED BY PILATE AS KING

In the early morning hours (possibly April 3, A.D. 33), the Sanhedrin ("high council") met again to give their night verdict some semblance of officiality (15:1). Jesus was then delivered up to the Roman authorities because the Jews had no authority to execute capital punishment. Pilate was the Roman prefect, or governor, of Judea who ruled from A.D. 26 to 36. He normally resided in Caesarea but was in Jerusalem to maintain control over the Jewish crowds at Passover.

Jesus admitted his claim to kingship, but he clarified what kind of king he claimed to be (15:2; cf. John 18:36-37). Jesus was silent before his accusers in fulfillment of prophecy (Mark 15:5; Isa. 53:7).

Pilate's response to the Jews (Mark 15:15), in contrast to his previous hostile dealings (cf. Luke 13:1), can be better understood in light of the A.D. 32 execution of Sejanus, Pilate's protector and supporter in Rome. Pilate's position as prefect was now insecure, and he did not want the Jews to raise trouble for him that might reach the ears of the emperor, Tiberius. For this reason, he reluctantly submitted to the demand of the Jews that Jesus be crucified.

15:16-47 The Crucifixion and Burial

15:16-21 LED TO THE CROSS

The term "headquarters" (15:16) is *praetorium* in Greek, which was derived from praetor, originally the name for Rome's highest magistrate, later called a "consul." The Praetorium was the praetor's tent or military headquarters. The term was used here to refer either to Herod's palace or, more likely, to the Antonia Fortress, located just north of the temple area. This fortress quartered the Roman "cohort," a battalion of six hundred soldiers. Simon was from Cyrene, the chief city of Cyrenaica in North Africa (15:21).

15:22-32 INSULTS AT THE CROSS

The "wine drugged with myrrh" (15:23) was intended as a sedative to ease the pain of crucifixion. All the details of the suffering borne by Jesus on the cross were recounted. Jesus was crucified with robbers; he bore insults regarding the temple; he chose not to vindicate himself by saving himself; and he did not show a miraculous sign to the sneering crowd.

15:33-41 RESPONSES TO JESUS' DEATH

Jesus quoted Psalm 22:1 in the Aramaic language (Mark 15:34). Apparently "Eloi" was misunderstood to be a reference to "Elijah," whose return the Jews expected (Mal. 3:1; 4:5). Josephus reported that the temple veil ("curtain," Mark 15:38) was thirty feet wide and ninety feet high (*Jewish War*, 5.5.5). The curtain is typical of the body of Christ (Heb. 10:19-20). Salome (Mark 15:40) was the wife of Zebedee and mother of James and John (Matt. 27:56).

15:42-47 BURIAL

Joseph was from "Arimathea" (Mark 15:43), a town of uncertain location. He was a member of the Sanhedrin ("high council"), which had condemned Jesus. Victims of crucifixion sometimes hung on their crosses a day or more (15:44). Jesus' death came after six hours. The burial of Jesus in the tomb of Joseph (15:46-47) was done in fulfillment of Isaiah 53:9.

16:1-20 Resurrection Events

Some Greek manuscripts of Mark end with 16:8. Others add two or as many as twelve verses to the text. The vast majority of Greek scholars today would say that the last twelve verses are not authentic since they are not supported by the two oldest and complete manuscripts of the New Testament. Not everyone agrees, however. In fact the vast majority of the surviving Greek manuscripts have the traditional ending, and the evidence supporting the inclusion of the traditional ending is older than the manuscripts that omit it. Until scholars settle this debated issue, it would be wise to retain the text but not develop any peculiar doctrines from it.

Mark 16:16 has been used by some to prove that baptism is necessary for salvation. But more careful observation reveals that the only basis for condemnation is a refusal to believe. Therefore, the only basis for salvation is faith (cf. Eph. 2:8-9).

LUKE

HISTORICAL SETTING

Luke was written for a certain prominent individual named Theophilus (Luke 1:1). The Greek meaning of the name "Theophilus" is "lover of God." Some interpreters theorize that the name may be symbolic for all Christians rather than referring to an actual person. But without clear proof for symbolism, "Theophilus" should probably be understood to be a real person to whom Luke addressed his two-volume work of the Gospel and Acts. The reference to this individual, however, was really a dedication characteristic of Greek and Roman literature. The work was clearly written for the benefit of Gentiles in general and Greeks in particular. As a result of Paul's missionary journeys the gospel spread through the Greek world, and there developed a need for a gospel record that would speak to the Greek mind.

The Greek nature of the book can be seen in the fact that the genealogy was traced to Adam, the father of the human race, rather than Abraham, the father of the Hebrew nation. Luke avoided the use of Jewish terminology like "rabbi" and instead used "master" or "teacher." Luke placed less emphasis on the fulfillment of prophecy, and he substituted Greek names for Hebrew names (cf. Luke 6:16; 23:33 with Mark 3:18). Abundant evidence indicates that Luke addressed his Gospel to Greek Gentiles.

AUTHOR

Although the Gospel of Luke is anonymous, both internal and external evidence point to Luke, the Gentile physician and companion of Paul, as the author. Internal confirmation of Luke's authorship is assumed by the close relationship between Luke and Acts. Acts was clearly authored by Luke, for only he could have written the "we" section of Acts, having joined Paul at Troas (Acts 16:10-17; 20:5–21:18; 27:1–28:16). Both Luke and Acts were addressed to the same man, Theophilus (Luke 1:3; Acts 1:1), and both use medical terminology. That strongly suggests that Luke, the author of Acts, also authored the Gospel of Luke. The writings of the early church fathers also attest to Luke's authorship.

Luke was a Gentile convert (Col. 4:10-14), possibly of the church at Antioch, as stated by Jerome and Eusebius. Luke joined Paul at Troas (Acts 16:10) during his second missionary journey and accompanied him to Philippi. Luke later accompanied Paul to Jerusalem (Acts 20:5–21:15) and finally to Rome (Acts 27:1–28:15). He was referred to by Paul as "Dear Doctor Luke" (Col. 4:14), and was his last friend to remain with him during Paul's second imprisonment (2 Tim. 4:11). Luke was an able historian, physician, missionary, and author.

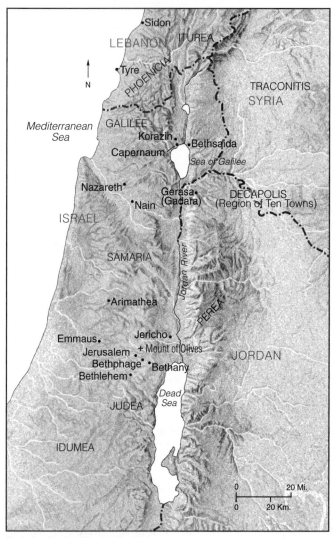

The broken lines (— · —·) indicate modern boundaries.
Copyright © 1986, 1988 by Tyndale House Publishers, Inc.

DATE

The Gospel of Luke was written before Acts (Acts 1:1) and after the development of Christianity to the point where it would attract the attention of a Gentile inquirer like Theophilus. The abrupt ending of Acts indicates that Luke concluded his writing at the end of Paul's imprisonment in Rome in A.D. 62. The Gospel was composed prior to that, probably about A.D. 60. Paul's two year imprisonment at Caesarea would have afforded Luke an opportunity to research and write the Gospel.

PURPOSE

The book of Luke was designed to promote certainty concerning the historical events and facts that form a foundation for the Christian faith (Luke 1:1-4). It did that by presenting Jesus' life in its historical context and by the great amount of detail gained by Luke's research. The heart of the book's teaching can be seen in how Jesus' life prepared believers for the power of the Spirit, who came at Pentecost after Jesus had been exalted to God's right hand.

GEOGRAPHY AND ITS IMPORTANCE

The book of Luke begins and ends in the Jerusalem temple. In between, Luke emphasized a long journey section that moves from Galilee down to Jerusalem—a journey that focuses on Jesus' victorious ascension from Jerusalem up to his Father's right hand. The progression from the spiritual state of God's people in the temple at the beginning of the book to the happy disciples praising God in the temple at the end of the book involves a journey that reveals the greatness of Jesus, outlines the costs of following him, and teaches the central place of the Holy Spirit in the lives of Jesus and the believers.

GUIDING CONCEPTS

THE UNITY OF LUKE WITH ACTS

Luke and Acts are parts of a two-volume set. Therefore, they need to be interpreted recognizing the connections between the two. The first volume, the Gospel of Luke, was a record of all that Jesus had done during his life—from his birth to his ascension (Luke 1:1-4). The second volume, the book of Acts, continued the record of the acts of the risen Lord through the work of his apostles (Acts 1:1-2). The Gospel of Luke began with the announcement in the temple of the coming of the Lord and his forerunner (Luke 1:13-17). The book of Acts ended with Paul in Rome preaching the gospel unhindered (Acts 28:30-31). Throughout the two books, whether Luke or Acts, the author presented one undivided message about the person and work of Jesus. Therefore, this study on Luke's Gospel will often recognize the connection between Luke and Acts.

THE FOCUS ON THE ASCENSION OF JESUS

Luke made the ascension of Jesus into heaven the central focus in both Luke and Acts. Luke made special reference to Jesus' ascension at his transfiguration (Luke 9:31) and put the major part of his account of Jesus' ministry (9:51–19:28) into a journey to Jerusalem, a journey that would find its completion in the ascension (9:51). So important was the Ascension that Luke described it twice, once at the end of Luke and again at the beginning of Acts.

Only in Acts 2 did Luke clarify why he found the Ascension so important (Acts 2:34-36). At that event, God the Father exalted Jesus to his right hand in heaven. But more important, the Ascension was where Jesus promised the community of believers that the Spirit would soon be poured out upon them (Acts 2:33). Peter quoted Psalm 110:1 (Acts 2:34-35; quoted first by Jesus in Luke 20:41-44). From the beginning of his Gospel, Luke built toward the event of Jesus' enthronement and the subsequent "pouring out" of the Spirit upon God's people. The goal of Jesus in Luke was not simply to die on the cross but also to be exalted to the right hand of God, to send his Spirit, and to powerfully enable his people to continue proclaiming the gospel. The Gospel of Luke builds toward the event of the Ascension and the gift of the Spirit. The book of Acts illustrates the unhindered witness to Jesus Christ through the power of the Spirit. The Gospel looks ahead to the Ascension; the book of Acts looks back to it. The Ascension and its resultant power for witness is at the very heart of the Luke-Acts account.

BRINGING GOOD NEWS

Luke used the concept of bringing good news or proclaiming the gospel twenty-five times in the Luke-Acts account. Mark and John did not use it at all, and Matthew used it only once. Old Testament background for that phrase can be found in 1 Kings 1:42; Isaiah 52:7; Jeremiah 20:15. The phrase is used in contexts of joy, the expectation of the end times, and the inclusion of Gentiles in salvation. The book of Luke gives a special focus on how the Good News came to the world in the person of Jesus. Acts shows how the Good News spread through the power of the Holy Spirit. In Luke the gospel was proclaimed by the perfect man of the Spirit, Jesus. In Acts it was proclaimed by believers empowered by the Spirit.

POWER AND SPIRIT
Power and Spirit are nearly synonymous in Luke-Acts (see especially Luke 1:35 and 24:49). Both found their source in God the Father and were given to Jesus or to his followers through the Spirit. Luke used the word for Spirit 109 times in Luke-Acts (Matt., 19 times; Mark, 22 times; John, 22 times). Luke introduced Jesus as a person conceived by the Spirit (Luke 1:35), as the man of the Spirit (3:22; 4:18; Acts 10:38), and after his resurrection, as the Lord of the Spirit (Luke 24:49; Acts 2:33). Therefore, on earth the Spirit was not the instrument of Jesus' power. Jesus was the instrument of the Spirit's power. And from that model believers can discover the nature of true discipleship. True disciples do not use the Spirit; the Spirit uses them.

PRAYER
Luke used the words for prayer thirty-four times in Luke-Acts (Matt., 15 times; Mark, 4 times; John, zero times). Luke recounted a number of special contexts for Jesus' prayers (Luke 3:21; 6:12; 9:18, 28; 11:1). Luke alone told his readers that at Jesus' baptism Jesus was praying when the Spirit descended upon him (3:21), that Jesus spent the night in prayer before he chose his disciples (6:12-13), that Jesus was praying before he told his disciples of his impending death (9:18), and that Jesus was praying as he became transfigured (9:28-29). Luke wanted his readers to know that at the critical new movements of Jesus' ministry he was in prayer and God answered. The same pattern would become evident for the disciples in the book of Acts. When they prayed, God's Spirit moved in powerful ways.

BIBLE-WIDE CONCEPTS

JESUS' USE OF THE OLD TESTAMENT
Jesus' own method of interpreting the Old Testament was taken up by Luke and the rest of the New Testament writers. Luke 24:27, 45 and Acts 1:3 show how Jesus' interpretations were impressed upon the minds of his followers and provided a foundation for their approach to the message of Old Testament Scripture. Throughout the New Testament, the Holy Spirit continued to guide the writers to show how Jesus the Messiah fulfilled the prophecies of Old Testament Scripture. Such fulfillment ratified the claims of Jesus and his followers and became the heart of the gospel proclamation.

THE LINKS WITH ADAM
Luke's genealogy tied Jesus all the way back to Adam's sonship from God (Luke 3:38). As such, it set up two poles upon which the human race was strung: Adam and Jesus. From Luke's perspective, only those two men were critical to the history of the world. Paul also saw a similar relationship between Adam and Jesus (cf. Rom. 5:17; 1 Cor. 15:45). For Luke, Jesus was the Man who could stretch across the uncounted centuries of human sin and restore humanity's sonship with God.

THE KINGDOM OF GOD

In Luke-Acts, Luke laid the foundation for answering how Jesus could come and go and the kingdom of God still not be fully established on earth. The disciples had expected the Messiah to come and establish the visible kingdom of God. Luke explained that the Messiah came first to redeem humanity by his death on the cross. Later he would return in power and glory to reign forever (2:35; 5:35; 9:22; 9:31; 9:44, 51; 17:25; 20:17; 22:19-20; 24:25-26, 46; Acts 5:31; 10:38-43). The surprise was that in between his first and second comings would come the age of the Spirit—an age marked by a fellowship of humble suffering and spiritual power modeled after Jesus' life on earth. Jesus reigned at the right hand of God and ministered his rule through the outpoured Spirit on earth. Such was the present form of the kingdom that Luke sought to explain.

NEEDS MET BY LUKE

Luke's audience needed truth that would make their commitment to Christ more solid and complete. They needed a stronger faith because believing in Jesus during Luke's day often brought persecution. Luke began his task by answering questions his readers had about Jesus' life on earth, knowing that by doing this he would strengthen their faith in Jesus. Next, Luke helped to deepen his readers' confidence in Jesus by showing how Jesus fulfilled Old Testament truths and prophecies. Finally, Luke built all of his two-volume work around the great day of Pentecost when Jesus sent the Holy Spirit to earth. Luke knew that faith and confidence in Jesus was dependent on the indwelling power of the Spirit among his readers. Jesus had come and gone. How could people maintain a solid commitment to an invisible Savior, especially during times of persecution and hardship? Only through the fact of the fulfilled Old Testament, the experience of the invisible but potent Holy Spirit, and the reminder and instruction brought by a book like Luke. Luke let his readers know what needs he wanted to meet (1:4). He wanted to give the reader the exact truth—that which was needed for assurance. Luke laid down the foundation for certainty (1:4) and provided facts that would inspire his readers to confidence and faith in Jesus the Messiah. The following questions reflect some of the thoughts of those who sought certainty in their relationship with Jesus.

- How did John the Baptist's parents respond to John's birth?
- How did God confirm that he was behind John's birth?
- How did John the Baptist and Jesus fit in with Old Testament prophecy?
- What were some of the events surrounding the birth and early life of Jesus?
- How do the events of Jesus' birth and life relate to Old Testament prophetic hope?
- How did Jesus relate to the Holy Spirit?
- What was Jesus' prayer life like?
- What did Jesus teach regarding discipleship?
- What happened to the kingdom Jesus proclaimed?
- How could Jesus come and go and the kingdom still not be fully established?

Luke's goal that his readers might know the certainty of the things they had been taught (1:4) meets more than a need to know simple facts. Certainty is a condition of the heart as well as of the mind. It is an inner confidence that grows out of the facts of Jesus' life and becomes a foundation for a believer's consistent Christian living and witness. Without confidence, Christian obedience will not survive the pressures of daily life and the potential problems Jesus' absence creates. Luke helps believers cope with a redemption gained but a kingdom still awaiting its perfection. He shows that Jesus' life was a journey through real time and history and that he made that journey successfully only by complete dependence on the Holy Spirit. The Holy Spirit is the key to having the needs of believers met as well. It is only through the Spirit's power that believers can realize the full potential in their own lives.

OUTLINE OF LUKE

I. PROLOGUE: PRAYER AND ANOINTING (1:1–3:38)
   A. The Purpose of the Book (1:1-4)
   B. Two Pregnancies Predicted (1:5-56)
   C. Two Sons Are Born (1:57–2:52)
   D. John's Ministry of Preparation (3:1-20)
   E. Jesus' Ministry: The Anointed One (3:21-38)

II. SPIRIT AND POWER IN GALILEE (4:1–9:50)
   A. The Testing of Jesus (4:1-13)
   B. Proclamation and Power (4:14-44)
   C. Power Interpreted and Focused (5:1–6:11)
   D. Power and God's Purposes: Rejection and Acceptance (6:12–7:50)
   E. Power and the Soils (8:1-56)
   F. Ministry in a Hostile World (9:1-9)
   G. The Crucial Interpretation of Jesus' Ministry: Passion (9:10-50)

III. TOWARD THE GOAL: DEBATES AND INSTRUCTION (9:51–19:27)
   A. Preparation for Departure (9:51–13:21)
   B. On the Journey: Faith during Conflict (13:22–17:10)
   C. On the Journey: Perseverance (17:11–19:27)

IV. THE GOAL ATTAINED: JERUSALEM (19:28–24:53)
   A. The Entrance into Jerusalem (19:28-48)
   B. The Religious Opposition to Jesus (20:1–21:38)
   C. The Passover (22:1-38)
   D. Arrest and Trial (22:39–23:25)
   E. Crucifixion and Burial (23:26-56)
   F. The Resurrection (24:1-53)

LUKE NOTES

1:1–3:38 PROLOGUE: PRAYER AND ANOINTING

Overview: In Luke 1–3, the author shifted between the stories of John the Baptist and Jesus. Two pregnancies were announced: Elizabeth's (1:5-25) and Mary's (1:26-38). Two births were recounted: John the Baptist's (1:57-80) and Jesus' (2:1-52). Two ministries were followed: John the Baptist's ministry of preparation (3:1-20); Jesus' ministry as the Anointed One (3:21-38). Throughout, the Spirit was behind the acts and speeches of those involved: pregnancy of Elizabeth (1:15, 41-42); pregnancy of Mary (1:35); Zechariah at the birth of John (1:67); Simeon at his recognition of Jesus (2:25). Luke gave insight to his readers concerning the people who awaited the Messiah and the Spirit's work that was accomplished through them.

1:1-4 The Purpose of the Book

The prologue of Luke is similar to the prefaces used by such classical historians as Herodotus and medical writers like Hippocrates. This reveals something of the method Luke used in composing his Gospel and what he intended to accomplish with it. The purpose of his Gospel was assurance (1:4, "reassure"). Reading this Gospel should bring assurance of the truth of Jesus the Messiah's life, death, and resurrection. And that assurance is only strengthened by the meticulous process of writing and research that Luke described. Assurance is built upon the events seen by eyewitnesses, handed down to Luke and others, and finally carefully researched and written by Luke. Luke wrote for the confirmation of the faith. He wrote to correct problem areas with regards to the facts and implications of Christianity.

The words "from the early discples and other eyewitnesses" (1:2) referred to the beginning of Jesus' ministry at his baptism by John (Acts 1:22). Luke was not an eyewitness but a historian who researched the facts "carefully" (Luke 1:3) and composed a point by point account of the information. The book was dedicated to "Theophilus," apparently a person of rank or nobility. Theophilus may have assisted in financing Luke's research and writing.

1:5-56 Two Pregnancies Predicted

1:5-25 THE CONCEPTION OF JOHN THE BAPTIST

"Herod" (1:5) was a king of Idumean descent who ruled Palestine from 37 to 4 B.C. under Roman auspices (see note on Matt. 2:1). The "order of Abijah" (1:5) was one of the twenty-four orders into which David divided the Levites (cf. 1 Chron. 24:10). Both Zechariah and Elizabeth were of priestly descent. Their characters (Luke 1:6) were

noted to show that they were part of the righteous remnant awaiting the coming of the Messiah.

An angel appeared to Zechariah (1:8-23). The temple location is significant. This was a once-in-a-lifetime opportunity for Zechariah to be in the temple. Lots (1:9) were cast (cf. Prov. 16:33) to determine which priest would have the privilege of burning incense in the Holy Place during the hour of prayer (Exod. 30:7-8). According to the Jewish Mishnah, this was a rare privilege. The angel referred to Zechariah's petition (Luke 1:13), probably for a child. Zechariah's response was the same as Abraham's (1:18; cf. Gen. 15:8). The angel was Gabriel (1:11; cf. 1:19). Gabriel had made earlier appearances in Daniel 8:16 and 9:21. He is the angel of mercy. John the Baptist would function as the Messiah's forerunner (Luke 1:17). Ministering in the "spirit and power" of Elijah (1:17), he fulfilled the prophecies of Malachi 3:1 and 4:5. The name "Gabriel" (Luke 1:19) means "man of God." He is one of two angels mentioned by name in Scripture. The other is Michael, the archangel. Gabriel is associated with the bearing of messages (1:26; cf. Dan. 8:16; 9:21). According to custom, the priest who had offered the incense was to pronounce a concluding benediction (Luke 1:22). But Zechariah was mute. As the angel promised, Elizabeth became pregnant (1:24-25).

1:26-38 GABRIEL ANNOUNCES MARY'S PREGNANCY

Mary was troubled at Gabriel's greeting (1:26-29). The announcement to Mary was made in the insignificant little village of Nazareth six months after John the Baptist's conception (1:36). Mary was "engaged", or betrothed, to Joseph (1:27). Betrothal was a formal relationship that existed for six months to a year before the marriage was consummated. There was no sexual union during that period (cf. Matt. 1:18). In Luke 1:27, 32-33 the author emphasized that the child was a descendant of David and thus the heir through whom the Davidic covenant would be fulfilled (2 Sam. 7:12-16). Mary submitted herself as God's servant, completely obedient to the will of her Master (Luke 1:38). The angel's message was full of messianic promises and predictions (1:30-33). The name "Jesus" is a Greek translation of Joshua, the one who led Israel across the Jordan into great military victories during the initial conquest of Israel. The references to sonship, throne, and David (1:32) and to reign and kingdom (1:33) all refer to the fulfillment of the Davidic covenant for a perfect king to rule over Israel in an eternal kingdom (2 Sam. 7:12-16). Note the coupling of "Holy Spirit" and "power" (1:35) and compare this with Acts 1:8

where the same coupling was made. Unlike that of Zechariah, Mary's response (1:34-38) carried no request for a sign.

1:39-56 MARY'S VISIT TO ELIZABETH

The "town" in Judea (1:39) was not specifically identified, although tradition associates this event with En Karem, a town located several miles west of Jerusalem. Various Christian denominations have built churches and monasteries there to commemorate the birth of John the Baptist. Mary's "Magnificat" (1:46-56) drew upon a series of Old Testament quotations to magnify the Lord. It resembles Hannah's prayer in 1 Samuel 2:1-10. This section brought both confirmation and exultation to the promise of Jesus. It was a prophetic confirmation of the events that had been given in Old Testament covenantal contexts. Elizabeth's song (Luke 1:41-45) spoke of being "filled with the Holy Spirit." That concept occurred in the Old Testament (cf. Num. 11:24-30; Deut. 34:9; Mic. 3:8) as well as in Luke's writings in the New Testament (Luke 1:15, 41; Acts 2:4; 4:8, 31; 9:17; 13:9). The filling with the Spirit was closely associated with the act of speaking. It took the sense of prophetic utterance involving the sovereign work of the Spirit of God. For Elizabeth, this filling was for a particular task, to praise the work of God in Jesus the Messiah.

The words of Mary's song (Luke 1:46-55) recognized that God's work through Jesus fulfilled the promise God made to Abraham (1:55). Mary praised God's acts of exalting the humble and bringing humiliation upon the proud and rich. In Jesus, God had reversed the means of attaining greatness in the world.

1:57–2:52 Two Sons Are Born

1:57-80 THE COMING OF JOHN THE BAPTIST

1:57-66 Controversy over the Name of the Son
It was common to call a son by his father's name. But Zechariah's willingness to name the baby John confirmed the work of God in his birth. According to the law, a male child was to be circumcised on the eighth day after his birth (1:59). It was a common Jewish custom to name the firstborn son after his father, but Elizabeth emphatically rejected that idea and followed Gabriel's instructions (1:60; cf. 1:13). The name "John" means "God is gracious."

1:67-80 The Song of Zechariah
Note the background of Malachi 4:1-6 (Luke 1:76) and Isaiah 9:1-2 (Luke 1:79). Mercy, remembrance, and oath are key Old Testament concepts. This prophetic hymn of Zechariah is known as the "Benedictus" from its opening word in the Latin translation. Zechariah's use of Isaiah 9:1-2 (Luke 1:79) was used by Matthew to introduce the impact that Jesus would have upon the Gentiles (Matt. 4:16). John grew up in the desert, outside of both the Levitical system

and established Judaism (Luke 1:80). He would be calling a people out of that system to come to the Messiah and the promised kingdom.

2:1-52 THE COMING OF JESUS

2:1-7 The Time and Place
Caesar Augustus (27 B.C.–A.D. 14), who brought great reform to the Roman Empire, commanded the registration of his subject population for the purpose of assessing the value of property and levying taxes. Quirinius (2:2) was governor of Syria twice (3–2 B.C. and A.D. 6–7), but neither of his governorships fit with what is known to have been the date of Jesus' birth (around 5/4 B.C.). Many solutions have been offered for this problem. It is possible to translate 2:2, "This census took place before Quirinius was governor of Syria." This would place the census around 6/5 B.C., a year or two before Herod's death. It is likely that Augustus would have wanted to have an estimate of the condition of the state before Herod's death.

The journey to Bethlehem was necessary to fulfill messianic prophecy (2:4; Micah 5:2). Jesus was born in either an enclosed courtyard or, as tradition says, a cave, because there was no room in the inn (Luke 2:7). The point is that he was born in obscurity and poverty as a son of David.

2:8-20 The Worship of the Shepherds
The Mishnah indicates that some flocks around Bethlehem were out all year, and those to be used at Passover were in the fields thirty days before the feast, as early as February (2:8). Shepherds were of low social status and were a people shunned by the rich and famous. The Lord was announced to the shepherds, illustrating his importance for "everyone" (2:10). What makes one exalted in God's sight is faith and obedience, not worldly might. See, for example, Mary's song (1:52-53). Notice the importance of divine signs in Luke's Gospel so far. Signs have been given to Zechariah (1:18-20), Mary (1:34-35), and to the shepherds (2:12). Those signs further Luke's purpose to establish certainty and assurance concerning the coming of Jesus the Messiah. God's message of peace was directed to "all whom God favors" (2:14).

2:21-40 Purification and Presentation
See Numbers 18:15-16 and Leviticus 12:8 for the Old Testament background to purification. For "circumcised" (Luke 2:21), see 1:59. The "time for the purification" (2:22) was a reference to the uncleanness of childbirth (cf. Lev. 12:1-8), which required that a sacrifice be offered for cleansing forty days after the birth of a male child. The offering of birds reflects the poverty of Joseph and Mary (Luke 2:24). They could not afford a sacrificial lamb.

Simeon's recognition and adoration of Jesus (2:25-35) further confirmed to Luke's readers that Jesus was the promised Messiah. Simeon had been looking for the coming of Messiah to "come and rescue Israel" (2:25). He invoked a blessing on the holy family and predicted the world's response to God's provision of salvation (2:35). His message confirmed Jesus' identity as God's Messiah. It showed that he would be salvation, light to the Gentiles, and that he was appointed to fulfill the promises of Isaiah 8:14 and 42:6. Simeon was another block in Luke's presentation of assurance and certainty.

Luke continued his presentation with the adoration of Anna (Luke 2:36-38). Simeon and Anna illustrate the godly character of the righteous remnant. They were faithful to God's promises and were looking for God's redemption. Anna was a descendant of one of the northern tribes, Asher, which had gone into captivity in 722 B.C.

2:41-52 Jesus' Youth
It was at the age of thirteen that Jewish boys became "sons of the law" and assumed adult responsibilities. Jesus became a son of the law and was eligible to keep feasts, fasts, and so forth. These first recorded words of the Messiah (2:49) served as the capstone to the infancy narratives. They set the tone for his coming ministry and for the believers' responsibilities as his disciples. He asserted the authority of his divine sonship.

Mary asked why Jesus had treated them that way, saying that they both had been anxious (2:48). She expressed all the normal emotions of parents who have lost their children. This is the interpretive key to this section. Mary and Joseph were acting like they had a normal parent-child relationship with Jesus. They were not living in the light of the great miracles and prophecies they had experienced concerning their son. He was the Son of God, not just an average teenager. In 1:49 Jesus answered Mary's why with another why question. Jesus' response implies that they should not have been looking all over Jerusalem for Jesus but should have known where he would be because of who he was. The Son would be found in the Father's house. Mary and Joseph had to learn to think of Jesus as the Son of God who had come to do his Father's redemptive will, not as an average person.

Although his parents misunderstood his mission, Jesus clarified the relationship between himself and his parents. All his concerns were Father-centered. Such a misunderstanding of his person and mission is possible for all believers. Joseph and Mary returned to Nazareth, in Lower Galilee, where Jesus grew to adulthood (2:51). Nothing more was recorded about Jesus' youth. The record of Jesus' life was not resumed until he was baptized by John.

3:1-20 John's Ministry of Preparation
3:1-18 JOHN'S MESSAGE
Luke the historian places the beginning of John the Baptist's ministry in the context of the politi-

cal and religious leadership of the day (3:1-2). The "fifteenth year" of Tiberius Caesar (A.D. 14–37) would be between August 19, A.D. 28, and December 31, A.D. 29 (reckoned from the Julian calendar or Tiberius' regnal year). Assuming Jesus had a three-year ministry and an A.D. 33 crucifixion, John's ministry would have begun in A.D. 29, and Jesus' ministry shortly thereafter. Pontius Pilate served as governor of Judea (A.D. 26 to 36). Herod Antipas (a son of Herod the Great) ruled Galilee and Perea (4 B.C.–A.D. 39). Philip, another son of Herod, ruled territories northeast of Galilee (4 B.C.–A.D. 34). Annas was high priest (A.D. 6–15) before being deposed by the Romans. His son-in-law, Caiaphas, was later appointed to the position (A.D. 18–36). John warned the Jews against trusting merely in their religious ancestry to secure a good relationship with God (3:8). John called the people to repentance. Repentance reveals itself by producing fruit—deeds for God. Note the thrice-repeated question asked by the hearers of John the Baptist's message concerning what they should do to show repentance (3:10-14; cf. Acts 2:37).

John the Baptist used the imagery of harvest to describe events of the Second Coming—deliverance of the righteous into God's kingdom and punishment of the wicked in the fires of hell (Luke 3:17; cf. Matt. 25:46; Isa. 30:24). John had been preaching the gospel of the coming kingdom (3:18) and called the people to repent of all sin.

3:19-20 JOHN'S REMOVAL
Because of his criticism of Herod Antipas's marriage to Herodias, John the Baptist was put in prison (Luke 3:18-20). Herodias had been the wife (and niece) of Herod's brother Philip (3:19). Herod Antipas divorced his wife and married Herodias in violation of the Mosaic laws against incestuous marriage (Lev. 18:6-18).

3:21-38 Jesus' Ministry: The Anointed One
3:21-22 JESUS' BAPTISM
John's role was played down in order to focus on Jesus. This was the only Gospel account to mention the heavens being opened and that Jesus was praying when the Spirit descended upon him.

3:23-38 JESUS' GENEALOGY
The genealogy that Luke chose to include in his account must have had a special purpose because every human being can be traced back to Adam. But perhaps that was just the point. The genealogy allowed Jesus to take his place in and identify with the human race. Also, Adam provided a universal link with Jesus and God for the Gentiles as well as the Jews. As Adam was a son of God, Jesus was the Son of God. As the sin of Adam destroyed the human race, Jesus would open up the way for its

redemption. The genealogy was inserted at this point because Jewish literature often placed the genealogy before the start of a man's ministry (see for example, Exod. 6:14-27).

How could Joseph be called the son of Jacob in Matthew 1:16 and the "son of Heli" in Luke 3:23? It has been suggested that this genealogy was really that of Mary who was the daugher of Heli. Joseph would have been the "son of Heli" by marriage (as son-in-law). One ancient explanation is that Heli died childless, and Jacob, his half brother, in accordance with the law of levirate marriages (Deut. 25:5-6), took his widow as wife and became the father of Joseph. While Matthew's genealogy descends from Abraham to Jesus, Luke's genealogy ascends from Jesus to God, linking Jesus not only with Israel but the whole human race. Both genealogies demonstrate Jesus' right to the throne as an heir of David (Luke 3:31; cf. Matt. 1:1, 6).

4:1–9:50 SPIRIT AND POWER IN GALILEE
Overview: The section of 4:1–9:50 emphasizes several key points. Jesus was anointed by the Spirit (Luke 4:18-21) in accordance with Isaiah 61:1. He came to build a community of witnesses (Luke 5:9-11). The power of his words was set in the context of the power of his acts (cf. 6:19; 20-49). Love for Jesus was related to the forgiveness of sins (7:47). And finally, a series of miracles and the sending out of the disciples led up to the confession of Peter (9:20) and the transfiguration (9:28-36). The climax was in God's own proclamation, "This is my Son, my Chosen One. Listen to him" (9:35).

4:1-13 The Testing of Jesus
Jesus was "full of the Holy Spirit" (4:1). That means he was in full submission to the Spirit. The "wilderness" (4:1) was a reference to the twelve-mile wide desert region southeast of Jerusalem paralleling the Dead Sea. The "highest point" (4:9) of the temple referred to the southeast corner overlooking the Kidron Valley. Luke left the testing of Jesus open-ended (4:13). Satan would return at a later time of opportunity.

4:14-44 Proclamation and Power
4:14-30 THE FIRST REJECTION AT NAZARETH
A linking phrase moves the reader from an account of the people's praise (4:14-15) to an account of those who did not praise him (4:16-30). Matthew moved from the temptation to selecting the disciples and then on to the first major discourse in Matthew 5–7. In contrast, Luke moved from the temptation of the Spirit-filled Jesus to his Nazareth sermon on the anointing by the Spirit spoken of in Isaiah 61:1. For Matthew, Nazareth was the fulfillment of prophecy (Matt. 2:23). For Luke, the Spirit's presence upon Jesus was the fulfillment of

prophecy. In Luke 4:18-19 Jesus said the purpose of his anointing was the proclamation of the gospel to the poor and handicapped. Jesus offered physical and spiritual healings (4:18). God's mercy was given to those who saw themselves in need.

Nazareth was located in lower Galilee just north of the Valley of Jezreel and four miles south of Sepphoris, the capital of Galilee until A.D. 18 (see introductory map). The synagogue was an institution that arose during the Babylonian exile and was a place where Jews gathered for worship, study, and prayer. Jesus stopped reading from Isaiah 61:1-2 in the middle of 61:2 indicating that "the day of God's anger" (Isa. 61:2) would be an event associated with his second coming and not his present ministry (Luke 4:18). Two specific elements of the prophecy were fulfilled (4:21). Jesus, the one who was "anointed," had come and Jesus' audience was about to prove itself blind to the gospel. Only the first line of Jesus' message was recorded by Luke. Luke jumped ahead to show how the hearers responded to Jesus' message.

The rejection of Jesus by the people of Nazareth (4:25-30) was preceded by a statement of the basic problem (4:23-24). How could Jesus say he was not "accepted" (4:24) when 4:22 seems to say that he was well received? Jesus defined "accepted" as his hearers receiving the gospel in faith from the heart. All other responses or praises were worthless and not accepted. Jesus illustrated the hardness of the people's hearts by recalling events of Elijah's day (4:25-27). Elements of "hardheartedness" from ancient Israel remained in the Israel of Jesus' day. The nation of Israel was like the people of the "hometown." With Elijah and Elisha, God went to the Gentiles before going to the faithless in Israel. Similarly, Jesus would not be accepted by people of his own hometown. That was a slap in the face to the Jews of Jesus' day. The people initially responded with wonder at Jesus' preaching, but were not willing to take it to heart (4:28-30). They would not admit to having hard and faithless hearts and thus failed to cry out to God in repentance.

4:31-44 HEALINGS AT CAPERNAUM
Capernaum (4:31), a tax collection station on the Via Maris, was located on the northwest shore of the Sea of Galilee (see introductory map). Contrast what the demons knew about Jesus (4:34) and the ignorance of the men of Nazareth (4:22).

5:1–6:11 Power Interpreted and Focused
5:1-16 POWER OVER HUMANITY
Jesus demonstrated his power to catch people by showing his power to catch fish. Another name for the "Sea of Galilee" (5:1) is the "Lake of Gennesaret" (see introductory map). The name "Gennesaret" was taken from the name of the large plain that lies along the northwest shore of the lake. This time, instead of

demons (4:34), a disciple acknowledged Jesus as Lord (5:8). It was God's power that enabled Jesus to catch people for his kingdom—a power that would be more fully revealed in Acts 2.

Jesus also used his power as a testimony to the leaders of Israel by healing a leper (Luke 5:12-16). Leprosy is a skin disease, certain forms of which are described in Leviticus 13. Lepers were regarded as "unclean" on the basis of Levitical law (Lev. 13:45-46). The words "as a testimony to them" (Luke 5:14) are important. This miracle of cleansing was designed to alert the religious establishment in Jerusalem that there was someone up in Galilee exhibiting Messianic credentials.

5:17-26 POWER OVER SIN
Jesus used his healing of a paralytic to illustrate and demonstrate his power to forgive sins (5:17-26). In doing this, Jesus identified his miracles of physical healing as signs that pointed to his power to work the greater miracle of forgiving sins (5:24).

5:27-39 POWER OVER TRADITIONS
"Levi" (5:27) was another name for Matthew. Jesus demonstrated his power over the traditions of Judaism (5:27-39). He showed that spending time with tax collectors and sinners was not sinning, but a means of bringing salvation to those in need. He showed that following the traditions of fasting did not make one spiritually acceptable to God. In the following section, Jesus will show that it is more important to serve others than to fulfill the requirements of Sabbath observance. The problems of "sin" (5:17-32) and the keeping of the "Sabbath" (6:1-11) were rooted in the old Mosaic system—a system that would soon be replaced. The parable of new and old clothes and wineskins means that people should adjust their behavior to what fits a new situation, not try to continue on with old and inappropriate ways. The new situation here is the presence of Jesus the "groom" (5:34-35). While he was on the earth, fasting was inappropriate. When he left, fasting would resume (5:35). Jesus required flexibility as he began his new work on earth. Those who held to the old ways ended up rejecting the very God whom they thought they were honoring. They were the ones in the parable who would rather continue using the old wineskins (5:39).

6:1-11 POWER OVER THE SABBATH
For "what King David did" (6:3), see 1 Samuel 21:1-6. Jesus was demonstrating that it was more important to fulfill the higher commands to bring love and justice by serving people's needs than to follow the traditions of men. To claim to be Lord over the Sabbath (6:5) was the same as claiming to be equal with the Creator of the Sabbath (Gen. 2:1-3).

6:12–7:50 Power and God's Purposes: Rejection and Acceptance
6:12-49 MINISTRY OF THE DISCIPLES IN LIGHT OF REJECTION
6:12-19 Prayer before Choosing the Disciples
The link to the historical context is in 6:11-12. In direct response to his trouble with the Jewish leaders resulting from the Sabbath conflict (6:1-11), Jesus began to build his community of apostles (6:13). Luke emphasized the importance of prayer in all that Jesus did, and choosing the twelve apostles was no exception (6:12).

6:20-49 Preparation for Kingdom Entrance
Jesus' sermon has the following structure: blessings and curses (6:20-26); the obligation to love (6:27-36); refraining from criticism (6:27-45); the importance of obedience (6:46-49). Luke's "Beatitudes" is quite similar to the "Sermon on the Mount" recorded by Matthew (Matt. 5–7). However, they are located at different times in Jesus' life chronologically, and Matthew's account was considerably longer than Luke's (107 verses in contrast to 30). It is probable that Jesus repeated the essential message of the Sermon on the Mount several times during his ministry. Luke recorded a similar sermon but with more brevity and slightly different language and phraseology. Luke's use of the phrase "Kingdom of God" (Luke 6:20) and Matthew's "kingdom of heaven" are virtually equivalent. "Heaven" was a respectful, Jewish form of reference to God.

7:1-50 PITFALLS IN INTERPRETING JESUS' POWER
7:1-10 The Centurion's Faith
In 7:1-17 the context is given for John's questions in 7:18-23. This miracle shows Jesus' ability to heal even though he was far away. This long-distance power for good would be especially important after Jesus ascended into heaven. Although far away, his power for good would still be available everywhere. The "Roman officer" (7:2), or "centurion," was an officer in the Roman army who was in charge of approximately one hundred men (a century). They were responsible for training their men, leading them into battle, keeping track of military equipment, posting guards, and making inspections. Jesus said the centurion's faith was greater than any Israelite's he had found. This contrast between a Gentile centurion and the Jewish nation continues the theme of Jesus' special inclusion of Gentiles in his ministry and the pronounced rejection of Jesus by his own people (see 4:14-30).

7:11-17 A Widow's Son
"Nain" was located in the Valley of Jezreel at the foot of the Hill of Moreh, about six miles south of Nazareth (see introductory map). The widow was an example of the troubled and needy kind of person to whom Jesus came to minister (4:18). Luke 7:15 describes one of three resurrection

miracles of Jesus (cf. Mark 5:41; John 11:44). It was this kind of miracle, contrasted by Jesus' own humility, that would give John the Baptist doubts about who Jesus was (Luke 7:18-19).

7:18-35 Expectations of the Messiah
John the Baptist doubted Jesus' identity (7:18-19). For "everything Jesus was doing" (7:18) that caused John to doubt if Jesus was the Messiah, see 4:14, 37, 44; 5:14-15; 6:17; 7:1-17. The Old Testament had predicted that the Messiah would bring relief from physical suffering even as Jesus was doing (7:22; cf. Isa. 35:5-6). Old Testament prophecy also looked forward to the poor having the Good News preached to them (Isa. 61:1). Jesus' answer to John's disciples essentially quoted Isaiah 66:1 (cf. Luke 4:18). Even the disciples needed to watch their preconceptions of what Jesus the Messiah would do, otherwise they might stumble or be "offended" (7:23).

In his discussion of John the Baptist (7:24-35), Jesus showed how the Jewish leaders had rejected John and would reject Jesus himself because John and Jesus did not fit with their preconceived ideas of what they should be like. Jesus clearly linked John the Baptist to the prophecy of Malachi 3:1 (Luke 7:27; cf. Matt. 17:10-13). That was how his baptisms were to be understood. However, for both Jesus and John, their association with sinners brought rejection.

7:36-50 Two Examples of Forgiveness
This event and its subsequent parable show how those who receive forgiveness for great sins will be likely to return great love to the person who forgave them. Jesus was talking about the relationship between loving him and appreciating his forgiveness. Those who see the awfulness of their sin along with the greatness of God's forgiveness will have the greatest love for Jesus. This incident must not be confused with the similar one involving Mary, sister to Martha and Lazarus, which took place during the last week of Jesus' life (cf. Matt. 26:6-31).

8:1-56 Power and the Soils
8:1-3 LINKING PHRASE: SUPPORT OF JESUS' MINISTRY
Note the linking phrases in the progression of his ministry (4:14-15, 44; 8:1-3). These women were ministering to Jesus and the disciples. Mary "Magdalene" (8:2) was from the village of Magdala located in the Plain of Gennesaret north of Tiberias. Joanna's husband, "Chuza" (8:3), was identified as "Herod's business manager." The reference was to Herod Antipas. Chuza had some position of rank as an administrator in Herod's government.

8:4-21 THE REASONS FOR PITFALLS IN INTERPRETING JESUS' POWER
For a note on parables, see Matthew 13:3. The parable of the sower and the soils dealt with the reception of

God's word. Luke added some clarifying details in 8:15 concerning a good heart. Jesus was interested in how people listened to the word of God.

8:22-56 MIRACLES
The function of these miracles was to show faith and its opposition. The audience's response was given at the end of each of the miracles.

8:22-25 Calming the Storm
The "lake" (8:22) was the Sea of Galilee, a body of water situated 680 feet below sea level and noted for its sudden storms that occur when the Mediterranean winds rush through the narrow valleys of Galilee onto the lakeshore. This miracle revealed Jesus' unbelievable power to his disciples. Their reaction was one of fear and amazement (8:25).

8:26-39 Healing a Demoniac
The disciples' question about Jesus, "Who is this man?" (8:25), was answered by the demon in 8:28. A "legion" (8:30) in the Roman army consisted of 5,300 men. The "Bottomless Pit" (8:31) was apparently a reference to a place of imprisonment for wicked spirits destined for the lake of fire (cf. Matt. 25:41; Jude 1:6; Rev. 20:3). The people who saw this miracle reacted with great fear (Luke 8:35).

8:40-56 Healing a Sick Woman and Jairus's Daughter Raised
In section 8:40-56, Luke looked at faith in two different ways. First, the faith of a woman was hidden because of her fear (8:50). Second, the faith of a man, shown by his inviting Jesus to come heal his daughter, was openly laughed at (8:53). Faith and fear are in opposition to each other. For in the person of faith, there is no reason for fear. The "fringe" (8:44) of Jesus' cloak was probably a reference to one of the four blue tassels that were worn by strict Jews according to Levitical law (Num. 15:38-40). Jesus said that Jairus's daughter was "asleep" (Luke 8:52), knowing that she would be raised from death. "Asleep" is a common euphemism for death. This term carries with it the assumption that people can look forward to being resurrected after they die (1 Thess. 4:13).

9:1-9 Ministry in a Hostile World
Jesus shared his power with his twelve disciples. He shared that authority even more broadly when he sent the Spirit to all his disciples (Acts 2). Herod Antipas (9:7) was the ruler of Galilee and Perea (4 B.C.–A.D. 39). He was also called "Herod the tetrarch." The Greek for "tetrarch" means "ruler of a fourth part."

9:10-50 The Crucial Interpretation of Jesus' Ministry: Passion
9:10-17 FIVE THOUSAND FED
"Bethsaida" (9:10) was located on the northeast shore of the Sea of Galilee, just east of the Jordan

River's entrance (see introductory map). See the note on Mark 6:45 for more on this miracle.

9:18-27 CONFESSION AT CAESAREA PHILIPPI

The feeding at Bethsaida was linked to the question, "Who do the people say I am?" (9:18) by the use of "people" in 9:16 and 9:18. The central issue was not bread, but understanding the identity of Jesus as the Son of God. Again, only Luke recorded that Jesus prayed just before he revealed his destiny to die on the cross (9:18). Luke 9:21-22 clearly reveals why his messianic identity had to be kept secret. Jesus had the goal of the cross and ascension before him, not great public recognition. He would leave the worldwide spread of his reputation up to his Spirit-empowered followers.

9:28-36 TRANSFIGURATION

Images from Israel's exodus from Egypt are prominent in the events surrounding the transfiguration. Moses and Elijah were talking with Jesus about his own exodus (departure) from Jerusalem. That happened at his ascension (24:51; Acts 1:9). The "mountain" (9:28) probably referred to 9,200 foot-high Mount Hermon (see note on Matt. 17:1). The "three shrines" (9:33) apparently were intended by Peter for the observance of the Festival of Shelters. This feast was to be observed in the messianic kingdom (cf. Zech. 14:16), which Peter anticipated would come soon.

9:37-43 A DEMON-POSSESSED BOY HEALED

For the reason the disciples were unable to drive out this demon (9:40), see Mark 9:29.

9:43-45 PASSION PREDICTION

Although the crowds marvelled at his miracles, Jesus wanted his disciples to grasp the fact of his upcoming death. The disciples, expecting Jesus to usher in his kingdom immediately with power and glory, had difficulty accepting Jesus' passion predictions. Jesus' time for bearing the cross was fast approaching; this was not a time to receive permanent praise. There was only one thing on Jesus' mind regarding his purpose on earth: the cross and the empty place waiting at the Father's right hand.

9:46-50 SECULAR PRIDE

The disciples argued within their ranks and denied acceptance to other followers of Jesus. Their pride revealed that they still did not understand the nature of the kingdom Jesus promised. They were still seeking power and riches. This attitude was obvious in their inability to understand Jesus' predictions of his upcoming suffering and death. They still had to learn to accept Jesus' and later, their own, bearing of the cross. They still had to learn that "Whoever is the least among you is the greatest" (9:48).

9:51–19:27 TOWARD THE GOAL: DEBATES AND INSTRUCTION

Overview: This section of the Gospel has long been a problem for biblical scholars. Luke specifically indicated that Jesus was traveling to Jerusalem (Luke 9:51, 53; 13:22, 33; 17:11; 18:31; 19:11, 28). The difficulty is in trying to trace the course of this journey. The vast majority of scholars see no literal journey in Luke's account, believing that the author arranged miscellaneous material into a "journey motif" to provide a place to record researched material Luke wanted to preserve but did not know its original historical or geographical context.

Another possibility, however, is to suggest that Luke's three main geographical notices (9:51; 13:22; 17:11) correspond with Jesus' three journeys to Jerusalem (recorded by John) that took place in the last months of Jesus' ministry (John 7:2, 10; 10:22; 12:1). Several passages show Jesus on the move (Luke 9:57; 10:1, 17, 38; 11:1; 13:10; 14:1, 25). Other passages focus on Jesus' destination (9:51; 13:22, 33; 17:11; 18:35; 19:1, 11). In light of the debate on the issue, it should be pointed out that it is not essential to the interpretation of this material to know the precise geographical setting in which it was originally given.

The ascension was Jesus' goal in going to Jerusalem (9:51). His death and resurrection were subordinate to the primary goal: Jesus' exaltation to the right hand of the Father and the subsequent pouring out of the Holy Spirit to empower the ongoing proclamation of his gospel. The focus of this long section was not on suffering and rejection at Jerusalem, but on discipleship in the shadow of the cross. Suffering is presented as an opportunity for full consecration and for following Jesus at all points of life. This section is in the form of a travel narrative to show the conflicts and lessons to be learned while the disciples walked with Jesus in this life. It recounts instruction in and opposition to the gospel proclamation.

The section divides into three cycles: (1) resolution to depart (9:51–13:21); (2) lessons on faith, conflict in the kingdom (13:22–17:10); and (3) lessons on perseverance (17:11–19:27). The key subjects covered are faithfulness, courage, service, the cost of discipleship, humility, riches, and stewardship. There is also a stress on how the "self" and the world's goods can be hindrances to devoted discipleship (9:23; 10:4; 12:15; 14:27; 16:14, 19; 17:27; 18:23; 19:2). This section emphasizes discipleship in the shadow of the cross.

9:51–13:21 Preparation for Departure

9:51-56 REBUFF AND REBUKE

Jesus focused on his ascension. He did not speak here of his death or resurrection. The Samaritans (9:52) were descendants from the idolatrous foreigners brought into the northern kingdom after the fall of Samaria in 722 B.C. and some of the Jews who had remained there (cf. 2 Kings 17). Although claiming adherence to the Torah, they were regarded by the Jews as religiously and ethnically impure. This section shows the character and attitude of a witness and how one should respond to rejection. One should continue to offer salvation and leave judgment for later (cf. Luke 6:35). Pride and exclusivism were behind the disciples' question in 9:54. The disciples were looking for a repeat of the miraculous judgment recorded in 2 Kings 1:10-12.

9:57–10:24 THE SEVENTY ARE INSTRUCTED: WITNESS AND REJECTION

Halfhearted discipleship is condemned (Luke 9:57-62). For a discussion of the term "Son of Man" (9:58), see note on Matthew 8:20 and the Guiding Concepts for Mark. The meaning of Luke 9:60 is "Allow the spiritually dead to bury those who are physically dead." Jesus was emphasizing the demands, priorities, and importance of God's kingdom program.

In 10:1-24 Jesus extended his ministry through seventy-two men (10:1, 17). Only Luke recorded this mission of the seventy-two. It was similar to the mission of the twelve recorded in Matthew 10:1–11:1. Note the definition of true joy (Luke 10:20). That joy is elaborated in 10:21-24. "Falling from heaven" (10:18) was a phrase that reflected a loss of power and authority (cf. Isa. 14:12-15). Satan's counterfeit kingdom was subject to a major setback as a result of the disciples' ministry.

10:25-37 THE GOOD SAMARITAN

The parable of the Good Samaritan illustrated the depth of God's love, while also calling everyone to show compassion in the same way. The "expert in religious law" (10:25) was one of the scribes, who spent their time studying and copying the Jewish law. It was a dishonest disciple who asked, "Who is my neighbor?" (10:29). New Testament or Herodian Jericho (10:30) was located in the Jordan Valley just north of the Dead Sea about 1,300 feet below sea level. The route through the Wadi Qilt is rocky and rugged with many places for robbers to hide in wait of travelers. For "Samaritan" (10:33), see the note on 9:52. The Samaritan was the least expected traveler to assist the injured Jew. The "pieces of silver" (10:35) were Roman and worth about a day's wage. Jesus showed that a neighbor is anyone who is in need (10:37). The point of the parable of the Good Samaritan (Luke 10:25-36) was made in 10:37. All are called to show compassion to those in need.

10:38-42 LISTENING TO THE WORD

In this account about Mary and Martha, the disciples' and Martha's priorities were examined and corrected. Martha questioned Jesus' care for her in

10:40 and commanded him to tell Mary to help with the chores. But Jesus cut through the "details" (10:41) pressing in on Martha and focused on one thing. Jesus showed his care for Martha by helping her see what was truly important and of eternal value. Rather than commanding Mary to get busy, Jesus instead emphasized the better choice Mary had made. Seeking to be with Jesus and listening to him was of the highest priority. The "village" (10:38) was Bethany, located about half a mile from Jerusalem on the east side of the Mount of Olives (see introductory map).

11:1-13 ON PRAYER: PERSISTENCE

Luke placed this discourse on prayer directly after his account of Mary insisting on staying at the feet of Jesus (10:39-42). Thematically these two events are related. Jesus was making it clear that it was important to be persistent in prayer. In the contrast made between earthly and heavenly fathers (11:13), the gift promised by God was the Holy Spirit. The Holy Spirit is the only crucial gift needed by believers in this age.

11:14–13:21 DEBATES WITH LEADERS: HYPOCRITES

11:14-28 Obedience to the Stronger Man
The section of 11:14-28 encourages obedience to the one who is "stronger" (11:21-22), Jesus the Messiah. Notice the people who are truly blessed: "all who hear the word of God and put it into practice" (Luke 11:27-28).

11:29-36 The Sign of Jonah
For a discussion of the sign of Jonah, see comments on Matthew 12:22-45. Without faith, many simply sought signs and miracles with unclear eyes (11:29-36).

11:37-54 Six Woes for the Jewish Leaders
The unclean leaders were condemned for their hypocrisy (11:37-54). It was customary in the biblical period to recline on cushions around a low table when eating (Luke 11:37). Contact with a dead body would bring ceremonial defilement upon a Jew (11:44; cf. Num. 19:16). To avoid this, tombs were usually marked with whitewash (cf. Matt. 23:27). Unmarked tombs would result in contamination. For the death of Zechariah (11:51), see the discussion on Matthew 23:35. Jesus' strong words against the Jewish leaders led them to plot his death (11:53-54). As he turned to address the crowd (Luke 12), they waited for him to say something they could use against him.

12:1-12 Courage during Attack
The word "meanwhile" (Luke 12:1) showed that while Jesus was speaking to the Jewish leaders (Luke 11), a crowd had gathered. Jesus then turned and addressed the crowd. The setting was similar to that of the sermon on the plain (6:19). "Yeast" (12:1;

"leaven," NASB and KJV) is known for its ability to permeate bread dough and work great changes in it. Just as yeast permeates bread dough, the disciples were urged to beware of the hypocrisy of the Pharisees, which was having a similar influence on the nation of Israel. The Pharisees were teaching falsehoods about Jesus to maintain their own security in Jewish society. For "blasphemies against the Holy Spirit" (12:10), see Matthew 12:31.

12:13–13:9 Serving with an End-Time Life Perspective
Jesus encouraged his followers to get their hearts in the correct place (Luke 12:13-34) in view of the fast approaching end times. He called his listeners to center their energy and service on God. When a man asked Jesus to tell his brother to share an inheritance (12:13-15), Jesus refused to arbitrate the matter. Jesus apparently recognized the man's selfishness and lack of concern for the things of God (cf. 12:16-21). To impress upon this man the importance of reorienting his values, Jesus told the parable of the rich fool (12:16-20). For treasures to last, they had to be eternal treasures gained in service of God, not self (12:21-34).

Jesus called his followers to serve in readiness (12:35-48). He emphasized the importance of being prepared—watchful and ready—for his second coming (12:40). Peter questioned Jesus (12:41) as to whether the thoughts of 12:40 applied to the disciples or to everyone. The stringent demands were for all who desired to follow Jesus. Jesus was setting the tone for all who await his return in the present age. The temptations of the long-term absence (12:45) of Jesus could cause some to forget their master's return and thus result in their destruction. Jesus emphasized that his followers were not only to be watchful, but also caring for the Master's own (12:42, 45).

Serving the Messiah in this age would include undergoing hostility (12:49-53). The "fire" (12:49) referred to the judgment on Satan and his domain that would commence at the cross (John 12:31). Jesus' "baptism" (Luke 12:50) referred to his sacrificial death on the cross (cf. Mark 10:38-39).

Despite all the harsh warnings of judgment, Jesus would allow time for repentance (Luke 12:54–13:9). The theme of this section is the necessity for repentance in a limited time. The incident involving Pilate (13:1) is not known from any other source, but it fits well with what is known of Pilate's character. This brutal act against the Galileans undoubtedly contributed to the enmity between Pilate and Herod Antipas (cf. 23:12). In 13:2-3 Jesus pointed out that this incident did not fall on the Galileans because they were exceptionally sinful. God's judgment would fall upon all who failed to repent, not just the exceedingly sinful. The "Tower of Siloam" (13:4) must have been located in the vicinity of the pool of "Siloam" (cf. John 9:11) just south of Jerusalem near the junction of the Kidron and Tyropoean valleys.

13:10-21 Establishment of and Entrance into the Kingdom
On the Sabbath, Jesus healed a daughter of Abraham (a Jewess) who had been crippled by a spirit for many years (Luke 13:16). The Abrahamic promises found fulfillment in this woman's life, not in spite of, but especially, on the Sabbath. Therefore, 13:18-21 should be read in that light. What better day than the Sabbath to give rest to this woman who had probably not enjoyed a truly restful day for eighteen years. The "mustard seed" (13:19) was the smallest of the garden seeds. This image was used frequently in Jewish rabbinic literature to represent something small. The function of "yeast" (13:21; "leaven," NASB and KJV) was to cause dough to rise. A little yeast is known to permeate and transform a whole lump of bread dough.

13:22–17:10 On the Journey: Faith during Conflict
13:22-35 INVITATION AND LAMENT OVER JERUSALEM
Jesus stressed the need for obedience (13:27) and not just acquaintance (13:26) when it came to salvation (13:23). Jesus called his followers to travel a narrow and difficult road. After receiving death threats from Herod, Jesus lamented over Jerusalem and again predicted his passion (13:31-35). This "Herod" (13:31) was Herod Antipas who had murdered John the Baptist (cf. Matt. 14:1-12). Herod was likened to a "fox" (Luke 13:32), a creature that lacks real power and dignity but accomplishes evil by cunning schemes. The lament of 13:34-35 was also recorded by Matthew after Jesus' royal entry into Jerusalem (Matt. 23:37-39). Jesus' prediction in Luke 13:35 anticipated the A.D. 70 destruction of Jerusalem by the Romans. It also looks forward to the Jews' recognition of Jesus' Messiahship at his second coming (cf. Zech. 12:10–13:1).

14:1-35 THE NATURE AND COST OF DISCIPLESHIP
14:1-11 Humility
Dropsy is a disease where the person suffers from swollen "arms and legs" (14:2) due to the retention of excessive fluids in body tissues. Jesus noticed how the Jewish leaders lived in contrast to the way of humility that he exemplified (14:7) and told a parable to illustrate their folly (14:8-10). The truth that the exalted will be humbled and the humble will be exalted (14:11) was exemplified by Jesus' own humiliation and then exaltation to the right hand of God. Jesus' healing of the man with dropsy was his seventh and last Sabbath healing. Jesus made it clear that humility (14:11), not

self-exaltation, was the passport to promotion in the kingdom of God.

14:12-14 Generosity

Jesus called his followers to give without any hope of return. This continued the theme of selfless discipleship already touched upon in his call to humility. The "resurrection of the godly" (14:14) promised to the generous was distinguished from the resurrection of the wicked (cf. John 5:29; Rev. 20:11-15).

14:15-35 Qualified Discipleship

Jesus continued his comments on the selflessness of the true disciple with a parable about a great wedding banquet (14:15-24). Many refused to come because of their worldly concerns. What was the purpose of Jesus' statement in 14:24? He desired to make it clear that only those willing to give up everything to enter the kingdom would find a place at God's table. Relate the discussion of the banquet to Isaiah 61:1. After the parable, Jesus continued his call to count the cost of following him (Luke 14:25-35). Following Jesus had to have priority over all other relationships (14:26). The words "more than" (14:26) expressed a disciple's turning from others in preference for God's kingdom when called to choose between family loyalty and discipleship.

15:1-32 THREE PARABLES OF THINGS LOST BUT FOUND AGAIN

The three parables of Luke 15 must be understood in the context or life setting given in 15:1-2. Jesus was showing the "sinners" that salvation was available to even them (15:7, 10, 32), while also answering the complaints of the Pharisees about Jesus spending time with sinners (15:2). Note the ending statements for each of the parables (15:7, 10, 32). Jesus was giving hope to the "sinners," while also calling the "righteous" Pharisees to rejoice with the hosts of heaven over the fact that someone who had been lost was found.

The three parables of Luke 15 (the lost sheep, the lost coin, and the lost son) were directed to the Pharisees, who did not share God's loving attitude toward sinners. True to their name (Pharisee means "separate one"), they believed in separation from sinners because God obviously hated such people. The parables were designed to correct the error of the Pharisees, showing how God loves sinners and takes delight when a lost sinner is restored. Readers of Luke's Gospel are forced to ask, "Where do we line up in our attitude toward sinners? Do we condemn them as did the Pharisees, or do we love them as God does?"

The "coin" (15:8) that had been lost was probably part of the woman's dowry and had sentimental value in addition to monetary worth. Luke 15:11-32 is often called the parable of the Prodigal

Son. "Prodigal" means "addicted to wasteful expenditure." The story reveals the heart of the father, representative of God, watching, loving, and rejoicing at the return of his lost son. The angry son who had remained at home (15:28-32) was representative of the "righteous" Pharisees.

16:1–17:10 DISCIPLESHIP: FAITH AND STEWARDSHIP

16:1-13 Men's Love for the Father Is Contrasted with Riches

Jesus used the parable of the shrewd steward (16:1-8) to make a comparison between the handling of earthly and spiritual affairs. These verses are closely linked with the three parables in Luke 15. Luke 15 concerned Jesus' response to the Pharisees' criticism of his welcoming sinners (15:1). God's love for sinners caused him to seek them out as the three parables in Luke 15 demonstrate. In Luke 16 Jesus brings his lesson home to the Pharisees. The parable concerns a servant who does everything he can to smooth his way with potential masters. Jesus encouraged his listeners to work just as hard to keep the way smooth with their heavenly Master. But because of the Pharisees' love for money (16:13-14), they were, in reality, the same as the sinners they condemned in 15:2. But the Pharisees, like everyone else, were sought after by the loving Father and would also have to conform to all of God's unchangeable law (16:16). The master commended the steward, not for his dishonesty, but for his wise foresight in preparing for the future (16:8). Similarly, the believer is to make wise use of material resources so that they will bring eternal benefit and reward. Jesus also warned his listeners that they needed to recognize the danger of money becoming the master and God taking second place (16:13). The transition from 16:13 to 16:14 shows that the following section also concerns the use of money.

16:14-18 Jesus Rebukes the Pharisees As Manipulators of God's Law

The Pharisees' love of money caused further animosity between them and Jesus (note the link between 16:13 and 16:14). The "smallest point" (16:17) was a reference to the very small mark that distinguishes the Hebrew letter *dalet* from the letter *resh*. Jesus was saying that he did not come to take away the law; he came to give the law new life. Jesus' teaching on divorce was presented in Matthew 5:32; 19:1-12; and Mark 10:1-12 (see the notes there). Since marriage can be terminated only by death (1 Cor. 7:39), Jesus taught that remarriage after divorce constitutes adultery (16:18).

16:19-31 The Rich Man and Lazarus

What was the point of the story about Lazarus and the rich man? Abraham appeared a number of times in this story (16:22, 23, 24, 25, 27, 29, 30, 31). There is debate about whether this was a parable or an actual historical incident. It was probably a parable intended to correct the Pharisees (16:14), who were lovers of money. Being rich was not necessarily a sign of God's blessing—it could signal a faithless heart bound for hell. "To be with Abraham" (16:22; "Abraham's bosom," NASB and KJV) was a figurative reference to "paradise" or the presence of God (cf. Luke 23:43; 2 Cor. 12:4). Like the Hebrew *sheol* in the Old Testament, "hell" (or "place of the dead," Luke 16:23) refers to the abode of the departed dead. "Hades" (Greek for "hell") was never used in the New Testament as the place of the righteous. Rather, it was used like the Greek term *Gehenna* for a place of flames and conscious torment (16:24, 28). Care should be taken to avoid building a detailed theology of the afterlife based solely on this parable.

17:1-10 Learning to Serve and Avoiding the Leaders' Hardness
A "millstone" (17:2) was a circular stone used for grinding grain into flour. The disciples realized that in order to receive powerful forgiveness (17:4), they needed a powerful faith (17:5). Unlimited forgiveness was the standard for those who had been forgiven much. The disciple's proper self-image was to be a servant (17:10)—one who is there to serve, not be served (17:5-10). The obligation of a slave was never discharged, neither was he to expect any commendation. Similarly, even the Christian's best and most selfless service would not place God under any obligation.

17:11–19:27 On the Journey: Perseverance

17:11-19 THE PROPER FOCUS OF GLORY: TO RETURN TO GIVE PRAISE
The words "between Galilee and Samaria" (17:11) apparently referred to the Valley of Jezreel in which the official border between the regions was situated. It was necessary to present themselves before the priests to demonstrate that they had been healed and to offer the sacrifice of purification (17:14; cf. Lev. 14:1-32).

17:20-37 THE SON OF MAN'S COMING
At the request of his followers, Jesus described the coming of God's kingdom. Jesus confirmed that his return would be like that of a thief in the night (Luke 17:20-21, 30-31; cf. 12:39). He desired to make it clear that the kingdom would catch everyone off guard, warning his followers to be continually faithful. Jesus, the King, was offering his kingdom to those who would respond and believe (17:21). In a real sense the kingdom was present in the person of Jesus Christ ("among you"). In "Noah's day" (17:26-27) people were going about

their everyday tasks and not heeding God's warning. They were unprepared for judgment and were destroyed. So shall it be before the second coming of Jesus. The background for the terse warning given in 17:32 is found in Genesis 19:26. Many manuscripts omit Luke 17:36 although it appears with certainty in Matthew 24:40. The "vultures" (Luke 17:37) will feed on the bodies of the slain at the second coming (Rev. 19:17-18).

18:1-8 THE DISCIPLES' PREPARATION
In Jesus' parable of the persistent widow, the judge had the responsibility of settling disputes and avenging wrongs, but he cared little for those who made appeals before him (Luke 18:2). The term "quickly" (18:8) does not necessarily mean "immediately," but "in due time," according to God's economy and timing. Notice the question in 18:8. The Son of Man will come looking for faith and wonders whether or not he will find any. He will judge the faithless (17:37) and reward the faithful.

18:9-14 HUMILITY IN PRAYER AND IN THE KINGDOM
The context for the parable of the Pharisee and the tax collector is set up in 18:9 and rounded out in 18:14. Jesus was speaking to some Jews who thought themselves beyond reproach. The ancient Israelites fasted on the Day of Atonement (18:12; cf. Lev. 16:29-34). Other fasts were added by Jewish tradition (cf. Zech. 8:19). The Pharisees had advanced this practice to excess (cf. Matt. 6:16-18). Regarding their "tithes," see Deuteronomy 14:22-23 and comments there. The tax collector requested that God's wrath against his sin be satisfied and that he be extended mercy. Jesus Christ, "the sacrifice for our sins" (1 John 2:2), would soon become the answer to his prayer.

18:15-17 JESUS AND THE LITTLE CHILDREN
Receiving the kingdom like a little child contrasts with the arrogance and pride in the surrounding acts of the indignant disciples (18:15), the Pharisee (18:11-12), and the religious leader (18:22-23). Jesus' call to be like children was not a call to be ignorant or naive. It was a call to believers to be humble, that is, willing to see themselves as God sees them and accepting that perspective (like the tax collector in 18:13) and then moving on in obedience to do what he wants (like the disciples in 18:28).

18:18-30 FALSE AND TRUE RICHES WITH REGARD TO ENTERING THE KINGDOM
A rich young man came seeking eternal life. Jesus pointed out the significance of his use of the word "good" (18:19). In essence Jesus was saying, "Why do you call me 'good' if you do not recognize my deity?" The rich man's problem was that he would not obey Jesus' final command (18:22). His riches were only the surface problem; the real problem lay

in the love he had for his wealth. For the word "needle" (18:25) Luke the physician used the Greek term for "surgeon's needle."

18:31-43 THE BLIND MAN HEALED

In recounting the healing of the blind man, Luke also emphasized the spiritual blindness of Jesus' disciples (18:31-34). They continually failed to accept Jesus' predictions of his upcoming death (18:34) and other teachings as well. Many of Jesus' teachings were understood only after he sent the Holy Spirit (18:34; cf. John 16:12-15). Matthew 20:29-34 indicates that the miracle took place as they were leaving Jericho. The account in Luke says it took place as they approached the town (Luke 18:35). Apparently the miracle took place as they were leaving Old Testament Jericho and were nearing New Testament or Herodian Jericho. The sites are about one-half mile apart. "Son of David" (18:39) was a Messianic term (2 Sam. 7:12-16; Isa. 9:7) showing a general awareness of Jesus' Messianic identity.

19:1-27 A TAX COLLECTOR CONVERTED: ZACCHAEUS

As a tax collector, Zacchaeus had enriched himself at the expense of his fellow Jews by charging excessive taxes (Luke 19:2). Collaborating with the Romans, he had worked himself up to a prominent position as "one of the most influential" (19:2). Zacchaeus proved the sincerity of his repentance by making restitution far beyond that which was required by the law (19:8; cf. Num. 5:6-7).

Note the relationship of the story of Zacchaeus (Luke 19:1-10) and the parables that begin in 19:11. They grow out of Zacchaeus's confession and proclamation that he would return what he had wrongly taken (19:8). For the significance of Zacchaeus's relationship to Abraham (19:9), compare 3:8 and 13:16. The parables of 19:11-27 clearly corrected the misconception that the kingdom was going to come immediately (19:11). Jesus asked that his followers continue in faithful service no matter how long it might take before Jesus returned. Jesus taught regarding the rejection of the king (representing himself) and announced judgment on the rejecting generation (19:11-27). "Ten pounds of silver" (19:13) was a measure of money worth one hundred *drachmas* or *denarii*. It amounted to about three months' wages.

19:28–24:53 THE GOAL ATTAINED: JERUSALEM

Overview: Luke's travel narrative (9:51–19:27) ends in 19:28 (see comments introducing this section). Next, Luke follows the sequence of events of the last week of Jesus' ministry recorded also by Matthew and Mark. This section was designed to show the innocence of Jesus before his judges. In line with Luke's purpose of presenting the exact truth so that the readers would find certainty in the faith, the book ends with proofs of Jesus' resurrection. Luke concludes his Gospel with the disciples in the temple praising God, waiting for the Spirit and power from on high.

19:28-48 The Entrance into Jerusalem

19:28-40 APPROACH IN PRAISE

Although Bethphage (Luke 19:29) has not been precisely located, Bethany was situated just east of the Mount of Olives about half a mile from Jerusalem. Bethphage was probably located in the immediate vicinity (see introductory map). The quotation in 19:38 was from Psalm 118:26, one of the Hallel psalms (Pss. 115–118) sung at Passover. The cry of the crowds (Luke 19:38) echoed the cry of the angels at Jesus' birth (2:14). An inspiring encouragement for witnessing in the face of rejection is found in 19:39-40.

19:41-44 JESUS' LAMENT OVER JERUSALEM

The "today" (19:42) of Jesus' royal entry into Jerusalem had been predicted by Daniel 9:25-27. The Messiah would be "killed" sixty-nine weeks (of years) after the issuing of the decree to rebuild Jerusalem. The "sixty-nine" weeks calculates to be 173,880 days (69 x 7 x 360). Jesus' royal entry took place on March 30, A.D. 33, exactly 173,880 days after the issuing of Artaxerxes' decree to rebuild Jerusalem, March 5, 444 B.C. (cf. Neh. 2:1-8). The "ramparts" (Luke 19:43) was a siege wall designed to prevent citizens from fleeing and to keep supplies from being smuggled in. The Romans built such a siege wall around Jerusalem when the city was attacked by Titus in A.D. 70.

19:45-48 THE FIRST CRISIS AND ITS RESULT

Upon entering the temple and seeing its courts being used as a marketplace, Jesus accused the traders of making the temple "a den of thieves" (19:45-46). The temple area (the Court of the Gentiles) had become a place for selling animals for sacrifice and changing Roman coin into the Jewish half-shekel (19:45). In demonstration of his Messianic authority, Jesus began to "drive out" those who were misusing the worship center. He quoted Isaiah 56:7 and Jeremiah 7:11 to support his actions (Luke 19:46). Luke took note of the multitude's acceptance of Jesus and how that had a restraining effect on the Jewish leaders who were bent on destroying him (19:47-48; cf. 20:19).

20:1–21:38 The Religious Opposition to Jesus

20:1-19 OPPOSITION REGARDING AUTHORITY

Jesus linked his authority to John's baptism (20:2-8) and to the "stone" predicted in Psalm 118:22 (Luke 20:17). Jesus told a parable about vineyard tenants to show how he would be rejected by the religious leaders just as they had rejected the prophets before him. The "vineyard" (20:9) imagery was familiar to first century Judeans. The same imagery was used by the prophet Isaiah to describe God's dealings with his people (Isa. 5:1-7). Jesus was to be the "cornerstone" (Luke 20:17; cf. Ps. 118:22) bringing unity and completion to God's redemptive program. Yet he was rejected by the Jewish religious leaders ("the builders").

20:20-26 OPPOSITION REGARDING POLITICAL RESPONSIBILITY
Behind the leaders' questions concerning the payment of taxes to Rome was a plot to accuse Jesus (Luke 20:20). Everyone would agree that a legitimate government has the right to tax its citizens (20:22). The question really concerned the legitimacy of the Roman government in Palestine. This was an attempt by the Jewish leaders to make Jesus say something against Rome and thus come into conflict with the authorities. On the other hand, if Jesus defended the legitimacy of Rome's authority, he would be taking a position unpopular with the Jewish people and would likely lose popular support. Jesus' answer amazingly avoided both pitfalls.

20:27-40 OPPOSITION REGARDING RESURRECTION
The question the Sadducees asked Jesus concerning levirate marriage and the resurrection of the dead was ironic because this Jewish sect rejected the idea of resurrection. Thus, they did not seek an honest answer but only desired to test Jesus. There is a note on levirate marriage (20:28) in Deuteronomy 25:5-10. The point Jesus made in Luke 20:35-36 was that marriage is an institution limited to life on this earth. There will be no marriage or procreation in heaven. The Sadducees rejected the idea of resurrection because they could not find the idea in Mosaic Law, the only Scriptures they accepted as authoritative. But Jesus pointed out evidence for the resurrection in Mosaic Law (20:37; cf. Exod. 3:6), leaving them speechless. He showed that the resurrection of the dead was implied by the fact that God continued to be the God of the patriarchs long after they had died.

20:41-44 OPPOSITION RESULTING FROM MISUNDERSTANDING THE MESSIAH
In Luke 20:42-43 Jesus quoted Psalm 110:1 to clarify his identity as the divine Son of God. He pointed out that the only way David could call his son (or descendant) "Lord" was if his son (that is, Jesus) was divine (Luke 20:44). Thus, David's statement prophetically looked forward to a descendant who would be divine, that is, Jesus. Psalm 110:1 was later used by Peter in Acts 2:34-35 to validate Jesus' deity and exaltation to the right hand of God.

20:45–21:4 PRIDE AND GENEROSITY
Luke set in contrast the deeds of the proud Pharisees (20:45-47) and the deed of a poor and humble widow (21:1-4) and showed the widow to be the one who was truly righteous. The value of giving was based on the amount of sacrifice and the attitude of heart, not on the amount given or the ostentation.

21:5-38 THE END OF THE TEMPLE AND THE AGE
Luke's version of the Olivet Discourse begins with some mention of the eschatological signs of the final tribulation (Luke 21:8-11) but then provides a parenthesis on Jerusalem's more immediate future—the Roman attack and destruction of the city in A.D. 70 (21:12-24). The sermon from 21:25 and following parallels Matthew's account describing the events of the Second Coming (21:25-28) and giving exhortations to watchfulness (21:29-38). The discourse is a straightforward encouragement to perseverance (21:19) and strength (21:36). The key elements are perseverance of witness in persecution (21:10-19) and exhortations to enable recognition of the returning Messiah (21:29-33) and readiness for that return (21:34-36). Apparently Jesus and the disciples were used to sleeping in the open air on the Mount of Olives (21:37).

22:1-38 The Passover
22:1-6 THE PLOTTERS UNIFY
According to Jewish law, Passover was observed on Nisan 14 and the Festival of Unleavened Bread followed, being observed on Nisan 15-21 (cf. Exod. 12:1-28; Lev. 23:5-6). The two feasts emphasized the removal of leaven or yeast, and the term "Unleavened Bread" was often applied to the whole season including Passover and Unleavened Bread (cf. Luke 22:7). The Jewish leaders, looking for a way of getting rid of Jesus, found Judas Iscariot willing to participate. The role of Satan was mentioned (22:3), reminding the reader that though Satan had failed to stop Jesus earlier (cf. 4:1-13), he had not stopped trying (cf. 4:13).

22:7-23 THE PASSOVER MEAL
A man carrying water would have been an unusual sight in the ancient world since this was normally a woman's job (22:10). The man may have been John Mark. It was probably in his mother's house that the disciples observed the Last Supper with Jesus (Acts 12:12). In the first century meals were taken around a low table where the guests reclined on cushions (Luke 22:14). The "bread" (22:19) was to serve as a memorial ("remembrance") of Jesus' sacrificial death on the cross. The "cup" (22:20) was to serve as a memorial to the shed blood of Jesus, the sacrifice that made the new covenant possible (cf. Jer. 31:31-34). The death of Jesus on the cross was scandalous and surprising. He clearly

emphasized that his death was in accord with what God had previously determined in the Old Testament Scriptures (Luke 22:22; cf. 24:44-47; and Acts 2:23; 4:28; 10:42; 17:31).

22:24-38 SERVANTS IN A NEW SERVICE
The section of Luke 22:24-38 can be subdivided further: greatness through service (22:24-30); preservation through failure (22:31-34); preparation for persecution (22:35-38). The term "friends of the people" (22:25; "benefactors," NIV) was often inscribed on coins along with the name of the ruling official. For most, it was a hollow and worthless title. The word "sift" (22:31) was an agricultural term that referred to the process of separating the kernels of grain from the chaff. The reference to the "sword" (22:36) was a bit confusing since Jesus apparently did not intend for his disciples to use force to deliver him (22:49-51; cf. Matt. 26:52). Perhaps Jesus used the term figuratively to speak of the perilous and difficult days ahead. The disciples apparently took him literally and produced two swords (Luke 22:38). Jesus' words "That's enough" (22:38) may simply mean "Enough of this talk" (see in that regard, 22:51).

22:39–23:25 Arrest and Trial
22:39-53 PRAYER AND ARREST IN THE GARDEN
Luke 22:43-44 are omitted in certain important manuscripts. However, their presence in many manuscripts as well as their citation by many church fathers proves their antiquity. The text does not say that Jesus sweated blood (22:44). Rather, Luke the physician observed that Jesus' perspiration was so profuse that it was "like" blood dripping from an open wound. The name of the servant of the high priest was Malchus (22:50; cf. John 18:10). At his arrest, Jesus noted with irony that the Jews had arrested him when no one could see them, though they had had numerous opportunities at the temple in broad daylight (22:53). This was because the religious leaders feared the general population who revered him (cf. 19:47-48), but Jesus also noted that coming in the darkness reflected on the religious leaders' character.

22:54-65 DENIALS AND BEATING
Matthew began his passion account with the beating of Jesus by the soldiers (Matt. 26:67). Luke's passion account started out with the denials of Peter and was followed by the beating. Luke's account tells the reader that Peter denied Jesus to his face (Luke 22:61). The place was the house of Caiaphas (22:54; cf. Matt. 26:57). The crowing of the rooster (Luke 22:61) signified the end of the third night watch, 12:00 to 3:00 A.M.

22:66–23:25 BEFORE PRIESTS AND KINGS
The "high council" (22:66) was a reference to the Sanhedrin, the highest court of the Jews. Jesus

made an undeniable affirmation of his deity (22:70). The listeners understood his claim and wanted to put him to death. Since the Sanhedrin had no authority to execute the death penalty, the case had to be brought before the Roman authorities (23:1). Pilate was the Roman prefect, or governor, of Judea (A.D. 26–36). The case the Jews made against Jesus concerning Jesus' opposition to Roman taxes (23:2) was a distortion of the truth (cf. 20:20-26). The "Herod" (23:7) mentioned was Herod Antipas (23:7) ruler of Galilee and Perea (4 B.C.–A.D. 39) who had murdered John the Baptist. He had no authority to decide the case against Jesus. The gesture was politically motivated and resulted in better relations between Pilate and Herod Antipas (23:12). The robe (23:11) signified for Pilate that Herod thought Jesus' claim to be king was a joke and not to be taken as a serious threat to the rule of Rome (23:13-15). Many manuscripts omitted 23:17. It may have been inserted to explain the basis for the release of Barabbas (23:18, 25). Luke made it plain that Jesus was innocent of any crime (23:14, 20, 22).

23:26-56 Crucifixion and Burial
Simon (23:26) was from Cyrene, the chief city of Cyrenaica in North Africa. The women were weeping for the wrong reason. The suffering of the Righteous One was only a foreshadowing of the awful persecution of the saints and the judgments of God that would happen in the future. Compare 23:30 with Hosea 10:8 and Revelation 6:16. The cryptic words of Luke 23:31 may mean "If they act so shamefully when the nation ('tree') is prospering ('green'), how will they act during times of difficulty ('dry')?" For the same imagery, see Ezekiel 20:47.

"The Skull" (Luke 23:33) is a translation of the Aramaic term "Golgotha" (cf. Matt. 27:33). "Sour wine" (Luke 23:36) was a common drink often used by laborers and soldiers. "Paradise" (23:43) was derived from the Persian word for a "king's garden." It was used here by Jesus to refer to heaven, the dwelling place of God. Again, Jesus' righteousness was stressed (23:41, 47). Jesus also framed his last words in the words of Psalm 31:5. All had happened according to the Scriptures. The "veil" (Luke 23:45) separated the Holy Place from the Most Holy Place. According to Josephus it was ninety feet high. Its tearing symbolized the opening up of the Most Holy Place, which symbolized God's very presence, to the saints of Jesus Christ (Heb. 10:19-20).

Joseph (Luke 23:50-51), a member of the Sanhedrin, was from Arimathea, a town of uncertain location. The term "day of preparation" (23:54) referred to Friday, the day of preparation for the Sabbath rest that began Friday at sunset. The commandment not to work on the Sabbath (23:56) is found in Exodus 20:10.

24:1-53 The Resurrection

24:1-12 AT THE TOMB

The reports of Jesus' resurrection were first met with disbelief (Luke 24:11). In 24:6-8 Luke reveals the reason for Jesus' passion predictions. They were to give assurance that his death was according to God's plan. That was the assurance Luke set out to give to his readers (1:4). It was customary in ancient Palestine to use a circular stone about one foot thick as the door for a tomb (24:2). It was rolled along a groove in the rock to seal the tomb.

24:13-35 ON THE ROAD

These verses are unique to Luke. One of the "two" (24:13) disciples was identified as Cleopas (24:18). The other, perhaps his wife, was not identified. If this Cleopas was the same person as mentioned in John 19:25, his wife was named Mary. "Emmaus" (24:13) was said to be "seven miles" (lit., "sixty stadia") from Jerusalem. The traditional site of 'Amwas is approximately twenty miles from Jerusalem. Perhaps a better location is el-Qubeibeh, situated just sixty-three stadia or seven miles north of Jerusalem (see introductory map). The site is marked by the ruins of a Crusader basilica and perhaps a Byzantine church. Jesus' appearance to Simon Peter (Luke 24:34) was also mentioned in 1 Corinthians 15:5. The point of this story was to show why people might not believe that Jesus had been raised from the dead—foolishness and slowness to believe the word of God (Luke 24:25).

24:36-53 IN JERUSALEM

Again, Jesus' appearance was designed to dispel all doubt that he had risen from the dead (24:38-39). The certainty Luke desired to build in his readers was rooted in understanding how the Old Testament spoke of the Messiah (24:44-47). Many Greek manuscripts do not contain 24:40. Jesus alluded to the common Jewish divisions of the Old Testament: the Law of Moses, the Prophets, and the Psalms, which were representative of the Writings. Luke ended his book where he began it—in the temple. This time the disciples were in the temple praising God and waiting for the power of the Spirit to come. "Just as my Father promised" (24:49) was a reference to the promise of the Holy Spirit, an event that was realized at Pentecost (cf. Acts 1:1-4; 2:33). "Bethany" (Luke 24:50) was located about half a mile from Jerusalem, just east of the Mount of Olives. Luke recorded the details of Jesus' ascension (24:50-53) in Acts 1:6-11 and the coming of the Holy Spirit in Acts 2:1-42.

JOHN

BASIC FACTS

HISTORICAL SETTING

The uncertainties in dating the book (see below) make a discussion of the precise historical setting difficult. The book's contents placed the earthly life of Jesus the Messiah into the context of his eternal preexistence. He was with the Father; he came to earth; and then he returned to the Father. Historically, this revelation spoke against criticisms that Jesus was just a mortal man or that he was just a man who was, for a time, empowered by God. John's desire to convince his readers to "believe" in Jesus' divine Messiahship was not only appropriate in John's day but is appropriate in any historical setting. He desired both believers and unbelievers to allow the signs that Jesus performed to reveal his eternal glory and create initial or deeper faith.

AUTHOR

Although the Gospel of John is anonymous, both internal and external evidence point to John the apostle, the son of Zebedee, as the author of the work. From internal evidence it is clear that the author was a Palestinian Jew, for he quoted the Old Testament (John 6:45; 13:18; 19:37), and had firsthand knowledge of Palestine's geography (1:44; 2:1; 5:2; 9:7; 11:18). The author was an eyewitness of the events he recorded (1:29, 35, 43; 2:6; 4:40, 43; 5:5; 12:1, 6, 12). John 21:20, 24 indicates that the author was the "disciple Jesus loved," the one who leaned on Jesus' breast at the Passover supper (cf. 13:23; 19:26; 20:2; 21:7). The author was one of the inner circle of Jesus' disciples. This group was comprised of Peter and the brothers James and John, the sons of Zebedee (13:23, 24; 20:2-10; 21:2, 7, 20). Since James was martyred not long after Jesus' ascension (Acts 12:1-5), and Peter appears as a different person from the beloved disciple (John 21:7), only John is left to be the beloved disciple and author of the Gospel.

External evidence from the time of the church fathers has confirmed the authorship by the apostle John. Irenaeus (A.D. 120–202) wrote, "Afterwards, John, the disciple of the Lord, who also had leaned upon his breast, did himself publish a gospel during his residence at Ephesus in Asia" (*Against Heresies*, 3.1.1). As for the reliability of Irenaeus, Eusebius said that his authority was Polycarp (A.D. 70–155/160) who had personally known John the apostle (*Historia Ecclesiastica*, 4.14). Theophilus of Antioch (A.D. 115–188), Clement of Alexandria (A.D. 190), Origen (c. A.D. 220), and Hippolytus (A.D. 170) all agree that John wrote this Gospel.

DATE

The discovery of the Rylands fragment of John's Gospel in Egypt (dated c. A.D. 135) requires that the date of John be sometime in the first century. Some scholars suggest that the Gospel was written around A.D. 85–90. They would argue that John's Gospel was written after the other Gospels as a supplement to them. But John's lack of reference to the fall of Jerusalem in A.D. 70 may indicate a date of writing some time before that event.

Some scholars conclude that the Gospel should be dated before A.D. 70. They feel that John wrote as if he had not seen Matthew, Mark, or Luke's Gospels. They also note that John referred to the followers of Jesus as "disciples" rather than "apostles" ("apostles" being a later designation). Perhaps the strongest argument for a date before A.D. 70 is in 5:2 where, in some translations, John wrote "there is . . . a pool" (KJV, NIV) not "there was a pool." This may indicate a composition before the fall of Jerusalem (A.D. 70). Later in 18:1 he wrote, "there was a garden" (KJV, NIV), probably referring to the King's Garden that was located just outside the city. These verb tenses would allow John's writing before or even

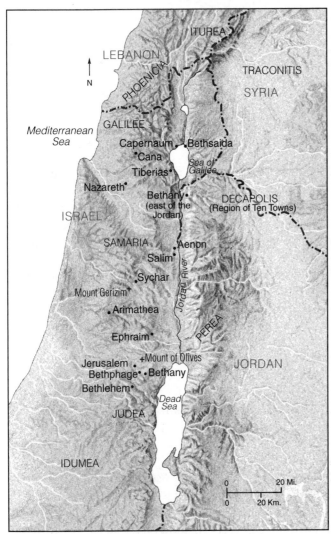

The broken lines (— - —) indicate modern boundaries.
Copyright © 1986, 1988 by Tyndale House Publishers, Inc.

during the time Jerusalem was under siege by the Romans, but before the city had actually been destroyed (c. A.D. 68–69). However, precise dating of the book is not necessary to appreciate its many contributions to the Christian's life of faith.

PURPOSE

The Gospel of John was designed to convince those who had not seen Jesus to believe in him (John 20:29-31). Believers were to read John's Gospel to bring about a deepening of their faith. Unbelievers were to read it so that they might come to believe in Jesus Christ. Both groups were addressed through John's arrangement of Jesus' signs, which progressively ascended in importance to the resurrection of Lazarus and then to Jesus' own resurrection. The reader was to receive the spiritual bread, drink, light, and life that Jesus offered.

GEOGRAPHY AND ITS IMPORTANCE

Although Jesus moved in the surrounding areas, John's major geographical focus was on Jerusalem. Jesus always returned to Jerusalem, specifically, to participate in various temple feasts. He returned from the Jordan and Cana of Galilee to the Feast of the Passover (John 2). His trip to the Jordan, Samaria, and Cana of Galilee ended with his return to another, unknown feast in Jerusalem (John 5). John even linked Jesus' feeding of the five thousand in the wilderness to the Passover celebration in Jerusalem (John 6:4-5). Jesus returned to Jerusalem for the Festival of Shelters (John 7) and Hanukkah (John 10). After raising Lazarus in Bethany (John 11), which was just over the Mount of Olives from Jerusalem, Jesus returned to Jerusalem for his final Passover (John 12). The geographical focus on Jerusalem and its feasts undergirds John's purpose to reveal that Jesus was the fulfillment of all the feasts and, especially, represented the perfect Passover Lamb of God. Around him alone, not the temple with its festivals, are believers to worship, celebrate, and find their redemption.

GUIDING CONCEPTS

JOHN'S COMMENTARY ON GENESIS 1

In his Gospel, John stressed the creative and powerful Word of God. Jesus himself was the Word (1:1). And when he spoke, his word was powerful to create and redeem. That pattern of creation by God's Word relates back to Genesis 1 and the creation of the world. John 1:1-13 takes up the themes of Genesis 1 and applies them to Jesus the Messiah. As the Word, Christ existed before the creation in close relationship to God and was himself God (John 1:1). He was the agent of creation (1:3). He was light in the darkness (1:4-5), and that light was symbolic of life itself (1:4). Jesus, the Life, was connected to God's Word, the Creator (1:4), and was given as the Mediator by which all men could have true life as children of God (1:12). As the Word created the world in the beginning, Jesus the Word came to recreate what had been broken by sin.

Throughout Scripture there is a relationship between wisdom and creation (1:3; cf. Prov. 8:22). Proverbs makes it clear that wisdom was at God's side at creation as a master workman (Prov. 8:22; cf. also Col. 1:16; 2:2-3). The first creation saw light separated from the darkness and brought both physical and spiritual life. The new creation account portrayed by John shows the light in the midst of darkness—a light not from the sun or stars, but from the presence of eternal life itself.

The "world" is presented in John 1:1-18 as all that is opposed to the "Word," Jesus the Messiah (1:10). In 3:16, the world that opposed Jesus is shown to be the very thing he came to save. For the Greek Gentiles, the Word represented the rational principle of the universe and the link between God and man. In Jewish usage, the Word was understood as the effective word of God and was sometimes used as a reverential substitute for his holy name. John 1 serves as a commentary on Genesis 1, but it also points toward a second creation by the Word by which the first creation would be redeemed.

Creation themes of "Word," "light," and "life" all find their fulfillment in the life of
Jesus the Messiah.

SIGNS AND BELIEF

John began and ended his Gospel by presenting events within the context of one-week
periods. John counted out some of the days that represent the first one-week period
(1:28, day one; 1:29, day two; 1:35, day three; 1:43, day four; 2:1, the seventh day, three
days after the day mentioned in 1:43). The seventh day contains the first of Jesus' seven
preresurrection signs or miracles—the creation of wine out of water. It is as if John
wanted his readers to recognize in the life and works of Jesus a reenacted seven-day
creation account (cf. Gen. 1); this time the new creation would be worked by Jesus the
Messiah as he made possible his Father's offer of eternal life. At the end of the Gospel
John detailed another week (12:1); one that would end with the resurrection of the
Light of Life (20:1).

Only John called Jesus' miracles "signs." He recounted seven signs that were
performed before Jesus' death and resurrection: (1) the turning of water into wine at
Cana (2:1-11); (2) the healing of the official's son (4:46-54); (3) the healing at the
Bethesda pool (5:1-15); (4) the feeding of the multitude (6:5-14); (5) the walk on
water (6:16-21); (6) the healing of the blind man (9:1-12); and (7) the raising of Lazarus (11:1-44). These signs formed the backbone of John's presentation of the person of
Jesus. They revealed Jesus' character as the Son of God and were designed to cause the
reader to believe in his glory (2:11, 23; 4:48; 11:47-48; 12:37; 20:30-31). A sign points
away from itself to something else. In the case of Jesus, the signs he performed pointed
to his glory, a glory that would be transferred from himself to those who believed in
him (17:20-22).

MISUNDERSTANDINGS IN JOHN

Throughout the book, John showed his readers how people misunderstood the words
and actions of Jesus. Jesus taught his audience by using illustrations from things they
understood in order to reveal things they did not understand. He used the ordinary
physical things of life to teach them about God and the eternal kingdom he promised.
He came as a man so that he might truly and clearly reveal the nature of God. The
misunderstandings of Jesus' listeners concerned (1) the identification of Jesus' body
with the temple of God (2:18-22); (2) the possibility of a second and spiritual birth
(3:3); (3) the nature of spiritual, living water (4:10); (4) the nature of a spiritual bread
of obedience to God (4:32); (5) the authority of Jesus (5:44-47); (6) the nature of the
true bread of life (6:30-36); and (7) the true origin of Jesus (7:25-29).

In all these misunderstandings there was movement from the physical to the spiritual. The misunderstandings took place when the people failed to move beyond a
merely physical understanding of Jesus' words to a spiritual understanding; from
seeing the outer meaning to discovering the inner one; from knowing Jesus, the man,
to knowing Jesus, the Son of God. The purpose of the signs and witness of Jesus was to
help those who saw and heard him to see beyond the physical miracles, like the turning of water into wine, to see that to which those signs pointed—the presence of the
creative Word of God to bring eternal life. These "misunderstandings" are related to the
theme of "incomprehension" examined in Mark (see the Guiding Concepts section for
the book of Mark).

BIBLE-WIDE CONCEPTS

THE WILDERNESS

John showed how Jesus reenacted and fulfilled several Old Testament events and concepts. Most of these came from the exodus and wilderness period of Israel's history. Jesus was presented as the true tabernacle (1:14); the true bronze snake (3:14); the true manna of God (6:49-50); the true rock of water (7:37-38); the true light of the cloud of glory (8:12); and the true Passover Lamb (1:29; 19:14). These links of Jesus to Israel's wilderness experience showed that the promises that had been made to Israel were fulfilled in him. On the one hand, the subtlety and pervasiveness of these themes from Israel's past mark John's Gospel as deeply Jewish in origin. On the other hand, his roots in the creation of the world (cf. John 1 and Gen. 1) mark John out as vastly universal in scope. And that is as it should be. From the beginning, God promised that all nations would be blessed, but that that blessing would come through the Jewish line of Abraham (Gen. 12:3).

BELIEF

Ever since the Garden of Eden humans have been responsible to believe what God tells them. Abraham believed God and acted upon his word (Gen. 15:6). Israel in the wilderness was given several tests of belief (cf. Deut. 8:1-3). Throughout the history of the Bible, belief was defined as trust that leads to obedience (Ps. 78:21-31). Behind the Hebrew verb for "believe" stood the ideas of stability, reliability, and faithfulness. Believers can believe in God because he is stable and faithful, but God also calls believers to be faithful and worthy of trust as well. The book of John was designed to enable belief (John 20:30-31). It was not just a tool for evangelism; it was also designed to strengthen the belief of those who already believed. For the one who already had eternal life, the Gospel of John would serve to increase the power and experience of life in Jesus Christ. The signs he presented were to convince his readers to believe and rely upon Jesus as the Son of God—the provider of eternal life.

NEEDS MET BY JOHN

John wrote to believers who were suffering persecution and conflict. Different groups within the early Christian church held faulty ideas about who Jesus was, and unbelievers from outside the church also persecuted the Christians. John provided comfort and faith-strengthening answers to questions about where Jesus came from, why he was rejected by most people while he was on earth, how he was with believers in Spirit though bodily absent, and where he would take believers in the future. The structure and content of John's Gospel show that his readers were asking the following questions.

- How is Jesus related to the beginnings of the world?
- What does Jesus have to say about the present sufferings of believers?
- Why does the world reject Jesus if he really is the Son of God?
- How is God's glory revealed on earth today?
- What does it really mean to have eternal life?
- What is the believer's relationship to Jesus and to God?
- What is Jesus' relationship to his Father in heaven?
- Where is Jesus going to finally take those who believe in him?

Jesus' physical absence after his resurrection and the perceived delay of his kingdom is always a potential crisis for his followers. Where is God? How can those
who seek him see his glory in the midst of day-to-day life? Continually, the New
Testament writers try to increase the faith of Jesus' followers by making God's presence more vivid and real. But the visions of faith are easily overcome by the all too
real visions of the world. With this problem in mind, John's Gospel reveals a Jesus
who first existed in glory before the world's creation, then in a humble life on
earth, and finally in resurrected glory forever at God's right hand. To the question
of how believers can see Christ's invisible glory today, John's Gospel replies that
the glory is seen in the lives of Jesus' followers—in their love for each other and
their witness to the world. The Spirit is with them and is making God's glory
known to the world.

But John's Gospel speaks to another more pressing question. If Jesus was God's glory
and believers now share in that glory, why does the world hate Jesus and his followers?
John helped his readers to understand world hatred and to cope with rejection and
suffering. The heart of this understanding centers on defining what is the best kind of
life. John showed that the best life is eternal and related to the life of God that flows
out through Christ. The stark contrast of eternal life with the world's limited life
should help believers cope with worldly problems. They can view all short-lived
human problems from the perspective of eternity. Jesus is not physically present, but
believers are not alone. As they let the Gospel of John increase their belief, their faith
will find deep roots and steadfastness in the vision of Christ's glory at God's right hand
and in his believing church on earth.

OUTLINE OF JOHN

V. THE SIGN OF THE RESURRECTION (12:1–20:31)
A. Focus on Death and Rejection (12:1-50)
B. Focus on Departure and Disciples (13:1–16:33)
C. Prayer following the Instruction (17:1-26)
D. The Passion of the Passover Lamb of God (18:1–19:42)
E. The Resurrection (20:1-29)

VI. ASSURANCE AND COMMISSION (21:1-25)
A. The Galilean Appearance (21:1-23)
B. Postscript (21:24-25)

JOHN NOTES

1:1-18 THE POSSIBILITY OF WITNESS IS EXPLAINED

Overview: The function of the prologue was to show how the hidden Word of God was able to be known; how the Word moved from hiddenness into openness; how the Word was able to be observed and spoken about. Three sets of key words progressively show how the knowledge of God came through Jesus. The first set of words concerns Christ's existence before the world and his life-giving power (1:1-4: "was," "with," "life"). The second set shows Christ's reception in the world and the results of rejecting or accepting him (1:5-13: "didn't recognize him," "light," "testimony," "accepted," "believe," "children of God"). The third set of words shows how the message about Christ was transmitted from the original eyewitnesses to the ever larger circle of believers (1:14-18: "we have seen his glory," "benefited," "blessings," "told us about him"). Each of the three sections of the prologue was designed to show how the coming of Jesus enables believers to know the Father. The knowledge of the Father through the Son was the foundation of the book's evangelistic purpose (20:30-31).

1:1-5 From Unknown to Known

The term "Word" was an established philosophical concept that John used, added to, and enriched, to communicate the nature of Jesus Christ. John's presentation of the "Word" incorporates both Greek and Jewish ideas.

Philo, the Alexandrian Jew who sought to bring about a synthesis of Greek philosophy with Old Testament thought, used the concept of the "word" to denote how God created and communicated with the material world. In keeping with Greek thought, Philo conceived of the philosophical "word" as a bridge between the transcendent holy God and the material evil universe. To the Greek of the first century, the word was a mediating principle between God and the world of created matter.

But John's usage of the term was also centrally located in the Old Testament Scripture's account concerning God and creation. Using the concept of the "Word," points were made in 1:1 concerning Christ's eternal existence, relationship to the Father, and character as God. Jesus the Messiah was the "Word," the Creator, come to bring about the redemption of the fallen creation—to recreate what had been broken by sin. John used the concept of the powerful and creative Word, a concept familiar to both Jews and Greeks, and gave it greater meaning, identifying the Word as the divine Person, Jesus, who came to reveal God to man. He was God's creative presence, present to redeem what had fallen into the bondage of sin and to mediate between the Creator and creation.

In the Old Testament the "word of God" is often personified as an instrument for doing God's will (Pss. 33:6; 107:20; 119:89; 147:15). Jesus, the Word, came to earth expressly to do God's will by bringing about God's plan for redemption. John repeats the statement that Christ was with God in order to show his close relationship with God (1:2). Jesus, the Word, was the creative and effective extension of God, given to show God's love to lost mankind.

In Genesis 1 God spoke (his word) and the entire universe came into being. In the Bible generally, the "Word" is the personification of God's revelation. Throughout Scripture *creation* and *salvation* are closely linked as forms of God's self-revelation (1:3). God revealed himself first as Creator (Gen. 1) and then as Redeemer or Recreator in the person of Jesus Christ. John presents Christ's work as the beginning of a new creation. Similarly, Paul calls the Christian a "new creation" in Christ (2 Cor. 5:17).

The themes of light and life, both describing God's work in the creation, are related to the person of Christ (1:4-5). Light shines in the darkness of creation. Light was the first element (cf. Gen. 1). All that will follow in John's account of Christ's life is done with a comparison of the creation account of Genesis in mind. For example, the first miracle, the sign of water changed into wine, receives the evaluation of "very good" by the master of the banquet ("best," 2:10). That parallels God's evaluation of his creation in Genesis 1 where he calls all "very good" (Gen. 1:31). In addition, this miracle comes as the culmination of a week of creative activity by Jesus the "Word," further paralleling the Genesis account (see "Signs and Belief" in the Guiding Concepts section).

"Light" and "darkness" (1:5) are frequently used metaphors in John's Gospel. Jesus was the source of spiritual light (cf. 8:12; 9:5). "Darkness" referred to the realm of spiritual evil—the satanic world system set against God (1:5; 3:19; 8:12). John tells his readers right at the beginning of his Gospel that the darkness could not extinguish the light of Christ.

1:6-13 John the Baptist: Witness and Belief

The function of John 1:6-13 is to explain how the "world" did not comprehend Jesus the Messiah. John the Baptist's purpose was to be a witness to the world (1:29, 36; note the repetition of witness in 1:7-8). John 1:7 has the first of ninety-eight occurrences of the word "believe" in the Gospel of John. The word essentially means "trust" and suggests not just an intellectual agreement with facts, but a committed reliance upon the truth concerning Jesus. "Light" (1:9) is here used differently than in Matthew 4:16, where Isaiah 9:2 is quoted. Matthew and John both suggest a close relationship between light and life as the remedy for darkness and death. But while Matthew portrays light as the dawning of the Messiah's presence near the end of the age, John presents light as the dawn of the original creation light and the first burst of mankind's life upon the earth.

Three connected statements (1:10) centered on the "world" reveal the good news of God's presence in the "world" (the incarnation) and the tragedy of the "world's" rejection of that presence. The only birth narrative about which John was concerned is in 1:12-13. He was concerned with the Christian's spiritual birth, not Jesus' physical birth. To "believe" (1:12) is a belief that results in a new birth into God's family.

1:14-18 The Object of Witness Enters the World

The section 1:14-18 makes the point that God took on human flesh in the person of Jesus. Jesus came to reveal and explain the nature of God (1:18), and everything he said and did revealed something of the nature of God the Father. John 1:14-18 serves as a bridge from the prologue to the narrative of Jesus' life. It shows that Jesus was a reliable representative of God the Father and that because of his presence among men, the record of which is to follow in the rest of the book, the believer can also bear witness to God's work on mankind's behalf. It also reveals that the circle of witnesses to the powerful work of

God is exclusive. Not everyone is able to bear witness, but only those who have seen and believed God's glory and witness through Jesus.

The incarnation of the Word is observed (1:14). This is a reference to the tabernacle in the wilderness and its link to glory. The Greek word translated "lived here on earth" pictures living in a tent. Jesus, in becoming a man, tented on earth with the rest of mankind. John systematically shows how Jesus fulfilled many of the events of God's glory to Israel in the wilderness of Sinai (see "The Wilderness" in the Bible-Wide Concepts section for John). This suggests that this little reference to Jesus' glory being seen while he "tented among us" ("lived here on earth among us," 1:14) is a reference to how Jesus was the fullness of what was begun when God's glory tented with Israel in the tabernacle in the wilderness. Some examples of how John speaks of glory are 1:14; 2:11; 5:41, 44; 7:18, 39; 8:50, 54; 9:24; 11:4, 40; 12:16, 23, 28, 41, 43; 13:31; 14:13; 16:14; 17:1, 4-5, 10, 22, 24; 21:19. The most frequent occurrence of the word is in John 17. The term "only" (1:14, 18) is best understood as implying "unique" or "one-of-a-kind" (cf. Heb. 11:17 where the same word is used of Isaac, not Abraham's only son, but his unique, special son of promise).

The mention of Moses, the law, and grace is a supporting witness to the greatness of Jesus Christ (1:16-17). This is the introduction to the wilderness concept in John (see Bible-Wide Concepts). In the Old Testament God sometimes displayed his glory by a vision (Isa. 6:1) or in some physical way (Exod. 34:5-8; Judg. 13:22). But through the person of Jesus Christ, God would make himself known in a new and personal way (1:18). Compare the revelation of God in Jesus Christ with his revelation in Exodus 33:7-8, 10-11, 20, 23.

But God is spirit (cf. John 4:24) and has no physical body. Jesus, in his incarnation, is the most complete revelation of the Father. This is the climax of John's introduction (1:18). Moses never really saw God, but Jesus did. And Jesus, as God's incarnate Son, revealed to mankind the very person of God. He is the bridge between God and man. This is the foundation of Christian faith—God revealed and explained in the person of the Messiah, Jesus.

1:19–2:11 A WEEK OF WITNESS: THE SIGNS BEGIN

1:19-42 John's Witness

1:19-28 THE WITNESS TO THOSE IN DARKNESS
1:19-23 John Functions As a Witness to the Light
The "Jewish leaders" (1:19) were the religious leaders in Jerusalem who had heard about his preaching and baptism of repentance. They wanted to know how John saw himself in relationship to God's prophetic program. John denied being "Elijah" (1:21), yet the

angel Gabriel (Luke 1:17) and Jesus (Matt. 11:10, 14; 17:10-13) clearly viewed John as fulfilling the Malachi 3:1 and 4:5 prophecies of Elijah's return. If Jesus confirmed John's identification with Elijah, why did John himself deny it? Since the Jews of the first century believed that Elijah would actually return in the flesh, John denied being the physically reincarnated Elijah that they anticipated. Although he did fulfill the prophecy of Malachi 3:1 and 4:5, he did so in an unexpected way. He came and ministered in "the spirit and power of Elijah" (Luke 1:17). In 1:23 John quotes Isaiah 40:3 with reference to the place and purpose of his ministry.

1:24-28 THE IDENTITY OF THE COMING ONE
There is here no explicit reference to Jesus' "water" baptism mentioned, for example, in Matthew 3:11. John simply notes the surpassing worth of the One to come, a worth that forms the basis for John's witness in John 1:33. This Bethany (1:28), the place where John baptized, is distinguished from the Bethany near Jerusalem (cf. Mark 11:1). The Bethany where John baptized was a village east of the Jordan about five miles north of the Dead Sea. The changing course and flooding of the Jordan over the years has completely obliterated the site so that no ruins exist today (see 3:22, 26; 4:1-2; 10:40).

1:29-34 THE WITNESS TO THE LIGHT
The actual event of Jesus' baptism was not mentioned by John. The writer's focus was on the witness to Jesus' identity as Son and Lamb of God. The phrase "Lamb of God" (1:29) contains much Old Testament imagery, taking the Jewish mind back to Genesis 22:8 when Abraham said, "God will provide a lamb." A ram was provided as a substitute for Isaac, but God's Lamb was yet to come.

The Passover lamb (Exod. 12:3) pointed the way to the full and final provision of God's sacrificial Lamb, Jesus (1 Cor. 5:7). John did not emphasize the repentance element of John the Baptist's preaching. Instead, he emphasized Jesus as the one on whom the Holy Spirit would remain—the very Son of God, who would baptize in the Spirit.

1:35-42 THE WITNESS TO THE DISCIPLES
Compare this event with Matthew 16:13-20. From the first meeting, Jesus was identified as the Messiah and had identified Simon as Peter (1:41-42). The Hebrew term "Messiah" (1:41) means "Anointed One" and was translated into the Greek as "Christ." "Cephas" (1:42) was an Aramaic name; "Peter" was the same name in Greek. Both words mean "stone."

1:43–2:11 Jesus' Initial Witness
1:43-51 HIS CAPACITY AS REVEALER OF HEAVEN'S GLORY
This section shows the growth of the results of Jesus' witness. Bethsaida (1:44), also known as

Bethsaida-Julias, was a double site with a fishing village on the shore of the Sea of Galilee about one and a half miles south of the fortified city. It was located just east of the Jordan near the northeast shore of the Sea of Galilee. Nazareth (1:46) was not highly regarded because it was not even mentioned in the Old Testament and because it was in the immediate proximity of Sepphoris, the old Roman capital of Galilee. Nathanael, not Peter, was the first to identify Jesus as the divine "Son of God" and "King of Israel" (1:49). He was the first to recognize what John the apostle was trying to communicate in his Gospel (cf. 20:30-31).

The focus in this section was on Jesus' origin, not on his exact links to the law and prophets. His hometown origin, Nazareth, became insignificant in the light of his supernatural origin, recognized by Nathanael. Exactly what happened between Philip and Nathanael under the fig tree is not important The point was that Jesus had been supernaturally there and already knew Nathanael (1:48-49).

Jesus described the "greater things" (1:50) in terms of Jacob's ladder at Bethel (1:50-51; cf. Gen. 28:11-17). Jesus was making the point that he was the revealer of heavenly things and the medium through whom heaven and earth would meet. Jesus was the one who would fulfill Jacob's dream, providing access and communication between God and man. The words "The truth is" occur twenty-five times in John and nowhere else. They serve to introduce a truth of special solemnity or importance.

2:1-11 HIS CAPACITY DEMONSTRATED IN THE FIRST SIGN
In the dialogue between Jesus and Mary (2:1-5), Jesus intended no disrespect. The phrase "How does that concern you and me?" (see a similar phrase used in Matt. 8:29; Mark 1:24; 5:7; and Luke 8:28) indicates a new relationship between Jesus and his mother. Cana (John 2:1) was located in Galilee, a three day's walk (about seventy-five miles) from Bethany (see introductory map). The exact site is debated. Kefr Kenna is popularly regarded by tourists as the place of Jesus' miracle, but there is little substantial evidence for this recent tradition. The better choice is Khirbet Kana, about nine miles north of Nazareth. This identification is supported by geographical references in Josephus, archaeological evidence, and early pilgrim itineraries.

The concept of Jesus' "time" (2:4) relates to the time for a display of his messianic powers and glory either by miracle or by death and resurrection (cf. 7:6, 8, 30; 8:20; 12:23, 27; 13:1; 17:1). The water had been brought for the "ceremonial purposes" (2:6), the ritual cleansing of hands before eating (cf. Mark 7:1-4). The word "wine" (2:9) refers to an alcoholic beverage. There is some doubt that Jesus would have made an intoxicating drink. But that is a cultural, not a moral, problem. Wine was the most frequently used beverage in the first century. Also, wine was commonly diluted, one part wine to three parts water. It was considered barbaric to drink undiluted wine.

Jesus' miracle should be understood in light of kingdom expectations. According to Joel 3:18, the mountains of Judah will "drip with sweet wine" in the messianic kingdom. Jesus' miracle was a sign of his messiahship and a foretaste of kingdom blessings. The master of the banquet was quoted (2:10) to show how good the wine was. That qualitative evaluation was the key to this miracle. It was "very good," or "the best," like God's creation in Genesis 1. That creative act displayed Jesus' glory. This revealed glory would result in belief for those who witnessed it. His glory was manifested to show people what the Father is like (cf. John 1:18).

In the Bible, creation is linked to salvation and God's communication of blessing. In his Gospel, John bore witness to the Creator at work; light in the darkness was forming a "new creation" through the work of his glorious Son (cf. 1 Cor. 5:17). The good wine was the first example of the Creator's presence and the goodness of his second creation. This was the first sign (2:11), that is, there were more to come. The signs of bread, healings, and resurrection life were still ahead.

2:12–4:54 JERUSALEM, SAMARIA, AND BACK TO CAPERNAUM: A SECOND SIGN
2:12–3:21 To Jerusalem
2:12-25 PASSOVER
2:12 The Stay in Capernaum
Capernaum, a fishing village and tax collection station, was located along the northwest shore of the Sea of Galilee.

2:13-22 The Cleansing of the Jerusalem Temple
The temple businessmen were selling animals and changing money so that the worshipers would have supposedly "pure" offerings. Some of the money was used for the offerings and some for the temple tax. Note the two things remembered (2:17, 22): (1) the Scriptures (Ps. 69:9 quoted in John 2:17) and (2) Jesus' words. This event clearly shows the transfer of significance from the temple to the body of Christ.

This "Passover" (2:13) has been dated April 7, A.D. 30. The Passover Feast commemorated the deliverance of Israel from Egypt (cf. Exod. 12) and foreshadowed Jesus' sacrificial death on the cross (1 Cor. 5:7). This is the first of two temple cleansings—one at the beginning and the other at the end of Jesus' ministry (cf. Matt. 21:12-17).

Herod began to refurbish the Jerusalem temple in 20/19 B.C. (2:20), and while the sanctuary was completed after one and a half years of work, the project was not finished until around A.D. 63. The "forty-six years" (2:20) was the period during which the sanctuary had stood. The question would probably be better translated, "How can you destroy and rebuild in a mere three days such a structure that has stood for forty-six years?"

2:23-25 Summary of His Ministry: Aspects of Trust
John showed that the basis of trust was in knowing the trustworthiness of the object of that trust. Jesus revealed his distrust of the crowds that had begun to follow him. Jesus came to reveal the Father, not to rely on humans. Although humans might believe, Jesus did not trust in them because of the witness he had regarding humans. Jesus saw this belief, based only on miracles, as superficial (2:24). He did not trust himself to these people and accept them as his disciples. The only fame he sought was in doing the will of his Father (4:34).

3:1-21 JESUS IS THE UNIQUE SON, NOT ANOTHER TEACHER
Jesus' encounter with Nicodemus (3:1-21) is related to the preceding verses concerning Jesus' trust of those who followed him (2:23-25). The encounter with Nicodemus was an example of Jesus not entrusting himself to humans. He knew people and knew their need for a new birth. He did not need Nicodemus's authority as a religious leader. He needed to tell him about being born again. John 3:1-21 describes a Jew's questions about Jesus. The section comprises the dialogue of Jesus and Nicodemus (3:1-15) and John's commentary on Jesus' words (3:16-21). John sought to show how entrance into the kingdom came by regeneration (3:1-8). The content of the entire book concerns the offer of a second birth from God (1:12-13) and the things in this world that try to block that new birth. John 3 is yet another example of the offer and its conflicts. The historical context for this conversation is given in 2:23-25, the feasts of Passover and Unleavened Bread.

The Pharisees were a sect of Judaism that came into existence during the intertestamental period. They were middle-class separatists, associated with the synagogue and characterized by legalistic interpretations of the law. Nicodemus was a member of the Sanhedrin, an aristocratic supreme court possessing jurisdiction over the Jews in both civil and religious matters. The signs that Jesus had performed were seen as pointing to God and establishing Jesus as a great teacher but not as the Son of God. But would Nicodemus, or anyone, take the next logical step and learn from this Teacher? That is the question of John's Gospel.

John 3:6 expresses a central theme of the book. The labor of Jesus was to teach the spiritual dimension of life so that, with the difference between flesh and spirit clearly drawn, people might believe in his offer of eternal life. Water and Spirit (3:5) define the "born again" of 3:3, 4, 7. The Greek word for "again" is also found in Galatians 4:9 (see "from above" in John 3:31; 19:11).

The concept of being "born again" must also relate to the physical versus spiritual birth from God discussed in 1:12-13. Although the kingdom of God is mentioned (3:3, 5), the concept of eternal life is the most emphasized truth in John's Gospel. Note the emphasis that is made with the statement "The truth is."

The one "born of the Spirit" (3:8) is like the wind to the unregenerate person. The unbeliever does not know the origin of the life that is in him nor his final destiny. God's working in regeneration is not explainable by natural laws. Like the wind, the effects can be seen, but not explained.

Nicodemus struggled with the parables of the new birth (3:9-15). He was locked into thinking on the level of the flesh. But only a new spiritual creation could bring salvation. Jesus had been teaching some of the basic truths about the new covenant (Jer. 31:31-34; Ezek. 36:26-27; Joel 2:28-32), concepts that Nicodemus, "a respected Jewish teacher," should have understood (3:10).

John included in his account an explanation of the relationship between the first and second births (3:11-15). Jesus was qualified to speak of heavenly things because he had been in heaven and was there to share the heavenly glory with humans (3:11). John again brought up the wilderness theme from Israel's history. Jesus' glory would be seen through the humiliation of being lifted up on the cross. What to people was a disgrace, to God would be the manifestation of his glory. The "bronze snake on a pole in the wilderness" (3:14) referred back to Numbers 21 where Moses prepared a bronze serpent to deliver the people from death by poisonous snake bites. The bronze serpent was an Old Testament illustration of the Messiah, Jesus. As the serpent was "lifted up," so would Jesus be lifted up on the cross, that people might look upon him with faith and receive spiritual healing.

In Jesus' elaboration on new birth, belief, and judgment there was a heavy emphasis on personal choice (3:16-21). John 3:20-21 implies the element of free choice and personal responsibility with reference to human actions after the initial confrontation with the light.

3:22-36 To Judea

3:22-30 AUTHORITY TO PURIFY: JOHN'S PARTICIPATION

The section of 3:22-30 describes the dialogue of John the Baptist and a Jew, and 3:31-36 is the apostle John's commentary on John the Baptist's words. The question of 3:25 concerns whose baptism, Jesus' or John's, is approved by God. "Aenon near Salim" (3:23) was a site located near the junction of the Jordan and Jezreel valleys. The site of Salim was located about eight miles south of Scythopolis and Aenon, although the location is uncertain. John the Baptist was later imprisoned by Herod Antipas at Machaerus, a fortress east of the Dead Sea (cf. Matt. 14:1-12). John the Baptist recognized that his place was that of a servant who would of necessity decrease, for it was his place to exalt the Master (John 3:30). John had introduced Jesus and thus had fulfilled his mission. These are the last words by John the Baptist recorded in this Gospel.

3:31-36 AUTHORITY TO MAKE ALIVE: JESUS' PREEMINENCE

These verses probably come from the mind of the author of this Gospel and again stress the thoughts of 3:6. Jesus was from heaven, stood above all earthly authority, and opened the doors of spiritual understanding and rebirth into eternal life.

4:1-42 To Samaria

Overview: This section links back to the question concerning Jesus' authority and his Jewish opposition (3:25-26). Jesus left Judea and began traveling north to Galilee (4:3-4). While it was common for more scrupulous Jews, like the Pharisees, to travel through Perea (east of the Jordan), Josephus says that some Jewish travelers went through Samaria because it was the most direct route. The necessity ("had to," 4:4) is not directly explained in the text. The results of Jesus' passing through Samaria (4:39-42) indicate that the necessity was related to bringing the word of redemption to the Samaritans. As the "light of the world," it was necessary for Jesus to take his message to Samaria also.

4:1-4 THE TRIP TO SAMARIA

The background of the Samaritans can be found in 2 Kings 17 where it is recorded that after the fall of the northern kingdom in 722 B.C., the Assyrians exiled the Israelites and brought in foreigners to occupy their land. These foreigners brought their own gods, and a syncretistic religion developed in which the God of Israel was worshiped along with other gods. The Samaritans developed their own Pentateuch in which scribes emended the text to legitimize their place of worship on Mount Gerizim, rather than Jerusalem. The leading Israelites were taken by Sargon. The remaining Jews continued to worship God and maintained close relationships with Judah (see 2 Kings 23:19-20; 2 Chron. 30:1-5; Jer. 41:4-13).

Under the Persian influence in 537 B.C. the returning Jews clashed with the Samaritans concerning the rebuilding of the temple. The drives of Ezra and Nehemiah for the purity of the Israelite race heightened tensions. This may have been the period in which the Samaritans, rejected from Jerusalem, built their own temple on Mount Gerizim.

Around 128 B.C. Jewish forces zealous for the purity of the Jerusalem temple captured Shechem and destroyed the Gerizim temple. In A.D. 6–9 the Samaritans defiled the Jerusalem temple on Passover by scattering bones in the temple precincts. This strife between Jews and Samaritans was not significant to the Romans. Under Roman rule both Jews and Samaritans together suffered Roman oppression.

As far as doctrine and practice were concerned, the Jews viewed the Samaritans as schismatics, not Gentiles. Their main problem was with the Gerizim temple. Here are some New Testament references to the Samaritans: Matthew 10:5-6; Luke 9:52-56; 10:33; 17:16; John 4:7-42; 8:48; Acts 1:8; 9:31; 15:3. In the first century A.D., the relations between the Jews and Samaritans continued to be quite strained. Jews regarded Samaritans as unclean religious apostates.

4:5-30 ANOTHER MISINTERPRETATION: JESUS AS JUST A PROPHET

4:5-9 Jesus Is Misunderstood As Only an Ethnic Jew
Sychar (4:5) was located at the modern village of Askar, about half a mile north of Jacob's well. The Old Testament site of Shechem that lies nearby was in ruins at this time. The water of "Jacob's well" (4:6) is noted for its fine quality—cold, pure, and refreshing. It produces a softer water than other springs in the area. The site can be visited today in the crypt of an unfinished church. "Noontime" was not the usual time to carry water. Note the irony of the Samaritan woman's statement (4:9) as she mistakes the Creator of the universe for a simple Jewish man.

4:10-12 The Source of Spiritual "Water"
The woman, like Nicodemus, must move from thinking on the physical level to the spiritual level. The woman must move from the figure of physical water to its spiritual counterpart, eternal life. The gift of living water relates to the gift of life-giving bread from heaven (6:30-35) and the ongoing theme of Israel in the wilderness. Spiritual thirst and hunger are satisfied by the living water and bread from heaven. The term "living water" (4:10) was a common reference to spring water in contrast to that which was found in a cistern (cf. Jer. 2:13). Jesus took this common term and filled it with new meaning—spiritual cleansing and refreshment through Christ. The well is 120 to 200 feet deep (John 4:11).

4:13-26 The Woman's Life Is Exposed
Jesus exposed the woman's life in order to bring her to the point of receiving the living water (4:13-18). Due to Jesus' insight into her private life the woman thought that he had the divinely given insight characteristic of a prophet (4:19-20). But Jesus raised the issue, not of his identity, but of the location and nature of true worship. Jesus only identified himself as the Messiah (4:26) after the woman herself raised the issue of the coming Messiah (4:25). The Samaritans believed God had designated Mount Gerizim (4:20) as the proper place for worship. They had built a temple there to rival the worship center in Jerusalem. The Samaritans believed in a coming Messiah who was to be primarily a teacher, a priest, and a restorer of true worship on Mount Gerizim. Jesus articulated the difference between worship that was expressed in external rituals alone and true worship in spirit (4:23). The term "spirit" refers to the sphere of worship. True worship happens when a believer's spirit is connected with God's Spirit, not when a believer is in any particular physical place like Jerusalem or Samaria. God's Spirit is everywhere, therefore worship can happen anywhere. The term "truth" implies that the human worshiper is open and conforming to God's revealed ways of worship and life, specifically Jesus' call to repentance and honest, spiritual worship.

4:27-30 Light Exposes Darkness
The disciples were surprised that Jesus had been speaking with the woman since it was not the custom for rabbis to converse with women in public (4:27). The woman was tentative as to Jesus being the Messiah (4:29). He had great knowledge—a point that had also impressed Nathanael with Jesus' deity (1:48-49; cf. also 4:39).

4:31-38 MISUNDERSTANDINGS CONCERNING "FOOD" AND "HARVEST"

Jesus used the symbol of food to represent doing God's will (4:34) and used the acts of eating and drinking as symbols of eternal versus earthly life. Jesus made statements that confused his disciples in order to go on to make his contrasting spiritual points. That same contrast was presented concerning the earthly versus spiritual harvests (4:35). The date may be calculated as January/February, A.D. 31. The grain harvest in April/May would have been four months away.

4:39-42 FIRSTHAND FAITH

The Samaritans believed because they had heard for themselves (see Thomas in 20:29). Their confession is the high point of this story. Jesus is Savior of the world (4:42), not just of a small ethnic handful of Israelites or Samaritans. The universal scope of Jesus' redemption is rooted in his role as Creator and Son of God (cf. 1:1-18).

4:43-54 To Capernaum

4:43-48 SIGNS AND SINCERITY

Jesus again examined the relationship between seeing and believing. Receiving Jesus because of his miracles (4:45) was not the kind of faith Jesus saw as honoring him (4:44). Jesus desired belief based on faith, not just in miracles, but in his word alone (20:29). This explains why the nobleman's request for his son's healing was criticized by Jesus (4:48). The royal official was an officer in the court of Herod Antipas (4 B.C.–A.D. 39), ruler of Galilee. Was it not natural to want his son to live? Certainly. But Jesus used a plural "you" in 4:48. He moved beyond the father and spoke to all his hearers. He knew human hearts and their desire for flashy externals like miracles rather than sincerely taking Jesus at his word. At that moment, heart belief in Jesus was more important than a dying son. For Cana of Galilee (4:46), see note on 2:11.

4:49-54 FAITH IN WORD AND FAITH IN DEED
The nobleman believed in Jesus' word alone, without proof (4:49-50). When the hour of healing was discovered, the man again believed, having seen the proof of Jesus' word (4:53). The movement was from believing the words of Jesus to seeing and believing the deeds of Jesus. The man first believed in Jesus' word. Then he believed in the deed and character of Jesus. That was a second sign (4:54). This event showed that Jesus' signs were not presented simply for evangelism. They were also for those who had already believed, yet needed to believe in Jesus on a more deep and sincere level.

5:1–11:57 FROM JERUSALEM TO JERUSALEM: THE FATHER'S WITNESS TO HIS SON
Overview: The section of 5:1–11:57 develops around Jesus' words in 5:21, 24-26, 28-29. In John 5 Jesus moved from the healing of the man by the Bethesda pool to proclaiming a future time when he would call all to a resurrection of life or of judgment (5:28-29). In John 11 Jesus called one man, Lazarus, to a resurrection from the dead. In between, Jesus used several figures to illustrate his ability to give eternal life. Jesus described himself as bread from heaven (6:32, 35, 51); the living water of life (7:38-39); the light of life (8:12; 9:5); the gate and good shepherd 10:9-11; and the resurrection life (11:25-26).

Jesus stressed throughout that his words and actions reflected the nature and will of the Father (5:19-20; 6:46; 7:15-18; 8:26; 9:3-4; 10:18, 37-38) and were the basis for receiving the life he offered. This illustrates the point made in 1:18, that Jesus explained what the Father was like.

5:1-47 The Witness Patterns of the Father in Jesus
Overview: In John 5, the author shows how Jesus redefined the Sabbath day as a time for saving people. He went on to reveal how all that Jesus said and did was a reflection of the Father's will (5:17, 19); every word and deed of Jesus on earth found its source in his Father (5:19, 30). Jesus' glory also found its source in the Father. These verses prepare the reader for Jesus' words in John 17.

5:1-18 A CRISIS: CAN GOD WORK ON THE SABBATH?
5:1-9 The Work Is Done: A Third Sign
This feast (5:1) is not identified. It was probably in the fall because the next feast mentioned is the Passover the following spring (6:4). The pool of Bethesda (5:2) was located just north of the temple area near the Sheep Gate (Neh. 3:32) and may have been used for washing sheep before Passover sacrifices.

John 5:4, omitted in many manuscripts, clarifies why there were so many ill people gathered around the pool and the reason behind the sick man's words in 5:7. The questionable material of 5:3-4 may have come to be deleted by a copyist concerned about what seemed to him to be a pagan or superstitious influence. Thus, it can be argued that all of 5:3-4 may have been included in the original manuscripts.

The question "Would you like to get well?" (5:6) was geared to encourage an expression of the man's desire, not his faith. That would come later. Jesus asked the man to get up and walk in order to provide a highly visible sign on the Sabbath (5:9). Jesus wanted to provoke the dialogue with the Jewish leaders concerning what should be allowed on the Sabbath day (5:10-47).

5:10-18 The Proposition Is Stated: God Is Working
Oral traditions advanced by the Pharisees forbade carrying certain things on the Sabbath (5:10). While Jesus associated the man's sickness with sin, the story of Job illustrates that this is not always the case (5:14). Jesus was criticized by the Jews on two counts: (1) healing on the Sabbath and (2) claiming equality with God (5:18). Had he not intended this, Jesus could have easily corrected their notion. Jesus' startling revelation was that his Father worked on the Sabbath and so Jesus would work as well (5:17). This brings out the true meaning of Sabbath—not inactivity but activity to restore and redeem. Jesus identified himself with the divine worker, and through his work he revealed the nature of God (1:18). Sabbath activity is the same as the saving work of God (cf. Matt. 12:1-8; Mark 2:23-28; Luke 6:5).

5:19-47 THE PATTERN OF JESUS' SONSHIP
5:19-23 Patterned after the Father
Requirements for Sabbath observance were patterned after the example of God the Father who works even on the Sabbath. Jesus quickly moved from his deed of healing on the Sabbath to the hope of resurrection and life (5:21). Greater things (5:20) are life and judgment with a view to honoring the Son's authority. Jesus only did what he saw his Father do. To look at Jesus was to see God the Father in action (1:18). The fact that Jesus did the will of his Father without question established the

reason for the glory of his ministry and the stumbling block for those who would not receive him.

5:24-29 Functioning As a Judge

In 5:24-29 the "life" and "judgment" offered by Jesus are elaborated. His hearers were not to marvel at his earthly acts like healings or knowledge (5:28) because they simply pointed to the ultimate and eternal resurrections to either life or death (5:29). His hearers already knew about the last judgment. But they would also find out that Jesus would be the one in charge.

5:30-37a The Authenticating Witness to Jesus

Note the link of 5:30 with 5:19. According to Jewish tradition, self-testimony without supporting witnesses was not regarded as legally valid (5:31). Jesus' witness was not "true" in the sense that it was not legally acceptable in a court of law. But Jesus never intended to be his own authority (5:30). Nor was John the Baptist Jesus' authority (5:33-35). His authority found its source in the Father (5:36-37). It was the Father who gave the works and words to his divine Son, Jesus. Jesus did not receive the witness of people (5:34, 41; cf. 2:24-25). Jesus presented five witnesses to the truth of his divine Person and authority: himself (5:30-31), John the Baptist (5:33-35), his own works or miracles (5:36), the Father (5:37-38), and the Old Testament Scriptures (5:39-47). The greatest witness of the five was the Father's authority (5:36). All of those focus on Jesus as the source of eternal life.

5:37b-47 The People's History of Rejecting God's Witness

The people had rejected God's witness in history (5:37-38), in word (5:39-40), in true devotion (5:41-42), in self-glory (5:43-44), and in Moses' words (5:45-47). Scriptures that bore witness to the truth of Jesus include Genesis 3:15; 12:1-3; 49:10; Numbers 24:17; and Deuteronomy 18:15-18. The rejection was based on preferring human over divine glory (John 5:43-44), an example of loving darkness instead of light (1:10-11).

6:1-71 The Implications of Bread Developed: The Old Testament and Manna

Overview: The heart of this chapter is Jesus' comparison of his feeding miracle with the manna God gave to Israel in the wilderness after the exodus from Egypt (6:31-32). During the temptations of Jesus (Matt. 4:4), he quoted Deuteronomy 8:3 with reference to making bread in the wilderness. The broader context of Deuteronomy 8:1-3 is crucial for understanding the ongoing significance of manna. The purpose of manna was to test the hearts of the people for faith and obedience to God's ways. The same was true in John 6. Note the use of "humbled" in Deuteronomy 8:3; Exodus 10:3;

Leviticus 16:29-31; 23:27, 32 (see also Mark 9:20; Exod. 16:4, 8, 12, 15, 22, 32; Ps. 78:24-25).

John 6 focuses on Jesus as the only way to life by election (6:65) and by faith (6:35). Jesus stressed the spiritual over the physical ("The truth is," 6:26, 32, 47, 53), but only those chosen by the Father believed him. The others misunderstood the sign of feeding (6:26) and the Old Testament sign of manna (6:32). Jesus defined true bread as himself and true eating as faith in him (6:35, 47).

6:1-15 THE POPULAR INTERPRETATION OF THE BREAD SIGN

6:1-6 Bread and Testing

The miracle of feeding the five thousand took place near the time of Passover, mid-April, A.D. 32. Because the Passover celebration was at hand (6:4), this incident should also be related to the idea of Jesus as the true Passover Lamb (1:29, 36; cf. 1 Cor. 5:7). The feeding of the five thousand took place on the east side of the Sea of Galilee near Bethsaida (Luke 9:10) in a remote place (Mark 6:35). The word "testing" in 6:6 was the same word used to describe what Satan did to Jesus in Matthew 4:1. That word was also used in Genesis 22:1 in the Septuagint (the Greek Old Testament) for the testing of Abraham. Jesus intended to test his disciples' insight and faith and to show them that he was the true bread of life.

6:7-9 Two Failures of the Test: Philip and Andrew

Philip and Andrew did not pass Jesus' test. The people of Israel failed a similar test given to them by Moses in the wilderness (Num. 11:13-15, 20-23).

6:10-15 The Miracle of Bread from Heaven: A Fourth Sign

The people associated Jesus (6:14) with the prophet of Deuteronomy 18:15. But they assumed that prophet would break Roman rule over Israel as Moses had broken Egypt's (1:21; cf. Deut. 18:15; Acts 3:22; 7:37). Jesus withdrew because they had missed the point and not accepted him on his terms. The crowd intended to force him to become king. He knew that this offer of kingship was superficial, motivated by a desire for bread rather than as a result of true recognition of his person. They wanted bread for physical life and independence for political life. But Jesus offered himself as the foundation for a new spiritual and eternal life.

6:16-21 THE SIGN OF WALKING ON WATER: A FIFTH SIGN

John placed this sign in the middle of his discussion of Jesus as the bread of life. It strengthened the disciples' faith. Jesus had just rejected earthly kingship, but he was still full of divine power and greatness. The disciples were crossing from the northeast side of the sea toward Bethsaida (Mark 6:45) with Capernaum on the northwest side of the sea as their destination. Their fears were changed to receptivity when they understood that it was Jesus (John 6:20-21). As God had power over the waters of the Red Sea and the Jordan River in the Old Testament, so his Son had power over the Sea of Galilee.

6:22-71 THE CAPERNAUM SYNAGOGUE: THE FULL INTENTION OF THE BREAD SIGN
6:22-40 *Jesus Gives a Clear Invitation to Believe and Receive*
Tiberias (6:23) was the Roman capital of Galilee built between A.D. 18 and 22 by Herod Antipas in honor of the Roman emperor Tiberius. The city was located on the west side of the sea and was famous in ancient times for its hot springs. Jesus' response (6:26) to the people's question (6:25) relates to their mistaken notion that Jesus came to meet all their physical needs. The problem Jesus sought to correct concerned the people's inability to see that the signs he performed pointed not to material prosperity but to spiritual wholeness and eternal life.

The people wanted Jesus to do what Moses did— give them manna (6:30-31). But Jesus helped the people realize that the ultimate source of manna was not Moses, but the Father (6:32). Then he identified himself as the Father's true bread (6:35). For more on the manna in the wilderness, see Exodus 16:15 and Numbers 11:8. Jesus contrasts Moses' manna, which was life sustaining but not life giving. He is the true bread, which is life-giving and permanently satisfying. Note the phrase "raise them to eternal life at the last day" (John 6:39, 40, 44, 54). Throughout, the option of resurrection to eternal life or resurrection to eternal judgment lies behind Jesus' words.

6:41-59 *Jewish Grumblings over Jesus' Origins*
The people could not believe Jesus was from heaven because they could only see his earthly parentage. They were grumbling because they were caught up in the "how" of his descent from heaven rather than in his sufficiency (6:42). John 6:45 refers to the time of the new covenant mentioned in Jeremiah 31:34 and also to the universal extension of God's redemption mentioned in the Abrahamic covenant (Gen. 12:3). Jesus' claim that he was the "living bread" (6:51) raised the objection of cannibalism (6:52). Again the people were unable to see beyond the literal, physical meaning of Jesus' words.

The words "eat" and "drink" (John 6:53-54) are figures of speech that denote the operation of the mind or spirit in receiving, understanding, and applying teaching or instruction. People today also think in terms of "digesting" ideas. This does not refer to the Last Supper, which had not yet taken place (cf. Matt. 26:20-29).

6:60-71 *The Disciples Grumble or Confess*
Those who were not drawn to Jesus withdrew (John 6:60-65), but those who were chosen remained (6:66-71). The characteristic that separated those who left and those who stayed was a Godgiven ability to discern between the things of the flesh and the things of the Spirit (6:63). Jesus did not give these people a second taste of his miraculous physical bread. He had made his point about the bread of life, of which, by faith, people could have as many tastes as they desired. The lesson was to linger, because the true bread of life remained.

7:1–11:57 Jerusalem
Overview: Jesus was either rejected or received as he presented himself in the images of water (John 7), light (John 8–9), the shepherd (John 10), and the resurrection (John 11). As light, Jesus illuminated and exposed. As the shepherd, Jesus guided and sacrificed. Those images were preparing the readers of John's Gospel for the intimate words of the shepherd to the sheep in John 13–17. As the resurrection, Jesus was the very life of God; a new life over which death had no power.

7:1-53 THE FEAST OF TABERNACLES
7:1-9 *Pressures in Judea and Galilee*
Opposition sets the tone for John 7–8. The date was September 10-17, A.D. 32, about half a year before Jesus' crucifixion. The "Festival of Shelters" (7:2) was one of the three pilgrim festivals (Deut. 16:16) that the Jews attended in Jerusalem. The feast originally involved thanksgiving for God's preservation of Israel in the wilderness (manna and water, for example). As a fall harvest festival it commemorated the first harvest in the land after the wilderness wanderings. Jesus' relatives felt he was staying too long in the shadows. They wanted him to act in a grand public way. That manipulation of Jesus may sound pious, but John calls it unbelief (John 7:5). Jesus' brothers did not believe at this point, but later they would (1 Cor. 9:5; 15:7). Jesus explained why the world hated him (John 7:7). It was becoming clear that the rejection of Jesus noted in 1:11 would lead to murderous hate. The seeming confusion about Jesus not going (7:8) and then going (7:10) up to the feast was avoided by understanding Jesus' "time" (7:6, 8). Jesus followed the pattern that God had laid out for him (5:19); he rejected going when his brothers wanted him to, and then went later.

7:10-13 *Secret Speculation about the Messiah*
The people "were afraid of getting in trouble with the Jewish leaders" (7:13, 26).

7:14-24 *Public Exhortation to Judge Rightly*
This relates to the Sabbath controversy of the healing at the Bethesda pool (5:2-9, 16). Jesus used this opportunity to authenticate his origin and authority (7:14-18). Jesus had never attended the leading rabbinical schools, yet all had to admit that he was an eloquent and knowledgeable teacher (7:15). He

defined a teachable spirit as one with willingness to do his will (7:17). He attacked narrow vision and defined righteousness (7:19-24). Jesus desired to clarify the intent and emphasize the application of the law of Moses (7:23-24). Jesus pointed out that since circumcision was allowed on the Sabbath (Lev. 12:3), then certainly it should be permissible to do a deed of mercy on the Sabbath (7:23).

7:25-36 Response to Signs
Jesus claimed God as his Father (7:25-30). Some of the people held to the unscriptural tradition that the Messiah's origin would be unknown and that he would be an unknown individual until anointed by Elijah (7:27). Because the people of Jerusalem knew all about Jesus, they were sure that he could not be the Messiah. Those people that did believe, believed because of the signs Jesus had performed (7:31-36). The paragraph ends (7:35-36) with an unanswered question, showing a misunderstanding regarding Jesus' arrival and future absence. The disciples would soon have similar questions (John 13–14).

7:37-52 The Last and Great Day of the Feast
Jesus gave the promise of the Spirit (7:37-39). It had become the custom during the Feast of Tabernacles for the priests to bring a vessel of water each day from the Pool of Siloam and pour it out at the base of the altar in Jerusalem. The ceremony was a symbolic confession of physical thirst and looked forward to the end of the dry season and the coming of the winter rains. For seven days the libations were made. The eighth day ("last day") was observed as a Sabbath and no water was poured. It was on this day that Jesus invited the people to have their spiritual thirst satisfied in him (7:37). Jesus had already used the image of springs of water with the woman from Samaria (4:13-14). The Old Testament mentions springs of water in significant ways (Exod. 17:6; Num. 20:11; Ps. 78:15; Isa. 48:21; 35:6-7; 41:17-18; 44:3; Jer. 2:13; Ezek. 36:25; cf. also Rev. 21:6; 22:1, 17). Note in John 7:39 "because" and its implication that the Spirit could not be given until he had been glorified. The glorification of Jesus was directly related to the giving of the Spirit. Peter would clarify the link between Jesus' ascension and the outpouring of the Spirit in Acts 2:33 (see also Peter's use of Ps. 110:1 and Joel 2:28 in Acts 2:16-21, 34-36).

There was division over Jesus' geographical origin (John 7:40-43). Ironically, they did not know Jesus was indeed born in Bethlehem (7:42; cf. Mic. 5:2; Matt. 2:5-6). They were blind even to the facts because they were blind to God and not willing to do his will (John 7:17).

7:53–8:11 THE FUNCTION OF LIGHT
This story is omitted in many manuscripts, yet there seems to be substantial evidence that this was part of John's original text. The stylistic trait of short

explanatory phrases that appear elsewhere in John (6:6; 6:71; 11:31; 11:51; 13:11, 28) also appear here (8:6). The same type of legal language that appears in John 1–12 also appears here. And the evidence for inclusion of the story is very early (Jerome and Augustine), mid-fifth century A.D. About 450 Greek texts include the story.

If Jesus had advocated stoning the woman, he would have gone against the official policy of Rome that prohibited the Jews from executing the death penalty for adultery (8:6). If he advocated her release, then Jesus would be accused of contradicting Mosaic Law (Lev. 20:10; Deut. 22:23-24). By his response (8:6-11), Jesus escaped the trap set for him. They could not accuse him of showing disrespect for either Roman authority or Mosaic Law. Jesus' response in 8:11 did not condone the woman's sin and cannot be used as an argument for the validity of situation ethics. Jesus named sin for what it was. He granted forgiveness, not permission to sin (note the relation to 8:15-16). This relates to a constant theme of Jesus: the necessity of inner, rather than merely outer, purity. His point was that stoning was only a part of God's government, and if one was guilty of sin, all were guilty.

8:12-20 THE LIGHT OF THE WORLD
This teaching was probably presented at the Festival of Shelters (7:2). In the Court of the Women in the temple were four golden candelabras that burned brightly throughout the festival (8:12). The light symbolized the pillar of fire in the wilderness and the glory that had once filled the temple. At the close of the feast, after the lights had been darkened, Jesus made the impressive claim, "I am the light of the world" (8:12).

Light in Jewish literature is often a reference to the Messiah (cf. Isa. 9:2). The Jews could not have mistaken the meaning of his words. Self-testimony (8:13) was not regarded as acceptable in a Jewish court of law.

8:21-30 THE LIGHT'S REMOVAL
Jesus had much to say about his glory and departure (2:19-22; 7:36; 13:33-37; 14:1-4, 18-19, 28-29; 17:24). The hearers believed Jesus' words (8:30), but, as 8:31-59 will show, they were not willing to abide in his words (8:31).

8:31-59 JESUS' FOLLOW-UP FOR NEW BELIEVERS: TRUE FATHERHOOD
Even while under Rome's subjection, the Jews claimed that they were servants of God, not of Rome (8:33; see Josephus, Jewish War, 7.323). The Jews were Abraham's physical offspring, but were not his spiritual children because they did not share the justifying faith of Abraham (8:39). It is ironic that they claimed never to have been enslaved, especially since they had been under the thumbs of Egypt, Assyria, Babylon, Greece, and finally, Rome.

The characters of the two fathers, God and Satan, were being manifested by the actions and words of their followers (8:43-47).

Jesus' accusers misunderstood what Jesus meant by death, and thus were unable to understand or believe in Jesus (8:48-53). The foundation of life is the keeping of Jesus' word. Jesus had already spoken about death in sins (8:24). The way to life was to hold to his teachings (8:31) and obey (8:51) his words. He spoke of eternal life; the hearers could only think of physical life and death. Physical death may come for the believer, but it won't be the final victor (8:51; cf. 1 Cor. 15:54-57).

Jesus clarified what life meant (8:54-58). His eternality was the only basis for the believers not seeing death. Again, their claim to be children of Abraham was exposed for the sham it was (8:53). With the words "I existed" (8:58), Jesus laid claim to the great Old Testament revelation of God's personal name, the One who eternally exists (cf. Exod. 3:14, "I am"). Jesus claimed to be the Old Testament God. There was no doubt in the mind of the Jews that this was a claim for deity (8:59). When Jesus explained his true nature, they responded in hate. But true believers, from John the Baptist on (1:31), believed in Jesus' eternal existence (1:2).

9:1-41 THE LIGHT AND TRUE BLINDNESS
9:1-3 The Reason for the Blindness
John 9 continues the theme of light and darkness, sight and blindness. It was held, though not widely, that the soul of a man could sin in a preexistent state (9:2). Others held that the offspring would be punished by God for the sins of the parents. But the reason for this man's suffering was not that anyone had sinned; this man's blindness was allowed so that through his life God's glorious light might be displayed.

9:4-12 The Light Enlightens
Jesus, the Light, came to relieve both physical (9:11) and spiritual (9:39-41) blindness. This was a clear example of the Light coming to his own people and either being received or rejected (1:11-12). The blind man had spiritual sight, but the Pharisees were spiritually blind, and thus rejected Jesus. The pool of Siloam (9:7) was located at the south end of Mount Zion, the City of David in the Tyropoeon Valley. The pool was fed by the Gihon Spring through Hezekiah's tunnel. The miracle of giving sight to the blind should have brought to the minds of the observers Isaiah's prophecies that in the kingdom, the blind would see (Isa. 29:18; 35:5; 42:7, 16). The miracle was a foretaste of kingdom blessings, both physical and spiritual.

9:13-34 The Healer's Nature Is Debated
To be "expelled from the synagogue" (John 9:22; that is, excommunicated) was a most serious punishment because it involved forfeiting one's social relations and religious privileges as a Jew. The words "give glory to God" (9:24) imply "give glory to God by telling the truth." Again, the question of Jesus' origin (9:29) arises. The Jewish leaders looked to his earthly origin. The healed man worked backwards from his healing to recognize the divine origin of his Healer.

9:35-41 The Light Is Worshiped and Rejected
Jesus did not come into the world for the purpose of condemnatory judgment (cf. 3:17), but his coming represented a judgment since the people who met him had to decide how to respond to his person (9:39). The Pharisees rejected the light Jesus offered and thus cast a dark shadow over their nation. Jesus not only sought to bring healing to the physically blind; he also desired to bring healing light to the spiritually blind.

10:1-39 THE SHEPHERD AND TRUE GUIDANCE
10:1-18 Intimate Sheep and Shepherd Relationship
The good shepherd presented in John 10 stands in contrast to the blind leaders of 9:41 who were in reality Satan's children (8:44). The author intended this chapter as part of the preceding discourse (10:21; reference to the blind man). Jesus' discourse on the good shepherd needs to be understood in light of the Old Testament references to the good and bad human shepherds (cf. Ps. 23:1; Isa. 40:11; 56:9-12; Jer. 23:1-4; Ezek. 34:23; Zech. 11:1-17). Jesus used this familiar image to communicate important truths regarding himself.

The "sheepfold" (10:1) was usually a rock enclosure designed to protect and shelter the sheep. The shepherd would actually lie down across the entrance of the sheepfold and become the "gate" (10:7). Note the editorial comment in John 10:6. It again reminds the reader that not seeing the spiritual truth behind Jesus' earthly words and acts was the main block to understanding him. In contrast to the Jewish leaders, Jesus leads his followers sacrificially (10:11, 15). On "one flock" (10:16) see 11:52 and 17:20-23. The "other sheep" (10:16) are the Gentiles who would be brought into God's family as heirs of the promise by faith (Eph. 2:16). The implications for the hearers are: Jesus is the good shepherd (10:11); God gave authority regarding the sheep and the sacrifice of Jesus (10:18); and obedience to Jesus' voice is necessary for those who desire to be one of his flock (10:27).

10:19-21 The Debate over the Source of Jesus' Power
The people debated the source of Jesus' power as they struggled to understand the implications of the healing of the blind man.

10:22-39 Feast of Dedication: Plain Statement of Identity
Hanukkah, or the Festival of Dedication, commemorated the cleansing and rededication of the temple by Judas Maccabeus in 164 B.C. after the defilement

by Antiochus Epiphanes (1 Macc. 4:52-59; 2 Macc. 10:5). It was also called the Feast of Lights because when the temple was cleansed, the lamps in the temple burned miraculously for eight days when the oil was sufficient for only one. The date was December 18, A.D. 32. "Solomon's Colonnade" (10:23) was the column-lined, covered porch along the east wall of the Court of the Gentiles. Belonging to and believing in Jesus is directly related to being given to Jesus by God (10:29). Jesus clearly stated his "oneness" with the Father (10:30). The security and comfort for his sheep lies in the essential link between Jesus and the Father. Jesus still tried to help the people even when they were about to stone him. He attempted to help them reason from the signs he had performed to their real significance (10:37-38). In 10:34 Jesus cites Psalm 82:6 to support his claim to deity.

10:40-42 BELIEF BEYOND THE JORDAN: CONFIRMED WORDS
This section, in which Jesus goes out into the wilderness (10:40), sets the stage for John 11:1-57. The hostility in Judea became so great that Jesus withdrew across the Jordan to Bethany, the place where John the Baptist had baptized (cf. 1:28). This Bethany must be distinguished from the Bethany near Jerusalem, where Mary, Martha, and Lazarus lived. The truth of John the Baptist's words, confirmed by Jesus' acts, brought about belief in the hearts of those who followed Jesus there.

11:1-57 THE SIGN OF LIFE
11:1-16 Background: Death and Threats
This sign of Lazarus's return to life is a fitting climax for the seven signs recorded by the apostle John. They all relate to the central truth of Jesus: that he is eternal life (1:4; 20:30-31). Note the relationship of love (11:3, 5, 11, 36) and glory (11:4, 15, 26, 40) in these verses. The ultimate way for Jesus to show love in this situation was not by rushing back to heal Lazarus before he died. It was to reveal the greater love and glory of resurrection.

The word "Although" in 11:5 is important. The delay was for God's glory and in the best love for Martha, Mary, and Lazarus. Compare 11:15 with 11:21, 32 regarding Jesus being there or not. Jesus' actions were designed to encourage belief (11:15). This "Bethany" (11:1), identified as the village of Mary and Martha, was located just east of the Mount of Olives, about half a mile from Jerusalem.

The disciples feared returning to Judea because of the opposition to Jesus that was growing there (11:7-16). But Jesus taught his disciples to see circumstances from the perspective of divine light (11:9-10), not from the perspective of the dark (11:8). Again the disciples felt and thought on the physical, rather than spiritual, level and therefore misunderstood Jesus' words (11:11-13). Jesus

referred to death (cf. 11:14) as being "asleep" (11:11) since a resurrection to life was anticipated for those who believed in him. The benefit of Jesus' absence (11:14-15) was resurrection for Lazarus and a great sign of the eternal life that was promised in Jesus the Messiah.

11:17-37 Two Interviews
Both Martha and Mary thought that Jesus could have kept Lazarus alive if he had been there (11:21, 32). But the implication of their statements is that now that Lazarus was dead, Jesus' being there could do no good. The "four days" (11:17) were significant, since it was held by some Jews that the spirit left the body only after the third day. In her talk with Jesus (11:17-29), Martha learned that he is a present power for life whether a person is in need of life for healing or resurrection life. She had faith in spite of her partial understanding of what Jesus said (11:23-27). The point is that Jesus is the resurrection to eternal life. Lazarus's physical resurrection, like the other physical healings by Jesus, points to a spiritual and eternal resurrection to life.

The Jews with Mary (11:30-37) also took up the sisters' questions concerning why Jesus had not arrived when Lazarus was still alive (11:37). The implication is that if Jesus really loved Lazarus, he could have kept him alive. Jesus would make a much greater point. Notice how the crowd took Jesus' ability to heal the blind man as proof that he would have been able to heal Lazarus too. See Luke 19:41-42 for another time Jesus cried (11:35).

11:38-44 At the Tomb
"God's glory" (11:40) was seen in the life given by God. Jesus prayed out of concern for the believer (11:42). He was giving an object lesson in prayer that emphasized that God had sent him. This miracle of resurrection (11:44) exhibited the kingdom condition excluding death (cf. Isa. 25:8) and vindicated Jesus' claim to be the bringer of life (John 11:25; cf. 5:21). Lazarus eventually died again. But this sign of physical resurrection was to point to the greater truth of resurrection to eternal life. This same point was made in the feeding of the five thousand. The people got physically hungry again, but the greater promise was the spiritual bread of eternal life.

11:45-57 The Sign's Impact
Two responses to Jesus can be found here: the response of belief (11:45) and the response of rejection (11:46). The Jewish leaders feared that Jesus would spark political upheaval that would result in further subjugation by Rome (11:47-48). Caiaphas (11:49) served as high priest from A.D. 18 to 36. Caiaphas thought that it would be better for one man (that is, Jesus) to die than for the nation to be subject to a heavier Roman yoke (11:50). Note 11:52 with reference to 10:16. The "village of

Ephraim" (11:54) has been identified as et-Taiyibeh, fourteen miles north of Jerusalem. The Passover of A.D. 33 was fast approaching, and many Galileans were going up to Jerusalem to participate in the festival (11:55).

12:1–20:31 THE SIGN OF THE RESURRECTION

Overview: Jesus returned to Jerusalem (12:1), despite knowlege that the Jewish leaders had given orders to seize him (11:55-57). The entire passion account is introduced with Jesus' willful movement to Jerusalem (cf. 2:19; 10:18). He was the Lamb of God willfully giving up his life for his sheep.

12:1-50 Focus on Death and Rejection

12:1-11 MARY ANOINTS JESUS

This may have been a thanksgiving party for Lazarus's resurrection. John puts this event into its historical time frame—the night before (12:12) Jesus' entry into Jerusalem. For "Bethany" (12:1), see note on 11:1. Judas was the treasurer and regularly stole funds (12:6). The result of Jesus' resurrection of Lazarus was belief for those who had seen the miracle (12:9-11).

12:12-19 INSIGHTS INTO THE JERUSALEM ENTRANCE

The royal entry took place on Monday, rather than Sunday. It was March 30 (Nisan 10), A.D. 33. John's use of Zechariah 9:9 (12:14-15) resulted from his looking back on Jesus' life from a time after Jesus' resurrection (12:16). There were mysteries about parts of Jesus' earthly life that were solved only after he was glorified and had sent the Holy Spirit to teach and remind his followers (14:26, 29).

12:20-26 FRUIT FOR THE GENTILES: FALLEN SEED

Note the link of 12:19 to 12:20. The "whole world" (12:19) was represented by the "Greeks" (12:20). "The time has come" (12:23). The "time" was that long-awaited time (2:4; 7:6, 30; 13:1; 17:1) in which Jesus would be glorified through his crucifixion and resurrection. Jesus was about to begin the culmination of his ministry as the Lamb of God. Jesus used the illustration of the fallen seed (12:24) to predict his death and its results; his death would bring salvation to the world. Jesus' death could easily have been

seen as defeat. But the gospel message claims that his death was necessary and of eternal benefit to the world (12:24). The gospel calls believers to give up their lives to God that his kingdom of light and life might take root in a dark and dying world. Love of life in this world can be a block to eternal life (12:25).

12:27-36 MISUNDERSTANDINGS CONCERNING JESUS' DEATH

God's authenticating witness to Jesus' person and authority (12:27-30) was for the crowd's benefit to help them believe (cf. 11:42). The crowd misunderstood the most important role of the Messiah—his responsibility to be lifted up as a sacrifice for sin. They only understood his permanence (12:31-36). Jesus used the phrase "Son of Man" to help educate them about his crucifixion. That is why they wondered who the Son of Man was (12:34). A crucified Messiah was a new and difficult concept for them to grasp (cf. 12:25-26).

12:37-50 PASSIONATE PLEA FOR BELIEF

This section serves to expand and explain the words of John's prologue (1:1-18) concerning light, life, and belief. The crowds listening to Jesus were still confused about who he was (12:34, 37, 42, 43). The words of 12:39-41 were quoted from Isaiah 6:10. In Jesus' last appeal to the crowds (12:44), he gave reasons for belief and emphasized the people's responsibility to believe. The divine person whom Isaiah saw (Isa. 6:1-4) was none other than the preincarnate Christ. The words concerning God's commands to Jesus (12:49-50) formed the foundation for Jesus' call to obedience and abiding in John 13–17.

13:1–16:33 Focus on Departure and Disciples

Overview: The four Gospels contain three great discourses of Jesus. In the Sermon on the Mount (Matt. 5–7) Jesus detailed the demands of righteousness and repentance. That sermon was given to those who wanted to know how to enter the kingdom. The stress was on fulfilling the law and Jesus interpreted the law for the present.

The second major discourse, the Olivet Discourse (Matt. 24–25; Mark 13; Luke 21), described the end times and the endurance that would be required of the faithful. That discourse was given to the

---

THE UPPER ROOM DISCOURSE

    I. A. Jesus' Example of Humility (13:1-20)
        B. The Prediction of Jesus' Betrayal (13:21-30)
   II. A. The Command to Love (13:31-35)
        B. Comfort in Absence (13:36–14:31)
  III. A. The Command to Love in the Face of World Hatred (15:1-27)
        B. Comfort in Absence (16:1-33)

disciples and centered on personal stability during a time of great temptation to depart from the faith. It was future oriented.

The third discourse, the Upper Room Discourse, defined the love of God. It was instruction concerning the new relationship between God and humanity brought about by the start of the new covenant founded in Jesus' blood. This discourse forms the key link to the "in Christ" emphasis of the epistles, especially Paul's writings. This instruction was Jesus' response to those few who believed and were insecure about living life after he had gone away.

The purpose of the Upper Room Discourse was to prepare the disciples for Jesus' death, resurrection, and absence (John 13:14; 14:2-3, 18, 21, 23; 15:18-27; 16:5, 16-22, 28-33). Jesus instructed his disciples about their future. Unlike the Olivet Discourse's emphasis on the end-time events of tribulation and apostasy, the Upper Room Discourse viewed the future from the perspective of how God would be present with them even though Jesus had gone away. It focused on the elements of abiding and love, so important for the life of faith during his absence.

The promise of the Holy Spirit was one of Jesus' central concerns (14:16-18, 26; 15:26-27; 16:7-15). The Holy Spirit would be the one who would help believers cooperate with God. The return of Jesus was discussed (14:1-3), but the coming of the Holy Spirit was viewed as the bridge of God's presence until Jesus returned. Jesus made it clear that there would be conflict with the world (15:18-27). But the believer's response to the world was to be controlled by love. Similarly, conduct between believers was to be governed by love (13:3-35; 15:1-17). Love contrasts with how the unbeliever responds to the light—with hate and hostility.

Finally, Jesus prayed for the preservation, sanctification, and unification of his disciples (17:1-26). Jesus' followers were to be assured that if anyone's prayers would be answered, Jesus' would. Every word in his prayer in John 17 will be answered for those who believe in him.

The accompanying chart shows the basic content of the discourse. It contains three sections that divide into two subsections each.

The key concepts are (1) finding comfort through Jesus' peace and the coming of the Holy Spirit; (2) the importance of remaining faithful to (abiding in) Jesus' commands; and (3) showing love for one another by following Jesus' example. These three concepts spoke to the disciples on the levels of emotion, the will, and behavior.

13:1-30 THE PREPARATION FOR THE INSTRUCTION

13:1-20 Illustration of Humiliation

Before Jesus could go on to speak of the disciples' glory, he first clearly illustrated the humble service

that would lead to glory. The lines of rejection (Judas) and acceptance (the disciples) were drawn. Jesus' departure would be the start of his disciples' continuance of expressing his love. Just before the Feast of Passover Jesus purposed to give his disciples a very practical demonstration of his love. The "full extent" of Jesus' love (13:1) referred to both the time and quality of his love. Feet were usually washed before the meal. But Jesus waited until during the supper (13:2) to make the act stand out as noteworthy. Jesus knew that he could take a servant's role without losing anything (13:3). The purpose of this action was to fix in their minds the nature of true greatness.

The background of this event can be found in Luke 22:24-30. The disciples were in the midst of a dispute over who was going to be the greatest in the kingdom. Jesus had taught them that greatness in the kingdom comes through serving others (Matt. 20:26-27), but they had not learned the lesson. Thus, he gave them this unforgettable illustration.

At first Peter rejected Jesus' humble service of foot washing (13:6-11), which pointed toward Jesus' humble, cleansing work on the cross. But when Peter saw that this foot washing was symbolic of cleansing from sin, he wanted to be washed from head to foot. Peter had discovered the spiritual aspect of the foot-washing ceremony but would need to think about the more literal aspects of service. He misunderstood Jesus the Messiah's servant role and therefore his own role as disciple. In 13:10 Jesus came back to the literal point. The spiritual point had already been understood. They were already clean. Jesus was also showing his disciples what it meant to serve—what it meant to be great in the kingdom of God.

As teacher, Jesus should be believed (13:12-15); as Lord, he should be obeyed. The teacher is the one from whom truth is learned; and the Lord is the one to be obeyed (13:13). Jesus explained his act of foot washing as a symbol and linked it to 13:34 and his new command to love. He linked being a servant of God to salvation and to the perfecting of discipleship. Jesus explained the significance of the foot washing in terms of a pattern of humble service that the disciples needed to follow.

Many view this act as an illustration of the "washing of rebirth" ("He washed away our sins and gave us a new life," Titus 3:5) and the "cleansing" of 1 John 1:9. Others prefer a more literal reading of humble service pictured by foot washing (13:15). John 13:17 is the classic passage on the relationship between knowing and the blessing of doing. In 13:18 Jesus quoted Psalm 41:9 as finding its ultimate fulfillment in Judas. That was a sign of Jesus' knowledge to encourage belief in him and a relationship with God the Father (13:9-20).

13:21-30 The Separation of the Son of Perdition
The separation was to get the unbelief (Judas) out in order to make room for instruction to the immature (disciples). The disciples ate while lying on their sides. John was "sitting next to Jesus" (13:23; cf. 21:20, 24). The words "next to" literally mean "in the sphere of." As the disciples reclined around a low table, they turned on their sides, propping themselves up with an elbow. The "bread" (13:26) was like a small sandwich with a bit of lamb with bitter herbs folded in a small piece of what is known today as Middle Eastern pocket bread.

13:31–16:33 THE PARTICULARS OF THE INSTRUCTION
Jesus made it clear that he was the exclusive means of salvation. The comfort he left behind was founded on his promises: he will return (14:3); he prepares a place for us (14:2); he answers prayer (14:13-14); he sends the Comforter (14:16); our obedience manifests the Father's love (14:21); the Spirit will instruct (14:26); and Jesus leaves peace with believers (14:27).

13:31–14:31 Instruction Regarding God's Presence
The prologue to this section is in 13:31-35. Jesus addressed the problem of his absence (13:33). Behavior during his absence is to be governed by love (13:34).

The problems centered on comfort in Jesus' coming absence (13:36–14:24). Jesus' statement in 13:33 about his absence provoked insecurities and questions from the disciples. Peter asked the first questions: where? (13:36) and why? (13:37). Peter's claim that he would lay down his life for Jesus was serious (13:37). Later that night he attempted to defend Jesus against those who arrested him in the garden (cf. 18:10). Peter wondered why he could not follow Jesus (13:36-38). Jesus' reply (14:1-4) shows what was behind Peter's question—a troubled and insecure heart. Jesus taught Peter and the others about the importance of love during Jesus' coming absence. Another aspect of comfort can be found in Jesus' foreknowledge (14:29).

Note especially 14:2, 23. Jesus will prepare a dwelling place for those who believe, and he and the Father will dwell with the obedient believer on this earth (14:23). The preparation of the place is certainly not heavenly carpentry but relates to Jesus' ascension and sending forth of the Spirit to take up his dwelling place with believers, whether now on earth, or later in heaven.

The cross was a stage in the glorification of Jesus. That symbol of shame was also a symbol of glory (see 1 Cor. 1:17). Jesus' departure (13:33) was the central issue of his ministry here. He emphasized the children's immaturity and the Father's care.

Thomas wondered how they would know how to find the Father if Jesus was not there to show them the way (14:5-7). Behind Thomas's questions was a burning desire to be where Jesus was and not to be left behind and alone. Philip (14:8-21) asked specifically for a demonstration of who the Father was (14:8). Jesus taught that he was the link between man and God. To see Jesus was to see the Father. John 14:11 presents the central idea of John's entire Gospel—belief (cf. 20:30-31).

The context would indicate that the "greater works" (14:12) are those things accomplished by Jesus' disciples through prayer in his name (cf. 14:13-14). In the biblical period, one's name represented the person; it was a summary statement of someone's character or reputation (14:14). The name of Jesus pointed to his attributes, his person, and all that he had accomplished. It was no mere magical formula, but a confession of dependence, trust, and confidence in the person and work of Jesus the Messiah. Again the obedient saint would be the one who experiences God in this earthly life (14:21). Jesus' answer to Judas' questions (14:22-24) brings the discussion around full-circle back to 13:34 (cf. 14:23).

In the epilogue (14:25-31), Jesus continued to show concern for the believers' comfort in his absence. He gave the promise of the Counselor (14:25-26). Jesus' promise of the Holy Spirit's power for remembrance meets the disciples' needs for insight and strength of faith after Jesus had gone (especially 2:22; see also 2:17; 7:39; 13:19; 14:20, "you will know"; 15:20; 16:4; 17:13; 19:35-37; 20:8-10).

The promise of peace (14:27) was a positive blessing (cf. Isa. 54:10; Ezek 34:25; 37:26). The promise of parting was in John 14:28-31. Jesus could have banished the "prince of this world" (14:30). But he did not because he wanted to show God's love and his own obedience to the world (14:31). See 14:31 for the relationship between love and keeping commandments.

The words "let's be going" may mean that Jesus and the disciples were departing from the Upper Room and that the discourse was finished along the way to the garden. Others suggest that Jesus made the statement at this time but did not leave until after his words in John 17. John included this statement in order to mark off a major division in the discourse.

15:1–16:4 Instruction Regarding the Harvest
In the section of 15:1–16:4, Jesus elaborated on keeping the Father's word (14:23), especially the commandment to love (13:34; 14:31). The cause of the disciple's fruit-bearing was explained by using the metaphor of the vine (15:1-11). This metaphor was common in the Old Testament (cf. Ps. 80:8; Isa. 5:1-7; Jer. 2:21; Ezek. 15:1-8; Hos. 10:1). Israel was the vine in the Old Testament passages. In John's Gospel Jesus was depicted as the true vine.

Two types of branches were described: fruit-bearing and fruitless (John 15:2). The fruit-bearing branches were "pruned" (lit., "cleansed") while the fruitless branches were cut off and destroyed.

What would happen to these fruitless branches was revealed in 15:6. Fruit was what the vinedresser intended for his vines—in this context, the keeping of God's commands. Pruning, in this context, would increase the disciple's obedience to the word of Jesus for a greater harvest. The harvest, in this context, would be acts of obedience that follow Jesus' acts of obedience and love. For a similar illustration, see Jeremiah 15:1-8. It appears that the fruitless branch was in fact a lifeless branch that had no life-giving connection with Jesus, the vine.

The vineyard image was simply another way of expressing the teaching of John 1:1-8. Jesus the Messiah is the light of the world. Some will accept him and gain eternal life. Others will reject him and gain death. Jesus is the vine to whom some will respond and bear fruit. Others will not respond to him and will gain death. The "in me" (15:4) is not the same as Paul's "in Christ." It is the place where the light of Christ shines on everyone (cf. 1:4, 9). The benefits of "remaining" or "abiding" (NASB and KJV) are obedience and joy (cf. 15:10, 12).

Jesus exemplified the totally honest friend who would be willing to lay down his life for his friends (15:13-16). The term "friends" (15:14) was used both in a general sense and a technical sense in the Roman period. In the technical sense, to be a "friend of Caesar" meant that you held the highest position possible in relationship to the emperor and the Roman government. Such "friends" of Caesar knew the emperor so well they actually opened his mail and carried out his correspondence. In addition, they were willing to go wherever the emperor commanded to conduct his affairs. Who is a "friend" of Jesus? Those who know him intimately and obey him willingly.

Jesus also taught his disciples how to relate to their enemies (15:18–16:4). This section taught them to show love in the face of hatred. The disciple would be equal to Jesus in showing love and in bearing the world's hate (15:20; 13:16). In Greek grammar, the "when" describes a condition that is assumed as true (15:18). The phrase *"When the world hates you"* could also be translated, *"Since the world hates you."*

The witness of the Holy Spirit and the disciples (15:26-27) was behind the writing of the Gospel of John in the first place (20:30-31). That witness in Jesus' name would produce the same hatred as John and Jesus experienced. Jesus warned of these negative things to keep his followers from stumbling after experiencing this hatred from the world.

Excommunication from the synagogue involved being cut off from all normal dealings with the Jewish community (16:2; cf. 9:22). The term "service" (16:2) referred to "religious service." Like Paul, they would persecute the Christians, thinking they were serving God in doing so (Phil. 3:6).

16:5-33 Revelation Regarding Comfort
The Holy Spirit would work during Jesus' absence. Jesus' departure was necessary for the sending of the Holy Spirit (cf. Luke 24:49; Acts 1:4-5; 2:1-40). The Holy Spirit would work in the world as prosecutor and as comforter (John 16:8-11). The word "convince" (16:8) was a legal term meaning to cross-examine for the purpose of convincing or refuting an opponent. It involved the setting forth in a clear and convincing manner the true character of a person or thing. The disciples would also be the recipients of the guiding and revealing work of the Father by means of the Spirit (16:12-15). The outcome of the resurrection would be Jesus' absence, but he would someday return (16:16-24).

Jesus promised to give peace during the times of tribulation. The section of 16:25-33 is foundational for 17:7-8. Jesus' stay on earth was just one half of a circle that began and ended with the Father. The way down, through obedience and the cross, was the way back to glory. In John 17 Jesus would include his followers in that journey back to the glory of God. Up to this time in Jesus' ministry he had spoken enigmatically—through parables, allegories, and figures with implications not easy to understand. From this point on, things would be different (16:25; cf. 16:29).

17:1-26 Prayer following the Instruction
Overview: This prayer was, in part, the basis for John's meditation that was presented in the prologue (1:1-18). Compare 1:1 with 17:5, 11, 24; 1:3 with 17:2; 1:4 with 17:2; 1:9-10 with 17:14; 1:12 with 17:3; 1:14 with 17:4, 24; and 1:18 with 17:3, 6, 26. Jesus used many purpose statements that added up to a powerful world mission (note the use of "so"; 17:1-3, 11, 13, 19, 21-23, 26). Along with the purpose statements, Jesus used comparison statements between himself and his followers (17:11, 14, 16, 18, 21-23). The purpose of unity is world witness. This was communicated by comparing the disciples and Jesus and by the transference of Jesus' glory to the disciples (17:22-23).

17:1-5 THE LORD AND THE FATHER
John 17 is the longest of Jesus' recorded prayers and was spoken in the presence of the disciples in the Upper Room or somewhere along the way to the Garden of Gethsemane. Jesus prayed for himself (17:1-5), his disciples (17:6-19), and for future believers (17:20-24).

17:6-19 THE LORD AND THE DISCIPLES
The essence of what Jesus did for his followers was to convince them that he was a true reflection of the

Father (17:7). This explained his words in the prologue (1:18). Jesus gave the reason for his petition for the disciples (17:6-8) and then requested their preservation (17:9-16). The "one headed for destruction" (17:12) was Judas, whose betrayal was anticipated in Psalm 41:9 (cf. John 13:18). The way to sanctification is through God's Word becoming reality in a believer's life (17:17; cf. 13:17). The "evil one" (17:15) referred to Satan. "Holy" (17:17) meant to "set apart." Jesus prayed that the disciples would be "set apart" for God and his purposes by the truth. Jesus' commission of the disciples was an extension of God's commission of Jesus (17:18). The disciples would be Jesus' representatives.

17:20-26 THE LORD AND THE FAMILY

Jesus prayed for the unification of future believers (17:20-23; see also 20:29). The purpose of the glory spoken of in 17:22 was for worldwide evangelization. This prayer for unity had an evangelistic purpose—so that the world may believe that God the Father sent his divine Son. The glory of believers is the unity shared between the Son, the Father, and themselves (17:22). Jesus wanted the disciples to behold his glory as proof of his eternal oneness with the Father (17:24). On this earth Jesus promised to continue to make the Father's name known (17:26). Sharing God's love (17:26) was the purpose of both his prayer and the entire section of John 13–17.

18:1–19:42 The Passion of the Passover Lamb of God

Overview: The Passion was the last aspect of the wilderness theme in John (Jesus as the tabernacle, John 1; the bronze snake, John 3; manna, John 6; rock of water, John 7; light, John 8; and Jesus as the Passover lamb, 18:28; 19:14; 1:29). Notice what Jesus knew during the passion events. He was seen as in full control of the situation. He knew his hour had come (13:1), what was about to happen (18:4), and that all was completed or accomplished (19:28). His hour of glory was related to the Greeks (12:23) and to Judas' exit (13:31).

18:1-11 THE ARREST

Darkness and light meet in these verses. Jesus' actions revealed the character and will of the Father (1:18; 17:6-7). His movement to the cross was the climax of explaining the loving heart of God. The "Kidron" (18:1) is a small north-south valley with a stream that flows during the rainy season. The valley is situated between the Temple Mount and the Mount of Olives. The "grove" referred to Gethsemane (cf. Matt. 26:36). A Roman "battalion" (18:3) consisted of a company of six hundred soldiers. The text does not indicate that the whole company came to arrest Jesus. Like the modern expression "the police came," so representatives of

the Roman military forces went to the garden. John 18:8-9 shows the fulfillment of 17:12. On 18:10 see Luke 22:51 for the healing of Malchus's ear.

18:12–19:16 THE TRIALS

18:12-27 The Jewish Trial

John contrasted the denials of Peter with the strong witness of Jesus. This gave the reader a good example to follow and completed Jesus' mission of explaining the Father through faithful witness. The examination by Annas (18:13), the high priest (A.D. 6–15) was unique to John's Gospel. Although he had been removed from office by the Romans, he was still regarded as a person of authority by the Jews since the high priest was to hold office for life. Caiaphas (John 18:14, 24), the son-in-law of Annas, was officially serving as high priest at that time (A.D. 18–36). Details of the trial before Caiaphas were recorded by Matthew. After questioning Jesus, Annas gave permission to proceed with the trial before Caiaphas (John 18:24).

Peter provided a negative example for the believer's witness in the world (18:15-18). Jesus provided a just question for all who would be unjustly persecuted in his name (18:23). John, known to the high priest, secured Peter's entrance (18:15). Since his mother, Salome, may have been the sister of Mary (John 19:25; Mark 15:40), and Mary was related to Elizabeth, a daughter of Aaron (Luke 1:5), John was of priestly descent. This is confirmed by Polycrates as recorded by Eusebius (*Historia Ecclesiastica*, 3.31).

18:28–19:16 The Roman Trial

More of the Roman trial is seen here than in Matthew, Mark, and Luke. The emphases are (1) the innocence of Jesus; (2) the attempted release by Pilate; and (3) the hardened unbelief of the religious leaders. The "headquarters" (John 18:28) was the governor's residence, perhaps Herod's Palace, but more likely the Antonia Fortress located just north of the temple area. The Jews did not want to enter the fortress, the dwelling of Gentiles, lest they be defiled and rendered unfit to eat the Passover meal.

How was it that Jesus and the disciples ate the Passover (the "Last Supper") on the day before his crucifixion (Matt. 26:20; Mark 14:17; Luke 22:14; John 13:2) and the Jews yet expected to eat the Passover on the evening of Jesus' crucifixion? Many solutions have been offered to solve this problem. It may be that there were actually two Passovers observed on the basis of two different methods of reckoning a day. The Galileans and Pharisees may have begun counting their day at sunrise whereas the Judeans and Sadducees may have begun their days at sunset. Thus the disciples from Galilee would have begun their Passover in the morning, but the religious leaders in Jerusalem would have not begun their official Passover until that evening, with their major preparations not starting until the following morning, the morning of Jesus' trial and crucifixion.

With the Galileans, Jesus and his disciples observed Passover on Thursday, Nisan 14. The Judeans sacrificed their Passover lambs Friday afternoon, Nisan 14 according to their reckoning, and observed the feast that evening. There is no explicit statement of Scripture to support the theory of two Passovers except for the evidence for two Jewish ways of reckoning a day. This view does explain John 18:28, allowing Jesus to be the Passover Lamb in fulfillment of Old Testament typology (John 19:36; 1 Cor. 5:7), and harmonizing the data found in the Synoptics and the Gospel of John.

Following the expulsion of Herod's son Archelaus in A.D. 6, Judea became a Roman Imperial Province governed by a prefect (John 18:29). Pontius Pilate served as prefect from A.D. 26 to 36. He normally lived in Caesarea but stayed in Jerusalem during Jewish festivals to help maintain order. The Jews, under Roman rule, were denied the authority to execute capital punishment except in situations that violated the sanctity of the Jerusalem temple (18:31).

In 18:34-35 Jesus inquired whether Pilate had been prompted by the Jews and was therefore thinking of a king as a Messianic person, or whether his question was strictly political. Pilate's response (18:35) reflects the fact that he was only interested in finding out if Jesus had done anything to warrant prosecution by Rome. Jesus admitted to having a kingdom, but not one that was a threat to Rome (18:36).

Pilate made the first of several attempts to free Jesus (18:38-40). Josephus wrote of a man whose ribs were laid bare by scourging (19:1). Pilate was unable to save Jesus. Note the three "not guilty" remarks (18:38; 19:4, 6). Pilate was obviously using sarcasm with his words, "You crucify him" (19:6). In fact, the right to execute capital punishment was the most jealously guarded privilege of the Roman government. The Jews had no such authority (18:31). The fear of losing his status as "friend of Caesar" (19:12; see the note on John 15:14) convinced Pilate that it was necessary, for his own sake, to allow the Jews to put Jesus to death. Pilate had been sent to Palestine to keep the peace at all cost.

Pilate had been a ruthless ruler (Luke 13:1), but in A.D. 32 his friend and protector (Sejanus) in Rome who had been covering up his abuses had been executed. Pilate was no longer secure and comfortable in his relationship with Caesar. He had to guard against any negative reports coming to the emperor's ears. The Jews knew that he was vulnerable at this point and forced Pilate's decision to crucify Jesus.

The "Stone Pavement" (John 19:13) was located in the Antonia Fortress. The crucifixion took place at 9:00 A.M. (Mark 15:25). In John 19:14-15 there may be yet a fourth attempt by Pilate to set Jesus free.

19:17-42 THE CRUCIFIXION
19:17-22 The Inscription
Golgotha was probably located at the site of the Church of the Holy Sepulcher, situated about one quarter mile southwest of the Antonia Fortress. The site was identified by Helena, the emperor Constantine's mother, when she visited the Holy Land in A.D. 326. A church was built over the site. This structure was later destroyed and rebuilt several times. The present church was completed in A.D. 1149 by the Crusaders.

19:23-27 Gambling and Adoption
Crucifixion, a horrible and prolonged means of execution, was perfected by the Romans. Having been hung with arms stretched wide above the head on an upright wooden post, the victim eventually succumbed to asphyxiation as his diaphragm became distended and lost its ability to fill the lungs with air. "The disciple whom Jesus loved" (13:23; 19:26; 20:2; 21:7, 20) was John, the author of this Gospel. Jesus assigned to him the responsibility of caring for his mother.

19:28-42 The Death of Jesus
"Sour wine" (19:29) was a common drink, often used by soldiers and laborers. "Hyssop" is a plant with stems two to three feet in length. Even Jesus' thirst was related to the fulfillment of God's word through the Old Testament Scriptures (19:28).

The Sabbath (19:31) was to be a "special Sabbath" in that it would coincide with Passover. Breaking the legs (19:32) was intended to bring death by preventing the victim from using the legs to raise himself up in order to breath. Victims often surged and plunged on the cross for amazingly long periods before dying of respiratory failure. However, Jesus had died early. Even the time of his death honored God and fulfilled his word (19:36). Joseph was from Arimathea, a town of uncertain location (19:38). Nicodemus's (19:39) visit with Jesus was recorded in 3:1-15. Matthew also recorded that the tomb belonged to Joseph of Arimathea (Matt. 27:57-60).

20:1-29 The Resurrection
20:1-10 THE EMPTY GRAVE
The "other disciple" (20:2) referred to the apostle John, the author of this Gospel. The orderly state of the tomb implied that a supernatural exit of Jesus from his burial wrappings had taken place (20:6-7). The effect was the same for the next group of eyewitnesses (20:8-10). What did John believe? Apparently he believed in the resurrection of Jesus. John 20:9 indicates that this belief preceded an understanding that the resurrection was foretold in Scripture (cf. Pss. 2:7; 16:10; Isa. 52:12-13). The disciples were convinced of the resurrection first and then later came to an understanding of the Old Testament prophetic Scriptures. This suggests that they did not manufacture a resurrection story to agree with their interpretation of prophecy.

20:11-18 THE LORD APPEARS TO MARY

This was the first of five appearances of Jesus on resurrection day: to Mary Magdalene (Mark 16:9-11; John 20:11-18); to the other women (Matt. 28:9-10); to Simon Peter (Luke 24:33-35; 1 Cor. 15:5); to the two disciples on the road to Emmaus (Mark 16:12-13; Luke 24:13-32); and to the eleven apostles (Mark 16:14; Luke 24:36-43; John 20:19-25). The words "Don't cling to me" (20:17) indicate that Mary needed to realize that Jesus' presence was not permanent. He explained that he had not yet ascended to the Father. That ascent was on the surface a sad departure of Jesus from those who loved him. On a deeper level, Jesus' ascent to the Father opened up the new presence of Jesus and the Father with the believer through the Holy Spirit.

20:19-23 THE LORD APPEARS TO THE DISCIPLES

In his first resurrection appearance Jesus reconfirmed his words of comfort, his promise of the Holy Spirit (20:19-20), and his commission to them (20:21-23). The disciples were commanded to receive the Holy Spirit (20:22). Jesus breathed on his disciples as he commanded them to receive the Spirit. (When the Day of Pentecost came, the disciples would complete their obedience to this command to receive the Spirit and would see the Spirit as the very breath of the risen and ascended Lord.) As they had received Jesus, so they would receive the Spirit. The next verse (20:23) unpacks the full implication of receiving the Spirit: it was the reception of God's authority to announce forgiveness and judgment in the name of Jesus.

20:24-29 THE SECOND APPEARANCE: FROM DOUBT TO BELIEF

The climax of the Gospel has two aspects. First, Thomas's confession of Jesus as Lord and God (20:28-29) was the perfect expression of faith and worship by a disciple of Jesus. Second, Jesus clarified the relation between faith and sight. Faith was not dependent on actually seeing the risen Lord. The next section made this very clear.

20:30-31 THE CALL TO DECISION

Here John disclosed the purpose of his Gospel—to encourage belief in the truth that Jesus was Israel's divine Messiah. The signs presented by John were to stand as the basis for belief. Unlike Thomas, the reader would not have access to seeing and touching the risen Lord before belief could take place. See 2:21-22 for how the signs operated for even the faith of the eyewitnesses.

21:1-25 ASSURANCE AND COMMISSION

21:1-23 The Galilean Appearance

21:1-14 THE CATCH OF FISH AND BREAKFAST

This was the third appearance of the risen Lord. In this narrative, Jesus told his disciples how they were to function as apostles. The catch of fish and the breakfast were certainly miracles and related to encouraging the disciples in their lives of faith. But this appearance had special significance for Peter and John. The "Sea of Tiberias" was another name for the "Sea of Galilee" (21:1). This name was derived from the name of the prominent town built by Herod Antipas and named for Tiberius Caesar. For "Cana in Galilee" (21:2), see note on 2:1.

21:15-23 PETER'S INSTRUCTIONS

In this section Jesus spoke with his disciples concerning love and service (21:15-19). Jesus had already met with Peter privately and probably dealt with his denial at that time (Luke 24:34; 1 Cor. 15:5). Here Jesus instructed Peter concerning his ministry and motives as a church leader. There is debate as to whether John intended a distinction between the two Greek words for "love," *agapao* (Jesus' word) and *phileo* (Peter's word), or whether John used the variation without intending any distinction. Those holding that a distinction is being made suggest that *agapao* is a volitional love that can be commanded. It seeks the good of the object loved even to the point of personal sacrifice. The other word, *phileo*, was understood to refer to an emotional love based on personal affection. Jesus was asking Peter about the depth of his commitment, and the apostle was responding by expressing affection. In his third question (21:17), Jesus used Peter's word (*phileo*), asking if his professed affection was real and sincere. Peter assured Jesus that it was. But 21:17 recounts Jesus asking three similar questions "a third time." In that light neither Jesus, Peter, nor John saw any significant difference between the two words for love in this context. The crucial point of this passage was that Jesus was highlighting Peter's responsibility of feeding and caring for Jesus' sheep, the believers. Peter's love for Jesus would be essential to being faithful to the task.

In 21:18-19 Jesus revealed that Peter would die a martyr's death, a death that would glorify God. Eusebius reported that Peter was crucified head down in Rome under the persecution of Nero in A.D. 64. John's future (21:20-23) was in God's hands. Peter's task was to follow Jesus.

21:24-25 Postscript

The conclusion concerns the true witness (21:24). That witness was claimed by the author ("I," 21:25) and by his circle of friends ("we," 21:24). Those other acts of Jesus were lost to history, but the signs included in John's Gospel would be sufficient to bring its readers to believe in Jesus, the Son of God.

ACTS

BASIC FACTS

HISTORICAL SETTING
The book of Acts covers the period from the ascension of Jesus (around A.D. 33) to Paul's first imprisonment in Rome (from around A.D. 60 to 62). Some of the events recorded in the book of Acts were also recorded in secular history, making it possible to build a basic chronology: the death of Herod Agrippa in A.D. 44 (12:20-23); the expulsion of the Jews from Rome by Claudius in A.D. 49 (18:2); the proconsulship of Gallio in A.D. 51 or 52 (18:12); and the procuratorship of Festus in A.D. 59 (24:27).

AUTHOR
Although the author of Acts is not named, the evidence points to Luke. The Muratorian Canon indicates that as early as the middle of the second century A.D., the church believed Acts to be written by Luke the physician, the friend and fellow traveler of Paul. The church fathers, Irenaeus, Clement of Alexandria, Tertullian, and Origen, support the view of Lukan authorship. No evidence in the other New Testament books conflicts with the view that Luke was the author.

The book indicates that the author is also the author of the Gospel of Luke (Luke 1:3-4; Acts 1:1). The dedication to Theophilus links the two works. The medical vocabulary used in Acts supports the tradition that Acts was authored by Luke. Luke is the apparent writer of the "we" sections of Acts (16:10-17; 20:5–21:18; 27:1–28:16), having joined Paul, Silas, and Timothy at Troas (16:11).

Luke was a Gentile convert (Col. 4:14), possibly of the church at Antioch (claimed by Jerome and Eusebius). Luke joined Paul at Troas (Acts 16:10-11) during his second missionary journey and accompanied him to Philippi. He later accompanied Paul to Jerusalem (20:5–21:15) and finally to Rome (27:1–28:15). He was called by Paul "dear doctor" and "co-worker" (Col. 4:14; Philem. 24) and was his last friend to remain with him during his second imprisonment (2 Tim. 4:11). Luke was an able historian, doctor, missionary, and theologian.

DATE
The book of Acts was probably written in Rome during or following Paul's first imprisonment there (A.D. 60–62). That the work was published around A.D. 63 is indicated by the lack of reference to the fall of Jerusalem (A.D. 70) or the persecution of the Christians by Nero following the fire of Rome in A.D. 64. There is no hint in Acts that Nero's

anti-Christian policy had yet manifested itself. The fact that Paul's imprisonment and death (A.D. 67 or 68) were not recorded is also evidence that Acts was written around A.D. 63.

PURPOSE

The book was designed to be the second half of a two-volume work by Luke, completing the story begun in Luke's Gospel. Acts shows how the coming of the Holy Spirit was the initial goal of Jesus' ascension; he was the continued presence of Jesus on earth to proclaim his kingdom. Acts solidly demonstrated how the Spirit would preserve and empower the gospel message through people who followed the sometimes hard road of worldwide evangelization.

GEOGRAPHY AND ITS IMPORTANCE

The book of Acts follows the geographical pattern mandated by the risen Lord (Acts 1:8). Beginning in Jerusalem, the geography expands to Judea, Samaria, and to the remote parts of the earth—in this case, to Rome, the book's geographical and thematic goal. The expansion of Christianity from Jerusalem to Rome exposed Christians to different cultures, but the responses to the gospel followed along two consistent lines. People either embraced the faith, or, for political and religious reasons, rejected the faith. Some of the rejections were extremely hostile, even fatal. But nothing stopped the geographical and spiritual spread of Christianity—not human hostility, political intrigue, storms, or illness. The power behind the spread of the gospel across the miles of mountains and seas was the Holy Spirit, who came at the beginning of the book and never ceased to empower the proclamation.

Modern names and boundaries are shown in gray.

GUIDING CONCEPTS

STRUCTURE

The unhindered gospel
The events in the book of Acts move in a straight line from Jerusalem to Paul's unhindered preaching of the gospel in Rome. The entire book can be summed up in the words "no one tried to stop him" (Acts 28:31). Although the believers sometimes suffered in chains, shipwreck, or martyrdom, the power of the gospel was not hindered. From Jerusalem in Acts 1 to the triumphal proclamation of the gospel in Rome in Acts 28, the book is about the power of the Lord through his Spirit to spread the message of redemption worldwide.

Key places
The spread of the gospel in Acts follows the geographic plan laid out by Jesus in 1:8. The book begins in Jerusalem (1:1–8:3), moves to Judea and Samaria (8:4-40), and concludes in the remote (from the viewpoint of Jerusalem) regions of the world (9:1–28:31).

Key people
The book also presents the lives of two famous missionaries, Peter and Paul. Peter receives the first focus (1:1–8:40). Then the book introduces Paul and moves back and forth between the ministries of these two great men (9:1–12:24). The book's largest and final part focuses on Paul's ministry (12:25–28:31).

THREE MAJOR PROBLEMS
The book of Acts focuses first on the spread of Christianity and its resultant problems within the Jewish community (1:1–8:25). Then the book shows the problems inside and outside Christianity when the gospel spread to the Gentiles (8:26–12:24). The last part of the book focuses more on the impact of the gospel on Gentile communities. In this section opposition comes from the Jewish and the civil realms (12:25–28:31). Overall, the book of Acts deals with the following three problems:

The problem of Jesus of Nazareth as the exalted Messiah
The Jews of the first century viewed Christianity as a new religion. The first part of Acts focuses on the problems within the Jewish community concerning the Christians' claim that Jesus was the Messiah and exalted Lord (1:1–8:40). It was difficult for the Jewish establishment to believe that a humble man from Nazareth could be the promised Messiah, much less God in the flesh. As Lord, he brought a new perspective on obedience to God's commands.

The problem of new perspectives on law and covenant
The new way in which the Christians understood the Mosaic Law aroused anger and persecution from the religious authorities. The new changes in the conditions for how humans had fellowship with God were hard for the Jewish religious leaders to accept. The book of Hebrews gives the most complete explanation of the movement from Moses to the Messiah. God had replaced Moses' covenant with Christ's. But he had not thrown away his demands for obedience and personal purity. The Christians believed that though the old covenant in Moses had been replaced with the new covenant in Christ, the perfect law of God still remained and had to be obeyed.

The covenant structure was certainly different between Moses and Christ. To be sure,

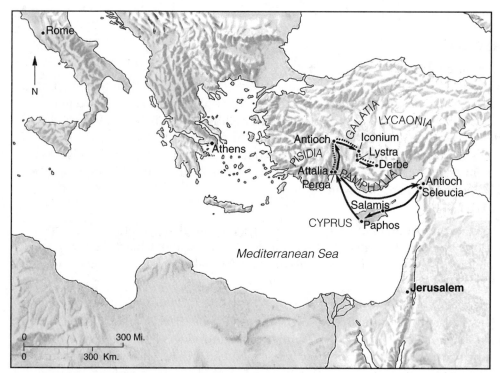

PAUL'S FIRST MISSIONARY JOURNEY (ACTS 13:1—14:28)

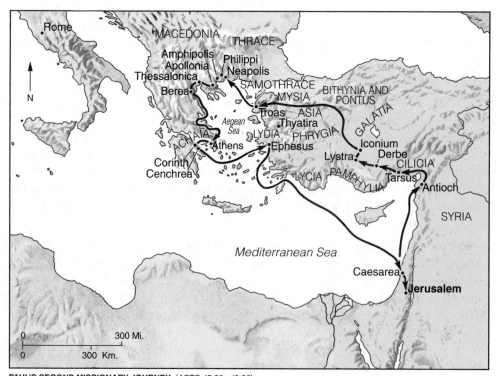

PAUL'S SECOND MISSIONARY JOURNEY (ACTS 15:36—18:22)

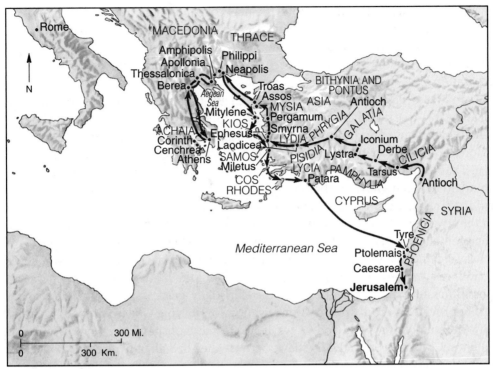

PAUL'S THIRD MISSIONARY JOURNEY (ACTS 18:23—21:16)

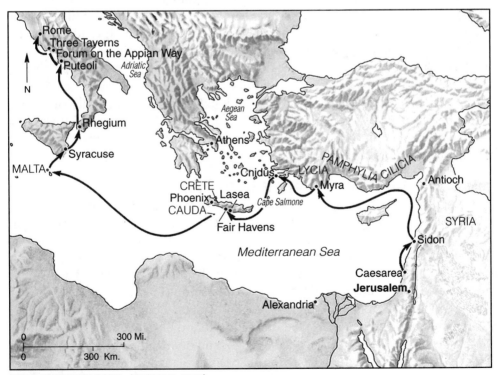

PAUL'S JOURNEY TO ROME (ACTS 21:17—28:31)

instead of ritual sacrifices at the temple, the new covenant had but one perfect and eternally effective sacrifice, the Lord. But the new covenant also had its laws. While Christians did not have to follow the dietary and cleansing laws of Moses, they were duty bound to obey the original and deeper intentions of those laws, calling believers to separation and personal purity.

Even in Moses' day it was never good enough just to cleanse the hands and allow an unclean heart—to eat kosher foods but feed the mind with unclean thoughts. The covenant had changed and some external rituals had found their spiritual fulfillment, but God's laws for morality and purity were, as always, still binding on the believer in Christ. The covenant structure around the law was subject to change—for example, from Adam to Noah, or from Abraham to Moses—but the essence of godly behavior remained. The religious leaders argued, however, that the Christians had thrown away both the covenant of Moses and his law and were therefore dangerously lawless.

The problem was that Christianity's critics had wrongly interpreted the Old Testament as teaching that salvation was gained by keeping the law of Moses. They believed that God was gracious, but salvation by grace without the merits of lawkeeping was an impossibility for them to accept. But for the Christians, grace was God's gift of redemption that provided the only powerful motivation for obeying God's commands. Christianity did not do away with God's laws, it simply reestablished grace as motivation for obedience. Christians obeyed God's laws because they had already received God's grace—not in order to gain grace.

The problem of Gentile and Jewish equality
The misunderstanding concerning how law related to grace led to a third problem addressed in Acts and most other New Testament books as well. If the Mosaic Law was done away with as a standard for gaining salvation, then a non-Jewish Gentile person could be saved without going through the process of conforming to the Mosaic commands such as circumcision, temple rituals, cleansings, and dietary restrictions.

That freedom from Mosaic laws was profoundly disturbing to the Jewish religious establishment and brought about much persecution. It also was a bitter pill for some Christians from Jewish backgrounds, who also caused bitter disputes within the fold of Christianity. These people were known as Judaizers, Christians who tried to make other Christians conform to the Mosaic Law (15:1).

THE USE OF THE OLD TESTAMENT IN THE SPEECHES
When Jesus instructed his disciples to be witnesses "to the ends of the earth" (Acts 1:8), he was quoting from Isaiah 49:6. He used the Old Testament to describe the spread of Christianity around the world. Indeed, Jesus' entire life fulfilled God's will as laid down in the Old Testament Scriptures. Luke recorded in his Gospel that Jesus explained how his life related to the Old Testament Scriptures (Luke 24:27) and opened the disciples' minds to understand his explanation (Luke 24:44-45).

Jesus passed down that method of using the Old Testament to his disciples. He taught them about the kingdom of God during the period of forty days following his resurrection (Acts 1:3). Paul himself was so taught and quoted the same Isaiah 49:6 passage in Acts 13:47 to describe the Scriptural basis for his ministry. Paul thus showed that he had also been taught by the risen Lord (26:22-23).

Throughout Acts the speeches that were made by Jesus' followers show that they were taught how to relate the Old Testament Scriptures to Jesus' life and the Christian mission by the Holy Spirit. Even after the Ascension, Jesus continued to teach them through his Spirit how to use the Old Testament.

BIBLE-WIDE CONCEPTS

JESUS RELATED TO DAVID, MOSES, AND ABRAHAM

Jesus and David: resurrection

In Acts 2:25-35 Luke gave the two most important links between Jesus and David. The first was in the quotation of Psalm 16:8-11 (2:25-28), which speaks of Jesus' resurrection. Because many Jews thought that passage related in some way to David, Peter had to explain its true meaning in 2:29-32.

Jesus' resurrection was directly related to Jesus being seated on the throne of David according to God's promise to David (2:30). That was the promise of the Davidic covenant made in 2 Samuel 7:1-29. And though Acts 2:25-28 spoke of Jesus' resurrection, it also spoke of the humiliation and pain of the death he had to suffer. But through that humiliation of death came the exaltation to the throne of God's promise.

Jesus and David: exaltation

The second major link between Jesus and David was in the quotation of Psalm 110:1 in Acts 2:34-35. That passage spoke of Jesus' exaltation to the right hand of God. After resurrection came exaltation. That was how the disciples understood Jesus' departure up into the cloud (1:9)—as a coronation procession. Now Jesus was at God's right hand, ruling according to the promise of David. Jesus now functioned as the administrator of the great promises of God to Abraham and Moses.

But that promise involved a certain time period noted in the phrase "until I humble your enemies, making them a footstool under your feet" (2:35). Jesus was and is reigning in the "until" period of conflict and of subduing his enemies. That sets the scene for the conflicts throughout Acts, the New Testament, and the history of Christianity as a whole. The present is a time for conflict as God's enemies are subdued. The final conflict and establishment of God's perfect kingdom is still future.

The startling revelation was that the Messiah had come, died, had been raised and exalted to the right hand of God, yet still the kingdom had not come in its historical fullness. Evil could still have temporal victories; flesh could still aggravate spirit. As Jesus, and David before him, had to undergo attacks from their enemies, so Christians would have to follow in the same path of humble obedience, but always knowing they would also follow in resurrection and exaltation.

Jesus and Moses

Jesus was the greater prophet whom Moses foretold. Peter quoted Deuteronomy 18:15, 19 in Acts 3:22-23. That meant that Jesus had now replaced Moses as the one to listen to (3:23, 26). Throughout Israel's history the Mosaic Law had been broken and ignored time after time. In Jeremiah's day God had spoken about making a new covenant sometime in the future (Jer. 31:31-34). It was Jesus who had inaugurated that new covenant (Luke 22:20).

Now Jesus was the greater prophet and lawgiver. God had spoken about the new covenant as including putting his Spirit within the hearts of the people (Ezek. 36:26).

Jesus as the exalted prophet would send that Spirit forth to baptize his followers (Acts 1:4-5; 2:3-4). From that time on, the believer in Jesus would have to hear *his* voice for the final decision on matters of God's law, not Moses'.

Jesus and Abraham

One of the most difficult problems faced by Christians as well as their critics in Acts was the inclusion of Gentiles in salvation and worship. Most zealous Jews allowed for Gentiles to be included in Judaism, but with clear discrimination against them. Never would the Gentile be viewed as an equal participant in salvation with a Jew. Even after a Gentile had undergone the rituals such as circumcision, cleansings, and dietary laws, he would still not be viewed as equal with one born of Abraham's line. And that mentality was naturally brought into Christianity by the first Jewish believers. But God would not let those cultural biases last for long.

God made both the Jews who did not believe in Jesus the Messiah as well as the Jewish Christians rethink their bias against Gentiles. God gave his Spirit to Gentiles on the basis of faith alone (Acts 15:8-9). Unlike the Jews, God did not show partiality (10:34-35). That meant that the Lord who reigned at God's right hand was sending his Holy Spirit upon Jew and Gentile alike. There was no distinction between them when it came to salvation. All were equal in need and were accepted on the same terms. That truth of equality would become Paul's central theme as he spoke against a return to the old standards of law and racial discrimination within the church.

That act of giving the Holy Spirit to the Gentiles clarified what God had intended all along when he first gave a covenant to Abraham (Gen. 12:1-3). All the world would someday be blessed in Abraham (Gen. 12:3). Peter quoted that promise in Acts 3:25-26. When God raised Jesus up and exalted him to his throne, that was the moment when the blessing to all families of the earth took a giant and final step forward.

No longer would there be Jews and Gentiles. All were equal candidates for direct blessing, not through the Mosaic conditions, but through the conditions of the greater prophet, greater son of David, and final fulfiller of the promise to Abraham, Jesus the Lord. Acts upholds the ethnic equality of all races in the new covenant of Christ. This realization provided the foundation for the necessary geographic spread of the message from Jerusalem to the ends of the earth (1:8).

RELATIONSHIP TO THE GOSPEL OF LUKE

As was said in the introduction to Luke's Gospel, Luke and Acts form a two-volume set. Each needs to be read with an awareness of the relationship between the two books. Acts builds on the truths of Luke's Gospel and continues the ministry of Jesus through the work of his Spirit and his body, represented by the church.

The place of the genealogy

Luke placed Jesus' genealogy right before the account of Jesus' ministry (Luke 3:23-28). Placing a person's genealogy before the recorded events of his life was an Old Testament pattern (cf. Exod. 6:14-27 regarding Aaron and Moses). Luke developed Jesus' ministry from this Old Testament pattern, thereby placing Jesus' works clearly within God's acts of salvation in history. Jesus was the Anointed One of God who had come to proclaim God's salvation (Luke 4:18-19). Jesus followed the pattern of the great ancestors in his genealogy by devoting himself to prayer at the great turning points of his life (Luke 3:21; 9:18, 28).

Jesus was the Man of the Spirit

Luke's Gospel highlighted how God gave his Spirit for prophecy to Elizabeth (Luke 1:41-42), Zechariah (Luke 1:67), Simeon (Luke 2:25-28), and Jesus (Luke 4:17-18). Acts shows God's next great advance in the gospel through the Spirit. He gave his Spirit to believers in Jesus the Messiah to enable them to proclaim the gospel. The Spirit is viewed as coming from the exalted Lord who sits at the right hand of God (Acts 2:33-36). The Spirit is the person through whom God touches and rules the world.

THE PRESENT AND FUTURE KINGDOM

The early believers struggled with how the Messiah could have come without ushering in the kingdom. Jesus explained how the kingdom was present in a hidden but powerful way (Matt. 13:1-52). The Messiah had come and so had the kingdom, but not in the way people had expected. It was a matter of misunderstanding how the kingdom was present, not of its postponement or delay.

In the book of Acts Jesus reigns over his kingdom from God's right hand. The kingdom was present, but not in the way it would be in its full historical manifestation at the end of the age. It was a time of sowing both wheat and tares, of leaven hidden in a lump of dough, of a mustard seed slowly growing to maturity.

The kingdom had not been delayed. Its present hidden but powerful presence was the way the kingdom would come to fullness. The visible physical kingdom, though now absent, was the hope of the Christian. The challenge was to see its glorious presence in the Spirit by faith and faithfully obey the King who reigned from God's throne until he came again. The present and the future manifestations of the kingdom are linked by a common bond: doing the will of God, on *earth* or in *heaven* (Matt. 6:10). The spread of the gospel was the only acceptable occupation for those who awaited the coming kingdom.

The gospel of the kingdom was the essence of the gospel message throughout Acts (3:19-21; 28:23, 31). The universalism of the Abrahamic blessing was becoming a reality. The shift from Moses to Jesus was debated and described (13:39; 15:9). The Spirit was poured out to provide strength for witness, comfort, and obedience (1:8; Ezek. 36:26-27; John 14:25-26; 15:26-27).

THE RELATIONSHIP OF ACTS TO THE OTHER NEW TESTAMENT BOOKS

As the books of the New Testament were written, they were first collected into two groups: the Gospels and the Epistles. The book of Acts filled the gap between what was recorded about the earthly life of Jesus (the Gospels) and the work of the risen Lord recorded through the Epistles. Acts gives both historical and theological links. It is at once a sequel to the Gospels and the background to the Epistles. Therefore, it is a crucial book for understanding the continuity between the earthly and resurrected life of Christ.

NEEDS MET BY ACTS

Times were not easy for the original readers of Acts. Many faced religious persecution from Jewish or civil organizations. Many lost their jobs and social standing and others were beaten or even killed for their faith. Luke wanted his readers to gain a deeper certainty about their faith in Christ—a certainty that would keep them faithful to God during hard times. The heart of that certainty was a need to understand where Christ went after his resurrection and how he could still be present with his followers. Christ had been exalted to the right hand of God, but his Spirit was poured out among his believers on earth. The certain presence of God's Spirit brought believers power for certainty in their faith and for witness.

Other needs addressed by Luke relate to how the followers of Christ were supposed to relate their new faith to the ancient ways of Israel. Throughout the book, Luke shows the deep Old Testament roots of faith in Jesus. The kingdom of God would come and be ruled by the Messiah as promised. Until then, the Messiah's people, both Jews and Gentiles, were to witness in the power of the Spirit. The structure and content of Luke's Gospel show that he was answering questions like these for his readers.

- How can Jews give up the Mosaic Law to follow Jesus?
- If Mosaic Law and Jewish tradition are unimportant for salvation, what good are they?
- How do Jesus and his teachings relate to God's promises to Abraham, Moses, and David?
- Does Jesus annul the Old Testament promises or does he somehow enlarge or modify them?
- How can it be possible that Gentiles do not have to follow the Laws of Moses in order to be saved?
- How is the kingdom of God operating now that Jesus is no longer on earth?
- What does it mean for the Holy Spirit to be here?
- How does the presence of the Holy Spirit relate to Christian life and witness?
- What is the connection between the Spirit and the rule of the risen Lord?
- Has the coming of God's kingdom somehow been put off or delayed?
- Is the Christian faith a threat to the Roman Empire?
- Should Christianity be a legal religion?
- What should believers be doing while they wait for Jesus to come back?
- Can hostility from religious and civil authorities hinder or even stop the spread of the gospel?

Luke's long narrative of Christ's acts after his resurrection helps meet three key needs for believers today. First, and most important, Acts explains how God is present with believers in his Spirit. That divine presence is the foundation for joy in life, awe in worship, and power in witness.

Second, Acts provides great insight into how Christians are to relate to the Laws of Moses. When Luke wrote, there was much controversy about how Christians were to relate to Old Testament laws. Luke described how the early church handled some of these difficult questions. And these point the way to how believers today are to relate to the laws of the Old Testament and contemporary pressures to false legalism.

Third, Luke helps believers understand why the kingdom did not come immediately after Christ's resurrection. God's plans for the kingdom were not somehow derailed. Luke showed that the present is fully part of God's plan and is pervaded with essential kingdom blessings because Christ is ruling from his place at God's right hand and his Spirit is present to work his wonders of power and blessing. Persecution then or now does not diminish the truth that the proclamation of the kingdom continues on without hindrance ("no one tried to stop him," Acts 28:31). God's work may experience opposition and hostility, but it will not be stopped. And until faith is replaced by sight, Acts helps meet the needs of believers for a pattern of prayer, witness, and worship.

OUTLINE OF ACTS

I. WITNESS POWER: MESSIANIC EXALTATION (1:1–2:47)
   A. The Final Departure (1:1-11)
   B. The Community of Prayer (1:12-26)
   C. The First Witness in Power (2:1-47)

II. THE JERUSALEM CAMPAIGN: HOSTILITY AND DIVINE PROTECTION (3:1–8:1)
   A. Events at the Beautiful Gate (3:1–4:4)
   B. The Interrogation of Peter and John (4:5-22)
   C. The Empowered Community (4:23–5:16)
   D. The Imprisoned Apostles (5:17-42)
   E. Ethnic and Administrative Squabbles (6:1-7)
   F. Stephen Is Arrested and Murdered (6:8–8:1)

III. THE SCATTERED WITNESS: THE DIRECTION AND DIRECTOR (8:2–9:31)
   A. Rise of Persecution (8:2-3)
   B. Philip in Samaria (8:4-25).
   C. Philip Preaches to an Ethiopian (8:26-40)
   D. The Conversion of Saul (9:1-31)

IV. THE GENTILES: INCLUDED BY GOD (9:32–11:26)
   A. Two Miracles in Neighboring Towns (9:32-43)
   B. Confirmation of Gentile Salvation (10:1–11:26)

V. JERUSALEM PERSECUTION: THE KING VERSUS A KING (11:27–12:24)
   A. Famine Relief (11:27-30)
   B. Herod's Final Atrocities (12:1-24)

VI. PAUL'S LONG-RANGE MISSION: JEW AND GENTILE CONFLICT (12:25–14:28)
   A. Commission and Preparation (12:25–13:3)
   B. Cyprus (13:4-12)
   C. Asia Minor (13:13–14:25)
   D. Return and Report to the Antioch Community (14:26-28)

VII. TOWARD A JEW AND GENTILE RESOLUTION (15:1-35)
   A. The Problem Arises (15:1-5)
   B. The Problem Debated and Solved (15:6-21)
   C. The Answer Is Formulated (15:22-29)
   D. The Response to the Answer (15:30-35)

VIII. THE SECOND MISSION: GENTILE EXTENSION INTO EUROPE (15:36–18:21)
   A. The Personnel Selected (15:36-41)
   B. The Journey to the Edge of Europe (16:1-10)
   C. In Philippi (16:11-40)
   D. Thessalonica and Persecution (17:1-9)

ACTS NOTES

1:1–2:47 WITNESS POWER: MESSIANIC EXALTATION

1:1-11 The Final Departure

1:1-5 THE COMMAND TO WAIT FOR THE SPIRIT

This introduction to the book emphasizes two aspects: (1) Christ's ministry from its beginning to his ascension and (2) his task of giving instructions by the Holy Spirit to his apostles after his resurrection. The rest of the book is the result of the apostles carrying out these instructions given by the risen Lord. These instructions (Acts 1:2, 4) and the Holy Spirit stand behind all the great acts of witness throughout the book.

Note the central place of the Spirit. Even the orders of the risen Lord were "from the Holy Spirit" (1:2). Although the author of Acts is not named, all the evidence points to Luke. The dedication to "Theophilus," the mention of the "former book" (the Gospel of Luke), and the medical vocabulary support the tradition cited by Irenaeus, Clement of Alexandria, Tertullian, and Origen that Luke authored the book. The reference to Theophilus, some prominent individual who may have assisted in the publication of Luke's research, is a dedication characteristic of Greco-Roman literature.

Jesus had promised that the coming of the Holy Spirit would be indicative of the kingdom's presence (1:3-5). This postresurrection teaching about the kingdom of God is foundational for the book. Jesus appeared and ministered to his disciples for a period of forty days between Jesus' resurrection and ascension. The "Kingdom of God" was the major subject of his teaching. The book of Acts begins and concludes with this subject (28:31).

The speeches of Peter (Acts 2–3) and Stephen (Acts 7) reflected their schooling during this forty-day period sitting under the teaching of the risen Lord as he told them the details about the kingdom (1:3). Acts 1:3 follows and guards the "day he ascended" (1:2) by showing that Jesus was alive, well, and seen by his apostles for a long time before he disappeared. What the Father "promised" (1:4) was the indwelling ministry of the Holy Spirit to be given as divine enablement (cf. Luke 24:49; John 14:16-17; Acts 2:33; Ezek. 36:27; Joel 2:28). The baptism performed by John the Baptist was about to find a new fulfillment in the coming of the Holy Spirit (Acts 1:5).

1:6-11 THE PROMISE OF CHRIST'S RETURN

1:6-8 The Commission of the Disciples

The disciples linked the coming of the Spirit (1:5) to the coming of the kingdom (1:6). They would find out that though the Holy Spirit would soon come, the fullness of the kingdom would not. They had to learn a balance between rejoicing in the power of the Spirit and humbly waiting through the conflicts of this age for the kingdom to come. In spite of Christ's rejection, the disciples still anticipated a literal Messianic kingdom (1:6). The word "restore" (1:6) implied a pattern that had existed before—the rule by kings in the Old Testament.

Acts 1:8 provides the outline for the entire book: (1) witness in Jerusalem (2:5–8:3), (2) witness in Judea and Samaria (8:4–12:25), and (3) witness in the Mediterranean world (13:1–28:31). The Spirit's function was to provide power for witness worldwide. The redeemed believers were being told what their primary function would be while they waited for Jesus to return. This is similar to the Olivet Discourse in Matthew 24–25. There the believers were told to be faithful and spread the gospel to the whole world (Matt. 24:14).

The phrase "the ends of the earth" (1:8) is a quotation of Isaiah 49:6. This showed that the mission of Israel, of Jesus, and the church was to spread the news of God's redemption. Paul applied the same passage to his ministry to the Gentiles in Acts 13:47.

1:9-11 Christ's Glorious Departure
The Ascension (1:9), an event prophesied in Isaiah 52:13, took place on the Mount of Olives and demonstrated that Jesus was the perfect pattern of righteousness acceptable to the Father (John 16:10). A cloud (1:9) had also enveloped Jesus and the disciples during his transfiguration (Luke 9:34) and was an image mentioned in relation to his second coming (Luke 21:27; Mark 14:62).

Jesus' visible departure upward was different from his other disappearances during the forty days following his resurrection (John 20:19-29; Luke 24:31, 36). It made a clear point as to where he went—up, in simple human terms, to the right hand of God (Ps. 110:1). Peter used Psalm 110:1 to describe this event (Acts 2:33-35).

The point behind the conversation with the angel (1:10-11) was to assert that Jesus could go and would someday come again, but the task of witness still remained. The unknown time of his return had nothing to do with a lessening of the command to witness. For his second coming, see Matthew 24:26-31; Revelation 19:11-16; Zechariah 12:10–13:1; 14:1-4.

1:12-26 The Community of Prayer
1:12-14 RETURN TO JERUSALEM FOR PRAYERFUL WAITING
A "half mile" (Acts 1:12) is also referred to as "Sabbath day's walk" (NIV, KJV). This limit had been calculated by the rabbis on the basis of Exodus 16:29 as interpreted by Numbers 35:5. The disciples were told to wait for the promise of the Spirit (Acts 1:4). The disciples waited prayerfully (1:14), presumably for the Spirit's coming. The disciples may have been following Jesus' prayer (Matt. 6:10) that the kingdom would come. The book of Acts shows how the believers' desire for God's power from the Holy Spirit impacted their obedience and witness.

1:15-19 JUDAS'S DESTRUCTION
Within the context of expectant prayer, Peter's thoughts were led to Scriptures instructing how to complete the original number of the Lord's twelve apostles. This book tells about the apostolic spread of the gospel, and the first step was to complete the original apostolic body. Matthew 27:6-7 notes that the temple priests bought the potter's field. For "Scriptures" (1:16), see 1:20 and the use of Psalms 69:25 and 109:8. The word "hanged" in Matthew 27:5 may be literally translated "strangled" and is used of Ahithophel in the Septuagint version (the Greek Old Testament) of 2 Samuel 17:23.

1:20-26 JUDAS'S REPLACEMENT
The fulfilled Scripture (Acts 1:20) came from two of David's psalms (Acts 1:16). It affirmed two principles that were applied to Judas: the judgment on rejectors (Ps. 69:25) and the replacement of defectors (Ps. 109:8). Psalm 69 is thoroughly Messianic. Other portions of it are used elsewhere in the New Testament (see Ps. 69:9 in John 2:17 and Rom. 15:3; and Ps. 69:21 in Luke 23:36). Psalm 109:22 is quoted in Matthew 27:39 ("shaking their heads," also see Ps. 22:7-8). The name of the field, "Blood" (Acts 1:19), implied that no one was to live there. The "position" (Acts 1:20) was not just a position. It demanded the experience of the full period of Jesus' earthly ministry (1:21-22).

To be qualified (1:21-22), this new leader was to have witnessed the resurrection (1:22) and experienced Jesus' life from his baptism to the ascension (1:22). Simply having seen the risen Lord, as for example, the five hundred of 1 Corinthians 15:6, was not sufficient for qualification as an apostolic witness. That witness demanded the experience that would enable him to put the risen Lord's appearance into the context of his whole life and teaching concerning the kingdom.

The apostles used a method of both rational and supernatural selection (Acts 1:23-26). Lot casting (1:26) was a means of determining the will of God (Prov. 16:33). It does not appear again in the Bible after Pentecost (cf. Rom. 8:14). Some have argued that the apostles were wrong in recognizing Matthias and should have waited until God filled the vacancy with Paul. However, Paul would not have been qualified on the basis of Acts 1:21-22, and the choice made was God's, not man's (1:24).

2:1-47 The First Witness in Power
2:1-4 THE FILLING OF THE SPIRIT FOR PROPHECY
The Holy Spirit's coming was accompanied by a sound (2:2) and a symbol (2:3). The Day of Pentecost was celebrated on the fiftieth day after the Festival of Harvest (Lev. 23:15; Exod. 34:22). This spring celebration commemorated the first of the grain harvest. The Spirit's coming at Pentecost signaled the presence of God predicted by the Old Testament prophets, John the Baptist, and Jesus (Acts 1:5). The fire appeared on the believers (2:3), much like the flames of God's holy presence appeared on the burning bush for Moses (Exod. 3:2).

With the coming of the Holy Spirit came also enablement to communicate God's message supernaturally (Acts 2:4). The believers were filled with the Spirit for the specific function of proclaiming the gospel (2:11). The disciples were all filled with the Spirit, baptized into the body of Christ, and indwelt by the Holy Spirit (1 Cor. 12:13; cf. Ezek. 36:27; John 14:17). Luke's Gospel presented people being filled with the Spirit to speak (Luke 1:41-42, 67). But the difference in Acts from the early chapters of Luke is the speaking in foreign languages—"in other languages."

2:5-12 AMAZEMENT

There were Jews from every nation in Jerusalem for the feast (Acts 2:5). They became the first illustration of the Lord's intentions to bring the gospel to the ends of the earth (1:8). They were amazed at hearing the message in their own language. The tongues were known languages (2:6, 8) used to communicate the gospel. The hearers could speak Greek or Aramaic so they did not need to hear the message in their own language. But God provided a special sign to communicate his gospel.

Peter's explanation of the phenomenon of tongues (2:14-42) appears to have been in a single language, probably Aramaic or Greek. The sign came in many tongues—an unusual act of God to highlight and define the scope of his message. But the explanation and invitation to believe came in one language.

The countries mentioned in 2:9-11 are the lands of the Jewish dispersion in the eastern Mediterranean. The message was about "the wonderful things God has done" (2:11), a first definition of the content of the gospel. "Converts to Judaism" (2:10; "proselytes," NASB and KJV) were Gentiles who kept the Jewish law and were admitted into full fellowship with the people of Israel. Three steps were required: (1) circumcision, (2) purification through self-baptism, and (3) the offering of a sacrifice. Many Gentiles were content with a more informal attachment to the Jewish religion and were called God-fearers (cf. 10:2).

2:13 MOCKING

Some people made fun of the miracle of tongues (2:13; cf. 1 Cor. 14:23). The communication of the great acts of God was clear (Acts 2:11). What needed explanation was how the believers could speak in other languages. That sign and its mocking by some of the listeners formed the transition to Peter's speech of interpretation. His speech explained the sign through teaching and evangelism.

2:14-36 PETER'S EXPLANATION OF THE SIGN OF TONGUES

The introduction (2:14) set the tone by being formal and impressive. Then Peter explained the languages (2:15-21). Jews engaged in worship on feast days and customarily abstained from eating or drinking until 10:00 A.M.

2:14-21 Peter's Use of Joel 2:28-32

In 2:16-21 Peter quoted Joel 2:28-32 in order to explain the miracle of tongues. There are three basic views regarding how Peter viewed the fulfillment of Joel 2:28-32. (1) The nonfulfillment view holds that Peter used the prophecy only as an illustration of what was transpiring in his day, not as a fulfillment. The only fulfillment would come later at the second coming of Christ. (2) The partial fulfillment view regards the part of Joel's prophecy that concerns the Holy Spirit as fulfilled (Acts 2:28-29), but the signs in the sky (2:30-32) as still to be fulfilled in the tribulation. (3) The full fulfillment view regards the essence of the prophecy as being fulfilled with additional fulfillments in the future (cf. Isa. 32:15; 44:3; Zech. 12:10–13:1).

Whatever the overall view taken, the essence of Peter's use of Joel can be better understood by examining the quotation in its original context. Joel presented a message about how God calls people to himself. He called upon the people to return with all their hearts, before the terrible day of the Lord came (Joel 2:11-12). Salvation would come to any who called upon the name of the Lord (Joel 2:32). But actually, God himself was calling the people to himself through the great signs and wonders (Joel 2:32). So the context was God calling people to himself by means of signs and wonders.

Peter's purpose in his sermon was similar to that of the prophet Joel. That is, Joel shared the same overall context with Peter's speech in Acts 2. Peter wanted his listeners to call upon the name of the Lord (Acts 2:21), but he ended with acknowledging that God was ultimately calling people to himself. The people's faith in God was a response to God's call through the signs and wonders in Jesus' life and the miracle of tongues. Seeing signs was to issue in faith and repentance.

Joel predicted that God would pour out his Spirit (Joel 2:28) and present signs and wonders (Joel 2:30) in order to cause people to call upon him for salvation (Joel 2:32). That was precisely Peter's point. Tongues showed that God had poured out his Spirit (Acts 2:15-17). God had presented signs and wonders through the life and resurrection of Christ (Acts 3:19, 22, 43). Therefore, the people should repent and respond in faith to God's call (2:38-39).

Peter linked the speaking in tongues to the Holy Spirit by adding "will prophesy" (2:18) to his quotation of Joel 2:29. He linked the signs and wonders predicted in Joel 2 to the work of God in Jesus' life on earth (Acts 2:19, 22). Prophecy was the pouring forth of the Spirit. Signs and wonders were seen in the life of Christ and would continue through the work of the apostles (2:43). Peter linked his present time to the time of threat and urgency that will surround the end of the age (2:20-21). The tongues were a sign confirming the predicted advance in God's redemptive and prophetic program.

The speaking in tongues was directly linked to the outpouring of the Spirit (2:16-17). The pouring forth of the Spirit was directly linked to the exaltation of Jesus to the right hand of God (2:33). Thus, the signs of the apostles, whether healings or tongues, were confirmations that God had exalted his Son to his right hand and now summoned people to respond in faith to his redemptive call. This sign was not simply a miracle; it was a sign pointing to the power and call of the risen and reigning Lord.

2:22-36 New Elements in Proclaiming the Christian Gospel

A radical shift was being presented. Now, for the Jew and the Gentile, the only acceptable response to God was to believe in his Son. That response of faith would then unlock forgiveness and the gift of the Spirit. Peter went on to show how Jesus was approved by God (2:22-23). "Miracles, wonders, and signs" (2:22) link back to 2:19. Although Jesus was approved by God, the people nailed him to the cross, but God was behind it all (2:23).

Appealing to Old Testament quotations, Peter presented three proofs that Jesus was the Messiah: (1) his miracles (Acts 2:22-23; cf. Joel 2:28-32), (2) his resurrection (Acts 2:24-32; cf. Ps. 16:8-11), and (3) his exaltation (Acts 2:33-35; cf. Ps. 110:1). Christ's resurrection and exaltation were presented as fulfillments of God's promise to David.

David spoke prophetically of the resurrection and reign of a future son according to the Davidic covenant (Acts 2:30; cf. Ps. 16:8-11). As that future son, Jesus experienced what was predicted for David's son, exaltation to the right hand of God (Acts 2:33-36; cf. Ps. 110:1). Peter viewed the raising up and exaltation of Jesus as one and the same event. See Matthew 22:43-45 and 26:64 for Jesus' use of Psalm 110:1. The conclusion (Acts 2:33) clearly links the pouring forth of the Spirit with Joel's prediction (2:17).

This first proclamation by a Christian prophet contains some basic elements of early Christian preaching. (1) The age of fulfillment has arrived as initially described by the Joel 2 context. (2) The message is universal but always comes to the Jew first. The speech focuses on devout "God-fearing" (2:5) Jews and Gentile converts (2:10). (3) The life, death, and resurrection of Jesus is recounted. Its essence is to show that the man Jesus was the promised Messiah (2:36). (4) The Old Testament is used as proof for Jesus' Messiahship. The next speeches expand the message to include the impending kingdom (Acts 3), the Messiah as Savior (Acts 4–5), and the longstanding Jewish resistance to God's affirmation of his prophets (Acts 7).

2:37-47 THE RESPONSE.

2:37-40 Direction Is Sought and Given

Direction is sought by the listeners (2:37) and given by Peter (2:38-40). Repentance and baptism enabled the believer to receive forgiveness and the Holy Spirit (2:38). Forgiveness of sins always came through faith in Jesus (Eph. 2:8-9). Baptism was a rite of identification by which new believers became associated with Jesus and his followers. The benefits of repentance were called a promise for Jews and Gentiles alike (Acts 2:39; cf. Eph. 2:11-13). Luke only recorded the gist of Peter's message; his many other words (Acts 2:40) were not recorded.

2:41-42 Community Growth in Numbers and Maturity

The rapid growth mentioned here was related to the repentance and belief of new members (2:41-42). Community teaching and fellowship was the only acceptable result of belief in Jesus as Messiah.

2:43-47 Growth and Maturity Is Elaborated

The wonders and signs (2:43) link back to Joel's prediction (2:19-20) and the life of Jesus (2:22). Certain aspects of Joel's prediction of signs and wonders were still future, like the prediction of a radical change in the sun and moon. But enough signs and wonders were performed by Jesus and his disciples after him to demonstrate that the time of Joel's prediction had begun—the time of special awe (2:43).

The communal sharing was voluntary and met the needs of believers who lingered in Jerusalem after Pentecost or lost jobs due to persecution. It was the natural expression of spiritual unity. The

---

SOME IMPLICATIONS OF THE NEW RELIGION

The linking of Jesus and the Spirit to the Old Testament and the end of the age was a giant step forward in God's plan of redemption. Christianity claimed that the Messiah had been identified: Jesus. As a result, to the extent that the existing Jewish religion rejected Jesus as Messiah, it was now insufficient with respect to salvation. Therefore God's approach to the sin problem had been radically advanced. Forgiveness was now to be found exclusively in Jesus.

A mind change was needed regarding Jesus in order to avoid rejecting the authority of Judaism. Mainline Judaism was apostate from God's perspective, to the extent of its resistance to the new proclamation. That resistance would grow stronger over time. Passages like Matthew 13 and Romans 9–11 explain why the Jews as a whole did not receive Jesus as God's Son. But their rejection of Jesus would be used to bring light to the Gentiles (Matt. 4:15-16).

spontaneous sharing of personal property was consistent with other principles of Scripture. The intentions behind God's distribution of manna would be taken up by Paul with reference to supplying the needs of the Christians (Exod. 16:18; 2 Cor. 8:14-15). The Mosaic Law had much to say about supporting the poor, needy, and widows (Deut. 10:18; 14:29; 16:11, 14; 24:17, 19-21; 26:12-13; 27:19).

3:1–8:1 THE JERUSALEM CAMPAIGN: HOSTILITY AND DIVINE PROTECTION

3:1–4:4 Events at the Beautiful Gate

3:1-10 THE LAME BEGGAR HEALED

Peter and John continued to follow the customs of temple worship (Acts 3:1). The events that took place there form the second major witness to Christ. Three o'clock (3:1) in the afternoon was the time for the prayer service that accompanied the evening sacrifice (cf. Exod. 29:39-46).

Peter healed the lame beggar with power granted by the Holy Spirit through the *name* of Jesus (Acts 3:2-8). Alms giving in the New Testament period was regarded as a meritorious act with sacrificial and atoning value. It was regarded above prayer and fasting as a means of attaining rightousness. The Beautiful Gate was located east of the sanctuary and gave access to the Court of Women from the Court of Gentiles.

The people who saw the healed beggar responded in amazement (3:9-10). The man had been lame from birth and known by many. The miracle became an occasion for preaching the gospel and for the first arrest of Christians.

3:11-26 PETER INTERPRETS THE SIGN

The controling image of this sermon is Jesus as servant. The "servant" image begins and ends this sermon (3:13, 26) and cements not only Jesus' role in God's plan for world redemption but the believers' as well. They must be servants of God's salvation blessings. The book of Acts describes the glories and the costs of that servanthood. The Old Testament supports the idea that the Messiah was to be a servant and a blessing for all nations in Abraham (see Gen. 22:18 in Acts 3:25-26) and in the raising up of the prophet greater than Moses (see Deut. 18:15, 19 in Acts 3:22-23).

The source of the healing was Jesus (3:11-16). The power for healing came through faith in his name. Scholars are divided as to whether the faith for healing was granted on the part of Peter or the lame man. "Solomon's Colonnade" (3:11) was a covered, colonnaded porch that ran the length of the Court of the Gentiles on the east. As servant, Jesus had been glorified (3:13) by the exaltation to the right hand of God as described in Acts 1–2 (cf.

Isa. 42:1; 52:13–53:12; Luke 1:54-55). The servant theme will be taken up again in Acts 4:25, 27, 30.

Peter proclaimed the coming kingdom (3:17-26). His logic was that the predicted suffering of Jesus was in the past. Therefore the people needed to repent and receive the coming time of restoration (3:18-19). The words "turn . . . and turn" mean "change your mind about Jesus and return to God." The time of restoration (3:21) was a reference to the future blessings of the Messianic kingdom.

Acts 3:20-26 contains four key themes: (1) Jesus' return is for the Jews in a special way ("for you," 3:20; and "first to you," 3:26). (2) The prophets predicted that time ("prophets" repeated three times 3:21, 24, 25). (3) God has raised up a prophet greater than Moses ("raise up," 3:22; and "raised up," 3:26). (4) Jesus' raising up begins the special blessing promised to all the nations through Abraham ("blessed," 3:25; "bless," 3:26). The people are to return to God (3:19), so that Jesus might return and restore (3:20-21). In the present, God had already sent the risen Jesus to the people (3:26) through the proclamation of the gospel and the presence of his Spirit.

The key Old Testament passages in this speech are Deuteronomy 18:15, 19 and Genesis 22:18. The "until" of Acts 3:21 reflects Psalm 110:1, which was also used in Acts 2:35 ("until I humble your enemies, making them a footstool under your feet").

4:1-4 THE FIRST PERSECUTION BEGINS

Peter and John were arrested (4:1-4), ushering in the first persecution. The "captain of the Temple guard" (4:1) was responsible for maintaining order in the temple and was second only to the high priest. The Sadducees were theological conservatives associated with the temple and priesthood. They objected to Jesus being called the Messiah and the concept of resurrection (Matt. 22:23-33). The ruling Sadducees may have presented a pious front, but they were motivated by jealousy. Luke links their jealousy (Acts 5:17) with a longstanding jealousy within Israel of God's chosen leaders (7:9). The initial persecution did not stop the effectiveness of the gospel message (4:4). That is one key point of Acts—prison could not imprison the power of the gospel.

4:5-22 The Interrogation of Peter and John

4:5-7 THE QUESTION OF AUTHORITY

This is the third major act of witness in the book. It took place before all the major religious rulers in Jerusalem (4:5-6). This was a meeting of the Sanhedrin (4:5, 15), the highest religious court of Judaism. Annas (4:6) was high priest (A.D. 6–15) before being deposed by the Romans. His son-in-law, Caiaphas (A.D. 18–36), was later appointed to the position. Nothing is known of John and Alexander (4:6) except that they were members of the high priest's family.

4:8-12 PETER'S REPLY

Peter's bold reply to the accusations of the Sanhedrin exemplified the prophetic enabling of the Spirit to proclaim God's message with boldness (cf. Luke 1:15, 67; Acts 4:31; 13:9). The core of the message concerned the resurrection (4:10) based on the Scripture of Psalm 118:22. The resurrection was seen as God's affirmation of Jesus the Messiah. Humans rejected the stone; God put it back in place permanently. The key themes were Jesus' humiliation at human hands and exaltation by God's hands (Ps. 118:22). See the themes of humiliation and exaltation in Psalm 118:22. Jesus quoted the same passage in Matthew 21:42-44, possibly before the very same people. Peter inserted "you" (Acts 4:11) before "builders" to make the passage more pointed. Peter explained the nature of the miracles. They were to move the onlookers from the physical healing of the lame man to the spiritual healing offered by Jesus the Messiah. Salvation was to be found in Jesus alone (4:21).

4:13-22 THREAT AND RELEASE: NO GUILT

The religious leaders ordered Peter and John not to witness (4:13-18). The leaders could not deny the miracle, but they did deny that Jesus did it. The words "no special training" (4:13) simply means that Peter and John had not been formally trained in the rabbinic schools (note 4:13). The disciples had been with Jesus and now sounded like him, especially after his forty-day resurrection teaching ministry and the sending of the Holy Spirit. Their motivation to witness was the demand of truth from eyewitness authority and doing right in God's sight (4:19-22).

4:23–5:16 The Empowered Community

4:23-31 EMPOWERED IN PRAYER

This section builds to the disciples' again being filled with the Holy Spirit to speak the word boldly (4:31). The power behind that filling was prayer based on Scripture. They confessed God as Creator of all (4:24). They also confessed that their persecution had been predicted, that is, that their pain was not a surprise to God. He was in total control. Hostility against Jesus the Messiah and Christians was part and parcel of God's intentions for the spread of the gospel in Acts and beyond (note Ps. 2:7; Acts 13:33). The believers related the Scripture (Ps. 2:1-2) to their own circumstances (see "nations" and "people" in Acts 4:25, 27). Psalm 2:7 will be quoted in Acts 13:33 to refer to Jesus' resurrection. For "Herod Antipas," see Luke 23:7-12. For "Pontius Pilate" (4:27), see note on Matthew 27:2. Their next step was to ask for "boldness in their preaching" (Acts 4:29) and miracles

(4:30). That request was right in line with Jesus' commands to witness (1:8). The result was that the believers were again filled for bold sharing of the gospel (4:31). But more, it was a confirmation from God of his continued control and presence with this little band of believers, even though it was cursed by the religious leaders.

4:32–5:11 EMPOWERED IN GIVING

4:32-35 The Believers Share Their Possessions
The acts of giving in 4:32-35 were the result of the believers' prayer and the powerful work of the Holy Spirit (4:23-31). The great power of the Spirit led to great acts of grace. The same Greek word translates "great" with reference to the apostles' power and grace ("favor") upon them all (4:33).

4:36-37 The Positive Example of Joseph (Barnabas)
Acts 4:36–5:11 gives two specific examples of giving, one negative and one positive. Joseph's nickname was "Barnabas," Aramaic for "son of refreshment" or "son of a prophet." The word "son" (4:36) was used in the Semitic sense, as a reference to the man's character. The word "encouragement" (4:36) may mean "consolation" or "exhortation." He was a Jew and a Levite, from Cyprus (4:36). Joseph freely gave the purchase price of the land to be distributed by the apostles to meet the needs of the community (4:37).

5:1-11 The Negative Example of Ananias and Sapphira
This couple lied to God (5:3-4), specifically the Holy Spirit (5:3, 9). Their sin was not in withholding some of the proceeds of the sale, but in pretending to give all they had received. Satan desired this kind of prideful deception among the Christian community. They pretended greater devotion than was real in their lives. In the biblical period, burial normally took place on the day of death in view of the rapid deterioration of the body in the hot Middle Eastern climate (5:6).

Their testing of the Spirit (5:9) became another of the first-time lessons provided by God in Scripture (see the Fall, Gen. 3; the Flood, Gen. 6–8; and the sin of Achan, Josh. 7). In 1 Corinthians 10:9 Paul also spoke of Israel testing the Lord. The essence of testing God was to push God to prove his presence, either to judge or to bless (cf. Matt. 4:7; see also Deut. 6:16; Exod. 17:7). Ananias and Sapphira "test the Spirit of the Lord" (Acts 5:9) by presuming his unwillingness to judge sin. In this case God indeed was with the Christian community both to bless and to judge.

Others have doubtless lied in a similar manner since then. But God had made his lesson at the first occurrence and continued to move on in grace. Here the emphasis was on giving rather than witnessing. The character of the witnesses had to be pure. In this flash of judgment it became clear that God was the audience for ministry, not men. To pervert the great grace (4:33) was to pervert the witness concerning Jesus Christ. The result of this judgment was great fear (5:5, 11).

5:12-16 EMPOWERED IN GEOGRAPHICAL EXTENT
God produced great awe through his miracles (2:43), great favor (4:33) and great fear (5:5, 11). These led to a purity of lifestyle among the believers that brought high esteem from unbelievers (5:13) and an increased spread of the gospel. For "Solomon's Colonnade" (5:12), see note on Acts 3:11.

5:17-42 The Imprisoned Apostles
5:17-25 THE MIRACULOUS RELEASE
All twelve of the apostles were arrested by the Jewish leaders. The source of the hatred shown was the jealousy of the religious leaders—jealousy based on the high esteem in which the Christians were held (5:13). The "high priest" (5:17) was Caiaphas (A.D. 18–36). For the "Sadducees," see note on 4:1. The miracle of release (5:19-20) was another confirmation of God's blessing and presence with the believers. Humans locked the door on the gospel's progress, but God opened it. This continues the tone set in 4:23-30.

5:26-32 SECOND ARREST AND DEFENSE
The continued threat of imprisonment was restated (5:26-28). At the heart of Peter's response to the Jewish leaders was the exaltation of Jesus to God's right hand, justifying their belief and witness (5:29-32; cf. 2:33-35). The end of Peter's response implied that the religious leaders were not obeying God because they did not believe in Jesus as Messiah (5:32).

5:33-40 GAMALIEL'S PROPOSITION
The response of the leaders was to kill all twelve of the apostles (5:33). "Gamaliel" (5:34), a respected Jewish rabbi often quoted in the Mishnah, was Paul's teacher and the grandson of Hillel (Acts 22:3). He gave a "wait-and-see" proposition (5:34-40). A certain Theudas (5:36) was mentioned by Josephus with reference to later historical events around A.D. 44 (Josephus, *Antiquities*, 20.5.1). It is possible that Josephus was wrong in the dating of Theudas or that there were two men with the same name. Judas the Galilean (Acts 5:37) inaugurated a religious and nationalist revolt in A.D. 6, but the rebellion was crushed by Rome.

Note Gamaliel's skepticism, which reveals an attitude toward Christianity common among Jews of that day. Gamaliel had seen many false religious leaders come and go, and he placed Jesus among them. But his skepticism was tempered with a healthy understanding of God's sovereignty. He had an attitude, not of faith in Jesus, but of waiting to see if the small group of Jesus' followers would survive and grow. But Gamaliel ignored the best

proof he would ever get—the resurrection of Christ. The proof of Jesus' claims is in his resurrection, not in the relative prosperity or growth of his followers. Flogging (5:40) was the same punishment that Jesus had received (John 19:1). Pilate also attempted to follow a punish-and-release pattern with Jesus (Acts 5:40; cf. Luke 23:16). The end of this second crisis with Jewish leadership was the result of their having no basis for convicting the apostles (Acts 4:21) and the impossibility of fighting against God (5:39).

5:41-42 TEACHING CONTINUED
The disciples continued to witness, and the split between Christianity and Judaism continued to widen. The command to stop sharing the gospel did not invalidate God's commission to witness (1:8; 5:20).

6:1-7 Ethnic and Administrative Squabbles
6:1 THE MATERIAL AND ETHNIC PROBLEM
The heart of the problem was racial tension over the daily ration of food for widows. This was a breakdown of the kindhearted sharing of goods seen in 2:44-45 and 4:34-37. It was a violation of a prime biblical command to care for widows while also being an ethnic slur against the Greek Christians. The common good had to be maintained. Compare with 2 Corinthians 8:14-15 and Exodus 16:18 regarding the equality in the distribution of manna.

But the overall thrust of this story was in surmounting this hindrance to prayer and the ministry of the word. This section moves from the possible neglect of the word of God (Acts 6:2) to the continued spreading of that word (6:7). The problem may have been material or racial, but the real problem was how this squabble could have kept the apostles from praying, preaching, and spreading the gospel. The book of Acts reveals that neither persecution from unbelievers nor squabbles with believers could hinder the spread of the gospel. The Hellenistic Jews were those of a Greek background; they spoke Greek rather than Aramaic.

6:2-6 THE NEED IS MET
The expression "food program" (6:2) was a figure of speech referring to the ministry of providing food for the widows. The phrase "full of the Holy Spirit and wisdom" (6:3) meant that the person's life was characterized by the virtues and power of the Holy Spirit, in this case the quality of wisdom was emphasized.

This movement to care for the Gentile Greek Christians was just a small taste of the massive Gentile movement to come. The laying on of hands (6:6) identified this already spiritual man with the blessing and authority of the apostles. In the biblical period, the laying on of hands was a rite of identification that signified the link or association between the parties involved (cf. Lev. 3:2). It is interesting to note that the names of the men chosen to mediate this racial problem (6:5) indicate that these men were of Greek or Hellenistic backgrounds. The deacons were chosen from among the Hellenistic Christians to balance the representation of the two groups (Hellenistic and Judaistic) in leadership.

6:7 THE INCREASE OF DISCIPLES IN JERUSALEM

This verse functions not only to show how the word was unhindered by human problems and that the number of believers had grown; but it contributes to the building of tension between the believers and the religious leaders who were already hostile and jealous (Acts 5:17-18, 33). This relates most closely with the following section concerning one of the Hellenistic deacons, Stephen. Note some other linking phrases in Acts (9:31; 12:24; 16:5; 19:20; 28:30-31).

6:8–8:1 Stephen Is Arrested and Murdered

6:8–7:1 BROUGHT BEFORE THE HIGH PRIEST

Stephen, one of the deacons, had been gifted with the signs and wonders shared by Jesus (2:22) and the apostles (2:43). The "Freed Slaves" (6:9) were Jews who had once been slaves of Rome but had been set free and settled in Jerusalem. They built their own synagogue in Jerusalem. Stephen, like Jesus, suffered a farce of a trial built on false accusations. Those accusations centered on the temple building, the temple customs, and the Mosaic Law (6:13-14).

7:2-53 STEPHEN EVALUATES HIS JUDGES

Stephen's message was designed to show that God's presence was not limited to the temple nor its customs. He pointed out that the leaders' rejection of the Holy Spirit was just like that of their ancestors, which had resulted in exile and punishment. Stephen's discussion of God's presence and redemptive purpose was based on God's promises to Abraham. His discussion of the temple and the laws was based on the Mosaic covenant. Finally, his second discussion of the temple and law was based on the Davidic covenant. The whole speech was a brief but complete interpretation of Israel's history based on Jesus' teachings about the Old Testament. Stephen argued that God was not restricted to one nation or one building. He also showed the religious leaders that rejection of God's ways had been a pattern with Israel throughout history.

7:2-16 Abraham to the Exodus

Stephen's sermon has been criticized for supposed historical inaccuracies. While it does contain some difficult interpretive problems, they are not beyond solution. Stephen's point in 7:2-8 was that Abraham had God's presence even without the Promised Land or the temple. The thrust was that Abraham had the word of promise that said God would give the land but only after a time of oppression in and deliverance from a foreign land (7:5-6).

The problem in Acts 7:2 is that Genesis 11:31-32 records no divine call of Abraham at Ur in Mesopotamia. Genesis 11:31–12:4 reveals a call from Haran. However, Genesis 15:7 and Nehemiah 9:7 record that Abraham was first called at Ur. Apparently he was first called to leave Ur (Gen. 15:7; Neh. 9:7; Heb. 11:8) and then from Haran was called to go to Canaan (Gen. 11:31–12:4). Stephen referred only to Abraham's first call at Ur.

Many have accused Stephen of an inaccuracy in Acts 7:6 when he referred to the period of Egyptian bondage as being "four hundred years" in length. Exodus 12:40 and Galatians 3:17 speak of the period as 430 years. Was Stephen in error? No. Genesis 15:13 refers to four hundred years of Egyptian bondage. Evidence from Genesis 15:16 suggests this was a rounded number. Stephen was probably thinking of the Genesis 15:13 text with the rounded number, or else he may have been calculating the period from a different starting point.

In Acts 7:9-16, Stephen used the jealousy shown against Joseph as an example of the kind of jealousy shown against God's leaders, especially Jesus, that was present in Stephen's day (cf. 5:17). Like Jesus, Joseph was rejected as a brother, rescued by God, exalted, and eventually received by his people. In 7:14, Stephen said that seventy-five of Joseph's relatives went with him to Egypt. Exodus 1:5, however, records the number "seventy." Was Stephen wrong? No. The Septuagint and the Dead Sea Scrolls support the reading "seventy-five." Stephen was probably following these texts, which apparently included Joseph's five grandsons in the final sum (cf. Num. 26:29, 35).

In Acts 7:16 Stephen appeared to confuse Jacob's purchase of property at Shechem (Gen. 33:18-19; Josh. 24:32) with Abraham's purchase of the cave of Machpelah at Hebron (Gen. 23:16-18). The problem was that Stephen named Abraham when the transaction at Shechem involved Jacob. One approach views the two purchases of land as telescoped in the same way the two separate calls of Abraham were telescoped in Acts 7:2. Another position points out that Abraham was in Shechem long before Jacob (Gen. 12:6) and perhaps made a first purchase of property there. Later it was reoccupied and purchased again by Jacob (Gen. 33:19). This is a reasonable hypothesis and would adequately explain Stephen's statement in Acts 7:16. The historical data presently available is insufficient to make a final judgment on this matter.

7:17-44 Moses and the Law

With Moses, as with Joseph before him, his brothers failed to understand his role as their deliverer. This would be mentioned again in 7:35. God's rejected ruler and deliverer was rescued and exalted at God's own time (7:35). The people of Israel rejected God's chosen one. Note Stephen's use of Deuteronomy 18:15 in Acts 7:37 (cf. 3:22). The people were neither obedient to Moses (7:39) nor to the prophet raised up after him, Jesus the Messiah.

The nation indeed had the tabernacle, but they did not worship God (7:42-44). Amos 5:25-27 was quoted to support the continued idolatry among the people in the wilderness. "Molech" (Acts 7:43) was the name of a Canaanite god whose worship included child sacrifice (Lev. 18:21). "Rephan" (Acts 7:43) was the name of an astral deity associated with the planet Saturn.

7:45-50 Dwellings As Symbols of God's Presence

Stephen used Isaiah 66:1-2 to show that the tabernacle and temple were only symbols of God's presence, not the substance or actual residence of God. Throughout Israel's history, the people had thought the temple or its equipment had a special ability in and of itself to save or bless. But that was just a pagan attitude toward the temple as a good luck charm. Even though they had the tabernacle and after that the temple, they were exiled from the temple and the land to Babylon (Acts 7:43). Jesus had reminded his people of what the real temple was (John 2:20-22; 4:21-24; cf. also 1 Kings 8:26-27). It is important to remember that Stephen was speaking to the accusation that he was destroying respect for the temple and its customs.

7:51-53 Application to the Hearers

Remember the charges against Stephen? They accused him of blaspheming Moses and God (6:11) and of destroying respect for the temple (6:14). But Stephen said that the leaders, his very accusers, had blasphemed and ignored God's true intentions for the Mosaic covenant and the temple regulations.

7:54–8:1 STEPHEN IS MURDERED

Filled with the Spirit, Stephen related a startling vision (7:55-56). The disciples had seen Jesus ascend up into a cloud (1:9), and Peter had preached that Jesus had ascended to sit at the right hand of God (2:33-35). But this was the first time Jesus' presence there was actually revealed. And it came from the final vision of the first martyr for Jesus Christ. Jesus stood to receive Stephen. Stephen's prophecy echoed the words of Jesus spoken before the same group (cf. Mark 14:62; and Jesus' use of Ps. 110:1 and Dan. 7:13). The presence of the Messiah at God's right hand provided a more universal and satisfying way of access to God and comfort during persecution.

Capital punishment was a carefully guarded privilege in Roman government (Acts 7:57-58; cf. John 18:31). This was not a punishment the Jews had the authority to inflict, with one exception—when the case involved the sanctity of the temple. In the temple a barrier wall separated the Court of the Gentiles from the area restricted only for Jews. Accordingly, Gentiles who crossed the barrier could be stoned—even if they were Romans (Josephus, *Jewish War*, 6.126). The Jews may have justified their actions against Stephen because of what he said about the temple (6:13) or this may have simply been a case of mob violence. The reference to "witnesses" (7:58) suggests that they sought conformity to the requirements of a legal execution (Deut. 19:15). Saul (7:58), who would soon figure prominently in the record of Christian history, was introduced as an enemy of the faith. Stephen's last words echoed those of Jesus (Acts 7:60; cf. Luke 23:34). It was as if Jesus was suffering all over again through his first martyr.

8:2–9:31 THE SCATTERED WITNESS: THE DIRECTION AND DIRECTOR

8:2-3 Rise of Persecution

The primary result of the growing persecution of believers in Jerusalem was not death to the new faith, but the spreading of the church to Judea and Samaria in obedience to the Lord's command in Acts 1:8. It appears that Saul was the chief mover behind the persecution (8:3) because when he stopped, the church enjoyed a measure of peace (9:30-31).

8:4-25 Philip in Samaria

8:4-8 INITIAL SUCCESS

Although there was no indication that the church was complacent, God used the pain of persecution to scatter the witness from Jerusalem. Samaria was the first example of the preaching ministry of those scattered. The elements confirming God's work abroad were attention ("crowds listened intently," 8:6), "miracles" (8:6) and "great joy" (8:8). This prepared the way for Simon the sorcerer's problem with materialism and the Samaritans' receiving of the Holy Spirit. Samaria had traditionally been a rival center of worship to Jerusalem and was hated by the religious Jews (see John 4 for Jesus' witness to the Samaritans). From Jerusalem, Philip went to the city of Samaria (8:5). This city, about thirty-five miles north of Jerusalem, had been rebuilt by Herod the Great and named "Sebaste" in honor of Augustus Caesar. It was in the heart of the region occupied by the Samaritans, a people of low regard in the sight of the Jews (see note on John 4:3-4).

8:9-13 SIMON THE SORCERER IS INTRODUCED

Simon's belief (8:13) was later seen to be superficial (8:20-23). It apparently was based on miracles alone and did not issue in faith unto salvation (James

2:20-24). His title (8:10) was a direct affront to the real power of God in Jesus, poured out through his Spirit. The Samaritans received the Good News about the kingdom of God and the name of Jesus.

8:14-25 SAMARITAN MINISTRY CONFIRMED
The interest in this section is in Simon's materialistic attitude toward the gift of the Holy Spirit. It compares with the story of Ananias and Sapphira's materialistic lies concerning their property (5:1-11). The simple authority given to Peter and John (8:17) was contrasted with Simon's desire to buy the same authority as if it were another magic spell (8:9, 18-19). But the divine cost and the glory that led to the simple act of laying on of the apostles' hands had already been paid for. Behind that act lay the death and exaltation of Jesus, something that could not be bought with mere money.

The Spirit coming upon the Samaritans confirmed God's presence and blessing on this next crucial advance in the unhindered spread of the gospel (1:8). As at Pentecost, this new outpouring of the Spirit was preceded by prayer (8:15; cf. 1:14).

Simon was reprimanded for his commercial attitude toward the gift of the Holy Spirit (8:20-23). Throughout 8:9-24 Simon's praise by the people around him was stressed ("great," 8:9; "Great One," 8:10; "influential," 8:11). When he lost that praise to the apostles, Simon became jealous, not for God's glory, but for his own (8:23). This continues the theme of how those within the community responded to the Holy Spirit. Simon desired the status of authority without the required knowledge and purity. Normally the Spirit was given at the moment of faith (cf. 10:44; Eph. 1:13), but this situation was unique (8:17).

The Jews had no dealings with the Samaritans. Had the Spirit been given while Philip was preaching, the Jews might have regarded Samaritan Christianity as distinct from the Judean brand; thus there would have been two churches. The laying on of hands by Peter and John associated the Samaritan believers with the Jerusalem church. That preserved the unity of the body of Christ and clearly marked out the next extension from Jerusalem to Judea and Samaria. The linking phrase (Acts 8:25) supplied the purpose of Peter and John's trip: to proclaim the word of the Lord.

8:26-40 Philip Preaches to an Ethiopian
8:26-28 PREPARATION
The Ethiopian was reading and wondering. Gaza (8:26) was located on the coastal plain about thirty-five miles west of Hebron (see introductory map). The Ethiopian eunuch (8:27) was a court official of the queen who ruled the northern region of modern Sudan. Eunuchs were in a position to secure the trust of royalty. They could have no children to begin a new usurping dynasty and were thus commonly promoted into positions as court officials.

8:29-35 PRESENTATION
The Ethiopian was baffled by the Scriptures (8:34). He was reading Isaiah 53:7-8, about the suffering servant of God. Philip followed Jesus' own interpretation of the Old Testament (8:35; cf. Luke 24:27, 44, 48).

8:36-40 BAPTISM
In a startling way, God gave a sign to the Ethiopian by snatching Philip away. Most Greek manuscripts do not contain Acts 8:37. Azotus (8:40), known as Ashdod in the Old Testament, was about twenty miles north of Gaza. Caesarea was located on the Mediterranean coast about fifty miles north of Azotus (see introductory map).

9:1-31 The Conversion of Saul
9:1-19 SAUL'S SALVATION
9:1-9 Saul's Confrontation with Jesus
Saul had authority to arrest Christians as far north as Damascus (9:1-2). Note the great change between rage (9:1) and peace (9:31) that resulted for the Christians because of Saul's conversion. "The Way" (9:2) was an expression used in the first century to refer to the Christian faith, that is, "the way of salvation" (cf. John 14:6; Acts 19:9, 23; 22:4; 24:14, 22). Damascus was an important oasis and caravan stopover east of the Anti-Lebanon mountains, about sixty miles north of the Sea of Galilee (see introductory map).

As he approached Damascus, Saul had a vision in which Jesus validated the claims of his gospel (9:3-6). The key question Jesus asked was, "Why?" Saul responded, "Who are you?" The divine response (9:5) linked Jesus and the Lord as one and the same. This confrontation with the risen Lord brought radical change to Saul's life. Saul had discovered that the man Jesus from Nazareth was in fact the promised and exalted Lord. Saul's conversion continues the theme of how God overcame all hindrances to the gospel message. Under God's power, the worst persecutor of the church was changed into its most influential evangelist.

Saul spent three days fasting (9:9). It is not known what Saul was thinking during this time, but when he again opened his mouth it was to proclaim Jesus as the Son of God (9:20, 22). This time was spent making the basic connections between Old Testament Scriptures predicting the coming of the Davidic Son of God, Jesus of Nazareth. Saul's conversion was also recorded in Acts 22:4-21 and 26:12-23 (cf. also 1 Cor. 9:1; 15:8; Gal. 1:15; Phil. 3:12; 1 Tim. 1:13). The conversion of Saul took place in the summer of A.D. 35.

9:10-19 Saul's Commission
In the dialogue between Ananias and God, Saul's mission to the Gentiles was foreseen (9:15). Saul was chosen to witness and suffer. The laying of

Ananias's hands on Saul was a means of identifying him with the Christians whom he had been persecuting (19:17). Saul's baptism identified him further with the movement. His filling with the Holy Spirit was his commission as God's prophet.

9:19-22 SAUL'S PERSUASIVENESS

Saul amazed all groups (9:19-21), the Christians and Jews alike. Proving that Jesus was the Messiah (9:22) was at the core of Saul's early thought and preaching.

9:23-30 INITIAL PERSECUTION AGAINST SAUL

9:23-25 Persecution in Damascus

Saul's escape from Jewish persecution in Damascus took place somewhere between A.D. 37–40. Galatians 1:17 reveals that immediately after his conversion Saul had spent three years in Arabia. This may be alluded to in the words "After a while" (Acts 9:23). Saul's return to Damascus after a three-year absence was greeted by this death plot. He used this incident in 2 Corinthians 11:32 as his final example of weakness and humiliation.

9:26-31 Persecution in Jerusalem

After Saul arrived in Jerusalem, he faced initial opposition from the Christian community. Barnabas befriended Saul because all the other Christians remembered Saul's past hatred toward the church and were slow to accept him (9:26-27). For more on Barnabas, see 4:36. Hellenistic or Grecian Jews (9:29) were those who spoke Greek and were at home with Greek culture and customs. The Hellenistic Jewish Christians were referred to in an earlier conflict within the church (cf. 6:1). Here the Hellenistic Jews tried to kill Saul (9:29) as they had done to Stephen (6:9). Saul was sent to Tarsus (see introductory map) by the Christian community to avoid the death plots against him (9:30). His aggressive style seems to have stirred up stronger opposition to the Christian community; after Saul left, the church enjoyed a measure of peace (9:31; cf. 9:1). Caesarea (9:30) was located on the Mediterranean coast about sixty miles northwest of Jerusalem. Tarsus (9:30) was Saul's hometown and was situated on the Cilician plain (cf. Gal. 1:21) about ten miles inland from the Mediterranean (see introductory map).

9:32–11:26 THE GENTILES: INCLUDED BY GOD

Overview: The section of 9:32–11:26 relates to the preceding section (8:2–9:31) in two ways. It resumes the account of the work of the original apostles, Peter in particular. And it introduces the expansion of the church among the Gentiles—a necessary precedent to Saul's later work among them.

9:32-43 Two Miracles in Neighboring Towns

Overview: These two miracles show how the message spread in two more areas of Jewish population (9:35, 42). The miracles of healing and resurrection mirror the signs and wonders of Jesus (2:19, 22, 43). Peter was traveling only to the Jewish people. With Dorcas's death, her friends came and called for Peter to come. He came willingly and Dorcas, who was already a believer, was raised. Peter's willingness to bring salvation to the Jews stands in contrast to his unwillingness to bring the message of spiritual life to the Gentiles. Peter's unwillingness was corrected by the great lesson of 10:9-16, 28.

9:32-35 AENEAS HEALED: LYDDA

Lydda (9:32), Old Testament Lod, was located about eleven miles southeast of Joppa (see introductory map). Sharon (9:35) was a reference to the fertile plain that extends for about fifty miles along the Mediterranean coast from Joppa to the Crocodile River (just north of Caesarea).

9:36-43 TABITHA RAISED: JOPPA

"Tabitha" (9:36) means "gazelle." "Dorcas" is the Greek rendering of the name. Joppa (9:36) was an important port city on the Mediterranean coast located about thirty miles northwest of Jerusalem (see introductory map). The ancient city, now called Jaffa, has been completely surrounded by modern Tel-Aviv. Peter was staying in the home of a "leatherworker" (9:43)—one who preserved the skins of dead animals. This was considered an unclean profession by the Jews in view of the leatherworker's regular contact with dead bodies. This may reflect Peter's increasing emancipation from Jewish ceremonial traditions; an emancipation that will be completed when he brings the gospel to the "unclean" Gentiles (Acts 10).

10:1–11:26 Confirmation of Gentile Salvation

10:1-8 THE GENTILE IS INTRODUCED

Cornelius is introduced by his character (10:1-2), prayerfulness and compassion (10:3-6), and obedience (10:7-8). Caesarea (10:1), located twenty-seven miles north of Joppa, was a major seaport and the seat of the Roman procurators of Judea. Cornelius was a centurion who commanded around one hundred (a "century") soldiers. A regiment was a military unit of six hundred men. Five regiments were stationed in Caesarea and one in Jerusalem. Cornelius was not a Jewish proselyte but accepted the Jewish religion and revered their God (10:2).

10:9-16 PETER'S VISION

The point of this vision was that God is not partial to any one ethnic or racial group (10:15). To eat all foods was symbolic for fellowshiping without discrimination with people of all races and people groups (10:28, 34). This was a direct fulfillment of 3:25-26 and all families being blessed in Abraham (cf. Gen. 12:3). The cleanness problem came from the commands of the Mosaic Law (Lev. 11). But Jesus had replaced the Mosaic covenant with the new covenant. The old was now fulfilled, but Peter was still learning what was old and what was new. This explains how Peter could disobey God's thrice repeated command to eat, while still thinking he was obeying the Mosaic Law (cf. Acts 11:8).

It seemed to Peter that God was contradicting his own law (but see Mark 7:19). But the dietary laws of the Mosaic covenant served, in part, to visualize the separation of Israel from the unclean nations. Now that Jesus had broken down that dividing wall, the old food restrictions were no longer needed. God had changed the covenant and ended the food distinctions. In Christ, no person was unholy or unclean (Acts 10:28; cf. Eph. 2:11-22).

10:17-33 PETER GOES TO CAESAREA
The message arrived from Cornelius (Acts 10:17-23), and Peter began to understand (10:23-33). The vision was about "food," yet it really concerned "race" (10:28). He understood that God's cleansing of the impure foods (10:15) related to his cleansing of the Gentiles. There were six believers who went with Peter to Caesarea (10:23; cf. 11:12). Peter had grasped the meaning of the vision (10:28). The primary point was not that Peter should change his diet, but that God had dissolved the traditional distinction between Jew and Gentile. This concept would become foundational for the unity of the church, proclamation of the gospel, and mission outreach.

10:34-43 PETER'S ADDRESS
Peter's words at this primarily Gentile gathering revealed a new understanding of how God relates to humans through the gospel. Peter summarized the life of Jesus (10:37-41). The emphasis was on Jesus' anointing with the Holy Spirit and power (10:38), the exact terms used for Christians' anointing (1:5, 8; Luke 24:49). Note the carefully selected witnesses (Acts 10:41). The resurrection ministry of Jesus before his ascension was to prepare witnesses. The orders to preach (10:42) had been given in 1:2. The forgiveness of sins (10:43) was given through the work of Jesus, the author of the new covenant.

10:44-48 THE SPIRIT EMPOWERS NEW WITNESSES
The key words are "amazed" and "too" (10:45). There was no difference in the way God confirmed faith in Christ, whether to the Jew or Gentile. Therefore, ethnicity was no longer of any consequence. They were cleansed by faith in Jesus' name. Baptism identified this group of Gentiles with the community of the redeemed (10:47-48). The outpouring of the Holy Spirit and speaking in tongues served to authenticate that these Gentiles had truly believed and were to be regarded no differently than Jewish believers.

11:1-18 THE LARGER COMMUNITY'S RESPONSE AT JERUSALEM
But the issue of Jewish and Gentile distinctions had to be further resolved (11:1-3). Those "other believers" (11:2) referred to Jewish believers who were unhappy at the report that Gentiles were being saved without becoming Jews (that is, circumcised) first. Peter explained the changes that were coming about (11:4-17). The "beginning" (11:15) referred to the day of Pentecost (Acts 2) when the church began. The essential issue was human versus divine, water versus Spirit (11:16). Spirit baptism was God's final word of acceptability (11:17). The church was satisfied with Peter's explanation (11:18), but the issue later came to a climax in Acts 15. This was a direct granting of repentance to Gentiles without the practices of Judaism and the Mosaic covenant as a middleman. Not all would stay quiet over this issue.

The door was now open to carry the gospel from Jerusalem to the ends of the earth (1:8). From this point on the book provides examples of how the gospel was not hindered and clarifications about how Christianity related to Mosaic Law and Gentile ways.

11:19-26 GENTILE RESPONSE AT ANTIOCH
Some Christians continued only witnessing to Jews (11:19). Phoenicia is the coastal plain region stretching about 120 miles north from Mount Carmel. Cyprus (11:19) is the large island (140 x 60 miles) located in the northeast corner of the Mediterranean Sea. Antioch (11:19) was the capital of the Roman province of Syria and the third largest city in the empire. It was located on the Orontes River about fifteen miles from the Mediterranean Sea. Cyrene (11:20) was the chief city of a district of North Africa called Cyrenaica. (For the locations of these cities, see introductory map.)

Other Christians ventured out to the Gentiles, and God encouraged them with large numbers of believers (11:20-26). The Gentile community was strengthened by Barnabas (11:22-24) and by Saul (11:25-26). This was Saul's first appearance in about six years (9:30) and can be dated around A.D. 43–44. Saul came to Antioch in A.D. 43 to begin a teaching ministry in the city (11:26). It was in Antioch that the disciples were first called "Christians," or "Christ-people."

11:27–12:24 JERUSALEM PERSECUTION: THE KING VERSUS A KING
11:27-30 Famine Relief
The function of the famine relief was to forge a link of fellowship between Gentile Antioch and the predominantly Jewish church of Jerusalem. The

link with Jerusalem was important for establishing apostolic foundations and connections to Jesus' earthly life. The Gentile church was not a mere "off-shoot" of Christianity, but was an integral exten-sion of Christ's international body. Luke linked Agabus's prophecy of the famine (11:28) to the reign of the emperor Claudius (A.D. 41–54). Josephus reported that the great famine did, in fact, occur during Claudius's reign, about A.D. 46.

12:1-24 Herod's Final Atrocities

12:1-2 JAMES IS PUT TO DEATH
"King Herod" (12:1) is a reference to Agrippa I (A.D. 37–44) who was the grandson of Herod the Great. In A.D. 37 Caligula endowed him with Philip's tetrarchy, and in A.D. 39 he received Galilee and Perea as well. In A.D. 41, Claudius added Samaria and Judea to his charge. Thus he ruled practically the same territory as his grandfather, Herod the Great. The apostle James was the first of the twelve to be martyred (12:2). Jesus had predicted James's harsh death in Mark 10:35-39. Herod's desire to please the Jews (12:3) by persecuting the believers was later repeated by the governors Felix (24:27) and Festus (25:9).

12:3-19 PETER IS DELIVERED
Peter was imprisoned (Acts 12:3-5) and released through God's power (12:6-11). The significance of this and the other releases from prison was to show God's power to overcome physical hindrances and God's verdict of "not guilty" on the activities of his witnesses. For Passover (12:4), see the note on Matthew 26:17.

After his release, Peter reported to the local gather-ing of Christians and then left Jerusalem for a safer place (12:12-17). James (12:17) is the brother of Jesus and the author of the book of James. The apos-tle James, the brother of John, had recently been murdered (12:2; cf. Mark 10:35-39). The "home of Mary" (12:12) was probably the location of the upper room where the Last Supper was observed (Mark 14:13-16) and where the early church met for prayer (Acts 1:13-14). John Mark (12:12) was the cousin of Barnabas and participated in Paul's first missionary journey (cf. 12:25). John Mark is proba-bly best known for writing the Gospel of Mark. "His angel" (12:15) might have been a reference to Peter's guardian angel (cf. Matt. 18:10) or his helping angel (cf. Heb. 1:14). At any rate, the believers could not believe that their prayers for Peter's release had actu-ally been answered (Acts 12:15).

Herod killed the guards who had allowed Peter's escape (12:18-19). According to Roman law, a guard who allowed a prisoner to escape became liable to the same penalty the prisoner would have suffered.

12:20-24 HEROD IS JUDGED
This section graphically demonstrates how the gospel could not be hindered even by a great and powerful king (note the contrast of 12:24). He died after Passover in A.D. 44. Tyre and Sidon (12:20) were the major port cities of Phoenicia (see intro-ductory map). While the Phoenicians were noted for their shipping and trade, they depended on the grain of Galilee for their food supply.

12:25–14:28 PAUL'S LONG-RANGE MISSION: JEW AND GENTILE CONFLICT
Overview: The expeditions of Paul share several char-acteristics: First, Paul went to the Jews first. That was not a reversal of God's mission to the Gentiles. It was a continued pattern that dated back to Abraham. It was not just to the Jews or just to the Gentiles. It was to the Jews first, but certainly also then to the Gentiles (cf. 13:46-47). The new covenant opened up the no-distinction ministry to Jews and Gentiles. Second, persecution of Christians came first from the Jews and then from the Gentiles. The Jewish persecu-tion reflected the ancient conflict within God's chosen community (Esau and Jacob). Gentile perse-cution related to questions of the Roman govern-ment and reflected the concept of the nations rising up against God's people (4:25-26). Third, Paul returned to strengthen the communities he had already planted (cf. Matt. 28:20). Fourth, Paul returned to his home base.

The geographical spheres of Paul's expeditions reflected the progressive nature of Jesus' commis-sion in Acts 1:8. Paul moved through Asia Minor, to the Aegean regions, and finally to Rome.

12:25–13:3 Commission and Preparation
Paul and Barnabas escaped the trials experienced by Peter while in Jerusalem (12:1-19). John Mark, who returned to Antioch with Paul and Barnabas, had been introduced in the context of the Jerusalem persecutions (12:12). The church in Antioch sought God's direction (13:1-2) and prayed for his blessing (13:3). The Holy Spirit represented God's sending power (13:4) and was behind all Paul's expedi-tions. The Latin name "Niger," meaning "the black man" (13:1) probably indicates that Simeon was a black man. For "Cyrene" (13:1), see the note on 11:20. Apparently Manaen (13:1) was the foster-brother of "King Herod Antipas," ruler of Galilee and Perea (4 B.C.–A.D. 39). The laying on of hands (13:3) symbolized the relationship between the church at Antioch and the missionaries sent out as their representatives. Essentially, it was a rite of identification.

13:4-12 Cyprus
13:4-5 TO THE JEW FIRST
Sent out by the Spirit, the apostles mirrored Christ's ministry (cf. 13:47; Matt. 4:15-16; Luke 4:18). Cyprus (Acts 13:4; see the note on 11:19) is located in the Mediterranean Sea about eighty miles south-

west of Seleucia, the port of Antioch (see map of *Paul's First Missionary Journey* on page 486). The island was about a twenty-four hour journey from Seleucia by boat. Salamis (13:5) was a major port and commercial center on eastern Cyprus. It boasted the largest marketplace in the Roman colonial Empire. For "John Mark" (13:5), see 12:25.

13:6-12 SERGIUS PAULUS

Bar-Jesus, or Elymas, an attendant of the proconsul Sergius Paulus, tried to oppose the ministry of Paul and Barnabas (13:6-8). Paphos (13:6) was the capital of Cyprus in Roman times and a worship center for Aphrodite, the Greek goddess of love. Governor (13:7) was the title given to the official chosen to rule a senatorial province such as Cyprus.

Elymas, an enemy of the gospel, was miraculously blinded. This miracle served as a sign for Sergius Paulus pointing to the truth of the gospel (13:9-12). God had used blindness in Paul's own life. "Saul" (13:9) was a Jewish name and "Paul" a Roman name. Both were probably given at birth, but Paul apparently began going by his Roman name as he began ministering in a Roman environment.

13:13–14:25 Asia Minor

13:13-52 PISIDIAN ANTIOCH

No reason was given for John Mark's return (13:13). In 13:16-41, Luke recounted the longest of Paul's recorded sermons. It was quite similar to Stephen's defense (Acts 7). Paul recounted Israel's history (13:14-22). He started with the Abrahamic covenant (13:17), moved to the Davidic covenant (13:22), and concluded by presenting Jesus as the Messiah promised by the Davidic covenant (13:23-25).

Paul addressed Jews and God-fearing Gentiles (13:16, 26). Perga (13:13), located in Pamphylia, a coastal district of Asia Minor, was about twelve miles from Attalia, the probable port of entry for the missionary team. Entering the region of Galatia, the missionaries came to Antioch of Pisidia, an important commercial and religious center (13:14). The city served as a major stop on the trade route from Ephesus to the Euphrates River. Antioch was near the district of Pisidia, but actually in the lesser known district of Phrygia. "Pisidia" distinguishes this city from "Syrian" Antioch, the city Paul had come from. The 450 years (13:19) was apparently a rounded figure that included the years of bondage (400 years, cf. Acts 7:6), wandering (40 years), and conquest (7 years).

Paul concluded his sermon with an application and warning (13:38-51). Note the use of the Old Testament in Acts 13:33-35, 41, 47 (Ps. 2:7; Isa. 55:3; Ps. 16:10; Hab. 1:5; Isa. 49:6). Compare the use of Psalm 2 here with its use in Acts 4:25-26. Compare the use of Habakkuk 1:5 (Acts 13:41) with Habakkuk 2:4 in Romans 1. Paul received the typical twofold response (Acts 13:42-43). For

"godly converts" (13:43), see the note on 2:10. The split from the synagogue (13:44-52) was caused by jealousy (13:45; cf. 5:17; 7:9).

In Acts 13:47 the fuller significance of the phrase "to the ends of the earth" (1:8) is revealed. It was a quotation of Isaiah 49:6 that Jesus had applied to the mission of the church. Previously, Simeon had applied the passage to Jesus when he was brought into the temple (Luke 2:32). Here, Paul applied the same passage as a command of God to his own mission (Acts 13:47; see also Matt. 4:15-16 and its use of Isa. 9:1-2). It was a commission in terms of the universal Abrahamic blessing.

Despite strong persecution from the Jews, disciples multiplied quickly (13:50-52). A Jew returning from travel in Gentile lands would shake off his garments to prevent carrying any "unclean" dust back into Israel. This action was commanded by Jesus (cf. Matt. 10:14) and symbolized the rejection of those who had rejected Christ. It was an acknowledgment that those who refused the gospel were like unbelieving heathen.

14:1-7 ICONIUM

After arriving in Iconium, persecution again arose from Jewish leaders who stirred up the leading citizens (14:2). This opposition came because so many of the Jews believed the gospel message (14:1). In order to protect their interests, the Jewish leaders had to get rid of the upstart missionaries. As in 8:1-4, persecution grew out of the generally favorable response to the gospel, not because the overwhelming majority opposed it (14:5-7). Despite the persecution, the gospel was spread.

Iconium (14:1; modern Konia) was located about eighty miles southeast of Pisidian Antioch. Iconium was a prosperous Greek city and was situated on a well-watered plain in the Galatian heartland of Asia Minor. Lycaonia (14:6) was a region of southern Asia Minor north of Cilicia. Its major cities were Lystra and Derbe.

14:8-20 LYSTRA

After seeing a miracle performed by Paul and Barnabus, the people of Lystra began to worship them as gods (14:8-13). Paul was forced to reinterpret this miracle for them (14:14-18). He began with their understanding of gods and from there taught them of the real God. He did this by using illustrations from creation, God's control of history, and nature. He stressed the unity and singularity of God.

Lystra, once a military outpost of Rome, was located about twenty miles southwest of Iconium. After the area was subdued by Rome, the city declined in population. It was so far off the main road that most of its inhabitants did not even speak Greek (14:11). It was probably at Lystra that Timothy was converted (cf. Acts 15:41–16:3).

Zeus (14:12) was the chief god of the Greek

pantheon. Hermes was the patron god of orators. It may have been as a result of this stoning that Paul bore the "marks" of Jesus (14:19; Gal. 6:17; cf. also 2 Cor. 11:25). Derbe was located seventy miles southeast of Lystra. Only recently has the city been identified with certainty, and little is known about it.

14:20-25 DERBE TO ATTALIA
After moving on to Derbe (14:20), Paul returned to establish the churches he had already planted (14:21-23). Paul's message to the churches established during the first missionary journey was summarized in 14:22. Persecution was not a hindrance to the kingdom of God. Paul called persecution the very gateway for entrance into God's kingdom (14:22). This statement contributes to the book's purpose of bringing encouragement to those suffering persecution. Elders (14:23) were appointed early on in Paul's ministry. For the appointment of elders, see the qualifications given by Paul in 1 Timothy 3:1-7. Pisidia (14:24) was a mountainous district of Asia Minor south of Phrygia. Pamphylia was the coastal district south of Pisidia. Perga, located about eight miles inland from the coast, was the chief city of Pamphylia. Attalia was an important seaport in Pamphylia.

14:26-28 Return and Report to the Antioch Community
Paul's first journey took about one and a half years (A.D. 48–49) and involved about 1,250 miles of travel. In this journey Paul and Barnabas widened the open door for including the Gentiles in the Christian church. Thus, Paul's first missionary journey continued the work already begun by Peter's first opening of the door to Gentile faith at the home of Cornelius (Acts 10).

15:1-35 TOWARD A JEW AND GENTILE RESOLUTION

15:1-5 The Problem Arises
The Christians who had once been Pharisees (15:5) asserted that Gentile Christians had to obey the Laws of Moses. They believed in the resurrection and Messiahship of Jesus, but placed that faith within the Mosaic covenant rather than the new covenant. The dispute centered upon the question of how salvation is received (15:1, 5). Jesus had anticipated this conflict between old and new in Matthew 13:51-52. The book of Hebrews presents a more elaborate discussion of this conflict.

Judea (15:1) was the central district of Palestine. These Jewish believers came to Antioch insisting that circumcision according to Mosaic Law (Gen. 17:11; Exod. 12:48; Lev. 12:3) was necessary for salvation. The church was faced with the question, Is a Gentile acceptable to God without becoming a Jew? For Phoenicia (15:3), see note on Acts 11:19. Samaria

(15:3) was the district north of Judea. For more on the Pharisees (15:5), see note on Matthew 3:7.

15:6-21 The Problem Debated and Solved

15:6-11 PETER CLAIMS GRACE ALONE
The Holy Spirit was God's affirming witness of approval for Gentile inclusion in the fold of Christianity (15:8). Those of Jewish background were demanding external signs, like circumcision, to prove inclusion, but Peter pointed out that God proved his acceptance of the Gentiles through the witness of the Spirit (15:8). Peter recounted how God's Spirit had been given as completely to uncircumcised Gentile converts (cf. Acts 10) as to the circumcised Jews. This divine witness confirmed that salvation came by faith, not by keeping the Mosaic Laws (15:9). Salvation by anything else tested God (15:10) and his salvation through grace (15:11).

15:12-21 JAMES ADDS OLD TESTAMENT SUPPORT
Again, God's signs and wonders were used to show his approval of the believing Gentiles (15:12; cf. 2:19, 22, 43; 14:3). Amos 9:11-12 was used (15:15-18) to show that the inclusion of Gentiles was a long-standing part of God's promised restoration of Israel according to his promise to David. The prophecy concerned God's future blessing on disobedient Israel. The Davidic dynasty ("the fallen kingdom of David," 15:16) would be restored in the kingdom, and then even the Gentile nations would know and worship the Lord. James was saying, "What God is doing today in blessing Gentiles is in harmony with his program for the future."

The suggested prohibitions of 15:20 were common-sense items—the reason being given in 15:21, "For." There was no need to wave red flags in front of those Jews who were culturally steeped in the Laws of Moses. However, those prohibitions were not at all connected to the issue of salvation; they were to increase community between Jews and Gentiles. The prohibitions come from Leviticus 17 and 18 and include idol sacrifices (Lev. 17:8-9), eating blood (Lev. 17:10-12), eating animals that had not been properly butchered and the blood drained, that is, "strangled animals" (Lev. 17:13-14), and "sexual immorality."

15:22-29 The Answer Is Formulated
The letter written here (15:23-29) became the official word from the apostles concerning the place of the Mosaic system in relation to salvation for Gentiles. By implication, it also became the official word on the sufficiency of faith in Jesus alone to bring salvation. Judas and Silas were chosen by the church in Jerusalem to return to Antioch with Paul and Barnabas to announce the decision of the Jerusalem church. Silas later joined Paul on his second missionary journey (cf. Acts 15:40).

15:30-35 The Response to the Answer

The people of the Antioch church rejoiced in the decisions made at the Jerusalem council (15:30-31). The nature and work of the New Testament prophets was revealed in the work of Judas and Silas (15:32-33). Their work was primarily that of encouragement and strengthening. The party from Jerusalem returned, but Paul and Barnabas remained to minister in the Antioch church (15:34-35).

15:36–18:21 THE SECOND MISSION: GENTILE EXTENSION INTO EUROPE

15:36-41 The Personnel Selected

15:36-39 THE CYPRUS MISSION

The argument between Paul and Barnabas about whether John Mark should accompany them on the second journey carried no judgment as to who was right or wrong. It simply described how Silas came to be Paul's companion rather than Barnabas. The account of Mark's desertion during the first journey (15:38) is found in 13:13. Despite Paul's negative feelings toward Mark at this point, Paul later found him to be useful for the ministry (cf. 2 Tim. 4:11). Cyprus (15:39; see note on Acts 13:4) was the native homeland of Barnabas (4:36).

15:40-41 PAUL AND SILAS GO TO ASIA MINOR

Paul and Silas traveled north from Antioch through the provinces of Syria and Cilicia into Asia Minor (15:41). (See map of *Paul's Second Missionary Journey*, page 486.) Silas's Roman citizenship turned out to be very helpful (16:37). Perhaps the dispute that resulted in Silas's selection was allowed by God for just this reason.

16:1-10 The Journey to the Edge of Europe

16:1-3 TIMOTHY CHOSEN AND CIRCUMCISED

It was probably at Lystra that Paul asked Timothy, apparently converted through Paul's ministry on the first journey (1 Tim. 1:2), to join the missionary team. Timothy was circumcised in the spirit of Acts 15:21, i.e., to avoid offending the sensibilities of the Jews (16:3, "in deference to the Jews"), not as a means of gaining saving grace. The act would help regularize Timothy's status as a Jew and enlarge his usefulness in ministry. Compare Paul's dealings with Titus (Gal. 2:3). For the cities of Lystra, Derbe, and Iconium, see notes on Acts 14:1, 6, 19.

16:4-5 THE DECREE IS DELIVERED

The important decisions, "as decided by the apostles and elders in Jerusalem" (16:4) were those reached at the Jerusalem council and recorded in their official statement (15:23-29). Paul and Silas were spreading the news that salvation came through faith alone and not by following the Laws of Moses. The result of this message was that the churches were strengthened and the believers grew in number (16:5).

16:6-10 THE DECISION TO GO TO MACEDONIA

The Holy Spirit led Paul to Troas by denying him entrance to other areas (16:6-7). The "go ahead" for God's choice came through a night vision (16:9). The Phrygian and Galatian regions (16:6) were located in central Asia Minor and would include within them the cities Paul ministered to on his first journey. Asia (16:6) referred to the Roman province located in western Asia Minor. Mysia (16:7) was the district of northwestern Asia Minor. Bithynia (16:7) was the district of northern Asia Minor bordering the Black Sea. Troas (16:8) was the major port on the Aegean coast of western Asia Minor. Macedonia (16:9) was a Roman province that encompassed much of northern Greece.

16:11-40 In Philippi

16:11-15 LYDIA: HOME BASE CHURCH

Samothrace (16:11) was a small island about halfway between the two ports of Troas and Neapolis. Neapolis, located on the northern shore of the Aegean, was the major port of Philippi. Philippi (16:12), ten miles inland from Neapolis, was a Roman colony. It was a leading city of Macedonia both politically and economically. The city commanded a fertile plain and was strategically located on the Egnatian Way, the major east-west travel route through Macedonia. Lydia (16:14) was from Thyatira, a city in Asia Minor noted as a textile center (see note on Rev. 2:18). In the ancient world the color purple was a mark of high rank and nobility. A special purple dye was extracted from the murex shellfish found in the east Mediterranean region.

16:16-18 A DEMON IS CAST OUT

The slave girl's prophecies were an annoyance to Paul because they blurred the fact that salvation came through Jesus alone. The girl was possessed by a spirit, literally a "spirit of Pythia." Pythia was the priestess of Apollo at Delphi who was believed to be inspired by the god to speak oracles when sitting over a sacred rock in his temple. The young girl at Philippi was apparently demon possessed.

16:19-34 SALVATION IN PRISON

Here a new element of resistance to the gospel is experienced by the missionaries—arrest by the civil authorities, not the religious Jews. It was important that Christianity not be seen by Rome as an illegal religion. The false accusations (16:19-21) sought to brand Paul and Silas as Jewish subverters of Roman law and order (16:20-21). The initial punishment (16:22-24) was reversed by the power of God (16:25-26). Again, not even prison could hinder the movement of God's message in this new region.

In fact, God used this difficulty as an opportunity to bring the jailer to salvation in Christ (16:27-34).

16:35-40 RELEASE AND ENCOURAGEMENT FOR THE CHURCH

In order to avert Roman retaliation, Paul clearly emphasized his Roman status (16:37). This secured a footing for the church within the Roman Empire. A similar judgment was made by Gallio in Corinth (18:14-15). Roman law exempted Roman citizens from degrading forms of punishment. A Roman citizen could claim his legal rights by declaring "I am a Roman citizen." Acts 16 should also be read as background for Paul's letter to the Philippians.

17:1-9 Thessalonica and Persecution

17:1-4 IN THE SYNAGOGUE

Amphipolis and Apollonia (17:1) were cities located on the Egnatian Way west of Philippi. Thessalonica, about one hundred miles from Philippi, was the capital of Macedonia. It was a large city (about 200,000). Situated on the Thermaic Gulf and the Egnatian Way, the city was very important commercially. The "three Sabbaths" (17:2) does not seem to have been the duration, but only the beginning of Paul's ministry in Thessalonica (Phil. 4:16; 1 Thess. 2:9; 2 Thess. 3:8).

17:5-9 JEWISH JEALOUSY BRINGS PERSECUTION

Again in Thessalonica, Jewish jealousy created problems for the church (Acts 17:5; cf. 5:17; 7:9). The charges were treason against Rome (17:7). Jesus was also accused of being a king to challenge Caesar (cf. John 19:12). The "bail" (17:9) was probably a sum of money that would be forfeited should there be further trouble. The account clarifies that Christianity did not cause the problems that followed it wherever it went. The problems were caused by unfounded religious, social, or civil hostility.

17:10-15 Berea and Persecution

17:10-12 INITIAL SUCCESS

The noble-mindedness of the Bereans came from comparing human thoughts with God's word. They compared the human words of the gospel with Old Testament Scripture and found it to be true. Berea (17:10) was a small city about forty miles west of Thessalonica. Located a considerable distance from the Egnatian Way, it was a place of no particular political or historical importance.

17:13-15 THE FOCUS OF PERSECUTION

Most of the persecution in Berea was focused on Paul. Silas and Timothy were able to remain for further ministry after Paul left the city. Paul left for Athens by sea, leaving Silas and Timothy to complete the work in Berea. They later joined him in Athens (17:16; 1 Thess. 3:1-2). This section is helpful background for understanding Paul's letters to the Thessalonians (see also comments on 18:5-11).

17:16-34 Athens

17:16-17 ACTIVITY AROUND THE SYNAGOGUE

The personal context for this section was Paul's spiritual distress over the idolatry of Athens (Acts 17:16). Athens was located about two hundred miles south of Berea, just five miles from the Aegean Sea. Athens, the birth place of democracy, was a cultural and intellectual community and was the worship center for Athena, the Greek goddess of wisdom. The road from the port at Piraeus, where Paul arrived, was lined with idols devoted to the many Greek deities.

17:18-21 PAUL GAINS A HEARING

The initial opinions of his hearers were negative (17:18). The "Epicurean" philosophers believed that the avoidance of pain was the chief end of life. The "Stoic" philosophers were those who embraced a philosophy of stern self-denial. The "Council of Philosophers" (17:19) was a council of men entrusted with the oversight of matters pertaining to religion, culture, and education in Athens. They met on the Hill of Ares (Mars, the god of war), a rock knoll northwest of the Acropolis.

17:22-31 PAUL'S ADDRESS

In his sermon, Paul promised to identify the "Unknown God" (17:22-23). Paul's calling the Athenians "very religious" was not a compliment, just a statement of fact. The emphasis of the message was actually on their ignorance (17:23, 30). Around 600 B.C. a terrible plague hit Athens (17:23). It was believed that one of the many gods of Athens had been offended and thus brought the plague. Sacrifices were offered, but the plague continued. Then Epimenides suggested that the Athenians had possibly offended an "unknown" god. It was ordered that a number of sheep be released in Athens, and that wherever they lay down, a sacrifice would be offered. The sheep were sacrificed to the "unknown" god and the plague lifted. Paul had observed one of the altars to this "unknown god" and used it as a cultural analogy in presenting the gospel to the Athenians.

After establishing a starting point, Paul went on to present the true and exalted God (17:24-28). Paul presented God exalted as Creator (17:24), exalted in sufficiency (17:25, no service needed), exalted in life-giving (17:25), and exalted in ordering the creation toward himself (17:26-28); and although God is partially hidden (17:27), he has also partially revealed himself (17:27-28). The poet (17:28) quoted by Paul was Aratus of Cilicia.

Paul gave a reasoned conclusion to his sermon (17:29-31). Because mankind is related to God, they should not think he is like gold or silver or stone

(17:29). The image of God is seen in human beings. Paul taught that in trying to find out about the real God, people should start by looking at themselves rather than creating nonhuman images of stone. Paul made it clear that the time for repentance was then (17:30-31; cf. 2 Cor. 6:1-2). Paul ended as he had begun, by offering a solution to their ignorance (Acts 17:23, 30). The mention of the resurrection was decisive and brought either radical rejection or acceptance of the gospel (17:31).

17:32-34 THE RESPONSE
The response to Paul's message in Athens appears to have been small. There is no record of a church being established in Athens as a result of Paul's ministry, but according to Eusebius, Dionysius became the first bishop of the city.

18:1-17 Corinth
18:1-4 PAUL FINDS HIS TRADE
Corinth was located about sixty miles west of Athens and was situated beside the isthmus that links the Peloponnesus with mainland Greece. Corinth was an important trade center with two fine ports: Cenchria on the Aegean to the east and Lechaeum on the Adriatic to the west. The city was also the worship center of Aphrodite, goddess of love. A temple dedicated to Aphrodite was situated on the 1,886 foot high Acro-Corinth. Paul ministered for one and a half years in Corinth (18:11).

For other references to Aquila and Priscilla (18:2), see Acts 18:18, 26; Romans 16:3; 1 Corinthians 16:19; and 2 Timothy 4:19. The imperial edict of Claudius (A.D. 41–54) commanding the Jews to leave Rome was issued around A.D. 50. The ancient historian Seutonius indicated that it was because "the Jews were indulging in constant riots at the instigation of Chrestus." He apparently wrongly imagined that Chrestus was the leader of these riots when in fact they were riots about Chrestus, a reference to Christ. Paul continued his pattern of starting his ministry in the Jewish synagogue and then speaking to the Greek Gentiles (18:4).

18:5-11 EIGHTEEN-MONTH GENTILE MINISTRY
Notice how separate the Jews and Greeks were as Paul left the synagogue and went next door to the Gentiles (18:6-7). Because of the great hostility in Corinth, God gave Paul special encouragement to minister there (18:7-11). This ministry in Corinth was the time during which Paul wrote the letters of 1 and 2 Thessalonians. When Silas and Timothy joined Paul in Corinth, they brought an encouraging report concerning the church at Thessalonica (1 Thess. 3:6-7). Having received this report, Paul sat down and wrote 1 Thessalonians (A.D. 51). He probably wrote 2 Thessalonians several months later.

18:12-17 GALLIO LEGITIMIZES THE NEW RELIGION
Christianity was a new religion in Rome's eyes and therefore shared the protection of Roman law. Gallio (A.D. 51–65) was a well-loved proconsul in Achaia. He apparently viewed Christianity as a branch of Judaism and therefore refused to become involved in the sectarian dispute. He later became involved in a conspiracy to overthrow Nero and was either forced to suicide or put to death. Sosthenes (18:17), who had succeeded Crispus as ruler of the synagogue (18:8), was beaten. If this is the same Sosthenes of 1 Corinthians 1:1, he eventually became a Christian.

18:18-21 From Corinth to Ephesus
Paul left Corinth from Cenchrea, Corinth's seaport on the Aegean, after one and a half year's of ministry. The cutting of his hair apparently concluded a Nazirite vow (Num. 6:1-21) voluntarily undertaken during his ministry in Corinth. The exact reason for this vow (Acts 18:18) is not known. The vow may have been for Paul's prosperous ministry at Corinth. At any rate, the vow shows that aspects of Old Testament worship were acceptable within the Christian faith. Paul would also conform to temple procedures in 21:24. Paul made a brief stopover at Ephesus, a place he had been denied entrance to earlier (16:6-7). He would come back to Ephesus on his next journey for a long and successful ministry.

18:22–21:16 THE THIRD MISSION: STRENGTHENING
18:22-23 Rest and Strengthening: Summary
Paul's second missionary journey had lasted two and a half years (A.D. 50–52) and included two thousand miles of travel. In the spring of A.D. 53, Paul set out from Antioch for Asia Minor (18:23) by the same land route he and Silas had followed on the second journey. (See map of *Paul's Third Missionary Journey*, page 487.) Having passed through Galatia and Phrygia, he headed for Ephesus (19:1).

18:24-28 Apollos Strengthened
The pre-Pentecost teaching of Apollos was corrected by Priscilla and Aquila (18:25-26). Apollos was from Alexandria, an important seaport and educational center on the western edge of Egypt's Nile delta. The city had a large Jewish population that had been strongly influenced by Greek culture and philosophy. The power of Apollos's witness was based on his use of the Old Testament Scriptures to prove that Jesus was the Messiah (cf. Luke 24:27, 44-47).

19:1-41 Paul in Ephesus
19:1-7 DISCIPLES STRENGTHENED
Paul advanced this little group's knowledge of salvation from John's baptism to the baptism of the Holy Spirit based on the resurrection and exaltation of

Jesus. Ephesus became a new center of Gentile ministry. The speaking in tongues indicated a new advance in the spreading of the gospel. The link was to the Samaritan mission of Acts 8:15-17. As usual, the tongues served as a sign to the Jewish community that God was working at Ephesus (cf. 1 Cor. 14:22; Isa. 28:11-12). Ephesus, a port city located near the Aegean Sea on the Cayster River, was the foremost city of Asia Minor. It was at the west end of the caravan route that linked Mesopotamia with Asia. Ephesus was also the worship center of Artemis, the many-breasted mother goddess of Asia (Acts 19:35). "Diana" (KJV) is a Romanization of Artemis. The temple of Artemis was one of the Seven Wonders of the ancient world. It was 425 feet long, 220 feet wide, and 60 feet high.

19:8-20 WONDERS IN EPHESUS AND ASIA
19:8-9 The School of Tyrannus
After being rejected by the Jews in the synagogue, Paul rented the lecture hall of Tyrannus as a place to instruct the growing body of believers. One Greek text indicates that he instructed them from the fifth to the tenth hour of the day (from 11:00 A.M. to 4:00 P.M.).

19:10-20 Evil Overcome by God's Power
From this lecture hall all of Asia Minor heard the gospel over a two-year period. Apparently Paul taught for two of the three years he minstered at Ephesus (20:31). It was during Paul's ministry at Ephesus, around the spring of A.D. 56, that he wrote the letter now known as 1 Corinthians. The exorcists professed to have the power to exorcise demons (19:13; cf. Matt. 12:43-45). The "books" (Acts 19:19) had magic spells written on them. Again, the section ends with the book's major theme, the prevailing of the gospel—in this case over the powers of black magic.

19:21-22 THE END OF THE AEGEAN MINISTRY
Two major aspects of Paul's ministry arise—the desire to see Rome and the plan to take an offering to the Jerusalem church. The desire to see Rome caused Paul to write the Epistle to the Romans from Corinth. The plan to collect an offering for the Jerusalem church figured largely in the problems Paul faced as he wrote 1 and 2 Corinthians.

19:23-41 RIOT OVER THE CITY PATRON DEITY
Christianity started to threaten the business and reputation of Ephesian idolatry (19:23-27). The small silver shrines housed minature figures of Artemis that worshipers would purchase and dedicate in the temple. Gaius (19:29) was from Derbe (20:4) and Aristarchus from Thessalonica (27:2).

The two-hour shouting match in the stadium (19:28-34) ended with the mayor persuading the crowd to disperse (19:35-41). The mayor was the most important man in Ephesus. His argument that truth should order their action (19:35-36, 40) provides a most eloquent sermon from an idolator. Again, Christianity was shown to be innocent of causing riots or spreading sedition.

20:1–21:14 The Return to Jerusalem
20:1-6 EPHESUS TO TROAS
Paul left Ephesus in the spring of A.D. 56 and headed for Macedonia. It was there in the fall of A.D. 56 that he wrote 2 Corinthians, preparing them for his next visit. Paul spent the winter of A.D. 56/57 in Greece, probably mostly at Corinth (20:3). There he wrote the great doctrinal treatise, the Epistle to the Romans. In the spring, Paul returned to Asia by way of Macedonia (20:6). "As soon as the Passover season ended" (20:6) refers to the seven-day festival following Passover (early April, A.D. 57). Troas was the Aegean port city from which Paul received his Macedonian call (cf. Acts 16:8-10).

20:7-12 THE SERMON AT TROAS
The "first day of the week" (20:7, Sunday) became the regular day of worship for the Christians. This day commemorated the day of Christ's resurrection from the tomb. The incident of Eutychus's healing served as yet another sign that confirmed God's presence and blessing on his gospel ministry.

20:13-38 MILETUS
Paul hurried to make it to Jerusalem by Pentecost, the anniversary of the day when God poured forth his Spirit upon the church (20:13-16). Pentecost was due to be observed in Jerusalem on May 27, A.D. 57. Leaving Troas (20:13), Paul decided to walk the twenty miles to Assos, a strategic port city in Mysia, while Luke and the other travelers went by ship. Mitylene (20:14) was the chief city on the Aegean island of Lesbos. Kios and Samos (20:15) are small Aegean islands just off the coast of Asia. Miletus, a port city located at the mouth of the Meander River, was situated about thirty miles south of Ephesus.

At Miletus Paul made his final farewell address to the Ephesian elders (20:17-35). This farewell message was similar to those given in Deuteronomy 29–31, Joshua 24:2-27, and Matthew 24–25. It contains the elements of farewell, blessing, and warning against falling away from the faith. Paul discussed past faithfulness (Acts 20:17-21), the uncertainty of the future (20:22-24), and the potential of the present (20:25-31). The "elders" were the leaders of the church at Ephesus. The term "elder" suggests the maturity of those who hold that office. The elders were responsible to shepherd (that is, pastor) God's "flock," the church (20:28).

Paul ended his farewell sermon with a commendation (20:32-35). The words of Jesus quoted by Paul (20:35) are not found in the Gospels, although the substance is there (cf. Luke 6:38). The gospel of

grace (Acts 20:24) is the same as the preaching of the
kingdom (20:25). God's kingdom is the framework
within which Paul preached the gospel. Acts 2:33-35
established that Jesus was already reigning at God's
side in this period of subduing his enemies. Even
though it created hostility from both Jews and
Greeks, Paul did not shrink from telling the whole
gospel (20:26-27). He never gave in to temptations
to water down the message in order to escape
conflict. This farewell causes those who read it to feel
the sadness and emotions along with Paul and the
Ephesian leaders (20:36-38).

21:1-6 MILETUS TO TYRE
From Miletus Paul and his associates sailed to the
island of Cos, and then to the island of Rhodes.
From Rhodes they sailed east along the southern
coast of Lycia, putting in at Patara. From there they
arranged a cross-sea voyage to the Phoenician port
of Tyre.

Some regard Paul's decision to continue on to
Jerusalem (21:4) an act of disobedience, and that
his imprisonment in Caesarea was God's discipline
for this disobedience. Yet the Holy Spirit only
warned of suffering and never said, "Do not go."
And Paul never referred to his imprisonment as
suffering for disobedience. The warnings (21:4, 11-
12) may have been designed to test Paul's commitment. He proved himself willing to go in spite of
the cost (cf. 20:22-24). The prophecies surrounding
his original calling also included great suffering in
the name of the Lord (9:16).

21:7-14 CAESAREA WARNINGS
The warnings here continue the warning theme of
21:1-6. Ptolemais (21:7, Old Testament "Acco,"
Crusader "Acre") was a port city on the north side
of the Bay of Haifa. Caesarea (21:8), located about
fifty-five miles northwest of Jerusalem, was a major
port in New Testament times and the center for the
Roman government in Judea. Philip the evangelist
(6:5; 8:5) had come to minister there. Agabus
(21:10) may have been the same prophet who foretold of the famine in Palestine (11:28). Paul's
comment in 21:14 summed up the thrust of his life
as well as that of the book of Acts. In all that he
did, Paul sought to do the Lord's will.

21:15–28:31 THE FOURTH MISSION: TOWARD THE GOAL
21:15–26:32 Arrest and Defense to Kings
21:15-26 THE VOW PROBLEM
Paul completed his final lap to Jerusalem. Paul's
arrival in Jerusalem marked the end of his third
missionary journey, a trip that had taken four years
(A.D. 53–57) and had involved 2,700 miles of
travel. Paul recounted to the believers in Jerusalem
his successful witness among the Gentiles (21:17-

19). The Jerusalem Christians, in turn, related
Jewish successes (21:20-21). Thousands had
believed and many tenaciously held on to the
Mosaic Law. Acts 21:21 provided an excellent
description of the Judaiser mentality that believed
that all Christians should keep the Mosaic Law.
Reports of Paul's ministry among the Gentiles were
interpreted by Jewish believers in Jerusalem to
imply that Paul was against the Mosaic Law! Of
course this was untrue (cf. Rom. 7:12), but how
could Paul prove it?

Paul demonstrated his relation to the old Mosaic
system (Acts 21:22-26). Paul was asked to join four
Jewish believers in a purification rite and pay the
expenses of their temple offering (not necessarily a
blood sacrifice, see Lev. 2). This was intended to
prove that Paul was not against the Mosaic Law.
Paul's motive in making this vow is reflected in
1 Corinthians 9:20. He saw no problem in observing a Jewish ritual as long as it was viewed in the
light of Jesus Christ and was not seen as a means of
salvation.

21:27–22:30 ARREST AND ADDRESS
21:27-36 The Arrest of Paul
Paul received the same accusations from the Jewish
leaders as Stephen had earlier (cf. 21:28 with 6:14).
And only rescue by the Roman troops saved Paul
from the same fate. Paul was falsely accused by the
Jews of bringing Gentiles into the temple area.
There were strict prohibitions against Gentiles
entering beyond the barrier that separated the
Court of the Gentiles from the courts that only Jews
could enter. Notices around the barrier read, "No
foreigner may enter within the barricade that
surrounds the temple and enclosure. Anyone who
is caught doing so will have himself to blame for
his ensuing death." The "Roman regiment" (21:31)
was a unit of six hundred Roman soldiers. One
regiment was stationed at Antonia Fortress, just
north of the temple area, at all times.

21:37–22:21 Paul's Address
Paul spoke to the Roman commander and gained a
hearing (21:37-40). The commander had thought
Paul was the Egyptian rebel leader who had led
Jewish rebels out to the Mount of Olives. Felix, the
Roman procurator, had put down that revolt. The
Jewish historian Josephus recorded the incident
about the Egyptian (Josephus, *Jewish War*, 2.261-
263). Paul's knowledge of the Greek language
(21:37) proved to the Roman commander that Paul
could not have been that Egyptian rebel (21:38).
The "Assassins" (21:38) was a reference to the
"sicarri," from *sica*, Latin for a "curved dagger."
This radical group of Jews mingled with crowds at
festivals and stabbed their pro-Roman opponents
with hidden daggers.

Aramaic (21:40) was the common spoken

language of first century Jews. When Paul spoke in this language, the Jews became silent and listened. Paul began his defense before the Jews by recounting his testimony (22:1-21). He recalled his persecutions (22:1-5), salvation (22:6-11), commission (22:12-16), and vision (22:17-21). Acts 22:16 does not teach baptismal regeneration. As the arising precedes the baptism, so calling on the name of the Lord precedes the forgiveness. The vision of 22:17-21 probably took place during Paul's first visit to Jerusalem after his conversion (9:26-30). It amplified and confirmed the commission he had received on the Damascus road (26:17). The command to go to the Gentiles (22:21) related to previous warnings that Paul would have no success in Jerusalem (22:18-19; cf. 13:46).

22:22-29 Paul Is Arrested As a Roman
A Roman citizen was entitled to certain rights, including a public hearing before the application of any punishment. Somehow Paul's parents in Tarsus had earned this right before his birth. Even the Roman commander was afraid of what would happen to him if it was found out that he had treated a Roman citizen the way he had treated Paul (22:29).

22:30–23:10 PAUL'S ADDRESS BEFORE THE JEWISH COUNCIL
The Sanhedrin was the same Jewish court that had tried Jesus. The court attempted to find the basis of Paul's crime. Paul showed his accord with the Old Testament law of respect for rulers (23:1-5). The high priest (23:2) was Ananias (A.D. 47–66), who was very pro-Roman and was executed by insurgents at the beginning of the Jewish revolt. Paul's failing eyesight (Gal. 4:15; 6:11) may have accounted for his failure to recognize the high priest (Acts 23:5). Or perhaps he was simply saying, "I didn't believe the high priest would speak like that."

Paul caused a split between the religious parties, finding support with his past group, the Pharisees (23:6-10). While the Pharisees affirmed the doctrine of resurrection, the Sadducees denied it (23:7; see the note on Matt. 3:7). Paul used this difference of opinion to his advantage before the Sanhedrin.

23:11-22 THE PLOT TO KILL PAUL
God gave Paul a special word of comfort assuring him of the opportunity to witness in the city of Rome (23:11). This vision explains why there was so much detail given in Acts 21–22 concerning Paul's escape from harm and his innocence before the religious and civil leaders. Paul was taking his place alongside Peter and Stephen. This was the Lord's fourth appearance to Paul (cf. Acts 9:5; 18:9-10; 22:17-18). From this point on, Luke focused on how God sovereignly worked the circumstances to move Paul to Rome.

Paul's journey to Rome (23:12-30) began with his escape from forty murderers in ambush. The large number was needed to overcome Paul and the Roman soldiers guarding him. Through God's providence Paul was saved. This event again showed how the gospel was unhindered, in this case by forty radical murderers. Acts 23:16 is the only reference in Scripture to Paul's immediate relatives.

23:23–26:32 PAUL IN CAESAREA
23:23-33 Paul Is Transferred to Caesarea
Arrangements were made to transfer Paul to Caesarea, the center of Roman government in Judea (23:23). Antonius Felix served as procurator, or governor (A.D. 52–58), of Judea and resided in Caesarea (23:24). The ancient historian Tacitus reported that "He exercised the power of a king with the mind of a slave." Lysias (23:26) was the military tribune over the Roman forces in Jerusalem. The letter to Felix (23:26-30) continued to support the book's theme of the innocence of the Christians from plots to overthrow the Roman government. This element of innocence gained greater detail as Paul got closer to Rome. This may indicate that Acts was written for a Roman audience. Antipatris (23:31) was located on the coastal plain about thirty-five miles from Jerusalem.

23:34–24:21 The Initial Interview with Felix
Paul's home province of Cilicia (23:34) was located in southeastern Asia Minor. Herod's "headquarters" (23:35) was the palace built by Herod the Great, which at this time served as the official residence of the Roman provincial governor.

Paul was forced to defend himself under Felix against accusations made by the Jews (24:1-21). The Jewish accusation was made (24:1-9). For Ananias (24:1), see the note on 23:2. Tertullus was a lawyer hired by the Jews to prosecute Paul. The "Nazarenes" (24:5) was a reference to those who followed Jesus of Nazareth. Acts 24:6-8 is absent in many manuscripts.

Paul's rebuttal (24:10-21) emphasized his obedience to God's word (24:14) and his innocence of any civil crime (24:12-13). The "Way" (24:14, 22) was a reference to the "Way of Christ," that is, Christianity. Paul protested the absence of appropriate witnesses at his hearing (24:19).

24:22-27 Felix's Procrastination
It is not known how Felix obtained this special information about Christianity. It may have been through his present wife, Drusilla, a member of the Herodian family. Drusilla (24:24), the third wife of Felix, was the youngest daughter of Herod Agrippa I (A.D. 37–44). She had been wooed by Felix from her first husband, king of Emesa. When Felix was recalled by Nero in A.D. 58, he left Paul in prison as a favor to the Jews (24:27). Porcius Festus succeeded Felix and served as procurator until his

death in A.D. 61. Paul's imprisonment was used by God to afford two years of witness in Caesarea (24:24-27).

25:1-12 Paul's Defense under Festus
The preparation was made for Paul's trial (25:1-5). Festus (25:1) became procurator at a time of considerable unrest including a breakdown in law and order. His visit to Jerusalem, the religious capital of Judea, was intended to placate the Jews. While in Jerusalem, the Jewish leaders sought to reopen Paul's case.

At the Jews' request, Festus prepared to try Paul (25:6). Festus did not want to alienate the Jewish population of Judea and sought to make concessions to those who accused Paul (25:9). The "appeal to Caesar" (25:11) was one of the most ancient and cherished rights of a Roman citizen. The right applied only to extraordinary cases, that is, those not specifically defined by statute laws. It was usually used to appeal the verdict of a lower court but could be exercised at any stage in the proceedings. The case would then be transferred to Rome and a verdict rendered by the emperor. This allowed Paul to realize his ambition to witness in Rome. At this time, the ruling Caesar was Nero.

25:13-26:32 Agrippa Joins Festus
Festus sought Agrippa's advice on Paul's case, and as a result, Agrippa asked to see Paul (25:13-22). Herod Agrippa II (25:13; A.D. 50-100) was the son of Herod Agrippa of Acts 12:1. When his father died, Claudius decided to rule Judea by procurators. Herod Agrippa II received the tetrarchy of Philip and was later given authority to rule virtually all the territory that had been in Herod the Great's domain. Bernice was Herod Agrippa's sister with whom he was living incestuously. Herod Agrippa, a Jewish king, was interested in Paul's case, and Festus was happy to gain his insight into the charges against Paul in order to write a proper statement regarding the appeal to Caesar (25:22).

Paul addressed Agrippa (25:23-26:23) and asserted that there was no basis for the accusations made by the Jews (25:23-27). This is the fullest address by Paul recorded in Acts (26:1-23). The length of the address was implied in Paul's opening statements (26:3). The address was delivered to one who knew a great deal about the Jewish religion. Paul described his previous early life (26:4-5), God's promise (26:6-8), his persecution (26:9-11), and his conversion on the Damascus road (26:12-18). His conclusion (26:19-23) again asserted his conformity to God's word, to the Law of Moses, and to the prophets.

It is debated whether the words "cast my vote against them" (26:10) indicate that Paul was a member of the Sanhedrin, or simply that he was in agreement with their decision. The expression "It is hard for you to fight against my will" (26:14) was used of Paul's resistance against God's prodding in his life.

Paul sought the conversion of the king (26:24-29). Agrippa's words can be paraphrased, "In short, you are trying to persuade me to become a Christian" (26:28). By appealing to Caesar, Paul had put himself into a new relationship with the Roman government (26:32). In order for the law of appeal to proceed, Paul was required to go to Rome. The final verdict confirmed Paul's innocence (26:30-32), but since he had appealed to Caesar, he was required to go to Rome for a further hearing.

27:1–28:31 The Expedition to Rome
27:1-44 FROM SAFETY TO A SHIPWRECK
27:1-8 The Voyage to Fair Havens
The detail in this account of Paul's journey to Rome was not given simply for excitement. It was to give a graphic example of the power of the book's last word: "And no one tried to stop him." When God wanted a proclamation to be made, he enabled it to be made by removing all hindrances.

The officer (27:1) was a commander of around one hundred soldiers in the Roman army. A "regiment" was a battallion of six hundred men. This particular regiment was named for the Roman emperor Augustus (27 B.C.–A.D. 14). The "we" (27:2) indicated that Luke sailed with Paul. The ship (27:2) was from the city of Adramyttium, on the west coast of Asia Minor, southeast of Troas. Note the sites along Paul's sea route on the map, *Paul's Journey to Rome* (page 487).

Sidon (27:3) was an ancient Phoenician harbor located seventy miles north of Caesarea. The ship sailed along the east coast of Cyprus to get shelter from the winds blowing from the west. The ship sailed along the coast of the Asian provinces of Cilicia, Pamphylia, and Lycia, landing at Myra, one of the chief ports of the grain fleet that brought wheat from Egypt to Rome (27:4-5).

At Myra (27:6), Paul transferred to a ship that had Alexandria, Egypt, as its home port. From Myra to Cnidus (27:7) sailing was slow because of the strong wind blowing out of the northwest. There they made the decision to sail south to Crete and then along the lee side of the island where they could be sheltered from the northwest wind. Fair Havens (27:8) was located on the island of Crete. Unfortunately its harbor faced west and would not provide suitable protection against the easterly winter winds. Because it was inadequate as a winter harbor, the sailors decided to move on to a better winter port.

27:9-26 Paul's Advice Goes Unheeded
It was fast appproaching the end of the winter sailing season on the Mediterranean (April–August). Mid-September through mid-November, and

February to March were regarded as dangerous times for sea travel (27:9). Mid-November to January was the off season when there was no safe sailing on the Mediterranean.

It was already October, for the Day of Atonement ("so late in the fall," 27:9; cf. Lev. 16:29-34) had past. Paul's warning was based on plenty of experience (cf. 2 Cor. 11:25). The harbor at Phoenix (Acts 27:12) promised greater protection against the winter winds. The "northeaster" (27:14; "Euraquilo," NASB; "Euroclydon," KJV) referred to the strong winter wind that blows onto the Mediterranean from the northeast. Blown southwest of Crete (26:16), the ship found shelter off the island of Clauda, about twenty-three miles to the south. The ship was undergirded with cables to prevent the hull from breaking apart in the rough water (27:17). The "sandbars of Syrtis" (27:17) were located off the coast of North Africa.

27:27-44 The Shipwreck
The ship's "lifeboat" (27:30) was a small dinghy that was normally towed, but in bad weather it was taken aboard in case it was needed. The "Sea of Adria" (27:27) was the ancient name applied to the Mediterranean Sea east of Sicily. Do Paul's words in 27:31 contradict his encouragement in 27:24? No, for God's will would be accomplished, but this never annuls the fact of human responsibility. Paul was insisting that all the ship's hands be available to help get the passengers safely ashore. They lightened the ship so that it would draw as little water as possible and run aground well up on the beach (27:38).

28:1-6 SNAKEBITE DOES PAUL NO HARM
Even a bite from a poisonous snake could not hinder God's proclamation. The small island of Malta (28:1) is located just south of Sicily. Paul's surviving the snake bite led the islanders to conclude that he was a god, a misidentification he had experienced previously (28:6; cf. 14:11).

28:7-10 MALTA MIRACLES
The Christians found honor and respect (28:10) on Malta. That is, they did nothing to support the accusations that they were criminals.

28:11-16 ARRIVAL AT ROMAN SUBURBS
After three months on Malta, Paul set sail around the first of February for Rome (28:11). The "twin gods" on the ship's figurehead were Castor and Pollux, sons of Zeus, who were regarded as the patrons of navigation. Sailing from Malta, Paul traveled north to Sicily and landed at Syracuse on the east coast of the island (28:12-13). After three days, they made their way to Rhegium on the toe of Italy.

When a favorable wind came up, they sailed along the coast of Italy and landed at Puteoli, the principal port of southern Italy, in the Bay of Naples. Hearing of Paul's approach, some Christians came from Rome to escort him to the city (28:15). Some met him at the Market of Appius, forty-three miles south of Rome. Others met him at Three Inns, thirty-three miles south of Rome. Paul was under the watch of the palace guard (Phil. 1:13), the elite soldiers of the Roman military whose primary function was to guard the imperial palace (28:16).

28:17-28 PAUL INTRODUCES HIMSELF AND THE "SECT"
28:17-22 Paul Is Given a Cool Reception
Paul centered his remarks around facts proving that he had done no wrong against Israel (28:17) and that he had no grievance against his people (28:19). The "hope of Israel" (28:20) was an eschatological expectation focusing on the resurrection, the Messiah, or the kingdom. Paul was received as an unknown stranger representing a sect with a bad reputation (28:21-22).

28:23-28 Paul Speaks of the Way
Paul used the Old Testament to link Jesus to the kingdom of God, the law, and the Prophets, a technique taught by the risen Lord (Luke 24:27, 44-45; Acts 1:3). The book ends with one parting word (28:25) that was an application of Isaiah 6:9-10 to the Jews in Rome (Acts 28:26-27). Jesus had used Isaiah 6 in Matthew 13:14-15. The unbelief of the Jews moved the focus of the Christian witness to the Gentiles (Acts 28:28). Many manuscripts omit 28:29.

28:30-31 SUMMARY OF PAUL'S TWO-YEAR ROMAN MINISTRY
The book concludes with two verses that cover the two full years of Paul's Roman ministry. During those two years Paul preached, unhindered, the kingdom of God (28:31) and sought to persuade visitors that Jesus was the Messiah of Old Testament prophecy.

Luke recounted nothing of Paul's trial or hearing before Caesar. There does not appear to be any first-century evidence for a procedure permitting a case to lapse automatically by default. It may have been that his accusers never appeared or it may have taken two years for his case to clear the courts. Whatever the precise circumstances, Paul was released after two years and then had an opportunity to continue his ministry in the Mediterranean world until his death in the spring of A.D. 68. The exalted Lord had poured forth the Holy Spirit and enabled a witness to Jesus Christ that neither death, persecution, corruption, shipwreck, lies, nor hostility could hinder.

Throughout the book, the clashes between Christianity and Rome clearly revealed to Jew and Gentile alike that Paul's religion did not subvert Roman law. The problems of social unrest stemmed from trumped up charges by Jews against Christians. Because of its ending (28:26-28), Acts stands as a final appeal to the Jews to convince them that God was behind the movement that claimed Jesus to be the Messiah.

Acts is a foundational record of Christian experience during the time spoken of in Jesus' parables (Matt. 13). These were the times when the believer was hurt by hostility and persecution. It was the time when the very power of God through the Holy Spirit seemed to be hidden in the shadows of world hatred. It was the time when the Spirit was accomplishing an unhindered witness that would one day issue in the coming of God's kingdom. The book of Acts revealed that God's salvation did not discriminate on the basis of race or politics. All had been brought near by the reigning Christ, and all could be saved through faith in his name.

ROMANS

BASIC FACTS

HISTORICAL SETTING

The letter to the Romans was written in Corinth toward the end of Paul's third missionary journey. Paul had collected and was about to deliver an offering for the Jerusalem church (Rom. 15:25-27; 1 Cor. 16:3-5; 2 Cor. 8). Paul had never visited Rome. After his visit there, he desired to move on to Spain (15:22-33). Paul had recently worked through severe problems with the Corinthian church (cf. 1 and 2 Corinthians). And it was from Corinth that he wrote his letter to the Romans—a letter which described the power of the gospel and the problems of human pride and the weakness of the flesh.

The city of Rome was founded in 753 B.C. on the Tiber River at a ford that was indispensable for traveling between northern and southern Italy. The ridges surrounding the Tiber River valley provided hilltop fortifications for times of attack. In Paul's day, Rome had a population of approximately one million (the largest city in the world) and was the political hub of the vast Roman Empire.

The church at Rome was not founded by Paul. Perhaps some Jews and proselytes from Rome who were in Jerusalem on the day of Pentecost (Acts 2:10) became believers and carried the gospel back to their city. The church was predominately Gentile (Rom. 1:5-6, 13; 11:13; 15:15-16), yet Paul's frequent quotations from the Old Testament and other references indicate that believing Jews would also read his letter (2:17).

AUTHOR

The Pauline authorship of Romans is almost universally accepted. Internal evidence of authorship abounds (1:1; 15:25; 16:3). The external testimony of the church fathers who quote Romans, among whom are Clement, Ignatius, Polycarp, and Justin, confirms the view that Paul was the author. The actual writing of the letter was done by Tertius, the secretary to whom Paul dictated the letter (16:22).

Paul as tentmaker and Pharisee

Paul was a strict Pharisee of the tribe of Benjamin (Phil. 3:5). Although he was born in Tarsus, he was educated in Jerusalem under Gamaliel (Acts 22:3). He was born in Tarsus with the privilege of Roman citizenship (Acts 22:28). Paul was a tentmaker by trade and used that craft to support himself while ministering in Corinth on his second missionary journey (Acts 18:1-3).

Paul may have been a member of the Sanhedrin (Acts 26:10) and was so zealous for his Jewish faith that he persecuted the church (Acts 26:9-11; Phil 3:6). Paul was first mentioned as Saul at the stoning of Stephen (Acts 8:1), an execution with which he was in hearty agreement (Acts 26:10).

Paul's conversion
Paul's conversion took place on the road from Jerusalem to Damascus (Acts 9:1-7), probably in A.D. 35. He remained in Damascus witnessing to the deity of Jesus in the Jewish synagogues (Acts 9:20). When it was learned that the Jews were plotting to kill Paul, he escaped from the city (Acts 9:25) and lived in Arabia for several years (Gal. 1:17).

Paul's early ministry
After revisiting Damascus, Paul went to Jerusalem where he visited with Peter and preached to the Hellenistic, or Grecian, Jews (Acts 9:26-29; Gal. 1:18-20). Threatened in Jerusalem, Paul went to Tarsus (Acts 9:30) and visited the regions of Syria and Cilicia (Gal. 1:21). Later while Barnabas was ministering in Antioch, he invited Paul to join him (Acts 11:25). The two ministered together for an entire year at Antioch (Acts 11:26). During the famine predicted by Agabus (Acts 11:28), Paul and Barnabas took relief aid from Antioch to the believers in Jerusalem (Acts 11:30). Paul and Barnabas then returned to Antioch, taking John Mark with them (Acts 12:25).

Paul's missionary journeys
Paul's three missionary journeys all began at Antioch. His first journey (Acts 13–14), from A.D. 48 to 49, was followed by another visit to Jerusalem (Acts 15). The second journey lasted from A.D. 50 to 52, and the third from A.D. 53 to 57. It was following Paul's third expedition that he was arrested in Jerusalem (Acts 21:27-36) and then imprisoned in Caesarea for two years (Acts 23:23–26:32) from A.D. 57 to 59. Having appealed to Caesar (Acts 25:11), Paul was transferred to Rome where he was confined for approximately two years (Acts 28:30-31).

After two years in Rome, Paul was released, apparently because no Jews had appeared to bring a charge against him (cf. Phil. 1:19, 25; 2:24). Paul then went east through Ephesus, where he left Timothy (1 Tim. 1:3), and then to Colosse (Philem. 1:22). From there he proceeded to Macedonia where he wrote his first letter to Timothy (1 Tim. 1:3). Paul may have at that time realized his desire to journey to Spain (Rom. 15:28; 1 Clement 5:7).

Paul again journeyed east and visited Crete (Titus 1:5), where he left Titus to set the church in order and appoint elders in A.D. 66. Paul wrote Titus concerning his responsibilities just before he journeyed from Asia Minor (2 Tim. 4:13, 20) to Nicopolis, where he spent the winter of A.D. 66/67 (Titus 3:12). Having spent spring and autumn in Macedonia and Greece (1 Tim. 1:4; 2 Tim. 4:20), Paul was arrested a second time and brought to Rome, where he was martyred in the spring of A.D. 68 (see the *Date* section below).

DATE
Early church fathers such as Clement of Rome, Eusebius, and Dionysius of Corinth generally support the second arrest of Paul and his martyrdom sometime near the end of Nero's persecutions. The date for Paul's death is based on early church tradition and is not certain. The letter was probably written from Corinth around A.D. 57.

PURPOSE
The letter to the Romans was designed to pave the way for Paul's visit to Rome by giving a straightforward presentation of the gospel. But the goal was not the conversion

of the readers. They were already Christians. The goal was to show the implications of the gospel for Christians who mixed ethnic bigotry, fleshly works, and stubborn pride with the pure word of redemption in Christ alone. Paul desired to wean his readers away from self-sufficiency with its source in human achievement and pride, whether religious or secular. The goal was to bring the readers to the point of being living and acceptable sacrifices to God (Rom. 12:1-2).

GEOGRAPHY AND ITS IMPORTANCE

From Corinth to Rome

At the time Paul wrote this letter to Rome from Corinth, he planned to return to Jerusalem, with an offering for the Christians there. After his journey to Jerusalem he planned to set out for Rome and possibly Spain. The letter to the Romans outlined Paul's beliefs about Jesus Christ so that the readers would be informed about him when he finally arrived.

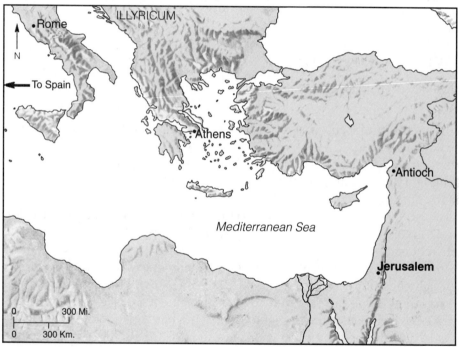

GUIDING CONCEPTS

CORINTH AND THE LETTER TO THE ROMANS

Paul's letter to the Romans is often viewed as a formal presentation of Christian doctrine, as if in it Paul organized his beliefs in a timeless way, untouched by the usual problems and debates with his readers found in all the rest of his writings. On the contrary, Romans throbs with real-life needs and carries the still glowing heat of Paul's most recent problems with the Corinthian church.

Paul had spent three years of his third missionary journey (A.D. 53–57) ministering in

Ephesus. After the riot in Ephesus (Acts 19:23-41), Paul departed for Greece and spent three months there (Acts 20:2-3) before his departure for Jerusalem with the contribution for the saints (Rom. 15:25-26). Paul spent a good part of that three months in Corinth and wrote his letter to the Romans from that city. This is clear from his reference to Gaius in 16:23 and 1 Corinthians 1:14. Paul's recommendation of Phoebe from Cenchrea, the eastern seaport of Corinth, is another indication that Corinth was the place of writing (Rom. 16:1). Perhaps Phoebe carried the letter to Rome.

Paul's letters to the Corinthians provide the best immediate background to the problems and the passion behind his letter to the Romans. The Corinthians had problems with pride and arrogance (1 Cor. 4:5-6; 2 Cor. 3:5-6, 15-16; 11:21-22). And they were not sure they needed to believe in a physical resurrection (see 1 Cor. 15; 2 Cor. 5 concerning the resurrection and the nature of flesh). Compare that with the problems of arrogance spoken of in Romans 11:18, 20, 25; 12:3, 16. Romans also dealt with the problem of causing other Christians to stumble (cf. Rom. 14 with 1 Cor. 8).

Romans is not an abstract formal presentation of doctrine. It is a throbbing presentation of the impact of Jesus Christ on the most cherished but fatal presuppositions of Jew and Gentile alike.

BIBLE-WIDE CONCEPTS

THE FOUNDATIONS OF REDEMPTION

The nature of God
Paul recounts a number of God's characteristics and brings God's character directly to bear on the Romans' needs.

God is the Creator. As Creator he is free to act upon and within his creation. He makes the rules for his creatures, not the other way around (Rom. 1:20, 25; 4:17; 8:18-23; 9:19-21).

God is also just. This characteristic of God is crucial at several points in the letter (for example, see 2:11; 3:3-4, 25-26; 9:6, 14, 19; 11:1-2) and is supported by numerous Old Testament quotations.

God is completely righteous. Paul used the Old Testament to show how God has always been righteous (for example, see Rom. 3:21; also, 3:4 and its quotation of Ps. 51:4). Paul stressed that the possibility of human righteousness is based only on the fact that God is righteous. Human righteousness is a participation in God's righteousness. That is the foundation of righteousness in Jesus Christ. Any righteousness must be linked to a relationship with him. Paul's point throughout Romans was that righteousness is a relationship with God himself, not simply external obedience to a set of rules.

The nature of human beings
Paul laid down several truths about the nature of human beings. Humanity is suffering under the effects of Adam's sin (5:12-21). People come to God by faith and receive salvation through the promises to Abraham (4:1-15). They are under the rule of the King of the line of David (1:3; cf. 1 Kings 11:36; 2 Kings 8:19). The human race is stretched out between two men, Adam and Christ. People live either in the first man, Adam, or in the last man, Christ (Rom. 5:15). And the movement from Adam to Christ is through the doorway of faith in the redeeming work of Christ, not by means of law,

ethnic background, religious tradition, or worldly tokens of status. Paul's letter to the Romans directly assaults human aversion, whether Jewish or Gentile (1:16), to salvation by faith alone.

THE CONCEPT OF RIGHTEOUSNESS
The big picture
Righteousness is the central concept in Romans; and the key element of being right with God is being like God. Righteousness involves obedience to God's commands (power for life) and a remedy for disobedience (forgiveness for sin). But Paul wrote to people who either wanted to do away completely with any standards or laws for living righteously (the Gentiles) or wanted to put every Christian back under all the laws of the Mosaic covenant (the Jews). So Paul presented a full-orbed view of how righteousness is achieved and how it relates to righteous living.

Righteousness has its beginning in the power of God to declare a believer righteous on the basis of faith in Christ (1:16-17). Everyone is equal in being declared unrighteous so that they all may be equally exalted in the righteousness of Christ (3:9, 21-24).

The middle phase of righteousness involves God's gift of strength and endurance to live righteously. That power comes not from self-effort but from the powerful work of the Holy Spirit (8:1-4, 12-13).

The final phase of righteousness is the realized power of resurrection and judgment in the life of the believer (2:5-6, 14-16; 8:23; 16:20). In Judaism, justification would only be known in the future judgment. For the Christian, justification is a fact based on the past act of God in Christ, the present power of the Holy Spirit, and the future hope for resurrection and reward.

Covenantal appearances
Righteousness stems from the character of God. God has always given specific commands that let believers know what a truly righteous life is. Those commands do not create righteousness; they define it. For example, Noah's righteous acts showed that he was righteous in his character (Gen. 6:9). The commands given to Abraham gave him a description of how he, as a righteous person, should behave (Gen. 12:1-3; 15:6; 18:19). The letter to the Romans gave extensive explanations about how the Christian receives the fulfillment of God's promises to Abraham. The commands given in the Mosaic covenant put God's laws into clear statements that give a clear gauge of one's righteousness.

Even people who did not have God's commands in the Mosaic Law could behave righteously (Rom. 2:14-16). Righteousness is an inner transformation brought about by the Holy Spirit. In Romans 5:21 righteousness is that which acquits mankind of sin and is the living power given to break sin's bondage.

The new covenant in Jesus Christ solves two problems that have been present since the fall of Adam and Eve in Eden—forgiveness for sin and ability for righteous living. Isaiah 53:11 spoke of God's act of justifying man on the basis of the Servant's suffering. The new covenant passages of Jeremiah 31:31-34 and Ezekiel 36:26 spoke of God putting the law and the Spirit inside believers to instruct and enable their obedience. The Old Testament and New Testament order was always forgiveness first, instruction in obedience second. The entire question of lawkeeping concerns not what people have to do to be saved, but what they are compelled by gratitude to do because they have been saved. Such was the answer Paul set out to give in Romans.

NEEDS MET BY ROMANS

Paul wrote to meet several key needs of his readers. First, he addressed some of their political questions by affirming that Christianity supported Roman laws and was not out to overthrow Roman rule. An early way to bring persecution upon Christianity was to claim that the religion was against the laws of Rome and sought to depose Caesar.

Second, Paul addressed the question of possible ethnic superiority. The Romans were experiencing some conflict between the Gentile and Jewish elements of the church. But neither being Jewish nor Gentile put someone in a better standing before God. Paul wanted the jealousy and fighting between Jewish and Gentile Christians to stop. He stressed that no ethnic group had special salvation standing before God. Jews and Gentiles all equally needed Christ's redemption. In that connection, Romans addressed the new role of the Old Testament Laws of Moses since the coming of Christ. Were Christians bound to keep the Laws of Moses? If not, then how was Christianity connected to all of God's Old Testament promises of redemption? Jews were pressuring the Gentile Christians to keep all of Moses' laws. Paul had to carefully explain the role of Old Testament law within Christ's redemption.

Third, Paul showed how two invisible things, faith and the Holy Spirit, were needed for gaining a secure salvation. Paul stressed that the entire witness of the Old Testament confirmed faith and the Spirit as the only means to salvation. Although Paul may not have known his readers in Rome, he knew from experience the kinds of problems they were having. These problems ranged from religious to civil matters. The structure and content of Romans show that Paul was answering questions like the following for his Roman readers.

- Does Christianity respect the laws of Roman government or does it promote rebellion?
- How can something as intangible as faith be a more secure way of salvation than the more tangible obedience to Mosaic Law?
- How can Jesus do away with the Mosaic Law and yet require his followers to obey the laws of God?
- How does complete forgiveness in Christ relate to his demands that people live righteously?
- What is the role of the Holy Spirit?
- Why are Jewish people not better off with God than Gentiles?
- Does not the heritage of Jews automatically give them special standing before God?
- How is the Christian supposed to relate to the civil authorities?
- How are Jews and Gentiles supposed to relate to each other within the church?

Throughout Romans Paul worked to break through the kind of human pride that insists on gaining salvation through human works rather than accepting the perfect righteousness God offers in Christ. The book seeks to do away with any thoughts of superiority believers might harbor based on their race or religious obedience, no matter how well-intentioned. Paul wanted all ethnic groups to take an equal place on the level ground around the cross of Christ and live in peace.

Believers may face frequent pressures to obey religious laws and be judged by their external conformity to religious norms—some biblical, others not. If believers just focus on these external rules, it is easy for them to become satisfied with giving good impressions to the people around them, when in reality God may not be so pleased with their inner spiritual life. To this situation Romans opens up the world of God's perfect righteousness revealed in his character and his laws, impossible for believers to achieve on their own, but freely given in Christ. Paul proclaimed that in Christ believers are free to obey God, not as a means of becoming righteous, but because they have already been made righteous.

Often what believers can see seems more substantial than what they can hear. Romans shows how the seemingly uncertain facts of faith and the Spirit, heard but not seen, are eternally secure grounds for their redemption. Visible obedience to God's laws may seem to be a more substantial way to certify merit before God. But Paul argued that the presently invisible rewards of faith and the Spirit are the only true grounds for eternal redemption. In Christ, God had brought to perfection all the Old Testament ways and promises of salvation.

OUTLINE OF ROMANS

I. RIGHTEOUSNESS FOR ACCEPTANCE BY FAITH (1:1–8:39)
   A. The Introduction of Paul and His Message (1:1-17)
   B. Righteousness Rejected by All Men (1:18–3:20)
   C. Righteousness Accepted by Faith (3:21–5:21)
   D. Righteousness and Personal Sin (6:1–8:39)

II. RIGHTEOUSNESS IN GOD'S ACTS WITH ISRAEL (9:1–11:36)
   A. God's Righteous Election of Israel (9:1–29)
   B. God's Righteous Witness to Israel (9:30–10:21)
   C. God's Righteous Restoration of Israel (11:1-36)

III. RIGHTEOUSNESS IN HUMAN OBEDIENCE UNDER GOD (12:1–16:27)
   A. The Renewed Mind: Proper Perspectives on Self, Church, and Society (12:1–13:14)
   B. The Renewed Mind: Acceptance and Edification of the Weak (14:1–15:13)
   C. The Trip to Rome: Reasons (15:14-33)
   D. Final Remarks: Friends and Enemies (16:1-24)
   E. Ascription of Glory (16:25-27)

ROMANS NOTES

1:1–8:39 RIGHTEOUSNESS FOR ACCEPTANCE BY FAITH

Overview: This entire section of 1:1–8:39 explores the relationship between faith and redemption linked to Abraham versus the merits of obedience to the Mosaic Law. Faith was always the way of salvation before and during the time of Moses. As seen in Acts, Christ's new covenant opened up salvation by faith in new ways to both Jews and Gentiles alike.

With or without the Mosaic Law, Jews and Gentiles are under God's condemnation (Rom. 1–3).

Because both Jews and Gentiles were used to thinking of salvation in terms of religious merit through works, Romans 4 demonstrates how secure redemption through faith can be, especially when it is a faith like Abraham's. Romans 5 continues the theme of the security of faith by showing how faith alone removes believers from death in Adam to life in Christ. Believers are much more secure in Christ than they would be in Adam 5:9-10, 15, 20). In light of the security in Christ by faith, Romans 6–8 addresses how the demands of the law and the flesh relate to the power of Christ and the Holy Spirit.

1:1-17 The Introduction of Paul and His Message

1:1 PAUL'S CHARACTER AND CALLING

This introduction clarifies Paul's identity and the nature of his message. He called himself an apostle of Christ to the Gentiles to bring the gospel of righteousness by faith in Christ. His personal role was that of being a servant of Christ (see Phil 1:1; Titus 1:1).

1:2 THE GOSPEL'S FOUNDATION: PROMISE

This greeting was designed to elaborate how the gospel in Christ was related to Old Testament promises (Rom. 1:2). Note the connecting first words in each verse (1:2-6). They build an elaborate description of how Jesus relates to Old Testament promises. This will also serve as a foundation to the arguments concerning promises in Romans 4 and 9–11. The promises of God, from Abraham to Christ, form the foundation and definition of present experience and future hope.

1:3-6 THE GOSPEL'S SUBJECT

The subject of the gospel is Jesus from two perspectives. He was the human seed of David (1:3) and the divine Son of God (1:4). As such, he is the ultimate King according to Davidic promise (2 Sam. 7)—eternal, divine, and exalted at God's right hand (Ps. 110:1; Acts 2:33-35). But he is also the Son of God in the flesh. Christ's identity as a human being will be foundational for the comparison between Adam and Christ in Romans 5 and the role of the Spirit in the Christian's life (Rom. 6–8).

Although consistent with Old Testament promise, Christ's kingly and divine nature combined with his humiliation and crucifixion broke all the Jewish presuppositions and expectations about how the Messiah would come. It also cut against their presuppositions about how the Messiah's followers should conduct themselves.

Jesus the Messiah's resurrection (1:4) was God's declaration of his sonship in power. That power was the Spirit of holiness—the foundation for all this letter's comments concerning the Christian's war with sin and victory in resurrection. Paul's ministry found its potency in the power of Christ's resurrection. The same power that raised Christ from death operates in the Christian's righteousness, Christ's lordship, Israel's hope, and the world's release from bondage. The entire book's perspective on power for salvation and Christian victory is based on the person and work of the Holy Spirit.

The instrument ("through Christ") of Paul's calling (1:5-6) is the risen Lord who commissioned him. That idea of mediation ("through") is foundational to all of the letter. Every forgiven sin, every gift of the Spirit, every act of power in ministry comes mediated from God the Father, through the risen Lord, and by the enabling power of the Spirit.

Notice, for example, the great stress on mediation in Romans 5:1-2, 5, 9-12, 16-19, 21.

In Romans 1:5, Paul's solid base of identity and authority is presented. The "us" here focuses generally on the Gentiles (1:5). The readers have an equality with Paul; both are considered "called" ones (1:6).

1:7 THE ADDRESSEES ARE FURTHER IDENTIFIED AND BLESSED

In expressing their calling and nature (1:7), Paul broadened his address to include the Jews as well. On saints (1:7; "very own people"), see 1:4; 12:1-2. The content of Romans 12–15 was founded on the fact that Christians are to behave in accordance with their nature as God's "own people."

1:8-17 PAUL'S DESIRE TO VISIT ROME AND REASONS FOR DELAY

The purpose of this section was to clear the air for his visit. Paul was positive and gracious; he had a message of encouragement that they needed, but he never talked down to them.

Paul's thanksgiving for the faith of the Romans (1:8) blends with the main body of the introduction. Compare what Paul wrote to the believers in Rome with Acts 28:15. Paul emphasized his interest in the Romans both in prayer and in his desire to visit them (1:9-15). He had long desired to travel to Rome (Acts 18:21; Rom. 1:13; 15:32), but his desire was ministry-oriented (1:11-12). He wanted to do them some spiritual good. Community sharing and encouragement is the vehicle of growth and stability.

As Paul affirmed his travel plans (1:13) he was not simply sharing a travelog. He was assuring them that he had not purposely been staying away from Rome. He was not embarrassed to come to the great city of Rome but had wanted to come for a long time. His visit was part of his Gentile calling and was an obligation from God (1:14-15). Paul was aware of the obligation that God had committed to him (cf. 1 Cor. 9:16-17; Acts 9:15).

The "people in our culture" (1:14) were those who spoke Greek in contrast to the "people in other cultures" (1:14; "barbarians," NASB and KJV) who did not. Note that Paul wanted to preach the gospel to the Christians (1:15) in Rome. But the "good news" (Isa. 52:7; 61:1-2) was a message for the saved as well as the unsaved.

Paul gave another reason for his desire to see them (1:16-17). The possible accusation that Paul was ashamed (1:16) to come to Rome was contrasted with his eagerness (1:15). Paul had not stayed out in the provinces because he was weak. On the contrary, he had the very power of God— the gospel (1:16). Although Paul was commissioned to witness to the Gentiles (Acts 9:15), he recognized an obligation to carry the gospel to the Jews first. That was in line with the great covenant with Abraham that promised redemption for the world through Abraham first (Gen. 12:3).

The words "God makes us right in his sight" (1:17) is the righteousness that God approves and provides. The words "from start to finish by faith" (1:17; "from faith to faith," NASB and KJV) mean that God's provision of salvation is by faith from start to finish. This illustrates Paul's desire in 1:15. He will pass the gospel on from his faith to the faith of others. Paul used Habakkuk 2:4 to support his point (cf. also Gal. 3:11; Heb. 10:38). This use of the Old Testament speaks to possible Jewish resistance to this message. This relationship between faith and righteousness is leading up to the conclusion of Romans 3:28.

1:18–3:20 Righteousness Rejected by All Men

Overview: This section, which reveals man's sinfulness, lays the foundation for the line of thought that moves through 3:31 and leads finally to God's promise of mercy (11:32). In the section 1:18–11:32 an explanation is given of how all people, Jew and Gentile, are included in and impacted by sin. It calls all ethnic groups to recognize their sinfulness and to understand God's promise that in Abraham all the nations of the world would be blessed. This obligated the readers of the Roman letter to receive all peoples as equal candidates for God's redemption.

This section functions in two ways. First, it shows how all are equally needy of God's remedy for sin. Second, it shows the great need that people have of the Holy Spirit's power in order to live righteously. Paul will present remedies to these problems in order. Here, Paul was speaking of the present exhibition of God's wrath, not the final wrath to come.

1:18-32 WRATH REVEALED AGAINST GENTILES

Romans 1:18 presents God's wrath, the opposite of God's revealed righteousness (1:16-17), and begins the long section that shows why faith is the only way to righteousness. Wrath is God's attitude toward sin. Note the links to Habakkuk's context (Hab. 2:4). Wrath is revealed by the "giving over" of man to his sin; it is the twisting of God's image into its opposite.

1:18-23 Mankind's Willful Rejection of God
God made his truth evident (1:18-20), but humans suppressed and rejected it (1:18-19). Romans 1:18 is added to begin Paul's thoughts on how all humanity is responsible for their sins. The core of the law is summed up in 1:19: "For the truth of God is known to them instinctively" (cf. 1:32). That basic knowledge about God is available by simply viewing God's creation (1:20). People are without excuse. This statement implicates Paul's audience—people who made excuses for why they

were exempt from God's wrath (cf. 9:19-20)—in mankind's universal guilt. Mankind rejected the true God (1:21-23) for its own image (see Acts 14:11-13, Lystra; Acts 17, Athens; Acts 19, Ephesus). The source of this data was the Old Testament and Paul's own experience.

1:24-32 God's Willful Rejection of Humanity
Because man rejected God's truth, he "let them go ahead and do whatever shameful things their hearts desired" (1:24-27). The "so" (1:24) links the punishment that follows with the just-mentioned sins. The words "let them go ahead" speak of God's judicial abandonment of sinners to their wicked ways. This was the divine penalty for rejecting God. Their life was based on a lie—the opposite of God's character and ways (1:24-25). The due penalty (1:27) was to suffer the consequences of the perversion itself.

Because man forgot his knowledge about God, God "abandoned them to their evil minds" (1:28-32). This is a severe marring of the image of God. It involves being controlled by the fleshly mind (1:28-31). This is a list of vices that lead to the willful disobedience to the ordinances of God (1:32). Note the split between knowing and practicing.

2:1–3:8 WRATH REVEALED AGAINST "MORALITY"

Paul had the Jews in mind primarily, though not exclusively, in this section. Paul had this section in mind when he wrote 1:18—"all" are under God's wrath. To convince the Jews of their need for redemption, much less a redemption through faith in Jesus, was a difficult task. Paul began by attempting to wean them, and any others, away from the self-righteousness of lawkeeping. The issue was not in knowing the laws of God (1:32) but in keeping them (2:1). It is in keeping God's law that all fail. In Romans 2, Paul showed, first subtly (2:1-16) and then openly (2:17-29), that the Jews, like the Gentiles, are without excuse (1:20; 2:1) and stand under God's condemnation.

2:1-16 God Judges according to Deeds, Not Words
Deeds, not words, are the object of God's judgment. The concept of "do" links Romans 1 and Romans 2 (1:32; 2:1-2; 2:25, "obey"; 2:26-27, "keep"). Some give hearty approval to sin (1:32), and some condemn it (2:1). But they both do it—and that is the fatal flaw that brings humanity under the wrath of God. Neither the wallowing in nor the judging of sin can overcome the universal and fatal flaw—the practice of sin.

Therefore, the "wallowers" and the "judges" receive the same condemnation (2:2-10). Paul is building to 2:29. The externals of race or the hurling of pious judgments cannot bring the internal cleanness granted by the Spirit; it is only the cleanness given by the Spirit that merits God's praise

(2:29). Romans 2:7-8 defines the concept of rewards based on deeds (2:6). God's judgment of deeds is not partial (2:11) to Jew or Gentile. His judgment is ethically, not ethnically, defined. Paul was quite clear that good works do not save (Eph. 2:8-9) but are the product of regeneration. The Jews were first in privilege, but also first in guilt and responsibility (2:9).

God will give impartial judgment to all (2:11-16). Paul was revealing that obedience was a criterion used in God's judgment of mankind, not because he supported salvation by works, but in order to establish that mankind, Jew or Gentile, does not have what God requires—a life of perfect righteousness.

Paul was being general here in regarding the principle of "obedience" as being essential before God. James 2:10 says that just one sin breaks all the law. Those who sin "even though they never had God's written law" (2:12) are the Gentiles who had not been entrusted with the Mosaic Law. Romans 2:13 is key to Paul's argument showing that it is not in hearing the law that righteousness is achieved but in the doing of it. This shows that the Jews who have heard the law are no better off than the Gentiles who have not heard it, for both have failed to do it. The Gentiles, nevertheless, do have a "law" of conscience that commends or corrects their actions (2:14).

2:17-29 The Externals of Judaism Are Negated
Paul asked those who had the Mosaic Law where their confidence was— in words or in lives conforming to the law (2:17-25). He addressed those who relied on law (2:17, 23) and boasted in God but did not obey either the law or God. And this was precisely what the Jews and Gentiles had in common—rejection of the truth and light God had given them. Note Isaiah 52:5 quoted in Romans 2:24.

Circumcision (2:25, lit., "a cutting around") is a reference to the removal of the foreskin of the male penis. This was common practice among Semitic peoples, including the Hebrews. In the Old Testament, God introduced the custom as the sign of the Abrahamic covenant (Gen. 17:10-14; cf. Exod. 12:48; Lev. 12:3). The rite was a sign that one had entered the covenant community of Israel. All too frequently, the real meaning of the rite was lost and it became an external practice without any spiritual content.

Because of that, externals such as circumcision were of no value (Rom. 2:26-29). Spiritual circumcision (Ezek. 36:26) of the heart (see Deut. 10:16 and context; Deut. 30:6; Jer. 4:4; 9:25-26) was an Old Testament concept. Paul's thoughts echoed Jeremiah's words regarding a circumcision of the heart (Jer. 4:4; 9:25-26). It was the inward reality, not the outward sign, that counted most with God.

The Spirit and letter contrast (Rom. 2:29) was central in Paul's most recent letter (2 Corinthians) preceding his writing of Romans (2 Cor. 3:6). Note the link of Romans 2:29 with 3:1.

3:1-8 Promises for Judaism Are Upheld
Paul will elaborate further on God's faithfulness to Israel in Romans 9–11. At this point, Paul provided a correction to a possible misunderstanding that he was implying that it was no longer of any worth being Jewish—that somehow, with the coming of Christ, God emptied the nation Israel of all worth and promise. However, the issue was not the failures of Israel, but the faithfulness of God (3:3). Paul responded to the question, "What is the benefit of being Jewish if it doesn't save me from sin and presents no advantage over heathenism?" He made it clear that God's promises would be upheld in spite of human unfaithfulness (3:3). Paul stressed Jewish disobedience to God's Messiah, though he began the stress on what the Jewish future would be. Paul met two objections (3:5-8). The first concerned the justice of God (3:5). The second concerned the false accusation of lawlessness hurled at Christians (3:8).

3:9-20 GOD'S WRATH REVEALED AGAINST ALL HUMANITY
In light of 3:1-8, is the Jew better off when it comes to escaping God's wrath (3:9)? Paul answers no, because sin has brought everyone to the same level. The "we" (3:9) referred to the believers, with a possible Gentile emphasis. Paul had "already shown" that all have sinned (Rom. 1–2).

The organizing image for the string of Old Testament quotations (3:10-18) were the parts of the human body. This revealed the numerical (none) and particular (parts of each one) pervasiveness of unrighteousness. The basic cause of this state of sin was a lack of fear in God (3:18). Paul appealed to the testimony of Old Testament Scripture (Pss. 14:1-3; 53:1-3; 5:9; 140:3; 10:7; Isa. 59:7-8; Ps. 36:1) to confirm that both Jew and Gentile were under sin and guilty.

Paul had already revealed how the law could not bring salvation, and next he revealed the purpose of the law (3:19-20). On 3:20, see Psalm 143:2. No one could in reality keep the law. Everyone knew that. What they missed, and what Paul was trying to teach, was that knowledge of sin did not equal a knowledge of damnation. The problem was serious. While everyone might have admitted they were not perfect, Paul had to convince them that their imperfections, minor as they might be, were fatal.

In 1:18–3:20, Paul established the universal guilt of both Jews and Gentiles by stacking their deeds up against God's revealed law. But Paul also did this to show that the law was inadequate. Mankind would need more than the law to achieve righteousness before God. They would need the grace of God.

Paul showed that all people had sinned in order to speak to the necessity of justification by faith. The problem was not so much that people were hell-bound, but that they were arguing that they were not. Their self-righteousness had blinded them to their sin. This blind self-righteousness was shared by the non-Christian as well as by the Christian. Because of this, Paul would bring the message of the gospel to both groups (1:8, 15).

3:21–5:21 Righteousness Accepted by Faith

3:21-26 RIGHTEOUSNESS MANIFESTED

Paul answered the question, If it is impossible to keep the law perfectly, where can righteousness be found? The manifestation of righteousness returns to the topic of 1:17. Righteousness is manifested apart from the keeping of the Mosaic Law (3:21). The words "not by obeying the law" (3:21) are key to Paul's theology of justification. Righteousness is attained through faith (3:22) and witnessed to by the Law and the Prophets (as Paul's Old Testament quotations throughout the letter confirm). Justification is free to people but cost God an infinite price (3:23-26). Redemption ("freed us," 3:24) is a price paid as a ransom. Jesus Christ was the price; God was the one who paid. All people were in bondage. The word "redemption" means "to purchase and set free." The word contemplates mankind's bondage to sin and God's provision of grace to release them from that bondage. The word "justified" ("not guilty," 3:24) means "to be declared righteous" as by a judge. This righteousness is not something earned, but something given as a gift on the basis of faith. For an Old Testament illustration of imputed righteousness, see Zechariah 3:1-5.

The sacrifice Jesus made in "sacrificing his life for us" (3:25) is a satisfactory sacrifice (1 John 2:2; 4:10). Such a sacrifice has God's wrath in full view. The need for the sacrifice and the cause of God's wrath were painfully explained in Romans 1:18–3:20. God sent Christ to satisfy that need of a sacrifice. The atoning sacrifice or propitiation contemplates mankind's liability to God's wrath against sin and is God's gracious provision to deliver them from that wrath. Christ is the believer's atoning sacrifice, satisfying with his blood God's holy demand that sin be judged.

God has demonstrated and satisfied his righteousness through the sacrifice of his Son (3:25-26). Some ask what God is doing about sin. Why doesn't he fully deal with it? Does his passing over sins mean the sinner is justified? Paul answers no. Ever since the Noahic covenant God has pledged himself to long-suffering and patience (Gen. 8:21–9:17). Humans had not become more holy, but

God would not immediately judge each and every sin. He waited for Christ to do that (see Acts 17:30). God suspended judgment on sins during the Old Testament period in anticipation of Christ's full and final sacrifice for sins (Rom. 3:25; cf. Hebrews 10:1-18).

Yes, God judged sin in the Old Testament, but sin's offense against God was infinite and his Old Testament judgments were merely finite. It was only in Christ that God showed his justice in matching the infinite crime with an infinite punishment. Sin's infinite offense has now been satisfied—justly and perfectly. That satisfaction is the foundation for God's justice in declaring all forgiven. Since Christ's death, God could be just in judging sin perfectly, but could also be the justifier of those for whom Christ died (Rom. 3:26).

The section of 3:21-26 emphasizes faith as the only way to justification. It clarifies the relationship of God's forgiveness of sin to his inherent justice. Paul could have ended his letter right here. But at this point another critical issue was addressed—boasting (3:27-31). Relate this to 2:17; 3:1, 9, and Paul's recent experience with the Corinthians' boastings (1 Cor. 4:18; 5:2; 8:1; 13:4).

3:27-31 BOASTING EXCLUDED

Salvation by faith excludes boasting (3:27-28). Where there is no room for self-effort, there is no room for boasting (cf. 1 Cor. 4:7). Take note of Romans 3:28. Because God is sovereign over Jews and Gentiles, there is a unity in his chosen means of redemption by faith (3:29-30).

Paul had to defend and describe his claims about what had happened to the law (3:31). This problem was hinted at in 3:1, 5-8. The law had been both done away with and established in a new way (3:31). This showed that Paul did not advocate a lawless life. On the contrary, he established the importance of the law. Two views of the law surface in Paul's discussion. The wrong view thought that keeping the law could bring salvation. The correct view saw the law as a set of directions for those who had already been brought into a saving relationship with God through faith.

Paul's references to the law (3:20, 28) could lead his readers to conclude that it was useless. On the contrary, it fulfills a vital role in confronting people with their sin and accountability before God. The law is vital and currently operative as a means for conviction (3:31; cf. 1 Tim. 1:8) but not as a means of salvation.

Romans 5–8 will further relate to establishing the law. See Matthew 5:17. Surprisingly, to maintain the law is to maintain faith. The law continually reveals mankind's need for Christ and reminds them of their forgiveness and perfection in him. Paul's work of establishing the law was to help his readers see the law, not as a way of attaining righteousness, but as a means of discovering their sinfulness and need for God's gracious forgiveness.

4:1-25 JUSTIFICATION THROUGH FAITH AS AN OLD TESTAMENT PRINCIPLE

4:1-8 For Abraham in Faith

Paul demonstrated in Romans 4 that justification by faith was nothing new. This section is a powerful exposition of Genesis 15:6 (quoted in Rom. 4:3, 9, 22) and how God has always forgiven his people on the basis of faith—whether Abraham before the law (4:3) or David within the time of the law (4:6-8). Both Abraham (4:3-5) and David (4:6-8) were justified in this manner. The entrance of the law in Moses' day did not interrupt this way of righteousness by faith. The two pillars of Genesis 15:6 are "faith" (Rom. 4:3, 5, 9, 11-13, 16, 18-20, 24) and "declared" (4:3, 5, 9-11, 22-23).

This explanation of faith and its righteousness explains what Paul meant in 3:20 and 3:31. The law was never designed to save, just to instruct and condemn (3:20). And to see faith's priority over the law was to set the law into its proper perspective, thus establishing it properly (3:31).

4:9-12 For Abraham in Uncircumcision

This section clarifies what Paul meant in 2:29. Circumcision was a sign (4:11), that is, its real meaning pointed away from the physical act to something else, in this case a heart of faith. See, for example, Acts 15:9. The point here (4:9) is that Abraham was declared righteous before (Gen. 15:6), not after, his circumcision (Gen. 17:9-14). The fact that Abraham was justified apart from circumcision opens the doorway of faith to Gentiles—"those who have faith but have not been circumcised" (Rom. 4:11).

4:13-25 For Abraham and His Worldwide Seed

Abraham was promised the world as his inheritance, not through the law, but through faith (4:13). Paul shows that the law of circumcision came after Abraham's justification by faith. Again, this established the proper framework for the law. It came to those who were already righteous by faith; therefore it must have a purpose other than justification. Its purpose was to correct and condemn where needed, thus driving its followers to God's grace through the offerings of the tabernacle, then the temple, and finally, Christ.

Law was not the vehicle of promise (4:13). Paul's use of Genesis 17:5 and 15:5 (Rom. 4:17-18) was Old Testament proof that Abraham was "the father" (4:16) through God's promise to him and through his own faith. The resurrection and creation themes of 4:17 are the foundation both for Paul's faith that God would do something with his "too old" body (4:19) and for the faith of all believers that God raised up the dead body of Jesus (4:24).

5:1-21 THE PEACEFUL SECURITY OF RIGHTEOUSNESS

For Paul, justification through faith was not just a matter of sound doctrine. It was also a source of great blessing (5:1-11). In Romans 1–4 Paul explained the correct way to God's righteousness through faith. This was an explanation of 1:17. But Paul established law, not as a way to gain salvation, but as a means to find condemnation.

For many, faith did not seem to be a very secure mark of salvation. How could something so intangible bring security? Paul answers that question here. He offsets insecurity by showing how much (5:9-10, 15, 17, 20) they have in Christ. Salvation through faith is as secure as the work of God through Christ (5:1-2, 5, 9-12, 17, 19, 21).

5:1-11 Security Is Based on God's Demonstration of Love

The "therefore" of 5:1 indicates that a logical inference is being drawn from the preceding discussion (3:21–4:25). The text of 5:1 may be paraphrased, "Let us keep and enjoy peace with God." Justification brings peace, not wrath, and is mediated by the Lord (5:1-2). It brings a future hope of glory (5:2). The Greek word translated "rejoice" in 5:2-3, 11 is translated "brag" in Romans 2:17, 23, where the element of self-centered boasting is present. In 5:2-3, 11 the element of self-confidence is removed. The substitute is accepting the mediation achieved "because of" God's sacrifice.

Even difficulties and hardships exhibit the love of God (5:3-11). Paul made it clear that there was great benefit in trials (5:3-4). Note the relationship of weakness in tribulation and God's manifested glory through earthen vessels. This removes the validity of any boasting in law-keeping. Another proof of security is the presence of the love and Spirit of God (5:5).

The term "restored" means "to change" (5:10-11). Restoration of a relationship with God by the

---

ADAM AND CHRIST

Death in Adam	Life in Christ
Sin	Righteousness
Condemnation	Justification
Death	Life

death of Christ means that man's state of alienation from God is changed so that he is now able to be saved (2 Cor. 5:19).

5:12-21 The Security Is Based on God's Free Gift
Paul concluded his consideration of justification by faith with an analogy demonstrating that while all men are in fact sinners (in Adam), all are potential beneficiaries of Christ's death and justification. The links are drawn between Adam and Christ. Paul's point was that security in Christ is even more secure than damnation in Adam.

Paul showed that even before the law, people died because of Adam's sin. Adam infected humanity with death. In a greater way Christ injected humanity with life. The human race is directly related to Adam and his sin. The theology of this verse is based on the concept of the corporate solidarity of the human race (cf. Heb. 7:9-10). With or without the law people sinned and died (Rom. 5:12; cf. 3:23). Because of Adam's disobedience, humanity "became sinners" (5:19; cf. 1 Cor. 15:21). Sin could not be charged as a violation of a specific command where there was no law. But sin existed, nevertheless, before the law was given at Sinai, as was evidenced by universal death from Adam to Moses.

Paul used Adam as a "contrast" (5:14) between him and Christ, indicating that while he had a place and purpose historically, he was also divinely intended to teach by means of analogy something about Christ. Paul took Genesis 3 and the curse of God on Adam's sin very seriously. Humanity's death was rooted in Adam's sin. Paul used that certain root to compare and contrast with the certain rooting of life in Christ. See the accompanying chart.

The key to seeing "everyone sinned" (5:12) as meaning "in Adam" is the "yes" of 5:13. What is it explaining? All are reckoned as sinners by Adam's one sin. Again, Romans 5:20-21 continues to establish the law (3:31) in its proper perspective.

6:1–8:39 Righteousness and Personal Sin
Overview: In Romans 6–8 Paul deals with how righteousness is imparted to people through sanctification. The word "sanctify" means to "set apart" for God's possession and use. There are three aspects: (1) positional—all believers are set apart for God at redemption (1 Cor. 1:2, 30); (2) experiential—conforming the believers' experience of righteousness to their position of being righteous in Christ (John 17:17; Rom. 8:3-4); and (3) final—when the believers see the Lord and are made holy like him (1 Cor. 15:54; 1 John 3:2). Romans 6–8 focuses on the second, experiential aspect of sanctification.

6:1-14 DOES SIN ENLARGE GRACE?
The link between Romans 5 and 6 can be found in how the heightened awareness of sin due to the

law's condemnation (5:13, 20; 6:1) is met with abounding grace (5:20).

6:1-2 Sin Is a Moral Contradiction to Salvation
Paul was forced to answer the criticism already mentioned (3:8) that Christians did not bother keeping rules (6:1). This criticism came primarily from Jewish Christians who wondered what would happen to people who claimed freedom from the law. But Paul moved the issue away from law-keeping to the Christian's new nature, in this case, his death to sin (6:2-3). The words "died to sin" (6:2) indicate that those who have believed in Christ have been separated from the ruling power of sin. Sin is no longer the master of one who has given his allegiance to Christ. Thus, the answer to the question in 6:1 is "Of course not!"

6:3-4 Identification with Christ through Baptism
Paul used the imagery of baptism to illustrate the vital union that the believer has with Christ. The Greek word for "baptize" was used in the dyeing trade for dipping cloth into dye. This dipping process brought about a change in the cloth's color and identity. Christian baptism also brings a change in identity—an identification with a new community.

Paul used baptism as a picture of the believer's change in identity—separated from the old life in Adam and united with Christ. The words "baptized to become one with Christ" mean "identified and united with Christ." This begins to explain more fully the believer's solid link with Christ as opposed to Adam. It was man's link to Adam, not to the Law of Moses, that was fatal. Therefore, it was man's link to Christ, not to the Law of Moses, that would bring redemption. This is all based on the implications of chapter 5 for those who are in Christ rather than in Adam. Two "rules" (5:17, 21), the rule of death in Adam and the rule of grace in Christ, are in view.

Paul returned to the question regarding law for the justified (6:4; "live"). The Christian's walk is not defined by any particular set of laws but by conformity to the resurrected life of Christ. Conformity to a law code has been replaced with conformity to Christ's death and resurrection.

6:5-11 Identification with Christ's Life
The function of this section is to clarify 6:3-4 by the example of Christ. This also relates back to Romans 5 and the believer's links to Adam and Christ. Paul continues to deal with the criticism that Christians can continue in sin in order to enjoy more and more grace (6:1). The issue here is conformity to Christ, not only in his resurrection power, but in the purpose of his death—to do away with servitude to sin (6:5-6). The believer's union with Christ in his death is designed to free him from sin's mastery. The term "old sinful selves" (6:6) refers to

the unregenerate person, the condition of the human race in Adam before having faith in Christ.

The words "so that sin might lose its power in our lives" (6:6) refer to the physical body as conditioned and controlled by sin. Paul concludes his first words on sin and the believer by reinforcing the model of Christ (6:10)—dead to sin, alive to God (6:10-11). The word "consider" (6:11; "count," NIV) is a mathematician's term and means "to add up" or "calculate." Paul is saying, "Add up the facts and live accordingly."

6:12-14 Willful Presentation of the Body

Paul's use of "control" (6:12) continues the topic's discussion from 5:17, 21. Two reigns are in view—the reigns of sin and grace. Although sin can plague all believers, they are to consider themselves dead to sin and choose to walk in the reign of resurrection grace rather than the reign of Adamic death. Reign equals obedience to the call of either sin or grace. It is the presentation of oneself (cf. 12:1) in response to one or the other.

The entire Christian life is a response to one reign or the other. Paul implies that sin has been reigning over the physical bodies of believers. Now he says, "Stop! Don't place your physical body at the disposal of sin. Rather, present yourselves to God for his service."

Compare 6:14 with 5:21. Romans 6:14 shows that the believer has already been judged a perfect person in Christ; therefore, questions of law-keeping are not relevant. Paul is trying to keep a careful balance between affirming the Christian's completed righteousness by faith in Christ and the expectation that a believer will live a holy life, not in order to get righteous before God, but because he is already righteous.

"No longer subject to the law" (6:14) means believers are not alone and faced with the insurmountable mountain of keeping God's law. Paul puts it another way in 8:15. There is no fear of condemnation. Being "subject to the law" in this sense is to be liable to God's retribution in a final sense of eternal wrath.

6:15–7:6 THE IMPLICATIONS OF BEING A BONDSLAVE

6:15-23 Should Believers Sidestep the Law

Triggered by his statement that believers are not subject to the law (6:14), Paul continued to assert both the righteousness of believers and their absolute mandate to live holy lives. Paul's critics assumed that those who were under grace alone would have no standard for behavior. They claimed it was the law that was the motivation to obedience. But Paul showed that those justified by faith were motivated to love and obey God by grace, not the law. Paul came to the conclusion that believers do not need the law to love righteousness. The lives

of believers in Christ are not determined by the limited provisions and resources of the "law," but rather by the redeeming and renewing resources of "grace."

The believer, not under the threat of condemnation for failure, is enabled to obey God from the inside ("heart," 6:17). It is in that internal sense that the believer becomes a slave to righteousness (6:18). Paul appealed to a familiar principle: you are a slave to the one you serve. People are either slaves to sin resulting in death, or slaves to righteousness resulting in life.

Paul continued by showing the consequences of being enslaved by either sin or righteousness (6:19-23). Paul showed that true believers are not lawless. Actually, their slavery to Christ results in sanctification. Paul's illustration of the two types of presentation ("slaves," 6:19) needs to be taken seriously. Little more than this (6:23) can be said once salvation by faith has been elaborated. Verse 6:23 contains a fundamental law of God's moral universe. Sin ends in death, and grace ends in eternal life. Death is earned as a consequence of sin; eternal life is received as free and unmerited favor.

7:1-6 The Death of Believers to the Demands of the Law

Paul continued to establish the law (3:31) by showing that through Christ believers have died to the law's condemnation so that they might live lives of righteousness. Apart from Christ, the demands of the law are upon the flesh. This continues the thrust from Romans 4. First, faith precedes and makes possible the way to righteousness (Rom. 4). Second, faith is secure (Rom. 5). Third, through the death of Christ believers are free to present themselves to God (Rom. 6). There is a standard for behavior under grace (6:1, 15-17).

Paul showed one exception to his observation in 7:1; one can live and still be free from the law's demands. In 6:14 Paul made the statement "you are no longer subject to the law," and now he returns to develop that subject. The major point that he makes is that death dissolves the dominion of the law. Paul used marriage to illustrate the concept (7:2-3) and then applied the teaching (7:4-6). Believers have died to the law and have been joined to a new master, Christ. Paul consistently taught that death brings an end to a marriage (7:2; cf. 1 Cor. 7:39). Used in this context, the word "binds" (7:2) means married. What is the parallel being drawn here? Just as a woman and man become one flesh in marriage (Gen. 2:24), people are bound to the law while living as sons of Adam. Just as the woman is free from her husband when he dies, believers are free from the law when they have died to the law and sin. The death to sin and the law experienced by believers opens them up to a new state of freedom from the law. They are free to live out the death and resurrection of Christ through the Holy Spirit's power.

To match the Christian experience of dying to sin and living to God, Paul used an illustration in which someone is set free by death, but still lives. Jesus Christ acted both as the husband in the believer's bondage to the law and as the new and living husband in righteousness. The human illustration requires two husbands to make its point. But the great truth of Romans 7 is that Christ is at the same time the one husband who dies to the state of bondage and the one who brings his bride, the church, into a new state of freedom. Romans 6 shows that believers are dead to sin; Romans 7 shows they are dead to their old relationship to law.

7:7-25 THE LAW'S TRUE FUNCTION
7:7 The Law Reveals Sin
These are Paul's final words on the law, completing the thought begun in Romans 6. The key question of 7:7 continues the line of thought from 6:1-2, 15 concerning how law is to be viewed from the standpoint of grace. Paul's point here is that the law reveals what sin is and must be distinguished from the sin itself. The law is not sin (5:20; 7:4-6), just as light is not that which it illuminates. Paul attacked legalism, not the law (7:14). Paul kept the situation in Romans 5 behind his discussions of law and righteousness. The believer could never escape his deathlink to Adam by keeping the law.

7:8-12 Sin Uses the Law
Paul's focus in these verses was not on whether the person is regenerate or unregenerate. The power of sin is present in any person who tries to keep the law on his own. Note Galatians 5:17-26 as a summary of Romans 7–8.

7:13-20 Sin, Not the Law, Causes Death
Does the law cause death? Sin is based on the reality of being in Adam (Rom. 5). The presence of sin is what creates the inherent tension within people. This paves the way for the explanation in Romans 8 regarding this time of groaning (8:22-23, 26).

Who is this person who struggles so much with sin? Among the most prominent views, it is held that these verses describe (1) Paul's life either before or after he became a Christian, (2) the experience of all people in Adam, (3) the experience of any person who relies on the law and his own efforts for sanctification, or (4) the experience of someone whose "true self" is struggling with the flesh (physical desires of the human body). It is likely that Paul was using himself as a picture of every human's struggle with good and evil.

7:21-25 The Power of Sin
How does this relate to the Christian? Romans 7 is talking about a walking-in-the-flesh approach to being righteous. After describing the believer's

struggle with the flesh, Paul affirms that believers are not without hope for deliverance (7:25). The answer comes generally in 7:25 and more specifically in Romans 8.

8:1-39 THE SPIRIT ILLUMINATES THE NEW BONDAGE
In Romans 3–5 Paul presented how the powerful union of faith in Christ makes all who believe righteous. In Romans 6–8 Paul tells how to live righteously through the power of the Spirit. To say it another way, faith, not law, brings about righteousness (Rom. 3–5) and the Spirit, not self-effort, brings about righteous living (Rom. 6–8).

Paul was still speaking to the issue of continuing in sin (6:1) versus living obediently to God's commands. See Paul's use of "give" (6:13), "follow" (8:4), "think about" (8:5-7), and "led" (8:14). The underlying structure is the process and path to holiness and glorification. Paul noted that believers still have unglorified bodies (8:23). But the Spirit gives them comfort in suffering, freedom from a condemned conscience, and freedom from the inability to do right.

8:1-11 God Meets the Law's Requirements in Christ
Christ met the law's requirements and thus set all believers free (8:1-11). Believers do not need to work to gain standing before God. Romans 8:2 sums up the thrust of Romans 5–7. The directing power of the believer drawing on new covenant resources is not the flesh, but the Holy Spirit. The principle of a Spirit-produced life ("power of the life-giving Spirit") brings release from the sin principle ("power of sin") that produces separation from God ("death"). The law is established (cf. 3:31) in its proper way in the Christian's life (8:4).

The mind (8:5-11; cf. 7:22-23; 8:5-7) is allowed to have its way in the Spirit. There is an absolute separation between being in the flesh and in the Spirit. In this section the potency of life in the Spirit is stressed, not the details of how such a life comes about. These verses expand and elucidate the contrast between the mind conditioned on and patterned after the flesh and the mind conditioned on and patterned after the Spirit. The provision of the Spirit is universal for all believers (8:9). No one who belongs to Christ lacks the Holy Spirit (cf. 1 Cor. 12:13). Believers can experience Christ's resurrection life now (8:9-11).

8:12-17 Sons of God through the Spirit
The cause of release from the law and sin is that believers have become sons of God (8:13-14). Turning from sin (8:13) is what was described in 6:19. The "fear" (8:15) is a fear of penalty in terms of God's final wrath at the end of the age. Note especially 8:11, 17. Being "adopted" (8:15) was a very significant matter in Roman law and culture. The adoptee was taken out of his previous state and

placed in a new relationship as son to a new father. As such, all his former debts were cancelled and he was able to start a new life. As adoptees of God the Father, believers are freed from their debt of sin and receive the rights, privileges, and responsibilities of God's own children.

8:18-30 A Focus on Future Hope
Paul addressed the potential discouragement faced by all Christians in suffering and in waiting for complete redemption from pain in the world. The Christian has great promises for the future (5:2). Romans 6–8 address how believers are to live until then. Paul deals with the question and problem of the "not yet" aspects of Christian experience (8:17).

Creation groans (8:19-22). In the Old Testament the Spirit hovered over the creation (Gen. 1:2). God cursed the world (Gen. 3) and opened it up to futility (Eccles. 3:20-22). Creation was subjected to futility as a part of God's curse on sin (cf. Gen. 3:17-18). Here, creation is personified as longing for deliverance from the consequences of the fall. One day this longing will be realized (cf. Rev. 22:3).

Christians groan (8:23-25). Why? Because they want glorified bodies. The believers' present bodies cause the groaning. The Holy Spirit (8:23) is God's pledge of the ultimate completion of the salvation process—the bodily resurrection.

The Spirit groans (8:26-30). Why? He groans for the needs of all believers and groans to lead them to redemption glory. The Spirit helps in the believers' prayers (8:26-27) by going beyond their conscious words to express their needs. While divine foreknowledge (8:29) emphasizes God's love and points to the initiating cause, predestination (8:29) emphasizes God's choice and points to ultimate destiny (8:29-30). Those who are summoned to God for salvation ("called") are declared righteous ("right standing") and will be given "his glory" at the Rapture or resurrection (1 Cor. 15:43, 49; Phil. 3:21; 1 John 3:2).

8:31-39 The Ultimate Statement of Security
In light of religious and civil persecution ("accuse," 8:33; "condemn," 8:34; "separate," 8:35), Paul summed up God's security in Christ. Nothing can separate the believer from God. Note that 8:32 sums up Romans 1–5, and 8:33-34 sums up Romans 6–8. Paul proclaimed the believer's ultimate and eternal victory: justification by God (8:31-33), security in Christ (8:34), and conquest in all things (8:35-39). In 8:36 Paul quotes Psalm 44:22.

In Romans 1–8 Paul has presented the gospel (1:15). He has clarified the relationship between faith and law as a means of righteousness. He has shown how faith is secure and the Spirit accomplishes God's desires for the believer's obedience and prayers.

9:1–11:36 RIGHTEOUSNESS IN GOD'S ACTS WITH ISRAEL

Overview: In Romans 9–11 the emphasis is on the question of a future for Israel. All that God promises is in line with his righteousness. Paul is clearly speaking to a Jewish criticism that Christianity evaporates the wonderful promises of God specifically for the nation of Israel. This discussion of the potential failure of God's promises to Israel (9:6) directly relates to God's promises of love and security for Christians generally (8:31-39). If it could be shown that God dropped his promises to Israel, then he might do the same to the church. Paul deals with the criticisms and supposed insecurities of God's failure (9:6), injustice (9:14), bullying (9:19), and rejection of his people (11:1).

In light of the seemingly radical shift of God's blessing from Israel to the church, Paul labors to show that the blessing of God on his church in no way violates his previous blessing or promise for Israel. Romans 9–11 forms the link between Paul's statements of the believer's great security in Christ through faith (Rom. 1–8) and his specific responsibilities of righteous sacrifice in everyday life (Rom. 12–15).

Romans 9–11 justifies God's righteousness regarding Israel, and 9:6 gives the thesis. Salvation indeed moves from the Jew first and then to the Gentile (1:16). But Paul clarifies who exactly is the Jew (9:27, quoting Isa. 10:22). He clarifies the distinction between the Israel of flesh and the Israel of promise. Paul expounds on the unbelief of Israel. He makes liberal use of Old Testament quotations to answer such questions as the following: Why are the Jews refusing the gospel? Has the purpose of God been frustrated? What does the future hold for Israel? How do the Gentiles fit into God's plan of salvation?

In this section Paul also speaks to a possible Gentile arrogance and pride in being selected for God's blessings (Rom. 11:17-18, 25). He had seen such arrogance and its sad social consequences in the Corinthian church, the setting from which he wrote this letter to the Romans. This section builds up to the exhortation to believers in 12:1-3 to renew their mind and not to think more highly of themselves than they should. This kind of arrogance regarding believers' standing before God could spill over into and damage relations with the Jews (Rom. 9–11), the body of Christ (Rom. 12), the government (Rom. 13), and the weaker Christians (Rom. 14–15). For the Gentile Christians to think that God's plans began and ended with them was a grave and short-sighted error.

9:1-29 God's Righteous Election of Israel

9:1-5 PAUL WOULD SEPARATE FROM CHRIST FOR HIS BROTHERS

For more on "chosen to be God's special children" (9:4), see Romans 8:15. Paul declared that if it were possible (which it is not, 8:39), he would gladly have traded his own salvation for Israel's (9:3; cf. Exod. 32:32). Romans 9:4-5 gives more details regarding the benefits of being a Jew.

9:6-13 ONE QUALIFICATION: ISRAEL OF PROMISE

Being recipients of the promise involves God's selective will. The "true" Israel had received all God's promises so far. See 9:13 regarding the continual conflict between the true and false people of God. Romans 9:6 gives the thesis of Romans 9-11. The promise of 9:8 relates to the Abrahamic covenant (cf. 4:13). The Israel spoken of in the Old Testament promises is not identical with the natural and physical descendants of Jacob. In Romans 9:7 Paul quoted Genesis 21:12 to prove the point of 9:6 that physical descent does not in and of itself make one a child of God and a recipient of the promise. Both Isaac and Ishmael were physical sons of Abraham, but Isaac was designated Abraham's heir. In Romans 9:9 Paul quoted Genesis 18:10, a prophecy of Isaac's birth. In Romans 9:12-13 Paul quoted from Genesis 25:23 and Malachi 1:2-3 to illustrate that God's elective purposes are often contrary to human expectation.

9:14-18 DOES GOD'S SELECTION FOR SALVATION IMPLY DIVINE INJUSTICE?

The concept of promise (9:8) by divine selection (9:11) leads to the question of 9:14. The source of the selection is God's mercy (9:15; cf. 12:1). This reveals how good God is to show any mercy at all. What part do humans play? See Exodus 7:3, 14, 22 regarding God and Pharaoh. Romans 9:16 is given in the context of all humans being in Adam (cf. Rom. 5). There is nothing believers could have done to attain their salvation. It would be a cruel trick if God made believers jump through hoops of righteousness in order to gain redemption. In 9:15 Paul quoted from Exodus 33:19 to illustrate God's sovereignty in the bestowal of his mercy and compassion. The hardening of Pharaoh's heart (Rom. 9:17; Exod. 9:16) was part of God's sovereign purpose.

9:19-29 DOES DIVINE SELECTION MAKE DIVINE JUDGMENT UNJUST?

The Creator has full rights over his creation (9:20). We have no basis to question the acts of God; he is beyond human evaluation. He is not accountable to his creatures. In 9:22-24 the point is that God's judgments and decisions are ultimately a display of and context for the riches of his mercy.

The Old Testament quotations support the idea of God choosing some for mercy. Hosea 2:23 and 1:10 in Romans 9:25-26 illustrate God's call to the Gentiles for salvation. Paul quoted Isaiah 10:22-23 and 1:9 to show that it was prophesied that only a remnant would be saved. Paul quoted Isaiah 1:9 in Romans 9:29. The point is that unbelief, not a failure on God's part, is what kept Israel from salvation blessings. How this personal unbelief fits together with God's sovereignty is one of the difficult questions in Christian theology.

9:30-10:21 God's Righteous Witness to Israel

9:30-33 THE ELECT WILL RESPOND IN FAITH

This section pits the "stumbling stone" (9:33) of salvation through faith against salvation sought through works of the law. This is based on the Old Testament quotation of Isaiah 28:16 ("believes in him," Rom. 9:33; 10:11). Paul quoted Isaiah 28:16 to specify Israel's problem—unbelief in Jesus the Messiah. To summarize: God's promises relate to his elect (Rom. 9:6-29), and the elect will respond in faith (9:30-33). Therefore God has not been unjust with Israel. Israel has simply not responded in faith to God.

10:1-15 THE ACCESSABILITY OF RIGHTEOUSNESS BY FAITH

In Romans 10 Paul develops the concept of righteousness that comes by faith, not by works, and shows Israel's failure in that area. Jewish unbelief is not due to God withholding his grace, but to Israel's own failure to appropriate God's provision of righteousness by faith. Romans 10:3 is the key verse (cf. with 1:17). This elaborates 9:31-33. For "law" (10:4), see 9:31.

The words "whole purpose" (10:4) combine the idea of aim (goal) and termination (see the use in 1 Pet. 1:9; 1 Tim. 1:5). The law points to Christ (Luke 24:44; Gal. 3:24) and is fulfilled in Christ (Matt. 5:17-18). The new covenant in Christ has ended the law as a contractual obligation. Yet the law as a reflection of God's values and standard has abiding significance for the new covenant believer. Note the bracket of Isaiah 28:16 in Romans 9:33 and 10:11. This section emphasizes the importance of faith over lawkeeping.

In Romans 10:6-8 Paul quoted from Deuteronomy 30:12-14 to reflect his own thoughts concerning the fact that faith-righteousness simply accepts what God has provided. In Romans 10:11 Paul quoted from Isaiah 28:16 as further proof that salvation is by faith. The ideas tied to "confess," "heart," and "mouth" (10:7-8) are drawn from the quotation of Deuteronomy 30:14. This continues the concept of Romans 9 regarding personal unbelief as the cause for condemnation. In 10:11-12 Paul linked "believes" to "calls on," which leads into the Joel 2:32 quotation of 10:13 (cf. Acts 2:21,

39). Paul quoted from Joel 2:32 to emphasize the universal application of salvation by faith. The text quoted in Romans 10:15 (Isa. 52:7) refers to those messengers announcing deliverance from Babylonian captivity. The idea is that the swiftness of the messenger's pace revealed the character of the message being delivered.

10:16-21 THE INCLUSION OF THE GENTILES

Quoted in Romans 10:16, Isaiah 53:1 anticipated Israel's rejection of the Good News of salvation. In Romans 10:18 Paul applied Psalm 19:4 to the proclamation of the gospel, which was just as effective and far reaching as the proclamation of nature. In Romans 10:19-20 Paul quoted Deuteronomy 23:21 and Isaiah 65:1, which predicted Gentile acceptance of the provision of faith-righteousness. In Romans 10:21 Paul quoted Isaiah 65:2 to show that God never ceases to plead with his people to repent and believe. But his immediate concern is to reinforce that the Gentiles have God's blessing because of Israel's unfaithfulness.

11:1-36 God's Righteous Restoration of Israel

Overview: The section of 11:1-36 shows the consequences for Gentiles as a result of Jewish disobedience and the promise of Israel's future restoration. The discussion in Romans 10 may lead some to conclude that God is through with Israel. Paul responded to this idea with an emphatic no. Salvation issued from Israel's rejection (11:11-24). But that is quite different from saying God had rejected his people (11:1). God's inclusion of the Gentiles should not result in their pride (11:18, 25; 12:3, 16). And Paul goes on to show that Israel's rejection is only partial (11:1-10) and temporary (11:25-32).

11:1-10 IN THE PRESENT REMNANT

Note the key questions in 11:1, 11. Foreknowledge (11:2) equals certain salvation. The present remnant of believing Israel (11:5) confirms God's faithfulness to his promises. Note the quotation of 1 Kings 19:18 in Romans 11:4. God had a remnant even in the dark days of Elijah (1 Kings 19:10, 18). In Romans 11:8-10 Paul quoted from Isaiah 29:10 and Psalm 69:22-23 to show that Israel's rejection and spiritual blindness was predicted by Scripture.

11:11-32 IN THE FUTURE REVIVAL

In Romans 11:11-24 Paul revealed the good that came as a result of Israel's rejection—the provision of salvation for the Gentiles. The first piece of dough (11:16; cf. Num. 15:17-21) and the root (cf. Rom. 9:5; 11:28) refer to Abraham and the patriarchs. The holiness attributed to the part is applied to the whole. Israel was consecrated by virtue of its patriarchal heritage; thus, its rejection was not final. The branches (11:17) represent Israel; the wild

olive shoot, the Gentiles; and the root of fatness, the Abrahamic covenant—the source of blessing for Israel and all nations.

The promise of future restoration shows God's equal mercy to Israel (11:25-32; also note 11:25-26, 29). Note 11:32 as the end of the presentation of the gospel. A divine "mystery" (11:25) is something hidden in the counsels of God, not accessible except as God is pleased to make it known. In Romans 11:26-27 Paul quoted from Isaiah 59:20-21 and perhaps Isaiah 27:9 to show that Israel would one day be saved and enjoy the benefits of the new covenant. Romans 11:32 is a restatement of all Paul tried to assert in Romans 1–3.

11:33-36 IN PAUL'S ESTIMATION OF PRAISE

Paul quoted from Isaiah 40:13 and Job 35:7; 41:11. This serves as the climax and benediction for the first half of the book (Rom. 1–11).

12:1–16:27 RIGHTEOUSNESS IN HUMAN OBEDIENCE UNDER GOD

Overview: The key concept in Romans 12–16 is the renewal of the believer's mind. See 11:34 for the mind of the Lord. Note what 1:21-22, 28 have to do with the need for a renewed mind (cf. Eph. 4:23).

12:1–13:14 The Renewed Mind: Proper Perspectives on Self, Church, and Society

12:1-2 EXHORTATION TO A TESTED PRESENTATION AND TRANSFORMATION

The mercies of God are those of which Paul spoke throughout Romans 1–11. The "And so" of 12:1 is a conclusion based on the entirety of the first eleven chapters. The word "give" (12:1) is the same as in 6:13, 16, 19. True worship is seen as a presentation of the self to God. The body is the vehicle of presentation. Remember what was said about the body in Romans 6–8.

The specifics of mind renewal (12:1) involve the proving of God's will (law) in everyday experience (12:2). Rather than being conformed to the world's mold, the believers are to be transformed (lit., "metamorphosis") from the inside out.

12:3–13:14 COMMANDS TO HUMILITY AND LOVE

12:3-8 Humility

Humility is the key to remaining in the root of Abraham (cf. 11:17-24). This call to humility links back to Jewish (Rom. 2–3) and Gentile (11:18, 25) tendencies toward arrogance. Paul desired that believers find their proper place in the body of Christ, using the gifts of God's salvation (cf. 1 Cor. 12–13). They are to be interdependent. Their exercise of gifts is limited (12:6-8). The exercise of gifts needs to be done without envy or pride; believers should not seek to get gifts in order to stay within

God's measure of grace. God gives the different gifts according to his will.

12:9–13:14 Love

Love in this context is recognizing one's proper place in society and the Christian community—humility before God and people. Love must be honestly applied (12:9-16), not like that of Ananias and Sapphira (Acts 5:1-11). Romans 12:9-21 gives extensive illustrations of what unhypocritical love looks like. In 12:19-21 Paul quoted Deuteronomy 32:35 and Proverbs 25:21-22 to demonstrate that vengeance is God's prerogative. Kindness, like the penetrating intensity of burning coals, is the Christian's means of conquering evil.

Love calls believers to be subject to the civil authorities (13:1-7). The word "obey" (13:1) means "to place oneself under" and refers to support as well as submission (cf. Titus 3:1; 1 Pet. 2:13). Paul said nothing about certain forms of government being ordained by God. It is significant that these instructions were given during the reign of the emperor Nero, a particularly evil ruler in his later years. Paul's words concerning government are important in light of accusations that Christianity was rebellious and anti-Roman. Taxes (13:7) are tribute paid by subjects of a ruling state; customs are levied on goods being transported for sale.

Love stands as a bridge between the Testaments (13:8-10). This section shows that Paul is still describing the nature of true love (begun in 12:9). Love fulfills the law (13:8). Paul's words on Christ being the "whole purpose of the law" (10:4) do not mean that the law has no application for the believer (13:9). Paul said that the law (cf. Exod. 20:13-17) can be summed up in the commandment of love (Lev. 19:18; cf. John 13:34). Paul continued his exhortations on love by pointing out the end-time motivation (13:11-14). Knowing that the time is near is a foundational motivation to show love.

14:1–15:13 The Renewed Mind: Acceptance and Edification of the Weak

14:1-12 THE LORD, NOT MAN, WILL JUDGE BOTH THE WEAK AND THE STRONG

Rome was a cosmopolitan city, and the believers there came from differing backgrounds and cultures. Some practices of the Jews and the Gentiles were mutually unacceptable. Here Paul provided guidelines for believers' actions where there had been no specific revelation. He called these believers from different backgrounds to mutual acceptance (14:1-12) and brotherly obligation (14:13-23). The issues are different for modern believers, but the principles are still applicable.

The "weak" (14:1) is the believer whose faith is not strong enough to enable him to perceive the full liberty he has in Christ to partake of all things.

"We" (15:1) refers to the strong believer whose faith is mature enough to appreciate and apply his full liberty in Christ, while at the same time not demanding the exercise of this right. In Romans 14:11 Paul appealed to Isaiah 45:23 to support the fact that God would judge all men (cf. 1 Cor. 3:10-15; 2 Cor. 5:10). In Romans 14:13 Paul appealed for believers to do nothing that would cause a brother to fall spiritually or become ensnared by a temptation to sin. The kingdom of God (14:17) is focused not on outward but on inward realities.

Note the link between 14:3 and 14:10 concerning looking down on or showing contempt toward "weaker" Christians (cf. also 15:1, "please ourselves"). The focus is on the end (service to God), not the means. The "weak" here were for the most part Jews who still held to strict obedience to the Mosaic Law without understanding how it was fulfilled in Christ. The stronger believers should always seek to live with and encourage those who are weak in faith.

14:13–15:13 THE RESPONSIBLE SUPPORT OF THE STRONG FOR THE WEAK

One way of supporting the weaker Christian is to remove activities or objects that might cause him to sin (14:13-23). Paul moved to a consideration of stumbling as in Romans 12. Another way of support is by living out the Christlike perspective of pleasing others before self (15:1-13). Believers are exhorted to follow Christ's example of self-denial in order to edify others (15:1-3). In 15:3 Paul appealed to Psalm 69:9 to support his exhortation. Throughout, the Old Testament is used to support Paul's words. Having "complete harmony" (15:5; "the same mind," NASB; "likeminded," KJV) does not mean total uniformity. It means unity regarding the object of the believer's love and glory (15:6).

The conclusion of this section on acceptance (15:7-13) clearly shows how Jew and Gentile Christians must be unified. Christ was a servant to both Jew and Gentile (15:8-9). Paul used a series of quotations from the Old Testament to demonstrate God's plan to include Gentiles in his plan for world blessing (cf. Ps. 18:49; Deut. 32:43; Ps. 117:1; Isa. 11:10). Romans 15:13 serves as the conclusion for section 12:1–15:13.

15:14-33 The Trip to Rome: Reasons

15:14-21 REASON FOR WRITING

Paul knew of their ability to instruct one another (15:14), but he desired to extend his own ministry (15:15-21). Illyricum (15:19) was located in present-day Yugoslavia, along the eastern shore of the Adriatic. The visit may have taken place toward the end of Paul's third missionary journey when he visited Macedonia (Acts 20:1-2). In Romans 15:21 Paul appealed to Isaiah 52:15 in support of his desire to preach the gospel where Christ was unknown.

15:22-29 REASON FOR DELAYING
Paul was completing his ministry in Asia (15:22) and was tending to the Jerusalem offering (15:23-29). This discussion of what hindered Paul from coming to Rome returns to the thought of Romans 1, where Paul asserted that he had not stayed away because of fear or shame of the gospel. One purpose for writing was to enlist Roman support for Paul's projected visit to Spain (15:24). According to 1 Clement 5:7 and the Muratorian Canon, Paul eventually made the trip. The offering for the Jerusalem Christians (15:26) was the subject of Paul's lengthy exhortation in 2 Corinthians 8–9. The believers in Macedonia and Achaia responded positively to Paul's instruction.

15:30-33 REQUEST FOR DELIVERANCE
Paul knew of potential trouble in Jerusalem. He desired to come to Rome and find rest. This is the end of the body of his letter (15:33).

16:1-24 Final Remarks: Friends and Enemies

16:1-2 COMMENDATION OF PHOEBE
Phoebe (16:1), a member of the church at Cenchrea (the eastern port of Corinth), is believed to have carried the letter to Rome. The term "deacon" (16:1) leads some to conclude that Phoebe was a deaconess (cf. Eph. 6:21; 1 Tim. 3:11).

16:3-16 GREETINGS TO FRIENDS IN ROME
Just how Priscilla (Prisca, NASB) and Aquila (16:3; cf. Acts 18:2, 26; 1 Cor. 16:19; 2 Tim. 4:19) had risked their lives for Paul (16:4) is not disclosed. It is debated whether "Junia" (16:7) was a male or female. Rather than being included as apostles, Andronicus and Junia may have been "well known to the apostles" ("relatives," 16:7). "Christian love" (16:16; cf. 1 Cor. 16:20; 2 Cor. 13:12; 1 Thess. 5:26) is often translated as "a holy kiss" (KJV, NIV) and was a culturally accepted Christian greeting that corresponds in Western culture to the handshake.

16:17-20 AVOIDANCE OF ENEMIES IN THE CHURCH
In 16:20 Paul saw the second coming of Christ as the final end to the conflict between the seed of the woman and the seed of the serpent prophesied in Genesis 3:15.

16:21-23 GREETINGS FROM FRIENDS IN CORINTH
Tertius (16:22) was Paul's amanuensis, or stenographer, who did the actual writing of the letter (cf. 1 Cor. 16:21; Gal. 6:11; Col. 4:18). Romans 16:24 is not found in many ancient manuscripts and is most likely not original.

16:25-27 Ascription of Glory
The book ends with a final confession of the power of God through the gospel—a gospel in full accord with God's Word and universally the standard for faith.

1 CORINTHIANS

HISTORICAL SETTING

The recipients of 1 Corinthians were the believers at Corinth (1:2). Corinth was strategically situated on the isthmus that links the Peloponnesus with mainland Greece, about sixty miles west of Athens (see introductory map). The city lay at the foot of the 1,886 foot high Acro-Corinth and thus could be easily defended. In ancient times the city controlled the land route between the Peloponnesus and the mainland. Because of its control over that land route, Corinth was considered one of the most strategically located cities in the ancient world. Corinth was also a great trade center that could boast of two very fine ports: Cenchrea on the Aegean to the east, and Lechaeum on the Adriatic to the west. Mariners avoided the treacherous two hundred-mile trip around the Peloponnesus by moving their ships on rollers across the narrow isthmus. Corinth was a commercial center known for its wealth, indulgence, and immorality. In addition to being an important commercial center, Corinth was the worship center of Aphrodite, the goddess of love.

Paul first visited Corinth in March of A.D. 51, during his second missionary journey after his visit to Athens (Acts 18:1). There he met Aquila and Priscilla and joined them in their trade of tentmaking while he ministered in the synagogue on the Sabbath. He was later joined in this Corinthian ministry by Silas and Timothy (Acts 18:5). Paul had a very successful ministry for a year and a half at Corinth (Acts 18:8, 11). It was during this time that Paul wrote 1 and 2 Thessalonians.

Paul left Corinth in A.D. 52 for Jerusalem (Acts 18:18-19). Apollos (Acts 18:26) was invited by the Corinthian believers to minister in Corinth, and he helped the church there in a significant way (Acts 18:27–19:1). Apollos later joined Paul in Ephesus (1 Cor. 16:12) and reported to him about the situation at the church in Corinth.

The occasion for 1 Corinthians was that Paul had received a letter asking about certain problems (7:1, 25; 8:1; 12:1; 16:1). Paul replied in writing before he could come and deal with the problems in greater detail (16:3-7).

AUTHOR

The Pauline authorship of the epistle is clear from 1:1 and 16:21 and is practically uncontested. Paul made at least three visits and wrote at least three letters to Corinth. Scholars debate exactly how the letters and visits of Paul to Corinth are to be arranged.

For example, did Paul's second visit to Corinth (mentioned in 2 Cor. 13:2) occur before or after he wrote 1 Corinthians?

The following order of events appears most likely. Approximately three years after his first visit to Corinth, Paul heard of some new Corinthian problems when he arrived in Ephesus on his third missionary journey (Acts 19:1–20:1). Paul then made a second visit to Corinth (not recorded in Acts but mentioned in 2 Cor. 2:1; 12:14; 13:2), where he did what he could to gain a hearing and solve the problems. But Paul's attempt failed, and he left them with an ultimatum: if he returned, he would "not spare" those who had been sinning on his second visit (2 Cor. 13:2). Then soon after his departure, he sent a letter telling the Corinthians to avoid immoral Christians (the letter mentioned in 1 Cor. 5:9), most likely speaking to the primary problem encountered on his recently completed second visit. Soon after, Paul wrote 1 Corinthians to clear up some new and some persistent problems. Second Corinthians was written later, within six months of 1 Corinthians.

This order of events is based on several conclusions. (1) First Corinthians 16:5-7 presents Paul's "Plan B" itinerary, a change from his original travel plans. (2) Second Corinthians 1:15-16 explains why Paul changed his travel plans. On or before his second visit, Paul had spoken of a final double visit, passing through Corinth both going to and coming back from Macedonia (2 Cor. 1:15-16). But the pain of his second visit caused him to change his original plans and to stay away as long as possible, returning only after he had passed through Macedonia. The change is announced in 1 Corinthians 16:5-7 and explained in 2 Corinthians 1:15-16. (3) If 1 Corinthians 16:5-7 is a change from Paul's original double-visit plan, then his statement in 2 Corinthians 1:23, "I didn't return to Corinth," meant that he had not been to Corinth since he wrote 1 Corinthians. A visit between the writing of 1 and 2 Corinthians is thus excluded. The letter mentioned in 2 Corinthians 2:3-9 and 7:8-12 is therefore best explained as being 1 Corinthians, and the visit mentioned in 2 Corinthians 2:1, 12:14, and 13:1 is Paul's second visit, made prior to writing 1 Corinthians.

This view of 1 Corinthians 16:5-7 and 2 Corinthinans 1:23 produces the following order of events: Paul makes his first and second visits to Corinth; Paul writes the letter mentioned in 1 Corinthians 5:9; Paul writes 1 Corinthians, and then 2 Corinthians; and finally, Paul makes his third visit.

DATE
Paul wrote his letter to the Corinthian believers from Ephesus (16:8) toward the end of his three-year ministry there, during his third missionary journey (spring A.D. 53 to May A.D. 57). It is probable that the letter was written in the winter of A.D. 55 or spring of 56.

PURPOSE
This letter to the Corinthians was designed to give Paul's corrections to a number of concerns that had arisen in the Corinthian church. These concerns were based on two singular problems: human arrogance and denial of the importance and power of the cross of Christ. Paul's reply called the church to unity and selfless love motivated by God's love in Christ.

GEOGRAPHY AND ITS IMPORTANCE

From Ephesus to Corinth

Paul had spent two years in Ephesus, right across the Aegean Sea from Corinth. During that time he had made a second visit to Corinth that ended badly, and Paul left Corinth under unfair criticism and humiliation. He planned to pay a third visit to Corinth, but until the problems there were resolved, he wanted to stay away and try to solve the problems by letter and a visit from one of his coworkers, possibly Titus.

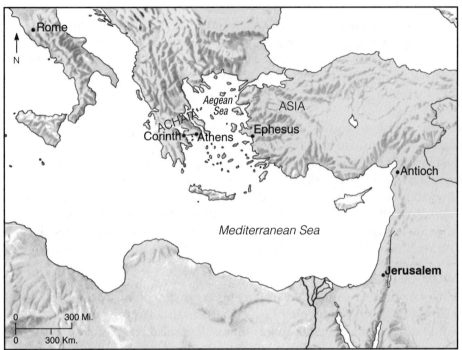

Copyright © 1986, 1988 by Tyndale House Publishers, Inc.

GUIDING CONCEPTS

PROBLEMS ADDRESSED

The Corinthian church had many problems. The believers there divided up into parties following different religious leaders (1 Cor. 1:12). They still participated in immoral practices (5:1). Some were involved in lawsuits (6:1). They abused the Lord's Supper and squabbled over spiritual gifts (1 Cor. 12–14). Some denied the resurrection (15:12). Earlier, Paul had written a letter (5:9) and sent Timothy to minister to the needs of the church (4:17; 16:10).

The problems may be summarized as follows. The Corinthians had fallen into serious errors based on arrogance developed from worldly wisdom that focused on riches, social standing, and personality traits. Paul was judged as an inferior apostle, one who could be left behind (4:6, 8) as the Corinthians marched on in their kingdom living. Paul's simple speech and lifestyle were criticized by the ostentatious Corinthians.

Paul mentioned his upcoming visit twice—at the beginning and end of the letter (4:18-21; 16:3-9). Paul placed his pending arrival before his readers in the hope that they would solve their problems before he arrived. Therefore, the discussions of purity (5:1–7:40), idols and sacrifices (8:1–11:1), traditions (11:2-33), spiritual gifts (12:1–14:40), the resurrection (15:1-58), and the offering for Jerusalem (16:1-4) were framed with the fact that Paul would soon be coming to visit the Corinthians—either in love or in discipline.

BIBLE-WIDE CONCEPTS

WISDOM

Throughout the Old Testament, wisdom was considered insight into the mind of God for physical and spiritual matters. Proverbs portrays wisdom as the very blueprint for how creation operates (Prov. 8). Thus, wisdom is knowledge of reality as God intended it, whether physical or spiritual. Also, humans have consistently tried to replace God's wisdom with a wisdom constructed of their own making. But God calls that human wisdom foolishness.

Paul mentioned wisdom and foolishness over thirty times in 1 Corinthians. The words "wisdom" or "wise" are used twenty-three times in chapters 1–3 and three more times in the remaining thirteen chapters. The first chapters of the letter contrast the Old Testament concepts of wisdom and foolishness. Paul drew from Isaiah and Jeremiah for the backbone of his assault on the false wisdom of the Corinthian believers (1:19, 31; see also 3:19-20 for his use of Job and Psalms). He contrasted their foolishness with the true wisdom and mysteries of God (2:7; 4:1)—mysteries that were hinted at in the Old Testament but only fully revealed by Jesus Christ through the Spirit.

THE KINGDOM OF GOD

The kingdom of God was a central Old Testament way of describing God's rule. It was a partial reality in the earthly kingdom of Israel and was also a future hope. The day of the Lord would usher in the kingdom in its fullness. Jesus also presented the kingdom as both here now in part (Matt. 13:11, 19, 24, 31, 33, 38, 44-45, 47; 28:20) and yet future in its final fulfillment (Matt. 6:10). Peter proclaimed that Christ was presently reigning over the world from the right hand of God (Acts 2:33-36). Paul also preached the gospel of the kingdom of God (Acts 14:22; 28:23, 31).

In 1 Corinthians Paul continued to proclaim how the great Old Testament truths of the kingdom had to be hoped for in the future and worked out in the present. Paul addressed the Corinthians' infatuation with pride and schisms within the framework of the kingdom of God (4:20). Although the kingdom was not realized among the Corinthian Christians perfectly, it was there spiritually in the power of the Holy Spirit sent from the risen and exalted Christ (Acts 2:33).

Looking toward the future aspect of the kingdom, Paul said behavior in the present could exclude entrance later on (1 Cor. 6:9-10; cf. Matt. 5:1-10). In the future, Jesus will deliver up the kingdom to God (1 Cor. 15:24). For now, the church enjoys the privileges and liabilities of Israel of old. Believers now have the greater blessing of the Spirit dwelling within them, not just in the tabernacle or temple (3:16-17). Israel's Passover and exodus have been fulfilled in Christ, the present believer's Passover (5:5-8). Like Israel, the church has been baptized into Christ and now enjoys the spiritual food and drink of Christ (10:1-4). Also like Israel, the church is subject to God's discipline (10:5-13; 11:28-31).

NEEDS MET BY FIRST CORINTHIANS

The Corinthians had problems with arrogance and pride. They tended to see themselves as the beginning and end of God's concerns (4:7; 14:36-38). That self-infatuation warped several of God's good gifts. It turned seeking the best for others into selfish status seeking. It turned the spiritual gifts of God into prizes to be gloated over or envied. It turned forgiveness into revenge and replaced the cross of Christ with partisan pride in flashy human ministers. Paul tried first to solve the problem of their arrogance and then to deal with each of the specific problems that had been mentioned to him. The structure and content of 1 Corinthians show that Paul was answering questions like these.

- What is wrong with having a favorite Christian leader?
- Should believers not have a high and lofty view of their leaders?
- Do their followers not have a share in the leaders' status?
- How can believers know who are the truly spiritual among them?
- Should Christians take other Christians to court?
- Do sexual relations with an unsaved spouse defile a believing spouse?
- Is marriage good or bad?
- Do strong Christians have to alter their behavior just to keep weaker Christians from copying them?
- How can believers live in unity with the great diversity of spiritual gifts in the community?
- Is it necessary for Christians to believe in a physical resurrection?

Although Paul addressed many different topics ranging from eating idol-sacrificed meat to partaking of the Lord's Supper, from immorality to marital relationships, from spiritual gifts to his travel plans, just one central truth informed each of his solutions—the Cross of Christ. Believers today can, along with the Corinthians, discover how the Cross of Christ is the answer to their problems. In regard to the problems of jealousy, pride, and division, the Cross puts all believers on the same level and teaches them to forgive each other and wait for Christ's perfect evaluation of them all at the end of the age. In regard to the tendencies of believers toward immorality, the Cross teaches them to purify their lives and celebrate Christ's sacrifice in holiness. The Cross shows believers the way to resolve their conflicts out of court and to appreciate the work of the Holy Spirit for edification. The specific situations have changed from first-century Corinth to the lives of believers today, but the issues addressed by Paul—pride, immorality, care, and generosity—are still the same.

OUTLINE OF FIRST CORINTHIANS

I. SPIRITUAL ENRICHMENT WHILE WAITING FOR CHRIST (1:1-9)
   A. The Greeting: Unity with All the Churches (1:1-3)
   B. The Thanksgiving: Enrichment in All the Gifts (1:4-9)

II. THE PROBLEM OF DIVISION: ARROGANCE IN THE COMMUNITY (1:10–6:20)
   A. The Exhortation to Unity in the Light of Partisan Quarrels (1:10–4:21)
   B. Community Purity versus Arrogant Liberty (5:1–6:20)

FIRST CORINTHIANS NOTES

1:1-9 SPIRITUAL ENRICHMENT WHILE WAITING FOR CHRIST

1:1-3 The Greeting: Unity with All the Churches

Sosthenes (1:1) was Paul's associate and may have once been the ruler of the synagogue at Corinth (Acts 18:17). In spite of their many problems, the Corinthians were "holy" (1:2), that is, set apart for God's possession and use. There are three aspects of the believer's sanctification—positional (made right before God at the moment of salvation, Acts 20:32; 1 Cor. 6:11), progressive (being conformed to Christ in word and deed, John 17:17), and final (transformation at the return of Christ, 1 John 3:2).

Paul's greeting was extended to "all Christians everywhere" (1:2), in order to begin correcting the Corinthians' narrow preoccupation with them-

selves (1 Cor. 4:7; 14:36). This hinted at the problem Paul sought to correct throughout the epistle. Paul placed the Corinthian church in the much larger context of all the churches of God (7:17; 11:16; 14:33; cf. also 2 Cor. 2:14; 1 Thess. 1:8; 1 Tim. 2:8). By using the word "grace" (1:3), Paul was recognizing that everything of worth that the Corinthians had was given by God (cf. 4:7) and was thus no ground for boasting.

1:4-9 The Thanksgiving: Enrichment in All the Gifts

1:4-7 ENRICHED EXPECTATION

The Corinthians' gifts were given (1:4), not earned. The people were enriched by God (1:5), not self-made. Paul was already seeking to correct the tendency of the Corinthians to boast in the gifts they were given by God. The gifts were given for the edification of the church during the time of waiting for Christ's return (1:7; cf. 13:8-13). Paul was emphasizing that the ultimate goal and hope of the believer was the return of Christ, not the spiritual gifts given during the time awaiting that return. The Corinthians had forgotten the ultimate goal of Christ's return (cf. 4:5).

1:8-9 DIVINE SECURITY
Until that day of Christ's return, God would do the confirming of character. God would keep his people "strong right up to the end" (1:8). Again, the fact that God did the work was emphasized. This began a corrective to the Corinthians' judgmental and prideful tendencies. Paul emphasized that "being invited" and "friendship" (1:9) were not exclusive experiences for just one part of Christ's church. These blessings belonged to all believers in the church of Jesus Christ. Paul made it clear that the security found in Christ related to him keeping believers blameless till the end. The fact that salvation is a work of God, the faithful one, is the true ground for security.

1:10–6:20 THE PROBLEM OF DIVISION: ARROGANCE IN THE COMMUNITY
1:10–4:21 The Exhortation to Unity in the Light of Partisan Quarrels
Overview: The first four chapters move between (1) Paul's statement of facts concerning the Corinthians' problems and his actions when he was with them, and (2) God's view of the implications of those problems.

Facts (1:10-17) The problem of religious cliques—Paul's original preaching of the Cross.

Implications (1:18-31) God's method: wisdom only found in the Cross.

Facts (2:1-5) Paul's original preaching of Christ crucified.

Implications (2:6-16) God's medium: wisdom through the Spirit.

Facts (3:1-4) Paul's inability to speak to them as spiritual people.

Implications (3:5-17) God's evaluation of final work: what conforms to the foundation, Jesus Christ.

Summary exhortations (3:18–4:21)

1:10-17 THE ISSUE: MAKING THE CROSS OF CHRIST VOID
In this section, Paul was concerned with the growing disunity in the Corinthian church. The people were forming religious cliques and making them the objects of their faith rather than finding unity in the cross of Christ. The Cross was to be the focus of the Christian life and an illustration of what it meant to follow Christ. The Corinthians were enjoying spiritual exaltation to the point that they

were ignoring the implications of sacrifice and service found in the cross of Jesus Christ.

The word "divisions" (1 Cor. 1:10) referred to internal dissensions over the leadership of the church. Paul appealed to the people to make adjustments that there might be unity in the church. The believers were giving spiritual allegiance to different leaders (1:12). Paul expected that each of the questions in 1:13 would be answered with a resounding no! Paul was careful not to distort the truth of the gospel by embellishing it with clever rhetoric because he desired to avoid diminishing the cross of Christ (1:17). Paul's concern focused on "the cross." This focus emphasized that God alone had worked man's salvation, not the various leaders who preached the word of God. It also called the Corinthians to identify with the Cross, through service and self-sacrifice. The Corinthians' problems needed the corrective emphasis of the Cross; the Cross needed to be the focus of their ways because it exemplified God's way. The next section develops this principle. Voiding the Cross was the mistake that led the Corinthians to exalt themselves and various leaders. Paul returned their minds to the crucified Christ, through whose suffering they were saved, and in whose steps they needed to follow.

Although Paul dealt with many subjects in this long letter, the underlying concepts that guided him were few. In evaluating ideas that stretched from idol-sacrificed meat to the Lord's Supper, from immorality to marital relationships, from spiritual gifts to travel plans, only one thought directed his conclusions—the Cross of Christ (1:17). Each solution Paul presented came from his discernment of a problem's relationship to that great truth.

1:18-25 THE CROSS: FOOLISH AND POWERFUL
The central thesis statement for this letter was given in 1:18. The two groups, those "on the road to destruction" and the "saved," were mentioned in order to cause the readers to identify with one or the other group when it came to the strife between the religious parties (1:12). Paul used Isaiah 29:14 to support his claim (1:19) that preaching a crucified Christ was considered foolishness in the eyes of the lost world. The worldly views of the Corinthian church also fell under Paul's condemnation. History supports this view (1:20-25). The wise of this world are made foolish by God bringing salvation to those who believe. This is paralleled in 1:22-24.

Paul used paradoxical language (1:25) because of the Corinthians' involvement with wisdom that was really foolishness. True wisdom is found in the salvation power of the Cross. Any other means of salvation or supposed wisdom makes void the cross of Jesus Christ and in God's eyes is actually "foolish."

1:26-31 THEIR CALLING: FOOLISH AND WISE

This relates to 1:18-25 as another example of Isaiah 29:14 in action. Their calling was considered foolish according to the flesh (1:26-31). Note the broader context of Jeremiah 9:12-24. To boast in the Lord is to boast in the cross of Christ. Paul emphasized God's choice three times (1:27-29, cf. 1:9, "invited"). Contrary to the world's approach, God chose to use not the wise, but the foolish and the weak to convey the Good News (1:26-29). Paul emphasized this fact to deny the Corinthians any occasion of boasting about their salvation.

Boasting (1:30-31) was a problem among the Corinthian Christians. They boasted of their salvation and spiritual gifts. Paul wanted them to realize that because their salvation was a gift from God, all their boasting should center in him. Their pride in their spiritual gifts was being cloaked in a guise of wisdom. Christ and his work on the cross had lost its hold on their thoughts and actions. In 1:31 Paul quoted Jeremiah 9:24 in support of his point.

2:1-16 PAUL'S COMING: WEAKNESS AND WISDOM

2:1-5 Wisdom and Power in Evangelism

Paul admitted his lack of human wisdom (2:2), not because he was unlearned and foolish in the world's terms, but to bring to focus the mystery of God's work on the cross and to reestablish faith in the power of God. Why did Paul come to Corinth in "weakness" and fear (2:3)? He had recently been run out of Thessalonica (Acts 17:1-10) and had not had a very encouraging experience in Athens (Acts 17:15-34). But Paul came to every city in "weakness" and fear (cf. 2 Cor. 7:15; Eph. 6:5; Phil. 2:12). Paul's attitude of "weakness" and fear was the way he ordered his ways in humility and awe before God, rather than in the self-reliant and cocky manner of worldly wisdom. Paul came to them humbly to show them that wisdom was not in him but in the power of God through Christ's work on the cross.

2:6-9 Wisdom and the Mature

In these verses, Paul explained how he could be rejected or misunderstood, even if his way was God's way. He revealed that the hidden mind of Christ is above human understanding and evaluation. The "rulers of this world" were contrasted with God and his wisdom (2:6-8). These "rulers" had failed to understand God's mysterious wisdom

and would be excluded from his kingdom. Those with the "wisdom that belongs to this world" even crucified the Messiah, Jesus. The "secret wisdom of God" (2:7), the truth of the gospel, was a divine secret—a truth undiscoverable apart from divine revelation. Paul's quotations of the Old Testament (2:9; Isa. 64:4; 65:17; Jer. 3:16) were used to defend the nature of the gospel, not simply to describe future glory in heaven (see Isa. 6:9-10 in Matt. 13:14-15).

2:10-16 The Communication of This Wisdom

Paul revealed that the things long hidden are now revealed by the illuminating work of the Holy Spirit, not by human wisdom. Only spiritual people could receive this revelation. The spiritual person is one who thinks like Christ.

The meaning of the last phrase, "using the Spirit's words to explain spiritual truths," (2:13) is uncertain. Among the possible interpretations are: (1) giving spiritual truth a spiritual form, (2) comparing spiritual truths with spiritual truths, (3) interpreting spiritual truths to spiritual men, (4) explaining spiritual truths with spiritual words (that is, filled with spiritual meaning).

In 2:14–3:3 Paul described people in four ways: (1) the "people who aren't Christians" (unsaved) (2:14; "natural man," NASB and KJV); (2) those "who have the Spirit" (mature Christian) (2:15-16); (3) "infants" (having characteristics of the flesh; spiritually weak or immature Christian) (3:1-2; "carnal," KJV); (4) those "still controlled by . . . sinful desires" (composed of a fleshly nature; characterized by a willful refusal to grow) (3:3; "fleshly," NASB; "carnal," KJV).

3:1-23 PAUL'S PERSPECTIVE OF LEADERSHIP

Note the concept of "pride" (cf. 4:6, 18-19; 5:2; 8:1; 13:4; cf. also Col. 2:18; Rom. 11–12, "mind"). In the Corinthian church was a growing puffed-up attitude that, if not immediately stopped, would ruin much of God's work in the church.

3:1-4 Paul's Inability

The problem for the Corinthians was not doctrine but lack of spirituality. The people only thought they were spiritual. Paul was not able (3:1) to talk to them as mature believers because they were not able (3:2) to relate to such a mature address. The mode of ministry had to be as to babes, not as to mature Christians. Their inability was related to

---

SUMMARY OF FIRST CORINTHIANS 1–3

Chapter 1	God did not send his wisdom through great men in order to level all people. The Corinthians were not great.
Chapter 2	God sent his message to people by the Spirit.
Chapter 3	The Corinthians were not spiritual.

---

their worldly or fleshly nature. They had been fleshly to begin with, and they were "still" in that state (3:3). They had not grown since they had come to Christ.

Paul continued his analogy of "infants" versus "mature" Christians with the illustration of feeding with "milk" or "solid food" (3:2-4). Paul sought to respond appropriately (3:1, "as" two times) to the needs of the Corinthians. He did not want to teach them truths they could not handle or understand. He had already spoken of the "secret" (2:7) to them and of the "lofty words and brilliant ideas" of God's message (2:1). Paul had not held back deep spiritual truths from the Corinthians. But he had limited his manner of speaking to them for their good. He gave them only milk.

3:5-9 The Corrective: God's Perspective

God's view of servants (3:5) was that they were channels "through" whom God worked. Their work was limited to Christ's gifts through the Holy Spirit within them. Any success they had was a gift from God. While Paul planted the church at Corinth, Apollos came to Corinth after Paul's visit and helped the ministry to grow (3:6; cf. Acts 18:27–19:1). But God, not the workers, caused the growth.

The unity of the workers was a result of their "same purpose" (3:8) and the fact that they all belonged to God. God was mentioned three times (3:9). The phrase "partners who belong to God" may mean either "fellow workers with God" or "fellow workers who belong to God." The context favors the latter.

3:10-17 Responsible to God for the Work

In this section, the builders were being warned about the quality of their work. The foundation of the church is a Person, not a doctrine (3:11). True building of the church involves a person's participation in the very life of Christ. This cuts against the "I am of Paul" mentality. For the final evaluation (3:12-15), see Amos 4:11 and Zechariah 3:2 regarding being saved through fire.

Paul shifted from God's building (the church) to his dwelling (the individual Christian) (3:16-17). Paul reminded the Corinthians that their work would be evaluated at the judgment seat of Christ (2 Cor. 5:10; Rom. 14:10). Paul did not explain the nature of the reward (1 Cor. 3:14) but elsewhere referred to "crowns" as representative of the believers' reward (1 Thess. 2:19; 2 Tim. 4:8; cf. also James 1:12; 1 Pet. 5:4).

3:18-23 Do Not Boast in Men

The people of Corinth had deceived themselves concerning the nature of the building (the church) and its builders (the church leaders). In 3:19-20 Paul quoted from Job 5:13 and Psalm 94:11 as a warning to those who thought themselves to be wise. This was the high point of Paul's discussion of the problem of division in the church. He ended the discussion with the focus on God, not God's servants. If they had had the choice, the "proud" in Corinth would probably have ignored 1 Corinthians 3:23 because for them to "belong to Christ" would put them under his authority, and they wanted to be under no one's authority. To add "and Christ belongs to God" was to put the Corinthians even one more level down from the top of the authority chain. They would want to stop with the statement "Everything belongs to you" (3:21). They would have agreed with 3:21 but would not have seen its fuller implications until this point in the letter. All things were theirs but only in the context of taking their place of submission under Christ and under God. Some of the Corinthians mistakenly conceived all things as being theirs in a selfish sense—an attitude that Paul sarcastically criticized in 1 Corinthians 4:8. To claim to have great spiritual riches as a Christian also includes the obligation to take a humble and submissive place under Christ and God.

4:1-21 EXHORTATIONS FROM PAUL'S PERSPECTIVE ON LEADERSHIP

4:1-5 Paul and Personal Criticism

These verses are concerned with the evaluation of humans by humans. Although the term "servants" (4:1) denotes subordination, "put in charge" (4:2) emphasizes privilege and responsibility. The call to leadership was a call to a pure and trustworthy character (4:2). The Corinthians acted as if they were the judges at the last day, but they had judged much too early (4:5, "before the Lord returns"). Their judgments of Christians were not for edification, but to put a final tag of good or bad, in or out, on the ones they judged. It was a nonministry judgment that had its source in pride.

4:6-13 Paul Applies His Message

Paul spoke of himself and other leaders to illustrate to the people their problems in the area of arrogance (4:6). Paul's concern for the problem of pride is reflected throughout the book (cf. 4:18-19; 5:2; 8:1). He used himself and Apollos as illustrations of leaders in the Corinthian situation and probably omitted the names of the real culprits to avoid their resentment.

Paul used the tool of sarcasm to reveal the pride of the Corinthians (4:7-13). The readers were acting as if the coming of the Lord and his judgment were already behind them. It is easy to see how this wrong perspective could grow out of the doctrine of the judgment of sin at the cross. If they were forgiven, how could there be any future evaluation? But this was a misunderstanding. Who regarded them as superior (4:7)? Only themselves. The answer to the second question of 4:7 is "nothing." The answer to the third question reveals the self-centered pride of the readers.

Paul, during much persecution, had left Thessalonica, passed through Berea (Acts 17:10) and entered Athens. He sarcastically used his persecuted lifestyle to show how far he had been left behind by the exalted and reigning Corinthians (4:8-14).

4:14-21 Paul Clarifies His Attitudes
As a loving father (4:14-17) Paul admonished the Corinthians; he did not seek to shame them. Tutors ("others to teach you," 4:15) were slaves and guardians responsible for the general supervision of children until they reached adulthood (cf. Gal. 3:24). Timothy (4:17), who was ministering with Paul in Ephesus (Acts 19:22), was sent to Corinth to remind the believers of Paul's teachings.

5:1–6:20 Community Purity versus Arrogant Liberty

Overview: First Corinthians 5–6 is part of a larger section that also includes 1 Corinthians 7. All three chapters are concerned with how individual purity affects the community. The emphasis moves from sexual purity (1 Cor. 5) to social purity (6:1-11), then back to sexual purity (6:12–7:40). The subject of immoral actions, sexual or otherwise, is traced from 5:1 through 6:8-10 to 7:2, 28, 36.

5:1-8 CLEANSING COMMUNITY IMPURITY
The problem in 1 Corinthians 5 was immoral sexual union. The words "father's wife" (5:1) was an Old Testament and rabbinical phrase for stepmother (Gen. 35:22; 49:4; 2 Sam. 16:22; 20:3; 1 Chron. 5:1). Marriage to a stepson was forbidden by both Jewish and Roman law.

5:1-2 The Response: Puffed Up Boasting
Removal from the assembly was the final step of church discipline outlined by Jesus in Matthew 18:15-18.

5:3-5 Paul's Response
The concept of "judgment" may be traced from 5:3 to 5:12-13. See 1 Corinthians 5:11 for a fuller description of handing someone "into Satan's hands" (5:5). Deliverance over to Satan is equivalent to being removed from the assembly, that is, excommunicated. Delivered into Satan's domain, the offender would no longer enjoy the protective fellowship of the church. The "destroyed" sinful nature (5:5) may refer (1) to the ruin of one's physical body through sickness, even death, or (2) the destruction of the fleshly hold over the person. The context (cf. 3:1-3) gives credence to the latter view. This view is more consistent with the ultimate purpose of church discipline, which is to restore the offender to fellowship with God and his people.

5:6-8 Paul's Critique of the Corinthians' Response
Paul used the leaven proverb to illustrate how "boasting" can soon permeate and destroy the church (5:6). For more on Old Testament Passover

concepts (5:7-8), see Exodus 12:15, 19; 13:7; and Deuteronomy 16:3-4. Leaven was cleaned out of all Israelite homes before the Passover sacrifice could be made. Paul characterized the whole Christian life as a celebration in the purity of Passover.

The Jewish feasts of Passover and Unleavened Bread (Exod. 12:1-28) served as the background for Paul's remarks. Just as leaven was removed from Jewish homes to celebrate these religious festivals, so the Corinthians should remove the leaven of unholiness from their assembly. This was especially appropriate since Christ, who fulfilled the typical significance of Passover, had been sacrificed. The Christian life was likened to a continual observance of the Festival of Unleavened Bread (1 Cor. 5:8). The leaven of unholiness had to constantly be removed.

5:9-13 CLARIFYING COMMUNITY PURITY
Paul mentioned here (5:9) a lost letter. The earlier epistle that Paul wrote to the Corinthians has not been preserved. While daily contact with the unbelieving people of the world is unavoidable, Christians should not have familiar fellowship with professing Christians who are involved in sin and refuse to respond to church discipline (5:11). Paul appealed to the Old Testament principle of the removal of the wicked (5:13; cf. Deut. 13:5; 17:7, 12; 21:21).

6:1-11 CRITICIZING FALSE RIGHTS
First Corinthians 6 continues the theme of judging others (5:3, 12-13; 6:2-3, 5). Paul had earlier emphasized judging the sinful among them (5:1-8). At this point he examines the need for church members to work out disputes among themselves within the church (5:9-13). He did not want them seeking judges from outside the church. If needed, they were to go before Christian arbiters (6:1-6). In 6:2-4 Paul pointed out the incongruity of believers appealing to civil courts when the saints would someday judge the world (6:2) and angels (6:3; cf. Isa. 24:21; 2 Pet. 2:4; Jude 1:6; Rev. 20:10). The question "why do you go to outside judges who are not respected by the church?" (6:4) might be better translated "do you appoint as judges men of little account in the church?" (NASB and KJV). The saints should not be judged by those "who are not respected," that is, by unbelievers.

Paul wondered why judgment should even be needed among Christians living holy lives (6:7-11). It was a sign of defeat to get even that far (6:7). The questions Paul asked pierce to the heart of how worldliness can void the work of Christ on the cross (1:17). In 6:5-8 Paul presented two alternatives to appealing to civil courts: (1) have a believer judge the case (6:5-6) or (2) be wronged rather than wronging others and destroying one's testimony in the community (6:7-8).

Paul gave a list of vices that were apparently evident in the Corinthian church (6:8-11). These vices are in sharp contrast to the life of true believers. The term "washed" (6:11) was a reference to the "new life" (Titus 3:5).

6:12-20 FOCUSING ON PHYSICAL PURITY
This section elaborates the principle behind 1 Corinthians 5:1–6:11 and reveals the root problem. The Corinthian Christians were willing to live with someone else's sin (5:1) because they were living with sin in their own lives (6:12-20). Apparently, some Corinthian believers were trying to use Christian freedom to justify their sins. Paul insisted that Christian liberty was limited by expedience and self-control. Their formal right to freedom did not equal the right to do anything they desired. Paul would not, however, substitute a new or old legalism. The way out of this problem was in a different direction.

Paul put forth a principle that applied to belly and body (6:13-20). Freedom in eating food does not equal freedom for immorality. The body is an eternal aspect of the person. It cannot be treated as separate from the real person.

The questions of 6:15-16 are not about physical possibility but ethical incompatibility. In 1 Corinthians 6:16 Paul used Genesis 2:24, a foundational text on marriage, to show that even in an adulterous relationship a union is established. A sexual union in and of itself does not make a marriage (cf. Gen. 2:24), but sexual intercourse does result in a one-flesh relationship and undermines the uniqueness of the one-flesh relationship of marriage.

Paul gave the Corinthians a strong warning to run from sexual immorality (6:18-20). Such sin is a sin against one's own body, which is the temple of the Holy Spirit (6:19), bought with the price of Jesus' suffering on the cross (6:20). It is sin against a body that will someday be resurrected from the dead through God's gracious gift of grace. Paul has moved his readers away from an attitude of fleshly arrogance and has prepared them for answers to the various questions they had sent to him.

7:1-40 FALSE AND TRUE SEXUAL PURITY
Overview: Note the word "now" in 7:1, 25; 8:1; 12:1; 16:1, 12. It introduces the various questions the Corinthians had sent to Paul. The general questions at issue in 1 Corinthians 7 are "Is it bad to be married?" and "Are sexual relations with unsaved or even saved spouses unholy?"

7:1-16 Marriage and Purity
1:1-7 THE GENERAL PRINCIPLE
The general principle is stated in 7:1. The phrase "it is good" probably reflects a Corinthian slogan Paul wanted to modify. Then Paul applied the principle

to marriage (7:2-7). Monogamy, not celibacy, is the norm for Christians (7:3). Marriage, just as much as celibacy, is a gift of God (7:7). Paul was in agreement with the principle of celibacy, but not because he advocated sexual asceticism in marriage. Marriage is good but not required. And temporary sexual abstinence is not commanded.

"As I do" (7:7) means Paul was sexually controlled—not just unmarried, but having the character to stay both unmarried and pure. While most Orthodox Jews were opposed to celibacy and regarded marriage as a duty, there were apparently some ascetics at Corinth who advocated celibacy and wanted Paul to approve it as a duty for all.

7:8-16 TRUE AND FALSE PURITY IN MARRIAGE
To the unmarried men and widows, Paul approved, but did not command, the single life (7:9). In 7:10-11 Paul addressed the issue of marriage and commanded, on the authority of Jesus, that married believers ought to maintain their marriage relationship. In the case of separation, Paul presented the believer with two options: (1) remain unmarried or (2) be reconciled to one's partner. Paul's teaching summarized previous revelation that married people are not to be divorced (Matt. 5:32; 19:3-12; Mark 10:1-12; Luke 16:18).

Unbelievers cannot defile a believing spouse (7:12-14). Here Paul dealt with the possibility of one partner becoming a believer after marriage. While Christ did not give any teaching concerning spiritually mixed marriages, Paul did ("I do not have a direct command from the Lord"), and his teaching is authoritative. Four times he instructed Christians to continue to live with their unbelieving partners. The "holiness" and "godly" (7:14) influence is limited to the one who does the sanctifying—in this case the believing spouse. Therefore, the issue in 7:14 is not God's saving and sanctifying work through Christ, but the blessed efforts of the believing spouse to provide an atmosphere of holy words and deeds.

Is the believer required by the command of Jesus and teaching of Paul to preserve the marriage at the cost of becoming a slave to the unbelieving spouse (7:15)? No. Paul says that if the unbeliever demands separation, the believer may accept it and be at peace with the situation. In such a case the believer is left with the two options mentioned in 7:11.

7:17-24 The Guiding Principle
7:17-19 STATED ONCE: WALK AS CALLED
No religious changes were needed to make a believer better off before God. Is a change of marriage status advisable for the believer? Paul repeated the principle three times: remain in your present condition; lead the life that God has assigned you. How could someone become "uncircumcised" (7:18)? The author of

1 Maccabees 1:15-16 recorded that under Hellenistic influence, certain Jews in the time of the Seleucid ruler Antiochus Epiphanes (175–164 B.C.) disguised their circumcision.

7:20-23 STATED TWICE: REMAIN
No social alterations should be made simply on the basis of worry about religious status. Apparently some of the Christians in Corinth were taking on various ascetic activities, even putting away their wives, so that they would have greater "spiritual" status among the people of the church there.

7:24 STATED THRICE: REMAIN
Paul reemphasized that there was no need to maneuver out of marriage, circumcision, or social position. God's call and salvation were not based on physical or social status but on Christ alone.

7:25-38 Marriage and Virgins
7:25-26 HISTORICAL CONCERNS
The next question Paul responded to concerned virgins—"young women who are not yet married." The point Paul made was that celibacy is desirable but not demanded. It is not a sin for a virgin to marry (7:28). The word "crisis" (7:26) should read "constraint" or "compulsion." The same Greek word is translated "urgency" in 7:37 and "compelled" in 9:16. Paul defined the nature of the "present constraint" in 7:28-31 (cf. also 2 Cor. 9:7; Philem. 1:14). Paul's mind was on constraints that came to the married, not on political or social upheavals. The main constraint Paul had in mind here was that being married cut into one's all-too-little time to serve the Lord (7:32-35). Because of the present shortness of time before the return of the Lord, men and women need to maximize their service to God.

7:27-34 CORRECTIVE FOR BALANCE
Paul again advised, "stay as you are" (7:27-28). He emphasized that the issue he was addressing was not one of sin. Paul recognized that with marriage come additional cares and concerns (7:28). First Corinthians 7:28 could be paraphrased, "But if you, a man, should marry, don't think you have done anything sinful. And the same applies to a woman." The nature of the times (7:29-31) called for unhindered service to the Lord (cf. Matt. 6:25, 27-28, 31, 34).

7:35 THE REASON FOR THIS ENTIRE SECTION
Paul desired that all Christians "serve the Lord best, with as few distractions as possible" (7:35). This idea was behind all his statements concerning marriage and celibacy in this section. Distracted versus undistracted devotion has a parallel in the lives of Mary and Martha in Luke 10:39-42.

7:36-38 ON FATHERS AND THEIR VIRGINS
Apparently the Corinthians had asked Paul about the duty of a father to a daughter of marriageable age (7:38). Paul advised that if there is no evidence of the gift of celibacy, the father should let his daughter marry.

7:39-40 Marriage and Widows
Bound in life and freed in death. The last issue Paul dealt with here is the question of widows. Paul recognized that since death ended a marriage, the widow was free to remarry. Yet, in his opinion, it would be better to remain single.

8:1–11:1 LIMITATION AND EDIFICATION: IDOL MEATS
Overview: This section concerns food that had been sacrificed to idols. Could a Christian eat that food? The focus of 1 Corinthians 8–11 is on the use of Christian liberty (8:9; 9:4-6, 12, 18; 10:23). Christian liberty had to be balanced with concern that other Christians not be led into sin. Paul used the specific example of idol meats to show the Corinthians how their freedom was being misused and was ruining fellow Christians (8:11). In 1 Corinthians 9 Paul cited his own refusal to accept pay for his ministry as an example of how Christian liberty should be curbed by concern for other Christians and a desire to spread the gospel. Finally, in 1 Corinthians 10 he used the illustration of ancient Israel to show that membership in God's redeemed community was no automatic guard against avoiding his displeasure. First Corinthians 10 uncovers the real and potentially disqualifying truth behind the exercise of the Corinthians' freedom: they were participating with demons.

8:1-13 Limitation Described
8:1-3 ORIENTATION TO THE BASIC ISSUE
Read 10:23-33 for the overall perspective. Paul's immediate concern was the use and limitations of knowledge (8:1-4, 7, 10, 11). Paul admitted that knowledge alone was not the solution to the problem. Just setting a brother or sister straight about the facts would not achieve the edification and love God desired. Paul's thesis that "while knowledge may make us feel important, it is love that really builds up the church" (8:1) was supported by two examples (8:2-3). Paul showed that the problem was how knowledge was used, not how much was known.

Paul introduced a new subject—meat sacrificed to idols. In Paul's day when portions of an animal were offered to heathen gods, part of the meat was eaten. If offered as a private sacrifice, the meat might be used for a banquet to which the offerer invited friends. If the offering was a public sacrifice, the meat could be sold in the markets to the people of the city. Should Christians buy and eat meat that has been offered to heathen gods? When invited to the home of a friend, should Christians eat meat that has been offered to idols?

In answering these questions, Paul developed important principles that enable believers to make the right decisions on questionable or debated matters: (1) Is it profitable? (6:12); (2) Is it enslaving? (6:12); (3) Will it hinder the spiritual growth of a brother or sister? (8:13); (4) Does it edify? (10:23); and (5) Does it glorify God? (10:31).

8:4-6 THE "WE KNOWS" ARE LISTED
Paul began his solution to the problem of meat and idols by recognizing that idols are not true gods (8:4). All "gods" are excluded from the realm of power. Although Paul granted that there were "so-called gods," such as those recognized in Greek and Roman mythology, there was only one true God with divine and sovereign power.

8:7-13 THE "DON'T KNOWS" ARE DEFENDED
But some still believed that eating meat sacrificed to idols was wrong (8:7). On the northern slopes of the Acro-Corinth was a temple dedicated to Demeter, the Greek goddess of agriculture, marriage, and fertility. Located within the temple were a number of dining rooms where worshipers could eat their sacrifices. Some of the Corinthian believers had once dined there in honor of this goddess and thus they associated the eating of this meat with idol worship. Because of this association, eating the sacrificed meat probably defiled the consciences of many of the Christians there. Paul illustrated the power of example (8:10-11), which could cause others to sin against Christ and their consciences (8:12-13). Those who flaunted their Christian freedom would not have seen that their actions, though not wrong in God's sight, might cause a weaker brother or sister to sin. First Corinthians 8:13 provides the principle that should regulate Christian conduct in morally neutral matters. The believers' use of liberty must be regulated by love for God and other Christians and governed by self-restraint.

9:1–10:13 Limitation Defended
Overview: Paul had thought through one area of possible criticism, his work and financial support, long before he went to Corinth. In the Thessalonian correspondence he argued that Christians ought to work for their food (1 Thess. 2:7-10), and he used himself as a model of self-support (2 Thess. 3:6-15). Paul addressed this issue at length in 1 Corinthians 9.

Paul had worked with Priscilla and Aquila in making tents (Acts. 18:3) in Corinth, an endeavor that had been thrown back in his face as an indication that he was neither strong nor using his full apostolic rights (1 Cor. 9:6, 15; 2 Cor. 11:7-9; 12:13).

9:1-2 THE NEED FOR THE DEFENSE: TO THOSE TO WHOM PAUL HAD NOT MINISTERED
Note the four questions. They all expect a yes answer. Paul established his absolute right to receive full financial support for his work. But he had set aside his right to receive support to avoid the criticism that he was preaching for money, not for God. Paul used this setting aside of his freedom to illustrate the truth that at times Christian freedom had to be set aside for higher service. Paul refused to be paid so that people could not be offended by it, and thus more people could be saved through his ministry (9:19-22).

9:3-12 THE DEFENSE: "I HAVE ALL THE RIGHTS ANY APOSTLE HAS"
Paul addressed the problem of other people making incorrect evaluations of his person and authority (2:14-15; 4:3; 9:3; 10:29-30). Paul asked eleven questions about his rights (9:4-12). The central issue was liberty (cf. 8:9; 9:4-6, 12, 18). Paul argued his right to receive financial support for his ministry. First Corinthians 9:5 reveals a little about the family life of the apostles. Peter and the rest of the apostles, including the half brothers of Jesus, were married. In 9:9-10 Paul quoted Deuteronomy 25:4 in support of the right to receive remuneration for one's ministry.

9:12-27 THE DEFENSE: "I DO NOT USE ALL RIGHTS IN ORDER TO WIN MORE TO CHRIST"
Paul presents two views of ministry. The issue was one of entrustment, not salary. For Jesus' teaching that the laborer is worthy of his hire (9:14), see Luke 10:7 and Matthew 10:10. Paul clarified his reason for giving up his various apostolic rights: to "bring them to Christ" (9:19-23). Note the use of "bring" (9:19-22). In 9:19-23 Paul revealed the whole scope of his ministry, of which the Corinthians had seen but a part. They had accused him of being limited because they concluded he was less than qualified to be an apostle. But Paul showed that his limitations were self-imposed and ministry-oriented. The Corinthians had made a value judgment without seeing the context of Paul's whole life. Paul's reward (9:18) was the privilege of presenting the gospel without accusations that he was doing it for personal gain.

Paul explains his regimen in the terms of running a race (9:24-27). Paul drew upon the cultural background of Corinth. Seven miles to the east was Isthmia, home of the Isthmian games held every other year in honor of the sea-god Neptune (Gk. *Poseidon*). In light of this background, Paul knew that the athletic imagery of running and boxing would be very familiar to the readers. The disqualification Paul feared (9:27) was that of being rejected with regard to his reward, not with regard to his salvation.

10:1-13 THE AVOIDANCE OF DISQUALIFICATION

Paul moved on from the challenge to avoid disqualification (9:27) to address the avoidance of disqualification with respect to their specific problem of idolatry (10:20). His drive to "bring them to Christ," no matter what freedoms had to be given up, should have been their drive as well. Any lapse in this drive might subject them to the displeasure of God. First Corinthians 9–10 shows how to avoid standing in the way of the ongoing thrust of the cross of Christ.

10:1-4 Privileges of the Forefathers

Here Paul set forth the example of the Israelites who, although greatly privileged (10:1-4), through lack of self-restraint (10:6-10) died in the wilderness, being disqualified (cf. 9:27) from entrance into the Promised Land. Paul used Israel's experiences as an example that the Corinthians would be wise to heed. Paul was making it clear that being a member of God's community did not insure against disqualification.

Paul singled out the key factors of baptism (10:2) and the Lord's Table (10:3-4) as signs of membership in God's community. The Israelites were identified and united with Moses ("baptized in the cloud and the sea," 10:2) by the crossing of the Red Sea. The rock that provided water (10:4) for the people in the wilderness was really a manifestation of Christ's presence. Paul did not believe the rabbinical legend that a material rock rolled along after the tribes, sending forth springs of water whenever the march stopped. Rather, Christ, the supplier of the water, was with them all along the way.

10:6-10 Israel's Experience in the Wilderness

Israel's experience in the wilderness provided an example for the Corinthians. Drawing upon the Old Testament illustration, Paul warned the Corinthians to beware of lust (10:6; Num. 11:4), idolatry (10:7; Num. 25), immorality (10:8; Num. 25), testing God (10:9; Num. 21:4-6), and grumbling (10:10; Num. 16:41-50). First Corinthians 10:7 gets Old Testament support due to the special Corinthian problems with temples, idols, meat, and the Lord's Supper of 1 Corinthians 11. The list of problems drawn from Israel's history was a perfect match to the problems at Corinth.

10:11-13 The Escape from Failure

After outlining the sins problematic to both Old Testament Israel and the Corinthian church, Paul assured the Corinthians of God's faithfulness to give initial endurance and a path of escape from falling into sin (10:13). God in his faithfulness always arranges a way of escape from temptation (lit., "a way out") and before that, gives strength to endure it.

10:14–11:1 Limitation Encouraged

10:14-22 LIMITATION IN IDOL FEASTS

Paul linked the Corinthian idolatry problem to the other temptations of 10:13. He set forth specific applications of Christian liberty to the issues facing the Corinthians. Partaking in a religious feast meant fellowshiping with the one worshiped at that feast (10:14-22). Since fellowship with God and with demons is incompatible (10:20), believers must not participate at pagan feasts. Pagan religious feasts are regarded as "the table of demons" (10:21).

10:23–11:1 LIMITATION IN IDOL FEASTS: SEEKING TRUE EDIFICATION

Paul put forth his central thesis in 10:23. He advised that believers may eat meat sold in the marketplace without asking questions that might perplex one's conscience. He appealed to Psalms 24:1 and 50:12 for support. As for eating meat in the home of an unbeliever, Paul advised that the believer not ask questions and just enjoy the meal (10:27-30). But if a fellow guest should inform the believer that the meat has been offered to idols, then he should abstain for the sake of the other man's conscience. Liberty to eat the meat was not in question—edifying other Christians was. Christian liberty must always be subordinate to God's glory and the spread of his gospel (10:31).

11:2–14:40 ORDER IN WORSHIP AND SERVICE

11:2-16 The Order of Authority for Women

11:2-3 BASED ON A DIVINE ORDER

All creation has levels of honor and authority. Within the Trinity, the Father is supreme (cf. 15:23-28). Although the Father, Son, and Spirit are equal in essence and worth, the Son and Spirit carry out different subordinate functions. The Son is under the authority of the Father, and the Spirit is under the authority of the Father and Son. Likewise, God has made male and female of equal worth but has given them different functions. The man has authority over the woman, not because he is better, but because God has given him that function.

According to Jewish custom, a bride went bareheaded until her marriage, but when she married, she wore a veil as a sign that she was under the authority of her husband. It is quite probable that both Jewish women and respectable Greek women wore head coverings in public. There were those at Corinth who were not wearing the traditional veil (11:5, 10). Paul, who was otherwise quite careful not to subject new converts to old traditions (Gal. 2:11-14), here ruled that the tradition needed to be followed.

Superior rank and authority does not imply

inequality (11:11), for Christ is subordinate to the Father, yet they are equal (John 10:30; 14:9; 5:18).

11:4-6 APPLIED TO A PRACTICAL EXAMPLE OF ORDER

It is uncertain if Paul was acknowledging the praying and prophesying of women as appropriate and indicating his approval (11:5; cf. 14:34-35; 1 Tim. 2:12). Scholars differ in how they compare this section with 11:33-36. Some see it as addressing the question of female prophesying outside (11:3) or inside (14:33-36) the formal church assembly. Others conclude that the issue of female prophesying, whether in or out of the church (11:3), and the problem of female silence in the assembly, relates to only one specific type of speaking—thoughtless chatter and needless interruptions. But whichever view is taken, this section on head coverings must be seen as an answer to a minor problem, one that could be finally concluded with an appeal to common sense (11:13), the natural order (11:14-15), and church tradition (11:16). Also, this discussion is within the context of "praise" ("glad," 11:2) rather than "no praise" ("I cannot praise you," 11:17). The overall point of his argument, however, was that women need to show proper respect for headship as do men. Although the woman was under the headship of the man, that was a subordination of function only and, therefore, maintained the essential equality of male and female. This equality is similar to the way Jesus, though subordinate in his function as servant to his Father, was nevertheless still fully equal to God in essence.

11:7-12 WOMEN NEED A VEIL: CREATION ORDER

The "angels" (11:10) must refer to the elect angels who know of no insubordination (Col. 1:16; Eph. 1:21). Male and female share essential equality in their origin from God (11:12).

11:13-16 BASED ON AN INTUITIVE SENSE OF ORDER

Paul's appeal to the "obvious" (11:14) reflected the general principle that throughout the world men wear short hair and women wear their hair long. He appealed to an intuitive general sense that male hair is shorter than female. He was not appealing to nature in the sense of zoology or botany. There are, of course, exceptions, just as the Spartans wore long hair, but tied it up for battle. Paul did not mean that the woman's hair was provided in place of a head covering and that she needed no veil (11:15). This would render most of the preceding discussion nonsensical. The long hair answers to the need for a covering.

11:17-34 The Order of the Lord's Supper

11:17-22 SPLIT BY THE MANIFESTATION OF PRIDE

The rest of 1 Corinthians 11 is devoted to the Corinthians' participation in the Lord's Supper (cf. Matt.

26:26-29; Luke 22:19). The believers would meet together "in fellowship meals celebrating the love of the Lord" (Jude 1:12), following which they would pass the bread and cup, observing the Lord's Supper (11:20). Unfortunately, many of the Corinthians were intent on getting filled up, overindulging in food and drink, rather than sharing in spiritual fellowship.

11:23-26 FOCUSED ON THE HISTORICAL EVENT

Paul emphasized the importance of remembrance (11:25-26), the essence of which is personal conformity to the body and blood of Christ. This relates to the problem in Corinth. They tended to misuse the body and avoid conformity to Christ and the shedding of his blood on the cross. The new covenant (11:25; Jer. 31:31-34; Ezek. 36:25-28; Heb. 8:6-13) amplifies and confirms the blessing promises of the Abrahamic covenant (Gen. 12:3). It also promises regeneration and the forgiveness of sin through faith in Christ and his sacrificial death for sins. The Lord's Supper is a dramatic sermon that looks back to Christ's death and forward to his return. In addition to remembrance, it calls all believers to actually participate in Christ's death and resurrection (11:26; cf. Matt. 26:29).

11:27-34 ACHIEVED BY PASSING THE TEST

Paul warned the Corinthians against profaning Christ's person and work by partaking in the Lord's Supper in an unworthy manner—with unconfessed sin (11:27). Christ was potently present to judge the snobbish and hasty eaters of the Lord's Table. Paul had other items to address, but he would wait to handle them in person (11:34; 4:18-21). But the next item could not wait—the issue of spiritual gifts was doing too much damage to the church and its witness to unbelievers.

12:1–14:40 The Order of Spiritual Gifts

Overview: First Corinthians 12 helped the Corinthians realize that different gifts did not mean a different spiritual source or a position of lesser worth (12:14, 19-20, 29-31). Diversity in function did not annul spiritual worth and unity. First Corinthians 12 teaches that all spiritual gifts are worthy of equal honor. Therefore, the Corinthians should not exalt one gift over another. First Corinthians 13 collects the majority of the Corinthians' problems under the solution of love. It shows the necessity of love operating behind each gift. First Corinthians 14 teaches that the application of love in the specific gift of tongues should always bring about edification.

To look at 1 Corinthians 12–14 another way, see the accompanying chart.

12:1-3 THE FOUNDATION

Paul asserted that there was a standard in ecstasy—the glory of God. The word Paul used for spiritual gifts in 12:1 is literally "spirituals," that is, "spiritual things or matters." In 12:4 he used the word "gifts," a term that is sometimes translated "grace." Spiritual gifts are God-given abilities for service. Every believer possesses a spiritual gift, but not all possess the same gift. Lists of spiritual gifts are found in Romans 12:6-8 and 1 Corinthians 12:8-10. These gifts are to be used in serving others (1 Pet. 4:10). The problem at Corinth was that certain spectacular gifts were emphasized and people were seeking the spectacular gifts for the sake of personal glory.

12:4-31 THE CONTROL AND VALUE OF THE GIFTS

Believers are not to exalt one gift and despise another. The divine source of all the gifts determines their equal worth. All gifts are from God and therefore may have differing functions, but all are of equal worth. There is a unity of origin behind the variety of effects. The purpose, not the source, of the gifts is emphasized: the common good (12:7). Note the use of this concept in 6:12; 7:35; 10:23; 10:33. A spiritual gift is the manifestation of the Spirit for the common good. Spiritual gifts are bestowed, not on the basis of merit, but according to God's sovereign purposes (12:11).

Paul used the human body to illustrate how the church was to function—with a unified diversity of gifts (12:12-26). This takes up the themes of 12:7 (common good) and 12:11 (as he wills). Paul wanted the Corinthians to accept the diversity of gifts given by God. The Corinthian problem was living with this diversity. They sought a false unity that was based on everyone seeking the same gift. Such a quest was not the basis for true unity.

Using the illustration of the human body, Paul described the relation of the gifted believers to one another and to Christ and explained how each was necessary and important. By the baptizing work of the Holy Spirit (12:13), believers were united with the universal body of Christ. The word "baptized" was used metaphorically here and carries the sense of "identification with." The Spirit is the criterion for identifying God's gifted people and for evaluating the worth of the gift. The worth is dictated by source, not function (12:15-26). Membership in God's community is not based on the type of gift he has given.

All members are equal (12:19-26). The nature of the church demands a variety that leads to interdependence and appreciation, not schism (cf. 12:14, 20). Some in Corinth had a foot-and-ear complex. They said or were told that they were not impor-

tant. Others had an eye-and-hand complex. They boasted that they did not need anyone else. But Paul sought to show them that they all needed each other and were given diverse gifts so that they could care for each other (12:25).

Paul applied the illustration of the body to the Corinthian church (12:27-31). In 12:29-30 Paul used a series of rhetorical questions to emphasize the point that God never intended to give the same gifts to all believers. Paul was showing that the function of the spiritual gifts was to express and be driven by the all-encompassing nature of love (12:31). In 1 Corinthians 13 Paul would present a way of life superior to a life spent in seeking and displaying spiritual gifts.

13:1-13 THE PRIORITY AND CONTROL OF LOVE

13:1-3 The Superiority of Love
Paul made it clear in these verses that the spiritual gifts were a means, not an end. The gifts were merely the means by which love was shown and edification brought about. Paul revealed the inadequacy of the gifts and knowledge without love, an idea already noted in 8:1. When angels speak in the Bible, they speak in the languages understood by their human hearers. Paul's distinction between tongues of humans and angels implied that the angels spoke another language among themselves. In Paul's day there was speculation about what languages the angels spoke among themselves and in God's presence. Paul covered the entire range of language, from the languages spoken in heaven to the languages of men, in order to stress that the form of any language without the content of edifying love is worthless.

13:4-7 Then Paul Shows the Way of Love in the World
This is a practical definition of love in the daily routine of life. Note how these descriptions relate to the Corinthians' problems: jealousy (3:3); bragging (4:7); arrogance (4:6); seeking their own (10:24); taking wrong into account (6:7); rejoicing in unrighteousness (5:2).

In the exercise of spiritual gifts, it is necessary to understand their place in relationship to God's priorities. Christ's new commandment (John 13:34-35) is to love one another. Christian love is preeminent, permanent, and most noble. The spiritual gifts are subordinate to love.

13:8-12 The Eternality of Love
In 13:10 Paul explained that the temporal gifts would pass away when the "end" came. There are

---

SUMMARY OF FIRST CORINTHIANS 12–14

Chapter 12   Diversity does not imply inferiority. Unity does not demand uniformity.
Chapter 13   Love is preeminent, to be practiced, and permanent.
Chapter 14   Therefore, gifts are to be used for other-oriented, not self-oriented, purposes.

three main views on the identity of the "end": (1) the complete canon of Scripture, (2) the second advent of Christ, and (3) the maturity of the body of Christ. The third approach is broad enough to embrace the relative maturity implied in the illustration of 13:11 as well as the absolute maturity that is depicted in 13:12. The church would be mature at the return of Christ (13:12) or at the point where continuing revelation would no longer be necessary (13:11). The spiritual gifts are for the present period of immaturity; the period before believers see God face to face.

14:1-19 THE VIRTUES OF PROPHECY
Paul cautioned the Corinthian believers not to exercise any gifts without love. He zeroed in on a specific gift, tongues.

14:1-2 The Exhortation
Paul discussed the regulation of the speaking gifts and set forth guidelines for the use of tongues. Tongues were given as a genuine spiritual gift on the Day of Pentecost (Acts 2:4) as a sign to the unbelieving Jews (14:22) and for the purpose of building up the body of Christ (12:7). Tongues were known languages, understood by men on earth (Acts 2:4, 6, 8, 11). Not everyone in the early church had this gift (12:30).

14:3-5 Two Contrasts Showing the Superiority of Prophecy
"Greater" (14:5) is determined by the ability of the gift to bring edification (14:3; cf. 12:31; 13:13; 14:39). Gifts (1 Cor. 12) plus love (1 Cor. 13) equal edification (1 Cor. 14).

14:6-8 Three Examples of Sounds That Profit
Edification determines the use and priority of the gift of tongues. Words spoken in public worship should always be clear so people will understand.

14:9-19 The Application
Paul desired that everyone listening understand what was spoken (14:9). This takes the thought back to 12:1-3. Knowing the content allows hearers to know if the utterance proclaims Jesus as Lord (12:3). Paul urged that zeal for gifts equal zeal for edification (14:12). The mind is the controlling factor (14:13). The context for Paul's remarks was the assembled church (14:19).

14:20-25 THE PURPOSE OF TONGUES
In 14:20-21 Paul called for mature thinking with regard to tongues and gave the criterion. Paul quoted

the Old Testament (Isa. 28:11) to show the result of hearing tongues spoken in a disorderly manner—unbelief. The sign was not the result of loving edification and would bar their access to the kingdom. Paul provided here the only direct statement regarding the specific purpose of the gift of tongues. Paul used the quote from Isaiah 28:11-12 to show that tongues are a sign of God's judgment. The tongues of Isaiah's day were the tongues of the Assyrians, which the people would hear if they rejected Isaiah's message. The Assyrian tongue was a sign of judgment to a generation of Israelites rejecting the word of God. So, Paul explained, tongues are a sign of coming judgment for rejecting Jesus the Messiah and the gospel of grace (cf. Matt. 23:37-38).

Paul recounted the results of mature thinking (14:22-25). The gift of tongues should be valued in proportion to the edification it brings to the church. Tongues spoken without interpretation are forbidden since they have a negative effect on the body of Christ and bring division and confusion without bringing edification.

14:26-40 THE ORDER FOR TONGUES AND PROPHECY
All that is done in worship is to be for edification (14:26). This is the theme of Paul's letter. There is an order given for speaking in tongues (14:27-28), for prophesying (14:29-33), and for women in the church (14:34-36). Compare 1 Corinthians 11:2-16 and 1 Timothy 2:11-15 with 1 Corinthians 14:34-35. Paul's reference to "the law" (14:34) probably reflects Numbers 30 (on vows), which sets forth the principle of subjection of wives and daughters.

15:1-58 THE IMPLICATIONS OF UNITY WITH CHRIST'S RESURRECTION
Overview: The structure of 1 Corinthians 15 surrounds a lively question and answer format. See the accompanying chart, "Questions and Answers about the Resurrection."

The ultimate problem in this passage centers on the question of whether believers need to be changed to enter the kingdom.

15:1-11 The Fact of the Resurrection of Christ
15:1-2 THEIR COMMITMENT TO THE MESSAGE OF THE GOSPEL
One of the problems the Corinthian church faced

QUESTIONS AND ANSWERS ABOUT THE RESURRECTION

15:1-11	Christian facts about the resurrection.
15:12-34	Resurrection of the dead is established. The problem is raised by a question (15:12).
15:35-49	The nature of the resurrected dead is defined. The problem is raised by a question (15:35).
15:50-58	The necessity of all being changed.

was that some were saying, "There will be no resurrection of the dead" (15:12). It has been suggested that these were Sadducees (Matt. 22:23-33), but this is unlikely since the Sadducees were associated with the Jerusalem temple, which was far from Corinth. They were probably Gentiles influenced by Greek philosophy. To the Greeks, immortality was a spiritual concept, and they had no place for the resurrection of the physical body. Since matter was considered essentially evil, release from a physical body was regarded as liberation, and a physical resurrection would amount to a return to bondage. Paul addressed these views through implications drawn from Christ's resurrection.

15:3-4 THE GOSPEL PRIORITIES

Paul put forward two foundations of the Christian faith (15:3-4). Each foundation was accompanied by two proofs—Scripture and a verifying historical fact. Paul set forth the two essential elements of the gospel: (1) the death of Christ for sins, authenticated by his burial, and (2) the resurrection of Christ on the third day, authenticated by his appearances.

15:4-11 THE REASON FOR EMPHASIZING THE RESURRECTION OF CHRIST

The resurrection of Christ was not an isolated event but the opening of the door to the resurrection of the dead in general. The appearance to James, Christ's half brother and a leader in the Jerusalem church (Acts 15:13), and to Paul, is recorded only here (15:7). James apparently did not come to faith until after the resurrection of Christ (cf. John 7:5; Acts 1:14). Paul viewed himself as one untimely born, prematurely converted in relationship to unbelieving Israel (1 Cor. 15:8; cf. Rom. 11:26). In 1 Corinthians 15:9-10 Paul corrected a possible attack on his past by providing the balancing view of God's grace.

15:12-34 The Fact of Bodily Resurrection

15:12-19 THE PROBLEM REVEALED BY A QUESTION

In this section Paul revealed the necessity of belief in the historical event of Jesus' resurrection. Paul's question implied that there was a close link between the resurrection of Christ and the salvation and resurrection of the believer. The resurrection of Christ was linked to the very fiber of faith (15:13-19). The false teaching of no resurrection could give hope only in this life (15:19).

15:20-28 THE RESURRECTION OF CHRIST INITIATES THE BELIEVER'S RESURRECTION

Paul explained the connection of Jesus' resurrection to the resurrection of believers by looking at Jesus' resurrection as the firstfruits of what was to come (15:20; cf. 16:15; Rom. 16:5). Paul drew upon a metaphor from Jewish worship, "the first crops" (Lev. 23:10-11). According to the law, the firstfruits

of the harvest were to be brought to the temple and offered to the Lord. The firstfruits implied that more of like kind was to follow. Because Christ is the firstfruits, his resurrection implies that the resurrection of believers will follow. Christ has initiated a new order. Now resurrection is as certain as death.

Paul put forward a certain order of exaltation (15:23-28). This explained the various stages experienced before final glorification. A problem was present as to how one could be saved but not yet glorified. Paul referred in 15:24 to the termination of the messianic kingdom when Christ will deliver his earthly rule up to God the Father who will rule for all eternity (see Ps. 110:1). It shows that the subjection of death is a process of time ("reign until," 15:25). When Christ rose to God's right hand, he began a period of time in which God would put "all his enemies under his feet" (15:25, 27, quoting Psalm 8:6). The revelation of that reign is rooted in Psalm 110:1, which notes that the reign lasts "until" Christ's enemies are subdued. Because the church is now in that period and is waiting until Christ finishes the battle with his enemies, believers are not to be surprised when they experience that intense warfare's conflicts and pain.

15:29-34 RESURRECTION AS A MOTIVE FOR SUFFERING

To deny the resurrection was to give a false power to death. Dying and rising again are inseparable concepts. What did Paul mean when he referred to "people being baptized for those who are dead" (15:29)? Some have taken Paul to refer to baptism "in behalf of" dead believers. That vicarious baptism did not necessarily have Paul's approval, but he referred to it to argue the logic of the resurrection. However, Christian baptism was normally administered without delay (cf. Acts 2:38; 16:31-33), and it is unlikely that Paul would have referred to such a practice without condemning it. It is probable that Paul was referring to believers who were being baptized "in place of" the dead—to fill up the ranks of those dying or being martyred. Baptism is being used figuratively to refer to what it signified—people coming to faith in Christ and being identified with his church on earth. The point is, the progress of such faith and church growth is to no avail if the dead be not raised.

In 1 Corinthians 15:32 Paul quoted Isaiah 23:13, a parody of the message of Solomon in Ecclesiastes 2:24. With no hope for the resurrection, life offers little more than eating and drinking.

15:35-49 The Nature of Bodily Resurrection

Paul continued to emphasize the believer's certain link to a glorified body. A question reveals a problem (15:35). There was a basic problem with the concept of raising a dead body (cf. Acts 17:32) or the possibility of flesh being glorified (15:36-49). Paul's distinctions between flesh and glory show that distinctions apply also to the next life as well as this one. The resurrection body is up to God, as are the gifts. Paul illustrated from nature that there are various kinds of bodies, each uniquely suited to the existence of the particular living thing. A body suited for life in the eternal kingdom must be different from a body of this present age. That follows the pattern of Adam and Christ (15:45). Adam, the first man, was a source of physical life for all men (Gen. 2:7). Christ, the last Adam, is a source of spiritual life for all who would believe.

15:50-53 Transformation in Place of Resurrection

Although not all will go through the process of death, all need to be changed. The parallel thoughts that stress the concept (15:50) answer more fully the question of 15:35, especially concerning what kind of body. If there were no resurrection, then the Corinthians were ready as they were to enter the kingdom.

A question also arose about believers who would be living at the last trumpet (15:52). The "last trumpet" does not correlate with the "seventh trumpet" of Revelation 11:15. Paul was drawing upon the practice of the Roman army to illustrate the removal of the church from the earth. The "first trumpet" signaled the troops to break camp. The "last trumpet" was the signal to begin to march (Josephus, *Jewish War*, 3.89-92). The "last trumpet" will signal the removal of the church to heaven.

15:54-58 Final Triumph in Immortality

Note the use of the Old Testament in 15:54-55. "Sting" means the potency of death. On 15:57, see Romans 7:24-25. Paul used Isaiah 25:8 and Hosea 13:14 to expound the believers' ultimate triumph over death.

Summary of 1 Corinthians 15: The resurrection of Jesus Christ is essential to the gospel (15:1-11). Take away Jesus' resurrection and you take away salvation (15:12-19). Add Jesus' resurrection and you add the believers' resurrection (15:20-28). Take away the resurrection and you take away the motivation to keep on in godly living (15:29-34). Add the resurrection and you add the believers' resurrection in glory (15:35-49). The new body is a necessity—all believers need to be changed (15:50-58).

16:1-9 THE JERUSALEM OFFERING
16:1-4 The Order for the Collection
The collection to which Paul referred (16:1) was for the believers in Jerusalem (Acts 24:17) who had endured famine and extensive persecution. Paul had instructed the churches of Galatia similarly on his first journey through that region (Gal. 2:10).

16:5-9 The New Order for Paul's Itinerary
The groundwork for some of the problems in 2 Corinthians resulted from this change of travel plans (2 Cor. 1:15-24). Paul's new plan was to travel from Ephesus across the Aegean to Macedonia, and then travel on to Corinth, where he planned to spend the winter. Paul planned to remain at Ephesus until Pentecost, when travel on the Mediterranean would be safe once again (see note on Acts 27:9).

16:10-24 EXAMPLES OF EXCELLENT LEADERS
16:10-12 The Itineraries of Timothy and Apollos
Although Paul encouraged Apollos (cf. Acts 18:24–19:1) to go to Corinth, the eloquent Alexandrian Jewish believer did not desire to do so at the time. Apollos's decision may have been based on the leadership problems in Corinth (1 Cor. 1:12).

16:13-18 Exhortations Regarding Traveling Leaders
Paul touched on the key elements mentioned here elsewhere in his letter: be alert (16:13), love (16:14), and be in subjection (16:15-18). Stephanas, Fortunatus, and Achaicus (16:17) may have brought Paul the letter from Corinth to which he was making this reply (7:1).

16:19-24 Final Greetings
The words "in Christian love" (16:20) was an expression of Christian love and fellowship, corresponding to today's handshake (cf. Rom. 16:16; 1 Pet. 5:14). The Aramaic phrase *Marana tha* is behind the words of 1 Corinthians 16:22, "Our Lord, come" (cf. Rev. 22:20). The personal handwritten note from Paul (16:21-24) again returns to the overall theme of the letter and Paul's life—love for the Lord.

2 CORINTHIANS

BASIC FACTS

HISTORICAL SETTING

See the Historical Setting for 1 Corinthians. Second Corinthians was written about six months after 1 Corinthians. Paul had made two previous visits to Corinth—his first visit and a second, follow-up visit to try to solve some painful problems. Paul's second visit is only briefly mentioned in 2 Corinthians 13:2-3, but that brief mention has great importance for understanding Paul's relationship with the Corinthians. The passage in 2 Corinthians 13:2-3 uncovers several problems Paul addressed. First, the problems were so bad that during Paul's second visit he had to threaten severe discipline. Second, Paul made that threat with his return in view, not as something he would do during that visit. With the problems still uncorrected by his second visit, Paul chose to leave and try to solve the problems from a distance. Third, the central problem related to Paul proving that Christ spoke through him (13:3). Some argued that Paul did not have divine approval and authority.

But Paul did not plan on staying away from Corinth forever. He sent Timothy and Erastus to Macedonia (Acts 19:22) and endured hard times in Asia (2 Cor. 1:8) before he left for Greece to hear the news from Corinth (Acts 20:1). Not finding Titus at Troas, Paul went to Macedonia (2 Cor. 2:12-13), finally finding Titus somewhere there (2 Cor. 7:6). Paul spent much time there exhorting believers (Acts 20:2), collecting the Macedonians' offering (2 Cor. 8:1), and writing 2 Corinthians.

During this time, Paul heard some good and bad news from Corinth through Titus and others (2 Cor. 10:2, 10; 11:4). Outsiders had come and worsened the problems (2:17–3:1; 11:4). They were promoting excessive punishment (2 Cor. 2:11) and were false apostles (2 Cor. 11:13-15, 18, 23) challenging Paul's adequacy (2 Cor. 12:14-18). They also used Paul's change of itinerary for another barrage of criticism, which took Paul seven chapters of 2 Corinthians to answer. Paul's motive in staying absent was to spare the Corinthians (2 Cor. 1:23), but his change of plans became fuel for his critics.

AUTHOR

The Pauline authorship of 2 Corinthians is clearly seen in the salutation (1:1) and throughout the epistle. The Pauline authorship of the letter is practically uncontested. See the Author section in 1 Corinthians for a discussion of the order of Paul's letters and visits to Corinth.

DATE

Second Corinthians was written during Paul's third missionary journey (A.D. 53–57), after his departure from Ephesus (Acts 20:1; 2 Cor. 2:13) for Troas and Macedonia. Paul spent some time in Macedonia (Acts 20:1-2) where he wrote 2 Corinthians, probably in the fall of A.D. 56. The letter was written a few months before Paul returned to Corinth (2 Cor. 12:14; 13:1) in the winter of A.D. 56/57.

PURPOSE

The letter of 2 Corinthians was designed to cement Paul's bond of love with the Corinthians after they had repented of their hard attitudes toward him and God. This was accomplished primarily by Paul's sharing of his pastoral calling under the new covenant and his pastoral love for God's people. But the letter also presented Paul's last words of warning to those who still persisted in doubting his authority. Even his warning, however, was couched in his strong desire to avoid fighting and return to Corinth in love and peace.

GEOGRAPHY AND ITS IMPORTANCE

The background for Paul's encouragement and warnings in 2 Corinthians was his past journey from Ephesus and his impending journey to Corinth. After Paul was asked to leave Ephesus, he went to Troas to find Titus and receive word about the situation in Corinth. Not finding Titus in Troas, Paul pushed on into Macedonia, where he finally found Titus, heard the good news about the Corinthian church, and wrote 2 Corinthians. The physical strains of the journey were used to support Paul's claims of deep concern and affection for the Corinthians. Paul let the Corinthians know that physical distance was acting as a buffer between them and his discipline. That distance was also proof that Paul wanted peace and was not rushing across the miles to fight and to bring harsh discipline.

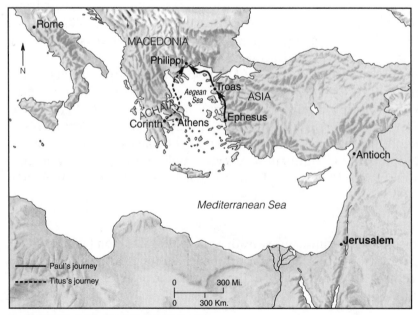

GUIDING CONCEPTS

PAST VICTORIES AND FUTURE VISIT

Two events cast their shadows over this letter: one past, one future. In both areas Paul presented a picture of true apostolic adequacy and pleaded for full reconciliation. Adequacy and reconciliation are the foundations of the letter.

Past victories

Paul used his travels with all their ups and downs to provide the framework for his correctives to the Corinthians' disdain for weakness and preoccupation with externals. Paul wrote 1 Corinthians from Ephesus, and it announced his intended visit to Macedonia and Corinth (1 Cor. 16:5-6). The Corinthians had caused Paul much pain and sorrow. He had written and visited the church there but still had made no major breakthrough.

Although Paul planned to stay in Ephesus until Pentecost (1 Cor. 16:8), he was forced to flee the city on account of the riot caused by the silversmiths (Acts 19:23-31). He proceeded north to Troas (2 Cor. 2:12-13) where he hoped to meet Titus (2:13), whom he had recently sent to Corinth to solve some serious problems (12:18).

Paul went on to Macedonia where his afflictions and troubles increased (7:5). While helping the Macedonian churches with their offering for the Jerusalem church, Paul was greatly encouraged by the arrival of Titus and his favorable report concerning the church at Corinth (7:6-7, 13-15). With this encouragement, Paul wrote 2 Corinthians.

Second Corinthians 1–7 focuses on the present implications of past problems and successes. Paul stayed away from Corinth for one reason. He wanted to spare them from his authority to severely discipline (1:23). In fact, he remained absent and wrote 2 Corinthians for the same reason—they were still not ready for him to come in peace. The theme of sparing concludes in 13:2, where Paul reasserted that when he came again, he would spare no one. Until then, he wanted the Corinthians to focus on the things of the heart, not of outward appearance (5:12). Paul used his journeys, with all their hopes, fears, and failures, to correct lingering problems in Corinth: problems that inhibited the Corinthians from giving him the full commendation he deserved and the full blessing available to them as believers.

Future visit

Second Corinthians 8–13 focuses on the problems relating to Paul's upcoming visit. Overall, 2 Corinthians is preparatory for Paul's visit. He was close to returning and wanted to prepare his way from one specific perspective; the perspective given in 12:19-21. Paul knew that the readers would think he was being defensive and self-protective (2 Cor. 12:19), but he was actually speaking for the sake of their "benefit." What may appear to be Paul protecting or defending himself is in reality his effort to build up his readers in order to avoid the conflicts and humiliation he experienced during his second visit (2 Cor. 12:20-21). Paul's point was that everything in the letter was for the readers' good, not for his own justification or defense. Paul rejected a defense rooted in self-exaltation and external accomplishments. Nevertheless, Paul spoke quite a bit about his personal adequacy, a touchy matter that could easily be misinterpreted as self-serving. Perhaps for that reason, he always carefully noted that he was not qualified in and of himself, but only as a result of receiving God's gifts (3:5; 4:7; 10:18; 12:9; 13:7). He spoke only to build up his readers and to glorify God, not himself (2:14; 4:5). This should be kept in mind throughout the letter.

The expectation of Paul's approaching (future) visit to Corinth—his third visit—pervades the entire letter. Second Corinthians 1–7 shows how Paul had to change his original plans (1:15, 23; 2:12-13; 7:5). Second Corinthians 8–9 speaks of Titus's work with the Corinthians to complete their offering for Jerusalem. Paul wanted the matter to be settled before he arrived (8:6; 9:4). Second Corinthians 10–13 focuses on Paul's upcoming arrival. He hoped for a solution to their problems, but he would not spare discipline for anyone who persisted in rebellion (10:2; 12:14, 20; 13:1-2, 10).

PROBLEMS

The major problem of the letter is summed up in 6:12—interpersonal friction bred by the Corinthians' hard hearts. The solution was to replace arrogance with weakness and see God's grace alone as the source of adequacy and sufficiency (12:9).

AUTHORITY

Some were not convinced that Paul was a qualified apostle (1 Cor. 9:1). He did not use his right to be paid for his services (1 Cor. 9:1, 6, 11-12, 18), and that opened him up to slander. Second Corinthians 10:8 and 13:10 begin and end with Paul's reply to slanders against his status as an apostle and his honesty in money matters. His authority was based on God's grace, not his own personal talents and status (2 Cor. 12:9).

TEST

The Corinthians tested Paul's divine authority. By questioning Paul's God-given authority, the Corinthians opened themselves up to false apostles (11:12-15). They wanted proof that Christ was speaking through Paul (13:3). One Corinthian test of proper lifestyle involved accepting their financial support (11:7). They expected formal letters of commendation (3:1). They wrongly assumed that God's apostles would have smooth, trouble-free lives (4:7-10). None of this was true for Paul.

Some accused him of walking according to the flesh (1:17; 10:2) and of being full of crafty schemes to get their money (4:2; 12:16). Paul offered proof for these tests of authority, but not the kind his readers expected. The true test was graded by the Lord, not the people (10:18). In the end, Paul commanded them to test themselves (13:5).

COMMENDATION

Second Corinthians almost has a monopoly on Paul's use of the word "commendation." The perspective on commendation that pervades the book is in 12:11. But the readers were not mature enough to recognize God's blessing on Paul (cf. 3:1; 4:2; 10:12, 18). The Corinthians boasted in appearance rather than in the issues of the heart (5:12). Paul had tried to correct this wrong boasting (2 Cor. 1:14, 21; 7:4, 14; 5:12; 8:24; 9:2; cf. also 1 Cor. 1:29, 31; 3:21; 4:7; 5:6). Paul boasted only in relation to the work God was doing through him (2 Cor. 10:1, 13, 15-17; 11:10, 12).

WEAKNESS

Above all, Paul's greatest commendation came through boasting in his weakness (cf. 11:16-18, 30 with 12:1, 5-6, 9). The Corinthians were infatuated with a superficial and worldly outlook (5:12; 6:14–7:1). But weakness was the way to true adequacy. Weakness was a topic in 1 Corinthians 8:7, 9-12; 9:22. The weakness of fear and trembling before God was commendable (2 Cor. 7:15; Eph. 6:5; Phil. 2:12). In 2 Corinthians weakness was also a means of glorifying God (10:1; 11:21, 30; 12:5, 9-10).

COMFORT

Second Corinthians 1 and 7 focus on how the Corinthians' repentance gave Paul great comfort. Comfort comes from the Corinthians' earnestness for Paul and forms the basis for the continued ministry of the offering (2 Cor. 8–9) and the last-minute discipline for those who still needed it (2 Cor. 10–13).

BIBLE-WIDE CONCEPTS

DIVINE PRESENCE, PURITY, AND SONSHIP

Paul believed that all the promises of God throughout the Old Testament were fulfilled in Christ. In him all the promises of God are answered with "Amen" (1:20). These Old Testament promises involved the presence of God for salvation and the indwelling Spirit. Paul specifically mentioned three Old Testament promises that would be central to solving the Corinthians' problems (6:14–7:1). They were (1) God's presence (6:16, quoting Lev. 26:12), (2) the exodus from the Babylonian captivity (6:17, quoting Isa. 52:11), and (3) becoming sons and daughters of God (6:18, quoting 2 Sam. 7:14). Paul understood that the great Old Testament events of God's dwelling among Israel in the tabernacle, redeeming them out of captivity, and adopting the line of David as his special sons were fulfilled in Christ and extremely relevant to the needs of Christ's church.

Paul continued to apply the Old Testament patterns of how God dealt with his redeemed community when he applied the equality God showed in providing manna in the wilderness to the equality to be shown through the Jerusalem offering (8:15, quoting Exod. 16:18).

PAUL AS SERVANT OF THE NEW COVENANT

Paul saw himself as a servant of the new covenant in Christ (2 Cor. 3:6, 14). Jeremiah had predicted a coming new covenant, and Jesus had proclaimed its inauguration (Jer. 33:31-33; Luke 22:20). Paul showed the implications of that new covenant for understanding true, but hidden, glory and how people could reject such a glorious covenant. The Old Testament background of the new covenant was crucial for accepting the genuine version of Christianity in the face of false apostles.

THE RIGHTEOUS SUFFERER

Throughout Scripture, people such as Abel, Joseph, David, and Job suffer unjustly—usually because of the fact that they were righteous. Jesus the righteous sufferer was the one through whom God expressed his favor and accomplished redemption. The pattern that Jesus set for suffering unjustly was uncompromisingly followed by Paul and urged upon his readers (1:5; 4:6-10). It was that very pattern of humiliation and righteous suffering that was the mark of Christ and the Christian—a mark totally avoided and shunned by the false apostles who attacked the reputation and authority of Paul.

NEEDS MET BY SECOND CORINTHIANS

Fleshly desires for money and status were the continual problems Paul faced at Corinth. The Corinthians cloaked their status-seeking in the guise of wisdom and maturity but actually opened themselves to immoral relations, a disregard for God's words through Paul, and ultimately a rejection of the reconciling power of the cross of Christ. Some of the Corinthians unfairly attacked Paul's free ministry as a cover for second-rate qualifications and a sneaky way to get money by means of his associates. Second Corinthians presents a moving example of a spiritual response to difficulties by means of a fusion of praise and correction. This letter to the Corinthians attacks the attitude that takes pride in appearances rather than in purity of heart. Paul sought to overcome the attitude that looks only on the outside for commendation and criticism (5:12). This attack answers a number of questions and meets many needs.

- How can suffering and low status reflect the glory of God?
- Is Christianity not supposed to bring exaltation and superiority?
- How can believers judge what makes a minister adequate?
- How can believers learn to view people in Christ rather than according to their external demeanor and abilities?
- What are the best motivations for giving money to Christian needs?
- What is the place and purpose of boasting in personal blessings given by God?
- How do personal weaknesses relate to God's great power and adequacy?

Christians face a great paradox. On the one hand, they are greatly gifted and exalted in Christ. On the other hand, they are not to exalt themselves over others, and, in comparison to God's holy adequacy, they soon sense their own great weaknesses. The desire of believers to boast pridefully directly conflicts with the Spirit's desire that they be humble and admit their weaknesses. Second Corinthians should help believers avoid either covering their weaknesses with prideful boasting or becoming so depressed by their weaknesses that they cannot enjoy their great blessings in Christ. Second Corinthians provides the balance between pride and depression by answering the questions above— questions that have been asked by Christians for two thousand years.

OUTLINE OF SECOND CORINTHIANS

I. A TEST PASSED: CONFIDENCE FOR CONTINUED OBEDIENCE (1:1–7:16)
  A. Mutual Trust Reaffirmed: A First Defense (1:1–2:17)
  B. Adequacy in Ministry Commended: A Second Defense (3:1–5:19)
  C. Exhortations to Reconciliation (5:20–7:16)

II. A TEST FOR THE SINCERITY OF LOVE: GIVING FROM THE HEART (8:1–9:15)
  A. Motivation by Example (8:1-7)
  B. Exhortation to Sincere Love (8:8-15)
  C. Commendation of the Administrators (8:16–9:5)
  D. Motivation by Principle (9:6-15)

III. TRUE VERSUS FOOLISH COMMENDATION: THE REAL SOURCE OF STRENGTH (10:1–13:14)
  A. Warning to Recognize Paul's Authority (10:1-18)
  B. A Demonstration of Paul's Authority (11:1–12:13)
  C. A Plea to Avoid Pending Judgment (12:14–13:14)

SECOND CORINTHIANS NOTES

1:1–7:16 A TEST PASSED: CONFIDENCE FOR CONTINUED OBEDIENCE

Overview: This section contains three mentions of Paul's travels from Ephesus to Macedonia with two corrective sections layered in between. See the chart below for the structure of 2 Corinthians 1–7.

The central problem in the first seven chapters is the Corinthians' restraint in their own affections (6:12). Paul offered the solution in 5:17, 6:13, and 7:1-2. The overall perspective is given in 5:12. The root of the problem was in their worldly affections, which had closed their hearts toward God and Paul. Paul's solution encouraged the readers to make room for God in their hearts (6:13; 7:2). Although Paul claimed great glory for his ministry (2 Cor. 3), the treasure was in earthen vessels (2 Cor. 4). Therefore, true glory could easily be missed if one focused on the container rather than its contents. This is why Paul only related to realities of people's hearts in Christ (5:12, 16).

As Paul drove his point home, he exposed the core of the problem. It was a problem of the heart (6:12) and could only be remedied by perfecting holiness in the fear of God (7:1). The entire discussion concerning Paul's ministry in weakness and glory must not be seen as a defensive reaction but as a loving correction (12:19).

1:1–2:17 Mutual Trust Reaffirmed: A First Defense

1:1-2 GREETING

"Greece" (1:1) refers to "Achaia," which was the Roman province south of Macedonia comprising most of central and southern Greece. Timothy (1:1) was Paul's associate during his ministry in Corinth (Acts 18:5) and was with him when he wrote this letter.

1:3-11 MUTUALITY IN SUFFERING AND COMFORT

1:3-5 Individual Enablement
The Lord Jesus Christ (1:3) is the medium for comfort and compassion. Paul also became an expression of God's words of comfort. His comfort had the purpose of being shared with others (1:4). Second Corinthians 1:5 restates and emphasizes the balance between sufferings and comfort. Paul

reflected on his recent difficulties in Ephesus (cf. Acts 19:23-41) and on how God had been his comfort. He recognized that God had given him a ministry of giving comfort just as he had received comfort from God.

1:6-7 Mutual Fellowship
Paul stressed that even his sufferings were designed to give benefit to the Corinthians. He was building to 2 Corinthians 7 and the full expression of fellowship. His sufferings did not point to weakness and lack of qualification or love—just the opposite. On "patiently endure" (1:6), see 1 Corinthians 10:13. The point is that comfort works simultaneously with suffering.

1:8-11 Sharing the Sufferings
Here Paul is sharing his experiences of suffering to give a lesson in encouragement. The sharing of Paul's weaknesses was not idle storytelling. It was the vehicle for sharing comfort. Ignorance is the block to sharing comfort. To hide his weaknesses from the Corinthians would only pander to those who thought weakness equaled disqualification. Part of the affliction Paul had experienced in Asia is recounted in Acts 19:23-41. The focus is on God's purpose of comfort, not the trouble itself. This was a lesson needed by the readers. Another description of God follows (1:10). Paul's appreciation for the effectiveness of intercessory prayer (1:11) is evidenced also in Romans 15:30-31; Philippians 1:9; and Colossians 4:12.

1:12-22 PAUL'S GOOD INTENTIONS FOR HIS FIRST TRAVEL PLANS

From this point on the purpose expressed in 2 Corinthians 5:12 controlled Paul's thoughts as he corrected the Corinthians' attitude of pride in appearances rather than purity of heart. He supplied internal standards of commendation and adequacy rather than the externals in which his opponents boasted.

1:12-14 Paul's Confidence: Clear Conscience
Paul's letters were as honest as his life. Paul desired a mutual appreciation with the Corinthians in the Lord (1:14). He wanted them to join him in boasting in the works accomplished by the Lord, rather

---

SUMMARY OF SECOND CORINTHIANS 1–7

1:8-11	Itinerary: Affliction in Asia
1:9–2:11	A Corrected Perspective on Paul's Change of Itinerary
2:12-13	Itinerary: Troas to Macedonia
2:14–7:4	A Corrected Perspective on Paul's Adequacy
7:5-16	Itinerary: Arrival in Macedonia and Titus's Good News

than quibbling about the external accomplishments of various people.

1:15-16 Paul's Change in Travel Plans Is Described
While Paul was still in Ephesus, he had written to Corinth and said that he would come soon "if the Lord will let me" (1 Cor. 4:19). Paul's original travel plans are noted in 2 Corinthians 1:15-16. His plan was to visit Corinth, travel north to Macedonia to gather the collection for the Jerusalem church, and then return to Corinth again to get help for his travel back to Jerusalem. But his plans had changed.

His change from those plans is recorded in 1 Corinthians 16:5-7. Instead of traveling first to Corinth, Paul had gone directly to Macedonia (2 Cor. 2:12-13; Acts 20:1). Now Paul had to defend himself against accusations of insincerity and vacillation.

1:17-22 The Charge and Its Implications Are Described
Paul responded to criticisms about his change in itinerary not defensively, but theologically. His defense was God's consistency—which Paul followed rigorously—based on God's faithfulness in the gospel and on the foundation of the character of Christ. Essential to the thrust of the letter are the establishment of the believers by God and the internal pledge of the Spirit in the heart (1:21-22).

Paul asserted that he followed a consistent God, and therefore his own actions, done only at the Holy Spirit's leading, were consistent. It is clear that Paul saw a potential link between the charge that his actions were fickle with the more devastating charge that the gospel he preached was not consistent. One so-called charge of fickleness had great implications from Paul's perspective. Why would this one change in plans tend to void his credibility? Because some people were just waiting for an excuse to discredit Paul (cf. 2 Cor. 10–13). "Silas" (1:19) was a variant for the name "Silvanus" (cf. Acts 17:1-9; 1 Thess. 1:1; 2 Thess. 1:1).

1:23–2:11 THE REASON FOR HIS CHANGE OF PLANS
1:23-24 Paul's Desire to Spare the Corinthians
The link to the previous section is mutual pride and joy (1:24) in the day of the Lord (cf. 1:14). If joy is to be the future's aim, it must also be the present's reality. This explains Paul's change of plans. He would remain absent as long as possible to ensure mutual joy when present. Because of the highly sensitive situation in Corinth, Paul had to be defensive and careful.

Paul stayed away to spare them grief (1:23) and to share joy later (1:24). This is key to Paul's ministry. He saw his readers as objects of joy (cf. John 17:13; 1 John 1:4). Paul had made a second visit to Corinth (2 Cor. 13:2), and it had been a sorrowful experience. Now Paul wanted to spare the Corinthi-

ans and himself another such sorrowful experience (cf. 2:1-2).

2:1-4 The Reversed Situation
Instead of another visit, Paul had written a stern letter to correct the believers. This letter may have been lost. Some hold that these verses refer to 1 Corinthians, which certainly contains subject matter that caused Paul grief and sorrow. Paul desired to show love, not judgment (1 Cor. 4:21; 12:20–13:1).

2:5-7 The Goal of Discipline Is Restoration
Paul's last words to the Corinthians, probably in 1 Corinthians, were words of sorrow and correction. One problem that may have given rise to Paul's severe letter was the failure of the church to deal with the gross immorality Paul had rebuked in 1 Corinthians 5:1-13. Now they had responded, and the sinner had been disciplined. Yet they had failed to forgive and restore the repentant offender. They were to avoid sorrow that overwhelmed the benefits of the discipline (2 Cor. 2:5-7; cf. 5:4 and 1 Cor. 15:54 for the Greek word translated "swallowed up").

2:8-11 Avoid Deception by Satan
Excessive discipline is one of Satan's schemes. Paul exhorted the Corinthians to restore the brother to fellowship and thus prevent Satan from using the situation to his advantage.

2:12-17 THE CONTINUED CONCERN OF PAUL
2:12-13 Resumption of Itinerary
Paul mentioned his lack of rest in spirit to reinforce his genuine concern for the Corinthians. After leaving Ephesus, Paul traveled north to Troas, a port city on the Aegean (2:12). There he waited for Titus whom he had sent to Corinth (7:6-7). When Titus failed to arrive, Paul departed for Macedonia where the two were reunited (7:5-7).

2:14-17 A Digression to 7:4
From 2:14 to 7:4 Paul launched out into a discussion that contrasts true Christian adequacy of the heart and the superficial adequacy of appearances (5:12). Paul used a number of concepts to illustrate this contrast: heart versus appearance, spirit versus stone, new covenant versus old covenant. Paul's point in 2:14-17 is that victory in his ministry did not equal news of success from Corinth. In earthly victory or defeat, Paul's success was gauged by his manifestation of Christ, not human response or acceptance.

The concepts of 2:15-16 lead to the broader concept of adequacy. Paul showed his sincere love toward the Corinthians even in his seemingly erratic itinerary. In 2 Corinthians 2:17 Paul both defended himself and attacked the "many" false apostles in Corinth (11:12-15). Second Corinthians 3:1–7:4 reveals the genuine quality of Paul's ministry. As Paul corrected the misunderstandings created by his change in itinerary, he provided tremendous insight into his own life, ministry, and motivation.

3:1–5:19 Adequacy in Ministry Commended: A Second Defense

Overview: The section of 3:1–5:19 presents the heart of Paul's answer to the question, "Who is adequate for such a task?" (2:16). Note the threefold mention of adequacy in 3:5-6. The contrasts of 2 Corinthians 3 are rooted in the life-or-death reactions to his ministry (2:16). Paul used such responses to reach his goal in 5:12, to assure the Corinthians of his love, and to expose true glory through the Spirit. Second Corinthians 3–4 show the surpassing greatness of Paul's ministry, though it operated in "perishable containers" (4:7).

3:1-11 NEW COVENANT ADEQUACY

The truths of this section are built upon a number of different concepts: (1) letters of commendation, (2) tablets of law, (3) old and new covenants, and (4) worthiness. The questioning of Paul's credentials always led him back to fundamentals in his own defense. Three interconnected lines demonstrate the superiority of the new covenant over the old: (1) the superior nature of the new covenant, (2) the resultant superior new covenant ministry, and (3) the superior benefit for those who receive that ministry.

In view are two kinds of ministry, not just the contents of the two covenants. Paul did not call the Mosaic covenant itself "condemnation" and "death" (3:7-9; cf. also Rom. 7:12, 14, 16). He kept the content of the covenant distinct from the concept of "written laws" (3:6). Here his focus is on how God's word was communicated—in the old covenant by the "written laws" written on stone, in the new covenant by the Spirit's writing on the heart. The new covenant's ministry far surpasses the great, though fading, ministry of the old covenant. It produces a change of heart as well as changes in external behavior.

Some itinerant teachers were circulating among the churches, bearing letters of commendation from other congregations (3:1-3). Paul wrote that his life and ministry spoke for themselves. He needed no such commendations. The Corinthian converts were his "letters of recomendation."

Note the contrasts of stone/flesh, ink/Spirit, old covenant/new covenant. Paul's ministry was one of the Spirit and the greater glory of the new covenant (Jer. 31:34; Heb. 8:6-13). The radiance of the old was fading (3:12-18).

3:12–4:6 NEW COVENANT INTIMACY

3:12-18 The Removal of the Old Covenant Veil

Paul did not not need letters of commendation because of his firsthand intimacy and its ensuing

boldness (3:12) and stability (4:1). Paul's boldness in speech is elaborated in 3:12-18.

Paul compared his own speaking with the speaking of Moses (3:12-13). But the comparison is really between two ministries, not just two ways of speaking. Skip from 3:13 to 3:18 in order to see that 3:14-17 is an explanatory digression. The "but" of 3:14 is then put in perspective. The continual use of the veil blinds, deafens, and dulls the minds of the people to God's glory in Christ (see 2:11; 4:4; Rom. 11:7, 25). The Corinthians should have realized the temporary nature of the old covenant's glory.

In 3:13 Paul explained the purpose of Moses' veil—to conceal the reality that the glory was fading (cf. Exod. 34:33-35). The "veil" (3:13-18) also had been used to interrupt the people's vision of God's glory. Moses put his veil on after he had spoken to the people of Israel (see Exod. 34:29-35). But in the new covenant, the veil is no longer needed (3:16). The glory is given through the Spirit, hidden but powerful (2 Cor. 3:3, 6, 8, 16-18; cf. 1 Cor. 15:45). The Spirit is the new means of covenant ministry. Moses beheld God's glory and his face was changed temporarily (2 Cor. 3:18; cf. 3:13). New covenant believers behold the glory of the Lord, though imperfectly, and are supernaturally transformed into the same image of glory. The idea of reflection (3:18) best fits the context of Moses' reflection of glory and Paul's reflection of the glory in perishable containers (cf. 4:7).

4:1-6 Stability in Heart

Take note of 4:1, 7, 16. The subject of stability was Paul's launching pad for the mention of despair and restlessness in spirit (2:13). Since Paul was adequate in Christ, rejection and persecution did not cause him to lose heart. Surpassing glory (3:1-11) and veiled hearts (3:12-18) explain the context and problems surrounding new covenant glory. In 4:6 Paul was loosely quoting from Genesis 1:3. The God who created physical light can illumine the minds of his spiritually blinded creatures. What then could be the reason that not all acknowledged and understood Paul's great adequacy?

4:7-15 NEW COVENANT SUFFERING

The answer to the final question in the previous section is: because the great glory of new covenant adequacy is within the earthen vessels of human frailty. This contrast between glory and weakness finds its source in a lesson Paul previously learned from God, which he waited until the end of the letter to recount (12:7-9). Weakness allows the glory of God to be revealed. To point to difficult physical circumstances was not to point to spiritual inner despair or inferiority (4:8-12). Both the psalmist and Paul spoke of their trials in order to glorify God (4:13, quoting Ps. 116:10). Paul poured out his heart with reference to his suffering for the sake of Christ. He shared a divine perspective on suffering that has been an encouragement to many in the straits of affliction.

4:16–5:10 NEW COVENANT IMMORTALITY
4:16-18 The Promise of Renewal and Eternal Glory
Why did Paul not lose heart? First, he knew the difference between the problems of an earthen vessel and the strength found through the glory within (4:1-15). Second, he looked forward to an eternal state in which a body of glory would replace the mortal body of weakness (4:16–5:10). This is building to his point in 5:12 that commendation must be made on heart realities, not external abilities or personality. Paul found strength of heart because of the promise of his future eternal state (4:16-18).

5:1-5 Physical Death Is Not a Reason to Lose Heart
Second Corinthians 5:1-10 shows that one's attitude toward the future life is fundamental to one's ethical conduct on earth. "For" (5:1) is a link back to 4:18 (cf. 4:1, 16 and the use of "And so" and "That is why"). Paul provided one example of the eternal things that are not seen (5:1-5). Again, Paul confirmed that his groanings were not because he was weak or unqualified but because he longed for the eternal and perfect body (5:4, 6; see the same groaning in Rom. 8:23).

Because of the burdens of life lived in a physical body, the believer longs, not to be bodiless ("naked" or "unclothed"), but to live in a resurrected, glorified body. The "guarantee" (5:5) is a down payment that renders further or final payments obligatory. The Holy Spirit is God's guarantee or pledge of the believer's future and complete redemption. Paul explained that even the threat of physical death is no reason to lose heart.

5:6-10 Continued Good Courage
Excavations in ancient Corinth have uncovered a raised platform known as the *bema* ("judgment") seat (5:10). It was there that Paul was accused before Gallio (A.D. 51–65), proconsul of Achaia (Acts 18:12). Paul used this terminology and imagery to describe the future judgment of the works of believers (cf. 1 Cor. 3:13-15).

5:11-19 ADEQUACY AS AN OPPORTUNITY FOR GENUINE PRIDE
The purpose of 2 Corinthians 1–7, if not of the entire letter, is revealed in 5:12. At this point Paul gave an answer to pride in appearances (5:11-15). The struggle was to communicate the hidden message, the veiled glory (3:14-15), the treasure in earthen vessels (4:6-7). Although not manifest to humans, Paul's adequacy and approval were manifest to the only one who counted—God. The fear of the Lord is a major theme of Old Testament Wisdom Literature (5:11; cf. Prov. 1:7). The fear of the Lord is expressed, not so much in trembling

knees, but in obeying God (Eccles. 12:13) and departing from evil (Job 28:28). The contrasts in 2 Corinthians 5:13 will take full expression in 2 Corinthians 10–12, where Paul will play the fool to teach true wisdom.

Paul continued his discourse on adequacy in Christ by putting forth his means of regarding people (5:16-19). The key "heart" versus "appearance" distinction (5:12) was used to regard people in light of God's grace in Christ, not according to the flesh (5:16-17). Paul no longer judged from a perspective that limited itself to what the eyes could see and the mind deduce. Paul saw all men according to their potential as having "new life" in Christ. To reconcile (5:18) implies "to change." Reconciliation by the death of Christ means that humanity's state of alienation from God is changed by the death of Christ (Rom. 5:11) so that all are now able to be saved.

5:20–7:16 Exhortations to Reconciliation
5:20–6:10 GODWARD RECONCILIATION
5:20-21 A Return to 5:14-15
From the world's perspective, the paradox of Christian glory is that Christ's sin-bearing suffering accomplished righteousness for the believer. Second Corinthians 5:21 declares the essence of Christ's work. The sinless Savior has taken mankind's sins in order that believers might share in God's righteousness.

6:1-10 Specific Application to the Corinthians
To receive grace in vain (6:1) is similar to the concept of emptying the cross of its power (1 Cor. 1:17). It would thwart the full intended purpose of God's redemption in Christ—in this case, renouncing God's ways of true glory through weakness and suffering. In 2 Corinthians 6:2 Paul quoted the Septuagint translation of Isaiah 49:8 to provide scriptural support for the exhortation of 6:1. Isaiah promised that God would hear and help his people. Paul interpreted and applied the promise to his own day. Isaiah's words to Israel become God's words to the church. Note the context of Isaiah's frustration in ministering to Israel (Isa. 49:4).

The descriptions of Paul's life ("that no one will be hindered," 6:3; "show that we are true ministers," 6:4; "live close to death," 6:9; "give spiritual riches to others," 6:10; "have everything," 6:10) all hinge on the "we beg" of 6:1 and show the manner of the exhortation. Paul provided very personal insight into his own experiences in his service for Christ. All that Paul said and did took into account the readers' best interests.

6:11–7:16 MANWARD RECONCILIATION
6:11-13 Paul's Yearning for Reconciliation with the Corinthians
Paul's reconciliation with the Corinthians was based on purity from sin (6:11–7:4). Paul provided

an example of restraint in affection (cf. 6:12). He made a plea for full fellowship (6:11-13) based on his character of good faith (6:1-10). The real problem in Paul's relationship with the Corinthians lay, not with Paul's attitude or qualifications, but with the Corinthians' own affections—their inner attitudes toward Paul (6:12).

6:14–7:1 Avoiding Being Yoked with Unbelievers
The unbelievers in view (6:14) were the false apostles who were trying to take over the affections of the Corinthian believers (11:3-4, 12-15, 18-21). Much of the trouble at Corinth stemmed from the believers' association with impure believers and unbelievers. The five questions of 6:14-16 all expected a negative answer and were intended to stress the incompatibility of Christianity with heathenism. The Devil (6:15; "Beliar," NIV) is a transliterated Hebrew term that means "worthlessness." In later Jewish writings the term became a proper name for Satan.

In 6:16 Paul quoted Leviticus 26:11-12 which gave God's promise to move into a new stage of intimacy with his people as he came to dwell in his tabernacle. See Leviticus 26:1 for the need to separate from idolatry and Leviticus 26:13 for the concept of yoke (cf. also Deut. 22:10; Lev. 19:19 for unequal yokes).

In 6:17 Paul quoted Isaiah 52:11, which was a call to Israel to come out from the impurity of the Babylonian captivity and reenter the holiness of life in the Promised Land. It was a second exodus from bondage into life centered around the presence of God in the temple.

Paul's third quotation (6:18) was from 2 Samuel 7:14 which originally was God's promise to take the sons of David and give them a special Father-son relationship with God as they served as kings of Israel. Paul broadened out the thought by the addition of "and daughters" to show that what was originally a promise to the male Davidic line of kings had, in Christ, become a reality of divine relationship for male and female believers.

Paul claimed that the above Old Testament quotations were promises for the Christian as well (7:1). In Christ, God's presence in the temple (6:16), his call for purity after release from bondage (6:17), and his relationship as Father to his children (6:18) are all realities (cf. 1:20). As God was present with Israel in the Old Testament tabernacle, so the presence of God through the Spirit is seen in the church. As God brought Israel out from bondage in Babylon, God would also bring about the greater exodus from sin and death into purity through Christ's sacrificial death. As God had chosen to bless the royal line of David, God would also view believers as royal sons and daughters. This grand understanding of the Old Testament

promises as they relate to New Testament believers illustrates the truth that in Christ every believer is a "new person" with a "new life" (5:16-17). God had taken what was old and made it new in Christ.

7:2-16 Joy over Repentance and Fellowship
Paul's primary focus in 2 Corinthians 1–7 was the need to correct the Corinthians' alignment with the worldly ways taught by the false apostles. But these chapters were written with Paul's full knowledge of the readers' repentance. Next, he spoke specifically of that good news. He made a confident plea for reconciliation (7:2-4) based on the Corinthians' proper repentance from sin (7:5-16).

Paul recounted his separation from and search for Titus (7:5-12; cf. 2:12) and resumed the discussion regarding his travel and ministry itinerary (cf. 2:13). Having left Ephesus, Paul traveled north to Troas, crossed the Aegean to Macedonia, and looked for Titus whom he had earlier sent to Corinth (7:5-7). From Titus Paul received the encouraging report about the Corinthians. Proper sorrow brought repentance without regret (7:8-10) that was centered on God, not self.

The letter that caused the Corinthians sorrow (7:8) is believed by most scholars to be a letter written after 1 Corinthians and delivered by Titus. Others believe it refers to 1 Corinthians. Although the letter brought sorrow, there was genuine repentance on the part of the Corinthians (7:9-10) and other beneficial results (7:11-12).

Paul revealed the results of proper sorrow (7:11-13). Why was Paul comforted? Because the Corinthians' sorrow at his rebuke had brought about repentance and obedience to God. The one "who did the wrong" (7:12) referred to the immoral man who was disciplined by the church (cf. 1 Cor. 5:1; 2 Cor. 2:6). Because of the Corinthians' repentance, Paul had full confidence in them (7:13-16). Titus had a very positive ministry with the Corinthians, and they grew in mutual affection for one another.

8:1–9:15 A TEST FOR THE SINCERITY OF LOVE: GIVING FROM THE HEART
Overview: Paul waited until this point to mention the offering because he could not speak about money when he knew some of his readers, though obedient in one area, were still yoked with unbelievers in their hearts. Not only was he being condemned by the false apostles for having a supposedly erratic and uncaring ministry, he was also being criticized for being dishonest. In 2 Corinthians 1–7 Paul addressed these and other issues in a caring and reconciling way. He tried to do the near impossible: to combine his personal defense and correctives for their worldliness with praise for their innocence in the matter of immorality (7:11).

The Corinthian problems with the Jerusalem offering concerned equality in giving. They asked why they should have to give up their money for others. What if they should need that money later on? Paul answered their question by discussing God's long-standing emphasis on equality dating back to how manna was divided up for the Israelites in the wilderness (8:10-15).

The second problem concerned covetousness (9:6-14). Paul's readers needed to learn how to give freely from the heart, trusting God to provide for their own needs. The third problem dealt with the trustworthiness of the bearers of the offering (8:16-24). This section represents part of the entire epistle's concern for financial matters (cf. 2:17; 4:2; 11:7-12; 12:13-18).

Paul clearly presented the problem (8:11), the solution (8:15; 9:9), and the purpose of his discussion (8:8). In 2 Corinthians 8–9 Paul commended those who would deliver the collection for the poor in Jerusalem. Charges of greed and thievery against Paul had blocked the progress of the collection (1:17; 2:17; 4:2; 10:2; 11:7; 12:13-18). Paul tried to correct two problems: (1) the question of equality (8:13-15) and (2) the question of giving freely from the heart (9:7-9). He wanted the offering to issue from sincere love (8:8), not from guilt or pride.

8:1-7 Motivation by Example
Second Corinthians 8:1-6 was written as one sentence in the original Greek. Paul spoke of the offering here, just after his warm-hearted commendation of their repentance and just before he made a final attack on the false apostles (2 Cor. 10-13). The offering was a duty (Rom. 15:25-27; cf. Gal. 2:10, "the poor"). Paul had instructed the Corinthians concerning giving to the needs of the saints (1 Cor. 16:1-4; cf. Acts 11:29; Gal. 2:10). Now he encouraged them to complete the preparations for their gift to the Jerusalem church. Their positive response to this exhortation is evidenced in Romans 15:25-26.

The churches of Macedonia (2 Cor. 8:1), the province of northern Greece, included Philippi, Thessalonica, and Berea. These churches were cited as examples in sacrificial giving (cf. Phil. 4:15-18). Paul's concern was that the work on the collection for the Jerusalem church (2 Cor. 8:6), a project begun a year earlier (8:10), be brought to completion.

8:8-15 Exhortation to Sincere Love
This exhortation to sincere love was based on a divine example (8:8-11). For an application of Christ's selfless example in 8:9, see Paul's experience in 6:10. The Corinthians were to continue that line of enriching and sacrificial giving.

Sincere love was also based on human equality (8:12-15). Paul's quotation of Exodus 16:18 showed that God always intended for needs to be met on the basis of relative need. The one who needs much should receive much (cf. 1 Cor. 16:2). When God gave the Israelites manna in the wilderness, those who gathered more than others were not able to save it, and those who gathered less had a sufficient amount. Equality was a sign of divine intention and provision. Paul's use of the term "equality" (8:13) did not mean that everyone had to have the same amount. Rather, everyone's basic needs were to be met; those in need were to be helped by those with plenty.

8:16–9:5 Commendation of the Administrators
The motivation of Titus, 8:16-23, came from God putting earnestness within him. The Macedonians' motivation to give their offering also came from God (8:3). Paul continued to support his views with Old Testament Scripture (8:21, quoting Prov. 3:4). The "brother" (8:18) is not identified, although it has been suggested that he was perhaps Luke or Trophimus.

Paul's purpose for sending the Christian brothers (9:1-5) was that he desired the churches to see his reason for boasting (8:24). Macedonia (9:2) was the Roman province of northern Greece, and Achaia was the province of southern Greece. Paul encouraged giving that was unaffected by covetousness (9:5), that is, given with a view to helping others, not motivated by the thanks or recognition one might receive.

9:6-15 Motivation by Principle
Overview: Paul set forth four principles of Christian giving: the principles of harvest (9:6), willingness (9:7), divine grace (9:8-10), and thanksgiving (9:11-15).

9:6 GIVING IS SOWING
In giving, the harvest is always in view. The farmer does not plant seed and then walk away, saying, "Well, I'll never see that again." Although it is out of sight and given away to the ground, he knows he will someday see the harvest.

9:7 GIVING IS FROM THE HEART, NOT THE PURSE
Note the quotation (9:7) from Proverbs 22:9. The first place to look when giving is how much honest willingness is in the heart, not how much money is in the wallet.

9:8-15 GIVING ENRICHES FOR FURTHER GIVING
Paul used Psalm 112:9 (9:9) and the quotation and broader context of Isaiah 55:10 (9:10) to show that the giver shall be provided a means of giving. Paul also connected the thoughts of Hosea 10:12. The farming images of sowing and harvesting illustrate the fact that if righteousness is sown, a great harvest of righteousness will be given in return. Thus, it conveys the realities of moral living after repentance.

10:1–13:14 TRUE VERSUS FOOLISH COMMENDATION: THE REAL SOURCE OF STRENGTH

Overview: Second Corinthians 10–13 successfully holds two seemingly contradictory attitudes: edification and sarcasm. Paul's sarcastic attack on his opponents is clear throughout (10:1; 11:4, 8, 11, 19-21; 12:13, 16). But that strong offense is set within a context of the meekness and gentleness of Christ (10:1). The harsh and critical content must be read within the intentions of humble and temperate emotion. If Paul's goal had been to put down the Corinthians and justify himself, his sarcasm could not have been called meek and gentle. But because his motives were for the upbuilding of the Corinthians (12:19), his words, though strong, were intended to nurture, not destroy.

The content of 12:19 is behind all of these words. Although some of Paul's words could be mistaken as defensive backlashes, the clear framework of "gentleness" (10:1) and "benefit" (12:19; "upbuilding," NASB; "edifying," KJV) alerts the reader to the true heart and point of this section: edification.

Paul put forward the problem (10:2), the solution (12:9), and the purpose of his discussion (12:19). In this section he commended himself as an eminent apostle. However, his boasting in weakness was quite different from that of his opponents. He corrected their assertion that he lived by the standards of this world (10:2).

Also, he pointed out that his free service of ministry should not have branded him as inferior or as a person cunningly trying to cheat them. The Corinthians needed their appearance-oriented evaluation of Paul turned around (12:11). They would only be able to follow the correct pattern of godliness after they understood what made a person commendable before God (11:3).

Second Corinthians 12:19-21 is the core of this section. Paul defended himself against attacks by certain opponents and false apostles (11:3). The Corinthians had been taken in by these criticisms. As a result, their evaluation of the apostle was appearance-oriented (10:7). They were focused on external matters rather than internal issues. Paul had to defend himself against these criticisms to prevent his ministry and teaching from being undermined (13:3).

10:1-18 Warning to Recognize Paul's Authority

10:1-6 REQUEST FOR COMPLETE OBEDIENCE

Paul desired no punishment for the readers (10:1-2), but he would punish those who needed it (10:3-6). On 10:5, see 1 Corinthians 1:17 concerning the opposition to the knowledge of God. This shows how the spiritual person wages war.

10:7-11 REMINDER OF HIS SUFFICIENT AUTHORITY

Apparently the false apostles had spread doubt about whether Paul belonged to Christ (2 Cor. 10:7, 11; 13:5). Again, Paul corrected the outward-oriented judgments (10:7; cf. 5:12). Paul boasted (10:8) because of the extravagant boasting of his opponents. He did not like to boast (cf. 10:13, 15; 12:1) but was forced to do so because of the criticism he had received. His boasts were not about what he had done, but what God had done. In the apocryphal Acts of Paul and Thecla, Paul was described as, "baldheaded, bow-legged, strongly built, a man small in size, with meeting eyebrows, with a rather large nose, full of grace, for at times he looked like a man and at times he had the face of an angel." It is believed by some scholars that this plain and unflattering account embodies a very early tradition.

10:12-18 REMINDER OF THE PROPER SPHERE OF COMMENDATION

All of Paul's boasting and commendation were based on what the Lord gave him. His opponents commended themselves (10:12-18). Paul quoted Jeremiah 9:24 to reinforce this idea (10:17; cf. 1 Cor. 1:31). The words of 2 Corinthians 10:17-18 should have been enough, but the situation in Corinth was out of hand. Paul had to continue. The subject returns to that of 3:1 and 5:12.

11:1–12:13 A Demonstration of Paul's Authority

11:1-6 THE PROBLEM PRECIPITATING PAUL'S FOOLISHNESS

Paul's "talking like a fool" (11:1) grows out of 10:12; to commend oneself is to be without understanding, a fool. Because Paul was going to commend himself, he called this foolishness. When compared with 10:8, this forms a startling conclusion. Paul would not be put to shame if he boasted because he would speak the truth. But even though he would speak truth, it would still be foolishness. Paul was saying that what makes boasting foolish is not the truth or falsity of the boast but the self-serving attitude motivating it. The goal of Paul's "foolishness" was to bring about edification (12:19).

Paul began by expressing his wish that his readers would put up with his foolishness (11:1). He asked that they bear with him (11:1, 4, 19-20) and made it crystal clear that he was acting the fool. The foolishness to which Paul referred was that of boasting. Self-commendation is foolish, but Paul engaged in it briefly to make a point.

Paul continued his argument by exposing and illustrating the problem (11:2-4). In 2 Corinthians 11–12 Paul was waging spiritual warfare according to his definition in 10:5. Paul was seeking to demolish the falsehoods that had taken root in the

Corinthian congregation (cf. 2:11; 3:14; 4:4; 10:5; 11:3). For the deception of Eve (11:3), see Genesis 3:4, 13 and 1 Timothy 2:14. Paul gave a reasoned evaluation of himself in 11:5-6. In this case, the message was more important than the medium.

11:7-15 THE ISSUE OF "FREE" MINISTRY
Note the reason why Paul had to be "foolish": accusations by false apostles and the acceptance of false apostles by the Corinthians. He raised a question relative to his being unskilled in speech (11:7). Paul's critics rudely implied that the Corinthians got what they paid for. But Paul did not work for free—it had cost someone besides the Corinthians. Paul "robbed" (11:8) other churches in the sense that he received gifts from them in order that he might not be a financial burden on the church at Corinth. Macedonia (11:9) is the northern province of Greece. Paul served the Corinthians freely out of love (11:10-11) in order to cut off opportunity from his enemies (11:12-15). They wanted to be regarded like Paul, but Satan was behind their deception.

11:16-29 FOOLISHNESS DISPLAYED
11:16-21 Sarcastic Opening
Paul continued his attack on his enemies by using sharp sarcasm (11:16-21). He spoke to the wise and unwise (11:16) and recounted his experiences of personal suffering as evidence of his apostolic authority (cf. John 15:18-25). He disassociated his boasting from anything God might do (11:17). He was making it clear that he was acting the fool (cf. 11:16-18, 21, 23, 30, "let me"; 12:1, 6, 11). Boasting according to flesh was well received in Corinth (11:18-21).

11:22-29 Foolish Boasting
Paul's pedigree (11:22) made it likely that his opponents were Judaizers, probably with a Jewish ethnic background. Paul continued by recounting his past performance (11:23-29). The thirty-nine lashes (11:24) referred to beatings Paul had received at the hands of the Jewish religious leaders. The law called for forty lashes (Deut. 25:1-3), but only thirty-nine were administered to avoid the possibility of exceeding the limit by miscounting. Paul had been shipwrecked (11:25) three times before his shipwreck on the island of Malta en route to Rome (Acts 27:40-44).

11:30-33 THE FOCUS OF PAUL'S BOASTING
Paul's boasting was in his very weakness (11:30-31). His glory was in earthen vessels (4:7, "perishable containers") in order to glorify God. He gave another example of his weakness in the account of his escape from Damascus (11:32-33). Paul's experience in Damascus is recorded in Acts 9:24-25. The term "governor" (11:32), meaning "ruler of a people," was the title of a leader of a town or coun-

try. This ruler was a subordinate of the Arabian king Aretas IV (9 B.C.–A.D. 40), the father-in-law of Herod Antipas. During the years A.D. 37–40 Aretas was given power to appoint an ethnarch by the emperors Caligula and Claudius.

12:1-10 FURTHER FOOLISHNESS DISPLAYED
12:1-6 Paul's Visions and Revelations
Paul continued his "foolish" boasting by recounting the visions and revelations he had received (12:1). These revelations did not illustrate Paul's weakness (11:30), but they set the context for the weakness of his "thorn in [his] flesh" (12:7). The point was that even though Paul had extremely privileged knowledge, he did not flaunt it. His visions had occurred fourteen years earlier, and yet Paul had kept them secret. The visions (12:2) Paul recalled took place around A.D. 42 (A.D. 56 minus 14 years) while Paul was still in Tarsus before Barnabas brought him to Antioch (Acts 11:25-26). The "third heaven" (12:2) and "paradise" (12:4; Luke 23:43; Rev. 2:7) refer to the place where God dwells. Paul's credentials were based on firsthand witness, not past glories (12:6).

12:7-10 Under God's Direction
Paul's sphere of boasting was in his weakness (12:5-10; cf. 5:12; 11:16-33). No one knows for sure what Paul's "thorn in the flesh" (12:7) was, but it has been speculated that it was some kind of eye disease (cf. Gal. 4:13-15; 6:11).

The focus in these verses is on Paul's weakness. He had asked God for deliverance from a specific weakness three times. Finally, a direct word from God showed Paul that he was, in reality, trying to throw away God's gift that kept his fleshly nature from boasting of his privileged position. Paul may have been caught up to heaven, but during his time of struggle with his "thorn," God had kept him in the dark. His affliction had to meet grace in order to bring about its God-intended result.

Paul thought God's grace would include the removal of the suffering. But God's grace was related to his sufficiency at all times, not to the presence or absence of suffering. Paul wanted to increase his power by the removal of the "thorn." God showed him where his true sufficiency was. Power came through seeing weakness as the very vehicle for manifesting the power of Christ, not through gradually eliminating mortal weaknesses. Weaknesses show the inadequacy of the vessel and affirm the ever-present grace and power of the Spirit within. This had been Paul's argument throughout the letter (1:9; 4:7, 11, 16-18).

12:11-13 THE NEEDLESSNESS OF THE DISPLAY
The Corinthians should have commended Paul, but instead they condemned him and forced him to defend himself. Miracles (12:12) had the specific purpose, in biblical times, of authenticating

messengers and their message. Paul's miracles authenticated his apostleship. Paul had given patient exhortations throughout 2 Corinthians 1–7. In 11:1–12:10 he gave a most intimate look into his private reasons for boasting in weakness. Here, his sarcasm (12:13) is still set in the context of patient and careful exhortation.

12:14–13:14 A Plea to Avoid Pending Judgment

12:14-18 PAUL'S CONTINUED DESIRE FOR TRUE MINISTRY

In 12:15-18 two elements introduce the conclusion of the letter: (1) Paul was about to make his third visit, and (2) he sought the Corinthians, not their money. Titus had gone to Corinth in Paul's behalf (12:18; cf. 2 Cor. 7:6, 13; 8:6). The slander against Paul in this section was that he used his friends to take people's money while he himself came off as self-sacrificing and innocent.

12:19-21 THE PURPOSE OF THE LETTER: EDIFICATION, NOT DEFENSE

Paul's purpose was edification in God's sight, not self-seeking defense (cf. 2:17). The Corinthians thought Paul was on the defensive, trying to vindicate himself from a wrong that he had committed. But he had done no wrong.

The concepts of defense and commendation (3:1; 4:2; 5:12; 6:4; 7:11; 10:11-12) are closely related. In 12:19 Paul clarified the difference between how the letter might be perceived (defensive) and how it was actually designed (for edification). The letter's many defensive and sarcastic sounding passages just show how extreme the situation was. Paul had to go to extreme lengths to get through to the Corinthians.

13:1-10 THIRD-TIME WARNINGS

13:1-3 Warning

All the sarcasm and foolish boasting of 2 Corinthians 10–12 comes to an end here. Paul's third visit

would bring talking to an end. In 2 Corinthians 1–12 Paul hoped that he would be able to come and find obedience. In 2 Corinthians 13 he vowed he would come and punish disobedience. Paul said he could come with punishment or with scolding (1 Cor. 4:21). Now was the time to see which one he would use. In 2 Corinthians 13:1 Paul quoted from Deuteronomy 19:15, which requires two or three witnesses to secure a conviction against a defendant (cf. Matt. 18:16; 1 Tim. 5:19). The issue to be proved was not the Corinthians' sins but Paul's authority in Christ (2 Cor. 13:3). His third visit would bring proof that he was God's appointed apostle.

13:4 Explanations

Paul presents a perfect model of ministry in 13:4. This verse gives a perfect outline of the letter's major themes of God's power becoming evident and active despite the weakness of its vessels.

13:5-10 Warning and Explanation

Paul turned the tables on his critics (cf. 10:7, 11). He instructed the Corinthians to examine their character and conduct to see if they were truly Christian (cf. Titus 1:16). Paul again asserted his desire for the Corinthians' approval even if he could not win it (2 Cor. 13:7-10).

13:11-14 FINAL GOOD WISHES

"Christian love" (13:12; cf. 1 Cor. 16:20; Rom. 16:16; 1 Thess. 5:26; "holy kiss," NIV) was a culturally accepted Christian greeting and corresponds in Western culture to the handshake. In this particular case it symbolized the reconciliation and peace needed in the Corinthian situation. Paul concluded the epistle with a great trinitarian benediction (13:14), emphasizing the grace that finds its source in the Son, the love manifested by the Father, and the fellowship established and sustained by the Holy Spirit. This letter contains Paul's longest benediction.

GALATIANS

BASIC FACTS

HISTORICAL SETTING

The term "Galatia" (1:2) can be understood in two different ways. One refers to the area inhabited by the Galatian ethnic group in northern Asia Minor—a place visited by Paul, if at all, on his second or third expeditions. A second usage refers to a political division of central and southern Asia Minor that became part of the Roman Empire in 25 B.C. Most scholars favor the view that this letter was addressed to the churches in the southern cities of this region—cities visited by Paul on his first and second missionary expeditions.

AUTHOR

The Pauline authorship of Galatians is confirmed by internal and external evidence. The author is named in 1:1 and 5:2. The early church fathers, from Clement of Rome on, affirm the Pauline authorship and authenticity of Galatians.

DATE

Scholars are divided as to the date and location of the original recipients of this letter. Some believe that Paul addressed the epistle to Galatia proper, which he did not personally visit until his second journey on his way to Troas. If this was the case, the letter would have been written after his second missionary journey any time from A.D. 53 to 56. Others hold that Paul addressed the letter to the churches of southern Galatia, which he had established on his first missionary journey. Identifying the recipients thus would put the writing of the letter at an earlier date, around A.D. 49.

The key issue in dating Galatians has to do with how Paul used the term "Galatia," whether he referred to Galatia as the official Roman province or as the more general pre-Roman territory founded by the Gauls. The provincial use of the term "Galatia" would direct the letter to the churches Paul founded on his first missionary journey. The territorial use of the name would date the letter later, with its addressees being the churches Paul founded during his second and third missionary journeys. Paul's writings show the use of both regional (Rom. 15:31; 2 Cor.1:16; Gal. 1:17, 21; 1 Thess. 2:14) and provincial names (1 Cor. 16:1, 5, 15, 19). No completely conclusive argument for Paul's use of Galatia as the provincial or territorial name has been made, though more recent scholarship has favored the southern Galatian view, and thus the earlier date. The decision to adopt either view does not materially alter the interpretation or application of the letter to the Galatians.

PURPOSE

The letter to the Galatians was designed to correct legalistic approaches to Christianity by demonstrating the priority of righteousness by faith over the works of the law. Paul made his argument by showing the priority of the promises to Abraham over the covenant with Moses. The goal of both the Abrahamic promise and Mosaic obedience was fulfilled in the righteousness brought through faith in Jesus Christ.

GEOGRAPHY AND ITS IMPORTANCE

Cities in Galatia

Paul passed through Galatia on all three of his missionary journeys. The four cities of Antioch, Iconium, Lystra, and Derbe received several visits from Paul during these journeys. Although it is not known exactly which of these churches were being addressed in Paul's letter to the Galatians, the letter makes it clear that the readers shared a common problem of falling to the pressures of legalism.

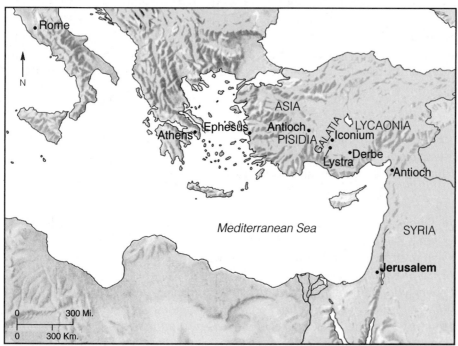

Copyright © 1986, 1988 by Tyndale House Publishers, Inc.

GUIDING CONCEPTS

The major problem presented in the letter to the Galatians was the challenge to Paul's gospel that believers are justified by faith in Christ alone, apart from the works of the law. Among the Galatian believers were false teachers who insisted on a Judaistic model for Christianity (Gal. 1:7; 4:17; 5:10).

The practical result of these doctrinal debates was an atmosphere of critical fighting (5:25), snobbish dismissal rather than restoration of sinning believers (6:1, 3), and a general tendency to give up and lose heart (6:9). The Galatian squabbles were not simply doctrinal niceties. They were damaging the fiber of the believers' compassion and perseverance.

BIBLE-WIDE CONCEPTS

Paul viewed Christians as the true Israel of God (6:16). This concept sums up all the Old Testament connections made in the letter. Paul contrasted the work of the Holy Spirit in the church with the work of the law under Moses (3:3, 5, 14; 4:6, 29, 5:16-18, 22-25). The Spirit is the Christian's link to the family of God (4:6). The sonship found in the Spirit was the link to Paul's discussion of the relationship between Abraham and the law (3:14-29).

The historical conflict between Isaac and Ishmael foreshadowed the conflict between the children of Spirit and promise (Christians) and the children of flesh (the hostile Jews, cf. 4:29). But that conflict also had a personal counterpart within each Christian in the form of hostility between flesh and Spirit (5:15-17).

Thus Paul's words reflect the line of conflict and hostility predicted by God in Genesis 3:15, where enmity between the seed of the woman and the seed of the serpent would wind through history. That enmity first took form with the murder of Abel by Cain and will take its final form when Jesus returns and casts Satan into the lake of fire. In between, all the conflicts between good and evil, flesh and Spirit, whether on the national or personal level, reflect the ongoing conflict between Satan and Jesus.

NEEDS MET BY GALATIANS

The question concerning who had true authority from God pressed hard against the Galatians. They admired both Paul and the Jewish leaders who were also Paul's critics. To complicate matters, both Paul and his critics claimed the authority of God and the Scriptures. But the issue for the Galatians was much deeper than a theological squabble between Christian leaders. Paul's critics claimed that the Law of Moses could save people from hell. But to imply that the law brought salvation denied the power of what God had done through Christ's death and resurrection. The legalistic stance of Paul's opponents also missed the point of God's work through Abraham. More personally, legalism left the Galatians in bondage to the fear of failure. It bound them to trying to save themselves through obedience rather than allowing them to relax and enjoy the freedom of fully won forgiveness in Christ. The central issue in this letter had to do with how much obedience was needed to merit salvation. The structure and content of Galatians show that Paul intended to answer questions like the following for his readers.

- How could God throw out the Mosaic law and replace it with a gospel of grace?
- If God's grace through Christ was sufficient for salvation, what was the purpose of the law?
- Does a Christian not have to obey the laws of Moses in order to be saved?
- How do faith in Christ and lawkeeping go together?

Christians must struggle on two fronts. They must admit their tendencies to sin and thankfully acknowledge God's complete and rich forgiveness by faith in Christ alone. But they also need to evidence their saving faith with good actions and deeds. While doing this, it is very easy to fall into replacing honest acts of faith with works of law that are subtly motivated by the desire to gain favor with God. There is a conscious effort at times for believers to earn at least a piece of their own salvation by doing good and piling up merit. The struggle between humbly receiving and legalistically meriting God's grace can be complicated by God continually asking his people throughout Scripture to obey him. What are believers to make of God's continual commands to keep his laws. What does he have in mind? Must believers keep laws to gain his favor? Or do they keep his commands because they already have the full measure of his favor?

Galatians opens the way to understanding how faith and lawkeeping go together. It shows believers how faith alone realizes the complete riches of God's grace in their lives. And, once believers are inside of God's grace, they fulfill the law's demands by reliance on the Spirit and through love (5:13-14). Galatians shows that obedience is given to God, not in order to merit his grace, but because by faith it has already been obtained. Galatians provides an important balance. It emphasizes the proper place of faith for salvation and the necessity of loving obedience to God as a response to that grace.

OUTLINE OF GALATIANS

I. INTRODUCTION: AUTHOR AND AUTHORITY (1:1-9)
   A. Greeting (1:1-5)
   B. The Problem of Another Gospel (1:6-9)

II. AUTHOR AND HIS AUTHORITATIVE MESSAGE (1:10–6:10)
   A. The Authority from a Revelation-Gospel (1:10–2:21)
   B. The Faith of Abraham: Primacy and Permanence (3:1–4:7)
   C. Personal Application and Exhortation (4:8-20)
   D. Freedom from the Yoke of Slavery (4:21–6:10)

III. THE FINAL EXPOSURE OF THE JUDAIZERS (6:11-18)
   A. Insights into Enemies (6:11-16)
   B. Final Warning and Benediction (6:17-18)

GALATIANS NOTES

1:1-9 INTRODUCTION: AUTHOR AND AUTHORITY

1:1-5 Greeting

1:1-2 COMMON IDENTIFICATION

Paul began this letter with an unusual description of himself. He described how he was commissioned as an apostle—not through men, but through Jesus and God. This immediately addressed one of the problems at hand. The Galatians apparently wondered if Paul was a divinely authorized apostle, or if he preached a merely human message. The term "apostle" (1:1) means "special representative." An apostle was commissioned and sent with authority to carry on a

task. Paul emphasized that his apostleship did not originate from man, but from God. Along with these words defending his authority, Paul also stressed God's great resurrection power through Christ that was available for the believer's benefit (1:1). The "Christians" with Paul (1:2) would have included Barnabas, Paul's fellow missionary to Galatia, and other believers at Antioch (Acts 13:1).

1:3-5 BENEDICTION

Jesus Christ was characterized as the one who gave himself for all believers. He brought deliverance from this present evil age, and all that he did was done according to the will of God his Father. This set the foundation for Paul's arguments in this letter: (1) Paul was divinely authorized; (2) his message embodied the pure will of God; and (3) he spoke his message in an age of evil conflict.

1:6-9 The Problem of Another Gospel

Overview: This letter does not have the usual section of thanksgiving for the readers' spiritual growth. Instead, it plunges directly into the problem.

1:6-7 DESERTION FROM GOD

Paul used the word "astonished" (1:6) in an ironic way. The "soon" (1:6) could be paraphrased "easily." Paul was not referring to the time since their conversion. He was amazed that they could slip so quickly and easily into the lies of another gospel. They had deserted a person, not a doctrine ("from God," 1:6). The issue was personal. They had left the one who called them. Paul had described the context of their calling in 1:3-5. The Corinthians faced a similar temptation to follow another Jesus and a different gospel (1:6; cf. 2 Cor. 11:4). The words "turning away," or "deserting," is used elsewhere to describe a military revolt. This desertion was in process; it was not yet an accomplished fact. The two results of the problem among the Galatians were: (1) the believers were being troubled and (2) the true gospel was being distorted. These are two areas that Paul developed throughout the letter.

1:8-9 CURSING THE PREACHER OF ANOTHER GOSPEL

The source of the other gospel does not matter (1:8). Paul presented a hypothetical situation. The phrase "forever cursed" (lit., "anathema") means "devoted to destruction" (cf. Josh. 6:17; 7:12). Paul was praying divine judgment on those who would pervert the truth. The repetition (1:9) was for emphasis. Paul had already given a previous warning about some who would present a different gospel. Paul's strong language shows the severity of the problem.

1:10–6:10 AUTHOR AND HIS AUTHORITATIVE MESSAGE

Overview: In this section Paul discussed why the gospel of Christ did not need the addition of the Mosaic law for salvation. Paul built his argument on (1) his own firsthand revelation from God (1:1–2:21); (2) the priority of the promises to Abraham by faith over those to Moses through law (3:1-29); (3) the priority of Abrahamic sonship over the law (4:1–5:15); and (4) the priority of the way of the Spirit over the way of the law (5:16–6:10). Clearly, Paul's opponents in Galatia were urging Christians to conform to the Mosaic law; a situation seen also in Acts 15:1.

1:10–2:21 The Authority from a Revelation-Gospel

1:10 NOT FOR PLEASING PEOPLE

Paul's critics accused him of being out to gain human approval at any cost. But Paul was out to please God, not other people.

1:11-17 NOT FOR SUPPLEMENT BY HUMANS

The gospel Paul preached came by revelation from God (1:11-12), not from men. That revelation began with the vision of Christ near Damascus. Paul asserted that he received his gospel, not by fallible man, but as direct revelation from the risen Christ (Acts 9:1-9; 2 Cor. 12:1-11). Jesus Christ was both the source and subject of the revelation.

Paul's mention that he stayed away from Jerusalem reinforced his lack of need to supplement his revelation with insight from the leaders in Jerusalem (1:13-17). His gospel needed no human confirmation. The "traditions" (1:14) mentioned by Paul referred to the *Halachah,* the Jewish oral law that applied the written law to new circumstances. These laws were collected and now appear in the Jewish Talmud. God had set Paul apart for his ministry from birth (1:15). See Isaiah 49:1 and Jeremiah 1:5 for the same sense of calling.

After his conversion on the Damascus road (Acts 9:1-7), Paul did not immediately return to Jerusalem but traveled first to Arabia and then back to Damascus (Gal. 1:17). The visit to Arabia was not mentioned in Acts but probably took place between Acts 9:21 and 9:22. The term "Arabia" (1:17) probably refers to the kingdom of the Nabateans, a territory of Transjordan extending south from Damascus to the northwestern part of Arabia. During his time alone in Arabia, Paul was able to reorient his theology and understanding of the Old Testament Scriptures in light of his encounter with the risen Christ.

1:18–2:10 NEEDS NO ALTERATION BY HUMANS

1:18-24 A First Short and Polite Meeting in Jerusalem
This account of Paul's travels reinforced the fact that he had authority independent of the Jerusalem leaders. This is in contrast with Paul's usual claim to close ties with Jerusalem (Rom. 15:25-27). He stayed away from Jerusalem for three years following his conversion (1:18). After his three-year absence, he returned once again to Jerusalem and had a brief visit with Peter and James, the half brother of Jesus. This visit to Jerusalem is dated around A.D. 37.

After this brief visit, he was still basically unknown in the Judean churches. But he brought glory to God anyway (1:24). The point was that Paul had virtually no contact with the Jerusalem leaders concerning the content or authority of his gospel message. After his brief visit in Jerusalem, Paul traveled north through Syria and Cilicia to Tarsus, his hometown, where he remained until his call to Antioch (Acts 11:25-26).

2:1-10 A Second Visit to Jerusalem:
No Change Required
Paul was in no rush to return to Jerusalem. He waited fourteen years and then returned to

Jerusalem to talk with the leaders regarding what he "had been preaching to the Gentiles" (2:1-2).

This section of Galatians contains one of the historical puzzles of Paul's life. Was Paul recounting his famine relief visit to Jerusalem (Acts 11:29-30) or his experience at the Jerusalem Council (Acts 15)? Those who believe that Paul was writing believers in northern Galatia understand this as a reference to the Jerusalem Council. Those who believe that Paul was writing to believers in southern Galatia view this as a reference to the earlier famine relief visit.

There are at least two convincing evidences for the latter view: (1) Paul mentioned that it was "because God revealed" to him that he should go to Jerusalem. This appears to refer to Agabus's vision of the forthcoming famine (Acts 11:28-30). (2) Had the Jerusalem Council already met, Paul would certainly have appealed to its decision as a strong argument against those Judaizers who were advocating circumcision and the keeping of Jewish traditions. The point of Galatians 2:1-10 is that Paul had contact with the Jerusalem church, but it added nothing to his message. The Jerusalem church simply recognized and approved Paul's ministry to the Gentiles.

The "fourteen years" (2:1) date from Paul's conversion (A.D. 35) until the autumn of A.D. 47. Actually, there are twelve complete years and a fraction of a year at the beginning and end of this period. The Jews regarded any portion of a time period as equivalent with the whole (see note on Matt. 12:39-40). What "God revealed" (2:2) referred to Agabus's prophecy of a coming world famine (cf. Acts 11:27-29).

Paul recalled the case of Titus as a test case for Gentile salvation apart from circumcision (2:3). He was building evidence for his claim that salvation was gained through faith in Christ alone, not by following the law. He showed how this true gospel was also upheld by the leaders in Jerusalem.

Paul also reported how the gospel had been distorted by false brothers (2:4-5). The implication was that the criticisms Paul faced in Jerusalem should not be entertained as possibly coming from God. The same false thoughts were apparently being pawned off as gospel in Galatian churches.

The gospel was not supplemented by the authorities or "pillars" of the church (2:6-10). The same God effectually worked in both Paul and Peter (2:8). Peter, James, and John recognized the God-given ministry of Paul and Barnabas (2:9). James was not the apostle (cf. Acts 12:2), but the half brother of the Lord and one of the leaders in the Jerusalem church (1:19).

2:11-21 PETER IS OPPOSED BY PAUL IN ANTIOCH
Having established that he was independent of Peter and the rest of the Jerusalem leaders, Paul

showed his equality to them in God's power and authority. At this point, he recalled a time in which Peter failed to uphold the true gospel. First, Paul continued to demonstrate that he was not out to please men, not even the great Peter. Second, Peter was claimed as the great champion of Jewish Christianity (2:8). Paul showed that even Peter did not maintain strict orthodox separation from the Gentiles. When Peter did separate from the Gentiles, Paul corrected his hypocrisy (2:13-14). Paul viewed Peter's actions as inconsistent. Paul opposed Peter (2:11) because Peter twisted the implications of the gospel (2:14, "not following the truth"). The men from James were Jewish Christians from Jerusalem. Peter's hypocrisy had public consequences, and therefore the issue needed public clarification. Although Peter had not been teaching that Gentiles should adopt Jewish customs, his actions had implied that they should.

There was no other mention in the New Testament of Peter's visit to Antioch and his clash there with Paul. This probably took place after the famine relief visit (Acts 11:29-30; Gal. 2:1-10) and either before or just after Paul's first missionary journey (Acts 13:1; 14:26-28).

How were the Jews saved (2:15-16)? Paul referred to the Gentiles (from a Jewish perspective) as sinners, that is, unbelievers. Galatians 2:16 contains the key thought of this letter. Notice how many times Paul asserts here that a man is not justified (that is, declared righteous) by the works of the law. But Paul did not totally reject the law (2:17-19). He stated strongly that freedom from the law does not promote sin—"Of course not!" (2:17). Paul explains 2:17 in 2:18. Those who had died to the law were not to try to live again to the law (cf. Rom. 6:1, 15).

Paul then made a transition to his debate in Galatians 3 (2:20-21). This debate concerned the relationship between faith and the law. The phrase "crucified with Christ" (2:19) means identified with Christ in his death (Rom. 6:3-8) and thus freed from the authority and penalty of the law. The fact of the resurrection implies a new life—a life in perfect righteousness. Since this is the case, Paul could not see why one would return to trying to keep the law to gain righteousness that is already achieved in Christ. Paul was alert to anything that might void the necessity that Christ die on the cross. To nullify the grace of God was to assert that Christ died needlessly (see Gal. 5:11; 6:12-14).

3:1–4:7 The Faith of Abraham: Primacy and Permanence
3:1-5 FAITH AS THE SOURCE OF SALVATION
Paul cried out to his addressees by name (3:1). Paul suggested that the Galatians had been put under an "evil spell." He forced the image of Christ on the

cross into their minds to bring them back to their senses. Paul asked a series of pointed questions in 3:2-5 as he relied on the Spirit to convict them as they thought about their answers. It was foolish to begin the Christian life by faith and then revert to slavery to the law's demands (3:3).

3:6-9 ABRAHAM AND LAW: SONSHIP BY FAITH
Paul built his arguments on the foundation of Old Testament Scripture, which when applied to the life of Christ, provided a sure support for faith. Note the key concept of promise in 3:14, 16, 21, 29. Notice that the gospel had been preached even to Abraham—the promise of God's redemption by faith. Paul appealed to Genesis 15:6 to show that even Abraham, the chief patriarch of the Jews, was reckoned righteous on the basis of faith (3:6). Those who share Abraham's faith are his spiritual descendants (3:7). Gentile justification by faith was not Paul's innovation (3:8) but was anticipated long ago in Genesis 12:3. Gentiles may receive the blessing of justification by faith just as Abraham did.

3:10-14 SALVATION FROM THE CURSE OF LAW
Having expounded the doctrine of justification by faith positively (3:6-9), Paul next presented the negative counterpart: the impossibility of justification by the law. In this section Paul compared lives lived by faith and lives lived by the law. Law is work-oriented, demands perfect obedience, and results in a curse if even one commandment is broken (3:12-13). Faith is belief-oriented and conforms to the means of Abraham's blessing (3:14), bringing justification by grace (3:11).

Paul appealed to Deuteronomy 27:26 to show that those living under the principle of the law were also under the law's curse (3:10). Paul quoted Habakkuk 2:4 to show that the Old Testament itself taught that men are justified by faith (3:11). Paul appealed to Leviticus 18:5 to show that the law is antithetical to faith for it demands "doing," while faith involves receiving what Christ has done (3:12). Paul quoted Deuteronomy 21:23 as proof that Christ became a curse for believers (3:13). The hanging of a criminal indicates his accursed state.

3:15-18 THE PERMANENCE OF RATIFIED FAITH
God's promise to Abraham is viewed from one perspective only—from the perspective of its fulfillment in Christ. No other person in the line (seed) of Abraham qualified as the bringer of promise. The promise stretches in an unbroken line from Abraham to its fulfillment in Christ. The next section develops how the law, which came in between Abraham and Christ, is to be understood. Israel was in bondage (3:17) for 430 years (cf. Exod. 12:40): from the time of Jacob's entrance into Egypt (c. 1876 B.C.) until the Exodus (c. 1446 B.C.). The covenant was ratified to Jacob just before his departure for Egypt (Gen. 46:1-4).

3:19–4:7 REASONS FOR THE LAW
3:19-22 The Law Reveals Mankind's Sin
The curse of the law came because the principle of the law demanded perfection, something no human could attain. One sin brought a curse on a person's life. The law trapped all people in sin (3:19-22). The law as an ethical standard existed before its codification at Sinai (cf. Gen. 18:19). But at Sinai the law was "added" as a contractual obligation with blessings promised for obedience and discipline promised for disobedience. The angelic involvement in the giving of the law is not fully explained in Scripture but is referred to elsewhere (Ps. 68:17; Acts 7:53; Heb. 2:2). Deuteronomy 33:2 mentions thousands of holy ones, probably angels, at the giving of the law at Mount Sinai.

If people cannot be justified before God by the law, then why did God institute it in the first place? Paul pointed out that the purpose of the law was to reveal sin (3:19) and lead people to Christ (3:22-25). A mediator, Moses, was needed because two parties were involved, the people of Israel and God. This made the Mosaic covenant conditional on human obedience—something that had failed up to that point in Scripture. But with the Abrahamic covenant there was no mediator bringing God and people into a conditional relationship. God alone was the one on whom the fulfillment of the conditions and promises rested (cf. Rom. 1:21-22).

3:23-29 The Law Leads to Sonship in Christ
Paul used "until faith" (3:23) to refer to "believe in Jesus Christ" (3:22). Faith itself existed before Christ, as Paul's discussion of Abraham's faith emphasized. The image of the law as "our guardian" (3:24) is of a slave in charge of his master's children. His job was to ensure the safe arrival of the children at school. So, the law is a childminder to lead people to Christ, the Savior and Teacher.

Galatians 3:28 has been used by some to deny the biblical concept of role-relationships within ethnic, social, and gender groups. However, the focus here is on spiritual equality in Christ. Equality of spiritual position and privilege does not necessitate that there be identical secular or spiritual activity (cf. Eph. 5:22, 27; 6:1, 5). Even Gentiles could be Abraham's spiritual offspring and heirs of God's promise by faith in the person of Christ (3:29).

4:1-7 The Law Leads to Sonship
In Galatians 3 Paul showed that faith was the only way of salvation from Abraham to Christ. In Galatians 4 he continued this thought by showing that faith brings mature sonship and law brings slavery. It considers heirs (3:29; 4:1) as children and as adults to explain the progression of time from Moses (the child period) to Christ (the adult

period, 4:7). The term "Father" (4:6) suggests both intimacy and reverence.

Paul answered the question of why the law was not binding as a contractual obligation as it had been on the Old Testament saints. The law's guardianship ended with Christ's coming. Believers in Christ enjoy the full status of sonship and are free from the legal limitations of slavery. Christ's redemption releases believers from the law's claim and confers on them the rights of sonship. In the first century, adoption meant that all old debts were cancelled and the adoptee started a new life as part of a new family (cf. note on Rom. 8:15).

4:8-20 Personal Application and Exhortation
4:8-11 CONCERNED APPLICATION
The Galatians were turning back to old ways (Gal. 4:8-9; cf. 4:3 with 4:9), and Paul feared his work among them had been in vain (4:10-11). What made it vain was the lack of the formation of Christ in their lives (4:19). The days, months, seasons, and years (4:10) refer to such Jewish celebrations as Sabbaths, new moon festivals, other religious festivals, and the year of Jubilee.

4:12-20 EXHORTATION TO MUTUALITY
4:12-15 Paul Pleads for Mutuality
Paul made it clear that he was not taking these ministry problems personally (4:12). The Galatians had not wronged him. Quite to the contrary, they had given much to him. Acts does not recount what Paul's bodily ailment was. Some have speculated that Paul contracted malaria in the lowlands around Perga and was compelled to go to the higher elevations of Pisidian Antioch in order to recover.

The reference to the Galatians' willingness to have "taken out" their eyes (4:15) has been interpreted by some to suggest that Paul had poor eyesight. Eyes are a priceless possession (Deut. 32:10; Ps. 17:8; Zech. 2:8). The expression suggests the Galatians' willingness to give up anything for Paul. But that original warmth toward Paul had now turned to hostility (4:16).

4:16-20 Desire for Face-to-Face Ministry
Does the truth make enemies? Yes (4:16). A key statement about the false teachers in Galatia is in 4:17. The false teachers desired to alienate the Galatians from Paul and the other true apostles. These teachers desired to force the Galatians to rely on their false instruction and help.

Paul called the Galatians to return to the basic truths of the Christian faith (4:19-20). The "tone" Paul desired to change ("gentle," 4:20) pervades the entire book. It was a tone of amazement and fatherly distress over children who were throwing away life itself.

4:21–6:10 Freedom from the Yoke of Slavery
4:21-31 FREEDOM BY SONSHIP
4:21-23 Past Children of Flesh and Promise
Here Paul vindicated his gospel by using an Old Testament incident to contrast the principle of law with the principle of grace. Abraham had two sons—Isaac and Ishmael—but only one (Isaac) inherited God's promises to Abraham. Paul wanted the believers to realize that they were spiritual heirs of Abraham by faith and thus needed to repudiate their bondage to the law.

4:24-28 Present Children of Flesh and Promise
Paul continued his image of two covenants, the Abrahamic and the Mosaic (4:24). He showed how the Mosaic law was for the immature and how faith in Christ according to Abrahamic faith would set believers free from sin and law. Galatians 3 reveals who Abraham's true sons are and the temporal nature of law. Galatians 4 explains the slave nature of the Ishmael line and its conflict with Isaac's line. This can all be seen under the concept of the "slave" and the "heir" (3:29; 4:1, 7).

What did Paul mean by giving an "illustration" (4:24)? He was certainly not suggesting that Genesis contains allegory, not history. Nor was he interpreting the Old Testament allegorically as did the Jewish rabbis. Rather, he was appealing to a historical situation (Gen. 16–17; 21) that had application to the Galatian crisis. The value of Paul's use of allegory was twofold: (1) Paul defended the principle of grace from the Old Testament, the chief authority of the Judaizers. (2) If the Judaizers were employing allegorical methods of interpretation, Paul answered them with their own method.

The two covenants represented by Ishmael and Isaac were characterized as being "born in a human attempt" (according to flesh) and being "born as God's own fulfillment of his promise" (4:23), or by "the Holy Spirit" (4:29). The mother of Ishmael, Hagar, represented Mount Sinai, the Mosaic law; and Jerusalem, Judaism of Paul's day (4:24-25). False teachers in Galatia were claiming the necessity of obeying the law as was being done in Jerusalem by the Orthodox Jews. The other mother in the passage is the "heavenly Jerusalem" (4:26), a reference to God's abode in the heavenly city that will one day appear on earth (Rev. 21:2). In Galatians 4:27 Paul cited Isaiah 54:1, which describes the restoration of God's people.

4:29-31 Conflict between Flesh and Promise
The conflict between flesh and promise existed among the believers in Galatia (4:29-31). Paul appealed to Genesis 21:10, 12 as the basis for his command that the believers abandon legalism (4:30). This directly condemned the false teachers as being according to the flesh and persecuting the

work of the Spirit. But this was not only an attack on false teachers. This also explained that persecution was not the Galatian believers' fault and did not imply something was wrong with them and their original faith in Christ. They were not to change beliefs and start following the law in order to avoid persecution. Their very beliefs showed that they were right in the middle of God's truth. In fact, Paul would show that this desire to avoid persecution was the very reason why the false teachers acted the way they did (6:12).

5:1 DIRECTION AND MAINTENANCE OF CHRIST'S WORK
Paul exhorted the Galatians to stand firm in the liberty that Christ has provided. The present imperative, "Make sure that you stay free" (5:1) could be translated, "Keep on standing firm."

5:2-12 FREEDOM FROM LEGAL OBLIGATION
This section relates back to the two sections on Abraham in Galatians 3–4. The discussion continues along the two lines, flesh and Spirit, law and promise. Paul argued that freedom was not found under the law. Paul was not talking about losing one's salvation. He was simply saying that turning to law was falling away from grace (5:4). This would amount to alienation from Christ. Falling into legalism was falling from grace. Paul used other terms to describe the fall from grace: "turning away" (1:6); "evil spell" (3:1); "trying . . . by your own human effort" (3:3); "tied up again in slavery" (5:1).

The source of the wrong persuasion was not from God (5:7-11). Source determines authority, and Paul had already belabored the truth that the source of his authority was from God (1:1–2:10). The source of the Galatians' problems was human, not divine (5:8). God was calling them (5:8). On "yeast" (5:9; "leaven," NASB and KJV), see 1 Corinthians 5:6. "Salvation through the cross alone" (5:11) was exactly what the legalists wanted to avoid (6:12). Paul made a strong statement against the Judaizers. The verb "mutilate" (5:12) refers to castration or similar mutilation (cf. Deut. 23:1). Such physical mutilation for religious purposes was commonly practiced in the worship of Cybele, the Phrygian goddess of nature. Paul expressed his wish that those who advocated circumcision should go all the way.

5:13-15 A WIDENING OF SCOPE TO LOVE
The false teachers pressured the Christians to keep all of the law. Paul argued that this should be done through love, not by wrangling over legalistic applications of the law (5:13-15). Galatians 5:13 is central to the exhortations in 5:26 and 6:1-10 because it describes the problem that led to 5:26 and the exhortations in 6:1-10. These hostilities and interpersonal problems were linked to the debates over the false teachings.

5:16-26 FREEDOM FROM FLESH
The illustration of the two lines of Abraham—one flesh, the other Spirit—became an image that revealed the internal state of the believer. The same hostility between the flesh and Spirit takes place inside each believer. The false teachers said, "Obey the law." But Paul argued that this command always finds an impossible barrier in the flesh. Only the Spirit could overcome it, and the Spirit only comes through faith in Christ, not legalism. Paul urged his readers to have a faith/Spirit approach to life, not a law/flesh attitude.

The present imperative "live" (5:16) could be translated, "keep on living." By continually depending upon and yielding to God, the believer can live under the control of the Holy Spirit and does not need to carry out the desires that seek to hold sway over his physical body (the "sinful nature"). Paul recognized that there was a continual war going on between the physical flesh and the Holy Spirit to control the life of a believer (5:17). In light of the Galatian conflict over keeping the law, Paul was saying that walking by the Spirit is living by grace, not by lawkeeping. It is living because of God's grace, not in order to gain it. Paul contrasted the acts of the sinful nature (5:19-21) with the fruit of the Spirit (5:22-23) in order to show that the way of the Spirit actually accomplishes the goals of the law.

6:1-5 MUTUAL FORGIVENESS
The conflicts over law had led to "conceit" and "jealousy" (5:26). The law did not inspire gentleness and the bearing of each other's burdens (6:1-2). Paul had to instruct them how to restore the power of the Spirit in their lives. The legalistic perspectives of the false teachers had no room for gentleness or restoration (4:17). They compared themselves to others (6:4; cf. 6:13) and were hindered by pride (6:3). This is the outcome of legalism—false pride and lack of compassion.

Paul dealt with the subject of church discipline (cf. Matt. 18:15-18). When a believer falls into sin, those who are spiritually mature should deal with the matter in a spirit of gentleness. The words "overcome by some sin" (6:1) could mean (1) overtaken and surprised by the transgression, (2) surprised in the transgression, that is, caught "redhanded", or (3) simply caught up in sin, with no reference to being seen or caught by others. While every Christian should bear his own part of the common load (6:5), believers should assist those excessively burdened.

6:6-10 FOCUSING ON THE GOOD THINGS IN LIFE
This section directly relates to the problems of the letter. False teachers were taking the support that was due true teachers. They caused the Galatians to distrust and not support the true representatives of

God. The obligation of believers to support their teachers financially and materially was a frequent Pauline theme (cf. 1 Cor. 9:3-14; 2 Cor. 11:7-9; Phil. 4:10-19; 2 Thess. 3:7-9; 1 Tim. 5:17-18). While believers should be willing to help all those in need, there is a priority (6:10). Their first responsibility is to those of the Christian family of faith.

6:11-18 THE FINAL EXPOSURE OF THE JUDAIZERS

6:11-16 Insights into Enemies

6:11-13 ENEMY MOTIVES

The false teachers demanded that Christians be circumcised in order to avoid persecution from Jews; they argued that Paul's way was the way of needless persecution (6:12). Paul openly exposed the real motives of the opponents. They were full of pride in their adherence to the law, but were failures at their own game (6:13; cf. 6:4). Paul took the pen from the scribe and wrote the closing words of the epistle himself. The large letters mentioned by

Paul served to authenticate to the believers that this letter was genuinely Pauline.

6:14-16 MOTIVE OF THE TRUE TEACHERS

Paul moved from the crucified Christ to the "new life" (5:6; cf. 1 Cor. 7:19; 2 Cor. 5:17). For Paul to call Christians the "people of God" is his final blow against the Judaizers. Some believe that Paul was distinguishing two groups of believers in Galatians 6:16—believing Gentiles and Christian Jews ("people of God"). It seems unlikely that Paul would distinguish two branches of Christianity in light of his remarks about the Gentiles being heirs of the promise by faith (cf. 3:7, 14, 29; 5:6; 6:15).

6:17-18 Final Warning and Benediction

Paul would stand for Christ to the point of suffering. The brand marks on Paul's body were the scars he had suffered as a result of persecution for the sake of Christ (6:17; cf. Acts 14:19). These were more impressive than the mark of circumcision that the Judaizers sought to impose. Paul ended his letter with its central theme: the grace of Christ.

EPHESIANS

BASIC FACTS

HISTORICAL SETTING

The words "in Ephesus" (1:1) are absent from the oldest Greek manuscripts. This may be accounted for in two ways: (1) The epistle may have been addressed to a single church but was later adapted to a general reading by the omission of the name, or (2) the epistle was originally written for general publication or for many churches, and one particular copy was addressed to the church at Ephesus.

Because Marcion knew this letter in the second century as the Epistle to the Laodiceans, copies of the letter may have been possessed originally by both Laodicea and Ephesus. The letter may have been intended to be read by a larger circle of Christian communities. Without the words "in Ephesus," the address reads "to the saints who are also faithful in Christ Jesus."

Paul first visited Ephesus on his second missionary journey (Acts 18:19). He also spent between two and three years of his third journey in Ephesus (Acts 19:8-10; 20:31). He left the city during a riot caused by silver craftsmen who felt their religion and trade were being threatened (Acts 19:24-28; 20:1). Paul later visited with the Ephesian elders at Miletus on his journey to Jerusalem (Acts 20:17-38).

The city ranked with Alexandria and Antioch of Syria as one of the most important cities of the eastern Mediterranean Roman world. It was a port city located on the Cayster River, three miles from the Aegean. It was an important city commercially as the starting place of a great overland trade route to the east.

Ephesus was the worship center of the Greek goddess Artemis (Diana in Latin). The temple of Artemis was 340 feet long, 160 feet wide, and richly decorated with 100 columns more than 55 feet high. The city was the guardian of the sacred image of Artemis, which was believed to have fallen from heaven (Acts 19:35).

AUTHOR

The Pauline authorship of Ephesians is attested both by internal and external evidence. Paul names himself twice in the letter (Eph. 1:1; 3:1). Pauline authorship was also attested by the early church fathers. Only in recent times have liberal critics questioned Paul's authorship of the letter to the Ephesians. They conclude that someone other than Paul was the author because the letter addressed the Ephesians as if they did not know Paul (3:2), and it did not mention anyone by name except the person who delivered it (6:21). But the letter may have been written by Paul to be read in several cities in the area of Ephesus. The oldest manuscripts of the letter do not have the phrase "in

Ephesus" (1:1) but do contain Paul as the named author. This would explain the general nature of the letter and still maintain Pauline authorship.

DATE
Ephesians is the first of Paul's Prison Epistles, the others being Philippians, Colossians, and Philemon (3:1; 4:1). Paul was in prison several times: Philippi (Acts 16:23); Jerusalem (Acts 23:18); Caesarea (Acts 23:33; 24:27; 25:14); and Rome (Acts 28:16, 20, 30). The imprisonments in Rome and Caesarea gave enough time for considerable correspondence. Since Paul anticipates in Philippians 1:19 and Philemon 1:22 his forthcoming release, and no such release was anticipated at Caesarea, it is most probable that Paul wrote the Prison Epistles, including Ephesians, during his first imprisonment at Rome, which lasted from A.D. 60 to 62.

PURPOSE
Paul's letter to the Ephesians was designed to deepen the walk of Christians who had no major spiritual problems. Paul sought to enlighten them by recounting the greatness of their past sins, God's great redemption, and the present power of the Spirit for waging victorious spiritual warfare.

GEOGRAPHY AND ITS IMPORTANCE

The City of Ephesus
Paul spent over two years in this strategic city. Ephesus was the largest city in the province of Asia, with a population of around 300,000 people. The city had the best seaport in Asia and was an important trade center. It also boasted a refined culture and

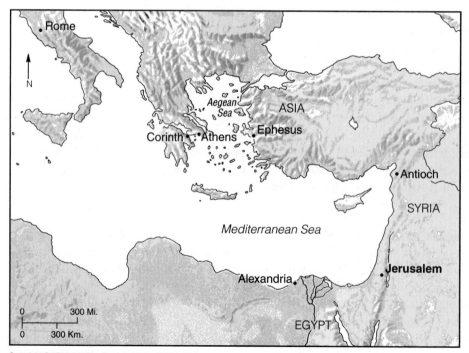

a well-known religion that worshiped in a massive temple built to honor the goddess
Artemis, a daughter of Zeus.

GUIDING CONCEPTS

PROBLEMS

Ephesians does not present the severe problems found in books like Romans or
1 Corinthians. But it does deal with critical problems for the Christian life. It is a book
designed for those with a need for a deeper and more consistent fellowship with God
and his people. Paul's desires for the Christians at Ephesus, that they might have
wisdom and intimate knowledge of God (Eph. 1:17-19), reveal the weaknesses he was
seeking to correct by this letter.

The readers needed to learn more of the racial unity brought through Christ (2:11-18;
3:4-10). They needed to provide a more settled place for Christ in their hearts (3:16-17).
They needed to learn how to cope with suffering (3:13) without losing heart. They
needed to discern truth from error concerning a walk that would please God (5:6, 15).
And they needed to understand where strength for the struggle with the flesh is found
(6:10). All these problems are summed up in Paul's first great prayer that their hearts
would become more enlightened about God's salvation (1:18). They needed their inner
darkness changed to light. The light will only come as the believers wake up and let
Christ shine on them (5:14-15). Throughout the letter Paul sought to bring to fruition
his prayer for the enlightenment of the Ephesians and all believers generally.

THE HEAVENLY REALMS

Paul mentioned the concept of the heavenly places throughout the letter. The concept
involves the place of Christ's reign (1:20-21) at God's right hand, the place of the
believers' exaltation with Christ (1:3; 2:6), and the place of the believers' conflict on
earth (6:12). Therefore, believers should not think of themselves as being here and the
heavenly places as being far distant. The heavenly places are a reality on earth, and
believers find themselves in a spiritual realm where both God's exalted Son and spiritual forces of wickedness exist. The idea is not that wickedness and Christ exist in the
same place, but that they exist in the realm of the spirit, not of flesh and blood. Christ
can only be enjoyed and wickedness overcome in the realm of the spirit through the
Holy Spirit (6:12).

BIBLE-WIDE CONCEPTS

THE BLESSINGS OF ONE SHARED WITH THE MANY

Throughout the Old Testament, human leaders like Moses, Joshua, the judges, David,
and Solomon functioned as God's saviors of his people. But all along there was the
expectation that one day God would send the perfect and final Savior, in whom his
people would find victory and rest. Each individual human leader only expressed in
part what the promised Messiah would achieve in full. The promise of victory through
conflict (Gen. 3:15) would then find its fulfillment (Rom. 16:20). But the critical need
at each point in God's history of salvation was that God be "in" his appointed leader,
that is, that the leader be under the blessing of God working through him, whether he

STOP.

OUTLINE OF EPHESIANS

I. GREETING (1:1-2)

II. THANKSGIVING (1:3-23)
   A. Thanksgiving to God: Praise (1:3-14)
   B. Thanksgiving for Humans: Petition (1:15-23)

III. REMEMBERING: PAST AND PRESENT (2:1-22)
   A. Separation: Restoration (2:1-10)
   B. Separation: Unification (2:11-22)

IV. STRENGTHENING: PRESENT TRIBULATION (3:1-21)
   A. Prison: Strengthening the Heart (3:1-13)
   B. Prayer: Strengthening the Inner Person (3:14-19)
   C. Praise: For Unrequested Power (3:20-21)

V. WALKING WORTHILY (4:1-6:9)
   A. Gifted for Maturity (4:1-16)
   B. Putting on the New Self (4:17-24)
   C. Laying Aside Sins (4:25–5:14)
   D. Wise Submission (5:15–6:9)

VI. STANDING FIRMLY (6:10-20)
   A. The Focus of Strength and Attack (6:10-12)
   B. Alert and in Armor (6:13-20)

VIII. PAUL'S MESSENGER OF COMFORT: TYCHICUS (6:21-22)

IX. BENEDICTION (6:23-24)

EPHESIANS NOTES

1:1-2 GREETING
Paul addressed his letter to the "faithful followers." Thus the purpose of his letter was not to correct flagrant disobedience. Paul desired to teach the believers in Asia Minor about seeking the deeper spiritual life. The words "in Ephesus" are absent from the oldest Greek manuscripts (see the Historical Setting section).

1:3-23 THANKSGIVING
Overview: This section (1:3-23) is made up of two sentences in Greek: the first in 1:3-14 and the second in 1:15-23. The first section of the letter (1:1–3:21) has around sixteen Greek sentences, while the second section of the letter (4:1–6:24) is made up of around forty-two Greek sentences. Paul's thoughts in the first three chapters are expressed in broader and grander scope than the short and to-the-point statements of Ephesians 4–6.

1:3-14 Thanksgiving to God: Praise
Overview: This grand expression is made up of three sections (1:3-6, 7-12, 13-14). The first proclaims the believers' being chosen by God for "sonship" (1:3-6). The second describes the believers' redemption (1:7-12). The third affirms the believers' present pledge of the Spirit for future hope (1:13-14). Each section ends with "praise our glorious God." Christ, the Son, is the central link in the praise to the Father, Son, and Holy Spirit. The spiritual blessings (1:3) stem from the believers' father/child relationship with God (1:5) and their resultant inheritance (1:11, 14).

1:3-6 SPIRITUAL BLESSINGS: CHOSEN ONES
Paul brought praise to God for the blessings he gives to believers in Christ (1:3). For the "heavenly realms," see 1:20; 2:6; 3:10; 4:8; 6:12 (see also the Guiding Concepts section). The riches promised to believers in the heavenly realms throughout this letter prepare them for a successful battle with the

forces of evil who are also part of the "heavenly realms" (6:12).

Paul next introduced the foundation of God's blessing: the fact that believers are chosen by God (1:4-6). The spiritual blessings are described. God's choosing of believers is directly related to their holiness in behavior (1:4). The doctrine of election ("chose us") must be balanced with man's responsibility (cf. John 3:36) and undergirded with the teaching that God is loving, sovereign, and just. "Predestined" ("His unchanging plan," 1:5) means to mark out by boundaries beforehand. For "adopt" (1:5), see note on Romans 8:15. The words "praise our glorious God" (1:12, 14) reflect the most important consideration in the universe—the glory of God (cf. Isa. 43:7; 1 Cor. 10:31). The "dearly loved Son" (1:6) is a reference to Christ.

1:7-12 SPIRITUAL BLESSINGS: FORGIVEN BY GOD

Part of the spiritual blessing believers receive is redemption through Christ's blood (1:7). The focus here shifts from God the Father to Christ and the present fact of redemption through his work. The words "purchased our freedom" (1:7) mean "redemption," and denote release from a state of bondage and servitude effected by the payment of a ransom. The word "redemption" was used in the first century A.D. for purchasing a slave out of the marketplace and setting him free.

God not only paid the price for man's redemption, he also graciously made it known (1:8-9). The "secret plan" (1:9) is the full gospel of Christ. This introduction prepares the reader for a further discussion in 3:1-12. A divine mystery is something not previously revealed and therefore unknown apart from divine revelation. Paul referred to the "secret plan" in 3:6 as the union of believing Jews and Gentiles in one body in Christ.

The content of the mystery is the unity that can come through Christ and his gospel (1:10). Christ is the sum of all; he defines all thought, action, and rule. The corresponding result of the mystery is the redemption of all those who believe (1:11-12).

1:13-14 SPIRITUAL BLESSINGS: SEALED BY GOD

God identifies, or seals, believers with the mark of the Holy Spirit (1:13). The phrase "the Holy Spirit, whom he promised long ago" sums up the Old Testament hope that God would send his Spirit for power and wisdom (see, for example, Num. 11:29; Ezek. 36:26-27; Joel 2:28-29; Acts 2:33; 1 Cor. 12:13). The sealing (guarantee) is elaborated in Ephesians 1:14. In ancient times the term "sealed" was used of an identifying mark, like a brand on a donkey, suggesting both possession and security. "Identified . . . as his own," believers are possessed by Christ and secure in him. The words "just one more reason" (1:14) refer to the promises of 1:3-14.

1:15-23 Thanksgiving for Humans: Petition

1:15-16 UNCEASING PRAYER

What's left after the great truths of Ephesians 1:3-14? Unceasing prayer (1:15-16). Paul's prayer (1:15-23) is based on what God has accomplished for the believer through Christ.

1:17-23 ENLIGHTENED HEART

Paul prays for the Ephesians' full knowledge of God (1:17). The knowledge comes by the enlightening of the heart as to God's hope, glory, and power (1:18-23). These truths are empowered by the resurrection and exaltation power of God (1:20-23). The resurrection and exaltation of Christ to God's right hand (cf. Acts. 2:33-35) have great implications for the believer. They are the very center of the Christian's life and are foundational for all Paul says throughout the letter concerning Jew and Gentile relations and power for waging spiritual warfare. The church is Christ's body. In ancient times, being seated at someone's "right hand" (1:20) was regarded as being in a position of honor and influence (cf. Ps. 110:1).

2:1-22 REMEMBERING: PAST AND PRESENT

Overview: Ephesians 2 begins with Paul's answer to his prayer of 1:15-23 for the enlightenment of believers. His petition to God was complete, but Paul's advice continued and would serve as a part of God's answer to that prayer. Paul contrasted the believers' past lives of sin (2:1-3) with their new lives, raised up with Christ in the heavenly realms (2:4-10). Appreciation of God's grace always demands that believers begin with an awareness of their past sin. People most aware of their sin appreciate most their need for grace.

2:1-10 Separation: Restoration

Overview: Ephesians 2:1-10 is one long sentence in Greek.

2:1-3 OBJECTS OF GOD'S WRATH

Two kinds of "walk" are compared throughout the letter: (1) the dead person's walk in sin (2:1-3) and (2) the living person's walk in love (2:4-7; 5:1-2). Prior to regeneration, the Ephesians were spiritually dead (Rom. 5:12). The "mighty prince of the power of the air" (2:2) refers to Satan (6:12; cf. John 12:31). Those "who refuse to obey God" (2:2) are unbelievers who are characterized by disobedience.

2:4-7 EXALTED TO LIFE

Paul dredged up the dirt from the past only to show the grace of the present. The passage moves from "you were dead" (2:1) to "But God" (2:4) to "Don't forget" (2:11) to "But now you belong to Christ Jesus" (2:13). The past provides the context for the appreciation of the grace given by God in the present. When God's mercy meets mankind's deadness, his grace brings exalted life. Only that context of past sins can enlighten people's hearts to the wonderful power of God's present grace.

Salvation is based on God's attitude of mercy and motivated by his *agape* love (2:4; cf. John 3:16). Ephesians 2:5 contains the solution to the state of spiritual death set forth in 2:1. The parenthesis "by God's special favor that you have been saved" is expanded in 2:8. The key word "seated" (2:6) indicates the believers' position in Christ as partakers of a finished, accomplished redemption. By virtue of the union of believers in Christ, they are positionally already in heaven. Christ's exaltation was their exaltation (2:6). The believers' deep need for grace will form the context for their eternal praise of God in the ages to come (2:7). They will remember their former need so that they can, with perfectly enlightened hearts, praise God.

2:8-10 SALVATION IS GOD'S GIFT

The "gift from God" (2:8) refers to the salvation promised to all who believe. To get the overall thrust of this section, read 2:11 directly after 2:1-2. Salvation is provided through God's grace and received on the basis of faith in God's promise of forgiveness because of Christ's shed blood. Good works are also a gift (2:10) from the God who made all creation. While good works cannot save (2:9), they always accompany salvation and are the result and evidence of a genuine faith.

2:11-22 Separation: Unification

2:11-18 PEACE BETWEEN JEW AND GENTILE

In the rest of chapter 2, Paul expounded on the unity of mankind in Christ. He wrote first of the alienation of Jew and Gentile (2:11-12) and then of their reconciliation by the blood of Christ (2:13-16). He showed how believing Gentiles had entered into the family of believing Israel by faith, so that there was, as a result, one people of God united in the one body of Christ.

Paul used Isaiah 57:19 (quoted in 2:17) and Psalm 118:22 or Isaiah 28:16 (alluded to in 2:20) to show how Christ, as the cornerstone, brought those who were near and far together into one holy temple in the Spirit. The words "But now" (2:13) introduce a contrast with the Gentile's previous position (2:11-12). Christ brought peace (2:14) by joining the two groups into one. The "wall" (2:14) is an allusion to the wall on the temple grounds that separated the court of the Gentiles from the court that only Jews could enter. The death penalty would be inflicted if a Gentile passed that barrier. That wall of hostility had been broken down in Christ.

2:19-22 THE RESULTANT EFFECT

Both Gentiles and Jews are now members of God's household (2:19). On the contrast with "citizens" (2:19), see 2:12. A "cornerstone" (2:20) provided the proper angles and perspective for a building's construction. It can refer to a stone in the foundation, the keystone of an arch, or the capstone of a pyramid. It is the stone that brings unity and completion.

3:1-21 STRENGTHENING: PRESENT TRIBULATION

3:1-13 Prison: Strengthening the Heart

3:1-7 THE GIFT OF A MYSTERY

Paul was a prisoner on the readers' behalf (3:1). The thought is interrupted from 3:2-13 and resumes in 3:14. Paul wrote this epistle while he was a prisoner in Rome (Acts 28:16). Paul's "special ministry" (3:2) was the message of God's grace given to him as the apostle to the Gentiles (Gal. 2:7). Paul next began to develop the concept of the "secret plan" that he introduced in 1:9. Paul made no claim to be the sole recipient of this revelation (3:5). His digression on the place of the Gentiles in Christ stressed their equality in the mystery of Christ. The "plan" (3:4) was not that Gentiles would someday be included in salvation. That had been known since Genesis 12:3 ("all the families of the earth"). The mystery, or "secret plan," centered on Gentile status as fellow heirs (3:6) to God's promises to the Jews. Note the words "both" and "together" in 3:6 to drive the point of equality home. The mystery was not that Gentiles would receive spiritual blessing (cf. Joel 2:28; Amos 9:12), but that Jew and Gentile would be united on an equal basis in one body, sharing a spiritual inheritance in the promises of God.

3:8-13 A WORD ABOUT PAUL'S PURPOSE

Paul went on to point out that sufferings are a glory, not something to be avoided. In light of all that God had done for the believing Gentiles (3:2-12), Paul asked that they not let his problems cause them to lose heart. Instead he enlightened their hearts to the glory hidden in tribulation. Paul also spoke of not losing heart in 2 Corinthians 4:1, 16.

3:14-19 Prayer: Strengthening the Inner Person

The first section of the epistle (Eph. 1–3) concludes with the apostle's second prayer for the spiritual lives of the believers. He returned to the themes of power (3:18; cf. 1:19) and the importance of a Christ-indwelling heart (3:19; cf. 1:18). It takes the power of the Spirit to allow the unhindered dwelling of Christ in the heart. Sin is unsettling. To "understand" (3:18. 19) the love of Christ could only come from the settled presence of Christ in the believers' lives. That fullness is the purpose of this letter regarding "hearts . . . flooded with light" (1:18).

HUGHES AND LANEY ◆ 594

3:20-21 Praise: For Unrequested Power

Paul's praise of God and his power pushed the perspective of his readers beyond what they could ask and conceive—to the infinite capabilities of God's power. God can do far more with and through those who believe in him than those people can ask for or even think about.

4:1–6:9 WALKING WORTHILY

Overview: In Ephesians 1–3 Paul revealed the wonderful benefits of believing in Christ: the unity found in the Spirit, the heavenly dimension of the Christian walk, and edifying speech and behavior among believers. All of these characteristics were modeled by Paul, and at this point (4:1–6:9) Paul urged the readers to live out the benefits of salvation. Paul desired that the lives and "walk" of the believers would be worthy of their calling as Christians.

4:1-16 Gifted for Maturity

4:1-6 CALLED IN THE UNITY OF THE SPIRIT

This section is built around Christ's ascension (4:8), an event that marked the believers' ascension as well (2:6). Ephesians 4:1 introduces the exhortations that build on the doctrines set forth in chapters 1–3. The key word is "lead" (4:1), a term used frequently by Paul to describe the believers' manner of life. Paul's main point was that believers should conduct themselves in a manner worthy of their high calling in Christ.

The believers' high calling in Christ called for unity in the body of Christ (4:2-6). Believers were in fact united positionally through their spiritual bond in Christ. They needed to be diligent to maintain this unity (John 17:21), allowing its implications to be lived out in their lives. The unity demanded of Christians comes from the "Holy Spirit" and with "peace" (4:3). This builds on earlier words about the "Holy Spirit," the divine seal of redemption (1:13-14), and "peace," that wholeness with humans and God bought by Christ's blood (2:13-14). The unity of believers is grounded on what they share in common through Christ. The "baptism" (4:5) referred to here is the baptism by the Holy Spirit into the body of Christ (1 Cor. 12:13).

4:7-8 VARIOUS GIFTS FOR THE UNITY OF THE FAITH

Paul used Psalm 68:18 to describe the resultant gift-giving of Christ's ascension. Here Paul discussed spiritual gifts—the abilities given by God for service in the Christian community (cf. 1 Cor. 12–14). Although there is unity in the body (4:1-6), there is a diversity of gifts given by Christ for the edification of the body (4:7, 11). Paul quoted and somewhat adapted Psalm 68:18 to show the biblical basis for the giving of spiritual gifts. There are two possible backgrounds for this quote: (1) A victorious warrior is elevated when he returns with a group of prison-

ers. Having received gifts from the conquered people, he distributes them to his followers. (2) The Levites were taken from among the Israelites as captives for God's service and given as gifts to Aaron to serve the priesthood (cf. Num. 8:6, 19). At Christ's exaltation (Acts 2:33) his gifts were spiritual. The point is that the believers needed to be enlightened concerning their experience of the Spirit. The grace they all experienced was a direct evidence of the gifts given by Christ.

4:9-10 CHRIST'S DESCENT AND ASCENT

Paul again presented Christ's humble life on earth, by which readers would better appreciate Christ's exaltation (John 3:13; 6:38; 16:28). Christ's exaltation came after his time of humiliation, and the same will be true for his followers. This is the meaning of Paul's statement in 3:13.

The parenthetical comment in 4:9-10 on "he ascended" (4:8) was written to show that only Christ fits the description. Some interpret 4:9 as evidence of a descent into hell by Christ between his death and resurrection (cf. 1 Pet. 3:19-20). More likely, 4:9 simply refers to Christ's coming down from heaven to earth. He descended to the "lowly" regions of the universe, that is, the "world." The phrase is used in Isaiah 44:24 for the earth; Psalm 139:15 for the womb; Ezekiel 32:24 for the netherworld; and Psalm 63:9 for the grave. The point is, however, that Christ alone fits the description of one who both "descended" and "ascended." Thus, he is able to give gifts to men.

4:11-16 GIFTS THAT BRING MATURITY FOR STABLE GROWTH

These are the gifts of Christ (4:7, 8, 11, "has given" and "gave"). The purpose of mentioning the gifts was to enlighten the readers to the value of the people mentioned in 4:11. They were literally Christ's gift to the church. Some hold that the terms "pastors" and "teachers" represent one gifted person, not two. Elsewhere, however, the ministries are separated (Rom. 12:7; 1 Pet. 5:2). Certainly a pastor should be able to teach (1 Tim. 3:2; 5:17), but there may be teachers in the church who do not function in the office or role of pastor. The purpose of these gifts is to equip the saints for ministry. The phrase "helps the other parts grow" (4:16), or "build itself up" (NIV), is used in ancient medical literature of setting a bone. It has the idea of "making fit." The Ephesians were being told that the way out of cunning, craftiness, and deceitful scheming (4:14) is to benefit from Christ's gifts to the church.

4:17-24 Putting on the New Self

4:17-19 THE NEGATIVE ASPECT

Paul had prayed for the enlightenment of their hearts in 1:18. The related concepts here are "minds" (4:18, 23, "thoughts"), "shut their minds" and "hardened their hearts" (4:18). One of Satan's goals is to so conform believers to the ways of the world that no one will know they are Christians. Paul described the believers' walk as a different walk. He contrasted the conduct of Christians with that of unbelieving Gentiles (cf. also Matt. 6:7).

4:20-24 BEING RENEWED IN MIND
Paul made the contrasts between the old and new self and darkened and renewed minds. "Throw off" (4:22, 25, "put away") means changing the "former manner of life" to a manner conforming to the "righteous, holy, and true" (4:24) likeness of God. That is only possible based on the prayers of 1:18-19 and 3:14-21.

4:25–5:14 Laying Aside Sins
4:25–5:2 SEPARATE FROM SINFUL DEEDS
Paul presented a contrast between the old and new manners of life. The new manner is directed in each case toward giving grace (4:29; cf. 4:7) to another person (4:25, "we belong to each other"; 4:28, "need"; 4:29, "helpful"; 4:32, "forgiving"). This is based on God's grace toward believers (4:32). They were to be appropriately angry over sin (4:26) like Paul was in 1 Corinthians 5:3-5, 12-13. But they were not to sin by not seeking to bring about forgiveness and restoration like the Corinthians did in 2 Corinthians 2:5-11. There is a place for a proper anger, that is, a righteous indignation, but one must be careful to avoid giving the devil opportunity. One of the Ten Commandments prohibited stealing (4:28; Exod. 20:15).

Paul warned against causing the Holy Spirit pain and sorrow through sin and a refusal to follow his leading (4:30). Christians grieve the Spirit when they do not "encourage" (4:29) themselves or others. Although the Spirit can be grieved by believers' sins, he will never abandon those who belong to him (Rom. 8:9).

As children imitate their earthly fathers, so believers are to imitate their heavenly Father (5:1), and 5:2 tells how. The exhortation of 5:2 could be translated, "Keep on walking in love." The words "fragrant offering" (5:2) look back to the sweet savor offerings of Leviticus 1–3, which prefigured Christ's voluntary sacrifice of himself.

5:3-14 SEPARATE FROM SINFUL PEOPLE
"Those who disobey" (5:6) are unbelievers who are characterized by disobedience to God. Paul admonished the believers to walk in the light, a metaphor for a life of holiness. While spiritual darkness is the realm of unbelievers, light is the realm of Christians (Col. 1:12-13; John 8:12; 12:35). Believers "expose" the things of darkness (5:11) by living differently (4:17-24), walking with God (1 John 1:7), being a light (Matt. 5:14-16), and rebuking sin (2 Tim. 3:16). Paul's quotes in Ephesians 5:14 were

probably taken from Isaiah 26:19 and 60:1. This verse contains a sample of how one might reprove a sinner.

5:15–6:9 Wise Submission
Overview: The essential elements of a renewed walk as Paul presented them were: (1) unity in love, (2) gifts in proper use, (3) a renewed mind, (4) separation from sin, and (5) submission. It was the last one, submission, that Paul focused on in Ephesians 5:15–6:9.

5:15-17 IN LIGHT OF EVIL DAYS
Since the time is short and the days are evil, a Christian's use of time needs redeeming or he will use it as most do—for evil. "Make the most of every opportunity" (5:16; "Redeeming the time," KJV) means to "buy it back"—to use wisely the short time that believers do have (cf. John 9:4). This demands an understanding of what evil is in the first place and an understanding of God's will. From this knowledge should follow action; Christians should use their time pursuing that which avoids evil and works to fulfill God's will.

5:18-21 AS A RESULT OF FULLNESS
Paul had already shown that the Spirit's power was behind the Christians' victories (1:13-14; 1:19-21; 2:18; 3:16; 4:4, 30). Ephesus was a center for the cult of Dionysus (Greek, "Bacchus"), the god of wine. Celebrations in honor of Dionysus emphasized fertility, sex, and intoxication. Intoxication would allow Dionysus to control the body of the worshiper. Thus the worshiper would do the will of the deity. Paul was saying in 5:18, "Don't be filled with the spirit of Dionysus through wine, but be filled with the true and living God by his Spirit." Paul's key illustration of being wise was to be filled with the Spirit for all the behaviors he described in 5:19–6:9. Paul described that fullness in several ways: speaking and singing (5:19), thankfulness (5:20), and submission (5:21).

The last point, submission, receives detailed development (submission in marriage, 5:22-33; submission of children to parents, 6:1-4; submission of slaves to masters, 6:5-9). In each area of submission Paul was careful to exhort those commanding the submission to show love to those under them, not to abuse them (husbands, 5:25-33; fathers, 6:4; masters, 6:9).

This passage further explains what Paul meant by laying aside the old self and putting on the new self (4:22-25). The acts of speaking, thankfulness, and submission show what believers should "put on" in the fullness of the Spirit's power and intention for their "walk" with God in Christ. They are visible manifestations of the grace and power that belong to believers in the "heavenly realms." Paul desired that the believers wake up and, with enlightened hearts, realize the power for life that God has given (3:14-21). All Christians possess God's fullness through Christ (1:23).

In 5:21 many have thought that Paul was teaching the principle of mutual submission of all believers to each other. Rather, Paul enjoined believers to submit themselves to and obey rightful authorities. He then proceeded to give some specific examples of proper submission—wives to husbands, children to parents, slaves to masters (5:22–6:9)—examples that ought not be reversed.

5:22-24 FOCUSED ON WIVES AND HUSBANDS
The submission of the wife to her husband does not suggest inequality, for Christ was in submission to the Father but was also his equal (John 14:9; 17:22; 1 Cor. 11:3; Phil. 2:6-8). The relationship between the husband and wife is one governed by unselfish love, where both meet the needs of each other.

5:25-33 FOCUSED ON HUSBANDS AND WIVES
Husbands are to have a Christ-like passion to bring their wives into deeper purity and holiness before God. Christ's sacrificial love for the church is set forth as the pattern for the husband's love for his wife. Husbands ought to consider whether they are loving their wives according to this pattern. Paul quoted Genesis 2:24, the scriptural basis for marriage (5:31). There is a symbolic purpose in marriage (5:32). The union is designed to be a reflection of the relationship between Christ and his church.

6:1-4 FOCUSED ON CHILDREN AND PARENTS
Obedience to parents can amount to obedience to God (Exod. 20:12; cf. also Deut. 5:16). A child's obedience led to a long life. This was especially true in the Old Testament where disobedience leads to death (Exod. 21:15, 17). Paul also described the father's proper relationship to his children (6:4). Fathers are to be gentle and patient like the Lord and are to avoid provoking their children.

6:5-9 FOCUSED ON SLAVES AND MASTERS
The Bible does not advocate slavery but rather assumes it as part of the cultural setting. Slavery was not instituted by God but by sinful and fallen man. What God does through his word is to regulate this evil until such a time as it is recognized as morally wrong and is changed. What Paul emphasized is one's perspective on slavery (cf. Gal. 3:28; 1 Cor. 7:20-23). Paul's word of admonition to the masters is like his word to fathers in Ephesians 6:4. Paul added a command for seeing the position of master in perspective. Paul reminded them that slave and slave owner alike are servants to the Master in heaven.

6:10-20 STANDING FIRMLY
6:10-12 The Focus of Strength and Attack
What kind of armor is available to protect believers from the evil in this world? (cf. 6:14-20). The armor comes from the "Lord's mighty power" (6:10). Paul called believers to arms so that they would be able to stand firm against the attacks of the devil. The God who calls believers to receive blessings in the "heavenly realms" (cf. 1:3) also provides armor for the struggle with evil in that same realm (see note on 1:3).

6:13-20 Alert and in Armor
Note the pervasive use of the Old Testament throughout this section: Isaiah 11:5 and 59:17 in 6:14; Isaiah 52:7 in 6:15; Psalm 7:10, 13 in 6:16; Isaiah 59:17 in 6:17; and Isaiah 49:2 in 6:17. These passages speak of God's great and promised redemption through his Messiah. The armor of God is not something the believers put on to fight on their own. The armor is Christ himself. Putting on the armor is equivalent to putting on Christ. The power of Christ is sufficient to stand against all evil and temptation that a believer will encounter.

Paul wrote this letter from Rome where he was under the custody of Roman soldiers (cf. Acts 28:16). Knowing that his readers would be familiar with the dress and armor of Roman soldiers, Paul used this imagery to communicate a spiritual message. Roman soldiers used a sturdy belt (6:14) to fasten their sword to their body. A soldier girded in such a manner would be recognized as being on active duty. Paul wanted believers to gird themselves with "truth," the foundation for all spiritual activity.

The soldier's body armor (6:14), made of bronze scales or plates sewn on leather, protected his front and sometimes his back. Paul exhorted believers to find their protection in righteousness.

Roman soldiers prepared for battle by putting on shoes that had short nails in their soles (6:15). These enabled them to stand firm and avoid slipping on the ground. Paul wanted believers to prepare themselves for spiritual battle with the gospel of peace. The Old Testament allusion is to Isaiah 52:7.

Two types of shields were used by Roman soldiers: a large shield that protected the whole body and was carried by the infantry, and a smaller shield, made of wood overlaid with leather, which was carried by the archers (6:16). Paul wanted the believers to take up the shield that consists of faith.

In 6:17 Paul quoted Isaiah 59:17. The soldier's helmet, made of metal or leather, was designed to protect his head, the most vital part of the body. The helmet of "salvation" is the helmet that consists of salvation and protects the believer's spiritual destiny. The sword, a two-foot, double-edged blade, was the soldier's most important weapon. He was trained to stab instead of swing and cut. The "sword of the Spirit" is the only offensive weapon mentioned. It is supplied by the Holy Spirit and is identified as the utterance or spoken word of God (cf. Heb. 4:12). Although Paul was under house arrest during his Roman imprisonment (Acts 28:16), he was probably chained to a Roman soldier and had these images before him as he wrote this letter (Acts 28:20).

6:21-22 PAUL'S MESSENGER OF COMFORT: TYCHICUS

Tychicus apparently carried the letter to the readers in Ephesus and Asia Minor for Paul (6:21; Col. 4:7). Paul's report as to how he was doing was linked to his situation as "God's ambassa-

dor" in "chains" (3:1; 4:1; 6:20). Paul, who was in a situation that most would consider difficult, was sending a letter and messenger to bring encouragement and comfort to the Ephesian Christians.

6:23-24 BENEDICTION

Paul wished that the Ephesians would have "love with faith" (6:23). The readers had faith, but they needed love with it. Paul's final benediction (6:24) summarized all the important elements of life in Christ.

PHILIPPIANS

BASIC FACTS

HISTORICAL SETTING

The readers of the letter are named in 1:1. Paul referred to them as "friends" (3:13, 17; 4:1, 8). The Philippian church may have been largely a Gentile church because there was apparently no synagogue at Philippi when Paul first arrived there (Acts 16:13, 16).

The city of Philippi, named after Philip of Macedonia (the father of Alexander the Great), was strategically located on a fertile plain ten miles north of Neapolis, the city's nearest port. Through the plain passed the Egnatian Way, an important ancient highway that ran through Macedonia linking the Aegean and Adriatic Seas. Travelers to Rome would cross the Adriatic and continue up the boot of Italy on the Appian Way. The city was famous in antiquity for its gold deposits and became a Roman colony in 42 B.C. The city had a famous school of medicine and may have been the home of Luke or perhaps the place where he studied as a medical student.

Paul established the church in Philippi during his second missionary journey in A.D. 50 (Acts 16:11-40). Philippi was the first European city in which Paul preached, and Lydia was the first convert. Paul and Silas were imprisoned there and miraculously released. Some believe that Luke, previously a resident of Philippi, remained at Philippi to work among the churches of Macedonia while Paul went on to Thessalonica (Acts 17:1; 20:5). The Philippian church became a significant source of financial support for Paul (4:15-16; 2 Cor. 11:9).

The church at Philippi was around twelve years old when Paul wrote this letter. Epaphroditus had recently arrived to bring Paul some aid (2:25; 4:18). The immediate occasion of the letter was the return of Epaphroditus following his illness (2:25-30). This gave Paul an opportunity to commend his fellow worker and encourage the readers.

AUTHOR

The Pauline authorship is attested by internal and external evidence. Paul is named as the author (1:1). Although Timothy was also mentioned in the greeting, the use of the first person throughout the letter indicates that Paul alone was addressing the believers. The biographical references are distinctly Pauline (3:4-11; 4:10-16), and the entire letter bears the stamp of Pauline thought. Early church fathers such as Polycarp and Irenaeus support Paul's authorship of the Philippian letter.

DATE

Philippians is one of Paul's prison letters (1:7, 13, 17; cf. Ephesians, Colossians, and Philemon). For the possible location of Paul's imprisonment, see the Date section for

Ephesians. A Roman imprisonment explains the references to the praetorian guard (1:13, "palace guard") and to Caesar's household (4:22). Because Paul anticipated his release (1:19; 2:24), the letter was probably written late in his first imprisonment, possibly during the spring of A.D. 62.

PURPOSE

The letter to the Philippians was designed to encourage joy and unity among the Christians there. It achieved this by exhibiting Paul's example of joy in Christ even during his imprisonment and by giving the supreme example of Christ's own humiliation and exaltation.

GEOGRAPHY AND ITS IMPORTANCE

THE CITY OF PHILIPPI

Philippi was named by the father of Alexander the Great, Philip II, after he enlarged and renovated the city. In 42 B.C. Philippi was made into a Roman colony. The city was on the Egnatian Way, the major overland route to the west.

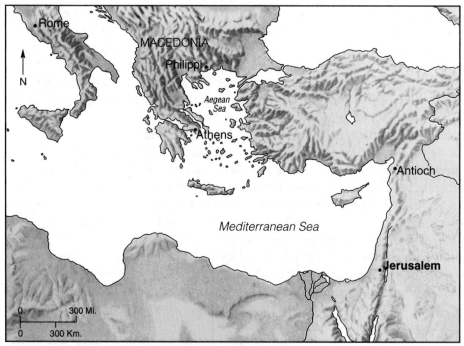

GUIDING CONCEPTS

STRUCTURE

The letter was designed to dispel any depression and discouragement surrounding Paul's imprisonment. It was no easy matter for Christians to accept persecution and imprisonment. Such treatment seemed to stand in stark contrast with the gospel of blessing and exaltation promised in Christ. It may have been a source of doubt among believers. They may have wondered if they had made the right choice in following Jesus into such persecution. Paul urged a divine perspective on suffering that leads from discouragement to rejoicing.

In this light, Paul showed how his prison sentence was really a cause for rejoicing (1:12-26), how the Philippians should live in the encouragement of Christ's model (1:27–2:18), how they should resist the pressures to conform to false doctrine (3:2-21), and how they should receive Paul's gratitude for their support in a balanced manner (4:10-20).

BIBLE-WIDE CONCEPTS

THE DAY OF CHRIST
Paul's desire was that the Philippian believers would be blameless in the day of Christ (1:6, 10; 2:16). That day was the broad time period of resurrection, evaluation, and reward for God's people (cf. also 1 Cor. 1:8; 5:5; 2 Cor. 1:14; 5:10; 1 Thess. 5:2; 2 Thess. 2:2). Jesus linked this day to his coming as the Son of Man. This involved the entire period of his second coming, a period of judgment and restoration mentioned throughout the Old Testament. The essence of this period is the process in which the faithful are rewarded, the rebellious are judged, and the eternal kingdom of God is established (broadly described in 1 Cor. 15:23-28). Only at that time would believers move from their period of groaning into resurrection glory (Rom. 8:23).

"GOD WITH US"
Paul's great joy and hope for victory was to have God with his people. Paul desired to have the joy of being with Christ in heaven (1:23; 3:20-21) and, before that, on earth (3:10-11). He desired for believers to have the God of peace with them (4:9) so that they could live lives of peace and joy no matter what the circumstances.

Ever since Adam and Eve were sent from God's presence in the Garden of Eden, humans had been longing for God to be with them once again. God's repeated promise to Abraham, "I am with you," hinted at a time of restored and unhindered divine presence. God dwelt with Israel in the tabernacle and temple, and through the Spirit, now dwells within Christian believers in a more intimate and complete way. The entire structure of Matthew's Gospel begins and ends with the fact of God being with the believers (Matt. 1:23; 28:20).

Paul's desire for God to be with the Philippians (4:9) echoed a theme prominent in the entire Old Testament by implying more than simple redemption. Yes, God had redeemed the Philippians, and his Spirit was indeed with them. But Paul was speaking of the experience of God's presence that comes from the "practice" (4:9) of truth, a firsthand experience of the sufferings and power of Christ (3:10; 4:13). God has always desired to be with his people firsthand in the difficulties of life.

HUMILIATION AND EXALTATION
Paul urged his readers to follow Christ's pattern of humility in order to attain a subsequent exaltation (2:8-9; 3:10-11). The order was always humiliation first, exaltation second. But some Christians lived as if they could skip the humiliation and go directly to the exaltation (1 Cor. 4:5-7). As a result of their faulty attitude, their suffering was a potential cause for alarm (1:28) and disunity (2:1-4; 3:17–4:3). But the pattern of the righteous sufferer who humbly waits in humiliation for God's timing of exaltation

pervades the Old Testament and is perfected in Christ (cf. for example Mark 8:31; 9:31; 10:33-34; 1 Pet. 2:21-23; 4:12-19). The believers in Philippi were to follow this model.

NEEDS MET BY PHILIPPIANS

When Paul first came to Philippi, he was thrown into jail for casting a demon out of a slave girl who then could no longer tell people's fortunes and make money for her masters (Acts 16:11-40). Paul, with his companion Silas, then sang praises to God in the jail. As he wrote this letter to the Philippians, Paul was again suffering imprisonment, but this time in Rome. He called the Philippians to rejoice even as he suffered imprisonment. Persecution against Paul was a potential cause of discouragement for the Philippians. But Paul presented them with a new way of looking at suffering. He showed them that it could be the grounds, not for discouragement, but for rejoicing. The structure and content of Philippians reveal that Paul intended to answer the following questions for his readers.

- Has Paul's arrest stopped the progress of the gospel?
- How is Paul feeling during his imprisonment in Rome?
- Is he discouraged and depressed because he cannot be out preaching?
- How does he feel about those preaching the gospel from envy and strife?
- How does he maintain a positive attitude about Christ?
- How do Christ's humble earthly life and final heavenly exaltation relate to peace and unity among Christians?

The readers needed to understand the significance of Christ's experience of suffering for their own experiences of persecution. Only then would they be able to experience the significance of Christ's exaltation in their own eventual reward. The Philippians needed to understand that their blessed position before God did not make them immune to pain and suffering. To think that suffering was a sign of some defect with themselves or God would open them up to the very discouragement and bickering Paul was trying to get them to avoid. In that light, the Philippians needed to be reminded that the pleasure of knowing Christ was not diminished by circumstances—a difficult truth to accept during times of persecution. Paul showed the Philippians how to live in joy and in peace with each other no matter what the circumstances.

OUTLINE OF PHILIPPIANS

I. GREETING (1:1-2)

II. THANKSGIVING: PARTICIPATION IN THE GOSPEL (1:3-11)
   A. Mutual Participation (1:3-8)
   B. Prayer for Fullness in the Day of Christ (1:9-11)

III. FROM PRISON: OBEY AND REJOICE (1:12–2:30)
   A. Release: For Joy and Progress (1:12-26)
   B. Exhortations to Joy and Progress: Unity (1:27–2:18)
   C. Mutual Joy by Messenger (2:19-30)

IV. EXHORTATIONS TO FOLLOW GODLY PATTERNS (3:1–4:1)
   A. Beware of Fleshly Boasting (3:1-16)
   B. Focus on Good Patterns (3:17–4:1)

V. FROM PHILIPPI: REPORTS FROM EPAPHRODITUS (4:2-20)
   A. Helps for Standing Firm (4:2-9)
   B. Rejoicing for the Offering (4:10-20)

VI. FINAL GREETINGS AND BENEDICTION (4:21-23)

PHILIPPIANS NOTES

1:1-2 GREETING
The greeting is friendly and casual. Paul does not call himself an apostle but links himself equally with Timothy. Paul had no need to defend his apostolic authority as he did when writing to some of the other churches (cf. Rom. 1:1; 1 Cor. 1:1; 2 Cor. 1:1; Gal. 1:1). While Paul is clearly the author of the epistle (3:4-11; 4:10-16), Timothy was Paul's amanuensis and cofounder of the church at Philippi (Acts 16:1-4). For the terms "elders" and "deacons," see the notes on 1 Timothy 3:1, 8. Paul singled out the leadership to emphasize the responsibilities they had in being good examples to those who followed them (2:29; 3:17).

1:3-11 THANKSGIVING: PARTICIPATION IN THE GOSPEL
1:3-8 Mutual Participation
The focus of Paul's thanksgiving was mutual fellowship in the gospel ("partners," 1:5; "shared together," 1:7). Paul thanked God for the Philippians' partnership in the progress of the gospel. The word "partnership" (koinonia) refers to what is shared in common, in this case, a joint ministry in the gospel of grace.

Paul's confidence was in God's continual work (1:6). The words "prison," "defending," and "telling" were courtroom terms that reflected Paul's circumstances in Rome (1:7; cf. Acts 28:16, 20).

Paul longed for fellowship with the Philippians in Christ (1:8). Prison did not depress Paul into a "me-centered" wallowing. His longings still conformed to his Lord's desires for the Philippians' perfection (1:9-11). The longings of Paul's heart (1:7) matched those of Christ. Prison did not deflect Paul's desire to know Christ or to make him known (3:8).

1:9-11 Prayer for Fullness in the Day of Christ
Paul prayed that the Philippians would abound with love (1:9). But that love needed to be channeled in "knowledge and understanding." They needed to find discerning ways to exercise love and righteousness. The elements of real knowledge brought out in the

letter are knowledge of Paul's own circumstances as causes of rejoicing rather than being depressed (1:12); standing firm rather than alarmed by opponents (1:27-28); being of one mind in the face of selfishness and conceit (2:1-4); putting confidence in Christ when pressured to put confidence in the flesh (3:2-4); standing firm in the face of disharmony (4:1); and knowing how to face circumstances of prosperity as well as need (4:10-13)—a return to the first perspective on Paul's prison circumstances. Throughout the letter Paul taught knowledge and discernment for choices and action that would produce love. On the day when "Christ returns" (1:10), or the "day of Christ," see the Bible-Wide Concepts for this book.

1:12–2:30 FROM PRISON: OBEY AND REJOICE
1:12-26 Release: For Joy and Progress
1:12-14 CIRCUMSTANCES SPREAD THE GOSPEL
Paul's joy and success were not based on where he was but on how effectively Christ was being proclaimed, again the emphasis of 3:10. Paul related how his circumstances had turned out for the greater progress of the gospel. Rather than thwarting the proclamation of the gospel, his imprisonment actually advanced the cause of Christ. The word "spread" (1:12) was used in ancient times of a pioneer cutting his way through the brush. The "palace guard" (1:13; "praetorian guard," NASB) was an elite corps of Roman soldiers that functioned as the imperial palace guard. They were responsible for prisoners who had appealed to the emperor. They heard the gospel when they were on duty guarding Paul.

1:15-26 DELIVERANCE FOR EXALTING CHRIST
1:15-17 Two Attitudes Regarding the Gospel
Even in the face of bad motives for preaching Christ, Paul found good in the situation (1:18). To the discerning, the success of ministry transcended personality. While some were preaching Christ out of love, others were motivated by selfishness. They apparently wanted to outdo Paul's evangelistic ministry while his activity was limited by his imprisonment.

Paul disagreed with their motives as believers today sometimes disagree with different methods of spreading the gospel. But Paul's one concern was: Is Christ being proclaimed?

1:18-26 Confidence in Future Release
Paul did not imply that his "deliverance" (1:19) would be from prison. He was ready to die (1:20). He meant continued deliverance from distress (1:17) and any hindrance to the proclamation of Christ (1:18). He was confident that he would be able to continue to exalt Christ (1:20). Release from prison would be desired only for the benefit of ministry (1:25-26). Paul allowed that he might remain absent (1:27), possibly permanently (2:17). For Paul, Christ was the one who gave meaning and significance to his existence. His life was wrapped up in Christ—witnessing, fellowshiping, and serving. Christ was the focal point and culmination of Paul's life experience.

Paul was confident that he would be delivered for the profit of the Philippians (1:22-26). Life for Christ (1:21) was a life given over to others (1:24). This reference (1:26) provides a clue as to Paul's travel plans. He anticipated a visit with the Philippians after his release from Roman imprisonment.

1:27–2:18 Exhortations to Joy and Progress: Unity
1:27-30 UNITY OF SPIRIT AND MIND
The Philippians' unity of spirit and firm standing in the face of their opponents was a sign of God's blessing on them and his displeasure of their opponents. Opposition to the gospel would result in ultimate divine judgment, while being persecuted was an indication of being among the redeemed (John 15:18-25). The believers were to resist the idea that questioned God's care and control. This potential idea and lapse of faith was the major problem Paul sought to avert in his letter.

Philippi was a Roman colony, and the people there were recognized as Roman citizens with the same legal position and privileges as those living in Rome itself. But they also had certain obligations and responsibilities—loyalty to the emperor and obedience to the law. Likewise, believers are citizens of heaven (3:20), and with that citizenship they also have obligations. Paul explained that believers were responsible as citizens of heaven to conduct themselves in a manner worthy of the gospel that they represented.

2:1-11 UNITY: MAINTAINED BY HUMILITY
2:1-4 Paul's Exhortation
Paul presented the one who exemplified perfect love and who exercised it with true knowledge and discernment: Christ. Paul focused on the mind (2:1-2) and on the mind's tendencies during times of need and trouble. Paul's exhortation in this passage is in keeping with Christ's prayer for unity among believers (John 17:21-23). The three "any"s of Philippians 2:1

represent conditions that are assumed as true and could be translated "since." The first verse sets forth the grounds for the believers' unity in Christ (2:2).

Apparently some believers at Philippi were characterized by vain conceit and selfish ambition (2:3-4). They thought more highly of themselves than they ought to have and neglected their responsibility to serve others (cf. John 13:1-17). Humility ("be humble") might be defined as a proper evaluation of oneself in the sight of God and others (2:3; cf. Rom. 12:3; 1 Pet. 3:8; 5:6).

2:5-11 The Example of Christ
The best example Paul could use to exemplify the qualities demanded by his exhortation (2:1-4) was the person of Jesus Christ (2:5-11). Christ emptied himself in order to be filled up with obedience. The emphasis was on the two modes of Christ's existence: the first in divine glory and splendor, the second as humble servant. Paul presented the supreme illustration of humility: Christ's example of sacrificing himself for others. Although in his preincarnate state Jesus possessed the essential qualities of God, he did not regard his status of divine equality a prize to be selfishly hoarded (2:6).

There are various interpretations regarding what Christ actually did in becoming a man (2:7): (1) he emptied himself of some aspect of his deity (cf. James 1:17; Mal. 3:6); (2) he veiled his glory (cf. John 17:5; Matt. 17:1-2); (3) he laid aside the independent exercise of some of his attributes (Acts 10:38; Matt. 24:36); (4) he received the form of a servant and became a man. The last view is most commended by the context. Christ lost nothing in his incarnation. He simply received the essential nature of a man and became a servant.

The result ("Because of this," 2:9) of Christ's humiliation was exaltation (2:9-11). Paul made free use of Isaiah 45:23 (cf. Isa. 45:21-25), making it a universal and Christ-centered statement. The purpose of Christ's exaltation was to secure for him universal worship. All will someday acknowledge his lordship (cf. Rev. 5:13). The words "Jesus Christ is Lord" (2:11) probably reflect an early creed of the Christians. But Jesus' exaltation is mentioned not as a hope for the believer's own future glorification. Rather, it is mentioned to cause the believer in the present to bow and confess Christ's authority in times of prosperity or opposition. In this context, Paul was recognizing Christ's authority to command humility and unity of mind among believers.

2:12-18 UNITY: THE FRUIT OF OBEDIENCE
2:12-13 Obedience and Salvation
Paul's "presence" or "absence" ("with you" and "away," 2:12) is linked to Philippians 1:27. Paul's emphasis in these verses was on "deep reverence and fear," not "obeying God." This fact is evidenced in Paul's emphasis on the awesome glory of the exalted

Lord and the presence of the Creator in the following verse (2:13). Paul was not advocating salvation by works in contradiction to Ephesians 2:8. There are three aspects of the believer's salvation: (1) past (justification), (2) present (sanctification), and (3) future (glorification). Paul was speaking of the present aspect of salvation: deliverance from the troubles the believer faces, such as complaining and arguing mentioned in the very next verse (2:14). God works in the believer, supplying the will to obey and then helping him do the things that please God.

2:14-18 Exhortations

Paul gave these commands only after he mentioned that believers are given the ability to do them. Each act of disobedience to Christ's lordship makes ministry in his name vain and meaningless (2:16). Paul employed the language of Jewish offerings to illustrate his sacrificial service and ministry to the Philippians (2:17). Paul viewed his life as a drink offering, or wine libation. Such an offering normally accompanied the burnt and peace offerings (Num. 15:1-10; 28:7) and was mentioned with the daily offering (Exod. 29:40-41). Verses 2:17-18 link Paul's exhortations (2:14-18) to his words about Timothy and Epaphroditus (2:19-30). Even if Paul might not be able to come to them, he would try to send Timothy as a middleman to minister to them.

2:19-30 Mutual Joy by Messenger

2:19-24 TIMOTHY

Timothy would function as a reporter to Paul (2:19) and as a helper to the Philippians (2:20-21; cf. 1:17). He was a tested worker (2:22-24). Paul planned to send Timothy to Philippi immediately and hoped that he would be able to visit the believers himself. This reference provides an indication of Paul's travel itinerary after his departure from Rome.

2:25-30 EPAPHRODITUS

Epaphroditus had been sent from Philippi with a gift for the apostle Paul (2:25; cf. 4:18). After delivering the gift, he had remained to minister to Paul. While in Rome, Epaphroditus became very ill and was delayed from returning to Philippi. His illness was not described, but it caused both Paul and the Philippians much concern. Paul regarded Epaphroditus highly because he followed Christ's pattern of humble service to the truth. Epaphroditus had done for Paul what the Philippians had not been able do for him because of their distance.

3:1–4:1 EXHORTATIONS TO FOLLOW GODLY PATTERNS

3:1-16 Beware of Fleshly Boasting

3:1-6 CONFIDENCE IN HUMAN ACHIEVEMENT GAINED

3:1 Rejoice in the Lord

The Lord alone is the focus of rejoicing (3:1). This rejoicing is inseparably linked to the avoidance of evil (3:2). The focus is on the Lord, not self-interest. The phrase "Whatever happens" (3:1) is an indication of an impending conclusion. Paul did not hesitate to repeat himself.

3:2-3 True Worship

A continual temptation for believers is to work for the advancement of self, not the Lord (cf. 1:17). Paul was referring here to the Judaizers and described them from three points of view. As to their character, they were "dogs" (3:2), a term used by Jews for Gentiles. As to their conduct, they did "evil." As to their creed, they advocated "circumcision" as a vital part of Christianity and necessary for salvation. Paul contrasted true circumcision and the false circumcision advocated by the Judaizers (3:3). Paul made it clear that true circumcision was not of the flesh, but of the heart (cf. Rom. 2:25-29). The true Jews are Abraham's descendants by faith, not by the flesh.

3:4-6 Confidence in the Flesh

To illustrate the sufficiency of faith-righteousness apart from legalistic Judaism, Paul set forth his previous grounds for confidence—his Hebrew heritage and Pharisaic practices. Paul had been a Pharisee of great status. He brought up this fact to show that status and self-motivated achievement can indeed be gained. But Paul gave up these achievements that seemed great in the world's eyes and in return gained real knowledge and discernment. Everything he once thought worthwhile he now considered "worthless because of what Christ has done" (3:7).

3:7-16 CONFIDENCE IN HUMAN ACHIEVEMENT REPLACED BY CHRIST

3:7-11 Knowing Christ

Paul "considered" all that was "important" (3:7), the righteousness he could claim as a Pharisee, to be worthless (3:7-8). See the same concept in 2:6, where Christ "did not demand and cling to his rights as God." Paul wanted to know Christ (3:8, 10; cf. 1:9, "knowledge and understanding"; 2:13, "working in you, giving you the desire to obey him"; and 1:11 "the fruit your salvation"). While it would be natural to be proud of his Jewish heritage and attainments, Paul counted it all loss (worse than useless) for the greater gain of knowing Christ. Paul gave up Judaism to gain a righteousness based on faith (3:9), a knowledge of Christ and his resurrection (3:10), a sharing with Christ in his sufferings (3:10), a likeness to his death (3:10), and a participation in the resurrection (3:11).

3:12-14 Pressing on

In this section Paul was referring to the moral and spiritual perfection spoken of in 3:8-10, not the resurrection of 3:11. Paul forgot the past, Christian and non-Christian, because his goal was continual present-tense obedience that yields the knowledge of Christ.

Each new moment is fresh and powerful for gaining the fruit of righteousness. Paul used the image of a runner with hopes of winning the prize stretching for the finish line to describe his Christian walk.

3:15-16 The Mature Attitude
The mature person is able to understand Paul's perspective on humility, rejoicing in difficult circumstances and desiring to know Christ afresh each day. Paul suggested that if the Philippians did not agree with him, God would assuredly correct their views.

3:17–4:1 Focus on Good Patterns
3:17-19 THE BAD PATTERNS
Paul and the leaders (1:1), Timothy and Epaphroditus, were good models contrasted with their opponents. Paul exhorted the Philippians to join with one another in imitating him.

3:20–4:1 THE PATTERN OF CHRIST
The end of the enemies of the Cross (3:19) is contrasted with the end of the Christian (3:20-21). All believers share in Christ's past humble state (3:21; 2:7-8) but will also share in his exalted state (3:21; 2:9). Although they lived on earth, the Philippian believers were also citizens of heaven. The Philippians would immediately grasp Paul's point. As Roman citizens living in the outpost of Philippi, a Roman colony, they were entitled to the same rights and privileges as those living in Rome. In the same way, Christians, who were citizens of heaven, lived on earth with all the rights and responsibilities of heaven's citizens.

Philippians 4:1 looks back across the previous verses and sums up the entire letter. In view of their heavenly citizenship and future transformation, believers are to be steadfast and are not to defect from their faith (cf. 3:2-3).

4:2-20 FROM PHILIPPI: REPORTS FROM EPAPHRODITUS
4:2-9 Helps for Standing Firm
4:2-3 RESTORE HARMONY
Disharmony in the church is often a by-product of personal conflicts, so Paul directed the readers to the matter of inner joy and peace. The comrade Paul addressed here, although possibly Epaphroditus, was not identified. The book of life records the names of the redeemed (cf. Exod. 32:32-33; Rev. 3:5; 13:8; 20:12).

4:4-7 REQUEST FROM GOD: PEACE
Rejoicing is linked to being "considerate" (4:4-5; "gentleness," NIV; "forbearing spirit," NASB). Gentleness and forbearance issue from knowing the truth regarding this world and the next; this is real knowledge and discernment (1:9-10). The imperative could be translated, "Keep on rejoicing" (4:4).

The return of the Lord serves as a motivation for gentleness and forbearance.

Paul called believers to have peace in all circumstances (4:6-7). On anxiety or worry (4:6), see Matthew 6:25, 27-28, 31, 33-34. Worry implies that God is not present. To pray with thanksgiving shows a spirit of humble submissiveness. God does not promise to answer all the prayers of believers. But he does promise peace. The word "guard" (4:7) is a military term meaning "to keep under guard as with a garrison."

4:8-9 DWELL AND DO: PEACE
Right thinking is the first step toward righteous living (4:8). But thinking, learning, receiving, and hearing demand practice (4:9) if one desires to experience the God of peace.

4:10-20 Rejoicing for the Offering
4:10-14 THANKSGIVING FOR THE GIFT
This can sound like a thankless thanksgiving for their gift. Paul essentially said that he was quite content without their gift; he did not need it. But Paul was not being thankless. He was making a crucial point. His thanks arose, not because the gift had moved him from discontent to contentment, but because the Philippians had done a compassionate and good deed (4:14) that brought them profit before God (4:17-18). Paul did not want them to think he was emotionally or spiritually deprived without their gift. Lack of freedom or lack of goods was not critical for Paul's contentment or joy. His contentment came from inward self-sufficiency in Christ (1:21; 4:13), not from outward circumstances. Paul was saying, "I can do all things through the one who continually empowers me" (see 2:13 for the power of God working within the believer). While this verse is applied to many situations, the immediate context indicates that Paul was acknowledging God's enablement to find contentment in all circumstances, in plenty or in poverty.

4:15-20 THE VALUE OF THE GIFT: FRUIT
The Philippians sent more than one gift while Paul was ministering in Thessalonica (Acts 17:1-10). This suggests that he stayed there longer than just three weeks (cf. Acts 17:2; 2 Thess. 3:8). God promises to meet all the "needs" of believers, not necessarily all their "wants" (4:19; Ps. 34:10; Prov. 10:3; Matt. 6:25-34; Rom. 8:32). Paul gave the perspective of discernment. Their gift to Paul was in reality a gift to God.

4:21-23 FINAL GREETINGS AND BENEDICTION
"Caesar's palace" (4:22) probably referred to slaves or employees in the emperor's palace rather than members of the imperial family. There is no evidence of Christians within the family of Nero (A.D. 54–68) who ruled at this time.

COLOSSIANS

HISTORICAL SETTING

The Christians at Colosse were mostly Gentiles. Paul seemed to equate "you Gentiles" and "in you" in 1:27. Later, he classed them among the uncircumcised, (2:13) indicating a Gentile origin. Paul also intended that the Laodiceans read this letter (4:16).

Colosse was located in the Lycus Valley about 120 miles east of Ephesus. The Lycus Valley, branching off from the Neander River, served as the natural gateway to Lydia and Phrygia, placing Colosse on an important trade route. Colosse's sister cities, Laodicea and Hierapolis, were located about ten miles northwest of Colosse.

The Greek historian Herodotus mentioned Colosse as a place of strategic importance. The city may have found its origin as a military base. The chief article of commerce, for which the city was well known, was *colossinus,* a peculiar wool that was somewhat purple in color.

There was a distinctive Jewish element at Colosse, but the majority of the citizens were Gentiles. The gospel was introduced to Colosse as a result of Paul's long and influential ministry at Ephesus (Acts 19:10, 26; 4:12-13). Epaphras, who brought the news of the church to Paul in Rome, may have been influential in bringing the gospel to Colosse (Col. 1:7-8). Archippus was also actively ministering there (Col. 4:17; Philem. 1:2). From all indications, it appears that Paul had not visited Colosse before he wrote to the believers there, and many in Colosse had not met Paul (2:1).

The occasion of the letter was the arrival of Epaphras from Colosse (1:7-9; 4:12) with the information about the growth of the church in witness and love (1:3-8). But opponents had come into the area as Paul had predicted (Acts 20:29) and were presenting false doctrine.

That false doctrine combined two main elements. The first was drawn from Old Testament ordinances of the Mosaic covenant (Col. 2:8, 11, 16), human thinking (2:8), and the worship of angels (2:18). The second was drawn from a philosophy that claimed special privileged knowledge and insight into the nature of the universe (2:4, 8, 18). The result of that doctrine was to demean the completeness and sufficiency of the nature and work of Christ.

Paul's response stressed Christ as Creator and head over the church (1:16-18); the source of all wisdom and knowledge (2:3-4); the fullness of the Deity and head over all authority (2:9-10); and the only source of hope for future resurrection glory (3:1-4). All believers, who are Christ's body, are connected to Christ, their head (2:19). They are to seek after heavenly things (3:1-2), put on the new self (3:9-10), and let the word of Christ dwell in them richly (3:16).

AUTHOR

Pauline authorship is clearly indicated by 1:1 and 4:18. The use of the first person throughout (1:24; 2:1, 4; 4:4) and the personal tone of the letter (1:7, 9; 3:18-21; 4:7-18) support Pauline authorship. The autobiographical material intertwined with the argument of the book (1:24-25, 29; 2:1; 4:18) and the similarity of Colossians with Paul's other letters bring additional support to his authorship.

DATE

Colossians is one of Paul's Prision Epistles. For a discussion of the possible location of his imprisonment, see the Date section for Ephesians. The Roman location has the strongest support. Also, Luke's use of "we" in Acts 28:16 indicates that he was in Rome with Paul, a fact mentioned in Colossians 4:14 as well. The letter was probably written in A.D. 62.

PURPOSE

The letter to the Colossians was designed to help the readers understand that there was no power greater than Christ. Paul did this by showing how Christ is responsible for maintaining the entire universe, redeeming the world, and overseeing his church. Thoughts and activities based on anything less than Christ's supremacy were to be corrected and conformed to his truth.

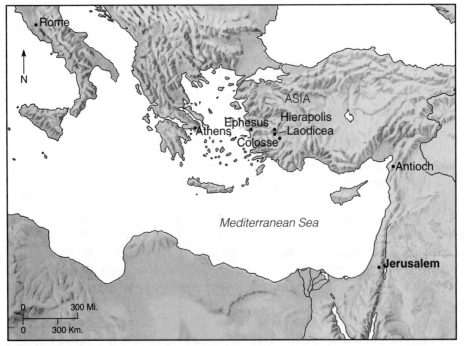

GEOGRAPHY AND ITS IMPORTANCE

THE CITY OF COLOSSE
Originally on a main road running eastward from Ephesus, Colosse diminished in importance when the road was moved westward through Laodicea. Paul had not been to this city when he wrote Colossians, but his influence probably reached the city during his long stay in Ephesus.

GUIDING CONCEPTS

Throughout the letter Paul confronts two problems that had arisen in the Colossian church. The first was a combining of legalism with Christianity. The second was an incorporation of mystical philosophies with Christianity. Both issues are compared and contrasted with the character and works of Christ. Now that Christ had been exalted to the right hand of God (3:1; Acts 2:33-35), all things were reconciled to Christ and had to be evaluated according to his wisdom. Paul stressed that Christ alone was now the measurement of knowledge and wisdom (Col. 2:3). The believer was raised with Christ (2:12; 3:1) and shared in his exalted wisdom. The believer was moved from hostility to peace. And that peace through reconciliation (1:20; 3:15) was the source of wisdom for the Christian in speaking (1:28; 3:16) and witnessing to unbelievers (4:5).

BIBLE-WIDE CONCEPTS

CREATION AND KINGDOM
Paul presented a black and white contrast between the kingdoms of light and darkness (1:13). From Genesis 3 onward God's history of redemption involved moving people from the darkness of Satan's kingdom to the light of Christ's. In Christ, believers could live and work for the kingdom of God (Col. 4:11).

But Christ was not one source of power and wisdom among many. Paul identified the exalted Christ as the Creator of the universe (1:16-17). Throughout the Old Testament creation and wisdom were closely related. God's creation was very good (Gen. 1:31). So to follow the natural laws set up in God's creation was to follow the way of wisdom (Prov. 8:22-36). The wisdom and knowledge found in Christ were not simply one mortal's ideas but expressions of the very imagination and knowledge that conceived and created the universe.

THE NEW COVENANT AND THE HIDDEN KINGDOM
One problem with living in Christ's present kingdom was the fact that it is hidden. The treasures of wisdom and knowledge were hidden in Christ (2:2-3). Christ was in the believer (1:25-27) and the believer's life and Christ himself were hidden in God (3:3). The mighty power at work in the believer (1:29) came from this hidden spiritual source.

But the hidden nature of the kingdom and God's covenant had long been predicted. Jeremiah had spoken of a new covenant by which God's commands would be placed in the heart (Jer. 31:33; quoted in Heb. 8:10). Ezekiel further revealed that the power to keep those commands would come from the Spirit placed within the believer (Ezek. 36:27).

To be sure, the kingdom of God would someday be visible for all to see (Col. 3:4).

But Jesus inaugurated a time period where the kingdom would be present but hidden. In his parables he compared the kingdom to a small seed or yeast hidden in a loaf of bread (Matt. 13:31-33). That hidden but potent existence of Christ's kingdom tempted some to look for more obvious outward manifestations of religion and wisdom (Col. 2:23). For others the hidden nature of the kingdom was a cause of groaning and eager expectation (Rom. 8:23). But Paul drove his readers back to the long-standing descriptions of the hidden kingdom of God in the Old Testament as fulfilled by Christ. Paul reminded his readers that though God's kingdom was hidden, it was still present, providing a basis for stability and hope.

NEEDS MET BY COLOSSIANS

The Colossians needed to be convinced that Christ was the supreme and final mediator between God and mankind. No other heavenly or earthly being was to control the lives of believers. Therefore, worrying about right days or right foods to appease unseen angels was actually an insult to Christ's supremacy. Life was not to be seen as an intricate maze of angelic powers through which only those initiated in secret wisdom could navigate. Life was simple, a negotiation of daily events with Christ alone. But the Colossians were faced with a conflict of authority between Christ and the non-Christians. The Colossians were tempted to treat Christ's teachings as debatable and subject to being compared and modified with other positions. Paul argued the absolute superiority and completeness of Christ and his wisdom. The structure and content of Colossians show that Paul intended to answer the following questions for his readers.

- Can believers draw from both Christ and other sources for spiritual wisdom and knowledge?
- How does Christ compare with other voices of religious authority?
- How can believers tell if a suggested religious behavior is good or not?
- How can believers know which authority figures should be listened to?

The Colossians faced problems quite like those faced by believers today. People are seeking answers to questions about how the spiritual world works. What spirit beings live in heaven? How do they move between earth and heaven? Do they ever communicate with people? How might they influence the lives of people? Continual interest in fortune-telling, seances, and astrology confirms the world's desire to see more clearly into the unseen spirit world. People want to feel more in control of their lives and destinies, to have more insight and direction in winding their way through the seen and unseen elements of life. But to that need Colossians clearly presents two facts. First, believers are not to concern themselves with understanding or submitting to whatever angelic orders of rank and authority that may exist. Second, believers are better off submitting to Christ's control of their lives rather than seeking to control their own lives. Christ alone is perfectly capable of guiding believers safely through life, a life that he sovereignly designed and will sovereignly accomplish.

OUTLINE OF COLOSSIANS

I. INTRODUCTION: CHRIST AS SOVEREIGN AND PEACE (1:1-23)
   A. Greeting (1:1-2)
   B. Thanksgiving (1:3-8)
   C. Petition (1:9-23)

II. CORRECTIONS AGAINST DIMINISHING CHRIST (1:24–4:6)
   A. The Purpose of Apostolic Concern (1:24–2:5)
   B. The Fact of Continual Completeness (2:6–3:4)
   C. The Acts of Reckoned Completeness (3:5–4:6)

III. CONCLUSION: NEWS ABOUT THE MINISTERS (4:7-18)
   A. Sharers of the News (4:7-9)
   B. Closing Greetings (4:10-17)
   C. Benediction (4:18)

COLOSSIANS NOTES

1:1-23 INTRODUCTION: CHRIST AS SOVEREIGN AND PEACE

1:1-2 Greeting

This is a standard Pauline greeting (cf. Rom. 1:1; 1 Cor. 1:1; Gal. 1:1; Eph. 1:1). Timothy, Paul's faithful associate, was with the apostle when he penned this letter.

1:3-8 Thanksgiving

Colossians 1:3-8 is one sentence in the Greek. Paul's gratitude to God for the Colossian believers is expressed in the three graces that he bestowed upon them: their faith, love, and hope (1:4-5). Paul's global perspective (1:6, 23) reveals the global power and scope of God's work in the gospel. The Christian faith was not just a localized religious cult. Paul needed to establish this to combat the Colossians' tendency to see Christianity as just another religion.

The gospel had been communicated to the Colossians by a faithful servant (1:7-8). The gospel message reached Colosse through Paul's coworker Epaphras, who apparently planted and organized the church. Epaphras is the only coworker of Paul designated a fellow bond servant. While Epaphras had undoubtedly reported to Paul in Rome concerning the errors threatening the believers, he also told of the love fostered in their hearts by the Holy Spirit.

1:9-23 Petition

1:9-12 WALK WORTHILY OF GOD

This petition comprises two long thoughts (1:9-20 and 1:21-23). Paul desired that their walk match the worth of the Lord (1:9-12). They had understood the gospel (1:6). Now they needed to deepen their knowledge of his wise will, a will that is spiritual and unseen. Paul's unceasing prayer for the believers was that they might attain a full knowledge of God's will. He made a subtle contrast between the partial knowledge advocated by the false teachers and full knowledge that is available in Christ. The result of being filled with knowledge is practical, a worthy life (1:10; cf. Eph. 4:1) accomplished in the power of God (Col. 1:11).

The thanksgiving of 1:12 is for complete and present qualification to share in salvation. This was foundational for arguing against the opponents who implied that such qualification had to be earned by progressively gaining knowledge. Light and dark symbolize the kingdoms of God and Satan. Believers have moved from darkness to light under the same God who moved the original creation from dark chaos to enlightened goodness.

1:13-17 WALK IN A MIGHTY REDEEMER

The Father's deliverance and the Son's reign are central for the Colossians' understanding and wisdom regarding their walk. Believers have been delivered from Satan's domain of darkness (Eph. 2:2) and brought into the kingdom of God's beloved Son (1:13). As those who have submitted to Christ the King, believers are in Christ's kingdom now, though the full realization of this fact is yet future (Rev. 20). The Son is the means of redemption (1:14). Redemption speaks of a release from slavery based on the payment of the purchase price or ransom.

Paul continued the letter by emphasizing the priority of the Son's creation (1:15-17). Christ is the Creator and Sustainer of all creation. The primary characteristic of the Colossian error was a deficient view of Christ and his work. Rather than attacking the Colossian error outright, Paul wisely began by setting forth the person and work of Christ and the believers' completeness in him. The word "image" (1:15) means "archetype," like the stamp that makes the impression on a coin. Christ is the one on whom the Father has set his mark. The word "supreme" (1:15) may have a temporal (first of many to come) or a positional (chief heir) emphasis. Here the emphasis is on primacy of position. The Colossians thought that angels had similar authority to Christ. But Paul showed that even the levels of angelic authority were under Christ's sovereign power. Paul's use of "kings, kingdoms, rulers, and authorities" (1:16) may appear to refer to human authorities. But in this context these words refer to unseen angelic powers, as other Pauline passages confirm (e.g., 2:15; Eph. 1:21; 3:10; 6:12).

1:18-23 LIVE UNDER CHRIST'S RECONCILING HEADSHIP

The progression of thought is from Christ as the image of God (1:15), to his rank in creation (1:16-17), to his rank in the church (1:18). His rank in the church comes from his fullness of deity (1:19). Paul declared that all the "fullness" of God (1:19) dwells in Christ. The word "fullness" was apparently used by the false teachers at Colosse (and in later Gnosticism) to denote the divine nature distributed among numerous intermediaries between God and the world. Paul insisted that Christ alone embodies the full measure of deity. Reconciliation and peace can come only through him (1:20; 3:15).

Paul applied the fact of God's reconciliation with man to the lives of all believers and declared himself a servant of that truth (1:21-23). The "But" (1:23) does not cast doubt on the security of truly saved people (John 10:28) but stresses the fact that the proof of the genuineness of the believers' salvation is their continuance in faith and hope.

1:24–4:6 CORRECTIONS AGAINST DIMINISHING CHRIST

1:24–2:5 The Purpose of Apostolic Concern

1:24-29 INTRODUCTION OF PAUL'S MINISTRY

Paul's goal was the completion of the Colossian believers in Christ (1:28). This goal led him into sufferings which, rightly seen, were the completion of Christ's sufferings. But Paul was not completing the vicarious suffering of Christ for sin (Heb. 9:28). Because of the unity between Christ and the church, Paul's sufferings for the sake of the church could be called Christ's sufferings as well.

Paul was the servant of a mystery that had been disclosed through the person and work of Christ (1:25-29). The exalted Creator (1:16-17) and head of the church (1:18) had revealed himself and lived within all the believers (1:27). That truth was an assault on those who implied that Christians needed knowledge and rituals to supplement the revelation of truth through Christ (2:4). Paul labored for their maturity (1:28-29).

2:1-5 APPLICATION OF PAUL'S MINISTRY

The city of Laodicea (2:1; see note on Rev. 3:14) was located in the Lycus Valley about ten miles northwest of Colosse. Paul was concerned that the Colossians would be deceived by the persuasive arguments of the false teachers. He admonished them to continue to live focused on Christ rather than pursuing less stable and speculative theories. Since in Christ the believer has the treasures of wisdom and knowledge, there is no reason to pursue philosophical speculation (Col. 2:3). The "persuasive arguments" (2:4) are elaborated in 2:16-23.

2:6–3:4 The Fact of Continual Completeness

2:6-15 INITIAL COMPLETENESS

The Christians needed nothing else but to continue on in faith. The second step was the same as the first ("just as" they had received, so they should live). There was not a switch from the first step of faith to some supposed second step of legalistic or mystical ritual (2:23). Paul used two metaphors to describe the relationship of believers with Christ. Like a firmly rooted tree (2:7), they were grounded in the truth of Christ. Like a house with a solid foundation (2:7), they were founded on their faith in Christ and were continually being built up in him.

To avoid being led astray by "empty philosophy," Paul emphasized the need to be deeply rooted in Christ (2:8-15). Two ways of living are identified: according to the world or according to Christ (2:8). Paul warned the believers against getting side-tracked by persuasive arguments and speculative theories. He emphasized that Christ alone is sufficient for salvation and spiritual growth. "Philosophy" (2:8) means "love of wisdom" and refers here to any system of thought that does not recognize the centrality of Christ. The problem with philosophy is that it has no basis of authority other than man's reason. Paul used the vocabulary of the false teachers to show how Christ epitomizes all they hoped to find in philosophy.

Paul continued by giving reasons for living according to Christ (2:9-15). Christ has the fullness of deity (2:9) and believers can find fullness or completeness in him (2:10) and live above all lesser rule and authority. The results are freedom from human judges and hollow rituals (2:16, 20). Spiritual circumcision (2:11) takes place when a believer is identified with Christ through personal faith.

Paul reminded the believers that they once stood as debtors, condemned because of the law (Eph. 2:15; Gal. 3:10). But Christ fulfilled the requirements of the law (Matt. 5:17) and by his death liberated believers from its condemnation (Col. 2:14). He erased the legal ordinances that condemned, nailing the document that was against believers to the cross. Not only was the debt of sins cancelled, but Satan's forces were conquered and humiliated through the cross (2:15). Paul drew on the imagery of a triumphant Roman procession where the victorious general and his troops led captives and captured booty in public display through the city streets. Similarly, Christ defeated Satan and led him in triumph through his resurrection.

2:16-19 CONTINUED COMPLETENESS

Believers are not subject to any authority and judgment except Christ's. "Eat or drink" referred to the ceremonial food laws observed by the Jews (Lev. 11); "festival" referred to the Jewish holy convocations (Lev. 16); "new-moon ceremonies" referred to a minor festival that was observed monthly (1 Sam. 20:5; Isa. 1:13); and "Sabbath" referred to the law of Sabbath-keeping (Exod. 20:8). These ceremonies were to be regarded by Christians as shadows of the realities now available in Christ. Their observance could not add to or subtract from the believers' completeness in Christ (2:17). The opponents were motivated by selfish pride (2:18-19).

2:20–3:4 CONTINUAL FOCUS ON CHRIST

Paul was describing man-made religion in any form. It could not overcome fleshly or sensual indulgence (2:23). Paul warned against asceticism, self-denial as a means of gaining acceptance by God. All human decrees and prohibitions have the appearance of wisdom but are of no eternal significance apart from the knowledge of God.

The man-made facade of glory (2:23) is not to blind believers as to where their true glory resides, hidden in God (3:4). This glory will be revealed when Christ is revealed. Paul instructed the believers to set their affections on things above, things consistent with one's position in Christ, not the things that were earthly and had no eternal significance. Believers are to become in experience what they already are in Christ positionally.

3:5–4:6 The Acts of Reckoned Completeness

3:5-17 PUTTING ON THE NEW SELF

Paul revealed the absolute deity and authority of Christ and affirmed that Christ resides in the believers, making them complete and above man-made religious efforts. Next he gave specific examples of conduct worthy of the Christians' salvation.

Paul showed that believers should be dead to old ways and alive to the new (3:5-14). With the "so"

(3:5) Paul made a transition from doctrine (1:1–3:4) to practice (3:5–4:6). (Paul made such a transition in most of his other letters as well.) The doctrine of Christ and the believers' completeness in him provides the basis for a discussion of proper Christian conduct. In the face of temptations that might lead to sin, Paul used a striking image of viewing the body as dead to sin. How the believers' death with Christ works out in practice is explained by more images in the following verses: "get rid of" (3:8; "put . . . aside," NASB; "put off," KJV); "stripped off" (3:9; "laid aside," NASB; "put off," KJV); "clothe yourselves" (3:12; "put on," NASB and KJV); "let . . . peace . . . rule" (3:15); and "let . . . Christ . . . live" (3:15-16).

The "old evil nature" (3:9) refers, not to the unregenerate nature, but to the flesh's disposition to follow physical desires and leave God out of the picture. The "brand-new nature" (3:10) refers to the disposition created in the believer by the Holy Spirit to obey God and live consistently with his spiritual inheritance. Paul exhorted the believers to put on new virtues that were more consistent with their new nature in Christ.

Christ's rule of peace (3:15) pulls believers together in unity (cf. 1:15-18). When differences threaten the unity of the body, the peace of Christ must be accepted as arbitrator. This peace was defined by Christ's words (3:16-17). This section has close parallels with Ephesians 5:18 where submission in marriage, family, and work flowed from the fullness of the Spirit. Here, the same groups were addressed from the perspective of the rich indwelling of Christ's word (3:16). Christ's teachings are to "live" in the believer. The context suggests that this may be accomplished through teaching, admonition, and singing. In 3:17 Paul was saying that believers' activities ought to be consistent with the reputation of Christ. Could they participate in this activity in association with Jesus' reputation (cf. 1 Cor. 10:31)?

3:18–4:1 SPECIFIC RELATIONSHIPS

Note the motivations for keeping these commands (3:18, 20-25). This section is closely parallel to Ephesians 5:21–6:9. Here Paul illustrated how the principles of Christian living may be expressed in everyday affairs. For submission (3:18), see note on Ephesians 5:22. For slavery (3:22), see note on Ephesians 6:5-9.

4:2-6 SPEECH PATTERNS

On the subject of prayer (4:2-4), see Ephesians 6:18-20. Paul recognized the power and potential available through prayer (Phil. 4:6-7; 1 Thess. 5:17). Here he exhorted the believers to continue steadfastly in prayer. For Paul's imprisonment in Rome (4:3), see Acts 28:16, 23, 30-31.

Wisdom to outsiders (4:5) is the context for

effective conversation (4:6). The believer's speech is to be "gracious and effective" (4:6). Here Paul was probably referring to speech that is "appetizing," a witness to unbelievers that is well prepared and focused on the individual needs of each person.

4:7-18 CONCLUSION: NEWS ABOUT THE MINISTERS

4:7-9 Sharers of the News
Tychicus (4:7; cf. Acts 20:4; Eph. 6:21; 2 Tim. 4:12; Titus 3:12) apparently carried this epistle to the church at Colosse. Onesimus (4:9), Philemon's runaway slave, accompanied Tychicus back to Colosse (cf. Philem. 1:10).

4:10-17 Closing Greetings
Many of the names mentioned in Paul's greetings are also mentioned elsewhere. Aristarchus (4:10; cf. Acts 19:29; 20:1-4; 27:2; Philem. 1:23-24) may have shared Paul's imprisonment on a voluntary basis, perhaps passing as his servant. John Mark (Acts 13:13; 15:36-40; 2 Tim. 4:11; Philem. 1:24), author of the second Gospel, having been restored to Paul's favor, was to be welcomed at Colosse should he travel there. Jesus, also called Justus (4:11), is not mentioned elsewhere. Epaphras (4:12-13; 1:7-8; Philem. 1:23) was influential in bringing the gospel to Colosse. Laodicea and Hierapolis were located in the Lycus Valley about ten miles northwest of Colosse. Luke (4:14; cf. 2 Tim. 4:11; Philem. 1:24), the author of Acts and the third Gospel, is referred to by Paul as "Dear Doctor Luke." Demas (2 Tim. 4:10; Philem. 1:24) was a helper who defected.

With his greetings Paul included circulation instructions (4:15-16). Paul not only greeted the Laodicean believers (cf. Rev. 3:14) but asked that this letter be shared with them and that his letter to Laodicea be read to the Colossians. Some take it that the letter from Laodicea was the encyclical letter now known as Ephesians (see note on Eph. 1:1). The church met at Nympha's (or Nymphas; masculine) house (cf. Acts 12:12; Rom. 16:5, 23). It wasn't until the third century that separate buildings were used for church worship.

Archippus (4:17), Paul's fellow worker (Philem. 1:2), was actively ministering in Colosse. Paul encouraged him to give this letter his full attention.

4:18 Benediction
Paul's greeting with his own hand confirms the genuineness of the epistle. For Paul's Roman imprisonment, see Acts 28:16, 20, 23, 30-31. The remembrance of Paul's bonds was not for sympathy. It was a reminder to see trials from the proper perspective (1:24-25) and, in that light, stand firm no matter what the situation (4:3-5).

1 THESSALONIANS

BASIC FACTS

HISTORICAL SETTING

Thessalonica, named in 315 B.C. by Cassander for his wife, the half sister of Alexander the Great, is strategically located on the Egnatian Way, which stretched across Macedonia to the west. Located on an excellent harbor at the northeastern corner of the Thermaic Gulf, Thessalonica was commercially very important. Due to its location, the city has been called "the key to the whole of Macedonia."

In Paul's day Thessalonica was a large city with as many as two hundred thousand people, the largest city of Macedonia. It had a sizable Jewish population, and Paul recognized it as a strategic place to begin a ministry (1 Thess. 1:8).

Luke gave a detailed account of Paul's ministry in Thessalonica (Acts 17:1-10). Paul taught in the synagogue for three Sabbaths. He worked to bring in support (1 Thess. 2:9; 2 Thess. 3:8) and also received offerings from the Philippian church (Phil. 4:16).

Paul was forced out of the city and went to Berea (Acts 17:11-12). Jews from Thessalonica disrupted the ministry in Berea, forcing Paul to depart (Acts 17:13-15). Paul moved on to Athens and left Silas and Timothy in Berea to continue the work. Silas and Timothy eventually joined Paul in Athens (1 Thess. 3:1-2). From there Paul sent Timothy to Thessalonica. Paul had gone on to Corinth where Timothy again caught up with him and brought news from Thessalonica (Acts 18:1-5). Paul wrote 1 Thessalonians from Corinth.

AUTHOR

Pauline authorship of this letter is attested both by internal and external evidence. The letter presents itself as being from Paul (1:1). His named companions were known to have been with him on his second journey (1:1; 3:2, 6; Acts 15:40; 16:1-3, 19; 17:4, 10, 14; 18:5). The form, vocabulary, and theological thought are clearly Pauline. Finally, the major early church fathers (Origen, Clement of Alexandria, Tertullian, and Irenaeus) testify to the authenticity of the letter.

DATE

Paul first visited Thessalonica on his second missionary journey (A.D. 50–52). The letter was written in A.D. 51, about six months after Paul left Thessalonica.

PURPOSE

Paul's first letter to the Thessalonians was designed to give comfort and encourage steadfastness in their commitment to Christ. This was done by reminding the believers of the past powerful realities of Christ in their lives and by clarifying some of the future events of Christ's return. Whether discussing the past or the future, Paul's purpose was to increase their present faithfulness and joy in Christ.

GEOGRAPHY AND ITS IMPORTANCE

THE CITY OF THESSALONICA
Paul was in Corinth when he wrote to the Thessalonians. Thessalonica was the major port for Macedonia. Cassander founded the city around 315 B.C. and named it for his wife, Thessalonica, who was also the half sister of Alexander the Great. During Paul's time Thessalonica was the capital and largest city of Macedonia.

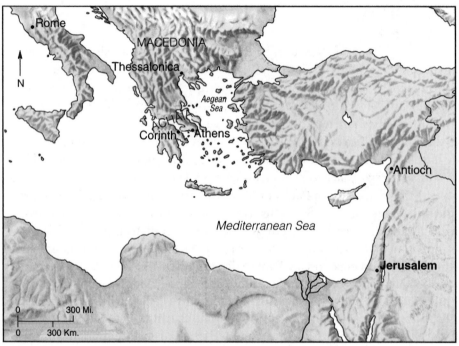

GUIDING CONCEPTS

DISTINGUISHING BETWEEN HUMAN AND DIVINE WRATH
Paul clarified the difference between human and divine wrath. The Thessalonians were undergoing great afflictions from Jewish opposition (3:3). Paul said they were destined for this human type of tribulation (3:3; see Acts 14:22). But they were not destined to undergo God's wrath in the future (1:10; 5:9). The suffering believers confused human and divine wrath. This error opened them up to misunderstandings in their conception of Christ's second coming, which would be their ultimate relief from suffering, and a potential lapse of steadfastness.

EXCELLENCE AND SANCTIFICATION
Paul wanted his friends to excel in their Christian lives (4:1, 10). He also wanted them to live sanctified lives (3:13; 4:3-4, 7; 5:23). All the instructions concerning persecu-

tion, morality, and the second coming were geared toward enabling excellence and sanctification. Even the section where Paul defended the integrity of his ministry among them (1:2–2:20) was designed to strengthen the foundation of the believers' faith and obedience.

BIBLE-WIDE CONCEPTS

THE DAY OF THE LORD

The day of Christ's return forms a constant background for Paul's thoughts in this letter (1:10; 2:19; 3:13; 4:13–5:11; 5:23). A correct understanding of that day was essential for accomplishing the sanctification of the believers. In the Old Testament, the day of the Lord was presented as having a number of distinct characteristics.

"Thy will be done"

First of all, because it is the day of the Lord, it implies that all the other days of history are not the Lord's in the way this one will be. History's days are permeated with the ungodly acts of rebellious humanity. The day of the Lord will be a day that begins a new eternal era in which the perfect will of God will find exact fulfillment.

Supernatural and worldwide

Second, the day of the Lord will bring supernatural interventions. The righting of wrongs in that day will not be dependent on human effort. Throughout the Bible, the day of the Lord is revealed as a day that cannot be accomplished by people, only by God. Third, the day of the Lord will be worldwide. It looks back to creation and to the fullness of the Abrahamic promises to all nations (Isa. 51:1-8).

The day of the Lord stretches on into the promised golden age for Israel and the earth. Isaiah moves through a whole series of end-time events as if through a single grand day. Daniel includes both judgment and the establishment of the Messiah's kingdom in that day (Dan. 7:10-14). Note Jesus' use of that Daniel passage as recorded in Matthew 26:64 and Mark 14:62. The day of the Lord will bring international judgment and an eternal kingdom for the saints. There is a close interrelationship between the kingdom to come, the Son of Man, and the saints of Christ's church.

A process of redemption and judgment

Fourth, the day of the Lord will involve both redemption and judgment (Isa. 24:20-23; 25:6-9). It will be a day when the faithful are received into the fullness of their redemption. It will be a day when unbelievers are rejected into the fullness of their damnation. Thus, the day of the Lord will actually be a broad period of time that stretches from the time of antichrist and tribulation through the Millennium and final judgments. The Old Testament views the day of the Lord as the final conquest over evil; it will be a day when faithfulness is rewarded and the heavens and earth recreated.

The day of the Lord is not simply a future historical fact. It will bring a moral evaluation of people's lives by Christ. And that future evaluation impinges on the present. The promise of future judgment should encourage believers to live properly now (Amos 5:18). God has given many days that prefigure the final day of the Lord (for example, Zeph. 1:11-18; the downfall of Judah to Babylon; the locust plague of Joel 2:1-11).

Nearness

Fifth, the day of the Lord is near. It is near because the Judge is near. Christ reigns at God's right hand and is present with power. All he needs to do is to start his judgments and restoration. He is not far away. He can begin in an instant. That is what makes the day near, that sense of instant possibility.

The concept of nearness is not built on nearness in the sense of time, a short or long time. The day of the Lord has been near for close to two thousand years because it is like death. All people know they are going to die. They do not know when they will die, but they do know it could happen at any minute. In that sense, death and the day of the Lord are always near.

Summary

The day of the Lord is God's future visible entrance into history and retribution for people who have rebelled from his way. That history has stretched from the fall of Adam to the present. At present, the kingdom of God is like a tiny mustard seed. And the conflict is between the people of God and those who hate them. When Christ returns, the conflict will be directly between himself and his opponents will result in a visible kingdom. The seed will have become a mature tree spreading around the world in the fulfillment of God's promises to Abraham (Isa. 51:1-8).

THE RULE OF THE LORD

The Lord to whom the day belongs is both the Suffering Servant (Isa. 53:1-12) and the exalted Son of Man (Isa. 9:1-7; Jer. 33:14-18; note Daniel 7:13 and Ps. 110:1 combined in Matt. 26:64). The hope for the day of the Lord is hope for redemption based on the suffering of the Lord. There could be no kingdom without the Cross (Matt. 16:21; Mark 10:45). The doctrines of future things and salvation must always go together (2 Sam. 7:14-15; Isa. 11:1-9; Zech. 6:12-13). Those who believe must always look back to the Cross and ahead to the Second Coming.

NEEDS MET BY FIRST THESSALONIANS

The Thessalonians' blessings in Christ had come up against the realities of life. They were being persecuted by religious and civil groups and some Christians had already died. They wondered why they should be so blessed by God and at the same time be so cursed by the world. The doctrinal truth of the line between relief for the saints and divine wrath on God's enemies had blurred. The pain of their hard circumstances could have blinded them to the broader realities of God's plan for history. By clearly distinguishing between human and divine wrath, Paul enabled the Thessalonian readers to go on in faith and steadfastness. The content of the letter indicates that the Thessalonians were probably asking questions like these.

- Have believers made the right and secure choice in accepting a Savior who has led them into persecution?
- With all the religious and civil leaders criticizing Paul, can believers be secure in accepting his authority?
- How can believers know that the persecution and tribulation they are suffering is not a result of God's wrath?

- How can believers feel secure about what has and will happen to deceased Christians?
- How can believers see this troubled life as designed to deepen their sanctification?

As with the Thessalonians, life's pain can cause today's believers to doubt that God is in control and wants the best for his people. Present conflicts can make believers insecure about the future and dull their perception and enjoyment of God's present goodness. When friends or relatives doubt the faith of believers and criticize their trust in the authority of the Bible, this letter encourages them to see beyond the problems to God's ultimate control of history. God's ordination of a process of time that involves some pain and injustice should not diminish the absolute certainty that the process will inevitably lead to righting all wrongs and rewarding the faithful. Believers need to hold fast to the future while living in the present. This combination will give them the perspective to maintain their personal purity, joy, and witness in an often joyless and hostile world.

OUTLINE OF FIRST THESSALONIANS

I. INFORMAL GREETING (1:1)

II. THANKSGIVING FOR AN EFFECTIVE INITIAL WITNESS (1:2-10)
A. For Manifested Character (1:2-3)
B. For Assurance of Election and Witness in Affliction (1:4-10)

III. DEFENSE OF PAST WITNESS (2:1–3:13)
A. A Witness of Integrity (2:1-12)
B. Paul's Thanksgiving for a Receptive Hearing (2:13-16)
C. Paul's Thanksgiving for Timothy's Good Report (2:17–3:13)

IV. REQUEST FOR INCREASED EXCELLENCE (4:1–5:24)
A. Exhortations to Excellence (4:1-12)
B. Concerning Those Who Died (4:13-18)
C. Concerning the Day of God (5:1-11)
D. Specific Community Relationships (5:12-24)

V. CLOSING REQUESTS (5:25-28)

FIRST THESSALONIANS NOTES

1:1 INFORMAL GREETING

The focus in Paul's greeting was on the three who ministered in Thessalonica, not on Paul and his apostleship (see 2:6). "Silas" is the shorter form of the name "Silvanus" (Acts 15:40). In 315 B.C. Cassander reconstructed Therma, a harbor city located on the Thermaic Gulf, and named it "Thessalonica" after his wife, the daughter of Philip of Macedon. Paul, Silas, and Timothy visited the city on Paul's second missionary journey (Acts 17:1-9) in A.D. 50. His ministry for "three Sabbaths" (Acts 17:2) was probably only the beginning of his ministry there rather than the full extent of it (cf. 1 Thess. 2:9; 2 Thess. 3:8; Phil. 4:16).

Because of the persecutions they were suffering, Paul identified this church closely with God and his Son who had also suffered. The believers were not alone in a hostile world. And despite the hostility of the world, they had peace with God. Although the people around the Christians may have been offended or threatened, God was not.

1:2-10 THANKSGIVING FOR AN EFFECTIVE INITIAL WITNESS

Overview: The section of 1:2–3:13 moves between Paul's ministry and its reception by the Thessalonians (reception, 1:2-3; ministry, 1:4-5; reception, 1:6-10; ministry, 2:1-12; reception, 2:13-16; ministry, 2:17–3:13). Clearly Paul was trying to reaffirm his godly ministry and the readers' godly responses in the light of critical hostility (cf. 2:3; 3:4-5; Acts 17:9; Phil. 4:16). It was customary for ancient letters to open with a word of gratitude, but Paul's thanksgiving is no mere formality. He is thankful for the believers virtues (1:2-3), conversion (1:4-7), and testimony (1:8-10).

1:2-3 For Manifested Character

Paul answered his critics point for point (cf. 1 Thess. 3:4-5; 2:3; Acts 17:6-9; Phil. 4:16-17): greed, 2:8-9; cowardice, 2:1-2; not caring, 2:7-8; mistaken message, 2:13-16; persecution, 3:1-4. "Continual anticipation" (1:3) is sometimes translated as "endurance" (NIV), which literally means "to abide under," that is, to hold up under trial with a positive and optimistic outlook. This outlook is inspired by hope.

1:4-10 For Assurance of Election and Witness in Affliction

The "full assurance" (1:5) relates to Paul's own affirmation of his sincerity (1:5). His sincerity was matched by the Thessalonians' commitment (1:6). The Greek word translated "imitated" (1:6) is related to the English word "mimic." Paul's integrity and their commitment cemented Paul's knowledge of their election (1:4). They reflected Paul and the Lord (1:6). Macedonia (1:7) was the province of northern Greece where Philippi was located. Achaia was the province to the south where Corinth was situated.

Paul noticed how the Thessalonians' witness confirmed what a positive and godly influence he had had. The hostility some of the Thessalonians felt toward him could not overshadow what God had done through him (1:9-10). The strategic location of Thessalonica on the Egnatian Way and at the head of the Thermaic Gulf undoubtedly did much to further the rapid spread of the gospel. Repentance (1:9) refers to a "change of mind" and involves a turning from sin and self to God. It is a synonym for believing, not a condition for salvation (Acts 26:20; Rom. 2:4; 2 Pet. 3:9).

The process of waiting (1:10) involves hope ("anticipation," 1:3). "From" is used three times (1:10) and outlines the past, present, and future hopes of believers ("Son from heaven," "raised from the dead," "rescued us from the terrors of the coming judgment").

"The coming" (1:10) is added to "judgment" in order to delineate between present tribulation and future judgment. For "rescued us from," see Matthew 6:13; 27:43; Romans 7:24; 2 Corinthians 1:10;

Colossians 1:13; 2 Thessalonians 3:2; 2 Timothy 3:11; 4:17-18; and 2 Peter 2:7, 9. The return of Christ is a very prominent theme in 1 Thessalonians. Paul concluded every chapter in this letter with some reference to the coming of Christ (1:10; 2:19; 3:13; 4:17; 5:23).

2:1–3:13 DEFENSE OF PAST WITNESS

2:1-12 A Witness of Integrity

2:1-6 NOT A VAIN ENTRANCE

The words "visit" (2:1) and "welcome" (1:9) are from the same Greek word. Paul recalled his first work among them. The gospel had been spoken after and amidst persecution (2:1-2). This showed the sincerity of Paul's work among them. A false minister would not have persevered in the persecution Paul had experienced. Paul defended the missionary team against criticism from some who believed that Paul and his associates were motivated by selfish desires (2:3; 5:6).

In refuting the accusations, Paul used the method of letting the record of his ministry speak for itself. When evaluated in the light of truth, the malicious charges being made against the missionaries could not survive. For Paul's experience in Philippi, see Acts 16:12-40. Paul, a Roman citizen, had been beaten and imprisoned without a trial. The apostle had also experienced opposition in Thessalonica (Acts 17:5-9).

Paul spoke to please God, not people. His message was true, pure, and without deceit (1 Thess. 2:3). This verse reflects three charges that had been made against the missionaries: (1) their preaching was based on "deceit," (2) they gained followers by "impure purposes," and (3) they used "trickery" on them. The word "trickery" means "to catch with bait" and suggests deception. "Flattery" was given as an example of methods used by those seeking "praise" from men (2:5-6). First negatively (2:5-6) and then positively (2:7-8), Paul recounted the missionaries' previous conduct among the Thessalonians.

2:7-12 A SACRIFICIAL ENTRANCE

Paul was full of affection for the Thessalonian Christians (2:7). He was not selfish or disinterested. His professional expertise was combined with the love of a mother for her children. He shared his life, not just words (2:8). The image of a caring mother points to the word "gentle." The phrase "as a mother feeding and caring" is a technical term for a professional wet nurse. But in this case the professional wet nurse is nursing her own children—the combination of professional expertise with personal love.

Paul continued to remind the Thessalonians of his irreproachable behavior (2:9-12). Paul early on had sized up the situation in Thessalonica and realized it was best not to receive money or gifts from the believers there. Because of this, Paul and his associates worked hard not to become a burden to them. They also received gifts from Philippi to support themselves financially (Phil. 4:16). This strategy is further explained in 2 Corinthians 11:7-11. Paul had the right to receive remuneration for his ministry (1 Cor. 9:3-14) but gave up that right so that no one would charge him with greed.

Paul mentioned three aspects of his preaching ministry: encouraging, comforting, and urging (2:11). Once again (cf. Eph. 4:1), Paul used the word "live" to describe the believers' conduct or manner of life (2:12).

2:13-16 Paul's Thanksgiving for a Receptive Hearing

Paul wanted the Thessalonians to look toward God, not men, as the end of true ministry (2:13). The preachers would come and go, but God would always remain. Ministers must eventually hand their work over, but God energizes. The work accomplished by the word of God (2:13) was a church that remained faithful in persecution (2:14-16). For a glimpse of how the Thessalonians suffered at the hands of their own countrymen, see Acts 17:5-9. The main offense of Paul's opponents was that they hindered the gospel (2:15-16). For "anger" (2:16), see Romans 1:18.

2:17–3:13 Paul's Thanksgiving for Timothy's Good Report

2:17-20 PAUL'S DESIRE TO SEE THE THESSALONIANS

Paul had been kept away from this church because of Satan (2:17-18), not because he had a careless attitude (2:3-4, 7). After Paul left Thessalonica, the believers there were out of sight, but not out of mind. Several times Paul planned to return to Thessalonica, but his efforts were thwarted by Satan. Happily for believers today that satanic thwarting resulted in Paul having to write this very letter.

Paul answered the accusation that he did not care about them by telling of his desire to see them and that one day they would be together with the Lord forever (2:19; cf. Matt. 24:3, 27, 37, 39; 1 Cor. 15:23). Paul emphasized Jesus' bodily presence at the coming of the Lord.

3:1-10 PAUL'S SUBSTITUTE MINISTER

Timothy was sent to strengthen and encourage the Thessalonians (3:1-5). Paul had left Silas and Timothy at Berea to complete the work there (Acts 17:13-15) and had traveled on to Athens (Acts 17:16) by sea where he was later rejoined by his associates. After several attempts to return to Thessalonica, he decided to go on alone to Athens and sent Timothy (and probably Silas, Acts 18:5) to

strengthen and encourage the believers. The Thessalonian believers were destined to suffer (3:3-4). But suffering at the hands of hostile people is radically different from suffering the wrath of God (5:9). They were destined for affliction but not destined for wrath. "Useless" work (3:5; "vain labor," NASB and KJV) would be the silencing of the Thessalonians' witness due to satanic temptations in persecution. The "Tempter" (3:5) refers to Satan by his characteristic activity.

Timothy brought good news back to Paul (3:6-10). After Paul had traveled on to Corinth (Acts 18:1), he was joined by Silas and Timothy who brought an encouraging report from Thessalonica (Acts 18:5). Paul was so thankful for their continued progress in the faith that words could barely express his joy (3:9). The expression "fill up anything that may still be missing" (3:10) was used of repairing a fishing net (Matt. 4:21). Paul wanted to build up the believers' faith so that they would not be deficient in any way.

3:11-13 PAUL'S DESIRE FOR THEIR ESTABLISHED HOLINESS

Paul prayed that God would remove the obstacles that Satan had put in his way (3:10) so that their fellowship could be renewed (3:11).

4:1–5:24 REQUEST FOR INCREASED EXCELLENCE

Overview: The key words are "blameless" and "holy" (3:13; 4:3-4, 7; 5:23) and "more and more" (4:1, 10; "excel," NASB). This entire section from 4:13 to 5:23 reveals important elements in the process of sanctification. The Thessalonians needed encouragement; their faith lacked strength. Paul would at this point seek to begin correcting them in the areas in which they were deficient. He would talk about personal purity (4:3-8) and comfort (4:9–5:11); he would continue talking about living with leaders who probed them about what they lacked (5:12-14). The main thought in all of this section is holiness (3:13; 5:23) and the means by which it is attained.

4:1-12 Exhortations to Excellence

4:1-8 EXHORTATION TO EXCEL IN PURITY

The word "finally" (4:1) does not indicate the close of the letter but serves to introduce a new subject (Phil. 3:1). Paul passed from matters of personal history to practical application. The sanctification referred to here is the believer's present sanctification—being set apart to God from the controlling influence of sin (4:3; see note on 1 Cor. 1:2).

The idea of men confining sexual intercourse to marriage was foreign to Greek morality of the first century A.D. Men were said to have mistresses for pleasure, harlots for casual sex, and wives for marriage and children. Although pagan religions knew nothing of sexual purity, and some even encouraged cultic prostitution as part of their fertility rites, God's will for Christians is sexual purity (1 Cor. 6:12-20).

Paul emphasized the importance of self-control (4:4-6). Some interpret "body" (4:4) as referring to one's own body (cf. 2 Tim. 2:21) or to one's own wife (1 Pet. 3:7). Since "control" may also be rendered "acquire," Paul could be referring to premarital chastity during courtship and the contracting of marriage. The word translated "body" normally meant "body" in Greek usage and "wife" in Jewish usage. Either way, believers were to be the masters of their desires, not controlled by them.

4:9-12 EXHORTATION TO EXCEL IN LOVE
On brotherly love, see John 13:34. Paul encouraged the believers to work to supply their own needs while doing ministry so that their witness might not be suspect. This followed Paul's own model for ministry (2:9).

4:13-18 Concerning Those Who Died
Overview: This passage revealed the fact that deceased and living believers would meet again at the Lord's return. This focus uncovered a confusion among the Thessalonians. They wondered what would happen to already dead believers when it came time for Christ to return. Comfort and encouragement (4:18; 5:11) were Paul's aim in these verses. The dead may have been lost to their relatives, but they were not lost to God (4:13-14). They would be seen again when Christ is revealed. Perhaps some thought that the dead would not be raised to resurrection bodies (4:14, 16). But the main issue concerned how they would all come together again at Christ's coming. Note the concepts of "bring back with" (4:14), "ahead of" (4:15), "first" (4:16), and "with them" (4:17). Sanctification would be greatly hindered by people depressed over lost loved ones whom they were not sure they would ever see again. Paul wrote to give hope to the grieving believers.

4:13-14 THE PATTERN OF CHRIST'S DEATH AND RESURRECTION
The believers at Thessalonica were apparently upset because they mistakenly thought that those who died before the Lord's coming would miss out on it completely. Paul wrote to clarify the relationship between the living and the dead at the time of Christ's return. His point was that the living would not precede the dead (4:15). The Lord's coming will begin with the dead believers but will also include the living saints, for they are all part of the one body of Christ. The certainty of the believers' resurrection is based on the fact of Christ's resurrection (4:14; 1 Cor. 15:20-22). "We believe" (4:14) reveals that the Thessalonian Christians did believe that the resurrection of Christ was true.

4:15-18 THE SEQUENCE OF APPEARANCE AT HIS COMING
The "Christians who have died" (4:16), the believers who had died and are present with Christ (2 Cor. 5:8) will be physically resurrected and receive their glorified bodies at the time of Christ's return (1 John 3:2). The word translated "caught up" (4:17) literally means "to seize" or "to snatch." It is from the Latin translation of this word that the term "rapture" is derived. The words "to meet" (4:17) were used of meeting a dignitary paying an official visit to one's city. The leading citizens would go out to meet the honored guest. Paul's instruction concerning the Lord's coming and believers' resurrection was to be a source of comfort and hope to the Thessalonians (4:18).

5:1-11 Concerning the Day of God
5:1-3 CERTAIN DESTRUCTION
See Matthew 24:36-44. The day of the Lord is one of the major themes of the Old Testament prophets (cf. Isa. 13:6, 9; Joel 1:15; Zeph. 1:14-18). The day of the Lord is that period of time during which God will deal with Israel and the nations through judgment and deliverance. According to Peter, that day will conclude with the purging of the heavens and earth in preparation for the creation of the new heavens and earth (2 Pet. 3:10-13; cf. Isa. 65:17; 66:22). The expression "like a thief in the night" (5:2) emphasizes the unexpectedness of the event and the unpreparedness of those to whom he comes. The expression "as a woman's birth pains" (5:3) is a common figure for increasingly intense pain and sorrow (Matt. 24:8).

5:4-11 CERTAIN SALVATION
Paul encouraged the Thessalonians to conform to God's light, not the darkness that leads to destruction in the day of the Lord. Since the day of the Lord will result in judgment for the wicked and deliverance for the righteous, self-examination was important. Believers are associated with "light" (spiritually enlightened because of the new birth) rather than "darkness" (the realm of sin and spiritual emptiness). The coming of the Lord should motivate believers to be mentally alert and morally vigilant. Paul used an illustration of a Roman soldier on duty (5:8). The believer must be on guard against a hostile world, putting on spiritual armor as protection against Satan's attacks (cf. Eph. 6:13-17). God has not appointed believers to be the subjects of divine wrath, but rather to be delivered from the day-of-the-Lord judgments by the coming of Christ (5:9). Whatever pain the Thessalonians would experience, they were not to think they had been abandoned to God's wrath (see the problem worsen in 2 Thess. 2:1-2). First Thessalonians 5:10 shows that 4:13-18 has not been far from Paul's mind. The issues of discouragement (5:11) and

sorrow (4:18) were definite threats to sobriety, faith, love, and hope (5:8). The point of speaking about the future coming of Christ was to give them hope and strengthen their present witness and sanctification.

5:12-24 Specific Community Relationships

Overview: Paul taught about living with people when the going gets rough. He had just encouraged them to build each other up (5:11). Next he asked that they honor those whose primary task is to do the building up—the church leaders (5:12).

5:12-14 APPRECIATION OF LEADERS

Paul explained that leaders are there to push believers to maturity. But their legitimate criticisms, no matter how difficult to accept, should result in peace and appreciation. Paul provided a helpful summary of the responsibilities of spiritual leaders (5:12). They are to "work hard" ("diligently labor," NASB), rule or govern ("among you"), and "warn" ("give instruction," NASB). They are to match their ministry to the particular needs of the people. "Warning" is appropriate for the unruly, "encouragment" for the fainthearted, and "care" for the weak. The ministries match the needs. "Lazy" (5:14) is a military term signifying the marching soldier who does not keep in proper step. Thus, it refers to those who are out of line.

5:15-22 PRAYER AND DISCERNMENT

This section provides the framework for seeking after being "good" (5:15, 21). In the original Greek, 1 Thessalonians 5:16 is the shortest verse in the Bible. The Christian who will "keep on praying" is living in constant communion with God and is always ready to pray. "Stifle" or quenching the Spirit (1:19) is illustrated in the next verses: "scoff" (1:20) rather than "test" (1:21) spiritual truths. This was probably going on in Thessalonica and is reminiscent of what went on in Corinth (1 Cor. 14:23, 27, 29, 33, 39). To "scoff" means to despise and count as nothing. Paul did not advocate an uncritical acceptance of every person that claims to be of the Spirit. Teaching must be carefully examined to determine what is true and what is not. Sound doctrine must be retained and unsound doctrine rejected (5:22).

5:23-24 PRAYER FOR COMPLETE SANCTIFICATON

Paul's closing prayer covered all the areas addressed in 1 Thessalonians 4–5, especially regarding sanctification (3:13; 4:3-4, 7; 5:23). Paul prayed for complete sanctification among the believers. He elaborated further by praying that the immaterial (soul and spirit) and material (body) parts of the believers might be presented blameless at the coming of Christ.

5:25-28 CLOSING REQUESTS

In Paul's closing words he made requests for prayer, sent greetings, and gave instructions for sharing the letter. The term "in Christian love" (5:26; "holy kiss," NIV) was a common oriental greeting in ancient times and corresponds to the practice in Western culture of shaking hands (cf. Rom. 16:16).

2 THESSALONIANS

BASIC FACTS

HISTORICAL SETTING

For the founding of the church at Thessalonica, read Acts 17:1-10 and the Historical Setting section for 1 Thessalonians. The immediate occasion of 2 Thessalonians was a report that Paul received concerning the positive faith and love of the Thessalonian Christians (1:3-4) and their misunderstandings concerning the day of the Lord which were caused by false teachers (2:2). Some believers thought they were in the day of the Lord and had given up working to live in idleness (3:6-12), apparently waiting for the Lord's return.

AUTHOR

Paul is identified as the author in 1:1 and 3:17. The authenticity of the letter was recognized by Irenaeus (c. A.D. 170). The objections to Pauline authorship by some scholars are based on criticisms that have little substance compared to the certainty that the early Christians showed as to the letter's genuineness.

DATE

Because Paul, Silvanus (Silas), and Timothy were still together when the letter was written, it is probable that the second letter was written from Corinth not long after the writing of 1 Thessalonians. The close connection between the two letters makes it unlikely that a long interval separated them. It is generally held that two or three months passed between the writing of the two letters. In harmony with the date of 1 Thessalonians (early summer of A.D. 51), 2 Thessalonians may be dated in the summer of A.D. 51.

PURPOSE

Paul's second letter to the Thessalonians was designed to encourage believers that all their persecution and suffering would ultimately be worth it all. Throughout the letter, the question of how all their pain could be a good and righteous part of God's plan is addressed.

GUIDING CONCEPTS

This letter deals with three basic concepts, one in each chapter. The first concerns whether or not it was right for believers to be undergoing such persecution as they were experiencing (1:1-12). The second concerns whether or not the readers had fallen under the wrath of the day of the Lord (2:1-17). The third relates to whether following Christ under such persecutions was really worth all the pain and effort (3:1-18).

BIBLE-WIDE CONCEPTS

THE RIGHTEOUS SUFFERER

One problem addressed in 2 Thessalonians was the question of God's justice in the suffering of the righteous believer (1:5-8). Job could not understand why he suffered unjustly. Hebrews 11 is full of examples of those who suffered unjustly because they were righteous. Jesus became the supreme example of the righteous sufferer (1 Pet. 2:22-24). The question for the righteous sufferer throughout Scripture was how to keep going on with God and believing in his goodness (1 Pet. 2:20-21). Unjust suffering can easily cause a believer to lose steadfastness (2 Thess. 3:5) and become weary of doing good (3:13).

CONFLICT BETWEEN GOD AND SATAN

The letter also explains the conflict between the children of God and Satan that began at the fall of Adam (Gen. 3:15). The description of the antichrist (2 Thess. 2:3-12) contributes to the revelations in Scripture concerning the end times (see, for example, Dan. 7:23-27; Matt. 24–25; Rev. 12:9-17). Throughout the Bible, the reason for discussing the day of the Lord was to show that the Lord of that day is present now, whether that day is near or far. It also serves to remind believers that their future evaluation is built on their actions in the present.

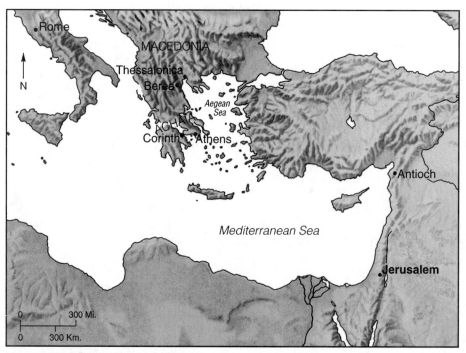

NEEDS MET BY SECOND THESSALONIANS

The Thessalonians went through much criticism and hostility because they had believed Paul's message about Christ. The message of great blessing in Christ seemed a bit contradictory to their experience of persecution. Not only did they have questions and worries about what God was doing, they also needed confirmation that Paul, the one who first brought the gospel to them, was trustworthy. Paul's brief second letter to the Thessalonians met three crucial needs. These needs are reflected in the following questions that were probably being asked by the Thessalonians.

- Is God doing the right thing by allowing believers to suffer so much?
- What is God doing about the evil people who are persecuting believers?
- Have the terrible days of the antichrist already arrived?
- Is it really worth being godly when it brings so much pain?

The joy the Thessalonians experienced at the beginning of their Christian walk soon met with the painful and unjust realities of life. And when this happens, believers today, like them, have some pressing needs to be met. This letter should help believers to become honestly and deeply convinced that what God is allowing to happen is part of his process of justice. The temptation is to quietly think that God is not being fair. But the proper balance will come when believers learn to be content with present suffering without blaming God. They must anticipate the future judgment of their enemies while still witnessing to them and seeking their salvation. Another need the letter addresses is how to keep going during the tough times. The goal is not a tight-fisted teeth-clenched resignation to life's problems, but rather a joyful, optimistic, and very wise assessment of the good and the bad in life with a view to maximizing all the good for Christ. This letter should help believers learn to keep their eyes both on the realities of this age and the rewards of the next.

OUTLINE OF SECOND THESSALONIANS

I. INFORMAL GREETING (1:1-2)

II. THANKSGIVING FOR THEIR BEHAVIOR IN TRIBULATION (1:3-12)
    A. Faith and Love in Affliction (1:3-10)
    B. Prayer for Fulfilled Desires (1:11-12)

III. A CORRECTED CHRONOLOGY FOR THE DAY OF THE LORD (2:1-17)
    A. Its Futurity and Components (2:1-12)
    B. Exhortation to Hold to the Traditions (2:13-17)

IV. CLOSING REQUESTS FOR PRAYER AND DISCIPLINE (3:1-15)
    A. Request for Prayer (3:1-5)
    B. Command for Discipline in Work (3:6-15)

V. BENEDICTION AND CLOSING (3:16-18)

SECOND THESSALONIANS NOTES

1:1-2 INFORMAL GREETING
In his greeting, Paul recognized a personal relationship (1:1) based on a divine source (1:2). Timothy and Silvanus were Paul's associates during his ministry in Thessalonica (Acts 17:10, 14). "Silvanus" is the longer name for "Silas" (see note on 1 Thess. 1:1). For matters concerning the city of Thessalonica, see note on 1 Thessalonians 1:1. Second Thessalonians was sent by Paul from Corinth in the summer of A.D. 51, not long after the writing of 1 Thessalonians.

1:3-12 THANKSGIVING FOR THEIR BEHAVIOR IN TRIBULATION
1:3-10 Faith and Love in Affliction
1:3-5 WHAT GOD THINKS OF THEIR SUFFERINGS
There is a cause and effect relationship between their love (1:3) and their perseverance in afflictions—a key theme of the letter (1:4). The idea behind perseverance is putting up with negatives in order to achieve another more constructive end. Because of the steadfastness of the Thessalonians under trial, Paul seized every opportunity to praise them.

God's verdict concerning the Thessalonians was: "He will make you worthy" (1:5). Their worthiness was the verdict built on their perseverance and faith under suffering (1:3-4). Their perseverance rendered them worthy. God would be right in judging them worthy to enter his kingdom. The church at Thessalonica was born in persecution (Acts 17:1-9) and grew in spite of continued persecution (1 Thess. 1:6; 2:14; 3:1-3). Some believers were beginning to question the righteousness of God in all this. Paul declared that their response in suffering was proof that God was working in them and that their faith was genuine.

1:6-10 WHAT GOD WILL DO ABOUT THEIR SUFFERINGS
The question of how God could be doing right regarding those who suffer or cause suffering had to be related to the question of when God would act. The question of God's justice in the Thessalonians' suffering would not be completely answered until Christ was finally revealed (1:7). Paul declared that at Christ's coming there would be a reversal of present circumstances. God would bring judgment on the wicked who were persecuting the Thessalonians and would provide rest for those who had endured such hostility. The word translated "rest" (1:7) was used to describe relief from tension, like that which comes from relaxing a taut bowstring. Old Testament appearances of God were frequently marked by the presence of fire (1:7; cf. Exod. 3:2; 19:18; 24:17; Ps. 18:12). A fiery manifestation of God's presence would be displayed at Christ's return. The

words "everlasting destruction" (1:9) do not suggest the annihilation of the wicked but rather their everlasting ruin by reason of their eternal separation from the presence of God.

1:11-12 Prayer for Fulfilled Desires
Knowledge of Christ's future return was to encourage powerful works of faith. The believers were to glorify Christ in the present (1:12), and he would be glorified in the believers at his return (1:10). For now, the believers are to glorify Christ by proclaiming his great love and holy purposes. At his return, Christ will glorify the believers by proclaiming their exalted, vindicated, and holy nature as children of God. The combination of those two glories, Christ in Christians now and Christians in Christ then, was vital for maintaining hope for the future and a vigorous witness in the present.

2:1-17 A CORRECTED CHRONOLOGY FOR THE DAY OF THE LORD
2:1-12 Its Futurity and Components
2:1-2 ASSERTION: IT IS IN THE FUTURE
Paul referred to the subject of Christ's second coming throughout the first chapter of this letter. His coming would mean rest for the saints (1:7). During Paul's stay in Thessalonica he had explained many of the details of prophecy to the believers (2:5; cf. 1 Thess. 4:13-18; 5:1-11). Paul had taught that the believers would have no part in the day of God's wrath (1 Thess. 5:9). Now, due to intense persecution and some misinformation (2 Thess. 2:2), some of the Thessalonians had come to believe they were in the midst of the day-of-the-Lord judgments. Paul wrote this letter to clarify that Christ's coming was still in the future.

Paul sought to clarify the fact that Christ's return and the day of the Lord were future events. He wanted to further explain that particular aspect of Christ's return that involved the believers' gathering together to meet their returning Lord. The potential problem (2:2) was that some claimed the day of the Lord was present. Had Paul changed his teaching regarding when that day would come? The Thessalonians were confusing present tribulation from men with the promised future judgments from God. They thought the day of the Lord had come and they were suffering under God's judgment. They also wondered why Jesus had not returned to redeem them out of the tribulation. They were disturbed due to a seeming change in the inaugural events of the day of the Lord. Paul explained that the day of the Lord had not yet arrived and that their suffering was not judgment from God but persecution from evil men. He turned the focus to how they should deal with the persecution they were experiencing. Paul explained that suffering severe tribulation should not be a cause of distress for them (cf. 1 Thess. 3:3).

2:3-12 INSTRUCTION: HOW THE DAY OF THE LORD WOULD COME
The Greek word translated "rebellion" (2:3) is only used again in Acts 21:21 to describe a political or religious "turning away." Here the context relates the word to the general events of the revelation of the antichrist (2:4-12) and the gathering of the church to the Lord (2:1). The Antichrist's works parallel the works of Christ. He will "come" (2:9; cf. 2:1), and he will have a revelation (2:3; cf. 1:7-8) and a gospel, a "great deception" (2:11; cf. 2:10). Paul wrote that two events needed to take place before the day of the Lord's judgments began: (1) the apostasy and (2) the revelation of the man of lawlessness (cf. Dan. 7:25; 8:25; 11:36). The term "rebellion" literally means "departure" and may refer to a departure from doctrine or the departure of the believers to meet Christ at his return. The "man of lawlessness" (2:3, 8-9) refers to the "little horn" of Daniel 7:8, the Antichrist of the end times (cf. Rev. 11:7; 13:1-10).

After the restraint's removal, the lawless one will seek to deceive and destroy (2:5-7). While the identity of this restrainer may be debated, its function is to show that this is the time of restraint, of grace for belief. The evil of this age has the stamp of the Antichrist's lawlessness (2:7). Yet the Antichrist cannot be revealed until "what is holding him back" (2:6) has been removed. The restrainer has been identified by some to be the Roman government, but there was no appearance of the Antichrist after the decline of the Roman Empire. The restrainer must be more powerful than Satan who empowers the lawless (Rev. 13:4). It may be that Paul was referring to the restraining ministry of the Holy Spirit.

After the restraint of the lawless one is removed, the Lord will move to destroy the Antichrist (2:8-12). This is the actual day of the Lord. Paul provided a description of the character and activity of the Antichrist. The Antichrist's career will be terminated at the second coming of Christ (2:8; Rev. 19:20; 20:10). The Antichrist, empowered by Satan (Rev. 13:4), will demonstrate signs and false wonders in order to deceive people into following him (2:9).

2:13-17 Exhortation to Hold to the Traditions

2:13-15 PRAYER IS BASED ON BEING CHOSEN FOR SALVATION
Paul turned from the punishment of the antichrist and his followers to the bright prospects of the Thessalonians. Here he thanked God for the believers and for what God had done in their hearts (2:13-14). Compare 2:13 with 1:3. A proper understanding of the day of the Lord would help the

believers to stand firm (2:15). The purpose of the believers' election was their ultimate salvation (glorification), and that would be achieved by the sanctifying work of the Holy Spirit.

2:16-17 PRAYER FOR THOSE CHOSEN
Paul desired that the Thessalonians would let truth push its way into their daily lives. The promise of the truth of future deliverance would give them steadfastness and faith in the present. God might let them suffer under persecution and tribulation, but that would serve to prove their perseverance and the evil of their persecutors.

3:1-15 CLOSING REQUESTS FOR PRAYER AND DISCIPLINE
Overview: Second Thessalonians 1 showed that God had just and blessed reasons for allowing the believers to be persecuted. Second Thessalonians 2 explained that the Thessalonians were not to be shaken from good works by thinking they had been misled and had fallen under God's judgments in the day of the Lord. In 2 Thessalonians 3 Paul encouraged them to be steadfast and not grow weary of doing good.

3:1-5 Request for Prayer
Paul requested that the believers pray for deliverance (3:2) and strength (3:3) so that Paul and the believers might continue in Christ's "love" and "endurance" (3:5; "steadfastness," NASB). Paul desired that the gospel "spread rapidly" (3:1), a metaphor taken from the athletic arena (cf. 1 Cor. 9:24). Paul undoubtedly had in mind his Jewish opponents in Corinth (3:2; Acts 18:1-18). This chapter presents the commands of Paul (3:4, 6, 12) for endurance (3:5) and discipline (3:6, 7, 11, 14).

3:6-15 Command for Discipline in Work
Doctrinal error often leads to practical misconduct. The misunderstanding concerning the day of the Lord led some to think that since the Lord was coming soon, there was no need to continue working. Some had quit their jobs and were leading undisciplined lives.

There was a connection between lack of discipline and the problem of perseverance (3:6, 7, 11; see "lazy" in 1 Thess. 5:14). The strain of persecution and the misguided pressures of thinking they were in the day of the Lord led to weariness in doing good (3:13). That weariness resulted in unruly and undisciplined living. Paul used the future events of the day of the Lord to drive his readers into a clearer present world-mission. The function of Paul's command was to drive them to a world redemptive ministry (cf. 1 Thess. 4:11-12).

Paul set himself forth as an example for others to follow (3:7-9). He reminded the Thessalonians that while he had a right to receive support for his ministry (3:9; cf. 1 Cor. 9:1-18), he had worked night and day to avoid being a financial burden on them.

Paul clarified his original command concerning the necessity of work (3:10). While Christians have a responsibility to help those in need, Paul corrected misguided charity that only encourages idleness. The problem and the cure (3:11-15) were similar to those in 1 Thessalonians 4:11; 5:14. Life's strains caused some to tire of trying to do good (3:13). In Ephesians 3:13 the Greek word for "tire" is translated "despair." Note the common factor in Luke 18:1-8; 2 Corinthians 4:1, 16; Galatians 6:9; and Ephesians 3:13. People lost heart because they somehow misunderstood the future blessed results of life's trials.

Paul ordered the church to keep away from and not have social contact (3:14; lit., "mix themselves up") with the disobedient and disorderly. This coincides with the final step of dicipline described by Jesus—excommunication (cf. Matt. 18:15-17). The discipline was designed to cause them to "turn inwardly" ("be ashamed," 3:14), reflect on their conduct, and repent of it. Second Thessalonians 3:15 emphasizes that the whole procedure is with a view to reformation and restoration to usefulness in the church.

3:16-18 BENEDICTION AND CLOSING
Although Paul dictated the letter, the final greeting was written in his own hand (cf. 1 Cor. 16:21; Gal. 6:11; Col. 4:18). This was an indication that the letter was genuine and was particularly important since some forged letters had been circulated in Paul's name (cf. 2:2). "Peace no matter what happens" (3:16) is the theme of this letter, and Paul gave several clear examples of how such peace could be found.

1 TIMOTHY

HISTORICAL SETTING

This letter was addressed to Timothy (1:2) but speaks to a broader audience (6:21 has the plural form of "you"). Timothy was first met by Paul on Paul's second missionary journey (Acts 16:1-3). Lystra was apparently Timothy's home. His father was a Greek, and his mother, Eunice, and grandmother, Lois, were devout Jews (Acts 16:1; 2 Tim. 1:5). Timothy had been trained in the Old Testament Scriptures (2 Tim. 3:14-15) and may have been converted by Paul on his first visit to Lystra (Acts 14:6-7; 1 Cor. 4:17; 1 Tim. 1:2). The words "my true child in the faith" suggest that Timothy was converted under Paul's ministry. Timothy worked with Paul on his missionary journeys (Acts 16:3; 17:14-15; 19:22; 1 Cor. 4:17; 16:10; 1 Thess. 3:1-2). He joined Paul and Silas when they traveled through the region of Lystra and Derbe on the second missionary journey (Acts 16:1-3) and faithfully served Paul during his second and third missionary journeys as well. He was with Paul during his first Roman imprisonment (Phil. 1:1; 2:19-24; Col. 1:1; Philem. 1:1). Timothy was his close companion and is associated with him in writing Philippians, Colossians, and Philemon. After Paul's release from Roman imprisonment, Timothy was appointed to lead the church at Ephesus (1 Tim. 1:3; 2 Tim. 1:16-18; 4:19). Timothy was also imprisoned (Heb. 13:23). Timothy was a prime example of a servant of God (Phil. 2:20-22). At the time Paul wrote 1 Timothy he expected to return to Ephesus, but he wrote this letter to give Timothy some directions for his ministry in case he should be delayed (cf. 1 Tim. 3:14-15).

AUTHOR

The letter names Paul as the author (1:1), and the autobiographical remarks fit his life (1:12, 13). The early church fathers accepted the letter as genuine. A possible reconstruction of Paul's travels after his first Roman imprisonment can provide the background for the Pastoral Epistles (1 Timothy, 2 Timothy, and Titus). The chart on the next page, "Paul's Travels after His Roman Imprisonment," attempts to reconstruct a likely itinerary based on the biblical data.

Since Paul had announced his coming to the Colossians, he probably left for the east upon his release from Rome (spring of A.D. 62). He apparently went to Colosse (Philem. 1:22) and then to Ephesus where he left Timothy (1 Tim. 1:3). From there he proceeded to Macedonia where he wrote to Timothy (1 Tim. 1:3) and visited Philippi (Phil. 1:25; 2:24). Paul may have then returned to Ephesus as he had hoped would be possible (1 Tim. 3:14). Paul may have then realized his desire in the spring of A.D. 64 to journey to Spain (Rom. 15:24).

After a possible stay of two years in Spain (A.D. 64–66), Paul again journeyed east and visited Crete (Titus 1:5), where he left Titus to set the church in order and appoint elders (A.D. 66). Paul may have then journeyed to Asia Minor to visit Miletus (2 Tim. 4:20) and Troas (2 Tim. 4:13). He probably wrote Titus concerning his reponsibilities before traveling to Nicopolis, where he spent the winter (Titus 3:12). Paul may then have spent the spring and autumn of A.D. 67 in Macedonia and Greece, perhaps visiting Corinth (2 Tim. 4:20). Paul was then arrested a second time and brought to Rome. There he wrote 2 Timothy, requesting that Timothy join him in Rome before the winter of A.D. 67/68. Paul's martyrdom is placed by Eusebius in the thirteenth year of Nero. Paul's death probably occurred in the spring of A.D. 68.

The occasion for writing 1 Timothy was the possibility of Paul's visit to Timothy at Ephesus being delayed (3:14-15). Timothy needed the instructions concerning specific matters of church policy and practice that only Paul could give.

DATE
The letter was written after Paul's release from his first Roman imprisonment (A.D. 62) and before his death in the spring of A.D. 68. First Timothy appears to have been written soon after his release and after his visits to Ephesus (1:3) and Colosse (Philem. 1:22) and his journey to Macedonia (1 Tim. 1:3). The letter was probably written in the autumn of A.D. 62.

PURPOSE
Paul's first letter to Timothy was designed to give the church clear directions for establishing the kind of leadership and decorum that would most effectively establish and support

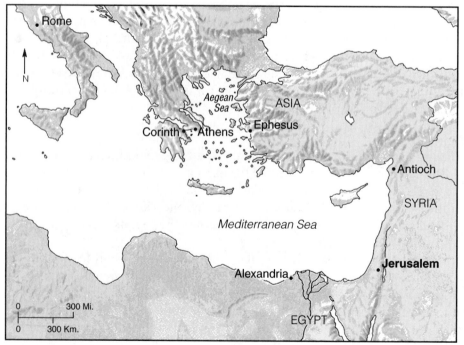

the truth of God in the gospel. This was done by focusing on love rather than speculation, salvation rather than squabbling, and true rather than false leadership. Throughout the letter Paul sought to encourage family love and respect among the believers.

GUIDING CONCEPTS

SUPPORTING THE TRUTH OF CHRIST
The key section for this letter is 3:14-16. It shows that the entire enterprise of the church is to be a pillar and support for the truth. That truth is embodied in the incarnation of Christ and lived out in the various practical issues dealt with in the letter. Everything Paul said about church life and leadership comes from the need for leaders to teach the wonderful truth about godliness in Christ.

BIBLE-WIDE CONCEPTS

PAST CORRESPONDENCE WITH EPHESUS
The Ephesian Christians tended to withhold their prayers for Gentile Christians in preference for Jews (2:1-7). But Paul had already shown the Ephesians that because the old covenant had been done away with (Eph. 2:15), the Gentiles were now fully included in the promise of salvation (Eph. 2:15). On that basis Paul continually pleaded for unity within the body of Christ (Eph. 4:16). Unity needed to be shown in an aggressive desire to match God's desire for the spread of salvation (1 Tim. 2:3-4). Paul had commanded that all anger and bitterness be put away (cf. Eph. 4:31 with 1 Tim. 2:8). And he had also warned that false teachers would come bringing deception and conflict (Eph. 5:6; Acts 20:29-31). The section of 1 Timothy 5:1–6:2 deals at length with the problems of submission and order within the family of God.

ISSUES FROM THE OLD COVENANT
The errant teachers of the law in Ephesus misunderstood and were abusing several Old Testament concepts. Paul dealt with these misunderstandings in his first letter to Timothy.

PAUL'S TRAVELS AFTER HIS ROMAN IMPRISONMENT

Place	References	Key Phrases
To Asia Minor	Philem. 1:22	"keep a guest room" in Colosse
To Ephesus	1 Tim. 1:3	"stay there in Ephesus"
To Macedonia	1 Tim. 1:3	"left for Macedonia"
To Philippi	Phil. 1:25; 2:24	"will come . . . soon"
To Ephesus	1 Tim. 3:15	"if I can't come for a while"
To Spain	Rom. 15:24	"planning to go to Spain"
	1 Clement 5:7	"the extreme limit of the west"
	Muratorian Canon	"the journey of Saint Paul to Spain"
To Crete	Titus 1:5	"I left you on the island of Crete"
To Asia Minor	2 Tim. 4:13	"the cloak I left . . . at Troas"
	2 Tim. 4:20	"I left Trophimus sick at Miletus"
To Greece	Titus 3:12	"meet me at Nicopolis"
	2 Tim. 4:20	"Erastus stayed at Corinth"
To Rome	2 Tim. 1:16-17	"When he came to Rome, he searched everywhere until he found me"

Law and faith

There was a conflict between law and faith. The foundational Old Testament passage on faith is Genesis 15:6. But the false teachers did not emphasize faith (1 Tim. 1:3-5) and thereby missed the original point of the law (1:7-10).

Riches

The Old Testament has much to say about the Ephesians' problem with riches (6:3-10, 17-19). Some key Old Testament passages are Deuteronomy 8:1-18; Jeremiah 9:23-24; 17:11; and Micah 6:12. Other important New Testament references are 1 Corinthians 1:26-31; 2 Corinthians 10:17; Mark 10:23-24, and James 5:1-6.

Widows

Paul dealt with the important Old Testament subject of widows in 1 Timothy 5:3-16. The Old Testament viewed the treatment of widows as a prime indication of a believer's devotion to God (cf. Exod. 22:22-24; Deut. 10:12-22; 14:29; 24:17-18; 26:13; 27:19; Isa. 1:17, 23; Jer. 7:6; Prov. 15:25; Zech. 7:8-10; Mal. 3:5). The New Testament also addresses this problem in James 1:27.

Truth

The false teachers misunderstood the nature of truth. For Paul truth was the very person of Christ (1 Tim. 3:16). All laws and conduct were to mirror God's ways as revealed in Christ. Anything that did not reflect Christ was not truth (cf. 2:4, 7; 3:15; 4:3; 6:5). For key Old Testament passages on truth (sometimes translated "faithfulness"), see Exodus 34:6; Nehemiah 9:13; and Psalm 31:5. In the New Testament see John 1:17; 14:6; 17:17; 18:37; and 1 Corinthians 5:8.

NEEDS MET BY FIRST TIMOTHY

Timothy had his work cut out for him when Paul left him to minister at Ephesus. Some Christians were trying to get rich by assuming roles of leadership in the church. Various social groups such as widows, elders, masters, and slaves were at odds with each other. And worst of all, status-seeking men were trying to become church leaders while teaching false doctrine and being completely inept at interpreting God's word. The Ephesian Christians needed to understand some basic distinctions between the proper and improper use of Scripture within the Christian community. The structure and content of 1 Timothy show that Paul intended to answer the following questions for his readers.

- When Scripture is quoted to support someone's position, how can believers know if the right interpretation is being made?
- Are believers supposed to pray for even the most ungodly national leaders?
- What else, besides a strong desire for leadership, is required for someone who wants to have authority in the church?
- How are believers supposed to relate to the various age and social groups in the church?
- What is the godly perspective on being wealthy?

For the Christians in first-century Ephesus, and for believers today the issues concerning how Christians should live together are the same. This letter to Timothy helps believers to know how to test a person's claim to being a Christian leader. Desire for leadership must be matched by depth of character and skill in interpreting the Bible. The letter also gives advice as to how various social and age groups are to live together in harmony. The heart of church life is revealed to be the person of Christ. All church activity should further Christ's purposes and reflect his character. The letter also gives great insight into developing a balanced Christian perspective on spiritual and financial wealth.

OUTLINE OF FIRST TIMOTHY

I. FORMAL GREETING (1:1-2)

II. THE INSTRUCTION TO KEEP SOUND DOCTRINE (1:3-20)
   A. The Instruction to End Fruitless Teaching (1:3-11)
   B. The Gospel Entrusted to Paul (1:12-17)
   C. The Command Entrusted to Timothy (1:18-20)

III. THE INSTRUCTION APPLIED: COMMUNITY TRADITIONS (2:1–6:19)
   A. Prayer: Adopt God's Desires (2:1-15)
   B. Leadership: Serve God's Truth (3:1–4:16)
   C. Honor for Household Members (5:1–6:2)
   D. Correctives to Materialism (6:3-19)

IV. CLOSING CHARGE (6:20-21)

FIRST TIMOTHY NOTES

1:1-2 FORMAL GREETING
Although Paul addressed the letter to Timothy as an individual, it was clearly meant for the edification and instruction of the whole church. Paul stressed his divine authority for the church leaders in Ephesus as well as for Timothy. They were not to take Paul's call by God lightly.

God is portrayed as Savior (1:1). Paul was stressing to Timothy the fact that his call to the ministry should remain fresh. Timothy was said to be Paul's "true" child in faith (1:2), probably reflecting his conversion under Paul's ministry. The greeting in this letter adds "mercy" to Paul's standard "grace and peace." On God as Father (1:2), see Deuteronomy 32:6, 19; 2 Samuel 7:14 compared with 2 Corinthians 6:18.

1:3-20 THE INSTRUCTION TO KEEP SOUND DOCTRINE
1:3-11 The Instruction to End Fruitless Teaching
Overview: After his release from his first Roman imprisonment in the spring of A.D. 62, Paul traveled to Asia (cf. Philem. 1:22) and then to Macedonia (cf.

Phil. 2:24). When he departed for Macedonia, Paul left Timothy in Ephesus for the specific purpose of correcting certain false teachers. For a description of Ephesus, see the note on Ephesians 1:1.

1:3-7 THE GOAL OF PAUL'S INSTRUCTION
Paul desired to turn fruitless teachings into acts of love (1:3-7). Some in Ephesus were addicted to strange myths. Paul may be referring here to Jewish myths and legends that are found in the noncanonical books of the Apocrypha (hidden writings), Pseudepigrapha (false writings), and Talmud. Books such as the Assumption of Moses, the Life of Adam and Eve, the Secrets of Enoch, and the Book of Jubilees relate speculative events, conversations, and prophecies.

The false teachers were focusing on these useless speculations rather than sound doctrine. Myths gave rise to speculation. The false teachers' hearts were not searching for godliness. They were just exchanging words. Speculation provided no foundation for acts of faith. The Greek word translated "speculation" (1:4) indicates an exchange of words rather than a true search (see also Titus 3:9). God's administration (lit., "house rules") operated on the basis of faith, not speculation. That is, God wants believers to have clear and solid facts to believe in and act upon, not just words to debate over.

The context of being pure in heart (1:5) contrasts with what speculation could not accomplish. It did not accomplish purity in heart, a clear conscience, or faith. A good conscience is related to being pure in heart. True faith emphasizes how God feels toward believers, not how believers feel they are doing in relation to others. A sincere faith shows outwardly what is true in the inner life before God.

First Timothy 1:6-7 shows the results of neglecting character growth. The men desired to be teachers of the law (cf. Acts 5:34 regarding Gamaliel) but did not have the character to back up their desire. Paul dealt more fully with the relationship between desire and character in 1 Timothy 3.

1:8-11 THE VALUE OF THE MOSAIC LAW FOR THE LAWLESS

Paul's words stood in contrast to the useless words of the false teachers (1:9). The law was not for the righteous. It was a corrective for the lawless (2 Tim. 3:16; Rom. 3:19-20; Gal. 3:24). Paul pointed out that the law was good if used correctly because some in Ephesus had been using it ignorantly. The law was not being used according to its intended function, that is, to correct error. It was not for playing around with (1:3-4) or for teaching error (4:1-5). The proper use of the law was application in light of its purpose (1:9).

The list of sinful deeds elaborates upon those subject to the law (1:9-10). If they had been righteous, they would not need the law. The law's function was now defined by the gospel of grace in Christ (1:10-11). Paul used the expression "right teaching" frequently (1:10; 6:3; 2 Tim. 1:13; 4:3). It refers to teaching that is healthy and wholesome in contrast to that which is false. The gospel, not the law, is what now fully and clearly reveals the will of God to redeemed people.

1:12-17 The Gospel Entrusted to Paul

Paul brought up his past life to show one example of the proper use of the law—to bring sinners to salvation in Christ. But he also showed how the gospel came to bring redemption after the law had brought condemnation. He showed that law had to be combined with patience and grace. Paul had been a blasphemer as a persecutor of Christians. The law brought condemnation upon him as a blasphemer. But God came to Paul, not by the corrective of the law, but in mercy (see Acts 3:17; 17:30). In that light, Paul told his readers to stop playing with the law, unless it was needed (1:8-11). And even if it was needed, the correction that the law demanded was to be tempered by the gospel of grace (1:12-17). The essence of salvation was to be found in understanding grace in Christ.

The Old Testament made a distinction between sins of ignorance and sins of defiance (1:13; Lev. 4:2; Num. 15:27-31). Atonement was available for the former, but not for the latter. Paul's sins against Christ and the church were in ignorance but still needed God's atoning mercy. The expression "true saying" (1:15) is literally "faithful is the word." This was a formula used by Paul in 1 and 2 Timothy and Titus to introduce important truths (3:1; 4:9; 2 Tim. 2:11; Titus 3:8).

1:18-20 The Command Entrusted to Timothy

The command to stop teaching false doctrines had been stated in 1:3. The goal of that command was godly character (1:5). This command had been entrusted to Timothy and was a major purpose for his going to Ephesus. Fighting the "Lord's battles" (1:18) had to do with moving others to love and disciplining the rebellious. The means of fighting are stressed: keeping faith and a good conscience. Fighting the Lord's battles is moving people on to a pure heart, good conscience, and sincere faith.

The false teachers were excommunicated, but the purpose was corrective, not final, judgment. This was a proper use of the law according to the gospel. Paul dealt with the false teachers by delivering them over to Satan. This remedial discipline, also known as excommunication (cf. Matt. 18:17), was designed to destroy their fleshly attitudes and drive them back to Christ (see note on 1 Cor. 5:5).

2:1–6:19 THE INSTRUCTION APPLIED: COMMUNITY TRADITIONS

Overview: The central thought behind this instruction is found in 3:14-15—proper conduct in the house of God. Notice the support of the truth and proper use of the law. The discussion of prayer (2:1-15) was designed to help the readers adopt God's desires for world salvation. The section on leadership (3:1-16) urges men and women to adequately serve God's truth. The condemnation of the lying teachers (4:1-16) comes because they have denied God's truth.

2:1-15 Prayer: Adopt God's Desires

2:1-2 EXCLUSIONS IN PRAYER
"First of all" connects this section with the previous verses. First Timothy 2:2 elaborates the "them" of 2:1. Paul was revealing possible areas being excluded in prayer. Paul's instruction to pray for kings was especially significant in light of the fact that Nero (A.D. 54–68) was in office at this time. Love that comes out of a pure heart, good conscience, and a sincere faith reaches out beyond the community. Paul used four terms to describe the ministry of prayer: "requests"—specific petition or supplication; "pray"—a general word for prayer emphasizing worship and reverence; "plead"—a

technical term for approaching a king, suggesting intercession on behalf of others; and "give thanks"—an attitude of thankfulness and gratitude that should always accompany prayer.

2:3-4 GOD HAS A UNIVERSAL DESIRE TO REDEEM HUMANITY

Paul's desire for universal prayer was based on the universal desire of God—the salvation of all the human race. God's desire defines and shapes the nature of this age and should also shape the behavior of believers. Paul desired that the Ephesian believers would pray sincerely for the salvation of all people. This would provide the link between praying and having a quiet life. Prayer for the world's salvation would also bring peace and righteousness. Salvation is characterized as "good" and pleasing to God (2:3). Sadly, in their disputes the believers were excluding some from their prayers who needed salvation. God is not partisan (cf. 1:16; 4:10). This fact is the reason why it is good to pray for the salvation of all people (cf. 1:13).

2:5-7 THE UNIVERSAL RANSOM

The "for" of 2:5 explains why it is good to pray for the salvation of others (2:3) and why God desires all to be saved (2:4). A "mediator" (2:5) is one who stands between two parties to remove a disagreement or reach a common goal. The mediator must perfectly represent both parties. Christ, the God-man, is the perfect mediator, representing both God's interests and man's without prejudice or compromise. This verse supports the doctrine of *hypostatic union*—that the deity and humanity of Jesus Christ were united in one person forever without the mingling of attributes.

Paul indicated that their prayer life did not reflect the character of God who desires all to be saved. Adopting God's attitude toward the world issued in truth, redemption, and prayer. Blocking God's desire by refusing to pray for unbelievers would issue in God's wrath and dissension in the church.

Paul had already given three reasons to pray for all people: all people have one God, one mediator, and one ransom. But he returned to his own experience (2:7) to provide the fourth reason of why prayers should be made for all: God had assigned Paul to work with the Gentiles, the group disregarded by most Jewish Christians.

2:8-15 PROPER CHARACTER IN PRAYER

2:8-10 Effective Prayer and Holy Living
Believers are to live holy lives (2:8). To "pray with holy hands lifted up" was a common posture for prayer in the biblical period (cf. 1 Kings 8:22; Pss. 28:2; 63:4; 134:2). The "holy hands" symbolized a pure and holy life. Prayers of believers should reflect what has been said about God, Christ, and Paul's worldwide ministry. Truth is now applied to

the community. God wants all people to know the truth. Prayer is related to the pure heart and should reflect God's desire for universal salvation.

Women should also live holy lives. The "clothing" of a godly woman is to be respectable and they are expected to behave with self-restraint. Their good works spring from inner goodness (2:10). Regardless of popular fashion, discreet and modest apparel is the standard for Christian women. The expression "by the way they fix their hair" refers to "gold-braided hair." In Paul's day it was the custom of dancing girls to braid their hair with golden bangles that shimmered as they moved. Hands are viewed as symbols of life; clothing is viewed as a symbol of character. People mirroring God's desire for universal salvation cannot come to prayer in an unholy way.

2:11-15 Leadership and Proper Order in the Church
Paul moves from strife between people regardless of gender (2:8) to strife between men and women (2:11-15). Paul encouraged women to receive doctrine and instruction with a teachable and submissive attitude. In Paul's day, Jewish men and boys were required to learn the law, but there was no such requirement for women. Paul did not want Christian women to be ignorant of the Scriptures and encouraged them to learn. The word "submissively" (2:11) literally means "under orders." As they learned, women were to listen to and respect those whom God had placed in positions of church leadership.

Paul's words in 2:12 do not mean that women should never teach. They are encouraged to teach in certain contexts (cf. Titus 2:3). Although debated, this appears to prohibit women from holding permanent positions of authoritative teaching in the church. "Have authority" (2:12) is to act as one's own authority, to have mastery over, or to exercise dominion. Teaching in the meeting of the church is apparently viewed by Paul as an exercise of authority (cf. also 1 Cor. 14:34-35). Women are to maintain their proper relationships with their husbands. To "learn quietly" refers to an outer expression of an inward state.

The focus of 2:13-14 is on Genesis 1–3. Eve overstepped the bounds set by Adam and God (cf. Gen. 3:17, "because you listened to [obeyed] your wife"). See also Genesis 3:13; 16:2; and 2 Corinthians 11:3. In this context the woman was deceived into usurping the authority placed over her. Paul sought to show that if she had listened to Adam she would not have sinned. Eve and women generally, by accepting their God-given functions, can be saved the trouble that results from overstepping their bounds. Although equal in spiritual privilege (1 Pet. 3:7), men and women have different roles in terms of ministry. God's created order establishes these role relationships for men and women which, if bypassed, lead to disaster as illustrated by the fall.

"Through childbearing" (2:15) is Paul's way of summarizing the role of the woman (cf. 5:14). It refers to the whole process and related activities of bearing and raising children. Many evangelicals believe Paul is referring to salvation through the incarnation of Christ. But this seems like an obscure way to refer to this doctrine. Contextually, Paul seems to be referring to physical salvation or deliverance from the temptation to usurp authority (the problem of 2:12). Such deliverance is possible for the woman who gives herself to the ministry of home and family life.

3:1–4:16 Leadership: Serve God's Truth
3:1-16 THE QUALITIES OF TRUE AND FALSE LEADERS

3:1 Choosing Appropriate Leadership
True and effective leadership supports and serves God's truth. The point of this section is to make sure that a person with a great desire for leadership (3:1) has the appropriate character. The problem was not with desiring to be a leader. It was with being qualified to be a leader. Leadership is not something a person gets just because he wants it. "Elder" (3:1) emphasizes the responsibility of giving oversight and emphasizes the dignity and maturity required for the office (cf. Titus 1:5, 7). The stress on these qualifications was the moral and spiritual qualities necessary to give leadership to God's people. The first and last qualifications are foundational (3:1, 7). The others are more specific.

3:2-7 The Man: Overseer
"Whose life cannot be spoken against" (3:2) summarizes all the qualifying characteristics that follow. "Must be" (3:2) controls all the traits that follow. "Faithful to his wife" refers to a character trait: a faithful husband or a sexually controlled single person. The expression literally reads "one wife's husband." The grammar also suggests that character, not just a head count of wives is in view. To be qualified for the office of elder, a married man must be faithful to his one wife. With reference to women, see 1 Timothy 5:9, 14-15. The temperate man knows his functions and limitations and is able to exercise his abilities accordingly. "Enjoy having guests in his home" (3:2) is related to Exodus 22:21-22. The elder must have a household that can be run similarly to the household of God. The home always reflects the character and ability of its leader.

3:8-10 The Man: Deacon
The deacon is just as important as an overseer. The word "deacon" literally means "servant." The term can be used of an officer in the church or in an unofficial sense of anyone who serves (cf. Eph. 6:21). The origin of the office of deacon can be traced to Acts 6:1-6. The qualifications are similar to those of the elder. Dignity is related to that which produces worship. A deacon is dignified if signs of a higher order can be detected in him (cf. also 1 Tim. 2:2; 3:4). Three negatives follow which further define and explain dignity. Conscience (3:9) is the source of love (cf. 1:5, 19). The deacon also is worthy of being tested to ascertain that he is blameless. The "in the same way" (3:8) presumes the testing of elders. Lest some should think that the "lesser" office of deacon does not require this, Paul adds this emphatic command.

3:11 The Woman: Deaconess
The women mentioned in 3:11 are logically related to deacons. But the Greek word for women does not necessarily mean wives. It is debated whether the women mentioned here refer to the wives of deacons or to deaconesses. If they were deaconesses, one would expect that they would be mentioned after the discussion of deacons. The placement of the verse in the middle of the paragraph about deacons seems to suggest that they were the wives of deacons. Yet one wonders why this qualification would be mentioned for deacons and not for elders (cf. 3:1-7). It has been suggested that deacons could be men or women and that verse 11 just adds qualifications relevant for those deacons who are female. It is oriented to an office of deacon relative to women. Phoebe is called a deaconess (Rom. 16:1), but this may reflect the unofficial use of the word ("service") as in 1 Corinthians 16:15.

3:12-13 The Man: Deacon
Paul returns to the office of deacon to stress further qualifications (3:12) and rewards (3:13).

3:14-16 The Reason for Writing: Conduct in God's Household
Paul revealed at this point the purpose of his letter to Timothy: it was to inform his associate and the church at Ephesus concerning the proper conduct of members in the local church. The "mystery of our faith" (3:16) is the bringing together of the spheres of heaven and earth in the incarnation of Christ. It focuses on Christ, who is able to produce a life of godliness in those who trust him. This verse may have been an early creed or perhaps a Christian hymn. This verse details the "truth" that is upheld by the church. That definition functions to underscore the importance of qualified church leadership. Leaders support the truth of Christ by their lives.

4:1-16 FALSE AND TRUE LEADERSHIP MANIFESTED

4:1-5 False: Fallen from the Faith
Paul set forth instructions for dealing with false teachers. God has a certain intention for those

who believe and know the truth: the enjoyment of creation. But false leaders have rejected what God called good, his creation (Gen. 1–3 is still on Paul's mind). These teachers are liars and hypocrites. The "last times" (4:1) is a term virtually equivalent to "the last days" (2 Tim. 3:1; Heb. 1:2; James 5:3; 2 Pet. 3:3) and refers to the latter days of the present age, the age of promise, which anticipates the age to come, the age of fulfillment. The false teachers' consciences were "dead" so that they had lost sensitivity to moral issues (4:2). The practices of celibacy and fasting are not meritorious in themselves; in fact, their practice may imply unbelief in the complete and free salvation God does provide (4:3). Paul's words, along with Acts 10:15 and Mark 7:19, demonstrate that the Jewish distinctions in food (Lev. 11) are no longer valid (4:4).

4:6-16 True: Discipline in the Faith
Paul explained the nature of beneficial discipline. Timothy was to feed on the word of God. He was to be constantly nourished in and trained by its teachings (4:6). "Godless ideas and old wives' tales" (4:7) refer to the Jewish myths mentioned in 1:4. Satan loves to get believers sidetracked to speculations on religious trivia. The phrase "training yourself" (4:7) comes from the Greek verb from which the English word "gymnasium" is derived. Like the disciplined athlete, the Christian is to pursue the development of his spiritual life. This is a continued corrective to the asceticism of 4:3. Profitable teaching, not fables, is needed.

First Timothy 4:9-10 refers back to 2:3-4. Timothy was to strive for the maturity that counts (4:11-16). The verbs in 4:11 encourage Timothy to keep on prescribing and teaching these things. Paul kept going back to the basics. Modeling is an essential component to education (4:12). Paul listed five areas in which Timothy should serve as an example. Note the "work" words, 1:3, 18; 4:6-7, 10. Timothy's young age was not of ultimate importance. All three terms of 4:13 describe an area of public ministry: "reading" Scripture in worship services, "encouraging" people to respond, and "teaching"—formal instruction based on the word of God.

In 4:14 it is debated whether Paul was referring to Timothy's spiritual gift or his spiritual office. Spiritual gifts are divine enablements for service in the body of Christ (see notes on 1 Cor. 12:1–14:20). The laying on of the elders' hands, an act of identification (Acts 13:3), accompanied Timothy's prophetic training. The result of Timothy's training and "gift" was a transparent character (4:15-16). "Save" (4:16) refers to deliverance from the reigning power and influence of sin, the present aspect of salvation (also referred to as sanctification).

5:1–6:2 Honor for Household Members
5:1-16 HONOR AND CARE BY AGE GROUPS
5:1-2 The Family Perspective
This section teaches how to view members of the congregation while trying to move them on to maturity. The family perspective is based on God's desire to save all people. Dealing with people in the body of Christ is a practical extension of what it means to be thinking like God. The section covers honor for widows (5:3-16), leaders (5:17-25), and masters (6:1-2). The key word throughout is "respect," and Paul encouraged Timothy to show respect appropriately to each group of people in the church (5:3, 17; 6:1). Timothy is to continue appealing to the older men rather than issuing sharp rebukes (lit., "to strike with blows"—in this case referring to words rather than fists).

5:3-16 Widows
Believers have an obligation to care for widows in the church. This is first a family responsibility (5:4, 8, 16) but becomes a church responsibility when there is no family available (5:16). Not all widows were qualified to receive financial support from the church. Those who did qualify took a "pledge" (5:12) and were placed on a "list" (5:9). These widows were apparently prayer warriors who committed themselves to serving the church. The age qualification would mean that there would be no chance for remarriage (5:9; cf. 5:14). The phrase "served other Christians humbly" (5:10) is a reference for sacrificial service to others (cf. John 13:1-17). On the phrase "faithful to her husband" (5:9), see the male counterpart in 3:2. Some young widows had already allowed Satan to lead them into sin (5:15). The final case (5:16) is a woman, probably a widow herself, with dependent widows.

5:17-25 HONOR FOR FAMILY LEADERS
5:17-21 Showing Honor to Elders
The use of the words "care" (5:3) and "respect" (6:1) show that "paid well" (5:17) refers to high esteem, not money (Matt. 10:10; 1 Cor. 9:1-14). "Elders" (5:17; cf. 3:1) have the responsibility of superintending the affairs of the church. The quotations of 5:18 are taken from Deuteronomy 25:4 and the words of Christ in Luke 10:7 and Matthew 10:10.

Honor must also relate to a leader's reputation (5:19-21). Although high standards had been set for elders (3:1-7), Paul knew that their office would not make them immune to sin. Here Paul applied the principles of church discipline (Matt. 18:15-18) to the case of a sinning elder. Discipline of leadership must be founded on fact, not rumor. The requirement for several witnesses was a Mosaic command (Deut. 17:6; cf. Matt. 18:16; 2 Cor. 13:1). The purpose of the public rebuke was to give a warning (5:20). It is debated whether the public rebuke (a reproof that brings conviction) applied only to the elder who continued in sin or to any elder who sinned on a particular occasion. The purpose "that others [of the elders] will have a proper fear of God" may favor the latter viewpoint.

No partiality was to be shown to certain elders of the church (5:21). This relates to allowing accusations to be received for some and not others, publicly rebuking some and not others, laying hands on some and not others.

5:22-25 The Importance of Purity in Church Leaders
The section of 5:22-25 concerns freedom from sin and care in ordination. Timothy was careful to avoid any appearance of evil and totally abstained from alcoholic beverages at the expense of his personal health (5:23). Paul explained that keeping himself free from sin (5:22) did not necessitate his abstaining from a medicinal use of wine (cf. Prov. 31:6-7; Luke 10:34).

Paul warned against the hasty appointment of an elder to office (5:24-25). While many have understood Paul to be forbidding a hasty ordination, the context seems to suggest that the concern was over a hasty restoration of a leader to his former position after discipline. The principle of caution would apply in both situations. The key idea here was that an elder is known by his fruits. While some men's character immediately disqualifies them from the office, the character of others will be revealed only with the passing of time. Both the good (5:24) and the bad (5:25) will ultimately be apparent. The judgment of 5:24 concerns the evaluation of a person's qualifications for leadership, not the final judgment of God.

6:1-2 HONOR IN WORKING ROLES
Slaves were to show respect to their masters for the sake of Christ's name. Slaves with Christian masters were to show respect for their masters even though they were also brothers in Christ. Slavery was an accepted social and economic institution during the biblical period. Rather than seeking to abolish the institution, Paul sought to improve the situation by giving directives to servants and masters (cf. 1 Cor. 7:21; Eph. 6:5-9; Col. 3:22–4:1; Titus 2:9-10).

6:3-19 Correctives to Materialism

6:3-10 THOSE WHO WANT: FALSE TEACHERS
Materialism was the motivation for the false teachers' ministries (6:3-5). "False teachers" (6:3) are those not in agreement with the teachings of Jesus

and that teach things that do not lead to godliness (Gal. 1:6-7). The results of refusing the path of contentment are given in 6:9-10. In contrast to the materialistic motives of the false teachers, Paul pointed out that godly Christian living does result in gain, both material and spiritual (Ps. 34:10; Phil. 4:19). The key is the development of "contentment" (6:6)—an inner satisfaction no matter what the situation God has ordained (Phil. 4:11-12). The focus of contentment is on God's gifts. People are born and die with nothing, except the life God has given. Anything else a person might add is temporary or optional and should not affect contentment with God's gifts. The "love of money," not money itself, is the root of all sorts of evil (6:10).

6:11-16 THE CHARGE TO FLEE MATERIALISM
The flight from materialism is achieved by pursuing godly character traits. The person consumed with seeking righteousness will not have time to be consumed by materialism. Paul's words in 6:12 are taken from the athletic arena. Timothy was challenged to fight on in the arena entered by all who become Christians. He was to grasp life as opposed to wandering from it (6:10). See also 1:6, 19 for a similar concept. For Jesus' confession before Pontius Pilate (6:13), see Matthew 27:11; Mark 15:2; Luke 23:2-3; and John 18:36-37. Paul linked a good life to the good confession of Christ. The unseen God (6:16) was the center of Paul's life. God alone possesses immortality by his divine nature, and believers inherit it by their new birth. This grasp of eternal life is the foundation for purity in leadership and community life.

6:17-19 THOSE WHO HAVE: THE RICH
The wealthy have special challenges in the area of pride and contentment. They are to see their wealth as given by God, not by their own abilities. The purpose for their wealth is to enjoy by giving, not to covet or hoard. If the rich are free to give (6:18), they will be able to take hold of true riches (6:19). The material goods of this life are a mere shadow of the eternal reality to come.

6:20-21 CLOSING CHARGE
Paul repeated his charge to guard the truth in true knowledge. Paul's final admonition to "avoid godless, foolish discussions" (6:20) reminded the readers of the central problem of the letter (cf. 1:3-4; 4:1-3, 7; 6:3-5).

2 TIMOTHY

BASIC FACTS

HISTORICAL SETTING

The primary recipient of this letter was Timothy (1:2). For information on Timothy, see the Historical Setting section for 1 Timothy. Since his first letter to Timothy, Paul may have visited Ephesus (1 Tim. 3:14) and ministered in Asia Minor, Macedonia, Spain, and on the island of Crete. The persecution of Christians in Rome began shortly after Rome burned in July of A.D. 64. Nero blamed the Christians for that catastrophe, and Christianity was made an illegal religion. It was probably in the summer of A.D. 64 under the persecution of Nero that Peter was martyred.

Paul knew that his death was imminent and that his work on earth was done (4:6-8). He was alone in Rome except for Luke (4:11). Apparently some had deserted him at his first defense before the Roman authorities (4:16). Paul desired Timothy and John Mark to join him before winter (4:9-13).

The immediate occasion for writting this letter was the need to encourage Timothy to stand fast in the face of opposition and apostasy. Paul could not be sure Timothy would arrive in Rome before his death, and he wanted to present some final instructions to his most intimate disciple.

AUTHOR

The letter identifies Paul as the author (1:1), and the letter contains autobiographical material that fits the life of Paul as recorded elsewhere (2 Tim. 3:10-11; 4:10-11, 19-20).

DATE

The letter was probably written while Paul was a prisoner in Rome (1:8, 16-17) for the second time. Paul was martyred in the spring of A.D. 68, so the letter may be dated around autumn of A.D. 67.

PURPOSE

Paul's second letter to Timothy was designed to encourage the readers by showing how Paul was able to cope with his impending death by his security in God's commitment to the spread of the gospel. Paul desired the readers to be more concerned with the ongoing success of the gospel than with their own personal status and comfort.

GUIDING CONCEPTS

GOOD WORKS

In this letter, Paul stressed good works (2:21; 3:17; cf. also 4:5, 7, 17). Good works are designed for the profit of the individual, but their end is the furtherance of redemption. Good works are based on the truth of God's word (3:16-17), which is profitable (3:16) and offers eternal life (1:1, 10; 2:10). Paul gave Timothy insight into wisdom in a crisis situation and helped him find stability in God's control over all of life's crises.

OPPOSITION

Opposition is seen in relationship to shame and suffering. The concept of shame occurs frequently (1:8, 12, 16; 2:15; 4:16). The opposition mentioned in 2 Timothy stems primarily from within the Christian community. The purpose of suffering is seen throughout the letter (1:8; 1:12; 2:3, 7, 10; 3:11; 4:5, 14, 18). Opposition is to be met with solid preaching of God's word (4:2) and consistent purity of character (2:21-22).

USEFULNESS

Three parables are used to describe a faithful person (2:2-6). The focus is on service that pleases the master, in this case God. The useful person is described as one who can use the word of God accurately, that is, apply God's word as he intended. Usefulness is grounded in following the will of God through his word (2:14-15, 21, 26; 4:11).

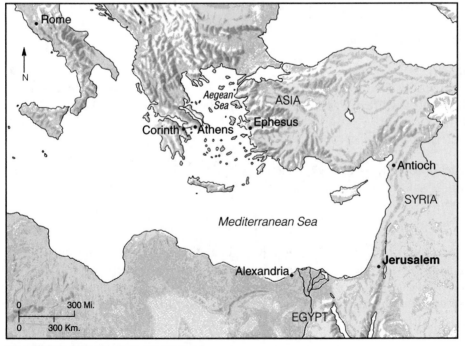

BIBLE-WIDE CONCEPTS

THE KINGDOM PROMISED TO DAVID

In a section on endurance in suffering hardship, Paul asked Timothy to remember two things about Jesus: that he was risen from the dead and that he was descended from David (2:8). The link between Christ's death and resurrection and David reveals the Old Testament perspective through which Paul viewed his sufferings. Jesus was the risen and exalted King who now reigned in the kingdom promised to a son of David. The pattern of death, resurrection, and reigning can be followed by Christ's faithful followers (2:11-12). If Christ's disciples die with him, they will reign with him. This Davidic link belongs to all believers through Christ. Finally, Paul looked forward to entering the kingdom of the greater Son of David (4:18). The reality of the Davidic kingdom, predicted from 2 Samuel 7 onward, was an essential part of Paul's encouragement and commands to Timothy (2 Tim. 4:1).

CONFLICT IN THE LAST DAYS

Throughout this letter Paul spoke of events in the last days (specifically mentioned in 3:1). The opposition and hypocrisy of the last days is a pervasive theme in the New Testament (Matt. 24:24; John 2:17; 15:18-25; 16:33; Acts 14:22; 20:29; 1 Thess. 3:3; 1 Pet. 2:21; 4:19), and it was also foreseen in the Old Testament (Ps. 69:1-12).

NEEDS MET BY SECOND TIMOTHY

This very personal letter, written toward the end of Paul's life, was directly aimed at meeting specific needs for Timothy. Paul wrote to strengthen the church in Ephesus, to encourage Timothy's own perseverance, and to remind Timothy of the central place of Scripture in his ministry. Paul assured Timothy that Christianity would survive in the face of Roman persecution because God, not just people, was ultimately guarding his gospel and preserving those who responded in faith. Paul reinforced God's unwavering personal commitment to Timothy to strengthen his desire to maintain a vital relationship with God. Finally, Timothy's focus was to be on the Scriptures—the document that had been for generations the authoritative guide to salvation and proper living. Paul's words of advice met a number of needs felt by Timothy in particular and the church in general. The content and structure of 2 Timothy show that Paul intended to answer the following questions for his readers.

- What truths will help believers resist the pressures of opposition to the truth of the gospel in Christ?
- How can believers avoid being ashamed of the gospel?
- How central should the Scriptures be for guidance and instruction in godliness?

As Paul met the personal needs of Timothy, he also met the needs of Christians throughout the ages. As in so many other Biblical books, the central issue concerns believing in God when life is difficult and unfair. Second Timothy gives two vital reasons for remaining faithful to God during hard times. First, Paul shows steps to affirming that God has not abandoned his people. Not only is God perfectly guarding the continuance of his worldwide spread of the gospel, he is also noting every individual good deed believers do and will justly reward them. Second, hard times must not distract believers from rigorous attention to God's word. They must counter fuzzy thinking about God and misinterpretations of the Bible by accurate teaching. They must resist feeling ashamed of their position in Christ and letting fear of hostility silence their witness to the world.

OUTLINE OF SECOND TIMOTHY

  I. GREETING (1:1-2)

 II. THANKSGIVING FOR A SINCERE FAITH (1:3-5)

III. REKINDLED CONVICTION AND DISCIPLINE (1:6–2:26)
   A. On the Basis of Attitude: Controlled Boldness (1:6-7)
   B. On the Basis of Attitude: Commitment to Suffer (1:8-11)
   C. On the Basis of Attitude: Suffering and Shame (1:12-14)
   D. Guarding the Trust: Discipline and Purity in Suffering (1:15–2:26)

IV. FAITHFULNESS AMIDST OPPOSITION TO THE TRUTH (3:1–4:8)
   A. Biblical Commitment in Difficult Times (3:1-17)
   B. Paul's Solemn Charge: Preach the Word (4:1-8)

 V. PAUL'S CONTINUED NEED FOR FAITHFUL MINISTERS (4:9-18)
   A. Need for Friends (4:9-13)
   B. A Warning about an Enemy (4:14-15)
   C. The Lord's Faithfulness (4:16-18)

VI. CLOSING GREETINGS (4:19-21)

VII. BENEDICTION (4:22)

SECOND TIMOTHY NOTES

1:1-2 GREETING
Timothy was Paul's "child" in the sense that Paul had led him to the Lord and nourished him in the faith (cf. 1 Tim. 1:2). For more on Timothy, see note on 1 Timothy 1:2. The author (1:1) is an apostle; he is not to be taken lightly, even by his dear friend Timothy. The promise of eternal life is an important theme of this letter (1:1, 10; 2:11; 4:8, 18; cf. with John 6:31-33). The concept of the "promised" (1:1) takes the reader back through the ages to God the Father who has been consistently working to bring about man's redemption.

1:3-5 THANKSGIVING FOR A SINCERE FAITH
Paul longed to see Timothy (1:3-4). Note the clarity of Paul's conscience despite the fact that he was facing criminal charges in a Roman prison. Paul's forefathers had served God with clear consciences. Paul displayed a strong sense of continuity with the Old Testament remnant through his piety and reverence for God. "Tears" (1:4) had been shed at Paul's last parting from Timothy, as in Acts 20:37. Paul's remembrance of Timothy's tears colors this letter.

Timothy had a sincere faith (1:5). Paul made a link back to the God of Timothy's mother and grandmother. He wanted to remind Timothy of all the people throughout history who had served God properly. Timothy was "sincere" (cf. 1 Tim. 1:5) in continuity with his ancestors. Timothy's faith had been cultivated by his godly grandmother, Lois, and mother, Eunice, who had trained him in the Old Testament Scriptures (cf. 3:14-15). The faith of his mother and grandmother represented the long line of those who had truly believed in the God of Israel (cf. 3:15).

1:6–2:26 REKINDLED CONVICTION AND DISCIPLINE

1:6-7 On the Basis of Attitude: Controlled Boldness

1:6 FAN THE FIRE INTO FLAME

The historical context for Paul's words in this verse was persecution. Paul saw Timothy as one who was going to have to carry on in this situation (cf. 1:3-5). As the coals of a fire need to be stirred to keep it from dying out, so Timothy needed to constantly exercise the spiritual gifts that God had bestowed upon him. The phrase "fan into flames" (1:6) is better translated "keep it hot." Timothy had not let his fire go out. The laying on of Paul's hands did not procure the gift but was the accompanying circumstance associated with the announcement of Timothy's gift (cf. 1 Tim. 4:14).

At the time he wrote 2 Timothy, Paul was a prisoner in Rome. He was chained as a criminal (2:9) in the Mamertine prison adjacent to the Roman forum. He knew that his death was imminent and that his work on earth was done (4:6-8). Paul recognized that though individuals will die, Christianity will live on.

1:7 THE NATURE OF THE GIFT IS DESCRIBED

The effect of God's gift should not result in cowardice but power. Of the three characteristics of God's gift, "power" is the ability to accomplish what God wants, "love" is the focus of and end result of power, and "self-discipline" is sound judgment to know how to combine power with love in a time of crisis. Paul urged Timothy to think about who was with him (1:6-7) and then urged him to think about what he was doing in the world (1:8-11).

1:8-11 On the Basis of Attitude: Commitment to Suffer

Paul warned Timothy never to be ashamed of the gospel (1:8; cf. 1:12, 16). The "strength of God" (1:8) is power to endure suffering and 1:9-11 defines that power: it is the power of God's gospel of grace.

1:12-14 On the Basis of Attitude: Suffering and Shame

The words "what I have entrusted" (1:12) literally read "my entrustment." This may refer to what Paul had entrusted to Christ, that is, his faith or commitment. But it most likely refers to what Christ had entrusted to Paul, that is, the gospel. The context on the concept of entrustment relates also to what had been entrusted to Timothy (1:14) and what he would entrust to others (2:2; cf. also 1 Tim. 6:20). God will guard the entrustment of the gospel until the day of Christ's return when all dangers for the believer have past. Paul knew that God had every intention of preserving and maintaining the gospel ministry on the earth. Security is not founded upon human effort but upon God and his work of grace through Christ.

1:15–2:26 Guarding the Trust: Discipline and Purity in Suffering

1:15-18 AN EXAMPLE OF ONE WHO REMAINED FAITHFUL

These verses give positive and negative examples of those who had been entrusted with the gospel. Christianity had become an illegal religion. Paul referred to those now in Asia, a Roman province in Asia Minor (western Turkey), who refused to speak on his behalf in Rome. Onesiphorus stands in stark contrast to the defectors. He had ministered to Paul in Ephesus and had sought him out in Rome despite the persecution he might suffer as a result.

2:1-2 TIMOTHY'S TASK: TEACH THE FAITHFUL

Paul's circumstances during his second Roman imprisonment (2:9) were quite different from his first imprisonment as described in Acts 28:16, 23, 30-31. Paul's conclusion in 2:1 was based on the preceding examples. Timothy must have strength (Eph. 6:10; Phil. 4:13; 2 Tim. 4:17) for passing on the truth. Paul used seven illustrations in chapter 2 to emphasize the need for diligence and sacrifice in serving Christ: a son (2:1), a soldier (2:3), an athlete (2:5), a farmer (2:6), a worker (2:15), a utensil (2:21), and a bond-servant (2:24). Paul's concern was for the faithful proclamation of his teaching without addition or subtraction. The key was to find those who were faithful (trustworthy, reliable) and capable (competent, qualified).

2:3-7 TIMOTHY'S TASK: SUFFER HARDSHIP

In 2:2 Paul presented two important concepts: faithfulness and the necessity of transmitting the gospel message. Paul used three parables to describe a faithful person. Male images were used because he was discussing the pastoral role. The Christian life involves warfare (2:3; cf. Eph. 6:10-17), and the Christian soldier must regard hardship as inevitable in a world that is hostile to Christ (John 15:18-25). Paul emphasized that hardship, struggle, discipline, and labor precede the enjoyment of reward. For any working person the master's pleasure is most important. The soldier always seeks to please his commander (2:3-4). The athlete abides by the rules for his event to win the prize (2:5). Only after the farmer has worked his fields long and hard may he accept his privilege to feed himself first (2:6). Paul made it clear that the prize to be won in the Christian life would only come after hardship and sacrifice.

2:8-13 TIMOTHY'S FOCUS: REMEMBER

God's promises to David as fulfilled in Christ were the foundation of Paul's hope for deliverance after suffering. The present suffering and opposition could not deter God from keeping his promises

(2:9). The word Paul used for "criminal" (2:9) was a strong word used to describe the two criminals who hung beside Christ at his crucifixion (cf. Luke 23:32-33, 39). Paul's chains did not hinder his proclamation of the gospel (2:10).

Paul appealed to a familiar Christian poem or hymn to emphasize that present suffering was necessary for future glory (2:11-13). The four lines are built around an "if-then" logic. It is a powerful and uncompromising statement of the commitment of God to furthering his gospel message. Even if many (like the examples in 2:17-18; 3:1-5) should end up denying Christ, Christ will be faithful to continue to proclaim his gospel through someone else. The fact that some "deny" Christ (2:12) may indicate that their initial faith was not genuine. Such a denial would be the evidence of unbelief. It is also possible that Paul was referring to a temporary denial of Christ such as Peter's (Matt. 26:69-75). The character of God is the foundation for faithfulness and strength. He is faithful (Rom. 3:3) to his mission of world redemption and judgment. Believers may disown him, but he will not disown those who believe in him. The faithful person is the one who acts like Jesus to bring redemption to the elect. The believer's strength is found in Christ Jesus and his strength and commitment to the task.

2:14-19 CORRECTING THE UNFAITHFUL: SPEAKING GOD'S WORD ACCURATELY

God's laborers were to handle his word accurately, proclaiming and applying it to life (2:15). The expression "correctly explains" (2:15) literally means "to cut straight" and may have it's background in Paul's tent-making business. At any rate, it is the opposite of the condition described in 2:16-18. These two false teachers taught that the resurrection was already past, apparently suggesting that the resurrection was a spiritual rather than a physical reality. The "solid foundation stone" (2:19) describing "God's truth" refers to the foundation of the church (Matt. 16:18; 1 Tim. 3:15; Eph. 2:19-22). This foundation is based on God's faithfulness in fulfilling his promises.

2:20-26 CORRECTING THE UNFAITHFUL: PURITY IN GOD'S HOUSE

Honored vessels are cleansed vessels (2:20-21). Paul gave three descriptions of how to find cleansing: flee lusts (2:22); refuse arguments or speculations (2:23); and be patient and gentle (2:24-26). These attributes describe a useful vessel (2:21) and one that will keep the gospel, not self-interest, in mind (2:10). The command of 2:22 is a present imperative, "Run from anything." "He" (2:26) could refer to God or Satan. It may be that the capturing is parenthetical: those having been held captive by Satan will come to their senses and do God's will.

3:1-4:8 FAITHFULNESS AMIDST OPPOSITION TO THE TRUTH

3:1-17 Biblical Commitment in Difficult Times

3:1-9 EVIL HEARERS BRING DIFFICULTY FOR GOD'S MINISTER

Paul reminded Timothy that men will love themselves (3:1-5). The "last days" refers to the last part of this present age (the age of promise), which anticipates the age to come (the age of fulfillment). The New Testament writers regarded Christians as living in the "last hour" (1 John 2:18; Acts 2:16-17, "last days"). The apostates referred to in 3:2-5 were the unsaved who met with the church.

Paul continued by showing that these opponents to truth would come to a bad end (3:6-9). Jannes and Jambres (3:8) are not named elsewhere in Scripture, although they are named in the Targum of Jonathan on Exodus 7:11, 22. The Jewish Targums are free renderings of the Hebrew text into Aramaic. These men were Egyptian magicians who performed counterfeit miracles in opposition to Moses. Their names were preserved by Jewish tradition and thus known to Paul.

3:10-17 ABIDING IN WISDOM BRINGS SALVATION

Timothy was to follow Paul's example (3:10-13). But he also had the greater example of the Scriptures (3:14-17). Timothy had a lifetime acquaintance with the Scriptures due to the faithful teaching of his mother and grandmother (3:15; 1:5).

Second Timothy 3:16 is a very important verse for the doctrine of Scripture. Paul declared that "all" (not some) of Scripture is inspired by God. This term refers to the source of Scripture. It came from God (as if it were his breath) to the men who wrote it (cf. 2 Pet. 1:21). This means that God so directed the human authors of Scripture that, using their individual interests and literary styles, his complete thought for man was recorded without error. As a result, the Bible is inerrant (an accurate record) and infallible (a reliable guide).

In theory the doctrine of inspiration relates only to the original manuscripts. But Paul was not being theoretical here. He was saying that even the Greek translation of the Old Testament, the Septuagint, which he consistently used in his quotations, was inspired by God. His point was not a technical discussion of original versus present copies of Scripture. His point was to emphasize the God-breathed profitability that comes from opening up the Scriptures and humbly applying them to life. Because it finds its source in God, it is profitable. And it was that profitability that was being eroded by the careless attitudes fostered in the last days (3:1-13). But the Bible has the wisdom that leads to salvation (3:15) and profitability in godly living (3:16-17).

No element of doubt exists. When believers go to Scripture, they will be met with divine profit.

4:1-8 Paul's Solemn Charge: Preach the Word

4:1-2 PREPARED TO PREACH

Paul reminded Timothy that the certainty of Christ's appearing and his coming kingdom were incentives to faithfulness. The preaching of God's word was to be powerful (reprove, rebuke, exhort), but the preacher was to be patient. Content must be delivered through pure character. Whether the time was opportune or not, Timothy was to preach the truth of God recorded in Scripture.

4:3-8 PAUL'S EXAMPLE OF FAITHFULNESS

Paul took opportunities to speak without worrying about the interest of the listeners. His eloquent and confident testimony (4:6-8) touched on his present readiness for death, his past faithfulness in service, and his future reward in glory. Paul used a metaphor taken from the custom of offering a wine libation as the concluding act in the sacrificial rite (4:6; cf. Num. 15:1-10). Paul drew upon athletic imagery to refer to his past faithful service to Christ (2 Tim. 4:7). Like a wrestler, he had agonized through the fight. Like a runner, he had finished the foot race. Paul kept the faith by defending it from attacks and by observing its obligations. At the end of the race course there awaited a laurel wreath that would be placed on the head of the victor (4:8). It was a perishable wreath (1 Cor. 9:25), but Paul's reward was an imperishable crown. For other crowns, see 1 Thessalonians 2:19; James 1:12; and 1 Peter 5:4. Paul emphasized the appearing of Christ at both the beginning and end of this section (4:1, 8).

4:9-18 PAUL'S CONTINUED NEED FOR FAITHFUL MINISTERS

4:9-13 Need for Friends

For Thessalonica, see the note on 1 Thessalonians 1:1. For Galatia, see the note on Galatians 1:2. Dalmatia was located in the southern part of Illyricum (Rom. 15:19), modern Yugoslavia. Mark's earlier failure in his Christian life (Acts 13:13; 15:37-40) did not destroy his usefulness for Christ (4:11). For Ephesus, see the note on Ephesians 1:1. Troas (4:13) was a port on the Aegean coast of western Asia Minor (cf. Acts 16:11). Paul's "books" (4:13) were papyrus rolls; his "papers" were skins of vellum, perhaps portions of the Old Testament.

4:14-15 A Warning about an Enemy

The description of Alexander as "the coppersmith" (4:14) may be intended to distinguish him from the Alexander mentioned in 1 Timothy 1:20 (cf. Acts 19:33).

4:16-18 The Lord's Faithfulness

At Paul's first defense, or preliminary hearing, before the Roman court, no one came to vouch for him. Luke may not have arrived yet. Others may have feared for their own lives. The "certain death" (4:17; cf. Ps. 22:21) may refer to an immediate danger from which Paul was spared. But Paul knew his Lord (1:12). And he would keep Paul from every "evil attack" (4:18; "evil deed," NASB; "evil work," KJV), that is, the temptations to sin arising from Paul's difficult circumstances—temptations to compromise his life and message in order to avoid persecution. Others have taken this to refer to deliverance from all the attacks of various people against Paul.

4:19-21 CLOSING GREETINGS

Prisca (or Priscilla) and Aquila (4:19) were Paul's fellow workers (Acts 18:2; Rom. 16:3; 1 Cor. 16:19). For Onesiphorus, see the note on 1:16-18. For Erastus (4:20), see Acts 19:22. He is probably not to be identified with the city treasurer of Corinth (Rom. 16:23). Trophimus was from Ephesus (Acts 20:4; 21:29), one of two Asians to carry the collection with Paul to Jerusalem (Acts 20:4-6; 21:29). Since Paul did not leave Trophimus in Miletus on their visit recorded in Acts 20:15, this incident must have happened after Paul's release from his first Roman imprisonment. Nothing is known of the four faithful persons (4:21) named here who had not deserted the apostle Paul.

4:22 BENEDICTION

Paul's words of benediction in 2 Timothy were his last recorded words. According to Eusebius, Paul's martyrdom took place in the thirteenth year of Nero, which commenced in October, A.D. 67. Jerome places Paul's death in A.D. 68. Paul probably died in the spring of A.D. 68, for he was hoping that Timothy would join him for the winter. According to tradition, Paul was beheaded with a sword, a method of execution used for Roman citizens, on the Ostian Way, a road leading south from Rome. According to tradition, he was buried in the catacombs south of the city.

TITUS

HISTORICAL SETTING

The recipient of this letter was Titus (1:4), one of Paul's partners in ministry (1:5; cf. 2 Cor. 7:6; 8:16-18, 23; 12:18; Gal. 2:1, 3). Titus, a Greek Gentile, accompanied Paul and Barnabas to Jerusalem during the famine relief visit (Acts 11:29-30; Gal. 2:1). Evidently, Paul took him along as a test case for Gentile salvation apart from circumcision. The fact that Titus was not compelled to be circumcised confirmed the believer's liberty and freedom from the law (Gal. 2:3).

Paul's first visit to Crete was on his voyage to Rome (Acts 27:7-8). About four years after Paul's release from his first Roman imprisonment Titus accompanied Paul to the island of Crete, where he was left to set the church in order and to appoint elders in every city (1:5). Titus later joined Paul in Rome for awhile. Second Timothy 4:10 speaks also of Titus having left Paul in Rome for a journey to Dalmatia. Eusebius (A.D. 339) indicated that Titus returned to Crete where he was made bishop and remained there until his old age. Paul apparently took the opportunity to visit Crete on his return voyage from Spain (A.D. 66). The immediate occasion for writing was that Titus was facing a difficult assignment (1:5) and Paul wanted to encourage him.

AUTHOR

Titus is one of the three Pastoral Epistles of Paul (cf. 1 and 2 Timothy). The letter itself identifies Paul as its author (1:1). The personal tone of the letter (1:4; 3:12-13, 15) also points to the genuineness of Pauline authorship. In addition to this internal evidence, the church fathers added their support to Pauline authorship.

DATE

The letter was probably written in the summer of A.D. 66, after Paul's return from Spain in the spring of that year. He probably wrote Titus before traveling to Nicopolis, where he spent the winter (3:12).

PURPOSE

Paul's letter to Titus was designed to establish the basic elements of church order and witness. It achieves this by emphasizing the need for purity in leadership and soundness in doctrine.

GEOGRAPHY AND ITS IMPORTANCE

The Island of Crete

It appears that after Paul's imprisonment in Rome, mentioned at the end of Acts, he was released and continued his missionary travels. Traveling to the island of Crete with Titus appears to have been one such mission. The mountainous island is around 156 miles long and from 7 to 35 miles wide.

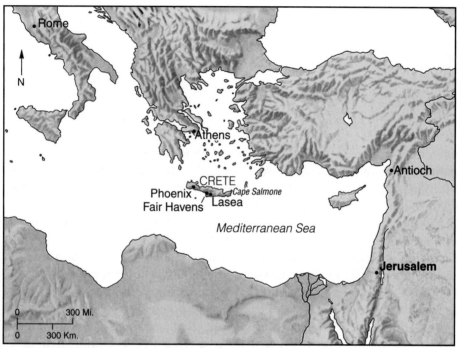

GUIDING CONCEPTS

SOUND DOCTRINE

Throughout the letter Paul stressed the importance of sound doctrine (1:1, 3, 9, 13; 2:1, 7).

THE APPEARANCE OF GOD'S GRACE

The letter is structured around three different appearances of God's grace: (1) God's grace manifested in his word (1:3); (2) God's grace manifested in Christ who will appear yet again at the end of the age (2:11-13); (3) God's grace shown in his kindness and love (3:4). Each one of these appearances functions as the basis for instruction and behavior. God's word was promised and revealed and now forms the basis of the Christian's entrustment (1:3). The appearance of God's grace (2:11) instructs believers to live sensibly (2:12). Finally, the kindness of God (3:4) is foundational to the behavior of believers commended in 3:1-2.

GOOD DEEDS

Considering the smallness of the book, Paul mentioned "good deeds" many times (1:16; 2:7, 14; 3:1, 8, 14). There is a close link between sound doctrine and good deeds

(2:7). Doing good works springs from the very heart of why Christ gave himself for mankind's redemption (2:14). The movement in 2:14 is from lawless deeds to good deeds.

BIBLE-WIDE CONCEPTS

Three topics show the deep connections of this letter with the Old Testament. First, there is a heavy emphasis on correcting false teaching from the law (1:10-11, 14, 16; 3:9) bred from misunderstandings concerning the role of the law in the Christian's life. Paul called the believers to do good deeds but insisted that those deeds be directed by faith, not by a legalistic attitude toward the law. Second, the threefold mention of Christ's redemptive appearance is placed within the age-old promise of God from the Old Testament (1:2-3). The promise of redemption in Christ had priority over the manifestation of the law. Third, the relationship of sound doctrine and good deeds was Paul's understanding of how Christ's appearance both freed believers from the law and yet bound them to a life of obedience. God's desire to make Israel his special possession (Exod. 19:5; Deut. 14:2) was fulfilled in the people of Christ (2:14).

NEEDS MET BY TITUS

The Christians on the island of Crete experienced the same problems with doctrine as did the major cities of Asia Minor and Greece. False teaching, spread by those not qualified to minister God's word, tended to move believers away from a clear and secure focus on the hope, discipline, and power stemming from the imminent return of Christ. Paul's letter to Titus met some basic needs of the church for security and direction in the face of opposition. The structure and content of Titus show that Paul intended to answer the following questions for the Christians on Crete.

- What kind of people do church leaders need to be?
- How should believers answer those who argue about the law and want them to keep it?
- How should the appearance of God's grace in Christ affect the behavior of believers?

The question of what and who believers should believe is always difficult to answer. Christian leaders may or may not be trustworthy. At times they may even ask believers to do things that contradict what others are teaching. Paul, in his letter to Titus, set out to give guidelines for evaluating leaders and their teaching. He also called believers to scrutinize themselves under the same tough evaluation. First, believers need to have an honest and accurate assessment of the leader's character. Are his motives good or based on desires for material gain? Second, they need to observe the results of the leader's teaching. Does it issue in Christian growth in grace or does it end up in pointless debates? Third, believers themselves are to have a deep understanding of what the appearance of Christ's grace means for the everyday events of life. These three guidelines are not easily followed, but Paul placed the challenge before the believers on Crete to continually probe character, evaluate results, and compare all things against the yardstick of grace alone.

OUTLINE OF TITUS

I. GREETING: THE RELATIONSHIPS IN PAUL'S COMMAND (1:1-4)
   A. Paul's Relationship to the Father and to Christ (1:1)
   B. Paul's Relationships with People (1:2-4)

II. THE SEARCH FOR COMMUNITY ORDER (1:5–3:15)
   A. A Basic for Order: Irreproachable Leaders (1:5-16)
   B. A Basic for Order: Family Love and Honor (2:1-10)
   C. The Model for Community Order: Grace and Obedience (2:11-15)
   D. A Basic for Order: Wise Subordination (3:1-11)
   E. A Basic for Order: Meeting Pressing Needs (3:12-15)

TITUS NOTES

1:1-4 GREETING: THE RELATIONSHIPS IN PAUL'S COMMAND

1:1 Paul's Relationship to the Father and to Christ

In chapter 1 Paul informed Titus of the administrative matters that would serve as the solid foundation for sound doctrine in the church. He encouraged Titus to set things in order in the church and appoint qualified elders (1:5). This was especially important in Crete because of the false teachers that were there.

Paul's introduction shows the scope, function, and nature of his apostleship and message. Paul used the term "slave of God" (1:1; "bond-servant of God," NASB) only in this letter. This term emphasized Paul's function of doing God's bidding. Paul presented the major concern of this letter here: he desired to teach the "truth that shows them how to live godly lives." Paul insisted that the truth of the gospel should result in personal godliness in the lives of believers.

1:2-4 Paul's Relationships with People

"Truth" (1:1) and "confidence" (1:2) are founded on God's eternal promise (1:2; cf. Eph. 1:4; 2 Tim. 1:9) and God's revelation in history (1:3; cf. Rom. 5:6; Gal. 4:4; Eph. 1:10). The designations "God our Savior" (1:3) and "Christ Jesus our Savior" (1:4) cluster around the three mentions of the appearance of God's grace (1:3-4; 2:11, 13; 3:4, 6). The designation "true child" (1:4) would indicate that Titus was one of Paul's converts. Titus was a Greek Christian (Gal. 2:3) and one of Paul's travel companions and fellow workers (1:5; cf. 2 Cor. 8:23; 12:18; Gal. 2:1; 2 Tim. 4:10).

1:5–3:15 THE SEARCH FOR COMMUNITY ORDER

Overview: In Titus 1:5-16 good works are related to usefulness in faith and truth. In 2:2-15 they are related to works stemming from instructive grace. In 3:1-11 good deeds grow out of compassionate grace. The emphases are different, but the basic foundation is the same in all three sections.

1:5-16 A Basic for Order: Irreproachable Leaders

1:5-9 THE BASIC QUALIFICATIONS

The island of Crete (156 miles long and between 7 and 35 miles wide) forms the southern boundary of the Aegean Sea. The center of the island is formed by a mountain chain rising to the height of 8,193 feet (Mount Ida, birthplace of Zeus) which is fringed by lower valleys along the coast. Jews from Crete were present at Pentecost (Acts 2:11) and may have carried the gospel message back to the island. The culture of these island people was strongly influenced by Cretan myth and legend.

Paul's first visit to the island took place on his voyage to Rome (Acts 27:7-8). He had suggested to the captain of the ship that they spend the winter there. Since he probably had not had the opportunity to evangelize the island during his first visit, he took the opportunity to return to Crete sometime after being released from his first Roman imprisonment. This letter indicates that Paul and Titus had a successful ministry there.

Paul's directive was twofold: set things in order and appoint irreproachable elders (1:6). Paul then set forth the qualifications for irreproachable elders (cf. 1 Tim. 3:1-7). The term "elder" (1:5-7) emphasizes the dignity and maturity required for the office. The determining factor for qualification stems from being God's minister (1:7). The church leader had to be one who held fast to the word of God, promoting truth and refuting error. Pure character was a necessity for the people with the roles of teaching and correcting. Good character plus sound doctrine were necessary to enable a ministry of exhortation and correction.

1:10-16 THE CORRECTIVE TO DISORDER

1:10-12 The Source of the Disorder: Greed
The character traits described in 1:10-12 are opposite to the traits of a qualified leader. Here Paul gave the reason for Titus's assignment and revealed the need to appoint qualified elders. There were false teachers among the Cretans. Paul used a strong expression, saying that these false teachers must be "silenced" (1:11). Paul cited the testimony of a Cretan poet and self-styled prophet, Epimenides (1:12; c. 600 B.C.). According to tradition, Epimenides slept for fifty years and then became a prophet. He possessed great knowledge of medicine and natural history. His statement concerning the Cretans was apparently very accurate.

1:13-16 The Corrective: Establish Soundness in the Faith
The command "rebuke them as sternly as necessary" (1:13) is a present imperative and could be rendered: "*keep on* rebuking them sharply." This severe rebuke matches a correspondingly severe problem. Such a rebuke was designed to bring conviction. It had to be sharp but was designed to be restorative, not vindictive. For "Jewish myths" (1:14), see the note on 1 Timothy 1:4. The concept of purity (1:15) was brought up to contrast the false way of purity that was represented in the "commands" of 1:14. True purity in Christ does not come from obedience to the law or Jewish myths.

Titus 1:16 expresses the major theme of Titus: "A believer's character and conduct must be consistent with his confession." This is the basic message of the epistle of James: faith without works is a fallacy.

2:1-10 A Basic for Order: Family Love and Honor

2:1-2 OLDER MEN
This section details the elements that are necessary to sound teaching (2:1). Character and behavior are the object of the teaching (cf. 1 Tim. 1:5). In contrast with the conduct of the false teachers, Paul insisted that the gospel must be graced with a godly life. The command "promote the kind of living that reflects right teaching" (2:1) is continuous and could be rendered, "Keep on teaching." The virtues of 2:2 are appropriate for all Christians but are especially imporant for older men who are naturally looked to as leaders in the church whether or not they hold office.

2:3-5 WOMEN
The older women are to be teachers of younger women, a task that mature Christian women are admirably suited for (2:3-5). The general character of godly women is stated first, then is followed by specific illustrations. Paul not only gave the mature Christian women the responsibility to teach, he also assigned a specific curriculum (2:4-5). In 2:5 the wife and mother has her primary sphere of responsibility in the home. Yet Proverbs 31:10-31 indicates that the home is not necessarily the limit of her sphere of activity.

2:6-8 YOUNG MEN
Paul's request that the conduct of the young men be exemplary was intended to quiet any criticism or attacks from outside the church (2:6-8). Paul emphasized the need, in the face of false teachers and others who desired to give Christianity a bad name, to be self-controlled (2:2, 5-6, 12).

2:9-10 SERVANTS
For a note on slavery, see Ephesians 6:5-9. Paul insisted that even the lowest slave of the Roman social order could adorn God's truth by manifesting Christian character in keeping with his confession. The servant was to make God as Savior look good in the real and present world.

2:11-15 The Model for Community Order: Grace and Obedience
The grace that saves believers (Titus 2:11) and instructs them (2:12) also gives them hope for the future (2:13). Grace as an instructor is seen throughout Scripture (Deut. 8:5; Prov. 1:2; 3:11-12 quoted in Heb. 12:4-7; Eph. 6:4; 2 Tim. 2:25; 3:16). The provision of salvation has been presented to all and is effective for all who believe. This is a universal provision (John 3:16; 2 Cor. 5:19), not a universal salvation. The "wonderful event" and the "glory" are one event (2:13)—the coming of the Lord Jesus for his church.

Paul's combination of Old Testament truths in 2:14 relates Christ to cleansing (Ezek. 37:23) and redemption (Ps. 130:8; cf. Mark 10:45 and Exod. 19:5-6). The imperatives of Titus 2:15 are in the present tense, "encourage and rebuke." Titus's authority was in accord with God's purpose in sending Christ.

3:1-11 A Basic for Order: Wise Subordination

3:1-2 "OTHER-CENTERED" CONSIDERATIONS
Paul considered the practical implications of sound doctrine and commanded Titus to keep on reminding the believers of the importance of good deeds. Paul's remarks were especially appropriate for the Cretans. The Greek historian Polybius remarks that they tended to be a seditious and rebellious people (cf. also Rom. 13:1; 1 Pet. 2:13). Paul, knowing the Cretans to be this way, made the godly qualifications in 3:1-2 a call to civil obedience. The purpose of this inward focus of godliness was also evangelistic. Through their godliness, the believers would exhibit God's grace to the people around them.

3:3-8 GOOD DEEDS FROM JUSTIFICATION BY GRACE
Paul reminded the believers on Crete of their sinful past (3:3) to inspire them to show kindness and consideration toward others. Paul cautioned them

not to become spiritual snobs who were insensitive to their continuing need for God's grace. This was foundational for Paul's discussion of God's act of kindness toward the world (3:5-7). Paul set forth a capsule summary of the doctrine of salvation and expounded on several of the provisions of the new covenant (Ezek. 36:25-28). Salvation is not merited by any righteous works, but wholly determined by God's mercy. "Washed" (3:5) speaks of the spiritual cleansing experienced in the new birth (cf. Ezek. 36:25; Acts 22:16). "New life" (3:5; "regeneration," NASB and KJV) is the supernatural imparting of spiritual life to believers in Christ (John 3:7). The "new life through the Holy Spirit" (3:5) refers to the Spirit's regenerating and indwelling ministry (cf. Ezek. 36:27). God's rich outpouring is to be mirrored in the believers' rich outpouring of kindness to others. To be "not guilty" (3:7) means to be declared righteous (Rom. 5:1).

3:9-11 THE ORDER FOR INSUBORDINATION
A person who causes "divisions" (3:10; "factious man," NASB; "heretic," KJV) is one who argues foolishly without accurate Scriptural support. See Acts

24:14 where Paul explained that Christianity was not a sect (a factious group) because it was in complete harmony with the Old Testament Scriptures. Paul's instructions for dealing with divisive people (3:10) reflect the teachings of Jesus concerning discipline in the church (Matt. 18:15-17).

3:12-15 A Basic for Order: Meeting Pressing Needs
In this section Paul brought up his need for companionship (3:12) and emphasized the importance of helping Christian travelers (3:13-14). Tychicus was a close friend and fellow worker of Paul (cf. Acts 20:4; Eph. 6:21; Col. 4:7; 2 Tim. 4:12). Nicopolis was located in the province of Achaia on the Adriatic coast. Zenas the lawyer and Apollos the well-known preacher (3:13; cf. Acts 18:24) were on their way to Crete. They may have been carrying this letter to Titus. Even in his final words, Paul once again emphasized the important theme of good works (3:14). The Cretans were to take the lead in good deeds; they were to be fruitful, not fruitless.

PHILEMON

BASIC FACTS

HISTORICAL SETTING

This letter is the only source of information about Philemon. He was a slaveholder who had been converted, possibly as a result of Paul's ministry (Philem. 1:19). At least, Philemon was indebted to Paul in some way. Because the church met at his house, he must have been a person of wealth and influence. Apphia is not specifically identified. Paul calls her a sister (1:2), and this is evidence that she was a believer. Archippus was a believer at Colosse and a fellow soldier with Paul and Timothy (1:2; cf. Phil. 2:25). Although the letter contains personal matters, it is also addressed to the church (1:2). Paul wanted to make this a public matter, perhaps to encourage other slaveholders to follow Philemon's example, or to apply social pressure on Philemon so that he might heed Paul's request.

Paul wrote this letter to Philemon on behalf of Philemon's slave, Onesimus of Colosse (Col. 4:9), who had run away to Rome. There he had evidently been converted under Paul's ministry. Onesimus had become a useful servant of the apostle in his imprisonment (Col. 4:9), and Paul desired to keep Onesimus with him to continue his ministry. But Paul recognized that Onesimus was the property of Philemon and must be subject to his master (cf. Eph. 6:5). Paul sent Onesimus back to Philemon with Tychicus (Col. 4:7-9) with a letter requesting Philemon to demonstrate grace and receive Onesimus as a brother in the Lord.

AUTHOR

Paul's letter to Philemon indicates that Paul was the author (1:1, 9, 19). The historical setting of the letter fits that of Colossians (1:23-24; cf. Col. 4:10-14).

DATE

The close connection of Philemon with Colossians makes it virtually certain that the two letters belong to the same period. Tychicus, accompanied by Onesimus, probably carried both letters to Colosse at the same time, probably in A.D. 62 (Col. 4:7-9).

PURPOSE

The letter to Philemon was designed to encourage a simple yet profound personal trans-action—the substitution of forgiveness and acceptance for the legal rights of ownership. The letter encouraged seeing relationships in light of the deep bonds created in Christ, rather than the earthly social structures of status and self-achievement.

GUIDING CONCEPTS

SLAVERY IN THE ROMAN WORLD

Slavery was universally taken for granted in the first century A.D. It was practiced in Jewish, Roman, and Greek cultures, although the institution varied in some degree from culture to culture. Jewish slaves had certain privileges and were under legal protection. The Jews prided themselves in the fact that they never treated their slaves with cruelty. Slaves among non-Jewish peoples did not receive such protection. The Greek civilization was built on the institution of slavery. Greek slaves were used for industrial purposes and worked in the mines under terrible conditions. Roman slaves, although considered the legal property of their master, could obtain freedom and become legal persons. They were generally used in houses or on farms. A slave could not be legally married or own property. Any children born to a female slave would become the property of her master.

The main sources of slavery were: (1) birth, being borne by a woman who was a slave; (2) the practice of exposing unwanted children whom anyone could claim; (3) the sale of one's own children into slavery; (4) voluntary slavery as a means of paying a debt; (5) penal slavery as punishment for a crime; (6) kidnapping and piracy; (7) military conquest and capture of peoples. Slave dealers often followed military campaigns, buying captured prisoners and shipping them off to the slave markets to be sold at a nice profit.

Cruel punishments were inflicted upon slaves for mistakes and disobedience. Slaves were often beaten with sticks or whipped. Runaway slaves and thieves were branded on the forehead with a mark. Others were imprisoned. Although many died as a result of mistreatment, it was illegal to take the life of a slave without a court order.

The rights of a master over a slave were in no way affected by a slave's running away. It was the duty of civil authorities to aid in the recovery of slaves. Some citizens made it their business to capture and return runaway slaves for a profit. It was a serious criminal offense to harbor a runaway slave.

The chief way a slave might become free was by a legal act of the owner called manumission—the act of setting a slave free. This was accomplished by either the payment of a ransom, or by an act of the state. In Rome, manumission was often granted in a slave owner's will. At times legal limits had to be placed on the release of slaves to prevent too rapid an integration of Rome with persons of foreign extraction. In Greek states emancipated slaves became resident aliens, but in Rome they could be granted citizenship. This resulted in a great flow of slaves to Italy, especially in the last two centuries before Christ. This could account for Onesimus's traveling to Rome. He was undoubtedly aware that there were many freed slaves in the city who might be willing to offer him some assistance.

Rather than trying to overthrow the cultural institution of slavery, Paul sought to work within the system, requiring that slaves obey their masters (Eph. 6:5-8; Col. 3:22-24) and that masters not mistreat their slaves (Col. 4:1; 1 Pet. 2:18-20). Although Paul seems to have been supportive of emancipation (cf. 1 Cor. 7:21), he was definitely more concerned with spiritual freedom than with the release of slaves. He remarked in 1 Corinthians 7:22 that a believing slave is "free" and that a free believer is "a slave of Christ."

BIBLE-WIDE CONCEPTS

Paul's letter to Philemon is a powerful cameo illustration of God's grace exhibited in the Bible-wide movement from the offense of human sin to repentance and reconciliation. This movement is based on God's willingness to receive sinful people as his brothers (cf. Heb. 2:11) by charging their debts of sin to Christ's account (2 Cor. 5:19). Paul commended this pattern to Philemon, and through him to believers today. All believers should be willing to receive past offenders as brothers and sisters in Christ (1:16) and forgive them (1:18-19).

NEEDS MET BY PHILEMON

Paul's letter to Philemon meets some basic needs that apply to situations beyond the specific needs of Philemon and Onesimus. The Colossian believers probably wondered how Christianity should affect the relationships between Christians of different social classes. The structure and content of Philemon show that Paul was answering questions like the following.

- How can Christian leaders encourage people to reconcile relationships without commanding them harshly?
- How should Christ affect the way believers view their relationships with people of differing social and vocational status?

Behind the issue of how Christians are to relate to others of various ethnic and social backgrounds lies their need to give up certain rights in order to display forgiving grace. God has every right to punish people for their sins. He has every right to put an end to a world that does not care about him. But he has given up his rights in order to display his grace in forgiveness and an intimate relationship of love. Likewise, the letter to Philemon encourages believers to choose grace and deeper relationships rather than insisting on formal rights and relationships of social status.

OUTLINE OF PHILEMON

I. GREETING (1:1-3)

II. THANKSGIVING (1:4-7)

III. PAUL'S RETURN OF ONESIMUS (1:8-16)

IV. PHILEMON'S RECEPTION OF ONESIMUS (1:17-22)

V. CLOSING GREETINGS (1:23-25)

PHILEMON NOTES

1:1-3 GREETING
Paul wrote to Philemon during his first Roman imprisonment (cf. Acts 28:16-31). Timothy (see note on 1 Tim. 1:2) is associated with him in writing the epistle, but Paul is clearly the sole author (cf. 1:9, 19). Philemon was a slaveholder (1:15-16) who had been converted, possibly as a result of Paul's ministry (1:19). He was fondly regarded by the apostle and had worked with Paul or helped him in the ministry (1:1). A careful comparison of the letter of Philemon with Colossians indicates that they were written at the same time to people of the same city. Philemon resided in the Lycus valley in the city of Colosse.

Apphia (1:2), some have speculated, may have been the wife of Philemon, although this is not specifically stated in the text. Archippus (1:2), a believer at Colosse, is regarded as a "fellow soldier" of Paul and Timothy. (For a note on the city of Colosse, see Col. 1:2.) The term "fellow soldier" is used figuratively as an expression of honor and appreciation for some sacrificial or risky service (cf. Phil. 2:25). Archippus resided at Colosse and was involved in the ministry there (Col. 4:17). The letter, while being personal in content, is also addressed to the church at Philemon's house. Perhaps Paul wanted to encourage other slaveholders to follow Philemon's example, or to apply pressure to Philemon that he might heed his request to forgive Onesimus.

1:4-7 THANKSGIVING
These verses begin with Paul's encouragement of Philemon to be gracious toward Onesimus. Paul reminded Philemon first to consider all the good things Christ had given him so that he would have an effective sharing (fellowship) of his faith, in this case goodwill toward Onesimus.

1:8-16 PAUL'S RETURN OF ONESIMUS
Paul could have used his apostolic authority to command Philemon to do what was right, but instead he appealed to the principle of "love" to encourage Philemon to show kindness to Onesimus. The name "Onesimus" means "useful." As a runaway, Onesimus was useless, but now, returning as a believer, he had become "useful," both to Paul and to Philemon. Onesimus left as a mere slave but would return as a beloved brother in Christ. Paul's request on Onesimus's behalf was the practical outworking of his prayer in Philemon 1:6.

1:17-22 PHILEMON'S RECEPTION OF ONESIMUS
Paul asked that any debts or damages charged to Onesimus be placed on his own account. Paul promised to pay them in full. The word "charge" (1:18) means to "impute" or "reckon" (cf. Rom. 5:13). This well illustrates Christ's work for the Christian. The debt of the believer's sin has been charged to Christ's account. Now God the Father receives all who believe in him as he would his own dear Son. Philemon 1:21 may indicate that Paul was hoping that Philemon would release Onesimus from slavery. Philemon 1:22 provides an important clue regarding Paul's travel plans after being released from his first Roman imprisonment. His first destination appears to have been Colosse.

1:23-25 CLOSING GREETINGS
Epaphras (1:23) was a native of Colosse and was apparently the founder of the church (Col. 1:7). The term "fellow prisoner" suggests that he voluntarily remained with Paul during his house arrest in Rome (Acts 28:16, 23). Mark (1:24) refers to John Mark, author of the second Gospel (cf. Acts 13:5, 13; 15:37, 39). Aristarchus was a Thessalonian and traveling companion with Paul (Acts 19:29; 20:4; 27:2; Col. 4:10). Demas was a companion of Paul's (cf. Col. 4:14) who deserted him during his last imprisonment (2 Tim. 4:10). Luke was the Gentile physician, companion of Paul, and author of the third Gospel and Acts (Acts 16:10; Col. 4:14; 2 Tim. 4:11).

HEBREWS

HISTORICAL SETTING

The ancient title of this letter designates the readers as Hebrews, but the letter does not mention the readers as either Jews or Gentiles. Most conservative scholars agree on the basis of internal evidence that the readers were Hebrew Christians. Some believe the readers resided in Jerusalem because of the references to the temple and temple institutions. Closer observation, however, reveals that the author writes of the tabernacle (Heb. 9:2), not the temple. Furthermore, the Jerusalem Christians were known for receiving charity, not giving it (6:10; 10:34). It has also been suggested that Alexandria was the place of residence of the readers due to a temple located nearby at Leontopolis. The letter also reflects an Alexandrian influence as seen in the quotations of the Septuagint.

Others have suggested on the basis of 13:24 that the readers resided in Rome. The salutation could be that of Christians originally from Italy sending back greetings to their friends. On the other hand, the phrase could merely refer to the present location of the writer and greeters. Because the letter was first known in Rome where there appears to have been an influential group of Hebrew Christians (Rom. 9–11; cf. Acts 28:17-31), it was either addressed to Hebrew Christians at Rome, or possibly somewhere else in the Roman world.

AUTHOR

The author is not identified in the letter. Tradition has variously ascribed the letter to Paul, Barnabas, Apollos, Luke, Silas, Philip, Priscilla, or John Mark. Because of the dispute regarding the authorship of Hebrews, the letter was not regarded as fully canonical by the Western church until the fourth century A.D.

DATE

Because Hebrews was quoted by Clement of Rome in his Epistle to the Corinthians, it had to have been written prior to A.D. 96. Hebrews would have been written at a time when Timothy was still alive (Heb. 13:23), but some of the original leaders of the Hebrew Christian assembly had died (13:7). The readers were apparently second generation Christians (2:3). The indications are that the Jewish sacrificial system was still in operation (7:8; 8:4; 10:1-2, 8, 11). This would demand a date prior to A.D. 70 when the Jerusalem temple was destroyed.

If the letter was written from Rome, and Timothy was able to come to Rome as Paul requested (2 Tim. 4:11-13) and was also imprisoned at that time (Heb. 13:23), then the date of writing would have followed his release, about A.D. 68 to 69. But the reference in 12:4, if interpreted literally, would indicate that the letter was written before the persecution of Christians under Nero, which began in July of A.D. 64. Thus, a date of origin in the sixties accords well with the available data.

PURPOSE

The letter was designed to correct the readers' desires to substitute old religious ways for the greatness of the new revelation of God in Christ. Although the geographical setting and date of the letter are uncertain, the spiritual condition of its readers is clear. The believers had demonstrated Christian love (6:10) and had endured persecution (10:32-34). In spite of these favorable traits, there were some areas of weakness.

The letter encourages the readers to make spiritual progress (5:11-12). Their failure to grow in the Lord was reflected in their Christian conduct (10:25; 13:2-17). The Hebrew Christians were looking back to their Jewish ways instead of ahead to Christ, the author and perfecter of faith (12:2). Facing the hardships of the Christian faith, they were in danger of drifting away (2:1) from the substance, Christ, to the shadow of the Old Testament sacrificial system (8:5; 10:1). It was to deal with such spiritual stagnation that the author wrote his letter to the Hebrew Christians.

GUIDING CONCEPTS

The first ten chapters of the book are built around five groups of Old Testament quotations. This amounts to a sermon about Christ based on Old Testament passages. Clearly the writer wanted to show how Christ related to well-known Old Testament themes and promises. The Old Testament passages are listed in the accompanying chart.

The key Old Testament passage in the book of Hebrews is Psalm 110:1, 4 (cf. 1:3, "sat down in the place of honor at the right hand"; and 1:13). It is also used in 5:5-6; 7:17, 21 and 10:11-14 where it is combined with the new covenant. Psalm 110 speaks of the eternal order of Melchizedek and the sitting down of the Son at God's right hand, the two key themes of the book. The entire book of Hebrews shows the implications of the answers to two questions: Why is Jesus sitting at God's right hand? And what does it mean for him to be a priest like Melchizedek?

CHRIST IN THE OLD TESTAMENT

Hebrews Passage	*Quoted Old Testament Passages*
Hebrews 1:2-14	Psalms 2:7; 104:4; 45:6-7; 102:25-27; 110:1; 2 Samuel 7:14; Deuteronomy 32:43 from the Greek Old Testament (the Septuagint).
Hebrews 2:5-18	Psalms 8:4-6; 22:22; Isaiah 8:17-18.
Hebrews 3:1–4:13	Psalm 95:7-11.
Hebrews 4:14–7:28	Psalms 2:7; 110:4.
Hebrews 8:1–10:39	Jeremiah 31:31-34; Psalms 40:6-8; 110:1; 26:11; Habakkuk 2:3-11. (The Jeremiah passage is the longest Old Testament quotation in the New Testament.)

BIBLE-WIDE CONCEPTS

The first ten chapters of the book reach back into the Old Testament to show how Moses, the law, and the priesthood have been completed in the new covenant inaugurated by Jesus. The rest of the book, Hebrews 11–13, is a series of exhortations built upon the message of Hebrews 1–10. The entire book is an exposition of how the Old Testament is fulfilled in Christ. But several Bible-wide concepts deserve special mention here.

First, Hebrews 1:2-14 clearly shows in its interpretations of Psalm 2:7, 2 Samuel 7:14, and Psalm 110:1 that Jesus was the long-awaited promised son of David, the King who would rule God's people and mediate between them and God. Adam was the first man, and he represented all humanity as he chose to sin rather than obey God. The chosen man Abraham was the recipient of a promise that mediated the blessing of all nations through him. The great leader Moses was also the mediator for God's people and several times saved them from destruction. God promised King David that a son of his would be the eternal Mediator between humanity and God. That greater son of David would be an eternal King ruling under God's unceasing loving-kindness. Hebrews shows how Jesus fulfilled that ancient promise of kingship and blessing.

Second, the interpretation of Psalm 95:7-11 in Hebrews 3:1–4:13 links those who profess faith in Christ to ancient Israel as they wandered in the wilderness from Egypt toward the Promised Land. And the Promised Land functions throughout the Bible as the middle ground between the Garden of Eden and the new heavens and earth. Like Eden, the Promised Land was a place of new beginnings and potential blessings. It represented a return to what had been lost when Adam and Eve were thrown out of Eden. But the path to the new Eden of the Promised Land had many pitfalls and barriers for the faith and steadfastness of God's pilgrims. All the weaknesses and forces that resulted in Adam and Eve's original loss of Eden's blessings still plagued those who journeyed across Sinai to the anticipated beauties of the Promised Land. Some pilgrims made it. Others fell by the wayside. Eden and the Promised Land were but preludes to the permanent place of God's blessing, the new and eternal heaven and earth. Hebrews links the journey through the desert of Sinai to the journey of believers through this age into the next. Some will make it into the new heavens and earth. Others will fall by the way.

Third, the letter to the Hebrews shows how Christ is the fulfillment of God's new covenant promised in Jeremiah 31:31-34 and other Old Testament passages. All the various promises and covenants God had previously used to restore his relationship with his creation pointed to and were fulfilled by his new covenant in Christ. The promise of victory over the seed of the serpent (Gen. 3:15), the perfection of God's promise to Noah to withhold his global wrath, the blessings promised through Moses' covenant, the inauguration of worldwide blessings through Abraham, and the perfect rule promised through David's greater son all come to fulfillment and perfection in Christ's new covenant. The new covenant remedied the problem of guilt now. The covenant's provision of inner change and power through God's Spirit would also help diminish disobedience now and would finally end all disobedience in the future. The details of how Hebrews elaborates these Bible-wide concepts will be seen in the following Notes section.

NEEDS MET BY HEBREWS

The original readers of the letter to the Hebrews faced a crisis of authority. The Jewish leaders they had trusted before believing in Jesus as the Messiah had seemed so wise and so true to God's revelations. Then Christian prophets had presented a convincing message that God had brought a new revelation of his will through Jesus of Nazareth. But now the new believers were having second thoughts. Their old Jewish leaders put pressure on them to return to the fold of Judaism. Some of the pressure was severe persecution, some was simple social shunning. But the real issue lay in the question of how an unknown man like Jesus from an obscure town called Nazareth could be accepted as being greater than famous leaders and prophets like Abraham and Moses.

To any who needed to be convinced of Jesus' absolute supremacy over Moses and Abraham, this letter demonstrated that the Bible itself predicted and identified that such a One would come. But the need to believe that Jesus' covenant was better than Moses' was just the foundation for the author's goals. He also sought to establish his readers' love and stability before God and their holy living and witness before the world. The issue began with doctrine but ended with an increased effectiveness in spreading the wonderful message of God's redemption in Christ. The book of Hebrews speaks to crucial needs felt by those under religious and cultural pressure to return to pre-conversion commitments. The structure and content of Hebrews show that the author was answering questions like the following.

- In what way is Jesus better than all the great heroes of the Old Testament?
- How does Jesus' new covenant improve upon Moses' old covenant?
- How can believers reconcile the hostility that comes their way because they are Christians with God's promises of security in his kingdom?
- What are some of the consequences of believers softening their commitment to Christ?
- What are some concrete ways of understanding the sometimes intangible reality of faith?

Many Christians face pressures to return to their old beliefs and life-styles. Family, friends, or just the flesh may pull them back toward living as they did before they met Christ. To correct this downward pull the writer of Hebrews presented a simple comparison between better and best. Christ is better than any of the old beliefs believers used to hold. His redemption is not only better, it is the only real salvation in the world. His forgiveness is perfect and eternal. Taken alone, who would not follow the best and choose Christ over what the world has to offer? The issue of who is the best is fairly easily settled. But that is only the first step to dealing with the more difficult issues met by Hebrews.

The writer was also aware that when a Christian chooses Christ as the only Redeemer, he also chooses to participate in Christ's sufferings. And when a Christian is suffering for Christ, it is tempting to end the pain by ending what caused it—the witness for Christ. The writer's argument for the supremacy of Christ on the basis of the Scriptures is but one support for persevering. His other argument is a more personal and less tangible matter. And that is how to make faith, that hard-to-grasp action, more solid and visible. Arguments for the supremacy of Christ are not going to produce steadfast Christian character without an accompanying faith that is strong and honest. The writer meets the needs of believers for stronger faith by providing a long list of people who believed that what God said, he would do. God's word promised many things, most of which, like God himself, are presently invisible. The writer of Hebrews used believers from the past to illustrate how God's invisible word had the power to move ordinary people to live obedient and even sacrificial lives. Only real things can affect the lives of believers, and only faith can make God a real force in their lives. The letter meets the need for a doctrinal presentation upholding Christ as the only supreme Redeemer. At the same time it seeks to deepen inner convictions so that believers will move from an intellectual assent that the doctrine is true to a committed lifestyle that can weather even persecution and hostility.

OUTLINE OF HEBREWS

I. THE EXALTED SON: BETTER THAN ANGELS (1:1–2:18)
A. Better by Nature (1:1–2:4)
B. Better by Empathy (2:5-18)

II. THE FAITHFUL SON: MORE GLORY THAN MOSES (3:1–4:16)
A. Greater Glory (3:1-6)
B. Conclusion: The Requirement of Consistent Belief (3:7–4:13)
C. Transition from Apostle to High Priest (4:14-16)

III. THE PERFECT PRIEST: ETERNAL AND EFFECTIVE (5:1–12:13)
A. Eternal: Melchizedek (5:1–7:28)
B. Effective: Better Covenant Administered (8:1–10:18)
C. Exhortations to Effective Faith (10:19–12:13)

IV. PATTERNS FOR MATURE PEOPLE (12:14–13:17)
A. Peace (12:14-29)
B. Love (13:1-6)
C. Obedience (13:7-17)

V. CLOSING REQUESTS (13:18-25)

HEBREWS NOTES

1:1–2:18 THE EXALTED SON: BETTER THAN ANGELS

Overview: In addition to being divinely inspired Scripture, the book of Hebrews is great literature. The first sentences are illustrative of the writer's lofty style, full of noble expressions and fine rhetoric. The book was clearly written by someone who was able and eloquent. Hebrews 1:3 sets out the two major themes of the book: (1) the purification of humanity's sin, which led to (2) Jesus taking his place at God's right hand.

Three points are made in Hebrews 1–2: Jesus is the Creator; angels are servants of the redeemed;

and Jesus is the brother of all those who believe. While the topics initially were of concern to Jewish believers, the truths of Christ's inherent greatness over creation and the world of spirit beings is important for all Christians. The excellence of Jesus is critical for those who might consider withdrawing from Jesus to return to their pre-Christian commitments.

Tradition viewed angels as being the mediators who gave the law to Moses (cf. Deut. 33:2; Gal. 3:19; Acts 7:38, 53). Christ is better than any other mediatorial agent God had used in his revelation. By using numerous quotations from the Old

Testament Scriptures, the writer demonstrates the superiority of Christ over angels. Angels were also highly regarded by the Jews as administrators of the nations (Dan. 10:20-21; 12:1). The writer does not disparage angels but simply shows how Christ is "better," a term used thirteen times in Hebrews to contrast Christ with the old order. Seven truths are stated about the Son that emphasize his greatness and show why the revelation given through him is full and final: (1) Heir of all things, (2) Creator of the world, (3) the radiance of God's glory, (4) the exact representation of God's divine nature, (5) the sustainer of creation, (6) the Redeemer of mankind, and (7) intercessor for believers.

1:1–2:4 Better by Nature
1:1-4 THE INHERITED NAME
1:1-2 Contexts of Divine Speaking
The author clearly recognized that God spoke both through his prophets (Old Testament) and his Son (New Testament). He viewed God's self-revelation through two eras (then and now) and two sources (the prophets and the Son). God was the source of the revelation that came to the forefathers of the nation Israel. But that revelation came bit by bit and by various methods: dreams, visions, signs, laws, institutions, and ceremonies. In contrast to the former revelation, the full and final revelation in these "final days" is in God's Son (John 1:18). Old Testament saints could say, "God speaks." Believers today say, "God has spoken."

1:2-4 The New Way Described
Jesus' supremacy is based on two facts: (1) he was appointed heir of all things and (2) before that he was the vehicle of creation (1:2). Here the writer emphasized the incomparable greatness, power, and majesty of the Son. Jesus has a better nature than angels. Christ is characterized as the Creator himself. His word sustains creation, and he has the very character of God.

1:5-14 BIBLICAL PROOF FOR THE SON'S NAME
1:5-6 Sonship
Jesus' excellence is confirmed by quoting Psalm 2:7 (cf. Acts 13:33) along with 2 Samuel 7:14. These are passages that speak of the coronation of God's chosen King according to God's promise to David. In view was Christ's exaltation to the right hand of God in resurrection power (cf. Acts 2:33-35). Christ is Son in terms of the kingship promised in 2 Samuel 7:14.

1:7-14 Vocation
This section shows that angels are ministers (see the beginning and end bracket in 1:7, 14) whereas Christ is the exalted Son (1:13 again quoting Ps. 110:1). The angels are servants (1:7 quoting Ps. 104:4) for the Christians (1:14). Therefore, Christians are not to worship angels. They are to be served by them.

Christ is better because of the worship he receives (1:6 quoting Deut. 32:43). Christ is better because of his eternal sovereignty (1:8-13 quoting Ps. 45:6-7; 102:25-27; and 110:1). Christ is better because of the work he accomplished at creation (1:10-12 quoting Ps. 102:25-27). And Christ is better because of the triumph he achieved (1:13 quoting Ps. 110:1). To sit at the right hand of royalty was regarded as a great honor and proved that someone was worthy of great respect. Treating one's conquered enemies as a footstool is a metaphor taken from the ancient practice of a conquering king placing his foot on the neck of a defeated king as a symbolic gesture of triumph. Why is Jesus sitting, rather than standing, at God's right hand? The book of Hebrews proceeds to answer this question. He has done his priestly work of purification for sin and now waits until the final judgment (Ps. 110:1). Jesus used Psalm 110:1 with reference to himself in Mark 14:62. Even the Jews of the first century A.D. understood Psalm 110 to refer to the Messiah.

The "salvation" mentioned in 1:14 looks to the final consummation of salvation where believers will be changed to full conformity with Christ (Rom. 8:29; 1 John 3:2). The writer has spoken about Christ as Creator and Sovereign over the angels. He next moves on to speak of something more personal than Christ as Creator; he reveals Christ's identity as brother to humanity.

2:1-4 STATEMENT OF NEED: PAY MUCH CLOSER ATTENTION
Here the writer presents the first of five warning passages (cf. Heb. 2:1-4; 3:7–4:13; 5:11–6:20; 10:26-31; 12:25-29). In this first warning, the writer shows that the Son's superiority to angels should not be neglected. Since the revelation through Christ is superior to that mediated by angels, and earlier disregard for God's revelation was duly punished, disobedience to the Christian message of salvation would not go unpunished.

Hebrews 2:1 reflects the major difficulty with the readers. They were drifting from the substance, Christ, back to the shadows of the old covenant system. They were failing to appropriate the blessings of their salvation (2:3). They would not be saved from the power of sin by drifting from grace back to the law and Judaism. The message of salvation was confirmed to the Hebrew readers by the apostles who heard firsthand; their message was certified to the Jewish hearers by apostolic miracles (2:4).

2:5-18 Better by Empathy
2:5-8 ALL IS SUBJECT TO HIM
The writer presents another example of the superiority of the Son over angels. The administration of the present world has been entrusted to angels (cf. Deut. 32:8; Dan. 10:20-21; 12:1; Eph. 6:12), but administration in the world to come is reserved for the Son (Heb. 2:5; 6:5). The writer refers to Psalm 8:4-6

(Heb. 2:6-8) in which the psalmist reflects on the original state of man and his dominion over creation (Gen. 1:26). The original psalm spoke of God putting all creation under the rule of humans (Gen. 1:28). That state of perfect rule will be a future reality. For now, believers have the vision of the Son of Man through his work of redemption to live by.

2:9-18 FAMILY RELATIONSHIPS
2:9 Jesus Made Lower than the Angels
In this verse the author goes from *son of man* (mankind) in Psalm 8 to the *Son of Man*. Jesus will give humanity the ability to completely subject the world in the future. The purpose of Christ being made a little lower than the angels was that he might taste death for all believers. The exposition interweaves with Old Testament text, especially Hebrews 2:9. The expression "tasted" is a metaphor for experience. The atonement is sufficient for all and effective for all who believe (John 10:15; 2 Cor. 5:18-19; Eph. 5:25; 1 John 2:2).

2:10 A Mutual Partaker in Humanity
Hebrews 2:10 presents the writer's thesis. It was fitting for Jesus to experience humility and death because it was in accord with God's plan to perfect him. The sufferings of Christ were necessary to complete his identification with humanity. Christ's sufferings made him truly qualified to be the perfect high priest.

2:11-13 Scriptural Proof
Both he who sanctifies and those who are sanctified are from one Father. That unity of source was a driving force in Christ's empathy for sinful mankind. The author used Psalm 22 to support his statement. All who believe are Christ's brothers and sisters; therefore, he is not ashamed to call believers family. But more pointedly, Psalm 22:22 (Heb. 2:12), along with the quotations of Isaiah 8:17-18 (Heb. 2:13), shows that as Mediator, Christ is God's King speaking of his royal family. The Isaiah 8:18 passage (quoted in 2:13) refers to children as signs of God's judgment and salvation ("Isaiah" means "salvation is of God"; the name of his son "Shear-Jashub" means "a remnant will return," Isa. 7:3; and "Maher-Shalal-Hash-Baz" means "quick to the plunder, swift to the spoil" in judgment, Isa. 8:3). As signs, Isaiah and his sons were pictures of Christ and his children. These quotations demonstrate the unity of Christ and the believers.

2:14-18 Conclusion
This conclusion takes up the "children" concept of Hebrews 2:13. The incarnation makes a difference in the believer's approach to the one who is the Creator. Again the contrast is between what is done for angels and for believers (Heb. 2:16). The delivery from fear of death (2:14-15) is elaborated with reference to Abraham's offspring (cf. Isa. 41:8-10). The

purpose of the incarnation of Christ was to defeat the prince of death (Heb. 2:14), deliver believers from the fear of death (2:15-16), and qualify him as a merciful High Priest (2:17). The topic of the High Priest is introduced (2:17; cf. Heb. 5–7). The term "offer a sacrifice" (2:17; "propitiation," NASB; "reconciliation," KJV) speaks of the satisfaction of God's wrath. The death of Christ satisfied God's wrath toward sin, enabling him to receive those who place their faith in Jesus (cf. Rom. 3:25).

Since Christ was tempted through his human suffering, he is able to sympathetically assist those who are spiritually distressed (Heb. 2:18). He understands the temptations of believers and is able to help them remain faithful. These exhortation passages help believers understand why the letter was written. They explained the new word from God, not from Sinai, but from the promised Messiah. These passages do not differ significantly from Paul's. They emphasize a worthy walk. The point the author wanted to make is this: if what God said through Sinai was impressive, think about what he has said through Jesus. The author is speaking about the world to come (2:5). That new world will end the present period of Christ's reign at God's right hand (1:13; Ps. 110:1, "until"). The world is moving toward the end of that period. The author was speaking of the coming age in Hebrews 1:2 and 2:3.

3:1–4:16 THE FAITHFUL SON: MORE GLORY THAN MOSES
Overview: Jesus is contrasted with Moses by using the metaphors Son versus servant and builder versus house. The exodus theme of Moses changes to the conquest theme under Joshua as the rest in the Promised Land is contrasted with the eternal Sabbath rest to come.

3:1-6 Greater Glory
3:1-2 THESIS STATEMENT: BOTH MOSES AND JESUS ARE FAITHFUL
Consider Jesus who was faithful like Moses. Moses was a great servant (Num. 12:7), but Jesus is the Son. Note the whole context of Numbers 12. In Judaism, Moses was regarded as the great prophet and leader of Israel, delivering the people from bondage in Egypt and leading them up to the Promised Land (Deut. 34:10-12). While careful to avoid deprecating Moses, the writer sets forth the superior person and position of Christ. The author addressed his readers as "friends who belong to God" (3:1), indicating that they were fellow Christians. The expression "are bound for heaven" (3:1) indicates that they have received an effective call of God to salvation.

3:3-4 JESUS' FAITHFULNESS AS BUILDER
Christ is Son and builder of the house of which Moses was just a part. As the real credit for a

building belongs to the architect and builder, so Jesus as the builder of God's house is entitled to more glory than Moses, who was merely an important part of the building.

3:5-6 JESUS' FAITHFULNESS AS SON

Christ's faithfulness is based on the relationship of being a Son, rather than a servant, in the house. The words "if we keep up our courage" (3:6) suggest that an abandonment of grace in favor of Judaism would demonstrate that the readers had never become genuine believers. True believers are those who persevere in the faith.

3:7–4:13 Conclusion: The Requirement of Consistent Belief

3:7-19 SCRIPTURAL COMMAND: DO NOT HARDEN YOUR HEART

3:7-11 The Principle

The writer warned that as the Israelites failed to enter into Canaan because of their sinful disobedience, an expression of unbelief (3:19), the believers also would miss out on a similar blessing if they did not continue steadfastly in their faith (3:12; 4:1). The reason for bringing up Moses was to talk about the wilderness and rest. The key elements are "today" (3:7) and "wilderness" (3:8). Having a great man like Moses did not stop the Israelites from great failure of faith and loss of rest in the Promised Land. Psalm 95 speaks of the rest in the Promised Land of Israel. Hardness of heart raised God's anger and blocked entrance into his rest. For the illustration of unbelief, the author quoted Psalm 95:7-11 (cf. Exod. 17:1-7; Num. 20:1-13) in which David warned his own generation against the rebellion and unbelief that had characterized God's people in the wilderness. A whole generation of the nation of Israel forfeited the privilege of entering the Promised Land (cf. Num. 14:22-23).

3:12-19 The Exposition

The basic problem for the original readers of this book was unbelief (3:12 and 3:19 frame this section). The writer warned the believers that as rebellion in the wilderness resulted in a forfeiture of God's rest in Canaan, so a retreat from Christ back to Judaism would also result in a forfeiture of God's blessing. Since they "share in all that belongs to Christ" (3:14), they should not be tricked into such apostasy. Professed Christians who, through a lack of trust in Christ, reverted to Judaism would be exhibiting the same unfaithfulness to God's revelation as their forefathers had in the wilderness. And the consequences could be equally disastrous.

4:1-13 APPLICATION: BE DILIGENT TO ENTER TRUE REST

4:1-10 The Need for Hearing Plus Faith

The Promised Land of rest was just a picture of a future entrance into God's rest that began on the first Sabbath, the seventh day of creation. It is a rest in the perfection and wholeness of a restored creation. God's creation Sabbath rest confirmed that everything was very good, just the way he wanted it. Psalm 95 is used to show the hard-heartedness of the people. The writer was answering the question of how there could be a rest other than that of the Promised Land. The writer demonstrated that "rest" was part of God's plan from the very beginning and that his plan for providing rest is still in effect. Hebrews 4:9 summarizes the conclusion of the arguments presented in 4:3-8.

God intends for believers to find rest (4:10). As God rested on the seventh day in light of the completion of creation, so his people may rest in the satisfaction that Christ's work of redemption is completed. The word translated "rest" may be translated "a Sabbath-kind of rest." The believer who rests completely in the finished work of Christ has ceased from self-efforts, human merit, and legalism as means of commending himself to God (4:10).

4:11-13 Exhortation to Diligence

Everyday is today in the believer's experience before God. The author was talking about the way believers think about God and respond to him. The exodus under Moses and the conquest under Joshua were not once-for-all events. They were pictures of an ongoing process of redemption and conquest that will lead ultimately into the eternal Promised Land of the new heavens and earth. Until then, there is no time to coast or retreat in Christian commitment. Believers either go forward or backward.

The discussion of the sharpness of the word (4:12) cements the certainty of a fall (4:11) for those who doubt God's interest or ability to keep track of his people's maturity. People cannot hide from God (cf. 1:1-2). The word of God is living and active, filled with God's vitality and energy. It is able to probe the deepest recesses of the human heart and leave nothing hidden. Confronted by God's word, people are confronted with God before whom they must give an account and from whom nothing can be concealed.

4:14-16 Transition from Apostle to High Priest

Jesus being a priest has always been in the writer's mind, but now in Hebrews 5–10 he will discuss it more clearly. Israel's high priest held the highest official religious office in the nation (4:14). The writer of Hebrews sought to show that Christianity also had a high priest, but one who was in every way superior to the priests of Judaism. The proof of Christ's ability to understand human weakness sympathetically is found in his own experience of temptation (4:15). Christ was tempted in all areas in which man is tempted (Matt. 4:1-11; 1 John 2:16), and with particular temptations suited for him. He experienced temptation to the full degree and yet did not sin.

5:1–12:13 THE PERFECT PRIEST: ETERNAL AND EFFECTIVE
5:1–7:28 Eternal: Melchizedek
Overview: The writer demonstrated Christ's superiority to prophets, angels, and Moses. Next he explained that Christ is superior to Israel's high priest, Aaron. The basis of his greatness is his exaltation by God (5:5) and his appointment as a priest according to the order of Melchizedek (5:6). The oath of God mentioned in Psalm 110:4 is linked to the oath he made to Abraham. In Christ the perfect priesthood of Melchizedek and the promises for Abraham are certain.

5:1-10 CHOSEN AND PERFECTED
5:1-6 Designated to Be Empathetic
Here the author set forth two general qualifications that any high priest needed to satisfy. He had to be taken from among humanity so he could sympathize with those he represented, and he had to be divinely appointed to the office. The author showed how Jesus met both of these qualifications. On the gentle (5:2) work of Christ, see Matthew 12:18-21, quoting Isaiah 42:1-4, and Luke 4:18, quoting Isaiah 61:1-2. Two Old Testament texts (Pss. 2:7 and 110:4) are cited as proofs of Christ's divine appointment to the priestly office. Aaron, Israel's first high priest, and his successors occupied their office by divine appointment (Exod. 28:1; Num. 20:23-29). The issue was the call of God and his public declaration of his designated priest (Heb. 5:4). Again Psalm 110:4 is quoted (5:6) in conjunction with Psalm 2 (5:5; cf. 1:5). The public declaration of Christ's lordship and priestly calling was his resurrection (cf. Acts 13:33). Jesus is a high priest after the order of Melchizedek.

5:7-10 Perfected for Eternal Priesthood by Suffering
The real suffering of the Son cannot be downplayed (5:7-8). Jesus' incarnation enabled him to meet the second qualification for serving as high priest: he was taken from among men (5:1). Christ met the qualifications for the high priesthood, but he would not have qualified as a priest of the Aaronic order because he was not of the tribe of Levi. Thus, Jesus fills the priestly office of the order of Melchizedek (cf. Gen. 14:18-20; Ps. 110:4). The writer develops the significance of this priestly order in Hebrews 7.

5:11–6:20 EXHORTATION TO DILIGENCE
In the third warning passage of Hebrews, the writer rebuked the believers for their lack of spiritual progress and encouraged them to press on to maturity.

5:11-14 The Problem Exposed: Dull Hearing
Lack of movement toward maturity was what made these people dull of hearing. Their hearing was not matched by character growth and maturity. The "this" (5:11) referred to Melchizedek (5:10). Melchizedek is mentioned in Genesis 14 and is prominent in the Dead Sea Scrolls. Sufficient time had passed since their conversion for them to have been well grounded in the faith so as to teach others, yet they were still in need of learning some of the basic principles of Christian growth. The readers had become sluggish in responding to God's word. They should have been able to communicate what was well-known about the person of Christ. The concepts of milk and solid food (5:13-14) match up with those of trained or untrained senses in discerning right and wrong (5:14). Lack of a consistent desire to apply doctrine, not complexity of doctrine, was the issue.

6:1-8 The Singular Solution: Move on to Maturity
Because of their spiritual immaturity, the writer encouraged his readers to move on to maturity. "Go on" (6:1) does not mean "repudiate" but merely "advance beyond the first step." The author mentioned six things (three pairs) that he regards as the fundamentals of Christianity. They relate to conversion, ordinances, and the doctrine of future events. As important as these matters are, they are foundational. After the foundation is laid, the house is built. One does not keep going back and relaying the foundation.

The author addressed true believers (cf. 3:1) and emphasized their deep experience in the things of Christ: they had been enlightened by the gospel, had experienced Christ, and had shared in the Spirit's indwelling ministry. He told them that it was impossible, when renewing their lagging commitment to Christ, to start all over again with a spiritual rebirth. They could not be born again— again. The offering of Christ was once-for-all. A falling away could not be remedied with a second regeneration. Even the worst-case example (6:8) could only be remedied by a pressing on to maturity. They were to get back on the road from where they fell off, not go back to the very beginning and start all over again.

Hebrews 6:6 has been understood to refer to saved persons who are subsequently lost (but see John 10:28-30), professing believers who have never really been saved (but see Heb. 3:1; 6:4-5), or saved persons who fail to go on to maturity. The context commends the third viewpoint. The sin involved a departure from grace back to Judaism. The writer pointed out that it was impossible to retreat to the Cross for repentance by recrucifying Christ. By seeking to return to the cross to get saved again, the Hebrew Christians were bringing public shame to Christ by slighting his person and work. Since beginning the Christian life again is impossible, the only option for the readers was to press on to maturity.

However, some were not interested in getting back on the way of Christ but were insisting on staying immature. This put them in grave jeopardy before God (6:8). The author drew an illustration from the natural world to show God's blessing on fruitfulness, progressing to maturity (6:7); he continued the illustration to show God's judgment on fruitlessness, regressing back to Judaism (6:8). The judgment on fruitlessness is the loss of reward at the judgment seat of Christ (cf. 1 Cor. 3:13-15).

6:9-20 Encouragement to Diligence

The writer commended the justice of God (6:10) in remembering the diligence of believers (6:10-12). The subject of becoming "dull and indifferent" (6:12) shows the continuation of the same thoughts and problems of being slow to learn (5:11), not paying careful attention (2:1-4), and hardening of the heart (3:7–4:13). Then follows an example of faith, patience, and divine justice (6:13-20). The writer quoted God's promise to Abraham (6:14; cf. Gen. 22:16-18), which is a promise for all who believe. In view of the faithfulness of God to Abraham, believers in Christ may have confidence that God will fulfill all he has promised.

But God wanted to prove his promise to believers even more than he did to Abraham (6:17). So he gave Christians both a promise and an oath (6:17-18). "Promised" (6:15) and "oath" (6:16) are the keys to this section. By God's granting both the oath and the promise, believers have the strongest encouragement for trusting God's promises (6:18).

The writer alluded to Israel's cities of refuge (6:18; cf. Num. 35:6, 9-32) that provided protection for Israelites who had slain someone accidently. So, too, the Christians have a place of refuge in Christ. An anchor (6:19) in a secure spot would keep a ship from drifting. Christ, the believer's anchor, is in the safest place possible. The anchor, a symbol for Christ, has been found engraved in early Christian tombs.

7:1-28 THE NEED FOR A NEW PRIESTHOOD

7:1-3 Melchizedek's Order: Perpetual

Melchizedek is mentioned in only two Old Testament passages (Gen. 14:18-20; Ps. 110:4). The writer of Hebrews was not interested in anything that might be known about Melchizedek outside of the biblical narrative. What he appealed to was true about Melchizedek in a limited, literary sense. The lack of biblical details about Melchizedek is used at several points to show the analogy between Christ and Melchizedek. Melchizedek prefigures Christ in that he was both a king and a priest, and his priesthood abides forever. Some have interpreted 7:3 to mean that Melchizedek had no parents and thus was a divine figure, an appearance of God. But all the writer was saying is that there is no genealogy for Melchizedek in Genesis and no record of his

death. The absence of this material is used by way of analogy with Christ's eternality. Hebrews 7:2 clarifies this by explaining Melchizedek's name in a symbolic manner. Hebrews 7:3 continues that symbolic explanation.

7:4-10 Melchizedek's Greatness

Abraham and Levi paid tithes. A new priestly order was needed because the first one was imperfect (cf. 5:10; 6:20). Melchizedek and Jesus after him were not dependent upon the qualifications for Levitical priests. The greatness of Melchizedek over Aaron is evidenced by (1) the fact that Abraham, the father of the Hebrew nation, paid tithes to Melchizedek, thus acknowledging the priest's superiority; (2) Melchizedek blessed Abraham; (3) there is no record of Melchizedek's death, whereas the Aaronic priests died and the office was passed to their heirs; (4) Levi, yet unborn in the loins of Abraham, paid tithes to Melchizedek.

7:11-17 The Imperfect Priesthood and Melchizedek's New Order

This section builds to another quotation of Psalm 110, this time 110:4. The emphasis was on a priesthood that will last forever. The first order was imperfect because it could not create a perfect people in God's sight (note the question of 7:11). This makes sense of 7:12. If the priesthood could be changed, so could the law because the priest administered the law. This brings in a new covenant. The Levitical priesthood was unable to make people acceptable before God, therefore a new order was necessary. The Levitical priesthood required the Mosaic law to support it. Any basic change in the priesthood required a corresponding change in the law. The writer was building to the transition from the old to the new covenant (cf. 8:13). What is "even more evident" (7:15) refers back to the need for a change in law along with a change of priesthood. Christ's priesthood is better than that of the Aaronic priests since it is not based on the law but according to the power of his resurrection life.

7:18-25 A Better Hope and Covenant

Again, Psalm 110:4 was quoted, this time with the emphasis on "oath." The concept of oath stems from the discussion of God's oath to Abraham in 6:13, 16-17. The "old requirement" (7:18) was the law (7:19). Since Christ's priesthood had been established by an oath, he guarantees a better covenant (7:22). His priesthood is eternal and perfect (7:23-25).

7:26-28 Perfection Described

The death of the high priests prevented them from continuing their ministry. Eighty-three high priests officiated from Aaron until the destruction of Jerusalem in A.D. 70. But Christ's resurrection means that he can hold his priesthood permanently. His perfection meets our "need" (7:26) in light of the oath that appointed him (7:28, referring to Ps. 110:4). The concept of meeting needs relates to Christ's work being fitting or proper, a concept that occurs elsewhere in 2:10; Matthew 3:15 at the baptism of Christ; 1 Corinthians 11:13 with reference to hair; Ephesians 5:3 regarding saints; 1 Timothy 2:10 regarding women; and Titus 2:1 regarding doctrine. Because of the obvious weaknesses of the Aaronic priests, the Old Testament itself anticipated a contrasting perfect and eternal order that would come "after the law" (7:28).

8:1–10:18 Effective: Better Covenant Administered

Overview: Levi administered an old law. It was a copy. The old covenant was administered to hearts of stone. This section sets out to answer the question of why Christ is sitting at God's right hand. See 8:1-3 and the "and since" of 8:3. The concept of offerings and where they were offered are also keys to understanding Hebrews 8–10. In this section contrasts were made between the offerings of the priests and the offering of Jesus and between the places of the tabernacle and the heavenly temple. Moses' tabernacle was a copy or a pattern (Exod. 25:40). The Levitical priests ministered only a copy (Heb. 8:4-5; 9:9-11).

Another question being answered in 8:1–10:18 concerns what creates a bad conscience. Note the division of earth (seen) and heaven (unseen) throughout. The subject of Christ's shed blood becomes the climax of the doctrinal section of Hebrews. Christ's sacrifice is superior because of its price (9:15-22), its finality (9:23-28), and its efficacy (10:1-18).

8:1-13 THE NEED FOR A CHANGE: IMPERFECT PATTERN OF MINISTRY

8:1-6 The Place of Ministry: a Copy
Christ is at the right hand of God in the heavens and in the true tabernacle. The crowning point of the discussion is that the believers do have a high priest at the right hand of God who discharged his ministry, not in an earthly shrine, but in the heavenly dwelling place of God. In contrast to the Aaronic high priests, Christ ministers in a heavenly sanctuary, the real tabernacle, as opposed to the earthly copy. The earthly tabernacle seems to have been a mere copy of the authentic tabernacle in heaven. This is evidenced by the fact that at Mount Sinai Moses was instructed by God to erect the earthly tabernacle after the pattern shown to him (cf. Exod.25:40). Moses saw something for which the verbal directions (Exod. 25–30) served as commentary. Christ's "ministry" (8:6) is that he is our Mediator. A "mediator" is one who stands in between two parties as an umpire or arbitrator and

negotiates a settlement. Christ's mediatorial activity was his atoning death that provided a basis for reconciling man to God. For the "better covenant" (8:6), see 6:17-18; 7:21.

8:7-13 Basis of Ministry: Imperfect
The copy administered by the Aaronic priesthood was imperfect; the covenant around which the priests ministered was imperfect. The essential problem was that the old covenant made demands that it could not help its followers to achieve (8:7). But the Old Testament spoke of a change in covenants (8:8-13). The writer contrasts the old covenant instituted at Mount Sinai with the new covenant enacted on the basis of Christ's atonement. The old covenant promised blessings for obedience and curses for disobedience. The new covenant secures unconditional blessings for believers on the basis of the finished redemptive work of Christ (cf. Jer. 31:31-34; Ezek. 36:25-28).

The writer quoted Jeremiah 31:31-34. The problem with the old covenant was that its followers continually broke it. Its laws stood outside of its subjects and they had little desire to follow them. The new covenant puts the law inside the hearts of its followers, leading ultimately to perfect, spontaneous, and heartfelt obedience. The old covenant could not accomplish that. The new covenant brings a new ability in relationship with God, not full of apostasy like the old covenant.

Christ is a high priest after the order of Melchizedek. He ministers the new covenant that gives new hearts. God's will is now internalized so that his people may instinctively do what he wants. He gives a new and intimate knowledge of himself. It is personal and individual rather than working through levels of priests and earthly leaders (8:11). The promise of a new covenant made the old covenant obsolete (8:13). From the writer's perspective, it was ready to "be put aside." This took place in A.D. 70 when the Jewish temple in Jerusalem was destroyed by the Romans, thus ending the Old Testament sacrificial system.

9:1-10 THE FIRST MINISTRY: THE HIDDEN HOLY PLACE

This section points out the need for the Most Holy Place to be hidden away. Verse 1 introduces this section on the general features of the tabernacle. The author presented a general description of the tabernacle (cf. Exod. 25–27, 35–40). He associated the incense altar with the Most Holy Place. The altar of incense actually stood in the Holy Place before the veil (Exod. 40:26-27), though its ritual use was connected with the Most Holy Place, especially on the Day of Atonement (Lev. 16:12-13).

The divine lesson (Heb. 9:6-10) is that these articles had no ability to cleanse the conscience. Why did the high priest have to enter the Most Holy

Place once a year when sacrifices were made all year long outside the Most Holy Place (9:7)? Because of sins done in ignorance. No matter how careful the nation was in offering sacrifices for their sins, they were always aware that some unconfessed and unsacrificed sin was probably out there putting the entire nation in jeopardy. This was the reason for the Day of Atonement (Lev. 16:16-17). While individual sins could be forgiven through the sacrifices, there always remained a consciousness of other unforgiven and unknown sins.

The fact that the priests daily entered the Holy Place to burn incense (cf. Exod. 30:1-8) and that the high priest yearly entered behind the veil to make atonement (Lev. 16) indicated that there was no final offering for sin under the Mosaic system. The old covenant provided only limited access to God (9:8) and limited cleansing from sin (9:9-10).

9:11-14 THE SECOND MINISTRY: A CLEANSED CONSCIENCE

Believers in Christ have access to the genuine Holy Place where God dwells. The sacrifice made for human sin was once for all and eternal. Christ fulfilled the ministry that was typified by the ministry of the high priests when he entered once for all into the Holy Place in the heavenly tabernacle, offering his own blood to obtain for believers' eternal (not to be repeated) redemption. Christ's sacrifice made a cleansed conscience possible, something animal sacrifices could never do.

9:15-22 THE SECOND MINISTRY: A CONFIRMED HOPE OF INHERITANCE

The inauguration of the new covenant came with the shedding of blood. The reason for the stress on blood was to show that it was not a negative in considering Christ as Redeemer. It was an established and crucial Old Testament truth. Almost everything needing ceremonial cleansing under the Old Testament law required blood. There were exceptions (Exod. 19:10; Num. 31:21-24). Apart from the shedding of blood (death) there is no remission (forgiveness) of sin. Believers have not been redeemed with perishable things like silver and gold but with the precious blood of Christ (1 Pet. 1:18-20). No animal sacrifice could have accomplished the perfect and final redemption effected by Christ's blood. As a last will and testament is valid only when the testator dies, so the new covenant was validated by Christ's death.

9:23-28 THE SECOND MINISTRY: APPLICATION OF THE TYPE AND ANTITYPE

The necessity of a better cleansing hinged on the better realities of the heavenly tabernacle (9:23). At the focal point of redemptive history ("the end of the age," 9:26), Christ put away sin "once for all time." There is no need for further sacrifice. This explains why Christ is sitting at God's right hand

(10:12; cf. Ps. 110:1). He has no further sacrificial priestly work to do. Christ's second coming will not be for the purpose of offering another sacrifice, but to take redeemed believers to himself in the consummation of their salvation.

10:1-10 THE NEED FOR A SINGULAR OFFERING

The writer emphasized that Christ's sacrifice was completely efficacious and final (10:10, 12, 18). It needs no repetition or supplement. The atoning value of the Old Testament sacrifices was temporary and typical. They expressed a need that in themselves they could not ultimately fulfill. Their efficacy depended upon Christ whose sacrifice they anticipated (John 1:29). In Hebrews 10:5-7 the author quoted Psalm 40:6-8 and interpreted it as being fulfilled in Christ. The inadequacy of the Old Testament sacrificial system is seen by the fact that Christ replaced it. He took away the "first" (10:9, the Old Testament system) to establish the "second" (Christ's atonement and new covenant). Jesus fulfilled the Old Testament types and provided the actual forgiveness that the animal sacrifices could only symbolize.

The fact that multiple offerings were needed in the Old Testament implied the inadequacy of those offerings. Psalm 40 was used to emphasize the singularity of Christ's offering. The first part of this psalm is an acknowledgment psalm with a transitional phrase in the middle followed by a lament psalm. It is this middle section that the writer of Hebrews uses with reference to the Lord.

Elsewhere Scripture emphasizes that God does not desire Levitical sacrifices when one's inner life is not right before him (cf. 1 Sam. 15:22; Ps. 51:16-17; Isa. 1:11-15; Jer. 7:2-23; Hos. 6:6; Mic. 6:6-8; Mark 12:33). God does want offerings because he has commanded them. However, those offerings are always seen in light of the offerer's purity of heart. The point of Psalm 40 is that God wants the person, not sacrifices. And what he especially desired was the body (10:5, 10) of his Son. The Greek Old Testament translated "ears" of Psalm 40:6 ("listen") as "body," and this is what the writer of Hebrews quoted to refer to the offering of Jesus' body once for the atonement of all.

10:11-18 FORGIVENESS FROM THE SINGULAR OFFERING IS CONFIRMED

Christ's singular offering (Ps. 40:5-8) resulted in his sitting down (Ps. 110:1, again quoted in Heb. 10:12) and the inauguration of the new covenant (Jer. 31:31-34). The fact that Christ "sat down" indicates that his work is completed. The writer confirms the finality of Christ's sacrifice (Heb. 10:15-17) by the witness of Jeremiah 31:33-34. Hebrews 10:18 provides the grand conclusion to the doctrinal section of the epistle to the Hebrews. From this point on the writer would give exhortations to appropriate the benefits secured for the believers by Christ. Sins are no longer remembered (10:17; contrast with 10:3) so there is no longer any need for sacrifice. The mention of "laws in their hearts" (10:16; Jer. 31:33) shows the extent of the perfection gained by Christ (10:14).

10:19–12:13 Exhortations to Effective Faith

Overview: The writer pleads for endurance. The heart of endurance is a faith that believes that what God says regarding unseen and unfulfilled promises will indeed happen. Hebrews 11 provides a long list of people who believed in the unseen promises of God.

10:19-25 THREE FUNDAMENTAL PROBLEMS

The new and living way in Hebrews 10:20 is through the perfect and complete forgiveness found in Christ and having God's law written upon one's heart. The writer now moves into a long section on exhortations. Three fundamental problems are dealt with: a clear conscience, a strong witness, and supporting the assembly. He first exhorted the believers to draw near to God by having a sincere heart, full assurance of faith and purity (10:19-22). The temple veil was typical of Christ, the only access into the presence of God. It is significant that at the crucifixion, the veil in the temple was torn (Mark 15:38), illustrating the inauguration of a new way of access to God through Christ. Second, believers were advised to hold fast to their confession based on God's faithfulness (10:23). Third, the believers were reminded that stimulation to love and do good deeds should occur when Chris-

tians continue to meet together and share their faith with others (10:24-25). The "day of his coming" (10:25) refers to the imminent return of Christ (1 Cor. 3:13; Phil. 1:10), which serves as a motivation to faithfulness.

10:26-31 THE PENALTY FOR WILLFUL SIN

In the fourth warning passage the readers are exhorted to beware of God's judgment upon deliberate disobedience to the truth. There is considerable debate regarding the identity of those who would "deliberately continue sinning" (10:26). Some have suggested that they were not Christians at all but were those who, though having made a profession, were not genuinely saved. But this view is not consistent with the view that Hebrews was written to believers (cf. 3:1). And note the references in Hebrews 10:29-30 to "his people." More likely, these are true believers who will be disciplined by God for sinning against a knowledge of the truth (cf. Heb. 12:5-11). Having made profession of faith, these believers were reverting to Jewish ritualism.

If Christ's sacrifice is viewed as inadequate, what sacrifice is there? Only judgment remains (10:27). For those who doubted God's judgment (10:30-31), the writer appealed to Deuteronomy 32:35 and Psalm 135:4. God's own people had not been exempt from accountability to act on what they knew. Willful sin is equivalent to not drawing near, not confessing, and not assembling. In this startling warning, even the penalties of the old and new covenants are compared. The writer compared the penalties from the lesser to the greater; if there was

---

HEROS OF FAITH IN HEBREWS

Heroes	Old Testament References
Abel	Genesis 4:2-5 (Hebrews 11:4 provides a clue as to why Abel's sacrifice was accepted and Cain's was not. Abel's sacrifice was an expression of faith.)
Enoch	Genesis 5:22-24
Noah	Genesis 6:13-22
Abraham	Genesis 12:1-4; 22:1-19
Sarah	Genesis 21:1-7
Isaac	Genesis 27:26-40
Jacob	Genesis 48:1-22
Joseph	Genesis 50:24-25
Moses	Exodus 2:1-15; 12:1-28; 14:13-31
Joshua	Joshua 6
Rahab	Joshua 2:1-21; 6:22-25
Gideon	Judges 6:11; 8:32
Barak	Judges 4:6–5:31
Samson	Judges 13:24–16:31
Jephthah	Judges 11:1–12:7
David	1 Samuel 16–17
Samuel	1 Samuel 7–10
Daniel	Daniel 6

judgment for breaking the Mosaic covenant, would there not be even greater penalties for breaking the greater covenant in Christ?

10:32-39 THE PROMISE FOR ENDURANCE
The writer encouraged the readers to remember their sufferings and victories of the past. He appealed to Habakkuk 2:3-4 to support the principle that those who are made righteous by God "will live," that is, "survive the ordeals of life" by the faith principle (10:37-38). The perseverance of 10:36 is defined by the Habakkuk quotation as living by faith (10:38; cf. also 6:9-20). See also Paul's use of Habakkuk 2:3-4 in Romans 1:17 and Galatians 3:11. The author reminded the believers that he knew they would endure as he elaborated what "hold tightly" (10:23) meant in light of God's faithfulness.

11:1-2 FAITH AS THE WAY TO APPROVAL
This chapter expands the thought of Hebrews 6:12. The time period covered by the first part of this list of faithful people is from the creation of the universe to Israel's entrance into Canaan (11:1-31). Having discussed the importance of maintaining faith and not turning back (10:32-39), the author illustrated from a number of Old Testament heroes the principle of enduring faith. The author began with a description of true faith. It is the "confident assurance" (the expression is used of a title deed that guarantees a future possession) that what is anticipated will be realized (11:1). Faith treats unseen things as realities, not mere wishes or hopes. Throughout this chapter the issue of faith hinges on believing in what is not seen or what is future (11:1, 3, 7-8, 11, 13, 19-22, 27, 39; cf. Rom. 8:24-25).

11:3-12 APPROVED EXAMPLES
Faith's bedrock foundation is belief that when God speaks, it will happen. And the consummate example of the power of God's word was when God's word created the universe out of nothing. Faith believes that God's word can make the invisible visible. This world was created out of nothing, without the use of preexisting materials. Each example that follows illustrates that belief in the unseen is based upon a promise of God. Hebrews 11:6 presents two unseen truths for faith: God's existence (that he is there) and nature (that he is consistent and good). Faith is the key to knowing God. As people respond by faith to the general revelation of God in nature (Rom. 1:19-21), God directs them to the special revelation of himself found in his Son through his word.

For the Old Testament references to these heroes of faith, see the accompanying chart.

11:13-16 EXPLANATORY ELABORATION
These people died in faith without receiving God's great promises for the future. But they were not bound to this earth (11:13). More than this physical life, they desired a better country and a city of promise (11:16).

11:17-31 FURTHER APPROVED EXAMPLES
Abraham (11:17-19) is the central figure of the list as the beginning of the nation of Israel, but especially because he believed in God's unseen power of resurrection. His belief was a signal of the actual resurrection of Christ and, through him, all those of faith (cf. 11:35). After making note of the patriarchs from Isaac through Joseph (11:20-22), Moses' exodus (11:23-29) forms the next high point (note 11:27). The section ends with the conquest of the Promised Land starting with Jericho (11:30) and faithful Rahab (11:31; for Rahab in the line of Christ, cf. Matt. 1:5; Josh. 2:1-24; 6:22-25).

11:32-40 APPROVAL BUT NO RECEPTION OF THE PROMISES
These last examples cement the critical truth of faith: they believed in the unseen realities of promise as defined by God's word. These believers suffered in pain, but they held fast to his word (cf. Heb. 1:1). One reason that these Old Testament saints did not realize the fulfillment of all God had promised was that the atonement of Christ had not yet taken place. The readers of this letter had something far better—the blessings of the new covenant (8:6-13). But believers still live with the unseen promise of Christ's return as a challenge to their worldly and faithless tendencies.

12:1-13 CONCLUSION: THEREFORE, ENDURE GOD'S DISCIPLINE THROUGH THE LONG RUN
The "crowd of witnesses" (12:1) refers to the heroes of the faith mentioned in chapter 11. Like a dedicated runner, Christians are to free themselves from entanglements and encumbrances so that there is nothing to hinder their life of faith. The expression "keeping our eyes on" (12:2) means to turn away from all distractions and to focus on just one thing. Christ endured through suffering. Again Psalm 110:1 is used, this time to describe Christ's reward after his suffering (12:2). His endurance is set forth as an incentive and encouragement for the believers also to endure.

This section shows that the original readers were under some form of persecution. Their only way to endure would be to heed all that had been said in Hebrews 1–11, especially maintaining faith in the unseen but powerful promises of God. Apparently none associated with these Hebrew Christians had yet suffered martyrdom (12:4). The writer appealed to Proverbs 3:11-12 to introduce the subject of divine discipline (12:5-6). As a father disciplines his children, so God disciplines believers. While God's discipline is sorrowful in its experience, it produces spiritual results—holiness (12:10) and righteousness (12:11). God's discipline is not intended to destroy believers but to produce endurance (12:2, 3, 7) and healing (12:12-13). The pain of discipline is only understood in a positive way when the connection is made between the all too visible discipline and the unseen love of the heavenly Father.

12:14–13:17 PATTERNS FOR MATURE PEOPLE

12:14-29 Peace

Peace is linked to sanctification and the concept of avoiding sin (12:1). The bitterness arises in the context of persecution. The persecuted person is likely to become bitter toward God, his people, and those who persecute. The result is a backing away from Christian commitment like Esau backed away from his birthright. The Esau illustration sums up the problem that arises throughout the letter—falling away from aggressive faith in Christ. The warning passages throughout have cautioned against facing a time when, like Esau, it would be too late to regain the blessing (cf. 2:1-4; 3:7–4:13; 5:11–6:20; 10:26-31; 12:25-29). Because of Esau's selfish, materialistic desires, he was rejected with respect to the blessing (Gen. 27:30-40).

Hebrews 12:18-29 uses the event of God's giving the law on Mount Sinai as an illustration of the even greater experience of coming to the real dwelling of God, the heavenly Jerusalem. Hebrews 12:18-24 is one long sentence in the Greek. Hebrews 12:18 looks back to 12:15-17 and applies the lesson of Esau to the readers.

In contrasting the old and new covenants, Mount Sinai serves as a symbol of law under the old covenant (12:18-21), and Mount Zion serves as a symbol of grace under the new covenant (12:22-24). The implicit question is, Do you want to return to the old? The "assembly of God's firstborn children" (12:23) referred to believers who belonged to the body of Christ. They were on earth, but their names were registered in heaven. The "spirits of the redeemed in heaven who have now been made perfect" was a reference to Old Testament saints who were yet to be raised (Dan. 12:2). The "blood of Abel" (12:24) referred to Abel's blood sacrifice (Gen. 4:3-5). Abel's sacrifice was good, but Christ's is better.

The writer pictured the history of God's grace from his speaking at Mount Sinai through Moses to his speaking from the heavenly mountain of Zion through his Son (cf. Heb. 1:1-2). Israel had only come as far as Sinai. To stay at Sinai was to fall short of God's revealed grace in Christ (cf. 12:15).

The fifth and final warning urged the readers to think seriously about heeding what God had spoken (12:25-29). A reminder of the awesome scene at Sinai was used to emphasize the importance of absolute compliance with God's word. The earth/heaven image of 12:26 was based upon the earth/heaven images in the quotation from Haggai 2:6 in 12:26. As God shook the earth in the past (Exod. 19:18), he will shake heaven and earth in the future at the second coming of Christ.

13:1-6 Love

The previous section (12:14-29) was an exhortation to pursue peace and sanctification (12:14). This paragraph exhorts God's people to love each other (13:1). For examples of entertaining angels without knowing it, see Genesis 18:1-3; 19:1-2; and Judges 6:11-24. The avoidance of love of money and what it brings is placed within the context of having possessions taken away during persecution (cf. Heb. 10:34). The writer appeals to either Deuteronomy 31:6 or Joshua 1:5 and Psalm 118:6-7 to encourage Christian contentment (cf. Matt. 6:24-34). Contentment is based on "what you have" (13:5). The scriptural quotations of Hebrews 13:5-6 show that what believers have is God himself. God has promised a permanent commitment to be with and help those who believe in him.

13:7-17 Obedience

This section begins and ends with a response to the teaching of Christian leaders (13:7, 17). In between, the content of that teaching is explained. While Christ's one sacrifice for sin stands for all time (cf. 10:12, 18), other kinds of sacrifices continue—praise, good works, and obedience (13:15-17). The "altar" (13:10) of Christians refers either to the cross or Christ's sacrifice made outside of the temple. As the bodies of certain sacrificial animals were burned outside the camp (Lev. 4:21; 16:27), so Christ suffered outside the gate of Jerusalem (John 19:17-20). The "city in heaven" (13:14) is the heavenly Jerusalem (cf. 12:22).

13:18-25 CLOSING REQUESTS

The author concluded his letter focusing on Christ as the Shepherd and his eternal covenant, the new covenant (13:18-21). Timothy had apparently been imprisoned but had recently been released (13:23). It was hoped that the author and Timothy would make a joint visit to the readers. The implication is that the author was not a prisoner at this time since his visit hinged on Timothy's coming. "The Christians from Italy" (13:24) could refer to those presently with the author who were from Italy (perhaps Rome), or those with the author who was presently in Italy.

JAMES

BASIC FACTS

HISTORICAL SETTING

The "Jewish Christians scattered among the nations" (James 1:1) were believing Hebrew Christians (1:2, 16; 2:1; 5:7). They were scattered as a result of the persecution in Jerusalem after the stoning of Stephen in A.D. 35 (Acts 8:1; cf. Acts 12:1-23). The letter indicates that the readers were suffering persecution and trials (James 1:2-4, 12; 2:6; 5:4). They were also lacking in fervor for good works and the practical application of truth to Christian living (1:26-27; 2:14-26).

AUTHOR

The author designated himself as the "slave of God and of the Lord Jesus Christ" (1:1). Little more is revealed about the author by the letter itself. Of the several men named James mentioned in the New Testament (Matt. 4:21; 10:3; Luke 6:16), James the half brother of the Lord (Matt. 13:55; Gal. 1:19) is the probable author. Eusebius and many others after him identify the author as the half brother of the Lord Jesus.

James grew up in Nazareth. He and his brothers remained unbelievers during the time of Christ's ministry on earth (John 7:5), but he had a significant role in the leadership of the Jerusalem church after Pentecost (Acts 12:17; 15:13-21; 21:18; Gal. 1:19; 2:9). The risen Lord appeared to James (1 Cor. 15:7), and shortly after that James appeared on the scene of the early church as a believer (cf. Acts. 1:14). Eusebius records that James lived as a perpetual Nazirite (Num. 6:1-21) and spent so much time in prayer that his knees became as hard as a camel's. The scribes and Pharisees of Jerusalem tried to persuade James to restrain the people who were following Jesus. He was taken to the pinnacle of the temple and told to speak against Christ. Instead, he took the opportunity to give testimony to Jesus. The enraged priests and Pharisees had James thrown from the temple. As the fall did not kill him, James was then stoned. Before his death, he prayed for his murderers, "Father, forgive them, for they know not what they do" (Eusebius, *Historia Ecclesiastica*, 2.23).

DATE

Josephus places the martyrdom of James in A.D. 62, so the letter must have been written earlier. An early date for the writing would be indicated by the use of the word "meeting" (lit., "synagogue," 2:2) for the place of the assembly of the believers and by the simplicity of ecclesiastical organization, which mentions elders alone (5:14). While difficult to date precisely, James was probably written between A.D. 45 and 49. This would make this letter the earliest book in the New Testament.

PURPOSE

The letter by James was designed to produce a vision for wisdom, good works, and the power of prayer. It did this by showing practical ways to live out the ethical implications of Christianity. Behind each of James's corrections are the unwavering holiness, goodness, and power of God.

GUIDING CONCEPTS

Three major themes shape the vigorous message of the book. (1) James insisted uncompromisingly on human equality in Christ. Watch for this in his discussions of wisdom (1:9-11), status (2:5), and wealth (5:1-6). (2) He was also a relentless activist. Words without actions to back them up are no better than what the devils say about God (2:19). (3) Finally, James was driven by a commitment to expose pride in all its awful and piously covered manifestations (cf. 4:1-3).

BIBLE-WIDE CONCEPTS

WISDOM LITERATURE

The book of James is a New Testament example of wisdom literature. Proverbs, Ecclesiastes, and Job are Old Testament examples. One characteristic of wisdom literature is its diversity. Life is diverse, and so wisdom instruction covers the whole range of life's situations. Another characteristic of wisdom literature is its unifying foundation: the fear of God. This is what allows the diversity of life to make sense. It is focused on God's character, not thousands of individual insights into life. The wise person is one who knows who God is. Knowledge of the character of God enables believers to act in a wise way in all of life's situations. Jesus' Sermon on the Mount (Matt. 5–7) and his parables (Matt. 13) are examples of New Testament wisdom literature. James has close affinities with the content of Jesus' Sermon on the Mount.

FAITH AND WORKS

James's argument that faith without works is useless (1:22-27; 2:14-26; 4:17; 5:19-20) is part of a pattern found throughout Scripture. God's people are to trust him and him alone for salvation and always affirm their trust by works of obedience. But James's letter is not an abstract theoretical discussion of salvation by works or by faith. He discusses faith and works as necessary and complimentary realities for any believer's life-style.

Faith reflects a person's valuation of God

From the very beginning of creation, the link between goodness and obedience was defined by doing what God wanted. God said something and it was done. Light, dry land, animals, and humans were all created when God commanded it to happen. That link between God's command and creation's follow-through was to be the same in human behavior. When God said to do or not do something, people were supposed to carry out God's will. Adam and Eve did not question whether or not God existed. The question was what value they placed on God's character and ability to run the world. If they valued God highly, they would obey him. If they did not value God, then they would disobey him. So, from the very beginning the issue of obedience revolved around the issue of how highly people would esteem God. And that is the essence of biblical faith—not the intellectual assent that God exists, but the heartfelt assent to the high value of the joys and regulations of being in a personal relationship with God.

Adam and Eve were to see God as the highest and last word on what they should think, do, or say. God noted Adam's lack of priority in that he listened to his wife (Gen. 3:17), implying that Adam should have listened instead to God. At the moment Adam took his wife's word over God's, he showed whom he valued the most. Faith is therefore a gauge of how much people value God and their relationship with him. But the only way people can exhibit their faith is through external and visible actions.

A person's claim of love for God has to be proven by appropriate visible actions. This is why throughout Scripture God showed disgust for people who claimed to love him but whose actions demonstrated nothing but hate. God criticized people who said good things about him but whose hearts were far from him (Isa. 29:13; Matt. 15:8; Mark 7:6). He even condemned the hypocrites who had what looked like godly devotion but in reality were motivated by selfishness (Matt. 6:1-2, 5, 16, 19-21). This adds another dimension to the relationship between faith (what people believe or claim to believe) and works (what people actually do); this is the dimension of underlying motives.

Actions should be motivated by a heart that loves and honors God. Love and honor for God are the essence of faith. Any works that look like they spring from hearts that love God but in reality spring from hearts that seek status and human praise are counterfeit and bring no pleasure to or reward from God. Throughout the Bible God desired his people to love him. He did not want them to obey him just because of promised punishments or rewards. Moses (Deut. 6:5; 11:13), Joshua (Josh. 24:23), Solomon (1 Kings 8:58), David (Pss. 37:31; 51:10, 17), Jehoshaphat (2 Chron. 20:33), Isaiah (Isa. 29:13; 51:7), Jeremiah (Jer. 31:33), Ezekiel (Ezek. 14:3; 36:26), and others all called for an obedience to God's laws that was motivated by a heart full of genuine love for God. People value what they love, and the more they value something, the higher will be their commitment to it during times of adversity. Behavior reveals people's values, and behavior is what the Bible calls "works." Aside from the hypocrite who masks his evil heart with religious works, works gauge where people are with God; they measure the love or lack of love people have for God (e.g. 1 John 2:4-6; 3:21-24; 4:7-11, 20-21; 5:2-3).

The link of faith and works to salvation

The Bible puts forth a very interesting paradox. No one who acts like the devil can be saved, and no one can save himself by acting like a saint. Both the proverbial saint and sinner are equally doomed under God's curse on Adam. But people are delivered from this doom by God's action in two different ways.

First, God pushes people to obedience. His laws of life are absolutes. God never allows believers to pick and choose among his laws. He demands moral conformity to himself and cannot live with people who sin. Abraham (Gen. 19:18), Moses (Deut. 30:11-16), and Jesus (Matt. 5:17-20) all insisted that believers must keep God's commandments. Adam's sin infinitely offended God. Because God's curse on the world sprang from that infinite offense, only an equally infinite sacrifice could reconcile God's offense. This makes any hope that works of obedience can bring salvation impossible. Yet God never stops demanding complete obedience to his laws from people who are hopelessly flawed. Clearly, obedience to God's commands is a separate issue from earning forgiveness or remedying the sin problem. Obedience is owed to God simply because of who he is. Salvation is God's business alone.

Second, God pushes people toward forgiveness. Throughout Scripture, God's push for obedience to his laws is kept clearly separate from his drive to bring believers into forgiveness. He shows that people cannot save themselves or make themselves acceptable to him by their works. God alone has brought the ultimate sacrifice for their sins, and they must accept that gift as complete, without a thought of bettering it by adding works of their own. Having received salvation by faith, believers keep God's laws, not in order to achieve forgiveness, but in order to show the value and honor felt for the one who already graciously saved them. Believers work to validate their claim of faith in God. That validation of their claim of faith is what James means when he speaks of works justifying or saving a person (James 2:14, 17, 21-22, 24-26). Without faith, works are hypocritical. Without works, a believer's faith is like the faith of demons, only intellectual (James 2:19). James's point is simple: just as fire gives off heat or the sun gives light, so faith will produce works.

NEEDS MET BY JAMES

James wrote to Christians who were suffering under the trials of family conflict and social ostracism. These difficulties pushed their belief in God's goodness to the limit. They found it tempting to respond to their problems with anger. They were tempted to hurt those who caused them pain. This anger even found its way into the Christian community where believers fought among themselves. Despite all the persecution the Christians were suffering, they still found it impossible to avoid acting like those who were oppressing them. They, like the worldly people around them, showed favor to the rich and ignored the poor; they sought the status of leadership without first being qualified; they had a soft attitude toward sin and exhibited little faith in prayer. The structure and content of James's letter shows that he intended to answer the following questions for his readers.

- What possible good can come from trials and suffering?
- How can believers continue to believe God is good when they are hurting so badly?
- Should believers look to worldly status and wealth as a protection against world problems?
- What is the relationship between a believer's beliefs and what he actually does?
- When believers are suffering, how can they resist striking back either verbally or physically?
- Is it possible that a believer's suffering is a result of personal sin?

The trials and sufferings experienced by believers today need the solutions James offered his readers. It is easy for believers to blame God when suffering is experienced. They may begin to think that God does not have their best interests in mind. Counter to this, James reminded his readers that God does only good. He is the Father of all good and never tries to cause his people to sin. To overcome the tendency of believers to base their joys on what the world has to offer, James taught that true joy comes from knowing God better and from growing in Christian character and witness. Instead of focusing on the material welfare of believers, James urged them to focus on how they could help others live purer lives. He helped them see the often wide gap between what they said and what they did. His advice for narrowing that gap relates to helping others live purer lives and living according to the law of love.

OUTLINE OF JAMES

I. GREETING (1:1)

II. EXHORTATION: BE JOYFUL IN TRIALS (1:2-27)
  A. The Purpose: Maturity (1:2-4)
  B. Desire for Insight: Asking in Faith (1:5-11)
  C. The Essential Insight: The Character of God (1:12-18)
  D. The Practice of Maturity (1:19-27)

III. EXHORTATION: BE IMPARTIAL (2:1–26)
  A. Implications of Partiality (2:1-13)
  B. The Practice of Impartiality (2:14-26)

IV. EXHORTATION: BE MATURE IN SPEECH (3:1–4:12)
  A. The Tongue as a Revealer of Maturity or Immaturity (3:1-12)
  B. The Practice of Maturity (3:13-18)
  C. The Source of Immaturity (4:1-12)

V. CONDEMNATION: ATTITUDES AND END OF THE RICH (4:13–5:6)
  A. Arrogance of the Will (4:13-17)
  B. Judgment on the Rich (5:1-6)

VI. EXHORTATIONS: MATURE ENDURANCE (5:7-20)
  A. Patient Endurance (5:7-11)
  B. Arrogant Oaths (5:12)
  C. Sharing in Prayer (5:13-18)
  D. The Essence of the Letter (5:19-20)

JAMES NOTES

1:1 GREETING

One of the key themes in James is the call to sinners to put their lives in order. The concepts of perfection and purity begin and end the letter (1:2; 5:19-20). James had a significant role in the leadership of the Jerusalem church (Acts 12:17; 15:13-21; 21:8; Gal. 1:19; 2:9). The "Jewish Christians scattered among the nations" (1:1) was a reference to the believing Hebrew Christians who, because of persecution (Acts 8:1-4), were scattered throughout the Roman Empire.

1:2-27 EXHORTATION: BE JOYFUL IN TRIALS

1:2-4 The Purpose: Maturity

"Trouble" (1:2) is a testing sent by God to prove the genuineness of the believer's faith (cf. with 1 Pet. 1:6). An attitude of joy is the proper perspective for such tests of faith. The command of James 1:2 is issued because joy in trials is easily missed. James spoke of trials and temptations in general. The letter specifically addressed the temptations arising from the flesh and from persecution. The way to finding joy while suffering trials is to see the direct result of endurance developed in one's life (1:3). Endurance means to bear up under any given situation, not to escape it. The author's exhortation was to stay in the testing so that it would result in endurance rather than sin. The result of endurance is maturity (1:4); the purpose of the testing is to produce maturity. A process is in view: enduring just one trial is not enough. James encouraged his readers to let the process of trials keep working to bring complete maturity; for this reason trials had to come in all areas of life.

1:5-11 Desire for Insight: Asking in Faith

1:5 GAINING INSIGHT THROUGH ASKING

Prayer makes available the needed wisdom to endure and profit from testing. The purpose of prayer is to gain the wisdom needed to see suffering as a gift, not to gain wisdom for making decisions. The focus is on viewing sufferings as a source of joy, not on general requests for what believers should do, where they should go, or what they should buy. Believers are to ask, Is suffering really joy in my life? In prayer they need to ask for the wisdom to see their suffering in this way. God is characterized as the one who gives generously to all men without reproach. God's generosity is the foundation upon which James builds his discussion about doubt (1:6-8) and the rich and poor (1:9-11). There are no hidden strings in God's dealings with his people. He does not reproach believers for asking or needing to ask.

1:6-8 DOUBTING GOD'S CHARACTER

The doubt of James 1:6 is not about whether or not God will give believers what they want. The asking of 1:5 was specifically for wisdom to see trials as joy. The doubting of 1:6 concerns whether or not God is generous and willing to hear his people without reproach (see the description of God in 1:5). James likened the doubter, the one who thinks God is stingy and reproachful, to the wind-tossed surf, blown here and there. This image describes a believer who is influenced by many different ideas about what God is up to: (1) whether God is of such a character as 1:5 asserts; (2) whether one really wants what God freely offers; and (3) whether God is giving the best to his people.

1:9-11 ASKING IN AN ETERNAL CONTEXT, NOT FROM EARTHLY STATUS

The poor are exalted and the rich are humbled. The point is that all people, whether rich or poor, are equal before God. No one receives special treatment on the basis of his earthly status, a point central to the readers' problems (cf. 2:1, 15-16; 4:1-2, 12). Since the readers of James's letter had trouble with "asking" and "doubting," James needed to explain what it meant to be a doubter or a double-minded person. Both rich and poor needed a proper view of the essential elements of life. The

poor may have thought their earthly circumstances determined their spiritual status before God. Thus, they may have "doubted" God's goodness and failed to "ask" for his gifts. The rich may have thought themselves above reproach spiritually because of their material wealth. But both rich and poor are equal in God's sight. All have equal access before God to ask and receive. James exhorted his readers to focus on the eternal rather than the earthly. God is not partial. The illustration concerning the transience of earthly wealth (1:10-11) is taken from Isaiah 40:6-7.

1:12-18 The Essential Insight: The Character of God

1:12 REWARD FOR PERSEVERANCE

The key ideas concerning trials and developing endurance (1:2-3) are again discussed. James's thoughts concerning joy amidst trials (1:2) and asking for help if lacking wisdom (1:5) are elaborated. Seeking heavenly reward (crown of life), not earthly riches, is the way of the wise. The "crown of life" (1:12) may refer to abundant life in its fullness and completeness or eternal life as the consummation of the believer's salvation.

1:13-15 FOUNDATION OF PERSEVERANCE: THE CHARACTER OF GOD

Asserting that God tempts believers to do evil (1:13) makes God responsible for their failures. After all, if God wants believers to fall, how can they resist? This wrong perspective is another example of doubting God's true character and therefore being double-minded. James returned to the crucial issue of how believers should view God when they are hurting (1:5). A proper view of God is the starting point for perseverance during times of trial. James 1:14-15 shows how temptation cannot have its source in God. Temptation has its source in mankind's own evil desires. It leads to sin and sin leads to death. James 1:14 shows more specifically what the various trials implied in 1:2 entailed. Evidently some of the believers thought that since God allowed trials in their lives, he was also the source of temptation. The fact that the same Greek word can be translated "testing" or "temptation," depending on the context, may have contributed to their misunderstanding. They thus excused their sin by declaring that God had brought the temptation. James corrected his readers by declaring that God was not the source of evil.

1:16-18 THE CONSISTENT PURPOSE FOR HUMANS

This section continues the thoughts concerning sin and its resulting in death (1:15). "God above, who created all heaven's lights" (1:17) visualizes God as the sovereign and perfect Creator of the sun, moon, and stars in Genesis 1. God wishes people well, not entrapment in sin and its resulting death. James told his readers that this God was also their Father (1:18). By his will believers are firstfruits of a new and sinless creation, not sinners. Sin comes from a will other than God's. This is a key insight into trials suffered by believers: God wills the best for his people. Again, see the description of God in 1:5. God, the source of all good things, does not change. He will not be different tomorrow, bringing evil instead of good. As Jewish believers, the readers were a "guarantee" to others that a fuller harvest of believers was yet to come (cf. 1 Cor. 15:20).

1:19-27 The Practice of Maturity

1:19-21 BUILT ON A TEACHABLE SPIRIT
The key ingredient in a teachable spirit is the willingness to listen. The person who listens is the person who is humble before God. The goal of humility is the righteousness of God, not the self-gratification gained by venting anger. A response of self-righteous anger during times of trial may feel good momentarily, but it will not accomplish the righteousness of God. This was a major problem addressed in the letter. God was blamed by believers for their temptations (1:13). Arrogance and anger were criticized by James throughout the book (2:1; 3:9; 4:2, 16; 5:6). The entire discussion concerning the tongue (1:26; 3:1-12) and fighting (4:1-12) arose because of human arrogance and anger. In putting aside all wickedness, believers are to respond to the word of God "planted" (1:21) in the hearts of believers by the Spirit (Heb. 8:10). This resource is able to deliver (1:21; "save") all believers from the reigning influence and dominion of sin (Phil. 2:12).

1:22-27 BUILT ON THINKING RIGHTLY ABOUT RELIGION
These verses show what the results of receiving the implanted word will be. Receiving God's word is doing what he asks, not just hearing what he says (1:22). The hearer who deludes himself is like a person who sees himself in a mirror, walks away, forgets what he saw, and then reconstructs a good image of himself (1:26). This person has forgotten his true self, then made up a false self to his own liking and pronounced himself pure and religious. But the essence of religion is humility. James mentioned orphans and widows as classic examples of how true religion makes room for the lowly. Throughout the Old Testament the widows and orphans were always test cases for Israel's humility, compassion, and obedience before God. But the readers were having trouble making room for the poor, as the discussions of the rich and poor show (see 1:9-11; 2:1-6; 5:1-6). The "perfect law" (1:25; "law of liberty," NASB and KJV) may refer to (1) the word of God which sets believers free in Christ (John 8:32); (2) the law of the new covenant written on the hearts of believers (Jer. 31:33); or (3) the Old Testament ethic as explained and developed by

Jesus (Matt. 5–7). This "perfect law" is a way of describing the application of God's love to life's circumstances. James was not thinking of "religion without God" but rather the outward expression of a genuine, inner faith. True religion involves ethical responsibilities.

2:1-26 EXHORTATION: BE IMPARTIAL
2:1-13 Implications of Partiality
2:1-7 THE IMPLICATIONS OF GOD'S MOTIVES IN SALVATION
James admonished his readers against playing favorites. They were to avoid showing special regard for people of position, wealth, or influence. Partiality, vividly pictured in James 2:2-4, is shown to be inconsistent with the Christian faith. Some in the church did not care for the lowly and made false distinctions between people. These distinctions came from evil motives (2:4). These motives were evil because they cut against God's motives in salvation (2:5). God gives generously to all (cf. 1:5, 9). To view people as less than God views them is to dishonor them (2:6). It is important that believers ask themselves if they are reflecting a ministry that gives generously to all men without reproach.

2:8-13 IMPLICATIONS OF THE ROYAL LAW
James placed the concept of law within the total context of God's salvation in Christ (cf. Matt. 22:40). The readers were somehow able to show partiality to the rich and snub the poor and still think they were religious (2:1-4; 2:9). They were deluded into thinking that some wrong things were not violations of God's will. They had not made the connection between showing partiality and God's demand that they love their neighbors. James helped them to see the full damage of sin; he refused to minimize it. The "law that set you free" (2:12) is the love of God applied to each particular circumstance in life (see the progression of thought in 1:12, 18, 21, 25). By contrast, God shows no mercy to those who are merciless (Matt. 18:21-35).

2:14-26 The Practice of Impartiality
Overview: At first glance it appears that James was directly opposed to Paul on the doctrine of justification. Paul insisted that "we become right with God, not by doing what the law commands, but by faith in Jesus Christ" (Gal. 2:16; cf. Rom. 3:20; Eph. 2:8-9). James, however, argued that "we are made right with God by what we do, not by faith alone" (James 2:24). But it is possible to reconcile these apparently contradictory viewpoints. James and Paul were confronting different issues. Paul was refuting those who advocated works, circumcision, and the observance of Jewish ceremonial law as necessary for justification. James, on the other hand, was challenging those who presumed that

mere intellectual assent to doctrine was sufficient for salvation. Paul was confronting Judaizers who wanted to add works to grace; James was confronting dead orthodoxy, which denied that a genuine faith was evidenced by works. Both agree that while faith alone saves, the faith that saves is not alone. It comes with good works (see Paul's comments in Eph. 2:9-10).

2:14-17 USEFUL FAITH

James gives a practical illustration of the person who is a hearer and not a doer of the word. This is the person who forgets what he has seen in the mirror of God's word (1:23-24). "What's the use" (2:14) refers to the obedience mentioned in 1:25. The claim of having faith (2:14) implies that the person is quite satisfactory in God's sight and does not need to worry about doing acts of obedience. Such people think they are religious but act like the person in 1:26 or 2:1. The implied answer to the last question of 2:14 is no. James allowed no special pleading. He was also not concerned with a theological discussion of faith. Rather, he was concerned with its practical aspects. Faith without works has no use for others, illustrated in 2:15-16 ("useless," 2:20; "worthless," 1:26). The passive verbs "stay warm and eat well" (2:16) imply that someone else will do the warming and filling. Their snobbery led them to shirk their works of faith and love. At the heart of the question is the issue: "Is an inactive, nonworking faith a genuine, saving faith?" James's implied answer is no! Such an "unworking" profession of faith is not a biblical faith! Faith without works is a fallacy (2:17).

2:18-26 EXAMPLES OF USEFUL AND USELESS FAITH

Good deeds are objective proof that faith is alive and useful. Without works, faith is useless (2:20; cf. 2:14) and dead (2:26). James's point is to have belief issue in helpful actions for others. Faith without works may expose an inner character that matches the character of demons (2:19). James was talking about the person who believes in everything that is good but does nothing that is good. The question hinges on a person's willingness (2:20), unlike the demons, to add good behavior to sound doctrine.

The concepts of "complete" (2:22) and "happened" (2:23) show how believers are to understand James's use of "right" (2:21; "justified," NASB and KJV). Paul used the term "justified" in a legal way, "to be declared righteous." James, however, used the term more in keeping with its use in the Greek translation of the Old Testament (the Septuagint), "shown to be righteous." Works fulfill and make visible one's claim to have believed in God. For Abraham to disobey God's command to offer Isaac and yet claim to be justified before God on the basis of Genesis 15:6 (quoted in 2:23)

would prove that he had not truly believed in the first place. This all relates back to the issue of believers hearing the truth but then forgetting to do it (1:22). Such people deceive their own hearts (1:26). Abraham heard and obeyed God's word. His faith was fulfilled, brought to its goal, thirty years later as Abraham obeyed God's command regarding Isaac. His works showed that he was indeed a friend of God (cf. Isa. 41:8). By the testing of Abraham's faith in Genesis 22, the patriarch was proven to be righteous. In like manner, the various testings of James's readers (1:2-3) were to have the same effect.

The comparison of Rahab with Abraham is another illustration of James's contrasts between the rich and the poor (cf. Josh. 2:4; 6:17; Matt. 1:5; Heb. 11:31), believers of high and low status. Read Rahab's great confession of the character of God in Joshua 2:8-13. James's examples of useful versus useless faith have ranged from demons to Abraham, a Jew, and Rahab, a Gentile. Again, James restated his thesis (2:26). Faith demonstrates its living and vital nature by what it enables believers to do for others.

3:1–4:12 EXHORTATION: BE MATURE IN SPEECH

Overview: James returns to the thoughts of 1:19-21 and emphasizes the importance of controlling one's tongue. The status-conscious readers would easily have desired the status position of teacher (see "jealous" and "selfish ambition," 3:14, 16). But James also included all acts of speaking, public and private, in this section. As works reveal the depth of people's faith, so words show the depth of their maturity. As belief without works is demonic (2:19), so also are words without heavenly wisdom (3:15; cf. also 4:7).

3:1-12 The Tongue as a Revealer of Maturity or Immaturity

Since the teacher's work is performed primarily through the use of his tongue, control of this instrument is of utmost importance. The greater the privilege in terms of knowledge and education, the greater the accountability for the use of that information (Luke 12:48).

The tongue is a symbol for the overall discipline and maturity of the whole person (3:2). The images of bridle, rudder, fire, untamed animal, poison, fountain, and fig tree all illustrate the cause and effect relationship between maturity and words. James has clearly shown the relationship between inner lust and outward expression (1:14-15). The images applied to the tongue illustrate the outward effects of inner lusts (cf. 4:2-4). The questions of 3:11-12 uncover the real issue: external behavior in sharp contrast with claims to purity and righteousness before God.

3:13-18 The Practice of Maturity

James gave two suggestions for handling the tongue. For the wise, he gave examples that revealed inner wisdom (3:13, 17). For the jealous and ambitious, he simply asked that they admit their arrogance and not try to cover up their evil with pious claims (3:14; and "sincere," 3:17). He directed both groups to pursue righteousness through making peace (3:18).

True wisdom is the practical and successful application of knowledge. Such wisdom comes from God and bears good fruit. The fruit, which consists of righteousness, produces peace, the very opposite of the sin and disorder of 3:14, 16 and 4:1-3.

4:1-12 The Source of Immaturity

4:1-6 GOD'S OPPOSITION TO PRIDE

James held up the mirror of God's word (1:23-25) to show his readers their true faces. The contrast with seeking peace (3:17-18) is seeking pleasure (4:1-2). James uncovered the heart of the readers' false claims to faith and righteousness: friendship with the world (4:4). They either forgot to go to God to meet their needs (4:2) or they tried to use God as a celestial shopping center for worldly goods (4:3). They either forgot the source or tried to manipulate the source. Either way, they were manifesting the ambivalent view of God that James had already addressed (1:5-18). Worldliness is an attitude that places self and the things of this world at the center of the believers' aspirations and activities. This attitude caused disputes among the saints.

James used the word "adulterers" (4:4) metaphorically, as did the Old Testament prophets who spoke of disobedient Israel as God's unfaithful wife (cf. Isa. 54:5; Jer. 3:20; Ezek. 16:15-17; Hos. 9:1). No specific Old Testament passage contains the words of James 4:5, but many passages express a similar sentiment—God is a jealous God (Exod. 20:5; 34:14; Deut. 32:16; Zech. 8:2). He will tolerate no rivals. He jealously desires the Spirit to dwell in believers.

But the heart of James's letter is found in the quotation of Proverbs 3:34 in James 4:6. The rest of the letter gives specific examples of what "humble" in Proverbs 3:34 means (see "humble," 4:7; "draw close" 4:8; "bow down," 4:10; "grief," 4:9; "weep," 5:1; "be patient," 5:7; "confess your sins," 5:16). The purpose is that God's grace, not his opposition, may be experienced.

4:7-12 GOD'S GRACE FOR THE HUMBLE

The way to exaltation is through mourning and humility (4:9-10), not through fighting and arrogance. The double-minded attitude has been in view from 1:8 throughout. A string of commands (4:7-10) is built around the Old Testament quotation of Proverbs 3:34 as James sets forth the remedy for worldliness. Resistance to the devil (4:7) is done by coming near to God (4:8). Submission to God and his will results in a heart purged from worldliness. James 4:9 issues a call to repentance in the face of the seriousness of sin. The cries of mourning and weeping reflect an attitude of sobriety in contrast with deluded and arrogant attitudes. The Beatitudes of Christ are behind this description of the one who truly sees the need for God (cf. Matt. 5:4). It is then up to God to deliver and exalt (4:10).

James 4:11-12 relates to the tongue analogy but more specifically to taking over authority that belongs to God alone. James exhorted believers to avoid slandering their brothers. He condemned a censorious, hypocritical judgment (cf. Matt. 7:1-5). He was not rejecting the appropriateness of judging others in proper contexts (cf. Matt. 18:15-18). His very letter is an example of proper, humble, and loving evaluations.

4:13–5:6 CONDEMNATION: ATTITUDES AND END OF THE RICH

4:13-17 Arrogance of the Will

The examples James presented in these verses reveal the opposite of a humble and teachable spirit under God. The key here is the inability of people to know what their lives will be like in the future (4:14). This prideful assumption of a prosperous future echoes the prideful arrogance against the poor, and the selfish ambitions of life seen earlier. James was not condemning intelligent planning but rebuking presumptuous planning that disregards God. When making plans, the Christian should acknowledge his dependence upon God and submission to his will. For Paul's example in this, see Acts 18:21, 1 Corinthians 4:19, and 16:7. Although some of James's readers disregarded God's sovereign and mostly unknown plans and were deluded as to their self-knowledge, they really knew better (4:17).

5:1-6 Judgment on the Rich

The "rich" (5:1) who were condemned by James were probably not Christians. At least their conduct would make their profession of faith suspect. They were laying up destruction for themselves in the last days (5:3). The corrosion of gold and silver reveals its worth for buying a safe standing before God in the judgment. The term "Lord Almighty" (5:4) is an Old Testament description of God. In this section James was probably referring to judicial murder—taking the poor to court to rob them of possessions that sustain and support their lives (5:6).

5:7-20 EXHORTATIONS: MATURE ENDURANCE

5:7-11 Patient Endurance

The two concepts of patient endurance (5:7-8, 10-11) and the Lord's coming (5:7-9, 11) are built upon the outcome of the Lord's dealings: compassion and mercy (5:11). James has returned again to perseverance during life's various trials (1:3-4). And again, the corrective to complaining and lack of perseverance is a firm grasp on the character of God. Patience is the inner quality that produces the outer manifestation of perseverance. The phrase "rains in the fall and in the spring" (5:7) refers to the two brief rainy periods that precede and follow the main season of rain in Palestine, November through April (cf. Deut. 11:14). The Lord's coming is a practical doctrine. James used it to encourage believers to exercise patience. Complaining against a Christian is taking over the prerogatives of the Judge (5:9). Job is set forth as an example of one who "endured" (5:11). In spite of his sufferings, he refused to renounce God (Job 1:21; 2:10; 13:15; 16:19; 19:25). The outcome of the Lord's dealings with him was Job's complete vindication (Job 42:7-17).

5:12 Arrogant Oaths

James is here concerned with oaths that are given in arrogance. He warned Christians not to make oaths merely to appear spiritual before others. He was also concerned that making such oaths was evidence of an even deeper spiritual disease—the belief that man could be holy without the grace of God. God swore (Heb. 6:17) and Jesus spoke under oath (Matt. 26:63-64). But James has in view the oaths arising from the prideful and mistaken notion of human sovereignty (cf. Matt. 5:34-37). James stressed dependence on God, not on self. Among the Jews, oaths were often made for reasons of spiritual pride, but then they were undone on the basis of technicalities in Mosaic law. But James called for constant honesty that could be depended on and could not be conveniently "recalled."

5:13-18 Sharing in Prayer

Rather than swearing when in trouble, James urged believers to pray and give praise. Rather than complaining to each other or praising themselves, James commended believers for lifting their pain and praise to God. In sickness, the patient is to call for the elders. Anointing with oil was a common practice (Mark 6:13). Here it is done in the name of the Lord. It is debated whether this passage commends a healing ministry for the physically sick or a spiritual ministry to those who are emotionally distressed or spiritually exhausted. The word "sick" (5:14) is used both of spiritual weakness and physical weakness. The word "well" (5:15) can refer to a healing of the heart. The connection of 5:16-18 is to do the praying and sin-bearing before one gets sick as well as in times of crisis. The reference to the incident in the life of Elijah (5:17; cf. 1 Kings 17:1; 18:1, 42, 45) confirms the power of prayer. In addition, while it is not always God's will for the sick to be healed (2 Cor. 12:8), it is always his will for the spiritually weak to be encouraged in their struggles against sin (5:15).

5:19-20 The Essence of the Letter

The essence of James's letter is a call to action (works) that allows truth to triumph over sin and error. This is the essence of everything he wrote. The individual under consideration (5:19, "anyone among you") is a Christian who has strayed from the truth. By turning that one back to God, the ultimate discipline of death (1 Cor. 11:30; 1 John 5:16) would be avoided. The multitude of sins covered were those that had been committed and those that would never happen because of a person's repentance. Through genuine repentence, forgiveness is appropriated and sins are hidden from the sight of God (cf. Ps. 32:1; 1 Pet. 4:8).

1 PETER

HISTORICAL SETTING

The letter is addressed to believers scattered throughout several Roman provinces (1 Pet. 1:1). Most were of Gentile background (2:10; 4:3), though some were Hebrew Christians (2:12; 4:3). They lived in a region north of the Taurus mountains where the apostle Paul had not preached (Acts 16:6, 7).

The suffering of persecution was a major background to the letter (1 Pet. 1:6-7; 2:11-12, 18-20; 3:13-17; 4:3-5, 12-19; 5:8-10). Such sufferings were common to most first-century Christians. The suffering was referred to as "many trials" (1:6) and appears to be of a more personal nature (2:15). Persecution arose from the believers' refusal to participate in their former lifestyles of sin (4:1-4). The place of the writing was referred to as "Rome" (5:13; "Babylon," NIV). Most scholars favor taking Babylon as symbolic for Rome (cf. Rev. 17:5, 9; 18:2, 10, 21). This view finds support in that Mark, who was with Peter (5:13), was also in Rome with Paul during his imprisonment (Col. 4:10).

AUTHOR

The apostle Peter was the author. Both internal evidence and the testimony of the early church confirms the statement in 1:1 that the apostle Peter authored this letter. He shows an intimate knowledge of the life and teachings of Jesus (cf. 1 Pet. 5:5 with John 13:3-5, and 5:2 with John 21:15-17). The author was an eyewitness of the sufferings of Christ (2:19-24; 3:18; 4:1; 5:1).

Simon Peter, originally from Bethsaida (John 1:44), was the son of Jonah (Matt. 16:17) and brother of Andrew, with whom he was a partner in a fishing business at Capernaum. Peter first met Jesus near Bethany beyond the Jordan when he was led to the Lord by Andrew and received his name "Cephas" (Aramaic), or "Peter" (Greek), meaning "rock" (John 1:42). Peter was chosen by Jesus as an apostle (Mark 3:16). Peter was a natural leader and often served as a spokesman for the Twelve (Matt. 16:15-16). With James and John he belonged to the innermost circle of the Twelve and was present at the raising of Jairus's daughter (Mark 5:37), the transfiguration (Matt. 17:1-2), Gethsemane (Matt. 26:36-37), and the empty tomb (John 20:6). He took a position of leadership among the disciples after Christ's ascension (Acts 1:15-22; 3:11-26; 5:1-11; 8:14-25, 10:1–11:18) and was the key preacher on the day of Pentecost (Acts 2). Peter was God's instrument to open the way of salvation to the Samaritans (Acts 8:14-15) and the Gentiles (Acts 10–11). In later years Peter traveled in an itinerant ministry with his wife (1 Cor. 1:12; 9:5).

According to tradition, Peter went to Rome around A.D. 62 and there was crucified during Nero's persecution, which began in A.D. 64. Peter's martyrdom is hinted at by Christ in John 21:18-19. According to early tradition, Peter insisted on being crucified head downward.

DATE

The letter reflected impending persecution, suggesting that it was written not long before Peter's death. But Peter's teaching that the government could be expected to administer justice (1 Pet. 2:13-14) and that a man who did what was right would be unharmed (3:13) indicate that this may have been written before the severe persecutions of Nero began in A.D. 64. Peter arrived in Rome in A.D. 62 and probably wrote this letter in A.D. 63 or 64.

PURPOSE

This letter by Peter was designed to exhort its readers to conduct themselves in accordance with the living hope they possessed as redeemed believers. The letter confirmed the believers' knowledge of salvation and encouraged them in their submission to authority and joyful response to suffering for Christ's sake.

GEOGRAPHY AND ITS IMPORTANCE

The Churches of Peter's Letter

Peter wrote to Jewish Christians who had been exiled from their homeland, Israel, because of their faith in Jesus (see Acts 8:1-4). Forced to spread out into strange lands, they no doubt also spread their faith. Paul extensively evangelized many of the areas mentioned by Peter.

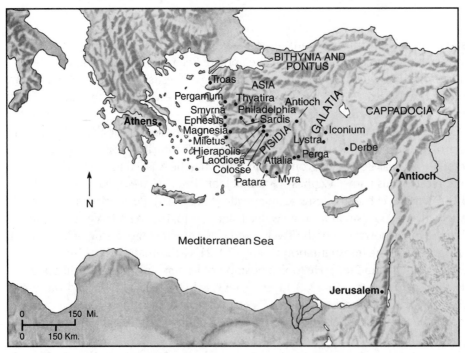

GUIDING CONCEPTS

HOPE AND SUFFERING

The two major concepts to look for in 1 Peter are suffering and hope. Throughout, the short letter speaks of suffering. But it does not simply discuss the pain of suffering. It places the fact of suffering within three contexts of hope. First, suffering takes place under the ultimate power of God to bring believers into full redemption (1:5-7; 5:6-7, 10). Second, those causing unjust suffering will someday face the judgment of God who judges all evil (1:17; 2:23; 4:5, 17). Third, as Christians suffer, they do so in the presence of the Christ whose example has gone before them (2:21; 3:17-18; 4:12-14). In addition to suffering, Peter continually raised the issue of godly conduct (1:6-7, 13-17, 22; 2:1-2; 2:12–3:17; 4:1-19; 5:1-10). All of his words about suffering and hope point toward one result: godly behavior in the present. But that behavior is not demanded in order to get into heaven. It is done because of the secure redemption of believers in Christ. Any hope they have for the future is secured, not by their actions, but by the resurrection of Christ (1:3).

GODLY CONDUCT IN THE MIDST OF SUFFERING

Peter called his readers to godly conduct (1:15, 17-18; 2:12; 3:1-2, 16). The problem Peter addressed was the real or potential complaining and disobedience brought on by unjust suffering. His readers were in danger of misunderstanding the source and reason for their trials (cf. 4:12-13). This misunderstanding could cause the believers to drift from their intimate relation with Christ. It would be easier for them to follow their hate and lusts (2:23; 4:1-3) than to follow the perfect example of Christ.

Peter met these problems by reminding his readers of the history of their redemption (1:3–2:3). Without being rooted in history, they could become rootless in holiness. He founded their witness upon the Rock of Christ's witness (2:4–3:7). He revealed the problem of unjust suffering (3:8-22) to be resolved in God's final evaluation (1:17).

BIBLE-WIDE CONCEPTS

STONE TESTIMONIES

Peter's use of "stone"

Peter linked together three Old Testament texts that spoke of the nature of Christ as "stone" (2:6-8; quoting Isa. 28:16; Ps. 118:22; Isa. 8:14). All three Old Testament passages are from contexts of judgment and restoration. All speak of God being a source of rest and safety. Isaiah 8 and 28 were already connected in the book of Isaiah itself. Both passages are built around similar events. Compare Isaiah 8:8 with 28:15-16; 8:15 with 28:13; and Isaiah 8:10, 14 with 28:15, 18. Both passages deal with judgment and with false and true refuge. The "stone" conveys the dual image of stability and judgment. That dual image is also seen in 1 Peter 3:10-12 where Peter quoted Psalm 34:12-16. Peter also made a passing reference to Isaiah 8:12-13 in 1 Peter 3:14-15. Peter's readers evidently needed some powerful words concerning Jesus as both a security to the believers and a liability to the opponents of God.

Broader Christian use of "stone" testimonies

Other New Testament writers also saw an important place for the three Old Testament "stone" passages that Peter used. Isaiah 8:14 is quoted in Romans 9:32; Isaiah 8:14-15 in Luke 2:34-35; Isaiah 8:17-18 in Hebrews 2:13; Isaiah 28:16 in Romans 9:33; 10:11. The parable of the vineyard is an example of how Christ used the "stone" testimonies. Mark 12:10 quotes Psalm 118:22. Christ, the rejected "stone," was connected to the rejected and then exalted Son. Matthew 21:42 quotes Psalm 118:22. Luke 20:17, 18 uses Isaiah 8:14-15 with Psalm 118:22.

Relation of "stone" to Psalm 34 (1 Peter 3:10-12)

Peter also quoted another Old Testament passage that rounds out the "stone" imagery. Peter used the "stone" to picture a divine anchor and example. He used Psalm 34 to portray the human response of obedience. The "stone" testimony draws on Israel's hope as completed in Jesus. Also the image gives the comfort of security and exhortation. Psalm 34 applies the truths portrayed in the "stone" image to believers.

THE FLOOD

Peter compared the flood of Noah's day with Christian baptism (1 Pet. 3:18-22). Noah went through the waters of the flood and was saved by being in the ark. The Christian goes through the waters of baptism and is saved by the power of Christ's own resurrection (3:21). The redemptive images of ark and cross point toward God's redemption in Christ.

NEEDS MET BY FIRST PETER

This letter from Peter met the needs of believers who were hurting and were tempted to lash out in pain and revenge. In contrast with their blessed salvation in Christ, believers faced unjust persecution and loss of their material goods in the world. God called them to lives obedient to his word. But it was that very obedience that brought on world hatred and persecution. The Christians faced a fork in the road. They could continue to obey and continue receiving the world's hostility or they could weaken their obedience to live more comfortable and persecution-free lives. The structure and content of 1 Peter show that Peter intended to answer questions like the following for his readers.

- In what way are believers protected by God's power (1:5)?
- What is the reason and purpose for pain in this life?
- What kind of perspective can help believers not respond with anger and hate to life's hurts at home and on the job?
- Why are believers experiencing so much distress if they are really God's children?

Peter tried to help his readers experience the reality of two events. The first was the past example of Christ during his life on earth. When Christ was unjustly treated, he was able to behave graciously and did not fall into the trap of seeking revenge. The second event was the resurrection of the saints that is yet to take place. During times of suffering, pain, and injustice, Peter encouraged believers to think about what their certain, though future, resurrection means for the present. Peter urged them not to let present sufferings blind them to these past and future truths.

OUTLINE OF FIRST PETER

I. GREETING (1:1-2)

II. THE FOUNDATION OF OBEDIENCE: THE LIVING WORD (1:3–2:12)
   A. Doxology: The Word's Focus (1:3-12)
   B. The Focus of the Believer's Calling: God's Holiness (1:13-21)
   C. Redemption's Foundation: Imperishable Word (1:22–2:12)

III. THE TESTIMONY FROM OBEDIENCE (2:13–4:11)
   A. In Life Relationships (2:13–3:7)
   B. Summary and Elaboration: Blessing though Maligned (3:8–4:6)
   C. Conclusion: The End Impinges on the Present (4:7-11)

IV. THE FOCUS IN OBEDIENCE: FAITHFUL CREATOR (4:12–5:11)
   A. The Suffering of Christ: God's Presence (4:12-19)
   B. Trusting His Appointed Leaders (5:1-5)
   C. Trusting His Powerful Grace (5:6-11)

V. CLOSING REMARKS AND BENEDICTION (5:12-14)

FIRST PETER NOTES

1:1-2 GREETING
This letter from Peter was addressed to the believers scattered throughout the provinces of Pontus, Galatia, Cappadocia, Asia, and Bithynia. For those who were suffering under persecution, the truth of God's foreknowledge was of great encouragement and gave them strength to persevere. Peter stressed the believers' election, obedience, and sanctification (1:2). While 1:1 refers to the addressees as "God's chosen people," 1:2 mentions that this election is according to divine foreknowledge ("chose you long ago"). While "chosen" points to God's selective choice, "foreknowledge" emphasizes the loving, personal aspect of that choice.

1:3–2:12 THE FOUNDATION OF OBEDIENCE: THE LIVING WORD
1:3-12 Doxology: The Word's Focus
1:3-5 PAST: SECURE SALVATION
The elements in this doxology move from God's past saving events to their present results and future perfection. God has caused believers to be born again to a living hope. Their faith rests on the resurrection of Christ. Peter contemplated the nature of salvation and poured out thanksgiving to God for this divine work accomplished through Christ's death and resurrection. He gave praise to God for the regeneration of the believers. He used the term "born again" (1:3; cf. John 3:3). This new birth leads to a "wonderful expectation" and an eternal

inheritance. The word "protect" (1:5) is a military term (see "guard" in Phil. 4:7) that means "garrisoned about." Throughout their earthly pilgrimage, God's divine power will protect believers.

1:6-9 PRESENT: PROVEN FAITH
God allows trials (cf. with James 1:2) in order to prove by testing the eternal quality of the believer's faith. As fire distinguishes true gold from the counterfeit, so trials distinguish genuine faith from superficial profession. The focus is on the present as well as the future outcome of a believer's faith (1 Pet. 1:7, 9).

1:10-12 PRESENT: FOCUS OF HISTORY
The focus is on the Messiah. The future element is mentioned once more. There are great glories to follow (1:11). Peter reflected on the revelation of mankind's salvation through the Old Testament prophets who, by the Spirit, predicted the coming of Jesus the Messiah (Luke 24:44). Although they sought the precise details regarding the coming Messiah ("when and to whom"), these matters were not revealed. The prophets did, however, predict the sufferings (Isa. 53) and glories of Christ (Isa. 11), without distinguishing his two comings.

1:13-21 The Focus of the Believer's Calling: God's Holiness
A practical conclusion ("so," 1:13) arises from the discussion of Christ's redemption in 1:10-12. History is the foundation of hope. The future revelation of Christ's grace should result in present godly behavior.

Peter reflected on the implications of the great cost of the believer's salvation for present obedience. The expression translated "think clearly" (1:13) refers to mental and spiritual preparation.

Holiness is based on God's character (1:14-16). The quotation in 1:16 is from Leviticus 11:44-45. Peter used the words "just as," "what's more," "also," and "too" throughout the letter to make critical comparisons between God and the believer (1 Pet. 1:15; 2:5; 3:18; 4:1). The character of God, the one calling the believers, is the standard for their behavior. The primary meaning of "holy" (1:15) is "separation." Moral purity is an outgrowth of the concept of holiness, for that which is separated unto the Lord must be in conformity to his righteous standards.

"Reverent fear" is the result of addressing God as an impartial judge (1:17). The future hope of believers is based on a redemption that God had in mind from eternity past. The relationship believers have with God does not diminish his demand for their holiness. It is the means whereby they have the ability to seek holiness. First Peter 1:18 deepens the motivation for obeying God. The concept of being chosen "long ago" (1:20) links back to 1:2. The broad sweep of God's redemptive history is the viewpoint for the security of believers while suffering unjustly. The words "paid a ransom" (1:18) mean to secure release by payment. Silver and gold are perishable in the sense that they can lose their value in a deflationary economy. They suggest temporary wealth, not eternal resources. As the Old Testament sacrifices had to be without flaw (Lev. 22:19-25), so Christ was unblemished and spotless, without sin (1:19; cf. Heb. 4:15).

1:22–2:12 Redemption's Foundation: The Imperishable Word

The great worth of salvation in Christ is the basis for sincere love (1:22-25). The "eternal" concept (1:23) is key to Peter's desire to encourage steadfastness in the face of potentially fatal human persecutions. It gives the future hope spoken of in 1:5, 7, 9. "Sincere love" (1:22) is the opposite of conformity to "evil" (1:14). It sums up all the exhortations to obedience throughout the letter. The means by which salvation was brought to believers was the word of God—the preaching of the gospel (Rom. 10:14). While to some the word of God may appear to be frail, Peter quoted Isaiah 40:6-8 in 1:24-25 to show that it will outlast all natural phenomena. Isaiah contrasts the transitory natural creation with the unfailing and abiding nature of God's word.

Peter pointed out that Christ's followers should expect rejection just as Christ was rejected. The issue is one of value, whether value is defined by people or God. Believers are to seek what God sees

as valuable—his rejected Son. The "so" of 2:1 looks back to 1 Peter 1 regarding the word of God. The word is not only the basis for spiritual birth but also for spiritual growth. A taste of God's goodness should produce an appetite for more (2:3).

In 2:4-10 Peter contemplated the privileges that accompany the believers' gift of salvation. As "living stones" believers are to worship God (2:4-8), and as priests they are to witness to the world (2:9-10). As Christ is the living Stone (2:4), believers are living stones (2:5) joined together to form one building. The metaphor shifts in the second half of 2:5. Here believers are consecrated "priests" who offer up spiritual sacrifices to God through Christ (cf. Rom. 12:1; Heb. 13:15-16). In 2:6 Peter appealed to Isaiah 28:16 to show that Christ is the primary foundation stone. In 2:7-8 Peter appealed to Psalm 118:22 and Isaiah 8:14 to show that Christ is a stumbling stone to those who refuse faith in him. In 2:9 Peter used several Old Testament terms (cf. Deut. 10:15; Exod. 19:6; Isa. 61:6) to declare what believers have become in Christ. The spiritual sacrifices (2:5) are summed up as proclaiming God's character and acts (2:9). In 2:10 Peter quoted Hosea 2:23. Paul used Hosea 2:23 linked to Isaiah 8:14 in Romans 9:25-26, 33. The Old Testament as fulfilled in Christ is the solid foundation for faith and hope.

In 2:11–3:12 Peter developed the doctrine of the believers' submission to appropriate authorities—kings, masters, husbands. Even in the light of severe persecution they must submit, as Christ did before them. Unjust suffering in Christ's name is a sign of God's Spirit resting on them and blessing (3:14; 4:14). And good works will glorify God (2:12). Even if unbelievers reject Christians now, they will glorify God later when he comes again. The most important relationship for Christians to be concerned about is the one between themselves and God.

2:13–4:11 THE TESTIMONY FROM OBEDIENCE

Overview: This section on submission comes out of the discussion of what it means to minister God's redemption to the world (2:9). The practical implications of being "living stones" and "priests" are developed. The focus is on the task of 2:12.

2:13–3:7 In Life Relationships
2:13-17 HUMAN INSTITUTIONS
The word "accept" (2:13) means to "place oneself under" and implies support as well as submission. Note that Peter said nothing about certain forms of government. He approved no special kind of government, but supported law and order in general. Peter referred to God in each verse ("Lord's sake," "sent them," "God's will," "God's slaves,"

"fear God"). Submission to civil authority was not only the will of God, it was also designed to "silence" (2:15) ignorant talk against Christians.

2:18-25 SERVANTS: UNJUST SUFFERING
What example did Christ give (see Isa. 53:4-9 quotation)? In 1 Peter 2:25 the apostle borrowed a sheep allusion from Isaiah 53:6. The principle of submission, even through unjust suffering, is supremely illustrated by Peter as he directed his readers to the death of Christ. First Peter 2:22-25 contains Peter's exposition of Isaiah 53. In 2:22 Peter quoted Isaiah 53:9. It was tempting to strike back while suffering unjustly, but Christ did just the opposite (cf. also 1 Pet. 3:9). This theology of Christ's sufferings was very relevant in this section on submission to authority because the authorities over the readers of this letter were often unjust. Here Peter reveals what it means for believers to be living stones (2:4-5). Christ as the stone (2:6-7) was an appropriate image for Peter to use because it was a perfect illustration of the prophetic certainty stressed in 1:10-12. For some, the stone is a problem and brings judgment. For believers, the stone is precious in God's sight.

3:1-6 WIVES: A WORDLESS WITNESS
This section continues the topic of submission ("in the same way," 3:1, 7). The submission of the wife to her husband does not suggest inequality, for Christ was submissive to and yet equal with the Father. In 3:3 Peter does not forbid jewelry or nice clothes. Rather he is pointing out by way of contrast what makes a really beautiful woman—the inner character qualities. Again, the contrast between what does and does not perish is made (1:4). Only the one who sees the difference will have the insight to build on the imperishable. Sarah called Abraham "master" (3:6; cf. Gen. 18:12), acknowledging him with the respect due a husband.

3:7 HUSBANDS: UNHINDERED PRAYERS
The husbands follow the pattern of submission ("in the same way"), though the word itself is not used. The issue is understanding and submitting to the requirements of any relationship, in this case between husband and wife. The husband submits to the requirements by meeting the wife's needs. How is the woman a "weaker" partner? Conclusions range from physical, spiritual, or emotional weakness. Although this is debated, the point of equality before God ("equal partner") that results in receiving honor is central. Note that the husband who fails to understand and honor his wife will have a hindered prayer life. What it means to have hindered prayers is explained in 3:12. A righteous person in relationship with his wife has the full attention of God in his prayers. God is against those who do evil to their wives, and their prayers will not be heard.

3:8–4:6 Summary and Elaboration: Blessing though Maligned
3:8-12 SUMMARY: HARMONY WITH GOD
Peter desired that believers give an honest blessing, not one muttered through clenched teeth, to those who persecuted them. The honest blessing should flow out of sincere love (1:22–2:12). There is a close relationship between giving and inheriting a blessing (3:9). Peter supported this point (3:10-12) with Psalm 34:12-16. Love of life and seeing good days (3:10) is the miraculous possibility of faith and obedience in the midst of life's problems.

3:13-16 SANCTIFY CHRIST AS LORD
The unswerving commitment to doing God's will at any cost (4:2) is the driving theme of this section. Christ is sanctified as Lord by doing the will of the Father (3:13-16). Peter continued the discussion in 2:20 concerning suffering for the sake of righteousness. He pointed out that believers who maintain a clear conscience while suffering unjustly will put their critics to shame.

3:17-22 REMAIN IN CHRIST'S ARK OF REDEMPTION
In 3:18-22 Peter presented the supreme example of undeserved suffering: the crucifixion of Christ. Jesus suffered death on the cross for the sins others had committed. In similar fashion, the suffering of the innocent could be God's will.

In 3:18 Peter reminded the believers of the suffering of Christ and what it accomplished. Christ's death for sins constituted a substitutionary judgment on behalf of sinners. His death prepared the way for the reconciliation of sinners with God ("bring us safely home to God," cf. 2 Cor. 5:18). But Christ's death was not a defeat. Having "suffered physical death," he was "raised to life in the Spirit." The two participles ("suffered physical death" and "raised to life") define the main verb "died." There is a balance and correlation between the two terms "physical" and "Spirit." Both terms emphasize quality and denote two contrasting modes of Christ's existence—his earthly sphere of existence as a man ("physical") and his heavenly sphere of existence as divine Spirit ("Spirit"). The point of 3:18 is that Christ's death was not a defeat but a triumph. While Christ died to his earthly sphere of existence, by resurrection ("raised to life") he entered into a fuller life and was liberated for greater ministry (Matt. 28:20; John 14:12).

One interpretive problem in 1 Peter concerns the identity of the "spirits in prison" (3:19), the location of this prison, and when Christ preached to them. There are several different viewpoints with regard to "the spirits in prison" and when Christ "preached" to them:

(1) The earliest view identifies the "spirits in prison" with the fallen angels ("sons of God") in

Genesis 6 (cf. 2 Pet. 2:4; Jude 1:6). But it is difficult to scripturally support the idea of the gospel being brought to demons.

(2) Some understand the "spirits in prison" to be unbelievers to whom the gospel was preached by Christ through the apostles after Pentecost. But this view fails to explain the reference to Noah.

(3) Others understand the "spirits in prison" to refer to those of Noah's day who are now dead and awaiting the final judgment. According to this viewpoint, Christ descended to hell between his death and resurrection. His preaching is viewed as being either condemnatory, no hope, or conciliatory, offering the antediluvians a second chance for salvation. However, there is no evidence in Scripture that anyone is offered a "second chance" after death (cf. Heb. 9:27). And why would Peter exclusively single out the people who lived before the flood to be the recipients of this pre-resurrection ministry of Jesus? The viewpoint is quite complex and requires a great deal of hypothesis and speculation.

(4) A view that can be traced as far back as Augustine holds that 3:19-20 refers to the preincarnate preaching of Christ through Noah (cf. 1:11 for the Spirit of Christ working within the Old Testament prophets). The preaching was accomplished by Christ's divine Spirit, the immaterial aspect of his person. The "spirits in prison" were the souls of those who heard the message, rejected it, and now find themselves in judgment. This view eliminates references to the obscure "doctrine" of Christ's descent into hell and the question of what his "preaching" might have accomplished there. It also has the advantage of clarity and simplicity.

But the point of the illustration in 3:19-20 is that Christ's past spiritual ministry in the Old Testament was resumed at his death. Christ's death was a victory, not a defeat. While death ended the physical, earthly dimension of his life and ministry, it inaugurated once again, and in a new and better way, his ministry as divine Spirit.

The ark built by Noah (3:20) is a symbol of the resurrection. It is the means of bringing people to God (3:18). The people in the ark were brought safely through the water (3:20). In a similar way, believers are brought safely to God through the cross. Water baptism and all it symbolizes is the picture of the believer coming to God through Christ. Like Noah, the people Peter was addressing had responded to God's message and were trusting Christ to bring them to God. The implication is that believers are not to jump out but wait patiently in their ark of Christ's cross through the storms of life. Believers are not to jump out of the ark to fight or retreat back into the world's ways.

4:1-6 OBEDIENCE TO THE JUDGE OF ALL
Obedience brings about a good conscience (3:16) and a good account in the last judgment (4:2, 5-6).

Peter brought up the subject of death and people being judged in the flesh in order to bring encouragement. His readers were suffering in the flesh, but they needed to know that even the threat of physical death was not a valid reason for losing sobriety and self-control (4:7-8). They might physically die, but they would have held on to true spiritual life (4:6). The approach is similar to that of 3:19-20. Peter looked back to Noah ("those who have died," 4:6) and probably included those believers after Noah's day up to the present. They had physically died, whether through martyrdom or other causes ("punished," 4:6). Peter was saying that the death and resurrection of Christ served to arm believers with the appropriate attitude for their daily battle against sin. The one who has identified with Christ's redemptive suffering is no longer responding to the lusts of the flesh, but to the will of God. The main point is that there is life, not condemnatory judgment, for believers who have died in Christ.

4:7-11 Conclusion: The End Impinges on the Present
The conclusion ("therefore," 4:7) calls for a total focus of life on glorifying God. Peter set forth the proper conduct of those experiencing suffering. Even during suffering believers were to meet the practical demands of Christian discipleship. Love, being ready to forgive again and again, covers the sins of others. Peter encouraged believers to use their spiritual gifts in serving one another (cf. 1 Cor. 12) and glorifying God.

4:12–5:11 THE FOCUS IN OBEDIENCE: FAITHFUL CREATOR
4:12-19 The Suffering of Christ: God's Presence
The thrust of this section was to explain the judgment of God. The Old Testament Scripture quoted here (4:18) is Proverbs 11:31. Some thought that judgment could only mean punishment for sin. To them, the "fiery trials" of persecution seemed strange and out of keeping with God's salvation. This had once been Peter's view of suffering when he told Jesus not to go to the cross (Matt. 16:21-23). This was a satanic view of life for believers. Others understood that judgment can be both punishment for unbelievers and purifying for believers. This perspective on judgment enables believers to submit in peace to God's ways of judgment, starting with the church first and then the world (cf. also 1 Pet. 5:10). Peter wanted his readers to understand that there was judgment for the family of God that follows the pattern of Christ's own sufferings. In that light, continued rejoicing is the proper response to suffering as a Christian (4:13). In 4:17 Peter alluded to Ezekiel 9:5-6. Persecution is divinely permitted to purge believers and

serves as a warning of judgment on the ungodly. The implication of the use of Proverbs 11:31 is that the ungodly face terrifying final judgment. Those who suffer according to God's will must place their confidence in God who is faithful and can be counted on to do what is right.

5:1-5 Trusting His Appointed Leaders

The concept of a faithful Creator (4:19) is pivotal to 1 Peter 5. As the Creator, God ordained the sufferings of Christ and his future glory (5:1). Leadership is to be carried out in conformity to that plan. In 5:1-4 Peter explained the way leaders were to shepherd their congregations. He exhorted the elders to shepherd (that is, feed and care for) the flock of God among them. The imagery of the shepherd and the flock was used by Jesus when instructing Peter (John 21:15-17). Faithful church leaders are promised a reward that they will receive from Christ, the Head Shepherd (5:4). In 5:5 Peter quoted Proverbs 3:34 to show the reason for humility. It reaches to the very character of God.

5:6-11 Trusting His Powerful Grace

The thrust of this letter concerning humility and subsequent exaltation is clearly stated in 5:6. The "good time" is when Christ returns (cf. 4:13). Until then, believers must cast their anxiety upon him only if they truly believe the great truths in this letter. The next contrast is suffering for a little time to gain perfection for eternity (5:10). But whether now or then, the dominion is always his (5:11).

5:12-14 CLOSING REMARKS AND BENEDICTION

Apparently Paul's companion Silvanus, or Silas (Acts 15:22; 18:5), is the scribe who wrote as Peter dictated the letter (1 Pet. 5:12). "Babylon" is often used here in some translations in the place of "Rome" (5:13). The earliest understanding of "Babylon" interprets it as referring to Rome. Other interpretations that were held later are the ancient city of Babylon, a city in Egypt named Babylon, or a cryptogram for a place of exile. The majority of scholars favor Rome as the place of writing and take "Babylon" as a symbolic designation for the city, as in Revelation 17:5, 9 and 18:2, 10, 21. "In Christian love" (1 Pet. 5:14) is often translated as "a holy kiss," which was a culturally acceptable Christian greeting.

2 PETER

BASIC FACTS

HISTORICAL SETTING
The readers of this letter were believers (1:1) and apparently the same group as addressed in 1 Peter (2 Pet. 3:1). See the Guiding Concepts section for 1 Peter. The problem facing the readers in 1 Peter was persecution. The problem facing the readers of 2 Peter was false teaching (2:1, 21). It was a teaching that advocated loose moral standards (2:10) resulting in enslavement to lusts (2:19). The false teachers denied the second coming of Christ (3:4). In contrast with the opponents' claims to knowledge, Peter emphasized the true knowledge of Christ (1:2, 3, 8; 2:20; 3:18).

AUTHOR
Although the authorship of Peter has been questioned, the letter itself names Peter as its author (1:1). The author referred to his approaching death (1:13-14). He witnessed the transfiguration of Jesus (1:16-18) as Peter had done (Matt. 17:1-4). A previous letter sent to the same readers is mentioned (3:1). The author had knowledge of Paul and his writings (3:15-16) as Peter must have had (Gal. 1:18; 2:9, 11, 14; Acts 15:1-29). There is nothing in the letter that might have motivated a forgery; it contains no heresy or new historical data about the life of Peter. The differences in form and style between 1 and 2 Peter may be due to his using a different scribe to actually put the words on paper. It is possible that he wrote this second letter himself but dictated the first one to a scribe.

DATE
Written after 1 Peter (2 Pet. 3:1), this letter was written shortly before Peter's death, which he believed to be imminent (1:14-15). The letter was probably written from Rome in the summer of A.D. 64.

PURPOSE
This letter from Peter was designed to warn its readers against false teachers in the church (2:1-2; 3:17). Peter intended for the letter to stir the readers to remembrance of the true teachings of their prophets and Savior (3:1-2) and encourage growth in knowledge of the Lord Jesus (3:18).

GUIDING CONCEPTS

DIVINE PROVIDENCE

Peter dealt with the concept of divine providence in 2:3-9; 3:7, 9-13. He was involved in an argument that was common in his day and one whose roots can be traced back to Epicurean philosophy. The Epicureans (from 300 B.C. on) were interested in having a trouble-free life. Because their god had to be the supreme model of being trouble-free, the concept of a god trying to keep the world together made no sense. He could not be trouble-free if he had to be concerned with the world. Therefore, there could be no divine providence.

Man's ideal also was to be trouble-free. He was to have the promise of freedom. In order to achieve this trouble-free state, the Epicureans denied the existence of a god who evaluated people after this life. Thus both the concept of an afterlife and that of judgment were done away with. The Epicurean argument was based on two premises. First, the wicked are not judged. Second, the righteous very often seem to be punished. From this, the philosophers reasoned there could be no sovereign god who was in control. The foremost enemy to the untroubled state of humanity was the concept of a sovereign and judging deity.

Some Jewish writings bring forth this same argument against Providence. In a Targum of Genesis 4:8, Cain and Abel debate about the justice of God. Cain claimed that God did not accept Cain's offering because he was partial toward Abel. Cain then went on to conclude that "there is no judgment, there is no judge, there is no other world, there is no gift of good reward for the just and punishment for the wicked." Scholars believe that this Targum reflects the thinking of the Sadducees, the Jewish sect that denied the concepts of resurrection, afterlife, and free will. This Jewish sect was in existence during New Testament times.

AFTERLIFE

Peter spoke of the afterlife in 2 Peter 3:7, 10-13. The statement in 3:4 that all things would continue as they always had implies that history would continue on in the same way. Thus, talk of divine intervention into history with a second coming and judgment did not fit the philosophers' theories. In talking about the afterlife and judgment, Peter desired to illustrate God's ability to keep and preserve his people. Passages that relate to this are 2:4, 9, 17; and 3:7. Deuteronomy 32:34-35 reveals that there are treasuries of judgment, but they are sealed. They are sealed for a future opening in order to give time for repentance now (3:9, 15).

JUDGMENT AFTER THIS LIFE

Peter spoke of judgment after death in 2:4, 9, 17; 3:7, 10. The false teachers in 2:1 were denying the return of the Lord. They were practical atheists. Practical atheists, seen also in Psalm 10:4, 6, 11, do not deny God's existence. They just live their day-to-day lives as if God does not exist. Psalms 14:1; 73:11; and Jeremiah 5:12 also relate to this idea. These people have no fear of God. They believe that they will not be punished because they think that God is not concerned.

BIBLE-WIDE CONCEPTS

This letter from Peter was an incredible collection of biblical references ranging from the beginning to the end of time. Peter's encouragement to purity and steadfastness was rooted in a deep appreciation of God's words and deeds throughout history. Peter brought to his readers' attention the hope of God's promises (2 Pet. 1:4; 3:9, 13). He viewed all as under God's sovereign kingdom (1:11). He revealed the present implications of the transfiguration of Christ (1:16-18). He pointed his readers to the words spoken by the Old and New Testament prophets and apostles (1:19-21; 3:2). He related present false prophets to the line of false prophets throughout the history of God's people (2:1). He graphically illustrated the present implications of ancient judgments upon angels (2:4), the world by flood (2:5; 3:6), Sodom and Gomorrah (2:6), and Balaam (2:15-16). Peter showed that obedience to God was demanded by his power as Creator and Sustainer of the heavens and earth. Finally, Peter reflected the words of Jesus (3:10) and Paul (3:15-16). Far from a casual collection of biblical concepts, this letter reveals a mind steeped in Old and New Testament truths and a heart of wisdom that knew precisely how to bring the right truths to bear on the particular problems at hand.

NEEDS MET BY SECOND PETER

This letter from Peter was designed to meet some continual and basic needs of God's people, especially as they were surrounded by conflicting and, without doubt, false teachings. Those conflicting doctrines bred insecurity and doubt, especially about the promise of Christ's return to establish justice and reward the faithful for their sufferings and witness. The structure and content of 2 Peter show that Peter was answering questions like the following for his readers.

- With so many contradictory views, how can sincere people know what to believe?
- What are believers to make of the fact that it has been many years since Jesus said he would come back and make things right?
- What does the long wait for Christ's return say about God?
- How can believers be sure that they are really called and chosen by God for redemption?

Peter wrote to people who needed to be certain about their salvation in the face of many conflicting doctrines. But he showed that security is obtained, not by theoretical teachings of doctrine, but by one's own personal growth in Christian graces and by conformity to God's nature. To have the "perfect doctrine" is no substitute for exhibiting godly qualities (2 Pet. 1:5-8). In today's society, which is so bent on gathering information, Peter urges believers to develop godly qualities. He also helps today's believers to cope with the long wait for Christ's return. Christ said he would be returning soon, but it has now been almost two thousand years. Peter revealed what this long wait says about humanity and, most important, what it says about God. Peter also sought to convince his readers that Christianity was not something that someone made up. He showed how to appropriate the apostolic witness of Christ's life (God's word) in one's personal experience to build a firm foundation for security and witness.

OUTLINE OF SECOND PETER

I. GREETING (1:1-2)

II. REMINDER: DILIGENCE TO PARTAKE OF THE PROMISES (1:3-21)
   A. Diligence in Growth (1:3-11)
   B. Attention to God's Word (1:12-21)

III. WARNING: FALSE TEACHERS (2:1-22)
   A. Consider Their End: Divine Destruction (2:1-16)
   B. Consider Their State: Slavery to Sin (2:17-22)

IV. REMINDER: DILIGENCE IN THE MIDST OF SKEPTICISM (3:1-18)
   A. Skepticism over Historical Continuity (3:1-7)
   B. Correction from Divine Chronology: Certainty (3:8-13)
   C. Concluding Exhortation from Divine Purpose: Salvation (3:14-18)

SECOND PETER NOTES

1:1-2 GREETING

Peter's greeting was based on a shared faith (1:1) within the sphere of growth in God's grace (1:2). Although the readers were apparently the same group of believers addressed in 1 Peter (cf. 2 Pet. 3:1), the more general address is used here because of the general applicability of the message to all Christians. The faith of the readers was the same kind of faith as was exhibited by the apostles; it was a true and genuine faith. The theme of the epistle (3:18) is introduced by the word "knowledge." The word Peter used means "full or true knowledge." His strong emphasis on true knowledge indicated that the false teachers also were claiming special access to divine truth.

1:3-21 REMINDER: DILIGENCE TO PARTAKE OF THE PROMISES

1:3-11 Diligence in Growth

1:3-4 A STATEMENT OF FACT: PARTAKING OF THE DIVINE NATURE
In these verses Peter considered the process of the believer's growth. Endowed with divine power, divine promises, and a divine nature, God enables the believer to grow in Christian virtue (1:5-7). Peter used philosophical terms and religious catch words that would grab the attention of the Greeks (1:3-4). The words "share in his divine nature" (1:4) refer to the believers as present sharers in the life of God through Christ (1:3) and future recipients of a glorified body (1:11). Peter's emphasis was not on the doctrine of salvation or on the doctrine of Christ. His letter was about God the Father. This gives further insight into the life-setting of the letter. Peter dealt with the readers' questions

about how it seemed that God was not doing much to bring his kingdom into the world.

1:5-9 ENLIGHTENMENT AND PURIFICATION
Because of the spiritual endowment believers had received, Peter urged the believers to cooperate with God's plan for producing certain virtues (1:5-7). Ultimately these virtues are produced by Christ (Phil. 2:13), but believers must be yielded to God's will and word for the growth to take place. In 1:8-11 Peter pointed out the positive benefits of having developed the virtues listed in 1:5-7. Believers who do not manifest these virtues are spiritually near-sighted (1:9). They have forgotten that their sins have been forgiven. These people have not really forgotten about their salvation, but they have forgotten the implications of past forgiveness on present behavior. They have been living as if their past forgiveness had no relationship to present holy living.

1:10-11 CERTAINTY FROM PRACTICE
The virtues listed in 1:5-8 provide true knowledge about God (1:8) and build a basis of certainty for believers about their salvation (1:10). Peter wanted his readers to be certain of their salvation so that they would stay true to the faith. But only their own firsthand experience of seeing God produce his character in their lives could create that certainty. Experiencing the divine nature of God now (1:4) will provide a rich reward later (1:11).

1:12-21 Attention to God's Word

1:12-15 AN ENDURING REMINDER
Peter and Paul both described their bodies as tents (1:13; cf. 2 Cor. 5:1). Peter wanted to leave a written record of reminder after he died (2 Pet. 1:15).

The Lord had spoken about Peter's death in general terms (John 13:16; 21:19). At the time of writing this letter Peter had been made aware by the Lord that his death was imminent.

1:16-18 EYEWITNESSES OF GLORY
Peter showed that true knowledge had its basis, not in cleverly devised tales, but in the testimony of the apostles (2 Pet. 1:16-18) and the prophetic word (1:19-21). In 1:16-18 Peter joined hands with the apostles James and John in his claim that they were eyewitnesses ("seen . . . with our own eyes," 1:16) of Christ's majesty at his transfiguration (Matt. 17:1-8). The term "eyewitnesses" was used by others as a technical term in various pagan religions of a person who had been fully initiated and allowed to watch a sacred ritual.

1:19-21 FIRM PROPHECY
The goal of this letter, protecting Christians from false teachings, depended on presenting the true authority to whom all believers would listen. Here, Jesus was the only one who had the Father's full approval, as seen in God's words quoted by Peter (1:17). It is debated whether Peter was saying that prophetic word (Scripture) confirms apostolic witness, or that apostolic witness confirms Scripture. Peter seemed to be saying that the truth of God's revelation is more certain, having been confirmed by two witnesses (Scripture and apostolic testimony) rather than just one. The phrase "until the day Christ appears" (1:19) probably refers to the coming of Christ to establish his kingdom. In 1:20-21 the apostle explained that no prophecy of Scripture was a matter of private origination. No true prophet thinks up a prophecy himself. The prophetic revelation comes from God through human instrumentality under the impulse of the Holy Spirit. This was why Peter spoke of the transfiguration and God's witness to Jesus as his approved Son. Only that which conforms to Jesus' words is acceptable teaching. Only God speaking through his Spirit, not ideas peculiar to a person's wishes, results in true divine prophecy. This prepares the reader for Peter's words about false prophets in 2:1-22. The chapter break would be more logical between 1:19 and 1:20 than it is at the end of 1:21.

2:1-22 WARNING: FALSE TEACHERS
2:1-16 Consider Their End: Divine Destruction
2:1-3 THEIR MESSAGE, JUDGMENT, AND AUDIENCE
Peter warned that false teachers would come among the believers, denying Christ and influencing others toward evil (2:1; cf. Acts 20:29-30). Peter emphasized the sure destruction of the false teachers (noted twice, 2:1, 3). The rest of the chapter outlines their judgment in graphic detail. By

contrast, Peter also encouraged his readers by pointing to the ultimate preservation of the faithful (2:9). Peter asserted that the judgment of the false teachers had been clouded by delay. Some thought that the lack of immediate judgment on these heretics showed an idleness on the part of God (2:3). But the issue with God's prophecies is never how long it takes them to be fulfilled, but how certain they are. Although these false teachers are seen to be unbelievers (2:12), salvation was available if they would but repent. The penalty for their sins was paid in full by Christ. The "true way" (2:2) refers to God's full salvation (cf. Acts 9:2; 16:17; 18:25-26; 19:9, 23; 22:4; 24:14, 22).

2:4-16 PAST EXAMPLE
Having pointed out the certain destruction of the false teachers (2 Pet. 2:3), Peter went on to give some examples of God's impartial judgment on the wicked. This is a long "if-then" idea that can be quickly seen by reading 2:4 and 2:9 together. Until the last judgment, God is able to keep good and evil sorted out, one for preservation, the other for destruction. The concepts of "rescue" (2:7, 9) and "spare" (2:4-5) are emphasized. The righteous are preserved through, not out of, times of evil (2:5, 7-9, "godly"). If God can really punish people and keep them for that purpose, he can also preserve the righteous. The implied logic is as follows: If God punished the wicked in the past, would he spare the false teachers now? Although debated, it is most likely that Peter was refering in 2:4 to the sin of the fallen angels of Genesis 6:1-4, who intermarried with mortal women and thus corrupted the human race.

The second example of God's judgment is the flood in Noah's day (2:5; cf. Gen. 6:5–8:22). The third example of judgment is God's wrath on Sodom and Gomorrah (2:6-8; cf. Gen. 19). The Genesis account gives the impression that Lot was not as righteous as Peter states (3:7). But Peter evaluated Lot's faith and belief. Lot did believe and obey God and did not condone the sexual perversion of the men of Sodom (Gen. 19:7). Peter's application (2:9) for the readers was that God would rescue the godly from temptation and bring judgment on the wicked. The "day of judgment" (2:9) referred to the great white throne judgment (Rev. 20:11-15). The basic elements of the judgment are elaborated in 2 Peter 2:10-16. The "way of Balaam" (2:15) referred to Balaam's materialistic motivation (Num. 22:5, 7; Deut. 23:4).

2:17-22 Consider Their State: Slavery to Sin
In 2:10-19 Peter proceeded to describe the character of the false teachers. He looked for the fruit of genuine faith and discovered that there was none. It is debated whether 2:20 refers to the false teachers

or the new converts ("who have just escaped," 2:18). According to the first view, the false teachers knew of the truth of Christ and apparently made some profession of this truth, but then strayed from it. They professed faith but never possessed it. In 2:21 Peter explained why their last state was worse than their first. Having been exposed to the truth, they had incurred a greater accountability (cf. Luke 12:47-48). According to the new convert view, Peter was pointing out the inconsistency of being delivered from sin's defilement and then returning to such slavery. Although applied in this case to believers, the impact of 2:21 remains the same. To return to previous sin after becoming cleansed by Christ is, in that context, worse than the preconversion state. Second Peter 2:22 shows in what way it is worse. It is worse because it is a great offense before God for believers to return to their old ways after receiving his cleansing. The two illustrations (2:22), one biblical (Prov. 26:11) and the other secular, show the inconsistency of being delivered from sin and then wallowing in it.

3:1-18 REMINDER: DILIGENCE IN THE MIDST OF SKEPTICISM

3:1-7 Skepticism over Historical Continuity

Peter referred to this as the "second" letter, 1 Peter being the first. Peter stressed two truths: (1) remember who brought the word of God (3:1-2); and (2) remember the potency of God's word to create and to destroy (3:3-7). From the viewpoint of prophecy (3:3), history divides into two periods: the present age (the age of promise) and the age to come (the time of fulfillment). The "last days" (3:3) refer to the end of the present age. One of the major doctrinal deviations of the false teachers was their denial of the second coming of Christ (3:4). They mocked the doctrine because so many years had passed since the promise had been given. But those who wondered whether God's promise would ever take place were forgetting God's creation of the world by his word and his act of judgment in the flood. Instead, they argued that God's seemingly present failure to judge world evil voided his promise that he would judge the world in the future. They were not the first to ask, "What happened to your promises, God?" (cf. Deut. 32:37; Judg. 6:13). But they were asking in sarcasm, not faith.

Peter claimed that those who said the world would continue as it always had, had forgotten to ask how the world came to be in the first place. Drawing upon biblical history (the creation and the flood), Peter pointed out that God was active in this world's affairs. He went on to appeal to biblical prophecy, the purging of the world by fire (3:7; cf. Isa. 66:15) and the judgment on the wicked (3:7; cf.

Dan. 12:2), as further evidences of God's divine intervention into the affairs of this world. Peter showed that the future is built consistently upon the past. Faith is built upon certainty based on the previous acts of God. Imposing a human time frame within which God is supposed to act leads to error.

3:8-13 Correction from Divine Chronology: Certainty

3:8-10 GOD IS NOT BOUND TO A HUMAN SCHEDULE

God's plan and timing are divine (3:8). Sovereignty, not slowness, is the issue. Appealing to the teaching of Psalm 90:4, Peter pointed out that what was regarded as a long time to people was like a mere day in God's reckoning. God is not bound by earthly time. The phrase "as some people think" (3:9) is intended as a slur against the opponents who say that delay functions as a prime argument against providential judgment. But, understood correctly, the present lack of God's full judgment is actually a proof for God's providence. God's so-called slowness is actually providing time to repent based on God's benevolent character. He is patient, not slow. That patience is clearly seen in God's covenant with Noah. Humans would continue to be as sinful as ever (Gen. 8:21), but God bound himself to withholding his full judgment so that he could show grace in Christ. A Jewish paraphrase of Genesis 6:3 notes that the 120 years God gave to Noah before the flood was for the people so "that they may work repentance and not perish." The Judaism of Peter's day understood the delay of God to be for repentance. This beautiful insight into the long-suffering nature of God is most clearly expressed in Exodus 34:6-7. Peter stressed this in 3:15. Peter's opponents had forgotten what should have shaped the God-centered person's worldview: God is compassionate and gracious and abounding in loving-kindness. They were not to have a black-and-white worldview that bound God to either instant retribution or no retribution. Both Christians and unbelievers receive the kindness of God leading them away from destruction (3:9).

Peter explained that the apparent delay of God's judgment was not an evidence of God's indifference regarding sin. The delay of Christ's return is redemptive in purpose; it is to allow more people to believe before judgment comes. The future day of the Lord is that period during which God will deal with his people through judgment and deliverance (3:10). It will include the tribulation, Christ's second advent, the millennial kingdom, and the purging of the heavens and earth (see note on 1 Thess. 5:2). Peter focused on the cataclysmic consummation of the day of the Lord, the purging of the earth by fire in preparation for the new heavens and earth (Isa. 65:17; 66:22; Rev. 21:1). This event will take place at the final revolt of Satan (Rev. 20:7–21:1).

3:11-13 EXHORTATION: BEHAVIOR AND HOPE
Peter set forth the coming judgments of the day of the Lord as an incentive to godly living. The "that day" (3:12) probably refers to that time when Christ hands over the reins of millennial government to God the Father, and the eternal state begins (cf. 1 Cor. 15:24-28; Rev. 21:1). For "promised" (3:13), see 1:4; 2:19; 3:4, 9, 13. The new heavens and earth were prophesied by Isaiah (Isa. 65:17; 66:22; cf. Rev. 21:1).

3:14-18 Concluding Exhortation from Divine Purpose: Salvation
The long wait for Christ's return displays the greatness of God's patience (3:14-15). Although Peter recognized that some of Paul's writings were hard to understand, he did regard them as Scripture (3:16). Peter hung the key to understanding his letter at the very end (3:18). There he put forth his central goal and theme: "Grow in the special favor and knowledge of our Lord and Savior Jesus Christ."

1 JOHN

BASIC FACTS

HISTORICAL SETTING

The readers are believers (3:1-2) of Gentile background (5:21). Because John spent his later years at Ephesus, it is likely that the letter was written from that city to a nearby group of Asian churches with which John was personally acquainted. The supposition of Augustine that the churches of Parthia are in mind has no foundation and probably arose from a corruption of the text.

False teachers appeared in the church (4:1) who drew some professing Christians from fellowship with true believers (2:19). The false teachers claimed a special illumination by the Spirit (2:27) that imparted a deeper spiritual knowledge. John combats this error by emphasizing the source and nature of true knowledge (2:3, 5; 3:16, 19, 24; 4:2, 6, 13; 5:2). The opponents also claimed to have reached a state of moral perfection (1:8-10). This ethical error brought pride and haughtiness, and John combats such attitudes by placing a strong emphasis on love for the brethren (4:7-21).

The major error among the readers was a denial of the incarnation of Christ (2:22; 4:2-3). This reflects an early form of Gnosticism known as Docetism, which claimed that Christ only "seemed" to take on an earthly human form. Many went farther to deny the reality of Christ's sufferings. In refuting the heresy, John did not attack the false teachers but carefully expounded the truth, encouraging his readers to continue in the faith and live consistent Christian lives with an awareness and concern for the errors that surrounded them.

AUTHOR

The author is not named in the letter. He claims to have been an eyewitness of the life and ministry of Christ (1:1). He expects not only to be heard but obeyed (4:6). Most scholars recognize the similarity in thought, vocabulary, and style between the Gospel of John and 1 John. Both works contain expressions such as "light," "love," "eternal life," "truth," "witness," "live," "comforter," "new commandment," "begotten of God," and "Savior of the world." Early church fathers such as Irenaeus, Clement of Alexandria, and later, Tertullian support John's authorship. See the Guiding Concepts section for the Gospel of John.

DATE

The date is related to the date assigned to John's Gospel (A.D. 85–90). First John was probably written after John's Gospel because the author seems to assume an acquaintance on the part of the readers with the facts of his Gospel. The absence of any reference to persecution may indicate that the letter was written before the persecution of Domitian (A.D. 81–96) against the church (ca. A.D. 95). The letter should probably be dated after John's Gospel, around A.D. 90.

PURPOSE

This first letter by John was designed to combat false teaching by a clear presentation of the truth. The primary purpose was to promote Christian fellowship (1:3) and knowledge in Christian truth and experience (5:13). John sought to promote fellowship in the family of God through instruction in true knowledge and by encouraging the believers in their love for one another.

GUIDING CONCEPTS

John corrects several problems that contrast with the heart of his desires for his readers. Some claimed to be able to have fellowship with God without practicing the truth (1:6; 2:3-4). But the heart of truth in practice was showing love to fellow Christians, something their opponents were not doing (2:9, 11; 3:23; 4:20). These false teachers also claimed that they had no personal sin (1:8, 10). Because of the confusion about who was and was not in fellowship with God, the believers' confidence in their own salvation was shaken (2:28; 3:21; 4:17; 5:14).

The problems and solutions of the letter may be summed up under three areas of question. First was the question of sin. Is it possible for believers to sin, and does sin destroy their relationship with God? Can or should believers pray for fellow believers who are in sin? Second was the question of incarnation. Did Jesus really come in the flesh or was it just an appearance? Do believers have to believe in a real flesh and blood experience of Christ on the cross? Third was the question of power. If believers are so hated by the world, where is the security and power to confirm them fully and ultimately as the children of God? The letter is to help believers know that they have eternal life (5:13).

The concept of "remaining" or "living" in God is the major theme of the letter. It is John's central desire for the believers and it penetrates all of John's arguments against his opponents. The Gospel of John uses "remain" ("abide," NASB and KJV) forty times, once for every twenty-two verses. First John speaks of "remaining" twenty-four times, once for every four or five verses (see for example, 2:24, 27-28). John shows how believers can know they "remain" or "live" in God. Such assurance will encourage them to continue in their love and prayer for other Christians.

BIBLE-WIDE CONCEPTS

WAITING FOR CHRIST'S RETURN

The letter examines how life can best be lived in this time of waiting for God's promise to be fulfilled (2:25; 3:2). This is the time of experiencing world hatred and inner conflict (3:13). This is the period when Christ reigns at the right hand of God (Ps. 110:1; Acts 2:34-35) and his people have times of groaning (Rom. 8:19-25). In 1 Corinthians 15:23-28 Paul made the clear link between the time of Jesus' reign and the time of the present in which believers have to cope with death and other problems that remain. All the promises of God are yes in Christ (2 Cor. 1:20), but believers must wait for some of them to be fully realized at the return of Christ.

THE NEW COVENANT

John shows the implications of being in the new covenant (1 John 2:18-29; 3:6; 4:12-16; 5:1-12). The new covenant promised a great and perfect sacrifice for sin (Jer. 31:34; cf. 1 John 2:2; 4:10). The new covenant promised the indwelling of the Holy Spirit (Ezek. 36:26-27; cf. 1 John 2:20, 27; 4:13). But it also provided a new way of obeying God, by placing the law in the hearts of all believers (cf. Jer. 31:33). It is that inner prompting of the Spirit that is behind all of John's discussion of keeping God's commands and knowing about him (1 John 2:4-6; 3:6-12; 4:13; 5:3).

CONFLICT BETWEEN THE CHILDREN OF GOD AND OF THE DEVIL

In Genesis 3:15 God predicted a continual struggle between the seed of Eve and the seed of the serpent. That conflict still existed in John's day (1 John 3:11-12). The world's hatred for God's people was not new. It reached all the way back into the Garden of Eden. Cain is the only mortal mentioned by name in the letter and is used as a model of the child of the devil. By implication, Abel is a model of the child of God who experiences hatred by the world. Also, like the serpent tempted Eve with divine knowledge apart from God's explicit commands, so those present-day antichrists sought to build a religion that claimed fellowship with God apart from his crucified and risen Son.

RELATION TO THE GOSPEL OF JOHN

In his Gospel John reported three appearances of Christ after his resurrection (John 20:11-18; 19-23; 24-29). By mentioning the fact of Christ's physical post-resurrection appearances, John was validating his claim of Christ's bodily resurrection. He could be seen, heard, and felt. He was really there. This made the link between the earthly and the resurrected life of Christ concrete. In his first letter John argued against some who had broken that link and had done away with the real body, death, and resurrection for Christ. The issue in the Gospel of John was that the man Jesus was also truly God (John 20:31). The issue in 1 John is that the divine heavenly Jesus is also truly man and lived on earth (1 John 4:2).

NEEDS MET BY FIRST JOHN

John wrote this letter to meet the needs of Christians who were wondering if they believed the right things about God and were really secure in his salvation. They were being told that if they were truly related to God they would not have any sin. They were also being told that it was foolish to believe that the Son of God would come in a literal physical body and that somehow his physical death could atone for sins. The content and structure of John's first letter show that he was answering questions like the following.

- How can believers have fellowship with God?
- What does sin do to the fellowship of believers with God?

- Is it important to believe that Jesus had a real human body and literally died on a cross?
- What is the mark of a true child of God?
- What is the mark of a true child of the devil?
- How can believers possibly cope with God's commands for righteousness?
- Should believers pray for other believers who are in sin?

Throughout Scripture people have tried to create religions that have all the trappings but do away with obedience to God's commands. Such an attempt is the target of John's words in 1 John. In the modern environment of competing religions, John meets the need of believers today to find security in their Christian faith (1 John 5:13). Today, as in John's day, believers face heresies that say salvation and a relationship with God can be had without worrying about keeping his commands. John makes it clear that the only way to salvation and a relationship with God is through the sacrifice of Christ and obeying God's commands.

Believers may find God's commands impossible to follow and almost oppressive in their demands. First, John encourages believers by confirming that their sins are already forgiven through Christ's sacrifice. He then points out that the commandments of God are not burdensome (1 John 5:3) because they are kept, not in order to gain salvation, but out of gratitude to God the Savior. In addition, the Holy Spirit instructs and enables believers to obey.

OUTLINE OF FIRST JOHN

I. THE LETTER'S PURPOSE: TO ANNOUNCE THE SOURCE OF FELLOWSHIP (1:1-4)

II. THE INCOMPATIBILITY OF FELLOWSHIP AND PRACTICED SIN (1:5–2:2)
   A. God Is Light (1:5)
   B. Fellowship and Sin (1:6–2:2)

III. VICTORY IN COMMANDMENT KEEPING (2:3-17)
   A. Specific Ethical Demand: Commandment Keeping (2:3-11)
   B. Victory by Present Knowledge of Christ (2:12-17)

IV. CONFORMITY TO THE MODEL OF CHRIST (2:18–3:24)
   A. Doctrinal: Jesus Is the Messiah (2:18-27)
   B. Living amidst World Hatred (2:28–3:24)

V. THE INCARNATION AND LOVE FOR EACH OTHER (4:1-20)
   A. The Doctrinal Battle: Jesus the Messiah Has Come in the Flesh (4:1-6)
   B. The Practical Battle: Loving One's Brother (4:7-20)

VI. ENABLEMENT FOR COMMANDMENT KEEPING (4:21–5:12)
   A. Ability through Faith (4:21–5:4)
   B. The Validation of Faith (5:5-12)

VII. THE INDISPENSABLE ADVOCACY OF CHRIST (5:13-21)
   A. The Resumption of Intercession for Sin (5:13-17)
   B. A Summary of the Work of God in Christ (5:18-21)

FIRST JOHN NOTES

1:1-4 THE LETTER'S PURPOSE: TO ANNOUNCE THE SOURCE OF FELLOWSHIP

Like his Gospel, John's first epistle begins with a prologue in which he sets forth some of the major ideas he will develop as the message unfolds. "From the beginning" (1:1) may refer to either the eternality (cf. John 1:1) or incarnation (2:7, 24) of Christ. The letter concerns the "Word of life" (1:1; 5:11-13). But "Word" and "life" are intangible and often wrongly defined. False teachers had come in and were redefining "Word" and "life" in heretical ways. To counter the problem, John began by noting that he and other eyewitnesses had heard, seen, and touched the very real and physical Word. John referred especially to the senses ("heard," "seen," "touched") in order to refute the denial of the incarnation of God in Christ (4:2). On this physical and bodily reality John based the rest of his truth regarding Christ's real death, resurrection, and ability to offer life. But only the group of apostolic eyewitnesses could validate the testimony concerning the "Word of life." Any other ideas about Christ not approved by the eyewitnesses of Christ's life were not to be received. John drew the line of truth around the testimony of the apostles.

John presented a process that moves from the abstract spiritual presence of the "Word of life" in heaven to the earthly experience of Christ's life. The "eternal life" (1:2, "Christ") was manifested to the world in the incarnation of God in Jesus. Christ was proclaimed by the apostles (1:3). The link between the Father and his people is the apostolic proclamation now recorded in Scripture. This section describes how the Word was manifested and the resultant unique authority of the eyewitnesses.

Fellowship is the thrust of the letter. There is no true fellowship with God apart from fellowship with the eyewitness community (1:3). Their fellowship was with God and with Christ. Christ was noted second because the opponents claimed to have fellowship with God and yet totally disagreed with John's testimony about Christ. Fellowship is sharing or participating in the life of God and the family of believers. Joy (1:4) was John's pastoral intent in writing the letter. Joy will come when the contents of this letter result in fellowship.

1:5–2:2 THE INCOMPATIBILITY OF FELLOWSHIP AND PRACTICED SIN

1:5 God Is Light

"Light" (1:7) is used by John to describe ethical character and spiritual illumination (2:9). God's character is light with no darkness. This sets the context for discussing which doctrines or practices

are suitable for a Christian. John began his message using the abstracts of light and darkness. But as long as light and dark remained abstract, it could not be proven that a person did or did not have fellowship with God. Therefore John immediately moved from the abstract to the specific by relating light to God's commands. John used love for Christians as the standard to prove whether a person conformed to God's light or not. John's admonition to walk in the light by showing love to fellow Christians was the cornerstone of his intention to bring about the joy of fellowship (1:3).

Because light and darkness could refer to either knowledge or ethics (cf. John 3:19-21), John took up both topics in the letter. He shed God's light on both false doctrine (knowledge) and false practices (ethics). The false doctrines about Christ had led to ungodly behavior toward fellow Christians. The rest of the letter explains the implications of God being light in the lives of believers.

1:6–2:2 Fellowship and Sin

1:6-7 WALKING IN THE LIGHT

This section makes the general ethical demand that fellowship not be accompanied by practiced sin. It begins by giving the conditions of fellowship: one's walk must match God's character (1:6). John contrasted saying with doing. To claim fellowship with God and yet persist in sin is to deny the reality of one's profession (1:6; cf. Titus 1:16). Some of John's opponents denied that evil could harm their enlightened spirits. They claimed to be righteous and did not acknowledge any sin in their lives (cf. 1:8). This first "if" test (1:6) formed John's foundational criticism of his opponents. The rest of the tests are elaborations on this one (cf. 1:8, 10).

John also reminded his readers of the positive results for those who walk in the light (1:7). Two things happen when believers walk in the light. They have fellowship with each other, and they are cleansed of sin. At this point, John was still focusing on the Christian "walk" in terms of commandment keeping. God's light shines forth his divine nature, which issues in his divine character. Because God's children partake of his nature, they should also display his character in godly behavior (note 4:17). John stressed fellowship with the eyewitness community of the apostles because they gave observable proof of true faith. The problem was that John's opponents claimed fellowship with God without having any fellowship with the community of believers (cf. 2:19).

John stressed behavior (live) by looking to the ultimate model of divine behavior, God in Jesus Christ (2:6). Christians can talk about righteous living because they have a model. To walk in the light is to live in active obedience to God's command to love as illustrated by Christ. When believers are in the habit of walking in the light (i.e., participating in the life of God), they will naturally confess their sins, and their consciences will be cleansed.

John brought up the problem of sin (1:7) because his opponents were against keeping God's clearly stated commandments (see "difficult," 5:3). They also did not believe in sin (1:8, 10). To speak of commandments was to speak of possible failure to keep them. But his opponents believed that their mystical brand of fellowship with God did away with the fact of any ongoing sin. Therefore, John commenced the attack by reminding his readers of God's commandments and the sins committed by failing to keep them.

John desired both to encourage the keeping of God's commands and to assure that occasional failure to keep the commandments was not fatal to the one cleansed by Christ's blood. He showed that such sin was done while living in the light (1:7). Therefore, in John's mind, being in the light does not mean perfection. And it also means that sin does not take a believer out of the light and into the darkness. For John, being in the light was a way to describe the believer's standing in Christ. It was not a way of describing any single act of obedience or disobedience for the believer. John placed all true believers in the light and all opponents in the dark. For John, being in the light and being in fellowship were one and the same. In John's terms, it is impossible for a true Christian not to be in fellowship. This is the basis of John's wonderful encouragement. His opponents were saying that people who sinned could not have fellowship. John taught that occasional sin does not take believers out of their saving relationship of light and fellowship with God. In fact, the sins of believers are forgiven and cleansed by Christ's blood.

The blood of Jesus was a literal sacrifice. But John's opponents did not believe in a literal flesh and blood body for Christ nor in literal commandments that were valid. So with no standard for sin and no literal body for sacrifice, the idea of a literal blood sacrifice was totally out of the question. Such was the heresy of the antichrists. Their false teachings took the life and merit out of Christ's death and blood.

1:8-10 FELLOWSHIP AND OCCASIONAL SIN
"Sin" in the singular (1:7, 8) means "guilt" (cf. John 9:41; 15:22, 24; 19:11). The claim here is to have done nothing that needed the blood of Christ's sacrifice. But believers are to admit that they do occasionally sin (1:9). Their sins and the sins of the world have been forgiven. For believers to confess sin is to admit the continual need of

Christ's cleansing blood. While occasional sin will not place them in darkness, they must always affirm and confess their need for Christ's sacrifice. Also, believers must always affirm their fellowship with the "light" by actions of righteousness that include practice of truth and dependence upon ongoing forgiveness. First John 1:8 is the opposite of 1:9; it speaks of those who deny sins rather than confessing them. Confession of sin is simply agreeing with God that the sin is wrong and inconsistent with one's participation in the life of God.

By saying "and to cleanse us from every wrong" (1:9), John drove home the point that sin is not to be denied in Christian lives but that its effects have been and will be completely dealt with by the blood of Christ. This is both a past and present experience of cleansing. God is faithful to his covenant promise. He is "righteous" because he indeed has perfectly dealt with sin. "Confess" (1:9) refers to public, not private, admission of having a continual need for the forgiveness and cleansing of Christ's blood. In this particular context it does not refer to the public listing of particular sins. The opponents said they no longer sinned or needed the blood of Christ. The believers were to publicly admit their need for Christ. On the public nature of confession, see Ezra 10:11; Leviticus 26:40-42; and Psalm 32:5. The idea is confession within the secure conditions of the covenant. In 4:2-3 "confess" has the idea of admitting or proclaiming or acknowledging that something is true. In 4:15 "confess" has the idea of profession (cf. Matt. 10:32-33; Rev. 3:5). Throughout the Old Testament confession is related to thanksgiving for forgiveness.

The response that one has never done specific acts of sin that need confessing (1:10) again reflects the error of John's opponents. John had just mentioned the importance of confessing sins (1:9). The assertion of 1:10 is nearly the same as the assertion of 1:8 but more emphatic and cutting. First John 1:8 speaks of self-deception and 1:10 shows that such claims make all that God said and did in Christ a lie.

2:1-2 A REALISTIC BALANCE
On the one side, the purpose of John's writing was to encourage his readers to avoid sin. His opponents left the door wide open to excessive sin, especially denying Christ and hating Christians. The "my dear children" draws the readers close to him. The opponents had chosen to escape the problem of sin (breaking commandments) by doing away with commandments. John's way was not only to affirm commandments and the rigorous avoidance of sin, but also to affirm the depths of forgiveness available when believers sin by breaking God's commandments. This is a present reality ("do") in the presence ("before the Father") of God. Jesus is the advocate of all believers, like a legal counsel for

the defense, someone called upon to speak in defense of another. When Satan accuses (Rev. 12:10), Christ defends.

First John 2:2 supports John's line of reasoning. Jesus also serves as the "sacrifice" (cf. Rom. 3:25), or satisfaction, for God's wrath on sin. While Christ's sacrifice was sufficient for the sins of the whole world, only those who believe may enjoy the benefits of his atoning work.The pronoun "He" takes the primary empasis here. The sacrifice is not external to Christ. John's point is that not only is sin to be an admitted reality, there is no limit to the potency of Christ's advocacy because of the effectiveness of his propitiation. John clearly says this, not to encourage sin, but to discourage fear and insecurity in admitting it.

2:3-17 VICTORY IN COMMANDMENT KEEPING

2:3-11 Specific Ethical Demand: Commandment Keeping

2:3-6 COMMANDMENTS MUST BE KEPT

John declared that true fellowship with God should be evidenced in the life of a believer by his obedience to God's word (2:3-6) and love for the brothers (2:7-11). First John 2:3-6 refers back to the assertion in 1:6 of having fellowship. What is new is the specific command to keep the commandments. Commandments are objective and verifiable statements passed on by apostolic tradition. The opponents' response is in 2:22 and 3:7. John discussed the sin aspect first (1:7–2:2) and then the subject of commandments because the commandments imply a failure from time to time. This idea of failure needed to be dealt with first. Believers have complete sufficiency in Christ.

Conformity to God as light is done by conformity to his nature as expressed in his commands. The perfection or completion of the love of God (2:5) takes place as a believer appreciates God's act of love and is thereby led to walk as Christ walked. One's profession is proved true by obedience and proved false by disobedience. Behavior provides an observable model for knowing if a person is in or out of God's light. In 2:6 John used the words "live in" ("to remain," or "continue in") as the equivalent to confessing Jesus to be the Son of God (4:15) and believing in him (2:24; 3:23-24).

2:7-11 A SPECIFIC OF CHRIST'S WALK: LOVE OF THE BROTHER

John gave new teaching for the new era ushered in at Christ's first coming (2:7-8). The teaching was not new regarding its source: the teachings of Christ. It was new regarding the quality of the age. The new age of grace was dawning, and the future age was already moving into the present. People may know whether they are in a right relationship

with God by their love for the Christian brethren (cf. John 13:34-35). This is in line with John's whole approach to the problem: a focus on observable behavior. Fear and insecurity in one's relationship with God vanish as his behavior reflects God's love in Christ (1:3; 1:7; 2:3). Thus in 2:10-11 John has come full circle back to the heretics' claim of fellowship (1:6). Fellowship with God is confirmed, not by sinless perfection, but by an orthodox confession of the deity and sacrifice of Christ, an open admission of a continual need for the blood of Christ, and a consistent walk that reflects the example of Christ. The term "darkness" (2:11) is used metaphorically to refer to the spiritual and moral condition of the unbelieving world. Unbelievers love darkness because it covers their evil deeds, but believers have no part in it (cf. John 8:12).

2:12-17 Victory by Present Knowledge of Christ

Continuous victory over the world is based on present knowledge and doing God's will (2:12-17). John used the term "children" to refer to all the believers (cf. 2:1, 28). Then John referred to both the old and young believers. The term "mature" refers to those who are older or more spiritually mature. The term "young" refers to younger members of the congregation. He repeated himself in 2:14 to emphasize why he wrote. He wrote, not because the readers were ignorant and weak, but because they were already strong and victorious. It was the opponents who viewed the believers as ignorant and weak. The sins of believers have been forgiven and continue to stand forgiven. The "world" (2:15) refers to the ungodly world and its wicked system, which is apart from and in opposition to God. Believers are not to love the world (2:15). Love of God the Father (2:15) is doing his will (2:17; cf. John 14:15). John's description of the world is also his description of the motives and attachments of his opponents.

2:18–3:24 CONFORMITY TO THE MODEL OF CHRIST

2:18-27 Doctrinal: Jesus Is the Messiah

John's opponents revealed their character by their action of leaving the church's fellowship. They also denied that Jesus was the Messiah and could not believe that the Messiah came in human form (2:22). In 2:18 John announced the coming of the Antichrist (cf. Rev. 13:1-10) and the presence of many antichrists. The term "anti" means that they opposed Christ and substituted themselves for Christ. The "last hour" (2:18) refers to the final period of the present age, the age of promise (cf. Dan. 2:28). John has prepared his readers for the exposure of his opponents as antichrists by clarifying the issues of sin and forgiveness (1:5–2:6) and by confirming the believers' victory in keeping the commandment to love (2:7-17). Next he reminded them of the time (the "last hour," 2:18), the character of his opponents ("antichrists," 2:22), and the anointing of the Holy Spirit ("received the Holy Spirit" and "what he teaches is true," 2:27). First John 2:27 indicates that the Holy Spirit is completely adequate for teaching believers, and they have no need to depend upon false teachers. The Spirit may use gifted teachers to expound God's word (cf. Eph. 4:11; 1 Cor. 12:28). What they all "know" (2:20) concerned the false claims of fellowship with God (cf. 1:8, 10; 2:4, 20, 24, 27). The anointing by the Holy Spirit (Rom. 8:9) would enable the believers to discern between truth and error (cf. John 16:13-15). John concluded chapter 2 by setting forth a threefold defense against doctrinal defection: adhere to the truth (1 John 2:24-26), rely upon the Holy Spirit (2:27), and anticipate Christ's return (2:28-29).

2:28–3:24 Living amidst World Hatred

2:28-29 RIGHTEOUSNESS AND CHRIST'S SECOND COMING

In 2:28 John encouraged believers to have confidence in Christ's coming despite criticism by the antichrists. John summed up his point in 4:17. A knowledge is spoken of in 2:28-29 in relation to and in the context of Christ's return. Christ is not just righteous in an abstract way. He is righteous and will come to seek those who are also righteous. This should motivate believers to lead godly lives so that they might have joy in anticipating his return. The practice of righteousness, not the knowledge of righteousness, is the assuring mark of one born of God.

3:1-3 THE MORAL IMPLICATIONS OF SONSHIP AND THE RETURN OF CHRIST

Being called children of God is a sign of God's love. With wonder in his heart, John marveled that believers should be called "God's children," an expression that emphasizes their relationship with God. Those who believe are his children now (3:2). This relationship to God results in the world not knowing them (cf. John 1:9-13); but it also gives believers confidence (cf. 2:28). John asserted that there was no progressive process by which believers gradually become God's children. Although the future does bring changes in believers' bodies, the future will in no way make them more God's children than they are today. In Christ believers are as related to God as they will ever be. When Christ appears to take his church to heaven, believers "will be like him," possessing glorified, resurrected bodies (Rom. 8:17, 29-30; 1 Cor. 15:51-53). The anticipation of Christ's return for the church is an incentive to purity. The words "keep themselves

pure" (3:3), given in the present tense, indicate that a continual, personal effort is involved. Purity is linked to the second coming. The present unglorified body should not block the expression of one's true relationship to God. Now is the time for purification. The coming of Christ will only be a change in the mode of the believer's existence, not a change in his position before God. But John's opponents had raised questions about a believer's present standing with God.

3:4-12 THE PURPOSE OF CHRIST'S FIRST APPEARING: TO TAKE AWAY SINS

In 3:1-3 John stressed that believers are children of God in the present. Next he emphasized that Christ came to take away the sins of all who believe (3:5). When John noted that true believers do not continue in sin (3:6, 9), he was describing the purifying efforts of 3:3. Christians will see Christ "as he really is" (3:2), so they are to purify themselves "just as Christ is" (3:3; cf. 3:7). The false teachers believed that knowledge was all important and conduct did not matter. John showed that conduct not only counts but is the essential ingredient in proving true knowledge and spiritual rebirth. The term "righteous" (3:7) was used by his opponents who were supposedly righteous irrespective of their behavior. John pointed out that righteous deeds spring from righteous character and are the proof of regeneration.

The believer should not practice sin. The expression "keep on sinning" (3:8) is in the present tense and suggests a continual practice, that is, "habitually sin." "Life" (3:9) may refer to the divine nature of those born of God (1 Pet. 1:3-4) or perhaps to the divine resources inherited through new birth (Jer. 31:31-34). But the specific sin that John warned believers not to practice is described at length in 3:10–4:21. The true believer should consistently practice love for God and his children. The children of the devil will consistently practice hate toward God and his children. In 3:9-12 John clarified what he meant by the antichrists (2:18, 22). They are children of the devil. John picked up the theme of brotherly love (3:10) and developed it. Cain (cf. Gen. 4:8) was set forth as a negative illustration of the concept of brotherly love.

3:13-24 SPECIFIC RIGHTEOUSNESS: LOVE THAT FOLLOWS CHRIST'S MODEL

John warned believers not to "be surprised" if the world's hate is experienced (3:13). One who has an attitude of hatred toward Christ and Christians is potentially capable of murdering Christians (cf. Matt. 5:21-22). Such a person demonstrates that he is not a possessor of eternal life. The readers had a problem with being hated. It made them wonder if they were really recipients of God's redemption. This explained why love of Christian brothers was so important to John. In a world controlled by the evil one's power, anti-Christian teachings and acts are to be expected. Only the children of God can bring comfort and instruct in truth. John showed that the teachings of both God and the devil centered on the truth of God's incarnation in Christ. See the accompanying chart for a comparison of true and false teachings.

In order to discern the source of the teaching, the believers were to examine the works that followed out of a set of teachings. This was John's approach. Assurance of salvation is based on conformity to the character of Christ who perfectly illustrated what it means to live by the law of love. And by discerning the validity of a teaching by examining its fruit, believers could avoid falling into error.

In 1 John 3:16-24 perfect love is related to the absence of fear. Christ's sacrificial death is a beautiful example of the love for others that should characterize believers. Assurance of salvation comes through loving in deed and truth (3:19-24). The false teachers sounded as if they knew God, but their deeds of hatred toward Christians betrayed them. Believers may be too strict or too lenient in their self-evaluations, but since God is omniscient, his evaluation will be just and fair (3:20).

Obedience confirms that believers are living in God (3:24). The witness of the Holy Spirit also serves to assure believers that they are God's own (cf. Rom. 8:9; 1 Cor. 12:13).

4:1-20 THE INCARNATION AND LOVE FOR EACH OTHER

4:1-6 The Doctrinal Battle: Jesus the Messiah Has Come in the Flesh

John moved from the importance of tangible obedience (3:24) to the experience of God's presence by his Spirit (4:1). He showed that the one who listens to God's truth is also of God's truth. Note the use of "believe" in 3:23; 4:1; 5:1, 10, 13. The emphasis throughout these verses is on how believers can be assured that they and others have truly believed in God. The reference to the Spirit (3:24) raises the question of how to distinguish between true believers and false teachers who claim that the Spirit abides in them. Here John presented tests for truth and error. The first test is confession (4:2-3): What do they say about the deity and incarnation of Christ? The second test is their crowd (4:4-5): Who are they associated with and who

listens to them? The third test is their consistency (4:6): Do they hear and obey the teaching of John and the other apostles (that is, apostolic doctrine)?

4:7-20 The Practical Battle: Loving One's Brother

4:7-10 THE SACRIFICE OF LOVE

John rounded out his test of truth regarding knowledge of God (3:14, 16, 19, 21, 24; 4:13, 17-18). He had already made the point that one must walk in the light, confess sin, keep God's commands, and love like Christ. At this point he added one more aspect: the true definition and motivation for love. The false teachers had redefined love according to the lusts of the world (2:15-16; 3:12). First John 4:7-21 contains John's classic exposition on the nature of love. Since God is love, the believer who is begotten by God should be characterized by the same kind of sacrificial love (4:7). The supreme manifestation of God's love was the giving of his unique Son that believers might enjoy life, both abundant and eternal, in him (4:9). For "sacrifice" (4:10; "propitiation," NASB and KJV), see the note on 2:2.

4:11-16 GOD'S PRESENCE IN LOVE

God has never been seen by humans, but when certain individuals show divine love, people come as close to seeing him as they can (4:12-13). Believers can know that they live in God and he in them because he has given them his Spirit. The love John was talking about was something concrete—something that follows the pattern of Christ. "Living" (4:15; "abiding," NASB and KJV) in God is the equivalent of confessing Jesus to be the Son of God; this includes keeping his commandments (3:24).

4:17-18 THE CONFIDENCE FROM LOVE

Confidence grows in believers as they match their acts of love in the world with God's loving nature. Believers should have confidence because they are like God. Perfect love is shown in acts that reveal God's character. See the concept of "as he really is" in 3:2-3. When God comes to judge the world, only that which conforms to his will and nature will remain. God will selectively destroy all that does not conform to his will. In 4:17 the relationship between God's will, his commands, and his character is clarified ("as he really is"). He will spare those from destruction who conform to himself. The believer who has practiced love during his earthly life will be able to approach the judgment seat of Christ without fear of punishment.

TRUE AND FALSE TEACHINGS

Two sources:	Evil One	God
Two teachings:	Anti-Christian	Christ/Apostolic Witness
Two acts:	Hate	Love

4:19-20 THE OBLIGATORY CIRCLE OF LOVE: GOD AND HUMANS

These verses link back to 4:10. People never love God directly from an original starting point within themselves. Whatever love they bring to God is but a response to his infinite and original love in Christ. This means that the love of believers must be like the love shown by God. Therefore, those who say they love God but hate the people God loves show themselves in error.

4:21–5:12 ENABLEMENT FOR COMMANDMENT KEEPING

4:21–5:4 Ability through Faith

The test of true love for God is whether or not a person keeps God's commandments (4:21–5:4). John set forth three tests for true faith: (1) belief in Jesus, God's Son and the divine Messiah (5:1), (2) love for the brethren and for God (5:1-2), and (3) obedience to God's commandments (5:3). The commandment is to love the one born of God. And that commandment is not burdensome (5:3). John returned to the concept of "commandment" (cf. 2:4) because it was the only standard by which believers could judge their security as God's children and confirm the anti-Christian nature of those outside. Commandments are burdensome to those who cannot or will not keep them. Commandments are burdensome to the one who denies the possibility of sin and failure. But, for the person of faith, commandments are the way to victory. Failures are forgiven and the model of God's love in Christ stands, not as a frustratingly impossible hurdle to surmount, but as an encouraging model to follow. Commandments are burdensome only to those not born of God. God has both required and enabled believers to keep his commands. Love for God is not mystical, as the false teachers argued, but behavioral—the keeping of God's commands. The present tense of "wins" (5:5) implies a continuous battle, while "defeats" (5:4) indicates an assured victory.

5:5-12 The Validation of Faith

5:5 OVERCOMING AND FAITH

The ideas of commandments not being burdensome (5:3) and overcoming the world (5:4-5) are closely linked. The pressures of the world are against obedience to God. Only the power and grace unlocked by the faith of believers can lift the burdens weighted against God's commands. The "overcomer" is identified as the one who is a believer in Jesus Christ, God's divine Son.

5:6-9 VALIDATION

John spent much time at the end of his letter proving that Jesus came in the flesh. This was because without a Christ who came fully in the flesh, believers do not have God's true witness. And without

God's witness they do not have his Son. And without his Son they do not have eternal life. The assertion, therefore, of Christ's flesh is no mere academic trifle. It makes a literal life or death difference for humanity. The three witnesses that are unified in their testimony concerning Jesus are the Holy Spirit (cf. Acts 10:38; Matt. 12:31-32), the water (that is, Jesus' baptism; Mark 1:9-11), and the blood (Jesus' death; Heb. 9:12). These three witnesses attest to the same truth about Christ and are therefore wholly reliable (cf. Deut. 19:15). The Holy Spirit is the divine and active force of witness in the community. The three witnesses are a single unit (1 John 5:9). Believers cannot reject a part of God's witness without rejecting the whole.

5:10-12 THE RESULTS

The security of believers comes back to the character of God. He is truthful and always faithful. Believers must follow Christ and exhibit his presence in their lives to prove the validity of their faith. Verse 5:12 summarizes all the testable aspects of salvation that John has elaborated on throughout the letter.

5:13-21 THE INDISPENSABLE ADVOCACY OF CHRIST

5:13-17 The Resumption of Intercession for Sin

There are two problems addressed in this section. The first is an insecurity concerning whether or not God hears prayer. The second is whether or not believers should pray for sinning Christians. What were in view were wrong judgments of sin that cause intercessory prayer to cease.

Here John linked the confidence of believers in God to their requests to him in prayer (3:21-22). Praying for sinning Christians is not an incidental concern used to illustrate praying with confidence. It was a very practical thrust of the letter. One purpose of John's letter was to give believers assurance of their eternal life (cf. John 5:24; 17:3). Now he showed them what to do with their confidence in God. False teachers, by claiming that a believer in true fellowship with God never sins, had created a problem. When Christians saw sin in another's life, they were not certain if they should pray for that person. So John had to clarify, in a way similar to 1 John 1:6–2:3, that the sins of Christians were to be confessed and prayed for.

John taught that there are two categories of sin—one leads to death, the other does not. He stressed that there was sin that did not lead to death possibly because his readers thought all sin led to death (5:17). For "every wrong," see 1:9. If every wrong is sin, then John had an exception in mind that led to death. It was perhaps a sin that was not to be prayed for (5:16), for John was noncommittal about praying for it (5:16).

There is considerable debate regarding the sin leading "to death." The basic views are: (1) A specific sin punishable by death (cf. Lev. 20:1-27); (2) renunciation of the faith and denial of Christ; (3) blasphemy against the Holy Spirit (Matt. 12:31-32); and (4) a state of persistent sin judged with physical death (1 Cor. 11:30). It is possible that John is contrasting spiritual life (5:13) with spiritual death (5:16). And he may be using the term "Christian" in a broad sense, like "neighbor" (2:9, 11; 3:16-17). These considerations, along with the context, suggest that John is referring to the persistent rejection of the gospel by the "antichrists," or false teachers. John does not explicitly forbid praying for such people, but he does not advise it.

Being an antichrist is the one class of sin in this letter that is clearly outside the usual bounds of human unrighteousness brought under the cleansing blood of Christ (2:18-22). Nowhere did John say that believers should pray for the antichrist's conversion or the salvation of his followers. Normal world hatred and denial of Christ was not in John's view here. In view was a group that claimed fellowship with God on the basis of Christ, used all the Christian terminology, and yet adamantly denied the truth of Christ's literal atoning death (cf. 2:26).

5:18-21 A Summary of the Work of God in Christ

The section of 5:18-19 gives the final context for the sin unto death. In view was the habitual sin of the antichrists, those who had been touched by the "evil one" and were children of the devil (3:10). It is apparent that John was not writing an evangelistic tract. He had clearly laid the lines of siege separating God and Satan (5:19). His concern here was not saving the lost but affirming and assuring the saved.

"The true God, and he is eternal life" (5:20) is often replaced with false replicas. This explains John's mention of idols in 5:21. It also reveals the essential error of the antichrists against which John argued throughout the letter. Antichrists are not those who deny Christ and substitute a deity of another name. The essence of anti-Christian heresy is to keep the name and acts of Christ but remove all reference to the atoning work of the reality of Christ's blood. The antichrists' idol looks like Christ on the outside but has the life of Satan coursing through its veins. The warning against idols is a most appropriate warning for readers in the ancient society of pagan Rome or for believers today.

2 JOHN

HISTORICAL SETTING

This letter from John the apostle was addressed to the "chosen lady and to her children" (1:1). This may refer to a church or an individual. Taking this as a metaphor carrying the idea of "church" seems out of harmony with the simplicity of the message (cf. 1:13). It is most likely that the addressee of this letter was an individual Christian woman and her family. She apparently had a sister whose children were in Ephesus and had contact with John's ministry there.

In Ephesus John had apparently become acquainted with the children of the "chosen lady" and was pleased to find them walking in the truth. From them John learned of the false teachers who were denying the humanity of Jesus (1:7). Second John is simpler than 1 John and makes a good introduction to it. The common elements between the letters form a needed repetition. The false teachers in both letters seem to be of the same heretical nature.

AUTHOR

The author's name is not mentioned in the letter in most translations. He is simply identified as "the elder," which has caused some to conclude that the letter was authored by someone other than John the apostle. The simple title, however, implies that the author had unique preeminence. A lesser author would have needed to begin his letter with authoritative titles. The letter bears a close resemblance in language and thought to 1 John (cf. 2 John 1:9 with 1 John 2:23; 4:20; 3:6). The reference to "truth" (1:1-4), "love" (1:5-6), and "antichrist" (1:7) are certainly typical of the apostle John.

DATE

The false teaching mentioned in the letter links it closely with the circumstances of 1 John. The references to the "new commandment" (1:5) and "the antichrist" (1:7) depend upon the fuller development of these concepts in 1 John. Quite probably it was written soon after 1 John had been sent, around A.D. 90.

PURPOSE

The letter of 2 John was designed to warn believers of the dangerous error infiltrating the church. John did this by exposing the nature of the false teachers and their doctrine. John also intended for the letter to challenge his readers to brotherly love and self-examination.

GUIDING CONCEPTS

This short letter vigorously hammers away at a single concept: participate only with those who love God and keep his commandments. Note the uses of "commandment" in 1:4, 5-6; "living in the truth" in 1:4; "teaching" three times in 1:9-10; "work" in 1:11; and notice the repetition of "truth," mentioned five times in 1:1-4.

BIBLE-WIDE CONCEPTS

The brief letter contatins references to Christ's new covenant teaching on love and commandment keeping. John revealed details of the kingdom struggle on a personal level, the struggle between antichrists and Christians, a struggle that goes all the way back to the struggle in Genesis 3:15.

NEEDS MET BY SECOND JOHN

This letter from John answered some basic questions about how Christians should draw the lines of fellowship with religious opponents. The original readers were faced with many traveling ministers who came in the name of Christ but were really imposters who taught lies about Christ, specifically that he never really came in the flesh. The denial that Christ had a human body led to the denial of Christ's physical death on the cross. Salvation became a matter of spiritual illumination rather than acceptance of Christ's death in payment for sin. The structure and content of 2 John show that John was answering questions like the following for his readers.

- What is the basic requirement for Christian belief and practice?
- What is lost if believers abandon the belief that Jesus came in the flesh?
- How can believers know Christian love when they see it?

While believers today often think that they are very sophisticated and able to tell whether someone is telling the truth about God or not, John warns that anyone is capable of being deceived (1:8). In the search for love (1:5-6) it is easy to miss the truth that love has a very specific sign: conformity to the commandments of God. John clearly revealed what lies at the heart of God's commandments: belief that Jesus came in the flesh. Without the link of Jesus to human flesh, it is easy to lose the link between believing Christian truth and living ("fleshing") that belief out in one's daily life. John's great desire was for believers to exhibit God's love, in true Christian behavior and not be religious counterfeits.

OUTLINE OF SECOND JOHN

  I. GREETINGS IN LOVE AND TRUTH (1:1-3)

 II. THANKSGIVING AND CONSEQUENT EXHORTATIONS (1:4-11)
    A. Thanksgiving (1:4)
    B. The First Exhortation: Love One Another (1:5-7)

C. The Second Exhortation: Watch Yourselves (1:8-9)
D. The Third Exhortation: Do Not Receive Them (1:10-11)

III. CONCLUSION: PREFERENCE FOR A PASTORAL VISIT (1:12-13)

SECOND JOHN NOTES

1:1-3 GREETING IN LOVE AND TRUTH
The term "Elder" (1:1), rather than "apostle," has caused some to conclude that the letter was authored by someone other than the apostle John. However, the title would be especially fitting for the apostle John who was advanced in years at the time of writing. John addressed the letter to the "chosen lady" (1:1). On "chosen," see John 15:16. This has been understood by some interpreters as a personification of the church as the bride of Christ (cf. Eph. 5:29-32). But the reference to her "children" seems to suggest an individual rather than the church. John appears to have been writing a Christian woman and her family. Perhaps a church met in her home and would have benefited from the letter.

John began his letter by laying out the framework for understanding "love in the truth" (1:1). He was concerned that truth have an impact on the deeds of those who claimed to believe it. They were not to love because they felt like it but because their love was true. The future (1:2, "will be in our hearts forever") gives believers an eternal model for present behavior. The truth "lives in us" now. The "truth" (1:2), a term used five times in the first four verses, is central to the message of this letter.

1:4-11 THANKSGIVING AND CONSEQUENT EXHORTATIONS
1:4 Thanksgiving
Living in truth is the key thought in the letter. It came as a command directly from God the Father (cf. 1:3, 9). John rejoiced to find some of the lady's children "living in the truth," a metaphor for godly living, ordering one's life by the truth of God's word.

1:5-7 The First Exhortation: Love One Another
Second John 1:5 gives a reminder and 1:6 defines it. The framework is the commands of God (1:4-6). The concept of walking in truth begins and ends in 1:4-6. The "new commandment" was taught by Jesus in John 13:34-35. Love is defined in terms of obeying Christ's commandments (cf. John 14:15). Second John 1:7 supplies a reason for the exhortation in 1:5 and specifies one aspect of the truth. The basic error of the false teachers was a denial of the incarnation of Christ (cf. John 1:14).

1:8-9 The Second Exhortation: Watch Yourselves
To deny that Christ came in the flesh would result in losing heavenly reward. Second John 1:9 critiques the wrong theology of the antichrists. They went beyond the limits of Christ's own teaching, as if he had only given insufficient teachings while on earth. The indispensible link between people and God is the truth of Christ. The presence of error calls for self-examination on the part of believers lest the false teachers hinder the work of the ministry, resulting in a loss of reward at the judgment seat of Christ (cf. 1 Cor. 3:10-15; 2 Cor. 5:10). Obedience, not mere profession, is the mark of true faith (John 3:36; Titus 1:16).

1:10-11 The Third Exhortation: Do Not Receive Them
Second John 1:10 describes a point-by-point examination of doctrine. John does not advocate fellowhip with heretics, those who substitute the teaching of Satan under the guise of Christ's. He is not speaking of a need to agree on every minor point of doctrine. To fellowship with antichrists is to fellowship with their destructive actions. Apparently, false teachers were being entertained in the homes of the believers in the name of hospitality. The command "don't invite him into your house" (1:10) relates to the heretic who seeks entrance among Christian communities in order to do his proselytizing among them. The apostle was referring to false teachers, not simply those who have been led astray and deluded by false doctrine. While hospitality is forbidden, mildness, politeness, and respectfulness to all mankind ought to be characteristic of those who know Christ. Verse 1:11 describes true guilt by association. To be on friendly terms with the evil, unbelieving, hostile world is to be God's enemy (cf. James 4:4).

1:12-13 CONCLUSION: PREFERENCE FOR A PASTORAL VISIT
The concept of joy looks back to 1 John 1:4 and before that to Christ's words in John 15:10-11. In his closing words, John anticipated a personal visit to complete his words of instruction. He would rather talk than write.

3 JOHN

BASIC FACTS

HISTORICAL SETTING

The addressee of this letter was the beloved Gaius. Three other men in the New Testament are known by this rather common name (cf. Acts 19:29; 20:4; Rom. 16:23; 1 Cor. 1:14). It is not likely that this Gaius is to be identified with any other in the New Testament. He was a "dear friend" of the apostle John. John had received a report from some of his itinerant representatives who had visited the district where Gaius lived (1:3). The apostle enlisted the help of Gaius to assure acceptance of and support for the ministering brethren who had been attacked by a man named Diotrephes (1:5-10).

AUTHOR

The author of this letter is not named in most translations. He is identified as "the elder." The style and thought of the letter unites it with 2 John and points to the authorship of the apostle John. Both letters stress "truth" (2 John 1:1-4; 3 John 1:1, 2-4, 8) and refer to hospitality (2 John 1:10-11; 3 John 1:5, 8). The author of both letters rejoices over those who are "living in the truth." In both letters the author expresses in almost identical launguage his intention to visit the readers (2 John 1:12; 3 John 1:14).

DATE

The letter was probably written about the same time as 2 John. It is unlikely that 3 John 1:9 refers to either 1 or 2 John. The letter referred to in 1:9 would have been intended for a small circle of readers and has probably been lost. It must be assumed that the second and third letters were written about the same time, around A.D. 90.

PURPOSE

This letter by John was designed to encourage the believers under the shadow of Roman persecution by reminding them of the ultimate victory of Christ over his enemies. John writes to commend Gaius for walking in the truth and to encourage the continued exercise of hospitality. The letter is also intended to censure the conduct of Diotrephes and to inform Gaius of the Apostle John's plan to visit the community and deal with the situation in person. He also warned the churches of the dangers of spiritual lethargy and apostasy. Another purpose was to bring the Old Testament prophecy and promises to full consummation, showing how God would deal with the nations, judge sin on the earth, establish his kingdom, and bring in everlasting righteousness. The final purpose is to present a picture of the glory of Christ in directing the churches, judging the world, and ruling his kingdom.

GUIDING CONCEPTS

As in 2 John, the apostle spoke of "living in the truth" (3 John 1:1, 3-4) and then illustrated the particular aspect of truth the readers needed to hear (1:8, 12). Here the need was for welcoming the true ministers of Christ. In 1 John the apostle warned not to welcome false teachers. In 2 John to welcome false teachers was to participate in their deeds (2 John 1:11). In 3 John to welcome true ministers was to participate in the truth (3 John 1:8).

BIBLE-WIDE CONCEPTS

Both 2 and 3 John give historical clues to understanding the situation of 1 John concerning the need to assert the truth of God's full incarnation in Christ. The commandment of Christ was that believers love one another (John 13:34). Third John gives a specific example of that love relating to traveling ministers of Christ.

NEEDS MET BY THIRD JOHN

This letter from John answered questions concerning church authority and traveling teachers. The readers faced a conflict between the apostle John and one of their church leaders. In that light, John showed them how to apply God's truth to the situation, thus avoiding a personal confrontation. The structure and content of 3 John show that John was answering questions like the following for his readers.

- Why should Christians be hospitable to traveling ministers of Christ?
- What is the basis for church discipline and authority?

John gives two good examples of how to apply God's truth to life's situations. The first was a simple application of truth to helping ministers traveling for Christ. The second illustrates the use of truth in church conflicts. The truth realistically states the problems involved but also drives the hearers to a deeper experience of God's love.

OUTLINE OF THIRD JOHN

I. INTRODUCTION: APOSTOLIC JOY (1:1-4)

II. APOSTOLIC CORRECTION: HOSPITALITY TO MISSIONARIES (1:5-12)
   A. Gaius's Faithfulness (1:5-8)
   B. Diotrephes' Challenge (1:9-10)
   C. Demetrius as a Model and an Ally (1:11-12)

III. CONCLUSION AND GREETING (1:13-14)

THIRD JOHN NOTES

1:1-4 INTRODUCTION: APOSTOLIC JOY

John hoped that the external prosperity of Gaius and the believers matched the prosperity of their souls (1:2). John referred to himself as the "Elder," a less authoritative designation than "apostle" (cf. 2 John 1:1). The letter was addressed to Gaius, possibly the Gaius of Derbe (Acts 20:4), the Gaius of Corinth (Rom. 16:23), the Gaius of Macedonia (Acts 19:29), or Gaius the bishop of Pergamos (*Apostolic Constitutions*, 7.40). Perhaps Gaius had been recently ill. John began the letter with a prayer for Gaius's health and prosperity. For the phrase "living in the truth" (1:3), see the note on 2 John 1:4. John used the term "children" to refer to his spiritual children, those who had been converted or discipled under his ministry.

1:5-12 APOSTOLIC CORRECTION: HOSPITALITY TO MISSIONARIES

1:5-8 Gaius's Faithfulness

John assured his readers of the correctness of Gaius's actions in caring for traveling ministers (1:5). The basis of their hospitality was the name of Christ (1:7). They were to participate with truth, not personalities. Hospitality is not only an opportunity but an obligation (Rom. 12:13) and a qualification for elders (1 Tim. 3:2). The missionaries went out to minister for the sake of Jesus' name (1:7). They accepted no support from "those who are not Christians" lest it should appear that they had compromised the gospel or were selling salvation. Paul's strategy was the same (cf. 1 Cor. 9; 2 Cor. 11:7-15). The work of the ministry is to be supported by believers, not unbelievers.

In 1:8 John presented the believers with an obligation and an opportunity; he asked them to share in the support of those proclaiming the name of Christ. Those who share financially in such a ministry are "partners" (1:8) for the truth. Giving allows them to have a ministry in other lands as colaborers with dedicated missionaries.

1:9-10 Diotrephes' Challenge

Diotrephes was characterized as being one who loved to be first. The particular problem revolved around interchurch relations with regard to receiving traveling ministers. He had apparently accused John with wicked words. The arrogance of Diotrephes was demonstrated by his ambition to be preeminent in the church and his rejection of apostolic authority. He had usurped authority by excommunicating (1:10, "puts them out of the church") believers who were exercising hospitality.

1:11-12 Demetrius as a Model and an Ally

Third John 1:11 calls Diotrephes' salvation into question. The evil deeds of Diotrephes evidenced that he did not really know God (cf. James 2:16-26). The contrast was Demetrius (1:12). He was probably the bearer of the letter and an ally with John. Demetrius received a good testimony from other believers and "even truth itself" (1:12), that is, his life squared with the truth.

1:13-14 CONCLUSION AND GREETING

John had more to say but would rather have preferred to say it in person rather than by letter. In some ancient texts, the phrase "May God's peace be with you" (1:15) begins a new verse.

JUDE

HISTORICAL SETTING

The specific locality of the readers of this letter is unknown. They had heard of the words of the apostles and were acquainted with the teachings of Paul (1:18-19). The letter dealt with an outbreak of false teaching. The problem is similar to that mentioned in 2 Peter 2:1-2, 10. The false teachers who had crept into the church were denying Christ and perverting the doctrine of grace, considering immoral indulgence perfectly legitimate (1:4). They were guilty of rejecting authority and preferred their own dreamings to God's revelation (1:8). These people were critical of the orthodox doctrine of angels and used language against good angels that even Michael the archangel did not dare use against evil angels (1:8-10). They were ruled by their passions (1:4, 16) and scoffed at the accepted Christian ways (1:17). The character and activity of the false teachers was certain evidence that they were devoid of God's Spirit (1:16, 19).

AUTHOR

Jude, the brother of James (1:1), was one of Jesus' half brothers (cf. Matt. 13:55; Mark 6:3). The author would not have been Judas the apostle, the son (or brother) of James (Luke 6:16) because the author seems to distinguish himself from the apostles (Jude 1:17). Little is known about him. Although he was not a believer until after the resurrection (John 7:5; Acts 1:14), he no doubt was influenced by his devout parents and the personal contact he had with Jesus. Jude and some of the other believing brothers of the Lord later engaged in some itinerant preaching (1 Cor. 9:5).

DATE

Jude 1:17-18 relates closely to 2 Peter 3:2-3. The lack of mentioning the downfall of Jerusalem may indicate a date before A.D. 70, possibly around A.D. 65–68.

PURPOSE

This letter from Jude was designed to encourage its readers to contend for the orthodox faith (1:3), to remind them of the certain divine judgment upon the ungodly (1:5), and to instruct the believers how to offset the evil effects of the false teachers (1:17-23). Jude did not refute the heretical doctrine of the false teachers, nor did he outline the specifics of orthodox belief. His purposes were simply to denounce heretical doctrine and to warn readers of the certain judgment that would come upon those who pursued such wicked ways.

GUIDING CONCEPTS

The basic elements of Jude center on contending (1:3) for the faith. But the letter immediately moves on to a long description of the opponents of the faith (1:4-16) with no specifics as to how to contend against them. This section is followed by a reminder of how these opponents were predicted by the apostles (1:17-19). But, again, Jude gave no specific information on contending with them. Next the readers are encouraged to be built up and kept in the love of God (1:20-21). Finally, Jude urged the believers to be merciful to those who doubted and who were sinning (1:22-23). All the while, they were to maintain a holy hatred for corruption (1:23).

Putting all of this together, believers can understand what Jude meant by "defend the truth" (1:3). Jude did not advise believers to argue hotly with the false teachers. Instead he told them to seek to understand the evil nature of their opponents and to remember their part in God's prophetic plan. He urged them to build themselves up in the love of God and mercifully try to correct and save those who would listen. In a word, contending is not winning a doctrinal argument. It is striving to win a brother or sister to Christ.

BIBLE-WIDE CONCEPTS

Jude pulled information from several Old Testament events such as the exodus (1:5), the destruction of Sodom and Gomorrah (1:7), and the wicked deeds of Cain, Balaam, and Korah (1:11). He also drew from the New Testament teachings of the apostles (1:17). This short letter shows that the events it describes are completely in line with God's perfect plan from the beginning of God's word. Jude's harsh condemnation of sinners coupled with his command to mercifully seek their redemption has affinities with James 5:19-20.

NEEDS MET BY JUDE

The letter from Jude provides helpful answers for those in the middle of debates about true belief and proper Christian behavior. The readers needed to know why the opponents could look so good and yet be so condemned by God. They also needed to know how to contend with the false teachers without falling into error and stumbling. The structure and content of Jude's letter show that he was answering questions like the following for his readers.

- Why are there so many false teachers in the church?
- The false teachers appear to be so good, but what are they really like?
- What priorities should believers maintain when they debate with false teachers?

Jude tells believers how to cope with the fighting and false teaching often found in the church. The first reaction of sincere believers may be to wonder how so many contentious people got into the church and why God let this happen. Second, they might want to respond with equally destructive hostility. But Jude reminded the believers to purify the church by avoiding the false teachers, and, if possible, by extending God's grace and offer of salvation to them.

OUTLINE OF JUDE

I. GREETING (1:1-2)

II. DESCRIPTION OF THE FALSE TEACHERS (1:3-16)
   A. The Problem and Past Examples (1:3-7)
   B. The False Teachers Described (1:8-16)

III. EXHORTATIONS TO HOLINESS AND MERCY (1:17-23)

IV. BENEDICTION (1:24-25)

JUDE NOTES

1:1-2 GREETING
The author identified himself as the brother of James. While there may have been another Jude with a brother named James, there was only one eminent, well-known James—the half brother of the Lord Jesus (James 1:1; Gal. 1:19; 2:9; 1 Cor. 15:7). Early church tradition confirms the view that this letter was authored by Jude, the half brother of Jesus. The readers were those who have been "called" to live in the "love of God" and "care of Jesus Christ." The rare greeting "mercy" (1:2) may be understood in light of the background of false teaching (2 John 1:3; 1 Tim. 1:2; 2 Tim. 1:2).

1:3-16 DESCRIPTION OF THE FALSE TEACHERS

1:3-7 The Problem and Past Examples
Jude had intended to write a doctrinal treatise, but upon hearing of the false teachers in the church, he decided it was more necessary to encourage and exhort the believers to contend for the faith. The word "defend" (1:3) suggests a striving as in an athletic contest. The false teachers had actually crept into the fellowship of the church and were using God's grace as a license to sin (1:4). In 1:5-7 Jude cited three examples of past divine judgment to demonstrate to the false teachers the principle that God does judge the wicked. The first example (1:5) was from the period of the exodus. The second example (1:6) related to the sin of Genesis 6:1-4 (see note on Gen. 6:1-4). The third example is the judgment on Sodom and Gomorrah (Gen. 19). All three examples illustrate the fact that God judges unbelief and disobedience.

1:8-16 The False Teachers Described
In 1:8-16 Jude turned from the examples of the past to the false teachers of the present. These apostates were following the same pattern of unbelief and disobedience and were destined for a similar judgment. The basic charges against these false teachers were: immorality, insubordination, and presumption (1:8). In 1:9-10 Jude contrasted the restraint of Michael the archangel with the presumption of the apostates. When Michael contended with the devil about the body of Moses, he did not presume to use insulting words or appeal to his own authority. If an angel was careful in what he said, how much more should mortals be careful. This incident is described more fully in the noncanonical, or apocryphal, book called the Assumption of Moses. Jude's reference indicates that he affirmed the truth of this incident. Both Jude and the writer of the Assumption of Moses may have drawn upon a common tradition. In 1:11 three examples of God's judgment on the wicked are presented: Cain (Gen. 4:4-9; Heb. 11:4; 1 John 3:12), Balaam (Num. 22–24; 2 Pet. 2:15; Rev. 2:14), and Korah (Num. 16).

In 1:12-13 Jude described the character of the false teachers. As Jesus said, "You can detect them by the way they act" (Matt. 7:16). The "fellowship meals" (1:12) were meals eaten in connection with the observance of the Lord's Supper (cf. 1 Cor. 11:20). In 1:14-16 Jude interpreted the prophecy of the noncanonical book of Enoch to be a prediction of the judgment that will fall upon such apostates and false teachers at the second coming of Christ. It is likely that the original prophecy was uttered by Enoch (Gen. 5:19-24; Heb. 11:5-6), and it was later incorporated into the book of Enoch. Jude knew of the prophecy and recorded it by divine inspiration.

1:17-23 EXHORTATIONS TO HOLINESS AND MERCY

In 1:17-19 Jude warned the believers to guard themselves from doctrinal error by remembering the apostolic teaching. The "last times" (1:18) are equivalent to the "last days" (cf. 2 Tim. 3:1). In 1:22-23 Jude reflected on three kinds of defectors and directed his readers in dealing appropriately with each situation. First, they were to "show mercy" to the doubters (1:22). The primary need was to convince the doubters of the truth. Second, they were to "rescue" those who could be saved (1:23). The "others" seems to refer to those who have already become involved in the false teaching but are not beyond help. No effort should be spared to snatch them from the error. Third, they were to separate from apostates those who were confirmed in their error. One can only pity them and take care not to become defiled by their false teaching. The phrase "contaminated by their sins" (1:23; Greek "the clothing stained by the flesh") may allude to the requirement of Leviticus 13:47-52 that a garment contaminated with leprosy was to be burnt.

1:24-25 BENEDICTION

In the benediction Jude praised God for his power to preserve and perfect the believers that they might one day stand faultless before the glorious person of Christ. This benediction takes its place with some other outstanding benedictions throughout Scripture. Aaron blessed the nation of Israel by invoking the character of God upon it (Num. 6:24-26). Paul emphasized the access of believers to God through Christ (Rom. 16:25-27) and the total power and control of God (Rom. 11:36). Jude's benediction contrasts stumbling with arriving safely "into his glorious presence" and places the lives and great hopes of believers squarely in the middle of God's past, present, and future glory and sovereignty.

REVELATION

BASIC FACTS

HISTORICAL SETTING

The original readers were seven churches of Asia (Rev. 1:4) identified as the churches in Ephesus (2:1), Smyrna (2:8), Pergamum (1:12), Thyatira (2:18), Sardis (3:1), Philadelphia (3:7), and Laodicea (3:14). These were the leading cities of the province of Asia and were connected by a road on which one could make a complete circuit from Ephesus to Laodicea, passing through all seven cities.

Revelation was received by John while he was in exile. Patmos was a small rocky island in the Aegean Sea off the coast of Asia Minor, about thirty-five miles southwest of Miletus. The island served as a place of banishment during the time of Roman rule. The small mountainous island measures only six by ten miles. John had been exiled to the island as part of Domitian's persecution against the Christians.

During the period of Roman rulers from Nero to Domitian, emperor worship became the official policy of Rome. Not all the emperors took their divine honors seriously, but Domitian did and took steps to enforce them. He took the title of "Lord and God" and proclaimed his infant son a god and his mother, Domitia, a goddess. The Christians refused to worship Domitian and as a result were severely persecuted under his reign. It was probably the refusal of John to submit to the imperial decree of emperor worship that led to his exile on Patmos. The persecution of the believers during the reign of Domitian is reflected in the message of Revelation (1:9; 2:10, 13; 6:9). Eusebius recorded that the apostle John returned to Ephesus upon being released from exile after the accession of Nerva in A.D. 96.

AUTHOR

Tradition ascribes the authorship of Revelation to John the apostle. The author calls himself John (1:1, 4, 9; 22:8). The author received his revelation while on the island of Patmos where the apostle John remained until after the death of Domitian in A.D. 96. There are also many resemblances between Revelation and John's Gospel. Only in Revelation 19:13, John 1:1, 14, and 1 John 1:1 is "Word" used for the person of Christ. Jesus is referred to as the Lamb in John 1:29, 36 and twenty-eight times in Revelation (and implied as the Passover lamb by the constant mention of the Passover in John 11:55; 12:1, 20; 13:1; 18:28, 39; 19:14, 31, 42). The expression "springs of life-giving water" or its equivalent is found only in Revelation 7:17; 21:6; and John 4:14; 7:38.

DATE

The weight of historical evidence points to a date toward the end of the reign of Domitian in A.D. 95 or 96. This later date allows for the growth and decline of the churches in Asia. The book reflects considerable persecution (Rev. 1:9; 2:10, 13; 6:9), and this certainly would have been the case during Domitian's rule. He initiated persecution against Christians who refused to worship him. Revelation is best dated toward the end of the reign of Domitian, around A.D. 96.

PURPOSE

The book of Revelation was designed to encourage believers under the shadow of Roman persecution by showing them the ultimate victory of Christ over his enemies and to warn churches of the dangers of spiritual disobedience. The book achieves this by bringing the Old Testament prophecy and promises to completion, showing how God will deal with the nations, judge sin on the earth, establish his kingdom, and bring in everlasting righteousness. Christ's glory in directing the churches, judging the world, and ruling his kingdom is the central feature of this book.

GEOGRAPHY AND ITS IMPORTANCE

THE SEVEN CHURCHES

The book of Revelation is a letter addressed to seven churches. The order in which those seven churches are addressed in the letter matches one possible route for its delivery. The seven churches were on a roughly circular road that connected the cities of the western part of the province of Asia. The letter may have left John's home on the

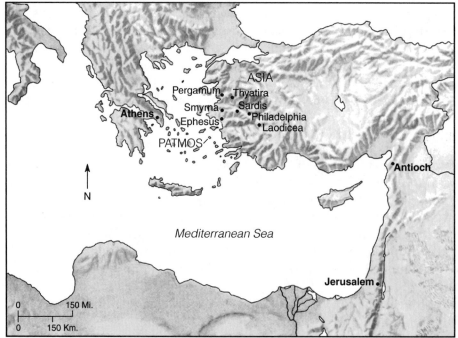

island of Patmos, arrived in Ephesus, moved on to Smyrna and Pergamum, and then circled southeast to Thyatira, Sardis, Philadelphia, and Laodicea.

GUIDING CONCEPTS

THE NATURE OF THE BOOK
One aspect of interpreting and applying Revelation concerns the exotic images it uses. Modern readers can easily identify with the control of God over history, his long conflict with Satan, and his coming judgment. But Revelation presents these events in a type of literature that makes little sense to today's readers. Trumpets, bowls of wrath, fire from heaven, mountains falling into the sea, beasts emerging from the smoke that issues up from the core of the earth, dragons, and many-headed beasts stand outside the usual ideas about God and his present work on earth. Such imagery sounds like science fiction and myth. Not only that, but understanding such imagery seems to lie beyond any interpretive scheme. What do these images mean today? The interpretation believers come to will be greatly enhanced if they first understand that the book represents three different literary forms.

THREE LITERARY FORMS IN REVELATION
First of all, the book is a letter (1:4), as seen by its form and style. This letter was written to meet a particular need or set of needs in the first-century church. It contains a greeting (1:4-7). It ends with a benediction (22:21). The fact that it was written as a letter sets Revelation apart from other prophetic and apocalyptic literature. John intended the book to meet the immediate needs of the first-century churches (cf. 2:10, 13).

Second, the book is a prophecy (1:3). As with all prophetic literature, this prophecy refers to the future's impact on the present comfort and obedience of its readers, in this case, believers in the first century A.D. (cf. 22:7, 10, 18-19). This revelation of the future was designed to meet the needs of honest curiosity and hunger for God. The future becomes the motivation to fulfill God's will in the present. In common with all prophecy, Revelation sets the call for present obedience within the context of the history of mankind's resistance to God's will. As prophecy, Revelation was given for the same reason prophecy was given throughout Scripture: because God's people were unfaithful.

Third, the book is filled with a literary form called apocalyptic. Apocalyptic contains the presentation, in highly figurative language, of a radical shift from this age into the next (1:1). The word "apocalyptic" means "that which is revealed." The subject of apocalyptic literature is always the day of the Lord.

The period between the Old and New Testaments was a time of silence. Although the people living during that silence had great faith in God, they were not seeing the promises for Israel fulfilled. The promises seemed far away, and the people were asking why there was so much evil in the world. This was the situation the writers of extrabiblical apocalyptic literature were addressing as well. They asserted that God was still at work among his people, and through their writings they called for a response of faith in adverse times. The righteous remnant of the Jews preserved these writings, and as Christianity arose, Christians identified with and preserved these writings.

CHARACTERISTICS OF APOCALYPTIC WRITINGS
The following are some characteristics of apocalyptic literature: (1) Apocalyptic literature found outside the Bible usually does not give the author's name. Biblical apocalyptic

literature does. For example, see Daniel and Revelation. (2) Historical events are described figuratively. The content concerns the end times. Beasts are used for people, and the use of numbers is also important, for example, 3, 4, 7, 10, 12. (3) In apocalyptic writings a great person from the past leads the author on a heavenly journey (e.g., Moses, Elijah, Adam, Enoch, Noah). In John's revelation, Jesus is the one who leads the author. (4) Extra-biblical apocalyptic literature presents a pessimistic worldview. Apocalyptic usually addressed a small group of the faithful, exhorting them to persevere despite the evil and suffering in the world. It brought comfort rather than castigation. In John's Revelation, the present world is shown to be hopeless. But the hopeless present is offset by a promise of future victory for those who stand firm and are "not afraid to die" (12:11). The Lamb gives present history meaning. Apocalyptic writings outside of the Bible answered the question, Why are we being persecuted? By contrast, the prophetic element in John's Revelation asks believers why they are sinning and commands them to stop it.

In summary, because Revelation contains the traditional imagery of apocalyptic, it is not concerned with detailing each event that will usher in God's future kingdom. Its concern is to impact its readers with a summary picture of future blessings and judgments. God used this medium because he wanted believers to be more impressed with the impact of the coming kingdom than with the identification of specific events that would come in the future. And though these events are described in figurative apocalyptic imagery, they also carry the message of all the Bible's prophets: the call to repentance and perseverance. The explosive images of prophetic apocalyptic emphasize the only logical remedy for sin: recreation on both a personal and cosmic level. See Amos 8:8-9; 9:5-6 (760 B.C.) and the book of Joel (835 B.C.) for early examples of prophetic apocalyptic in the Bible. The re-creation of the world will not come through the normal flow of historical events but only by God's direct replacement of the old universe with the new.

Apocalyptic literature is just one of many background areas of study that are helpful for Bible students in understanding John's Revelation. A study of the book also requires a sound knowledge of both the Old and New Testaments. But an appreciation of the aspects that Revelation and apocalyptic literature have in common clarifies the literary reasons for the complex imagery it contains. Such an appreciation also points the way to a proper interpretation of the book, helping readers apply its prophetic call to live lives of obedience in the present age.

INTERPRETING THE BOOK OF REVELATION

Figurative imagery is only meaningful to the one who knows the future and the reality behind the figures used. Throughout history believers have matched God's prophetic promises with current events seeking to identify specific fulfillments of prophecy. But only God can identify the meaning behind the images used in Revelation. But modern readers can, at least, appreciate the effect of specific symbols even if they cannot be certain of the reality behind the figures used. A number of different approaches to interpreting Revelation have been used throughout the church's history.

Contemporary-Historical

This approach takes the view that everything symbolized in the book of Revelation found its fulfillment in the downfall of Jerusalem (A.D. 70) or of Rome (A.D. 476). This position views the events symbolized in the book as having been fulfilled by events contemporary to its original readers in the first century A.D. The events were symbolic of the destruction of either Jerusalem or Rome and have all long been fulfilled.

Historicist
According to this approach, the events symbolized in Revelation began at the time John wrote the book, but they continue into the present. This was the view of people like Wycliffe and Luther. This approach interprets the book recognizing that the events recorded in Revelation reflect events throughout the ongoing history of the church as believers await the coming kingdom.

Futurist
The futurist view generally sees the majority of events in Revelation as happening in the future. Those who hold this view may find foreshadowings of the future judgments in present events, but they believe that Revelation 4–19 represents future events only.

There are three variations of this view. The first variation sees Revelation 1–3 as relating to the first-century church. The seven seals of Revelation 4–19 refer to a future period of tribulation climaxed by the return of Christ.

The second variation also sees Revelation 4–19 as referring to future tribulation and judgment but views the seven churches in 1–3 as symbols of churches throughout the ages and as possible stages in church history.

The third variation views the churches in the first three chapters as real historical churches but with lessons from which churches of all ages can profit. This view's main distinction concerns when the seven seals are opened. It holds that the opening of the seven seals began in the first century A.D., continues into the present, and will end at the future return of Christ. It does not see the seven churches of Revelation 1–3 as symbolic, and it places the severe tribulations and judgments of Revelation 4–19 in the future.

Timeless and Symbolic
In this view the churches and seals refer to the ageless conflict between God and Satan. The book is not to be interpreted with reference to any one set of historical events. The book presents the ageless struggle of the kingdom of God with the kingdom of Satan, concluding with God's final and complete triumph.

BIBLE-WIDE CONCEPTS

USE OF OLD AND NEW TESTAMENT THEMES
Revelation completes all the promises and predictions made throughout the Bible. It fulfills the promises for a new creation and a fully redeemed people who are able to dwell in the returned and unhindered presence of God. It also fulfills the promises for full judgment of sin and the vindication of God's holiness and justice. The themes of the temple and God's presence are fulfilled in the new earth. The central theme of God's redemption through the Lamb provides the power for both salvation and judgment.

EARTHQUAKES AND THE APPEARING OF GOD
The appearance of God is the foundation of the warnings and promises throughout Revelation. Throughout the Bible when God appears, the earth goes into convulsions at

his holy presence. This relates to God's appearance in battles (Judg. 5:4-5; Mic. 1:4), in his reign over the nations (Pss. 97:5; 99:1), in activities prior to world judgment (Isa. 13:13; Ezek. 38:19-20), at the giving of the Mosaic covenant at Mount Sinai (Exod. 19:18; Ps. 68:8), and at the day of the Lord (Isa. 64:1-7; Joel 2:10). In Revelation, the future appearance of God is modeled on his past appearances to save or to judge.

Earthquakes are part of the signs involved in making way for the new heavens and earth (Matt. 24:7; Mark 13:8; Luke 21:11; Heb. 12:27). In the book of Revelation earthquakes occur at the seventh seal (Rev. 8:1), trumpet (11:15), and bowl (16:17; cf. 8:5; 11:19; 16:18). The earthquakes are presented in words descriptive of the appearance of God at Mount Sinai (cf. 4:5; 6:12-17). Only one mountain shook in the desert of Sinai. But in Revelation God's appearance shakes the whole earth. Also, the divine appearance in Revelation is an appearance of Christ (1:7; 19:11-12).

NEEDS MET BY REVELATION

The book of Revelation speaks to the needs of the faithful believers and the unfaithful who are succumbing to the pressures of sin and persecution. Jesus had been away for what seemed like a very long time. The pain of persecution tempted some to wonder how God could be with them and how long it would be before he came back to set things right. The pleasures of wealth tempted some to abandon their zeal for Christ. They wondered why they should witness for Christ and risk losing everything they had worked so hard for and enjoyed so much. Faithful Christians wondered how much pain they would have to endure and needed to understand how their pain could be reconciled with God's love and justice. The structure and content of Revelation show that John was answering questions like the following for his readers.

- What does Jesus think about the present successes and failures of the church?
- What can believers expect in the period of time before Jesus returns?
- How will God ultimately be victorious over all of his powerful enemies?
- In what ways will believers be or not be protected from Satan's hostility?

The problems of the seven churches of Revelation 1–3 are identical with many of the problems of today's church. Believers today struggle with witnessing to unbelievers, keeping themselves morally pure, remaining steadfast through life's problems, and maintaining a vibrant love for God. All the overt and subtle forces of hell seem to stand against their attempts to give their best for God. Daily they find themselves attacked by evil forces, causing them to wonder if seeking God is really worth it. It becomes natural to lapse into moving mechanically through the motions of worship and Christian living.

Believers know the future holds an eternity of either reward and bliss or horrible suffering. But at times that future seems far off and unrelated to keeping people on track with God in the present. But John's Revelation breaks into the apathy and brings the future into crystal sharp focus. Revelation takes the vague and potentially non-motivating future and brings it alive in all its splendor and horror. It splashes a cold dose of reality over the church's apathetic attitudes. It wakes believers up to their materialism; it wakes them to their fears and apathy toward God and toward a world in need of the gospel. It also breeds a holy fear concerning how long people can continue in sin and apathy and how far they think they can push God's grace.

Revelation combines the need of believers to be evaluated by Jesus with their need to know about the trials of the future. Were it not for salvation in Christ, believers would suffer the judgments described in the book. That mixed sense of relief and fear should motivate those who are not truly committed to God to stop wasting time and despising God's grace. The book also meets the need of more faithful Christians by balancing the question, How long until Christ returns? with the concern about how a just God could allow world evil to go on for so long. The book clearly shows that Christians may experience unjust and evil deeds. But it also reveals the terror of God's judgment that is reserved for those who have rejected Christ.

OUTLINE OF REVELATION

I. THE SOURCE AND SETTING OF THE MESSAGE (1:1-20)
- A. Prologue (1:1-3)
- B. Greeting (1:4-8)
- C. Prophetic Commissioning (1:9-20)

II. PRESENT EXHORTATIONS TO THE CHURCHES (2:1–3:22)
- A. Ephesus (2:1-7)
- B. Smyrna (2:8-11)
- C. Pergamum (2:12-17)
- D. Thyatira (2:18-29)
- E. Sardis (3:1-6)
- F. Philadelphia (3:7-13)
- G. Laodicea (3:14-22)

III. FUTURE EXPECTATIONS FOR THE WORLD (4:1–22:5)
- A. The Perfect Source of Glory and of Judgment (4:1–5:14)
- B. Seven Seals Broken (6:1–8:1)
- C. The First Four Trumpets (8:2-12)
- D. The First Two Woes (8:13–9:21)
- E. The Little Book and the Two Prophets (10:1–11:14)
- F. Seventh Angel Sounds (11:15-19)
- G. The Dragon, the Beasts, and the Lamb (12:1–14:20)
- H. The First Bowl Emptied (15:1–16:2)
- I. The Second through Seventh Bowls (16:3-21)
- J. The Woman and the Beast (17:1-18)
- K. Babylon's Downfall Described (18:1-24)
- L. The Marriage of the Lamb (19:1-21)
- M. A Final Rebellion Is Put Down (20:1-15)
- N. The Perfection of Creation's Glory (21:1–22:5)

IV. BLESSINGS AND CURSES (22:6-21)

REVELATION NOTES

1:1-20 THE SOURCE AND SETTING OF THE MESSAGE

Overview: Revelation 1 sets the context for the book. The prologue (1:1-3) shows that Revelation came from God through Christ, an angel, and John. It also presents the purpose of the book: blessing from hearing and heeding the book's message. Throughout the book the hidden message of God is centered on the contents of a scroll with seven seals (5:5, 7; 6:1, 3, 5, 7, 9, 12; 8:1). It is the vision of Christ in 1:9-20 and the contents of the scroll that contain the revelation. The vision of Christ for the churches shows that he is at present the awesome and potentially lethal God who will in the future come to judge the world.

1:1-3 Prologue

The prologue was composed by John after he experienced the visions recorded in the book. He used this prologue to introduce his readers to what the book was about and how they were to respond to it. The book is first of all a revelation concerning Jesus Christ. "Revelation" means "disclosure" or "unveiling." Jesus is both the source and the subject of the revelation. The message is for his "servants." The book begins and ends by stressing Christ's return for his servants (1:1, 3; 22:3, 6-7, 10, 12, 20). For the concept of "soon" (or "quickly"), see Luke 18:8 and Romans 16:20. Also, consider 2 Peter 3:8-13. This is a letter to slaves encouraging them to obey their Master's commands in light of his expected return.

The message was presented largely in signs and symbols. Signs and symbols teach truth by transference. What is known about the sign in a known realm reveals something about the unknown realm toward which the sign points. Most of the symbols or signs in Revelation are explained in the context or in some other place in Scripture. A blessing is promised for those who read and heed the words of the prophecy.

What is there to "obey" (1:3) in the book of Revelation? Revelation 1:3 is a beatitude promising blessing for those who heed what is in the book. Revelation reveals other blessings in 14:13; 16:15; 19:9; 20:6; 22:7, 14 (cf. Luke 11:28). These blessings form a stark contrast with the curses at the end of the book (22:18-19). The essence of taking the message of the book into one's life is maintaining love for Christ and one's family. This will result in overcoming, or "victory" (cf. 2:7, 11, 17, 26; 3:5, 12, 21; 5:5; 11:7; 13:7; 17:14; 21:7; Matt. 24:13). For seeing the letter as "prophecy" (1:3), see 22:7, 10, 18-19.

1:4-8 Greeting

As with the prologue in 1:1-3, the greeting was written after John had experienced the visions of the book. It presents the major themes of the book: seven churches, the eternality of God, Jesus the faithful witness, and God's eternal glory and dominion. These themes will be illustrated throughout the book. John gave a standard blessing: "grace and peace." Revelation is addressed to the seven churches of Asia. The churches were in cities Paul had visited on his second and third missionary journeys. As elder, or bishop, of Ephesus, the apostle John was responsible for these churches. Note the structure of 1:4-8. It starts and ends with the eternality of God (cf. Exod. 3:14-15). The middle part describes the person and work of Jesus, which results in believers being "priests" (1:6). The servants of God do their priestly ministry in Christ surrounded by the eternal power and nature of the Father.

The "sevenfold Spirit" (1:4) is variously interpreted as referring to: (1) the seven angels (1:16, 20); (2) the fullness of the Holy Spirit in all his ministries (2:7, 11, 17, 29; cf. Isa. 11:2-5; 1 Cor. 12:4, 13); or (3) a heavenly entourage of spirits that have a special ministry in connection with the Lamb. It is always best to see if the book itself can shed light on an issue. In this case 3:1; 4:5; and 5:6 refer to the seven spirits. These verses show that the main emphasis is on the power and presence ("horns and eyes," 5:6) of God on the earth (cf. Zech. 4:2, 10). The number "seven" appears fifty-four times in Revelation. Throughout the Bible the number seven is associated with the idea of completion and perfection (cf. Gen. 2:2; Exod. 20:10).

Jesus Christ is described as "the faithful witness" (1:5; cf. 2:13; 11:3; 17:6) in order to encourage the same from the readers. This relates to the bookwide theme of "overcoming," or being "victorious" (2:7, 11, 17, 26; 3:5, 12, 21; 5:5; 11:7; 13:7; 17:14; 21:7; cf. Matt. 24:13), enduring to the end faithfully. The "first to rise from the dead" (1:5) refers to Christ (cf. Col. 1:15). He was the first to receive an immortal, resurrection body (cf. 1 Cor. 15:20). As such, he is able to resurrect those who die for their faith (cf. 20:6). The term "kingdom" (1:6) reflects the present unity of believers under their King ("the glory and dominion"). The term "priests" (1:6) reflects the service to God by believers (cf. 5:10; Exod. 19:5-6; Isa. 61:6; 1 Pet. 2:5, 9). This service will continue throughout eternity (cf. 22:3).

Revelation 1:7 breaks the flow of the narrative. It is an outburst that clearly presents the theme of the book. Daniel 7:13 and Zechariah 12:10 are combined. Their predictions will be fulfilled at Christ's return (cf. also Matt. 16:27; 24:30; and John 19:37). Note the two "amens" (1:6-7). This glorious picture was needed by those who looked forward to a future filled with uncertainty and tribulation.

God confirmed his eternal sovereignty in 1:8. For Alpha and Omega, see 21:6; 22:13; and Isaiah 41:4. While some take "the Alpha and the Omega" (1:8) to refer to Christ (21:6), in this context it refers to God who is verifying the contents of the prophecy. He is the "A" to "Z," that is, the complete God. "Almighty" is used only ten times in the New Testament and nine of its appearances are in this book (1:8; 4:8; 11:17; 15:3; 16:7, 14; 19:6, 15; 21:22; cf. 2 Cor. 6:18). Triumph in tribulation is based on trusting in God to be the most powerful of all.

1:9-20 Prophetic Commissioning

1:9-11 THE FIRST COMMAND TO WRITE
The first Roman persecution of Christians was under Nero in A.D. 64-67. He ordered the burning and mutilation of Christians and brought about the deaths of Peter and Paul. The second persecution was under Domitian, around A.D. 95. This persecution brought John to Patmos. At the time of writing Revelation, John was in exile on the island of Patmos, a six by ten mile island in the Aegean Sea about thirty-five miles southwest of Miletus. This island served as a place of banishment during Roman times.

Revelation 1:9 recounts the major themes of the book: suffering, the kingdom, and patient endurance in Jesus (cf. 3:10; 2 Thess. 3:5). The "Lord's Day" (1:10) may refer to Sunday, the first day of the week (cf. Acts 20:7; 1 Cor. 16:2). If this was the case, John had his vision on the day the seven churches he would address were meeting to worship. It is also possible that the "Lord's Day" may not refer to Sunday but to the kind of day (that is, a day totally given over to the Lord's words and acts) on which John received this revelation. For the phrase "in the Spirit" (1:10), see Acts 10:10; 11:5; 22:17; and 2 Corinthians 12:2-4. The loud voice was like a trumpet (1:10; cf. Exod. 19:16, 19; cf. Heb. 12:19; Matt. 24:31; 1 Cor. 15:52; 1 Thess. 4:16). The book was originally written as a prophetic exhortation to seven churches (1:11).

1:12-16 DESCRIPTION OF THE SPEAKER
John's vision was of the majestic person of Christ, the risen and glorified Lord, standing among the churches. The vision is similar to that recorded in Daniel 7:9-14. But this picture of the risen Lord is radically different from the picture presented in the Gospels, where the risen Lord was mistaken for a gardener and made breakfast for his disciples by the Sea of Galilee. In Revelation the risen Lord is revealed as the fearsome Judge, first of the churches and then of the world. The Lord is presented in this startling way in order to motivate the readers to pay attention. The "seven gold lampstands" (1:12) are

identified in 1:20 as the seven churches. The picture of seven lamps occurs in Exodus 25:37; 37:23; and Zechariah 4:2. The "seven stars" (1:16) are identified in 1:20 as seven "angels."

There are a variety of opinions regarding the identity of the seven "angels." Some have understood John to be referring to the human leader or pastor of each local church. Others have viewed them as guardian angels of the churches (1 Cor. 11:10). And others believe the term "angel" should be understood literally as "messenger," referring to the human messengers sent by the churches to visit John and receive Christ's letter to their churches (cf. 2:1; for other human messengers in Scripture see Hag. 1:13; Mal. 2:7; Matt. 11:10; Luke 9:52; James 2:25). The order in which the churches are addressed is strictly according to geographical arrangement.

1:17-20 THE SECOND COMMAND TO WRITE
John revealed his personal response to what he saw (1:17), and by doing this, called believers to share his feelings of awe at the vision of Christ among the churches. Jesus comforts John with his right hand (1:17). His charge of the "keys" (1:18) reveals his full power over death. The risen Lord exhibits his full authority to command (1:19; cf. Dan. 8:18; 10:10, 12). The commission in Revelation 1:19 is often seen as the key to understanding the structure of the entire book: "what you have seen" (referring to Rev. 1), "the things that are now happening" (referring to Rev. 2–3), and "the things that will happen later" (referring to Rev. 4–22). John was being instructed to write down the entirety of what he saw and to leave nothing out.

2:1–3:22 PRESENT EXHORTATIONS TO THE CHURCHES
Overview: Each message follows a standard format: (1) the charge to write to the angel of the church; (2) identification of Christ in terms of his appearance in Revelation 1; (3) the church's positive qualities; (4) words of exhortation; (5) a closing with an exhortation to hear and a promise to the "victorious." The closing to each message broadens the scope to all the churches. All seven messages are to all churches in every age. The impact of this format for the overall message and purpose of the book is that there is a critical need for Christians to endure a future period of terrible persecution. The churches are told to be "victorious" by returning to their original commitment and guarding against cultural conformity.

Each of the churches' letters begins with a vision or characterization of Christ similar to the vision of 1:9-20. The selection of each reference to the vision of Christ matches the special needs of each of the seven churches. See the accompanying chart on the seven churches.

Each message was intended to deal with the specific internal conditions of each individual church. The churches were commended for their good traits and condemned for their failings.

2:1-7 Ephesus

Ephesus, the foremost city of Asia Minor, was located near the Aegean Sea on the Cayster River and had a population of around 250,000 (see introductory map). The city was the guardian of the temple of Artemis (Diana) and of her image. According to legend, the image fell from heaven (Acts 19:35). The emperor cult flourished at Ephesus, and temples were built there to Claudius, Hadrian, and Severus. The magic arts and mystery cults also flourished there (Acts 19:13-19). Ephesus had a fine harbor, which served as an export center at the west end of the Asiatic caravan route. The city had a fine theater that seated 25,000 people. The church at Ephesus was founded by Aquila, Priscilla, and Paul (Acts 18:18-19). By the time of John's Revelation, the church had persevered through the trouble of false teachers but had lost its first love.

2:1 VISION OF CHRIST: HOLDS AND WALKS

The vision of Christ holding and walking (2:1) reinforces his intimate knowledge of their hearts and actions. The picture of Christ with a letter to each church relates to his intimate knowledge of the problems each church faces (cf. 1:12, 16; 2:4).

2:2-3 PRAISE

The Lord praised the Ephesian Christians for their deeds, perseverance, and endurance. Toil and patience characterized their overall lifestyle. They were doctrinally sound and had exposed false teachers (cf. Matt. 7:15; Acts 20:29). They had persevered and endured many trials and hardships.

2:4-5 PROBLEM

Although endurance is a key theme throughout the book, it is not the only or final criterion for pleasing Christ. The Lord told these believers that they had left their first love and exhorted them to repent. See Matthew 24:12 for Jesus' warning that the "love of many will grow cold." The idea of "love . . . as you did at first" (2:4) is purposely left

general to let the readers specify what their own first love for God was (cf. Jer. 2:2; John 13:35; 2 John 1:5). The remedy is to "look," "turn," and "work" (2:5). Doctrinal purity and endurance did not guarantee vital inner love for God. The remembrance by believers of their first state of love for Christ is potent for bringing about repentance and action. Christ's coming to judge (2:5) would be realized by his extinguishing the life of that particular church. There is a close relationship between Christ's coming to judge the churches (Rev. 2–3) and his coming to judge the world in the day of the Lord (Rev. 4–22).

2:6-7 EXHORTATION

According to the early church fathers, the Nicolaitans were the followers of Nicolas (cf. Acts 6:5). Others understand the name etymologically to refer to those who "conquer the people," that is, those who usurped authority and dominated the people. In context, their problem is linked to the teaching of Balaam (2:14-15) and may also be related to the works of 2:20-21 concerning food and idols. This also relates to the Jerusalem council's decrees in Acts 15:29. These exhortations to the churches of Asia Minor (2:7, 11, 17, 29; 3:6, 13, 22) are applicable to all churches and to individual believers as well (cf. Matt. 11:5). "Victorious" (2:7) is a combination of doctrinal purity, faithful witness, and vital love for Christ. Those who are "victorious" are not a special group of Christians but true believers who persevere faithfully to the end (21:7; 2:7, 11, 17, 26; 3:5, 12, 21; cf. 1 John 5:4-5). For the "tree of life," see Revelation 22:2 and Genesis 2:9; 3:22-24. "Paradise" signifies the place of Edenic fellowship with God.

2:8-11 Smyrna

Smyrna (modern Ismir) is located about thirty-five miles north of Ephesus (see introductory map). It was an important port city and trade center that also boasted of schools of science and medicine. Smyrna was also a center for the imperial cult of emperor worship. Temples at Smyrna were dedicated to the emperor Tiberius, Zeus, and Cybele. The gospel probably reached Smyrna at an early date, presumably from Ephesus (Acts 19:10). The church at

---

THE SEVEN CHURCHES OF ASIA

Ephesus (2:1)	See 1:12, 16.
Smyrna (2:8)	See 1:17-18.
Pergamum (2:12)	See 1:16.
Thyatira (2:18)	See 1:14-15.
Sardis (3:1)	See 1:16.
Philadelphia (3:7)	See 1:18.
Laodicea (3:14)	See 1:5.

Smyrna suffered from poverty and persecution by the Jews. Polycarp, one of the apostle John's disciples, served as bishop of Smyrna and was martyred there around A.D. 156 when he refused to recant his faith. He was burned alive on a wooden pyre.

2:8 VISION OF CHRIST
The vision of Christ's experience of suffering (2:8) matches the suffering and death that would be faced by the church in Smyrna (2:10; cf. the picture of Christ in 1:17-18).

2:9 PRAISE
The church at Smyrna experienced great affliction and poverty. Christ's words, "I know" (2:9), reveal the heart of the Christians' comfort. It is far from trite to say that God knows about the needs of his people. The spiritual riches of the believers in Smyrna contrasted with their material poverty. This stands in contrast with the state of the believers in the Laodicean church (3:17). For the concept of real versus false Jews, see Romans 2:28-29 and John 8:31-47. The "synagogue of Satan" referred to those who were Jews by birth but did not share Abraham's faith (cf. Rom. 2:28-29).

2:10-11 EXHORTATION
The "ten days" (2:10) refers to a brief period of suffering (Gen. 24:55; Neh. 5:18; Jer. 42:7; Acts 25:6). Satan was behind the suffering and tribulations of the saints throughout the book. Satan's work serves as a testing (2:10) for the saints (cf. 3:10). Faithfulness results in getting the crown of life, but only after death. The "second death" (2:11) is described in 20:6, 14 and 21:8. The "second death" refers to eternal separation from God in the lake of fire.

2:12-17 Pergamum
Pergamum was located about fifty miles north of Smyrna and about fifteen miles from the sea (see introductory map). To reach the city from the coast, one could travel up the Caicus River, which was navigable by small craft. Pergamum had a fine library and was the place where parchment was first used. The city was chiefly noted as the religious center of the province of Asia. It was the center of

four of the great pagan cults honoring Zeus, Athena, Dionysus, and Asclerius. Each of these deities had a beautiful temple. The first temple dedicated to the imperial cult (in honor of Augustus) was built at Pergamum in 29 B.C. The pagan temples and idolatry undoubtedly led John to refer to the city as the place "where that great throne of Satan is located" (2:13).

2:12 VISION OF CHRIST
The Lord is pictured as having a two-edged sword (cf. 1:16). This sword is seen in terrible use later (19:15, 21; cf. also Isa. 49:2; Heb. 4:12). The sword is related to the Lord's impending visit to the church (2:16).

2:13 PRAISE
The Lord praised the believers in Pergamum for having kept the faith. Antipas (2:13) is described as being a "faithful witness," an attribute he shared with Christ (1:5). Satan's work and throne are seen throughout Revelation 2 (2:9, 10, 13, 24; and also 3:9) and are connected to the Old Testament characters of Balaam (2:14) and Jezebel (2:20). Satan's work to destroy the church will extend into his terrible deeds recorded in Revelation 4–20.

2:14-16 PROBLEM
The Lord pointed out to them that they had allowed immoral teachings to come into their lives. The teachings were not a body of doctrine but a manner of behavior as described by the last part of 2:14. Their problem had two aspects: (1) They were eating food before idols in the temples; and (2) they were engaged in sexual immorality as pagan worship. For Balaam leading the Israelites into immoral activity, see Numbers 25:1-5 in connection with Numbers 31:16. They were involved in worship of false gods, which involved immoral sexual practices. Revelation 2:15 links the above sin to the teachings of the Nicolaitans and sheds light on the teachings of this basically unknown group. The center of their problem was that they were conforming to the ungodly activities of the surrounding society. "Come" (2:16) refers to Christ's second coming (cf. 3:11; 22:7, 12, 20).

THE SEVEN CHURCHES: REAL OR SYMBOLIC?
Some have viewed these churches as picturing seven successive periods of church history. But this view involves considerable speculation and subjectivity. As with any of the letters in the New Testament addressed to particular churches, the churches in Revelation should be understood as real first-century churches, but modern interpreters must also realize that the message is to all of Christ's churches throughout time. To defend the timelessness of the message is not to withold the original historical reality of the seven churches. The churches are like those addressed in Romans, Ephesians, Philippians, and so forth.

In addition, emphasis needs to be placed on the prophetic nature of the messages to the churches in Revelation. They are more like oracles than letters, and the command to write (repeated in 2:1, 8, 12, 18; 3:1, 7, 14) is used in the Greek Old Testament to announce prophetic messages. Thus, the letters are prophetic messages written to real churches with timeless messages to Christ's church throughout the centuries.

2:17 EXHORTATION

The "victorious" person is promised three things. The "manna that has been hidden" probably refers to the sufficiency of the person of Christ, the bread of life (cf. John 6:31-35). The theme of manna has its roots in the Old Testament. It is also seen in John 6 where Jesus indicated that he was the bread of life. The "hidden" concept may refer to the manna that was placed in the Ark for a memorial (Exod. 16:32-34; cf. Heb. 9:4). Tradition says that it was taken by Jeremiah at the time of captivity and hidden in the ground at Mount Nebo (2 Macc. 2:4-7). It was to remain there until the coming of the Messiah when the Ark would be brought to the new temple. Or it might refer to the "food of angels" (Ps. 78:25) that would descend from heaven during the Millennium to feed the blessed (2 Baruch 29:8; *Sibylline Oracles*, 7.149). A "white stone" was used in antiquity for voting and signified acquittal or acceptance. A white stone also was used as an admission ticket to a banquet, in this case the Messianic banquet. According to the rabbis, precious stones fell from heaven with manna. Christ received a "new name" after his resurrection (cf. Phil. 2:8-11), and believers will also. The essential contrast in this verse is between God's "hidden manna" and the unclean food and immorality offered by the false teachers at Pergamum.

2:18-29 Thyatira

This longest letter to the churches is addressed to the least known church. Thyatira was an important manufacturing center located approximately forty miles southeast of Pergamum (see introductory map). The city was situated in a valley on the road from Pergamum to Laodicea. Thyatira was especially noted for its trade guilds, which were more organized than in any other ancient city. Their meetings were bound up with acts of pagan worship and immorality. Dye manufacturing was an important industry in Thyatira. The purple dye was made from a root instead of from shellfish. Garment weaving, pottery making, and brass working were also trades known to have existed in Thyatira. In its early days, Thyatira had a temple dedicated to Tyrimnos, an ancient sun god. The gospel may have been brought to the city by Lydia of Thyatira who was converted under Paul's ministry in Philippi (Acts 16:14). The city is commended in Revelation for its deeds, love, faith, service, and perseverance, but it is rebuked for tolerating the false prophetess "Jezebel" (2:20).

2:18 VISION OF CHRIST

The eyes and feet of the Lord are stressed (cf. 1:14-15; 2:23; Dan. 10:6). The image of eyes like "flames of fire" indicates Christ's ability to search the minds and hearts of believers.

2:19 PRAISE

This church is praised for its works, love, faith, and perseverance. They had continued growing and were doing more for God than they had done during the the first days of their faith.

2:20-25 PROBLEM

Although this church was given high praise, it also had a problem with immorality. It tolerated immoral teachings. The reference to "Jezebel" (2:20) indicates sins of fornication and eating idol food, sins parallel to those practiced by the Israelites in their worship of Baal (1 Kings 16:29-33; 2 Kings 9:30-37). Again, the church was falling prey to cultural pressure to accommodate the pagan custom of idolatry. This pressure may have had its source in the commitment of trade guilds of that day to their patron deities. "Sickbed" (2:22) is a punishment for sin (cf. 1 Cor. 11:27-30). They will be cast into great tribulation so that the churches will know God as the one who tries hearts (17:2; 18:19; cf. Jer. 17:10; Matt. 16:27; Rom. 2:6).

"Depths of Satan" (2:24) may either be a sarcastic reversal of the claim to know the deep things of God, or a claim to have mystical power over Satan by entering into his realm and showing him powerless. "Until I come" (2:25) refers to Christ's second coming.

2:26-29 EXHORTATION

The Lord's exhortation to this church relates to rule in the Millennium. In 2:26-27 John quoted Psalm 2:9 indicating that "all who are victorious" will be associated with Christ in his kingdom reign (5:10; 12:5; 19:15; 2 Tim. 2:12; 1 Cor. 6:3). The context of Psalm 2 is very important, especially Psalm 2:7. True believers will share in Christ's rule. The "morning star" (2:28) refers to Christ himself (cf. 22:16). In the Old Testament the concept functions as an allusion to an evil being (Isa. 14:12) and to the immortality of the righteous (Dan. 12:3). Again, "hearing," and "listening," and "understanding" mark the end of this and all the letters to the churches. This is also how Jesus ended his Sermon on the Mount (Matt. 5–7).

3:1-6 Sardis

Sardis was situated in the western part of the Roman province of Asia about thirty miles southeast of Thyatira (see introductory map). The city stood on the northern slope of a mountain with a river flowing at its base. This setting rendered the city almost impregnable. Sardis was once the capital of the kingdom of Lydia. In A.D. 17 the city was destroyed by a great earthquake. Although rebuilt by Tiberius, Sardis never recovered its former glory and importance. The ancient city was noted for its fruits and wool. The making and dyeing of woolen garments was the chief industry of Sardis (cf. Rev. 3:4-5). Worship at Sardis had a sexual emphasis and focused on Sybele, a goddess similar to Diana in Ephesus. The church was probably founded during the time of Paul's ministry at Ephesus (Acts 19:10).

3:1 VISION OF CHRIST
The Lord is pictured as having the seven spirits and the seven stars (cf. 1:16).

3:1 PRAISE
The Lord praised the Christians at Sardis for their good deeds (see also 3:4).

3:1-3 PROBLEM
The Lord did not find the deeds of this church complete in God's sight. Although the church had a reputation of being alive, it was dead on the inside. This is similar to the loss of first love for Christ (cf. 2:4). Again, as in 2:5, the remedy was to "go back to" (remember), "hold to" original behavior and teaching, and "turn" to God. Throughout the Old Testament, Israel was also called to "remember" and "return" to God's redemption and commands. This is the most severe denunciation given to the churches. But this church had no named heresy or outside opposition, only incomplete acts of obedience to Christ (3:2).

3:4-6 EXHORTATION
The Lord talked about future rewards to be given to "all who are victorious." The righteousness of the "victorious" will be acknowledged by Christ before the Father (cf. Matt. 10:32). The "Book of Life" (3:5) refers to the book of the redeemed (cf. 20:15; 21:27). The concept of the "Book of Life" is seen in Exodus 32:32-33, Psalm 69:28, and Daniel 12:1. For "clothed in white" (3:5), see 3:18; 4:4; 6:11; 7:9, 13; and 19:14.

3:7-13 Philadelphia
Philadelphia, located twenty-eight miles southeast of Sardis, was a wealthy trade center in the wine producing district of Asia (see introductory map). The city was situated on a 650 foot terrace above the banks of the Cogamus River at the threshold of a fertile plateau from which its agricultural prosperity was derived. Philadelphia was called "little Athens" because of the magnificence of its temples and public buildings. Dionysus, the god of wine, was the chief deity of the city. The believers at Philadelphia were commended for their deeds, their obedience to God's word, and their loyalty to Christ (3:8). It is the only one of the seven churches of Revelation not subject to some measure of condemnation or criticism.

3:7 VISION OF CHRIST
The Lord is pictured as holy and true and as having the "key of David" (3:7; cf. Isa. 22:15-25). This is a change from the usual reference back to the vision of Christ in Revelation 1:18. The "key of David" refers to Christ's control over the messianic king-

dom. The content of this letter is similar to the one to Smyrna. The readers were assured that Christ could bring them safely through persecution and into God's kingdom.

3:8-10 PRAISE
The Lord praised the believers at Philadelphia for their deeds. They had an open ministry (3:8) and experienced victory (3:9). They were promised to be kept from the "great time of testing" (3:10) in contrast with "those who belong to this world," referring to the people who continue to reject the salvation of God (6:10; 8:13; 11:10; 13:8, 14; 17:8).

3:11-13 EXHORTATION
The believers are reminded to hold fast until Christ returns (3:11; cf. 6:9-11; John 16:33; 17:15; Rev. 7:1-8; 12:6). Satan is the chief accuser and persecutor of Christ's children (12:10; 2:9; John 8:44; 17:15; 2 Cor. 11:14-15). "All who are victorious" will gain a place in the new city (cf. 21:1-2). The "pillars" (3:12) may allude to the custom of honoring a magistrate by setting up a pillar in one of the temples of Philadelphia in his name. The writing of the name of God on those who are "victorious" identifies the believer as God's own possession.

3:14-22 Laodicea
Laodicea was located in the Lycus Valley on an important crossroads forty-five miles southeast of Philadelphia and about ninety miles east of Ephesus (see introductory map). The city prospered in banking, commerce, and the manufacturing of clothing made from the glossy black wool of the sheep raised nearby. It had a medical school and was noted for its production of a salve used to cure eye diseases (cf. 3:18). The church at Laodicea, with the other Lycus Valley churches of Hierapolis and Colosse, was probably established during Paul's ministry at Ephesus (Acts 19:10), perhaps through the work of Epaphras (Col. 4:12-13).

3:14 VISION OF CHRIST
The picture of the Lord in 3:14 looks back to that of Revelation 1:5. Christ's work is certain ("Amen") and his witness is faithful.

3:15-18 PROBLEM
Laodicea (3:16) had no local water supply, so water was brought in by conduit from hot springs some distance away. The water no doubt arrived lukewarm, like the spiritual condition of the Laodiceans. The point is that the cold and pure waters of Colosse and the hot and medicinal waters of Hierapolis both could be put to good use. But lukewarm water was good for nothing.

3:19-22 EXHORTATION
The Lord invites them to repent (3:20). Christ was depicted as outside the church, inviting the Christians within to receive him. In view is the final

invitation to Christ's messianic banquet (3:21). The believer is promised the privilege of sitting with Christ on his throne and reigning with him throughout eternity (22:5; cf. 2 Tim. 2:12).

4:1–22:5 FUTURE EXPECTATIONS FOR THE WORLD

Overview: The third section of Revelation looks ahead to the future (cf. 1:19). Revelation 4–5 forms a prologue to this major prophetic section by providing a heavenly perspective for the earthly events to come. These chapters move from earth to heaven to provide a glorious vision of God that will pervade all the following chapters. The source of glory and judgment comes from a God who deserves ceaseless worship. Against the background of the adoration of God in heaven, the awesome events of the last days are revealed.

This section shows the specific challenges involved in following Christ's call to be "victorious" (2:7, 11, 17, 26; 3:5, 12, 21). It provides consolation and courage in the coming tribulation (2:10; 3:10; 7:14). It also gives insight into how history is run—not by human political power but by a God who is active and enthroned. In light of human and satanic persecution, the church appears unable to overcome earthly powers. But the scroll is the key to the end of such injustice and the beginning of God's unhindered reign.

4:1–5:14 The Perfect Source of Glory and of Judgment

4:1-11 THE SOURCE OF GLORY AND THE RESPONSE OF CEASELESS PRAISE

"Then as I looked" (4:1) is a recurring phrase referring to a movement from one vision to another (cf. 9:13; 15:5; "After this," 7:9; 18:1; 19:1). John was invited to go to heaven for a preview of coming events. He did this by means of a spiritual vision. John was on Patmos but saw the glories of heaven. The "door standing open in heaven" (4:1) was used to show that John was going into a hidden realm to reveal what was unseen. These events are to be viewed from the perspective of heaven, not earth. John was "in the Spirit" (4:2), that is, caught up in a continued ecstatic state.

The vision of God closely resembles the vision of God in Ezekiel 1:22-28. It also has links to Isaiah 6:1-5; Psalms 47:8; 104:2; and 1 Timothy 6:16. All the terrible suffering of the saints is to be viewed through the perspective of this vision of God's glory and worthiness for worship. The "gemstones" (4:3) signify the first and last tribes of Israel in Exodus 28:17-21. In Ezekiel 28:13 these stones are counted among the treasures of the king of Tyre.

There is considerable debate as to the identity of the twenty-four elders (4:4). Some interpreters regard them as a special order of angels. Others

believe they represent the redeemed of all ages—twelve representing Israel and twelve representing the church. Since there were "twenty-four" orders in the Levitical priesthood (1 Chron. 24:4; 25:9-31), some have taken the number to be representative of believer priests. But in 5:9-10 the elders seem to be set off from those redeemed by Christ. In 7:13 one elder equals one being. It is probably best to regard them as human or celestial beings who have some responsibility for leading in heavenly worship (4:9-11; 5:8-12). Whatever their actual identity, their function in the book is clear. They were to reveal to the readers of John's revelation the proper response to God—ceaseless praise and worship.

For the "seven spirits of God" (4:5), see the note on 1:4. The thunder and lightning were reminders of how God appeared to his people at Mount Sinai (Exod. 19:16-18; cf. Pss. 18:7-14; 77:18). In Revelation the presence of thunder and lightning marks off important events and is always connected with the temple scene in heaven (8:5; 11:19; 16:18). The four creatures also function as leaders in unceasing praise for God as a background for the unfolding of his seven-sealed scroll of judgment (see also 5:9-10, 14; 11:16-18; 19:4). They are related to the cherubim of Ezekiel 1 and Isaiah 6:2-3. In Ezekiel's vision of the glory of God, he saw four "living beings" (4:6) who were later identified as cherubim (Ezek. 10:15), an order of angelic creatures. These creatures are additional to the traditional orders of heavenly beings. Each of the four creatures had a unique face. One had the face of a lion, another the face of a calf, another the face of an eagle, and the last had a human face. Whether these are to be taken as four actual creatures or as symbols, their function is clear. They were involved in ceaseless praise. The specific focus of praise was needed by the readers of this letter, especially those undergoing difficult times.

The creatures praise God for his holiness (4:8) and the elders praise God for his worthiness as Creator of all things (4:11). Seeing God in his holiness and Creator-sovereignty is indispensable for appreciating the upcoming judgment of the contrasting evil on the earth. The praise of a holy God results in seeing how bad it is on earth and how glorious it is in heaven.

5:1-14 THE SOURCE OF JUDGMENT

Revelation 5 is a continuation of the heavenly scene. John focuses his attention on a sealed book in the right hand of the one sitting on the throne. The question of worthiness for judgment (5:2) is answered. The fact that the scroll is written on the inside and on the back indicates that there was a lot to say (cf. Ezek. 2:10). The drama of seeking a worthy opener heightens the importance of the sealed scroll. To break the seals was to open the scroll. The function of seals in the ancient world was to protect important documents for private and select viewing. This scroll is so confidential that it has not one, but seven seals. Only when all seven are broken will the contents of the book be revealed. The "strong angel" (5:2) will appear again in 10:1 and 18:21. The one worthy to open the seals would have to match the worthiness of the Father (4:11). The revealing of God's judgment involves worthiness (5:2), not power. The challenge goes out to heaven above, earth beneath, and underneath the earth (5:3; cf. Exod. 20:4; Phil. 2:10). When the seven seals are broken, the judgments of God are poured out on the earth (cf. 6:1).

The question "Who is worthy to break the seals on this scroll and unroll it?" (5:2) is answered in 5:4-7. Christ conquered (5:5), and his triumph serves as the model for the believers' "victory." Christ's victory is explained in 5:9-10. Jesus the Messiah is the one who overcame death and thus demonstrates his right to open the book. The terms "Lion of the tribe of Judah" (5:5; Gen. 49:8-10) and "heir to David's throne" (Isa. 11:1, 10; Rom. 15:12) are Messianic. Christ is the royal figure coming from the tribe of Judah and the descendant of King David. His victory, and that of his followers, is victory through righteous suffering, sacrifice, and conflict. The "seven horns" (5:6) are an image of strength (Zech. 1:18). For the "seven spirits of God" (5:6), see note on 1:4. Lamb (5:6) is used of Jesus in Revelation twenty-eight times (cf. Isa. 53:7; "our Passover lamb," 1 Cor. 5:7).

The worthy one is worshiped (5:8-14). "The prayers of God's people" (5:8) relate to the prayers for the end of evil and the beginning of God's kingdom. This is especially true of the prayers noted in the fifth seal (6:9-11). Both Father and Son are praised. For "new song" (5:9), see Psalm 98:1 and Isaiah 42:10. For being made "God's kingdom and his priests" (5:10), see 1:6 and 20:6. The new song is sung by all heavenly and earthly creation (5:13). The universality of Christ's work calls for this universal praise.

6:1–8:1 Seven Seals Broken

Overview: Revelation 6:1–8:1 records the breaking of the seven seals of the scroll (5:2). It is important to realize that breaking only some of the seals does not open the book. The contents of the scroll are not revealed until after the seventh seal is broken. The events associated with the opening of the seals are simply an overture to the dreaded and final judgments of the scroll itself. The first four seals are the beginning of sufferings that lead up to the final great sufferings of the Tribulation and second coming of Christ. The first four seals relate to the events alluded to in Daniel 9, Matthew 24:4-31, Mark 13:4-37, and Luke 21:7-36.

6:1-2 A WHITE HORSE
The breaking of the first seal marks the coming of the antichrist, the "little horn" of Daniel 7:8 or the "man of lawlessness" of 2 Thessalonians 2:3. The "bow" (6:2) may refer to a rainbow as in Genesis 9:12-17 and symbolize a conquest by peaceful means and diplomacy. There are similarities with Zechariah 1:8-17; 6:1-8. The figures of riders and horses form a stark contrast with Christ on a white horse in Revelation 19:11-16.

6:3-4 A RED HORSE
This is the horse of war. The breaking of the second seal marks the removal of peace from the earth. The red color of the horse suggests bloodshed, and the "mighty sword" (6:4) confirms it.

6:5-6 A BLACK HORSE
This is the horse of famine. There is a cause and effect relationship between the taking of peace at the breaking of the second seal and the increase of famine and inflation after the third seal is broken. The "pair of scales" (6:5) symbolizes the coming inflation and famine. A "day's pay" (6:6; "denarius," NASB; "penny," KJV) is literally "a denarius," which was a Roman monetary unit worth approximately one day's wage.

6:7-8 A PALE HORSE
Death results from war and famine. Ezekiel 14:21 is quoted in 6:8. These four seals are separated from the last three. They are preliminary to the opening of the scroll's contents. The fourth seal reveals an ashen or yellowish-green horse that carries the horseman "Death," resulting in the destruction of one-fourth of the earth's population. Being eaten by wild beasts was one of the curses of the Mosaic covenant (Deut. 28:26).

6:9-11 SOULS UNDER THE ALTAR
The fifth seal is now opened. The location is the temple in heaven (cf. Hab. 2:20). At the opening of this fifth seal the souls of martyred saints are revealed. They represent those who were slain for their faith. Their location under the altar shows that they are seen as a sacrifice. The answer to their question "how long?" (6:10) is that they must wait "until" (6:11) the final number of martyrs have died. At present, they are praying for judgment that has not yet come but will justify God's reputation (cf. Pss. 79:10; 94:3; Hab. 1:2). The phrase "the people who belong to this world" refers to those who are against God (6:10; cf. 11:10; 13:8, 12; 17:2, 8; 3:10; 8:13). After the devastation accompanied by the first four horsemen (seals 1-4), the martyrs are revealed praying for God's vengeance (seal 5). The sixth seal begins the vengeance requested by the martyred saints. The seventh seal reveals the scroll's contents and the heart of God's judgments. This relates to the purpose of the book

by being a word of comfort for the redeemed during this and prior periods. The fifth seal is important because it implies that the first four seals were not divine wrath upon the unrighteous. This wrath would come, however, in the Great Tribulation seen in the sixth and seventh seals.

6:12–7:17 HEAVENLY CATACLYSM

The breaking of the sixth seal unleashes universal havoc in the heavens and on earth (6:12–7:17). These cosmic disturbances characterize the day of the Lord and are predicted in Isaiah 34:4, Joel 2:30-31, and Matthew 24:29. The imagery used in these verses is from Joel 2:28-32. For the earthquake, see 8:10; 9:1; and Matthew 24:29. For the moon and sun, see Acts 2:20, Joel 2:28-32, Isaiah 34:4, and Mark 13:25-26. For the mountains moving, see Nahum 1:5 and Jeremiah 4:24. Those trying to hide from all this know that the day of God's wrath has finally come (6:16-17). The term "wrath" (6:16-17) expresses a major characteristic of the day of the Lord (cf. 1 Thess. 1:10; 5:9).

Before the final devastation is unleashed, God sets apart 144,000 sealed ones (7:1-8). Revelation 7 records a parenthesis between the sixth and seventh seals. From the severity of the judgments it would appear that not a single person could be delivered (6:17). The question was "Who will be able to survive?" (6:17). But the God of wrath is also the God of mercy. Revelation 7 records the manifestation of God's grace in the face of his wrath by giving two visions of the sealed and the slain. This vision is between the breaking of the sixth and seventh seals, a pattern repeated between the sixth and seventh trumpets (10:1–11:13). For the "four winds" (7:1), see Daniel 7:2 and Jeremiah 49:36. There is a direct relationship between the sealing of these "servants" (7:3) and their safety. They are sealed for faithfulness and safety (cf. 9:4). The "seal" is a mark of ownership. It does not have to be visible to be real (Eph. 4:30). The 144,000 (7:4) are identified as coming from the twelve tribes of Israel. The tribe of Dan is missing, and Joseph is

included instead of Ephraim. The important thing is that they are drawn from twelve groups. Since John did not reveal the function of the 144,000, any view concerning their role is conjectural. The point is that they and a great multitude will be kept through the Tribulation and will make it safely into the eternal kingdom (7:15-17). This may relate to the prophecy of Joel 2:3 (cf. 14:1, 3-4).

John also sees a great company of Gentiles who were martyred (7:9-17) during the Tribulation (7:14). This is the group referred to in 6:11. In 7:15-17 John records the blessings to be enjoyed by the redeemed during the kingdom and the eternal state. For the Great Tribulation, see 3:10; 6:11; Daniel 12:1; and Mark 13:9. The concept of eternal service (7:15) is completed in 22:3. The tabernacle represents the new heavens and earth. For Jesus as the Lamb and shepherd, see Ezekiel 34:23 and Revelation 2:27; 12:5; 19:15.

8:1 THE SEVENTH SEAL IS OPENED

After the interlude of Revelation 7, the seventh seal is broken. The scroll's contents are now revealed, framed within the seven trumpet judgments of God's wrath (8:2–11:19).

8:2-12 The First Four Trumpets

8:2-7 HAIL, FIRE, AND BLOOD

Casting the incense burner to the earth initiates the next series of judgments. The first trumpet is a judgment of fire. A third of the trees and all of the grass of the earth is destroyed.

8:8-9 FIRE MOUNTAIN

The second judgment is upon the sea. A huge object is thrown into the sea that destroys one third of the sea life and one third of the ships. The mountain (8:8-9) and star (8:10-11; cf. Exod. 7:20) are from the coals of the altar (cf. Exod. 9:18-26).

8:10-11 FIRE STAR

The third judgment is on the fresh water. Wormwood is a plant with a strong, bitter taste and is used as a symbol of bitterness and calamity.

THE RELATIONSHIP BETWEEN THE SEALS, TRUMPETS, AND BOWLS
The seven seals build up to the revelation of the scroll's contents. The seven trumpets reveal God's judgments. The fifth, sixth, and seventh trumpets are called the "woe" judgments (8:13; 9:12; 11:14). The seven bowls are the terrible exposition of the seventh trumpet (note 10:6-7; 11:15-19; 15:1; 16:17-21). The imagery of seven trumpets relates to the seven trumpets that sounded before Jericho (Josh. 6:4-5). But here when the trumpets blast, the world, not just a city, falls apart. Like the first seven-day creation, another series of seven will precede the new heavens and earth. Like the exodus, bowls of God's judgment will bring release for God's people. Like at Mount Sinai, God's thunder, earthquake, and smoke (8:5) will signal his presence on earth. In the Old Testament, trumpets announced important events (cf. Zeph. 1:14-16). At Jericho, they announced the presence of God (Josh. 6:3). For the altar of incense (8:3), see Exodus 30:1-10; 1 Kings 6:22; and Hebrews 9:4. In Revelation 5:8 incense represents the prayers of the martyred saints for God's vengeance. There is a direct link with the beginning of the trumpets and the prayers of the saints in Revelation 5. The contents of the scroll are presented as the answer to the martyrs' prayers.

8:12 DARKNESS

God used darkness at several key points in his history of redemption (Exod. 10:21-23; Joel 2:2; Mark 13:24). The first four trumpets systematically unravel God's work of creation in Genesis 1. The fourth judgment affects the sun and stars. Not only will the light diminish, but it appears that the day and night cycle will be shortened. In Joel 2:10 a plague of locusts darkened the sun and the moon.

8:13–9:21 The First Two Woes

8:13 THREE WOES ANNOUNCED

The final three trumpets are trumpets of even greater woe than the first four. These signal the period of the great tribulation (Matt. 24:21-29).

9:1-12 TORMENTING LOCUSTS

The "bottomless pit" (9:1) is seen again in 9:11; 11:7; 17:8; 20:1-3 (cf. Luke 8:31; Rom. 10:7). The fifth trumpet, identified as the first of three woes, is a judgment of locusts. The locusts are not ordinary locusts, for they attack people, not just plants, and their "king" (9:11) is Satan, the ruler of the demons (Matt. 12:24). See Exodus 10:1-20 for the locust plague at the time of the exodus. The prophet Joel drew a close comparison between the locust plague and the day of the Lord (Joel 1:2-2:11). Locusts were referred to as symbols of judgment throughout the Old Testament. Here the locusts torment like scorpions, that is, they are like scorpions in their power, not their appearance. As in the first four seals, the image of horses in battle is used again (9:7; cf. Joel 2:4-5). The locusts are seen as a terrible combination of man and beast. They only hurt those who have not been sealed (9:4). The trumpets are God's wrath, which falls on none of God's redeemed community. See Israel's protection (Exod. 8:22; 9:4, 26; 10:23; 11:7). The locusts have power limited to five months (9:3-6). The point of this limited time is to still offer time for repentance (cf. Luke 21:25-26). Using the known reality of locusts, God has revealed the nature of the torment that is to come. "Abaddon" (9:11; cf. Job 31:12; 28:22) means destroyer. The Greek form of this name is Apollyon. Caligula and Nero claimed identification with Apollo, and Domitian, the persecutor of John, claimed to be his incarnation.

9:13-21 MURDERING HORSES

The sixth trumpet, and second woe, brings death and destruction to a third of mankind (9:18). The second woe is introduced by the sixth trumpet. It comes as a voice from the altar, the place of the prayers of the martyred souls (6:9-11). The horsemen are described in 9:13-21. They are called plagues in 9:18. The Euphrates functioned as a source of battle and destruction for Israel (Isa. 8:5-8). It was the northern boundary of the Promised Land (Gen. 15:18). Note the lack of repentance in

9:20-21. Believers are spared (cf. 9:4). Under the fourth seal one quarter of the earth's population had been slain, and here an additional third are to be destroyed. Though one-third of humanity is destroyed, the remainder still does not repent. The point for the readers in the seven churches of Revelation 2–3 is clear. Will Christ's sacrifice and words of warning be enough to cause them to repent of their sins?

10:1–11:14 The Little Book and the Two Prophets

Overview: Again, there is an interruption between the sixth and seventh elements in a sequence. Sandwiched between the sixth and seventh trumpets, Revelation 10:1–11:14 shows God's answer to the lack of repentance mentioned in 9:21. He will no longer delay the end (10:6), and he will force his enemies to give him glory through the resurrection of his two witnesses and the accompanying signs (11:12-13). People may not repent, but they will give God the glory. This section answers two questions. The first concerns how much longer it would be before the judgments were finished (10:6). The second concerns the elaboration of further prophetic details concerning the events of the Tribulation and the kingdom to come (10:11). Although the seventh trumpet marks the end of the Tribulation (cf. 11:15), the book does not conclude there. John is told to prophesy again, focusing this time on the major characters and movements of the tribulation (cf. Rev. 13–19).

10:1-7 DELAY NO LONGER

The "mighty angel" shows his signs of conquest (10:2-3, 5, 7). The mystery of the seven thunders (10:4) shows that there are still things to come that have not yet been revealed (see also 15:1; 16:17). The angel announces that there will be no further delay in the completion of God's wrath and the inauguration of God's kingdom on earth.

10:8-11 THE PROPHECY PASSED TO JOHN

Eating the little scroll (10:9) was an allusion to Ezekiel 2:8–3:3. The New Testament speaks of other mysteries of God (10:7; Rom. 11:25; 1 Cor. 15:51; Col. 2:2; 2 Thess. 2:7). Here, the mystery has to do with all that is unknown concerning God's prophecies of how he will triumph over evil and usher in his kingdom. The mystery of God refers to the program of God declared by the prophets that brings about the consummation of human history, specifically, the kingdom (cf. 11:15). Again, this is a message of exhortation to the present churches and an encouragement to those going through the tribulation.

11:1-14 THE TWO PROPHETS

This vision is given in anticipation of a major construction project during the Tribulation—the building of the Jewish temple in Jerusalem (cf. 2 Thess. 2:4). Reference is made to the Gentile domination (cf. Dan. 8:9-14; Luke 21:24). To measure the temple and its worshipers (11:1) is to claim sovereign ownership and protection of them. Similar measurements take place in Ezekiel 40:5–43:17; Zechariah 2:1-13; and Revelation 21:15-17. Revelation 11:6 describes the power of these witnesses. Links are drawn to Moses ("blood," Exod. 7:20, and "plague," Exod. 8:12), Elijah (no rain, 1 Kings 17:1; 18:41-45; 2 Kings 1:10-12) and the witnesses in Zechariah 4:3, 11, 14 (olive trees and lampstands). The actual persons of Moses and Elijah were seen with Christ at his transfiguration (Matt. 17:2-3) and were mentioned in Malachi 4:4-5. The witnesses are protected by God's power. They are presented as real people, though some interpreters view them as symbolic of the witnessing believers who are martyred during the Tribulation. The point is that God still continues to graciously offer salvation through men who genuinely mourn the evil state of the earth. The months and days mentioned in 11:2-3 may refer to the last three and a half years of the Tribulation. It is during the last half of the Tribulation that the Antichrist will overthrow Jewish worship and establish his own (cf. Dan. 9:27; 2 Thess. 2:4). The "beast" (11:7) refers to the antichrist (cf. 13:1). The names "Sodom and Egypt" (11:8) are used to refer to Jerusalem and suggest the spiritual condition of that city. God's overall sovereignty is designed to encourage the readers as they go through their own tribulations.

11:15-19 Seventh Angel Sounds

This trumpet introduces the third woe. With this trumpet, the kingdom of the world becomes the kingdom of the Lord. The content of the seventh trumpet is not immediately described. First, comes the great outburst of praise that summarizes the results of God's final judgments. The covenant (11:19) appears to be the archetype of all God's earthly covenants; it is the eternal covenant that asserts his right as Creator to be obeyed, to judge, and to redeem. Revelation 11:18 records different aspects of judgment based upon Christ taking his dominion over the nations. The wicked dead will be judged (cf. 20:11-15); the prophets and Old Testament saints will be rewarded (cf. 20:4-6); and the destroyers of the earth will be destroyed (cf. 19:19-21).

12:1–14:20 The Dragon, the Beasts, and the Lamb

Overview: This section is placed between the seventh trumpet and the execution of the seven bowl judgments. The narrative flow of the book breaks between the sixth and seventh seals (7:1-17), the sixth and seventh trumpets (10:1–11:14), and between the seventh trumpet and the seven

bowls (12:1–14:20). The breaks increase in length as the narrative moves closer to the climax of God's seven bowl judgments. Each break elaborates the nature of the times and how God is punishing evil and preserving his saints even through death (13:10; 14:13).

Revelation 12–14 contains explanatory prophecies and deals with the principle characters and major movements of the Tribulation period. These chapters elaborate the implications of the rage of the nations (11:18) for believers throughout history and especially during the Tribulation. Revelation 12 presents the persecution of Christians (12:17) by Satan. Its point is to stress the ultimate defeat of the devil and the triumph of faithful Christians (12:10-12). Revelation 13 details the persecution of Christians by Satan through his two beasts. Thus, in Revelation 12–13 the focus is on Satan's war with the saints (12:17; 13:7; cf. 11:7). Revelation 14 proclaims and then illustrates the terrible fate of those who follow the beasts and the triumph of those who follow Jesus.

12:1-17 THE DRAGON AND THE WOMAN

In Revelation 12 two signs are given. The first is a woman clothed with the sun, with the moon at her feet and a crown of twelve stars on her head (12:1; cf. Isa. 66:7-8). The second sign, an enormous red dragon, is given in 12:3. This imagery relates to an age-old desire for salvation. The slain Lamb (12:10-11) has a special place in Revelation 12. The victory is due to Christ alone, who is seen as the fulfillment of all pagan hopes. The conflict in heaven continues on earth. It unveils the activities of Satan and his angels in their attempt to destroy the Messiah and Israel. The woman with child represents Israel who gave Christ to the world (12:5) and will be severely persecuted during the tribulation (12:13). Satan's ultimate objective is to destroy the woman's child, Christ (12:4). The son of the woman (12:5) is Christ, as is seen by the fact that he is the ultimate ruler of the nations. Israel's flight to the wilderness is designed to avoid the persecution of the antichrist during the last three and a half years (1,260 days) of the Tribulation period (Matt. 24:15-21). In Revelation 12:7-12 the scene shifts from earth to heaven. Satan and Michael, the archangel, are involved in a conflict. Satan and his angels are thrown out of heaven and are confined to the earth (12:9) for the rest of the tribulation period. He will now vent his wrath on earth. In 12:13-17, having been cast out of heaven, Satan will center his hostilities on the "woman," Israel (12:5-6). His goal is to destroy Israel so that Christ will not have a people over whom to rule.

13:1-18 THE TWO BEASTS

The Beast, or Antichrist, is Satan's counterpart to what God offers the world in Christ. The Beast is a political figure who arises from the Gentile nations ("the sea," 13:1; cf. Dan. 7:3) and receives his power and authority from Satan himself (13:2). The miraculous healing of the Beast's death wound results in amazement and worship (13:3-4). The whole earth worships the dragon and follows the Beast to whom he had given authority (13:3-4). The Beast is given authority to engage in his evil exploits for forty-two months, the last three and a half years of the tribulation period. The "endurance" (13:10) is submission to the sufferings of the Tribulation without submission to Satan and his representatives.

The second beast (13:11-18) functions to witness to the Antichrist (2 Thess. 2:4). He is referred to as the "false prophet" (19:20). This would serve as a warning against false prophets to the original readers of John's revelation, just as it is for believers today. When God's purposes are finished through the beast, he will be judged (20:10). The assurance that God will punish evildoers sustains the faith of the persecuted. The number representing the beast is identified as "666" (13:18). Many have sought to identify the Antichrist on the basis of this number, but such attempts will be futile until the Tribulation begins.

14:1-20 THE TRIUMPH OF THE LAMB

These people, by way of contrast with those in 13:16, have the name of the Lamb and his Father stamped on their foreheads (cf. Joel 2:32). Revelation 14 continues detailing the age-old conflict between Satan and God. Although in Revelation 13 it may look like the corruption of the earth by the Antichrist is out of control, 14:1-5 tells the other side of the story. John tells of the 144,000 who have not defiled themselves with the beast's religious system. The words "pure as virgins" (14:4) are probably a reference to the Beast's religious system: the "prostitute" of Revelation 17. They are separated to God as women are separated to their husbands (cf. 2 Cor. 11:2).

The three angels (14:6-12) continue to extend God's grace for repentance (note Matt. 24:14). John recorded three angelic announcements intended to warn those on earth of God's impending judgment. The first angel announced the "everlasting Good News" (14:6-7); the second angel announced the doom of Babylon (14:8; cf. Rev. 17–18); and the third angel announced the judgment on those who worship the beast (14:9-13). The fall of Babylon (14:8) is initially described in terms drawn from Isaiah 21:9 and Jeremiah 51:7. Babylon is mentioned throughout the book (Rev. 16:19; 17:5; 18:2, 10, 21; cf. 1 Pet. 5:13) and seems to stand for the world system that is totally against God and his people.

John next recounts his vision of two judgments by God's sickles (14:13-20). In the middle of the devastation of the Tribulation period, God gives his verdict concerning the martyrs: they are blessed (14:13). Using the imagery of harvest, the judgment on the earth is detailed. These verses are a preview of the judgment at the Second Coming described in 19:17-21. These two reapings may relate to the two reapings mentioned by Christ in Matthew 13:24-30, 36-43. The "city" (14:20) most likely refers to Jerusalem (Dan. 11:45; Zech. 14:1-5).

15:1–16:2 The First Bowl Emptied

Another sign is now given. The wrath of God is completed in the seven plagues mentioned in 15:1. They are called seven bowls of wrath in Revelation 16. But before the final wrath, God provides a picture of final bliss for those who "had been victorious" (15:2-4). Those earthly saints are now connected with the place of God's glory mentioned in Revelation 4. Being in the very presence of God is the goal for the exhortations to be "victorious" throughout the book. "God's Tabernacle" in heaven (15:5) is the true tabernacle after which the earthly one was patterned (Heb. 8:5; 9:23-24). In Revelation 15:5-8 the temple is opened, the four living creatures again appear (cf. 4:6), and the temple becomes unapproachable in God's judgment glory (cf. Isa. 66:6). Judgment is an expression of God's righteous character (15:4; 16:7; 19:2). This chapter evokes images from the Exodus: the plagues, the sea, the song of Moses, the tabernacle of testimony, and smoke.

16:3-21 The Second through Seventh Bowls

16:3 SEAS OF BLOOD

The second bowl, like the second trumpet (8:8-9), is poured out upon the sea but is more severe. As

---

THE RELATIONSHIP OF THE SEAL, TRUMPET, AND BOWL JUDGMENTS
The seal and trumpet judgments brought partial destruction and afforded opportunity for repentance. But the seven bowl judgments dispense 100 percent judgment and zero percent opportunity for repentance. All is at an end; the evil are evil and the righteous are righteous (cf. 22:11). There are no pauses for elaboration. The bowls empty in rapid fire. This third series is explicitly called the "wrath of God" (15:7).

The first four bowls are similar to the first four trumpet judgments, but they are more intense and complete the wrath of God. These judgments are poured out during a brief period at the end of the tribulation just prior to Christ's second coming. The first bowl (16:1-2), like the first trumpet (8:7), is poured out upon the earth. This judgment of malignant sores falls upon the followers of the beast.

a result of the judgment, the sea is turned to blood.

16:4-7 RIVERS OF BLOOD

The martyrs' prayer of 5:8 is now being answered (16:6-7; cf. 2 Thess. 1:5-6). The third bowl, like the third trumpet (8:10-11) is poured out upon the fresh water so that it becomes blood.

16:8-9 SCORCHING SUN

The fourth bowl, like the fourth trumpet (8:12), affects the sun. The increased intensity of the sun scorches the inhabitants of earth.

16:10-11 DARKNESS

Even at this terrible point, people still resist God (cf. 13:1, 5-6; 10:10-11; 17:3). The fifth plague falls upon the throne of the Beast and brings darkness to his empire.

16:12-16 EUPHRATES DRIED

The sixth bowl judgment will dry up the Euphrates River to facilitate the crossing of the armies of the kings of the east (cf. Dan. 11:44) as they rush to involve themselves in the campaign of Armageddon. "Armageddon" is literally "the hill of Megiddo," referring to the hill upon which the ancient city of Megiddo was located. Megiddo was strategically situated at the foot of Mount Carmel to control travel through the Jezreel Valley.

16:17-21 EARTHQUAKE

The wrath of God is completed (16:17). The great earthquake (4:5; 8:5; 11:19) destroys the city of Babylon. The city's downfall is elaborated in Revelation 17–18.

17:1-18 The Woman and the Beast

Revelation 17 describes the downfall of Babylon (14:8; 16:19) in greater detail. Babylon probably refers to the religious, political, and commercial aspects of the Antichrist's empire. Revelation 17 focuses on the "prostitute," the false religious system controlled by the beast of 13:1. Revelation 18 will describe the judgment on the Beast and his empire.

The same angel will show the bride of Christ (17:1; 21:9). The Beast (17:3) appears to represent satanic influence throughout history. Its various heads are its attempts at world rule throughout history. The eighth head is the Antichrist of 13:1-10 (cf. Dan. 7:19-21).

The "prostitute" imagery is seen also in Nahum 3:4 and Isaiah 23:16-17. This woman is to be contrasted with the woman of 12:1-6 and the bride of Christ (21:9). The prostitute is given a name that reveals she is the representative of the false religious system that began in ancient Babylon (cf. Gen. 11:1-9). The name is "mysterious" (17:5), that is, the city of Babylon on the Euphrates is not meant. This is a secret, or symbolic, use of the name, the

exact understanding of which remains to be revealed (cf. 14:8; 16:19; 17:6, 18; 18:24). Names on foreheads (17:5) appear throughout the book for evil (13:16; 14:9; 20:4) and for good (7:3; 9:4; 14:1; 22:4). This vision answers a question asked by saints throughout the ages: Why do the enemies of God often seem so victorious instead of being judged? The vision shows that she will indeed be destroyed at God's chosen time. The Beast and harlot's descriptions function as guides to interpreting their destruction in 18:1–19:5.

The seven heads, horns, and hills have been variously interpreted as Rome, other countries and kings, or simply as a symbol for all the kingdoms of history. More specifically, the seven heads are seven mountains or kings; five have fallen, one exists, and the other is yet to come. The first five kingdoms would include Assyria, Babylon, Persia, Greece, and Egypt. The kingdom in existence while John wrote was the Roman Empire (sixth). The kingdom yet to come will be the final form of world government. It is identified in 17:11 with the Beast's own empire. The idea of "was alive and then died" arises from past and future expressions of Satan through rulers. "Ten kings" (17:12) may mean ten actual nations or may be symbolic for all the nations of the world.

For "waters" (17:15), see Jeremiah 51:13. The destruction of the prostitute is described in images drawn from Ezekiel 23:11-35. Once in power, the beast and his associates will reject the authority of the prostitute's system and throw off her rule. With that system destroyed, the Beast will then be introduced by the false prophet as the true god (13:12; cf. 2 Thess. 2:4).

18:1-24 Babylon's Downfall Described

18:1-3 THE ANNOUNCEMENT OF BABYLON'S DESTRUCTION

Revelation 18 describes the judgment on the final form of Babylon, the Beast and his empire. The imagery of Babylon falling is taken from Isaiah 21:9, where the ancient city of Babylon was destroyed.

18:4-20 LAMENT OF THE WORLD OVER BABYLON

Revelation 18:4-20 is a message from "another voice calling from heaven" (18:4). The message begins with a call to separate from the city (18:4) and ends with a call to rejoice (18:20). The heavenly rejoicing forms a stark contrast with the world's mourning (18:9-19). The prayer of the martyrs (6:10) is answered. The call to separate is to believers living in the Tribulation period who might be tempted to compromise their convictions and become associated with the Beast. The world's leaders give three laments over fallen Babylon (18:9-10, 11-17a, 17b-19). Compare this with Ezekiel's lamentation over Tyre (Ezek. 27). Half the commodities mentioned in 18:11-13 are mentioned also in Ezekiel. Mariners, kings, and merchants are also mentioned in the Ezekiel lamentation. The merchants mourn over the long list of commodities rather than their long list of sins. The judgment against Babylon is on behalf of heaven and the saints (18:20).

18:21-24 BABYLON DESTROYED
The reason for the destruction is Babylon's deception (18:23) and murder of the saints (18:24).

19:1-21 The Marriage of the Lamb
19:1-10 THE GLORY OF GOD AND THE MARRIAGE OF THE LAMB
Revelation 19 begins with rejoicing in heaven by the angels and the redeemed. "Hallelujah" (19:1) is transliterated from Hebrew and means "Praise the Lord!" The Old Testament context of the verse quoted in 19:2 is Deuteronomy 32:34-43. The blood of the saints has been avenged (19:2; cf. 6:10). The Old Testament context of 19:3 is Isaiah 34:10. Many biblical texts describe the relationship between God and his people under the metaphor of marriage (19:9; cf. Isa. 62:4; Hos. 2:19; 2 Cor. 11:2; Eph. 5:25-33; Rev. 21:2). Here, John describes the marriage of the Lamb and the marriage supper. The wedding feast (19:7-9) is a reference to the end of the long and sometimes painful engagement between Christ and his saints. It marks the beginning of the eternal unbroken marriage relationship of perfect fellowship and love. This vision is here to encourage the readers through their tribulations with the vision of their ultimate entrance into God's glory. The study of prophecy should witness to Jesus, giving believers a greater appreciation of his person and work (19:10).

19:11-21 THE WAR OF THE LAMB
This is the second coming of Christ. Jesus the Messiah returns with his heavenly armies to execute judgment on his enemies and to establish his kingdom (cf. Zech. 14:1-5; Matt. 24:29-30). Jesus is referred to as the "Word" (19:13; cf. John 1:1). There is debate regarding the identification of the "armies of heaven" (19:14). Some interpret them to refer to the saints. More likely, they refer to the angels of heaven who are under God's command (cf. Mark 8:38; 2 Thess. 1:7). The vision of the great banquet of God (19:17-21) describes the carnage resulting from Christ's judgment on his enemies. This event is similar to that described in Ezekiel 39:17-20.

20:1-15 A Final Rebellion Is Put Down
20:1-3 SATAN IS BOUND
Revelation 20 describes the duration, nature, government, and chronological sequence of events related to the Millennium. There are three main views regarding this chapter: (1) The postmillennial view interprets the chapter figuratively. The thousand years is understood to refer to a period of prosperity that will culminate in the second coming of Christ. (2) The amillennial viewpoint interprets the chapter symbolically. There is no literal period of a thousand years of Christ's reign after his return because the reign of Christ began in heaven after his ascension. (3) The premillennial viewpoint interprets the chapter as referring to an actual thousand-year period. Christ will return and inaugurate a literal thousand-year earthly reign during which peace and righteousness will prevail.

John observes that Satan is bound for one thousand years (20:1-3). This is so there will be no external source of deceit during the thousand years. Satan, the organizer of opposition against Christ, is removed so that righteousness and peace will flourish (cf. Isa. 11:3-5).

20:4-6 JUDGMENTS FOR ONE THOUSAND YEARS
The martyred believers and perhaps others (see Dan. 12:2, 13; Matt. 19:27-28; 1 Cor. 6:2; 2 Tim. 2:12) are resurrected to share in Christ's millennial reign. The rest of the dead are not raised until after the Millennium (cf. 20:11-15). This brief description covers one thousand years but emphasizes the blessedness of those who overcame temptation to give in to the Antichrist and thereby escape the horrors of the second death. Again, this encouraged the original readers of Revelation (and should encourage readers today) to view physical death as less important than risking the second and eternal death.

20:7-10 GOG AND MAGOG DEFEATED
Satan is released for a final period of deception (20:3), which is magnified by the contrast of its absence during the thousand years (20:4-9). The Old Testament background is Ezekiel 38–39. This event is similar in purpose to the one spoken of in Ezekiel 38–39 and therefore is also called "Gog and Magog." Satan's followers are apparently those who were born in the Millennium but did not have true faith in Christ. As a result of this final rebellion, Satan is thrown into the lake of fire where he will stay throughout eternity.

20:11-15 THE GREAT WHITE THRONE JUDGMENT
The Great White Throne Judgment involves the resurrection and judgment of what 20:5 called "the rest of the dead." The record books are consulted to demonstrate that the judgment is deserved (20:12), and then the book of life is opened to see if their names are within and their deeds have been covered by faith in the shed blood of Jesus. The absence of one's name in the book of life indicates that one's destiny is the lake of fire, the second death.

21:1–22:5 The Perfection of Creation's Glory

21:1-8 THE NEW HEAVENS AND EARTH

The last vision of Revelation describes the new Jerusalem, which will serve as the abode of the saints throughout eternity. John saw the new heaven and earth after the present earth had been purged from the effects of sin by fire (Isa. 65:17; 66:22; 2 Pet. 3:10-13). This completes God's promise to Abraham to give him a land. This does not refer to the partial fulfillment seen in the land of Palestine but to the advent of a new heaven and earth (cf. Heb. 11:10, 16; 13:14). The new Jerusalem comes down out of heaven to settle on the earth (Rev. 21:2). This city is to be occupied by "all those who are victorious" (21:7; cf. 2:7, 11, 17, 26; 3:5, 12, 21; 1 John 5:4-5). The judgments of the day of the Lord (cf. 2 Pet. 3:10-12) will melt into eternal peace. The glory of God's children will have released the creation from its futility (Rom. 8:19-22). God's presence will form the perfect and eternal tabernacle (cf. Lev. 26:11-12; Jer. 31:33; Ezek. 37:27; Zech. 8:8). The transformation of believers from glory to glory will be complete (2 Cor. 3:18; 4:16-18; 5:16-17). This functions as a motivating vision for overcoming the present temptations to deny Christ and his holiness.

21:9–22:5 THE NEW JERUSALEM

The "bride, the wife of the Lamb" (21:9) is a reference, not to the city itself, but to its inhabitants (21:24, 27; 22:2-5). For the twelve gates (21:12), see Ezekiel 48:30-34. The city is portrayed with equal dimensions like a cube, significant because the holy of holies in the temple was also a cube (cf. 1 Kings 6:20). The image is of the perfect tabernacle of God (21:3), built from the ground up with the most precious of materials. In Revelation 22 the images of Eden return once again; the river and the tree of life (22:1-2; cf. Gen. 2:9; 3:22; Ezek. 47:12) appear once again. The promises to David are fulfilled in the believers (21:7; cf. 2 Sam. 7:14; 2 Cor. 6:18). In the new Jerusalem the faithful will behold what Moses and all people after Adam were denied; they will see the very face of God (cf. Exod. 33:20, 23; Matt. 5:8). Zechariah 14:7 spoke of a time when there would be no night (Rev. 21:25).

The awful curse of God that fell upon the earth and humanity in Genesis 3 is now reversed (22:3). God's bond servants can now perform what God wanted from his people from the beginning; God had created man to serve him for eternity (22:3). Nowhere in Scripture is there a description of the complete details of the believer's eternal state (cf. 1 Cor. 2:9), but John provides believers with a foretaste of the glories to come. Heaven is in reality a new heaven and earth; it is a beautiful place where believers will enjoy fellowship with Christ, rest, joy, service, and worship.

22:6-21 BLESSINGS AND CURSES

This epilogue returns to the themes of the prologue (cf. 1:3) and serves as the conclusion of the book. The prophecy was authenticated by the angel (22:6), by Christ (22:7), and by John (22:8-9). John was commanded to leave the book unsealed, for the time was near when people would need understanding of what God was doing (22:10). Revelation 22:11 reveals that when Christ comes, there will be no further opportunities to change one's destiny. The term "dogs" (22:15) refers to persons of lower character. Jesus himself speaks again in 22:16. He identifies himself as the "heir to David's throne" (5:5), the one with whom God would fulfill Israel's covenant promises (Luke 1:32-33). An invitation by the Spirit and the bride was given to all who would thirst for the water of life (22:17; cf. Isa. 55:1). They were offered the free gift of salvation. In 22:18-19 John warned against additions or subtractions from the prophecy (cf. Deut. 4:2; 12:32; Prov. 30:6). The warning of 22:19 assumes that no genuine believer would tamper with the Scripture. For the third time in this chapter (22:7, 12, 20), the Lord said that he would come soon. John's reply is also that of his readers, "Come, Lord Jesus."

LOOK FOR OTHER BOOKS IN:

The Tyndale Reference Library
Bible Resources for Everyone's Library

The Tyndale Bible Dictionary
The Tyndale Handbook of Bible Charts and Maps
The Tyndale Concise Bible Commentary